A New Dictionary of Religions

A
New Dictionary
of
Religions

EDITED BY
John R. Hinnells

BLACKWELL
Reference

Copyright © Penguin Books Ltd 1984, 1995

The right of John Hinnells to be identified as editor of this work has been
asserted in accordance with the Copyright, Designs and Patents Act 1988.

First edition published by Penguin Books Ltd 1984
This revised edition first published 1995, by arrangement with Penguin Books Ltd
Reprinted 1997

Blackwell Publishers Ltd
108 Cowley Road
Oxford OX4 1JF, UK

Blackwell Publishers Inc
350 Main Street
Malden, Massachusetts 02148, USA

British Library Cataloguing in Publication Data
A CIP catalogue record for this book is available from the British Library

Library of Congress Cataloging in Publication Data
A New dictionary of religions/edited by John R. Hinnells.
    p.   cm.
Includes bibliographical references and index.
    ISBN 0–631–18139–3 (alk. paper)
1. Religions—Dictionaries. I. Hinnells, John R.
BL31.P48   1995   94–10302
200'.3—dc20   CIP

Typeset in 9.5 on 10pt Plantin
by Wearset, Boldon, Tyne & Wear
Printed and bound in Great Britain
by Hartnolls Ltd, Bodmin, Cornwall

This book is printed on acid-free paper

This book is dedicated to
Marianne, Mark and Duncan,
a much-loved family

Contents

Acknowledgements

My profound thanks go to the many people who have helped in the preparation of this *New Dictionary*. All contributors have been cooperative. Special thanks are again due to the bibliographer, Miss Nora Firby, not only for the exemplary care and characteristic thoroughness with which she has edited the bibliography, making it a major contribution to the book, but also for her considerable assistance with the index.

In the planning of the first edition invaluable advice was given by Lance Cousins and Trevor Ling, my erstwhile colleagues at Manchester; Richard Gordon, formerly of the University of East Anglia; John Clark of the University of Manchester; Jean Holm, formerly of Homerton College, Cambridge; Professor Geoffrey Parrinder, Emeritus Professor of the Comparative Study of Religion at London University; Professor Ninian Smart of the University of California; Professor Cyril Williams of the University of Wales at Lampeter; and Peter Woodward, former Inspector for Religious Education in Birmingham. Thanks are also due to the publishers for the honour as well as the stimulating challenge of being asked to think in terms of such a broad geographical and temporal canvas, and especially to Michael Dover, formerly of Penguin Books, who originally comissioned me.

For giving me the chance to bring out this *New Dictionary*, I would also like to record my thanks to Alyn Shipton of Blackwell and Ravi Mirchandani of Penguin Books, both of whom have become friends, not simply colleagues. Sincere thanks are due also to Gillian Bromley for her immense care, meticulous work and good will in dealing with such a complicated manuscript.

Above all, thanks are due in inexpressible measure to my family, Marianne, Mark and Duncan. Without their help, support, understanding and encouragement this task could not have been contemplated, much less completed. To them, this *New Dictionary* is dedicated as a token of thanks, and love.

J.R.H.

Introduction

This *New Dictionary of Religions* has grown out of the *Penguin Dictionary of Religions*, first published in 1984. It has, however, undergone such substantial change and expansion that it is properly called *A New Dictionary*. The original list of twenty-nine contributors has grown to sixty-five (from twelve countries around the globe). Completely new sections have been added, notably on Afro-Caribbean religious movements, modern North American developments, traditional religions in Latin America and Japanese New Religious Movements. An important additional theme is religions in migration (e.g. Hinduism in the Caribbean, in Africa, Britain and America, Islam in Europe, America and elsewhere, and various Sikh groups) and entries on groups found mainly in their respective diaspora such as Deobandi, Barelvi. Some major subjects have undergone large-scale change (especially Hinduism, Buddhism, and Eastern and early Christianity), others have been completely rewritten (Study of Religion, Jains, New Religious Movements in the West, Gnostics, Manichaeans, Mandaeans). Entirely new subjects have been introduced (Ahl-i Haqq, Implicit Religion, Yezidism, Zoroastrian Pseudepigrapha). Most entries have been updated in content and bibliography in order to take account of recent advances in scholarship and modern developments within the religions (for example in the New Religious Movements). Where existing sections have been expanded the new emphasis is mostly (though not wholly) on modern developments and practices (for example, new entries have been added on Jewish and Sikh practices, Hindu festivals and rites, and religious pluralism).

Essentially the task of a dictionary is to define terms, but sometimes it is convenient to group together explanations under an umbrella article and in some instances it was decided that the most effective 'umbrellas' are geographical entries (e.g. Islam in America or Africa, Christianity in Korea). This is particularly the case with the indigenous traditions of Latin America, where it was judged that the most effective way of handling such a mass of material from such a large continent was to have broad religious categories and entries on individual regions and their place within those broad categories (see the appropriate contents list). In the case of Christianity there has been 'positive discrimination' in favour of those aspects of the religion not well represented in many general publications, specifically Eastern Christianity, its spirituality and practices. A number of additional entries have been added to cover the terminology associated with cross-cultural issues, for example on gender, mysticism, pilgrimage, 'near-death experiences' and sexuality. In a number of areas (for example Hinduism) greater attention has been paid to terms concerned with religious iconography. Pieces have also been added on some of the scholarly approaches to the study of religion and their vocabulary (e.g. Psychology/Philosophy/Sociology/ Phenomenology of Religion).

There are two ways of defining terms: in very short accounts of individual terms or in longer entries which subsume various terms in a flowing text. This second alternative has been used rather more here than in the first edition with the addition of some comparatively long pieces (e.g. on the Study of Religion, Gender, Mysticism), both in order to make the *New Dictionary* enjoyable to read and because it is often the case that one term is best explained in conjunction with another and the longer entries facilitated this.

The allocation of wordage merits comment. On some subjects (notably Western Christianity) much published material is easily available and in such instances there is a greater proportion of shorter articles. Where little is known or available (as for example on the Hindu calendar) then a longer entry has been produced. The total wordage allocated to a religion is not, therefore, indicated by the number of articles on that religion, nor is the wordage necessarily indicative of the importance attached to a subject. Obviously the number of bibliographical entries is proportionately greater for the short entries on well-documented subjects. Although there are entries on some people (it would be odd to omit Jesus or Muhammad!) names have not generally figured as headwords because a reference work of biographies has been published in my *Who's Who of Religions* (Macmillan, 1991; Penguin, 1996). Although the bulk of the space has been allocated to the religions which spread around the world the term 'religion' has been interpreted broadly to include what have been described as the 'secular alternatives' of Marxism and Humanism, as well as astrology. In view of the growing interest in the occult, but the lack of reliable material on it, it was thought important to allocate a reasonable amount of space to that area here.

The team of sixty-five scholars come not only from different continents, from Latin America to Japan, Europe, the United States and Australasia, but also from a variety of academic disciplines – as historians, orientalists, classicists, archaeologists, sociologists, anthropologists, linguists, art historians, philosophers, theologians – reflecting the many aspects of the study of religions. Care has been taken both to make use of their respective specialist interests and yet to provide a reasonably consistent approach to the individual religions. Obviously, different emphases are necessary in handling subjects as different as, for example, the archaeological sources of ancient religions in Egypt and the contemporary evidence for New Religious Movements in the West. Nevertheless, it is important for the reader to have confidence that the *Dictionary* reflects a well-balanced approach to the subject as a whole and also to the specific religions. Authors were, therefore, provided with a matrix of thirty topics, including beliefs and practices, people and places, texts and arts, society and institutions, on which to model their material. The Editor wishes to express publicly his sincere thanks for the way all authors cooperated effectively in this important but difficult task.

The explanation of terms occupies the core of the *Dictionary*, but there are two extremely important additional sections to the book: the bibliography and the index. For the specialist moving outside his or her own field, and for the interested reader who wishes to pursue a particular topic in greater depth or breadth than a dictionary entry can provide, the extensive bibliography offers an invaluable guide to a wide network of information. The notation system which is used (see 'Using the Dictionary' below) permits reference either to books on quite specific details inside the entry or to general works relating to the overall theme of the piece. The intention is to enhance the value of the *Dictionary* as a scholarly aid, without detracting in any way from the broad interest of the text. Market research on the first edition suggested that readers particularly appreciated the bibliography. In the *New Dictionary* there are not only additions to reflect the latest scholarship but also some references to books in languages other than English and in a few cases to outstanding articles in 'mainline' journals for the specialist while retaining the majority of references for the general reader.

It is often difficult to define precise boundaries around subjects, as it is around religions. This problem looms particularly large in this book in respect of the bibliography (e.g. in the distinction between the categories on 'The Study of Religions' and 'Cross-cultural Studies') and index. The solution adopted has been to make copious use of the direction 'see also'.

An index may at first sight appear superfluous in a dictionary. It is, however, essential here if the reader is to be given reasonable access to the many thousands of terms explained within the 1,400 entries. In an entry of 200–300 words on one technical term, e.g. Confucius or Yoga, a number of important words will be explained. This is inevitable inasmuch as one word commonly needs explanation in terms of, or alongside, another. The 'headword' of an entry, therefore, often functions as an umbrella term below which a variety of terms are elucidated. This is, of course, particularly so when groups of terms are explained under general headings (e.g. in regional entries). The index provides a guide to these numerous explanations.

The index has an additional purpose. The headwords are usually technical terms from the religions concerned and not the common English word. For example, the Sikh doctrine of God appears under **Akal Purakh**, not under 'God (Sikh doctrine of)'. There are two reasons for this. First, the alternative would have meant that such general headings as 'God' or 'Ritual' would have required up to thirty versions of them relating to the different subjects encompassed in the *Dictionary*. Second, the use of such general English terms would have entailed the imposition of a Western conceptualization on the material and could therefore have distorted non-Western concepts. Sometimes authors have considered this not a danger but an aid, especially where a range of religions is subsumed under one heading, for instance the Ancient Near East, when no one technical term from a single appropriate religion exists. Given that it is generally desirable to have technical words as headwords, it was thought necessary to guide the reader who wanted to know what a particular religion taught on a subject when he or she did not know what the appropriate technical term was. The index, therefore, includes English terms in order that the reader may find the idea sought. In the Sikh example, **Akal Purakh** is the headword, but this is also referenced in the index under 'God'. It is thus possible to look up themes in the various religions without knowing in advance all the technical terms.

Considerable thought was given to the possible inclusion of a guide to pronunciation. In view of the many variations in the pronunciation of major languages this was eventually excluded, with reluctance, as highly desirable but impracticable.

Diacritical marks, which have not been used in the main body of the text, are included in the index for the interested reader.

Because of the religious assumptions underlying the abbreviations 'BC' and 'AD' ('Before Christ' and 'Anno Domini', which assume acceptance of Jesus as Messiah or Lord), these are unacceptable to many religious people who belong to other religions. In this *Dictionary* the alternative abbreviations BCE (Before [the] Christian Era) and CE (Christian Era) are used throughout. These make no assumption about a person's religious position. For readers not familiar with this usage it may be said that AD 1995 refers to the same year as 1995 CE: the date is constant, only the nomenclature changes. Similarly, the term 'Hebrew Bible' is used rather than 'Old Testament' because the latter is a specifically Christian term, implying as it does that there is a New Testament. From a traditional Jewish perspective it is not the *Old* Testament but the living Bible. 'Hebrew Bible' is a religiously neutral term for it does not indicate 'ownership' but refers simply to the language in which almost all of it is written.

As the world approaches the third millennium travel and communication are bringing its peoples closer together so that there is increasing contact between people and cultures. The growing interest in the study of religions is producing an expanding market for books on 'other' religions. With the growth of this literature, and the contact of people, so there is a commensurate need to understand the specialized vocabulary used by those who practise the religions and by those who write about them. One rather generous reviewer in a religious newspaper described the first edition as a 'godsend'! Although I appreciate such a compliment, I hope that this *New Dictionary* will be found of even more use than the first.

JOHN R. HINNELLS

Using the Dictionary

The Bibliography

Each subject area listed on pages xvi–xxxvii below has a separate bibliography. These are numbered from I to XXXVI. The number of the relevant bibliography is indicated in square brackets immediately after the headword in each entry. All the bibliographies are in alphabetical order with the books numbered in arabic figures. In the entries bibliographical references are in square brackets. The first arabic figure indicates the number of the book and a subsequent roman numeral indicates a chapter in that book, whereas a subsequent arabic figure refers to a page number. For example, [10: v] refers to chapter v of book number 10, whereas [10: 5] refers to page 5 of that book. In the rare cases where one author refers to a book in a bibliography other than his or her own, the relevant bibliography, in roman numerals, precedes each and every reference. In a limited number of cases the same book appears in more than one author's bibliography. Such double listings have been allowed to stand, because the text references are to different paginations in different editions.

The Index

To find where the meaning of a technical term is explained, and what the technical term for, and details of, a concept are in a given religion, consult the index. Important terms that cannot be located in the body of the *New Dictionary* under one spelling may be traced in the index under the variant spellings (for example, 'Koran *see* Qur'an', or 'Hasidism *see* Chasidism'), and roughly equivalent terms may be similarly traced (for example, 'Brotoi *see* Thnetoi Anthropoi').

To find all the terms covered by the *New Dictionary* on a specific religion, consult the 'List of Contents by Subject Area and Author' (pp. xvi–xxxvii below).

Variant Spellings

In a number of religions technical words appear in more than one language (e.g. in Zoroastrianism in both Avestan and Pahlavi, in Buddhism in Sanskrit, Pali and other languages, in Latin and Greek for some Classical Greek and Roman terms). The practice in the *New Dictionary* is to use the language which the author considers most appropriate in any given context. Cross-references are given in the index.

Abbreviations Used in the Text

b.	born	f (ff)	following page(s)
BCE	before Christian era	*fl.*	*floruit*
c.	*circa*	pl.	plate(s)
CE	Christian era	r.	reigned, ruled
d.	died	*s.v.*	*sub voce, sub verbo*

Cross-references are shown by printing the appropriate headword in SMALL CAPITAL LETTERS, with a large capital indicating the letter under which the entry will be found in the alphabetical sequence.

List of Contents by Subject Area and Author

Note: The roman numeral in square brackets after each heading refers to the corresponding section of the bibliography (see pp. 577–676)

African Religions [II]
Professor Adrian Hastings, University of Leeds

(*See also under* NEW RELIGIOUS MOVEMENTS IN PRIMAL SOCIETIES)

Afro-Caribbean Religions [III]
Kathy Williams, formerly University of Warwick

American Religions [IV]
Professor Martin E. Marty, University of Chicago

Amerindian Religions [V]
Dr Stephen J. Reno, Southern Oregon State College

Ancient Egyptian Religions [VI]
Dr A. Rosalie David, Manchester Museum

Ancient European Religions [VII]
Dr Hilda Ellis Davidson, formerly Lucy Cavendish College, Cambridge

Ancient Near Eastern Religions [VIII]
Dr A. Rosalie David, Manchester Museum

AFTERLIFE (ANCIENT NEAR EASTERN)
ANCIENT NEAR EASTERN RELIGIONS
ART AND SYMBOLISM (ANCIENT NEAR EASTERN)
ASSYRIANS
ASTROLOGY (ANCIENT NEAR EASTERN)
BA'AL
BABYLONIANS

COSMOLOGY (ANCIENT NEAR EASTERN)
DIVINATION (ANCIENT NEAR EASTERN)
ELAMITES
EVIL (ANCIENT NEAR EAST)
FESTIVALS (ANCIENT NEAR EASTERN)
GILGAMESH, EPIC OF
HAMMURABI'S CODE

HITTITES
HURRIANS
KINGSHIP (ANCIENT NEAR EAST)
MAGIC (ANCIENT NEAR EASTERN)
MARDUK
PHILISTINES
PHOENICIANS
SUMERIANS
TEMPLES (ANCIENT NEAR EASTERN)
ZIGGURAT

Arctic Peoples' Religions [IX]
Eric H. Pyle, formerly University of Queensland, Brisbane

LAPPS

(*See also* ALASKAN ORTHODOX *under* CHRISTIANITY, EASTERN; ESKIMO–ALEUT *under* AMERINDIAN RELIGIONS; SHAMAN *under* CROSS-CULTURAL STUDIES)

Astrology [X]
Professor Roger Beck, Erindale College, University of Toronto

ASTROLOGY

HOROSCOPE

STAR-WORSHIP (ASTROLATRY, SABAISM)

(*See also* ASTROLOGY *under* ANCIENT EGYPTIAN RELIGIONS; ANCIENT NEAR EASTERN RELIGIONS; HINDUISM)

Buddhism [XI]
L. S. Cousins (LC), formerly Victoria University of Manchester
Dr Rupert Gethin (RG), University of Bristol
The late Professor Trevor Ling (TL), formerly University of Singapore
Dr Valerie J. Roebuck (VR), Victoria University of Manchester
Dr Paul Williams (PW), University of Bristol

ABHIDHAMMA (LC)
ALAYA-VIJNANA (LC)

AMITABHA (PW)
ANAGAMI (TL)

ANAGARIKA (TL)
ANANDA (TL)

(*See also under* CHINESE, JAPANESE, TIBETAN RELIGIONS)

Chinese Religions [XII]
Dr Stewart McFarlane, University of Lancaster

Chinese Religions

Chinese Buddhism

(*See also* CHINA *under* CHRISTIANITY, ISLAM)

Christianity [XIII]
A.   Bible and Early Church

The late Professor Fred Bruce (FB), formerly Manchester
University, revised by
Dr George J. Brooke (GB), Victoria University of Manchester
Keith Munnings (KM)
Dr Henry D. Rack (HR), Victoria University of Manchester

B.   History and Doctrine

The late Professor Fred Bruce (FB), formerly Manchester
University
Dr Ben Pink Dandelion (BD), Society of Friends, London
Professor D. P. Davies (DD), University of Wales, Lampeter
David J. Melling (DM), formerly Manchester Metropolitan
University
Dr Henry D. Rack (HR), Victoria University of Manchester

C.   Philosophy and Theology

David J. Melling (DM), formerly Manchester Metropolitan
University
Professor David A. Pailin (DP), Victoria University of
Manchester

D.   Eastern Christianity

Dimitri Brady (DB), Manchester Metropolitan University
David J. Melling (DM), formerly Manchester Metropolitan
University
Dr Andrew Palmer (AP), School of Oriental and African
Studies, London University

Cross-Cultural Studies [XIV]

Professor Paul Badham (PB), University of Wales, Lampeter
Professor Ursula King (UK), University of Bristol
Dr Oliver Davies (OD), University of Wales, Lampeter
Professor John R. Hinnells (JH), School of Oriental and
African Studies, London University
Dr Keith Howard, School of Oriental and African Studies,
London University
Professor Martin E. Marty (MM), University of Chicago
David J. Melling (DM), formerly Manchester Metropolitan
University

Gnostics [XV]

Dr Erica C. D. Hunter (EH), University of Cambridge
Dr Samuel N. C. Lieu (SL), University of Warwick
Professor A. Van Tongerloo (AV), Catholic University of
Louvain

Greek Religion [XVI]

Dr Christiane Sourvinou-Inwood, University College, Oxford

ORPHEUS, ORPHISM   RITES (GREEK)   THEOI
PHILOSOPHIA   TEMENOS   THNETOI ANTHROPOI
POLITIKE

Hinduism [XVII]

L. S. Cousins (LC), formerly Victoria University of
Manchester
Dr Mark Juergensmeyer (MJ), University of California, Santa
Barbara
Dr Kim Knott (KK), University of Leeds
The late Professor Trevor Ling (TL), formerly University of
Singapore
Dr Valerie J. Roebuck (VR), Victoria University of Manchester
Simon Weightman (SW), School of Oriental and African
Studies, London University

SAMSKARA (SW)
SANT MAT (MJ)
SARASVATI (VR)
SATI (TL/VR)
SATSANG (MJ)
SHAKTI (VR)
SHANKARA (LC)
SHIVA (VR)
SHRUTI (TL/VR)
SOUTH-EAST ASIA,
    HINDUISM IN (TL)

SURAT SABD YOGA
    (MJ)
TANTRA (1) (VR)
TAPAS (TL/VR)
TIRTHA-YATRA (SW)
TRIMURTI (VR)
UPANISHADS (VR)
VAHANAS (VR)
VAISHESHIKA (LC)
VAISHNAVA VEDANTA
    (LC)

VARNA (TL/VR)
VEDA (VR)
VEDANTA (LC)
VISHNU (VR)
VRATA (TL)
WEST, HINDUISM IN
    THE (KK)
YOGA (LC)
YOGA-DARSHANA
    (LC)

Iranian Religion (Non-Zoroastrian) [XVIII]
Professor Roger Beck (RB), Erindale College, University of
Toronto
Professor John R. Hinnells (JH), School of Oriental and
African Studies, London University
Dr P. Kreyenbroek (PK), School of Oriental and African
Studies, London University

AHL-I HAQQ (PK)
MITHRAISM (JH)
YEZIDISM (PK)

ZOROASTRIAN
PSEUDEPIGRAPHA
    (RB)

Islam [XIX]
Professor Edmund Bosworth (EB), Victoria University of
Manchester
Dr Louis Brenner (LB), School of Oriental and African
Studies, London University
Dr Jorgen S. Nielsen (JN), Selly Oak Colleges, Birmingham
Professor A. Rippin (AR), University of Calgary
Elizabeth Scantlebury (ES), Liverpool Institute of Higher
Education
Professor James Thrower (JT), University of Aberdeen

ABRAHAM (IN ISLAM)
    (EB)
AFRICA, ISLAM IN
    (LB)
AHL-I-HADITH (ES)
AHMADIS (EB)
AKHIRA (EB)
AKHLAQ (EB)
AL-AZHAR (EB)
ALI, ʿALIDS (EB)
ALLAH (EB)

AMERICAS, ISLAM IN
    THE (AR)
ANTI-CHRIST (IN
    ISLAM) (EB)
AQ'IDA (EB)
ART (IN ISLAM) (EB)
AYATULLAH (EB)
BABIS (EB)
BAHAʿIS (EB)
BARELVI (ES)

BISMILLAH, BASMALA
    (EB)
CALENDAR (IN
    ISLAM) (EB)
CALIPH/CALIPHATE
    (EB)
CENTRAL ASIA AND
    KAZAKHSTAN,
    ISLAM IN (JT)
CHINA, ISLAM IN (EB)

Jainism [XX]
Dr Paul Dundas, University of Edinburgh

Japanese Religions [XXI]
Professor J. Edward Kidder, International Christian University, Tokyo

The following division of entries between Shinto and Japanese Buddhism is made to help readers, especially those wanting to study all the material on Buddhism. It must be stressed, however, that the separation of the religions is at some points artificial.

Shinto

Buddhism in Japan

Christianity in Japan

Folk Religion

(*See also under* NEW RELIGIOUS MOVEMENTS IN JAPAN)

Judaism [XXII]
Dr George J. Brooke (GB), Victoria University of Manchester
Dr Alan Unterman (AU), Victoria University of Manchester

Latin American Religion [XXIII]
Professor Robin M. Wright, Universidade Estuadal de
Campinas, Brazil

Magic and the Occult [XXIV]
The late Professor Fred Bruce (FB), formerly Manchester
University
Grevel Lindop (GL), Victoria University of Manchester
Keith Munnings (KM)

(*See also* VOODOO *in* AFRO-CARIBBEAN RELIGIONS; *and under* ANCIENT
EGYPTIAN RELIGIONS, ANCIENT NEAR EASTERN RELIGIONS)

Mesoamerican Religions [XXV]
Professor David Carrasco, Princeton University

New Religious Movements in Japan [XXVI]
Professor David Reid, Seigakuin University, Tokyo

New Religious Movements in Primal Societies [XXVII]
Professor Harold W. Turner, formerly Selly Oak Colleges, Birmingham

(*See also under* AFRICAN, AMERINDIAN *and* PACIFIC RELIGIONS)

New Religious Movements in Western Societies [XXVIII]
Professor Eileen Barker, London School of Economics and Political Science

Pacific Religions [XXIX]
Professor Brian E. Colless and Professor Peter Donovan, Massey University, New Zealand

Australian Religion

Melanesian Religion

Polynesian Religion

(*See also under* NEW RELIGIOUS MOVEMENTS IN PRIMAL SOCIETIES)

Prehistoric Religion [XXX]
Eric H. Pyle, formerly University of Queensland, Brisbane

Roman Religions [XXXI]
Professor John A. North, University College London

(*See also* MITHRAISM *under* IRANIAN RELIGION)

Secular Alternatives to Religion [XXXII]
Professor Stuart Brown, The Open University

Sikhism [XXXIII]
Professor Hew McLeod, University of Otago, New Zealand

Study of Religion [XXXIV]

Professor P. Antes (PA), University of Hanover
Revd Dr Edward Bailey (EB1), Network for the Study of
Implicit Religion
Professor Eileen Barker (EB2), London School of Economics
and Political Science
Professor Stuart Brown (SB), The Open University
Professor A. Dyson (AD), Victoria University of Manchester
Dr Gavin Flood (GF), University of Wales, Lampeter
Revd Professor Leslie J. Francis (LF), Trinity College,
Carmarthen, and University of Wales, Lampeter
Jean Holm (JH), formerly Homerton College, Cambridge
David J. Melling (DM), formerly Manchester Metropolitan
University
Eric Pyle (EP), formerly University of Queensland, Brisbane
Professor Ninian Smart (NS), University of California, Santa
Barbara
Dr Terence Thomas (TT), The Open University (in Wales)

ANCESTOR WORSHIP (EP)
ANIMISM (EP)
ATHEISM (EP)
CHTHONIAN RELIGION (EP)
DANCE (EP)
DEMON (EP)
DUALISM (EP)
ELIADE, MIRCEA (GF)
ENCOUNTER OF RELIGIONS (TT)
ENLIGHTENMENT, THE (TT)
EVOLUTIONISM (TT)
FOLKLORE (EP)
FUNCTIONALISM (EP)
HENOTHEISM (EP)
HISTORY OF RELIGIONS (PA)
IMPLICIT RELIGION (EB1)

LITERALISM (EP)
MONISM (EP)
MONOTHEISM (EP)
MYSTERY-CULT (EP)
NATURAL RELIGION (EP)
ORIGIN OF RELIGION (EP)
PANTHEISM (EP)
PHENOMENOLOGY OF RELIGION (PA)
PHILOSOPHY OF RELIGION (SB)
PILGRIMAGE (DM)
POLYTHEISM (EP)
POPULAR RELIGION (TT)
PSYCHOLOGY OF RELIGION (LF)
RELIGION (PA/TT)
RELIGIONSWISSEN-SCHAFT (PA)

RELIGIOUS EDUCATION IN SCHOOLS (JH)
RELIGIOUS STUDIES IN HIGHER EDUCATION (NS)
RITES OF PASSAGE (TT)
SACRIFICE (TT)
SALVATION (TT)
SECULARIZATION (AD)
SOCIOLOGY OF RELIGION (EB2)
SPIRIT (EP)
STRUCTURALISM (EP)
STUDY OF RELIGION (TT)
SYMBOL (TT)
SYNCRETISM (TT)
THEISM (EP)
TOTEM (EP)
TYPOLOGY (EP)

(*See also under* CROSS-CULTURAL STUDIES)

Tibetan Religion [XXXV]

Dr David Stott (DS), Manchester Metropolitan University
Dr Paul Williams (PW), University of Bristol

BARDO (DS)
BON (DS)
CHÖD (DS)
DALAI LAMA (PW)
GELUG (DS)
GESAR (DS)
JONANG (DS)
KADAM (DS)
KAGYU (DS)
KANJUR (DS)

LAM RIM (PW)
LHA–DRE (DS)
MANDALA
   (BUDDHIST) (PW)
MILAREPA (PW)
NYINGMA (DS)
RIMÉ (DS)
SAKYA (DS)
SHAMBALA (DS)

TANTRA (2) (DS)
TARA (PW)
TERMA (PW)
TIBETAN ASTROLOGY
   (DS)
TIBETAN RELIGIONS
   (DS)
TULKU (PW)
TUN-HUANG (DS)

Zoroastrianism [XXXVI]

Professor John R. Hinnells, School of Oriental and African
Studies, London University

AHURA MAZDA
AMESHA SPENTAS
ANGRA MAINYU
AVESTA
BUNDAHISHN
CHINVAT BRIDGE
DAXMA
FIRE (ZOROASTRIAN)
FRASHOKERETI
FRAVASHI

GAHAMBARS
INDO-EUROPEANS
MAGI
MANTHRAS
NAUJOTE
PAHLAVI
PARSI RELIGIOUS
   REFORMS
PARSIS

SHAH
SHAHNAME
TRIPARTITE
   IDEOLOGY
YASNA
YAZATA
ZOROASTER
ZOROASTRIANISM
ZURVAN

(*See also* MITHRAISM *under* IRANIAN RELIGIONS)

A

Abhidhamma [XI] The content of the third part of the Buddhist scriptures (TIPITAKA). *Abhidhamma* (Sanskrit *abhidharma*) probably arose as a non-sectarian movement in the 4th and 3rd centuries BCE, developing the earlier SUTTANTA approach, but with the formation of sects differing schools arose. Two distinct versions survive; others probably existed. For the north Indian *abhidharma* of the SARVASTI VADINS, *see* VAIBHASHIKA. In the south the THERAVADA preserved a canonical *abhidhamma-pitaka* attributed to the BUDDHA himself in the PALI language. The earlier works set out a description of mental processes and their interactions with the physical and the transcendent (LOKUTTARA) by giving elaborate accounts of specific events. These were seen as short-lived minds (*cittas*) related to specific sense objects and accompanied by a number of structures composed of basic mental elements (*dhammas*; cf. DHAMMA). These minds are viewed as constantly changing in level, object and content in a sequential stream. The aim of this *abhidhamma* analysis is not really theoretical; it is related to insight (VIPASSANA) meditation and offers a world-view based upon process in order to facilitate insight into change (ANICCA) and no-self (ANATTA) so as to undermine mental rigidity.

By the early centuries CE the chief centre of activity had moved from India to Ceylon. An elaborate system was worked out, specifying many details which had initially been left undecided. This was summarized by BUDDHAGHOSA (*c*.430 CE) in his *Visuddhimagga* and *abhidhamma* commentaries and at about the same time by Buddhadatta. A series of subcommentaries followed, notably those of Ananda (perhaps 6th century) and DHAMMAPALA, but the standard introduction was written later by Anuruddha (probably 11th century) [2]. Pali commentaries on *abhidhamma* have continued to be written down to the present century, especially in Burma.

Abraham (in Islam) [XIX] Abraham or Ibrahim, called the 'Friend of God', is the most important and, with MOSES, the most frequently mentioned of the former prophets in the QUR'AN. He is regarded as the rebuilder of the Ka'ba in Mecca (HARAMAIN), after its destruction by the Flood, and as the propagator of the original pure monotheism, the 'religion of Abraham', later restored and perfected by the Prophet MUHAMMAD (*see* HANIF). [20 s. v.; 38 'Ibrāhīm'; 137 index]

Acaranga [XX] The first of the 12 SHVETAMBARA JAIN scriptural texts known as 'limbs' (*anga*). The Acaranga consists of two parts, the second of which was accepted by the tradition as unquestionably later in date but which nonetheless remains of great significance because of the biography of the TIRTHANKARA MAHAVIRA it contains. The first part of the Acaranga is a composite work of nine chapters, with only the name of the seventh surviving. Dating in part from the 4th century BCE and perhaps even earlier, it provides important evidence for nascent Jain views on doctrine and practice, often somewhat different from what was to be their classical formulation, as well as a famous description of Mahavira's austerities prior to his enlightenment. [7: 1–213]

Adi Granth [xxxiii] The principal SIKH scripture, known by a variety of names. Originally called the *Granth Sahib*, or 'Revered Book', it became the *Guru Granth Sahib* after the line of personal GURUS terminated in 1708. It is also known as the *Adi Granth*, or 'First Book', a title which distinguishes it from the later DASAM GRANTH [8: III]. The volume was compiled in 1603–4 by Arjan, the fifth Guru. In it he included his own works and those of his four predecessors, together with a selection from earlier representatives of the SANT TRADITION such as Kabir (*see* BHAGAT BANI). Three recensions exist. The printed text used today represents the third of these, a slightly expanded version of Guru Arjan's original compilation incorporating compositions by the ninth Guru [26: 60–3, 73–9]. Although a substantial collection, the scripture communicates a consistent message of spiritual liberation (SACH-KHAND) through belief in the divine Name (*nam*). There is also a general consistency in terms of language. The Gurus, like their Sant predecessors, used a simplified form of early Hindi known as *Sant Bhasha* (*see* SIKH LANGUAGES). Guru Arjan had as a substantial source the Goindval *pothis* (or Mohan *pothis*), a collection of four manuscript volumes compiled on the instructions of the third Guru, Amar Das. Arjan produced the Kartarpur version which reached its final form when the works of the ninth Guru, Tegh Bahadur, were added. The entire volume was recorded in Gurmukhi, the script used for modern Punjabi. Consistency is also a feature of the volume's organization, its contents being carefully arranged according to metre, form and author [25: 286–8]. The hymns which comprise its contents are known as *bani* or *gurbani*, 'utterances of the GURU'. Sikh doctrine recognizes only one Guru, successively incarnated in ten individuals. When the personal line ended the functions of the Guru passed to the community (the PANTH) and to the scripture (the *Granth*). The scripture thus came to be regarded as the physical embodiment of the eternal Guru and as such is treated with impressive reverence. [9: 91–105; 28: 82–9; 31: IV]

Advaita Vedanta [xvii] The best-known school of VEDANTA, one of the classical Indian DARSHANAS (salvation-philosophies). The earliest extant writer is Gaudapada (perhaps 7th century CE), but SHANKARA is the principal ancient authority. 'Advaita' means 'non-dual' and the system of Shankara is a near monism, holding that there is in the last analysis only one reality: BRAHMAN – the divine power. Knowledge of *brahman* is devoid of any multiplicity or duality; such knowledge leads to liberation (MOKSHA). It is reached by contemplation on the received teachings of the Vedanta, ritual and devotion being merely auxiliary. There is a marked convergence with MADHYAMIKA Buddhism, which strongly influenced the early Advaita [47 vol. 16: 222ff]. The Advaita Vedanta is probably the most influential of all schools of Hindu thought, with a long tradition of writers and authorities. The 20th century has seen its revival in a modernized dress, with some success outside India through the work of the Ramakrishna Mission, such Vedanta-influenced writers as Aldous Huxley and Christopher Isherwood and, more recently, the Maharishi Mahesh Yogi (*see* TRANSCENDENTAL MEDITATION) [36: I, 406–94; 103: 207–28; 105: 28–38]

Advaitin Cosmology [xvii] By the medieval period in India the

ADVAITA VEDANTA had developed an organized 'cosmology', largely based upon combining the earlier VEDANTA tradition with the closely related SAMKHYA world-view. What was held to be an inferior or conventional understanding was distinguished from the salvific knowledge of ultimate reality (a distinction deriving from SHANKARA and ultimately from Buddhism). From the standpoint of this lower knowledge the world is hierarchic and emanationary, with gross, subtle and causal levels. The gross body experiences the gross world in the waking state through the senses; the subtle body experiences subtle images and forms through the mind, especially in the dream state (and in visionary experience); while the causal body experiences a more unified consciousness, especially in dreamless sleep (and in yogic experience – see YOGA). Underlying this account is an acceptance of the principle of correspondences between psychological states and the universe at large: the gross world emanates from a subtle world, the subtle from the causal; both the universe and the individual vary between a state in which the three worlds are emanated and one in which the gross and subtle are withdrawn into the unified causal realm.

BRAHMAN is in each of these realms both separately and in their totality, appearing on each level both as individual souls and as a collective soul or deity. From the conventional standpoint *brahman* is the creator (ISHVARA) or personal deity with positive attributes (*saguna*). Motivated by LILA he creates the cosmos through the power of MAYA (2). Nevertheless, from the ultimate point of view true reality is without differentiating attributes (*nirguna*); the appearance of separation is the result of ignorance (*avidya*), i.e. illusion on the individual level.

Adventism [IV] The Adventist movement in America, which took firm shape in the Seventh-day Adventist denomination, had two starts, one under William Miller and a second under Ellen Gould White. In the midst of movements expecting the imminent end of the world, Miller, an independent Bible student, proclaimed his deduction that all signs pointed to such an end in 1843, or at least by 22 October 1844. His followers abandoned their ways of life and in many cases their possessions and joined him in awaiting it, but suffered what Millerites called The Great Disappointment. In a second generation, however, people of Adventist faith reinterpreted the events of 1843–4 and claimed that something had happened, but had occurred in the invisible realm where the resurrected JESUS lived with his Father. So Adventists regathered. They continued to expect Jesus to come soon again, but did not set a date. Those were years of great religious experiment in America, and Adventists promulgated vegetarian and other health-supportive measures. In this climate Ellen Gould White began to record her visions, and became the effectual head of the church, organized in 1860. Adventists established publishing ventures, sanitaria and the hospitals for which they have remained known ever since. Adventists have been aggressive missionaries for causes of physical health, propagators of belief in the second coming of Christ and successful missionaries of their gospel. While they had only 733,026 adherents in the USA in 1993, their worldwide movement approaches 5 million Adventists. [19: 130–6; 21]

Aeon [xv] (from Greek *aiôn*) The Aeon-concept [28] is situated in ZOROASTRIAN speculations on the 'limitless time', the eternity (*zurvan akarana*) as opposed to a limited time period or cycle, referring to the divine and the created respectively. Under Iranian influences perhaps, a similar distinction is attested in the opposition between Aeon and *chronos* in Plato's *Timaeus*. In Hellenistic times, the concept of ZURVAN as the expression of the eternal God was exported westward [23] to Egypt through Syria, and finally to Rome and Constantinople where Aeon became identified with the ancient city gods as the founder and protective deity of the town (in order to secure the idea of the 'eternal city'). In this aspect the cult of Aeon in ALEXANDRIA influenced the concept of Christian Epiphany. A mutual influence between JUDAISM and Hellenism is found in the Aeon concept of the SEPTUAGINT. As a major deity in the cult of Mithras (*see* MITHRAISM) Zurvan–Aeon entered for a second time the Hellenistic-Roman world. The Gnostic concept of Aeon focuses on its personalized nature, in which the Aeon as entity or collectivity belonging to the higher world is mediator between the divine and this world, and it therefore plays a substantial role in descriptions of the ascension of the soul (*see* GNOSIS, GNOSTICISM) [14]. Christian Gnostics unsuccessfully tried to introduce their teachings on a personalized Aeon, but these were refuted by Irenaeus and Tertullian. Nevertheless, the New Testament definition of Aeon based upon the Septuagint is partially rooted in Iranian premises, as it is a world era between creation and last judgement, or this actual (transitory) era, in opposition with the future era (namely the Kingdom of God); cf. PAUL. Both eras are interrelated, as the Christian believer is already participating in the future era which works in this era as a pneumatic reality.

Aesir [VII] The Aesir (cf. *'Ansis'* of the Goths) [32: 190] are the main gods of Norse mythology, excluding Freyr, Njord and other VANIR deities. ODIN, the All-Father, THOR, LOKI, Heimdall [3: 172–6] and BALDER, together with an unspecified number of lesser gods, dwelt at Asgard, a stronghold of the gods [3:

VII] built with the help of a giant who was afterwards cheated out of his payment [3a: 72–3]. There are references to a war with the VANIR, ending in a truce [3a: 71–2], but a threat remained from the FROST-GIANTS, and Heimdall was on constant watch against attack, while THOR kept his hammer ready. In the Poetic EDDA [21: 1–13] the Aesir are described as builders and craftsmen, playing board games, establishing law, meeting at their Assembly (the 'Thing') and creating mankind, but they are doomed to perish at RAGNAROK. The idea of a group of divine powers must be old, and other words used for them are *regin*, *hopt* and *tivar*, but the picture of local deities dwelling together in Asgard is presumably a late development by poets and storytellers. In Iceland a new religious sect, the Asatruarmenn ('Believers in the Aesir'), was officially recognized in 1973, the aim of the founders being to restore the ancient rituals of pre-Christian Iceland.

Aetherius Society [XXVIII] Founded in London in 1955 by His Eminence Sir George King (1919–) after he received the instruction on 8 May 1954: 'Prepare yourself! You are to become the voice of Interplanetary Parliament' [33: 19]. Sir George claims to be in contact with Cosmic Beings (some of whom have come to earth in flying saucers); Aetherius, a Cosmic Master from Venus, is of particular importance. Members of the Society cooperate with Cosmic Sources to direct spiritual energy to save the planet from disaster, with specially trained Prayer Teams performing a ritual that enables concentrated amounts of energy to be directed into a Battery invented by Sir George. [5: 165–6; 33; 42: 728; 72: III; 75: II]

Africa, Christianity in [XIII.B] Roman Christianity in northern Africa was largely destroyed by the Islamic invasions. The major survivors are the Monophysite COPTIC churches of Egypt and Ethiopia (*see* CHRISTOLOGY). Elsewhere in Africa Christianity was largely produced by later MISSIONS. In west Africa, apart from Portuguese ROMAN CATHOLICISM in the 16th century, most work was done in the 19th century, first by PROTESTANTISM, then by Roman Catholics. The areas of activity of the two churches generally corresponded to the religious affiliations of rival European trading and colonial powers. The same is true of east Africa after exploration by David Livingstone (1813–73). In southern Africa Dutch settlement from the 17th century produced a local Reformed church (*see* CALVINISM) as well as missions. The apartheid policy (theologically supported by the local Reformed church) led to much tension with missionary churches. Local versions of European churches of missionary origin have achieved independence since the 1950s. In east Africa some groups of Christians have spontaneously converted to the Orthodox Church (*see* EASTERN ORTHODOX CHURCH). There are also numerous African independent churches of a messianic, PENTECOSTALIST type mixed with traditional African religion (*see* AFRICA, NEW RELIGIOUS MOVEMENTS). [87; 88; 92: IX–XII; 121 vol. 3: XVI, XXIII, vol. 5: XVII; 122 vol. 5: XI, vol. 7: IX]

Africa, Islam in [XIX] Islam spread very early along the Mediterranean shores from Egypt to Morocco, Islamization being well advanced by the 9th century, so that the northern shores of the continent belong essentially to the Mediterranean basin and the heartlands of classical Islamic civilization. Islam spread later into sub-Saharan Africa, brought initially by traders across the desert from the Maghreb to western and central Africa, and across the sea from south Arabia and the Persian Gulf to the east African coastlands. Muslim dynasties were established in west Africa from as early as the 11th century in Takrur and Kanem, and subsequently in the empires of Mali, Songhay and Borno. Militant Islam first appeared in the western Sahara with the Almoravids (11th century); from the 17th century, a sustained tradition of JIHAD emerged in the western and central Sahara, which then spread to the Senegal river valley in the 18th century and culminated in the *jihads* of 'Uthman dan Fodio (1754–1817) and 'Umar b. Sa'id al-Futi (1794–1864) and the Mahdist state in the Sudan in the 19th century (*see* MAHDI). Similar militant movements also occurred in the Horn of Africa, under Ahmad Gran (1506–43) and Muhammad b. 'Abd Allah (1864–1920), although not along the Swahili coast of east Africa, from where Islam moved into the interior only from the 19th century as a result of trade in ivory and slaves. SUFISM was of considerable influence in Saharan and Sudanic Islam; many of the *jihadi* leaders were Sufis, although formalized SUFI ORDERS did not appear until the 18th century in the central Sahara (*see* QADIRIS), from where they spread to the Sudanic zones. The TIJANIS would begin to rival Qadiri dominance during the 19th century. A similar impetus in eastern Africa, especially in the Sudan and Somalia, came from Ahmad b. Idris (1760–1837), whose teachings led to the formation of a number of influential brotherhoods (*see* SANUSIS, MIRGHANIS). Sufi orders spread from the Horn of Africa into Swahili areas during the 19th and 20th centuries. Closely associated with Sufism in sub-Saharan Africa was the veneration of holy men (*see* WALI) and the influence of the Muslim healing arts, such as Qur'anic erasures and protective AMULETS. During the 20th century, the spread of Islam in sub-Saharan Africa was facilitated by the new political order imposed by European colonial rule, the evolution of modern communications and the modernization of Muslim institutions, especially schools. [65 vol. 2: 209–405; 63; 106; 125]

Africa, New Religious Movements in [XXVII] Black Africa in its interactions with Christianity (but not with ISLAM) has produced perhaps 8,000 movements with some 9 million members, about a third of these being in South Africa alone (see AFRICA, CHRISTIANITY IN). Some seek to revive traditional religions in new forms with Christian borrowings; these would include the Church of the Ancestors in Malawi, the Religion of the Ancestors in East Africa [2: 119–21], the Reformed Ogboni Fraternity [2: 122] and Godianism in Nigeria and the Déïma cult in the Ivory Coast [12: 56]. Some model themselves on the Jews of the BIBLE, such as the Israelites under Enoch Mgijima in South Africa from 1912 [12: 42–3; 18: 72–3; 26: 61–3], the Bayudaya in Uganda since 1923, and the God's Kingdom Society in Nigeria from 1934. Most movements, and all the larger ones, would be regarded as independent churches since they use the Bible and intend to be Christian, however confusedly, and they fall into two broad classes: ETHIOPIAN CHURCHES and prophet-healing or ZIONIST MOVEMENTS. Among the more notable movements have been the Harrist churches of the Ivory Coast derived from prophet HARRIS; the Nigerian ALADURA churches and later revivalist and 'spiritual science' movements; the KIMBANGUIST CHURCH in Zaire; the African Apostolic Church of Johane Maranke and the Apostolic Sabbath Church of God of Johane Masowe in Zimbabwe [5]; the Lumpa Church of ALICE LENSHINA in Zambia; Reuben Spartas's African Greek Orthodox Church in east Africa (see EASTERN ORTHODOX CHURCH); the Kenya movement of MARIA LEGIO; in Malawi the PROVIDENCE INDUSTRIAL MISSION; and in South Africa Shembe's NAZARITE CHURCH and the Zion Christian Church with

some 300,000 members. Rather different are KITAWALA in central Africa, the various sections of the Bwiti cult among the Fang in Gabon with creative attempts at a synthesis of African and Christian elements [2: 27, 55; 12: 56], and those few movements regarding their founder as a new black Messiah replacing JESUS Christ [18: 323–37]. Altogether these developments represent a remarkable religious ferment among African peoples [2].

Africa, New Religious Movements in (Islamic-related) [XXVII] If we exclude mahdist and renewal movements (e.g. the recent MAITATSINE MOVEMENT in northern Nigeria) which are internal to Islam, black Africa has produced few new religious movements in its interactions with Islam in comparison with those arising from Christianity. There have been a few Islamic-influenced spirit-possession cults, such as the Zar cults in Ethiopia and the NILOTIC Sudan in the 19th century, the Kitombo cult of the Kamba in Kenya in the 1890s, the cult among the Lebu in Senegal in the 20th century, and more extensively the Bori cults among the Hausa of west Africa at the same time. Both the Lebu and Bori movements concerned women, who had a place in traditional tribal religion but were marginalized by the male-dominated Islam in changing societies. In the highly organized Bori cults ALLAH was vaguely recognized, but help came from a pantheon of spirits drawn from both Islamic and tribal traditions, with whom warm personal relations were established through possession by the spirit. These groups are of a new type in being voluntary societies rather than public cults, are essentially transitional means of meeting women's needs for fecundity, healing and support in troublous times, and they all appeared at the frontiers of Islam with black Africa. More Islamic in content was the Layé fraternity of

Seydina Limamu (1843–1909), a Lebu fisherman near Cape Verde who in 1883 experienced a call to revive and expand orthodox Islam, which fully accepted him. As the movement developed it became more Africanized and the Meccan pilgrimage obligation was jettisoned, wives were not limited to four, songs and poems in Wolof replaced the dominant Arabic and women were restored to the place they had previously held in the Lebu religious system. Although apolitical in intent, Limamu was persecuted by the French colonial authorities, but the movement has survived by closer relation with Islam through the Qadiyya order. Leadership passed through his sons to his grandson, Seydina Issa Thiaw, in 1971. The major movements have been more sophisticated and include the MOURIDES of Amadu Bamba in Senegal and the HAMALLISM of Mali and the Ivory Coast, which combine both Africanizing and modernizing changes. One of the main reasons for the comparative paucity of Islamic-related movements is the orthodox principle of preserving the QU'RAN in Arabic, whereas the Christian scriptures have been translated into hundreds of vernaculars. [21]

African Orthodox [XIII.D] A spontaneous movement to EASTERN ORTHODOX Christianity had emerged in east Africa by the 1920s. The Ugandans Reuben Spartas (later Bishop Christopher of Niloupolis), Obadhia Basjjakitalo and Kyrillos Pasha Kasule led the main group, first towards an 'African Orthodox Church' (based in the USA) and then into communion with the Eastern Orthodox Patriarchate of Alexandria (1946). Since 1959 EASTERN ORTHODOX MISSIONS have been invited to most African countries – notably to Zaire where Kosmas Aslanidis (d. 1989), an Athonite monk, was warmly received. The COPTIC Orthodox have also worked to develop closer

links with their fellow African Christians, particularly in South Africa. [10; 99] (*See also* ETHIOPIAN CHRISTIANITY; NUBIAN CHRISTIANITY.)

African Religions [II] There are as many African religions as peoples or 'tribes', that is, many hundreds. This *Dictionary* can refer only to a few, selected somewhat arbitrarily to illustrate different types or areas, or to an account of available literature in English. The following receive individual attention: AKAN, DOGON, FON, IGBO, MENDE and YORUBA in west Africa, and ZANDE in central Africa; DINKA, NUER and SHILLUK among the NILOTICS; GANDA, LOVEDU, SHONA and ZULU among BANTU.

A crucial factor in the differentiation between African religions is the deep diversity of African social and political systems. Religious belief and ritual both reflect and mould social structure and would be largely incomprehensible apart from the latter. Despite the contrasts there are also profound similarities. [General and thematic surveys: 8; 11; 14; 20.] African religions do not exist in a vacuum. They have influenced each other through human contact – migration, military conquest, marriage – and through the action of religious specialists. Within one people there could be significant differences in regard to religion, caused by the sectional activity of secret societies or local shrines: religion was thus in part associational. Equally, religion frequently crossed tribal frontiers, not only by borrowings, but also by the enduring sense of a wider community. Major territorial cults (MBONA, MWARI, Luak Deng) provided pilgrimage centres for people of different tribes [15; 18], while systems of divining, secret societies, cults of affliction and WITCHCRAFT ERADICATION often passed from people to people. So did the name of God.

African religions belonged to preliterate societies. This has affected their character and our knowledge; however, non-literate societies can possess an extensive oral literature, and many African religions have significant texts, some of which we now possess [23; 31; 32]. Non-literate religions change at least as much as literate ones, but changes go unrecorded, hence the mistaken view that African religions are unchanging. Their historical development may be partially plotted through analysis of layers within current ritual and myth, and from the evidence of earlier written sources [13]. There is some historical documentation available in Latin and Portuguese from the 16th century on, especially in regard to the Congo and Zambezi valleys, and much more in many languages dating from the wider entry of missionaries and other Europeans into Africa in the 19th century. The greatest problem in the study of African religions is that almost without exception books are the work of outsiders: sympathetic or unsympathetic, they inevitably import alien categories, even when written by Africans.

Much discussion has centred on belief in God. Some early observers denied any such concept; subsequently many missionaries and African scholars have pointed out, even over-stressing, an underlying African monotheism interpreted in rather Christian terms [8; 9; 17; 35; 42]. There has been some sharp reaction against this [12; 44]. There are certainly some peoples with either no conception of a supreme God or one so limited as to be effectively otiose (Acholi, Lango, LOVEDU, Nyakyusa, Swazi, ZANDE; JOK). These are significant exceptions. The great majority of African religions recognize a single supreme creator God, witness to whom in prayers [16], proverbs and creation myths is massive (IRUVA; KATONDA; LEZA; MODIMO; MULUNGU; NZAMBI). Nevertheless, the prayers of only a few are concentrated upon God (NUER; see also MWARI). More

characteristic is a pattern of intermediaries – ancestors or nature gods – to which most ritual and prayer are immediately directed, although direct access to the deity remains possible, especially in emergency (ANCESTOR VENERATION; MIZIMU; ORISHA).

Attention must also be paid to DIVINE KINGSHIP and RAIN-MAKING; to rituals of initiation (CHISUNGU) and secret societies (BAGRE; MENDE; NYAU); to SPIRIT-POSSESSION, so-called fetishes or objects of impersonal power (NKISI), systems of DIVINATION (IFA), witchcraft and sorcery (NGANGA; WITCHCRAFT ERADICATION movements; ZANDE).

It is impossible to describe the overall present state of Africa's religions. Many ethnographic studies using the present tense in fact give a picture 50 years old. The advance of CHRISTIANITY, ISLAM and modernization have greatly altered things, destroying the coherence of many systems (see also AFRICA, CHRISTIANITY IN). There have also been religious revivals (YORUBA), producing a neo-traditionalism, sometimes incorporating elements from the world religions, in which divination and spirit-possession cults particularly flourish (see also AFRICA, NEW RELIGIOUS MOVEMENTS IN).

Afro-Americans (Caribbean and South America): New Religious Movements [XXVII] The descendants of African slaves in the Caribbean and South America, especially in Brazil, have created new movements ranging from revivals of the old tribal religions with varying degrees of Christian influence to independent Christian churches. Best known is VOODOO in Haiti and the Dominican Republic [16: 64–71, 295–303]. In Grenada, Trinidad, St Lucia and Brazil Shango combines African and Catholic elements [16: 73–86, 103–6, 190–5]; likewise Santería in Cuba and the Maria Lionza cult in Venezuela [16: 86–94, 163–70, 308–9]. The Cumina and CONVINCE cults of Jamaica focus on ancestral spirits, with little Christian content [16: 98–102]. The three groups of Bush Negroes, Saramaka, Djuka and Boni, living in the interior of Surinam and French Guiana developed cults with some Christian borrowings. This influence produced reforming prophets such as Wensi in 1936, and Akalali from 1972 who further reformed the Gaan Tata or Masa Jehovah cult, itself a more Christian form from the 1880s [16: 204–11]. A similar range occurs in the AFRO-BRAZILIAN CULTS of coastal Brazil. Syncretistic movements resembling a more revivalist type of Christianity include the Revivalists, a general term in Jamaica for POCO-MANIA [12: 165; 26: 59–60], Revival Zion, etc., as well as the SHAKERS of St Vincent and the Shouters or SPIRITUAL BAPTISTS of Trinidad [16: 111–27]. In Guyana the Jordonites (from 1917) are strongly influenced by the Hebrew scriptures (see BIBLE) and by Jewish religious forms, as also are the House of Israel and various 'back-to-Africa' cults of which the most notable are the RASTAFARIANS of Jamaica. Traditional African SPIRIT-POSSESSION provides a congenial background for the great growth of Pentecostal forms of Christianity (see PENTECOSTALISM; and also WEST INDIES, CHRISTIANITY IN THE), some Western-influenced but much of local origin [16: 45–50, 309–10]. There are also many independent churches in orthodox or EVANGELICAL traditions and all types of Jamaican black churches have travelled with immigrants to Britain, such as the large New Testament Church of God [16: 274–80]. [12: 133–41; 22: 701; 26: 108–14]

Afro-Brazilian Cults [xxvii]
Many varieties of these cults have developed since about 1830, first among the descendants of African slaves in north-east Brazil and lat-

terly more widely. There are traditional YORUBA cults; Candomblé (known as Xango, Batuque or Pará in different areas) incorporating Catholic and west African elements; Macumba, with further BANTU African contributions and local Indian spirits and curative practices; and UMBANDA, drawing on all the above together with European SPIRITUALISM and OCCULTISM to form a nation-wide religious complex sharing its adherents with folk ROMAN CATHOLICISM. [16: 177–204, 158–63; 26: 108–14]

Afterlife (Amerindian) [v]
Despite a rather widespread lack of definition regarding man's postmortem fate, conceptions of afterlife differed greatly among Indian tribes of North America. Speculations were usually closely linked to conceptions of the SOUL as well as to a particular view of human life in this world. Most tribes held that humans possessed more than one soul (usually a 'free' soul and a 'life' or 'breath' soul), the former departing the body at death, perhaps lingering for some time near the corpse, before passing to its final disposition [8: IX, 134–9]. Among the Algonquian (see ALGONQUIN), Cherokee and IROQUOIS, for example, the soul might be required to pass a test before entering the land of the dead. A SHAMAN might serve as the soul's guide. Mortuary customs reflect varying conceptions of afterlife. In general, the dead were feared (though not by the SIOUX, a notable exception), and elaborate funeral rites were intended to effect the soul's smooth transition to the other world [24: VII–VIII]. With the exception of the PUEBLO tribes, who possessed a rather detailed conception of afterlife, most notions were of a vague, shadowy existence, often an indistinct continuation of earthly life. Among the nomadic tribes of the prairies and plains, the notion of a 'happy hunting ground' was common. Generally, however, human

life was viewed neither as a testing-ground nor as a preparation for eternal life, though later Christian influences may be noted.

Afterlife (Ancient Egyptian) [VI]
A belief in continued existence after death was common to all levels of ancient Egyptian society and, apart from the Old Kingdom (*c*.2600 BCE) when only the royal hereafter was clearly defined (*see* RE'), rich and poor expected an individual eternity. To this end, tombs were prepared with articles of daily and religious use (*see* FUNERARY PRACTICES), according to the individual's wealth; many were mummified (*see* MUMMI-FICATION) and provided themselves with elaborate coffins [5]. The complex concept of the personality that included, in addition to the body, the immortal elements – the *Ba* (soul) and *Ka* (spirit) – was the foundation of the funerary beliefs and practices. The Egyptians believed that the deceased would require a preserved body and tomb (*see* MANSION OF THE KA) environment to which the *Ka* could return to partake of sustenance (food-offerings provided by relatives and *Ka*-priests, or, later, by means of models of food, wall-paintings, and a menu inscribed on the tomb wall (*see* HIEROGLYPHS)).

A celestial afterlife was envisaged for royalty, and the wealthy lavishly equipped their tombs for a continued existence. The cult of Osiris (*see* OSIRIAN TRIAD), although originally associated only with royalty, underwent democratization during the Middle Kingdom (*c*.1900 BCE). Osiris achieved widespread popularity because he offered his followers, regardless of their status, the promise of resurrection and a continued existence tilling the land in the 'Fields of Reeds'. This was dependent upon a satisfactory assessment of the individual's life by the divine tribunal at the day of judgement, when the deceased recited the Negative Confession, affirming his moral fitness. His heart was weighed in the balance against the feather of truth; the final verdict was recorded by Thoth. Having been declared 'justi-fied', the deceased then passed to the Osirian underworld, but the hearts of the unworthy would be devoured by a mythological creature. [5]

Afterlife (Ancient Near Eastern)
[VIII] Fine funerary goods have been discovered at various ancient Near Eastern sites, such as: (1) the Royal Tombs at Ur (*c*.2500 BCE) [26: 74–81]; (2) a burial at Ashur, *c*.reign of Tukulti-Ninurta (*c*.1240 BCE) (both cremation and inhumation customs existed concurrently in HITTITE society [13: 164–9]); and (3) Ugarit, where provision was made to feed the deceased buried in subterranean vaults (*see* PHOENI-CIANS).

However, the mythology (*see* ANCIENT NEAR EASTERN RELIGIONS) in literary sources indicates a general belief that only the gods were immortal, although even they might die. Either humans had no hope of survival after death, or, as in SUMER-IAN mythology, their spirits would descend to a dark underworld, where life would dimly reflect the joys of earthly existence [16: 153–66]. The concept of individual resurrection seems to be missing, although a number of myths recall the story of a vegetation god who dies, thus depriving the earth of his bounty, but who finally returns to life and restores abundance to the land and its inhabitants.

Afterlife (Christian View of)
[XIII.B] Traditionally, the Christian view of humanity sees the individual's soul as surviving death. At death an interim judgement is made. This distinguishes between worthy souls destined for heaven, and the unworthy consigned to eternal punishment in hell. Limbo in Roman Catholic tradition has been seen as a place where pre-Christian holy peo-

ple and unbaptized infants are placed, free of punishment but excluded from the beatific vision. Pope John XXII (1316–34) taught that the souls of the righteous dead do not experience the beatific vision until the last judgement. This view, which resembles EASTERN ORTHO- DOX ideas of the afterlife, was con- demned by his successor, Benedict XII (1334–42) but a form of it was revived by Luther. ROMAN CATHOLI- CISM teaches that most saved souls undergo a period of purification in purgatory, but PROTESTANTISM rejects this. A few enter the immedi- ate presence of God (beatific vision; *see* COSMOLOGY, CHRISTIAN). At the end of time the Second Coming of JESUS Christ takes place and the New (Heavenly) JERUSALEM (the home of Christians) descends (cf. MILLENARIANISM). In a general RES- URRECTION of the dead, souls are clothed with a transfigured body. The last judgement settles the final destiny of the resurrected: eternal bliss in heaven or eternal torment in hell. Heaven is also the dwelling place of angels, i.e. immaterial beings who act as God's messengers and some as men's guardian angels. Catholics offer devotion to them as they do to SAINTS. The Devil (Satan) is the leader of evil angels fallen through pride. They tempt and torment Christians but are con- signed to eternal fire at the last judgement. (Belief in demon- possession was once common and exorcism to remove DEMONS is still occasionally practised [157: 493–4].) These teachings have been elaborated by legend, speculation, and folklore. During the 19th cen- tury heaven was increasingly seen in terms of an idealized family reunion rather than as a place simply for the perpetual worship of God, and there was increasing reaction against the idea of eternal punishment. The 20th century has seen a decline of speculation about the details of the afterlife (though cf. SPIRITUALISM). In EASTERN ORTHODOX tradition

two different themes are empha- sized: (a) no one is in hell except those who insist on remaining there, and (b) God's mercy is offered to all. Those who accept it are bathed in the light of his presence; to those who reject it is the fire of hell. Mod- ern Christian views of the afterlife emphasize that all language about it is highly symbolic, picturing the bliss of communion with God and the agony of separation from him (e.g. the 'flames' of hell). Some think of conditional immortality (the wicked being extinguished); others of uni- versalism (the ultimate salvation of all). 'Resurrection of the body' has also been very variously interpreted, e.g. not only as the resuscitation of the physical body but also as the survival of the personality in some form (*see also* ESCHATOLOGY). [114: xvii; 129; 170]

Afterlife (Greek) [xvi] In earliest eschatology all *psychai* (shades), even those of mythological HEROES, went to Hades, a subterranean, gloomy land of the dead. From the 8th century BCE the belief appeared, grew rapidly and became dominant, that select heroes inhabited a para- dise (Elysion, or *Makaron Nesoi*, Isles of the Blest). MYSTERIA and sects such as Orphism (*see* ORPHEUS, ORPHISM) promised a blissful after- life to those who underwent initia- tion and followed certain precepts – ritual and later (in most circles) also ethical. The notion of post mortem rewards and punishments after a general judgement spread into main- stream eschatology. Reincarnation (*see* ETHIKE; ORPHEUS) remained a marginal belief. Celestial/astral immortality in the sky appeared in the 5th century BCE and subse- quently grew in popularity. All these beliefs, and doubts about the after- life, coexisted. The Late Hellenistic craving for assurances of immortal- ity found satisfaction primarily in Mysteria and the belief in astral immortality. [3: 357–68; 4: 194–9,

285–301; 10: 261–8; 14: 48–76; 11: 50–66; 27: 62–3, 796–8]

Afterlife and Death (South American) [xxiii] South American myths often explain that death entered the world in the context of a trial – through the failure to pass a test or to undergo an ordeal, making a fatal choice or giving an inopportune signal. Special care is taken in disposing of the dead, the corpse being covered with shrouds, ornaments or some other wrapping (symbolism of the womb is often present in the coffin/tomb). Various forms of ritual strife, formal sport and games are enacted to accentuate the rupture between life and death. Food offerings and ritual hunts at or after burial establish proper relations with the dead. Mortal remains are disposed by inhumation, cremation, ingesting flesh (*see* CANNIBALISM) or imbibing ashes; secondary burial sometimes completes a process of multiple endings.

Important features of South American concepts of the afterlife include the following: the dead inhabit various parts of the cosmos; trial or judgement conditions one's entrance to life after death; such judgements are not made solely on the basis of the deceased's moral character but depend also on other personal qualities and on the manner of death; a guide often conducts the dead on their journey; the songs of mourners and pictographs along the route to the afterlife remind the deceased which is the safe road, for various obstacles lie in wait to block the way or to lure the dead from their goal; the land of the dead often presents a reverse image of this world. Metempsychosis and reincarnation are the main ways in which the transformation of the deceased's soul is achieved. [7; 25; 33: viii].

Aggadah [xxii] Aramaic term referring to the non-legal material in rabbinical literature (*see* RABBI), dealing mainly with theology, ethics and folklore [67: 253; 11]. All of the main elements of later Jewish belief are found in the Aggadah, but they are presented in the fluid form of PARABLES and stories, which have enabled Jews in very different cultural environments to interpret Aggadic teachings in a meaningful way [70: 55]. Some Jewish pietists accept Aggadic ideas as doctrinally binding, but most Jews adopt a selective approach [14 vol. 2: 354].

Agonshu [xxvi] Claiming some 300,000 members, Agonshu is a recent development among new religious movements in Japan. Agonshu was founded by Kiriyama Seiyu (1921–) in 1969, though legal incorporation under the present name did not occur until 1981. It stands in the Tantric, or esoteric, BUDDHIST tradition. After study of MAHAYANA sutras and experience in the SHINGON Buddhist monastic world, Kiriyama came to believe that 'attaining enlightenment in the present life' (*sokushin jobutsu*), a goal highly valued in esoteric Buddhism, was identical with the Nirvana set forth in the Agama (Japanese: *Agon*) sutra. He also taught that the Agama sutra shows the way to Nirvana, to release from the wheel of karmic cause and effect. Agonshu includes in its regimen such opportunities for self-discipline as meditation, fasting and standing under a waterfall. It also emphasizes performance of rituals to protect the living from ancestral spirits who, because of ritual neglect by their descendants, send punishments and misfortunes on the living. Agonshu is a computer-age religion that offers Japanese people not only an exotic mix of high-tech forms and universalistic ideas but also a reassuring emphasis on traditionalism. Once a year it holds its 'Star Festival' (*Hoshi matsuri*) in Kyoto. In the presence of half a million visitors Kiriyama and his helpers, dressed as *yamabushi*, or mountain ascetics, burn *gomagi*, or wooden paddles, which people purchase and inscribe with prayers and requests. Whipped up by chanting, drumming and dramatic music, people see two huge mounds of burning *gomagi*, one for the ancestors, another for the satisfaction of immediate needs. Held on 11 February, the National Foundation Day which for many still carries overtones of nationalism, the Star Festival is said to be for world peace. [16: VIII, 208–33]

Ahimsa [XVII] Meaning 'non-harming', 'non-violence', this is a central concept of Hindu and Jain morality, and the ideal, though not usually the term, is also important in BUDDHISM (*see* SILA). Jainism carried it furthest: JAINS seek to avoid harming even invisible forms of life. Its development in HINDUISM, in particular the rejection of Vedic animal sacrifice (*see* VEDA) and the widespread adoption of vegetarianism, was probably influenced by the other two religions, though it was clearly part of a general tendency in Indian culture. The *ahimsa* ideal seems to have spread through society from the BRAHMANS to the lower VARNAS, leading to the low status of those whose caste duties (DHARMA) involved killing, such as butchers and fishermen. For the KSHATRIYAS there was tension between this ideal and their duty to protect the state as warriors and rulers. In practice *ahimsa* did not rule out, for Hindu kings and law-givers, recourse to war, capital punishment or judicial torture [12: 118–19; 43: xxx–xliv]. Now, however, complete abstention from violence is seen as the ideal for all Hindus, and in this form, mainly through the influence of Gandhi, the concept of *ahimsa* has influenced pacifist thinking throughout the world [57: 178–80]. (*See also* ARTHA; BHAGAVADGITA.)

Ahl-i Haqq [XVIII] The 'People of Truth', nominally an ultra-Shi'ite sect (*see* SHI'ISM), some of whose beliefs, however, are of pre-Islamic Iranian origin. Another name for the group is Yarsan. Little is known about the early history of the sect; Sultan Sahak (or Ishaq), one of the divine incarnations who lived in Kurdistan (14th–15th century CE), is widely regarded as the founder [7: 12]). Iranian Kurdistan (Kirmanshah province) is still the heartland of the sect. Later, Ahl-i Haqq beliefs spread; there are now sizeable communities in various places in Iran and Iraq outside Kurdistan, and some in Turkey. Estimates of their numbers vary from over 500,000 [6: 39] to several millions.

The Ahl-i Haqq believe that, before creation, God dwelt in a pearl. Inside the pearl He created a Heptad (*Haftan*) of divine beings. He made a covenant with the leader of the Heptad. The covenant was accompanied by the sacrifice of a bull, and followed by the creation of the world from the pearl [6; 9]. History, according to Ahl-i Haqq teaching, is cyclical, and God and members of the Heptad manifest themselves again and again in human form; thus Sultan Sahak and Ali, the Prophet MUHAMMAD's son-in-law, are both manifestations of the Deity. Since Ali has a place in their mythology the group can present itself as a Shi'ite sect, although they do not normally perform the external duties or PILLARS OF ISLAM. The community is divided into eleven branches (*khandan*), each headed by a family of Sayyids. Every member must choose two spiritual leaders, a *pir*, who is a Sayyid, and a *dalil*, a member of another group of 'priestly' families. All Ahl-i Haqq must 'submit their head' (*sar sipurdan*) to their *pir* as a sign of complete obedience in a solemn ceremony of initiation. Another central ceremony is the *jam'*, which must be performed at least 17 times a year [6: 156]; it consists of the sacrifice of a male animal followed by a ritual meal, and of prayers and the singing of sacred texts (*kalam*) [6: 157–8]. The latter are full of arcane allusions and have to be explained by a trained 'reciter' in order to be intelligible. The singing of *kalams* is accompanied by the music of a sacred instrument, the *tanbur* (lute); *tanbur* music, together with dancing and meditation, can induce states of ecstasy which enable initiates to perform unusual feats [6: 160f].

There have always been differences between local traditions, notably between those of Kurdistan and Azerbaijan. A recent development was initiated by Hajj Ni'matullah Jayhunabadi (d. 1920 CE), who broke the traditional code of secrecy, writing down the ancient teachings and presenting them in a more contemporary light. His successors went further, seeking to bring Ahl-i Haqq doctrine more in line with mainstream Shi'ite ideas [2]. As a result the community is now split between traditionalists and reformists. Since the 1960s the latter have attracted a following among Iranian intellectuals of non-Ahl-i-Haqq background. Some Iranian Ahl-i Haqq now demand recognition as a religious minority, unconnected with Islam; others believe that theirs is the only true esoteric form of that faith, while most hold more moderate views.

Ahl-i-Hadith [xix] 'People of the HADITH.' A 19th-century Indian Islamic reform movement that emphasized the *hadith* as the only reliable source for interpreting the QUR'AN and the SHARI'A. Thus both the four classical schools of law (FIQH) and the teachings and authority of the SUFI ORDERS were categorically rejected. There were to be no intermediaries or guides other than the text itself, a rejection of both the orthodox, teacher-guide SUFISM of the DEOBANDIS and the mediator-*pir* system of the BARELVIS. As a result, the Ahl-i-Hadith developed their own distinctive form of SALAT, leading to high-profile altercations with other Muslims. Disputes between the different schools of thought resulted in court action and finally necessitated the setting up of separate MOSQUES. In common with the other Islamic movements at that time, the importance of MUHAMMAD was central. Love for the Prophet was pre-eminent and he was to be the model for all aspects of life, his SUNNA to be known directly from the *hadith*. However, the Ahl-i-Hadith rejected the notion of Muhammad as an intermediary between the believer and God and prohibited all pilgrimage, even that to the Prophet's tomb in Medina. They were referred to by other Indian Muslims as WAHHABI, a comment on their rejection of Hanafi law. The Ahl-i-Hadith movement was more extreme than that of the Deobandis but, although it drew support from the educated and well-born, had less influence. Its tighter organizational structure has resulted in a network of about a dozen Ahl-i-Hadith mosques in Britain with headquarters in Birmingham, from where the magazine *The Straight Path* is published. [92; 49; 99; 113]

Ahmadis [xix] The movement founded in India by Mirza Ghulam Ahmad (*c.*1839–1908), who claimed to have received divine revelations and who proclaimed himself the MESSIAH, the MAHDI, an AVATAR of KRISHNA and a reappearance of MUHAMMAD. Whether he claimed to be a new prophet is unclear, but orthodox Indian ISLAM regarded him and the mainstream Qadian movement of his followers as having placed themselves outside Islam. A more moderate minority, based on Lahore, has however maintained closer links with orthodoxy. The Ahmadis have carried on vigorous missionary work in Europe and Africa, and their aggressive methods in Pakistan have in recent decades caused considerable tension, and even public disorder, there (*see* SOUTH ASIA, ISLAM IN). [7: xix; 20 'Ahmadiyya movement'; 28: x; 38 'Ahmadiyya'; 78: xi; 142: 243–4]

Ahura Mazda [xxxvi] 'The Wise Lord' or 'Lord Wisdom', the term used by ZOROASTER and his followers for God. Zoroaster did not introduce a new God, but rather exalted one of the popular 'lords' (*ahuras*) to a unique position as the wholly good, sole creator who is alone worthy of absolute worship. Zoroaster claimed to have visions of Mazda, whom he spoke of as his friend and teacher, a judge and helper of man who is characterized by wisdom and benevolence. Mazda's first creations were the AMESHA SPENTAS, his helpers who reflect the divine nature and unite man to God, and the YAZATAS (beings worthy of worship), and finally he created the seven creations which together make up the whole of the Good Creation (namely man, cattle, fire, earth, sky, water and plants) [8 vol. 1: VII, VIII; 11: II; 30: 10–14].

In the PAHLAVI literature the two words 'Ahura Mazda' coalesce into 'Ohrmazd'. What Zoroaster implied about God, these texts clarify. The good creator Ohrmazd is opposed by an independent 'devil' Ahriman (ANGRA MAINYU). Both beings have existed from eternity. Ohrmazd is responsible for all that is good in the world – light, life, health and joy. Good is characterized by order, stability, harmony. The destructive forces of evil are outside Ohrmazd's control. He is not, therefore, all-powerful (omnipotent). The world, Zoroastrians believe, is the arena for the battle between Ohrmazd and Ahriman (*see* BUNDAHISHN). It is only when good ultimately triumphs that Ohrmazd will become omnipotent (*see* FRASHOKERETI) [63: I, IV; 64: XII]. Most PARSIS nowadays deny that Angra Mainyu is a being, declaring rather that the concept represents an evil tendency in man. Under Christian influence they have come to believe that Ahura Mazda is omnipotent, and so reject the traditional teaching of a wholly good but not all-powerful God [10: 202–4; 29: pt III].

Ajivaka [xvII] A member of an Indian religion founded by GOSALA (*fl. c.*500 BCE). The Ajivakas were influential during the Mauryan period (3rd–2nd centuries BCE) but largely disappeared from north India after the 2nd century BCE, surviving in south India on a small scale until about the 15th century. Ajivaka doctrines are known only from hostile sources, but they were evidently closely related to the JAINS and probably played some part in the evolution of the VAISHESHIKA. The Ajivakas were naked ascetics, undertaking severe austerities. A late source gives the four cardinal points of the faith as (1) the Lord, i.e. Gosala, (2) the categories (*padartha*), (3) the modifications and (4) the scriptures. The Ajivakas seem to have been the first Indian school to develop a form of atomism, involving seven kinds of permanent 'atoms'. [Standard work: 10]

Akal Purakh [xxxIII] ('The Eternal One') The Sikh doctrine of God is succinctly stated at the beginning of the ADI GRANTH in words attributed to GURU NANAK (the *Mul Mantra*). In an ultimate sense God is unknowable. There is, however, a sufficient revelation communicated by the grace of the GURU, the 'voice' of God mystically uttered within. Nanak begins by declaring the unity and creating power of God. Although God is *nirankar,* 'without form', his presence is visible to the enlightened believer, for God is immanent in all creation. The creation constitutes God's Name (NAM) and he who comprehends the *nam* grasps the essential means of release from transmigration (GURMAT). God is thus pre-eminently *Satnam,* the True Name. The other Nanak term which continues to be regularly used is *Akal Purakh,* the Eternal One [27: V; 28: 29–30, 49–50]. Nanak laid the foundation and as the Sikh PANTH evolved so too did its concept of God. The belief that justice may require resort to arms is reflected in a corresponding extension of the doctrine of God. For Guru GOBIND SINGH a characteristic epithet was *Sarab Loh*, 'All-Steel', he who is incarnated in the sword. A further development resulted from the ending of the line of personal Gurus in 1708. Although the personal succession had terminated, the eternal Guru remained, embodied in the scripture and present in the corporate community. As such the eternal Guru merges with the godhead. This development is reflected in the meaning attached to the important term VAHIGURU. Originally an ascription of praise to the Guru [25: 252], it became a noun designating the eternal Guru himself and eventually coalesced with *Akal Purakh*. Today God is called both *Akal Purakh* and *Vahiguru*.

Akali [XXXIII] During the 18th and 19th centuries the title *Akali* (devotee of AKAL PURAKH, God) designated SIKH warriors noted for their bravery and disdain for official authority. In this sense their modern descendants are the NIHANGS. Early in the 20th century the title was assumed by radical Sikhs agitating for freedom of GURDWARAS from private control. The Akali Dal (Akali Army), formed for this purpose in 1920, still continues as a major political party in the Punjab. [23: XIII, XVIII]

Akan Religion [II] The Akan form a large group of matrilineal peoples inhabiting southern Ghana, among them the Ashanti and Fanti. While their religions are not identical, there are common features. Nyame is the name of the supreme god (possibly related to the central African NZAMBI). The name probably relates to the sky. Nyame is by no means 'withdrawn'. In the past he has had altars, *nyamedva* (God's tree), outside many small homes. He is frequently invoked, but has little organized worship comparable with that of the many lesser gods, the

Abosum, Nyame's 'children'. Greatest of these is Tano, the river deity. Beneath Nyame but above the Abosum is Asase Yaa, the earth – female and his 'wife' – whose special day is Thursday, as Saturday is Nyame's.

As important as the Abosum are the Asamanfo, ancestors (*see* ANCESTOR VENERATION), of each clan and lineage. The symbol of Akan social and political identity is the sacred stool of each lineage, chiefship and kingship. The stool, resting in its stool-house, is the point where living and ancestors meet. The most important religious, but also political, activities of life are the installation of a new chief, 'upon the stool of the ancestors', and the stool festivals – the Adae (every 21 days) and the new year Odwira ceremonies. Through the stool, its symbolism and rituals, sacred chiefship is placed at the heart of Akan life from village to kingdom, and all the elements of belief – Asamanfo, Abosum and, above both, Nyame – are integrated into a unity at once social and religious. [6: VIII; 46]

Akhenaten [VI] PHARAOH Amenophis IV (*c*.1367–1350 BCE) repudiated the state-cult of Amen-Re' (AMUN), introducing instead the exclusive 'monotheism' of the Aten (ATENISM). His name changed to Akhenaten, he moved his capital to Amarna, and disbanded the traditional priesthoods (*see* MANSION OF THE GODS). His personal devotion is expressed in the 'Great Hymn to the Aten' (*c*.1360 BCE) [8: 282–8], the indirect inspiration of Psalm 104. Nefertiti, his queen, shared his cult [22: VI, 79] but the counter-revolutionary king, Horemheb (1335–1308 BCE), obliterated the cult after Akhenaten's death.

Akhira [XIX] The afterlife in ISLAM, contrasted with the present life, *dunya*. After the last judgement, the righteous will be separated from the damned (QIYAMA). Paradise is described in physical terms in the

QUR'AN and HADITH as a luxurious garden (*jannat al-firdaus*), with all sorts of sensual delights, and the vision of God (ALLAH) as its culmination (earlier Persian and Judaeo-Christian concepts seem to have had an influence here). Some later theologians, however, without denying the material joys, emphasized also the spiritual bliss. On the other hand, hell (*jahannam*) is a place of fire, sometimes pictured as comprising concentric zones for differing classes of sinners and manned by the keeper Malik and the demons of hell. There was much discussion on the nature of sin and whether consignment to hell was permanent or might be for a fixed term only (DHANB). [48: 53–5; 71: 197–250]

Akhlaq [XIX] The Islamic term for ethics. ISLAM took over many of the pre-Islamic Arab virtues (JAHILIYYA) and gave them moral and religious sanction, and as the spiritualization of the faith proceeded, theologians came to emphasize individual responsibility and morality. To these indigenous strains were added the practical, opportunist morality of the Persians, especially prominent in the sphere of statecraft, and an acquaintance with Greek ethics through Galen (*fl.* 3rd century BCE), Plato (428–348 BCE), Aristotle (384–322 BCE), etc. In recent times, ISLAMIC MODERNISM has favoured activist ethics rather than the quietist ones of traditional SUFISM, as familiarity with Western moral philosophy and ethics has increased. [20 'Ethics (Muslim)'; 34; 38 'Akhlāk'; 77: XIII; 80 v]

Aladura [XXVII] A YORUBA term ('prayer people') for various independent prophet–healing churches spreading from western Nigeria around west Africa and to Britain since about 1918. The main expansion came with Joseph Babalola's mass divine-healing movement in 1930, which issued under leaders like (later Sir) Isaac Akinyele in the Christ Apostolic Church. Other main sections are Oshitelu's Church of the Lord (*Aladura*), and the many Cherubim and Seraphim societies [12: 50–2], deriving from a prophet Moses Tunolase (1885?–1933) and a young Anglican woman Victorianah Abiodun Akinsowon (1907–), together with hundreds of later, smaller aladura movements. Among these a famous example has been the self-help *Aiyetoro* ('happy city'), built on piles on a lagoon mudbank east of Lagos by a group of persecuted Cherubim and Seraphim from 1947. Men and women lived separately, a strict ethic prevailed, a radical economic communism and diverse sophisticated business activities resulted in great prosperity for upwards of 2,000 members, and death was believed to have been conquered. By the 1970s internal dissension had appeared and the original utopian impetus had faded. Developments since the 1970s have been replacing the aladura form with EVANGELICAL/PENTECOSTAL REVIVALIST movements influenced by American models, such as the Church of God Mission in Benin City, and with 'spiritual science' movements. The latter meet needs similar to those fulfilled by the aladura by offering semi-secret knowledge of how to acquire spiritual power, and are modelled on exogenous examples beyond the Christian category such as SUBUD and the ROSICRUCIANS, which have been long present in Nigeria.

Alaskan Orthodox [XIII.D] Although a Russian presence was first established in Alaska in 1741, it was only in 1794 that a small group of monks arrived in the province from the Valaam Monastery in Karelia. From the start the Russo-American Company officials persecuted the monks for their direct support of the oppressed natives. In spite of opposition missionary work was extended. Inokenty Veniaminov (d. 1879) and Jacob Netsvetov devised Aleut and Tlingit alphabets, translated Christian texts and sought to preserve native cultures. Having developed a distinct Alaskan identity, the Orthodox community continued to grow even after the separation from Russia in 1867. In 1970 the EASTERN ORTHODOX CHURCH canonized the most outspoken champion of native rights, Herman of Serpukhov (d. 1837). This monk denounced the excesses of the governor, Baranov, and fearlessly continued to preach to the natives from his Spruce Island hermitage. In 1935 another hermit, Gerasim Schmaltz (d. 1969), revived the Spruce Island mission. [26; 29; 62; 80; 99] (*See also* NEW MARTYRS; SALOI)

Alaya-vijnana [XI] 'Store consciousness', the most fundamental of the eight consciousnesses of YOGACARA BUDDHISM. *Alaya-vijnana* is the well-spring from which all ordinary experience arises – a storehouse of tendencies accumulated over innumerable previous lives. Constantly taken from and added to in the present, it modifies itself to appear both as the world of mental experience and as the world of external things. In this light waking life is considered to differ from dream life only in degree, not in kind. Mistakenly taken as a stable core of selfhood, the store consciousness is in fact a continuously arising flux underlying apparent mental activity. Since it must be both correctly understood and transformed in nature for the mind to be liberated, the Yogacarins emphasized the necessity for deep meditation (SAMATHA), penetrating to the centre of being. [80a]

Al-Azhar [XIX] Possibly from an epithet, 'the shining one', applied to Fatima, daughter of the prophet MUHAMMAD and wife of 'ALI. It is the name of the MOSQUE in Cairo founded by the Fatimids in 972 as a training college for ISMA'ILI mission-aries. Over the centuries it has become the most famous educational institution of the Sunni Muslim world, in the past for the training of the ULEMA, but recently, under the influence of reformers from Muhammad 'Abduh onwards (*see* ISLAMIC MODERNISM), modern subjects such as Western languages and science have been introduced into what was essentially a theological curriculum, and women students have been admitted. Thus Al-Azhar now approximates in many ways to a modern university. (*See also* MADRASA) [38 s.v.; 66: VI]

Alchemy [XXIV] The quest for a substance (the 'philosopher's stone' or 'elixir' or 'tincture') which will transform ('transmute') base metals into gold or confer immortality on man, often accompanying or symbolizing the pursuit of spiritual perfection. Pre-scientific societies regarded gold as incorruptible, hence symbolizing or conferring changeless perfection in other spheres. Alchemy combines spirituality and chemistry, aspects which its practitioners have variously integrated, mixed or selectively ignored. Alchemy emerged as an art both in the Far East and in Western civilization (mainly in Alexandrian culture) in the last two or three centuries BCE. Chinese Taoist (*see* TAO CHIAO) alchemists (5th to 9th centuries CE) sought the elixir by chemistry and contemplative techniques reputed to confer spiritual harmony and immense longevity. Western alchemy descends from 2nd-century Gnostic (*see* GNOSTICISM) texts on metallurgy. Perhaps purely technological in intent, these nonetheless invited mystical interpretation: man was base metal; transmutation signified his spiritual perfection; the elixir was the means to the immortality of the soul. Laboratory procedure was an outer discipline corresponding to inner spiritual practices. [6] The process consists of taking the *prima materia* in a vessel (or alembic) and subjecting it to heat and distillation. It may take many years for the body, soul and spirit of the matter, known alchemically as salt, mercury and sulphur, to be freed from the base matter and transformed to perfection. The physical process (or outer discipline) differs from chemistry in its use of astrological timing of the operation and in the excessive repetition of certain stages. Alchemy spread (9th century) to the Arab world, later returning to Christendom, where it reached a high point between 1400 and 1700, stimulating scientific research (R. Boyle, 1627–91, and Sir Isaac Newton, 1643 1727, were both deeply interested) and generating a vast literature with a rich symbolism. Alchemical imagery informs the songs, poetry and drama of this period, in such works as Ben Jonson's *The Alchemist* (1610), the secular and religious poetry of the metaphysical poets, most particularly John Donne (c.1571–1631), and William Shakespeare's *Midsummer Night's Dream* (1595–6?). Alchemical principles and methodology are also evident in much of the medical practice of that period. With the secularization of science, alchemy lost much of its prestige and by the mid-19th century was almost dead in the West. Interest in the spiritual dimension was revived by the psychologist C. G. Jung (1875–1961), who argued that 'the alchemist projected . . . the process of individuation into the phenomena of chemical change' [17]. Alchemical ideas are still influential in the Western magical tradition (GOLDEN DAWN) and in contemporary psychology. Alchemy is still practised by a dedicated few in Europe and the USA and more widely in south-east Asia, where it shades off into traditional medicine and MAGIC.

Alchemy (Chinese) [XII] Alchemy in the Chinese context is almost invariably associated with the quest for immortality. The two basic forms

of alchemy were: (1) the compounding of the 'External Elixir' (*Wai Tan*) of immortality from chemicals, metals and drugs; (2) the compounding of the 'Inner Elixir' (*Nei Tan*) by controlling the vital substances or energies of seminal essence (*ching*), breath (*ch'i*) and spirit (*shen*) within the body. *Nei Tan* alchemy employs the terms and symbols of *Wai Tan* alchemy, while actually engaging in mental and physical disciplines such as meditation and control of the breathing. The distinction between *Nei Tan* and *Wai Tan* probably dates from the 6th century CE. [55: v, 128–43; 90: III, 55–78; 115: 126–35]

The forerunners of the early alchemists were the recipe masters (*fang shih*) of north-east China in the 3rd century BCE. They are said to have incorporated the YIN–YANG and WU HSING (Five Elements) theories with their own methods of controlling the spirits and transforming their bodies, in order to achieve a quasi-physical form of immortality. According to Ssu Ma Ch'ien (140 87 BCE) in the 'Historical Records' (*Shih Chi*), the Emperors Ch'in Shih Huang Ti (d. 210 BCE) and Han Wu Ti (d. 87 BCE) encouraged the *fang shih* in their arts, in the hope of achieving immortality for themselves. One famous *fang shih*, Li Shao Chun, advised Han Wu Ti that by sacrificing to the furnace he could transmute cinnabar into gold, and then by eating from vessels made from the gold he could prolong his life. Having achieved longevity he could undertake the voyage to P'eng Lai island to meet the immortals, sacrifice to heaven and earth, and achieve immortality himself. [79: XXXIII, 12–50]

The oldest extant treatise on alchemy is the *Ts'an T'ung Ch'i* (Kinship of the Three) written by Wei Po Yang between 120 and 150 CE. It describes in cryptic terms the method of preparing the elixir of 'returned cinnabar' (*huan tan*) by heating the dragon (lead) and the tiger (mercury) in a sealed crucible. It quotes extensively from the TAO TE CHING and *I Ching* and employs YIN–YANG theory. The treatise also advocates meditation, and the refining and circulation of the breath (*ch'i*) through the channels of the body. All these practices and methods are described in such vague and cryptic terms as to defy easy classification into internal or external alchemical categories. [79: XXXIII, 50–75; 93]

Alexandria, Early Christianity at [XIII.A] Christianity was established in Alexandria within two decades of the death of JESUS. Apollos (*Acts* 18: 24) is the first named Alexandrian Christian. In the early 2nd century Alexandrian Christianity had strong leanings towards GNOSTICISM. The Alexandrian school of theology, later exemplified in the writings of Clement of Alexandria (*c.*150–215 CE) and Origen (*c.*185–254 CE), was characteristically dependent on the thought of Plato, interpreted biblical texts allegorically and spiritually, and stressed the transcendence of GOD and the divine nature of Jesus. [11: I, 152–7; 13: II, 219–39; 18: 80–7]

Algonquin [V] The term denotes a North American tribe of the Algonquian linguistic stock, originally inhabiting the Ottawa valley and adjacent areas east and west. As with other Eastern Woodland tribes, the reality of MANITOU, an all-pervasive force in nature, was affirmed. In addition, a supreme being (often portrayed as a THUNDERBIRD), with intermediate divinities (brother sun, sister moon), and earth-mother, Nolomis, source and nourisher of life, were portrayed in myth. The WINDIGO and TRICKSTER-transformer culture-hero figured in shamanic practice (*see* SHAMAN), as did the VISION QUEST. [8: II–V, VII]

'Ali, 'Alids [XIX] 'Ali (*c.*598–660 CE) was the fourth CALIPH or 'suc-

cessor' to the Prophet, and since he was MUHAMMAD's cousin and son-in-law, his partisans in the civil warfare over political and religious leadership in early ISLAM regarded his claims as especially cogent (SHI'-ISM); they held that the Prophet himself had expressly designated 'Ali and his descendants the 'Alids as caliphs and IMAMS. Over the centuries, the 'Alids often sought political power through revolutionary outbreaks, with minimal success, but the consequent repressions did create a characteristic atmosphere in Shi'ism of emotionalism and sympathy with martyrdom (*see* PASSION PLAY (IN ISLAM)). The body of 'Alid descendants, eventually very numerous, were always regarded with respect by all Muslims of whatever sectarian affiliation, being called *sharifs* or *sayyids*, 'noble ones', and often in the past accorded social and financial privileges. [33; 38 s.v.; 69]

Allah [XIX] The name for God in ISLAM (meaning uncertain: perhaps *the* God). Allah was known as the supreme, but not sole, deity in Arabia before MUHAMMAD's mission, but it was the Prophet's task to proclaim him as the one, unique God. The QUR'AN accordingly stresses God's unity (*tauhid*) and makes polytheism (*shirk*) the supreme, unforgivable sin; the trinitarian Christians are thus to be condemned (*see* TRINITY). God is the creator of all existence (KHALQ), the controller of nature and the bestower of its fruits and the transcendent sovereign lord, and in the last days he will judge mankind (QIYAMA). Later theologians tried to define Allah's attributes, but stressed their difference from those of his creation. The fact of God's omnipotence created problems for these scholars over the degree of free will granted to mankind (*see* FATALISM (IN ISLAM)) [140: IV]. Notable for liturgical and devotional purposes (used e.g. by the Sufis in their sessions of *dhikr*: (*see* SUFI INSTITUTIONS) are the

'Ninety-nine most beautiful names' given to Allah. [20 'God, concept of'; 38 'Allāh'; 67 'God'; 71: 553–5; 137 index s.v. 'God']

Altjiranga [xxix] The Aranda word (sometimes written *alcheringa*) conventionally used to denote the concept of sacred time in AUSTRALIAN RELIGION. It refers to the beginning of time, when primordial mythical beings ('totemic ancestors'), in human or animal form, roamed the earth and made it habitable. Their spirits remain in the land, or in rocks (*see* WONDJINA), or in sacred objects (TJURUNGA), to be periodically incarnated in human foetuses. They also left tracks on the ground for people to follow in their everlasting search for food, and they laid down the correct rituals for ensuring its continuous supply. Thus there is an eternal aspect to the *altjiranga*, like a timeless dream state; hence the common translations, 'the eternal dream-time' or 'the Dreaming'. [10: 42–50; 27: 610–15; 28]

Alvar [xvii] Name of a type of ardently devotional Hindu saint of the Vaishnava (VISHNU) tradition meaning, literally, 'diver', that is, into the depths of mystical experience. They are particularly associated with the Tamil region of south India and date from about 500–1000 CE. Their hymns, the collection of which is called the *Prabandham*, had by the time of RAMANUJA acquired the status of sacred scripture, whose expositors were known as *acaryas*. The group of twelve Alvars, eleven men and one woman, cast in bronze, has an honoured place in the south Indian Vaishnava temple. *See also* NAYANNAR. [80: 258f, 263; 114; 38: 1–5, 87–129, 145–6]

Amaterasu-Omikami [xxi] Literally 'Heavenly-highest-shining deity', popularly, the sun-goddess, the chief KAMI in the native Japanese pantheon, a goddess created variously by the union of Izanagi and Izanami (*see* SHINTO MYTHOLOGY), from her father's left eye or from a mirror held in his left hand [3: i, 32–63; 19: 284–311; 34: 3–28]. Capable of spontaneous reproduction, she became the chief *kami* after the activities moved to earth, sending her grandson Ninigi-no-mikoto to secure the Eight-Island Country. She was, by tradition, enshrined at ISE JINGU in the reign of Emperor Suinin (*c.*4th century CE) and remains as a source of divine inspiration and guidance, a rather vague, ancestral spirit from whom all emperors are descended. She is not represented in the arts.

America/USA Religions [IV] [27] Religion presumably was represented on North American soil for thousands of years, as evidenced by archaeological findings, thanks to the presence of Native Americans (*see* AMERINDIAN RELIGIONS), descendants of people who had crossed a land bridge from what is now Siberia. Their spiritual understandings and practices were viewed almost entirely in negative terms by the Europeans who came in the 16th century, to whom these native peoples, called Indians, were seen as heathen and savage. Not until late in the 20th century were the beliefs and behaviour of Native Americans appraised positively by more than a few romantics. In recent decades, thanks to movements of Native American self-expression on the one hand and a search for alternatives to European influence in matters of the spirit on the other, Indian ritual and interpretation have received increasingly positive notice [3: i].

From 1492, after the encounters of Columbus with what came to be called the New World, until 1607, the predominant forms of European Christianity in the New World and eventually on the soil of what became the USA were ROMAN CATHOLIC. They were brought by explorers, conquerors and missionaries from the Iberian peninsula, chiefly from the newly self-conscious Spain. The Spaniards established missions in what is now the US south-west and in Florida [1: II, III]. The coming of British people for permanent settlement in Virginia in 1607 and in New England after 1620 and 1630 – the beginnings of the Puritan colonies at Plymouth and Massachusetts Bay (see PURITANISM) – did more than anything else to provide the framework for and strongest influence in American religiosity. In the northern colonies Puritan CONGREGATIONALISM was established by law, just as Episcopalianism was officially legitimated in the southern colonies. People from Great Britain, now including many Scots-Irish Presbyterians, also predominated in the middle colonies, but there they were not officially established. They also had to share Pennsylvania, originally a Quaker colony (see HOLY EXPERIMENT), with PROTESTANTS from the European continent, many of them German-speaking Lutherans (see LUTHERANISM), Reformed (see REFORMATION), and ANABAPTIST. Only Maryland began, and for a brief time only was settled, under Catholic auspices. The French Catholics arrived in 1608, and established New France in today's Canada. They explored the interior of today's USA, but did not remain a strong presence compared to the Catholic populations which arrived in the 19th century from elsewhere in Europe [1: IV, VIII, IX, XIII].

Africans began to arrive in 1619, most of them in slavery. While debate still continues about the degree to which slaves retained African spiritual understandings and practices, these forcibly imported people underwent traumatic change. In the course of the centuries, most were converted to Christianity, with BAPTISTS and METHODISTS long predominating both in the 'free-men's churches' before the Civil War (1861–5) and in the largely segregated African-American denominations since. Through the years numbers of non-Christian religious movements, often brought from the Caribbean, existed alongside these mainly Protestant groups, and since the middle of the 20th century large numbers of blacks have been attracted to the NATION OF ISLAM ('Black Muslims') and other Islamic groups. About 8% of Americans when polled identify with 'African-American Religion' [1: XLII; 13]. Jews arrived in 1654, first in new Amsterdam (New York), and were a small but visible presence ever after. However, after pogroms in Eastern Europe, large migrations of Jews began to arrive after 1881. Jews make up 2–3% of the American people, but exert influence beyond their numbers (see NORTH AMERICA, JEWS IN) [1: XXXV].

After the American Revolution and the development of the US Constitution, it became obvious that if a nation was to replace the 13 colonies, the Congress dared not try to choose which church to establish or which faith to privilege. The First Amendment of the Constitution forbade establishment just as it protected the free exercise of religion. By 1833 the last of the states had disestablished religion [20: VI]. From the Constitution and the First Amendment period (1787–9), the USA became a field of open competition for religious groups. Some came as immigrant blocs with their own churches; others developed renewed versions of older faiths (e.g. METHODISM out of Episcopalianism; Baptists out of Congregationalism; Disciples of Christ (Christian) out of PRESBYTERIANISM); still more participated in NEW RELIGIOUS MOVEMENTS (e.g. SHAKERS, Latter-day Saints [24], Seventh-day Adventists, CHRISTIAN SCIENTISTS, JEHOVAH'S WITNESSES) [20: VII–IX].

Social scientists who interview people find that about 25% of American people identify themselves as ROMAN CATHOLIC; fewer than 10%

have 'no religion' or 'no religious preference'; about 8% list 'other' as their preference (EASTERN ORTHODOX, MORMON, Asian religion, and the like). That leaves about half the American people identifying themselves as Protestant. However, this population group is divided into two almost equal cohorts. One is often called 'mainstream' or 'mainline', while the other is 'evangelical', which includes FUNDAMENTALIST, PENTECOSTAL, Southern Baptist and conservative Protestantism in general [23: IV, v] (*see* AMERICAN CHRISTIAN DENOMINATIONS).

The split within Protestantism occurred during the decades before 1925. One party was more predisposed to use revivalist techniques and to resist 'modernism' (*see* REVIVALISM). For half a century the mainstream parties were predominant in the public eye. However, more recently they have languished or declined statistically, while the evangelical sector has prospered and taken ever more active roles in political life.

The general absence of large identifiable atheist or agnostic population elements – more than 90% of US citizens profess to believe in God – strikes many observers as an anomalous situation in a nation of great religious freedom, affluence, mobility, higher education and technological prowess. A category of considerable interest in recent times is 'Other'. While statistically small, this sector attracts great attention, especially as immigrants from Asia have made their religious practices more evident and as new religions developed [23: 97–9]. The NRMs or 'new religious movements', called 'cults' by their detractors, attracted attention in the most recent third of the 20th century, at a time of great cultural upheaval. Some were attracted to transformed versions of Asian religion (NICHIREN SHOSHU, the UNIFICATION CHURCH, the HARE KRISHNA MOVEMENT and the like) in a pattern that rejected European

imports and long-established 'organized religion'. Others were drawn as part of a spiritual search, surprising in a society that is often called 'secular', that was not satisfied by traditional forms. Some scholars described the new search as part of 'privatization', a non-institutional form of religious practice that challenges inherited patterns. [6; 18; 1; 2; 7; 8; 14; 16; 19; 20; 27]

American Christian Denominations [IV] ROMAN CATHOLICS make up the largest single denomination in the USA; one-quarter of the people identify with Catholicism, while over 58 million are registered in the almost 20,000 parishes. American Catholics share the historic ROMAN CATHOLIC faith. The Catholic Church in America having been listed as a mission until 1908, Catholics in the USA tended to be dependent upon signals from Europe, often unquestioning in obedience to the Church, rarely experimental in theology, and – perhaps in part because they felt beleaguered by a sometimes hostile PROTESTANT majority – very loyal to Rome. Since the Second Vatican Council (1962–5), however, the American Church has seen the spread of internal varieties and great experiment as expressions of freedom, and there has been a feeling on the part of both an educated laity and the Church leadership that the times call for new forms alongside the more traditional [4: 9]. The Catholic Church was served by orders of religious men and women in setting up in America distinctive, parochial schools; these turned out to be a major instrument for keeping the loyalty of Catholics at a time when public schools often took on a Protestant guise, but remain strong now that the public schools have changed. These orders also established and maintain, now usually with significant lay and even non-Catholic participation, a system of colleges and universities. Because of migrations from many nations,

American Catholicism displays a great variety of internal ethnic differences, some of which have led to rivalries and resentments in the running of the Church.

Far fewer Eastern than Western Europeans migrated to the USA, so a second branch of Christianity, Orthodoxy, has far fewer members and less influence (*see* EASTERN ORTHODOX CHURCH). Approximately 2 million communicants are claimed by the Greek Orthodox, and there is a significant RUSSIAN ORTHODOX body, plus any number of smaller (e.g. Romanian, Serbian) Orthodox churches. They have tended to retain the liturgy in the various European languages and been perceived as traditionalist in church life, while becoming full participants in American citizenship and ecumenical Christian life [8: 334–5].

Protestant groups account for about 60% of the people; while thousands of African-Americans (*see* BLACK CHURCHES IN AMERICA) are in largely white denominations, racial segregation has marked these denominations descended from immigrants who came from Europe. While there are approximately 200 Protestant denominations in the *Yearbook of American and Canadian Churches*, most of the members can be viewed in several denominational families or clusters [12: v]. The most liberal trio are the Episcopalians, the United Church of Christ and the Presbyterians; in colonial times these were the dominant ones, but today claim only 8 or 9 million adult members together, plus an indeterminate number of 'fellow-travellers'. In recent times they have experienced membership losses. The Episcopalians are members of the Anglican Communion (*see* ANGLICANISM). In cultural life, they are influential beyond their numbers. They are thinly spread across the nation and have no area of dominance to call their own as they did Virginia and the Carolinas in colonial times. The United Church of Christ resulted from a merger in 1957 of the Congregational Christian and the Evangelical and Reformed churches. Theirs was the most significant merger of the century, because the membership cohorts were different, Congregationalists being heirs of New England PURITANISM, and the Evangelical and Reformed of originally German-speaking immigrants. Both had rich theological traditions typified by names such as that of the most honoured Puritan thinker, Jonathan Edwards, or the most respected 20th-century theologians, the brothers Reinhold and H. Richard Niebuhr. However, there is so much freedom and diversity in today's United Church of Christ that it would be hard to characterize its main strands of theology. PRESBYTERIANISM has seen schisms by a very small Orthodox Presbyterian Church, after the controversy over FUNDAMENTALISM, and a Presbyterian Church in America, formed in 1973 in reaction to liberalizing trends in the two main Presbyterian bodies. These merged in 1983 to form the Presbyterian Church (USA), the best-known group. Like the other liberal Protestant churches, this one has produced a disproportionate number of US Presidents, Supreme Court justices and people of influence in commerce. Its ancestry included chiefly Scots-Irish immigrants after 1706. Split into largely northern and largely southern bodies before the Civil War, Presbyterians have worked through a process of ten or more mergers to form this single group. While classified as liberal, this body includes great numbers of moderate and conservative leaders and members, who contend over loyalty to historic Presbyterian confessions of faith and modern transformations and experiments.

Moderate Protestants include METHODISTS, who derived from Anglicanism in England but swept the frontiers to become the largest

Protestant cluster until recently, when its United Methodist Church experienced losses; LUTHERANS, heirs of German and Scandinavian immigrants who formed many rival synods but have now either merged into the more moderate Evangelical Lutheran Church in America or remained in two large bodies, the Lutheran Church–Missouri Synod and the Wisconsin Evangelical Lutheran Synod, or in one of the numerous very small and ultra-conservative groups, all of them responsive to 16th-century Lutheran statements of faith; Christians (Disciples of Christ), a once very successful frontier denomination that stressed biblical 'primitivism' or simplicity and ecumenism; Northern Baptists, and Reformed, chiefly of Dutch heritage, in both a moderate and a conservative denomination [27].

The Southern Baptist Convention has passed the declining United Methodist Church to become by far the largest Protestant denomination; while it predominates in the south, it now has a national presence and is aggressive in its efforts to evangelize. Smaller Wesleyan bodies, heirs of the reforms of John Wesley, have grown, some in the forms of the Church of the Nazarene and various 'Holiness' bodies. But the explosive growth on Wesleyan and Holiness soil has been among PENTECOSTAL bodies formed in the 20th century, with the Assemblies of God being most prosperous. Add to these the 'historic peace churches' like the Quakers (see FRIENDS, RELIGIOUS SOCIETY OF), the Mennonites and the Church of the Brethren; the ADVENTISTS, who developed in the USA in the 19th century; the conservative Church of Christ, which professes to have no denominational structure; and the very liberal (and not always self-described as Christian) Unitarian-Universalist Association, and one has a register of the varieties of Protestant bodies which are constantly adapting to meet change in the American environment. [1: XLIV–LI; 8: XII; 4; 5; 9; 12; 14; 18; 22; 23; 27]

American Indian Movements (Christian Mission) [IV] [2; 3] Beginning with the members of ROMAN CATHOLIC religious orders who came with explorers and conquistadors in the 1540s, and continuing through the entire English colonial period, European Christians who came to North America professed and sometimes demonstrated desires to convert the people they called Indians. While they had utterly negative views of the 'heathen' practices of the 'savages', sometimes thinking they were children of the devil, at other times they were seen as special prospects for salvation. Catholics baptized thousands of them. PROTESTANT colonists in Virginia and even more in New England justified some of their ventures as extending the gospel through the conversion of Native Americans. They had meagre success. Roger Williams learned some languages and translated religious texts; some Moravians in Pennsylvania were quite sincere about living with the Indians they would convert; a family of ministers named Mayhew, through several generations on the island of Martha's Vineyard, helped evangelize 'praying Indians'; one David Brainerd, who died young, was memorialized as a hero who would convert them. But by the end of the colonial period almost no missionaries were left and there were few Christian Indians. So frustrating was Native American work, and so dangerous to life and health was it becoming, that New Englanders in particular began to put their missionary energies into foreign places. Yet as Protestantism moved west, with ever fresh encounters with Indians, some kept trying to Christianize them. After the Civil War, the Indian policy of President Ulysses S. Grant was supportive of church efforts on reservations. Catholics and Protestants alike were assigned to reservations, where they built missions and converted some of the inhabitants. [3: II–VI]

Numbers of well-known Native Americans were able to blend the symbolism and thought patterns of their Indian and Christian ways. Thus Black Elk, a notable articulator of the Native American vision through the poetic translation of John G. Neihardt in *Black Elk Speaks*, was also a Catholic catechist in the final decades of his life. In the latter decades of the century, as more and more Americans of European descent came to be critical of the Christianizing effort and appreciative of Native American ways, it became ever more evident that where Indians were not resistant they tended to fuse the motifs of their peoples' inherited ritual and understanding with selective elements of Christianity, but seldom accepting an unmediated transfer of European Christianity. [2: I]

Americanism [IV] 'Americanism' can mean a mere patriotic sentiment, but on many occasions it acquires a religious cast. Modern nationalism often comes with symbols (flags, monuments, rituals, pledges, marches) which echo or mimic religious ritual. Because of the extreme diversity of religious groups in America, none of them strong enough to provide a single set of symbols for everyone, the majority of Americans, according to polls, respond favourably to the elevation of the nation itself to a kind of spiritual status. The roots of Americanism as a religious sentiment or expression go back to the English colonists, who were convinced that their efforts were exemplary, 'God's New Israel', a 'city set upon a hill'. The founders chose as a motto, which still appears on money, *Novus Ordo Seclorum*; they were introducing a 'new order of the ages'. The language of 'manifest destiny', the sense that the USA ought to have

and indeed had a mission, a privileged direction, enhanced it, and the identification of the victorious Union forces with divine purpose in the Civil War further enhanced it [1: IX]. Times of warfare, of extreme political conflict, partisan suspicion or, sometimes, positive support for causes, lead people to accent the American Way of Life as the operating faith, even as they may remain active in churches whose theology asks them to call everything, including their nation and, in this case, their Americanism itself, into question. In classic terms, 'Americanism' is for some a word for a necessary bond among people; for others or at other times it can be a temptation to idolatry [16: XVIII]. Major figures in American history are invoked on both sides of controversies over Americanism. Most notable is President Abraham Lincoln, who had a kind of mystical vision of the Union cause and thus of Americanism – but who also taught caution about identifying nation or national sentiment with the exclusive favour of God. [2; 14; 20: XII]

American Indians (Central and South): New Religious Movements [XXVII] New religious movements developed early in Indian contact with whites, and have continued ever since. Some arose deep in the Amazon area, focused on young men regarded as reincarnated CULTURE HEROES in the form of 'new Christs', and were short-lived. In contrast, the HALLELUJAH religion among the Akawaio in the Guyana hinterland began in the mid-19th century. A succession of prophets with visionary experiences developed its emphasis upon prayer and moral discipline, with a holy village, Amokokopai (*see* NEW JERUSALEMS). The local Anglican missionaries have been cooperating with the movement since the 1960s. In Maranhão State, Brazil, a typical short-lived movement appeared among the Canela Indians in 1963, led by a prophetess promising the tribal culture hero's return to reverse their position in relation to the civilized and white peoples. The practices of folk ROMAN CATHOLICISM were adopted and whites' goods bought, but the birth of a messianic figure did not occur as expected and after a clash with a government agency the movement collapsed. In Panama a new movement appeared in 1961 among the Guaymi mountain people, where Mama Chi, after a vision of JESUS and the VIRGIN MARY, became woman leader of a syncretist religion that united the Guaymi and imposed a new lifestyle. Those organized more like independent indigenous churches prove longer-lasting and there are numbers of these in Peru, such as the Israelites of the New Universal Covenant (Israelitas del Nuevo Pacto Universal) among the Aymará Indians. There are Pentecostal movements (see PENTECOSTALISM) as among the Toba of the Argentine Chaco, but elsewhere these tend to shade into the *mestizo* or mixed-race inhabitants and into more orthodox Christian churches. (*See also* AFRO-AMERICANS.) [12: 141–53; 22: 701].

American Indians (North) and Eskimos: New Religious Movements [XXVII] North American Indians have maintained the three oldest continuing interaction movements found among any tribal peoples. At Charlestown, Rhode Island, the Narragansetts' one independent church has sustained tribal identity since it separated from the mission churches in the 1740s. In northern Mexico the Yaqui and Mayo have maintained independent churches ever since the Jesuits were suppressed in the 1760s and have taken them to new settlements in Arizona, as well as having produced a number of prophets and shorter-lived movements. The HANDSOME LAKE RELIGION goes back to 1800. In the 20th century the NATIVE AMERICAN CHURCH developed from the new

peyote cult (PEYOTISM), while the INDIAN SHAKER CHURCH began in 1881–2. Among the Apaches of New Mexico the Holy Ground religion founded in 1921 emphasizes morality and one God, absorbs JESUS Christ into traditional mythology and has a syncretistic symbolism and ritual. There are more orthodox independent Indian churches, usually derived from Christian missions; some are among urbanized Indians but most are on reservations, as among the Seminoles in Florida, the Creek and other Indian tribes in Oklahoma, and in Arizona especially among the NAVAJOS and HOPIS. Among the Plains Indians the traditional SUN DANCE has been revived in the 20th century, with some new forms and functions showing Christian influence. During the last century US movements have passed from resistance to peaceful coexistence, from millennial to non-millennial hopes and from nativistic to more Christian forms, despite current revivals of tribal religions in their original modes. Canadian and Alaskan movements have been more local and ephemeral, or have derived from the larger movements in the USA. The independent church form has been less common, although Albert Tritt's church lasted among the Kutchin in Alaska from about 1910 into the 1930s. Since 1970 a Pan-Indian Ecumenical Conference (see ECUMENICAL MOVEMENT) has met in Montana and on the Stoney Reserve in Alberta, uniting traditionalist and Christian leaders in seeking religious and cultural renewal for all Indians. ESKIMO movements go back to 1790 in Greenland, and include the Belcher Islands millennial movement that ended with police action in the early 1940s. [12: 101–32; 22: 701–2]

Americas, Islam in the [XIX] It is not known when the first Muslim set foot in the Americas. It cannot be determined with any certainty whether Arab explorers in the pre-

Columbus era ventured across the ocean. Some Muslims are thought to have come to the New World from Spain in the early period of European exploration, perhaps even with Columbus, but they were of no lasting significance to the history of ISLAM in the Americas. Within the last four centuries, however, there have been two major movements of Muslims to the area, one as a result of the slave trade and later mass importation of indentured labourers, and the other as a result of immigration from various parts of the Muslim world, commencing in the mid-19th century. Both of these movements, for different reasons, define the character of Islam in the Americas. The Atlantic slave trade from the 16th to the 19th century brought Muslims from various Islamicized African tribes (Yoruba, Fulani, Hausa) to the Caribbean, the American colonies and, especially, Portuguese-ruled Brazil. While Islam seems to have died out among the descendants of the imported slaves, this aspect of the African-American background has proved to be a potent symbol in more recent times, with conversions to Islam being linked to black nationalism and an African heritage on many occasions in the USA, as within the 'Black Muslim' movement (see NATION OF ISLAM). In the 19th century, the British and the Dutch imported labourers to work in their colonies, and many of these came from Muslim countries in Asia, especially India and Indonesia. Islam has continued among many of these groups, for example in Surinam, Guyana, and Trinidad and Tobago. The pattern of immigration, first from the Middle East and then from many other parts of the Muslim world, started in the mid-19th century. Many of the Arab immigrants were Christian, but a substantial portion in Argentina, Brazil, Canada and the USA was Muslim. The first MOSQUE in the United States was built as early as 1915. In the post-Second World War period Muslim immigration blossomed and the population is now very diverse in its origins, with Muslims from countries including Bosnia, South Africa, Pakistan, Palestine and the Sudan forming the Islamic community. Population estimates for Muslims in the Americas vary widely. The *1992 Britannica Book of the Year* provides the figures of 1,326,000 Muslims in Latin America and 2,642,000 in North America.

The majority of Muslims in the Americas are followers of the Sunni (see SUNNA) schools of law. SHI'ITES from Iran have become a more prominent group in the USA in the post-Khomeini period. ISMA'ILIS, followers of the Agha Khan, have also become a significant element in the Muslim population, first in the wake of their expulsion from Uganda in the 1970s, and then through continued immigration from east Africa in general. Muslims in the Americas diverge significantly among themselves on many religious issues and practices. This is to be seen especially in the difference in attitude between the second and third generation of American Muslims and the more recent immigrants. The former, on the whole, tend towards finding their Islamic identity within the wider context of society, assimilating to the extent felt necessary and identifying the ideals of Islam more closely with 'civil religion', especially in the USA. The latter tend to have been heavily influenced by currents in modern Muslim thought and are self-consciously Muslim in the maintenance of their notion of Islamic ideals. They do not consider the adjustments made by the older generations of immigrants to the secular (or Christian) society of the Americas to be desirable. IMAMS (prayer leaders) are frequently recent immigrants from the Middle East, due both to the lack of religious training facilities in the Americas and to the willingness of countries such as Saudi Arabia to finance their positions. This has tended to exacerbate the differences in religion between the acculturated and the immigrant groups, the former frequently complaining that religion as it is preached is not relevant to modern life, for example in standards suggested for male–female interaction.

A number of attempts at organizing Muslims in each country have been made, with varying degrees of success. In the USA and Canada, the Islamic Society of North America emerged in 1981 as an umbrella body bringing together a large number of special-interest Muslim groups. It sponsors conferences and an annual convention, provides materials for Islamic education, and issues guidelines for help in maintaining Islamic traditions. The American Muslim Mission, the legacy of the NATION OF ISLAM (the 'Black Muslims'), encompasses the main indigenous form of Islam in the United States. As that group becomes increasingly identified with 'orthodox' Islam, construction of bridges between the immigrant and the indigenous groups is considered more likely. [3; 60; 72; 73; 139]

Amerindian Religions [v] During a period extending over 25,000 years, from the time of the earliest migrations across the Bering land bridge to the present day, the religions of the aboriginal inhabitants of North America have displayed a vast variety of forms. These have ranged from simple hunting rituals, through more elaborate calendric rites (see CALENDAR ROUND) based upon settled agricultural economies, through the hunting and war-related cults of the nomadic tribes of the plains to more recent manifestations including the GHOST DANCE, PEYOTISM, syncretistic forms bearing Christian influence, the REVITALIZATION MOVEMENT, pan-Indianism and the Red Power movement. The great diversity of belief and practice, the relative scarcity of archaeological data, the near-absence of historical records, the virtual extinction of many tribes, the influence of missionary efforts and the general tendency towards acculturation present the scholar with a near-impossible task of reconstruction and generalization. Most Amerindian religions, however, affirm the existence of a supreme power (personal or impersonal), as well as the divine origin of the cosmos (see COSMOLOGY; CREATION MYTHS). The ontological good of this world, the possibility of direct human contact with the supernaturals through visions (VISION QUEST) and rituals, and humans' ability to acquire and direct supernatural power for their own ends are equally important. The 'sacramental' character of the physical world, the essential interrelatedness of the human, divine, animal (see OWNER OF THE ANIMALS) and vegetative realms, and the composite nature of the human individual (consisting of a body, plus a 'free' SOUL and a 'life' soul), are central themes of Amerindian religions. Most groups affirm the perfectibility of humanity in this life, through behaviour in keeping with fundamental relationships, as well as the possibility of some postmortem existence. Individual and collective rites seek to discern the significance of natural patterns (e.g. the movements of animals, celestial and seasonal variations, and the intentions of the supernaturals) in order to channel, influence or act in accordance with the sacred realities. Amerindian religions generally stress the priority of actions over belief and, although the centrality of individual religious experience is commonly affirmed, the consequences for the community are usually underscored. [2: I, II, IV, VI; 12; 17: V–VIII]

Amesha Spentas [XXXVI] The 'Holy' or 'Bounteous' Immortals in ZOROASTER's teaching. Their number is traditionally seven, but mod-

The Amesha Spentas

Avestan form	Later form	English 'name'	Creation protected
Ahura Mazda	Ohrmazd	Wise Lord	Man
Spenta Mainyu	–	Holy (Creative) Spirit	Man
Vohu Manah	Bahman	Good Purpose	Cattle
Asha	Ardvahist	Righteousness	Fire
Khshathra	Shahrevar	Power, Kingdom	Sky
Armaiti	Spendarmad	Devotion	Earth
Haurvatat	Hordad	Health	Waters
Ameretat	Amurdad	Immortality	Plants

ern scholars and PAHLAVI texts disagree on which Immortals are to be included in that number (see table). The fact that the number remains constant, while the identity of the beings changes slightly, suggests that the number seven was symbolically significant and/or a strong element of the tradition. In the Pahlavi literature Ohrmazd (AHURA MAZDA) is identified with Spenta Mainyu and so becomes one of the seven Amahraspands (the Pahlavi form of Amesha Spentas). Some scholars argue that this was also Zoroaster's belief [8 vol. 1: VIII], but others disagree [64: 43–51]. The Amesha Spentas are thought of as heavenly beings, somewhat resembling the archangels of Christian belief. Each Immortal is thought of as a guardian of one of the seven creations which constitute the Good Creation. All the Immortals are symbolically represented through their respective creations in the central rite, the YASNA, and when this is performed in total purity with devotion by a priest it is believed that the Amesha Spentas are powerfully present. They are described in human terms; for example some are male, some female and one of them, Vohu Manah, greets the righteous soul at the CHINVAT BRIDGE to conduct it to heaven. There is also an important abstract dimension to their nature.

Their 'names' are not personal ones, but denote aspects of the divine nature in which humans can and should share (except Spenta Mainyu, the Holy Spirit). So, by embodying the good purpose, by living a life of righteousness and devotion, human beings can share in the kingdom, enjoy health and immortality. The individual's religious duty can, therefore, be described as making the Immortals dwell within him or her. [10: 21–4; 64: 45–50]

Amida Worship [XXI] The Japanese combined AMITABHA (Infinite light) and Amitayus (Infinite Life) into Amida, the Buddha of the Pure Land (Jodo = Chinese CHING T'U) Western Paradise (Saiho) (see JAPANESE BUDDHAS AND BODHISATTVAS) [8: 74–87; 14: 61–3]. Within TENDAI, following ENNIN's return from China in 847 CE, meditation halls were built and the chanting of nembutsu (a contraction of Namu-Amida-Butsu) started. The Fujiwara aristocrats were ardent believers, erecting large Amida temples, some for retirement purposes. The priest Genshin (Eshin Sozu) (942–1017) wrote Ojoyoshu (Essentials of Salvation or Birth in the Land of Purity) in 985, stressing the practice of the repetition of Amida's name, with the mind fixed on the BUDDHA IMAGE.

Purely Japanese, it was the first reasoned exposition of Jodo, Pure Land doctrine.

All Amida worship was still under this-worldly Tendai until *Yuzunembutsu* was founded by Ryonin in 1124, the first Amida sect, based in Osaka. Genku (1130–1212) or Honen Shonin (Enko Daishi) left Mt Hiei for Kyoto and, using the *Ojoyoshu*, emphasized faith and the saving grace of Amida, initiating the concept of Pure Land as rebirth in the next existence. His teaching dates the formation of the Jodo sect from 1175 [36: 192–7]. His thesis *Senchaku Hongan Nembutsu Shu* (Collection of Passages on the Original Vow and the Nembutsu) of 1198 resulted in his banishment in 1206. On returning in 1211, he built the large Chion-in, the chief temple of the sect and the parent of many offshoots.

Shinran (1173–1262) broke the customary priestly celibacy and taught *akunin shoki*, grace for the inevitable sinner, drawing a large following among farmers. His successors separated into Jodo Shinshu (True Pure Land sect), the largest group today, for which later generations built the Hongan-ji in Kyoto, headed by the Otani family, now in east and west branches. Followers of Ippen Shonin (Chishin) (1239–89), known for the *odori-nembutsu*, the dancing *nembutsu*, built the sect around his name. Amida worship now thrives in many sub-sects, whose members revere the founders and recite incantations, in temples which assume most of the funeral business in Japan because of the generous promises they make for the soul's eternal bliss.

Amidah [xxII] The central prayer of the JEWISH LITURGY, the word meaning 'standing' since the prayer is said standing facing towards Jerusalem [70: 167]. It consists of 19 benedictions, and is also known as the *Shemoneh Esreh* ('Eighteen'), a benediction having been added in the 2nd century against heretics [29: 92; 64: 50]. The *Amidah* is recited thrice daily, and in a slightly different form on Sabbaths (SHABBAT) and festivals (CHAGIM) when an extra *Amidah*, *Musaf*, is added. [14 vol. 2: 838]

Amitabha [xI] A BUDDHA who dwells in Sukhavati, a Pure Land in the West. Amitabha was the most successful of a number of Buddhas who formed the focus of specific cults in Indian MAHAYANA Buddhism, often based on one or two MAHAYANA SUTRAS devoted to those Buddhas. The earliest was probably Akshobhya, and a cult centred on Amitabha seems to have developed by the early years CE. The name Amitabha means 'infinite light' and Amitabha is usually equated with Amitayus ('infinite life'), although they are distinguished by Tibetans. In a previous life, when he took the vows of a BODHISATTVA, Amitabha vowed that upon becoming a Buddha his Pure Land or Buddha-realm would be particularly superior and that all who repeated his name or thought of him even ten times would be reborn in this Pure Land after death and there in his presence meet with optimum facilities for becoming enlightened. Since he has become a Buddha all is now as he wished, and all bar those who have committed particularly heinous crimes can be reborn in that Pure Land. It is suggested that it is necessary to meditate on Amitabha and his Pure Land, and direct one's merit (PUNNA) to rebirth in that place, although in China and particularly Japan these additional factors gradually became less important, and devotion to Amitabha (known as Amida in Japan; *see* AMIDA WORSHIP) has become a form of religious practice and aspiration with a wide appeal, exemplifying the compassionate Mahayana desire to help as many people as possible. At the same time those who follow the Pure Land tradition, particularly Shinran in Japan, have developed a sophisticated doctrinal basis for complete reliance on Amitabha and his salvific vows. [101: 251–76] (*See also* AMIDA WORSHIP; CHINESE BUDDHISM; CHING T'U TSUNG.)

Amulets and Talismans [XXIV] Objects believed to be charged with magical power have been used to protect or give strength to their wearer in all parts of the world, probably since antiquity. Amulets are thought to ward off misadventure, disease and assault from malefic beings (human and demonic) – as may be seen in the many and widespread forms of protection from the evil eye. Some amulets make use of engravings of particularly terrifying monstrous creatures, as in for instance the ancient Greek depiction of the head of the gorgon, whose eye was supposed to petrify any likely assailant. Talismans, in contrast, of which good luck charms are a popular example, are believed to impel the beneficial and enhance a person's potentialities and good fortunes. The efficacy of a particular amulet or talisman is usually thought to reside in its form and in the substance from which it is made. Forms are often unusual, generally symbolic (such as the ankh, the hand, the cross and the phallus) and are sometimes inscribed with religious or magical formulae. Their value is often thought to be derived from their origin: bones or relics of saints or heroes, animal parts exemplifying particular animal characteristics (swiftness from a hare, strength from a bull) and substances thought to have special properties are all used. The amulet or talisman may then be empowered by some form of chant or blessing. A traditional use of amulets and talismans is in connection with burial to protect the soul journeying through the underworld. Their popularity tends to be a feature of folk belief rather than of more orthodox religious practice, but they are nonetheless often regarded sympathetically by established religions: the Roman Catholic Church, for instance, has long recognized their function, and they may be found throughout Buddhist and Hindu countries, sometimes commemorating famous teachers or holy men who have just died.

Amun [VI] Originally a local god of Thebes, Amun was elevated by the Theban princes (18th dynasty, *c.*1550 BCE) to become the great state-god of Egypt's empire. Associated with RE' as Amen-Re', Amun assimilated his powers; in the vast temple complex at Karnak, he was worshipped with his consort, Mut, and son, Khonsu. So great was his influence that his priesthood (*see* MANSION OF THE GODS) threatened the king's sovereignty, perhaps contributing to the 'revolutionary' Aten cult championed by Akhenaten (ATENISM).

Anabaptists [XIII.B] The nickname ('re-baptizers') of a variety of 16th-century sects, some pacific, some violent [203]. A common characteristic was baptism of mature believers, instead of infants, as a mark of church membership. The peaceful Mennonites (Menno Simons, 1496–1561) survive in America [157: 902].

Anagami [XI] In THERAVADA Buddhism, a 'non-returner', that is, a being who will not return to the earthly round of birth and death, but will be reborn in a heavenly sphere, where he will attain the state of an ARAHAT.

Anagarika [XI] The original form of the Buddhist life. The term designates one who has gone forth from his home in order to search for the truth about life. Such a person is called *an-agarika* because he is a 'non-householder', that is, a homeless wanderer. This practice of leaving the regular life of a householder was fairly common in ancient India, and is still practised. It was, and is, regarded as very honourable. Sakyamuni (the BUDDHA) himself left his home and family in this way, in order to attain supreme enlightenment, and became Buddha (GOTAMA). The order of BHIKKHUS (monks) which he later founded consisted of such *anagarikas*. Like other groups of this kind in northern India at that time, they depended on the goodwill of householders for their sustenance. Buddhist scriptures contain accounts of the reasons which prompt a person to become an *anagarika*, and the procedure for doing so, such as the following: 'The life of the household is full of obstacles. It is the path of impurity; it is not possible to lead the higher life which is extremely pure and clean by one living the life of a householder. How now, if I were to shave my hair and beard, put on the yellow robe and walk forth from home to homelessness.' (*Anguttaranikaya*, II.208)

Ananaikyo [XXVI] Founded in 1949 by Nakano Yonosuke (1887–1974), Ananaikyo is a Japanese new religious movement in the Shinto tradition. Its chief centre is located in the city of Shimizu, south of Mt Fuji. The sect claims nearly 100,000 adherents. Once a successful building contractor, Nakano came under the influence of Omoto in 1921. He gave up the world of business, joined Omoto and became an ardent missionary, devoting eight years to a type of spiritual training called *reigaku*. Nagasawa Katsutate, a SHINTO scholar of the Japanese classics and a *reigaku* adept, was his mentor – as he had been for the founder of Omoto, Deguchi Onisaburo. While meditating in 1899, Nagasawa had received a KAMI-message (*see* BYAKKO SHINKOKAI) that in 50 years a religious organization would be established in the city of Shimizu, that it would be called Ananaikyo, and that through this organization the way of the *kami*

would spread throughout the world. He asked Nakano to become his successor and to found the organization that had been foretold. Nakano, agreeing to do so, made *reigaku* central to the organization he founded in Shimizu in 1949. Because of a *kami*-message received in 1956, Ananaikyo holds that astronomical influences can help people resolve earthly problems. It is unique in having constructed observatories at several places in Japan in order to study heavenly bodies and interpret their influences. [10: IX, 187]

Ananda [XI] GOTAMA's personal attendant and one of his principal disciples (*see also* BUDDHA); a first cousin of Gotama and his exact equal in age (to the day). When other disciples were in doubt concerning the teaching, Ananda was frequently called on to explain, and his skill in doing so, which became known to Gotama, was highly praised. He also championed the cause of the women disciples and persuaded Gotama to admit them to the SANGHA. After Gotama's death he took a leading part in reciting the received version of the master's teaching.

Ananda Marga [XXVIII] Founded in India in 1955 by Shrii Shrii Anandamurti (1921–90). The movement spread to the West during the 1970s. Members are expected to follow ascetic spiritual practices relating to cleanliness, diet, posture, sexual relations and service, and to practise YOGA and chant *Ba'ba na'm kevalam* to 'focus the mind on the Supreme Consciousness'. The movement defines itself primarily as a philosophical or political organization that engages in social welfare and education, rather than as a religious movement. Protests over the imprisonment of their leader in India in the 1970s led to the self-immolation of some members. [5: 54–5, 167–8; 42: 906–7; 61]

Anargyroi [XIII.D] The 'Unmerce-nary Physicians' of EASTERN ORTHO-DOX tradition, a class of saints whose cult was established by the 5th cen-tury. The most revered are invoked in the liturgy; they include Kosmas and Damianos (3rd century), Samp-son Xenodochos (6th century), Aga-pit (11th century) and the martyrs Kyros and John (3rd century) and Panteleimon and Hermolaos (4th century). These Christian doctors used medicine and prayer to cure people and animals alike, steadfastly refusing any form of payment. The Anargyroi are commemorated sepa-rately and also as a group of 12, 22 or more (on 17 October). The as yet uncanonized Athenian doctor Dimi-trios Lekkas (d. 1979) is popularly acclaimed as a modern Anargyros. [3; 12; 44]

Anatta [XI] (Pali; Sanskrit: *anat-man.*) A term used in BUDDHIST thought meaning 'not-self'. Certain strands of Indian thought contem-porary with the BUDDHA assumed an unchanging, eternal self or ATMAN underlying and unifying an individ-ual's various experiences; this self, it was claimed, could be experienced directly in states of meditation. Early Buddhist thought, however, sugges-ted that the idea of a unitary, unchanging self is a mental con-struct we project on to the flow of consciousness. When experience is analysed and broken down into its constituent parts no 'self' is found, only various mental and physical phenomena (*see* DHAMMA) that can be classified in terms of five cate-gories or 'aggregates' (Pali: *khandha*; Sanskrit: *skandha*): body, feelings, recognition, volitions, conscious awareness. These five aggregates, continuously rising and falling in dependence on one another (*see* PATICCASAMUPPADA), constitute the sum total of an individual's experi-ence or world. Buddhist thought thus argues that there is nothing in experience that an individual can ever rightly claim as his or her unchanging 'self'. For Buddhism the notion of self is not a reflection of the way things are but a function of a deep-rooted attachment that perpetuates a distorted view of the world and thus leads to suffering (DUKKHA). Conversely, relinquish-ing one's ultimate (imagined) pos-session, the self, is the way to freedom from suffering. This under-standing forms the basis of Buddhist ethics and compassion: as long as one is bound and restricted by the notion of self, one cannot truly act selflessly for the benefit of others. Together with *dukkha* and ANICCA, *anatta* is one of the three marks (Pali: *tilakkhana*; Sanskrit: *trilak-shana*) of all conditioned existence. [34: 53–4; 12] (*See also* ABHID-HAMMA; EMPTINESS; VIPASSANA.)

Ancestor Cult (Chinese) [XII] The veneration of ancestors (*pai tsu*) is one of the most ancient, persistent and influential themes in Chinese religion and traditional Chinese society. From excavations of Shang dynasty sites (1500–1000 BCE) it is known that the Shang rulers pro-vided their dead with all the essen-tials for continued sustenance, and consulted their royal ancestors by means of ORACLE BONES for advice on ritual, military, agricultural and domestic matters [14; 17a: 1, 17–32; 114]. The principal deity, SHANG TI, was quite possibly a supreme royal ancestor in origin. The oracle bones and inscribed bronze ritual vessels are concerned almost exclusively with royal ancestors. By the time of the Western Chou dynasty (1027–770 BCE) the idea of the interdependence of the living and the dead was clearly established. The formal ritual and ethical requirements of the ancestor cult are described in the 'Classic of Rites' (*Li Ching*) [69; 96].

The motives and underlying ideas behind the beliefs and practices of the ancestor cult are varied and complex. Clearly the formal and cer-emonial expression of grief by the relatives serves an important function. The funeral and mourning rites serve to re-establish and maintain the unity and continuity of the family. The reverence and respect paid by a devoted son to his deceased father is clearly an application of the important virtue of filial piety (*hsiao*). There is also an element of self-interest or self-preservation. The *hun* (spiritual soul) and the *p'o* (gross soul) of the dead (*see* HUN-P'O) are dependent for their survival and happiness upon the offerings of spirit money, incense, and food and drink made by their descendants. In return the *hun* soul, as a spirit (*shen*), can achieve considerable benefits for the family by means of its supernatural contacts. In the case of ordinary beings this relationship is considered to last only for between three and five generations. The souls are then succeeded by more recent ones. The *p'o* soul normally resides in the grave, but if it is not accorded the proper respect and offerings it could emerge as a malevolent ghost (*kuei*); so it is very much in the interests of the family to supply them (*see also* FUNERAL RITES). [1; 17a: 3, 63–5; 45; 50; 53; 98: xx, 155–9; 99: III, 34–55; 122: II, 28–57]

Ancestor Veneration (African) [II] In most although not all African religions (among the exceptions are the Masai, NUER, and Tiv) ancestors play a major role; they are generally the immediate recipients of most prayers and sacrifices. This reflects the profound importance of kinship in the ordering of society. Ancestors protect the living, but insist also upon the maintenance of custom, punishing by sickness or misfortune those who breach it. There are, nevertheless, many major differences upon which it is unwise to impose a single model of interpretation. In general ancestors are seen as elders, named and approached in much the same way as the most senior of living elders: yet they have additional mystical powers and,

among many peoples, different or additional names (*see* MIZIMU). In more God-conscious societies ancestors may be approached simply as intermediaries to God, but where ritual, petition and sacrifice are regularly directed to ancestral spirits with little or no reference to God, it seems linguistically perverse to deny that this is worship – a word itself admitting a range of meaning. Among some peoples a clear verbal distinction is certainly made between reverencing ancestors and worshipping God; thus the Gikuyu use *gothaithaya* (their word for worship) for the latter but never for the former, as the Zulu use *ukukhonza* for worshipping God. The usual Zulu word for venerating ancestors, *ukuthetha*, means literally 'speaking with'.

In some religions a wide range of male and female ancestors – perhaps the collective dead – are venerated, in others a rather narrow jural line of authority-holders; in some, ancestors are seen as concerned chiefly (or only) with the supply of continued gifts to them, in others rather with the wider social behaviour of the living; in some, their individual characteristics may be remembered, in others these appear irrelevant. Ancestors normally enter into full status only after completion of various post-funerary rituals. In some west African societies (for example, Benin and the Ibo) ancestor veneration is combined with belief in their reincarnation in descendants.

It is in small agricultural societies which lack political structures beyond lineage heads (for example, Lugbara and Tallensi) that the worship of ancestors can be most clearly found. In larger kingdoms it tends to become a more varied communion with the dead, while among pastoralists it is often absent [7: 16–21, 122–42; 24; 30; 43]

Ancestor Worship [XXXIV] Devotion, going beyond veneration, to persons who have died [117: 56–7,

291–2; 124: 46–8, 61–3, 172–4]. To honour the dead and hallow their memory is common. Many peoples go further, believing that the dead (especially leaders and heroes) live on and can affect the life of later generations [11: 127–54; 43: 64–7]. Hence prayers and rites (see RITUAL), often SACRIFICES, are directed to them. Some theorists have claimed to find the ORIGIN OF RELIGION in such practices [145: 34] or in the deification of heroes (Euhemerism). [117: 18–19; 145: 6]

Ancient Egyptian Religion [VI] Geographical factors profoundly affected the development of religion in Egypt. The multitude of tribal deities in existence before the unification of Egypt (c.3100 BCE) formed the basis of the pantheon which consisted of state-gods (mainly cosmic deities with some elevated local gods) and local gods (each town had its own divinity). These had temples (see MANSION OF THE GODS) and received a cult, but the majority of people worshipped household gods at village shrines [5]. By the Old Kingdom (c.2600 BCE), the priests had attempted to rationalize the multitude of divinities, some were grouped into 'families', the most famous being the Great and Little Enneads (nine gods) of Heliopolis and the Ogdoad (eight gods) of Hermopolis. Later, divine triads (AMUN; OSIRIAN TRIAD; SETH) were established [17: VII, 142].

The twin forces of the Nile and the sun moulded FUNERARY PRACTICES and beliefs. The annual inundation revived the parched land and vegetation – a cycle reflected in the life, death and resurrection of Osiris, god of vegetation. Similarly, the sun died each night, renewing its birth at dawn. The Egyptian concept of human existence (life, death, rebirth – see AFTERLIFE) was inspired by the cyclic pattern evident in these natural phenomena [5].

The Egyptians called their country Kemet (the 'Black Land'), referring to the black mud deposited on the river banks by the inundation; with scanty rainfall, Egypt supports a thriving community only because of the Nile's inundation. Even so, irrigation provides only limited cultivable land, and in earliest times (pre-dynastic period, c.3400 BCE), the dead were buried outside this area, in the desert, where the heat and dryness of the sand naturally desiccated the corpses. This led the Egyptians to regard the artificial preservation of the body (MUMMIFICATION) as essential to the person's continued existence.

SYNCRETISM was an important feature of ancient Egyptian religion. In the pre-dynastic era, early religious development reflected political events. As communities were amalgamated, following intertribal conflicts, and larger political units were formed, so the characteristics and cult-centres of the deities of the conquered tribes were absorbed by the victors' deities [17: VII, 139]. Also, cosmic deities may have adopted the attributes and centres of older, tribal gods. Later, the deities of foreign neighbours or conquered peoples were sometimes incorporated into the Egyptian pantheon.

Ancient European Religions [VII] The main pre-Christian religions known to us, outside Greece and Rome, were those of the GERMANIC and CELTIC peoples. We know very little of the beliefs of the SLAVS and BALTS. Celts and Germans were in contact in Roman times [31: 42–9], and again in the British Isles in the Viking age. The Celts were converted by 500 CE, but the old religion survived up to the 11th century in Scandinavia, and ancient myths influenced Icelandic [3: 14–16] and Irish [17: 14–20] literature. Writing was limited in pre-Christian cultures to RUNES and early inscriptions, so for our knowledge of this subject we depend upon archaeological finds, Greek and Roman writers, early missionaries, material recorded after the conversion to Christianity, inscriptions identifying deities with their Roman counterparts, names of persons, places, and gods. While these religions were never centralized, a main outline can be discerned. There is a sky-god fighting monsters with club or hammer (DAGDA; Perkunas (see BALTS); Perun (see SLAVS); THOR); a god of eloquence, magic and the dead (LUG, ODIN); fertility deities (BRIGIT; MATRES; VANIR); a TRICKSTER figure (Bricriu [4: 213–14]; LOKI); and female battle spirits (VALKYRIES). Little is known of the Germanic priesthood, but the DRUIDS helped to preserve Celtic traditions [15: IV]. Sacred places were in forests, on hills and islands, near lakes and springs, and at burial places [4: 127]. Regular feasts were held (SAMHAIN [4: II; 3a: 88–93]), and sacrifices and offerings made for fertility and victory (VOTIVE OFFERINGS). There were simple temples and Celtic sanctuaries for healing [4: 27–35]. Divination was widely practised [4: V], and there was elaborate funeral symbolism (SHIP-FUNERAL [3a: 134–6]). Myths of creation and the world's ending (RAGNAROK), tales of exploits of the gods and journeys to supernatural realms (LAND OF YOUTH) survive in later literature.

Ancient Near Eastern Religions [VIII] Mesopotamia – the 'land between the rivers' Tigris and Euphrates – was the cradle of ancient Near Eastern religions. Although it was successively occupied by new peoples, who brought their languages, ideas and religious beliefs (ASSYRIANS; BABYLONIANS; SUMERIANS), there was a continuing civilization which passed on the earliest traditions [10; 16; 20; 23]. Central to this was the city-state [23: 13–14]; each city-state had its own deity and TEMPLE, which held a key position in the community and provided an indication of its wealth. At first loosely associated in a league

(see SUMERIANS), the cities eventually acknowledged a supreme overlord, and the Akkadians and Assyrians developed the concept of universal rulership, creating state pantheons to emphasize national unity. Local gods continued to exist alongside the great gods.

The Old Babylonian period was very important, for an extensive written literature now arose (see GILGAMESH, EPIC OF; MARDUK) [24], in which the earlier Sumerian elements – names and characteristics of gods, myths and legends, omens (see DIVINATION), and MAGIC – were preserved and eventually handed down to the Assyrians [11] and, through the HURRIANS [9], to the HITTITES, thus providing the basis of most primitive Near Eastern religions. Monuments [6; 26] and seal impressions (see ART AND SYMBOLISM) [5; 23: 27–32] amplify our knowledge of these gods and their temples.

It was generally accepted that men were created solely to serve the gods and to supply their basic needs – food, drink and shelter (TEMPLES). The Sumerians introduced the doctrine of the creative power of the divine word [16: 130–1] and this became widely accepted throughout the Near East. Similarly, most societies regarded KINGSHIP [7; 12; 19] as divine, and the king as the chief priest of the great state-god.

Comparatively little attention was given to the AFTERLIFE (see PHILISTINES; PHOENICIANS), and although some elaborate grave goods have been discovered, the concept of individual immortality was disregarded in these religions.

The main textual sources of knowledge concerning religion include the extensive literature of the Old Babylonian period, when myths and epics relating the proceedings of gods and men in earliest times were mostly written down in Sumerian; also recorded were the hymns and psalms addressed to gods and kings, and the incantations and prayers recited by private persons or priests to alleviate sickness and affliction (see MAGIC (ANCIENT NEAR EASTERN)) [24]. The Hittite literature includes Babylonian 'scientific works', as well as creation and resurrection epics such as the myth of 'Slaying the Dragon Illuyankas' and that of the 'Missing God' [13: 180–94]. Paucity of written evidence about other societies (ELAMITES; PHILISTINES; PHOENICIANS) limits our understanding of their beliefs.

Myths and legends relate the history of the gods since the first creation and the deeds of ancient heroes (see GILGAMESH, EPIC OF; SUMERIANS) [24]. They attempt to explain the world (see COSMOLOGY); and they return to the recurrent themes of the victory of good over EVIL ('Slaying the Dragon' – a New Year Babylonian and Hittite myth [13: 181–2]) (see FESTIVALS; MARDUK), and the disappearance and return of a vegetation god who deprives the earth of its fertility and then restores it [for the Hittite myth see 9; 13: 184–9; see also the Ugaritic myth of Aqhat, PHOENICIANS, 4: 27].

Anekantavada [xx] The 'many-pointed doctrine', evolved by JAIN philosophers as a relativistic theory which insisted on the necessity of taking a variety of perspectives into account before a judgement about any entity could be formulated. This relativism most likely takes its origin from two factors: Jainism's belief that any judgement not based on omniscience, the all-knowing, all-seeing state believed to have been attained by the religion's saving teachers (KEVALIN; TIRTHANKARA) is inadequate; and the fact that Jain doctrine regards reality as being characterized by the three factors of arising, permanence and disappearance. In its classical form, Jain relativism stipulates that judgements be based on seven standpoints (naya): the 'common' (naigama), in which the general and specific characteristics of an entity are taken together; the 'general' (samgraha), which looks at an entity from its general characteristics only; the 'transactional' (vyavahara), which looks at an entity with regard to its specific aspects; the 'straight-thread' (rijusutra), according to which an entity is judged in respect of its immediately manifest characteristics; the 'verbal' (shabda), which takes into account grammatical inflection; the 'subtle' (samabhirudha), which requires that the etymological derivation of words be taken into account; and the 'thus-happened' (evambhuta), which restricts a word semantically to the action or state which it denotes. To be correlated with this mode of analysis are seven statements which can be made about an entity and which signify their provisional nature by including the Sanskrit word syat, 'may be'. These constitute the 'doctrine of may-be' (syadvada). [4: 197–200; 11]

Relativism is Jainism's main intellectual claim to fame in India. Although possibly a natural doctrine for a religion which regards non-violence to all creatures (AHIMSA) as its central ethical attitude, it has very little direct relevance for the majority of Jains today.

Angakok [v] A term used among the hunting and fishing peoples of the central Arctic (Tonralik, in Alaska), referring in the most general sense to someone, male or female, who has a helping spirit; thus a SHAMAN or sorcerer. Those who, by a variety of traditional shamanic techniques or initiation, make contact with sila, the fundamental, elemental, and all-pervasive power of the universe, gain an angakog or qaumaneq, a 'lighting' or 'enlightenment' whereby they obtain divinatory and curative powers. [23: II] Through the tuition of an elder angakok (plural, angak ut), a youth was prepared for contact with the supernatural world by fasting and physical ordeals. At length, through dream or vision, a transformation of psyche and body was experienced, often symbolized by dismemberment and reconstitution at the hands of the *tunrag* (helping spirits). The ecstatic experience thus confirmed and supplemented by instruction in techniques of curing and divination, the neophyte assumed a public role, assisted henceforth by his spirit helper. Varying degrees of intensity of the initial experience, together with the importance of the helping spirits contacted (the benevolent spirits of the deceased were regarded as of lesser rank), resulted in a hierarchy, the *angakok* having a more intimate and personal relationship with the *tunrag* than others.

Angels (Biblical) [XIII.A] In earlier books of the BIBLE the 'angel of Yahweh' appears as the messenger of GOD to human beings. There are vaguer references to other angels. In post-exilic times, possibly under the influence of ZOROASTRIANISM, a hierarchy of angels emerges with four or more named archangels. Some of these angels control separate nations; others have charge of natural elements like fire and water; others are related to the processes of history and are expected to exercise a divine role in judgement. In non-biblical literature of the second temple period fallen angels (*Genesis* 6: 1–4) are sometimes blamed for the existence of evil. In the New Testament angels are specially active in the Apocalypse, representing the military might of God and exemplifying true worship. [7: I, 280–2; 11: I, 248–55]

Angels (in Judaism) [XXII] Despite the frequent references to angels in the BIBLE, there seem to have been some rabbinical sages who doubted the desirability of angelology in JUDAISM [30: 109]. The MISHNAH does not mention angels, and some Talmudic rabbis seem to avoid mentioning angels in their interpetations of scripture (*see* RABBI; TALMUD). This attitude is carried over into the Haggadah, the Passover liturgical

text, which emphasizes that the deliverance of the Israelites from Egypt was 'not through an angel, and not through a messenger' but by God himself, despite biblical evidence to the contrary. That this was a minority view is clear from the many, highly personified, descriptions of angels found throughout rabbinical literature (14 vol. 2: 956]. Angels also play an important role in Jewish MYSTICISM, the MERKABAH mystics confronting angels who guarded the entrances of the various stages of ascent to a vision of the divine throne. They also appear in Jewish folklore [22: 35].

Anglicanism [XIII.B] The established (*see* STATE, CHRISTIANITY AND THE) Church of England became independent of Rome through the REFORMATION, but contains 'Catholic' and PROTESTANT elements. (The Anglo-Catholic party originated in the Oxford (Tractarian) Movement in the 1830s; the Evangelical party during the Evangelical Revival.) Church government (*see* CHURCH ORGANIZATION) is by bishops. WORSHIP is primarily in fixed liturgies: the *Book of Common Prayer* (1662) and new services introduced since 1965. Doctrine was classically expressed partly in the Thirty-Nine Articles (1563), which covered points then in dispute with the Church of Rome (*see* ROMAN CATHOLICISM), partly in the Prayer Book and partly in Homilies (official sermons in 1563 and 1571), but later Anglicans see these as outmoded and in any case as not expressing the full range of Anglican doctrine (cf. CREEDS). Bishops of the worldwide 'Anglican Communion' (e.g. US Episcopalians) have met in Lambeth (in London) conferences since 1967. [148; 151]

Angra Mainyu [XXXVI] The 'Hostile Spirit', one of the twin (or opposed) spirits (the other being AHURA MAZDA) considered by ZOROASTER to be the source of all evil and good respectively (Ahriman in PAHLAVI literature). In order to destroy the good, Angra Mainyu created his own spiritual forces: the demons, *daevas* (usually male in later texts) and *druges* (later generally female). These may be represented in various forms – animal, insect, human, or as a monster (e.g. Azi Dahaka). Their 'names', however, reflect their generally abstract nature and function, e.g. Aeshma (Wrath). The characteristics of evil are violence, chaos, untruth, i.e. it is wholly negative and destructive. It is believed that Angra Mainyu has existed from eternity, wholly independent of Ahura Mazda. Evil is, therefore, a reality over which Mazda has no control, until the final victory (FRASHOKERETI). The world is essentially good; all the evils within it are the weapons by which Angra Mainyu seeks to destroy it, notably sin, disease, dirt, decay, and death (*see* BUNDAHISHN). The presence of such weapons of evil therefore pollutes the good creation. In ritual life it is essential to exclude all such impurity in order to worship Ahura Mazda in holiness. Evil exists in non-material or spiritual form (*menog*), like a parasite in people's bodies in the form of Wrath or Greed, or in harmful, repugnant forms (*khrafstra*) such as beasts of prey or snakes. It is humanity's religious duty to eradicate all evil, thereby making Angra Mainyu impotent and Ahura Mazda omnipotent. So the individual is Ahura Mazda's fellow worker (*hamkar*) in the battle against evil. [8 vol. 1: VIII; 10: 19–21; 14; 28: 59–62; 63: I–IV; 64: XII]

Anicca [XI] PALI (Sanskrit: *anitya*), 'impermanent'. In Buddhist thought impermanence is the first of three marks (Pali: *tilakkhana*; Sanskrit: *trilakshana*) that characterize all physical and mental phenomena (DHAMMA) (cf. SAMSARA); the second and third are DUKKHA and ANATTA. The teaching of imperma-

nence is in part a Buddhist counter to the Upanishadic teaching of an enduring, permanent self (ATMAN). For Buddhism such an 'eternalist view' (*see* DITTHI) is not in conformity with the way things are: all experiences and everything experienced exist only fleetingly. On the other hand, Buddhist thought is insistent that the teaching of impermanence is not to be understood as entailing the alternative 'annihilationist view'. The correct analysis of impermanence has thus been a matter of some consequence in Buddhist thought. Given the basic premiss that things endure only for a moment, some Buddhist schools, such as the SARVASTIVADA, tried to calculate the length of a moment (Sanskrit: *kshana*; Pali: *khana*). Others, such as the SAUTRANTIKA, argued that to do so undermined the very notion of impermanence. For the Sautrantikas impermanence meant continuous change, but if something endures, albeit for a very short period of time, then for that time at least there is no change. Strictly, the Sautrantikas argued, a moment can thus have no duration at all. Ultimately the proper understanding of impermanence is to be referred to the understanding of 'dependent arising' (PATICCASAMUPPADA). From a practical point of view, investigation of *anicca* is the task of VIPASSANA meditation, which aims at contemplating and experiencing directly 'the rise and fall' of all phenomena. [16: 34, 134–44; 34: 50]

Animal Cults (Ancient Egyptian) [VI] In prehistoric Egypt, many tribal deities had animal forms. During the earliest dynasties, anthropomorphization occurred gradually (Archaic period, *c.* 3000 BCE), but most towns continued to worship a particular animal deity [20: I, 8]. Regarded as repositories of the deity's divine powers, many animals, including cats, crocodiles and ibises, were revered and cared for.

They were mummified (*see* MUMMI-FICATION) [4; 14: 155–6] and buried in large cemeteries during the Late Period (*c.*800 BCE) – excesses which invited the ridicule of other countries.

Animal Slaughter (Jewish) [XXII] According to traditional JUDAISM meat may only be eaten if it comes from an animal of a kosher (KASHRUT) species which has been ritually slaughtered (*shechitah*) [23: VI]. This is done by the slaughterer (*shochet*) passing a sharp, smooth knife across the neck of the animal, thereby severing the windpipe, the oesophagus, and the jugular vein. The animal loses consciousness almost immediately. The slaughterer has to be highly trained and a reliable person. [66: 18; 70: 202]

Animism [XXXIV] (1) The belief that a SPIRIT (or spirits) is active in aspects of the environment. The term may cover *animatism* [118; 145: 67, 165], the belief that life, power and feeling are all-pervading, even in the physical environment. Animism, more strictly defined, has reference to belief only in personal powers [36: 62–72; 43: 49–58].

(2) The theory that the ORIGIN OF RELIGION lies in 'belief in spirits', which is the minimum definition of religion [135: 13; 145: 55–8; 158: 27–9; 166].

(3) A loose, misleading, designation for religion in any tribal culture.

Anselm [XIII.C] (*c.*1033–1109) A native of Lombardy who became a pupil of Lanfranc, succeeding the latter as prior at Bec in Normandy and later as Archbishop of Canterbury. His relations with the Norman kings were stormy since he refused to compromise the spiritual rights of the church. Intellectually he was a brilliant philosopher and theologian. His *Proslogion* and *Liber apologeticus pro insipiente* put forward the classical version of the ontological argument (*see* ARGUMENTS FOR THE EXISTENCE OF GOD) and his *Cur deus homo?* presents a classical expression of the satisfaction theory of the Atonement. (*see* SALVATION, CHRISTIAN DOCTRINE OF) [6; 26]

Anthroposophy [XXIV] Literally, 'wisdom of humanity': an esoteric movement founded by the Austrian Rudolf Steiner (1861–1925) in 1913 when he broke away from the THEOSOPHICAL SOCIETY in Germany. It shares the same tenets as THEOSOPHY but emphasizes the central place of humanity. Strongly influenced by Goethe, whose scientific works he edited, Steiner formulated his system in quasi-scientific terms. Anthroposophists believe that the universe and humans themselves, who are reborn many times, have evolved through three stages of mind and matter. The early phases ('astral' and 'etheric') were characterized by intuitive and clairvoyant modes of consciousness (*see* PSYCHIC POWERS) and rarefied forms of matter. These phases still exist but are now concealed by physical matter and intellectual consciousness. They may be recovered and used purposefully through mental, physical and spiritual exercises. The birth of JESUS Christ was the central event of human history: humans had evolved to a point where material existence had caused them to forget their spiritual capacities. Christ came to reverse this trend, inaugurating an era of spiritual regeneration. The celebration of the sacrament is central to the Anthroposophical Society's Christian Fellowships. Anthroposophists have used Steiner's ideas as a basis for experimental work in agriculture, education and other fields [14].

Anti-Christ (in Islam) [XIX] Known as *al-Dajjal* ('the deceiver'), Anti-Christ plays an important role in Islamic eschatology (*see* AKHIRA; QIYAMA) as the false Messiah whose appearance on earth will presage the end of the world and the last judgement. *Al-Dajjal* is pictured in HADITH (the idea is absent from the QUR'AN) as a one-eyed monster with the name Kafir ('unbeliever') branded on his forehead, who will appear from the East (certain sources localize this as Indonesia) and establish a reign of tyranny for 40 days or years before being vanquished by JESUS or the MAHDI in Palestine or Syria. [20 'Dajjal'; 38 'Dadjdjāl; 67 'Al-Masīhu'd-Dajjāl']

Antioch, Early Christianity at [XIII.A] Antioch on the Orontes (in Syria) was founded in 300 BCE. In the dispersal of Christian Hellenists from Judaea after Stephen's death (*c.*33 CE), several seem to have come to Antioch and spread their message there, first among the Jews and then also among Greek-speaking pagans. Those who embraced the new religion of CHRISTIANITY were first called Christians in Antioch (*Acts* 11: 26). Antioch was the centre from which Cilicia, Cyprus and central Asia Minor were evangelized in the following decades. From the 2nd century the Antiochene school of theology was characteristically dependent on the thought of Aristotle, interpreted biblical texts historically and literally, and stressed the oneness of GOD and the humanity of JESUS. [6: 129–33, 175–87; 11: I, 265–9; 18: 201–3]

Anti-Semitism [XXII] Antagonism to Jews on religious, economic or racial grounds [14 vol. 3: 87; 25; 44]. Prejudice against Jews was widespread in the pre-Christian era, but active persecution of Jews is inextricably bound up with Christian attitudes towards them. They were accused of being deicides, collectively responsible for the death of JESUS. They were thought to desecrate the consecrated wafer used in the EUCHARIST, and to perform the ritual murder of Christian children whose blood went into the unleavened bread eaten at Passover. This latter accusation, known as a 'blood libel', was often the excuse for Christian pogroms against Jews, ending in pillage, rape and massacre [36: 171; 43: 402]. During the middle ages Jews were expelled from almost every country of Christian Europe. They were forbidden to own land or engage in the crafts and were restricted to lending money at interest or to peddling. The influence of Christianity on anti-Semitism may be seen by comparing the situation of Jews in Christian lands with that of Jews in Islamic countries. In the latter they were second-class citizens, having to pay special taxes, but they were rarely forced to convert to another faith, or to live at the mercy of mob rule. Jewish attitudes to GENTILES have been shaped by the history of anti-Semitism, culminating in the Nazi HOLOCAUST of 1939–45. [35: VII, 70: XIV]

Anukampa [XI] The motivation which impels a BUDDHA and his ARAHAT disciples to teach. *Anukampa*, 'sympathy', which leads them to give help to the world at large, is distinguished from *karuna*, 'compassion', which refers to the meditational practice of extending compassion to all living beings. In later Buddhism, especially the MAHAYANA, *karuna* is used for both purposes and the concept of the wider compassion (*mahakaruna*) of a Buddha is introduced. [1]

Apocalyptic [XIII.A] From the Greek meaning 'revelation', the term Apocalyptic is used in three varying ways. Strictly it refers to pieces of Jewish and Christian literature from the 3rd century BCE onwards which contain the narration of a vision or audition; often the story is about the seer taking a guided journey around heaven. This literature is commonly divided into two groups: disclosures of the way the COSMOS really is, and apocalypses which are primarily concerned with the way the cosmos will be in the future or at its end. The term is also used of certain motifs which are commonly but not exclusively found in both cosmological and eschatological apocalypses. Among these are ANGELS and DEMONS, the language of judgement, descriptions of battles and unusual natural phenomena. Thus 'apocalyptic' is often used nowadays to refer to any cataclysmic event, even though nothing supernatural is involved. The term is also used of the social groups or movements within JUDAISM and CHRISTIANITY which composed and passed on apocalypses. Such apocalyptic movements may have comprised articulate minorities who coped with their negative experience of this world and their sense of marginalization by describing their hopes for divine intervention on their behalf so that the cosmos could become as God had originally intended it to be. [11: I, 279–92; 16: 95–125; 18: 56–64]

Apostles [XIII.A] In early Christianity the term 'apostles' (from the Greek word meaning 'to send out') was given to the 12 disciples whom JESUS had sent throughout Galilee. In the first days of the JERUSALEM church under PETER they were its leaders and the author of the *Acts of the Apostles* largely restricts his use of the term to them. Some, notably PAUL, applied the designation to themselves to assert the authority of their own commissioning by Jesus after his resurrection. Of the later careers of most of the original apostles nothing is known. [5: 168–9; 11: I, 309–11]

'Aqida [XIX] 'Creed', in ISLAM. The profession of faith in the unity of God and the prophethood of MUHAMMAD (SHAHADA) provides a simple basic creed for believers, and it is this alone which is used liturgically in the Muslim worship (SALAT). However, as Islam has developed, various theological schools and conflicting sects (FIRQA) have embodied their beliefs and principles in more formal documents, comparable e.g. to the Christian CREEDS. Although basically arising from within Islam itself, the wording and argumentation of some of these may have been influenced by techniques of Greek philosophical discussion (KALAM) [71: 339–71; 87: 294–370]. Both Sunni and Shi'i creeds exist (*see* SHI'ISM; SUNNA), but there is no consensus even within these two main groups of Muslims concerning one particular, supremely valid document. [20 'Creed (Islam)'; 38 "Akīda'; 140]

Arahat [XI] (Pali; Sanskrit: *arhat*) In early BUDDHISM and in THERAVADA Buddhism a term for one who has reached the goal of the Buddhist path and attained 'enlightenment' (*bodhi*) or NIBBANA by fully realizing the FOUR NOBLE TRUTHS and completely eradicating all forms of attachment, aversion and delusion; an *arahat*'s thoughts and actions are thus understood to be entirely motivated by wisdom, compassion and the absence of selfish desire. The *arahat* cuts the bonds that bind beings to the cycle of rebirth (SAMSARA) and after death is not reborn (*see* PARINIRBANA). Partial realization of the truths and incomplete eradication of the defilements lead to the lesser attainments of the 'stream-attainer' (*sotapanna*), 'once-returner' (*sakadagamin*) and 'non-returner' (*anagamin*); together with the *arahat*, these are the 'noble persons' (*ariya-puggala*) who constitute the 'noble SANGHA'. Consideration of the relative status of the enlightenment of a BUDDHA and that of his 'disciples' (Pali: *savaka*; Sanskrit: *shravaka*), namely the *arahats*, ended in the MAHAYANA criticism that the path to arahatship is marred by a selfish concern for one's own release from suffering, and is inherently inferior (*see* HINAYANA) to the path of the BODHISATTVA, which is based on the aspiration to become a Buddha and thereby bring release from suffering to others. [13: 93–5; 34: 64–5]

Arawak Religion [XXIII] Arawak-speaking peoples are widely distributed throughout the north and north-west of the South American continent. The best descriptions of their religions are from the Northern Maipure (Baniwa, Guajiro) and pre-Andean (Campa, Amuesha) peoples. In Baniwa religion, the salvific powers of the Creator/Transformer Yaperikuli overcome the primordial forces of chaos, creating order in the world (see CREATION MYTHS). The Creator's son, Kuwai, an extraordinary being whose body is the source of sacred music, represents ancestral power, invoked in initiation rituals today. The more powerful SHAMANS and chant specialists, key figures in religious life, have been considered saviours like the Creator. Guajiro religion centres on two divine principles in complementary opposition, manifest in the Lord of the Rains (Juya) and powerful female beings (Pulowi) associated with dangerous places and sickness. Through the way of the souls of the deceased, humans participate in the divine essence since the dead return to the earth in the form of rain or supernatural beings to perpetuate life and death. Most Guajiro shamans are women. For the Campa of eastern Peru, creation is the history of transformations that change the earth and its primal inhabitants into their present form. In their festivals the Campa seek a personal interaction with these transformative divinities through the use of the hallucinogen *ayahuasca*, fermented beer and music. As the world came into being through transformation, it will be destroyed at some time in the future by the will of the sun-god Páva. [25; 38; 42]

Architecture (Christian) [XIII.B] Early Christian worship was in houses, later specifically adapted for the purpose. There followed the basilica, a rectangular building with a semicircular apse for the altar at one end, and sometimes a separate baptistery for baptism (since early times 'altar' in Christianity has denoted the table where the 'elements' of the EUCHARIST are placed). In the East, domed churches developed which have remained characteristic to this day; and the building itself acts as an ICON. In the West the basic rectangle persisted, divided into a nave (for the congregation) and chancel (for the priest and main altar). Church plans then grew more elaborate (especially those of cathedrals and monasteries – see CHURCH ORGANIZATION) to allow for multiple altars and masses. They also reflected the increased numbers and enhanced status of the priesthood, and more elaborate worship. The medieval Gothic cathedral [71; 159: III, IV] was a complex symbol of the heavenly Jerusalem, expressed in the vertical emphasis of the building. Churches were filled with images which were the 'Bible' of the illiterate laity [64; 146: VIII] Renaissance centre-plan domed churches of the 15th century used styles influenced by classical antiquity. They have been accused of being merely 'humanist' [159: 182–4]. Their architects, however, explained them in religious NEOPLATONIC terms as symbols of God [207: 1]. The COUNTER-REFORMATION compromised between the centralized domed church and the basilican rectangle. Their luxuriant, even theatrical baroque ornament and images emphasized ROMAN CATHOLIC doctrine and devotion, unlike PROTESTANTISM, in a highly emotional way [159: VI]. Protestantism drastically purged images for theological reasons. The English Dissenters and their American followers used plain buildings suited to worship based on preaching rather than on sacraments [47 vol. 2]. Churches in ANGLICAN-

ISM reflected the use of sacramental worship, fixed liturgy and preaching. In the 19th century Anglo-Catholics pioneered a revival of Gothic. The LITURGICAL MOVEMENT encourages centralized church plans; and style is now influenced by modern architecture and materials [49: 21–41; 84]. Churches were formerly used for many social as well as religious purposes [48].

Ardas [XXXIII] The 'Petition', a formal prayer recited at the conclusion of Sikh RITUALS (*see* GURDWARA). It begins with an invocation extolling the 10 GURUS. This is followed by an intermediate section recalling past trials and triumphs of the PANTH. Finally there comes the actual prayer of petition. Although an approved Punjabi text has been published [30. 103–5], only the first eight and last two lines are unalterable. Elsewhere the wording may be varied and personal intercessions introduced. [8: 180–3; 34: x]

Ardhamagadhi [XX] The dialect in which the SHVETAMBARA JAIN scriptures are composed [4: 60–1; 6: 59–61]. Ardhamagadhi, literally 'Half Magadhi', is a Prakrit, one of a number of dialects of the Indo-Aryan linguistic group which stand in the same relation to Sanskrit as the medieval Romance languages do to Latin. Although regarded as the eternal language of the scriptures as well as the language of the gods in heaven, Ardhamagadhi most likely was an exclusively literary language based on some variety of dialect belonging to the region of Magadha in the Ganges basin which was originally spoken by MAHAVIRA and his disciples (GANADHARA) and subsequently regularized.

Arguments for the Existence of God [XIII.C] In Western thought there are generally considered to be five arguments for the existence of GOD: (1) The *ontological* argument, classically given by ANSELM and

R. Descartes (1596–1650) and recently reworked by Hartshorne (b. 1897) (*see* PROCESS THEOLOGY). It maintains that the concept of God as perfect entails that God be regarded as existing – for Hartshorne as existing necessarily – since otherwise God would not be perfect. The argument is mainly criticized for illegitimately inferring reality from a concept. (2) The *cosmological* argument, classically given by Aquinas (*c.*1225–74) (*see* THOMISM). It argues from the contingent or causal nature of reality that it must have a necessary ground, a 'first cause', identified as God. Critics argue that the contingent quality of reality does not show either that it had an absolutely first originator or that the qualities of such a primal entity must be those of 'God'. (3) The *teleological* argument, classically found in W. Paley (1743–1805). It argues from supposed evidence of design or purpose in the world to its having an intelligent creator. Critics question whether there is such evidence and, if there is, whether it indicates creation by a perfect being. The most famous critics of the above arguments are D. Hume (1711–76) and I. Kant (1724–1804). (4) The *moral* argument, offered by Kant and H. Rashdall (1858–1924). It asserts that moral obligation is only adequately understood when it is held to point to God as the source or justification of the moral sense. Critics question this interpretation of moral experience. (5) The *experiential* argument, as in A. E. Taylor (1869–1945) and John Baillie (1886–1960). It holds that God's reality is so self-evident that on reflection it cannot justifiably be doubted. Critics challenge the interpretation of the experience as being neither justified nor self-evident. [8; 11]

Arianism [XIII.C] A doctrine which held that JESUS Christ was not of one substance with GOD but had been created by 'God the Father' as the medium of creation. Christ, although not God by nature, was held to have received the status of 'Son of God' from God on account of his perfect goodness. The name 'Arianism' comes from Arius (*c.*250–*c.*336 CE), who maintained these views in ALEXANDRIA. Under the influence of Athanasius (*c.*296–373), Arian views were condemned at the Council of Nicaea (*see* COUNCILS OF THE CHURCH) in 325. [6; 10]

Arioi [XXIX] A pre-Christian fertility cult of travelling actors and actresses in the Society Islands, similar to Hawaiian *hula* dancers. Their mythical founder was the god ORO. Even commoners could rise through the ranks of *arioi* societies to gain divine patronage and great MANA (but only for themselves, as most members with offspring were required to practise infanticide). *Arioi* initiates believed that a heaven of sensual delights awaited their spirits after death. [16; 22; 30]

Arminianism [XIII.B] The Dutch theologian Jacobus Arminius (1560–1609) modified the doctrines of CALVINISM, especially predestination. His followers protested against Calvinism in the *Remonstrance* (1610) [19: 268–9]. This declaration allowed for free will in man's SALVATION and asserted that JESUS Christ died for all men. They were condemned at the synod of Dort (Dordrecht, the Netherlands, 1618–19). Later Arminians in Holland and England inclined to UNITARIANISM and questioned substitutionary views of the Atonement (cf. SALVATION). But by the 18th century most METHODISTS and ANGLICANS combined orthodoxy on these points with rejection of predestination. [157: 90]

Art (Hindu) [XVII] The term 'Hindu art' is in some ways a misnomer, since JAIN and BUDDHIST groups in any part of India, as well as Hindus, would commission images from the same professional artists, and much of what follows would be true of Jain or Indian Buddhist art, too. The differences in general lie in subject matter, not style. Although in Hinduism the highest form of the divine (BRAHMAN) is considered to be without qualities and inexpressible, for most worshippers it is more easily contemplated in the form of gods and goddesses, each with his or her own character, iconography and myth (*see* BHAKTI; ISHTADEVA). Both visual and performing arts are therefore of vital importance, not only in telling the stories of the gods but also in providing aids to contemplation. With a few exceptions (*see* LINGAYATA), the divine is pictured in terms of richness and exuberance rather than austere simplicity. Deities are visualized anthropomorphically, though not subject to the same physical restrictions as human beings. Often they have more than one pair of hands, whose gestures (MUDRA) and attributes symbolize their characters and powers, and sometimes more than one head, human or animal, suggesting their many aspects. Faces of deities, heroes and saints, though expressive, are not conceived as portraits, and distinctive attributes such as flowers, weapons and animal attendants (VAHANAS), and even distinctive colours, help to identify them. These attributes also represent facets of the divine character, and are sometimes themselves personified as minor deities: notable examples are the weapons of VISHNU, especially his fiery wheel (*cakra*), and the trident (*trishula*) of SHIVA and DURGA.

The language of symbolism draws not only on YOGA but also on classical Indian dance traditions such as *Bharatanatyam*. Some of the most distinctive forms of Hindu iconography show deities dancing, for example Shiva as *Nataraja*, 'King of Dancers', or playing musical instruments, for example KRISHNA with his flute. The idealized human body is of central importance: no conflict is seen between physical and spiritual beauty, and divine or saintly beings are normally depicted in terms of the current ideals of human beauty and proportion, formalized in craft texts such as the *shilpashastras*, composed from about the 5th century CE on. The forms are designed to touch universal human emotions. Images of beauty and delight, often including sexual imagery (MITHUNA/MAITHUNA), mark the temple as an auspicious place, a suitable dwelling (MANDIRA) for the deity.

Alongside the classical arts of India exists a lively tradition of folk art, which has nourished and been nourished by them [122]. In practice it is impossible to draw a clear line between the two traditions, especially in the case of such arts as pottery, which provides sometimes magnificent images of deities for those who could not afford stone or bronze [56: 191–201]. Today, too, the forms and legends of deities are taught by cinema and television as well as by the colourful prints found wherever Hindus live. (For iconography, *see also* the names of specific deities, e.g. GANESHA, LAKSHMI, PARVATI, SHIVA, VISHNU.) [4: 13–32; 58; 109]

Art (in Islam) [XIX] The fundamental religious feature of Islamic art is usually held to be the ban on depicting living forms. This seems to have arisen not so much from explicit Qur'anic doctrine (the QUR'AN attacks images, but as focuses for idolatry) as from both a fear of rivalling God's creative power and a general indifference to the representational and aesthetic side of religious experience, later given a retroactive legal basis by HADITH. An influence from Byzantine iconoclasm seems improbable [55: IV, VII; 80: 252–3]. In fact, representation of living beings has nevertheless flourished in the arts of e.g. Persia,

India and Turkey, despite pious disapproval; yet the archetypal decorative motifs in Islam have been vegetal and arabesque, seen especially in religious architecture such as MOSQUES, mausoleums [93], etc., with emphasis also on calligraphy [119] and artistic forms of the Arabic script. [10; 20 'Art, sacred (Islam)'; 41; 57; 74; 82: II; 116: IX]

Art (Jewish) [XXII] Jewish attitudes to representational art have differed down the ages, but one can trace a deeply held suspicion of the use of ICONOGRAPHY for religious purposes. The BIBLE associated the making of images with idolatry, and this attitude carried over into rabbinical and medieval JUDAISM. The remains of the 3rd-century Dura Europos SYNAGOGUE, with many murals of biblical scenes, indicate that some early Jewish communities were not averse to using art-forms as long as God himself was not represented [47: 1]. Synagogues in the middle ages tended not to portray human figures in decoration; abstract designs or animals like the lion were preferred. This is still the practice today. Jewish craftsmen devoted their creative energies to scribal arts, to illustrating manuscripts and to fashioning ceremonial objects in silver and gold. In general Jewish culture has influenced Jews to express themselves through instrumental MUSIC, song, literature and poetry rather than through representational art, which has no Jewish cultural roots. [14 vol. 3: 499; 34: I]

Art and Symbolism (Ancient Egyptian) [VI] Art-forms in ancient Egypt were primarily developed for religious purposes, and then extended for secular use. Architectural innovations were devised for tomb and temple architecture (*see* MANSION OF THE GODS; MANSION OF THE KA; PYRAMIDS); relief sculpture and wall-painting were developed for religious decoration; and craftsmen employed in the minor arts and

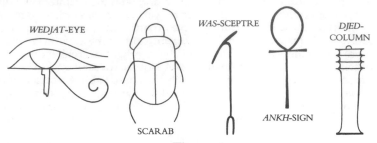

Figure 1
Ancient Egyptian symbols

jewellery-making supplied items for FUNERARY PRACTICES. Although often exquisitely executed, the prime function of all religious art-forms was to provide models and representations of animate or inanimate objects which could be magically activated.

Various symbols achieved widespread popularity and magical significance in Egypt (*see figure 1*); these included the *ankh* (life), *djed* (stability), and *was* (dominion) signs; the scarab or dung-beetle (renewal of life); and the *wedjat*-eye (spiritual and physical wholeness). Amulets in these forms were made for both the living and the dead, to give protection against evil and dominion (*see* MAGIC). Symbolism was present in many aspects of religion, including representations of Re' and Osiris (*see* OSIRIAN TRIAD) reaffirming their cyclic rebirth (*see* AFTERLIFE).

Art and Symbolism (Ancient Near Eastern) [VIII] Monuments, reliefs, sculpture and cylinder seals all provide additional information regarding ancient Near Eastern religions [5; 6]. Finest metalwork, shell-engraving and mosaic-work are evident in the grave goods from the royal cemetery at Ur [26]. Monumental stone bas-reliefs decorating HITTITE religious centres (1250–1220 BCE) indicate the debt they owed to earlier Mesopotamian sources [13: 195–214]. Seal impressions show the characteristics of many deities in the presence of their worshippers. Animals sometimes occur as the cult symbols of deities – a bull for the Hittite weather-god [13: 134], the dragon (*see* ANCIENT NEAR EASTERN RELIGIONS) as the symbol of EVIL [13: 181] and the serpent as an ELAMITE divinity [17: 38]. Other symbols sometimes replaced the human form: Hittite underworld deities were sometimes represented as swords and the *huwasi* stone (an inscribed or decorated stele) could replace a god's statue [13: 149]. Gigantic animals perhaps symbolized natural cycles, and semi-divine beings (half human and half plant or animal) probably represented the land's fertility in Elam [17: 37].

Artha [XVII] One of the four goals of life recognized in Hindu tradition (KAMA, DHARMA and MOKSHA being the other three). *Artha* represents the whole range of activities associated with material gain and the protection of it; in other words, the world as dealt with by economists and politicians. Hindu tradition includes a special classical treatise dealing with this realm of life (and others dealing with *kama* and *dharma*): this is the *Artha-shastra*, the authorship of which is attributed to Kautilya, the BRAHMAN minister of Candragupta, the Indian emperor of the 4th century BCE [12: 51]. It is a feature of *Artha-shastra* that it 'concerned itself primarily with the attainment of the ends irrespective of the nature of the means employed'. [12: index]

Asalha [XI] The BUDDHIST festival that commemorates the conception, great departure and, especially, the first teaching of the BUDDHA (*see* GOTAMA) and which falls on the full-moon day (*see* UPOSATHA) of the month of Asalha (Pali; Sanskrit: *Ashadha*), the fourth month of the Indian calendar corresponding to June/July. In Sri Lanka this month is also the time for the Asalha procession (*perahera*) in Kandy when the Buddha's tooth relic is paraded around the city in a procession of elephants, drummers and dancers. The Asalha full moon marks the beginning of the three months' 'rains retreat' (Pali: *vassa*; Sanskrit: *varsha*). According to the prescriptions of the VINAYA, monks (BHIKKHU) should remain resident in one monastery and not travel during these three months; this is a time of increased religious activity for both members of the SANGHA and lay followers (UPASAKA); in the THERAVADA countries of south-east Asia it is common for laymen to take temporary ordination for this period. [34: 193]

Asanga [XI] Indian BUDDHIST thinker, associated with the YOGACARA tradition of Buddhist philosophy. We know very little of Asanga's life or even when he lived, although there is a Tibetan legend which tells us something about MAHAYANA Buddhism. Asanga was devoted to MAITREYA and wanted to have a vision of him. After meditating for 15 years he had not seen Maitreya and decided to give up. Then when, full of compassion, Asanga stooped to help a diseased dog, the dog turned into Maitreya himself. Maitreya was always present, but seen only when compassion had burned away all impurities. Maitreya took Asanga to the Tushita heaven and there delivered a series of new texts. Asanga may have lived in the 4th century CE, and is said to have been the brother of VASUBANDHU.

Asceticism, Christian [XIII.D] The world in which the Christian gospel was first preached already knew the ascetic lifestyles of Cynic and Stoic philosophers, of the Egyptian priesthoods and, at least by repute, of the Indian 'gymnosophists'. Moral uprightness and austerity of life were respected as marks of virtue and self-control, signs of excellence of character. Christian preaching, too, emphasized the importance of an ordered, morally upright and self-disciplined life; it called the believer to die in Christ to this world and to look to the Kingdom of God and the coming judgement. Not surprisingly, individuals and communities responded to this preaching by taking up an ascetic style of life. Ascetic practice has several functions: training in control of the appetites and passions; training in detachment; training in awareness of transience and mortality; training in the appreciation of the divine benevolence; expiation for wrongs done; healing from the effects of sin; identification with the Passion and death of Christ; preparation for a new state of life.

MONASTICISM was greatly influenced by asceticism; indeed, the two versions of the Rule of St Basil, generally thought of as a handbook for monks, are probably rather a guide for ascetics living a common life. The monasticism of the DESERT FATHERS was strongly ascetic. Stylites and dendrites fasting and praying on pillars or in trees were visible signs of the call to the ascetic life. Leaders of the REFORMATION were generally opposed to the ascetic ideal as tainted with notions of meriting SALVATION. The ROMAN CATHOLIC response was a renewed emphasis on the value of ascetic practice, manifest in the strict rules and austere lifestyles of orders such as the Capuchins, the Passionists and the Trappists.

FASTING and celibacy are common elements of Christian asceticism. Practices such as wearing hair shirts and chains and self-flagellation, while once common, are now rare. Other ascetic practices include sleep-fasting, abstinence from meat or from alcohol, wearing poor clothes or no shoes, sleeping on the floor or in a chair, observance of prayer-vigils, PILGRIMAGES and sometimes the avoidance of washing (*alousia*). Christian asceticism is to be distinguished from forms of asceticism which see the material world and the body as evil; for CHRISTIAN THEOLOGY the world and the body are essentially good, though sometimes the rhetoric of ascetic teachers can create an ambiguous impression. In many older Roman Catholic texts on spiritual theology a distinction is made between 'ascetic theology', which deals with the normal path of Christian perfection, and 'mystical theology', which deals with the graces of mystical prayer and the union with God. [16]

Ashkenazim [XXII] Jews from Christian Europe. In the late middle ages, when the European and west Asian worlds were divided between Christian and Islamic countries, the Jewish people also found itself divided into two main groups. The term *Ashkenazi*, originally meaning 'German', was applied to Jews of central and eastern Europe [14 vol. 3: 719]. The main Jewish communities of the early middle ages were in the Franco-German Rhineland (*see* EUROPEAN JEWRY), whence they spread east to Poland and Russia: hence the name *Ashkenazim*. *Ashkenazi* Jewry, cut off from SEFARDI Jewry in Islamic lands, developed its own cultural complex, customs, traditions of interpreting the TALMUD, pronunciation of Hebrew, calligraphy, MUSIC, and its own lingua franca, Yiddish – an originally German dialect with Hebrew and Slavic accretions. *Ashkenazim* and *Sefardim* do not differ in theology or basic Jewish practice [70: 211; 73]. In modern times the vast majority of Jews are of *Ashkenazi* stock, and they have dominated Jewish intellectual and cultural life.

Ashoka [XI] An Indian emperor who reigned c.269–232 BCE and extended the Mauryan empire across nearly the entire Indian subcontinent. Ashoka's rock and pillar edicts, which have been found in various locations throughout India, indicate that after a particularly bloody military campaign in Kalinga (eastern India) he turned to BUDDHIST teachings and became a committed supporter (*see* UPASAKA) of the Buddhist SANGHA. The subsequent promotion of DHAMMA in his edicts is not to be seen as a bid to convert his subjects to Buddhism as such, but rather as an attempt to put into practice some of its principles in his role as emperor. Thus while his vision of Dhamma is not couched in narrow and exclusively Buddhist terms it does appear to owe much to his personal understanding of Buddhism. The edicts commend in particular the non-injury of living creatures (AHIMSA), the provision of medical care for the sick and tolerance among all religious groups; Ashoka highlights his own efforts in these directions and in promoting Dhamma throughout his empire and beyond. Buddhist tradition claims Ashoka as its own and many legends about his life are recounted in the *Ashokavadana* and the Sinhalese chronicles (*Dipavamsa* and *Mahavamsa*). According to Sinhalese tradition it was Ashoka's son, Mahinda, who, as a Buddhist monk, first brought Buddhism to Sri Lanka. [53: 184–202; 94; 91]

Ashrama [XVII] A stage of human life, of which there are four in the Hindu tradition: (1) the pupil, or *brahmacarin*; (2) the householder, or *grihastha*; (3) the forest-dweller, or *vanaprastha*; and (4) finally, when all human ties are ended with the total renunciation of the world, the stage of the *sannyasin*. Each of these ashramas has its own appropriate rule of life or DHARMA; there are thus four *ashrama-dharmas*. The four may rarely have been fully followed in reality, but the existence of the scheme emphasizes what is regarded as the ideal way of life. It has been suggested that the scheme affirms the necessity of the householder stage in order to counter the practice followed by some ascetic movements of omitting this stage and passing directly to homelessness, which thereby robs society in so far as families are not founded [12: 160]. Even among Hindus the four stages apply only to the 'twice-born' classes or VARNAS.

Asia, Christianity in [XIII.B] A few Monophysites and Nestorians (*see* CHRISTOLOGY) reached INDIA and CHINA in the early centuries CE. Monophysitism once had substantial churches in western Asia, but competition with other Christians undermined them in the face of ISLAM, and Christianity was permanently weakened in this area. Substantial penetration of India, China and JAPAN came with Roman Catholic (*see* ROMAN CATHOLICISM) MISSIONS of friars and Jesuits (*see* MONASTICISM) from the 16th century. They were decimated by persecution a century later. Fresh work in these areas came with PROTESTANT missions and renewed Roman Catholic effort in the 19th century. These efforts were most successful in the South Seas, less secure in China and not numerous in Japan [58]. Indigenous cultures and major religions (BUDDHISM; HINDUISM; ISLAM) have proved generally resistant to Christianity in Asia, except in the Philippines and Vietnam. Nationalism has also given an adverse image to Christianity as an alien Western religion. [121 vol. 3: XVIII–

XXII, vol. 5 XI–XVI; 122 vol. 3: X–XIV, vol. 6: IV–VII]

Asia and the Pacific, New Religious Movements in [XXVII] In Asia the Burkhan (meaning BUDDHA) millennial movement among the Altai Mountain kalmucks from 1904 was anti-SHAMAN and anti-Christian. Some 300 new religions have appeared in Korea since about 1860, when Tonghak (Eastern Learning) began, and one, T'ongil Kyohoe, has spread widely in the rest of the world as the UNIFICATION CHURCH. The hill and forest tribes of India in interaction with Hindu and Christian influences have produced many reforming and prophet movements [9], and in Burma, Thailand and Vietnam there have been similar reactions to Buddhism and Christianity. Indonesian movements are often messianic (*see* MESSIAH) and APOCALYPTIC, usually with traditional and Christian sources, but especially in Java drawing on Islamic and JAVANESE mysticism. Agama Islam Desjati (True Islamic Religion) from 1950 represents a rare anti-Arab syncretistic form. The Bungan cult in Kalimantan and Sarawak from 1947 has been a reforming Christian syncretism. In the PHILIPPINES [8] millennial revolts are endemic and include the intermittent syncretistic Colorum movements; also millennial but more nationalistic are the many Rizalist cults believing in a return of the national martyr, José Rizal (*see* RIZALISTAS); chief of these is the Watawat ng Lahi (Banner of the Race). The largest movement is the IGLESIA NI CRISTO (Church of Christ). MELANESIAN movements [27] often take the form of CARGO CULTS but there are also more political forms, such as Paliau's movement on Manus from 1946 and the Hahalis Welfare Society on Buka Island from the 1950s [26: 466–83], and independent churches such as Sila Eto's CHRISTIAN FELLOWSHIP CHURCH in the Solomon Islands from 1959. Hawaii and the POLYNESIANS also have independent churches such as the Congregation of the Poor and the Daku Community in Fiji; the main MAORI MOVEMENTS are Ratana and Ringatu. Australian (*see* AUSTRALIAN RELIGION) aboriginals have produced few movements apart from the peaceful Elcho Island cult from about 1958 and some Pentecostal churches (*see* PENTECOSTALISM) more recently. [12: v–vii; 22: 703–4; 26: 73–5]

Assyrians [viii] The classical age of Sumer (*see* SUMERIANS) was brought to an end by the conquest of the city-states by Sargon of Agade, a northern ruler. Sargon and these Akkadian kings created the idea of a universal empire and, many years later, the Assyrians adopted the same concept [18].

Ashur, a trading city in the Ur III empire, successfully maintained independence when the Kassites took Babylonia and the north fell to the HURRIANS. Although incorporated into the loose confederation of Mitannian states, Mitanni's weakness eventually enabled Ashur to assert its independence under Ashur-uballit I (1365–1330 BCE), the first real king of 'Assyria'; and with the later emergence of Assyria, Ashur retained its prominent position.

The idea of a universal empire was embodied in the concept of a universal deity. The cult of Sin, the moon-god, played an important role throughout Assyrian history, and he had many centres – Ur in Babylonia, Harran in Mesopotamia, in Lebanon and in Palestine. In the Neo-Assyrian period, he became royal patron (*see* KINGSHIP (ANCIENT NEAR EAST)), and Shamash the sun-god was also widely revered. However, the religion was overwhelmingly dominated by the national god, Ashur, who embodied the homeland and the capital city, as well as being a god of the region around Kanesh where many Assyrian merchants

lived. Ashur gradually supplanted MARDUK, the Babylonian god, as national deity. Other important deities were Enlil, Adad and Ishtar. Gods were remote from men, and this was frequently emphasized by the custom of representing them by symbols (*see* ART AND SYMBOLISM (ANCIENT NEAR EASTERN)) [10].

The Assyrians believed that events on earth reflected the recurrent groupings of the heavenly constellations. It was thought that the ten deities representing the fixed and moving stars took turns in ruling the universe. Thus, the king of all these lands was expected to reside in a city dedicated to the ruling deity of that particular time-span, and so the kings periodically changed their royal residences to satisfy this belief. There were four capitals: Ashur, Nineveh, Khorsabad and Nimrud. They acknowledged and preserved BABYLONIAN culture; Ashur-ban-apli (631 BCE) assembled a corpus of cuneiform literature, including religious and omen texts. In earlier times, Assyria employed scribes trained in Babylonia and built up libraries [25: 38].

Astrology [x] The art of predicting the future or of interpreting events, human lives and character from the positions of the heavenly bodies [general surveys: 2, 11; brief history: 15]. Astrology originated in the taking of astral omens for state purposes in Mesopotamia in the 2nd millennium BCE (*see* ASTROLOGY (ANCIENT NEAR EASTERN)). From about the 5th century it developed there, and subsequently in the Greek world (especially in Egypt after Alexander's conquest), into the technical system for predicting the fates of individuals (HOROSCOPE) which survives today [astrology in the ancient world: 3; 4; 6; 10; 13]. Contrary to popular belief, pre-Greek Egypt contributed virtually nothing. The art reached its definitive form in the Roman empire by *c.*100 CE. Refinements were made in the later empire, in the middle ages in Byzantium, Islam, and western Europe, in the Renaissance [1] and in modern times (e.g. the inclusion of the planets discovered since the 18th century). Astrology in India, though ultimately derived from Mesopotamian and Greek sources, has developed and flourished in a separate tradition [15: 223] (see ASTROLOGY (INDIAN)). An entirely independent system developed in China, largely concerned with correspondences between celestial events and the condition of the empire.

Historically, astrology has had links both with scientific astronomy and with religion. Astronomical data are necessary ingredients for astrological predictions, and generally the borderline between astronomy and astrology has been somewhat blurred. Though sometimes treated with scepticism, astrology was until the 18th century usually regarded as a valid branch of a single science (for example, Ptolemy, 2nd century CE, wrote both the greatest text of Greek scientific astronomy, the *Almagest*, and a treatise on astrology, the *Tetrabiblos*). In Mesopotamia, and subsequently in the Graeco-Roman world, STAR-WORSHIP fostered the growth and influence of astrology [6; 7; 10]. Logically, however, astrology is independent of religion, and in the West with the triumph of Christianity it was accepted that the stars were no more than the indicators, not the ultimate agents, of fate. Nevertheless, astrology has always raised quasi-religious questions, notably the problem of determinism: if the future can be foretold, it is presumably determined; what place then is left for human free will? It was on that ground that astrology was in the past most vehemently attacked (modern astrologers, though, concern themselves more with human character than with future events and so sidestep the issue). Modern criticism focuses more on the scientific implausibility of astrology [5]. Although it still enjoys a certain vogue (millions, with more or less credulity, follow in the daily newspapers forecasts which are astrologically very naïve) and is practised by a relatively few dedicated adepts [apologetics: 8; 16; manuals: 12; 14], educated opinion in the West now generally holds that astrology is outside the realm of intellectual respectability and thus valueless [critiques: 5; 7]. Recently, however, there have been attempts to re-establish at least parts of it on a statistical and empirical basis [8].

Astrology (Ancient Egyptian) [VI] The practice of astrology was imported into Egypt from Mesopotamia, perhaps in the Persian period (c. 500 BCE). The use of hemerology – the determination of lucky and unlucky days – was derived from mythology and not from astrology. However, the Egyptians had a long-standing interest in astronomy; 'star-ceilings', with charts of the heavens, occur in tombs and temples [6]. These were tables giving the movements of the stars at night. Also, a calendar, based on the agricultural year, was devised and used – at least from earliest historical times (c. 3100 BCE).

Astrology (Ancient Near Eastern) [VIII] Astrology [22] superseded extispicy (DIVINATION) as the favoured method for obtaining omens for political and military purposes in Mesopotamia in the 2nd millennium BCE. Individual fates could be determined by portents or warnings of the gods, or predicted by the HOROSCOPE, which was developed later. Both the Egyptians and the Greeks adopted some aspects of its study. According to the Epic of Creation [24: 60–71], each great god was assigned a position in the sky, and each star or constellation was allotted to one of these deities.

Astrology (Indian) [XVII] Indian astrology is a distinctive system, developed from around 100 CE, and combining late Vedic elements (ATHARVA-VEDA) with a structure derived from the Greeks [99: 8–12, 81–3; 113: 1–7]. It was shaped by the 6th-century astronomer/ astrologer Varahamihira [99: 84–6; 113: 9; 129] with later influences from the TANTRA (1) movement and Islamic science [113: 12–13; 99: 97–100]. It shares with Western schools the 12-sign zodiac and traditional planetary rulerships, though the zodiac used is a sidereal one, based on the constellations, rather than a tropical one, reckoned from the equinoxes [113: 17–21]. It gives special importance to the moon, and treats the lunar nodes (eclipse points) as invisible planets [113: 12–13, 71–3]. Whereas Western astrology today is concerned mainly with the individual psyche, Indian astrology is still used to forecast events. It is widely accepted in Indian society, fitting as it does with Hindu views of KARMA and the respect paid to the heavenly bodies as deities [119: 62–77, 125–136].

Asura [XI] In Indian mythology a class of non-human beings who are the enemies of the *devas* (heavenly beings), and thus represented as responsible for encouraging evil tendencies. There is controversy concerning the relation of these beings in Indian mythology with the Iranian *ahura* (see AHURA MAZDA; ZOROASTRIANISM). Both traditions descend from the Indo-Iranians (see INDO-EUROPEANS) but the roles of the *asuras* (Iranian *ahuras*) and *devas* (Iranian *daevas*) appear to be reversed. In the Rig-veda (see VEDA), *asura* is used also as an epithet for certain important gods, suggesting that *deva* and *asura* were originally the titles of two families of gods; but in the ATHARVA-VEDA *asura* is already used collectively to indicate hostile beings. In PALI BUDDHIST literature (see THERAVADA) the most frequent references are in connection with continual war between

asuras and *devas*. In MAHAYANA Buddhist literature they constitute one of the six forms of existence, together with denizens of hell, ghosts, animals, humans and *devas*. They are said to be motivated by envy of the *devas*, and constantly at war with them. [111: 21–6]

Atenism [VI] The Aten (sun's disc) is mentioned long before AKHENA-TEN's reign, but he elevated the god to an unprecedented status (c.1360 BCE). Atenism was a version of the Heliopolitan doctrine (see RE'), but the deity now became 'sole god' and a universal source of life. Atenism continued the 'monotheistic' trend already evident in AMUN's cult, but also expressed a uniquely close relationship between god and king. New, roofless temples (see MANSION OF THE GODS) were built at Thebes, Amarna and elsewhere [22: x, 122].

Atharva-Veda [XVII] A collection of ancient Indian hymns, chants and spells, which was later added to the existing collection of VEDA material. The contents are different in nature from the earlier collections (*Rig-veda*, etc.), which were mainly addressed to the gods of the Aryans (see INDO-EUROPEANS), whereas this consists to a larger extent of charms (of various kinds and for various purposes), exorcisms, magical spells and incantations. Some of the material contained in the *Atharva* is, however, of a cosmological nature. This is a later development of some of the speculative material about the origin of the universe which is found in the tenth and last book of the *Rig-veda*. Compared with most of the earlier Vedic material, however, there are few hymns in the *Atharva* addressed to specific gods, and the general stance is pantheistic.

These differences have been explained as being due to the extent to which the ideas and cultic practices of the immigrant Aryan pastoral tribes had been influenced by those of the more predominantly agricultural people of north-west India, whose territory they had invaded. [80: 57f; 111: 72–8; 139: 15–30]

Atheism [xxxiv] (1) Disbelief in the existence of any GODS or of GOD. This may take the form of: (a) dogmatic rejection of specific beliefs, e.g. of THEISM; (b) scepticism about all religious claims; or (c) agnosticism, the view that humans can never be certain in matters of so-called religious knowledge (e.g. whether God exists or not) [110: 110]. An atheist may hold belief in God to be false, or irrational, or meaningless [37: vi; 72: 160 1; 75: 3–4; 135: 238].
  (2) A form of religion which rejects the reality or ultimacy of all superhuman beings [75: 31; 110: 114–19].

Atman [xvii] A central and sometimes controversial term in Indian philosophy, connected with the vital question of who we are. In origin it simply means 'self' as in 'myself', 'yourself', but in the UPANISHADS it becomes the term for the true self or innermost nature of every living being, pure and unchanged even while the body and mind undergo change, death and rebirth as a result of external circumstances and KARMA. It is possible to experience it through spiritual practice (e.g. JNANA YOGA), though the Upanishads seem also to suggest that everyone touches it at times, for example during deep, dreamless sleep. The *atman* within the individual parallels the BRAHMAN within the universe, and spiritual liberation (MOKSHA) is seen as the realization of the union of *atman* and *brahman* [139: viii–xii]. This remains a typical HINDU view. BUDDHISM, on the other hand, rejects the concept of a permanent, unchanging essence within each being, preferring to speak of ANATTA (*anatman*), no-self. (*See also* VEDANTA.)

Atua [xxix] Gods and supernatural beings in POLYNESIAN RELIGION, other than the uncreated supreme being (TANGAROA or Io). Highest 'departmental' gods are TANE (light and forests), Tu (war), Rongo (cultivation), Whiro (underworld), Haumia (uncultivated food) and Tawhiri (storm). Hine, the first woman, formed from earth by Tane, becomes goddess of darkness and guardian of Po, the place of the dead. As the moon-goddess Hina she teaches crafts to women, giving her name to heroines in many legends. Pele is the great Hawaiian goddess of volcanoes [15; 22]. Lesser tribal *atua*, local gods, goddesses, and spirits regulate everyday life, punishing breaches of *tapu* (TABU) by sickness or accident. They guide devout worshippers through dreams and omens. Ghosts (*kehua*) and monsters (*taniwha*) are also *atua*, who guard their own people but can be used by sorcerers to harm others. When pleased by offerings and ritual chants (*karakia*), *atua* may communicate through a medium or prophet (*taura*), or become present in animals, images, or the TOHUNGA's carved 'god-stick'. Right relations with the *atua* result in MANA, the power which comes from kinship between gods and mortals. [6; 7; 16; 28; 30]

Augustinianism [xiii.c] A movement of Christian thought influenced by doctrines classically developed by Augustine of Hippo (334–430 CE). Against the MANICHAEANS, he maintained that GOD was the sole creator and that EVIL is a lack of some good; against the Donatists he argued that it was the purposes and not the character of its adherents that made the CHURCH 'holy'. He regarded the civil authorities as serving God's providence and as good so far as they acted justly. Against PELAGIANISM he developed doctrines of the fall, original SIN and predestination, holding that by heredity humankind is tainted by sin and that God, acting in inexplicable wisdom and justice, has chosen ('elected' or 'predestined') only some persons to be saved, the rest being consigned to everlasting damnation [6; 10; 12]

Auspicia [xxxi] The *auspicia* (auspices) were the special province of the Roman augurs (SACERDOTES) and were sent by Jupiter, as the chief state-god. The senior officials (magistrates) in charge, either in Rome or on campaign, had the right to take the *auspicia*, to consult the gods about the coming action; the augur was the expert adviser or interpreter [8: 598; 14: 2190–225]. The original *auspicia* were taken from the flight of birds, interpreted in relation to the appointed TEMPLA; other techniques were accepted later. The signs were divided into those sought deliberately by the magistrate (*signa impetrativa*) and those sent unasked (*signa oblativa*), which were held to be valid only if actually observed by the magistrate [8: 594–600; 13: 10–19; 14: 2195–208]. In early times all action, public or private, was supposed to be accompanied by *auspicia*, but by the late Republic (*c.*100–31 BCE) constitutional change had separated command from the old rituals, though the augurs continued to be of high importance in public life until the end of the 1st century BCE and existed, if without political influence, down to the 4th century CE. [13: 63–5]

Australasia, Christianity in [xiii.b] Christianity in Australia originated in British and, later, European churches, conditioned by colonial experience. Some Anglicans evidently carried church 'establishment' ideas with them, which failed in face of competition from other churches. Public money, which was often available for church buildings and schools, by the 1870s gave way to self-support. Churches gained independence from Europe at differ-

ent times, from ANGLICANISM as late as 1962; Englishmen have often been appointed to Australian bishoprics. ROMAN CATHOLICISM was originally strongly Irish and working-class, influenced by anti-English feeling, and involved in the founding of the Australian Labor Party. The Irish connection also influenced a strong devotion to the PAPACY as a fellow-sufferer at the hands of non-Catholics. Social differences between the churches today are much reduced. A notable recent development has been the introduction of a great variety of ethnic versions of Christianity (notably Roman Catholic and EASTERN ORTHODOX) associated with growing immigrant populations [6]. Australian missionary work is chiefly in Papua New Guinea [121 vol. 3: xiii, vol. 5: vi; 122 vol. 5: vii, vol. 7: viii]. New Zealand missions came with colonization in the 19th century, predominantly Anglican but with substantial elements of PRESBYTERIANISM and METHODISM. The indigenous Maoris eventually became officially Christian but some joined charismatic cults [100: 260–5]. (*See also* ASIA AND THE PACIFIC, NEW RELIGIOUS MOVEMENTS IN; MELANESIAN RELIGION; PACIFIC RELIGIONS; PHILIPPINES RELIGION.) [6; 121 vol. 3: xiv, vol. 5: vii; 122 vol. 5: vi, vol. 7: viii]

Australian Religion [xxix] The Aborigines of Australia have one of the oldest living religions, although Christian and Western incursions in recent times have been highly destructive of it. Tribal differences across the vast continent make a general description difficult, but the Aranda of central Australia have a typical system. It is based on 'totemic ancestors', supernatural beings who are *altjiranga ngambakala*, 'born of eternity' (*see* WONDJINA and DEMA DEITIES), who shaped the landscape into a habitable place filled with their various sacred animals, plants or natural phenomena;

and a concept of sacred time or eternity (ALTJIRANGA) expressed in sacred myths, rituals and objects (TJURUNGA). Each human being is an incarnation of one of these ancestors (the spirit having entered the foetus when the pregnant mother passed by the sacred spot where the totemic ancestor sleeps). The ancestor continues his or her slumber even though reincarnated and, indeed, in more than one child at the same time.

The person receives his or her totem from that particular ancestor (be it a plant, an animal or a heavenly body such as the sun). A male kangaroo person, for example, after being initiated into his totemic clan, is empowered and obliged to perform 'increase rituals' to ensure the constant supply of kangaroo meat to his community. Women have their own secret traditions and rites, but male relatives carry out totemic rituals for them. Initiation for boys, after puberty, was by physical ordeal, such as circumcision, subincision (cutting the urethra) and removal of a tooth.

Each person is in a sense his or her own priest, but the medicine-man has special powers of divination, healing and sorcery (e.g. the death-rite of bone-pointing; see TJURUNGA); his powers often come through visionary experience of the totemic ancestors and their insertion of quartz crystals in his body [11]. Everyone has two souls, one human and immortal derived from the natural parents, the other immortal and eternal which returns to the totemic ancestor at death. Although the existence of sky beings and even a sky father is widely recognized, they are considered to have no control over humankind: the totemic ancestors of the earth and the social group are the active forces working on a human being. [4; 10; 11; 21; 22; 27; 28]

Authority (Christian) [XIII.B] Christianity claims that its truth rests ultimately on a revelation from GOD through JESUS Christ, transmitted through scripture (BIBLE) and 'tradition' in the CHURCH. The early church regarded 'tradition' as Christian belief centred in the CREEDS of major church centres. For the EASTERN ORTHODOX CHURCH 'tradition' is the living authority of the church's whole life and teaching, which includes scripture. ROMAN CATHOLICISM sees Christian truth as contained in scripture and 'tradition'. The Catholic church's developing understanding of both is promulgated infallibly as 'dogma' (doctrines binding on Catholics) through COUNCILS and the PAPACY [36]. The Council of Trent (1545–63) asserted that scripture and 'tradition' were to be received as of equal authority; but the Second Vatican Council (1962–5) appeared to minimize the distinction [1: 114–18]. PROTESTANTISM originally appealed to the Bible alone for authority, interpreted by individuals under the guidance of the HOLY SPIRIT. However, Confessions of Faith and church authority soon provided a fresh 'tradition'. Christians have often claimed that reason can by itself discover some religious truths (NATURAL THEOLOGY) as well as interpret revelation. Since the 18th century in the West reason has sometimes (e.g. DEISM) seemed to overshadow church authority if not scripture, especially for LIBERAL PROTESTANTISM. But Protestant 'Fundamentalism' takes scripture alone as an infallible guide. [51; 114: II; 132; 188]

Avadana [XI] A type of Buddhist Sanskrit literature consisting in legends of past Buddhist heroes. In PALI literature the form *apadana* is used. Outside Buddhist literature the term denotes a 'heroic exploit', as applied, for instance, to RAMA.

Avalokiteshvara [XI] MAHAYANA Buddhist BODHISATTVA who is a focus of numerous devotional practices and seen as incarnating the supreme qualities of compassion (KARUNA). In Tibet, Avalokiteshvara is thought to have a particularly strong connection with the DALAI LAMAS. He is said to save from many dangers and to appear in whatever form is appropriate in order to help sentient beings. One late Indian MAHAYANA SUTRA has Avalokiteshvara giving birth to the HINDU gods and sending SHIVA as the Great Lord (*Maheshvara*). Avalokiteshvara is held to live on the mountain of Potalaka, sometimes said to be in the south of India, but also in China. In Chinese and Japanese BUDDHISM he is often portrayed as female (*see* KUAN (SHIH) YIN; JAPANESE BUDDHAS AND BODHISATTVAS). Avalokiteshvara is frequently portrayed with 11 heads and 1,000 arms, while a four-armed version is also popular in Tibet, where he is also associated with the MANTRA *om manipadme hum*, a mantra which is no clearer when translated. [101: 231–6]

Avashyaka [xx] The six 'obligatory actions' of the JAIN religion [4: 146–9; 10: 189–91]. Although there is possible evidence for the existence of some of these at an earlier period, the full context and significance of the Avashyakas are found for the first time in the Avashyaka Sutra (*c.* 2nd century CE), a text belonging to the scriptural canon of the SHVETAMBARA sect and on which there exists a voluminous commentary literature. However, these ritualized actions also find an important place in DIGAMBARA tradition and are performed by followers of all the main Jain sects, albeit sometimes with differences in the wording of the ritual formulae, the enumeration of the actions and so on. Practised by the Jain ascetic community both daily and on specific occasions, the Avashyakas have from the early medieval period also played a significant role in lay religious activity.

The Avashyakas are as follows: (1) 'equanimity' (*samayika*), quasi-meditative activity carried out for 48 minutes; (2) praise of the 24 TIRTHANKARA; (3) 'homage' (*vandana*) of the ascetic teacher, whether present in person or symbolically; (4) 'turning back' (*pratikramana*), formulaic utterances of confession and repentance for faults committed wittingly and unwittingly; (5) 'abandonment of the body' (*kayotsarga*), a temporary ascetic posture assumed in either a sitting or standing position; and (6) 'renunciation' (*pratyakhyana*), temporary abstention from a variety of substances and activities.

Avatara [xvii] The *avatara* is a HINDU concept, signifying the 'descent' (*ava* = down) to earth of the deity. The concept is peculiar to the tradition associated with the worship of the major deity, VISHNU [138: 91–2]. This deity is thought of as assuming human or animal form from time to time in order to save the world from imminent destruction, or chaos, or some other great peril. The forms which he is believed to have assumed in the past are conventionally listed as nine. The first three are non-human: fish, turtle and boar. The fourth is a hybrid, a man–lion. The remaining five are human, that is: a dwarf; Rama-with-the-axe (Parashurama); RAMA; KRISHNA; and the BUDDHA. The *avatara*-to-come is Kalkin. The last four of the past *avataras* are probably historical or semi-historical figures. Rama-with-the-axe was, according to tradition, a BRAHMAN who destroyed the KSHATRIYA class when there was a danger that they would dominate the world. The story probably reflects a conflict in early times between the Brahman class and the Kshatriyas for social and political supremacy. The seventh *avatara*, Rama, is the hero of the epic poem the RAMAYANA [138: 141–3]. The sixth, Krishna, is the hero of many legends and stories which deal with him as divine infant, boy, youthful lover and amorous companion of the *gopis* (milkmaids) and, finally, as the divine being who appeared to Arjuna on the eve of the great battle at Kurukshetra and urged Arjuna to do his duty disinterestedly as a member of the warrior class [139: 249–325]. The inclusion of the Buddha in this list of Hindu manifestations of the deity has been explained variously: as a way of subsuming the cult of the Buddha and bringing it under Brahmanical control, and as a subtle way of discrediting the Buddha by interpreting the appearance of the Lord Vishnu in the form of the Buddha (a heretic) as a means of leading astray evil men. To this list of nine past *avataras* has been added a tenth, Kalkin, who will appear at the end of the present age, a messianic figure combining elements of ZOROASTRIAN (*see* FRASHO-KERETI) and Hindu eschatology.

Avesta [xxxvi] The scriptures of ZOROASTRIANISM, traditionally believed to have been revealed in their entirety to ZOROASTER. Only 17 hymns, the *Gathas*, can, however, be attributed to him. Some parts of the Avesta, notably some ancient hymns, *Yashts*, are substantially pre-Zoroastrian in origin [24], whereas other portions date from approximately the beginning of the Christian era. But the contents can, as a whole, be considered pre-Christian in date because (at least by the 1st century) the language of the Avesta was a dead one, used only for recitation of prayers and not for new compositions.

The material was originally transmitted in oral form only. Writing was considered an alien art and therefore unsuitable for sacred words. The passages were memorized by priests. The first move to collect the diverse traditions was probably in Parthian times (early centuries CE), but it was a few centuries before a special, phonetically accurate, alphabet was devised which made it possible to commit the Avesta precisely to writing. The

written Avesta were composed in 21 divisions (*nasks*). Copies were preserved in important FIRE temples for scholar priests but these were, presumably, little used by most Zoroastrians because of the strength of the oral tradition [6: v]. The manuscripts were probably destroyed in the Arab (7th century), Turkish (11th) and Mongol (12th) invasions. The only portions of the Avesta now extant are the liturgical portions memorized and used regularly by priests (MAGI), but judging from ancient summaries this represents only a quarter of the original. Secondary to the Avesta were the translations from the sacred language with commentary. These were known as the *Zand*. The only surviving *Zand* is in PAHLAVI. The Avesta was partly translated into Sanskrit by early Parsi scholars, notably Neryosang Dhaval in the early 12th century.

The main liturgy is the YASNA [translation: 45]. The central section of this is known as the *Staota yesnya* and is considered by many Zoroastrians to be one of the most powerful prayers (MANTHRAS). It was probably one of the first fixed liturgies of the religion. At the heart of the *Yasna* are the 17 hymns of Zoroaster, the *Gathas* (*Yasna* 28–34, 43–51, 53). Encased within these hymns is the 'Yasna Haptanghaiti', substantially a pre-Zoroastrian liturgy adapted to the revealed religion and recited during certain offerings. Other main sections of the Avesta are the *Visperad* [translation: 45], a supplement to the *Yasna*; the *Vendidad*, or *Videvdat* (anti-demonic law) [16]; and the *Yashts* (hymns) [17; 24], a number of which are summarized as litanies (*Nyaishes*) [18]. These with other prayers are collected into the *Khordeh* (or smaller) *Avesta* intended for use in private devotions.

Avidya [xi] (Sanskrit; literally 'non-knowledge', or lack of understanding of the nature of reality.) In its

Pali form, *avijja*, it indicates lack of knowledge of the FOUR NOBLE TRUTHS. The inability to see the true nature of things is regarded in Buddhist tradition as the root of all evil.

Ayatullah [XIX] 'Miraculous sign from God', a title held by high dignitaries of the Shi'i religious hierarchy. SHI'ISM provides the nearest approach in ISLAM to what might be called a clergy, and among the body of scholars trained in the shrine-cities of Iraq and Persia/Iran (MASHHAD) there evolved in the upper echelons a group of *mujtahids* ('those who exert themselves in interpreting the faith') considered as qualified to give authoritative judgements in matters of faith and practice. Recently, the title of *Ayatullah* has been applied to outstanding leaders in this latter group, but its application seems to depend on the personality and charisma of the scholar concerned and his consequent recognition by the community at large. This process is seen clearly at work in regard to the Ayatullah Khumaini, who in the 1960s emerged as the main political opponent of the Shah of Iran, Muhammad Riza Pahlavi, and after the 1978–9 revolution became recognized as Vilayat Faqih or supreme temporal representative in Iran of the Hidden IMAM [38 Suppl. s.v.; 96]

Aztec Sculpture [XXV] (1400–1521 CE) Monumental stone sculpture was one of the finest achievements of Mesoamerican culture (*see* MESOAMERICAN RELIGIONS). The master sculptors of the Aztec traditions developed the aesthetic forms of their Toltec predecessors and decorated their temples and palaces with major and minor pieces [11: 53–67]. Some of these works were mass-produced in small and large sizes to express a standardized symbolic system concerning sacred warfare, fertility, solar worship and death [17: 108–35]. All carvings were part of a great sacred art related to the ceremonial cycles and myths of the religion. The largest number of carved objects were statues of male and female deities in nude or nearly nude appearance. Also, large numbers of animal and insect stone images were produced, including serpents, feathered serpents, jaguars, frogs, turtles and grasshoppers. Stone masks in various local styles were produced and sometimes buried at major ceremonies at the temples. Also remarkable were the year bundle stones called *xiuhmolpilli* (*see* NEW FIRE CEREMONY), which were deposited in ritual tombs at the end of a 52-year calendar cycle. The Aztecs also produced exquisite reliefs of deities, warriors and religious events. Most of these works display a combination of poignant realism and intricate entanglement of symbols decorating larger forms, along with technical polish. Among the most outstanding large pieces are the CALENDAR STONE, the statue of Coatlicue, the mother goddess, the mammoth *cuauhxicalli* ('eagle vessel') of King Tizoc, which held human hearts, and the oval of the goddess Coyolxauh-qui-Chantico, all of which appear to have been associated with the cult of the TEMPLO MAYOR in the centre of Tenochtitlan.

B

Ba'al [VIII] A central figure in many Ugaritic accounts (*see* PHOENICIANS), Ba'al was widely worshipped as a warrior-god in Canaan, the son either of Dagon, the corn-god, or of El, chief Ugaritic deity. Ba'al's consort was 'Ashtoreth (Ishtar), the goddess of battle; his daughters were Mist and Dew. Ba'al destroyed his enemies, including Mot, god of dryness and death, although his brief submission to Mot brought drought to the earth. Ba'al's revival, as rain-god, brought back the land's fertility. (*See* ANCIENT NEAR EASTERN RELIGIONS) [4: 27]

Babis [XIX] A Muslim sect arising out of Persian SHI'ISM in the early 19th century, and important as the precursor of the BAHA'IS. It arose from the atmosphere then current of messianic expectations (*see* MAHDI) under the leadership of Mirza 'Ali Muhammad (1819–50) of Shiraz, who in 1844 proclaimed himself the Bab ('gateway') to the Hidden IMAM and the inauguration of a new prophetic cycle after the Prophet MUHAMMAD, with his own message now abrogating certain prescriptions of the Islamic law or SHARI'A. Mirza 'Ali gathered round himself a band of enthusiasts who attempted to seize power in various parts of Persia. These outbreaks were bloodily suppressed and the Bab himself executed in 1850, but the movement continued both in Persia and in other parts of the Middle East, and under a new leader, Baha'ullah, evolved into Baha'ism in the second half of the century. [20 s.v.; 38 s.v.; 78: XI]

Babylonians [VIII] The remnants of the last SUMERIAN allegiance – the Ur III dynasty (*c.*2113 BCE) – were taken over by the Amorites. New dynasties arose at Larsa, Kish and Babylon, where King HAMMURABI, having devoted his early years to internal affairs, now took Sumer and Akkad in his 31st year, and Mari and Eshnunna thereafter [7; 24: 482–3]. This was a turning-point: the warring city states now became one country, and an area equal to the southern part of modern Iraq was united as 'Babylonia'. Babylon itself became a political and cultural capital.

In his Law Code (HAMMURABI'S CODE), Hammurabi states that the chief gods of Sumer had exalted MARDUK, god of Babylon, as supreme deity; he ordered the king to establish justice in the kingdom (*see* KINGSHIP (ANCIENT NEAR EAST)). Culturally, the 1st dynasty of Babylon (*c.*1792–1595 BCE) inherited and preserved Sumerian wisdom and religious lore. Scribes copied Sumerian texts, although this language was no longer spoken, and Sumerian myths were now compiled and set down as epics (*see* ANCIENT NEAR EASTERN RELIGIONS) [24: 37–57, 383–91]. Akkadian also flourished as a literary language [24: 60–149, 331–43]. The EPIC OF GILGAMESH [24: 60–71] was an important religious poem in praise of Marduk, which was recited in the course of the New Year rituals at Babylon (*see* FESTIVALS (ANCIENT NEAR EASTERN)) and told of the rebellion by the underworld gods against the great gods, and Marduk's eventual creation of the world (see COSMOLOGY (ANCIENT NEAR EASTERN)).

The Babylonians were famed for their astronomical observations (see ASTROLOGY) [22; 24: 449–51], and their science of DIVINATION to foresee events. In addition to oracular priests there were incantation priests who used MAGIC against EVIL or to obtain good fortune. Their TEMPLES incorporated ZIGGURATS which housed the god's shrine.

New Kassite rulers (c.1600–1200 BCE) replaced Babylonian kings, but they adopted Babylonian culture, incorporating their own gods into the pantheon. Later, Assyria (see ASSYRIANS) adopted and modified the Babylonian heritage [11], and finally, with the advent of the Neo-Babylonian Empire (700–500 BCE), Nebuchadnezzar (c.600 BCE) restored the city of Babylon and the ancient shrines.

Back to Africa Movements [III] In 1787 a group of colonists arrived in Sierra Leone from England. Their intention was to repatriate blacks to Africa, but also to rid England of a problem. Slaves brought to England from America and the West Indies, especially throughout the first half of the 18th century, were freed in 1772 after Justice Mansfield's ruling on the illegality of slavery. Even more complex and pressing was the plight of the emancipated blacks in the USA. Presidents Jefferson, Monroe and Madison all supported African colonization. The American Colonization Movement sent the first colonists to Liberia in 1820. In America, Bishop Henry McNeal Turner (1834–1915) constantly preached the value of going 'back to Africa', although his view of Africa was somewhat symbolic, being based on his interpretation of the Hebrew BIBLE. In the context of a response to racism and oppression, Africa represented not the wilderness into which Cain had been exiled, but the chosen home of the lost tribe of Israel, the chosen people. Africa offered a biblically sanctioned, noble and redemptive reference point. During the 19th century, therefore, the 'back to Africa' rhetoric was powerful, while actual repatriation was spasmodic and individual.

Some black missionaries from the diaspora worked in Africa during the 19th and early 20th centuries, but their attitude was ambivalent. The spirit of Africanity was fostered by the National Association for the Advancement of Colored People, founded by Booker T. Washington and others in 1909. Other influential educational institutions encouraged pride, even if initially counselling accommodation, such as the Tuskagee Institute, founded in 1900 by W. E. du Bois (1868–1964). A strong sense of African consciousness was a dominant element in the ideology of African American mass movements: the Liberia Exodus Association of Martin R. Delany and others before 1877; the Akim Trading Company of Chief Alfred Samuel until 1914; and the United Negro Improvement Association, founded by Marcus Mosiah Garvey (see GARVEYISM), in 1914. The UNIA profoundly influenced later movements including the NATION OF ISLAM and RASTAFARIANISM. In particular its theme of 'One God! One Aim! One Africa!' inspired proto-nationalist and religious movements throughout the black diaspora. The UNIA was used as a reference point for the growth of black identity, pride, rhetorical style, and alternative worship styles and expressions.

While the idea of journeying back to Africa has remained mythic for most enthusiasts, a group of Black Muslims has settled in Liberia, and the Ethiopian government has granted land to Rastafarians. Equally mythic are the views of some young Africans who, influenced by reggae/Rastafarianism, gospel and soul music, search for Afrika, disillusioned by their own experiences. [52; 63; 80; 91; 96]

Bagre [II] The Bagre is one of many special associations or 'secret societies' found in west Africa. It belongs to the LoDagaa people in north-west Ghana and has spread also into northern Ivory Coast and Upper Volta. Membership of such associations is optional, an additional dimension to the religious or social life which some never join. Unlike many secret societies the Bagre does not use masks, but it does possess what is probably the most lengthy and remarkable 'myth' text to be found anywhere in Africa. This is recited, and repeated by the neophytes, during the long series of ceremonies which constitute the initiation of new members (male and female) and are closely related to the agricultural cycle.

The LoDagaa are an acephalous people (i.e. without governmental institutions above the village level) whose regular religion, like that of Tallensi or Lugbara, appears to consist principally of ANCESTOR VENERATION. But the Bagre myth has little to say about ancestors, its orientation being strikingly theistic. While the myth is concerned to explain the many Bagre ceremonies, it does this in the context of a doctrine of creation, the relative remoteness of God (Naangmin) and the relationship between God, man and 'beings of the wild' – man's mysterious brothers in the world who taught him most of his skills. The Bagre provides one of the richest sources for African traditional theology and a warning to the student to recognize the great complexity discoverable in popular religion even in small societies. [32]

Baha'is [XIX] A faith arising out of the Islamic BABI movement in Persia. Baha'ullah (1817–92) was originally a Babi who in exile acquired the conviction that he was the prophet foretold by the Bab. His faith of Baha'ism developed subsequently from an authoritarian, post-Shi'i (SHI'ISM) sectarianism into a universalist religion of humanity, with stress on the essential unity of all faiths, education, sexual equality, monogamy and the attainment of world peace. It claims to be a scientific, undogmatic faith. It has no formal public ritual or priesthood, and no really authoritative scriptures. Local congregations hold informal devotional sessions and function within an administrative framework. There has always been an emphasis on missionary work, so that Baha'ism has been carried to Europe, the Americas, Africa, etc., while still remaining strong in Persia/Iran despite sporadic persecution, intensified in recent years. [20 s.v.; 22; 38 s.v.; 40; 78: XI; 103]

Balder [VII] The Icelandic story of Balder, slain by the blind god Hother with a shaft of mistletoe after other plants and substances had sworn not to harm him, is well known. It comes from a late source, the 13th-century Prose EDDA [28: 48–52]. There are some cryptic references to his death in earlier poems, and to LOKI's malice in causing it and punishment by the angry gods. In Saxo's 12th-century account [26 vol. 1: III, 65–76], Balder is ODIN's son by a human mother, killed by the Danish hero Hother after a battle in Jutland [3: 182–9]. Balder, like Freyr, means 'lord', and could be the title of a fertility god; this would be consistent with the legend that all creation weeps for Balder when a thaw comes after frost. However, Balder has close links with Odin, who tries to rescue him from HEL, and begets another son to avenge him; and Balder's death is a precursor of RAGNAROK. Balder's wife is Nanna, and his son Forseti was said to be worshipped in Frisia. Places were named after Balder in Germany, Norway and Denmark, and his name occurs in an early German spell, but no reliable evidence for a cult of Balder has been found [32: IV].

Balinese Religion [xxix] The religion of Bali (an island of Indonesia) is officially HINDUISM, but this is combined with indigenous practices and beliefs. The Balinese call it Agama Tirtha (Religion of Holy Water), indicating the centrality of sanctified water in their rituals. The water is blessed by a BRAHMAN priest (*pedanda*) reciting Sanskrit incantations (MANTRAS). He is a devotee of SHIVA or (in a few cases) the BUDDHA. Women are not entirely excluded from this role. Another priest (*sengguhu*) has a special relationship with VISHNU and he is concerned with the underworld. The village priest (*pemangku*) officiates at temple ceremonies, receiving offerings of food and flowers for the gods. Trance is a recognized means of communication with ancestors, spirits and deities; a special functionary (*balian*, male or female) acts as a trance-medium for divine revelation. Seasonal festivals revolve round the cultivation of rice in irrigated terraces. The Balinese temple is walled but unroofed. Ritual battles are staged there between the forces of good (led by Barong, a lion) and evil (Rangda, a witch), usually ending in a balanced compromise. Cremation, often preceded by temporary burial, is the normal funeral rite and an occasion for great festivity. [17; 26]

Ball Court [xxv] An outstanding feature of the ceremonial centres of MESOAMERICAN RELIGIONS was the ball court or Tlachtli, the scene of ritual ball games which in some traditions re-enacted the sacred drama of the sun's journey through the underworld and the struggle between the powers of light and darkness for its destiny [2: 8–12]. Played on a court shaped like an I, representing the four-quartered cosmos (CEMANAHUAC) and the night sky, with raised viewing platforms for spectators who wagered for their team, the ball-game cult was inspired by various local mythical traditions which, in part, focused on

solar motion and agricultural fertility. The game was determined when a small bouncy rubber ball was hit through a carved stone disc embedded in each of the long walls [7: 312–19]. In some regions, the captains of the losing teams were decapitated on a sacrificial stone to revitalize cosmic processes (*see* HUMAN SACRIFICE).

Balts [vii] The Balts were INDO-EUROPEANS, ancestors of the Lithuanians, Letts and Old Prussians [10: 1]. Their conversion to Christianity in the 14th century was slow, but little is known of their beliefs. Sixteenth- and 17th-century chroniclers like Grunau are often misleading. Something, however, may be learned from folk songs and traditional symbolism [1: 631–4; 10: viii]. A thunder-god, Perkunas, overcame evil spirits, established order and helped farmers. Zemepatis and his sister Zemyna were master and mistress of the earth, Kalvaitis the heavenly smith, and Laima a goddess of fate. There were many supernatural beings resembling Celtic fairy-women. Songs tell of Saule the Sun and her daughters, and Menuo, the fickle Moon. The Balts had powerful priests, and 'sacred' towns and villages. Their holy trees, particularly oaks, were destroyed by missionaries. Cremation continued until the 14th century; there were human sacrifices at funerals, and communities accepted voluntary death rather than defeat. [10: 188]

Bantu Religion [ii] The large majority of peoples in central and southern Africa can be classified, on a linguistic basis (use of the *ntu* root in the word for person), as Bantu; *see* GANDA, LOVEDU, SHONA and ZULU RELIGIONS. While Bantu religion has many diversities, as these different entries show, its most widespread features are the following: a great concern for ancestral spirits, who constitute the principal guardians of morality (so that some would describe its predominant characteristic as 'ancestralism'), a fear of witchcraft and a belief in one supreme God who, while seldom fairly described as otiose, is hardly ever the recipient of much public worship (*see* IRUVA; KATONDA; LEZA; MODIMO; MULUNGU; NZAMBI). The extensive sharing of religious beliefs and practices between different Bantu peoples is evidenced not only by the inter-tribal use of such god-names as Nzambi and Leza, but by the still wider spread of other basic religious terms such as NGANGA and MIZIMU.

Baptism (in Early Christianity) [XIII.A] The Christian initiation rite of dipping in water may have been taken over from the practice of JOHN THE BAPTIST, or even of the QUMRAN community, Christianized by the use of the words 'in the name of Jesus'. It betokened the convert's repentance and faith in JESUS, and was accompanied by the reception of the HOLY SPIRIT. In PAUL's teaching it denotes the believer's union with the risen Jesus in his death and burial and is the sign of incorporation into the 'body of Christ' (*see also* SACRAMENTS). [6: 280–3; 9: 152–61]

Baptists [XIII.B] Though once nicknamed 'ANABAPTISTS', Baptists trace their origin to John Smyth (*c.*1554–1612) who used baptism of mature believers only as a mark of church membership. Baptists strongly emphasize the independence of the local church, although individual churches are linked in associations of various kinds at various levels. Almost from their 17th-century beginnings there were 'General' Baptists (*see* ARMINIANISM) and 'Particular' ones (*see* CALVINISM) as well as varieties of each. The 18th-century Evangelical Revival (cf. REVIVALISM) made some of the Particulars enthusiastic missionaries.

The Baptists are a loose family of churches. Their main numerical base is in the USA (particularly among black Christians; *see* BLACK CHURCHES IN AMERICA), with an important north/south division. Periods of religious conflict or revival often produce new groups of Baptist churches. Although there are international bodies (such as the Baptist World Alliance, with its headquarters in Washington, DC, USA) and national bodies, many Baptist churches belong to neither. Hence there is a great diversity of belief and practice which makes generalization impossible. [62 vol. 2: 63–6; 189; 199]

Bar Mitzvah, Bat Mitzvah [XXII] Jewish boys and girls are considered adults on their 13th and 12th Hebrew birthdays respectively, when they become responsible for keeping the commandments, being called bar mitzvah ('son of the commandment') and bat mitzvah ('daughter of the commandment') respectively [5; 14 vol. 4: 243; 27]. Originally the mark of adulthood was the growth of two pubic hairs, but since hairs might grow and then fall out an average age of puberty was accepted. Since the middle ages [1: 32] it has been customary to celebrate a boy's bar mitzvah by calling him up for an *aliyah* to the TORAH reading, usually on a SHABBAT morning. This is followed by a celebratory kiddush after the service and a party after the Sabbath. A bar mitzvah boy begins putting on TEFILLIN on weekday mornings and can henceforth be included in a *minyan* quorum of ten adult males for public service [70: 142]. In modern times Reform and Conservative congregations introduced bat mitzvah ceremonies for girls, to parallel bar mitzvahs, and subsequently Modern Orthodox congregations also instituted ceremonies for groups of girls together, usually on a Sunday. More traditionalist Orthodox groups [cf. 39], however, reject the bat mitzvah ceremony altogether as a modernist innovation imitating Reform or Christian practice [69: 34].

Bardo [xxxv] The BUDDHIST doctrine of *bardo* refers to the intermediate state between death and rebirth. Although the doctrine is mentioned in ABHIDHAMMA and TANTRA (2), its most famous expression has been in the NYINGMA texts known collectively as *Liberation through Hearing in the Bardo*, which teach that liberation is attained by recognizing the peaceful and wrathful deities encountered in the *bardo* as manifestations of the luminosity and emptiness of one's own mind. [7; 11]

Barelvi [xix] (Alternative spelling: Brelwi.) A school of thought within Indian ISLAM that arose as a reaction to DEOBANDI reform. It gains its name from the town of Bareilly, the home of Ahmad Raza Khan (1856–1921). He championed the defence of the popular Islam of the villages and argued for the validity of *pirs* (Persian for SHAIKH; *see also* WALI) and shrine-based religious practice. Barelvis are renowned for their love of the Prophet and the doctrine of the 'light of MUHAMMAD' (*nur-i-Muhammadi*), said to be derived from God's own light and to have existed from the beginning of creation. The Prophet is believed to be present in all places, particularly at *maulid* celebrations (*see* 'ID). Opponents of the Barelvis accuse them of treating Muhammad like a deity. The *pirs*, who are often *sayyids* (*see* 'ALI, 'ALIDS), are considered to be possessors of *baraka* (blessing) derived from the Prophet. Their followers have mainly been drawn from the poor, illiterate strata of society. The *pirs* are called upon to treat all types of physical and mental illness, often in the form of exorcism from JINN possession. Followers of Ahmad Raza Khan are represented in the West, for example in the Raza Academy, Stockport, England, which publishes *The Islamic Times*. However, 'Barelvi' has come to be used more as a blanket term for Muslims from the villages of the subcontinent, typified by their love of Muhammad and their continued reliance on *pirs*. The presence in Britain of large numbers of Barelvis was a contributing factor in the depth of reaction to *The Satanic Verses* by Salman Rushdie. [35; 49; 92; 99; 113]

Basilides [xv] One of the earliest, best-known and most frequently refuted of all GNOSTIC teachers, Basilides flourished in the early 2nd century CE in Egypt. He claimed as his teacher Glaucias, an interpreter of the apostle PETER. He is said to have been the author of a gnostic commentary on the gospels which has not survived. Of the two versions of his teaching preserved by the Church Fathers Irenaeus (*c.*130–*c.*200 CE) and Hippolytus (d. *c.*235 CE), the second is generally regarded as the more authentic. Rejecting all idea of a pre-existing matter, Basilides derives everything from the supreme being, whom he considers to be so ineffable and inconceivably great that he would not even say he exists. He also rejected the idea of emanation common to most Gnostics; all things subsequent to the supreme being are in effect his generation. From the panspermia or seed-mass originally deposited by him emerges the First Sonhood, who gives light when needed to the lower parts of creation. This is followed by the Second Sonhood, which, emerging in like manner, rises not from its own unaided power, but with the assistance of a boundary spirit who is left as the demarcation between the visible and the invisible part of the universe when the Second Sonhood passes to the Ogdoad or Eighth Heaven. This Eighth Heaven is under the sway of the Great Ruler (Archon) emitted by the seed-mass for the purpose of governing this world (AEON) of perfection.

A second world-creating power is the maker of the seven heavens or Hebdomad. He, too, produces from the seed-mass a Son greater and wider than himself who assists the Father in the organization of the Hebdomad. This takes the form of 365 beings who are all 'dominions and powers and authorities' with a ruler called Habrazax (a secret paraphrase of the name of Yahweh written in four Hebrew tetragrams). Below this Hebdomad, however, comes this world of ours, called the 'Formlessness', everything happening in it as decreed by the supreme being from the first. Yet this Formlessness contains within it the Third Sonhood, whose mission is apparently to guide the souls of men to the place for which they are predestined, which it does by imparting to them some of its own nature. The coming of the Saviour took the form of a light from the highest heavens shining through the intermediate places to the Son of the Hebdomad and falling upon 'JESUS the son of MARY', who, after the crucifixion, ascended like the two first parts of the Sonhood to the divine presence. In due time the third part of the Sonhood will, it is said, follow him. When this happens, the soul predestined to the seven heavens will pass thither, those more enlightened (the psychic) will be admitted to the Eighth Heaven, and the most enlightened of all (the pneumatic) will probably ascend with the Third Sonhood to the Highest. A great ignorance will fall on the unenlightened classes of mankind (the hylic), an oblivion which will prevent them from remembering or otherwise being troubled in their beatitude by the knowledge of the still better things above them.

Basilides was also said to have taught docetism, alleging that it was not Christ but Simon of Cyrene who was crucified and that the soul could be purified through transmigration, although evidence for this is scanty.

His followers formed a separate sect which survived into the 4th century but whose influence rarely extended beyond Egypt. [7; 9; 10; 13; 24]

Batak Religion [xxIX] The Bataks are an Indonesian tribal group of northern Sumatra, now largely Christianized, with a Muslim minority. Long known internationally as anthropophagous, they had written texts and a religion partly influenced by India (e.g. *debata*, 'god'). The Toba Bataks believed in a three-tiered universe: men in the middle world; the fettered dragon Naga Padoha in the underworld; the gods in the upper world, notably the creator Mula Jadi and his three sons Batara Guru, Soripada, and Mangalabulan. Creation involved a struggle between the upper world and the underworld. Mula Jadi's tree, named Jambubarus, had leaves inscribed with fates (e.g. poverty, wealth, sorrow), and each soul (*tondi*) took a leaf as its lot. *Sahala* (the power of the *tondi*) resembled MANA; it could be increased by feeding on another person's *tondi* in ritual cannibalism. The priest (*datu*) had magic books, and practised healing and divination. [19; 26]

Bedwardism [III] Alexander Bedward (1859–1930), of August Town, Jamaica, is significant both for his role as a charismatic REVIVAL-IST leader and for his influence throughout Central America and Cuba, as well as Jamaica. He was originally a member of the Jamaican Native Baptist Church, which had a tradition of visions and prophecies. Such visions gave spiritual guidance as to practical behaviour, while prophecies reinterpreted the BIBLE as well as making personal and policy statements. Within the JNB Church he became a famous preacher and spiritual healer, and his Bedward Church incorporated these features. In 1895 he was arrested for sedition following his prediction that 'the black wall shall crush the white wall', but was soon released. In December 1920 a large crowd gathered at Mona, near Kingston, where he announced that he would fly to heaven. 'Flying' was a characteristic of Revival and Bedward churches, enabling people to spring swiftly from place to place. His ascension failed to materialize, and he was committed to a mental hospital. His followers were not disheartened, and many of them remained loyal to their notion of BACK TO AFRICA. Africa and Zion thus became closely associated in similar messianic cults.

Bedward's movement drew on both MYALISM and revivalism. The cult that he left behind has become far less dramatically APOCALYPTIC, and its worship style far less extravagant. Many Bedward followers became proto-RASTAFARIANS. [6; 85]

Bhagat bani [xxxiii] Compositions by persons other than the SIKH GURUS included in the ADI GRANTH. The bulk of the Adi Granth comprises works by six of the Sikh Gurus. Practically all of the small remainder consists of devotional hymns (*bani*) by poets of the SANT TRADITION (*bhagats*) which were in agreement with those of the Gurus. These Sants (or *bhagats*) were either contemporaneous with GURU NANAK or preceded him. Kabir is the best known, followed by Namdev and Ravidas (Raidas). [26: 71; 30: 53–4]

Bhagavadgita [xvii] A verse UPANISHAD included in the MAHABHARATA. At the beginning of the episode the hero Arjuna, on the verge of a decisive battle, revolts from the bloodshed of a civil war and refuses to fight. His charioteer KRISHNA persuades him to fight with arguments ranging from the mundane – that people would think him a coward – through the social – that Arjuna's failure to do his duty as a KSHATRIYA would lead to a breakdown in the moral order (DHARMA)

– to the philosophical – that in reality no one kills or is killed: the self that incarnates simply changes bodies as a person changes clothes. The implications go far beyond the tension between Kshatriya duty and AHIMSA, and the story is often taken as a model for the action that everyone must take on the field of life. Whereas the teachings of the earlier Upanishads are often attributed to GURUS who have withdrawn from worldly life, and are mainly concerned with the way of knowledge, JNANA YOGA, the Bhagavadgita teaches KARMA YOGA, the way of action, by which a person may live in the world without attachment, carrying out his or her duties without desire for reward. Moreover, in the culminating vision of the poem Krishna reveals his cosmic form as a great deity, teaching the way of devotion or BHAKTI YOGA [139: xv–xx, translation, 249–325; 137]. The Bhagavadgita has always been recognized as an important teaching, particularly by Vaishnavas (*see* VISHNU), but it has gained further popularity in recent years through its influence on Gandhi. The scene of Krishna teaching Arjuna in the chariot, occasionally depicted in painting in the 18th and 19th centuries, has now become a popular subject of Hindu iconography, represented in painting or sculpture in many temples (*see* ART, HINDU). [68]

Bhagavati [xx] Epithet meaning 'revered', used of the fifth text or 'limb' (*anga*) of the SHVETAMBARA JAIN scriptural canon [3]. Although near-impossible to date because of its composite nature, portions of it must certainly pre-date the common era. The more formal name of this scripture, the 'Exposition of Explanations' (Sanskrit: *Vyakhyaprajnapti*), relates to its main feature: detailed answers given in generally stereotyped language by MAHAVIRA to questions from his disciple (GANADHARA) Gautama relating to various aspects of his teachings. Vast in extent and near-encyclopaedic in range of reference, the 'revered' scripture is one of the most important sources, if also frequently one of the most difficult, for the development of Jainism into both a fully autonomous philosophical system with its own technical vocabulary and a soteriological path functioning within its own cosmology.

Bhajan [XVII] Literally 'adoration' or 'worship'. The term is commonly used of Indian hymn-singing sessions held, usually, by Vaishnavas (*see* VISHNU), at which there may also be some brief exposition of scripture. *Bhajans* are well-known features of Vaishnava religion in India, especially, for example, in Madras [118: 90–172] and Gujarat [100: 102ff], where *bhajan-mandali* (hymn-singing groups) are the commonest form of village religious devotion. In recent times they have been introduced by Gujarati immigrants into their new places of abode, for example in the West.

Bhakti [XVII] One of the three major recognized paths to salvation in HINDUISM. It is the attitude and activity of devotion to God; hence a *bhakta* is 'a devotee'. The other recognized 'paths' to salvation are ritual activity (*see* KARMA) and spiritual knowledge (*see* JNANA YOGA). The emphasis on worshipful devotion, as distinct from sacrificial rituals, is found in India at least as early as the 2nd century BCE; the cult of the god Vasudeva (a form of VISHNU) is attested by Megasthenes, then Greek ambassador at the Indian capital. Bhakti cults seem to have grown notably in the later Buddhist period in India and after, that is from about the 8th century CE. The *bhakta* is usually devoted to a particular manifestation of deity, such as RAMA, or KRISHNA, and thus adheres to a school of devotion. Among the Shaivas (*see* SHIVA), important *bhakti* schools include the LINGAYATA, while among Shaktas

(*see* SHAKTI) devotion is often centred upon formidable aspects of the Goddess such as DURGA or KALI. The *bhakti* schools have their great theologians, such as RAMANUJA (d. 1137) [138: 130–3; 12: 334f] whose role has been to expound theologically the nature of the relationship between the worshipper and the personal God. Other great exponents of *bhakti* religion are its poets, for example, Namdev (b. 1470), Tuka Rama (1598–1649), whose hymns are still sung in Hindu households in Maharashtra, and Caitanya (1485–1533), of Bengal.

Bhaktas draw upon every kind of human love to express their devotion: for the boy-saint Sambandar (a NAYANNAR) it is a child's love for Shiva and PARVATI, the father and mother of the world; for many Vaishnavas it is a mother's love for the naughty but lovable child Krishna. The Nayannar Sundarar, 'the Insolent Devotee', addresses Shiva with the affectionate rudeness of a close friend. Above all, perhaps, the language of romantic love is used, as when the ALVAR Andal speaks of Vishnu as her bridegroom, or the LINGAYATA saint Mahadeviyakka speaks of Shiva as the illicit lover to whom she longs to escape [38: 42 61, 117–29; 108: 111–42]. For many Hindus, the love story of Krishna and Radha, a model of human love in all its phases, provides an allegory of the mutual love between the deity and the devotee [90: 9–28].

Bhakti Yoga [XVII] 'The way of devotion' is one of three or four alternative routes of spiritual development (YOGA) widely recognized in Indian thought. The emphasis in this mode of practice is on loving devotion and self-surrender to the deity, leading to inner transformation through grace. Eventually elaborate BHAKTI theologies were developed (for example VAISHNAVA

VEDANTA). [35: 105–8; 133: 145–7; 137: 26–8]

Bhattaraka [xx] A type of cleric or caste GURU found among the DIGAMBARA JAINS. The institution of the *bhattaraka* probably has its origins in the early medieval period in India when some elements of the Digambara ascetic community abandoned wandering and naked mendicancy to live in monasteries endowed by lay supporters. The *bhattarakas* (the term possibly denotes a learned man: cf. Tamil *pattar*, 'priest'), who, although non-initiated ascetics, are celibate and wear orange robes, have traditionally been responsible for the overseeing of ritual and ceremonial among the Digambaras, the custodianship of libraries and the general promotion of Jain learning, while also serving as mediators between their local community and the temporal authorities. Of the various *bhattaraka* 'thrones' scattered around India today, the most important are those at Mudbidri and at Shravana Belgola in Karnataka and at Kolhapur in Maharashtra. [4: 105–7]

Bhavana [xi] What has become known as Buddhist meditation, *bhavana*, literally 'bringing into being', refers to the fourth truth (*see* FOUR NOBLE TRUTHS) – the bringing into being of the EIGHTFOLD PATH in its two aspects of SAMATHA (Sanskrit: *shamatha*) or stillness of mind and VIPASSANA (Sanskrit: *vipashyana*) or insight. Buddhist meditation practice is of two types according to which aspect is emphasized: calm meditation and insight meditation. These are ultimately harmonized and developed together in order to give rise to a higher order of mind (*see* LOKUTTARA). The precise relationship between the two approaches has been variously described, from an early date. One tendency is to view *samatha* meditation practice as preliminary to the practice of insight and as identical to Hindu DHYANA YOGA, whereas *vipassana* would be seen as more advanced or more efficacious and uniquely Buddhist. Earlier authorities (e.g. BUDDHAGHOSA) permit the less usual possibility of omitting all but the most preliminary stages of *samatha*, but more recently a tradition has emerged or been revived (especially in Burma) which sees this as a desirable short cut and emphasizes the danger of attachment to pleasant experiences in *samatha*. The alternative tradition, which emphasizes full development of *samatha* and sees disadvantages in premature development of advanced insight, remains widespread (especially in Thailand). The two approaches may be distinguished as the Insight and Calm schools respectively, but intermediate positions are often found and the two are frequently considered as complementary or suited to different psychological temperaments.

Manuals of *bhavana* have been written at most periods in different Buddhist countries. For THERAVADA Buddhism the most important non-canonical account is that of Buddhaghosa. For the Indian MAHAYANA the most influential writings are those attributed to ASANGA (*see* YOGACARA) and the work of Kamalashila (8th century CE), but most later Mahayana schools have their own manuals of instruction. [14: 11–44; 48; 69: 137–58; 79: 61–84]

Bhikkhu [xi] (Pali; Sanskrit: *bhikshu*.) A BUDDHIST monk. The *bhikkhu* is one who has given up the household life and entered the community of Buddhist monks (SANGHA). His lifestyle derives from that of the ancient Indian homeless ascetic living on alms; this was adapted (in part by the Buddha himself) to allow for a more communal and settled way of life which led eventually to monks' taking up more or less permanent residence in monasteries (VIHARA); however, the ideal of the monk who dwells in the forest practising meditation (BHAVANA) remains powerful [7; 92]. The *bhikkhu* does not technically officiate as a priest, although it is common practice for Buddhists to invite monks to give blessings and preach at marriages (an essentially secular matter) and funerals.

In a form approximating somewhat to the original, the monk's way of life survives most completely in THERAVADA Buddhism. One becomes a monk by undergoing the ceremonies of 'going forth' (*pabbajja*) and higher ordination (*upasampada*) which may be performed on separate occasions or together. A candidate for the first ceremony must be at least eight years old; the ceremony involves shaving the head, donning ochre robes, renouncing personal possessions (apart from such basic requisites as an alms bowl and robes) and undertaking to live by the ten precepts (*see* SILA) which include celibacy, not handling money and not eating after midday. The novice (*samanera*) becomes a candidate (but not before the age of 20) for higher ordination, which requires a quorum of five senior monks to be legitimately conferred. The fully ordained *bhikkhu* undertakes to regulate his life by the 227 precepts of the Buddhist monastic rule (*see* PATIMOKKHA; VINAYA). The vows of a Buddhist monk are not necessarily lifelong and in southeast Asia especially many men spend a short period as monks. [29: 87–117; 100]

Bhikkhuni [XI] (Pali; Sanskrit: *bhikshuni*.) A Buddhist nun. The order of nuns was founded by the BUDDHA (*see* GOTAMA) in response to questions concerning the ability of women to attain enlightenment. The TIPITAKA contains a number of important discourses (SUTTA) delivered by nuns, along with the 'Verses of the Women Elders' (*Therigatha*) [64], a collection of poems attributed to early female ARAHATS.

The lifestyle of the nun as laid down in the VINAYA essentially parallels that of the monk (BHIKKHU). The ancient order of nuns strictly survives only in the SANGHA's 'eastern' ordination lineage, although in the THERAVADA and Tibetan traditions many women still effectively live as nuns by permanently keeping either eight or ten precepts (*see* SILA); some are respected teachers of meditation (BHAVANA). [34: 221–4; 30: 274–95]

Bhudevi [XVII] 'Earth Goddess', or Prithvi/Prithivi, 'the Broad One', 'the Earth', has been revered in HINDUISM from the time of the VEDA, in which she is worshipped in a pair with Dyaus, 'Sky', an old INDOEUROPEAN deity (cf. Greek Zeus, Roman Jupiter – Dius + *pater*, 'Father Sky') [94: 201 7]. In the PURANAS she is closely linked with VISHNU, who becomes incarnate to save the earth in times of peril. As the boar AVATARA, for example, he is said to have rescued the earth by raising it above the flood waters: in images of this scene, the earth is generally personified as a small female figure clinging to the boar's tusk [58: 95–100]. Naturally Vishnu came to be seen as her lover [92: 185–97]. In south India, in particular, the link was formalized, and Bhudevi is regarded as one of Vishnu's wives, second only to LAKSHMI in importance [120: pl. 42], and accompanying him in some of his avataras: *see* RAMA; KRISHNA. The ALVAR Andal, who praised Vishnu in passionate love songs, is regarded as his bride and an incarnation of Bhudevi [38: 118–29].

Bible (Christian) [XIII.A] The Bible of the CHURCH comprises two collections, which Christians call the Old Testament and the New Testament. The Old Testament is substantially the Hebrew Bible with its three divisions (law, prophets and writings), amounting in all to 24 documents (in the traditional Jewish reckoning) or 39 (in the conventional Christian reckoning). The law, the first five books, is often called the Pentateuch (from the Greek meaning 'consisting of five scrolls'). While PROTESTANTS acknowledge the authority of these Old Testament books alone, the majority of other Christians admit that other works, mostly to be found in the SEPTUAGINT, which EASTERN ORTHODOX Christians accept as an inspired translation, are also of scriptural status. The New Testament comprises 27 documents, written within the century following the death of JESUS. These are five narrative works (four GOSPELS and the *Acts of the Apostles*), 21 letters (13 of which bear the name of PAUL) and the APOCALYPTIC *Book of Revelation*. In large measure the New Testament represents the written deposit of first-generation Christian preaching and teaching, in the light of which the Old Testament has traditionally been interpreted in the church.

The Bible has a unique status in the church, in the way it is read and used in public worship and private prayer, and in the way appeal is made to it as the standard for belief and conduct. The nature of its authority, how most suitably it should be interpreted and who may interpret it are all matters of ongoing debate. In ROMAN CATHOLICISM and the Orthodox churches the revelation of scripture has to be understood through the tradition of the church (*see* AUTHORITY). [3; 7]

Bible Belt [IV] The 'Bible Belt' is a geographical reference in American religion, but one will find it marked in no atlas. It is a colloquialism learned from the enemies of PROTESTANT FUNDAMENTALISM who perceived or thought they perceived a regional congeniality to extremely conservative religion in the south and the mid-west. The man who coined the term was H. L. Mencken, a journalist who reported on the

famed Scopes Trial in Dayton, Tennessee, in 1925. That trial pitted defenders of the teaching of evolution in high-school biology classes against BIBLICISTS and fundamentalists who wanted to exclude such teaching in favour of their interpretation of the biblical story of creation as having scientific warrant. Mencken was repelled by what he considered the ignorance and prejudice of these Tennesseans and those who sided with them; most of them came from the south. He was wrong about the origins of their movement, however, for fundamentalism was propagated first in northern cities like Chicago, Toronto, New York and Boston. It was true, however, that BIBLICISM did find its strongest support in the areas where Baptists and Methodists had taught literalism and where the culture was anti-urban and anti-cosmopolitan. The phrase worked its way into the culture, and remains a term of disdain, suggesting as it does that the populations who occupy this geographical 'Belt' will be unreasonable, ignorant and prejudiced. [5; 7; 15]

Biblical Criticism [XIII.A] The application to biblical documents, since the start of the 19th century and largely in the Western churches, of critical methods which are applicable to literature in general. It includes: (1) textual criticism, the ascertaining as far as possible of the original wording and the assessment of various readings in thousands of manuscripts; (2) source criticism, the investigation of literary sources lying behind the biblical documents; (3) tradition criticism, the examination of the stages by which the material in our documents was transmitted; (4) form criticism, the study of the forms and the typical life settings in which the traditions were cast while being handed down; (5) historical criticism, the investigation of the historical setting of the existing documents; (6) redaction criticism, the consideration of the contribution of the authors who finally received the tradition and incorporated it into their works; (7) canon criticism, the description of how a document has been placed into and treated as part of the canon of a believing community; (8) literary criticism, the analysis of the text as literature, often apart from historical or theological issues, but incorporating a set of questions based in the critic's approach, such as feminism, post-modernism, etc. [2; 4: 1113–65; 7: III, 238–338; 24]

Biblical History [XIII.A] Most of the narrative works in the Hebrew BIBLE received their final form in the 6th century BCE or later. The history they attempt to describe is ideological, though it is not entirely incongruous with what little may be known from archaeological evidence. The religious history of Israel is portrayed as originating with a migration from Mesopotamia to Canaan and Egypt in the first half of the second millenium BCE. With the return to Canaan (*see* EXODUS), probably in the 13th century BCE, the history of Israel as a nation properly begins with some kind of tribal confederacy. The threat from the Philistines may have provoked the establishment of a monarchy by the end of the 11th century BCE. The dynasty which David founded lasted in Jerusalem until it was crushed by the Babylonians in 587 BCE. Some of the elite were deported. This Babylonian exile lasted until Cyrus the Persian captured Babylon (539 BCE) and allowed the exiles to return home. The post-exilic Jewish community formed a temple-state living peacefully in the Persian empire and then under Alexander the Great and his earlier successors. An attempt by Antiochus Epiphanes (r. 175–164 BCE) to impose pagan religious uniformity provoked a rebellion under Judas Maccabeus and his family (Hasmoneans). The rededication of the temple in 164 is celebrated in the Jewish festival of Hannukah. The Hasmoneans established a dynasty of high priest monarchs which lasted until the country was taken over by Rome in 63 BCE. The Roman empire provides the context for the century of New Testament history. [4: 1219–52; 5]

Biblicism [IV] [15; 25] The BIBLE has played an uncommonly large role in the development of American religion. Since PROTESTANTISM dominated, and, lacking a pope or other single religious authority, needed a text for authoritative reference, its members turned to the Bible both for personal salvation and for the moral undergirding of society. Therefore, when any were perceived as tampering with biblical authority, they were threats to SALVATION and society. Liberals and modernists, by accepting forms of biblical criticism current in Germany and elsewhere, thus were regarded as subversive and calling for a counter-attack. The main weapon in the arsenal of those who reacted, therefore, was biblicism. If biblical authority could be absolutely assured, one could stand firm against theories of evolution and progress, immorality, and more. Because the integrity of the biblical text had been called into question, its defenders felt called upon to support their approach with especially strong undergirdings of philosophy – though few biblicists would have used the word philosophy; they would claim that they got their doctrines of biblicism from the biblical text.

Since the Bible was ambiguous about its own authority, and rich with apparent contradictions and ambiguities, biblicists had to show how there could be only one interpretation of the Bible, just as the Bible had to be the only reference book in the pursuit of truth in faith and morals. Biblicists used various syllogisms about the Bible being the word of God; God being perfect and incapable of error, as his book therefore also must be; God being loving and thus taking care to be revealed in a book that had plain meanings which could settle everything.

Whether associated with words like 'inerrancy' and 'infallibly' or not, the biblicist instinct has been to care for the letter of scripture and to insist that one's own party or church or self was assuredly presenting the one true reading, over against others who must necessarily be acting in bad faith. [15: vi, xiv]

Big Drum Dance [III] Found in Grenada and Carriacou, a small island just to the north of Grenada. The rites associated with it represent retentions from Africa, and are folk rituals which do not include spirit or ancestor possession. Other names for the dance are the Nation Dance or *saraca*, sacrifice. In Carriacou the dance is performed as a sign of respect to the ancestors and to avoid annoying them. 'Nation' refers in the eastern Caribbean to the original African nations/tribes before slavery, with which the participants identify. Dances are generally family affairs and may be arranged during marriage preparations, or at the threat of illness or misfortune. Collective ceremonies may be held at the launching of one of the famous Carriacou schooners. All parts of the ceremony are a symbolic representation of the life of earlier generations, and include a ritual meal, singing, libations and prayer, music and dance. [86]

Bismillah, Basmala [XIX] The words 'In the name of God, the Merciful, the Compassionate', which begin all but one of the *suras* of the QUR'AN. They are used by Muslims as a validating formula for solemn acts; as invocation of a divine blessing before many acts of daily life, such as eating; and as a frequent calligraphic motif in Islamic ART and the writing-out of talismans and amulets. [71: 556–9; 137: 60]

Black Churches in America [IV] The vast majority of African-Americans who are church members belong to black BAPTIST, METHODIST and, more recently, PENTECOSTAL denominations. In the *Yearbook of American and Canadian Churches* the largest Baptist groups, the National Baptist Convention, USA Inc., the National Baptist Convention of America and the National Missionary Baptist Convention of North America, list, respectively, 8 million, 3.5 million and 2.5 million members. The African Methodist Episcopal Church claims 3.5 million and the African Methodist Episcopal Zion Church 1.2 million; the (Pentecostal) Church of God in Christ lists 5.5 million members. Add to these the large number of small denominations and the independent (sometimes 'store front') congregations, and one can see that the black churches play a very large part in the economy of American religion. Almost all blacks who are Catholic are members of the ROMAN CATHOLIC church; a small schismatic group has attracted few. Blacks who are Muslim, whether in the NATION OF ISLAM ('Black Muslims') or in more conventional Islamic bodies, technically would not list themselves under 'black churches', so it is appropriate to concentrate on Protestants.

Theories as to why so many Africans became Baptist and Methodist are much contested. Some scholars suggested that the use of REVIVALIST techniques, the immersion rituals practised by Baptists, the legitimating of 'enthusiastic' forms of worship, the informality and the opportunities for lay participation in both provided a measure of good match with the memory of practices slaves brought with them from their African religious roots. Others have stressed the more simple explanation: Baptism and Methodism were the overwhelming religious affiliations of slaveholders and the rest of the citizens in the American south.

Whether they forced religion on slaves, made Christian teaching and practice an option or left slaves on their own to find their way by examples from the environment, it was natural that they would move to Baptist and Methodist forms [20: xiii].

Slavery was both an inhibitor of and a stimulus to the development of church life, not only because it could be an instrument of control but because slaves found meaning, dignity and hope through the message and practice of the church. Black churches had formed late in the 18th century. The Methodist movement provided a congenial home for free blacks, who trace its origins to a movement by Richard Allen and Absalom Jones to withdraw from a Philadelphia congregation in which whites practised discrimination in seating. They formed two bodies which replicated the structure and teaching of the white Methodist bodies. Pentecostalism took shape in racially integrated movements that began around 1906 in California and spread rapidly, especially across the south. The Church of God in Christ is by far the largest of the Pentecostal bodies.

The black churches were the most distinctive products of both slave and segregated African-American cultures. They demanded and produced much of the community leadership, and their organizations gave structure to the lives of blacks where white official society excluded them. Forced into segregation by white Baptist and Methodist bodies after the Civil War (1862–5), they then 'chose' it and protected their churches as zones of creativity. Most of them participated in the civil rights movement as it came to prominence after 1954. Some denominations have taken part in the ECUMENICAL MOVEMENT, cooperating with other Protestants. However, in recent decades various factors including criticism of 'Eurocentrism' in white churches, resentment over lingering racism and the expression of 'African-American consciousness' have led many black leaders to stress the 'African' dimensions of their faith [13: vii, viii]. While blacks who form distinct minorities in Catholic, Episcopal, Lutheran and other liturgical churches have often expressed preferences for formal ('high church') ritual, most African-American worship has been characterized by informal patterns of worship. Bodily movement has been less inhibited than in the churches of European descent; singing is often much more free-form; there is usually a lively response interrupting the sermons; choir and instrumental music marks the life of churches that have lived with first 'Negro spirituals' and later 'gospel' and 'soul' music.

The African-American churches have suffered because of slavery, segregation, rural and urban poverty, and the willingness of America to see a 'permanent underclass', usually predominantly black, take form. In the midst of the demoralization of the ghettos and the higher morale of middle-class life, the church has attracted millions of members with its vision of freedom, dignity and hope, and produced many of the religious leaders of America, most notably Martin Luther King, Jr, in the civil rights movement. [13]

Black Jacobins [iii] Napoleon Bonaparte attempted to put down a slave rebellion in San Domingo in 1803. The defeat of his expedition led to the formation of Haiti. This was the only successful slave revolt recorded, and its outcome was the result of the leadership of Toussaint L'Ouverture (d. 1803). San Domingo had been the greatest French colony and France depended on it for one-third of its overseas trade. The term 'Black Jacobin' was coined by C. L. R. James, a Trinidadian, whose seminal book of that title was, as the writer averred, the first history written in relation to the Caribbean people it concerned. In many ways it is prophetic and predicts the reclamation of culture and identity by the people of the Caribbean. In Haiti the strength of the Jacobins' faith in liberty was incorporated into the syncretism between ROMAN CATHOLICISM and African retentions in both the Rada and Petro Rites of VOODOO. [53]

Black Muslims *see* NATION OF ISLAM

Black Power [III] There is no one definition of 'Black Power', but it has been described as a force 'to organize the rage of black people, and put new hard questions and dreams'. During the 1960s and 1970s it was the militant secular wing which was visible, although the movement had its roots in the BLC. Richard Allen (d. 1831) of the early African Methodist Episcopalian Church in the USA constantly supported black empowerment through black institutions, and the demand for control over resources and leadership in both sacred and secular spheres has remained a focus of activity throughout. The term 'Black Power' was coined in June 1966 on the James Meredith civil rights march between Memphis and Jackson, USA, by Stokely Carmichael of the Student Non-Violent Coordinating Committee (SNCC). The civil rights movement was already under great stress, with considerable tension between those who continued to believe in the efficacy of non-violent action and those demanding direct action. From this time on there was a great growth of black nationalism. After the death of Martin Luther King on 4 April 1968, the constituency for Black Power was the huge population of the urban ghettos of the USA. There was a call for the control of resources, both in employment and in housing, together with a growth of

militancy. Personal pride and the reclamation of dignity were paramount, expressed in the Africanization of names and personal appearances. The African Methodist Episcopal Church played its part in articulating the views of Black Power, and in 1966 produced a national document on Black Power which was followed in 1969 by the Black Manifesto, presented by James Foreman to the National Economic Development Council in Detroit, Michigan, and adopted on 26 April. The Black Manifesto attacked white Christianity, and produced a theological crisis in BLC, white denominations and those with members from both communities. Black history and black experience were to be understood as sacred history: black theology was to be seen as being created through events and experiences.

Black Power spread into the diaspora, and in the churches took two forms. One was a demand for BLACK THEOLOGY [99] and the indigenization of worship and ritual. The other was a demand that the church play its part in attacking the oppression of poverty which so many blacks experienced. [82; 98; 99]

Black Theology [III] The concept may appear to be rooted in the US civil rights movement of the 1960s and 1970s, but in fact it has a long and honourable history in Africa and the Americas. Such men as Henry Macneil Turner and Marcus Mosiah Garvey (*see* GARVEYISM) read the BIBLE in the light of the black experience. Turner wrote in the 1880s: 'We have as much right biblically and otherwise to believe that God is a Negroe, as you buckra or white people have that God is a fine-looking, symmetrical, and ornamented white man' [99]. Garvey said: 'We Negroes believe in the God of Ethiopia, the everlasting God,— God the Father, God the Son, and God the Holy Ghost, the one God of all ages. This is the God in whom we believe, but we shall worship Him through the spectacles of Ethiopia' [43]. The history of black theology lies not in books but in the lives of its adherents, and that history has its roots in sermons, folk tales, dance and songs. It was only by creating their own theology that black people could make sense of a world that had treated them as things and made them the objects of the white man's trade. Not for nothing was the Atlantic slave trade referred to as 'that peculiar institution'. [4; 11; 12; 13; 21; 22; 24; 27; 28; 41; 43; 44; 60; 65a; 66; 92; 95; 97; 98; 99]

Bodhgaya [XI] The place of the BUDDHA's (see GOTAMA) enlightenment (bodhi) in Bihar, India. Bodhgaya is one of four principal Buddhist pilgrimage sites (cf. KUSINARA, LUMBINI, SARNATH); according to tradition, anyone visting these sites with sincere faith will be reborn in favourable circumstances. This site, venerated by the emperor ASHOKA in the 3rd century BCE, is now marked by the Mahabodhi temple built (c. 7th century) adjacent to a pipal tree (ficus religiosa) that is apparently a direct descendant of the original bodhi tree under which the Buddha is said to have sat in meditation on the night of his enlightenment when he finally defeated MARA. Today Bodhgaya is a flourishing pilgrimage centre with temples built by pilgrims from all over the Buddhist world. (See also VESAKHA.)

Bodhi-Pakkhiya-Dhamma [XI] (Pali; Sanskrit: bodhi-pakshika-dharma.) The later name for the 37 items, in a set of seven groups of mental qualities, given in the earlier BUDDHIST discourses (SUTTAPITAKA) as a mnemonic summary of the Buddhist path. The first three groups, foundations of mindfulness, right efforts and bases of psychic power (iddhi), are each fourfold. After them come the five qualities of faith, strength, mindfulness, concentration and wisdom, viewed either as exercising control (indriya) or as unshakable powers (bala). The sixth group lists seven factors of awakening (bodhi), while the last group is the EIGHTFOLD PATH itself. In later Buddhist writings the set is interpreted in two ways. The series of groups may describe the stages of the spiritual path in sequence [e.g. 83: 232ff]. Alternatively the 37 items may list the most prominent contents of the mind occurring simultaneously in a given moment of transcendent (LOKUTTARA) consciousness or partially in the later stages of insight (VIPASSANA) meditation. [96: 121–33, 417; 27]

Bodhisattva [XI] In BUDDHISM a bodhisattva (Pali: bodhisatta) is one who has taken the vow to attain perfect Buddhahood, and one who is actually on that path. All Buddhist traditions accept the concept of the bodhisattva, but in MAHAYANA Buddhism this is seen as being the highest aspiration and it is often stated that all sentient beings will eventually become bodhisattvas and finally fully enlightened BUDDHAS. Thus the higher aspiration of a bodhisattva who aims for Buddhahood for the benefit of all sentient beings is contrasted with what is for Mahayana a lower aspiration, that of the ARAHAT who aims simply for personal freedom from suffering and rebirth. The path of the bodhisattva is frequently stated to be very long (often given as three incalculable aeons), and begins with the 'enlightenment mind' or 'thought of enlightenment' (bodhicitta), portrayed as a revolution of the mind from self-cherishing to altruistic compassion. The stages of the bodhisattva's path have been mapped in some detail, proceeding through ten 'levels' (bhumi) which are related to another scheme of five 'paths' (marga), and involving the gradual attainment of the 'perfections' (PARAMITA), most frequently given as six. In Mahayana bodhisattvas are thought to be ever present and actively engaged in benefiting the world. Some, such as MAITREYA, AVALOKITESHVARA, MANJUSHRI and TARA, are said to have attained great powers through their meditations and merit, and use these powers to further help others.

It is often said in modern books that the bodhisattva postpones enlightenment in order to help others. The idea of postponing requires further research, but does not appear so far to be supported by the Indian texts. (*See also* KARUNA.) [101: 49–54, IX; 44]

Boehme, Jakob [XXIV] (1575–1624) Born near Gorlitz, Upper Lusatia, Germany, Jakob Boehme was a shoemaker and devout LUTHERAN. The depth and daring of his Christian THEOSOPHICAL speculations earned him the name 'Philosophus Teutonicus'; his writings are regarded by some as the greatest mystical prose, by others as the work of a fanatic. Between 1590 and 1610 he underwent a number of profound religious experiences [13]; for seven successive days he was in an ecstatic state, surrounded by what he termed 'the light of the spirit'. In 1600 he believed he was shown the innermost foundation of nature and acquired the capacity to see with the eyes of the soul into the heart of all things (a faculty which he was convinced remained with him), and in 1610 he came to see former visions which had appeared chaotic as a unity. After 12 years of reflection he composed an account of his experiences and beliefs, *The Aurora* (The Dawning Day), which was denounced by the local pastor (an orthodox Lutheran), and he was forbidden to write again. He obeyed until 1619, when he began writing again a series of visionary works on the divine mysteries, the nature of good and evil and their one source in the divine abyss. These culminated in the publication in 1623 of his last work, *Mysterium Magnum* (The Great Mystery), a commentary on

Genesis and an account of creation in terms of three divine principles called, using terminology from ALCHEMY, salt, sulphur and mercury (manifest in man as material body, spiritual body and soul).

His descriptions of the path to Christ and of the unitive mystical experience (*see* MYSTICISM) are powerful and controversial. His aim was to clarify the role of faith in the life of a Christian, though he faced ecclesiastical opposition to this. Boehme's theology is complex and forcefully poetic in expression: he uses symbols (alchemical, kabbalistic and GNOSTIC) and myths to indicate a wisdom grounded in relevation. Sophia, the personification of wisdom, is related to all three persons of the Trinity; she is the dwelling-place of the Spirit of God and the seat of divine contemplation. Evidence of Boehme's influence can be traced in the works of many 17th- and 18th-century writers, notably John Milton, Sir Isaac Newton, William Law and William Blake.

Bon [XXXV] The indigenous pre-Buddhist religion of Tibet. Although its relationship to SHAMANISM is a complex one, in the earliest form of the religion there seem to have been definite similarities. The term 'Bon' itself was probably derived from the ritual recitation (*bon*) of its practitioners. The developed form of the religion still in existence today is the result of a synthesis of the original doctrines and the BUDDHISM introduced in Tibet from the 7th and 8th centuries onwards. According to tradition the founder of the later 'purified' Bon was Shenrab Miwo, who hailed from the mystic land of Zhang Zhung and who in myth became an equivalent of Shakyamuni BUDDHA, being credited with the dissemination of *sutras* and *tantras* and the foundation of a monastic order [9].

Bon is said to have existed in Tazig (Iran) in ancient times, and indeed some accounts have suggested influence from ZOROASTRIANISM and in particular ZURVAN. Tibetan Buddhist scholars often identify Shenrab with Lao-Tzu, thus making Bon a derivative of Taoism (*see* TAO CHIAO). However, modern scholars postulate Shaivite (*see* SHIVA) influence from Kashmir as a factor in the development of Bonpo doctrine [24].

In its earlier forms Bon doctrine was both theistic and dualistic, suggesting that the creation of the world was brought about by coexistent good and evil principles. However, the doctrine of developed Bon is generally in accord with Buddhist non-theistic tenets. In particular it shares with the NYINGMA school the soteriological structure of nine *yanas* ('vehicles') [20]. The nine *yanas* climax in the meditation of 'the great perfection' which Bonpos claim was transmitted first by Shenrab and only later entered the Nyingma tradition.

Brahma [XVII] An important god in HINDUISM, the first member of the TRIMURTI or Triad, who creates the universe anew in each world-cycle. His name is the same word as BRAHMAN, denoting the unconditioned Absolute, but given masculine instead of neuter grammatical gender to denote a personal being rather than an abstract power. The name is connected, too, with those of the Brahman priests (BRAHMANS) and the texts which order their rituals (BRAHMANAS). Brahma is the archetypal priest, just as VISHNU is the king and SHIVA the ascetic.

Brahma is little mentioned in SHRUTI literature, though other priestly gods such as Prajapati, 'Lord of Offspring', play a comparable role; but he is an important figure in the epics (MAHABHARATA and RAMAYANA) and the PURANAS, often setting the action of a myth in motion, or appearing at the end to resolve it. He was formerly the centre of a BHAKTI cult, and still has an important TIRTHA at Pushkar in

Rajasthan, but today he is a relatively remote figure, less vivid in popular imagination than Vishnu, Shiva or the goddesses (*see* SHAKTI), including his own best-known consort SARASVATI [7: 1–36].

In art he is distinguished by his four heads, corresponding to the four directions and the four VEDAS. He generally appears as a stout, bearded man, elderly but vigorous, though in south Indian art he may be young and handsome like the other gods. He holds the prayer-beads and water-pot of a Brahman priest, or palm-leaf texts of the Veda. His animal symbol (VAHANA) is the *hamsa* or sacred goose [4: 198–9; 58: 171–2, 297, 299; 92: 34–55; 109: 63].

In Buddhist cosmology (CAKKAVALA), though the idea of a creator god is not accepted, Brahma becomes the title of a whole class of high-ranking gods, and Maha-Brahma (Great Brahma) appears to the BUDDHA after his enlightenment to entreat him to teach the DHAMMA to beings rather than immediately enter PARINIBBANA.

Brahma Kumaris [XXVIII] The Brahma Kumaris World Spiritual University (BKWSU) advertises itself as non-political, non-religious and non-sectarian. It was founded in 1937 in Karachi by Dada Lekh Raj (1877–1969) after 'Shiva, God the Supreme Soul, entered [his] body . . . to begin the task of creation of a new world order'. Over 200,000 people worldwide are now said to practise the Raja Yoga, which does not involve a mantra, or special posture or breathing techniques – or the worship of a GURU. Fully committed members are celibate; they usually wear white and are strictly vegetarian. Nearly all those in a position of spiritual authority are women. [5: 168–70; 42: 909–10]

Brahman [XVII] In HINDU thought *brahman* (neuter gender) is the abstract, impersonal Absolute. The

Absolute is said to be *nirguna* (beyond-quality), pure, eternal. When characterized with qualities, the 'qualified brahman' (*saguna brahman*) becomes the immanent cause of the universe [138: 51ff]. In the UPANISHADS the realization of the union of the self (ATMAN) with *brahman* is the ultimate goal, the attainment of which constitutes MOKSHA, or release from empirical existence and the round of rebirth. The earliest sense of the word *brahman* appears to have referred to the power of the sacred chant uttered by the Brahman priest (*see* BRAHMANS) at the time of offering the Vedic sacrifice (*see* VEDA). The sound itself was believed to be efficacious, and thus came to represent the power of the eternal sacred Absolute.

Brahmanas [XVII] Texts, dating from around 900 BCE, designed to guide the Brahman priests (BRAHMANS) in carrying out the Vedic sacrifices (*see* VEDA). In Sanskrit the name of these texts is identical with that of the Brahman class (VARNA), and embodies the concept of priestly power (cf. BRAHMAN, BRAHMA). They are composed in the form of commentaries on the Rig-, Sama- and Yajurvedas, the best known being the Shatapatha, one of the Yajurveda Brahmanas. They seek to explain the often obscure language of the Veda in terms of the sacrificial ritual, often by means of correspondences. For example, there is frequent reference to forming auspicious pairs (MITHUNA) between 'male' and 'female' ritual objects, with the aim of bringing about good fortune in the life of the person offering the sacrifice. The enquiry of the Brahmanas into the meaning of the Veda was taken to a more philosophical level in the Aranyakas ('Forest Teachings'), and the UPANISHADS [95: 2, translations, 10–25].

Brahmans [XVII] The most elevated of the four VARNAS or Hindu social classes. (Sometimes the name is anglicized to 'brahmins'.) The traditional occupations of the Brahmans are transmission of the Sanskritic sacred traditions (VEDA), and the performance of priestly sacrificial rituals. Only Brahmans were permitted to carry out these rituals, and only on behalf of members of the first three *varnas*. As composers of the ancient normative religious, social and legal texts, the Brahmans had great prestige and the three lower *varnas* had to follow the Brahmans' teaching. To kill a Brahman was one of the five most serious sins (the other four being to violate a GURU's bed, to steal a Brahman's gold, to associate with outcastes and to drink spirituous liquor). The king in ancient Hindu society, a KSHATRIYA, was an absolute ruler, with the exception that he was not the master of the Brahman, and could not take his wealth. In Hindu cosmology the Brahman is said, at creation, to have emerged from BRAHMA's head.

Having dominated Hindu society for many centuries, the Brahman class has in the 20th century become the target for attack by various lower-CASTE anti-Brahman movements. Some of the most notable of these have been in south India (in Tamil Nadu) and in Maharashtra. In modern India Brahmans are found as landowners, politicians, civil servants, teachers and in various other professional classes, and, sometimes (more usually in rural areas), pursuing their traditional occupation as priests. In the latter case they sometimes only eke out a bare existence.

Brahma-Sutra [XVII] The fundamental text of the systematic VEDANTA, attributed to Badarayana and probably dating from about the 1st century CE. The first two chapters aim to establish the Vedanta interpretation of the UPANISHADS (VEDA) and refute various rival systems, especially the SAMKHYA. The remaining two chapters are mainly concerned with the nature of the soul (ATMAN) and the divine power, destiny after death, methods of meditation, and liberation (MOKSHA). The individual statments (*sutras*) are very concise, sometimes even cryptic, and occasionally allow fairly divergent acceptable alternatives on matters of later theological importance. As a result many of the authoritative works of the different schools of Vedanta have taken the form of commentaries on the *Brahma-sutra*. [Summary: 40: 54–61; translation: 105: 227–564]

Brigit [VII] The Gauls worshipped a Celtic goddess equated with Minerva, associated with arts and crafts. Her equivalent in Ireland was Brigit ('High One'), the DAGDA's daughter, expert in poetry and prophecy. She was sometimes a threefold goddess. Like Brigantia, in northern Britain, she was associated also with flocks and herds, springs and rivers [25: 358–62; 17: 34]. The Christian St Brigid of Kildare took over traditions of the earlier goddess, and kept the spring feast, Imbolg (SAMHAIN), as her festival.

Britain, Christianity in [XIII.B] After the fall of the Roman empire, Celtic Christianity [137] and the Anglo-Saxon church developed on different lines. During the REFORMATION separate established churches developed as the Church of England [148] (*see* ANGLICANISM) and Church of Scotland [33] (*see* PRESBYTERIANISM). The Anglican church was disestablished in predominantly Roman Catholic Ireland (1869) and strongly Nonconformist Wales (1920). PURITAN critics of the Church of England displaced it after the Civil Wars (1642–8) but were persecuted after the restoration of the Church of England in 1660–2. However, religious toleration (1689) allowed substantial bodies of Dissenters (also known as Nonconformists and Free Churchmen) to develop [199] (*see* BAPTISTS; CON-GREGATIONALISM; METHODISM; PRESBYTERIANS; QUAKERISM). These have played an important part in English life. ROMAN CATHOLICISM, which survived as a persecuted minority after the Reformation, increased greatly from the 19th century, chiefly through Irish immigration. Since 1945 the British religious scene has developed in a multicultural and multi-faith direction, notably through immigration from the Indian subcontinent. Ethnic versions of Christianity have also increased through immigration from the West Indies and continental Europe. [89; 187]

Buddha [XI] The most usual title of Siddhattha GOTAMA, the historical founder of BUDDHISM. Often translated as 'the enlightened one', *buddha* means literally 'one who has woken up' – that is, from the sleep of the unenlightened mind, which is subject to the defilements of attachment, aversion and delusion – and gained knowledge of 'the way things truly are' (cf. ARAHAT, DHAMMA, ARIYA-SACCA). According to early Buddhist tradition Gotama was only one in a long line of similar Buddhas extending indefinitely back in time (cf. CAKKAVALA) – the early texts mention seven by name, while later tradition names 25 and then 28 – who all awoke to and then taught the same essential and eternal truth. While the number of previous Buddhas is theoretically indefinite, the appearance of a Buddha in the world is yet a rare and momentous event, for a Buddha is the one who, when the teaching of the previous Buddha has disappeared from the world, once more brings it to light and teaches so that the path to the cessation of suffering can again be followed by others. While such 'perfectly and fully awakened ones' (Pali: *sammasambuddha*; Sanskrit: *samyaksambuddha*) are not conceived of as omnipotent creators of the universe they are nevertheless reckoned to be its highest beings, the attainment of Buddhahood being the culmination of innumerable lifetimes spent as a *bodhisatta* (Pali; Sanskrit: BODHISATTVA) perfecting such qualities as generosity, patience, wisdom and loving kindness (*see* PARAMITA; cf. JATAKA). Yet, having attained perfect Buddhahood in their final life as a human being and having established the dispensation (*sasana*) of a Buddha, Buddhas disappear from SAMSARA (*see* PARINIBBANA). This early conception of Buddhahood (which is maintained in THERAVADA Buddhism) was developed and adapted by certain schools (*see* MAHASANGHIKA) and especially in MAHAYANA Buddhism, which recognizes the simultaneous and continued existence of numerous transcendent Buddhas in different parts of the universe (cf. AMITABHA). (*See also* BUDDHA, BODIES OF; PACCEKABUDDHA.) [34: 28–9, 125–30]

Buddha, Bodies of [XI] The word *kaya* (body) in Sanskrit is ambiguous, referring both to an actual body and also to any collection. Early Buddhist sources seem to have distinguished between the DHARMA (Pali: DHAMMA)-body (*dharmakaya*) of the BUDDHA, and his physical body (*rupakaya*). The dharma-body is superior, the actual qualities possessed by the Buddha which make him a Buddha – certain pure mental states and knowledges, etc. Sometimes *dharmakaya* may have referred to the collection of the Buddha's teachings, again superior to the physical body of the Buddha. Early MAHAYANA writers such as NAGARJUNA speak of the *dharmakaya* as the ultimate truth itself – EMPTINESS (*see also* MADHYAMAKA) – as understood by a Buddha's wisdom (PRAJNA) and exemplified in his being as a Buddha. This 'body' is said to be the result of the Buddha's wisdom, just as his physical body is the result of his merit (PUNNA). The YOGACARA school developed a theory of three bodies of the Buddha. His *dharma-*

kaya (sometimes called the 'essence body' – *svabhavikakaya*) is his (or her – see TARA) non-dual enlightened stream of consciousness, the ultimate truth, while he manifests to appearance in order to benefit others in two ways: (1) as an 'enjoyment body' (*sambhogikakaya*), which is in the form of a Buddha seated on a lotus in a Pure Land (*see* AMITABHA) teaching only the Mahayana to BODHISATTVAS; and (2) as numerous 'transformation bodies' (*nairmanikakaya*) emanating wherever needed in order to help all sentient beings in whatever way may be appropriate (*see* SKILFUL MEANS; TULKU). According to this theory, GOTAMA Buddha (Shakyamuni) is often said to be a transformation body emanating for a particular purpose, and the MAHAYANA SUTRAS are finally the teaching not of Gotama as such but of a Buddha in the form of an enjoyment body. Nevertheless, since in infinite time infinite beings must have become Buddhas, there is usually held in Mahayana Buddhism to be infinite enjoyment bodies as well as infinite transformation bodies manifested by each enjoyment body. [101: VIII; 61: x]

Buddha Image [XI] Buddhism initially avoided representing the BUDDHA in human form, presumably to emphasize the transcendental nature of the knower of NIBBANA. Symbols were employed both for devotional purposes (especially the STUPA and the *bodhi* tree) and in narrative iconography (e.g. the royal parasol and the DHAMMA wheel), probably recalling different episodes in the life of the Buddha. The Buddha image was created about the 2nd century CE in the Indian territories of the Kushana empire (*see* CENTRAL ASIAN BUDDHISM). Two artistic schools arose: one more Indian, centring on Mathura, and another in Gandhara in north-west India under Hellenistic influence. The canonical description of the 32 characteristics of a great man by which a Buddha could be predicted (probably intended for visualization meditation) was taken as the basis: hence features such as lengthened ears, a curl or mark on the forehead (the *urna*) and elongation of the crown of the head into either a topknot of hair or a protuberance (the *ushnisha* – originally a 'turbaned head'). The use of the Buddha image is not sectarian and spread rapidly. For cultic purposes it should enshrine relics, but in practice this is not necessarily the case (especially in east Asia). Both small and large images have been constructed as works of merit in very large numbers throughout the Buddhist world and an extremely rich artistic heritage has evolved. The various formalized gestures (MUDRA) tend to symbolize events in the life of the Buddha and (in the MAHAYANA) aspects of the nature of Buddha-hood. The Buddha image is sometimes known as the *Buddha-rupa*. [82; 85]

Buddhaghosa [XI] The most influential authority for THERAVADA BUDDHISM. Indian in origin, Buddhaghosa (*c.*430 CE) went to Ceylon to study at the Theravada monastic university (Mahavihara) in Anuradhapura. Existing commentaries in the local language, Sinhala Prakrit, were translated by him into PALI, which was more widely understood. His commentaries (*atthakatha*) were accepted as an authoritative interpretation of the Pali Canon (TIPI-TAKA). In the *Visuddhi-magga* ('Path of Purification'), intended as a general commentary to the Canon as a whole, Buddhaghosa outlined the stages and methods of the practice of Buddhist meditation (BHAVANA), together with a detailed account of ABHIDHAMMA theory. [5: xvff]

Buddha-Sasana [XI] Literally the 'Buddha-teaching' or 'Buddha-doctrine', this term is used in modern Asian contexts as an equivalent for 'Buddhist religion', as in the Buddha-Sasana councils and com-

missions set up by governments in countries such as Burma, Sri Lanka and Thailand.

Buddhism [XI] The religious and philosophical tradition that looks to the BUDDHA (*see* GOTAMA) as its founder. The Buddha, who lived in north India in the 5th century BCE, was part of a wider ancient Indian movement of wandering homeless ascetics and holy men. This movement was not unified, but embraced many different varieties and tendencies: some allied themselves closely with brahmanical traditions; others were advocates of extreme forms of asceticism; yet others developed varieties of meditative and contemplative disciplines (*see* YOGA). It is this last group from which early Buddhism emerges. While some of the basic assumptions of Buddhism, such as the law of KARMA and the goal of liberation (MOKSHA) from the round of rebirth (SAMSARA), are held in common with HINDUISM and other Indian religions such as JAIN-ISM, conceiving of Buddhism as splitting from Hinduism is something of a misunderstanding; what is generally meant by the term 'Hinduism' is a later synthesis of Indian religious ideas, one of whose formative influences was Buddhism. Already during the Buddha's lifetime a considerable following was established, centring on a monastic community (*see* SANGHA) supported by a lay community (*see* UPASAKA). During the reign of the emperor ASHOKA (3rd century BCE) Buddhism became a major Indian religion and was subsequently established across the whole subcontinent and beyond.

The earliest teachings (DHAMMA) were preserved in the SUTTAS (cf. TIPITAKA) and address the problem of universal suffering (*see* FOUR NOBLE TRUTHS); they expound a distinctive system of moral (*see* DANA, SILA), meditative (*see* BHAVANA, SAMADHI) and mental (*see* PRAJNA, VIPASSANA) training aimed at producing a transcendent knowledge that frees the individual from selfish concerns (*see* ARAHAT). This fundamental orientation underlies all Buddhist practice; the great variety of teachings are for the most part understood by the Buddhist tradition itself as fitting into this framework (cf. SKILFUL MEANS). In so far as it does not involve belief in one omnipotent, personal God, the Buddhist understanding of the world is non-theistic; however, belief in 'divine' or 'superhuman' beings of various kinds is a significant part of all traditions of Buddhism (*see* CAKKAVALA; BODHISATTVA). The Buddha's teachings were systematically presented by the various ABHIDHAMMA schools which gave rise to the later MAHAYANA philosophical schools of the MADHYAMAKA and YOGACARA. Dating from the 2nd century BCE, the Mahayana represents a movement that to a greater or lesser extent affected the whole subsequent history of Buddhism, though certain schools of Indian Buddhism, including the THERAVADA, resisted the wholehearted adoption of the Mahayana vision. The final development on Indian soil was the development of Tantric Buddhism (*see* TANTRA).

Having played a major role in the formation of Indian culture for some fifteen centuries, Buddhism had by the 12th century virtually disappeared from India. In the early centuries CE Buddhism was establishing itself beyond the confines of India in central Asia (*see* CENTRAL ASIAN BUDDHISM) and China. By the 6th century it had reached Japan, while the 7th century saw the beginnings of Buddhism in Tibet. In all these areas Buddhism developed distinctive cultural forms. Today there are three principal living traditions of Buddhism. The 'southern' or Theravada tradition is found in Sri Lanka (*see* SINHALESE BUDDHISM) and various countries of south-east Asia (*see* SOUTH-EAST ASIA, BUDDHISM IN); this is essentially a non-Mahayana

school using the PALI canon of scriptures. The other two traditions embrace a Mahayana outlook. The 'eastern' tradition is found in China, Vietnam, Korea and Japan (*see* CHINESE BUDDHISM; JAPAN, BUDDHISM IN) and its scriptures are preserved in the Chinese Tripitaka. The 'northern' tradition of Tibet and Mongolia (*see* TIBETAN RELIGIONS) preserves its scriptures in the Tibetan KANJUR and Tenjur. Within each of these major traditions there are numerous schools with distinctive teachings. Over the last hundred years many different forms of Buddhism have been established in the west (*see* WESTERN BUDDHISM).

Bundahishn [XXXVI] Creation in ZOROASTRIANISM. There is a PAHLAVI text of this name which deals with the origins, purpose and nature of creation. In its present form it dates from the 10th century CE, but essentially it represents a compilation of ancient teachings contained in the AVESTA [55: 40f; translation: 4].

AHURA MAZDA and ANGRA MAINYU (God and the 'devil') have existed independently of each other from eternity. Mazda dwells on high in light, but Angra Mainyu dwells down in darkest hell. Mazda, being omniscient (all-knowing), was aware of his adversary's existence but Angra Mainyu, being ignorant, did not have such knowledge. When he came to learn of it, then with characteristic violence he sought to destroy Mazda, and so the cosmic battle between good and evil began. Each side produced its own creations. Ahura first created the spiritual (*menog*) world (*see* AMESHA SPENTAS; YAZATAS) and later the material (*getig*) world. In Zoroastrian belief the spiritual and material worlds are not opposites. The material is the visible, tangible expression, almost fulfilment, of the spiritual.

In traditional Zoroastrian belief the world lasted for 3,000 years in spiritual form and then 3,000 in perfect material form before evil assaulted it. Against health Angra Mainyu created disease; against beauty, ugliness; against life, death. The archetypal man, Gayomaretan (Pahlavi Gayomard), and bull died from his attack, but as they did they emitted sperm from which grew humans and animals. Thus began what Zoroastrians know as the time of mixture (*Gumezishn*), the time when good and evil are mixed together in the world. The turning-point in the period of battle was the birth of ZOROASTER, occurring 3,000 years after Angra Mainyu's assault. He brought the revelation from God, which it is believed will inspire men to fight for the good. The 3,000 years following his death are the age in which we now live, a period when good and evil are locked in battle, but a time when good is gradually emerging triumphant. The final defeat of evil will take place at FRASHOKERETI. The world is therefore by nature perfect. All evils in it are due to Angra Mainyu. It is 'the Good Creation' of Ahura Mazda; consequently Zoroastrians are required by their religion to care for the world (they proudly and not unreasonably present themselves as the world's first ecologists) and to enjoy it in moderation. Hence Zoroastrian ethics are determined by 'the Golden Mean'; to reject the world through asceticism is as wrong as excessive indulgence in its mate-

rial pleasures. [8 vol. 1: IX; 28: 68–70; 53a; 63: V, X; 64: XV]

Bush Negroes *see* SARAMAKAS/ SARAMACCAS

Byakko Shinkokai [XXVI] A new religion of Japan, originating with Goi Masahisa (1916–80) and emphasizing prayer for world peace. It teaches that human beings derive from the universal KAMI, that for each person there are protective spirits (*shugorei*), or protective *kami* (*shugoshin*), and that directing one's thoughts towards these protectors facilitates their providing the help needed, such as restoration of health. What the *kami* desire above all else is peace among the peoples of the world. To pray for world peace, therefore, helps to bring about both individual salvation and peace in the world. Once a week, members assemble to hear tape-recorded messages that Goi made before his death and to pray for world peace. In token of its dedication to peace, Byakko Shinkokai distributes stickers and erects 'peace poles' that bear the words 'May peace prevail on earth'. It has also conducted world peace prayer ceremonies in Los Angeles, Assisi, Paris and Beijing. Byakko Shinkokai has its chief centre near Tokyo in the city of Ichikawa, Chiba Prefecture. The present leader is Goi's adoptive daughter, Saionji Masami. It claims approximately 500,000 members.

C

Cakkavala [XI] (Pali; Sanskrit: *cakravada*.) A term in BUDDHIST cosmology meaning 'world-sphere' or 'world-system'. Buddhist cosmology has much in common with the cosmologies of JAINISM and HINDUISM, all three being adapted in part from common ancient Indian traditions. The complete description of a world-system represents the detailed account of the Buddhist conception of the round of rebirth (SAMSARA). At the centre of the *cakkavala* is Mount Meru, surrounded by rings of mountains and oceans. Beyond these mountains, in the four cardinal directions, are four continents: the southern continent, Jambudipa, is the continent inhabited by ordinary human beings. Below are the 'descents' occupied by beings reborn as animals, ghosts, hell-beings and jealous gods as a result of bad actions (*see* KARMA), while rising above Mount Meru are six happy realms inhabited by *devas* or gods enjoying the results of good actions. These 11 realms comprise the world of the five senses (*kama-loka*). Beyond are the 20 realms of the form and formless worlds (*rupa-loka, arupa-loka*) inhabited by further classes of gods known as Brahmas, reborn as such as the result of various meditation attainments (*see* SAMATHA); each presides over thousands of world-spheres. These 31 levels of existence define the basic structure of the round of rebirth, but its full extent can be defined neither spatially nor temporally, nor in terms of numbers of beings. Thousands upon thousands of world-systems inhabited by countless beings, dying and being reborn again, evolve into existence and then contract across immeasurable spans of time. Not created by any god, the sufficient explanation for its existence is to be found in the principle of 'dependent arising' (PATICCASA-MUPPADA).

This cosmology tends to be presented by Buddhist tradition as at once a description of the world and an account of different mental states and levels of consciousness: the cosmos as a whole reflects the workings of the minds of individual beings. This assimilation of cosmological and psychological description follows from the precedence given to the mind in Buddhist thought, a precedence most explicitly articulated in the YOGACARA understanding of 'consciousness' alone as real. [34: 32–9; 49]

Calendar (Christian) [XIII.D] The Christian calendar is composed of four main elements: the cycle of the liturgical day; the weekly cycle of days, inherited directly from Judaism; the Paschal cycle of movable feasts which move with the date of Easter, a cycle which echoes the Jewish festivals of Pesach (Passover) and Shavuot (Pentecost) (*see* CALENDAR, JEWISH) but is calculated in a significantly different way; and the cycle of fixed feasts falling on fixed dates of the solar calendar.

From the 7th century the custom spread in the Western Church of dating years from the birth of Christ as calculated by the Scythian monk Dionysius Exiguus. The ecclesiastical year begins on the first Sunday of Advent, a penitential season preparing for the feast of the nativity of Christ (25 December), and the Epiphany (6 January), which celebrates the visit of the Magi and the revelation of Christ to the nations. The cycle of fixed feasts continues throughout the year: the Paschal cycle is superimposed upon it. The Sundays 'after Epiphany' give way to the three Sundays of Septuagesima, Sexagesima and Quinquagesima which precede Ash Wednesday and the penitential season of Lent. At the end of Lent, Palm Sunday ushers in Holy Week which culminates in the Sacred Triduum: Holy Thursday, the commemoration of the Last Supper; Good Friday, a solemn fast commemorating the Crucifixion; and Holy Saturday, the Vigil of Easter Sunday, the feast of the Resurrection. The Easter season continues until Ascension Thursday, 40 days after Easter, and Pentecost, Whit Sunday, the feast of the descent of the Holy Spirit on the apostles, celebrated seven weeks after Easter. The Sundays between Pentecost and Advent are dated 'after Pentecost' or 'per annum' in Roman use, and from the following Sunday 'after Trinity' in traditional English use. Other major festivals include Candlemas (the presentation of Jesus in the Temple) on 2 February, the Annunciation to the Blessed Virgin on 25 March, the feast of Saints Peter and Paul on 29 June, the Transfiguration on 6 August and the Assumption of the Blessed Virgin on 15 August.

Eastern Christian churches have their own distinctive religious calendars. Byzantine churches use both the BC/AD dating system and a system which dates the year *apo ktiseos kosmou*, from the date of the creation of the world implied by the SEPTUAGINT text of the BIBLE; according to the version of this calendar in contemporary use, the year from 1 September 1991 to 1 September 1992 CE was the year 7500 AKK. The ecclesiastical year begins on 1 September, and like the Roman Catholic and Anglican calendars has an annual cycle of fixed and movable feasts. The dates of fixed feasts do not fall on the same day for all Eastern Christians; some communities have retained the use of the Julian calendar (*see* OLD CALENDAR MOVEMENT) for religious purposes and celebrate fixed feasts 13 days later than those who use the Gregorian. The opening of the ecclesiastical year on 1 September (the feast of St Symeon Stylites) gives a particular significance to the Marian feasts: the Nativity of the Blessed Virgin on 8 September and the Dormition ('falling asleep', i.e. the death of the Virgin) on 15 August come at the opposite ends of the year, emphasizing her role in salvation. Other Marian feasts include 21 November, the Entrance of the Virgin into the Temple, and 9 December, the Conception of the Virgin by St Anne. As in the West, the birth of Jesus Christ is celebrated on 25 December; 1 January, the feast of the Circumcision of Christ, is also the feast of St Basil; Theophany (6 January) commemorates the baptism of Jesus; and 30 January, the feast of the Three Hierarchs, is also the festival of Greek Letters, celebrating the church's acceptance of Greek thought and literature as a vehicle for the Christian gospel. Movable feasts depend for their date on the calculation of Pascha (Easter), which is the same for all Byzantine Christians. The date is often later than Western Easter, not only because of the Julian calendar but also because the last days of Holy Week must not fall on or before the Jewish Passover. The movable cycle begins on the Sunday of the Pharisee and the Publican, four weeks before Lent; Lent itself begins on Pure Monday and ends on Lazarus Saturday, the eve of Palm Sunday. The cycle ends with the Sunday of Pentecost, which in the East is the feast of the Holy Trinity, and the Sunday of All Saints.

Another cycle begins at Easter and organizes the weeks of the year into sequences of eight, each using one of the eight musical tones and its characteristic poetical texts for its offices. Each day of the week of each tone has its own hymns and verses which are collected in the *Paraklitike* or *Oktoechos*.

The COPTIC Church dates years from the Year of the Martyrs (284 CE); Ethiopian and Armenian churches also make use of a calendar which divides the year into 12 months of 30 days each and a 13th month of five days.

Calendar (in Islam) [XIX] The religiously sanctioned system of dating in ISLAM is one of purely lunar months, so that a year comprises 354 days and the months do not correspond to the seasons of the solar year. There are approximately 103 Muslim lunar years to 100 in the Gregorian solar calendar. The Muslim era is computed from the Prophet MUHAMMAD's migration or *hijra* (*hegira*) from Mecca to Medina, which took place in September 622 CE, although the year actually begins from the opening of the lunar year in which the migration took place, i.e. 16 July 622. For practical purposes, such as the collection of taxes and agricultural operations, a lunar year was unsuitable, and over the centuries various solar adaptations were made, e.g. the Ottoman Turkish (*see* ISLAMIC DYNASTIES) fiscal year and the Persian solar year computed from the *hijra*. At present, the *hijra* year is used mainly for religious purposes. [37 'Zamān'; 45; 48: 182–4; 77: IX]

Calendar (Jewish) [XXII] The Jewish calendar consists of a year made up of 12 lunar months each of 29 or 30 days [14 vol. 5: 43]. In ancient times these months began when witnesses testified to the sighting of the new moon. From about the 4th century the calendar was calculated in advance, and eyewitness testimony

disregarded. The average lunar year of 354 days is just over 11 days short of the solar year. In order for the festivals (CHAGIM), which are based on the agricultural year, to fall at their appointed times as well as on their correct lunar date, the lunar year has to be brought into line with the solar year. An extra lunar month is intercalated in February–March seven times every 19 years. The religious year begins with the New Year festival, falling around September–October, when the world is thought to be judged on its activities during the past year (*see also* FASTS) [59: XIII; 70: 172]

Calendar Round (Amerindian) [V] Among the settled agriculturists of the North American south-west, calendric rites achieved their fullest development as emphasis on collective efforts to ensure fertility and social well-being gradually supplanted more individualistic forms. Thus major ceremonies of the PUEBLO tribes are intimately connected with calendric observances, notably the seasonal transitions, so critical to planting economies. Among the HOPI, for example, calendar rituals are elaborately structured. The yearly pattern of planting, growth and harvest microcosmically recapitulates the original stages in the creation of the world: pre-dawn, dawn and full sunrise – a pattern that is further reflected in the daily cycle (*see* COSMOLOGY). [26: III] The principal Hopi ceremonies of Wuwuchim, Soyal and Powamu still further reflect the basic pattern. Typically, these rituals include the following elements: preparation through isolation in the *kiva* (or underground ceremonial chamber); avoidance of food and sexuality; recitation of the creation narrative; use of prayer-sticks and tobacco; dry-paintings (SAND-PAINTINGS); and culminate in public dancing. The critical transitions, the summer and winter solstices and the spring and autumn equinoxes, are thus marked by the cooperative efforts of man and the supernaturals.

Calendar Stone [xxv] One of the finest pieces of MESOAMERICAN RELIGIOUS sculpture, the Calendar Stone (1500 CE) is 3½ metres in diameter and weighs 24 metric tons. It is more accurately called the Piedra del Sol, because it is a carved image of the cosmogony depicting the five ages or 'suns' of the universe (*see figure 2*) [12: 37]. At the periphery of a series of concentric circles are two giant fire-serpents whose pointed tails meet at the date (13 Reed) of the creation of the fifth sun. These serpents enclose a series of star-symbols and solar rays which are attached to 20 day signs of the Aztec calendar. The central section [11: 60] is divided into four square

panels signifying the four ages of the universe, Sun of Jaguar, Sun of Wind, Sun of Fiery Rain, and Sun of Water (*see* CEMANAHUAC), which surround and constitute the glyph for the Aztec age, Sun of Movement. The central face is probably the sun-god Tonatiuh, whose protruding tongue is a sacrificial knife. On either side of his face are jaguar claws holding human hearts. The symbolic meaning of the image is that the Aztecs considered their age to be the Age of the Centre, which incorporated all universal space and time within itself.

Caliph, Caliphate [xix] The institution of the caliphate dates from MUHAMMAD's death in 632, when caliphs ('successors') were chosen to lead the community, preserve and

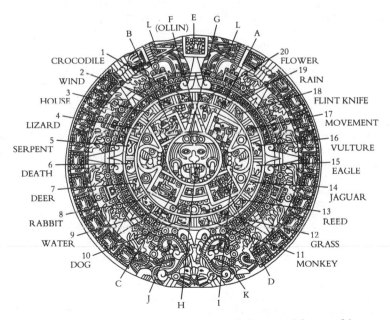

A Sun of Jaguar.
B Sun of Wind.
C Sun of Fiery Rain.
D Sun of Water.
E Sun of Reed (ritual date 13, or 1011 CE).
F *Ollin* motif (ritual date, 17 Movement)

enclosing central figures of the stone.
G Sun-god Tonatiuh.
H Sacrificial knife.
I Claws holding human hearts.
J K Fire serpents.
L Fire-serpent tails.

Figure 2
The Calendar Stone

extend its borders (*see* JIHAD) and ensure the canonical celebration of the cult (*see* SALAT) and the application of the SHARI'A [48: VIII; 80: VII]. It continued through the lines of so-called 'Rightly guided' or 'Orthodox' (632–61 CE), Umayyad (661–750) and Abbasid (750–1517) caliphs (*see* ISLAMIC DYNASTIES) until 1517, and the Ottoman Turkish sultans (or secular rulers) subsequently assumed, on their own initiative, the title, only abolished formally by Kemal Atatürk in 1924. The mainstream Sunni (SUNNA) community regarded the caliphate as a temporal necessity only, for there could be no divinely inspired figure after the Prophet; but the Shi'is viewed it rather as a divinely designated office or imamate (*see* IMAM; SHI'ISM). Hence the unity of the original caliphate, already impaired by sectarian quarrels over its exact nature (*see* FIRQA, KHARIJITES), was broken by the 10th century, when the Shi'i line of Fatimid caliphs arose in Egypt side by side with the official Sunni one in Baghdad. Yet its concept as a focus of loyalty for all Muslims continued until the 20th century, with a special appeal for Muslim groups away from the heartlands (*see* PAN-ISLAMISM), and its abolition called forth the evanescent and fruitless 'caliphate movement' in the 1920s, notably in Muslim India. It is in such areas as this, also, that the idea of the early caliphate as a golden age, whose simplicity and austerity should be restored, has recently been influential (*see* SOUTH ASIA, ISLAM IN). [11; 38 'Khalīfa'; 142: II]

Calumet [v] The original French designation of the 'reed pipe' found among the Miami and Illinois of North America is now generally applied to all ceremonial smoking instruments of Amerindians, and localized variations have been supplanted by pan-Indian custom. [17: VIII] Vouchsafed to humankind by the White Buffalo Woman (*oglala* is

the SIOUX variant), the pipe is a microcosmic symbol of the universe. The clay of the stone bowl represents the earth; the wooden stem represents vegetation; and the stem carvings symbolize animals and birds. The act of smoking is thus a reaffirmation of the cosmic network of relationships. [1: III]

Calvinism [XIII.B] John Calvin (1509–64) established a partial theocracy (*see* STATE, CHRISTIANITY AND THE) in Geneva backed by the theology of his Institutes of the Christian Religion [19: 212–14]. This inspired the Reformed Church type of PROTESTANTISM (e.g. Scottish PRESBYTERIANISM). Calvinism expressed the sovereignty of God in predestination but also in closely supervised church and civic life. Calvinistic CONGREGATIONALISM and Presbyterianism were influential in the American colonies and affected by REVIVALISM (e.g. Jonathan Edwards, 1703–58). Karl Barth (1886–1968) has been the most influential modern Calvinist theologian. [26; 131; 138; 201]

Canada, Christianity in [XIII.B] Canadian Christianity reflects its colonial origins. French colonization of the 17th century brought Jesuit missions to the Indians, hostile to Gallicanism (*see* STATE, CHRISTIANITY AND THE) and JANSENISM as well as PROTESTANTISM. Conquest by Britain (1763) brought various forms of Protestantism. The early establishment of ANGLICANISM with church lands ceased as other denominations grew. The United Church of Canada (1925) incorporated METHODISM, CONGREGATIONALISM and PRESBYTERIANISM. ROMAN CATHOLICISM of a conservative type remains strong in the French provinces as part of their cultural identity. [85; 121 vol. 3: X, vol. 5: III; 122 vol. 3: V]

Candomblé [III] The earliest Afro-Brazilian cult, largely female in membership and centred in Bahia. The name arises from the name of one of the three drums used in the ceremonies. The drums accompany the singing, dancing and rituals which lead to possession by the ancestors of favoured adherents. Macumba, another Afro-Brazilian cult found in Rio de Janeiro, is named after the central participants, who may become possessed. Possession by the ancestors is the central goal of the cult. *Ma-Cumba* were those elders of the cult in its early form, who were senior enough to be possessed. [9; 14; 86]

Cannibalism (South America) [xxiii] Consuming the dead was one of the most striking ways in which Native South Americans responded to intense ambivalence about the sacredness of human death. Cannibalism involves two mutually exclusive practices: consuming the pulverized bone-ash of close relatives, or ingesting the flesh of outsiders to one's group. Values (vengeance, memory, time) underlying the ritual sacrifice and consumption of the dead enemy lay at the heart of TUPIAN cultures. For peoples of the Orinoco and northwest Amazon, imbibing the bone-ash of dead kinsmen served at once to nourish life and to regenerate social institutions (the family). [33: viii]

Canon [xiii.a] The canon (from the Greek meaning 'measure') of the BIBLE is the Christian way of describing the list of books acknowledged variously by SYNAGOGUE and CHURCH as uniquely authoritative. The three divisions of the Hebrew Bible (law, prophets and writings) may represent three stages by which it received 'canonical' recognition. The main content of the Hebrew canon was recognized before the beginning of the Christian era and the form of its text largely decided in the 1st century CE. The Christian canon of the Old Testament was wider than the Hebrew Bible; it included also documents found in the SEPTUAGINT and elsewhere, though since the REFORMATION Protestants have adopted the Hebrew Bible alone. The main outlines of the New Testament canon were fixed during the 2nd century, largely through the controversy over MARCIONISM. Though there were disputes about the inclusion of some books such as *Hebrews* and *Revelation*, the canon of 27 books was widely agreed by 367 CE. [3; 4: 1034–54; 7: I, 113–59, 284–308; 11: I, 837–61]

Cantor [xxii] the prayer leader in the SYNAGOGUE, particularly on Sabbaths (SHABBAT) and festivals (CHAGIM), known in Hebrew as a *chazan* [19: 498]. The cantor is not a priest, and any layman can fulfil this role [70: 209]. In modern times, with the use of choirs in synagogues and the development of Jewish liturgical music (*see* MUSIC (JEWISH)), the cantor has become a full-time, paid synagogue official. Certain pieces of the LITURGY have become standard parts of the cantorial repertoire. [14 vol. 7: 1542]

Cargo Cults [xxvii] The name given to hundreds of new movements occurring primarily but not solely in Melanesia, expecting a new order of equality with whites and human fulfilment to be achieved supernaturally, and symbolized by the arrival of a cargo of Western-type goods by ship or plane, perhaps accompanied by returning ancestors. Wharves, airstrips and warehouses may be built, and to hasten the event new rituals and behaviour replace the traditional customs and economy. The social consequences form a problem for governments and churches, but most movements are short-lived, even though cargo thinking (that development depends on ritual and the supernatural) is deeply rooted in Melanesian cultures. Over 70 *koreri, mansren*, etc., movements have been recorded in Irian Jaya since the 1850s [10; 26; 199–206]. The earliest, much noticed, in Papua was the so-called 'Vailala madness' from 1919, but others include the Mambu cults from 1937, Yaliwan's Yangoru movement from 1971, and JON FRUM in Vanuatu. As cargo cults seek acceptance in modernizing nations they tend to develop into independent churches or exhibit more realistic economic activities, even though these too may fail, or be rescued by outside entrepreneurial interests. Cargo ideology, however, remains pervasive and may even underlie the movements of a PENTE-COSTAL or REVIVALIST nature that have been replacing the cults since the 1970s. These arise either spontaneously or prompted by visiting expatriate revivalists, and mostly remain within the older churches, both Catholic and Protestant. [19]

Cariban Religion [xxiii] Located primarily in northern South America, Cariban peoples share a number of themes in their mythologies, cosmologies and shamanism (see SHA-MANS AND RELIGIOUS SPECIALISTS) which identify a matrix of belief. World-destruction by flood ends the primordial world and gives rise to the differentiation of species. Often, the flood follows the felling of the Great Tree of Life in the centre of the world. Alternately, aquatic serpents cause the flood and the killing of these monsters gives rise to separate forms of life. Ceremonies central to Cariban religious life (the New Garden Festival for the Makiritare; the Shodewika girl's initiation rites for the Waiwai) commemorate these mythic events. The *Mawari*, widely found in Cariban cosmologies, are supernatural beings variously associated with aquatic serpents, animal people, the primordial jaguar, or spirits of the mountains visible only to shamans. Frequently, myths oppose a Supreme Being, source of light and

goodness, or benevolent CULTURE HEROES, to an evil being, a TRICK-STER who brings death, darkness and misfortune into the world. Extraordinary importance is given to sonic symbolism in shamanic practice, developed either as ritual blowing (as among the Akawaio) or as an esoteric language (the Kari'na); in both cases, sounds imitate the primordial reality of the spirits (*see also* HALLELUJAH). [8; 9; 12]

Caste [xvii] Strictly speaking this is not a religious concept, but it is closely related to HINDU religion and society. Portuguese in origin, the word 'caste' is normally used to refer to what in India is called *jati*, the social status which is one's inheritance at birth, whether high or low. *Jati* may be identified with a particular occupation; there is a *jati* of scavengers, another of weavers, of potters, ironworkers, leatherworkers and so on. All these *jatis* are regarded as low; some of them are regarded by high-caste Hindus as ritually polluting. The list of *jatis* runs into many hundreds, and varies greatly, not only from one region of India to another but also from one village to another. Not all follow their traditional occupation. This is often the case with BRAHMANS, and with some of the lower castes; for example, palanquin-bearers will nowadays more frequently be cultivators. With caste membership go certain restrictions on social intercourse, especially in such matters as intermarriage and interdining; in urban areas, at least, the latter is now difficult to observe strictly.

Caste therefore assumes a religious character, in that: (1) priesthood is, in orthodox terms at least, the prerogative of the Brahman caste: (2) the superiority of the Brahmans to all others is regarded as religiously sanctioned in the sacred texts of the VEDAS; (3) the theory of KARMA, i.e. the law of moral cause and effect, is regarded as providing an explanation of why some people are born high while others are born low; and (4) the distinction between 'unclean' and 'clean' castes (or castes which are ritually polluting and castes which are not) is to some extent (but only partly) a religious conception. 'Caste' sometimes refers also to the ancient theoretical scheme of VARNAS, and attempts are made to correlate *jatis* and *varnas*, but without clearly satisfactory results. In modern India it is found that the dominant *jati* (in practice) is not always that of the Brahmans (although it may be so in theory), and where some other *jati* is dominant the attitudes and values of that *jati* tend also to be dominant, rather than those of Brahmans. [12: 148ff; 124: 9–11, 89–93, 103–5; 131 vol. 1, 201–12]

Caste (Sikh) [XXXIII] In terms of status or privilege CASTE is explicitly rejected by Sikhs. NANAK denounced it, subsequent GURUS reinforced his message and ritual observance confirms it [34: 8–10]. At baptism all must drink the same water; and in GURDWARAS all sit together, receive the same KARAH PRASAD, and eat in the same LANGAR. Caste is, however, retained within the PANTH as a social order. The Gurus were married according to caste prescription and gave their children in marriage similarly. This convention has survived virtually intact, with the result that practically every Indian Sikh belongs to a particular caste. An absolute majority are JATS, members of rural Punjab's dominant caste.

Other important castes with both Sikh and Hindu sections are the Khatri and Arora. Distinctively Sikh castes are the RAMGARHIA (a composite artisan caste), Ahluwalia, Ramdasia and Mazhabi, the latter two comprising Sikhs from outcaste origins. The Gurus were all Khatris. [26: v]

Catacomb Church [XIII.D] Also known as the 'Tikhonites' or 'True Orthodox Church', the Catacomb Christians broke with Metropolitan Sergei Starogorodsky when he insisted that bishops and priests declare their loyalty to the Soviet regime (1927). Led by Metropolitan Joseph of Petrograd (executed in 1937), many Orthodox, including numerous bishops, refused to accept any concordat with the militantly atheistic state and continued to commemorate PATRIARCH Tikhon Belavin's successor Peter Polyansky of Krutitsy and Kolomna (executed in 1937). Persecuted by the communists, the Catacomb Christians refused on principle to register with the authorities or have any dealings with Soviet power and the increasingly compromised Patriarchate. The Catacomb Church maintained a strong hold on Siberia, the Caucasus and other outlying areas; it went 'underground' in the 1930s and has only partially emerged after the fall of communism. Many Catacomb communities have since united in the 'Free Russian Orthodox Church' connected to the RUSSIAN ORTHODOX CHURCH ABROAD, while others have sought links with the OLD CALENDAR MOVEMENT of Greece. [18; 23] (*See also* NEW MARTYRS.)

Cathars [XXIV] Catharism (Greek *katharos*, unpolluted or pure) is believed to trace its roots from 2nd or 3rd century CE GNOSTICISM via the MANICHAEAN TEACHINGS. Cathars were devoted to the pursuit of direct mystical experience of pure spiritual light whose true home is with the Good God in heaven. The Gospel of St John was the chief source of their doctrine and they (or some, at least) practised celibacy, rejected SACRAMENTS and held that good and evil had equal power in the universe. Catharism became widespread in Languedoc during the 12th century CE, and by the 13th century had so many adherents that Pope Innocent III took measures against the HERESY. Attracted as much by the prospect of looting the rich lands of southern France as by the desire to make war on a rival religion, barons and knights from all over Europe invaded Languedoc under the leadership of Simon de Montfort and by 1229 the Cathars surrendered the defence of their land. Other sects of similar origins, such as the Bogomiles from Bulgaria and the Albigenses from southern France, adopted local names.

Catholic [XIII.B] From a Greek word meaning 'general' or 'universal' and taken to be one of the four classic marks of the church (the others being unity, sanctity and apostolicity) (cf. CREED). The commonest uses of it by Christians today are: (1) to describe 'orthodox' as distinct from 'heretical' Christians (see HERESY, ORTHODOXY, SCHISM); (2) as the term preferred by Roman Catholics to describe themselves; (3) in contrast to PROTESTANTISM for churches such as ROMAN CATHOLICISM, the EASTERN ORTHODOX CHURCH, Old Catholics (see PAPACY) and ANGLICANISM, which emphasize church tradition (see AUTHORITY), episcopal MINISTRY, and SACRAMENTS in continuity with the early church.

Celtic Religion [VII] The Celts were established in central Europe by 500 BCE as nomadic warrior tribes. They moved eastwards into Asia Minor, where they were known as Galatians, and westwards into Gaul, Spain and Britain [22: 20–8]. Early Welsh and Irish literature preserves Celtic myths [23]. Religious practices are described by Posidonius (c.135–50 BCE) and other classical writers [30]. Art and archaeology also provide evidence for cults and religious symbols [22: III]. The religion had many local variations, but in the west the organized professional class of DRUIDS taught and preserved religious traditions [15: IV]. Teutates, Esis and Taranis (Thunderer) are said by Roman writers to have received

human sacrifice in Gaul [27: 29]. There was a goddess equated with Minerva (BRIGIT), and many fertility goddesses (MATRES) and goddesses of battle (VALKYRIES). Deities were frequently represented in sets of three. The chief gods remembered in Ireland were DAGDA, a primitive figure with club and cauldron, LUG, a warrior-god skilled in many crafts, and Manannan, god of the sea [17: 69–73], together with many powerful goddesses with both fierce and benevolent aspects [25: V; 27: III]. Two- or three-headed figures, as well as horned heads, have been found (see HEAD CULT). There were small local temples as well as more elaborate ones under Greek or Roman influence [20: 40–54], and many holy places in hills or by water. (see VOTIVE OFFERINGS). There were four main festivals with sacrifice at the quarters of the year (see SAMHAIN), and ceremonial feasting played an important part [24: 197–201]. The supernatural world was associated with the depths of earth or sea, or distant islands (see LAND OF YOUTH). Birds and animals, especially the boar, bull, horse, swan and raven, were symbols of divine power [25: VII; 12: VI].

Cemanahuac [XXV] The Aztecs (see MESOAMERICAN RELIGIONS) conceived of the world as a land surrounded by water, Cemanahuac, with their capital, Tenochtitlan, located at the *tlalxico* or navel of the earth from which extended four quadrants, *nauhcampa*, literally four directions of the wind. In an alternative version, the earth was conceived of as a giant crocodile floating in the primal waters. Each of the four quarters had specific names, colours and influences associated with it. Though the pattern varied from culture to culture, a typical Mesoamerican version was: east/ Tlacopan, 'Place of dawn', yellow, fertile and good; north/Mictlampa, 'Region of the underworld', red, barren and bad; west/Cihuatlampa,

'Region of women', blue-green, unfavourable, humid; south/ Huitzlampa, 'Region of thorns', white; centre/Tlalxico, 'Navel', black [2: 3–8; 12: 46–61] (*see figure 3*). The waters surrounding the inhabited land were called *ilhuicatl*, the celestial water, which extended upwards in a vertical direction, merging with the sky and supporting the lowest level of heaven. This cosmological pattern of a central space with four cardinal sections surrounding it became the organizing principle for a multitude of supernatural, political, tributary and economic conceptions in central Mesoamerican society.

The vertical cosmos was conceived of as a series of 13 layers above and nine layers below the earth [17: 406]. Each celestial layer was inhabited by a deity, a sacred bird and a specific cosmological influence and colour. The nine underworld layers were hazard stations for the souls of the dead, who, aided by magical charms buried with the bodies, were assisted in their quest for eternal peace at the lowest level, called Mictlan.

The Aztecs and their neighbours believed that they lived in the Fifth Sun or age of Nahui Ollin, Sun of Movement. This fifth age was preceded by four universal ages, Sun of Jaguar, Sun of Wind, Sun of Fiery Rain and Sun of Water, each named after the cataclysmic event which destroyed it. Each age was ruled by one of the great deities who became the sun during one age: TEZCATLI-POCA, QUETZALCOATL, TLALOC and Chalchuihuitlicue. [12: 25–46] This

Figure 3
The Aztec five world regions

cosmogony appears as a pictorial image in the centre of the CALENDAR STONE.

Central Asia and Kazakhstan, Islam in [XIX] From being, for almost a century, the forgotten lands of Islam, the now independent republics of former Soviet Central Asia and Kazakhstan (Turkmenistan, Uzbekistan, Tajikistan, Kyrgyzstan and Kazakhstan), which, with the exception of Kazakhstan, received Islam from their having been incorporated into the Arab empire in the 8th century, and which today have one of the largest concentrations of Muslims in the world (35 million, according to the 1989 Soviet census), are once again coming to the centre of Islamic affairs as Russia, Turkey, Iran and Afghanistan vie for influence with them. Closely allied to the Central Asian republics is the now independent republic of Azerbaijan where some 7 million (mainly Shi'ite) Muslims (*see* SHI'ISM) live. As is the case with Muslims in the Russian Federation, the Muslims of Central Asia and Kazakhstan do not constitute a homogeneous group, but exhibit wide ethnic and cultural diversity – the Kazakhs, for example, were largely nomadic until well into the 20th century and retain, along with Islam, many of their pre-Islamic shamanistic beliefs (*see* SHAMAN) and practices [143: 9–13]. While the majority of Muslims in these republics, which were somewhat artificially created out of older khanates by Soviet power in the 1920s, are Turkic-speaking, the Tajiks (who spill over into Afghanistan) speak a form of Persian. Almost all of the Muslims in Central Asia are Sunni (*see* SUNNA) and adhere to the Hanafi legal school, although small communities of Shi'ites (including 60,000–100,000 ISMA'ILIS) are found in the mountainous region of Gorno-Badakhshan in south-eastern Tajikistan [4: 313, 379; 15: 110]. From the 9th to the 14th centuries

Central Asia was at the forefront of high Islamic civilization and the MOSQUES and MADRASAS of Bukhara (the capital in the 10th century of the famous Samanid dynasty) and Samarkand were among the most renowned in all Islam. The buildings of these cities, which are among the most beautiful in the Islamic world, remain to this day a constant reminder to the inhabitants of this region of their once glorious status within the Islamic world. Al-Bukhari (810–70) and Ibn Sina (Avicenna) (980–1037) are just two of the many renowned Islamic scholars who were active in this region. The region was also a major centre of SUFISM and the now worldwide Naqshbandi order was founded in Bukhara in the 14th century by Baha'al-Din al-Naqshbandi. Other illustrious Sufis associated with the area were Yusuf Hamadani (d. 1140) and Ahmad Yasavi (mid-12th century); the latter's tomb in the city of Yasy in southern Kazakhstan is, together with the tomb of al-Bukhari in Samarkand, the most sacred shrine in the whole of Central Asia. However, by the 19th century, these regions had become a by-word in the West for fanaticism, bigotry and cruelty; during that century they were eventually incorporated into the expanding Russian empire and, after some resistance by the pan-Turkic and pan-Islamic Basmachi movement, into the Soviet empire in the 1920s. During the Soviet period Islam in the region divided into an 'official Islam', recognized and tightly controlled by the Soviet authorities and governed by a Spiritual Board with its headquarters in Tashkent, and an 'unofficial Islam', largely centred on popular and, in the opinion of many students of Islam, degenerate Sufi practices such as pilgrimage to the tombs of Sufi 'saints' (*mazars*). These republics are today seeking to recover their Islamic identity and are the object of intense Islamic missionary activity, mounted from a variety of countries and by a number of Islamic organizations; however, secularizing, as well as communist influences – an inheritance from the Soviet period – remain strong, particularly in Kazakhstan, where large numbers of ethnic Russians continue to reside, and in Tajikistan, where in 1993 the old communist leaders, after a bloody struggle with the 'Islamists', were still in control. Of the countries vying with each other for influence in this region, Turkey appears to be establishing the strongest cultural and economic ties with the new republics of Central Asia, although the influence of Iran, particularly in Tajikistan, should not be underestimated. This is a region where the politics of Islam will continue to be played for some time to come.

Central Asian Buddhism [XI] Buddhist missions reached China during the 1st century CE. By this time monasteries appear to have been established from India into northern Afghanistan, Tadzhikistan and Sinkiang (Chinese Turkestan) along the trade routes terminating near TUN-HUANG. The area was inhabited during the 1st millennium CE mostly by peoples speaking Middle Iranian languages such as Sogdian and Khotanese Saka. Buddhism in company with other religious traditions was well established in the area until after the coming of ISLAM. Local climatic conditions have preserved written materials, paintings, etc., which have contributed greatly to our knowledge of ancient Buddhism as well as of MANICHAEISM, Nestorian Christianity (see CHRISTOLOGY) and East Iranian languages and culture. Both MAHAYANA and earlier Buddhist schools were present, especially the SARVASTIVADA and the MAHASANGHIKA. Most Buddhist missionaries to China before 265 CE were from central Asia, which consequently had a formative influence on CHINESE BUDDHISM. [24a]

Cernunnos [VII] Horned male heads or figures occur frequently in Celtic art, a tradition going back to the Northern Bronze Age. On a Paris relief an antlered god sitting cross-legged is inscribed '(C)ernunnos' (Horned One), and the name has been adopted for this type of deity [25: 162–4; 17: 44–8]. He often has a neck-ornament and a purse, and is accompanied by a ram-headed serpent, a stag and other animals, as on the Gundestrup cauldron (probably 1st century BCE).

Chagim [XXII] Literally 'festivals'. The Jewish ritual year (CALENDAR) begins with the two-day New Year festival (ROSH HA-SHANAH), a time of repentance when the *shofar* or ram's horn is blown to awaken the Jews to turn back to God. Two weeks later (usually mid-October) is the festival of TABERNACLES (Sukkot), when Jews live in a temporary booth or *sukkah*, reminding them of the time the Israelites spent wandering in the wilderness. Tabernacles ends with a separate festival when the annual reading of the Pentateuch (*see* BIBLE) is concluded with a celebration of the Rejoicing of the TORAH (Simchat Torah). Two months later the minor festival of Chanukah commemorates the religiously inspired revolt of the Maccabees against the Hellenistic rulers of Palestine in the 2nd century BCE (*see* BIBLICAL HISTORY). Lights are lit in the Jewish home for eight days. Ten weeks later Purim commemorates the deliverance of the Jews as recorded in the Book of Esther. At the beginning of spring Jews celebrate the PASSOVER (Pesach), when the EXODUS from Egypt occurred. No leavened bread is eaten; unleavened wafers or *matzah* are eaten instead. At the beginning of Passover a Seder meal is held, at which four cups of wine are drunk and the story of the Exodus recited from a Haggadah text ('Haggadah' is the Hebrew equivalent of the Aramaic AGGADAH, and is generally used to refer to this text). Seven weeks later PENTE-COST (Shavuot) commemorates the revelation of God at Mt Sinai (*see* MOSES). [16: 170; 19: XI; 59: V–XXIX; 70: X–XI]

Ch'an [XII] The term *ch'an* (Japanese ZEN) is an abbreviation of *ch'an-na*, the Chinese transliteration of the Sanskrit DHYANA (PALI: *jhana*). In CHINESE BUDDHISM *ch'an* was used as a general term for meditation. The Ch'an school (Ch'an Tsung) is summarized in various texts as: 'A special transmission outside the scriptures;/No depending on words and letters;/Direct pointing to the human mind;/Seeing into one's own nature, and attaining Buddha-hood' [27: v, 67; 97: v, 176]. Although this summary is attributed to Ch'an master Nan Ch'uan (748–834 CE), most of the ideas were present in the teachings of Tao Sheng (360–434 CE) [35: VII, 270–84; 27: IV, 61–6; 28: v, 74–7].

Ch'an tradition regards Bodhidharma as its founder in China. He is said to have arrived in China from India in 520 CE. After attempting to teach the Emperor Wu the truth of EMPTINESS (*shunya*), he spent nine years in meditation facing a wall. He emphasized the teachings of the *Lankavatara-Sutra* (*see* YOGACARA). [27: III, 45–51, v, 67–87; 97: v, 163–228; 28: VI, 85–98].

The 'special transmission', and the Ch'an patriarchal lineage from Bodhidharma to the fifth patriarch, Hung Jen, was generally accepted; but the succession of Shen Hsiu (600–702 CE) as the sixth patriarch was publicly contested in 734 CE by Shen Hui, who claimed that Hui Neng (638–713 CE) had been the true sixth patriarch. He accused Shen Hsiu of deviating from true Ch'an by endorsing a gradual method of training. He insisted that Hui Neng's direct approach of sudden awakening, which rejects all distinctions between enlightenment and ignorance, and between ordinary beings and BUDDHAS, was the

true Ch'an teaching. Eventually Hui Neng's position became generally accepted. He was particularly associated with the Diamond Sutra (VAJRACCHEDIKA), a verse of which had stimulated his own 'inner awakening' (Chinese: *wu*; Japanese: *satori*). [7: XXVI, 425–49; 9; 15: XII, 350–64; 24: XIV, 346–68; 27: v, VI; 35: IX, 386–406; 28: VIII]

After the government persecution of Buddhism in 845 CE, Ch'an emerged as the strongest survivor. By this time five Ch'an sects had developed. Only the Lin Chi (Japanese: *rinzai*) and Ts'ao Tung (Japanese: *soto*) survived during the Sung dynasty (960–1126). During this period the Lin Chi masters developed the *kung an* (Japanese: *koan*) as subjects for meditation and systematic training, to bring their students to awakening (*wu*; *satori*) [91]. The Ts'ao Tung sect had developed the teaching of the Five Ranks on the relationship between relative and absolute, and they stressed the value of constant attention and formal seated meditation (*tso ch'an*; Japanese: *zazen*). [11; 27: VII, VIII; 91; 28: XI]

Chasidism (or **Hasidism**) [XXII] A movement founded in the late 18th century by Israel Baal Shem Tov, known as the Besht. The early centres of Chasidism were in the Ukraine and southern Poland, but within two generations it had spread throughout eastern Europe. Chasidic teachings were a popularized form of KABBALAH, emphasizing the importance of the inner service of God rather than the keeping of Jewish ritual laws [70: 107]. God can be served in everyday activities as well as through the *mitzvot* (*see* MITZVAH). The single most important aspect of this service is *devekut*, or cleaving to God, in joy. Chasidism gave new value to the life of the ordinary Jew who could not aspire to any great understanding of Jewish lore. The PARABLE or story, conveying its message to simple and sophisticated Jews alike, was widely used as a teaching medium. Many of these Chasidic stories have been retold by modern Jewish theologians [8; 9]. The Chasidic movement was strongly opposed by rabbinical conservatives, known as Mitnagdim, who suspected it of heterodox tendencies and put it under the ban of excommunication or *cherem*. Today Chasidic Jews are indistinguishable from their Orthodox co-religionists, except for the organization of their communities around the figure of the *tzaddik* or Chasidic leader [38; 39; 49: 37; 69]

Chen Yen [XII] The Tantric (*see* TANTRA (2)) school of BUDDHISM in China. The term *chen yen* (True Word) translates the Sanskrit term MANTRA. The school was introduced into China in 716 CE by Shubhakarasimha, who translated the *Mahavairocana-Sutra*, and was developed by Vajrabodhi (663–723), and by Amoghavajra (705–74). Although Amoghavajra gained the patronage of Emperor T'ai Tsung, the school was never generally popular. Tibetan Tantric Buddhism was introduced by the Yuan dynasty (1279–1368) and survived as the Tibetan Esoteric sect (Tsang Mi Tsung) (SHINGON). [15: XI, 325–37; 94: X, 135–6]

Cheyenne [V] A North American Indian tribe of the ALGONQUIN linguistic stock. Originally agriculturists of the central plains, its members later became nomadic hunters. Many of their religious rituals were associated with warfare. The annual Renewal of the Sacred Arrows (a cosmogonic ritual), founded on the Cheyenne story of creation according to which a bundle of sacred arrows symbolized the whole tribe (*see* COSMOLOGY), was intended to ensure regeneration and prosperity. Also practised were the SUN DANCE (occasionally still danced today), the Buffalo Head Dance and the GHOST DANCE. More recently, the Peyote

Cult (*see* PEYOTISM) has assumed prominence. [24: XIV]

China, Christianity in [XIII.B] Early Nestorians (7th century; *see* CHRISTOLOGY) and medieval Western missions to China died out in the 14th century. The Jesuit Matteo Ricci (1552–1610) began a tradition (condemned in the 18th century) of accommodating Christianity to Chinese ceremonies and religious language. A fresh start in the 19th century was facilitated by European political influence. Identification of Christianity with this influence aggravated traditional Chinese xenophobia and intellectual antipathy to Christianity, demonstrated in the Boxer rising (1900). The T'ai P'ing rebellion (1850s) included a measure of Christian SYNCRETISM [37 vol. 6: 286 8; 100: 266 75]. An important aspect of missionary policy was a Christian higher education system. The advent of a communist state (1949) soon led to the exclusion of missionaries, and necessity as well as government policy compelled churches to be self-supporting. The 'Cultural Revolution' of 1966 brought persecution but reports since 1981 suggest an easing of religious intolerance and more open worship which testify to the survival and even growth of Christianity. The period of persecution fostered cooperation between some churches but also created divisions over collaboration with the government. ROMAN CATHOLICISM has also experienced tensions due to the long break in contact with Rome. Christianity, however, has never been more than a minority influence in China. [100: IV, IX, XVII; 106; 121 vol. 3: XIX, vol. 5: XIII; 122 vol. 3: XIV, vol. 6: V, vol. 7: XIII]

China, Islam in [XIX] Islam arrived on the China coast in the 8th century through the efforts of Arab Persian traders, but the numerical strength of the indigenous Chinese Muslims today (called Hui in Chinese) is in the interior mountain and steppe areas of western and south-western China proper, such as Kansu, Ningsia, Shensi, Yunnan and Szechwan, where communities of Chinese Muslims have been established since at least the 13th century. In the westernmost province of the Chinese People's Republic, Sinkiang (the contemporary Uighur Autonomous Region), the indigenous Eastern Turkic population is wholly Muslim and is even longer-established, but its religious and cultural links are with western Turkestan, the Central Asian republics of the former Soviet Union, rather than with China proper.

The Chinese Muslim communities have often during the last two centuries been in revolt against imperial and communist Chinese attempts at centralization and religious uniformity. The 1936 China census counted 47 million Muslims out of a total population of 452 million; no figures are available for the communist period. Always cut off by distance from the mainsprings of Islamic piety and scholarship, the Islam of China proper, under its native religious leaders, the *ahungs*, had to coexist uneasily with Confucianism (*see* CONFUCIUS) and thus became in many ways eclectic, at least until the millennarian movement of the 'New Sect' in the later 18th century and the outbursts of militant, revivalist Muslim rebellion in Kansu, Szechwan and Yunnan during the 19th century. Since the communist revolution it has, like other religions, been persecuted, but the post-Mao period seems to have brought some relaxation of official disapproval, if only for diplomatic reasons; a trickle of Chinese Muslims make the pilgrimage to Mecca each year, and MOSQUES and MADRASAS are reopening on a limited scale.

China, The People's Republic of, Chinese Religion in [XII] The fall of the Ch'ing dynasty in 1912 meant the end of the great Sacrificial Rites (*Chi Li*) of imperial religion in China, and the official examination system based on the CONFUCIAN CANON had been abolished in 1905. The traditions of religious Taoism (TAO CHIAO) and CHINESE BUDDHISM and many features of popular or diffused religion in China continued to survive [122: XII, 294–330].

After the establishment of the People's Republic of China in 1949, public acts of ritual and worship were actively discouraged (even though freedom of religious belief was included in the constitution). In the 1950s official religious organizations such as the Chinese Buddhist Association, the Chinese Muslim Association and eventually the Chinese Taoist Association were founded, under the auspices of the Bureau of Religious Affairs. These were primarily intended to establish control over the religions and ensure political conformity. Such state control of religion is by no means a new phenomenon in China.

During the mid- and late 1960s anti-religious campaigns were pursued as part of the general policy of eradicating old values and customs. By 1970 many urban temples and monasteries had been closed down. Reports began to appear about violent anti-religious acts carried out by the Red Guards of the Cultural Revolution. Homes were searched for religious objects and monks and priests were publicly humiliated. More recently, official attitudes to religion appear to have relaxed. Many monasteries and temples have reopened, ostensibly as places of historical and cultural interest. As recently as October 1981 official concern was expressed at the attitudes of prayer and reverence adopted by some visitors to the temples. Sections of the Chinese press reiterated that while freedom of religious belief was protected under the constitution, people should be actively discouraged from practising religion.

Probably the most resilient traditional religious values and practices are those which have never been centrally organized. It is clear that many aspects of popular or diffused religion in China, such as reverence for ancestors, family and even communal festivals, and belief in local deities and spirits continue to survive, albeit in restricted forms, in the rural areas of mainland China. (*See also* ANCESTOR CULT (CHINESE); CHINESE PANTHEON; CHINA, THE REPUBLIC OF (TAIWAN), AND HONG KONG, CHINESE RELIGION IN; FESTIVALS (CHINESE)) [6a; 17a: 13, 221–6; 98: XXVIII, 231–41; 99: VIII, 114–22]

China, The Republic of (Taiwan), and Hong Kong, Chinese Religion in [XII] Many features of traditional Chinese popular or diffused religion flourish in Taiwan, Hong Kong and the New Territories, in spite of the influences of industrialization and secularization. One aspect of traditional Chinese life, the practice of FENG-SHUI (geomancy), has actually increased with the extensive building programmes in these areas. The annual cycle of communal and family festivals, such as New Year, the Bright and Clear Festival, and Serving All Souls, and the birthdays of particular deities are still celebrated with enthusiasm and sincerity (*see* FESTIVALS (CHINESE)) [99: VII, 108–13]. The traditions of family religion, such as reverence for ancestors and the honouring of gods on the family altar, continue to be observed, particularly by the elderly (*see* ANCESTOR CULT (CHINESE); FUNERAL RITES) [1; 53].

The two most popular deities in Taiwan are the Heavenly Empress, known familiarly as 'Granny' (Ma tsu), and the Goddess of Mercy (KUAN (SHI) YIN). Other important deities include the Jade Emperor (Yu Huang), the God of War (Kuan Kung), the local earth-god T'u Ti Kung, AMITABHA Buddha, and

Sakyamuni BUDDHA (*see* CHINESE PANTHEON) [53; 98: XXV, 198–209; 99: IV, 56–68].

The majority of Chinese see no conflict or disharmony between the three great traditions of Confucianism, Taoism (TAO CHIAO) and BUDDHISM. Most people accept ideas and practices from all three. In general the values of Confucianism provide the framework for public life and for family and social ethics, emphasizing qualities such as loyalty, propriety (LI) and filial piety (*see* CONFUCIAN CANON; CONFUCIUS).

The ostensible concern of the Taoist adept or priest is with the quest for immortality. In practice the Taoists have a much more important social role. They are the ritual manipulators of spirits, in healing and exorcism, and they regulate the important festivals which restore the balance of the *Yin* and *Yang* forces in nature and in society (*see* YIN–YANG). One such festival is the elaborate festival of cosmic renewal (*chiao*) which takes place in most villages once every 60 years (*see* TAO CHIA) [88–90].

For ordinary people Buddhism represents the virtues of abstinence and restraint, as exemplified by the relatively austere lives of the monks. It also offers the hope of salvation through rebirth in Amitabha's Pure Land (CHING T'U TSUNG). Buddhist monks frequently assist at funeral rites (*see* CHINESE BUDDHISM). In many villages the temple (*miao*) is the centre of social and cultural life as well as a place of religious worship and ritual. Most village temples are administered by a lay committee of directors who usually employ a Taoist priest to officiate. [99: IV, 62–9]

Chinese Buddhism [XII] There are various legends about the entry of Buddhism into China at very early dates, and there is some evidence of a Buddhist community in 65 CE at P'eng Ch'eng in northern Kiangsu [15: II, 27–32]. Buddhism entered

China via the trade routes from Central Asia (*see* CENTRAL ASIAN BUDDHISM). A memorial written in 166 CE criticizes Emperor Huan for worshipping at altars to Huang-Lao and the BUDDHA, and refers to a 'Sutra in Forty-Two Sections' [15: II, 34–6]. The close association between Buddhism and neo-Taoism (HSUAN HSUEH) is a distinctive feature of early Buddhism in China. It led to the interpretation and translation of key Buddhist terms with Taoist ones, and to the development of the *ko i* (extending the meaning) method of expounding Buddhist teachings by referring to texts such as the *I Ching* (Classic of Changes), TAO TE CHING, and the CHUANG TZU. Many Chinese in the 2nd and 3rd centuries regarded Buddhism as simply a foreign form of Taoism (TAO CHIAO) [15: II, 48–53].

An Shih Kao was an important Buddhist teacher in China. He arrived in Lo Yang in 148 CE and effectively founded what became known as the Dhyana school, which emphasized the rules of discipline of the VINAYA (PATIMOKKHA) and meditation. One of his early translations was the *Sutra on Mindfulness of Breathing (An Pan Shou I Ching)*. The other early interest in Chinese Buddhism was reflected by the PRAJNA school, based on the interpretation of the Perfection of Wisdom (PRAJNAPARAMITA), the earliest translation being of the *Perfection of Wisdom in 8,000 Lines (Ashtasahasrika Prajnaparamita)* by Chih Ch'an (Lokakshema) in 175 CE. This school was strongly influenced by neo-Taoist thought [7: XX, 336–42; 15: III, 57–80; 35: VII, 237–58].

Hui Yuan (344–416), the most eminent Chinese Buddhist of his age, established a famous monastery at Lu Shan, engaged in a lengthy correspondence with KUMARAJIVA [85: 181–95], defended the right of the SANGHA to remain independent of the state [24: XII, 280–6] and founded a cult of AMITABHA (15: III, 103–12]. Hui's disciple Tao Sheng

(360–434) studied with Kumarajiva for three years and developed his theories of the true self (*chen wo*) or Buddha nature (*fo hsing*) in humanity and sudden enlightenment (*tun wu*) [15: III, 112–20; 35: VII, 270–84].

The period between the 5th and 8th centuries CE was the time of the development and expansion of the major Buddhist schools and popular movements, such as CH'AN, CHEN YEN, CHING T'U, Chu She, FA HSIANG, HUA YEN, LU, SAN LUN and T'IEN TAI [7: XXII–XXVI; 15: XII, XII; 24: XIII, XIV; 94: X, 124–39]. By the Sung dynasty (960–1126) Buddhism had declined and only the Ch'an and Ching T'u schools remained active and popular. [15; 16; 83; 119; 123]

Chinese Pantheon [XII] The Chinese pantheon is so extensive that it is impossible to count all the gods and spirits in it. The regional and historical variations, the influence of gods from BUDDHISM, and religious Taoism (TAO CHIAO) make systematic classification difficult. Even the apparently obvious distinction between a Buddhist pantheon and a Taoist pantheon is problematic because of the extent of the early interaction between these two traditions [122: 1, 23–5].

From Chou times (1027–402 BCE) the official or state religion of China focused upon the abstract deity Heaven (T'IEN), and its counterpart Earth (*Ti*) and the Royal Ancestors (*Tsu Tsung*). These were almost exclusively the concern of the ruler and the feudal lords or, in imperial times, the Emperor. [2; 4: III, 54–68; 72: 93–111; 73: V, 70–6]

The popular and anthropomorphic equivalent of Heaven was the Jade Emperor (Yu Huang), who received the full title 'Jade Emperor Lord on High' (Yu Huang SHANG TI) during the T'ang dynasty (618–907 CE). He came to be regarded as the ruler of the heavenly court and bureaucracy during the Sung dynasty (960–1126 CE). These were regarded as heavenly versions of the earthly institutions, with departments run by their appropriate gods and spirits. The most important of these include the Ministry of Thunder (Lei Pu) and the Heavenly Ministry of Healing (T'ien I Yuan), run by the legendary first three Sage Emperors of China: Fu Hsi, Shen Nung and Huang Ti. The Ministry of Fire (Huo Pu) is run by a former Taoist sage and astral ruler of Mars, Lo Hsuan. The Ministry of Epidemics is run by another former Taoist, Lu Yo. The Ministry of the Five Sacred Mountains (Wu Yo) has the god of T'AI SHAN, the Great Divine Ruler of the Eastern Peak (Tung Yueh Ta Ti), as its chief minister. He is the Jade Emperor's grandson and chief assistant. He can determine a person's lifespan and their fortune and he assists Yama (*see* VEDA) (Yen Lo Wang) in presiding over the fate of those in the hells. [25: 262–302; 117: 151]

Other major gods include the god of the ramparts or city-god Ch'eng Huang, whose duties made him the supernatural equivalent of the city magistrate. The god of the stove, Tsao Chun, had a vital role in domestic life by keeping records of each person's actions and reporting at least once a year to the Jade Emperor. Fu Shen the god of Happiness, Shou Hsing the god of longevity, and Ts'ai Shen the god of wealth are now among the most popular Chinese gods. [22; 23; 25; 49; 117]

Ching T'u Tsung [XII] Pure Land school. Textually the school is based upon the *Larger Sukhavativyuha-Sutra* (translated in 252 CE), the *Smaller Sukhavativyuha-Sutra* (translated in 402 CE by Kumarajiva), and the *Amitayur-Dhyana-Sutra* (translated in 424 CE by Kalayashas). The *Sukhavativyuha-Sutras* contain a detailed account by the BUDDHA Sakyamuni (GOTAMA) of how the Buddha AMITABHA came to preside

over the 'Land of Bliss' (*Sukhavati*) or 'Pure Land' (*Parisodhana-Kshetra*) as a result of his practice and devotion in a previous age as the monk Dharmakara. The *sutras* repeat the great vows taken by Dharmakara to enable those devoted to him and to the Pure Land to be reborn there and attain enlightenment. The Buddha then projects rays of light from his body and illuminates the Pure Land for the assembly to see (a detailed description is given in the *sutras*).

The tendency towards devotion focused on Amitabha and the Pure Land developed very early in China. In 402 CE Hui Yuan, the head of an important monastery near Lu Shan, founded a cult of Amitabha and vowed to be reborn in the Pure Land [15: IV, 106–8]. The organizer of Ching T'u as a separate school was T'an Luan (476–542). He emphasized the practice of *Nien fo* (Japanese: *nembutsu*), literally mindfulness or recollection of the Buddha, which was usually practised by devoted repetition of the phrase, 'Namo Amitabha Buddha' (Chinese: *Nan-mo A-mi-t'o Fo*; Japanese: *Namu Amida Butsu – see* AMIDA WORSHIP). Tao Cho (562–645) argued that the practice of *nien fo* was the only effective method of gaining rebirth in the Pure Land and hence enlightenment, because ignorant beings in the age of the DHARMA's decline were incapable of other religious practices or higher understanding. He advised the constant repetition of Amitabha's name and he developed the rosary for this purpose. Shan Tao (613–81), in his commentary on the *Amitayur-Dhyana-Sutra*, advocates primarily the practice of *nien fo* with a pure and undisturbed mind, together with the chanting of *sutras*, meditation upon Amitabha, worship of his image and the singing of hymns in his praise. [15: XII, 338–50; 24: XIV, 334–45; 94: X, 125–7]

Chinvat Bridge [XXXVI] *Chinvato Peretu* (PAHLAVI: *Chinvat Puhl*) The 'Bridge of the Separator', the Bridge of Judgement in ZOROASTRIANISM. It is believed that for three days after death the soul (*urvan*; Pahlavi: *ruvan*) meditates on its life before proceeding to its judgement by the three YAZATAS, Mithra, Sraosha and Rashnu. Its good and evil thoughts, words and deeds are weighed in the balance. If the good predominate, then it is led by a beautiful maiden, the personification of its conscience (*daena*), across the bridge to heaven. If the evil predominate, then an ugly old hag leads the soul trembling across the bridge, which narrows so that the soul falls down into hell. This is the first judgement. The stay in heaven or hell is a temporary one for reward or corrective punishment for the soul until the day of the resurrection (FRASHOKERETI) when the whole person can be judged. [28: 64–5; 36; 40; 49; 54: IX]

Chisungu [II] Dancing the *chisungu* is the ritual of female initiation – girls' puberty rites – among the matrilineal Bemba of northern Zambia and neighbouring peoples. The ceremony could take many weeks, involves the segregation of the novices, makes great use of clay figurines and consists of a mass of symbolic usages whereby girls just prior to marriage are formally taught both 'the things of womanhood' and 'the things of the garden'. There is no form of circumcision. *Chisungu* is understood as a necessary handing on, sanctioned and required by the ancestors, of the norms required for marriage and good living.

The *chisungu* may be compared with the *nkang'a* of the Ndembu, another Zambian matrilineal people. For both peoples these are among the most important of rituals (*see also* NYAU). The Bemba have no male equivalent, but the Ndembu also have circumcision rites for their boys. Circumcision is part of the initiation of boys among many Afri-can peoples in all parts of the continent, but is by no means universal. Some, such as the Gikuyu, practise female circumcision (clitoridectomy) as well. For the Gikuyu, *irua* (initiation) provides entry at once into a particular age-set and to full maturity; it is the central ritual of personal and communal life. But just as other peoples, like the Bemba, have initiation rituals without circumcision, so there are peoples, such as the GANDA, who have no puberty rites whatever. Where such rituals exist their meaning is closely related to the structures of society, but equally they are rich in a mass of often apparently obscure symbolism and may throw much light upon underlying religious concepts. [47; 49: 198–268; 50: 86–129]

Chöd [XXXV] The Chöd ('cutting') tradition of Tibetan BUDDHISM originated with the Indian Dampa Sanjay (d. 1117) and his Tibetan disciple the yogini Machik Labdron (1055–1149). Chöd combines the theories of the PRAJNAPARAMITA with the methods of TANTRA (2). By meditation on Shunyata (*see* SHUNYATAVADA) and the visualized sacrifice of his physical existence to all sentient beings, especially those of a demonic nature, the Chöd practitioner 'cuts' or severs attachment to the notion of a truly existent self. Although Chöd no longer constitutes an independent sect its teachings have been preserved within the KAGYU and NYINGMA schools. [6]

Cholollan [XXV] (4th–16th centuries CE) At the time of the Spanish conquest (1521 CE), the city of Cholollan (also referred to as Cholula) was the religious centre of Mesoamerica, compared by the Spaniards to Rome and Mecca because of the great pilgrimages to its many shrines [10: 119–20]. This ceremonial and market city was one of the longest-occupied sites in Mesoamerican history and was organized around the Tlachihualtepetl, the largest pyramid temple in the world, which covered more than 16 hectares at the time of the conquest. This great shrine, famous as the oracle of QUETZALCOATL, was rebuilt at least four times during its existence. Historical records indicate that it was first settled by the Olmeca-Xicalanca, who constructed the early version of the ceremonial precinct. Following the fall of the great capital Teotihuacan in the 8th century CE, Cholollan became the pilgrimage and market centre *par excellence*, and drew pilgrims, merchants, nobles and kings to its fairs and innumerable religious shrines. This expansion was partly brought about by the Tolteca Chichimeca, who resettled the city following the fall of their capital, Tollan Xicocotitlan. The Tolteca Chichimeca renamed the city Tollan Cholollan Tlachihualtepetl, revitalized the cult of Quetzalcoatl, and dispensed sacralized authority to the many rulers of the land who travelled to the shrine for investiture ceremonies. Cholollan was governed by two priestly rulers: the Acquiach, Elder of the Above, and the Tlalchiach, Elder of the Ground. Historical records show that the city was used as a periodic truce centre for warring factions, which celebrated there together on special occasions.

Christadelphians [XIII.B] Founded by John Thomas (1805–71) in the USA, in 1848 this Christian SECT (the name means 'Christ's Brethren') aimed to revive original Christian belief and practice. The BIBLE is seen as infallible and central emphasis is laid on Biblical PROPHECY of the return of JESUS Christ to set up his rule on earth. Other beliefs include: rejection of the doctrine of the TRINITY; baptism by immersion only; true believers alone to be raised from the dead; and no separate MINISTRY. [205: 219–314; I, 7: 569–71; 125]

Christian Fellowship Church [XXVII] The largest independent church in Melanesia (*see* MELANESIAN RELIGION), founded about 1959 in New Georgia, Solomon Islands, by Silas Eto (b. 1905), who after education in the Methodist Mission (*see* METHODISM) had a series of visionary experiences. An admirer of John Wesley and J. F. Goldie, the pioneer missionary, Eto became dissatisfied with local Methodism and developed a well-organized church with PENTECOSTAL worship, healing, prosperous economic activities and a holy village, Paradise (*see* NEW JERUSALEMS). In the 1970s relations with Methodism and other churches were being re-established.

Christian Kabbalah [XXIV] The interpretation of KABBALAH as specifically confirming Christian doctrine. Pico della Mirandola (1463–94), who studied Hebrew under Jewish teachers, argued that Kabbalah proved the divinity of JESUS Christ and that the triadic structure of the *sefirot* (*see* SEFIRAH) confirmed the TRINITY. His views influenced scholars who saw in Kabbalah similarities to the Christian NEOPLATONISM of pseudo-Dionysius. The Hebraist Johannes Reuchlin (1455–1522) (notable for his defence of the TALMUD against Dominicans who demanded its destruction) wrote influential dialogues asserting the value of Kabbalah and expounding techniques of *gematria* (*see* NUMEROLOGY), *notarikon* (alphabetical symbolism) and *temurah* (mystical reinterpretation of words), which he applied to confirm Christian doctrine. He hoped such interpretations would aid the conversion of the Jews, and indeed a substantial number of conversions during the 16th and 17th centuries were justified by reference to Kabbalah. By the mid-17th century most Christian scholars had some knowledge of Kabbalah, but after 1700 its popularity waned and views that

Kabbalah 'proves' Christianity are now rare. [2]

Christian Science [XIII.B] The teaching of the Church of Christ, Scientist, founded in 1879 by Mary Baker Eddy (1821–1910) of New Hampshire, USA, based on her *Science and Health with a Key to the Scriptures* (1875). Special emphasis is placed on the destruction of sin and on healing the sick through prayer alone, based on the principle of the 'allness of Soul, Spirit and the nothingness of matter', which is often taken to mean, at least by outsiders, that physical suffering is an illusion to be conquered by the spirit-filled mind. The denomination comprises the First Church of Christ, Scientist in Boston, USA and its branches throughout the world. It has spread mainly in English-speaking countries, perhaps appealing more to the affluent than most SECTS. Worship is simple, including hymns, prayers and readings from the BIBLE and *Science and Health*. The church publishes an international newspaper, *The Christian Science Monitor*. Membership in 1970 stood at 623,579; 'affiliation' in 1980 at 1,654,546. [13: 14; 62 vol. 3: 442–6; 76; 104; 158]

Christian Theology [XIII.B, XIV] Discourse about God, or the discipline that treats of the divine. NATURAL THEOLOGY relies upon ordinary human experience and the operation of reason, while the theology of the world religions generally reflects upon divine revelation. In the case of CHRISTIANITY, this is the self-communication of God in JESUS Christ, as mediated to us through the BIBLE and Christian tradition. Theology is best understood as the expression or articulation of faith, or, as in the famous formula of St Anselm (d. 1109), 'faith seeking understanding'.

While the starting-point of theology is faith in revelation, the tools of theology commonly derive from the world of secular philosophy. Theology therefore stands between the static forms of revealed truth and developing philosophical traditions which are much influenced by the cultures of which they are a part. The function of theology is profoundly kerygmatic, therefore, in so far as it mediates revelation to a changing world. (*see* PHILOSOPHY OF RELIGION.)

Theologies can be divided into those which make greater or lesser use of philosophy, and into those which seek to critique the revealed tradition or simply to expound it. ROMAN CATHOLIC theologians have tended to make much use of philosophy, while remaining faithful to the revealed tradition (e.g. Thomas Aquinas). Some PROTESTANT theologians have shunned philosophy, appealing to the supremacy of historical revelation (e.g. Karl Barth), while others have fundamentally reinterpreted revelation in the light of philosophical concepts (e.g. Rudolf Bultmann). Orthodox theology is generally conservative and suspicious of philosophy, preferring to derive its concepts as far as possible from within the Christian world (e.g. Sergei Bulgakov).

Christian theologians today can be broadly divided into those who expound the tradition in new ways (Olivier Clément, Karl Rahner, Hans Urs von Balthasar); those who wish to reinterpret the tradition, applying it to political and liberationist ends (Gustavo Gutierrez, Leonardo Boff, Jürgen Moltmann), including feminist (Elisabeth Schüssler Fiorenza, Rosemary Radford Ruether), black (James Cone) and Third World (Choan-Seng Song) theologians; and liberal theologians (Hans Küng, John Hick), who reassess the Christian tradition in the light of modern rationalism and RELIGIOUS PLURALISM.

Christianity, Early [XIII.A] Christianity of the 1st century CE is known principally from the New Testament. Though JESUS may not have intended to establish a new religion, all varieties of Christianity from earliest times have appealed to his authority. Jesus' early followers preached that in the death of Jesus GOD had acted uniquely for the salvation of the world. The early Christian communities were pluralistic from the outset, reflecting the variety of contemporary Judaism of which Christianity was initially a part. The continuing significance of Jesus' teaching and healing ministry and of his death was proclaimed in a variety of ways. Early Palestinian Christian groups may be broadly categorized in three types: those associated with the majority of the APOSTLES in Jerusalem, largely continuing Jewish practice; those from a Hellenistic Jewish background, less tied to particular institutions and structures; and those who combined elements of both, such as PETER. As soon as Christianity had taken root among GENTILES (see PAUL), Jewish Christianity declined in influence. Unlike synagogues, Gentile churches were not permitted associations in the eyes of Roman law and from the time of Nero (64 CE) were often the target of attempts at suppression. The attractiveness of the Christian GOSPEL lay in part in its classless syncretism and philosophical respectability: based in the teaching of Jesus about the impartial rule of God, it assured believers of life after death, forgiveness and freedom from the power of DEMONS, and of their individual worth.

In 313 CE Christianity's right to exist was confirmed by Constantine's Milan edict of toleration. In 381 CE Theodosius established it as the religion of the Roman empire. [11: 1, 926–79; 13; 18]

Christianity, History and Character of [XIII.B] After the ministry of JESUS Christ in Palestine, Christianity spread through the Roman empire and beyond, to Persia, India and Ireland. It survived the fall of the Western Empire in 476 CE and converted the 'barbarian' invaders. The Eastern Empire survived as the Christian state of Byzantium until its fall to Islamic forces in 1453 CE. By the 11th century the church had divided into the Western and EASTERN ORTHODOX churches. The Western church under the PAPACY contributed much to the development of Western civilization, partly through MONASTICISM. It also experienced conflicts with heresies (see HERESY (MEDIEVAL CHRISTIAN)) and the state (see STATE, CHRISTIANITY AND THE). The 15th-century CONCILIAR MOVEMENT challenged papal authority. The 16th-century REFORMATION and COUNTER-REFORMATION split the Western church into ROMAN CATHOLICISM and PROTESTANTISM, Protestantism further divided into many churches and SECTS. European expansion and MISSIONS from the 16th century spread Christianity to the USA, AFRICA, ASIA and LATIN AMERICA; but religious observance in Western Europe has greatly declined in the 20th century. It has, however, grown substantially in parts of Asia and especially Africa, both in traditional churches and in new religious movements (see NEW RELIGIOUS MOVEMENTS IN PRIMAL SOCIETIES). Early Christian theology and medieval SCHOLASTICISM owed much to Greek philosophy as well as to the BIBLE. Even MYSTICISM has often been influenced by philosophical speculation. Later Western theology (unlike that of the Orthodox Church) has been much influenced by contemporary science and philosophy, especially in Protestantism. Despite a rich tradition of mysticism and ASCETICISM, Christianity has shown strong activist tendencies in social and political life (see SOCIAL MORALITY (CHRISTIAN)). Central to its teaching is the idea of GOD, as a TRINITY, who created the world and saves mankind through the work of the divine son Jesus Christ (see

Membership/affiliation of Christian churches

Group	Membership	Affiliation
Roman Catholicism	432,125,990	672,319,062
Orthodox	97,237,333	143,402,488
Lutheranism	23,347,633	60,000,000
Reformed/Presbyterian	18,989,088	32,434,522
Baptists	18,982,612	29,418,833
Anglicanism	16,403,751	47,556,975
Methodism	13,452,545	21,795,923

CHRISTOLOGY; SALVATION, CHRISTIAN DOCTRINE OF). Historically, Christianity has emphasized its claims to exclusive religious truth, but these have been less marked in recent times [8; 19; 37; 46; 57; 62 vol. 3: 348–430; 103; 105; 121; 122; 136; 145; 186]

Numbers given for different Christian churches are difficult to compare as some count whole nations while others have restricted 'membership' but many 'adherents'. Claims are made for Christianity at 1,000 million to be the largest world religion. The figures given in the table for adult 'membership'/'affiliation' (1970) suggest the relative size of the larger bodies, without defining the degree of commitment (and 'membership' is variously defined in different bodies) [13: 14, 792].

Christology [XIII.B] Teaching concerning the person of JESUS Christ (cf. GOD; TRINITY). As Christians traditionally believe that Christ is both human and divine, the problem has been to defend the idea of distinct, fully divine and fully human 'natures' in a single, unified personality. Explanations owed much to Greek thought. Early theologians saw Christ as the eternal Word (*Logos*) of God taking human form (Incarnation). In answer to the Arian view of him as a kind of subordinate being between God and man (*see* ARIANISM; HERESY (MEDIEVAL CHRISTIAN)), the COUNCIL of Nicea (325 CE) defined him as 'of one substance with the Father'

(*homoousion*). Theories proliferated in the 4th and 5th centuries, many being condemned as heretical. Apollinarians emphasized Christ's divinity but saw his humanity as merely physical. Nestorians upheld humanity in Christ so distinct from his divinity as to suggest a split personality. Eutychians thought that there were two natures before the Incarnation and one 'mixed' nature after it. The Council of Chalcedon (451) [19: 51–2] defined the limits of orthodoxy: 'Jesus Christ . . . truly God and truly man . . . of a reasonable soul and body; of one substance with the Father as regards his Godhead and . . . of one substance with us as regards his manhood . . . recognized in two natures, without confusion . . . without separation.' Dissident communities persisted, including Nestorians. Monophysites taught that only one nature existed after the Incarnation. Monothelites taught that only one will existed in Christ. Early PROTESTANTISM remained 'orthodox' except for UNITARIANISM and later DEISM. From the 19th century onwards changing philosophies and views of human nature produced further speculation. In general (unlike the early church) the humanity of Christ has been readily accepted; the divinity has been more difficult. *Kenosis* theories see Christ as 'emptying' himself of divine 'attributes' (*see* GOD, CHRISTIAN CONCEPT OF) to become man. The Chalcedonian definition has been widely criticized yet not replaced. [19: 35–52; 114: VI, XI, XII; 157: 281–2; 184]

Chthonian Religion [xxxiv] Devotion to GODS of the earth (ancient Greek *chthon*) as against those of the sky or heaven. The term is often used with specific reference to the nether-world (compare ANCESTOR-WORSHIP); but myths, rites (RITUAL) and cults centred on the earth and its fertility may also be called 'chthonian' (contrasting with 'Olympian' in ancient Greek religion).

Chuang Tzu [xII] The Taoist philosopher of the late 4th century BCE who provides the theme and inspiration for the treatise of the same name (TAO CHIAO). Only the first seven of its 33 chapters are thought to have been composed by Chuang Tzu [38: I, 3–5; 39: II, 172–6]. The work contains many of the same basic concepts and terms as the TAO TE CHING, but it gives a more detailed and systematic exposition of them. The *Chuang Tzu* embraces a much more personal and individualistic form of mysticism than that of the *Tao Te Ching*; in it one of the implications of naturalness (*tzu jan*) and non-doing (*wu wei*) is never to put oneself in a position in which one is called upon to govern or administer anything [110: vII, 93–4, xvII, 187–9]. Hence unlike the *Tao Te Ching*, the *Chuang Tzu* is not addressed specifically to the sage ruler. Chapter two of the *Chuang Tzu* includes a detailed exposition of the arbitrary and indeterminate nature of names, language, argument and all claims to valid knowledge. As an alternative its author recommends the embracing of all apparent opposites and contradictions [7: vIII, 179–90; 38: III, 8–14; 39: II, 176–83; 110: II, 36–76].

The work also devotes some attention to methods of mental discipline such as concentration, abandoning sense input and discriminatory thought, and achieving inner emptiness. These are summarized under the process called 'fasting the mind' (*hsin chai*) [7: vIII, 179, 201, 207; 110: IV, 57–8, vI, 90–1, vII, 97].

The *Chuang Tzu* advocates the value of yielding to change as part of the natural order of things, and this includes the sage's acceptance of his own death with equanimity. [7: vIII, 191–4; 19: vI; 21: I, II, III; 34: x; 38: 23–5, 110: vI, 77–80]

Church (Christian) [xIII.A] (Greek *ekklesia*) Both 'church' and SYNAGOGUE are terms used in the SEPTUAGINT of the community of Israel, and both are also used in the New Testament of a Christian community, but from an early date 'synagogue' has been reserved for Jews and *ekklesia* for Christians. In its Christian sense 'church' is used in two different ways in the New Testament: (1) of any particular local community of Christians in a city, such as JERSUALEM or CORINTH, or of the church meeting in someone's house; (2) of the universal worldwide community of Christians. At first the local churches were variously organized; in apostolic times (*see* APOSTLES) there was no overall organization for the universal church. It comprised Jews and GENTILES, although in some places its membership might consist entirely of one or the other. By the end of the 1st century it was predominantly Gentile (*see* CHRISTIANITY, EARLY). [4: 1338–53; 5: 195–221]

Church Discipline [xIII.B] Christian regulations for religious and moral life include systems of CANON law [157: 231]. This developed from rules of early COUNCILS, bishops and Popes, later elaborated as in ROMAN CATHOLICISM's *Corpus juris canonici*. The Eastern and Oriental churches developed their own system (*see* EASTERN ORTHODOX CHURCH). ANGLICANISM based its canons on medieval material last revised in 1969. Most churches have developed rules administered through hierarchies of church courts. Some, such as Roman

Catholicism, Anglicanism and PRESBYTERIANISM, have at various times made use of excommunication [157: 490] – the ultimate penalty of exclusion from the SACRAMENTS. This formerly involved civil penalties as well. The term *anathema* was formerly used of exclusion from the church for HERESY. 'Discipline' is also used to refer to systems of rules in MONASTICISM. It also refers to acts of physical self-denial (like fasting) to assist spiritual progress; and to the scourge, self-flagellation, sometimes used for PENANCE.

Church Music (Christian) [XIII.B]

Syrian, Byzantine and Latin Christianity inherited from Late Antiquity a family of musical modes organized into eight 'tones' and used for the psalms and hymns of the liturgy and the divine office. They also used musical declamation for the solemn reading of scripture. Psalms were sung in different ways to a variety of psalm-tones, some simple, near-monotone chants, some elaborate, complex melodies. In direct psalmody the singers sang the psalm together. In responsorial psalmody a cantor or a group of cantors sang the verses of the psalm while the choir responded to each verse with a refrain. The psalm verses sung before and after scriptural readings in the liturgy and the office, such as the Latin gradual or the Greek *prokeimenon* and the alleluia verses used in both traditions were originally sung to elaborate melodies in this manner. In antiphonal psalmody two choirs sing alternate verses of the psalm. Sometimes refrains are used in antiphonal psalmody too. The relatively simple melodies of the introit and communion verses of the Roman MASS and the *antiphona* of the Greek–Byzantine rite are fragmentary remains of antiphonal psalms [155]. A fourth form of psalmody exists in the Byzantine rite, used at *Hesperinos* (Vespers) and *Ainoi* (Laud), where the verses of a psalm or psalms are interleaved with hymn verses.

The COPTIC, SYRIAN, ETHIOPIAN and Byzantine churches retain the tradition of monophonic chant, a single melodic line, sometimes supported with a drone (*isokratima*) or, in Coptic and Ethiopian practice, with rhythmic instruments, such as the cymbals, systrum and triangle. Syrian chant tends to use simpler melodies than the Greek and Coptic traditions. In Romania and Serbia Byzantine-style chant, and in the Russian, Ukrainian and Bulgarian churches traditional medieval chant (*znammeny*) coexist with harmonized and polyphonic music. The Armenian Church has developed a rich choral tradition of its own. The traditional music of the Roman mass was Gregorian chant ('plainsong') – a single vocal line. But music for the mass regularly adopted secular changes in style and became increasingly elaborate. Masses by classical and romantic composers eventually entered the concert hall, as did 'requiems' (for the dead). The LITURGICAL MOVEMENT encouraged simplification and congregational participation.

The 'motet' (a polyphonal chant) was notably developed by G. P. da Palestrina (*c.*1525–94). From the 'cantata', a religious libretto with solos and choruses, developed the more elaborate 'oratorio'. This reached a popular climax with G. F. Handel's (1685–1759) *Messiah*. 'Passions' (commemorating Christ's sufferings) reached a summit in the work of J. S. Bach (1685–1750). Divorced from its religious setting, much of this music has become part of the Western musical heritage. Psalms (from Hebrew scripture; *see* BIBLE) and hymns have had a more popular and congregational role. Members of both Eastern and Western churches wrote them to teach doctrine and inspire devotion; and they came to have an accepted place in the EUCHARIST. PURITANISM preferred psalms, as divinely inspired, but hymns eventually became a staple element in Protestant worship. Major contributors included Martin Luther (1483–1546), Isaac Watts (1674–1748; *see* CONGREGATIONALISM) and Charles Wesley (1707–88; *see* METHODISM). Their strong theology and felicitous language degenerated in the 19th century into vagueness and sentimentality, notably in REVIVALISM. Religious songs of black Christians had stronger existential roots in slave experience. Modern church music and hymns reflect most levels of contemporary style and taste. [111; 167]

Church of Christ [xxvIII] More traditional Churches of Christ are anxious not to be confused with the worldwide branches of the Boston Church of Christ, an offshoot of the 1967 'Crossroads Movement' [42: 535–6], which are frequently known by the name of a city or town – such as the London (or Birmingham) Church of Christ. Strongly evangelical, with a heavy emphasis on baptism being essential for salvation, the movement expects a zealous commitment from its members. Members have 'Disciplers' to instruct them in their beliefs and monitor their actions. Those who do not live up the movement's strict expectations are liable to be expelled. [5: 186–8]

Church of Scientology [xxvIII] Founded in 1954, the Church of Scientology is based on the teachings of L. Ron Hubbard (1911–86), a successful science fiction writer who invented 'Dianetics' [30]. Although having a mind and body, the individual is considered to be essentially a 'Thetan' – a soul or spirit of an immortal nature which goes from life to life. Scientologists say that their principal sacrament is 'auditing', the purpose of which is to 'clear' the Thetan of past painful experiences [66: xII]. A device called an E-meter is used by auditors to help them locate the 'engrams' or

blockages that are causing problems. The movement, which claimed over 10,000 staff members worldwide by 1990 [17: 458], offers a wide range of courses, is associated with a drug rehabilitation programme called Narconon [17: 470] and actively lobbies against what it perceives as social ills, particularly in the field of mental health. There is a long history of criticism from certain ex-members and the CULT-WATCHING movement [41: 196–9]. In 1968 the British government imposed restrictions on foreigners entering the UK to study or work for Scientology; these were lifted in 1980 after a government inquiry (the Foster Report). [5: 173–4; 6: 51–60; 11: v; 41: IV/B; 42: 744–7; 74; 75: VI]

Church of the East [xIII.D] Paradoxically, the church whose network straddled the largest area on the medieval globe was banned as heretical from the Christian empire of the Romans. Seven years before the Third Ecumenical COUNCIL (Ephesus, 431 CE) the Christian subjects of the rival Persian empire declared allegiance to the 'Katholikos' (bishop of Seleucia-Ctesiphon, the Persian capital) and independence from the Patriarch of Antioch in Syria. Branded unfairly as man-worshippers for their opposition to the Third Council, they were tarred with the same brush as Nestorius, the victim of that Council. In reality the Persian school of theology followed that of Antioch; for them, the Exegete *par excellence* was Theodore of Mopsuestia (d. 428). This school flourished at Edessa in Mesopotamia until 489; but in 457 it was divided and the Antiochene theologians under the poet Narsai (d. 503) established themselves outside the Roman Empire, at Nisibis. Theodore's work (which stressed the historicity of Scripture) was translated into Syriac, the Aramaic dialect of Edessa, and explained by Narsai and his successors. The School of Nisibis was superseded by that of Baghdad, which was founded in 830 and sponsored by the Muslim government, with the purpose of making the wisdom of the Greeks accessible to Arab scholars and scientists.

The Nestorian Monument is a large standing stone discovered near Hsi-an Fu in the 17th century with an inscription in Chinese and Syriac documenting the activities of the Church of the East in China in the 7th and 8th centuries, until 781. Five hundred years later a Chinese monk of the same church made his way from Peking to Paris and returned to Rome, where he failed to persuade the Pope to launch a new crusade against the Mamelukes with Mongol cooperation. From China to Persia the Church of the East was dependent on the tolerance of the Mongols; its network mirrored that of east–west trade and extended as far as southern India. In steady decline since the 14th century and briefly invigorated by Anglican missionaries in the 19th, the church survives, racked by strife, in a diaspora to which Chicago and London have become essential. The Assyrian Orthodox Church, to designate it by its chosen name, once had 230 bishops; barely a tenth of that number remains today. [6; 105; 110; 113; 114; 115; 118; 120; 121]

Church Organization [XIII.B] ROMAN CATHOLICISM, ANGLICANISM and the Orthodox churches (*see* EASTERN ORTHODOX CHURCH) have a hierarchical organization. For the first two the basic unit is the parish (usually a village or area of a town) [157: 1032–3]. Parishes are grouped in 'dioceses' [157: 404] under a bishop; and groups of dioceses in a province under an archbishop as 'metropolitan'. The cathedral as the chief church of the diocese and 'seat' (*cathedra*) of the bishop is usually governed by a 'chapter' of 'canons' (always priests) led by a 'dean'. In Roman Catholicism the structure is headed by the Pope (*see* PAPACY); but in the Orthodox church the

principle of autocephaly obtains. Systems of organization in PROTESTANTISM vary greatly. PRESBYTERIANISM and METHODISM have relatively centralized systems of local, regional and national representative bodies. Some Lutheran churches (*see* LUTHERANISM), MORAVIANISM and METHODISM in the USA have bishops, but without regarding them as a higher order of MINISTRY. CONGREGATIONALISM and the BAPTISTS have historically emphasized the independence of the local church. Most of the main Protestant bodies and Anglicanism have developed world representative bodies for consultation. (Cf. also COUNCILS.)

Church Universal and Triumphant [XXVIII] Founded as the Summit Lighthouse in Washington, DC in 1958 by Mark Prophet (1918–73), the Church Universal and Triumphant was incorporated in 1974 by his widow, Elizabeth Clare Prophet (1940–), who is now known to her followers as Mother or Guru Ma, and who acts as God's messenger, receiving revelations and instructions from the Ascended Masters, who include St Germain, Buddha, Jesus and the Archangels. The Church owns the 33,000-acre Royal Teton Ranch in Montana, where 500 members live and work, and where conferences of several thousand international 'Keepers of the Flame' meet and 'decree' – a prayer of rapid chanting which committed members practise daily. [5: 211–12; 41: IV/C; 42: 800–1; 50]

Circumcision (in Islam) [XIX] Though popularly regarded as one of the touchstones of the true believer, neither male circumcision nor female excision has any warrant in the QUR'AN. However, they were obviously ancient Near Eastern practices, and were soon hallowed by Muslim tradition as part of the SUNNA, so that male circumcision became regarded both as an initiation ceremony into the Islamic community and as a rite of passage into adult society. Normally, the operation is performed on boys after the age of seven or eight years and before the onset of puberty – in more advanced societies with a local anaesthetic – and is accompanied by festivities [38 'Khitān'; 48: 161; 67 s.v.; 77: II; 80: 251–2]

Circumcision (in Judaism) [xxII]
The rite of circumcision, *berit milah*, performed on Jewish male children and converts to JUDAISM, represents the sign of the COVENANT between God and the seed of Abraham (*Gen.* 17: 11). Circumcision takes place on the eighth day after birth, even if the day is a Sabbath (SHABBAT) or festival (CHAGIM), but may be delayed for health reasons. The child is placed momentarily on a chair set aside for the prophet Elijah, who is thought to attend every circumcision ceremony, and then on the lap of the person who holds the child, the *sandek* or godfather. Circumcision is performed by a *mohel* or trained circumcisor. He removes the foreskin of the penis with a sharp knife, then tears back the underlying membrane. The blood is sucked from the wound, either by mouth or in more modern times through the use of a glass tube to prevent infection. A celebratory meal follows. [14 vol. 5: 567; 64: 401; 70: 134]

Classic Maya [xxv] Among Mesoamerican cultures, the Classic Maya (200–900 CE) developed the most brilliant and complex religious traditions, expressed in elaborate networks of lavishly constructed ceremonial centres in southern Mesoamerica [9: VI, VII]. Classic Mayan cities were marked by a flowering of exquisite sculpture, monumental architecture, predictive sciences and religious ritual [4: III, IV; 11: VII, VIII].

Mayan culture was run by priestly and royal hierarchies which directed the social order through an elaborate ceremonial system of temporal cycles and renewals. Among their most outstanding achievements were their writing system, mathematical precision and astronomical observation. These developments were utilized in the worship of time, *kinh* (also signifying sun or day), which was measured in minute detail. *Kinh* and all important dimensions of life were recorded in a hieroglyphic writing system [13], still little understood, consisting of a hybrid mixture of pictographs, ideographs and syllabic forms which narrated calendric, historical and dynastic activities. This writing system survives in three codices, the *Codex Madrid*, the *Codex Dresden* and the *Codex Paris* (*see* CODEX (MESOAMERICAN)), in numerous temple inscriptions and on ceremonial architecture. The Mayan priesthood developed a mathematical system based on the concept of zero and positional notation, which was developed to measure astronomical cycles with precision [5: VII]. Time was computed through the intermeshing of a 260-day calendar with a 365-day calendar, both of which were renewed every 52 years. In this larger calendar system, each day was named for its position in both calendars. The Mayan solar calendar was more exact than the Gregorian year (brought from Europe in the 16th century) This great computation of sacred time had a fixed starting-point at 3113 BCE and prophesied the end of the universe in 2011 CE.

The Mayan cosmos was organized into 13 heavenly compartments and nine levels in the underworld where the nine gods of the underworld ruled. Horizontally, the earth had four quarters surrounding a central region (CEMANAHUAC). This universe had been destroyed and created a number of times. Among the most important deities reigning in this cosmos were Itzamna, the creator-god who fertilized the universe, Ah Kin, the sun-god, Ix Chel, the moon-goddess, and the Chacs, or rain-gods (*see* TLALOC).

Codex (Mesoamerican) [xxv] (10th–16th centuries CE) One of the most important sources for the study of MESOAMERICAN RELIGIONS is the surviving picture books from the Mayan (*see* CLASSIC MAYA), Mixtec and Aztec regions which carry examples of the writing system, consisting of pictographs and ideographs with different degrees of phoneticism [17: XII]. These codices carry narrative drawings consisting of pictures of gods [19: 107, 135], processions, battles, sacrifices, buildings, places and celestial events as well as ideograms associated with ideas and symbolic systems [11]. This writing system is also found in low-relief sculpture such as the CALENDAR STONE, the Tizoc Stone and the Teocalli de la Guerra Sagrada (*see* AZTEC SCULPTURE).

Mesoamerican codices include manuscripts called *tiras* (strips of animal skin or paper), or screenfolds called *amoxtlacuilolli* (which were folded *tiras*, long strips composed of sheets of animal skin or paper glued together), rolls and *lienzos* or canvas sheets on which paintings appeared. These manuscripts depicted a series of celestial or human events which were read and interpreted, with some flexibility, by oral specialists trained in the tradition. Every significant human event was influenced by consultation with the specialist in charge of these manuscripts. Surviving pre-Conquest codices fall into two categories: historical–genealogical books and ritual–divinatory books. Ritual–divinatory manuscripts like the *Codex Madrid*, *Codex Vaticanus B* and *Codex Borgia* depicted sacred almanacs (*Tonalpohualli*), divinities, divination and prophecies of future events. One codex even covers such topics as bee-keeping, rain-making, crop care and diseases. Historical–genealogical books like the *Codex Bodley* and *Codex Colombino* pictured the

history of kings and dynastic genealogies. The native pictorial tradition was transmitted into the post-Conquest culture and appears in the *Codex Mendoza* which, accompanied by Spanish glosses, pictures the history, tribute and daily life of the Aztec capital, Tenochtitlan. [15]

Communion [XIII.C] A term used in several contexts in Christianity.
(1) A synonym for the EUCHARIST.
(2) The act of receiving the consecrated bread and wine.
(3) The communion of saints, the fellowship of all Christians in heaven and on earth.
(4) A specific Christian church or family of churches, e.g. EASTERN ORTHODOX CHURCH or ANGLICANISM.
(5) To be in communion with a church indicates mutual recognition and acceptance of the SACRAMENTS and MINISTRY of respective churches.

Conciliar Movement [XIII.B] The Great Schism (1378 CE) between rival Popes (*see* PAPACY) was officially ended by the COUNCIL of Constance (1417 CE). Several reforming Councils (whose doctrine was typical of the Conciliar Movement) then upheld the doctrine that final authority in the church lies in a General Council. Though condemned by the papacy, the tradition of questioning the final authority of the Pope persisted until Vatican Council I (1869–70). [19: 135–7; 45; 157: 326]

Confucian Canon [XII] This achieved its present form (comprising the Five Classics and the Four Books) in the Sung dynasty under the direction of Chu Hsi (1130–1200 BCE). During the Former Han dynasty (206 BCE–9 CE) controversy arose between the Old Character school (*Ku Wen Chia*), which used editions of the Classics that had purportedly survived

Emperor Ch'in Shih Huang Ti's burning of the books in 213 BCE, and the New Character school (*Chin Wen Chia*), who used the editions of the Classics rewritten in the reformed script after the Ch'in persecutions [35: II, III, IV].

The Five Classics are:

(1) The *Shu Ching* (Classic of History), which is a collection of documents, speeches and counsels made by Chinese rulers and ministers purporting to date from the legendary rulers Yao and Shun to the early Chou dynasty (1000 BCE). Many of the supposedly older documents actually date from the Later Han dynasty (23–220 CE) [56; 66].

(2) The *Shih Ching* (Classic of Odes), a collection of 300 poems and songs dating mainly from the early Chou dynasty (1027–402 BCE) [57; 67; 103].

(3) The *I Ching* (Classic of Changes), a collection of texts on divination based on a set of 64 hexagrams made by various combinations of broken and unbroken lines reflecting the relationship between the two basic forces in nature and human society (YIN–YANG). Each hexagram is determined by casting 49 yarrow stalks, and each has a short cryptic interpretation. These have subsequently been expanded in the 'wings' or appendices, which are attributed to CONFUCIUS but which date from the Former Han dynasty [118].

(4) The *Ch'un Ch'iu* (Spring and Autmn Annals), extracts from the history of the state of Lu from 722 to 484 BCE, said to have been compiled by Confucius. They are accompanied by commentaries which date from before 200 BCE [68].

(5) The *Li Ching* (Classic of Rites), a collection of three books on the LI (Rites of Propriety): the *Chou Li* (Rites of Chou); *I Li* (Ceremonies and Rites); and *Li Chi* (Record of Rites). Although compiled during the Former Han dynasty, parts of these texts are much more ancient [69; 96].

The Four Books are: the *Lun Yu* (Analects) of Confucius, the *Chung Yung* (Doctrine of the Mean), *Ta Hsueh* (Great Learning) and the *Meng Tzu* (MENCIUS). [17a: III, 55–7; 51; 61; 62; 64; 99: 123–6]

Confucian State Cult [XII] The transformation of CONFUCIUS from a practical moralist, political adviser and educator into a focus of worship and eventually of a state cult was a complex process. There is an unsubstantiated tradition that Duke Ai of Lu built a temple in honour of the sage shortly after his death. The historian Ssu Ma-ch'ien (140–87 BCE) records that the Han Emperor Kao Tsu visited the temple in 195 BCE and offered sacrifices to the sage [92: VII, 93–7]. The first mention of a regular cult of Confucius apart from his veneration by descendants was during the reign of Kuang Wu of the later Han dynasty. He sent a minister to sacrifice at Confucius' grave in 29 CE and eight years later he granted titles to two descendants of Confucius [92: VII, 103–4]. In 59 CE the Emperor Ming Ti ordered that sacrifices should be made to Confucius in government schools. He visited the K'ung family ancestral temple at Ch'u Fu and made sacrifices to the Sage. Two later Han emperors followed his example. During the T'ang dynasty (618–907 CE) the examination system based on the Confucian Classics (*see* CONFUCIAN CANON), which had started in the Former Han dynasty (206 BCE–9 CE) was developed further as a method of selecting officials for office. Temples in honour of Confucius were built in all major towns, and the cult continued to flourish in the later dynasties. In 1530 CE, during the Ming dynasty (1368–1644 CE) Emperor Chia Ching, influenced by the rationalist wing of neo-Confucianism, reformed the state cult of Confucius. He simplified the titles of Confucius and the ceremonies, and replaced the images of the Sage with inscribed tablets. The Manchu rulers of the Ch'ing dynasty (1644–1911) carried out further reforms, but the cult declined after the founding of the Chinese Republic in 1912.

Confucius [xii] K'ung Fu Tzu (551–479 BCE). The best known and probably most influential thinker in Chinese history. He was born of an impoverished noble family in the state of Lu, now Shantung Province. At the age of 20 he began his official career as keeper of the grain stores. According to most accounts he became prime minister of Lu in 501 BCE, although this is unlikely, and he is said to have resigned from office four years later because he disapproved of the ruler's policies. For the next 13 years he wandered from state to state attempting to advise different feudal rulers and gaining a small following of disciples. He eventually returned to Lu to spend the rest of his life teaching [7: ii, 14–48; 17a: iii, 51–61; 19: iii, 39–59; 20; 34: iv, 43–75).

The most reliable source for Confucius' own ideas are the Analects or 'Selected Sayings' (*Lun Yu*), the earliest parts of which were composed shortly after his death [105].

Confucius was primarily an educator and a transmitter of knowledge rather than a creative thinker. In accepting students he did not apply any class distinctions, accepting the poor as well as the rich [105: vii, 124]. One of his major contributions was the redefinition of key ideas in Chinese life and thought along ethical and humanistic lines. The term *chun tzu*, literally meaning 'son of a ruler' or person of noble birth, was extended by Confucius to refer to anyone who was benevolent and modest of speech. Similarly he extended the use of the term Li (rites of propriety), which traditionally referred to the rules of proper conduct in anything from formal ritual procedure to detailed matters of etiquette. For Confucius, *Li* referred primarily to the correct spirit in which ritual and social behaviour should be conducted, and this involved cultivating an attitude of respect and restraint [39: i, 9–31; 105: viii, 132]. Confucius clearly regarded Heaven (T'IEN) as a positive and personal force in the universe [105: vii, 127, xiv, 189]: he was not, as some have supposed, an agnostic and a sceptic. His important contribution to political thought was his insistence on the identification of ethics with politics. He believed that government was primarily a matter of moral responsibility and was not simply the manipulation of power. [92; 95; 105: ii, 88, xii, 168]

Congregationalism [xiii.b] Churches historically emphasizing government through officers elected by the membership, and the independence (hence the name 'Independents') of each local church. In later times associations of churches developed for cooperation. Membership was defined in terms of a 'gathered church' of believers bound by a 'covenant'. Congregationalism strongly influenced the founders of the New England colonies (notably the 'Pilgrim Fathers') and the USA has continued to be a major centre [2: ix]. The majority of English Congregationalists and PRESBYTERIANS formed the United Reformed Church in 1972, but some Congregationalists continued as a separate church. Originally CALVINIST in doctrine, later Congregationalism has often been open to influence from LIBERAL PROTESTANTISM. [62 vol. 3: 42–5; 157: 332; 199]

Conjure [iii] A method of treatment and control found in black communities in the Americas and the Caribbean. The control is exerted by a negative practitioner in magic, who uses WITCHCRAFT, for instance, in gaining control of a man's double spirit (*see* DUPPIE/JUMBIE). Conjure may be part of an alternative health system where 'root medicine' from the traditional pharmocopaeia may be used alongside folk psychotherapies. Alternatively the conjurer may deal with magical transformations. In some ways he/she may parallel the functions of the *bocor* in VOODOO, or the *root doctor* in the southern states of the USA, who specializes in folk therapies which syncretize knowledge from Africa and the Americas. Tales told by slaves of African descent in the USA frequently subverted the powers of the slave owners, and those which involve transformations are also 'conjure' tales. [1; 25; 45; 86]

Conservative Judaism [XXII] A modern movement within JUDAISM concentrated mostly in North America. Conservatism began with early 19th-century responses to modernity in Central Europe. Jewish intellectuals, like Z. Frankel (1801–75), who were unhappy with wholesale reforms of Jewish life, wished to preserve elements of the tradition. They founded the so-called 'Historical School', whose purpose was to introduce changes into Judaism which were consonant with Jewish historical development. This attitude was transferred to the USA by traditionally minded immigrants, who established the Jewish Theological Seminary (1887) in New York to train RABBIS in a modern approach to tradition. Solomon Schechter (1847–1915) was brought over from England to head the seminary in 1902. An organization of Conservative rabbis, the Rabbinical Assembly of America, was formed at this time, followed by the association of Conservative congregations, the United Synagogue of America (1913). Conservative Judaism spread rapidly until it became the largest formal association of Jews, overtaking both REFORM and Orthodox Judaism [65: 254]. In 1922 a member of the seminary staff, Rabbi M. Kaplan, founded a more radical branch of Conservative Judaism known as 'Reconstructionism'. This has now

become a completely separate religious movement. [11; 14 vol. 5: 901; 19: 285; 21; 25; 44; 56: XIII, XIV]

Conversion (to Judaism) [XXII] Someone intending conversion to JUDAISM would at first be discouraged by a traditional Jewish law court (Bet Din). Should they persevere they would be expected to study Jewish teaching and familiarize themselves with religious practices. The ceremony of conversion (*giyur*) involves circumcision for the male and bathing (*tevilah*) in a ritual bath (*mikveh*) for both males and females. They are then considered as full Jews [11; 14 vol. 13: 1182; 60]. In REFORM JUDAISM conversion involves a simpler ceremony [70: 15].

Convince Cult [III] A very old form of MYALISM, found in Jamaica. It appeared just before emancipation (1833) which abolished slavery in British territories, and before the American Baptist missionaries had arrived. It appears that a sign of conversion is a fainting away. This physical sign is taken as a sign of 'convince'/genuine conversion. It is also known as Convince Fankee, and its adherents are Bongomen. Bongomen take their name from the spirits who possess them during devotions. These are of minor significance, influencing everyday life rather than having any cosmic stature. They may be departed Convince members, or ancestors. Since Myalism and MAROON religions have similarities, Convince may have arisen from one or other of them, or indeed from their interaction. It does not pay great attention to God the Father and the Son because they are thought to be too distant and inaccessible. It is thought that the strongest spirits come from dead slaves and Maroons. The next most powerful are dead *obeahmen* (see OBEAH). The behaviour of these spirits has many of the characteristics of other cults which syncretize Amerindian, African and Christian religions. Possession is central to ceremonies. Spirits are called down by drumming, and a spirit 'mounts' the devotee, as if he were a horse, and 'rides' the possessed person with great vigour (*see* VOODOO). Appropriate rituals are carried out for each spirit, and it is said that spirits use a particular form of English. In worship Christian elements are incorporated in the form of Bible readings and hymns, as well as calls to Bongo spirits, and call and response songs. The latter draw in style from the typical African pattern of a leader 'calling', and the congregation 'responding' to him, thus creating an antiphonal effect. [2]

Coptic Christianity [XIII.D] Tradition attributes the first evangelization of Egypt to St Mark. From an early period the Pope of Alexandria, chief bishop of Africa, stood second only to the Roman Pope in the Christian hierarchy, and ALEXANDRIA became a major centre of Christian learning. The Egyptian church dates its calendar from the 'Year of the Martyrs' (284 CE) in which Pope St Peter died, as the 'Seal of the Martyrs' in the last great persecution under Diocletian. Christian MONASTICISM first developed in an organized form in Egyptian Thebaid.

When the ARIAN controversy led to the use of COUNCILS to establish a state orthodoxy in the now Christian Roman empire, the Alexandrian Patriarchs Athanasius and Cyril became symbols of orthodoxy in their fight against Arius and Nestorius respectively. Loyalty to the exact formulae used by Cyril led the Egyptians to oppose the majority at the Council of Chalcedon (451 CE) and to adopt Monophysite doctrine. With imperial support a second line of (EASTERN ORTHODOX) PATRIARCHS was established who won support in the powerful Greek community, but not among the Copts, the native Egyptians. Both churches

survive today, together with smaller but important EASTERN CATHOLIC counterparts. Coptic, the last stage of the ancient Egyptian language, is still used in church services, and the Coptic church has preserved a version of the ancient Egyptian calender (*see* CALENDAR, CHRISTIAN). Under ISLAM the Copts survived and developed an important Arabic Christian literature. The election of a Copt, Boutros Boutros Ghali, as Secretary General of the United Nations from 1 January 1992 has widened awareness of the Coptic community. There is a growing Coptic church in America, Europe, Britain and Australasia. In recent years improving relations with the Eastern Orthodox have resulted in mutual recognition and acceptance. [6; 7; 35] (*See also* ETHIOPIAN CHRISTIANITY; NUBIAN CHRISTIANITY.)

Corinth, Early Christianity at [XIII.A] Corinth, refounded as a Roman colony in 44 BCE, was first evangelized by PAUL *c*.50 CE. He spent about 18 months there and built up a large and gifted, if volatile, CHURCH. Most of the problems inherent in the Christianization of pagans were evident in Corinth and are treated in Paul's Letters to the Corinthians. Further problems arose *c*.96 CE, when internal strife in the Corinthian church called forth an admonition from Clement, writing from Rome. [6: 248–79; 11: I, 1134–9; 15]

Corroboree [XXIX] A term used in Australian English for any Aboriginal festive gathering involving singing and dancing (*see also* SINGSING). The word was first used by 19th-century settlers in New South Wales, and was presumably borrowed from some local dialect. Because it covers sacred ceremonies and non-sacred entertainments alike, it is not a useful word in religious studies. In AUSTRALIAN RELIGION, religious ceremonies are ritual enactments of myths accompanied by song and dance, every movement being symbolic and meaningful, performed on sacred ground specially painted and marked for the occasion, as are the performers themselves. Non-religious dramatic performances with singing and dancing are for public entertainment and even instruction, as they sometimes include comment on social issues. The best-known instrument for musical accompaniment is the *didjeridu*, a long hollow drone-pipe with a wax mouthpiece [4: 367–87; 28]

Cosmogony (Jewish) [xxii] The Pentateuch (*see* BIBLE) begins with the account of the creation of the world by God, and there are scattered references to the topic in other biblical books. In rabbinical literature (*see* RABBI) we already find some discussion of the idea that God created the world from nothing [14 vol. 5: 1059], and this theme of creation *ex nihilo* predominates in the work of the medieval theologians. Most of the latter reject the various notions of a pre-existing matter advocated by Greek philosophy [30: 94]. It is even stressed that creation *ex nihilo* is an essential part of Jewish doctrine (*see* THEISM) [28: 413]. Side by side with the philosophical interpretation of creation there were a number of medieval mystical teachings of a rather different nature. These see the created world as the end-product of a complicated process of emanation in which the unlimited Godhead, or *Ein Sof*, reveals Himself through ten stages or *sefirot* [61: 25] (*see* SEFIRAH). These stages represent continuity between the human and divine worlds.

Cosmology (Amerindian) [v] The wide variety of cosmogonic myths, the diversity of subsistence patterns, and the ever-present possibility of non-Indian influence upon aboriginal beliefs and practices make it difficult to generalize regarding AMERINDIAN RELIGIONS and their world-views. One may note, however, that Native American religions have usually placed greater emphasis upon action in this world than upon other-worldly speculations. The physical universe (although its origin is often a matter of conjecture; *see* CREATION MYTHS) is generally accepted as the proper arena of human existence and the context in which humanity is to realize its fullest development. Yet interpenetrating the visible, everyday world is its invisible, sacred, and powerful complement (*see* MANITOU). Although conceptions of transcendent deities are not unknown (e.g. among the SIOUX), greater emphasis is usually placed upon the possibility of human interaction with the supernatural through the medium of this world. Human life is conceived of as placed within a context of interlocking relationships wherein the divine, human, animal and vegetative forms influence one another (*see* e.g. OWNER OF THE ANIMALS). Thus there is a corresponding concern to discover these relationships and to establish correct patterns of behaviour in order to preserve the network and thereby realize fertility, long life and social stability (*see* CALENDAR ROUND). Rather than a sharp distinction between the sacred and profane, Amerindian religions emphasize a continuity of existence; rituals, individual or collective, are thus directed to the control of cosmic forces and the influence of personal fate. [23: viii, x, xi, xiii]

Cosmology (Ancient Near Eastern) [viii] SUMERIAN cosmology [24: 37–57] became the foundation of many Near Eastern concepts. The Sumerians speculated that the major components of the universe were heaven (a vaulted, hollow space) and earth (a flat disc) which existed, immovably, in a boundless sea from which the universe had come into being. Between heaven and earth was the atmosphere, from which the sun, moon and stars were fashioned [16: 127–52]. The separation of heaven and earth and the creation of the planets were followed by plant, animal and human life. Invisible, immortal gods guided and controlled this universe, according to prescribed rules.

Deities were immortal and sustained high moral values [16: 154], but they could also be negligent, ill or wounded, and even die [13: 157]. Whether city-gods or state-deities, they tended to represent the elements of nature (moon, sun, weather, agriculture) and the underworld. Many early Mesopotamian deities survived in Assyria or were introduced into the HITTITE pantheon through the HURRIANS. All had human forms and were attributed with human needs (see ISLAND OF CREATION; TEMPLES (ANCIENT NEAR EASTERN)).

Cosmology (Christian) [XIII.B] The early and medieval Christian picture of the universe largely follows Aristotle (384–322 BCE) and Ptolemy (85–160 CE), with additional material from the BIBLE. The heavens and the earth are taken to be created out of nothing by GOD. The earth was seen as the centre of several transparent concentric spheres which carried the sun, moon, planets and stars. Hell lay below or within the earth, and heaven beyond the outermost sphere (cf. AFTERLIFE (CHRISTIAN VIEW OF)). The lower reaches of heaven were the home of angels and saved souls, the uppermost area the home of God himself. The nature of heaven and hell and the life of souls there were variously pictured. Heaven, for example, was seen as a paradise garden and an idealized city, and various views were held of the relationships between souls and their placing in heaven. Some held that the earth would be renewed for a period before its destruction at the end of time. The development of scientific cosmology in the 17th century, dis-

placing the earth from the centre of the universe, did much to destroy this ancient picture. In the West, attempts to give 'scientific' explanations of the traditional pictures of the universe and of the earth were increasingly replaced by a decline of speculation about the location of heaven and hell and a tendency instead to concentrate on the nature of the afterlife and the fate of souls. [I.7 vol. 4: 74–107; 62 vol. 4: 74–107; 129; 154 vol. 4: 163]

Cosmology (South American) [XXIII] The complex spatial and temporal constructions of South American cosmologies permit only the broadest of generalizations. Vertical structures of the universe vary widely in composition from three-layer arrangements to the massive nine-layered cosmos, on the model of a whirling spindle, of the KOGI. Generally, upper worlds are associated with the creative and life-renewing principles of light, lightness and liquids (rivers, lakes); underworlds, with places of the souls of the dead; and this earth, with the centre of the universe and the locus of human life. Different kinds of space and places of being in the universe are systematically associated with one another so as to constitute a whole. Horizontal space highlights the centre (or centres), associated with a plethora of images (cosmic tree, mountain, ladder, vine, pillar) symbolizing communication between spatial planes; the periphery, or outer margin, which often expresses in altered form the same values found in the centre; and a variety of mediating elements, openings and penetrations connecting inner and outer realms. The places where sacred being first appears often become the model for innumerable constructs of space.

South American cultures recognize multiple kinds and units of time independently of chronological history. Cosmic, astrological and sonic cycles, the seasonal ripening of fruits, the appearance of animal species, etc., all represent different modes of time. Festival rounds, ordered in calendric cycles, maintain the order of the universe, reenacting the mythic events that created temporal order in the first place (*see* CREATION MYTHS). Here, distinct cycles of time are interwoven: solar and lunar cycles, rainy and dry seasons, flower cycles, the cycle of song and sounds, the human life-cycle, and periodic manifestations of emotions and colours. Ritual music, above all, is the symbol of complex time, transforming spaces into dynamic containers of changing life. Ritual drunkenness, combat and noise, all prominent aspects in religious festivities, refer to temporal constructs rooted in the primordium and its demise. [33: II; 26; 35]

Cosmos [XVI] Order, universe. The Greeks believed that the universe was ordered. Cosmic order, identified with justice (*dike*), was a fundamental concept. Cosmogonic myths took the form of theogonies. In the earliest (8th century BCE) and most influential, the original entity was Chaos. Then came Gaia (Earth) and other beings like Eros (Love). Gaia had many children from her son Ouranos (Sky), including the Titans. One Titan, Kronos, castrated and dethroned his father and became world ruler. He was himself dethroned by his son Zeus (*see* THEOI), whose rule was challenged by the *Gigantes* (Giants), Gaia's sons, whom the 'new' gods, Zeus and his contemporaries, defeated with Heracles' (*see* HEROES) help. Orphic (*see* ORPHEUS) theogonies diverged from the mainstream. Central was the murder by the Titans of the future world ruler Dionysos-Zagreus, Zeus' son, later reborn as Dionysos (*see* THEOI). [17: 318–20; 20: 113–19; 25: 73, 215–17; 38]

Councils of the Church [XIII.B] Official meetings of bishops and others at various levels of the Christian CHURCH to settle doctrine or discipline; at lower levels usually called 'synods'. General (Ecumenical) Councils represent the whole church. In ROMAN CATHOLICISM they are considered valid and infallible if summoned and confirmed by the PAPACY (but cf. CONCILIAR MOVEMENT). They recognize 21 such Councils. These include Nicea (325 CE), on ARIANISM and the TRINITY; Chalcedon (451), which summed up the limits of orthodoxy in CHRISTOLOGY; Constance (1414–17), which settled the Great Schism in the West; Trent (1545–63), which was concerned with the COUNTER-REFORMATION; the First Vatican Council (1869–70), which focused on the Papacy; and the Second Vatican Council (1962–5) [1], which wrestled with the modernization of Roman Catholicism. The Orthodox churches (*see* EASTERN ORTHODOX CHURCH) believe that Ecumenical Councils cannot err, nor is papal sanction necessary for them. They generally recognize seven as authoritative, but Monophysites only the first three and Nestorians the Council of Nicea. ANGLICANISM and PROTESTANTISM recognize the AUTHORITY of the first four Councils in varying degrees. [102]

Counter-Reformation [XIII.B] Also termed, more positively, the Catholic Reformation, this was a 16th-century movement of reform in ROMAN CATHOLICISM and a movement of defence and counter-attack against the REFORMATION. Doctrine was redefined and discipline reformed at the COUNCIL of Trent (1545–63) [19: 261–9]. The PAPACY recovered respect and authority. New religious orders (*see* MONASTICISM), notably the Jesuits [19: 258–60; 157: 734–6], encouraged MISSIONS and pastoral activity. Notable mystics appeared in Spain, e.g. St Teresa of Avila (1515–82) and St John of the Cross (1542–91) (*see* MYSTICISM). HERESY was repressed by the special tribunals of the Roman and Spanish Inquisitions [113] and the 'Index' (an official list of prohibited books) [157: 697]. Catholic princes strengthened the church politically against PROTES-TANTISM. [37: VIII; 53; 99]

Covenant [XIII.A] According to the BIBLE, from the time of Moses (*c.*1200 BCE) Israel considered itself to be a covenant community, bound to GOD by a solemn agreement in which he undertook to be their God and they undertook to be his obedient people. This covenant, which included the 'ten commandments', was their national constitution (*see* TORAH). In form it resembled the treaties between Near Eastern kings and their vassals. From time to time the people were recalled (as by the prophets) to their covenant loyalty. The reformation under King Josiah (621 BCE), based on the law code in the biblical book *Deuteronomy*, was a covenant renewal. The prophet Jeremiah's prediction of a new covenant (*c.*587 BCE) was taken up both in the QUMRAN community and in the Christian CHURCH, each of which regarded itself as the community of the new covenant, Israel restored. [11: I, 1179–1202]

Cow [XVII] For Hindus the killing of a cow is a serious crime. The ARTHA-*shastra* refers to the killing of cattle as a crime worthy of death, but this may refer only to royal cattle [12: 196–7]. Nevertheless, reverence for the cow (whose five products, milk, curd, butter, urine and dung, are regarded as purifiers) has grown steadily from the time of the BHAGA-VADGITA, to the extent that Gandhi (1869–1948) regarded it as part of the essence of HINDUISM. [138: 185; 131 vol. 1: 255–8]

Creation Myths (Amerindian) [V] Cosmogony is one of the major themes of North American Indian mythology. The possibility of early European influence cannot be dis-counted. A survey of the more than 300 major variations reveals the presence of seven primary symbolic types: earth-diver; world-parent; emergence; spider-creator; creation by conflict or theft; creation from a cosmic giant; and the creator pair. [20] The earth-diver motif (most common throughout North America) attributes creation to an animal-like figure who dives to the bottom of a primeval ocean to retrieve mud or sand from which a somewhat fragile cosmos is shaped; its completion is usually left to a CULTURE HERO or TRICKSTER. The world-parent motif (limited primarily to the south-west) develops the sexual relationship of sky-father and earth-mother so common elsewhere. The sexual act is preparatory to true creation, which usually occurs after their separation. Emergence myths (mainly in the south-west, and among some Plains Indians) portray a gradual metamorphosis of mankind, animals, etc., as they progress through successive worlds to entry into the present or final world. 'Spider'-creation narratives identify this figure as the first being, who spins the web upon which the world is suspended. Conflict myths (primarily in the west and north-west) attribute creation to the actions of a trickster figure who 'steals' or fights to gain control of the elemental factors of creation (sun, fire, earth, water). Less frequent is the motif of creation resulting from the redistribution of parts from the body of a fallen giant (there is some occurrence in the north-east and north-west). A seventh type, widely occurring, ascribes creation to the cooperation or competition of two primordial agents (HERO TWINS), variously represented as twin brothers, sisters, father–son, uncle–nephew, etc.

Creation Myths (South American) [XXIII] These may be grouped into three main scenarios, each of which includes a variety of themes.

In the first, creation springs from nothingness through the thought, dream or intention of divine, frequently supreme, beings, who later withdraw from creation after initiating its existence. In the second, perhaps the majority of cosmogonies, creation occurs through the transformations undertaken by primordial beings or a shifting succession of heroes, beginning with some prior state of affairs which undergoes transformation in the course of creation. In this scenario, one finds such themes as creation occurring through the pilgrimage and minstrel wandering of heroes; creation through the death of a primordial being which transforms or transfigures reality; creation through the sexual union of primordial progenitors, whose coupling produces creative transformations; and co creation where demiurges, CULTURE HEROES, TRICKSTERS and ancestors compete with one another or with the supreme being to complete creation. The third scenario marks the beginning of a new creative epoch with the cataclysmic destruction of the primordial world, one of the most important events in South American mythic history.

Countless narratives affirm the existence of other worlds that pre-exist the current one; each is imperfect and suffers catastrophic destruction by flood, fire, other natural disasters, putrefaction or petrifaction. From this destruction there arose a variety of SYMBOLS representing vehicles of SALVATION through which the new world would be created. At the same time as that catastrophe dispelled the chaotic, homogeneous and univocal existence of primordial beings, it produced periodicity, multivalent existence and systematic relatedness among multiple orders of being (animals, cardinal points and axes, colours, shapes, sounds). The primordial beings then took on hidden, partial, or periodic forms. Speech, sound and music appear,

rendering an ontological difference between primordial and mundane being. Human life, and the separate forms of multiple human experience, including existence in historical time, complete the scenario. Yet creation is not a closed account: the principles of divine order may occasionally intervene in history, offering the possibility that the status quo be obliterated in favour of a totally new order. [33: III, IV; 26; 31]

Creeds (Christian) [XIII.B] Short official statements of Christian belief, originally used at baptism (*see* SACRAMENTS). They are arranged in sections on Father, Son and Holy Spirit, with varying texts (*see* TRINITY). The so-called 'Apostles' Creed' [19: 23] was accepted in the West for use in baptismal liturgies and ordinary WORSHIP in ROMAN CATHOLICISM and ANGLICANISM. It has also been acceptable to a wide variety of other churches. The more elaborate Nicene Creed (based on that of the COUNCIL of Nicea) [19: 24–7] has been used at MASS or EUCHARIST. (Its *Filioque* clause, stating that the Holy Spirit proceeds from the Father and the Son, inserted later, was at first controversial even in the West and is rejected by the EASTERN ORTHODOX CHURCH.) The Athanasian Creed (of uncertain origin) is more elaborate in its CHRISTOLOGY and in modern times has been less used, because of its severe anathemas (formal exclusion from the church for HERESY). Early PROTESTANTISM produced 'Confessions of Faith' such as the Augsburg Confession (*see* LUTHERANISM) [19: 210–12] and Westminster Confession (*see* PRESBYTERIANISM) [19: 244–7]. The Thirty-Nine Articles had fulfilled a similar though more limited role for ANGLICANISM. In recent times (at least in Western Christianity) the traditional creeds and confessions of faith have often been radically reinterpreted or treated with far less respect as guides for doctrine, and some Christian churches (e.g. BAPTISTS) have generally been reluctant, even when strictly 'orthodox', to use formal creeds at all. [114: ix–xii]

Cremation (in Japan) [xxi] The priest Dosho (628–700 CE), an early introducer of Hosso sect (*see* NANTO ROKUSHU) practices who had studied under HSUAN TSANG in China, is the first recorded person to have been cremated in Japan, following a request made to his disciples. Cremation then received imperial sanction by Empress Jito, who was cremated in 704, a year after her death. In succeeding centuries the practice spread socially and geographically. Glass and inscribed gilt-bronze cinerary urns were later replaced as receptacles for the ashes by stone boxes and clay vessels. Following a medieval decline in the practice, perhaps because of the expense, it is now customarily carried out under BUDDHIST auspices, but is legally enforceable only in heavily populated areas.

Creole/Creolization [iii] The original meaning of Creole is 'one born away from home', and therefore the name may refer to a variety of peoples, different in origin, race, and geographical situation. The original Creoles came from west Africa. They were freed from slaving ships and landed at one of the fort areas, particularly in the Gambia, Sierra Leone, the Gold Coast and the Niger region. They had already lost their ethnic identity, since groups of individuals from a variety of tribes were sold together, and therefore the missionaries organized them into new communities. They were given or bought English names as they converted to Christianity. They formed an elite group along the west African coast, and in time others would join them and go through the process of creolization/assimilation. Out of such experience a particularly innovative and syncretic society would grow. Its characteristics were

adherence to CHRISTIANITY, westernization in dress and social manners, a high level of education, belief in a western legal system, and loyalty to the British Crown.

The Creoles in the Caribbean came from the slave-owner class, in that their children were 'born away from home' i.e. Britain or the other countries involved in Caribbean colonization. While wealthy slave-owners might return to the 'old' country, many of the plantation managers were not rich, and they would become permanent inhabitants of the Caribbean. Although they retained strong metropolitan links, these would become increasingly mythic, and in succeeding generations the Creole identity would become increasingly more ambiguous. The same level of syncretization between the culture of the slaves and that of their masters applied to all levels of culture and social relationships. Creolization became, and remains, particularly crucial in the realm of religion and language. In both cases it provides a manner of communicating either language or a religious belief-system where there was formerly no such possibility. Slaves were denied access to the master's language, and Europeanisms were of necessity grafted on to African structures and intonation. Parallel SYNCRETISMS occurred between Christianity and African religions.

It is useful in African–Caribbean religion and language to think of Creole as being a continuum, where people can function at several points along the line from Africa to Europe. Language, religion and worship always allow continuity and change. Just as the Creole speaker will generally be able to move along the continuum, having other language references, so the devotee may move along the religious continuum and select from more than one denomination, cult or religion. Choice may allow for the fact that denominations such as ANGLICANISM or ROMAN

CATHOLICISM may be status-rewarding, while African expressions provide greater possibilities for active participation in the decision-making of the church. In both language and religion there has been a tendency for adherents and outsiders alike to undervalue the strength of Creole institutions, which have been seen from the naturally distorting perspective of metropolitan cultures. [17; 36; 59; 74; 75; 96]

Crusades [XIII.B] European military expeditions to recover Christian holy places in Palestine from ISLAM. The First Crusade (1095 CE) captured JERUSALEM and established Christian states, which fell by 1291 despite further expeditions. Crusading motives included land hunger and commerce as well as religion. The fourth (1202–4) was diverted to capture Constantinople from the Byzantine Empire and dispossessed the EASTERN ORTHODOX CHURCH. Others attacked heretics (e.g. the Albigensians; *see* HERESY (MEDIEVAL CHRISTIAN)) and non-Christians in Europe. The crusades also produced military 'orders' (*see* MONASTICISM) such as the Hospitallers (*c.* 11th century) and KNIGHTS TEMPLAR (founded 1118 CE). [166; 171]

Culavamsa [XI] The 'Small' *vamsa* (or chronicle), a PALI work which takes up the narrative of the BUDDHIST history of Sri Lanka from the MAHAVAMSA (Great Chronicle). The *Culavamsa* deals with the period from 302 CE to the beginning of the 19th century, and is the work of at least three successive authors [57: 142]. It was translated into German by W. Geiger, and from German to English by C. M. Rickmers.

'Cult-Watching' Groups [XXVIII] Three overlapping but distinguishable groups have emerged since the 1970s to monitor the current wave of NEW RELIGIOUS MOVEMENTS (NRMs). The first is the 'anti-cult movement' (ACM), which covers a wide range of individuals and organizations concerned to expose and alert the public and governments to the perceived dangers of NRMs. The ACM began with parents who were anxious about their children's involvement with an NRM, but they were joined by 'deprogrammers' [5: XI, Ap.III; 12; 48], ex-members [29] and others interested in lobbying and helping those affected, either directly or indirectly, by the NRMs. There is now a network of anti-cult groups around the world which provide literature, speakers, 'exit counsellors' and 'expert witnesses'. Forcible deprogramming is illegal, but it continues to be practised for large sums of money by more extreme anti-cultists, although most of the groups officially promote 'exit counselling' without the use of physical coercion [29]. Many allegations made by anti-cultists are similar to those historically made about religions now generally considered socially respectable (e.g. CHRISTIANITY (EARLY), JUDAISM, METHODISM, ROMAN CATHOLICISM and the SALVATION ARMY). Allegations most frequently levelled at the contemporary NRMs include brainwashing or mind control [12; 22; 29], the splitting up of families [3: V], bizarre sexual practices, the amassing of large fortunes for leaders by exploited followers, tax evasion and political intrigue. Since the events surrounding the PEOPLE'S TEMPLE in 1978 [27], constant reference has been made to the possibility of mass suicide, with the deaths of Branch Davidians in Waco, USA in 1993 and of members of the Solar Temple in Canada and Switzerland in 1994 providing further ammunition for such fears. Among the most active and influential anti-cult organizations are the American Family Foundation and the Cult Awareness Network, both in the USA [11: XV; 13; 41: V/B; 44; 64; 65], L'Association pour la Défense de la Famille et de l'Individu (ADFI) in France, with affiliated branches elsewhere in

Europe, and Family Action Information and Rescue (FAIR) in England [4: xvii; 6: vii–ix].

Secondly, there is the 'counter-cult movement', consisting mainly of groups of Protestants, Catholics or Jews who are primarily concerned with exposing theological error in the hope of 'Evangelizing the Cults' [21; 41: v/A]. Examples include the Spiritual Counterfeits Movement in California, the Dialog Center in Aarhus (the Netherlands) and the Deo Gloria Trust in England [6: 227–30]. Since the 1980s, several counter-cult movements have been publicizing the alleged threat of a SATANIST conspiracy [54]. Not all members of traditional religions are necessarily opposed to the NRMs, some promoting the idea of dialogue [9].

Thirdly, there are groups closely associated with academics who have studied NRMs, their aim being to provide the public with objective information about the movements. Examples include the Institute for the Study of American Religion at the University of California, Santa Barbara [36; 41; 42; 43; 44], INFORM at the London School of Economics [5: Ap. I], CESNUR in Turin, RENNER at the University of Aarhus and CINR in Montreal. [59; 60; 64; 65]

Culture Hero (Amerindian) [v] Often the central figure in Amerindian myths, the culture hero continues the work of creation, transforming the landscape, regulating the cosmic patterns and defining the dimensions of nature and human existence (*see* CREATION MYTHS) [8: ii]. The figure frequently provides a link between the primordial time of beginning (e.g. the golden age of the past) and the present human condition. His actions (including teaching mankind necessary arts and crafts as well as instituting laws and ceremonies) serve as a bridge between the two periods [24: iv]. Numerous accounts portray the culture hero as having the form of an animal-being (raven, coyote and hare being common forms), while others speak of an anthropomorphic figure with SHAMAN-like powers, though the latter type is less frequent. Occasionally, the figure is placed in opposition to the supreme deity and through their interactions come the less desirable aspects of human life, including old age, disease, and death. The TRICKSTER-transformer presents a reversal of the more positive characteristics of this figure.

D

Dagda [VII] The Irish Dagda ('good god') is 'Father of All', a protective deity [27: 52–7]. His huge club, supported on wheels, can both kill and restore to life, while his cauldron of abundance provides inspiration and rejuvenation. He is a rough, primitive figure, with a huge appetite, resembling the Gaulish mallet-god Sucellos [17: 44] and the Scandinavian THOR [4: 204–7]. He mates with the Morrigan, the war-goddess, and various river-goddesses. Oengus, a youthful deity, and BRIGIT are his children.

Daimon, Daimones [XVI] The generic Greek meaning for *daimon* is 'divine power'. The word was used also to denote individual gods and, more narrowly, to mean 'intermediary beings between men and gods', hence 'individual destiny'. Some *daimones* received cult. There is one 5th-century reference to a *daimon* as an evil spirit, but it was Plato's pupil Xenocrates (*c.*395–314 BCE) who developed the concept *daimon* (demon), as seen in the growing Hellenistic popular demonology, where philosophical speculation met superstition. [4: 179–81, 329–32; 23: 171–5; 25: 282–4, 289–92; 27: 518–25, 871]

Dalai Lama [XXXV] The Dalai Lamas have been rulers of Tibet since the Fifth Dalai Lama in the 17th century, while remaining as Buddhist monks. Each Dalai Lama is held to be the reincarnation of the preceding Dalai Lama (*see* TULKU), while the Fifth Dalai Lama discovered through a revelation that the

Dalai Lamas also bear an especially close relationship to the BODHISATTVA AVALOKITESHVARA, known in Tibet as Chenrezik, the bodhisattva of compassion (KARUNA). This close relationship is usually explained as one of emanation, although the present (14th) Dalai Lama seems to favour the idea that the Dalai Lamas are human beings who through their intense vows of compassion have been blessed by Avalokiteshvara beyond their normal capacity in order to help others. The socio-political involvement of the Dalai Lamas is seen as an expression of the bodhisattva's wish to help others. This help is thought to continue throughout future rebirths, whether or not the Dalai Lama is recognized or installed as head of state. (*see* MAHAYANA; GELUG) [30]

Dana [XI] A BUDDHIST term meaning 'giving'. Psychologically the act of giving in general is understood as a powerful antidote to attachment and selfishness (cf. FOUR NOBLE TRUTHS; ANATTA), but the most potent kind of giving is that directed towards the three jewels (*see* TISARANA) of BUDDHA, DHAMMA and SANGHA; it is to this sort of giving that the term *dana* characteristically refers. Such *dana* is an important feature of lay Buddhist practice and centres on the offering of the traditional requisites (robes, food, lodging and medicine) to members of the SANGHA; in the countries of THERAVADA Buddhism *dana* is almost synonymous with the formal offering of alms to monks. *Dana* is seen as a significant and auspicious act (PUNNA) and as such forms the starting-point of the Buddhist path, paving the way to good conduct (SILA) and the practice of meditation (BHAVANA). [34: 198–9]

Dance [xxxiv] Rhythmic bodily movement. Ritual dancing has been a significant form of religious expression from ancient times (e.g. in PRE-HISTORIC RELIGION and its hunting and fertility rites; Egypt and the ANCIENT NEAR EAST; ecstatic MYSTERY-CULTS). It has great importance for tribal peoples; in religions of Indian origin wherever they have spread; and e.g. in the Japanese dancing religion (Odoru Shukyo), the Islamic order of dervishes (*see* SUFI ORDERS) and some REVIVALIST Christian groups. Indeed, the churches increasingly recognize its place in the liturgy, while theologians use the concept in some religious cosmology [118: xxxi; 130: 106–8, 361–3 (where a Christian writer refers to the dance of SHIVA, and quotes some physicists); 158: 92–3, 168].

Darshana [xvii] One of the six salvation-philosophies of classical HINDUISM. *Darshana*, literally 'seeing', means both 'view' and 'insight'. A world-view is implied, recognition of which will set one on the right path. As salvation results from overcoming a fundamental illusory understanding or ignorance (*avidya*), full recognition, as an experiential knowledge, is tantamount to liberation (MOKSHA). So *darshana* means not merely intuitive insight but also the system of thought which leads to this. The term has been used more widely. Jainism (*see* JAINS), the LOKAYATA, the Buddhist schools, even grammar and ALCHEMY have been recognized as *darshanas*. Eventually the notion became accepted that there were six affirming (*astika*) *darshanas*, as opposed to those denying (NASTIKA) the authority of the VEDA (but other

lists remained current in non-brahmanical circles). [General accounts of Indian philosophy: 36; 47; 51; 103; 121].

Although differing substantially on many points, the six orthodox Hindu *darshanas* accept the same social and ritual structure (orthopraxy) and the same general world picture (transmigration in SAMSARA). Listed with their subject-matter they are: (1) NYAYA, originally rhetoric and dialectic, later logic and epistemology; (2) VAISHESHIKA, ontology and metaphysics; (3) SAMKHYA, spiritual and 'occult' theory; (4) YOGA, spiritual practice; (5) MIMAMSA, ritual practice and requisite scriptural exegesis; (6) VEDANTA, the nature of the transcendent and appropriate scriptural exegesis. The first two differ mainly in subject matter, but share the same general viewpoint. The same is the case with Samkhya and Yoga. From the medieval period the first five *darshanas* were widely regarded as approaches to the sixth. Viewed as different levels of truth serving particular purposes, the six *darshanas* were reconciled into a single very rich Vedantic system, requiring great subtlety of interpretation. [12: 325–31; 121: 23–148]

Dasam Granth [xxxiii] In addition to its primary scripture, the ADI GRANTH, the Sikh PANTH recognizes a second collection, entitled the *Dasam Granth* or 'Book of the Tenth (Guru)'. Although the specific origins of this substantial work are obscure, its association with GURU GOBIND SINGH is well established (*see* GURU (SIKH DOCTRINE)). The traditional view holds that the entire collection was written by the Guru. A more cautious and convincing interpretation attributes a small portion of it to him and the remainder to poets of his entourage [22: 314–16]. Among the works attributed to the Guru himself are *Jap Sahib*, the paean *Akal Ustat*, an autobiographical work entitled

Bachitra Natak and *Zafar-nama*. The bulk of the collection comprises a retelling of the KRISHNA legends and a lengthy series of diverting anecdotes, predominantly amoral stories concerning the wiles of women (the *Triya Charitra*) [19: 52–9; 26: 79–81]. Most of the collection is written in Braj with little Punjabi (*see* SIKH LANGUAGES). The script, however, is Gurmukhi. [9: 105–13; 10: 139–47; 28: 89–92]

Dashavaikalika [xx] One of the most important texts of the SHVE-TAMBARA JAIN scriptures. The *Dashavaikalika* ('Ten Evening Recitations') is one of the 'root' (*mula*) scriptures, so called because they have to be studied by Shvetambara ascetics at the outset of their renunciatory career. Traditionally, the *Dashavaikalika* is regarded as having been written some time before the common era by the monk Shayyambhava as a summary of the scriptures for his son, although it most likely represents a selection of pre-existing texts. The *Dashavaikalika* contains concise statements of Jain doctrine and advice about normative ascetic behaviour and etiquette. [13: 199–239]

Da'wa [xix] An Arabic word meaning 'call' or 'invitation', often calling someone to ISLAM and thus translated as 'mission'. It is also used to mean 'propaganda', that is, an 'invitation' in a political context. The basic sense of *da'wa* is present in the QUR'AN (16: 25), '*Invite* [everyone] to the way of your Lord with wisdom and good counsel.' In early Islamic times, the word is associated with the propaganda leading up to the takeover of rule by the 'Abbasid family in 750 CE. In working towards the overthrow of their predecessors, the Umayyads, they organized a secret campaign of *da'wa* which urged that the person most qualified to lead the community must be a member of the family of the prophet MUHAMMAD.

The most famous use of the term in Islamic history is associated with ISMA'ILI Fatimid rulers of north Africa in the 10th century, and their efforts to convince fellow Muslims to give their allegiance to the Isma'ili line of IMAMS. This call to the fulfilment of Islam was led by a *da'i*, a propagandist or missionary. The aim of the call was to convince Muslims that the Isma'ili Imam was the only legitimate source of guidance in Islam in both spiritual and temporal matters. There was, therefore, a significant political element in the acceptance of this call, for it involved the acceptance of a political leader who, the propaganda suggested, would establish the legitimate Muslim theocratic state.

In contemporary times, *da'wa* emphasizes spirituality over politics, such that accepting the call comes to mean being transformed morally and spiritually by Islam on an individual level. This redefinition is in keeping with trends in contemporary Islam, especially among FUNDAMENTALIST groups, towards the personalization of religion, as well as reflecting an apologetic response to the impact of Christian missionizing among Muslims. The emergence of missionary organizations is also a part of this particularly contemporary aspect of *da'wa*. Such organizations provide a centralized administration of personnel working toward the spread of Islam, often paying some or all of the living expenses of such people. Active publication programmes are also characteristic of these efforts, along with the establishment of centres of worship and teaching. Starting in the mid-19th century, especially in India, organizations emerged which were dedicated to the spread of Islam, often targeting specific social groups such as the Hindu CASTE of untouchables. One such group which has based itself explicitly around the model of the mission is the heterodox Ahmadiyya (founded in India in 1889). The AHMADIS have put a great deal of stress in recent decades on translating the Qur'an into many languages and each of the leaders of the movement has been active in writing works about Islam and its response to modernity.

The impact of *da'wa* throughout the Muslim world has been felt mainly by Muslims themselves, who have been urged by their fellows to be more fervent in their faith in the face of the challenge of secularism. *Da'wa* has become a part of government policy in some places, for example in Indonesia, where in 1969 the government set up a centre for missionizing in response to an independent effort coordinated in 1967 by the Muhammadiya group, which aimed to establish a more fully Islamic society in Indonesia. The goal of such efforts is always stated to be the strengthening of the Muslim community and making nominal Muslims into active full participants in the faith. Efforts at conversion from other faiths are also an important and successful element of *da'wa* in contemporary times. A growth of Islam in the USA, for example, is frequently noted to be the result of conversion efforts, although there have not been many concerted and well-organized missionary endeavours with the goal of conversion in mind. [38 s.v. da'wa, vol. 3: 168–70; 43; 105]

Daxma [xxxvi] (*dakhma, dokhma*) Popularly known as a 'tower of silence'; a structure in ZOROAS-TRIANISM, in which the dead are laid for the flesh to be devoured by carrion-eaters (e.g. vultures). In ancient times the bodies were, it seems, simply exposed in a remote place with no structure. Death in Zoroastrian belief is the principal weapon of ANGRA MAINYU ('devil'), so that the locus of a dead body is considered a place where evil is powerfully present. To bury, cremate or dispose of the body at sea would defile the sacred creations of earth,

fire and water (*see* AMESHA SPENTAS); hence the rite of exposure. [8 vol. 1: XII] Strict religious regulations direct the treatment of corpses. Nowadays PARSIS remove a corpse quickly to *daxma* grounds. There it is washed, a priest prays over it, and a dog and sacred FIRE are present to keep evil forces at bay. The corpse is carried in the funeral procession by corpse-bearers (*nasasalars*) who walk in pairs (in *paiwand*), as do the mourners, to protect themselves from the evil of Angra Mainyu, whose influence is greatest where death, his apparent victory, is triumphant (at least until the resurrection – FRASHOKERETI). Only *nasasalars* enter the *daxma*; the mourners remain praying outside [29: pt III, 54–7]. Because they come into such contact with the impurity of death, *nasasalars* live apart and before re-entering society undergo the great nine-day purification ceremony, the *barashnum*. After attending a funeral mourners must also bathe to rid themselves of any contagion of impurity. Typically Zoroastrians do not commemorate the dead by lavish tombs but rather by charitable endowments declared after the *uthumna* or 'fourth-day ceremony' in memory of the deceased. From such bequests and through extensive donations at other times Zoroastrians have rightly earned themselves a considerable reputation for charitable giving, especially for medical and educational work and for general relief for the poor. [Hinnells in 7]. Zoroastrians living in countries where *daxmas* cannot be used (perhaps because there are no vultures) traditionally bury their dead in cemeteries (*aramgahs*) but increasingly in the Western world they practise cremation, arguing that modern methods utilize intense heat generated by electricity and therefore do not defile the sacred flame. They also argue that this is an ecologically sound practice. [9: 111–38; 14: 23–52; 46: 55–9; 47: III, v]

Dayak Religion [XXIX] 'Dayak' is a general name for the various tribal peoples of Borneo, notably the Ngaju in the south (in Indonesia) and the Iban or 'Sea Dayaks' in the north (in Malaysia). Borneo (or Kalimantan) has a long history of Hindu, Buddhist and Islamic kingdoms (e.g. the Sultanate of Brunei). Such influences can be seen in the Iban word for god or spirit, *petara* (Indian *batara*, 'lord'), and the name of their creator-god, Raja Entala (Indian *raja*, 'king', plus Islamic *Allah*?). Similarly, the two highest Ngaju gods are (male, upper world) Mahatala (Indian and Islamic mixture?) and (female, underworld) Jata (Indian). The cosmos is governed by *hadat* (Ngaju) or *adat* (Iban), from the Arabic word for 'custom'; its observance ensures cosmic and social harmony. *Muli* (Iban) or *puli* (Ngaju) is the equivalent of Polynesian *tapu* (TABU). As in Bali (*see* BALINESE RELIGION), the most lavish Ngaju ceremony is the second funeral, a few years after burial, but here the body is laid in a family shrine rather than cremated. A type of SHAMAN is found: the Ngaju *balian* (female, ritual prostitute) and *basir* (male, transvestite), and Iban *manang* (female or male transvestite); they procure healing with the help of their familiar spirits. [18; 24; 26]

Dead Sea Scrolls [XIII.A] The term refers to manuscripts found in six sites near the Dead Sea. The most famous and largest find comes from 11 caves near QUMRAN on the northwest shore of the Dead Sea. About 850 manuscripts were discovered there between 1947 and 1956; most of them are very fragmentary. The Qumran manuscripts fall into three groups: (1) texts of the various books of the Hebrew BIBLE which show that some books existed in more than one form in the precanonical period and that many variant readings are very ancient; (2) texts of non-biblical works commonly classed as INTERTESTAMENTAL LITERATURE, previously known almost exclusively in later Christian translations; (3) texts which describe the history, organization and beliefs of a community (*yahad*) which was established by an anonymous priest called the Teacher of Righteousness and which is commonly identified with the Jewish group described by JOSEPHUS as ESSENES. Though a few of the manuscripts are written in Greek, no part of the New Testament has been identified with certainty.

From the other sites, the most intriguing finds have included a substantial part of the Wisdom of Ben Sira in Hebrew at Masada, and in Nahal Hever correspondence from Bar Kosiba (Bar Kochba) together with an archive of legal documents belonging to a Jewish lady called Babatha. [4: 1068–79; 22: III, 380–469; 23: 483–550; 25]

'Death of God' Theologies [XIII.C] The 'death of god' slogan is taken from Nietzsche's story of the madman in *Die fröhliche Wissenschaft* (1882) and used to label a number of very varied radical theologies developed especially in the USA in the 1960s. Among the claims advanced are (1) that language about a transcendent GOD is meaningless for modern secular humanity, (2) that God is not experienced today, (3) that God is not significant in contemporary culture, (4) that God is not a dominating presence but has 'withdrawn' to give humanity scope for responsible freedom, and (5) that God is not an enslaving threat but an immanent creative force within life. Few of these theologies were thoroughly atheistic. Most sought to identify a faith centred on JESUS Christ that would be appropriate to a humankind 'come of age'. [1; 18]

Deism [XIII.C] Originally referred to belief in one God, as opposed to ATHEISM and POLYTHEISM. During the 17th century the word came increasingly to be applied to positions which were regarded as less than fully orthodox forms of CHRISTIANITY. 'Deists' were often accused of rejecting belief in revelation, miracles, providence and immortality. In fact the deism which flourished in the first half of the 18th century did not constitute a coherent movement. The so-called deists differed greatly over what they maintained, although they were united in seeking to hold only those religious beliefs which they considered to be rationally warranted. Generally they upheld the truth of some kind of NATURAL THEOLOGY. Among the leading deists are A. Collins (1676–1729) and M. Tindal (c.1657–1733) in England, F. M. A. de Voltaire (1694–1778) and J. J. Rousseau (1712–78) in France. Joseph Butler's *Analogy of Religion* (1736) was a classical reply to the English deists, arguing that revealed religion faced no greater problems than the natural theology accepted by the deists. Since the 18th century 'deism' has come to connote a belief that God created the world in the beginning but does not intervene in the course of natural and human affairs. [27; 28]

Dema Deities [xxix] The name *dema* comes from the Marind-Anim peoples of south-west Papua and has been used to refer to similar concepts in MELANESIAN RELIGION and elsewhere. *Dema* gods and goddesses are mythological figures (animal, human or superhuman) who have given to certain peoples their land, food-crops, totems and knowledge (how to cultivate crops, raise pigs, make canoes, perform dances and sacred rituals). From their dismembered bodies, blood, etc. came the different tribes that are now in existence, together with their territory. Both local culture and the natural environment remain permeated with the supernatural power of these creative deities. [23; 29]

Demon [xxxiv] A SPIRIT, below the status of GODS and subject to them, sometimes guardian of a human individual (Greek: DAIMON). The early concept was modified in a distinction between good demons (angels) and evil ones (devils). Sometimes, 'demon' was equated with 'evil spirit' (*see* DUALISM). However, the daimonic (an important notion in modern theology) has no necessary connection with malevolence or the negative aspects of existence. (*see also* AHURA MAZDA; ANGRA MAINYU; JINN.)

Demons (Biblical [xiii.a] In JUDAISM during the Hellenistic period there was a belief in individual demons. The influence of ZOROASTRIANISM may easily be recognized. In the story of Tobit a sinister part is played by Asmodaeus (Zoroastrian Aeshma-daeva, the 'demon of fury'). In the manuscripts from QUMRAN several texts speak of Belial and the angels of his lot from whom protection is sought in a number of ritual texts, including rites of exorcism. In the synoptic GOSPELS the leader of the demons is Beelzebul and exorcisms also feature. [11: II, 138–42; 22: III, 352–8; 26: 61–9]

Demythologizing [xiii.c] The method of interpreting the New Testament put forward by R. Bultmann (1884–1976). An exponent of the Form-Critical method (*see* BIBLICAL CRITICISM) of analysing the materials of the GOSPELS, Bultmann maintained that Christian belief was based on the Christ of faith rather than on the JESUS of history. He also held that since GOD's own nature was beyond human apprehension, theology must confine itself to describing human existence as it is confronted by God. His programme of demythologization is based on the claim that the New Testament does not merely contain specific elements which are untenable for modern people (such as the conception of a three-storeyed universe and stories of miracles), but that its presentation of the Christian faith is understood throughout in terms of a view of reality which is now unacceptable. Accordingly, Bultmann argues that if its content is to be grasped by people today, it must be thoroughly and radically reinterpreted in terms of an appropriate conceptuality. This for Bultmann is largely provided by Heidegger's EXISTENTIALIST categories. [2; 3; 18a]

Deobandi [XIX] A 19th-century reform movement in Indian ISLAM, taking its name from the town of Deoband. In the 1860s a group of scholars, under the leadership of Muhammad Qasim, established a college offering traditional Islamic subjects but in a format derived from British educational practice. Urdu replaced Arabic as the medium of instruction. They taught the need for a return to correct belief and practice as found in the classical texts and became renowned for the study of HADITH (traditions of the Prophet) and as a source of *fatwas* (legal judgments) derived from the Hanafi school of law (FIQH). The Deobandis also had strong roots in the orthodox *sufi* (see SUFISM) tradition, emphasizing the importance of a close relationship with one's spiritual guide. With their insistence on *tauhid* (the unity of God) as the central tenet of Islam, they sought to abolish popular customs that elevated the Prophet and the saints. The Deobandi movement had a wide appeal since it combined the two strands of intellectual learning and spiritual experience: SHARI'A and *tariqa* (see SUFI ORDERS). Its influence has spread far beyond its place of origin – in 1967 there were about 9,000 affiliated colleges. Muslim communities in the West have employed IMAMS from the Indian subcontinent. On occasion, there have been tensions between an *imam* trained in the 'puritanical' Deobandi tradition and his largely BARELVI-orientated congregation, leading to a proliferation of MOSQUES along 'sectarian' lines. [49; 92; 99; 113]

Desert Fathers [XIII.D] ASCETICS who fled from the life of the cities of the Roman empire once Christianity had become the state religion, and sought to live a life of prayer, FASTING and hard work in the Egyptian deserts. They are famous in the history of Christian spirituality for their austere common sense, their singleness of purpose and the luminous simplicity of their lives. Many collections of their lives and sayings exist. They had a seminal role in the development of Christian MONASTICISM.

The Desert Mothers are less well known but no less important. Many were spiritual teachers in their own right. A number of the Mothers were penitent ex-prostitutes, several of whom – St Mary of Egypt, St Thais and St Pelagia – are objects of great devotion and respect in Orthodox tradition, St Mary even having the fifth Sunday of Lent dedicated to her.

The common use of the ancient titles *abba* or *apa* (or, in the case of the Mothers, *amma*) has led certain writers to give all the Desert Fathers and Mothers the titles Abbot and Abbess respectively.

The desert has an important symbolic meaning in Christian spirituality (as also in Jewish and Muslim traditions). It represents the place where the individual stands alone, naked and fragile in the presence of God. Several religious orders have places where members can retire, temporarily or permanently, into an austere solitary or near solitary life of asceticism and contemplation, some retaining the name 'desert'. [6; 16; 20; 73; 78; 94; 95; 96; 97] (*See* STARETS.)

Dhamma [XI] The PALI form of the Sanskrit DHARMA. The basic sense of the term is common to both BUDDHISM and HINDUISM, though within each tradition it develops characteristic connotations and nuances as well as specific technical meanings. Dhamma is the underlying order or pattern of things; it is the way things truly are. For Buddhism this is primarily conceived of in terms of the law of 'dependent arising' (PATICCASAMUPPADA). The failure to see this Dhamma means that one's view of the world is distorted, and as a consequence one's actions are not in keeping with the way things are; this leads to suffering (DUKKHA). The BUDDHA's teaching, however, prescribes a way of practice that leads to the seeing of Dhamma and to actions that are in harmony with the way things are. Since the Buddha's teaching as handed down in Buddhist scriptures (see TIPITAKA) is in accordance with the way things are, it too is known as Dhamma; to follow the teaching is to practise Dhamma, and to attain enlightenment (bodhi) is to realize Dhamma (cf. NIBBANA). In this way Dhamma becomes one of 'the three refuges' (TISARANA) of a Buddhist.

A further technical sense of Dhamma derives from the particular way in which Buddhist thought, especially the ABHIDHAMMA, conceives of 'the way things truly are' in terms of specific classes of momentary physical and mental events. These events are the fundamental constituents of the way things are and are thus referred to as dhammas; to understand Dhamma is to see the world in terms of dhammas. The precise ontological status of dhammas became a matter of philosophical debate among Buddhist schools, with some arguing that the tendency (exemplified especially by the VAIBHASHIKA Abhidharma) to view dhammas as ultimately existing in themselves undermined the fundamental Buddhist teaching of dependent arising (cf. MADHYAMAKA). [16: 92–6; 8]

Dhammapada [XI] One of the books belonging to the SUTTA section of BUDDHIST scriptures (see TIPITAKA). This short book, whose title means 'sayings on DHAMMA', is an anthology of over 400 aphoristic verses which cover various aspects of Buddhist teaching and are traditionally attributed to the BUDDHA (see GOTAMA) himself. As such the Dhammapada has enjoyed considerable popularity especially, in its PALI version, in the countries of THERAVADA Buddhism. Ancient versions now less well known are the Gandhari Dharmapada, the Patna Dharmapada and the Sanskrit Udanavarga. [71]

Dhammapala [XI] The name of two important THERAVADA Buddhist commentators. Dhammapala I (probably 7th century CE) was the south Indian author of PALI commentaries (atthakatha) on various canonical and semi-canonical works, and adapted north Indian Buddhist ideas, especially those of ASANGA, to accord with Theravada tradition. Dhammapala II (probably 10th century) was the author of numerous sub-commentaries (tika) supplementing the works of BUDDHAGHOSA and Dhammapala I, notably the influential commentary to the Visuddhimagga. Later tradition and some modern scholarship identified the two. [4: 46ff, 254ff]

Dhanb [XIX] The general term for sin in ISLAM. The QUR'AN does not clearly propound a doctrine of original sin, but speaks of man's innate weakness and his sharing in Adam's sinfulness. All sins are regarded as disobedience to God and as ingratitude for His goodness. The supreme sin of shirk, polytheism and denial of God's unity (see ALLAH), is unforgivable. Below this, the Qur'an and tradition distinguish lesser sins, which do not affect a person's faith, from grave ones, which God may pardon or punish for a certain period. There was much discussion by later theologians and sectarians about what constituted a grave sin (kabira); one Prophetic tradition posits seven, echoing the seven deadly sins of Christianity. The KHARIJITES and Mu'tazilites held that grave sins entailed permanent damnation. All authorities, however, admitted God's complete freedom to forgive sins (except *shirk*), and the Sunni (*see* SUNNA) view came to be that this did not even require the sinner's prior repentance, for if God were to accept it, the divine pardon would be unnecessary. [20 'Sin (Islam)'; 67 'Sin'; 140 index s.v. 'Sin']

Dharma [XVII] The essentially untranslatable Sanskrit word for one of the central concepts of Indian religion, covering ideas of cosmic, natural and social order. It is the nearest equivalent to the Western concept of 'religion', though without the implied distinction between sacred and secular areas of life. In HINDUISM, in contrast to BUDDHISM (*see* DHAMMA), *dharma* is not seen as universal, though certain aspects of it, such as the avoidance of taking life (AHIMSA), may be proper to all beings. Rather, every being is seen as having a *svadharma*, 'own *dharma*', a proper way to live which would differ for people of different VARNAS, CASTES and stages of life (ASH-RAMA), and for men and women. *Dharma*, for Hindus, is intimately linked with life within society, and the performance of good KARMA to ensure a happy rebirth. In one common formulation, *dharma*, ARTHA (political and financial success) and KAMA (love and pleasure) form a group of three goals of life, in order of priority, each of which can be legitimately pursued, but not at the expense of the ones before it in the list. A fourth goal, MOKSHA, spiritual liberation, stands apart from the other three, since it means release from all worldly concerns [57: 55].

Dhimmis [XIX] 'Protected peoples', the term applied in pre-modern ISLAM to the Qur'anic 'People of the Book', those possessing written scriptures, originally

Christians and Jews, but later extended to Zoroastrians, Hindus, etc. included within the Islamic empire. *Dhimmis* were accorded legal status within Islam, but as second-class citizens, liable to a poll-tax (*jizya*) instead of military service, and were forbidden to proselytize. Their legal disabilities were not removed in most Islamic countries till the 19th and early 20th centuries. [38 'Dhimma'; 129]

Dhyana Yoga [XVII] The way of meditation, one of four main routes of spiritual development (YOGA) widely recognized in Indian thought. It emphasizes purification and stilling of the mind by means of meditative techniques. Influential examples of this approach are the classical YOGA-DARSHANA and Buddhist BHAVANA. The aim is to develop *samadhi* (ecstasy), a type of contemplative experience of alert absorption and unification. Different degrees and types of *samadhi* are elaborated in great detail in many Indian religious systems. *Dhyana* is more or less synonymous, sometimes used for an inferior stage, sometimes for a more advanced level. *Dhyana yoga* usually involves systematic and intimate instruction from a teacher (GURU) and is often, but not invariably, associated with some kind of withdrawal from general social intercourse. It is sometimes associated with the development of PSYCHIC POWERS (*siddhi/iddhi*).

Di Deaeque [XXXI] The gods and goddesses of Rome. These varied widely in character, from the high gods (such as Jupiter, chief of the state-gods, and Mars, god of war) down to the protectors of specific processes, such as one stage in the growth-cycle of corn [12: 208; 22: 16]. The naming of deities was important to successful prayer, but formulae allowed for extra unknown powers. Even major deities had no kin relations, no adventures, and little personality, until later borrowing from Greek counterparts. This has led to theories that the early Romans had no gods, only spirits (*numina; see* NUMEN), who developed personality late and under foreign influence [22: 15–16]. The theories are incompatible with the Romans' INDO-EUROPEAN inheritance [8: 18–46; 19: 573–82], but rightly emphasize the range of types existing contemporaneously. The Romans recognized no intermediate category between men and gods; even the dead were seen as unindividualized, but divine (*divi*). There were various means by which the number of gods and goddesses increased: they might be summoned from enemy cities by 'evocation' (as Juno from the Etruscan city of Veii) [10: 21–2]; or recommended by the SIBYLLINE BOOKS to be brought from abroad (as Apollo); or recognized as abstractions – Victory, Concord, Piety [8: 397–441; 19: 616–24]. This preparedness to accept the new continues to be evident in imperial times, when cults from Asia Minor, Syria and other parts of the East were accepted (*see* SYNCRETISM) [24]. Roman gods were rarely thought to speak or intervene directly in human affairs, but complex negotiations were undertaken through prayers and especially vows – which defined the conditions for fulfilment with quasi-legal precision [10: 14–16, 26–8; 19: 590–8]. The gods' response was thought to come through signs and PRODIGIA, but most importantly through success and victory. [2: 235–45; 21: 51–7]

Dialectical Materialism [XXXII] The name usually given to the outlook on human nature and on the world appropriate to MARXISM. The name did not originate with Marx (1818–83) or F. Engels (1820–95). Their account of the dialectical method was, however, expounded by Lenin (1870–1924) as 'nothing more nor less than the scientific method in sociology, which consists in regarding society as a living organism in a constant state of development, the study of which requires an objective analysis of the relations of production which constitute the given social formation and an investigation of its laws of functioning and development'. This statement by Lenin already implies a materialist standpoint, namely, that social change is governed by underlying material (economic) factors and not by ideas. So understood, dialectical materialism involves a hostile view of IDEOLOGY as a mere reflection of human social relations and an obstacle to basic changes.

Dialectical materialism has sometimes been taken to involve a particular view of what processes can take place in nature. The Soviet agriculturist T.D. Lysenko urged, in the 1930s, that the genetic theory favoured in the West was incompatible with dialectical materialism. The result of Lysenko's efforts was the suppression of the theory but not, as had been hoped, an increase in agricultural productivity. Dialectical materialism is now commonly interpreted by Marxists in such a way that a conflict between its principles and the findings of natural science is no longer possible. [22: II]

Digambara [xx] One of the two main JAIN sects [2: XII, XVII; 4; 9; 10]. The name Digambara means 'sky-clad' and derives from the nakedness assumed by male ascetics of this sect to signal the totality of their renunciation of worldly ties. Although it seems likely that the earliest Jain monks wore no clothes, options were introduced into the rules about ascetic behaviour, and the wearing of white robes was assumed by one section of the community, to be known as the SHVE-TAMBARA sect. This division in Jainism took place very gradually and the term Digambara does not seem to have been used in a sectarian sense until about the 6th century CE. The Digambaras differ from the Shvetambaras on a variety of points other than ascetic dress. As well as rejecting the Shvetambara scriptures, substituting works and compilations by their own ancient teachers, they deny that the enlightened individual (KEVALIN) needs food and also that women can achieve enlightenment.

The Digambaras have produced some of Jainism's greatest philosophers and poets. Among the most noteworthy are the logician Akalanka (8th century CE) and the epic poet Jinasena (9th century CE). The literature of the south Indian Kannada language gained much of its original impetus from Digambara writers. The Digambara community today is small, albeit extremely self-aware, and is largely restricted to the states of Karnataka and Maharashtra, although there are significant pockets in Madhya Pradesh and Rajasthan.

Din [XIX] The term used in ISLAM for 'religion' in general, so that one can have the *din* of Islam or earlier *din*s before the revelation of the faith. The term has connotations of indebtedness and obligation, i.e. of the believer's duties towards God. In Islamic theology, *din* comprehends both faith, *iman*, and the practice of the prescriptions of the law, the SHARI'A, and is often contrasted with the *dunya*, the sphere of secular life. [54, vol. 1: 1]

Dinka Religion [II] The Dinka are a NILOTIC people in the southern Sudan; among their neighbours are the NUER and SHILLUK. Nhialic (literally, 'the Sky') is the Dinka name for God. In comparison with the Nuer Kwoth, he is encountered far more through the experience of powerful spirits (JOK), of which the most important are Deng, Garang, Abuk and Macardit. They are known especially through possession. Deng, Garang and Abuk (who is female) are the names of the first Dinka and remain very common today, but the spirits are distingui-

shed from the Dinka progenitors. Macardit ('the great black one') is unique in being wholly bad and harmful. Oxen sacrificed to placate Macardit should be black.

Deng stands above all others so much that he seems almost to have the character of Nhialic. He is associated with rain, thunder and lightning. It is significant for the identification of Deng and Nhialic that the great and ancient shrine known to Nuer as 'Luak Kwoth' is called 'Luak Deng' by Dinka.

The Dinka also respect totemic spirits, among whom may be noted *Ring* (flesh), the spirit of the priestly clans, the Masters of the Fishing Spear. It is incarnate within them. Dinka religion, like Nuer, centres upon ox-sacrifice, but here sacrifice is both more ritualistic and more sacerdotal, normally being executed by Spear-Masters. The powers of Spear-Masters derive from the rich myths relating to Aiwel Longar, the miraculous hero who led the Dinka to their present home (compare Nyikang of the Shilluk). He was conceived in the river and led his people across it, but frequently dealt them death as well as life.

The health and prosperity of the people are symbolized by, and indeed seen as dependent upon, the life of the Spear-Master. *Ring* enables them, furthermore, to lead the people and speak absolutely truthfully, above all when invoking in sacrifice. Great Spear-Masters, when old, choose death voluntarily, being buried alive after giving final advice to their people. [39]

Dipankara [XI] A Buddha of a past age whom Shakyamuni Buddha, GOTAMA, the BUDDHA of the present age, met (in a previous life), and determined that, having honoured Dipankara, he would himself become a Buddha. Having so determined, he thereby became a BODHISATTVA, but had yet to pass through countless successive lives (some of which the JATAKA stories [41] are said to relate) before entering the Tusita heaven (the fourth of the six heavens, or Deva-worlds, in Indian cosmology, where one day corresponds to 400 years of human life [56: 1033; 58]), prior to his last birth (in Lumbini) as the Buddha [97: 335].

Dipavamsa [XI] One of the PALI chronicles (*vamsa*) (*see* CULAVAMSA) which relate the BUDDHIST history of the island (*dipa*) of Sri Lanka. The *Dipavamsa* deals with the period up to the middle of the 4th century CE. It was probably composed during the succeeding 100 years, but incorporates much older historical traditions, and is 'the outcome of a fairly large number of previous works', all of which were the work of groups or schools, rather than of individual authors. [25; 57: 131–8]

Disciples (Early Christian) [XIII.A] The GOSPELS mention disciples of the PHARISEES and of JOHN THE BAPTIST as well as disciples of JESUS. Apparently Jesus had many followers other than the APOSTLES. The Gospel of Luke describes how Jesus sent out 70 disciples to preach and heal. The disciples formed the nucleus of the CHURCH, in which 'disciple' became a synonym of 'Christian'. [9: 104–6; 11: II, 207–10]

Ditthi [XI] (Pali; Sanskrit: *drshti*) 'Views', or 'wrong views'; refers in early BUDDHISM to the one-sided or slanted attitude which underlies rigid opinions. This is seen as due to specific psychological forces – drives or cravings (*tanha*) – which involve some kind of partial or incomplete understanding following loss of mental balance. The two extreme views of 'eternalism' and 'annihilationism' give certain conviction of eternal life or post-mortem annihilation respectively. Other types of *ditthi* include fatalism, materialism, theism and views based upon a need to assert the self. Less frequent is the use of *ditthi* to refer to 'right view' as part of the EIGHTFOLD PATH. Various levels of understanding are mentioned. Fundamental is a basic knowledge of the law of action (*kamma*; Sanskrit: KARMA) and result which alone allows true moral responsibility. Higher are various degrees of insight culminating in transcendent right view (*see* LOKUTTARA) deriving from a permanent mental balance and contact with the unconditioned. (*see also* PATICCASAMUPPADA.) [4]

Divination [XXIV] The use of magical means to discover information inaccessible to normal enquiry (about the future, lost objects, hidden character-traits, etc.). Divination exists in all societies, often under the auspices of religion (e.g. the Delphic oracle, the Tibetan state oracles), but sometimes outside or in opposition to it (as under CHRISTIANITY, which has generally opposed divination).

The art of divination is to discern the future or the unknown by addressing, often through symbolic language, unconscious levels of the mind. A large body of divinatory methods exist for the diviner to interpret a question, their own or another person's. The practitioner trains to recognize the hidden realms and latencies within the question and, in the language of their own particular system, to present an interpretation. The study of divination can concur with the ideal its name implies, to know the divine [12: I]; equally, divination meets the desire to add questions on matters closer to hand like money, love, children and health. It takes two main forms: oracular, where the diviner enters a trance or other special state and relays the information; and interpretative, where random or enigmatic data are interpreted. In principle the interpretation of any apparent random or enigmatic data can be the basis of a divination system, as in, for example, the throwing of dice. For a system to be effective it has its own internal logic and the question should be asked sincerely and with clarity: many systems have inbuilt safeguards against misuse. The logic of any divination system is that the user in shuffling (or whatever action is involved) is part of the event of shuffling. In the shuffling process the inner state of the shuffler's being and the way the cards are mixed is interrelated via the unconscious. Thus the order in which the cards are dealt is a compound of outer event and inner state. The distinction is not clear-cut, however, for some interpretative systems (ASTROLOGY; TAROT) contain a powerful symbolism, others seem chosen to stimulate clairvoyance (*see* PSYCHIC POWERS), and the sheer flexibility of interpretation normally admits an element of the 'oracular'. The diviner needs a shrewd knowledge of human nature as well as intuitive gifts because his or her role, however humble socially, is inevitably a priestly one, mediating between worldly concerns and mysterious but purposeful higher powers. [22]

Divination (African) [II] Divination is important for many African religions, and believed to be a reliable method for obtaining the answers to particular questions (by whom one's child has been bewitched, what spirit is troubling one, which practical course one should pursue over a specific matter, etc.). It takes two main forms (among many), the first being that of oracles, such as IFA or the ZANDE poison-oracle, the second that provided by a medium when possessed (*see* NGANGA; SPIRIT-POSSESSION). The former depends upon a certain mechanical and objective technique, the latter upon contact with spirits, though this will be preceded by careful interrogation of the client. Many peoples make use of both, oracle operators tending to be men while mediums are often women. [23; 24: 136–96; 29]

Divination (Ancient Near Eastern) [VIII] Regarded as a supreme science, divination was used as a practical guide in all human affairs. Omens were consulted before battle, in personal matters or to determine a god's anger, and omen texts are an invaluable source of political and other information [13: 160–4; 23: 20–2; 24: 346, 449–51]. Probably first devised by the SUMERIANS, divination became increasingly important in the Old BABYLONIAN period (*c.*1700 BCE) and was inherited by the HITTITES. Augury (looking for signs in nature), lottery and extispicy (the excision and examination of animal entrails to foretell events) were employed, but later ASTROLOGY challenged extispicy as the favourite method.

Divination (Roman) [XXXI] Elaborate methods existed in Rome to establish the attitudes of the gods towards human events, but this involved little actual prediction of future events. AUSPICIA took the form of asking the gods' approval for a particular course of action, such as joining battle. PRODIGIA were essentially bad signs, whose menace could be averted by the piety of the state and the skill of the priests. [15; 19: 595–6, 617–18] Belief in divination is, however, implicit in myths and in later poetry, and must always have existed at all levels of society. In the late Republic (1st century BCE) the *haruspices* (diviners from Etruria, possibly representing a different tradition) began to be bolder in offering interpretations and this evidently reflects an increasing popularity of divinatory systems at the lower-class level as well. This tendency continued through the empire, when far more sophisticated systems of divination through MAGIC and ASTROLOGY gradually established themselves at the highest levels of power and culture. [2: 51–71, 252–5; 13: 119–39]

Divine Kingship (African) [II] Divine kingship can be well illustrated from Africa. Its characteristics are the relationship of dependence between the king and nature, the degree of seclusion imposed upon him, the primacy of ritual and sacerdotal over administrative action in his life, and the conceptual centrality of the kingship within the religious belief-system. Furthermore, the king may be seen as a reincarnation of a divine hero of the past and his death should be the effect of a deliberate choice on his own or his successor's part, not the consequence of sickness. Among the best examples are the SHILLUK *reth*, the LOVEDU Mujaji, the *lwembe* of the Nyakyusa [51: 17–48] and the *hogon* of the DOGON.

While the major monarchies of Africa, such as those of Ashanti, Benin, Dahomey and Buganda (*see* AKAN, FON, GANDA), may not have fallen fully into this category, most still combined profound sacrality with secular political expertise. Rituals of kingship, especially the installation of monarchs, the renewal of king and kingdom in new-year ceremonies and the cult at royal tombs are among the richest sources for African religious symbolism (examples of which are the Akan *odwira* and the Swazi NCWALA).

Dogon Religion [II] The Dogon of Upper Volta have a complex religious cosmology, much of it highly esoteric, and represent one of the most intricately sacralized societies in Africa. The basic belief is in the duality of Amma, the God creator, and Nommo, the totality of the universe, existing originally within an enormous egg. There is a basic male/female twinness in the Amma/Nommo relationship forever symbolized in subsequent relationships within Nommo. The perfect image of Nommo is, therefore, a pair of twins of opposite sex. The original ancestors of the Dogon were four pairs of twins, making eight into a particularly significant number in a vastly complicated NUMEROLOGY. The orderly development of the world was initially impeded by the bursting forth of Yurugu – the TRICKSTER or White Fox – the purely male part of an original Nommo. Yurugu, associated with death and night but also with DIVINATION, remains the unpredictable element in life: at times apparently evil, at others inspirational. Order was restored through the sacrifice of Lebe, the first man.

The whole of social life, cultivation, the shaping of villages and homesteads, and particularly the life of the chief of each village, the *hogon*, is so arranged as to symbolize the intricacies of cosmological belief: villages are built in pairs, eight storerooms preserve eight varieties of millet, the home of a living *hogon* contains eight stones for *hogons* of the past and eight for *hogons* of the future. The *hogon*, the high priest of Amma and successor of Lebe, controls all sides of life through his own ritualized existence, and stands as human symbol of the universal Nommo. [6: 83–110; 33]

Drama (Christian) [XIII.B] Early Christians condemned the drama, because of its 'pagan' or immoral associations, until the medieval Mystery or Miracle plays developed (apparently from dramatized elements in the liturgy). These dramatized the Creation, Passion (sufferings) of Christ and lives of SAINTS, mingled with popular comic elements. Some still survive, notably the Oberammergau Passion play in Germany. There are recognizable dramatic elements in the ceremonies of Holy Week (in Easter season), especially in ROMAN CATHOLICISM and the Orthodox churches (*see* EASTERN ORTHODOX CHURCH). PROTESTANTISM in general (notably PURITANISM) disapproved of drama, but religious drama is now widely used (as well as DANCE, which hitherto has played little part in Christian worship). [154 vol. 4: 1033–53; 157: 425]

Dreads [III] The Dreads of Domenica take their name from the RASTAFARIANS. The island has a very high level of unemployment, with some 60% of all land in the hands of ten planters or corporations, and the level of educational opportunity is very poor for the vast majority. The Dreads express their alienation through the wearing of locks, 'dreadlocks', and by generally deviant behaviour in defying the civil authorities in drug use and abuse. 'Dread' (fear/awe) means the power within man, and Dreads consider Domenica to be Babylon. Some Dreads believe that Haile Selassie was/is God, while others believe that it is their duty to redeem Domenica. Believers are vegetarian, and dress simply. Cannabis is considered the essential sacrament. [86]

Dreams and Visions in Modern Tribal Movements [XXVII] In most new tribal movements dreams and visions may have revelatory and mandatory qualities. Founders' visions often involve a visit to heavenly beings for a commission to found the new religion, together with details of its rituals, ethics and sometimes a new script or language. All dreams are potentially significant, but many need interpretation by a leader, or the application of moral, biblical (see BIBLE) or other critiques to eliminate those coming from evil spirits. Revelatory dreams can also be induced by sleeping in a sanctuary, fasting, rolling on the ground, or by hallucinogenic drugs such as peyote (see PEYOTISM) in the NATIVE AMERICAN CHURCH [26: 416–17, 430–2] or *iboga* in the Gabon Bwiti religion. For movements founded through visions or dreams see CHRISTIAN FELLOWSHIP CHURCH; ALICE LENSHINA'S church; NAZARITE CHURCH [18: 110, 112,

328–30]; the MAORI MOVEMENT Ratana; the HANDSOME LAKE RELIGION; and many CARGO CULTS. [5; 15: 123–7, 130–1, 206–7; 18: 265–75; 26]

Druids [VII] The Druids (the name is probably derived from a word meaning oak) were priests and learned men of Celtic Gaul and Britain. Many Greek and Latin writers refer to them, particularly Posidonius (1st century BCE) and his imitators [30]. They taught young men, organized religious rituals, including sacrifice, and were skilled in healing, astronomy, calendric calculations and consultation of omens [20: 94–6]. There is considerable argument as to their influence and the nature of their learning, which was not committed to writing [15: 104–21]. The Romans set out to suppress them in the 1st century CE. Interest in Druids revived in the 17th century, and the antiquary John Aubrey mistakenly assumed that Stonehenge and other megalithic sites were Druidic temples [20: 118–25]. A romantic, vaguely mystical picture of their ceremonies and secret wisdom was built up, and in 1819 Iolo Morganwg (Edward Williams) claimed an association with the National Eisteddfod of Wales, based on dubious evidence [20: 143–50]. The Ancient Order of Druids began in 1781 as a secret society in London, developing into a friendly society, but strangely attired groups of self-styled 'Druids' have continued to meet to celebrate the summer solstice at Stonehenge, Tower Hill and Primrose Hill in London, and other sites [20: 155–7].

Druzes (Druses) [XIX] A sectarian Muslim group, today found in the mountainous regions of Lebanon, northern Israel and southern Syria. Their numbers have been variously estimated at between 200,000 and 300,000. They stem from the Shi'i Muslim sect of ISMA'ILIS, as an offshoot in the 11th century of the Fatimid movement (*see* 'ALI, 'ALIDS; ISLAMIC DYNASTIES; SHI'ISM). In belief and practice they are considerably aberrant from the main body of Muslims, rejecting many of the prescriptions of the SHARI'A and emphasizing e.g. metempsychosis (transmigration of the soul). The Druzes have maintained their identity through endogamy and through the social leadership of a class of ascetic initiates to the faith, the *'uqqal'* ('sages'). [8; 20 s.v.; 38 'Durūz']

Du'a' [XIX] In Arabic, literally 'the invocation [of God]', the term in Islamic religion normally used (together with *munajat*) for private, individual prayer and intercession to God as opposed to the corporate worship or SALAT enjoined by the SHARI'A. It thus involves, essentially, requests to God for personal wellbeing or that of the Muslim community. Islamic piety has resulted in the compilation and publication of collections of these invocations and prayers. [67 s.v.; 100]

Dualism [XXXIV] (1) As a worldview, the belief that the 'real' is of two kinds, or in two ultimate controlling powers. Thus, metaphysical dualism (cf. MONISM) may oppose matter to SPIRIT, while dualistic religion involves belief in two eternally conflicting principles [43: 125–32]. Modified dualism holds God to be ambivalent, both benevolent and malevolent.
   (2) A view of man as consisting of two substances, physical (flesh, body) and mental or spiritual (mind, soul, spirit).

Dukkha [XI] (Pali; Sanskrit: *duhkha*) A term used especially in BUDDHISM but also in other religions of Indian origin to characterize the whole world of ordinary experience. Literally 'pain' or 'anguish', the term *dukkha* is most usually translated by the word 'suffering'. In its religious and philosophical contexts *dukkha* is, however, suggestive of an underlying sense of 'unsatisfactoriness' or 'unease' that is felt to mar even apparently pleasant experiences. These too are *dukkha* since they are unreliable and subject to loss; to rest one's hope of final happiness in such experiences can thus only lead to further suffering. In this way *dukkha* characterizes not only the obvious suffering of unpleasant experiences but the whole round of rebirth (SAMSARA), since anything experienced in *samsara* is compounded of unstable conditions and is thus ultimately impermanent (*see* ANICCA). The only final release from suffering is thus the 'unconditioned' (*see* NIBBANA). In Buddhism, along with *anicca* and ANATTA, *dukkha* is one of the three marks of all conditioned existence. (*see also* ABHIDHAMMA; ARIYASACCA; VIPASSANA.) [74: 16–28]

Duppy/Jumbie [III] In Jamaica 'duppy', and in Trinidad 'jumbie' are terms which describe that part of a person which is the spiritual 'other'. This is not the soul but rather the spiritual shadow. The duppy/jumbie becomes crucial at death, because a funeral which does not incorporate the duppy/jumbie into the other world lays it open to appropriation by a witch/*obeahman* (*see* OBEAH). (*See also* ZOMBIE.) [86]

Durga [XVII] 'She who is hard to approach', 'Unassailable'; one of the most important Hindu deities (*see* SHAKTI), embodying for many the supreme manifest form of Godhead. She is best known as *Mahishasuramardini*, Slayer of the Buffalo Demon (ASURA). Through asceticism (TAPAS) the demon had obtained the boon from BRAHMA that he could be slain only by a woman; then, thinking himself safe, he made war on the gods. However, the gods combined their energy (*shakti*) into the form of a beautiful 16-year-old girl, and placed duplicates of their own weapons – SHIVA's trident, VISHNU's discus, the noose of Yama, god of death, and so on – in her many hands. Thus armed, and riding on a lion (see VAHANA), she slew the demon, releasing him from his buffalo shape and granting him liberation (MOKSHA).

In art, Durga is represented with up to 18 arms, holding her divine weapons, but smiling gently on her worshippers, and with her foremost hands often making gestures that give reassurance (see MUDRA). Like Shiva, she has a third, vertical, eye in her forehead. In the more recent versions (since about the 18th century) her lion is often replaced by a tiger. She is regarded as an aspect of the goddess PARVATI; KALI is one of her emanations. [4: 449; 92: 238–49; 89: 48–59]

E

**East Indian Religion in the West
Indies** [III] Throughout the development of the plantation economy
in the Caribbean, the provision and
maintenance of an adequate and
economically viable workforce had
been a problem. Until the 1830s the
plantations' requirements were supplied largely by slave labour originating from west Africa. Some of these
slaves travelled with their masters
from other countries in the Americas. When Britain abolished slavery
in 1833, the slaves were emancipated, and it became necessary to
find cheap labour from other sources, because the freed slaves became
costly to employ, while some of
them began to work independently.
In Trinidad, Guyana and Jamaica
the problem was serious. Initially
islanders from the smaller islands in
the eastern Caribbean, like Grenada,
were introduced, but their numbers
were inadequate. Labour from the
USA and British colonies was unsatisfactory because few were willing to
work as hard as was necessary with
the sugar cane. Attempts were made
to import labourers from France,
Germany and Portugal, but with a
similar lack of success. Part of the
problem was that there was a general
belief that only Africans, or those of
African descent, could survive hard
labour in tropical conditions.

A small immigration from China
failed because the Chinese proved to
be more enthusiastic as petty traders, and left the plantations to open
shops. It seemed that India would
provide the only inexhaustible supply of agriculturally experienced
labour, and an indentured labour

scheme was initiated. Indians would
be brought to the Caribbean where
they would be guaranteed work and
subsistence wages, although these
would generally only be spent in
plantation stores. After a period of
work, initially five years, but extended to ten, those who chose would
be able to return to India, their
passages paid. The years 1844–1917
were the main period of immigration. By 1860 what had originally
been seen as a temporary measure
had become a regular and depend-
able flow, and by 1871 Indians composed 25.1% of the population:
there were 27,425 in Trinidad alone.
Most still worked on the estates, but
only 40% were indentured. The vast
majority stayed on in the Caribbean
as low-wage earners.

Obviously the racial, religious and
later political profile of that part of
the Caribbean was altered, although
the colonial authorities did not
acknowledge these variations. The
vast majority of the Indians came
from Calcutta ('Kalkutiyas'). A
smaller number originated in
Madras ('Madrassis'), the latter
being considered less industrious.
Most of these immigrants were HIN-
DUS, and were able to practise their
religion. By 1850 most estates had
their temples, with BRAHMANS officiating much as in India. There were
fewer Muslims, the minority group
being SHI'ITE. From the 1850s they
celebrated Hosein/Hosay, commemorating the death of the Prophet's
grandson. The Sunni Muslims (*see*
SUNNA) and Hindus joined in with
enthusiasm, so there developed
something that had the character-

istics of an 'Indian' festival, although the Creole and African groups joined in too. Nevertheless the religion and culture of the Indians contributed to their low status. They were not 'free'. Muslim and Hindu marriages were not recognized by the colonial authorities until 1945, and had to be registered instead, in Trinidad at the infamous Red House in Woodford Square, Port of Spain. Until 1945, therefore, all Indian children were born notionally illegitimate. Despite the range of African–Caribbean cults, the black communities considered themselves superior and Christian. Hindus were perceived as unclean and uncivilized and Islam was perceived if anything even more negatively. Both Hindus and Muslims resisted conversion to Christianity, although particularly the PRESBYTERIANS made inroads in the south-east of Trinidad. The Pathans, who had chosen to come as free men to Trinidad at the end of the First World War, were particularly resistant to incorporation in any other group.

Their religion proved a great comfort to all the Indians, and social and religious patterns of India were reinvented in the peasant Indian villages. Peasants were also part of the CREOLIZATION process. Indian social structures had been fragmented. Over time emphases had altered, and memories were adapted to a new situation. Entry into education came late in the Indian community, and there is debate as to how far social and religious distance contributed to this. However, the independence of India in 1947 created great pride in the community and suggested to them the possibilities of new identities.

While most studies of East Indian religions concentrate on the extraordinary persistence of a general sense of Indian religious and personal identity, what is striking is the survival in the West Indies of the culture of India in diet, customs, festivals and names: for instance, *roti*

is a Trinidadian national dish. In Indian families men still have considerable control over women. Parents still arrange most marriages, or at least are asked to approve love-matches. They arrange the *barat* (procession), *tassa* (drumming) and food. Hindu families avoid marriages between cousins, however distant, while Muslims permit them. Muslims brought the QUR'AN, while Hindus retain some sense of the CASTE system, and while all Muslims believe in equality before ALLAH, in Trinidad some sort of Muslim social hierarchy has been created.

Most Christian Indians are converts, generally Presbyterian, ROMAN CATHOLIC or ANGLICAN, but they may well retain considerable respect and interest in Hindu or Muslim beliefs. Some churches in the south of Trinidad are mainly Indian. On Good Friday, the VIRGIN MARY in the Roman Catholic church in Siparia is decorated by Hindus with bracelets of their hair. They petition her for help, particularly in illness, and thank her for favours received, and they celebrate Christmas.

The Vedic tradition (*see* VEDA) persists in Hindu homes; their houses can be identified by the prayer flags outside, and at Hindu burial sites. Divali, the Hindu festival of light, is celebrated as a national holiday. Bamboo arches called *deyas* are lit with many candles, and there is drumming and dancing. The celebrations of Hosay resemble carnival processions. [19; 29; 57; 79; 92]

Eastern Catholics [XIII.D] A family of churches in full COMMUNION with the see of Rome, but sharing the liturgical, calendrical and to some extent theological and canonical traditions of the EASTERN or Oriental ORTHODOX churches. Eastern Catholics are sometimes called 'uniates', a name they generally resent. A small number of Catholics of the

Byzantine rite in southern Italy actually belong to the Western patriarchate, and many other immigrant or refugee communities in the West are governed by bishops acting as exarchs of the Pope.

Most Eastern Catholic communities are the product of Catholic missionary work among the Orthodox interacting with the aspiration of particular Orthodox hierarchs and communities to strengthen or validate their position by union with Rome. Normally such Eastern Catholics are organized into churches, each headed by its own PATRIARCH. The Catholic patriarchates of Alexandria (of the Copts (*see* COPTIC CHURCH)), Antioch (of the Syrian Catholics), Babylon (of the Chaldeans) and the single Patriarchate of Antioch and All the East, Alexandria and Jerusalem (of the Melkite Catholics) are of this kind. The Major Archbishop of Lviv heads the large and historically important Ukrainian Catholic Church, brought into union with Rome at Brest-Litovsk in 1596.

The Maronites hold a unique position among Eastern Catholics as the sole Eastern Christian community the whole of which is in communion with Rome; in every other case there is an Orthodox counterpart church for each Eastern Catholic Church. The Maronites were recognized as a distinct community at least as far back as the reign of Khalifa Mar'wan (744–8 CE). In the period of the CRUSADES they asserted their adherence to Rome, and their Patriarch, Jeremiah II, was present at the Fourth Lateran COUNCIL in 1215 and in 1216 was recognized by the Pope as Patriarch of Antioch of the Maronites.

The Chaldean Catholics represent the major surviving fragment of the ancient Church of the East, the 'Nestorian' church.

Almost all Eastern Catholic Churches experienced the pressure to Latinization; this sometimes originated as much in a wish to distinguish themselves from their Orthodox counterparts as in the insistence of Latin clergy, though sometimes, as in the drastic 'reforms' imposed on the St Thomas Christians at the Synod of Diamper, the latter was the case. In recent years, many Eastern Catholic communities have been active in exploring their whole cultural and religious heritage, and in reforming and restoring worship, art, theology and religious life, rejecting Latin models and returning to their own traditions.

Catholic church leaders have frequently aspired to see the Eastern Catholic churches as a bridge between Rome and Orthodoxy. Some Eastern Catholics, most notably the late Melkite Patriarch Maximos IV Saigh, have played that role; the Orthodox, however, tend to see 'uniates' as a threat and to treat them with great suspicion. What the impact on this relationship will be of the rise of Western rite Orthodoxy in America and Europe remains to be seen. [6; 8; 99]

Eastern   Orthodox   Church [XIII.D] A family of self-governing churches following the doctrine of the Seven Ecumenical COUNCILS. The Orthodox communion includes the four ancient Patriarchates (*see* PATRIARCH) of Alexandria, Antioch, Jerusalem and Constantinople, and the churches of Bulgaria, Belarus, Cyprus, Georgia, Greece, Romania, Russia, Serbia and Ukraine, in each of which it is the major religious community; it also includes the Orthodox churches of Albania, China, the Czech Republic and Slovakia, Estonia, Finland, Japan, Latvia, Lithuania, Poland and the USA. Orthodox communities belonging to various jurisdictions exist in Western Europe, in Africa (*see* AFRICAN ORTHODOX) and Australasia.

Since the separation of the Nestorian and Monophysite churches (*see* CHRISTOLOGY), and the loss of

COMMUNION with the Western Church, the Orthodox Church is the main historical inheritor of the Byzantine tradition of Christianity (see EASTERN CATHOLICS; CHRISTIANITY, HISTORY AND CHARACTER OF). Orthodox theology is strongly trinitarian (see TRINITY) and apophatic. In his essence God is utterly unknowable but is present throughout creation in his energies. The energies are God and can be experienced. The human being is created in the image and likeness of God: by the SIN of Adam human nature is damaged and the likeness to God fades, but the image remains. Adam's sin brings death into the world, and because of death sin multiplies. JESUS Christ conquers death by his death and resurrection, undermines the rule of sin and pours out the gift of new life, sending down his HOLY SPIRIT. Enlivened by the Holy Spirit, the CHURCH already shares in the life to come.

Orthodox religious life centres on the MYSTERIES (SACRAMENTS) in which the acts of God in history become present realities by the power of the Spirit. The mysteries enlighten and transform not only the individual but also the whole community and are effective symbols of the final restoration of the whole of Creation to God. (See also AFRICAN ORTHODOX; ALASKAN ORTHODOX; MACEDONIAN ORTHODOX; OLD BELIEVERS; OLD CALENDAR MOVEMENT; RUSSIAN ORTHODOX CHURCH ABROAD; WESTERN ORTHODOX CHRISTIANITY.)

Eastern Orthodox Missions [XIII.D] The Constantinople Patriarchate, having assumed the title 'Ecumenical' in 587, sought to co-ordinate all Christian missions to the barbarians. For centuries this primarily involved evangelizing the various peoples who settled either within or along the frontiers of the Byzantine provinces. The Georgian and Abkhazian churches assisted in this project far beyond their Caucasian base. By 1000 monks like Nikon Metanoeite (d. 988) had brought Christianity to the Sklavenian tribes who had settled in the Greek lands since 580. From 858 PATRIARCH Photios the Great was able to send missions further afield, to Moravia, Bulgaria and Russia. Constantine-Cyril headed a mission to the Khazars (860) and another, with his brother Methodios, to Greater Moravia (862). These two scholars from Thessaloniki set about creating a Slavonic alphabet and liturgy; they were assisted in their translation work by Gorazd, Kliment and a group of native clergy.

The conversion of Khan Boris of Bulgaria (865) and the Serbs (867) was also supervised by Patriarch Photios. The disciples of Methodios, expelled by Frankish clergy after 885, helped consolidate these gains. Welcomed by the Bulgarians, Kliment (886) and later Naum (893) extended the mission to the Slavs of Outer Macedonia. In 988 Prince Vladimir of Kiev embraced Christianity and so opened the whole of Rus to Greek and Bulgarian missionary work. In their turn Kievan monks (particularly from the Caves Lavra) spread Orthodox Christianity among their Slav, Finnish and other neighbours. Notably, Stephen of Perm (d. 1396) evangelized the Zyrian peoples and, like Cyril and Methodios, devised an alphabet and translated sacred texts into the local vernacular. Others, like Gury and Varsonofy (from 1555), continued this work among the Tatars and related tribes.

Under Turkish domination Athonite monks (including Kosmas Aitolos, martyred in 1779) laboured chiefly to combat the advance of Islam among the Albanians and other Balkan nations. Their Russian counterparts established missions across Siberia (1702), in China (1715) and in Alaska (1794). Makary Glukharev (d. 1847) brought Orthodoxy to the Altay peoples, while Inokenty Veniaminov worked across the Russian Far East and in America. The latter coordinated the translation of Christian writings into Aleut, Tlingit, Yakut and Tungus; as Metropolitan of Moscow (1868) he also founded the Orthodox Mission Society. Nicolas Ilminsky (d. 1891) similarly worked on translations into the colloquial languages of the Tatars, Chuvash, Kirgiz, Kalmyks and others. In the same period missions were established in Central Asia and Iran, and the Palestine Society was set up to aid the Arab Orthodox.

The work of Nicolas Kasatkin (d. 1912) in Japan from 1860 provided a model for all subsequent Orthodox missions. Almost single-handedly, like Stephen of Perm, he founded a Japanese Orthodox community that soon became autonomous in all but name. Bishop Nicolas himself translated the Orthodox liturgy into Japanese and identified with his flock to the point of leading prayers for Japan's victory in the Russo-Japanese war. He also helped to set up a mission in Korea in 1898.

The 1917 revolution in Russia did not bring an end to Russian missionary activity. John Maximovitch (d. 1966) and others used the Orthodox diaspora as a base for mission among the host communities. Since the Second World War Greek missions have been invited to sub-Saharan Africa and the Far East (also to Indonesia in 1988). The tendency has been for Christians in the Third World to turn to the Eastern and Oriental Orthodox churches for missions that are free of the imperialist baggage of Western Christianity. The main thrust of Orthodox mission remains the creation of self-sufficient and self-governing churches centred on a liturgy in the contemporary spoken language. From Japan to east Africa this has generally been accomplished by incorporating those aspects of the national culture that are compatible with the Orthodox ethos and helping a local Orthodox tradition to emerge. [25; 27; 61; 62; 79; 84; 85; 87; 92; 99] (*See also* AFRICAN ORTHODOX; ALASKAN ORTHODOX; WESTERN ORTHODOX CHRISTIANITY.)

Eckankar [XXVIII] Founded in Las Vegas after John Paul Twitchell (1908?–71), who had previously been among the first Scientology 'clears' (*see* CHURCH OF SCIENTOLOGY) and an initiate of Kirpal Singh, declared himself in 1965 to be the 971st Eck Master. The present leader is Sri Harold Klemp. Eckankar teaching is considered an advanced form of SURAT SABD YOGA, concentrating on physical techniques and spiritual experiences to enable the soul to travel beyond the physical limitations of the body to the higher spiritual realms of the 'Sugmad' – the formless, all-embracing, impersonal and infinite equivalent of God in theistic religions. 'Chelas' (students or members) practise spiritual exercises in their own homes. [5: 174–6; 34; 41: IV/D; 42: 955–6; 69]

Ecumenical Movement [XIII.B] A movement, originally mainly in PROTESTANTISM, to promote understanding and in some cases union between Christian churches. The modern movement was stimulated by the International Missionary Conference at Edinburgh (1910). It grew through organizations for doctrinal and social discussion in the 1920s. The World Council of Churches has met periodically since 1948. Participation by the EASTERN ORTHODOX CHURCH, ROMAN CATHOLICISM and PENTECOSTALISM makes it broadly representative of various forms of Christianity, but not of FUNDAMENTALISM (*see* AUTHORITY). Its recent selective support for liberation movements (*see* LIBERATION THEOLOGY) has been controversial. Councils of churches are also common at regional and national levels. A major achievement of the movement has been the increasing theological discussion, understanding and practical cooperation that have marked the relationships between the main Christian churches since the mid-20th century. The Orthodox churches and PAPACY have removed the anathemas (*see* CHURCH DISCIPLINE) formerly levelled against each other, and the Orthodox and Monophysites (*see* CHRISTOLOGY) have been reconciled. Some church unions have been achieved (*see* CANADA; INDIA, CHRISTIANITY IN). A projected union of English ANGLICANISM and METHODISM failed in 1972. Although achieved in India, reunion between episcopal and non-episcopal churches (*see* MINISTRY) remains the most difficult to achieve. Optimistic reunion schemes characteristic of the USA and Britain during the 1960s appear to have given way to concern about political and social questions. Reunion schemes now tend to focus on local unions between individual local churches. Theological divisions today often cut across those traditionally dividing churches. Divisions are now often between radicals and conservatives both within and across churches rather than between them. [1: 341–66; 169]

Edda [VII] The title given to two Icelandic books providing most of our information about Norse mythology. Snorri Sturluson, poet, historian and politician (1179–1241 CE), retold in superb Icelandic prose many northern myths, with quotations from poems and explanations of mythological imagery [28: 1–164; 32: 21–7]. He intended to provide a handbook for poets so that the ancient lore would not be lost. The book is called *Edda* in one MS, and therefore known as Snorri's Edda or the Prose Edda. The word *edda* means 'great-grandmother', but the title may have been derived from Oddi in Iceland, where Snorri was brought up. In 1643 a 13th-century manuscript book known as the *Codex regius* was found in an Icelandic farmhouse, containing poems on gods and heroes. This collection, together with a few poems from other MSS, is called the Elder, Poetic or Saemund's Edda, after an 11th-century scholar [21; 32: 18–44]. Various dates from 800 CE upwards have been suggested for the poems, a number of which appear to be pre-Christian and may have been composed in Norway. Some deal with the exploits of Freyr, LOKI, ODIN and THOR, and they include riddle contests between gods and giants, and much about the creation and destruction of the worlds of gods and humans.

Eightfold Path [XI] Outside traditional BUDDHIST cultures this is probably the best-known summary of the Buddhist path (Pali: *magga*; Sanskrit: *marga*). According to tradition it was the Eightfold Path that formed the subject matter of the BUDDHA's (*see* GOTAMA) first teaching. Elsewhere in Buddhist texts the Eightfold Path is commonly presented as precisely defining 'the way leading to the cessation of suffering' (*see* FOUR NOBLE TRUTHS). The Eightfold Path comprises 'right' or 'perfect' (Pali: *samma*; Sanskrit: *samyak*) view (*see* DITTHI), intention, action, speech, livelihood, effort, mindfulness and concentration. These eight items embrace three dimensions of Buddhist practice – 'wisdom' (PRAJNA) (items 1–2), 'conduct' (SILA) (items 3–5) and 'concentration' (SAMADHI) (items 6–8) – which together are seen as capable of producing an inner transformation of the individual (cf. ARAHAT). When the eight items are developed to the point of producing this transformation they are said to constitute the 'noble' (Pali: *ariya*; Sanskrit: *arya*) path or way. The items of the Eightfold Path represent headings for aspects of Buddhist practice that are dealt with fully in other contexts; thus the

Eightfold Path is more a description of what the Buddhist aspires to develop than how he or she sets about doing it. (*see also* BHAVANA; BODHI-PAKKHIYA-DHAMMA.) [34: 68–72]

Elamites [VIII] Before the migrations of the Medes and Persians *c.*1000 BCE, the history of religious development in Iran (*see* ZOROASTRIANISM) concentrated on the Elamite kingdom (Old Elamite kingdom, *c.*2550–1860 BCE; Classical period, *c.*1330–1000 BCE) [21: III, 21–32; 22: III, 23–40]. Elam was regarded as a religious centre which always retained a distinct religious tradition [15], although the pantheon included Babylonian as well as native deities and there were many features in common with other Mesopotamian religions (*see* BABYLONIANS; SUMERIANS). Sources include dedicatory inscriptions, god lists, monuments, reliefs such as the famous religious procession at Kurangun, sculpture and seals, but these give an inadequate understanding of the essentials of the religion.

The kingdom was basically a tribal federation. Each tribe retained its deities, and each city-state worshipped a patron deity and consort. Only the strongest rulers sought to give the state a religious cohesion, elevating certain local cults to national status and making the capitals – Susa and Dur-Untash – sacred centres where the tribal gods had shrines, or 'resting-places'. Choga-Zanbil was also a great centre.

A divine ruler, who performed priestly duties (*see* TEMPLES (ANCIENT NEAR EASTERN)), the king held his authority from the gods. Royal descent passed through the female line; the society was characterized by matriarchal traditions; and the earliest pre-eminent deity was a mother-goddess, recognized for her powers in MAGIC and in the underworld. A male god, Khumban, later became supreme, and the great national god, In-Shushinak (origi-nally a local god of Susa), finally achieved prominence.

No temple or foundation has survived, but cylinder seal representations indicate that they followed the Babylonian type; however, a distinctive feature was the huge horns which decorated the tops of the temple walls. The temples employed many priests and servants, and housed votive statues and gifts made to the gods. Daily animal sacrifices were made, and an oracular priest probably read the omens (*see* DIVINATION (ANCIENT NEAR EASTERN)).

Elam was regarded as the home of witches and demons. The most important and distinctive Elamite symbol was the serpent, which represented an ancient god and perhaps the dark powers of the earth (*see* ART AND SYMBOLISM (ANCIENT NEAR EASTERN)). Religious art and inscriptions of gods' names indicate some features of this religion and its close association with Mesopotamian beliefs, but many of its essential and unique elements remain obscure.

Elan Vital [XXVIII] The Divine Light Mission (DLM) was founded in India in the 1930s by Shri Hans Ji Maharaj (1957–), then achieved rapid growth in the West after his 13-year-old son, Guru Mahara Ji, visited London. Thousands of 'premies' pursued self-realization by practising the 'Knowledge', four simple meditation techniques for experiencing Divine Light, Divine Nectar, Divine Harmony and the 'primordial vibration' which is the Holy Name or Word. Following Mahara Ji's marriage and his wresting control in the West from his mother, the DLM was disbanded and the more low-profile Elan Vital created. Members still meet together and travel to frequent festivals attended by Maharaj (as he is now called). [5: 176–8; 20; 22: VII; 25: 65–70; 26: III; 41: IV/E; 42: 956–7]

Eliade, Mircea (1907–86) [xxxiv] A historian and phenomenologist of religion associated with the 'Chicago School', Eliade was born in Romania and studied at the University of Bucharest and the University of Calcutta (1928–32) under the famous Indian philosopher, Surendranath Dasgupta. He also spent six months studying the theory and practice of Yoga in a Rishikesh ashram. He returned to teach at the University of Bucharest and published an influential book on yoga in 1936 which is arguably his best work [59]. During the Second World War he served as a Romanian cultural attaché. After the war he became a visiting professor at the Sorbonne in Paris and in 1957 went to the University of Chicago where he was Professor of the History of Religions until his retirement. He wrote many works on the phenomenology and history of religions [49; 51; 53; 54; 55; 56; 57; 58]. He founded the Chicago journal *History of Religions* in 1961 and was editor in chief of the *Encyclopedia of Religion* (1986). He was also a novelist, wrote a two-volume autobiography [50] and published his *Journals* in four volumes [52].

Eliade maintained that religion must be understood on its own terms and cannot be explained away by Sociology or Psychology. Put simply, Eliade's theory is that there is an irreducible Sacred dimension to human experience which is manifested in myth (*see* Mythology), Symbol and Ritual, particularly in pre-literate societies. This manifestation of the sacred he calls a 'hierophany' or an 'archetype'. Hierophanies express a sacred dimension beyond time or history, which is contrasted with the 'profane' world of modern human experience. The task of the historian or phenomenologist of religion (*see* History of religions; Phenomenology of religion) is to map out the recurring patterns or structures of religious consciousness, such as 'initiation' or 'mystical ascent'.

Myths are about creation and return to a timeless, sacred realm, while rituals re-enact this return. A ritual, claims Eliade, repeats an archetypal action of a god or ancestor *in illo tempore* (before history began), and so attempts to abolish time and the 'terror of history'.

Eliade, influenced by Jung, can be seen within a romantic and idealist tradition. He has been criticized for his implicit theology and for not paying enough attention to the historical particularity of religions, though he attempted to counteract this criticism in his last works. In emphasizing the inner experience of religion, Eliade has neglected its ideological and social functions which are of great significance, even in 'archaic' societies.

Emblems (Sikh) [xxxiii] Two devices are regularly used by Sikhs as auspicious emblems. The earlier of the two, a combination of the Gurmukhi figure 1 and letter O (*see figure 4*), is taken from the Adi Granth, where it is used as an invocatory symbol representing the unity of God (the 'One *Oankar*' or Primal Being). The second popular device is the Khanda, the Khalsa emblem, comprising a steel quoit flanked by two daggers (*kirpan*) with vertical two-edged sword (*khanda*) superimposed.

Emin [xxviii] The Eminent Way is said to have been conceived by Raymond Armin (1912?–), known as Leo, in 1924, but began to attract others beyond his immediate family in the early 1970s. The Emin now has several centres in Europe, North America, New Zealand and Israel [7: 17–33]. The beliefs are of an esoteric nature, incorporating a number of ideas from various occult and other traditions, with a major concern about becoming electrically polluted. Public lectures are offered on a diversity of subjects, such as geomagnetism; how to improve the way you think; the significance of dreaming; colour: a real influence in human life; astrology; theatre; and the value of family life. [2; 7: 17–33]

Emperor-Worship   (Roman) [XXXI] Alexander the Great (336–323 BCE) and his successors provided the model for the deification of Roman emperors, though human becoming god is not wholly alien to Roman tradition [20: 53–62; 25]. In the eastern provinces, the living emperor was worshipped as such, but in Rome itself deification (*consecratio*) was a distinct ceremony decreed after death for the emperor, if he was thought deserving [9: 3–25]. Complex in its origins, the institution was never imposed from the centre, except to some extent in the Latin west. Its diversity and wide extension suggest that it provided a symbolic resource of value to local city elites (who provided the priests and benefactions) and to the central authorities [20]. Jokes, some attributed to the emperors themselves (one allegedly died saying, 'I feel I am becoming a god'), and even more the silence of literature suggests scepticism among intellectuals [9: 177–206]. However, the silence may indicate simply that the institution, after initial awkwardness, became routine. For, although emperors did not manifest divinity by performing miracles, they were certainly recognized as gods in both language and ritual (in spite of the ambiguities of their position), the more so as time went by. [13: 238–44; 18: XLIX; 20]

Empiricism [XXXII] The doctrine that there is no knowledge of the world except what is derived from sense experience. Philosophers who have been empiricists, like David Hume (1711–76) and Bertrand Russell (1872–1970), have commonly been led into SCEPTICISM about religion. An extreme form of anti-metaphysical empiricism is LOGICAL POSITIVISM. In a broad sense, however, empiricism has by no means always been antagonistic to religion. Many theologians, including F. R. Tennant [26], have adopted an empiricist standpoint.

Emptiness [XI] Or voidness (Sanskrit: *shunyata*; Pali: *sunnata*), an important Buddhist concept. It may be used in reference to the successive meditations (*see* SAMATHA) to show their peaceful nature, quite empty of noisy distraction or subtle disturbance. Sometimes it refers to insight (VIPASSANA), where phenomena are seen as empty of self (ANATTA) or anything similar, and sometimes to NIBBANA or transcendent (LOKUTTARA) mind, as empty of greed, hate and delusion. In MAHAYANA BUDDHISM emptiness is frequently stressed, especially in the SHUNYATAVADA, signifying initially freedom from views and proliferating concepts. The realization that phenomena are empty of any substantial existence is distinguished as

IK-ONKAR: SYMBOL OF GOD

KHALSA EMBLEM

Figure 4
Sikh emblems

more profound. This should not be interpreted as nihilistic or as asserting the non-reality of ordinary experience; this would itself be a position and hence not 'empty'. What is envisaged rather is some kind of profound transformation of the understanding, leading to a type of relaxed fluidity of action. [16: 242–50]

Encounter of Religions [XXXIV] Religions are the social expression of the religious affiliations of peoples, and as peoples have migrated so religions have been in encounter throughout human history. The encounters have resulted in various outcomes. In some cases a dominant or powerful people have ensured that their form of religion has triumphed and reduced indigenous forms to minority status; or, in extreme conditions, the dominant religion has resulted in the extirpation of other forms of religion. This is clearly what happened as Christianity spread throughout the continent of Europe after gaining state dominance in the Roman empire. In north Africa EARLY CHRISTIANITY was more or less wiped out by the advance of ISLAM in the 7th and 8th centuries CE. In many instances the movement of a dominant religion has resulted in SYNCRETISM, by which the dominant religion absorbs or, occasionally, transforms more localized forms during the geographical or historical advance. Such a state is to be seen in certain aspects of CHRISTIANITY in Europe, in HINDUISM in south-east Asia, in BUDDHISM throughout Asia into Japan, and in Islam in the Indian subcontinent. Such movements and encounters, which for the most part have occurred without very much self-awareness on the part of the participants, are part of the whole HISTORY OF RELIGIONS and can be studied in retrospect. There have also been many encounters of religions which have resulted in conflict as religions have competed for space

and allegiance. One of the major conflicts in the history of religions has been, until recently, the continuing conflict between Christianity and Islam, dating back to the CRUSADES of the 11th–13th centuries and further exemplified by the final expulsion of Islam from Spain in 1492. In more recent times the encounter of religions has become a matter of creating some form of *modus vivendi* in an increasingly plural world as peoples and their religious affiliations have become much more mobile and as a self-awareness of the need to work together rather than compete has overtaken some religious groups which until the early part of this century were still engaged in missionary work aiming at the displacement of indigenous religions, a movement which has been part of the history of Christianity, Islam and Buddhism for many centuries. Especially since the 19th century, with the growth of such political forces as the British empire, there has been an increasing awareness of the viability of different forms of religion and of a greater need to study those religions which were formerly in competition and with which the peoples of one religion have increasingly been forced to live in harmony as far as this is achievable. Thus encounter has taken on a force of its own with strategies, such as programmes of dialogue between adherents of different religions, devised to ease the situation of encounter and increase cooperation and toleration. Historically this kind of movement, which grew out of a movement within Christianity to encourage cooperation between Christian denominations, the ECUMENICAL MOVEMENT, has sometimes been described as 'the wider ecumenism' [XIV 71], and has become part of the history of religions and thus a proper object of study in its own right, apart from its existence as a movement within a number of religions. Christian theologians have contributed to the attempt to create harmony between religions by formulating their theology on the premise of the plurality of religions, sometimes on the grounds of the need for the religions to cooperate against the threat of secular world-views and movements [162 vol. 3, 6; 163]. There have been a number of attempts at formulating a 'theology of religions' or a 'world' or 'global theology' [154]. Although the initiative has primarily been taken from within Christianity, leaders of other religions have increasingly responded [133; 120; 81; 141; xiv 24; xiv 20]. Officially, globally organized religions like Christianity have created bodies such as the Vatican Secretariat for Non-Christians and the section of the World Council of Churches, Geneva, entitled 'Dialogue with Men of Living Faiths and Ideologies' to advance creative encounter and dialogue with peoples of other religions. (see also RELIGIOUS PLURALISM.)

Enlightenment, the [xxxiv] The Enlightenment (German: *Aufklärung*; French: *Élaircissement*) was a European intellectual movement of the 18th century with its roots in 17th-century ideas in science and philosophy, especially the philosophy of John Locke (1632–1704), including his thoughts on the relation of reason to religion. The movement had its presence in France, Germany and Britain. Among the French thinkers were Voltaire (1694–1778), poet, playwright, philosopher and essayist, noted for his hostile attitude towards the Roman Catholic Church, clericalism and what he considered to be the superstition of traditional Christianity, but also for his appeal for religious toleration and rational piety; Montesquieu (1689–1755), historian and social and political theorist; and Diderot (1713–84). The last was editor of the 17-volume *Encyclopédie*, the monument to the French Enlightenment. It contained, apart from Diderot's own writings, the work of Voltaire, Montesquieu and Rousseau. Although the *Encyclopédie* did not have a single intellectual viewpoint, indeed it contained articles which attacked and defended religion, it generally sought political and social progress by promoting debate on morality, politics and religion. In Germany the movement was under the leadership of Christian Wolff (1679–1754) whose rationalistic theology, although not that radical, was sufficiently threatening to induce a violent response from German Pietists (see PIETISM). Gotthold Ephraim Lessing, playwright and theologian, opposed both Wolff's theology and the Pietists' irrational attacks on Wolff. Lessing coined the term 'bibliolatry' to describe the Pietists' attitude towards Christian tradition. Crucial to much later criticism of the foundation documents of the Hebrew religion and Christianity was the work of biblical critic, Hermann Samuel Reimarus (1694–1768). The most important German Enlightenment figure, however, was Immanuel Kant (1724–1804), philosopher, critic of religion and champion of rational autonomy over against the heteronomy of traditional religion. In Britain the Enlightenment is associated with the names of John Toland and Matthew Tindal, both DEIST in theology, and Joseph Priestley, Presbyterian minister as well as philosopher and scientist. Enlightenment thinking is also apparent in Jeremy Bentham (1748–1832), founder of utilitarian philosophy, Adam Smith (1723–90), author of *The Wealth of Nations*, and Edward Gibbon (1737–94), historian and author of *The Rise and Fall of the Roman Empire*. The philosopher David Hume also reflected at least the religious views of the movement, while being critical of reliance on human reason. The Enlightenment also had its American adherents: Thomas Paine, author of *The Rights of Man*, Benjamin Franklin and Thomas Jefferson, who was for a time a close correspondent of Joseph Priestley. The basic aim of the Enlightenment thinkers was to achieve autonomy for human thought and tolerance for individual perspectives. By comparison, 'Fundamentalist interpretation of the Bible was a millstone around the neck of the defenders of revelation' [116: 292]. Although the Enlightenment was an 18th-century movement in that this was the period of its flowering as an intellectual event, its influence only gradually permeated religious, social and political life in Europe and America. Many of the 19th century's controversies regarding critical studies of the Christian BIBLE and attacks on the questionable morality of much Christian dogma bear the influence of the Enlightenment. Traditionalists still regret the influence of the Enlightenment and regard it as an attack on piety, traditional ecclesiastical authority and simple devotion. However, the Enlightenment did have positive influences on Christianity. 'The ridicule heaped upon the Bible by the writers of the Enlightenment did Christians a great service by compelling them to begin the process of tracing the evolution of a lofty idea of God from crude primitive origins, as against their static picture, indiscriminately compiled, of a timeless tyrant. The Enlightenment did a further service to Christianity by ridiculing hell, the ironies of Voltaire and Diderot clinching the case already advanced by innovative Christian thinkers.' [116: 292] In many ways its influence is still not fully realized in the life of European states and the USA in matters relating to religion and political power and public morality, the modernizing of religion itself, the relationships between races and the freedom of expression and orientation in private and public life.

Ennin [XXI] (792–864 CE), posthumously known as Jikaku Daishi, was a priest of the TENDAI sect from Tochigi prefecture who trained under SAICHO on Mt Hiei from the age of 14. He travelled with Fujiwara Tsunetsugu to China when 46, keeping a detailed account, *Nitto guho junrei koki*, and returning about ten years later. His commentary on T'ang China is a valuable first-hand record. He became chief priest of the Tendai sect in 854, sponsoring *nembutsu*, chanting the name of AMIDA. His followers split into two opposing groups, vying for power within the sect.

Ephesus, Early Christianity at [XIII.A] Although CHRISTIANITY had reached Ephesus before PAUL resided there (*c.* 52–55 CE), it is to him and his colleagues that the thorough evangelization of the city and its hinterland is due. But in the Christian tradition of Ephesus the outstanding name is John, 'the disciple of the Lord', who is said to have settled there (with MARY) in old age and is commemorated by the ruined basilica of St John on the hill Ayasoluk (a corruption of *hagios theologos*, 'the holy divine'). [6: 286–99; 11: II, 542–9; 15]

Eschatology (Biblical and Christian) [XIII.A] The doctrine of the 'last things' (Greek *ta eschata*), whether personal or cosmic. Eschatological beliefs describe what will ultimately happen either in terms of restoration to an ideal original state or in terms of a new creative act by GOD. In either case God would vindicate the cause of righteousness and establish his rule or kingdom. The teaching of JESUS can be understood to include elements of both kinds of eschatalogy. Concerning death and its aftermath, in early Israel the dead were pictured as sharing an undifferentiated existence in Sheol. In post-exilic times, particularly from the 2nd century BCE onwards and in APOCALYPTIC writings, the belief in bodily resurrection, especially for the righteous, was held by many Jews, including the members of the

QUMRAN community and the PHAR-ISEES. This belief was inherited by the Christians, who held that the first stage in the general resurrection of the righteous and the wicked for judgement had taken place with the resurrection of Jesus. (Cf. AFTER-LIFE; FRASHOKERETI; RAGNAROK; for details *see* AFTERLIFE, CHRISTIAN VIEW OF.) [11: II, 575–609; 18: 87–96]

Eskimo–Aleut [v] Together, the Eskimo–Aleut (the latter a branch of the former, but having a distinctive culture of their own) occupy an area extending from the islands south-west of Alaska to the south-east of Greenland, including Newfound-land and Labrador. Little is known of early Aleut religion, missionary work having begun almost imme-diately after outside contact. Eskimo–Aleut religion is greatly influenced by a hunting and fishing economy. The powers of the uni-verse, *inua* (also *yua, tayaruu*), are conceived of as anthropomorphic beings. In Alaska these are identified as personal GUARDIAN SPIRITS and/ or 'owners' or 'persons' of the ani-mals. In central and eastern areas they are viewed primarily as female deities and as *tupilaks* (composite animal figures (*see* OWNER OF THE ANIMALS), helpers of SHAMANS). The cosmos is perceived as naturally harmonious, or at least neutral, calamities befalling humankind through its negligence or disobe-dience [24: VII–VIII]. Chief among the spirit powers are those ordering the forces of nature (*see* COSMOL-OGY). A masculine power is asso-ciated with the sky and upper regions, and a feminine power is associated with the sea and land. The latter, often designated Sedna (or Siitna), is the irascible ruler of the undersea world and the one who gave rise to all creatures of the sea. Myths relate that while escaping a seducer she was cast out of her father's boat. As she attempted to cling to its side, her father, in fear for

his life, struck at her hands with an ivory axe, cutting off her fingers, which were transformed into seals, walruses and other sea animals. Sedna herself retreated to the depths where she now resides, visited on occasion by the ANGAKOK (or sha-man) who seeks to persuade her to grant mankind good fishing [23: II]. Shamans also influence the move-ments of SOULS (*tarneg*), directing them back to their owners, who have suffered illness during their absence, or to the kingdom of the dead in the case of permanent separation. The autumn ceremonial, held among the Central Eskimo, seeks to placate Sedna and to establish the cosmos on a favourable course.

Esoteric Work [XXIV] Esotericism is the single name, used for the first time by Eliphas Levi in the mid-19th century, for the body of ideas includ-ing THEOSOPHY, ASTROLOGY, ALCHEMY and the many other tradi-tions or schools teaching 'OCCULT philosophy'. The first recorded use of the word 'esoteric' is by Lucian, who ascribed it to Aristotle as a classification of his own works into esoteric and exoteric, the latter sim-ply meaning popular or untechnical. Later writers employed the term esoteric to mean secret doctrines taught to a select few. The same breadth of usage exists today, and esoteric work encompasses all philo-sophical disciplines concerned with the inner (Greek, *esoteros*, inner or interior) transformation of man. Essential to esoteric work is access to 'knowledge' (not 'knowledge of', in the sense of information), which is apprehended at the interface between the known and the unknown. Central to modern eso-teric doctrine are the three lines of work – work for self, work for others and work for the work's sake. Although these may all have exoteric manifestations, the 'work' occurs within the individual, within the 'group' and within the mind of man as a whole. Esoteric work, often undertaken in groups, is usually conducted under highly disciplined conditions such as those concerning speech both inside and outside the group. The intention of this is to establish trust and to maintain integrity in the transmission of the teachings.

Essenes [XIII.A] A Jewish group mentioned by JOSEPHUS (and others) alongside the PHARISEES and the SADDUCEES. According to him they are of two kinds. One had a strict hierarchical order of communal living, sharing property and abstaining from sexual activity. Members were admitted after a three-year probationary period and a rite of initiation. The focus of their daily routine was prayer, work, ritual washing and a communal meal. The other kind combined these ideals and practices with marriage. The discovery of similar descriptions of the life and ordering of a community (*yahad*) in the DEAD SEA SCROLLS from QUMRAN has led many to identify those who lived at Qumran with the Essenes. Other texts there describe groups that marry and live throughout the land; these may be identified with Josephus' second kind of Essene. [11: II, 619–26; 21: 341–79; 22: II, 555–97; 25]

Ethike [XVI] Morality. The Greek gods, especially Zeus, were thought to protect justice. 'Bad' behaviour was punished, directly, e.g. through plagues etc. which would affect the community unless the offender were punished, or through action on, and in interaction with, the human mind that leads to catastrophe. The Erinyes (Furies) punished certain crimes. But bad men often flourish, so the notion arose that one could be punished in one's descendants and later also that one was punished in the afterlife. Some believed in retribution through reincarnation. *Nemesis*, divine retribution personified, punished human presumption (*hybris*). Mortals must, above all,

worship the gods, honour their oaths, respect their parents, and behave well to guests, suppliants, heralds and the dead. The moral content of religion – especially of Mysteric religion (*see* MYSTERIA) – increased progressively, especially in Hellenistic times, when philosophy and the cults of Asklepios and the oriental gods posited a higher ethical standard. This included the spiritual purity which had first been propounded at Delphi (*see* MANTIKE). [4: 246–54; 9: 150–2; 10: 246–68; 21; 27: 54, 64–7; 28: 99–100, 152]

Ethiopian Christianity [XIII.D] The Ethiopian Orthodox Church is the largest community surviving from the ancient Christianity of Africa. It was founded in the 4th century by two shipwrecked Christians, Frumentius (Abba Salama) and Aedesius, who won favour with the Axumite Emperor Ezana, and strengthened by the work of the 'Nine Roman Saints', Syrian monks who arrived around 500 CE. With the spread of ISLAMIC power, the Ethiopian Church was brought within the orbit of the COPTIC Patriarchate of Alexandria, to which it remained subject until the present century. It is now a fully independent national church, with counterparts in Eritrea and Tigre. The Ethiopian Church has a rich literary and musical tradition, and a unique architectural and iconographic heritage most visible in the many magnificent churches hewn from living rock. The monastic communities represent an archaic form of Christian MONASTICISM.

There also exist in Ethiopia significant communities of EASTERN CATHOLIC and EASTERN ORTHODOX Christians. [6; 7; 8; 35] (*See* AFRICAN ORTHODOX; COPTIC CHRISTIANITY; NUBIAN CHRISTIANITY.)

Ethiopian Churches [XXVII] African independent churches appearing from the 1880s, first in Ghana, Nigeria (here called 'African churches') and South Africa, often through secession from a mission or older church which they resemble in worship, polity and doctrine, with some African variations and cultural features such as polygamy. The term 'Ethiopian' used in southern Africa and as a classificatory term derives from biblical references to Ethiopia and from its ancient church, regarded as a model for independence. [12: 40–41, 45; 18: 53–9]

Eucharist [XIII.B] The chief SACRAMENT and central act of Christian WORSHIP (also called Holy Communion, Lord's Supper, and MASS). JESUS Christ at his final meal or 'Last Supper' with his disciples blessed bread and wine with the words 'this is my body', 'this is my blood'. Debate has centred mainly on the nature of the 'presence' of Christ in the rite; and its character as a Christian 'sacrifice'. In ROMAN CATHOLICISM 'transubstantiation' teaches that after consecration the 'substance' (inner reality) of the bread (the 'host') and wine becomes 'sacramentally' the Body and Blood of Christ, while the 'accidents' (their physical characteristics) remain unchanged. The EASTERN ORTHODOX CHURCHES and many ANGLICANS believe that the bread and wine become the body and blood of Christ without attempting to define the mode of change. LUTHERANISM teaches 'consubstantiation' (coexistence of the complete physical elements with the Body and Blood). Calvin (see CALVINISM) and some Anglicans deny any physical change but believe that the power of the Body and Blood is received (Virtualism). Some Protestants (e.g. Zwingli, 1484–1531 CE) see the rite as a memorial aiding faith. PROTESTANTISM rejected the notion of sacrifice in the Eucharist, but Roman Catholicism, the Orthodox Church and Anglo-Catholics see it as at least realizing and applying the original sacrifice of Christ's death for the living and dead. Eucharistic worship ranges from the elaboration of the mass and the Orthodox Church liturgy to the simplicity of the typical BAPTISTS or the PLYMOUTH BRETHREN and their 'Breaking of Bread'. QUAKERS (see FRIENDS, RELIGIOUS SOCIETY OF) and the SALVATION ARMY do not use it. Roman Catholicism has traditionally given only the bread ('communion in one kind') to the laity, but in recent years the wine has often been administered as well. The ECUMENICAL MOVEMENT and LITURGICAL MOVEMENT have reduced many of the traditional eucharistic differences between Christians. [48: 222–45; 114: 211–16, 440–58; 157: 475–8; 160]

Europe, Christianity in [XIII.B] After the fall of the Western Roman empire, and during the middle ages, Christianity became a predominantly European religion. The REFORMATION split in the Western Church left northern Europe dominated by PROTESTANTISM, southern by ROMAN CATHOLICISM; while the east was dominated by the EASTERN ORTHODOX CHURCH. Close relationships were established with the state (see STATE, CHRISTIANITY AND THE). European conflicts and empires (Spanish, French, British) have been reflected in the expansion of their brands of Christianity to the rest of the world. Christian theology, WORSHIP and CHURCH ORGANIZATION are still strongly marked by the European phase of world history. European-influenced Christianity has been extended and modified in the USA and thence to the rest of the world. In Western Europe since the 19th century, churches have tended increasingly to lose public influence to the state as well as suffering large losses in active membership. In Eastern Europe, however, under communist rule, churches were in some cases (notably Poland) foci for national feeling and resistance to state pressure. The situation has changed yet again with the collapse of communist rule in the 1990s. [8;

37 vols 2–5; 103; 121 vols 1, 2, 4;
134]

Europe, Islam in [XIX] In certain
parts of Europe there has been a
Muslim presence almost as old as
historical ISLAM, especially along the
Mediterranean coast. But the vast
majority of Muslims now living in
Europe have arisen out of three historical episodes.

During the 13th and early 14th
centuries the Turco-Mongols of the
Khanate of the Golden Horde,
based in the Volga basin, became
Muslim. As Mongol rule retreated in
the face of Russian expansion during
the 15th century, many of the Tatar
descendants of the Muslim Turco-
Mongols remained in the places of
settlement, especially in the Volga
basin and the area of Crimea. Their
subsequent history was a mixture of
tolerance and persecution. At the
height of the Russian empire in the
18th and 19th centuries, many
Tatars migrated as traders and
craftsmen within the empire, and
major Tatar settlements grew up in
the area today covered by western
Ukraine and eastern Poland. Other
communities settled in major cities
including St Petersburg, where a
mosque in the Central Asian style
was built at the end of the 19th
century, Moscow, and Helsinki.
Under Soviet rule all popular forms
of Islam were suppressed, and the
Tatars were particular victims of
Stalin's policies of ethnic suppression and deportation. Only gradually
was an official Muslim structure
established in the USSR, through
which the state sought to keep control. Of the four official Muslim
Religious Boards, one was based in
Ufa in the Bashkir autonomous
republic working in Tatar for a
mainly Sunni (*see* SUNNA) Hanafi
population.

During the 14th to 16th centuries
the Ottoman empire expanded out
of its eastern Anatolian bases east-
ward into the Caucasus and westwards into south-eastern Europe,
maintaining its rule and influence in
those areas for several centuries. As
a result Muslim populations established themselves in many of the
conquered regions, either through
settlement or through conversion. It
is estimated that the total Muslim
population of the European part of
the former USSR had reached well
over 15 million by the end of the
1980s.

In south-eastern Europe the effect
of Ottoman rule was the establishment of Muslim populations of
some significance. Internal migration and settlement led to the creation of mainly Turkish Muslim
communities in parts of Thrace and
elsewhere. Conversion and mixed
settlement also meant the creation of
major Muslim communities, principally the Albanians and the Slav
Muslims of Bosnia-Herzegovina and
parts of Thrace and the lower
reaches of the Danube. Today the
Turkish Muslim communities are
concentrated in the southern parts
of the former Yugoslavia, in Macedonia, parts of the Greek province of
Western Thrace and – the largest
group, of some half a million – in the
eastern Rhodope mountains of Bulgaria. Albanians make up significant
parts of the population of Macedonia and the Kosovo province, formerly of southern Yugoslavia, as
well as Albania proper. Slav Muslim
communities are concentrated in
Bosnia-Herzegovina, where they
were given status as a distinct 'Muslim' nationality in 1968, and in the
Rhodope mountains and the eastern
Danube basin in Bulgaria. By the
late 1980s the Muslim population in
the whole of former Yugoslavia was
about 4 million; in Bulgaria, 1 million; Albania, some 2.5 million; and
in Greece, about 150,000. The collapse of the communist regimes
throughout eastern Europe has
reopened questions of the relationship between religion, ethnicity and
nationality in ways which have contributed to destabilizing of the state
patterns established after the First

and Second World Wars. Particularly in former Yugoslavia, the Caucasus and in parts of the Russian Federation, the place of Muslims in nation states, as majorities or minorities, has become a cause of some tension.

The Muslim presence in western Europe comes out of a very different historical background, namely that of immigration to the metropolitan centres of 19th- and 20th-century European colonial systems. Early significant immigration took place into Britain and France from the mid-19th century; in the German states Muslims settled from south-eastern Europe. The main change took place with the recruitment of industrial labour in the decades after the Second World War. So far as Muslim immigration was concerned, the general picture was that Britain recruited from the Indian subcontinent, France from north Africa and West Germany from Turkey (although not a colony, Turkey had developed close economic links with Germany from the late 19th century). The smaller countries in between followed the lead of their larger neighbours in various mixtures. By the end of the 1980s the Muslim population of France was over 3 million, that of Germany some 1.7 million and of Britain over 1 million. Belgium, the Netherlands and Italy each had 300,000–400,000, Austria, Switzerland, Sweden and Spain each around 100,000–150,000 and Norway, Denmark and Portugal in the tens of thousands, giving a total for Western Europe in the region of 7–8 million. The circumstances of the immigration have meant that Muslim settlement has been concentrated in industrial centres. Differing contexts in the various West European countries have meant that Muslims live in varying conditions, in terms not only of their civil and political status but also of their religious status. In Austria, under a law of 1912, and in Belgium, by a law of 1974, Islam has official status on a par with the main churches, although the benefits accruing as a result are very different in the two countries. Most of the advantages granted to organizations in Germany are also available to Muslims, even though the vast majority remain Turkish citizens; but Muslim requests for a status equal to that of the recognized churches have been rejected. In most countries establishment of mosques and prayer houses has been relatively simple, and in the three main countries their number has reached 1,000 and more. Muslim organizations remain identified with those of the countries of origin, mostly Sunni (*see* SUNNA) and often of a religio-political nature. But there is also growing activity among the younger Muslims who have been born and brought up in Europe. This expresses itself in a growing number of youth associations as well as in the increasing involvement of young people in the existing organizations. As this happens, the priorities and programmes of Muslim organizations are beginning to concentrate more on issues relating to the country of settlement and wider Islamic issues, rather than on matters relating to the countries of origin. (*see also* RUSSIA AND THE NORTH CAUCASUS, ISLAM IN.) [49; 99]

European Jewry [XXII] There are records of Jews on the European mainland several centuries before the Christian era, but it was only after the Roman conquest of Palestine in the 1st century BCE that the Jewish population of Europe grew substantially. From the 4th century CE the Christian church imposed various discriminatory restrictions on Jews, and these have shaped the history of the Jews in Christian Europe up to the modern period. The Jews were expelled from England in 1290 [53: IV], from France in 1394, from different parts of Germany in the 14th and 15th centuries, from Spain in 1492 and from Portugal in 1499 [14 vol. 6: 1069]. Despite pogroms (organized attacks against Jews), persecution and expulsion (*see* ANTI-SEMITISM), European Jewry flourished spiritually, in particular in Poland and Lithuania (*see* ASHKENAZI). Great centres of Jewish scholarship were set up, and the Jewish community was a self-governing state within a state in the late middle ages [43: LXXI]. The Nazi massacres destroyed the old European communities (*see* HOLOCAUST), and since 1945 the centre of Jewish cultural life has shifted to ISRAEL and the USA. [32; 44; 52]

Evangelical [XIII.B] (1) A word derived from the Greek for GOSPEL (the Christian 'Good News' of SALVATION) and used today of groups in PROTESTANTISM claiming to declare this with special fidelity. (2) In German-speaking lands, an alternative name for LUTHERANISM. The term has been used in English-speaking countries since the 18th-century Evangelical Revival (*see* REVIVALISM) to denote those emphasizing such teachings as the infallibility of the BIBLE, justification by faith and personal conversion. They are generally hostile to ROMAN CATHOLICISM and Anglo-Catholicism (*see* ANGLICANISM). But some Evangelicals adopt more liberal views on the Bible and social questions. [14]

Evangelicalism [IV] Evangelicalism is a worldwide movement in Protestant Christianity that has taken decisive form in Anglo-America and acquired a special stamp in the USA. Since the mid-20th century, after the rise to prominence of evangelist Billy Graham, described as someone who moved from FUNDAMENTALISM to 'neo-evangelicalism', the 'neo-' came to be dropped, and movements associated with people like Graham came to be called simply 'evangelical'.

'Evangelical' means having to do with the evangel, or Christian gospel. The 16th-century Lutheran REFORMATION and LUTHERANS into contemporary times have cherished the word to stress their belief in a gospel of divine grace, and the word appears in the name of bodies such as the Evangelical Lutheran Church in America. In the 19th century evangelicalism represented a movement in British ANGLICANISM. But most people have let those associations of the word be obscured as they concentrate on the new evangelicalism. This can be described as the confluence of two main streams. One is simply '19th-century mainstream Protestantism', which called itself 'evangelical' before tensions grew within the churches. By the early 20th century it was clear that much of the seminary, mission board, journalistic and theological leadership was openly embracing 'modernity'. This meant that they were open to theories of evolution, were progressive in their outlook, and made use of BIBLICAL CRITICISM. Many moderates just did what they could to avoid controversy and stayed 'evangelical'. Those who did get involved in a controversy called 'fundamentalist–modernist' found themselves repulsed by what they thought was the crudeness and belligerence of the fundamentalists. Agreeing with them in doctrine, the evangelicals formed more moderate organizations and movements, such as the National Association of Evangelicals in 1942 [25: I; 11: V].

Such evangelicals take conservative views of the inspiration of the BIBLE and often describe themselves as 'literalist' in respect to doctrines that they see liberals treating symbolically. Once holding aloof from most political involvement – support of Prohibition (of alcoholic beverages) was a rare exception – since certain Supreme Court decisions of 1962 and 1963 (against prayer in public schools) and 1973 (permitting abortion), they have done an about-face and many of them are now participants in some of the most visible, controversial and sometimes effective political coalitions. While liberal churches never mastered radio or television, evangelicalism produced the phenomenon of 'tele-vangelism'. Evangelicals, as television demonstrates, put a high premium on converting others, 'evangelizing'. They send missionaries around the world, support many humanitarian ventures and see themselves as providing moral backbone for a pluralist America that they consider to be succumbing to relativism and humanism. At the same time, evangelicalism has acquired considerable breadth, and includes an 'evangelical left': theologians and activists who are critical of American evangelicalism's identification with national military might, *laissez-faire* free-enterprise economics and acquiescence in social policies that they believe leads to neglect of the nation's poor [10].

Apart from all the controversy over evangelical moralism and politicking, if evangelicals are asked what they are *really* in the world for, they would say something about saving souls, providing community, and themselves experiencing divine grace. [15; 25]

Evil (Ancient Near East) [VIII] MAGIC was used to combat evil forces, which were often personified as demons. Sometimes a sick person was identified with an animal, which was then killed [23: 21]. Myths and ritual combats (*see* ANCIENT NEAR EASTERN RELIGIONS; FESTIVALS (ANCIENT NEAR EASTERN)) depicted the victory of good over evil, but people's own sin and not the god's vengeance was regarded as the cause of their suffering. No human troubles were therefore considered unjust, and a renewal of the god's favour was sought through prayers and lamentations [16: 166].

Misfortune was regarded as the result of divine negligence or of a person's sin (or even that of his or her forebears); however, blame was never attributable to the gods, and prayer could gain salvation [16: 153–66].

Evil, Christian Doctrine of [XIII.B] Christians have endeavoured to explain the origin and meaning of evil and suffering, but especially to defend the goodness and omnipotence of God against objections arising from the existence of evil. Christian MONOTHEISM has been resistant to DUALISM and PANTHEISM, although these have sometimes influenced Christian philosophies and SECTS, e.g. the Albigenses (*see* HERESY (MEDIEVAL CHRISTIAN)). Satan as an evil power is ultimately subordinated to God (cf. AFTERLIFE). Origen (*c*.185–*c*.254 CE), St Thomas Aquinas (*c*.1225–74 CE; *see* THOMISM) and many others have explained evil as an abuse of human freedom necessarily allowed to achieve good. Leibniz (1646–1716) (who coined the term THEODICY for these matters) [157: 1358] saw the world as the best of all possible worlds with evil a necessary shadow to highlight its attractions. Modern treatments [91] have oscillated between optimistic and pessimistic views of human capacity for good and the possibility of overcoming evil in the world. These different views are partly related to changing views of HUMANITY and of SIN. Suffering has also been treated as an occasion of spiritual development in submission to God, following JESUS Christ's example, but there has been considerable revulsion against this view in recent times, especially since the HOLOCAUST.

Evolutionism [XXXIV] An anthropological approach to the study of religion, especially the ORIGINS OF RELIGION, based upon notions of the common development of humanity and human institutions from simple, or, as often described, 'primitive', to complex organisms and organizations. According to this approach, the origins of religion(s) are to be found in 'primitive' societies which manifested simple, fragmented attitudes towards the unseen powers that governed their lives, attitudes based on perceptions of the operative powers of such entities as the ghosts of ancestors. Such ideas were held to be evident from observations of isolated groups, such as Australian aborigines, who had not developed in the manner of more 'sophisticated' societies. Later developments, it was claimed, saw the evolutionary emergence of spiritual beings, GODS, many gods, hence a structure of POLYTHEISM, which in turn evolved into MONOTHEISM, the belief in a single all-powerful God. Scholars who adopted these views in varying ways included G. W. F. Hegel (1780–1831), in his *Phenomenology of Spirit* (1807), Herbert Spencer (1820–1903), in his essay 'Progress: Its Law and Cause' (1857) and E. B. Tylor (1832–1917), in his work *Primitive Culture* (1871). In the case of Spencer, like Auguste Comte, the culmination of the evolution of religious awareness was to be agnosticism, in which religion as such is superseded. Tylor was most clearly an 'evolutionist'. He defined religion as 'belief in Spiritual Beings' and it is to him that later generations owe the use of the term ANIMISM to describe religious orientation outwith the major world religions. Compared with later studies in religion two things stand against Tylor's theories. First, there is the fact that, as Andrew Lang (1844–1912) showed, the notion of a 'high god' can be found among some of the most so-called 'primitive' peoples; and secondly, Tylor's concentration on 'belief' and the 'mental connection', an intellectualist approach to religions, has been undermined by an awareness that religious behaviour is more complex than mere expression of belief and intellectual assent. While evolutionism [145] as a method of explaining religion has

been largely discredited, there remained scholars like Durkheim who retained certain aspects of the evolutionary approach. One such is Robert N. Bellah, who propounds not an evolutionist assessment of the development of religion as such but rather the evolution of religions as 'symbol systems' in which it is claimed that 'at each stage [of religious evolution] the freedom of personality and society has increased relative to the environing conditions' [18: 290]. Bellah acknowledges that engaging in such an exercise 'is an extremely risky enterprise . . . justifiable if, by throwing light on perplexing developmental problems they contribute to modern man's [*sic*] efforts at self interpretation' [18: 291].

Exile (Jewish) [XXII] The experience of exile is central to Jewish self-consciousness. The pattern of exile began when the Babylonian empire carried off the inhabitants of the Judaean kingdom in the 6th century BCE (*see* BIBLICAL HISTORY). That exile was only short-lived, and many Jews returned to rebuild their TEMPLE in JERUSALEM and live once again in their homeland. After the destruction of the second temple (70 CE) and the crushing of the Bar Cochba revolt against Roman rule (135 CE), Jewish life in Palestine deteriorated. The demographic centres of Jewry during the middle ages were in different parts of the diaspora (dispersion) [14 vol. 6: 8]. Since Jews saw themselves as the people of God, to whom the HOLY LAND had been promised, they interpreted their suffering in the diaspora as a consequence of the condition of exile itself. At the centre of their liturgy was the hope of a return to Zion in the messianic age (*see* MESSIAH; ZIONISM). [11; 64: 51]

Existentialism [XIII.C] A philosophical doctrine which largely derives from Kierkegaard, although its standpoint of radical concern for the individual person is foreshadowed in Pascal (1623–62). Søren Kierkegaard (1813–55) was a Danish philosopher and theologian who attacked the prevailing Hegelian metaphysical system and the interpretation of CHRISTIANITY as a dogmatic system. Affirming the essential link between authentic truth and its subjective appropriation, he criticized attempts to produce an objectively inferred system of belief, and emphasized the necessity of a leap of faith by the individual as one who stands alone before GOD. In the 20th century existentialist positions have been developed in various ways. Heidegger (1889–1976) and J.-P. Sartre (1905–80) maintain that the fundamental principle that 'existence precedes essence' (i.e. that individuals do not have an imposed nature but must decide their character for themselves) is necessarily atheistic while G. Marcel (1889–1973) and K. Jaspers (1883–1969) have developed Christian interpretations of the doctrine, stressing that faith is committed trust in a person rather than assent to dogmatic propositions. [23]

Exodus (in Judaism) [XXII] The redemption of the Israelites (*c.* 15th–13th centuries BCE) from slavery in Egypt, known as the Exodus from Egypt, is a fundamental motif of Jewish ritual. The major festivals (CHAGIM) – PASSOVER, PENTECOST and TABERNACLES – are built round events associated with the Exodus [59: IX, x, xx]. The belief in a Messianic age (*see* MESSIAH) to come is dependent on the idea of divine salvation, and this is represented in Jewish consciousness by God's acts in Egypt (*see* BIBLICAL HISTORY; MOSES), culminating in the Exodus *en route* for the Promised Land. [14 vol. 6: 1042]

F

Fa Hsiang Tsung [XII] The DHARMA Characteristics or 'Consciousness Only' (*Wei Shih*) school. This was the Chinese YOGACARA or *Vijnanavada* teachings, which were systematically developed in India by Asanga and VASUBANDHU (4th/5th centuries CE) and in China by Hsuan Tsang (596–664 CE). The last-named translated Vasubandhu's *Treatise in Thirty Verses on Consciousness Only* (*Ch'eng Wei Shih Lun*) with commentaries [60], and his *Treatise in Twenty Verses on Consciousness Only* (*Wei Shih Er Shih Lun*) [47] (*see* ALAYA-VIJNANA). The school was never popular in China. (*see* Hosso *in* NANTO ROKUSHU.) [7: XXIII, 370–95; 15: XI, 320–4; 35: VIII, 299–338]

Falsafa [XIX] The Islamic term for philosophy. Orthodox ISLAM was always uneasy about the utility of philosophy, often viewing it, because of the extraneous forces which moulded it, as inimical to faith and conducive to heresy and unbelief. Hence when philosophy developed in Islam through translations from Greek – Plato, Aristotle, NEOPLATONISM, etc. – it tended to be cultivated by scholars from trends of thought and sects outside Sunni orthodoxy (*see* SUNNA), such as the Mu'tazilites, Twelver Shi's (*see* SHI'ISM), ISMA'ILIS, etc. Such philosophical questions as the difference in created beings between essence and existence, God's knowledge of particulars, the materialness or spiritualness of punishment and reward in the next life (*see* AKHIRA) and whether creation was *ex nihilo* were discussed by al-Farabi (*c.*870–950), Ibn Sina (Avicenna) (980–1037) and others. The orthodox reaction came through the practitioners of KALAM and through the towering figure of al-Ghazali (1058–1111), whose refutation of the philosophers was in turn combated by Ibn Rushd (Averroës) (1126–98). Philosophy declined after the 13th century as the intellectual aspect of Islam became increasingly ossified. [38 'Falsafa'; 107: VII; 133]

Family, The [XXVIII] Originally known as the Children of God, and subsequently The Family of Love, the Family was founded as part of the JESUS MOVEMENT in California in 1968 by David Berg (1919–94), who later became known as Moses (then Father) David or 'Mo'. Members see themselves as FUNDAMENTALIST Christians espousing a 'godly socialism'. They believe that we are approaching the 'Endtime', when out of capitalism and communism (both being materialistic in practice and philosophy) there will emerge a world government with a single state religion, led by the Anti-Christ for a period of seven years; following this, the Second Coming of Jesus Christ will herald the wrath of God and the Battle of Armageddon, to be followed by the millennium (the thousand-year reign of Christ on earth). The movement's beliefs can be found in over 100 volumes, the main theological references being the BIBLE and 'Mo letters', tracts with cartoon illustrations covering subjects from prophecies of impending disaster to instructions on health, sexual practices and child care.

The movement grew fairly rapidly in the 1970s; then, in response to hostile reactions, it went underground for several years, although it has pursued a more open policy since 1992. Public antagonism arose partly as a reaction to the 'Mo letters' which were considered to be blasphemous and, in some instances, pornographic, and partly because of the practice of 'flirty fishing' – using sex to convince outsiders that they were loved by Jesus and the members – until internal complications and the fear of AIDS resulted in sexual 'sharing' with outsiders being banned in 1987. Raids by police in Australia and elsewhere were carried out in 1992, but the children were returned to their homes when no evidence supporting allegations of child abuse was found. Full-time members (Disciples) tend to live in communities and work full-time as missionaries, 'litnessing' (selling literature and witnessing), and carrying out various social ministries. There is also a category of 'lay' members, known as TRF Supporters. [5: 171–3; 6: 33–42; 11: VI; 22: II; 41: IV/F; 42: 1011; 70; 72: IV]

Fasting [XIII.D] Abstention from food, or from certain kinds of food normally eaten; or a restriction of the quantity of food eaten, or of the times at which food is eaten. (Fasting should be distinguished from the observance of dietary rules forbidding certain foods as unclean or sacred.) It is common for religions to have periods of fasting prescribed in the religious calendar e.g. Yom Kippur in JUDAISM, Ramadan in ISLAM, Lent in the CHRISTIAN tradition. MONASTIC communities frequently fast as a regular discipline; the Buddhist SANGHA restricts meals to the earlier part of the day, while EASTERN ORTHODOX monks and nuns normally abstain permanently from meat, and also from fish, dairy prod-

ucts, wine and olive oil on Mondays, Wednesdays and Fridays for most of the year. Fasting in preparation for religious ceremonies is common – e.g. fasting before Holy Communion in traditional Christian practice. Fasting is also practised as an exercise in self-discipline, as an expiation for wrongdoing, to sharpen concentration or to develop an enhanced awareness of responsibility for the natural world. [16]

Fasts (Jewish) [XXII] The most important of the Jewish fast days (*tzom* or *ta'anit*) is the Day of Atonement or YOM KIPPUR [70: 178]. This lasts for 25 hours, beginning at sundown on the previous day and continuing until nightfall. Jews spend most of this time in the SYNAGOGUE in prayer, and refrain from all food and drink. The only other fast of similar duration is the 9th of Av (Tishah Be-Av), remembering the TEMPLE destruction. Day-long fasts (sunrise to nightfall) are the 17th of Tammuz, when the events leading to the Temple's destruction began; the 10th of Tevet, remembering the siege of Jerusalem by the army of Nebuchadnezzar; the 3rd of Tishri or Tzom Gedaliah, when the Babylonian appointee as governor of Judah was assassinated in the 6th century BCE (*see* BIBLICAL HISTORY); and the 13th of Adar (Ta'anit Ester), in memory of the events recorded in the Book of Esther [59: XI, XIV]. The essence of all fasting is repentance. [14 vol. 6: 1189]

Fatalism (in Islam) [XIX] There was a persistent strain of fatalism in older Near Eastern religions which was carried into early ISLAM [109]. The QUR'AN speaks of God's eternal decree (*qadar*), but elsewhere it allows a place to human free will. It was the task of later theologians to formulate a doctrine which to some extent harmonized the two opposed views, so that orthodoxy came to allow humanity a certain liberty to acquire actions broadly foreordained by God (ALLAH) [140: 49–57]. The idea of resignation to the divine will has strengthened these tendencies towards a determinist emphasis on God's sovereignty. The term *kismet* stems from a Turkish form of Arabic *qisma* 'sharing-out', i.e. 'allotted fate' [67 'Predestination'].

Fatiha [XIX] The short opening *sura* of the QUR'AN, beginning, 'In the name of God, the Merciful, the Compassionate. Praise be to God, the Lord of the Worlds . . .'. It is held in special reverence by Muslims and much used liturgically, in some ways forming a parallel to the use of the Lord's Prayer in Christianity. It is an indispensable part of the worship or SALAT, being recited at the beginning of each prostration, and is further used as a prayer for the sick, the dead, etc., as an exorcism formula and as a component in the wording of AMULETS AND TALISMANS. [20 s.v.; 38 s.v.; 137: 46]

Feng-Shui [XII] Literally 'wind and water', usually interpreted as geomancy. Feng-Shui is the Chinese practice of determining auspicious sites for buildings and graves, in accordance with the natural forces and currents (*ch'i*) of the landscape. The *yin* force (see YIN–YANG) in nature is identified as the White Tiger, which should be found to the left of a proposed site; and the *yang* force is the Azure Dragon, which should be to the right. [31: 86, II, 21–5; 78: XIV, 359–63]

Fenriswolf [VII] The wolf Fenrir (Fenriswolf) is one of LOKI's monstrous sons. The tale of his binding by Tyr, who sacrificed his hand in Fenrir's jaws to save the AESIR, is probably an ancient Germanic myth [28 Gylf sec. 34: 26–9; 3a: 74; 32: 180]. Fenrir breaks loose at RAGNAROK and devours ODIN, but is slain by Odin's son Vidar. He may possibly be identified with the hound Garm at the entrance to HEL, and with the wolf pursuing the sun [3: 59; 32: 280–1].

Festivals (Ancient Near Eastern) [VIII] Cult-centres held periodic festivals which included sacrifices and libations to the deities (see ANCIENT NEAR EASTERN RELIGIONS). Some were local celebrations; others, probably performed by the king at the centre of the state-cult (see KINGSHIP (ANCIENT NEAR EAST)), were intended to benefit the whole country. Particularly important were the new year festival and the spring festival, at which in some instances a mock combat was enacted (see HITTITES) [13: 152]. This celebrated the annual victory of life over death, and of good over EVIL.

Festivals (Chinese) [XII] The great family and communal festivals (*Chieh Chi*) which were observed in traditional China and which are still observed in Taiwan and Hong Kong reflect many of the distinctive features of Chinese popular religion [122: IV, 86–99; 99: VII, 108–13].

Among the most important domestic celebrations and rites are those associated with the new year (*Hsin Nien*). The end of the old year and the expelling of the dark *yin* force (see YIN–YANG) is signified by cleaning and repainting the home. Two or three days before the end of the year the god of the stove Tsao Chun is dispatched to the heavenly court of the Jade Emperor (Yu Huang) (see CHINESE PANTHEON) to report on the behaviour of his hosts during the year. This act is signified by burning Tsao Chun's picture and making offerings of sweet rice and wine in order to sweeten his reports. His return on New Year's Eve is signified by mounting a new picture and setting off fire-crackers. On New Year's Eve, Heaven, Earth, and the household gods and ancestors are honoured by the family with offerings of food, incense, candles, spirit money and many bows. On the third day the festival of Ts'ai Shen, the god of wealth, is celebrated in the home by placing offerings of meat and fish before his picture. Another important New Year festival is the Li Ch'un, beginning of spring. In imperial times this involved the Emperor's symbolic ploughing of a field in the capital, followed by a procession led by the 'spring ox', which was then sacrificed. In modern times the procession is led by a paper ox.

The Ch'ing Ming (Clear and Bright) festival is celebrated in the third month of the year by visiting and repairing ancestral graves, and offering food and spirit money to the *p'o* (souls of the ancestors) (*see* HUN-P'O). A special offering is also made to the Lord of the Soil (T'u Ti Kung), who protects graves. On the eighth day of the fourth month the birthday of the BUDDHA is celebrated at Buddhist temples by chanting *sutras* and washing the BUDDHA IMAGES. Traditional Chinese and Buddhist beliefs and practices combine in the P'u Tu or 'Saving All Souls' festival in the seventh month when the ghosts (*Kuei*) of those who died without descendants, or who were not properly buried, wander in search of food. The gates of hell are believed to be open for most of this month. On the 15th day the ghosts and their nearest Buddhist equivalents the *pretas* are offered food, drink and prayers and in the Yu Lan Hui (Avalambana)

festival are saved, at least temporarily, from their torments. [3: 4; 49; 88: I, 16–31]

Festivals (Hindu) [XVII] The Hindu religious and ceremonial year is based on lunar months, each of 30 lunar days (*tithi*) divided into two fortnights (*paksha* or *pak*): the dark or waning fortnight (*krishna paksha* or *badi*) which begins after the full-moon day (*purnima*) and the bright or waxing fortnight (*shukla paksha* or *shudi*), which begins after the new-moon day (*amavasya*). In some regions (the south, Bengal, Maharashtra and Gujurat), the month begins with the bright half; in others (Uttar Pradesh, etc.), it begins with the dark half, which makes for a lack of correspondence in the names of the months in which the dark halves fall. In order to keep broadly in line with the solar year, every 30 months a leap month is added. The months are named as shown in the table.

Many Hindu festivals take their names from the Sanskrit ordinals which give their date in the month. Thus *Rama navami* is RAMA's ninth, which refers to the ninth day of the bright fortnight of *Cait* on which Rama's birthday is celebrated. *Janmashtami* is the birth eighth (of KRISHNA), that is, the eighth day of the dark fortnight of *Bhado* on which Krishna's birthday is celebrated. The major religious occasions of the

The Months of the Hindu Year

Sanskrit	Hindi	Season	Period
Caitra	Cait	Vasanta = spring	March–April
Vaishaka	Besakh		April–May
Jyaishtha	Jeth	Grishma = summer	May–June
Ashadha	Asharh		June–July
Shravana	Savan	Varsha = rainy season	July–August
Bhadrapada	Bhado		August–September
Ashvina	Ashvin/Kvar	Sharada = autumn	September–October
Karttika	Katik		October–November
Agrahayana	Agahan	Hemanta = winter	November–December
Pausha	Pus		December–January
Magha	Magh	Shishira = cool season	January–February
Phalguna	Phagun		February–March

Hindu year follow below, giving the months according to Uttar Pradesh usage.

Cait: *shudi* 1 is the start of the lunar year, which is celebrated variously as such; *shudi* 9 is Rama's birthday; *shudi* 1–10 is one of two periods of *navaratra*, nine nights, devoted to the Goddess; the full-moon day, *purnima*, is *Hanuman jayanti*, the birthday of HANUMAN the monkey deity. *Besakh*: *shudi* 3 is the *Akshaya tritiya* or Akti festival, which is the start of the agricultural year and auspicious for starting new enterprises; it is also the birthday of Parashurama, the sixth AVATARA of VISHNU; *shudi* 14 is the birthday of Narasimha, the man–lion *avatara* of Vishnu. *Jeth*: *shudi* 13 to *purnima* is a three-day fast observed by women to ensure conjugal happiness, ending with the worship of Savitri. *Asharh*: *shudi* 2 is *ratha yatra*, the Chariot Journey, which celebrates Krishna as Jagannath, Lord of the World, renowned from the ceremonies at the great temple complex in Puri, Orissa (*see* JUGGERNAUT); *shudi* 11 is *Devashayani*, when the gods go to sleep, and also the start of *caturmasa*, the four months to *Katik shudi* 11, which is the period for fasts and austerities, the manner of their observance depending on the traditions and affiliations of the families concerned; it is also one of two days on which the *Varkari* pilgrims in Maharashtra hope to reach the temple of Vitthala (a manifestation of Vishnu) at Pandharpur, the other being the last day of *caturmasa*. *Savan*: *shudi* 5 is *Naga pancami*, celebrated in honour of the serpent deities of mythology and also to seek protection against snake-bites; *purnima* is the festival of *raksha bandana*, the tying of AMULETS to seek brotherly protection. *Bhado*: *badi* 8 is *Janmashtami*, the birthday of Krishna; *shudi* 3 is *Hartalika* or PARVATI's festival, which is an important fast day for women: for the married, for the health and prosperity of their husbands, for the

unmarried, for obtaining a husband; *shudi* 4 is the first of ten days for the worship of GANESHA, the elephant-headed deity who removes difficulties; *shudi* 7–9 is devoted to the worship of Gauri (Parvati), usually by the lady of the household; *shudi* 14 is dedicated to Vishnu as Ananta, the Eternal Preserver. *Kvar*: *badi* is *pitri paksha*, the fortnight of the fathers, when food offerings are made, ideally by the eldest male, to the departed up to three generations, the ninth being reserved for the female departed; *shudi* 1–9 is the second *navaratra* devoted to the Goddess, with DURGA PUJA occuring on *shudi* 8; in the north, *Rama-lilas*, portraying the triumph of Rama over Ravana, are enacted during *navaratra*, concluding, together with the Goddess worship, on the 10th, *Dasara* or *Dassahra*, which is a major festival; *purnima* is a festival called *kojagara* devoted to LAKSHMI. *Katik*: *badi* 13, known as 'wealth's 13', is the start of the four or five days of *Divali*, the festival of lamps; *badi* 14 celebrates Krishna's victory over the demon Naraka with a day of festivities and the lighting of oil lamps in the evening; the new-moon day, *amavasya*, is for Lakshmi *puja* and the end of the financial year; *shudi* 1 is *Divali* itself, a day auspicious for new beginnings and the start of the new financial year, celebrated with festivities and present-giving; *shudi* 2 is the day brothers should visit sisters; *shudi* 11 is the last day of the austerities of *chaturmasa*, the day the gods reawaken and the second pilgrimage for the *Varkari* pilgrims to Pandharpur to worship Vitthala; *purnima* is known as *tripurni purnima* and is both a Shaivite (*see* SHIVA) and a Krishnaite festival. *Pus*: sometime in this month, always on solar 14 January, is *makara samkranti*, known as Pongol in the south, which marks the entry of the sun into Capricorn (*see* ASTROLOGY (INDIAN)) and is a particularly important day for ritual bathing, especially at Prayag. *Magh* is the important month for ritual bathing, especially *purnima*, and many *melas* (fairs) take place during it. *Phagun*: *badi* 14 is *mahashivaratri*, the Great Night of Shiva, a major Shaivite festival; *purnima* is *Holi* and the bonfire is lit in the evening; the following day, *Chait badi* 1, there is the throwing of coloured powder and the general mood of licence for which this final festival of the year is famous.

It must be remembered that no individual's or household's religious year will, in practice, resemble the above: perhaps few of these major festivals will be observed, the greater proportion of the calendrical rites performed being regional, local, or CASTE-, sect- or family-specific. There is great variation in the regional modes of observance, the mythologies associated with a given occasion, and the significance attached to a particular festival by the households of different castes and of different sectarian affiliations. These fasts, feasts and festivals that constitute such a large part of Hindu ceremonial life bring a renewal of values and a reaffirmation of relationships as they mark out the structure and the passing of the year. [5; 126]

Fideism [XIII.c] A term (from Latin *fides*, faith, belief) used to describe that kind of theological understanding which fundamentally denies that it is possible to establish the truth or reasonableness of religious beliefs by unprejudiced arguments and which consequently stresses the primary role of the commitment of faith in providing the basis for theological understanding. Initially the word was adopted by A. Sabatier (1839–1901) and E. Ménégoz (1838–1921) to describe their PROTESTANT interpretation of CHRISTIANITY as 'the religion of the Spirit' and of SALVATION as being by faith alone. The term is now generally used in a pejorative manner, particularly with reference to those views which have taken up the notion of a 'language-game' put forward by L. Wittgenstein (1889–1951) to argue that a religious or theological position is a self-contained system of understanding with its own presuppositions and rules that cannot be validly criticized or justified from outside the system. [13; 21]

Fijian Religion [XXIX] The Fiji islands have a mixed population of (1) Indian immigrants (mainly Hindu, but also Muslim and Christian) and (2) native Fijians (predominantly Christian, particularly METHODIST). The Fijians and their religion are said to exhibit a mixture of MELANESIAN and POLYNESIAN features. (Fiji stands on the dividing-line between the two regions and had trading relations with Tonga.) The supreme god was Ndengei (a serpent, a Melanesian trait), who lived in a cave on the north-east end of Vitilevu island. Earthquakes occurred when he turned over; he received food offerings and replied to requests brought to him by priests. Some priests were possessed by other deities (*kalou*) and in trance gave revelations on warfare, weather and healing (as in Polynesia). MALE CULTS relating to ancestors (as in Melanesia) were associated with stone enclosures (reminiscent of the Polynesian MARAE). Ritual cannibalism was sometimes practised against enemies (*see* MANA). *Mburu* was the land of the afterlife, under the sea. [21; 22; 28]

Fiqh [XIX] 'Knowledge', the technical term for the science of Islamic law, covering all aspects of human activity, from the religious cult to personal, criminal and constitutional law, hence including the SHARI'A proper and other sources of legal knowledge. After the 8th century, several schools of religious law (*madhhabs*) grew up, of which the four most important ones, still surviving today, are those of the Hanafis, Malikis, Shafi'is and Hanbalis. A

Muslim should follow one of these systems exclusively; only in recent decades have legal reformers selected items from different schools and combined them for modern legal proposals. In fact, the differences between the schools are slight. The Shi'is have their own body of law, again not greatly different from that of the Sunnis (see SHI'ISM, SUNNA). [38 'Fikh'; 80: 180–91; 107: IV]

Fire (Zoroastrian) [XXXVI] (*Adur*, older *atar*) One of the seven creations of AHURA MAZDA, protected by the AMESHA SPENTA of righteousness. Fire in all its forms, from the sun to the household fire, is sacred. The living warmth of the element of fire is thought to pervade all other creations. It has a unique ritual place in ZOROASTRIANISM, much of which derives from its role in Indo-Iranian tradition (see INDO-EUROPEANS), as recipient of the sacrificial offering and conveyor of it to the gods (cf. Agni in HINDUISM). Prayers were addressed to the fire itself [translation 18: 134–87]. In ancient times ritual offerings were made to the household fire but in Achaemenid times (*c.*4th century BCE) the temple cult of fire was introduced [10: 60–5, 85–90]. It is the fire, not the temple, which is the focus for worship. Fires may be moved from temple to temple, but they may not be extinguished. The three most famous ancient fires were those of Farnbag, Gushnasp and Burzenmihr. All were centres of pilgrimage. Gushnasp was the object of lavish royal patronage and the only one whose ruins (Takht i Suleyman) have been identified [27: 113–18].

In modern Zoroastrianism, especially among the PARSIS, temples have become increasingly important as they provide pure shrines for the sacred fires. Ritual fires are consecrated for private devotion and they are used in higher liturgies, but they are not used for congregational worship (YASNA) [30: 55–64]. Essentially temples consist of a sanctuary for the fire, a prayer-room, and a separate room (*urvisgah* or *yazishngah*) for the higher liturgies. There is no distinctive architectural style. The highest grade of fire is *Atash* (= fire) *Bahram* (see YAZATAS), the installation of which is so complex that it takes a year [47: IX]. Once installed it is enthroned and served with royal dignity. Two such temples exist in Iran, eight in India. The second grade is the *Adaran* fire, which is used in 'ordinary' temples, often called by the Persian name *dar-i Mihr* (Court of Mithra), or in India by the Gujarati term *Agiary*, meaning 'house of fire'. The lowest grade of fire, *dadgah*, can burn in the home but if it burns in a temple then it, like the others, must be ritually tended. The differences between the grades of ritual fires are determined by the rites of consecration. Worshipping before the fire, considered the son or representative of God, Zoroastrians believe they are standing in the presence of God. A fire is present at all Zoroastrian rites. The daily devotions of Zoroastrians in the temple consist basically of individual 'pilgrimage' in a state of purity and after the *kusti* prayers (see NAUJOTE). In the prayer room the worshipper pays respect to, prays and meditates before the fire burning in the *afarganyu* (clay or metal vessels, sometimes rather inaccurately referred to as 'fire altars'). The fire is 'fed' five times daily with sandalwood by the priest in the *boy* ceremony, at each of the five *gahs* (ritual divisions of the day). The burning sandalwood and frankincense (*loban*) add a delightful aroma to the powerful visual imagery and intense personal experience of worship in the temple. The layperson (*behdin*) cannot tend a fire in the temple, but may theoretically do so at home. The requirements of the purity laws make it practically impossible for Zoroastrians to keep a permanently burning fire at home; instead, many burn a *divo*, a glass container with oil and wick giving a small burning light. [20: II; 29: pt III, 44–53; 46: 60–5, 93–101; 61]

Firqa [XIX] 'Sect' in ISLAM. In early Islam, there were intense struggles over such basic theological and political questions as predestination and free will, the nature of God's attributes, gradations of sinfulness (DHANB), the createdness or uncreatedness of the QUR'AN, the nature of the CALIPHATE, etc., and corresponding sects formed, some purely theological and philosophical, others political and activist (e.g. ISMA'ILIS, KHARIJITES, SHI'ISM). Basing themselves on a tradition of the Prophet that 'differences among my community are a mercy from God', Muslim authorities did not regard the existence of sects as necessarily inimical to the basic unity of Islam, and despite their proliferation, Islam has always remained an essentially unified faith and institution. [52: VII; 78]

Five Ks [XXXIII] Amrit-dhari Sikhs (those formally initiated into the KHALSA) are required to wear the Five Ks, and many KES-DHARI Sikhs (lacking formal initiation but maintaining uncut hair) also do so. The Five Ks, so called because each begins with the letter k, are uncut hair (*kes*), a comb (*kangha*), a steel wrist-band (*kara*), a sword of varying size (*kirpan*) and a pair of shorts (*kachh* or *kachhahira*). [10: 14–17; 30: 83]

Flame Foundation [XXVIII] 'The Eternal Flame is a group of physically immortal people', based in Scottsdale, Arizona. Charles Brown (*c.* 1933–), BernaDeane Brown (*c.* 1934–) and James Russell Stole (*c.* 1949–) are the 'architects' and 'ministers' of physical immortality, Charles Brown having felt a completely new intelligence operating in his body when he realized in 1960 that JESUS spoke of *physical* immortality. Once people accept this revelation, immortal cells are said to

multiply to strengthen the immune system and eliminate death enzymes in the DNA. As physical immortality must be experienced 'cellularly', it must be learned through regular contact with other immortals at meetings that evoke 'passion, intensity and intimacy'. [5: 179–80]

Folklore [XXXIV] Traditions, customs and beliefs of the 'folk' or common people. Much that is studied by anthropologists in small-scale societies (rites – *see* RITUAL – tales, songs, sayings) would, as a survival in technologically advanced society, be placed in this category. The study of such traditional material has formed an important aspect of RELIGIONSWISSENSCHAFT [117: 172–4; 145: 51].

Fon Religion [II] The Fon, principal people of Dahomey (now the People's Republic of Benin), were organized under the powerful monarchy of Abomey, which developed after the 16th century. Their exceptionally complex religion borrowed much from neighbouring societies (particularly the YORUBA) without fully synthesizing the borrowings, so that the variations remain great in different parts of the kingdom and cult centres. The monarchy, a relative latecomer, influenced, but was hardly central to, Fon religion, which in this and other ways may be compared with GANDA.

Its most striking character lies in its sexual duality. The creator god is seen as double – Mawu and Lisa – though behind these is a shadowy Nana Buluku, recognized but seldom mentioned. Mawu is female, symbolized by moon and night; she stands for rest and the first stage of creation – fertilization. Lisa, the male partner, has as his symbols sun and day; his field is work, and the second stage of creation, its ordering. (Among Ewe peoples west of the Fon, Mawu is male and Lisa a little-used praise name for Mawu.)

Mawu is assisted in creation by

Da, a demiurge symbolized by rainbow and serpent; Lisa is assisted by Gu, the heavenly blacksmith. These are but two of a vast pantheon, the Vodun, the progeny of Mawu/Lisa, hierarchically responsible for every aspect of the world's ordering. The basic model of pairs of twins of opposite sex runs throughout the heavenly hierarchy and is seen as the ideal human condition. *Fa*, word of Mawu and symbol of destiny, is patron of a complex system of DIVINATION (IFA to the YORUBA).

The Fon are divided into clans, each of which has a divine founder, the Tohwiyo. Fon worship includes temples for Mawu/Lisa and also a remarkable system of convent initiation. [6: 210–34]

Founders of Religions [xxxiv] Many religions and religious groupings acknowledge a human person who occupies a significant place in the history of the religion as the person who in some way or other could be acknowledged to be the founder of the religion. In some instances this historical person actually set out to form a religious group which has persisted through history. In other instances it is not clear that the person did set out to form a religious grouping, but arising out of the person's activity the early followers acted in such a way that a group was formed, a movement grew, with the result that in later history the grouping which developed looks back to the person as the initiator and inspiration of the group's corporate life. In some instances we find that the institution which is formed out of the group recollection of the founder develops its own character, including a revaluation of the founder's life and teaching, arising from the 'routinization' of the 'charisma' of the founder [174: III, VI, XIX]. The group can be an identified religion such as Confucianism (*see* CONFUCIUS), BUDDHISM, CHRISTIANITY, ISLAM or SIKHISM, or a sect within the boundary of a religion, such as the Church of Latter-day Saints or the UNIFICATION CHURCH. A common feature of the category of founder is that the person claims to have received a special message, set of truths or vision, sometimes called a revelation, whether through meditation or by supernatural intervention. Founders can be classified into three broad types. (1) Those whose biographies can be fairly accurately reconstructed and whose role in the continuing life of the founded group is more or less in line with what the founder intended. MUHAMMAD [51: V, D;], Joseph Smith and the Revd Sun Young Moon [39] broadly belong in this class. (2) Those of whom not a great deal is known of their historical lives, whose biographies (or, more accurately, hagiographies) reflect not only what is known of the founder's life but also aspects of the significance of the founder, the founder's role and function, in the continuing life of the group which are edited into the hagiography in the form of legends and mythologically interpreted events, which though not historical are held to be consonant with the spirit and meaning of the founder's life. In this class would be included ZOROASTER, GOTAMA the BUDDHA, JESUS the Christ [180] and GURU NANAK. (3) Those whose 'lives' conform to some idealized type of person whose existence is essential for the spiritual well-being of the group rather than to any historical personal biography. Lord KRISHNA is such a person, and Lao Tzu. Confucius belongs in this class more than in any other.

Founders are significant for the various religious groupings since they represent various aspects vital to the group. Prominent among these are the exemplary nature of the 'life', understood as 'sacred biography' [98], the source of authority in the beliefs and actions of the group, exemplified often by miraculous actions or events, while in some instances importance is given to the 'presence' of the founder in spirit in the activities of the group. In most, if not all, cases there is a development in the significance of the founder over time so that eventually the picture of the founder differs quite radically from what may be historically known of the original life.

Four Noble Truths [XI] (Pali: *ariya-sacca*; Sanskrit: *arya-satya*) Essentially knowledge of the four 'noble truths' constitutes the content of the enlightenment (*bodhi*) gained by the BUDDHA (*see* GOTAMA) and his disciples (*see* ARAHAT); full realization of the four truths is thus the aim of BUDDHIST practice. In brief the four truths are suffering (DUKKHA), its cause, its cessation and the way leading to its cessation. These *ariya-saccas* are not propositional truths requiring intellectual assent, nor do they constitute a Buddhist creed. Rather, they indicate the orientation of Buddhist teaching – the Buddhist path is concerned with the understanding of just these matters. Indeed, that this is so is said to be the particular mark of the teaching of Buddhas. Prior to enlightenment there can only be a limited understanding of the truths, but at the moment of enlightenment the true nature of suffering is finally penetrated, its cause, namely craving (Pali: *tanha*; Sanskrit: *trishna*) (cf. PATICCASAMUPPADA), is abandoned, its cessation, namely NIBBANA, is experienced directly, and the way to its cessation, constituted by the items that make up the EIGHTFOLD PATH, is fully developed. [34: 47–72]

Frashokereti [XXXVI] (PAHLAVI: *Frashegird*) The 'making fresh' or renovation of creation at the end of the historical process in ZOROASTRIANISM. Because the world is the good creation of AHURA MAZDA, Zoroastrians do not look for the 'end of the world'; instead they look forward to the time when it will be cleansed from all the unnatural impurity with which evil has afflicted it (*see* BUNDAHISHN). The earliest traditions divided time into three great eras: creation, *bundahishn*; the period when good and evil are 'mixed together' (Pahlavi: *gumezishn*); and the final state after the renovation, the time of separation (*wizarishn*) of good and evil. But in the scholastic theology of the Pahlavi books the history of the world is divided into four periods, each of 3,000 years, the last of which, it is believed, began with Zoroaster (i.e. the present time is 'in the last days'). Zoroastrianism traditionally awaits the coming of a saviour (*Saoshyant*; Pahlavi: *Soshyant*), who will be born of a virgin, but of the seed of the prophet Zoroaster. He is expected to raise the dead and introduce the universal judgement. The first, or individual judgement, immediately after death (*see* CHINVAT BRIDGE) is for the soul only, but because the whole person is considered the creation of Ahura Mazda a second judgement after the resurrection is essential so that the person may be judged, rewarded or corrected in body as well as in soul.

Many scholars believe that this teaching, together with the idea of evil (*see* ANGRA MAINYU), heaven and hell, and the details of how evil attacks the world before the 'end' (e.g. earthquakes, wars, social and cosmic upheavals), all influenced Jewish, Christian and Muslim doctrines [29: pt II, 24–38]. After the resurrection the heavenly and demonic forces will pair off in final conflict. The world and its people will pass through a river of molten metal as a final test of purity. Then, when evil is finally defeated, heaven and earth will merge in what is literally the best of both worlds and humankind will dwell in perfection in the kingdom of Ahura Mazda for eternity. [8 vol. 1: IX, vol. 3: 361–446; 10: 42f; 15; 28: 68–70; 53a; 63: x; 64: xv]

Fravashi [xxxvi] (PAHLAVI: *Fravahr*) A person's eternal spirit, which according to ZOROASTRIANISM remains in heaven even during his or her life on earth. In the creation myth (*see* BUNDAHISHN) it is said that when AHURA MAZDA created the material world the *fravashis* of all people were consulted to see whether they chose to assume material form, and so take part in the battle with evil, or to remain in spiritual form and therefore stand apart from the conflict. The *fravashis* collectively chose to assume material form. The doctrine of free will is basic to Zoroastrianism and is developed to its logical conclusion in this myth, asserting that everyone has chosen to live in the material world. It is customary for Zoroastrians to invite the *fravashis* of the deceased to be present at community celebrations, for there is a strong sense of the unity of the living and the dead. The festival associated with the souls of the dead (*Fravardigan*; *see* GAHAMBARS) is a time not of mourning but of joyful celebration. [8 vol. 1: index; 9: IX; 53a]

Freemasonry [XXIV] An international all-male movement with a membership of some 6 million, devoted to charitable and social activities and the secret practice of certain rituals. Freemasonry is not a religion, although in most countries masons must acknowledge a supreme being, venerated as 'the Great Architect of the Universe'. Members of a masonic 'lodge' take three 'degrees' (Entered Apprentice, Fellow Craft and Master Mason), which are conferred with impressive rituals dramatizing the soul's progress from darkness to spiritual light and rebirth. (There are also many 'side degrees' to which a Master Mason may proceed, which include more specific work with ROSICRUCIAN and KNIGHTS TEMPLAR material.) In each degree the candidate is presented with 'working tools' symbolizing moral qualities he is expec-

ted to cultivate. Masonic teachings consist mainly of moral allegorization of the traditional implements of building and geometry, supplemented by legendary material imaginatively elaborated from the Hebrew scriptures (*see* BIBLE). [7]

Freemasonry derives from the craft organizations of the medieval British free-stone masons. In the late 17th century declining lodges of such 'operative masons' accepted as members antiquarians interested in architectural traditions. These 'speculative masons' took over the lodges, refurbishing their traditional rituals and ethical teachings. During the 18th century freemasonry spread widely in Europe and North America, and it has since proliferated into a wide variety of forms. In Europe it attracted radicals and DEISTS; it has generally been viewed with suspicion by both the communist parties and ROMAN CATHOLICISM. Orthodox freemasonry, however, has been remarkable mainly for its generous charities and its respectability (13 presidents of the USA have been masons, and since 1747 all Grand Masters of England have been noblemen). Masonic teachings and rituals have often been reported, but they remain little known among non-masons, and their aura of secrecy is an important source of their imaginative and emotional power.

Friday (in Islam) [XIX] This 'day of assembly' (*jum'a*) has religious significance in that congregational worship at the midday SALAT, provided that there is a quorum of 40, is obligatory. It is not in origin a Sabbath or day of rest, but in the modern Islamic world it has become an official holiday. (*see* ISLAM.) [20 s.v.; 67 s.v.]

Friends, Religious Society of (Quakers) [XIII.B] Established in the 1650s and originally called 'Children of the Light' or 'Friends of Truth', Friends were nicknamed

'Quakers' for the way adherents trembled during worship [28a: 57]. George Fox (1624–91) and Margaret Fell (1614–1702) are credited with being the main leaders of the early years (*see* QUAKERISM, HISTORY OF). Friends sought a return to 'primitive Christianity'. They saw churches ('steeplehouses'), a paid priesthood ('hireling ministers'), credal statements and outward sacraments as signs of apostasy. It had been revealed to Fox that everyone could have a direct, unmediated relationship with God. He and his followers travelled the country preaching and disrupting church services, often ending up in prison for their outspoken views and refusal to pay tithes [28b: 84].

Fox taught that, regardless of sex and class, all had the opportunity to 'turn to the inward Light'. This process culminated in an individual's ability to lead a sinless life under the guidance of God, witnessing to 'that of God in everyone' [115: 68]. Any time or place was deemed as sacred as any other; Quaker MEETINGS for worship were not restricted to particular days or buildings. Men and women were free to contribute vocally (to 'minister'), but the basis of worship was silence as participants sought the direct relationship with God. Friends refused to swear oaths, after *Matthew* 5: 33 and because to do so might imply that Friends did not tell the truth at other times. The Quakers adopted a pacifist stance around 1661.

It has been claimed that by 1660 there were 40,000 Quakers in Britain [28b: 512]. Under the new monarchy, the Quaker Act of 1662 was specifically passed to outlaw the group [29b: II]. After a decade of fervent proselytization, the group entered a more pragmatic period known as 'restoration Quakerism' [164: 107]. From this period, Quaker history diverges: Quakerism in Britain went one way, the HOLY EXPERIMENT and Quakerism in

North America another, with some Friends there later adopting a pastoral system, tolerating outward sacraments and initiating mission work [83], which underpins the history of Quakerism in the rest of the world (*see* QUAKERISM (WORLDWIDE)). Today, there are Quaker meetings which retain the traditional silent basis ('unprogrammed') and others which have a pre-arranged order of worship ('programmed'). Total membership for the group worldwide is just over 210,000. [62 vol. 12: 129–33]

Frost-Giants   [VII]   GERMANIC mythology differs from CELTIC in its greater emphasis on the adversaries of the gods. The AESIR were under continual threat from the frost-giants, apparently representing cold, chaos and sterility, and distinct from the fair giants, the VANIR. The EDDAS have many stories of their attempts to steal the gods' treasures, particularly THOR's hammer, the only weapon they feared, and the goddess Freyja (one of the Vanir [3: 39–45, 89–91]). Individual giants are Hrungnir, who fought a duel with THOR; Thiazi, who stole the apples of youth; Thrym, who hid Thor's hammer; Suttung, from whom ODIN stole the mead of inspiration; Geirrod and his daughters, who tried to destroy Thor; and Hymir, a sea-giant. These, with others whose stories are lost, were killed by Thor, but many giants survived to attack Asgard (the Aesir dwelling-place) at RAGNAROK, although they perished in the final conflagration. Their allies were LOKI and his monstrous sons, FENRISWOLF and the World-Serpent. [3a: 80–3]

Functionalism   [XXXIV]   (1) A mode of explanation, based on understanding of what something does or of the effects it produces rather than of what it is [12: 23; 117: XII]. RELIGION has been defined functionally (as that which promotes social solidarity or gives confidence).

The sciences of religion have sought to explain functionally the ORIGIN OF RELIGION or its persistence [11: 12–24, 106–22; 24: VIII; 33: II; 135: 20–4, 38–42].

(2) A way of understanding religious beliefs. Its objects (e.g. GODS) are regarded as SYMBOLS for functions or aspects of the divine or of ultimate reality.

[General survey in 171: 167–215]

Fundamentalism [XIV] Fundamentalism [65] is a worldwide modern religious phenomenon, particular to no religion but most at home in PROTESTANT CHRISTIANITY and ISLAM. The word 'fundamentalist' was coined in America in 1920 to describe parties in American Christian denominations – especially BAPTIST and PRESBYTERIAN – who militantly fought off assaults of modernity. In their case, modernity was represented by the teaching of evolution and BIBLICAL CRITICISM within the denominations and in the culture around them. Words like 'conservative' and 'traditional' no longer served for people who, as a pioneer said, would 'do battle for the Lord'. George Marsden, a notable American historian of fundamentalism, describes fundamentalists as evangelicals who are angry [61: 102–23].

Some scholars and many militantly reactive conservatives in other religions sometimes protest against the spread of the term 'fundamentalism' to cultures where it was not native. Speaking of 'fundamentalist-like' movements, or forces with 'family resemblances to fundamentalism' have satisfied some, but most scholars, mass communicators and participants in international politics have come to use the term generically, while taking pains to show how different each fundamentalism is from others [64: 814–42].

Geographically, fundamentalist influences are indeed represented almost everywhere on the inhabited globe. In north Africa, the Sudan is governed by fundamentalists, and militant religious parties are the majority in Algeria. Sunni Muslims (*see* SUNNA) of the Muslim Brotherhood (founded in 1928) have through terrorist activities against tourists brought down Egypt's tourist trade and thus most of its economy, and threaten its government. They were responsible for the assissination of Anwar Sadat. Small Jewish parties such as Gush Emunim, 'the bloc of the faithful', agitate on the West Bank in Israel, and throughout the Middle East both Shi'ite (*see* SHI'ISM) and Sunni parties have engaged in military activities. Best known was the Iranian revolution of Shi'ites who overthrew the government in 1979 and have been in power ever since.

Afghanistan, Pakistan and other central Asian nations have strong Muslim fundamentalist movements, while India has seen lethal action between HINDU and Muslim fundamentalists and SIKH fundamentalists are active in the Punjab. South America has seen the rise of large Protestant evangelical fundamentalist movements on traditionally ROMAN CATHOLIC soil. While there are reactionary, ultra-conservative Catholic movements, few are aggressively reactive fundamentalists. In the USA, fundamentalist parties, linking with conservatives, have formed movements like the MORAL MAJORITY and the Christian Coalition. They prospered nationally with the election of their favoured President Ronald Reagan. Today their influence is felt most at the local level, in anti-abortion, anti-pornography, pro-censorship, 'pro-family' activities. They control the Republican Party in some states. Fewer in number – perhaps between 15 and 25 million – than the more moderate evangelicals and more exuberant fundamentalists with whom they are politically allied, they have surprised scholars by their appearance and durability.

Fundamentalism was viewed as

pre-modern, a kind of fossilized religious form, when it developed in the 1920s, especially on Protestant and Islamic soil. (There are fewer fundamentalists in Asia, where BUDDHISM and Hinduism were historic faiths, because fundamentalists need specific texts and canons, which are harder to find in such faiths but are obvious in Qur'anic Islam and biblical Christianity and Judaism.) Yet it can also be seen as 'late modern' or 'post-modern'. Fundamentalists do not resist – indeed, they take advantage of – modern instruments such as mass communications media, which are favoured in all their movements. They advance through radio, television, computerized communications and high-speed mailing services [62: 313–557]. Some of them favour 'rationalist' methods and are not highly emotional in their worship.

What lies at the root of fundamentalism is the belief that absolute reliance on a completely reliable and assured holy book will provide the doctrines (for Protestants), the practices (for Muslims, who draw on QUR'AN and SHARI'A) and the stories or prescriptions (in Judaism devoted to literalist use of TORAH) in which believers will find identity, authority and purpose. They become instruments of the divine to work out God's intentions in the world. The world is sharply divided between the parties of good and evil, and thus between God and Satan, or Christ and Antichrist, or Allah's people and the infidel or imperialist.

Fundamentalism is always patriarchal; God is strongly male and governs through earthly male authority. It is family-centred, education-minded and often highly communal. Not all fundamentalists spend their time working to elect candidates or, certainly, bearing arms. In more quiescent states they can be law-abiding, quite nationalist where a regime satisfies them, and devoted to worship and teaching. While their literalism may offend

their non-fundamentalist co-religionists, they seem unobtrusive on the public scene. But in areas of cultural and social upheaval, for example Algeria, where a corrupt militarist regime inspires reaction, or the USA, where believers feel impinged upon by governmental activity and mass communications, they take shape as very active and, to others, unsettling forces that portend disequilibrium and upheaval in many nations. [63: 620–44]

Fundamentalism (Islamic) [XIX]
The legitimacy of applying the term 'FUNDAMENTALISM' to the Islamic faith has stimulated a great deal of discussion among scholars. The term has garnered widespread use in both the popular media and scholarly writing, and has been argued by some to be quite appropriate. The emotive and negative value judgements associated with the word in the popular mind are generally the bases for the objections to its use in the context of discussions about ISLAM. Some writers have also commented on the lack of complete definitional correspondence between the application of the word to Islam and its original coinage in American Protestant circles. Other terms that have been suggested in place of Islamic fundamentalism include radical Islamism, Islamic reformism, Islamic radicalism, Muslim neo-revivalism and Muslim neo-normativism. The aptness of the word fundamentalism, however, lies in many of the elements found in a general description of the fundamentalist phenomenon.

The activism of fundamentalists in general in combating secularist and liberal tendencies (but not generally modernism as a whole) in society is certainly salient in the Islamic case. The expressed concern is to retrieve the fundamentals of Islam in order to create a religious identity through a political and social order (thus providing Islam with an ideological focus) in the face of a modern situation which is perceived to be destructive of individual religious lives. This retrieval of Islam is accomplished by emphasizing certain beliefs and practices which serve to provide a means for those who embrace them to interact with the world outside on an Islamic basis. The dominant characteristic in this regard is the goal of implementing the requirements of Muslim law, the SHARI'A, with the aim of having Islam apply to all aspects of life. The public manifestation of Islam concerns fundamentalists, but the foundation of this manifestation is portrayed as stemming from a strong (and 'pure') personal faith. It must be noted, however, that the idea of the inerrancy of scripture as a distinguishing characteristic of fundamentalism in its Christian manifestation does not apply in the Islamic case, since that is a doctrine held in common by virtually all Muslims.

Fundamentalism in the Islamic world is often pictured as having started with the WAHHABIS in 18th-century Arabia, and it is even traced back further, being cited as a recurrent trend in Islam. In this way, fundamentalism is seen as an internal Islamic movement characterized by a revivalist and purificatory (anti-mystical, anti-philosophical) spirit and not a reaction to the concept of modernity alone. Contemporary fundamentalism is frequently located on the fringes of society, connected neither to the religious learned classes nor to the governmental policy-makers, and that serves to distinguish it from the earlier revivalist tendencies which tended to acquire an institutional legitimacy. Contemporary Islamic fundamentalism is generally a lower-middle-class, urban phenomenon, which expresses the frustration of economic and social expectations and desires felt by a newly educated and displaced group of young people.

Islamic fundamentalism refers not to a single movement but to a conglomeration of groups with similar inclinations. The Ikhwan al-Muslimun ('Muslim Brotherhood') of Egypt, especially as enunciated in the writings of Sayyid Qutb, and the JAMA'AT-I-ISLAMI, which was founded by Abu'l-A'la Mawdudi and became a significant force in Pakistan, are the most typical manifestations of this tendency, although it would certainly be possible to point to many more groups and individuals in order to variegate the description. Abu'l-A'la Mawdudi was born in 1903 and founded the Jama'at-i-Islami in India in 1941. He was a major religio-political leader in Pakistan until his death in 1979. He called upon Muslims to return to the Qur'an and a purified SUNNA ('example of Muhammad') in order to revitalize Islam. Islam had to become the constitution of the state in order for this to occur, and thus Mawdudi worked towards this political goal in Pakistan. He wrote extensively, and his books have had a significant impact on Muslims around the world. His urgings for a revived personal faith commitment from individual Muslims have resounded in many places within the Muslim diaspora especially, where the goal of a Muslim state seems unlikely to be achieved in the near future. The Egyptian Sayyid Qutb lived from 1906 to 1966, and his writings express the intellectual side of the Muslim Brotherhood. He championed the return to 'pure Islam'. He saw a necessity for moving away from the materialism and nationalism of the West, which he perceived as contaminating Islam. Personal allegiance had to be to Islam alone. For Qutb, Islam provides the perfect social system for all humanity, one which will cure all the ills of the modern world once it is fully implemented. With the establishment of a truly Islamic state, all aspects of life will fall into their proper place. This structuring of society according to the principles of the Qur'an is by no means an unobtainable ideal one: it is very practical, it is within reach and it is worth pursuing.

The sense of certainty in the fundamentalist position, which is often commented on by outsiders, stems from the absolute reliance on the firmness of their sources of authority: the Qur'an and the *sunna*. These authoritative sources of the past provide the only foundations through which change may be legitimized. Muslim fundamentalists argue that Islam is the basis for all life, is flexible and is non-superstitious (in keeping with contemporary rational norms). Islam also encourages independent reasoning (*ijtihad*), but this must be practised in a truly Islamic way on the basis of clear texts and only on the occasions when those texts need elaboration. Aspects of the modern world may be embraced, but not to the extent of modifying what are argued to be essential elements of the faith. Employment of modern technology and contemporary modes of political organization are traits often noted among fundamentalist groups.

Islamic fundamentalists have garnered a great deal of attention in the popular press in recent years and have become synonymous, in many minds, with Islam as a whole. However, as a movement, it represents only a small portion of the world Muslim population. The age-old conception of Islam, which values the communal expression of the faith most highly and sees the legal culture of the jurists as Islam's lasting achievement, remains strong, especially among those relatively unaffected by secularist tendencies. [79; 111; 121]

Funeral Rites (Chinese) [XII] The Funeral Rites (*Sang Li*), mourning and continued offerings are essential elements in the traditional Chinese ANCESTOR CULT. Generally the procedures follow those described in the Classic of Rites (*see* CONFUCIAN CANON; LI) [69; 94: VII, 88–91]. The elaborateness of the rites is deter-

mined by the status of the deceased in the family and the lineage. Their main intention is to assist the spirit (*shen*) of the *hun* soul (*see* HUN-P'O) on its dangerous journey through the underworld, and its safe transference to the spirit or ancestor tablet (*shen chu*). Only the very worth *shen* can ascend to heaven. The *p'o* soul, which normally resides in the grave, must also be ritually sustained and pacified to prevent it becoming a dangerous ghost (*kuei*). (*See also* FENG-SHUI; FESTIVALS (CHINESE).) [1; 44; 50; 75; 98: XXI; 99: III, 34–65; 122: II, 28–57]

Funerary Practices (Ancient Egyptian) [VI] At all levels of society, the dead were supplied with funerary goods for the AFTERLIFE. For the wealthy, these included anthropoid and rectangular coffins, face-masks, canopic jars (containing viscera), funerary jewellery, amulets, furniture, clothing, toilet equipment, and food and drink [5]. Also, there were model brewers, butchers and bakers to prepare a continuing source of victuals. Hundreds of *ushabtis* (mummiform figurines representing agricultural labourers) provided the deceased with a MAGIC work-force.

A specialized literature, read at funerals and during mortuary rites (*see* MANSION OF THE KA), relied on magical efficacy to overcome evil and to ensure the deceased's survival. First devised to obtain the king's immortality (the Pyramid texts, Old Kingdom, *c.*2500 BCE [10]), democratization of religious customs made them available to wealthy commoners (Coffin texts, Middle Kingdom, *c.*1900 BCE). Later, New Kingdom texts (*c.*1500–1100 BCE) include the Book of the Dead [1], and the cosmographic texts in the Valley of the Kings: the Books of Gates, Caverns, the Day and the Night, and *Am-Duat*. (*see also* MUMMIFICATION, PYRAMIDS.)

Fylgja [VII] This term is used in early Icelandic literature for a shape accompanying a man through life. It resembles an external soul, often in animal form, visible in dreams or to those with second sight, and is capable of journeys away from the body. *Fylgja* is also used, together with the term *hamingja*, for a female guardian spirit attached to a family, passed on through the generations and sometimes seen as a supernatural bride [32: 221–30]. VALKYRIES may appear in this role, and the term *dísir* (goddesses) is also used for such guardian figures. In the Icelandic legendary sagas a giantess may be represented as both foster-mother and bride of the hero, helping him in time of need. Such beliefs may originally have been associated with the VANIR goddesses, and with the MATRES of CELTIC tradition. The conception of the guardian spirit has left a considerable mark on heroic tales and poems, in both Irish and Icelandic literature.

G

Gaccha [xx] Term for a sectarian division among the SHVETAMBARA JAIN community [4: 119–24]. A large number of sub-sects appeared among the Shvetambaras in the 11th century CE on the basis of attempted doctrinal reform or preceptorial and regional connections. Only a very small number survive today, of which by far the most significant is the Tapa Gaccha, founded by the ascetic teacher Jagaccandra in 1228.

Gahambars [xxxvi] The six seasonal festivals of the religious year in ZOROASTRIANISM, which together with New Year's Day (*No Ruz*), comprise a sequence which all Zoroastrians are required to observe. Each festival is held in honour of an AMESHA SPENTA and the respective creation. They are: 'Midspring' (*Maidhyoi-zarema*), honouring Khshathra and the sky; 'Midsummer' (*Maidhyoi-shema*), honouring Haurvatat and water; 'Bringing in the corn' (*Paitishahya*), honouring Armaiti and earth; 'Home-coming' (*Ayathrima*), honouring Ameretat and plants; 'Midwinter' (*Maidhyairya*), honouring Vohu Manah and cattle; and *Hamaspathmaedaya* (meaning uncertain), which is in honour of AHURA MAZDA and his creation, humanity – a time for joyfully welcoming back to earth the FRAVASHIS of the departed. This last festival is known among the PARSIS as Muktad, a Gujarati term. *No Ruz*, New Year's Day, was celebrated in honour of Asha and fire.

The rites for each festival are similar, beginning with the ceremony of the YASNA in the morning, followed by feasting where all who have the means are bound by the traditional Zoroastrian duty to give charitably to others. [12: 245–55; 9: II; 30: 51–5, 72; 47: 419–27]

Ganadhara [xx] Disciple of the JAIN omniscient teachers (TIRTHAN-KARA). MAHAVIRA is portrayed as having, soon after his enlightenment, converted 12 BRAHMANS who were to lead the various groups (*gana*) of the Jain ascetic community and mediate their teacher's doctrine. Two are of particular importance for the SHVETAMBARA sect: Gautama, who is associated with auspiciousness and prosperity, and Sudharman, from whom virtually all Shvetambara sub-sects (*see* GACCHA) claim lineal descent. [4: 32–4; 10: II]

Ganda Religion [II] The Baganda live north-west of Lake Victoria, in Uganda. They formed for centuries one of the most powerful monarchies in the region of the great lakes. While the king (*kabaka*) closely controlled religious institutions, as all other sides of life, and the dead kings were venerated, each with his own shrine-tomb, Ganda religion was not intellectually centred upon the kingship, itself a secular rather than a religious institution.

Ganda religion shares the common BANTU characteristics: KATONDA, the creator-god; MIZIMU, ancestral spirits; *mayembe* (horns, of cow or buffalo), fetishes or objects with magical power (NKISI); *musezi*, the night-witch. Yet magic and witchcraft appear less important than among many peoples. Many proverbs show the strength and antiquity of belief in the one supreme Katonda. In practice organized Ganda religion came to pay little attention to Katonda, and was rather characterized by worship of the Lubaale, an extensive pantheon of nature heroes, similar to the Cwezi of the neighbouring Nyoro. In this it contrasted with the more emphatically monotheistic belief (in Imana) of two other nearby monarchies, Rwanda and Burundi.

The most powerful Lubaale were Mukasa (the lake-god) and Kibuka (war). Mukasa, god of water, fertility and healing, sustained life in all its forms and was wholly benign. In marked contrast Kibuka frequently demanded human sacrifice. All the Lubaale had main and secondary temples (*kiggwa*), each with priest (*mukabona*) and medium (*mmandwa*). The royal tombs (*masiro*) had *mmandwa* but no *mukabona*, a dead *kabaka* seeming to stand somewhere between *mizimu* and Lubaale.

Ganesha [xvii] 'Lord of Troops': one of the best-loved Hindu deities, invoked at the beginning of any enterprise to remove obstacles. With KARTTIKEYA, he is one of two sons of SHIVA and PARVATI, the 'troops' (*gana*) of which he is leader being Shiva's fierce but comical attendants. He is depicted as a genial, pot-bellied figure, distinguished by an elephant's head with one tusk broken off, his trunk often curling round to pick up a sweet from a bowl in his hand. There are many explanations of his appearance: in most, he lost his head either through the action of a malevolent planet or as a result of conflict with Shiva, who replaced it with the head of the first creature that he found. Symbolically the elephant embodies both strength and wisdom. As god of both luck and learning, Ganesha often appears in art with LAKSHMI and/or SARASVATI, or with his wives Buddhi and Siddhi, Intelligence and Success.

Sometimes he imitates the dance of his father Shiva, to humorous effect. His animal symbol (VAHANA) is a mouse, another creature good at passing through obstacles. [4: 223–4; 12: 314–15; 92: 261–9; 109: 48]

Ganga [xvii] The river most sacred to the Hindus (known to Europeans as 'the Ganges'). Many other rivers in varying degrees share the quality of sacredness attributed to the Ganga, which is regarded as flowing from the foot of VISHNU, and through the matted hair of SHIVA, who offered his head to prevent the world from being smashed to pieces by its descent. With the other major river of the north Indian plain, the Yamuna (Jumna), the Ganga is regarded as a goddess. So also is the 'invisible river' SARASVATI. (*See also* TIRTHA.) The three are associated with the three main gods of the Hindu pantheon. Sarasvati is the consort of BRAHMA, while Yamuna is strongly associated with Vishnu (KRISHNA grew up on her banks). Ganga is a constant companion of Shiva, resting in his hair in either river or goddess form. As such she is sometimes said to be his mistress, arousing the jealousy of her sister PARVATI. [4: 114–15]

Garveyism [iii] Marcus Mosiah Garvey (1887–1940) was born in Jamaica, and is one of the country's national heroes. He had a vast impact on the black diaspora, for his influence was even greater in the USA than in Jamaica. It is the sum of his philosophies and their impact that make up Garveyism. He founded the largest Pan-African Movement in history. He had learned from all the forerunners, and had a clear and enormous vision and an indomitable spirit. His main contribution was to nationalism and independence. He influenced Thuku in Kenya, and Nkrumah in Ghana. Nnandi Azikiwe, the first Governor-General of Nigeria, wrote of the effect Garvey had on him. Garveyism is the proof that West Indians were committed to the struggle for Africa, and gloried in their own Africanity. What he did was to plant the seeds of African consciousness within and outside the continent. These qualities make up Garveyism.

In 1964 Garvey's remains were brought back from England to Jamaica, and he was reburied in the National Heroes' Park. In 1980, when a bust of him was unveiled in the Hall of Heroes of the Organization of American States, he became the first national figure from an English-speaking nation to be so honoured.

Garvey's personal philosophy was pragmatic, and he believed that the discovery of blackness in the individual was like a religious conversion. In the 1920s he was influenced by New Thought, which incorporated self-mastery and mental healing. There were also elements from CHRISTIAN SCIENCE. Imprisoned in the USA, Garvey likened his experience to that of John Bunyan. Out of his experience arose a manifesto of racial unity and a quasi-religious rhetoric, published in 1920 as *African Fundamentalism*. He was also influenced by ZIONISM, and the parallels between the two movements are clear in ideology and the desire for a territory of their own. Garvey's views are summed up thus: 'God and Nature first made us what we are, and then out of our creative genius we make ourselves what we want to be. Let the sky and God be our limit, and Eternity our measurement' (1923). [30; 42; 48; 49; 63; 64; 93]

Gê-Bororo Religion [XXIII] In the complex dual organizations of Gê and Bororo societies of central Brazil, dichotomous classifications of reality are exhibited in ceremonial life. Each village is bisected by a system of halves (or moieties) or a series of such systems, opposed by dyadic classification and between which relations of logical complementarity are ritually played out, made formal through ceremony in elaborate ways. Society is in short a process within a specific cosmological scheme of things evident in ritual and circular or semicircular village layouts [15: 127]. Out of the antithetical ideas, categories and institutions that constitute their way of life, Gê and Bororo societies strive to create a harmonious synthesis, a balance and harmony through opposing institutions.

In essence, Gê-Bororo cosmologies and social philosophies emphasize both spatiality and repetition. The eastern Timbira, for example, seem to seek closure of time (the past, present and future world) through the circumscribed spaces of their villages. There, everything has its place and this unchangeable place exorcizes time. The village thus becomes a utopian microcosm englobing the totality of the external world. [7; 15; 19]

Gedatsukai [XXVI] Okano Seiken (1881–1948) founded Gedatsukai, or the Nirvana Association, in Japan in 1929. Its 'holy land' is located in the city of Kitamoto, Saitama Prefecture. Its adherents number approximately 240,000. After founding Gedatsukai, Okano took orders in the SHINGON Buddhist Daigo sect in 1931. The connection with the sect remained strong over the years, and on his death it bestowed on him the title Gedatsu Kongo, or the Diamond of Nirvana. Gedatsukai reveres the KAMI Tenjinchigi-okami, the source of all being. The divinity to whom people pray for help and protection is the same *kami* under the name Gochi Nyorai, a name borrowed from esoteric BUDDHISM. When Gedatsukai members pray for help, they utter an incantation meaning 'reverence to the Diamond of Nirvana', thus implying that in their eyes Okano is one of the Buddhas. *Ongoho shugyo*, one of the chief exercises in Gedatsukai, has to do with possession and mediation. One performing this exercise kneels before a *kami* or buddha altar, holding a special card between the hands, and begins to meditate. Spirits light on the card and present requests for purifying ritual and warnings. The messages, however, are interpreted not by the person engaged in the exercise but by a mediator posted alongside. Since about 1985, Gedatsukai has held training courses for people wishing to become mediators. Unique to Gedatsukai is the *amacha kuyo* ritual. On a card inscribed with the name of an ancestral or other spirit, one pours sweet tea, efficacious, it is said, for purifying suffering spirits. This ritual is to be performed morning and evening before the home altar. Though basically Buddhist, Gedatsukai does not deny the spirits or *kami* that people worship before becoming members, but includes them in its rituals and world-view. [5]

Gelug [xxxv] The Gelug tradition of Tibetan BUDDHISM was founded by the great scholar Tsongkhapa Lozang Dragpa (1367–1419 CE). In early life Tsongkhapa studied with masters of all the major Tibetan lineages, and received extensive training in philosophical and meditational teachings. Subsequently he attracted many disciples and founded the monastery of Ganden, which became one of the three principal seats of the Gelug tradition. The chief characteristics of the tradition are its strict adherence to the VINAYA rules of monastic discipline and its emphasis on the 'graded path' (*lam-rim*) to enlightenment, which was inherited from the KADAM school [23; 25]. In philosophy the Gelugs have upheld the viewpoint of the Prasangika MADHYAMIKA as interpreted by Tsongkhapa, in which emptiness is referred to as 'the negation of all predicates' (*med-gag*).

Although the hierarch of the Ganden monastery is officially the head of the Gelug school, the office of the DALAI LAMA, hierarch of the Drepung monastery, has attained preeminence. This is due to the Dalai Lama's position as head of the Tibetan state, a position attained in the lifetime of the fifth Dalai Lama, Ngawang Lozang Gyamtsho (1617–82), who unified the country under the authority of the Gelug sect [18]. The title Dalai Lama ('ocean-like guru') was conferred by the Mongol, Altan Khan, on his GURU Sonam Gyamtsho (1543–88), who was retrospectively recognized as the third in the line of incarnations. The political power of the tradition continued until 1959 with the exile of the 14th Dalai Lama, Tenzin Gyamtsho, as a result of the communist Chinese invasion and suppression of Tibetan independence.

Gender [xIV] Whereas the word 'sex' refers primarily to biological differences between women and men, the word 'gender' indicates the historically and culturally developed interpretations of what it means to be a woman or man in different religions and cultures. The understanding of sexual differences varies widely in terms of the different sexual roles and images ascribed to both sexes, and the power and status accorded to each. Many religious teachings and practices, especially scriptural statements, theological doctrines, official authority, representation and rites are closely associated with gender differences, often said to be normatively prescribed by sacred scriptures.

Critical gender analysis has become an important part of contemporary scholarship, including the STUDY OF RELIGION. Such analysis deals in principle with both men and women, but given the overwhelmingly male-orientated (androcentric) orientation of all previous knowledge, which took male experience and understanding as the universal human norm whereas women's experience was marginalized and neglected, there exists the urgent necessity for a radical critique of this imbalance. Thus current attention to gender issues tends in practice to be primarily focused on women. [74] Contemporary feminist scholars have developed a substantial body of new theory and knowledge, already institutionalized in many women's studies courses [14: 433–40]. Frequently, however, these make little or no reference to RELIGION. Yet the history of the modern women's movement has deep roots in religion. It originally drew much inspiration from the Judaeo-Christian belief that both male and female are created in the image of God and are called as equal heirs to God's kingdom. The feminist critique of society and culture centres on the pervasiveness of patriarchy, the all-male power structure visible in institutions, widespread assumptions and attitudes, but it is also concerned with sexism (whereby social life is organized according to sharply differentiated gender roles) and androcentrism or the male-centredness inherent in our thought structures, concepts and language [74: 272–6]. The feminist critique of religion has so far been addressed mostly to CHRISTIANITY and JUDAISM [16; 17], but a growing number of publications now also deal with the feminist transformation of BUDDHISM and other world religions [18; 29; 52; 80].

Feminist theology, both Jewish and Christian, has already produced a large body of literature, dealing with all aspects of theology in a new, critical perspective, from biblical studies to patristics (now balanced by 'matristics'), church history, systematic theology and ethics [58]. Central to all debates is the question of whether traditional symbols and teachings can be reformed or reconstructed, or whether they must be radically rejected and replaced by new ones. Much valuable work has

been done on the use of metaphor and language, especially in relation to the image and concept of God or, put more neutrally, in relation to the human constructs of ultimate reality in relation to gender models. Feminist theology is not just a Western development, but has to be seen in a global context. Women in Asia, Africa, Latin America and elsewhere in the so-called 'Third World' are developing new theological insights out of their own experience of oppression. They draw on specific understandings of liberation and develop newly emerging spiritualities [49].

If one looks at women in world religions systematically and comparatively, three perspectives can be singled out. The first concerns women's role and status in different religious traditions. (What is their participation in ritual and liturgy? What religious authority do women hold? What access are they given to priesthood, monasticism or religious leadership? What kind of religious communities and rites of their own have women created?) The second deals with the question of how women are represented in religious language and thought. (What do different sacred scriptures teach about women? Do they project empowering or debilitating images, emphasizing equality and partnership or subordination? Are feminine images and symbols used in relation to the transcendent?) The third and most important one concerns women's own religious experience. Its focus is not what world religions teach *about* women, but rather how women themselves have spoken. A rich historical task consists in rediscovering women's voices in the past and recovering women's experiences of and contribution to religion. How have women articulated their own religious experiences in rich devotional and mystical literature? How far is this experience different from that of men? How far has it been integrated or remained peripheral in the doctrinal and spiritual teachings of different religious traditions? So far studies on religious experience have paid hardly any attention to gender differences; the comparative study of female and male mystics is still in its infancy. Yet women saints and mystics from all religious traditions exercise a strong fascination on contemporary women and provide inspiring role models in terms of female identity, autonomy and strength [52].

Women's spirituality expresses itself in numerous ways and exists both outside and inside different religious institutions. It possesses a strongly experiential and experimental character expressed through new visions, SYMBOLS and RITUALS [72]. It is often connected with the search for feminine figures of the divine, especially the Goddess, and with a renewed understanding of WITCHCRAFT. But the search for spiritual liberation, connectedness and wholeness is not always explicit; it also represents an important implicit dimension of the contemporary women's movement, visible especially in the peace movement and in ecofeminism [52].

The feminist challenge to religion has led to a profound paradigm shift in theology and religious studies. Feminist scholars of religion are developing a different kind of methodology which involves a 'participatory hermeneutic' where the researcher's existential participation and commitment enter into the interpretation of what is being researched. In other words, feminism is not only a contemporary social vision with a profound influence on the practice and study of religion, but it is also part of an academic method which calls into question much of the assumed 'objectivity' of previous methods and calls for a new critical reflection on what religion is about.

Religion and gender studies [50] is a growing field where some of the liveliest, most challenging and most creative developments in contemporary religious studies are taking place. A growing number of women scholars help us to gain a better understanding of the gendered nature of the self, of religious experience and practice, of the gender variables affecting human behaviour and social relations, of the gendered nature of our symbols and constructs of ultimate reality. This work in turn raises fundamental questions about the nature of religion itself as traditionally defined by Western theology and philosophy.

Gentiles [XXII] The term Gentile is a translation of the Hebrew word *goi*, meaning member of a non-Jewish people. The Jews, seeing themselves as the children of Abraham with whom God had entered into a special COVENANT, made a sharp distinction between themselves and other nations. Their attitudes towards Gentiles have varied, depending partly on the attitudes of Gentiles themselves to the teachings of JUDAISM and to Jews [14 vol. 7: 410; 25; 35; 60]. The Gentile or Son of Noah has, according to Jewish teaching, to keep the seven Noachian laws: to maintain the rule of law; not to practise idolatry, blasphemy, homicide, sexual immorality and theft; and not to eat a limb torn from a living animal. The pious of the Gentiles have a portion in the OLAM HA-BA or world to come. The opinion of the RABBIS about Muslims was that they were ethical monotheists, but considerable reservations were felt about Christian monotheism (*see* TRINITY). [25; 70: XIV]

Germanic Religion [VII] Information about the religion of the Germanic peoples, in the area bounded by the Rhine, Vistula and Danube, comes from Julius Caesar (1st century BCE [2]). Tacitus (1st century CE [29: 101–41]) and other Latin writers, of varying reliability [31: I, VI]. Anglo-Saxon England was settled in the 5th century and converted to CHRISTIANITY by the 7th, but Scandinavia not until the 10th century. Evidence from missionaries, place-names, cult objects, amulets, grave goods and other archaeological finds (see SHIP-FUNERAL; SUTTON HOO) adds to our knowledge. The Icelanders retained an interest in earlier myths, and the Poetic and Prose EDDAS are the richest source for these, together with early skaldic verse [32: I]. In the VIKING age (9th–11th centuries) there were four main deities [3: II–IV]. ODIN (Germanic Wodan) was god of magic, poetry, riches and the dead, and ruler of VALHALLA. THOR (Germanic Donar), armed with his hammer, was widely worshipped as a sky-god, controlling the weather and protecting law and the community. Freyr and Freyja were fertility deities, with many different names (see VANIR). Earlier gods might be remembered as minor deities, like Tyr (Germanic Tiwaz [3: 59]). Numerous names of supernatural beings (FROST-GIANTS, FYLGJA) are preserved in Icelandic mythological poetry. There was an elaborate system of nine worlds of men and other beings round the World-Tree (YGG-DRASIL), doomed to destruction at RAGNAROK. Powerful religious symbols in poetry and art were the horse, boar, wolf, eagle and raven, as well as ship, spear and hammer [9: 139–76], and the mead of inspiration provided for the gods [3a: 72].

Gesar [xxxv] King Gesar of Ling is the greatest CULTURE HERO of Tibet. Traditionally he is venerated as an emanation of Padmasambhava and vanquisher of all the forces inimical to religion. [5] However, modern scholarship, while unable to date him, has suggested that Gesar might be a pre-Buddhist figure. His epic cycle, which was only finally systematized in written form in the 19th century by the great scholar Ju Mipham (1848–1914), spread in Tibet and Mongolia by the agency of wandering bards. A messianic hope has been inspired by the notion of King Gesar's triumphant return to rescue Tibet from its enemies and establish BUDDHISM throughout the world.

Ghost Dance [v] A revivalistic, prophetic movement among Amerindian tribes of the Great Basin and Plains of North America in the late 19th century. The founding prophet, a Paiute Indian, Wovoka, claimed it had been revealed to him in a vision that, if the Indians would dance, the dead would return and all native peoples would be restored to the happy way of life they had before the arrival of the white man [23: v]. As the movement spread among oppressed Indian groups, its eschatology was greatly embellished and its latent anti-white militarism blossomed [8: II]. Fanatical belief that 'ghost shirts' would protect wearers from the harm of enemy bullets prompted still further confrontation with whites. The movement subsided rapidly following the tragic massacre of Sitting Bull and his people at Wounded Knee in 1890.

Gilgamesh, Epic of [VIII] During the first dynasty of Babylon (c. 1760 BCE), myths about Gilgamesh were combined as a single epic (see ANCIENT NEAR EASTERN RELIGIONS). He was a pre-eminent figure in these accounts, which include tales of ancient kings and heroes of Sumer [24: 72–9]. This epic tells of his search for eternal life and of the origin of KINGSHIP. The introductory passage provides our main source for the SUMERIAN concept of the creation of the universe (see COSMOLOGY (ANCIENT NEAR EASTERN)). The epic also gives the earliest-known account of a universal flood [16: 200–5], which is thought to have influenced the flood narrative in the BIBLE.

GLA [xxvi] The God Light Association, regularly abbreviated to GLA, started in Japan in 1969 when people began to gather at regular times to hear the teachings of Takahashi Shinji (1927–76), a man said to have achieved enlightenment. Takahashi instructed people to 'go back to Jesus, go back to Buddha'. Both JESUS and the BUDDHA, he taught, were angels of light sent by the one and only God in order to save human souls. The differences that seem to separate them show that what Jesus spoke of as love and what the Buddha spoke of as compassion are identical, for both spring from the heart of God. GLA teaches that human souls originate in the universal source of eternal life. The purpose of human life is fulfilled as the soul grows and progresses, and as human souls, acting in harmony, create new kinds of harmony in the world. People die and are reborn any number of times, depending on their spiritual growth and their contribution to harmony and progress. Takahashi Shinji taught that people could verify the teaching that the soul originates in universal eternal life. According to him, the way to gain knowledge of one's series of lives was through speaking in tongues. His daughter and successor, Takahashi Keiko (1956–), teaches that people may now find such evidence through dialogue with the departed spirits of people they know well: parents, brothers and sisters, friends, etc. GLA has videotaped many such dialogues and claims to have confirmed their content objectively by follow-up research. It avoids sensationalism, but continues to gather evidence of the continuing life of the soul and seeks to win others to the truth. As of December 1992 it had over 14,000 members in Japan and others in Brazil and the USA. Its chief centre is in Tokyo.

Gnosis [xv] Within the variety of Gnostic circles (*see* GNOSTICISM) the basic concept of Gnosis implies a self-knowledge or self-understand-ing both on the existential and on the transcendental level. Gnostics have to know their origins, those true roots which do not belong to this immanent material world: in fact they share in their pneumatic aspect a divine status (consubstantiality). Unfortunately, through the action of the creator of *this* material world (the demiurge), they are cut off from their real roots through their corporeal being here in this world. But, as elects, they possess the knowledge to escape this perishable status and have the means to become perfect, on the pneumatic level. Therefore, the knowledge of true origins (the divine world), of the exact cosmogonical and cosmological evidence and of cosmic history ('Gnostic myth'), of this Gnosis which was revealed through a divine mediator, is truly redemptive. It is clear from the definition that there are anthropological consequences implied in this concept of Gnosis: the esoteric 'knowers' are elect or perfect and will find freedom and redemption (through transmigration), in opposition to the 'a-gnostics'; they have to deal with certain moral and ethical prescripts, as well as with a certain illuminated way of life. Among basic ideas of this Gnosis are the presence of the divine particles in humankind and nature, the necessity of the reawakening of these divine elements, and the dualistic nature of the world. The term Gnosis is therefore linked up in a particular way with the Gnostic systems of the first three centuries CE and plays a predominant role in MANICHAEISM, Mandaeism (*see* MANDAEANS) and certain Islamic esoteric circles; Buddhist, Hermetic and Neoplatonist concepts must also be considered. It is not surprising that certain anthroposophical doctrines of the 20th century, as well as more recent NEW AGE speculations, try to revive an adapted version of what they suppose to be the ancient Gnosis. [7; 13; 24a]

Gnosticism [XIII.A] The doctrine that knowledge (Greek GNOSIS) is the way to salvation, especially for human spirits thought of as particles of light or sparks from the upper world which have fallen into prison-houses of flesh (see PLEROMA; PRIMAL MAN). Those who are worthy (usually only men) receive the saving knowledge from a redeemer-revealer (see REDEEMED REDEEMER). This basic scheme was variously elaborated in the Gnostic schools of the 2nd century CE, most, but not all, of which had associations with CHRISTIANITY (see BASILIDES; MANDAEANS; MANICHAEISM; VALENTINIANISM). The possibility of a pre-Christian Gnosticism is not ruled out, but commonly the redeemer figure is JESUS; however, because the material world is evil, he is considered only to have indwelt a body temporarily and thus only seemed (hence Docetism, from Greek *dokeo*, to seem) to die on the cross.

The variety of Gnostic schools was such that Irenaeus of Lyons (*c.*180 CE) could say that there were as many systems of redemption as there were Gnostic teachers. But they shared the same basic principle that the material world is evil, while the world of spirit is good. This led to the belief that the two worlds owed their existence to two different creators, the creator of the material order (the demiurge, the GOD of the Hebrew BIBLE) being an opponent of the supreme god of truth (AEON). This cosmological dualism was variously set forth in mythological narratives and genealogical schemes, some of which depended on motifs in the Hebrew Bible, though the Bible as such was generally rejected because of its positive view of the created order (see PRIMAL MAN).

Though at one time particular Gnostics and their thought were known only from the writings of their opponents, the discoveries at NAG HAMMADI have provided us with many of their own works. Some Gnostic schools, e.g. the followers of Valentinus (*c.*140 CE), were not far removed from church orthodoxy. Others were directly opposed to it, in ethics and theology alike; such were the followers of Carpocrates (*c.*140 CE), who are alleged to have practised community of wives as well as property (see SIN, CHRISTIANITY AND; WOMEN (IN EARLY CHRISTIANITY)). Such libertine Gnosticism was a deviation from the norm. Another group of the same period, the Naassenes, took their name from the serpent (Hebrew *nahash*), which they regarded as the embodiment of wisdom. Forms of Gnosticism have appeared at various times in the history of the church, e.g. the Cathari; see HERESY (MEDIEVAL CHRISTIAN). [14; 17; 19]

Gobind Singh, Guru [XXXIII] (1666–1708) Tenth and last personal GURU of the SIKHS, the only son of the ninth Guru, Tegh Bahadur. From his father he inherited at the age of nine a small state in the Shivalik hills, north-east of the Punjab, and when he grew to manhood engaged in a series of wars with other hill chieftains. In 1699 he summoned his Sikhs to his centre at Anandpur for the most crucial event in Sikh history, the inauguration of the KHALSA. Increasingly Mughal (Mogul) forces intervened in the hill wars between states under their suzerainty and in 1704 they forced Gobind Singh to withdraw from Anandpur. In the conflict which followed the Guru lost all four of his sons. Eventually he found security in southern Punjab and while there the persecuting emperor, Aurangzeb, died. Gobind Singh accompanied his successor Bahadur Shah to the Deccan and while there was assassinated at Nanded. Shortly before his death he is believed to have declared the line of personal Gurus to be at an end and to have conferred the authority of the Guru on the ADI GRANTH (Guru Granth) and the PANTH (Guru Panth). [14: II–VIII]

God, Christian Concept of [XIII.B] Christianity formally teaches MONOTHEISM, rejecting both DEISM and PANTHEISM. (Elements of POLYTHEISM have, however, been common at popular folk level in various countries.) God has created the world distinct from himself, while remaining active within it. His attributes include eternity, unchangeableness (immutability), and unlimited knowledge (omniscience) and power (omnipotence). This monotheism is complicated (but according to Christian belief enriched) by the teaching that God shows himself to be a TRINITY in unity of Father, Son (JESUS Christ) and HOLY SPIRIT. [160a]

God (in Hebrew and Christian Scriptures) [XIII.A] Even in the earliest sources, the God of Israel is known as Yahweh. He was not only the God of Israel; he was acknowledged as the creator and sustainer of the universe and as the judge of all nations. It was their common allegiance to Yahweh that was the hallmark of the Israelites' religion. One of his fuller titles was 'Yahweh, the God of hosts' (i.e. the hosts or armies of Israel or heaven). The Israelites identified Yahweh with El, the head of the Canaanite pantheon. More particularly, in some narratives and several psalms, Yahweh was identified with El Elyon ('God Most High') who had been worshipped in JERUSALEM. The documentary evidence that Yahweh's worship was aniconic (*see* ICONOGRAPHY) is confirmed negatively by the absence of any artefact which can be recognized as his image. The prophets of Israel emphasized Yahweh's ethical character (explicit in the Mosaic COVENANT): he was a God of righteousness and mercy, and required those qualities in his people.

The God of the New Testament is identical with the God of the Hebrew Bible. JESUS is portrayed as having an intense awareness of communion with God. According to PAUL, the invocation 'Abba' (father) on the lips of Christians is a token that they have received the same spirit as indwelt Jesus. [11: II, 1041–55]

Gods, Goddesses [XXXIV] The objects of worship, adoration, fear and obedience and the sources of obligations, commandments and forms of acceptable behaviour who speak to, appear to, and generally occupy positions of sacred or deeply significant existence for those who acknowledge them. Gods and goddesses vary from very local unseen spiritual beings to cosmic and universal divinities, their influence sometimes malign, sometimes benign. These beings are held to control the cosmic elements – there are gods of sky, earth, air, fire, thunder and fertility – and to control the destinies of peoples, through protection against enemies or diseases, or through the prosecution of wars. Human existence itself is held to depend on the favours or disapproval of gods and goddesses. In order to gain favour or avoid disapproval devotees offer prayers, gifts, sacrifices. Special boons demand special gifts. In all religious contexts gods and goddesses, or at least supernatural spiritual beings, are present. Even in the non-theistic religious context of the teaching of the BUDDHA there are references to gods, but these are not the determining powers of some other religious contexts; rather, they are spiritual beings who themselves are in need of deliverance from the bonds of existence. In some traditions the same god or goddess can be seen as either benign or malign. The Hindu goddess KALI is such an example. Religious traditions may acknowledge the existence of more than one god or goddess, giving rise to the category of POLYTHEISM. HINDUISM is such a tradition. Hindus acknowledge gods and goddesses for virtually every aspect of human existence; cultic heroes or saints fulfil much the same functions in other religions. That Hindu gods and goddesses do function in this way alongside a strong tradition of there being only one supreme deity or primal being raises questions about the category 'polytheism' as applied to Hinduism. Other religious traditions may owe allegiance to only one god or goddess, out of a choice of such beings, giving us the category of HENOTHEISM. Some would argue that this was the status of the god of the early Hebrews. Other examples of henotheism would be certain tribal gods in Africa and the Pacific, and the allegiances of certain forms of the Hindu BHAKTI devotional tradition. Yet other religious traditions may acknowledge the existence of only one supreme, universal god, giving the category of MONOTHEISM. JUDAISM, CHRISTIANITY and ISLAM are such traditions. Among these last-named traditions belief in multiple gods, and especially in goddesses, is considered not merely heretical or pagan but also morally debased. Religious traditions vary from the iconic (see ICON), in which gods and goddesses are given representative form as images, as in Polynesian and African religions, in Hinduism and certain forms of BUDDHISM, to the aniconic, in which representations of gods are forbidden and condemned, as in Judaism, Christianity, Islam and SIKHISM. However, even in these so-called aniconic religions (apart from Islam) representations of the divinity (for example that of God in the Sistine Chapel in Rome), religious heroes (the saints in Christianity and the GURUS in Sikhism) or saviours (JESUS Christ, the Second Person of the Divine Trinity in Christianity, and GURU NANAK in Sikhism), are to be found in the homes of devotees and in official buildings used for rituals. There would appear to be one common feature of belief in gods and goddesses and that is that these beings exercise power over the believer's world, whether for good or ill. [113; 51: I, A, B; 89]

Goeteia, Mageia [XVI] The Greeks disapproved of witchcraft, whose goddess was Hecate, but made use of it. *Mageia* boomed in Hellenistic times, enriched as it was by new, Oriental material. Clients sought either to achieve some desirable result for themselves, health, wealth, victory, erotic success (through amulets, love potions, spells (incantations, *epodai*)); or to harm their enemies by means of spells and curses (*katadesmoi, katadeseis*) which were inscribed on tablets and buried, preferably in graves. Other practices were melting wax figurines or sticking them with pins, and placing bound lead figurines in graves. [17: 270–4; 27: 309–23; 13; 23: 3–131]

Golden Dawn, Hermetic Order of the [XXIV] The most influential Western magical organization of modern times, which made a significant contribution to the modern revival of interest in the OCCULT, not least through the substantial body of literature on its teachings [16] and rituals which has been published. Founded in 1888, it established 'temples' at London, Paris, Edinburgh and elsewhere whose members pursued an extensive programme of esoteric studies, including ASTROLOGY, KABBALAH, TAROT, meditation and ritual MAGIC. It was founded by S. L. MacGregor Mathers (1854–1918), Wynn Westcott (1848–1925) and Dr William Woodman (1828–91), all at the time members of the ROSICRUCIAN Society of England [16: II] which was open to Master Masons (see FREEMASONRY) only. The order had a 'grade' structure derived from the 'degrees' of Freemasonry, a member's progress through the grades being marked by a series of colourful initiation rituals drawing on Christian, Egyptian and Rosicrucian symbolism. Membership figures are unknown, but between 1888 and

1896 over 300 people joined. In 1900 Mathers's autocratic rule aroused dissent and the Irish poet and writer, W. B. Yeats (1865–1939) deposed Mathers and assumed leadership for several years [16: XVI]; but he could not prevent the order from disintegrating into factions. Central organization lapsed during the 1920s but several temples continued independently as late as the 1950s, including Dion Fortune's 'Society of the Inner Light'. Numerous organizations deriving from these or the original order still exist.

Gosala [XVII] The founder of the AJIVAKA religion (*fl. c.*500 BCE), often referred to as Makkhali ('staffbearer'). Gosala probably predeceased both his close associate MAHAVIRA (the founder of Jainism; *see* JAINS) and the BUDDHA. Believed to have attained both omniscience and liberation, Gosala taught that everything is predetermined by fate (*niyati*) and that final liberation (MOKSHA) is inevitable for all at the end of a long period of transmigration. [10: 27–79]

Gospel [XIII.A] An Old English word meaning 'good tidings', corresponding to Greek *euangelion*. In Christianity it is used first of the message JESUS proclaimed, then of the message about Jesus, and finally of the written records of Jesus' ministry. *Mark* (1: 14–15) says that Jesus preached the gospel of God, that God's rule is near at hand. *Luke* (4: 18–19) identifies Jesus' preaching with the good news announced to the poor by the anointed figure described in *Isaiah* 61:1. The good news about Jesus declared that in him, especially in his death vindicated by his resurrection, God had acted decisively for humanity (*see* SALVATION). When four 1st-century records of Jesus were first collected in the New Testament CANON, they were referred to collectively as 'the gospel'. Later came the practice of designating each of the four records

(*Matthew, Mark, Luke, John*) as 'a' gospel or referring to them together as 'the gospels'. On the model of these canonical gospels several other (apocryphal) gospels appeared from the middle of the 2nd century onwards. It was claimed they were written by APOSTLES and other associates of Jesus.

Gospel of Wealth [IV] [14: 1429–61] In 1900 the American industrial magnate Andrew Carnegie, though not personally a religious man, chose religious terms to describe and advocate an outlook on life. He called it the 'Gospel of Wealth'. It was but one among many such apologies being written around the turn of the century by industrialists who were making great wealth and who found a need to provide a rationale for their own fortune and a guide for others to prosper [16: 301–10].

Carnegie's Gospel of Wealth, and that of other writers, to be sure, had in common a dependency upon an outlook called social Darwinism. This was an extremely voguish interpretation of life that blended some features of Charles Darwin's notions of 'the survival of the fittest' with CALVINIST incentives to be morally earnest about earning and capitalist economics.

The Gospel of Wealth ran counter to one inherited and one contemporary interpretation. Historically, the PROTESTANTS who dominated American culture, while preaching responsibility and stewardship, also saw economic status to be a part of the determined aspect of life. That is, just as sons of noble people inherited nobility while peasants were to be content with their peonage, so the offspring of the landed and affluent were likely to inherit wealth. The message to them was not to trust in their riches or to hoard them; meanwhile, the poor were told to be content with their status.

With the rise of enterprise and the middle class this theology suddenly changed. Popular preachers like Henry Ward Beecher started promulgating the view that some measure of wealth was available to all, which meant that being poor was ordinarily a sign of indolence and sin. God favoured those who worked hard, and they would be blessed with riches. Carnegie's Gospel of Wealth did not need God; a kind of iron law of history decreed prosperity for the industrious, of whom generosity and investment were expected.

The Gospel of Wealth appeared against the background of a contemporary SOCIAL GOSPEL movement. Protestant clerics around the turn of the century criticized social Darwinism, *laissez-faire* capitalism and accumulations of great wealth, and favoured socialistic and cooperative life. This, to the authors of the Gospel of Wealth, represented a violation of nature's law and immoralism. [1; 14: 1429–61; 26]

Gotama [XI] (Pali; Sanskrit: *Gautama*) The family name of the historical BUDDHA and founder of BUDDHISM; his personal name was Siddhattha (Sanskrit: *Siddhartha*) but he is also referred to by the titles Bhagavat (Blessed One), Tathagata (Thus-gone/come) and Shakyamuni (Sage of the Shakyas). His dates are uncertain; recent research suggests that *c.*484–404 BCE is to be preferred to the usually quoted 566–486 BCE. The story of Gotama, in particular his struggle for enlightenment, represents one of the cornerstones of Buddhist culture and has inspired works of art of all sorts across much of Asia. As handed down by Buddhist tradition [15: 35–66; 39] it is in certain respects mythic, yet the general outline need not be regarded as inherently problematic as history. He was born on the borders of what is now India and Nepal (*see* LUMBINI) into a locally important family of the ruling class (*see* VARNA) and enjoyed a privileged upbringing. He married and had a son. His disenchantment with his comfortable life-

style is related in terms of his encounter with an old man, a sick man, a corpse and a wandering ascetic. Confronted with the seeming inevitability of suffering (DUKKHA), he left home at the age of 29 to become a wandering ascetic himself. After six years spent variously with teachers and practising severe asceticism, he rejected this path and, seated in meditation beneath the *bodhi* tree at BODHGAYA, finally gained 'enlightenment' (*see* ARAHAT; LOKUTTARA; NIBBANA). His first discourse at SARNATH marks the beginning of 45 years devoted to teaching 'the path to the cessation of suffering' (*see* EIGHTFOLD PATH) and organizing the Buddhist order (SANGHA). His pupils were other wandering ascetics, ordinary householders and occasionally local rulers. His teachings are preserved principally in the discourses (SUTTA) of the NIKAYAS and in the VINAYA-pitaka (cf. TIPITAKA). At the age of 80 he finally fell ill and died (*see* PARINIBBANA) at KUSINARA; his body was cremated and the relics were divided and enshrined in various STUPAS. Reliquaries which may contain portions of these relics have been recovered from archaeological sites in northern India; another apparently ancient relic is kept in the Temple of the Tooth in Kandy. [95; 6; 62; 81]

Grail, Legend of the Holy [XIII.B] In medieval legends and romances the Grail is portrayed as a cup possessing and conveying spiritual powers. The origins of the story are thought to lie in pre-Christian Irish myths, possibly associated with ancient fertility rituals involving a cup, sword and sacred king. Medieval writers gave it a Christian setting and meaning and several versions of it exist in European literature. It is a notable part of the developed legend of the British hero King Arthur whose knights went in quest of the Grail. One version of the legend explains that the Grail was the cup used by JESUS Christ at his last supper and that Joseph of Arimathea, having caught Jesus' blood in the Grail at the crucifixion, then conveyed it to Glastonbury in England. The Grail also figured in Richard Wagner's opera *Parsifal*. [62 vol. 6: 89–94; 127]

Great Awakenings [IV] Renewals, reforms and revivalists are regular features of religions; in the USA several such movements have acquired the name 'the Great Awakening', associated with numbers, through at least 'The First Great Awakening' and 'The Second Great Awakening'. Like other cultural phenomena, these are not events in the same way that beginnings and ends of wars, or earthquakes and passage of laws are. Rather, people take note of a complex set of events and give a name to it. So, many years after PROTESTANT religious excitements throughout the British colonies in America, some applied to these events the name 'the Great Awakening' [17]. In this telling, the Great Awakening began with some stirrings in New Jersey under Theodorus Jacobus Frelinghuysen, who began to attract crowds with his emotional style of preaching. Soon he was joined by members of the William Tennent family, PRESBY-TERIANS who trained ministers through a 'Log College' near Philadelphia. William's son, Gilbert Tennent, became a strong leader who encouraged new methods of winning converts. Meanwhile, in New England, a noted preacher and theologian, Jonathan Edwards, began to notice uncommon responses to his preaching and to discuss 'surprising conversions'. He was joined by many other local pastors, some of whom found their territories invaded by evangelizers who cared little for church establishment, public order or quietly rational preaching. They stirred people up, sometimes against their 'settled' preachers and official church. The purpose was to convince people of

their sins and turn them to the grace of God, after which they formed alternative congregations.

The biggest impetus may have come from George Whitefield, a British CALVINIST evangelizer who visited colonies from south to north on frequent tours, using his rhetorical gifts to command crowds in the tens of thousands and converts in the hundreds in each engagement. Whether or not the name Great Awakening should have ever been applied, it is clear that for a ten-year period in the 1730s and 1740s churches were dividing, ministers were arguing, crowds kept forming and people were converted. It was one of the few intercolonial events, one that some felt helped breed a common spirit towards the formation of the nation [17: III].

As these energies seemed spent, while efforts to convert people continued, there was a new surge of revival activity beginning in the 1790s. The West, across the Appalachians, was opening, and BAPTISTS and METHODISTS especially hurried to start churches there. They did this through large 'camp meetings' and invented New Measures to stimulate conversion. Thousands of people might gather for protracted meetings, and be energized by the preaching and singing. The Second Great Awakening also was promoted by individual pastors, most of whose names however never came to be well known. Charles Grandison Finney, who drew crowds in the 1820s, was among the innovators who tried to apply the techniques of modern psychology to produce conversions.

Only controversy surrounds the efforts of some historians to define Third and Fourth Awakenings. Suffice it to say that periodically, under evangelists like Dwight L. Moody, Billy Sunday and Billy Graham, each coming a half-century after the previous one; promoted by REVIVAL-IST techniques and local churches; commented upon by chroniclers of the culture; sometimes issuing in programmes of reform; Americans became convinced that extraordinary excitements occurred, moments in which their promoters were convinced that God was working remarkably to stimulate change in individual humans and society, to 'awaken' both. [17: IV–VI]

Greek Religion [XVI] It is in the 8th century BCE that 'historical' Greek religion began to crystallize into the forms that were to characterize it subsequently; in the preceding 'Dark Age' (which followed the collapse of Mycenaean palatial society in the 12th century BCE), circumstances were conducive to divergent local developments. In the 8th century Panhellenic sanctuaries (TEMENOS) and the epics of Homer and Hesiod became vehicles for crystallizing and systematizing belief, and radiated a Panhellenic religious dimension, which influenced, without suppressing, local variants (see THEOI). Greek religion had no canonical body of belief, no revelation, no scriptural texts (except for sects, which did have sacred books (see ORPHEUS)), no professional divinely anointed clergy claiming special knowledge or authority, no church; it was the ordered community, the *polis* (not just 'the state', but the ordered world of the citizens), that assumed a role comparable to that played in Christianity by the Church. It was each *polis* or *ethnos* (tribal group, e.g. the Thessalians) that set into place the religious system, the calendar, the cults, etc., that mediated human relationships with the divine. Most priests and priestesses were ordinary citizens appointed by the community or elected by lot for a year or for life; from the later 4th century BCE onwards in some areas priesthoods were increasingly frequently sold; some priesthoods were reserved for the members of a particular *genos* (see INSTITUTIONS). Priests served one (or sometimes more than one) cult and could not officiate beyond their prescribed domain. They were not obliged to dedicate themselves exclusively to priestly duties. Myth (MYTHOS) was constantly reshaped by the poets who articulated and elaborated belief. Piety was primarily expressed in cults (see HEORTAI; RITES; INSTITUTIONS). Alexander's eastern conquests created new circumstances, reflected in Hellenistic (323–31 BCE) religion. The popularity of the cult of Tyche (Fortune) reflected belief in life's unpredictability. Mostly, trends begun earlier intensified. Civic cults continued, often accommodating new needs as the Tyche-cult did. A festival sometimes imported notions from STARWORSHIP. Gods acquired epithets denoting benevolence and/or protection. A ruler-cult was important (see POLITIKE). Voluntary cult associations flourished, some involving MYSTERIA, which thrived in Late Hellenistic times, when traditional cults also enjoyed a revival. Oriental THEOI were adapted to Greek needs (a superficial syncretism related them to Greek deities). Eschatological salvation was a central preoccupation of the Late Hellenistic period. These trends developed further and crystallized under the Roman empire. [2; 4; 25; 27: 16–17, 51–67, 129–32, 327; 31; 34; 35]

Green Corn Festival [V] Known among the North American Seneca Indians as the *notekhwe'es* (literally, 'they gather food'), Green Corn is a major agricultural festival, especially among north-eastern Amerindian groups [24: XII]. Typically occurring in August, when the first corn is ripe, the ceremony is held in the longhouse (council-house) and lasts three days or longer. Recurring elements of the ritual include a thanksgiving prayer, a tobacco invocation (see CALUMET), recognition of the first appearance of the corn, dancing and a repetition of the thanksgiving prayer. The ceremony ends with a feast.

Guarani Religion [xxiii] The present-day Guarani live dispersed in small groups in southern Brazil, Paraguay and north-eastern Argentina. Their religion which, in its structure and function, perpetuates the religion of the ancient Guarani, can be defined as one of inspiration, sacramentalized in song and dance, guided by prophets in search of the 'Land without Evil' (*Yvy Marã'ey*), the celestial paradise of the Creator. All Guarani receive from the divinities a soul that is the word, the name. Its function is to confer on man the gift of language, divine wisdom that is represented in sacred hymns. The word, love, and the hymn that generates the loving word make the Guarani who he or she is; an individual who loses the word loses his soul and is no longer Guarani. Their cultural ideal is the mystical living of the divinity which depends on the spiritual disposition to hear the voice of revelation. Guarani prophetism, far from being an effect of contact (although this has contributed to its appearance), is rooted in traditional religion, myths of world-creation and destruction, and the extraordinary powers invested in the *carai*, SHAMANS/prophets, true priests whose lives are dedicated to inspiration and the search for perfection. [6; 21]

Guardian Spirits (Amerindian) [v] Belief in guardian spirits is widespread throughout North American Indian peoples, excepting those in the south-west. Typically, the term refers to a complex of beliefs and rituals regarding the acquisition of personal guardian spirits through dreams or visions. Such spirits are usually sought through VISION QUEST, and although they appear in a variety of animal forms are seldom to be identified with a particular species [8: v]. They usually bestow special power upon their devotee, often providing a tangible sign in the form of a MEDICINE BUNDLE.

Guna [xvii] As a term in Indian thought *guna* basically means a constituent strand or part, but it acquires the senses of 'quality' in VAISHESHIKA and 'modification' in grammar. VEDANTA distinguishes between *saguna* and *nirguna* BRAHMAN, i.e. the divine with and without attributes, but the most important use is in the originally SAMKHYA idea of the three *gunas* or modalities which constitute the primal ground or nature (PRAKRTI) from which the experienced universe evolves: *sattva* (goodness), *rajas* (passion) and *tamas* (darkness). Psychologically *sattva* makes lucid and gives joy, *rajas* arouses activity and gives misery, while *tamas* restrains and gives dullness. *Sattva* makes the body light and the faculties clear, *rajas* makes the body mobile and stimulates the faculties, while *tamas* makes the body heavy and clouds the faculties. Cosmologically *sattva* predominates in the realm of the gods (*deva*), *rajas* among men and *tamas* among animals and plants. One leads on to another and they act together in a multitude of ways in order to bring about through their transformations the complexity of the ordinary world. In the intervals between world cycles (*kalpas*) the three *gunas* are in equilibrium and nature is undifferentiated. [121: 77–80]

Gunasthana [xx] Series of 'stages of quality' on the JAIN spiritual path [10: 272–3]. Starting from an initial situation of wrong views, the embodied soul (JIVA) can with the right effort and karmic impulse rise through a variety of transitional stages until reaching the sixth *gunasthana*, in which the restraint of the ascetic state is attained. After the elimination of a variety of negative qualities, the series culminates in the 13th stage, in which omniscience is gained, and the 14th, which lasts for only an instant before death and final liberation (*see* MOKSHA (JAIN DOCTRINE)).

Gur-bilas [XXXIII] A variety of SIKH literature which praises the courage and fighting skills of the later GURUS. The two Gurus who attract attention in this regard are the sixth, Hargobind (1606–44), and the tenth, GOBIND SINGH (1675–1708). The Gur-bilases are quite distinct from the JANAM-SAKHIS, which relate the peace-giving qualities of the first Guru, NANAK (1469–1539). [30: 11–13]

Gurdjieff, Georgei Ivanovitch [XXIV] (1874–1949) A highly unconventional religious teacher whose system, expressed in his own idiosyncratic terminology, was apparently synthesized from diverse sources including BUDDHISM and KABBALAH. Born at Alexandropol, in Armenia, Gurdjieff spent several years in Central Asia and Tibet before teaching in Russia and, after 1922, at his Institute for the Harmonious Development of Man at Fontainebleau, France.   Ordinary people, Gurdjieff taught, are 'asleep' – they act mechanically according to ingrained habit-patterns, and the three 'brains' which govern the individual's activity and consciousness ('Thinking, Feeling and Moving Centres') are uncoordinated. He or she has neither a soul nor a true will, and must remedy these defects by 'conscious labours and intentional sufferings' – the strenuous practice of exercises designed to develop self-awareness and release untapped reserves of mental and physical energy. [30] Versions of Gurdjieff's system are taught by several organizations in Europe and America established by his followers or those of his associate, P. D. Ouspensky (1878–1947). Ouspensky recorded the content of Gurdjieff's teachings between 1915 and 1917 in his book *In Search of the Miraculous* [24]. Many were drawn to the Institute, including writers such as Katherine Mansfield and Jane Heap.

Gurdwara (Dharamsala) [XXXIII] In the Sikh JANAM-SAKHIS there are frequent references to rooms or buildings called *dharamsalas*. The *dharamsala* was the cult centre of the early PANTH. Each local community (*sangat*) gathered there as a conventicle (*satsang*) for pious discourse (*katha*) and singing of the Gurus' hymns (*kirtan*) [25: 107–8]. Early sources occasionally refer to the *dharamsala* as a *gurdwara* ('Guru's door'), and eventually this name became general. The shift was evidently associated with a developing belief that the GURU was mystically present wherever Sikhs gathered in *satsang*, a belief greatly strengthened by the custom of placing a copy of the ADI GRANTH in a *dharamsala* whenever practicable [25: 261–2]. Today the strict definition of a *gurdwara* is any place where the scripture is installed (*see* RITUALS (SIKH)). The *gurdwara* is, however, much more than a place of worship. Although its prime focus is the sacred volume and its principal function *kirtan* [30: 80–3], it is also a community centre in the wider sense [10: 169–72]. Every *gurdwara* should include a hospice and a refectory (LANGAR) at which meals are served free to all comers. The presence of a *gurdwara* is marked by a triangular flag (*nishan*) coloured saffron or dark blue. The functionary in charge is called a *granthi* (reader). [8: IV; 20: V; 34: 101–6, 112–17]

Gurdwaras (Historic Locations) [XXXIII] The number of SIKH holy places is very large. Most are concentrated in the Punjab, but several are scattered over other parts of India/Pakistan and beyond. Almost all are associated with incidents from the lives of the GURUS, beginning with NANAK's birth (Nankana Sahib, Pakistan) and ending with GOBIND SINGH's death at Nanded in the Deccan. With few exceptions all are marked by *gurdwaras* or clusters of *gurdwaras*, the more important of them bearing the honorific 'Sahib'.

The most famous centre is Amritsar, founded by the fourth Guru and developed by his successor. Pre-eminent among all *gurdwaras* is its Golden Temple (HARIMANDIR SAHIB) [20: 159–73]. Many shrines mark places which the JANAM-SAKHIS record as places visited by Nanak on his travels. These include Panja Sahib near Rawalpindi [25: 92–3]. Among the prominent shrines of the Delhi area are Sis Ganj and Rakab Ganj, commemorating the execution and cremation of Guru Tegh Bahadur. Second only to the Golden Temple in importance is Kesgarh Sahib, Anandpur, which marks the founding of the KHALSA. Other important *gurdwaras* associated with the tenth Guru are Harimandir Sahib in Patna and Hazur Sahib in Nanded [20: XIII–XVII]. Since 1925 the principal Punjab *gurdwaras* have been controlled by the statutory Shiromani Gurdwara Parbandhak Committee.

Gurmat [XXXIII] 'The teachings of the GURU', the correct and preferred term for what in English is called Sikhism. The two sources of Gurmat are scripture and tradition. The first of these includes the DASAM GRANTH, but in practice the substance of scripture-based doctrine derives from the ADI GRANTH. This component comprises the teachings of NANAK, confirmed and reinforced by the other GURUS whose works have been included in the Adi Granth. In their many hymns the Gurus repeatedly stress the need to recognize the divine in the created world (AKAL PURAKH) and to appropriate God's proffered grace by meditating on his immanent presence (NAM SIMARAN). [5: xx; 27: v] It is safe to assume that all who call themselves SIKHS accept Nanak's insistence on *nam simaran* and virtuous living. The same cannot be said, however, for the component which derives from tradition. Later tradition stresses the need to accept initiation into the KHALSA and to act

according to its code (RAHIT). This requires observance of external symbols (mostly visibly the uncut hair) and a distinctive rule of living. The Khalsa order was established by the tenth Guru and those who accept its discipline normally insist that it is an essential part of Gurmat [30: 136–41].

Gurpurab [XXXIII] Anniversaries of events associated with the SIKH GURUS are known as *gurpurabs*. Three of particular importance are the birthdays of GURU NANAK (November) and GURU GOBIND SINGH (December), and the martyr-dom of Guru Arjan (May/June). On all such occasions Sikhs attend GURDWARAS and hold *melas* or fairs. (*See also* SIKH FESTIVALS.) [8: 132–5]

Guru [XVII] In Hindu tradition, a person worthy of respect, such as a parent, and hence a teacher. The term, which originally indicated especially a BRAHMAN who instructed young *brahmans* in the sacred lore, has come to mean a religious teacher of any kind who has undertaken to give personal instruction to a pupil or disciple (*chela*). The *guru–chela* relationship is a very close one, and requires the utmost reverence and obedience towards the *guru* from the *chela*. [12: 164–5]

Guru (Sikh Doctrine) [XXXIII] The word *guru* means 'preceptor' and in HINDU society that has normally meant a human teacher. Within the SANT TRADITION OF NORTHERN INDIA, however, Guru came to be identified with the inner voice of God. This view was inherited and transmitted by NANAK, for whom the *guru* or *satguru* represented the divine presence, mystically apprehended and inwardly guiding the truly devout along the path of *mukti* (SACH-KHAND). Because Nanak communicated this essential truth with unique clarity he, as human vehicle of the divine GURU, eventually received the title of Guru [25: 251–3; 27: 196–9]. This role was transmitted to each of his nine successors (GURUS) in turn, the divine spirit successively inhabiting ten enlightened individuals. The death of the 10th Guru ended the personal transmission, but the immortal Guru remained. According to Sikh doctrine the Guru dwells eternally present in the sacred scripture (which thus became the *Guru Granth* – *see* ADI GRANTH) and in the corporate community (the Guru PANTH). [5: 297–301]

Gurus (Sikh Masters) [xxxiii] The SIKH community (the PANTH) with its distinctive doctrines (GUR-MAT) derives from a succession of ten Gurus who taught in the Punjab during the 16th and 17th centuries. NANAK (1469–1539 CE), first of the ten, was born a HINDU in an area ruled by Muslims. His teachings, delivered in hymns of superb quality, bear the characteristic SANT impress with little evidence of Muslim influence (*see* SANT TRADITION OF NORTHERN INDIA) [27: v]. An extensive hagiography (the JANAM-SAKHIS) describes his childhood and missionary travels [27: IV]. Eventually he returned to the Punjab and there attracted disciples, one of whom succeeded him as Guru Angad (1504–52). The third Guru, Amar Das (1479–1574), consolida-

ted the Panth, particularly in terms of pastoral supervision [26: 7–9, 41–2]. His son-in-law, Guru Ram Das (1534–81), founded the town of Amritsar (*see* GURDWARAS) and at his death confirmed the succession in his own family by choosing his youngest son Arjan (1563–1606) as fifth Guru. Arjan's term was important, partly because he compiled the principal scripture (the ADI GRANTH) and partly because the Mogul authorities began to taken an unfriendly interest in the Panth. Guru Arjan died in Mogul (*see* ISLAMIC DYNASTIES) custody, and the skirmishes which followed in the time of Guru Hargobind (1595–1644) strengthened those elements within the Panth which favoured a more militant policy [22: 56–7]. Guru Hari Rai (1630–61) enjoyed a peace which continued precariously through the brief term of the child Guru Hari Krishan (1656–64). Mogul hostility revived, however, and eventually led to the execution of the ninth Guru, Tegh Bahadur (1621–75). Open warfare followed during the period of his son Guru GOBIND SINGH (1666–1708). Meanwhile, Gobind Singh had formally instituted the KHALSA order (1699), conferring on the Panth its visible and distinctive identity [14: VI]. With his death in 1708 the line of personal Gurus came to an end. [8: II; 2: IV–XV; 3: III–IX]

H

Hachiman [XXI] A KAMI of fishermen and cultivators, the cult starting at Usa in Kyushu, Hachiman is popularly known today as the god of war [19: 426–40; 34: 41–5; 35: 23–4]. This deity, probably at first pronounced *Yawata* (Eight Banners), became associated with military men after being patronized by the Minamoto family in the 12th century CE, and was then identified with Emperor Ojin of the 4th century CE. From the 8th century, in the early blend of SHINTO and BUDDHISM, Hachiman was titled *Daibosatsu Hachiman* by the court, the Great Bodhisattva Hachiman (*see* JAPANESE BUDDHAS AND BODHISATTVAS), or *Hachiman Daimyojin*, Great Deity Hachiman. About one-third of all SHINTO SHRINES are dedicated to Hachiman.

Hadith [XIX] The 'story', the body of traditions in ISLAM, i.e. the sayings of the Prophet MUHAMMAD, his Companions and other prominent early Muslims, the whole constituting the SUNNA and being regarded as a source of law only second to that of the QUR'AN; the *hadith* literature thus provided guidance on aspects of law and life where Qur'anic warrant was lacking [80: 170–7; 107: III]. The form of the individual *hadith* is one of subject matter (*matn*) preceded by a chain (*isnad*) of oral repeaters and guarantors of the tradition. The traditions were later written down in collections, for, since fabrication of *hadiths* to justify particular sectarian or political doctrines became a flourishing industry, such scholars as Muhammad al-Bukhari (810–70) and Muslim (c.817–75) had to sift through and critically evaluate an immense corpus, said to number 600,000, reducing them to collections of about 4,000 *hadiths* each. These are known as 'the two *Sahihs*', i.e. sound collections, and are accorded complete credence. To these, four others of slightly less reliability were added, the whole achieving canonical status. [5; 38 s.v.; 48: 65 6; 54: III; 58; 71: 79–250]

Hafiz [XIX] In Islam, the title given to a person who has memorized the whole text of the QUR'AN; in premodern times this was especially the prerogative of the blind. In so-called Qur'an schools (*kuttab*), the text of the Sacred Book was taught either in its entirety or in a certain number of its component parts (*juz'*), so divided up for easy recitation of the complete text e.g. during the 30 nights of the fasting month of Ramadam (SAUM). The tradition behind the recitation of the Qur'an is an important one in Islam, and formerly there was a specific profession of Qur'an reciters (*qari'*). [115]

Hajj [XIX] The Islamic Pilgrimage, accounted one of the PILLARS OF ISLAM. The modern ceremony in the month of Dhu 'l-Hijja is a conflation of two earlier ceremonies held in western Arabia, the *hajj* and the *'umra*, and is centred on Mecca and its shrine the KA'BA, considered to be Abrahamic in origin (*see* HARAMAIN), with certain ritual acts done outside the city. Every adult Muslim should perform the pilgrimage at least once in his or her lifetime. The pilgrim wears a special, ritually clean garb (*ihram*), and observes certain TABUS during the days of the Hajj ceremonies. It has long been an occasion for Islamic solidarity and strengthening of brotherhood within the faith, and modern transport methods have meant that increased numbers of believers can fulfil this obligation (*see* 'ID). [20 'Pilgrimage (Islam)'; 38 'Hadjdj'; 47; 48: 81–102; 67 s.v.; 80: 161–2]

Halakhah [XXII] The legal side of JUDAISM, the texts dealing with Jewish law and ritual being known as *halakhic* literature. The term *halakhah* is of unknown origin, and is usually taken to mean 'the way of going' from a root meaning 'to go'. It has been explained as that which comes from the past and goes on, i.e. a traditional rule, or as that in which Israel goes, i.e. a religious norm. In more recent times it has been argued that the term originated with the name for a fixed land tax, which then came to mean a fixed religious rule [41: 83]. The term *halakhah* is used in the TALMUD and MIDRASH, where certain rules are described as '*halakhah* going back to MOSES at Sinai' or as 'a *halakhah* which is not publicized as a practical decision'. In the many cases of legal dispute it is often said that 'the *halakhah* is like RABBI X', 'the *halakhah* is like the later authority', or that 'this is a *halakhah* for the times of the MESSIAH', i.e. it has no practical application before then. *Halakhah* is contrasted with non-legal material, AGGADAH [14 vol. 7: 1156; 67: 248, 253; 70: VII]. There is some discussion of the relative weight to be given to a *minhag*, or customary practice, where this prescribes a different norm of behaviour from the *halakhah*. The traditional Jew is bound by codified halakhic decisions, while the GENTILE is thought to be commanded by God only to keep the seven Noachian laws. REFORM and CONSERVATIVE JUDAISM have introduced

modifications into *halakhic* rulings which are generally not accepted by Orthodox Jews. [5; 11]

Hallelujah (South American Religions) [XXIII] Prophetic movement among Carib-speaking peoples of the savannahs of British Guiana and northern Brazil. The movement originated in the mid- to late 19th century, largely due to Anglican missionary activity. The first prophet, Bichiwung, a Macuxi Indian, is said to have received divine inspiration for the words and songs of Hallelujah.

The doctrine consists of a reinterpretation of Christian theology in which the pantheon is incorporated into indigenous cosmology; SHAMANS have been key innovators and propagators of the teachings. As with Seventh Day Adventism, also important among natives of the region, the notions of a promised paradise and return of the CULTURE HERO/saviour are prominent. [5]

Hamallism [XXVII] This new Africanizing movement was one of the larger to emerge in west Africa and traces to Muhammad ben Amadu, a gentle mystic reformer of the ritual of the Tijaniyya, a SUFI ORDER, who formed a small brotherhood among the Wolof traders in what is modern Mali before his death in 1909. It was his successor, Shaikh Hamahu'ullah ben Muhammed (1886–1943), commonly known as Hamallah, who expanded the reformed Tijani order among the peasant population. Violent clashes with traditional TIJANIS led the French to deport Hamallah successively to Mauretania, the Ivory Coast and France, where he died in 1943. The fraternity he developed later declined, although it still numbered perhaps 50,000 in Mali by the 1970s and extended to Mauretania.

Deviations from orthodox ISLAM included omission of 'and MUHAMMAD is his prophet' from the profession of faith, or even substituting reference to Hamallah; rejection of the pilgrimage to Mecca and sometimes of the QU'RAN itself; replacing the prayer position towards Mecca with orientation towards Nioro, 'the Mecca of Hamallism'; and shouting the prayers themselves. Other opposition derived from its challenge to the social order by emphasis upon the equality of social classes – of young men against the elders, of lower classes against the elites, of slave tribes and to some extent of women in worship. In this way it contributed to the Africanization of Islam and to modernization, and therefore appealed to the *evolués* becoming active in political movements for independence and became allied with the main nationalist party, the Rassemblement Démocratique Africain. Two of its disciples became presidents of the emergent nations and one, Amadu Hampaté Ba, a member of UNESCO's executive council, who encouraged translation of the Qu'ran into Fulani and Bambara. Hamallism itself, like the Mourides, declined after serving its purpose.

An early disciple of Hamallism, Yakouba Sylla, a Soninke, deviated still further from Islam, after claiming a revelation from Fatima. He developed his own highly authoritarian movement, first in Mali in the 1920s and then, after being deported to the Ivory Coast, at Gagnoa from 1930. With a labour force committed to obedience, a puritan ethic and a millennial theology, and drawn from the discontented members of society, his businesses prospered and his influence reached as far as Mauretania, until his movement went into decline.

Hammurabi's Code [VIII] The gods, as guardians of Mesopotamian cities (*see* BABYLONIANS; SUMERIANS), gave laws to mankind; their role is made clear in Hammurabi's Code, where the king enacts their instructions [7]. Hammurabi, king of the first dynasty of Babylon (1792–1750 BCE), is credited with the compilation of the famous Code of Laws [23: 99–101], the most important single written document from Mesopotamia. Preserved on a black stone stele, the code states that the gods of Sumer had exalted MARDUK, and instructed Hammurabi to create justice in the land. He is shown before Shamash, the sun-god, who was also god of justice. Among laws governing society, the code also recognizes the social obligations of the TEMPLE [23: 18].

Handsome Lake Religion [XXVII] Also known as the Longhouse religion or Gui'wiio ('Good Message'), founded by an alcoholic Seneca chief, Ganioda'yo ('handsome lake') (1735–1815), whose heavenly revelations in 1799 transformed himself and the demoralized Seneca. Quaker beliefs (*see* FRIENDS, RELIGIOUS SOCIETY OF) were combined with traditional rituals and a puritan and modernizing ethic. The movement spread among the Iroquois tribes. Authorized preachers of the Code of Handsome Lake still serve some 5,000 adherents in Upper New York, Ontario and Quebec, and maintain Indian identity. [12: 101–7; 23: VIII–X; 26: 387–97]

Hanif [XIX] (adj. Hanafi) In early ISLAM, a term for one who follows the original, pure monotheistic religion, that of ABRAHAM and the first men. It is regarded in the QUR'AN as the religion to which mankind has an innate, natural propensity, and is contrasted with polytheism and idolatry and the corrupted monotheism of the Jews and Christians. Subsequently, it was often used as a synonym for 'Muslim', and Islam often called the 'Hanafi religion'.

Hanuman [XVII] Hanuman in Hindu myth is a monkey-god, son of Vayu the wind-god and a female monkey, celebrated for his staunch devotion (BHAKTI) to RAMA and Sita. In the RAMAYANA he uses his great strength and superhuman powers in Rama's service. In art he is shown as a monkey or ape of varying species, sometimes with a partly human body, but always with a long tail [4: 204–6]. As befits his monkey nature, he embodies mischief and humour as well as devotion, wreaking havoc in the palace of the demon Ravana who was holding Sita captive. In modern prints he often has the muscular torso of a bodybuilder, having become the patron deity of those who practise this sport.

Harae [XXI] Purification by exorcism – *harae*, *oharae* or *harai* – is the oldest of the current SHINTO practices. It is first mentioned in the 8th-century books (*see* SHINTO LITERATURE): when Izanagi was attacked by evil spirits while trying to extricate his wife from the land of the dead, Yomi-no-kuni, he retired to wash himself in a river (*see* SHINTO MYTHOLOGY). Purification was officially practised twice a year in early times, when the antisocial evils represented by Susano-o were washed away. *Harae* ceremonies (*see* MATSURI) are now performed to exorcize those evils which are thought to disrupt normal social behaviour, and to nullify the stigmas accompanying disasters, diseases, childbirth, death, sorcery, bad dreams and omens [general: 19: 79–91; 32: 51–2]. Running water or a neutralizing detergent is the preferred agent. The supplicant may also obtain purification by walking through a miscanthus ring; sprinkling salt at home or elsewhere; disposing of a small human effigy; or participating in or witnessing dramatic performances in which symbolic malign spirits are destroyed. Cleansing (*misogi*), at the entrance to a shrine or temple, is done by washing the hands and rinsing the mouth with water at a basin. In the shrine, the priest waves a *gohei*, a short stick bearing strips of white paper. Abstention (*imi*), once fol-

lowed by the community as a whole, then by a designated family, is now practised only by the priests, and, like *harae*, is intended to enable the supplicant, thus purified, to appear clean before the KAMI.

Haramain [XIX] The two sacred cities of ISLAM in western Arabia, Mecca and Medina, in which the Prophet MUHAMMAD received the divine revelations and successfully launched the new faith. Mecca had long been a trading town with an important shrine, the KA'BA, which Muhammad now cleared of idols and made the pilgrimage centre of the purified Islam (*see* HAJJ). It had always had a sacred enclosure (*haram*) around it, which could be entered only at times of pilgrimage, in a state of ritual purity. Mecca therefore continues to be the most sacred site of all for Muslims. Medina was the town where Muhammad established his base after the migration of 622 CE. For over 30 years it was the capital of the new Arab CALIPHATE, and always a centre of scholarship and piety, in particular for the study of law and HADITH. The location there of the Prophet's MOSQUE and his tomb makes it a goal of veneration, often visited by pilgrims who have made the Hajj to Mecca, though the Medina shrine may be visited at any time. Both remain closed to this day to nonbelievers. [39]

Hare Krishna Movement [XXVIII] The International Society for Krishna Consciousness (ISKCON), founded on his arrival in America in 1965 by His Divine Grace A. C. Bhaktivedanta Swami Prabhupada (1896–1977), was to become one of the most visible of the NEW RELIGIOUS MOVEMENTS that came from the East. In their colourful eastern dress, and the men with shaved heads except for their top-knot, devotees became a familiar sight on the streets and in public places such as airports as they sang and danced, selling records, books and their magazine, *Back to Godhead*. Additional publicity (and financial support) came through the interest of the Beatle, George Harrison. It is through their frequent chanting of their main MANTRA, *Hare Krishna, Hare Krishna, Krishna Krishna, Hare Hare, Hare Rama, Hare Rama, Rama Rama, Hare Hare* that the devotees became popularly known as the Hare Krishna. The theological basis of the movement is the BHAGA-VADGITA, as translated by Prabhupada. Devotees are expected to lead strictly ascetic lives: they may not take meat, drugs or alcohol and they must remain celibate except for the purpose of procreation of children within marriage. Many members of the Hindu community in the West (and in India) accept ISKCON as an authentic strand within their tradition. The movement did, however, come in for considerable criticism from the anti-cult movement in the 1970s and 1980s (*see* CULT-WATCHING GROUPS). The movement itself has brought about considerable changes in order to overcome the misuse of power exerted by some of the gurus whom Prabhupada left in positions of authority on his death. [5: 184–5; 6: 26–33; 11: IX, XIII; 26: II; 41: IV/H; 42: 920–2; 49; 63]

Harihara [XVII] A combined deity, half VISHNU (Hari) and half SHIVA (Hara), designed to overcome sectarian prejudice between Vaishnavas and Shaivas by showing that both are aspects of one reality. One half of the image has Shiva's attributes, such as his trident (*trishula*) and matted hair, while the other has those of Vishnu: discus (*cakra*), royal crown, etc. [4: 199]. A comparable, but even more striking, image shows Shiva as *Ardhanarishvara*, the Lord who is Half Woman, on the right male and on the left the female form of *Parvati* [4: 216; 89: 28–9; 109: 46–7]. Despite their anti-sectarian purpose, composite images seem to have been more popular among Shaivas than among Vaishnavas: cf. TRIMURTI.

Harimandir Sahib [XXXIII] Harimandir Sahib (the Temple of Hari, or God) in Amritsar, also known as Darbar Sahib (the Divine Court), the principal centre of the SIKHS. Westerners invariably call it the Golden Temple, referring to its gilding in the early 19th century by Maharaja Ranjit Singh. Amritsar was founded by Guru Ram Das (1574–81), who began excavations for the pool surrounding the temple. The original temple was completed by his successor Arjan (1581–1606). Hargobind (1606–44) was compelled to withdraw from Amritsar, but the Sikhs returned in the 18th century and by the middle of the century the temple had become the prime focus of Sikh devotion. In 1984 its surroundings were badly damaged by the Indian army's assault against Sikh militants led by Jarnail Singh Bhindranwale. (*see also* GURDWARAS (HISTORIC LOCATIONS); SIKH POLITICS.) [7: 58–9; 20: 159–73]

Harris Movement [XXVII] The largest mass movement towards Christianity in west Africa. It stemmed from William Wade Harris (*c.*1850–1929), a mission catechist in Liberia who led some 120,000 people in the Ivory Coast and western Ghana to abandon traditional religion and adopt an elementary Christianity between 1913 and 1915, when he was deported back to Liberia. British METHODIST missionaries, who discovered the movement in 1924, attracted many adherents in building up the large Methodist Church, but some 100,000 followers continue to practise in Harris churches. The spiritual head, John Ahui, who was a contemporary of Harris, died in 1992; current leaders plan to revitalize and publicize the church. [2: 10, 53; 12: 52–3; 26: 174–5]

Hatha Yoga [xvii] The branch of YOGA which specializes in methods of physical training. Its earliest surviving manuals (e.g. the *Hatha-yoga-pradipika* of Svatmarama) are not earlier than the medieval period, but many Hatha Yoga techniques are of much older origin. Hatha Yoga claims to be a beneficial preliminary to the more difficult mental training of the YOGA-DARSHANA. A basic moral and religious discipline was originally required for Hatha Yoga, but in some more modern forms the undertaking of bodily purification exercises is considered a sufficient prerequisite. Suppleness, flexibility and physical control are emphasized more than muscular development or speed of movement. The main methods are postures (*asana*), some very difficult, systematic tensing and relaxation of particular areas (*bandha*), breath control (*pranayama*) of various kinds, and the use of imagination and attention in order to control various bodily phenomena. More advanced is a colourful visualized physiology derived from TANTRA (1), involving the arousing of fundamental vital or sexual energy (*kundalini*) and the activation of various channels (*nadi*) and centres (*cakra*). Eventually this should lead to SAMADHI and DHYANA YOGA practice. [35: 17–75; 45: 175–93; 133: 148–50]

Haus Tambaran [xxix] A spirit-house of the Tambaran ancestor cult (Sepik area, northern New Guinea), but used generally to refer to ceremonial MALE CULT houses throughout Melanesia (*see* MELANESIAN RELIGION). In these, young men are secluded during initiation, taught the secrets of ritual and folklore, and admitted gradually to full status as adults [2]. In the past, a traditional *haus tambaran* (or *eravo* in the Papuan Gulf region) could tower to over 15 metres in height. [29]

Havdalah [xxii] (Hebrew, 'separation') The ceremony of separation between the end of the holy time of Sabbaths (SHABBAT) and festivals (CHAGIM) and the beginning of profane time, before work can be undertaken or food eaten. A full *havdalah* is made after Shabbat with blessings over wine, or other national drink, over spices, and over a multi-wicked candle as the hands are stretched towards its light [59: 26]. A blessing is then recited acknowledging that God divides between holy and profane, between light and darkness, between Israel and the nations, and between the seventh day and the six working days. The wine is then drunk and the candle extinguished [69: 91]. Shorter versions of this ceremony are performed at the end of YOM KIPPUR (no spices) and at the termination of festivals (no spices and no candle).

Hawaiki [xxix] The legendary homeland of Pacific island peoples. Modern Hawaii, though named after it, is not the Hawaiki of old. A more likely dispersal point for early migrations is Savai'i (i.e. Hawaiki) in Samoa. But in most island genealogies Hawaiki simply represents the distant birthplace of gods (ATUA), chiefs and men, from which great ancestors set sail. Spirits of the dead, seeking a resting-place, return there along the path of the setting sun. [3; 7; 15; 28]

Head Cult (Celtic) [vii] The taking of enemy heads in battle, to be preserved and set up in houses or fortresses, is frequently mentioned in early Irish literature. The Roman writers Diodorus Siculus and Strabo, deriving information from the Greek Posidonius (2nd century BCE [30]), describe similar practices among the continental Celts, and this is confirmed by art and archaeology [4: 71–8]. In sanctuaries of the 2nd century BCE, such as Entremont and Roqueperteuse in southern Gaul, there were carvings of heads, and human skulls were displayed [20: ii, 40]. Many stone heads from the Celtic period, some with horns, some with three faces, have been found in the British Isles [25: II]. Heads were apparently associated with sacred springs, and were revered by the Celts as a source of supernatural power, providing inspiration, fertility and healing. The head clearly played an important part in many rites of CELTIC RELIGION over a wide area and a considerable period of time.

Healing (in New Tribal Movements) [XXVII] Because interaction with Western societies usually results in more sickness for tribal peoples, already lacking adequate medical care, and because religion and healing have always been closely associated, many new tribal movements offer spiritual healing based on faith, prayer, vows, exorcism or laying on of hands. The methods include physical treatments (holy water or oil, fasting, herbs, purgatives or emetics) and psychological components (confession, reconciliation, community support). Some folk-healers, with varying degrees of religious SYNCRETISM, cater for the physically and mentally sick, as in the 'balmyards' of lower-class Jamaica, the AFRO-BRAZILIAN CULTS and the 'healing homes' of Nigeria, and through the rural folk-healers of the Philippines (see PHILIPPINES RELIGION). Many healers such as Babalola in the ALADURA, Kimbangu in the KIMBANGUIST CHURCH and Ratana in a MAORI MOVEMENT, have contributed to numerically large groups, and most of the movements contribute a valuable medical service for certain kinds of sickness. [5; 7: 377–87; 15: 175–7; 18: 220–37; 26]

Hel [VII] In Scandinavian tradition the name for both the realm of the dead and the sinister giantess ruling it, said to be LOKI's daughter. Hel is a vague image for death rather than a clearly defined concept, existing alongside the tradition of the dead

dwelling in mounds and the warrior paradise VALHALLA [3: 32, 149–62]. The emphasis is on the long road leading there, with dangerous rivers to cross and a great gate which the living cannot pass.

Hellenistic Judaism [XIII.A] The culture and religion of Jews in the Greek-speaking world after Alexander the Great (d. 323 BCE). Jews occupied one of the five wards of ALEXANDRIA; many settled in Cyrenaica. There was a large Jewish colony in ANTIOCH; others settled in Phrygia, Greece and Italy. Some forms of Hellenistic Judaism could also be found in JERUSALEM and throughout Palestine, though there were conservative reactions against its generally more universalistic outlook. In Alexandria the greatest Hellenistic Jewish thinker and writer was the philosopher Philo (20 BCE–50 CE). [13: I, 205–80; 16: 15–30; 22; 23]

Henotheism [XXXIV] Concentration of attention upon a single GOD where many gods figure in belief or myth. 'Kathenotheism', roughly equivalent, is, more precisely, concern with one god at a time; the god worshipped is effectively the only one to the worshipper. 'Monolatry' is also used for the worship of only one god, while the existence of other gods is admitted or not questioned.

Heortai, Panygereis [XVI] Greek festivals, in honour of one or more deities. *Heortai* were festivals within the city state, such as *polis* (city-state) festivals, and deme ('borough') festivals; *panygereis* were of inter-state importance. Cities sent embassies to each others' festivals and to the *panygereis*. Religious calendars varied between cities. Some *heortai* were peculiar to one city, others were celebrated by all (e.g. the *Thesmophoria*, in honour of Demeter and Kore (see THEOI; MYSTERIA)); yet others were celebrated by certain ethnic groups (e.g. the

Karneia were celebrated by the Dorians in honour of Apollo (*see* THEOI)). Each festival was a nexus of RITES spread over one or more days. These always included sacrifices, with feasts, processions, dances and songs (mostly narrating myths). In addition, they often included *agones*, competitions, musical and/or sporting. Tragedies (and comedies) were produced at dramatic competitions during the Athenian festivals of Dionysos. Many other rites (e.g. offering a robe to a deity, cleansing a statue, sacred ploughing, obscene behaviour) were also performed in some festivals. The greatest *panygereis* were the four Panhellenic *agones*. The Olympia (Olympic Games), the earliest and greatest, were in honour of Zeus (*see* THEOI) and involved a Panhellenic truce. The Pythia, founded in 582 BCE, were held at Delphi (*see* MANTIKE) in honour of Apollo. The Isthmia, founded in 581, were in honour of Poseidon; the Nemea, founded in 573, were in honour of Zeus. [4: 99–109; 25: 253–60; 11: 98–127; 31; 33]

Heresy (Medieval Christian) [XIII.B] Medieval Christian DUALIST sects included the Cathari ('the pure'), called Albigenses in southern France. They rejected the flesh and material creation as evil. The soul's salvation comes by liberation from the flesh, marriage and the eating of animal matter being forbidden for the 'perfect' minority. The rest postponed baptism into 'perfection' until near death. This movement (linked with a distinctive civilization in southern France) was suppressed by a CRUSADE and inquisition (i.e. special court for the trial of heretics) in the 13th century. The Waldensians in 12th-century France somewhat resembled later PROTESTANTISM and still exist today. The rather similar English Lollards originated with John Wyclif (*c.*1330–84). His emphasis on predestination and a purified church influenced the Hus-

sites (John Huss, *c.*1369/72–1415) [45]. This movement, affected by nationalist feeling, weakened Catholic influence in Bohemia. Some ('Bohemian Brethren') later linked up with the REFORMATION, and a remnant was revived by the MORAVIAN BRETHREN. [157; 193]

Heresy, Orthodoxy, Schism (Christian) [XIII.B] 'Orthodoxy' is Christian belief adjudged correct by a CHURCH AUTHORITY. 'Heresy' is denial of an officially defined doctrine of the Church. ('Heretics' sometimes, naturally, denounce the official church as heretical.) ROMAN CATHOLICISM nowadays allows for the relative innocence of those brought up in a heretical environment. 'Schism' is deliberate separation from the church without the involvement of doctrinal error [80]. For Roman Catholicism this means those out of COMMUNION with the PAPACY (the severity of this view was mitigated by the Second Vatican COUNCIL) [1: 355–66]

Hermeneutics [XIII.C] The theory of understanding or interpretation, especially of biblical (*see* BIBLE), philosophical and literary texts. Although interpreters had long been aware of the need to determine rules for valid exegesis if alien meanings were not to be read into texts, the development of historical consciousness, from the 18th century onwards, added a new dimension to the problem. It came to be questioned whether a person of one culture could grasp the original meaning of texts produced in a different culture. The classical hermeneutic response argues that an interpreter can re-experience the mental processes of a text's author and so apprehend the meaning of the text because both author and interpreter share a common humanity. Recently this hermeneutic principle has been questioned on the grounds that it may fail to reflect adequately the fundamental differences of awareness produced by different cultures. Other studies have argued that understanding is an art: it cannot be produced simply by observing rules, because of the so-called 'hermeneutical circle' – namely the recognition that the meaning of a text as a whole and the meaning of each of its parts are reciprocally related since the apprehension of the one depends upon the apprehension of the other. [19]

Hermetica [XIII.A] A body of Hellenistic mystical philosophy of the 2nd–3rd centuries CE, called after Hermes Trismegistus, 'Thrice-Greatest Hermes' (the Egyptian god Thoth). Hermes and others reveal this teaching to mortals as the way of wisdom and life. Some of the 18 treatises have the form of Socratic dialogues; others are epistolary in style. There is an element of Egyptian thought (*see* ANCIENT EGYPTIAN RELIGION) in their background. The Greek sources are partly Platonic, partly Stoic (*see* GREEK RELIGION); the SEPTUAGINT has also been drawn upon, especially for cosmogony. [17: 292–7, 300–7]

Hermetism [XXIV] Traditions derived from the HERMETICA, influential on European MAGIC, ALCHEMY and MYSTICISM. Texts of the Hermetica reached Europe in the late 15th century, when it was supposed that their legendary author, Hermes Trismegistus, was a real person, an Egyptian sage roughly contemporary with Moses. Elements from NEOPLATONISM and GNOSTICISM in the texts were mistaken for evidence that Trismegistus had anticipated Plato and foretold the coming of JESUS Christ. Hermetic discourses on talismans, astral magic and mystical GNOSIS thus became acceptable to some Christians. Hermetic cosmology, assuming a hierarchy of gods under the one supreme God and an elaborate structure of symbolic correspondences throughout nature, blended easily with Neo-platonist or KABBALISTIC views and stimulated the growth of Renaissance Christian OCCULTISM. Although shown in 1614 to be post-Christian, the Hermetica retained their authority for devotees of magic, and a fascination with ancient Egypt has characterized Western occultism ever since. [32]

Hero Twins [V] One of the most common and basic motifs of North American Indian mythology is that of the primeval hero twins. Usually conceived of as lesser divinities or as CULTURE HEROES, the twins are often the subjects of a miraculous birth (e.g. the NAVAJO and HOPI twin war-gods). In some versions of the myth, their mother is killed after their birth and their consequent exploits are to avenge her death. In still others, their father is portrayed as the sun-god, and their youth a period wherein they seek to learn his true identity. The twins may exemplify opposing characteristics (e.g. the one bringing benefits to mankind, the other introducing disease, old age and death), perhaps representing conflicting aspects of the more general figure of culture hero [8: III, 38–43]. In many accounts, the twins complete the process of creation by ridding the world of monsters, by shaping the physical landscape or by contributing to man's socialization. (*See also* CREATION MYTHS.)

Heroes [XVI] A heterogeneous category of Greek mythological figures and/or cult recipients. They were mortals who after death became semi-gods, able to help or harm mankind. Some heroes were nameless, being referred to simply as 'the hero'. Many heroes, named or not, did not figure in heroic myth. Most great mythological heroes were connected with cities as founders or kings; they were also appropriated as ancestors by the great aristocratic families. They received cult. Some had mortal parents, most important heroes had one divine and one mortal parent. A hero's power was centred on his grave. Cult was offered at the alleged graves of the heroes (which were sometimes rediscovered Mycenaean tombs); but not all hero shrines were believed to be associated with the hero's tomb. Heroic cult involved *enagismata* (*see* RITES), libations, prayers, votive offerings and sometimes lamentations. Heracles (the greatest Greek hero), Asklepios, the Dioskouroi and a few others received cult both as heroes and as gods. Some exceptional men were heroized after their death, as were, from some time in the 5th century BCE onwards, those Athenians who died at war in defence of their city. Heroization of the recent dead became routine in the Hellenistic period. [4: 199–208; 15: 82–98; 19; 20: 145–219; 25: 233–5; 26: 29–32; 27: 575–602]

Hesychasm [XIII.D] The most influential Eastern Christian mystical tradition (*see* MYSTICISM, CHRISTIAN). Although the great teachers of hesychasm are almost all MONASTICS, many clergy and laity have become hesychasts. Hesychasts seek deification (theosis) by constant prayer and moral and mental self-discipline. Following the teachings of St Gregory Palamas, hesychast tradition distinguishes between the unknowable essence of God and the outpouring energies which suffuse and sustain the cosmos: by God's grace, hesychasts seek to attain the experience of the Uncreated Light, a direct experential knowledge of God in his energies.

The *Philokalia* compiled by St Nikodemos of the Holy Mountain and St Makarios of Corinth is an encyclopedic collection of mystical and ascetic texts seen by the compilers as embodying the hesychast tradition. A version of the Philokalia was produced in Slavonic by St Paissy Velichkovsky and a Russian version by St Theofan the Recluse; both versions have the title 'Dobro-tolubye'. Valuable as the *Philokalia* is for hesychasts, it can easily mislead an incautious reader into the belief that the hesychast tradition is a single historical lineage going back to the earliest authors whose works it contains, such as Evagrius of Pontus and St Maximus the Confessor, and that this is the only mystical tradition in Eastern Christianity. [54; 60; 65; 83] (*See also* JESUS PRAYER; STARETS.)

Heyoka [V] A category of ritual specialists or intermediaries, found primarily among North American (Plains and some Eastern Woodlands) Indian tribes, who, by virtue of a vision of the 'thunder beings' (THUNDERBIRDS), are obliged to assume clown-like, anti-natural behaviour [17: VI]. Named after a minor deity, the adherents of this ancient, although still extant, form of the 'contrary' cult of the Plains characteristically engaged in such 'reverse' activities as masking, dressing warmly in summer, wearing no clothing in winter, backward speech and other shamanic (*see* SHAMAN) feats [23: VII]. Failure to behave in an atypical manner, it was believed, would be punished by lightning. Although much degenerated today, the cult survives in more conservative communities, providing, at the very least, an outlet for individual variation.

Hieroglyphs [VI] Egyptian hieroglyphs (consisting of phonograms and ideograms) first appear *c.*3100 BCE, apparently already fully developed as a writing system. This system was used for more than 3,000 years throughout Egypt and her empire, particularly for inscriptions on tombs, TEMPLES and religious objects. Two cursive scripts were derived from hieroglyphs: hieratic, used by the priests in compiling religious books, and also for literary and business texts; and demotic, evolved from hieratic from *c.*700 BCE, and used in the Graeco-

Roman period for ordinary, non-religious writing requirements. The earliest body of religious writings was the Pyramid texts (Old Kingdom, *c.*2500 BCE) (*see* FUNERARY PRACTICES [10]).

Hilal [XIX] Arabic 'crescent'. Now regarded as the quintessential symbol of ISLAM, it appears early in Islamic ART and architecture as a decorative motif, probably taken over from Sasanian Iran (*see* ZOROASTRIANISM) and subsequently used on blazons, flags, etc. of the Egyptian Mamelukes and Ottoman Turks (*see* ISLAMIC DYNASTIES). Western Christendom viewed it as the Islamic counterpart to the emblem of the cross, but only towards the end of the 18th century did the Islamic world gradually adopt it as a religious symbol. It now appears, together with a star, on the flags of many Islamic countries, and the Red Crescent is the Islamic equivalent of the Red Cross. [20 'Crescent'; 38 s.v.]

Hinayana [XI] A term used in MAHAYANA BUDDHISM in the sense of 'lesser' or 'incomplete vehicle' to characterize Buddhist practice that is seen as geared to the goal of the enlightenment of the ARAHAT rather than to the complete and perfect enlightenment of a BUDDHA. *Hinayana* is thus used by Mahayana writers to refer both to those ancient Buddhist schools (traditionally reckoned as 18) that did not conform to the outlook of the Mahayana, as well as to the practice of the preliminary stages of the Buddhist path, which is understood as being motivated by the desire to gain enlightenment for oneself rather than for the sake of all sentient beings. The only non-Mahayana Buddhist tradition to survive today is the THERAVADA, which is sometimes misleadingly referred to in modern writings as 'Hinayana Buddhism'. This implies an inappropriate Mahayana perspective; Theravada Buddhism would regard

any suggestion that its conception of the goal of the Buddhist path is deficient in either compassion or wisdom – and hence an 'inferior way' – as based on misunderstanding (cf. ANUKAMPA).

Hinduism [XVII] The name given to the highly diverse religious tradition that has evolved in India over the last 3,000 years and is today represented by the beliefs and practices of well over 500 million Hindus, of whom the majority live in India where they constitute 80% of the population. Diversity is the key to understanding the religious life of Hindus since Hinduism is not a unity, having no 'founder', no single creed, no single universally accepted scripture, no single moral code or theological system, nor a single concept of god central to it. It is rather a tradition that embraces a wide variety of religious positions, incorporating both small local cults that may be known to only a few villages, to major sects like Vaishnavism (*see* VISHNU), Shaivism (*see* SHIVA) and Shaktism (*see* SHAKTI) that have millions of adherents, rich mythologies, temples, iconographies and theologies, each of which could be considered a 'religion' in its own right.

There are certain presuppositions that sustain this diversity and constitute, as it were, the given, being universally familiar framework concepts. The first such construct is DHARMA, a class-linked concept meaning 'duty', 'religion', 'the right way of behaviour' for the particular class to which it is linked. Hinduism is sometimes referred to as *Hindu dharma*, the *dharma* of Hindus. At the cosmic level, *dharma* is *sanatana dharma*, the eternal *dharma*, the universal law of order which decrees that everything in the universe should be in its right place and behave according to its own nature. Coming to the human world, there is first the general *dharma*, *sadharana dharma*, which provides a general ethic enjoining meritorious acts like pilgrimage, charity, honouring the gods, etc. and prohibiting lying, causing injury, etc. Secondly, there is *varnashrama dharma*, which today means primarily the observance of the customs and rules of one's CASTE, particularly with regard to purity and pollution. The sum total of the duties and right behaviour for an individual is their *svadharma*, their individual *dharma*. Connected to *dharma* are two further concepts, SAMSARA, the endless cycle of birth and rebirth to which souls are subject, and KARMA, which is the doctrine that every action produces its own inevitable result, and that one's status in this life is determined by one's actions in a former birth. Actions in accordance with *dharma* produce merit (*punya*) and lead to good *karma*, and sin (*papa*) results in bad *karma*. *Samsara* sets the basic problem Hinduism poses: how to escape from the endless cycle of rebirth and obtain *mukti* or MOKSHA, liberation or salvation, the precise nature of which is variously defined in the theologies of the different sects. Another fundamental metaphysical presupposition is that of BRAHMAN, the impersonal absolute or world soul which underlies the phenomenal diversity of the universe and with which the individual soul, ATMAN, is united in some form of relationship when salvation or liberation is obtained. *Brahman* is often represented in a more personal way as ISHVARA or *bhagvan*, the Lord, and worshippers of Vishnu or Shiva, for example, will consider their respective chosen deity, ISHTADEVA, to be *bhagvan*, the Lord, in which case salvation is expressed more in terms of going to the deity's heaven. The doctrine of the *ishtadeva* states that, while there are many restrictions on conduct in Hinduism, in belief individuals have complete freedom to choose which manifestation of the divine shall be the object of their worship and their chosen path to salvation. Hinduism is sometimes considered to be *sadhana*, a

methodology for realizing salvation with three main approaches: the way of action, *karma*; the way of enlightenment, JNANA; and the way of devotion to the Lord, BHAKTI.

It is, then, around this framework of metaphysical presuppositions that much of Hinduism is articulated. The tradition of Hinduism began with the arrival of the Indo-Aryans in India some 3,500 years ago, although excavated statuettes of a male deity in a Shiva-like yogic posture (*see* YOGA) and female goddess figures are indicative of some form of INDUS VALLEY religion going back perhaps to 4000 BCE; this is sometimes called proto-Hinduism. The period from 1500 to 500 BCE is the Vedic period, named after the VEDAS, collections of hymns addressed to various gods which were used in the various fire and sacrificial rites the Indo-Aryans brought into India. The middle Vedic period was characterized by pure ritualism, exemplified in scriptural works called BRAHMANAS; but in the late Vedic period there was a transition to metaphysical speculation in scriptures called UPANISHADS in which the doctrines of *samsara*, *karma* and *moksha* appear for the first time. The period of classical Hinduism ran from 500 BCE to 500 CE, for which the two great Indian epics, the RAMAYANA and the MAHABHARATA, are rich encyclopaedic sources. The period is marked by a shift in the primary religious concern from *moksha*, escape from the world, to *dharma*, right living in this world, and saw the emergence of the *dharma shastras*, the religious law books, which laid down the principles of *varnashrama dharma* which established the four VARNAS, classes of society: the Brahmins, priests and educators; the KSHATRIYAS, rulers and warriors; the *Vaishyas*, merchants and cultivators; and the *Shudras*, the menials. New theistic cults came to the fore with the rise of the syncretic deity Vishnu, absorbing existing cults as his AVATARAS, and Shiva, also syncretic, while later in the period the Goddess cults began to flourish. The rise of these theistic cults brought a rich development of mythology and the construction of temples with associated ICONOGRAPHY. Middle or medieval Hinduism extends from 500 CE to about 1850. It is characterized by proliferation in almost every domain. On the social level there was a major proliferation of CASTES (*jatis*). In religious philosophy there was a significant evolution in VEDANTA from among the six DARSHANAS, schools of salvation, with the ADVAITA system of SHANKARA in the 9th century followed by the Vishistadvaita system of RAMANUJA in the 12th, which opened the way for THEISM, especially Vaishnavism, in Vedanta and led to the schools of Madhva (13th century), Nimbarka (14th) and Vallabha and Caitanya (16th), all proponents of *bhakti*, the devotional path to salvation. *Bhakti* was transformed from a restrained piety to an ecstatic experience by the Tamil devotional poets, the Vaishnava Alvars and the Shaiva Nayanars. This new attitude found expression in the Sanskrit Bhagavata Purana (9th century) which proved a major source of inspiration for Krishna *bhakti*, while devotion to the other important *avatara* of Vishnu, Rama, inspired one of the most loved works in the north, the Ramacaritamanasa of Tulsidasa (16th century). Numerous new sects and fine devotional poets appeared using the recently emerged vernacular languages like Hindi, Bengali and Marathi, which brought millions into direct contact with scriptural traditions for the first time. In Shaivism a new Vedanta-inspired school emerged in Kashmir; the devotionalism of the Nayanars was incorporated into a theological system called Shaiva-Siddhanta (12th century); and a new school called Vira-Shaivism (12th century) arose which rejected both caste and temple worship. Shaktism saw a major development with the appearance of Tantrism (*see* TANTRA (1)) which also influenced Shaivism and BUDDHISM. Tantrism, which is highly esoteric, has its own form of yoga and a psycho-physiological system and characteristic modes of worship and practice designed to lead to self-realization and liberation. Finally, from the 14th century the tradition of the SANTS developed, whose proponents, mainly from the lower castes, rejected the caste system and all forms of external religion and preached a form of interior religion based on the need for constant awareness of and love for an Almighty who was without attributes, *nirguna*. Namdev, Kabir, Raidas and Dadu were among its principal exponents, as was NANAK whose teaching later developed into SIKHISM. From the middle of the 19th century Hinduism was subjected to great self-examination as it confronted both Western culture and Christianity, and the outcome was a revival and response from within which has resulted in Hinduism becoming far more self-aware, self-confident, even self-assertive, as it claims its place among the other major world religions. Hinduism is not its history; but the history of the tradition explains its range, richness and diversity, and demonstrates the family relationships that hold between its various parts. That Hinduism is a single religious universe is affirmed whenever a Hindu accepts as a fellow Hindu someone with beliefs and practices that differ substantially from his or her own, and it is this self-identity, rather than a communality of doctrine and practice, that gives Hinduism the cohesion and coalescence of a great world religion.

Hinduism, Modern Developments [XVII] From the first half of the 19th century, the great changes that were occurring within India were matched by developments within the very diverse religious tradition of Hinduism which continue to this day. The factors that provoked such changes were legion and complex: British rule, the expansion of communications, the arrival of the printing press, the development of the modern vernacular languages, Western education, the use of English, the challenge of CHRISTIANITY and its missionaries (*see* MISSIONS, WESTERN CHRISTIAN), the growth of political and social awareness, nationalism, the pressure of both internal and international events that resulted in independence and the formation of Pakistan, and the experience of Hindus living abroad in a much enlarged diaspora. These were some of the significant external factors for change; but it was the diverse responses that took place within Hinduism that have produced its transformation into a self-assertive world religion. There were two major intertwined directions of change: the first, which has received the greatest attention in Western writing, is the Hindu 'renaissance', the evolution of 'neo-Hinduism', beginning with Ram Mohan Roy (1772–1833) in Bengal [73; 48; 117]; the second, more localized and less coherent and articulate, and hence much neglected if only because much of the material is in vernacular tracts, is the widespread revitalization and restatement of the existing tradition in many of its strands which can be thought of as a 'counter-reformation' of *sanatana dharma*, the eternal or 'old style' religion of Hindus [83]. Ram Mohan Roy [31] founded the Brahmo Samaj [32] in Calcutta in 1828. He was Western-educated and much influenced by Christianity: he advocated a theistic approach, rejected idol worship and reincarnation (*see* SAMSARA), and campaigned against SATI, the self-immolation of widows on their husband's funeral pyres, and for Western education, equally for women and men alike. He was followed by Debendranath Tagore, the

father of the poet, and then by Keshab Chandra Sen [20]. Under their leadership the Samaj campaigned against child marriage and for inter-CASTE marriage, for the remarriage of widows and for the education of women. Its influence lay not so much in its theological position as in its role in self-examination and in awakening the Hindu social conscience. A not dissimilar organization in Maharashtra, the Prarthana Samaj, under Mahadeva Govind Ranade, was equally concerned for social welfare and campaigned effectively on behalf of the depressed castes. Quite different from these movements was the Arya Samaj founded by Dayananda Sarasvati (1824–83) in 1875 [66]. Dayananda sought to remove from Hinduism all the 'corruption' and accretions which, in his own idiosyncratic view, had entered it since the VEDAS. He also fiercely attacked both ISLAM and Christianity, which he saw as threats to Hinduism in attracting converts from the lower castes, a process the Arya Samaj sought to arrest by introducing a ritual of 'reconversion' to Hinduism and investing the lowest castes with the sacred thread. The Arya Samaj aroused much opposition for its militancy and dogmatism, but it met with some success and made a further contribution in the field of education. In retrospect perhaps its major function was in Hindu confidence-building, a process further advanced by Madame Blavatsky and Mrs Besant of the THEOSOPHICAL SOCIETY who were uncritically lavish in their praise of everything Hindu. The next major influence was a man of deep spirituality and mystical experience, Ramakrishna Paramahansa [79], who saw the divine in every person and every religion, concluding that everyone should follow their own path to realization, but also advocating service to one's fellow humans. One of his disciples was Vivekananda [41], who went as the representative of Hinduism to the World Parliament of Religions in Chicago in 1893; here he presented Hinduism for the first time to the world as a universal faith and in doing so raised its status both within and without India. He also established the Ramakrishna mission in various parts of the world. Other major figures in the Hindu 'renaissance' were Aurobindo [104], who began preparing India for the spiritual leadership of the world in 1910, and Shivananda, a *sannyasin* who in 1936 founded the Divine Life Society, now a worldwide organization, and produced many works of a morally improving nature [75]. But it was Mahatma Gandhi (1869–1948) [50] who called himself a follower of *sanatana dharma*, who sought to liberate the soul of India from its vices before liberating the country from the British. In an extraordinary way he embraced the people of India and imbued them with his own deep spirituality, in the process bringing Hindu self-awareness and self-identity to a new level of maturity. There have been many other 'renaissance' voices, e.g. Radhakrishnan [84], the former President of India, but Gandhi did inwardly what Vivekananda had only spoken of: he effected the realization of Hindu spiritual values on a prodigious scale. Alongside the 'renaissance' ran a counter-reformation, bringing new life, self-examination and redefinition within the existing traditions. Many organizations on different scales were formed in Hinduism's defence, some, like the Rashtriya Swayamsevak Sangh [3] and the All India Hindu Mahasabha, underpinning political parties and movements, and ultimately leading to Hindu militancy and religious chauvinism [55]. New movements evolved, like the Swami Narayana movement [135], a form of Gujarati Vaishnavism, which has grown to be very influential both within Gujarat and among Gujaratis abroad; the Radha Swami Satsang [86] within the SANT tradition; and the Krishna Consciousness movement, which is a form of Gaudiya Vaishnavism [102]. A number of GURUS and 'God-men and women' fully within the Hindu tradition have become influential on varying scales, some, like Sai Baba [97] within India; others, like Maharishi Mahesh Yogi, bringing TRANSCENDENTAL MEDITATION to the West [85]. Finally, there is now an active global Hinduism movement devoted to identifying and representing the considerable religious and spiritual riches of Hinduism to the now much expanded Hindu diaspora and to the spiritually needy of the world. (*see also* NEW RELIGIOUS MOVEMENTS IN THE WEST.)

Hindus [XVII] Inhabitants of the 'land beyond the Indus river' were called 'Hindus' by the invading Muslims who, in the 8th century, entered India from the north-west. The term therefore designates primarily an inhabitant of India [80: 142]. Some of these inhabitants (fewer than 20% in 1971) follow religious traditions (mostly foreign to India) which require their adherents to differentiate themselves by the use of such terms as Muslim, Christian, Sikh, etc. Those who do not specifically so designate themselves constitute the 'Hindu' population, both of India and of those territories elsewhere to which such Indians have migrated (*see* HINDUISM). Hindus follow a number of different cults: of DURGA, KALI, KRISHNA, RAMA, SHIVA, VISHNU and many others. A distinctive feature of Hindu cults is that many of the deities are female (*devi*). In India, Hindus constituted 82.64% of the total population at the census of 1981.

History of Religions [XXXIV] A sub-discipline of RELIGIONSWISSENSCHAFT in the German-speaking world. In English, however, the term is often used to translate the German word *Religionswissenschaft* as in the case of the International Association for the History of Religions (IAHR), being thus the equivalent of what is called the STUDY OF RELIGIONS by others.

As a sub-discipline of *Religionswissenschaft* it is the discipline which provides all relevant data concerning religious traditions of humankind. Consequently, it is not restricted to the historical development of religions alone but is also concerned with the presentation of their respective doctrines and behavioural codes, as well as with the interpretation of holy scriptures, if there are any, and the development of ritual forms up to the present. With regard to the adherents of religions the history of religions has an interest in social strata, in the political options in society and, to some extent, in the influence of religions on the psychological development of their followers, though other sub-disciplines of *Religionswissenschaft*, such as SOCIOLOGY OF RELIGION and PSYCHOLOGY OF RELIGION, treat these in greater detail. The wide range of study interests indicates that the history of religion(s) is neither exclusively historically oriented towards a pure listing of historical facts nor limited in its interests to aspects of the past. It covers both particular religious traditions as a whole (e.g. BUDDHISM, HINDUISM, CHRISTIANITY, ISLAM) and singular movements within religions (e.g. Twelver Shi'ism within SHI'ISM or Islam).

The main difference between history of religion(s) and doctrinal interpretation within religions, such as Christian theology, for instance, lies in the exclusiveness of academic principles applied by the former. While in the latter religious conviction is a main source of the interpretative framework, there is no such reference for the history of religion(s). All data known are put together on the basis of intersubjectively verifiable results arrived at by historical, philological and socio-empirical methods, without any preference being accorded to religious options made within any one of the movements studied. Consequently, a descriptive history of the adherents' convictions and mentalities is the main interest of these studies. No preference is given to any group, so that neither mainstream apologies nor divergent positions gain disproportionate importance. With regard to doctrinal interpretations stemming from these religious traditions themselves, the contribution of the history of religion(s) is neither to favour certain positions nor to hide religious facts in order to maintain a certain doctrinal line. In this sense the history of religion(s) has no declared aim within the development of religions but it may have an incidental effect on that process.

The difference between the history of religion(s) and theological research is obvious with regard to the function of church history as a theological discipline. Originally, the latter served as an auxiliary discipline of homiletics, providing hagiographical material for exhortation regarding ideal Christian behaviour. Later on, it took the lead in the apologetic attempt to defend the church against criticisms of its historical role; and, in more recent times, it has been mainly concerned with historical material bearing on hitherto unknown reform claims, showing that these have historical prototypes. The history of religion(s), by contrast, has no such function as its declared aim. This, however, does not exclude side-effects on the religious traditions concerned. A good example of such an effect is the work of the *Religionsgeschichtliche Schule* of late 19th-century Protestant theology in Germany. It embedded biblical texts from both the Hebrew Bible and the New Testament in their socio-cultural surroundings, thus paralleling the 'holy texts' with similar texts of the ancient Orient or of Hellenism respectively. The result of these studies was that the 'holy scriptures' proved to be more time-related than when viewed on the basis of the concept of doctrinal revelation as information coming only from God. The deluge, for instance, was thus viewed as a story reported in Mesopotamia, part of the cultural heritage of that region. This type of research, argued the opponents of the *Religionsgeschichtliche Schule*, takes away from the Bible its exclusiveness and reduces it to an ordinary text with all the characteristics of its time. Obviously, such a history of religion(s) had side-effects on both Protestant and Catholic theologies. In both it led, first, to anti-modernist reactions, and then to new reflections on the theological concept of revelation, nowadays conceived of in terms different from pure verbal inspiration. More recent examples of side-effects are doctrinal systematizations of teaching data in Native American or African religions or in NEW RELIGIOUS MOVEMENTS, which are often picked up by these religions and thus become part of their own teachings. In spite of these unintended consequences, the history of religion(s) tries to pursue its task as described above. [59a, vol. 6: 399–408; 100; 104]

Hittites [VIII] The Hittite empire equalled the power of Egypt, Babylonia and Assyria for some 200 years in the 2nd millennium BCE (Hittite Old Kingdom, *c.*1740–1460 BCE; Hittite empire, *c.*1460–1190 BCE). There is indication of an INDO-EUROPEAN strain in the language and physical appearance of some of the population, but the religion mainly incorporated elements of the original tradition. Isolated city communities were unified under the king at Hattusas (*see* KINGSHIP (ANCIENT NEAR EAST)), but independence in local religious matters was preserved [12; 13]. Civil and military concerns were centralized at Hattusas, but the king allowed virtual religious auton-

omy, although he was regarded as the great chief-priest.

Some syncretism occurred, however, and the state and kingship were placed under the protection of a group of national deities who received elaborate rituals at Hattusas (*see* FESTIVALS (ANCIENT NEAR EASTERN)). The sun-goddess, 'queen of heaven and earth', was supreme patron of the state, and the sun-god, the 'king of gods', was lord of righteousness and justice. The weather-god of Hatti was the official consort of the sun-goddess. The nearby shrine of Arinna was an important cult-centre. The myths reveal something of the character of the state-gods (e.g. storm-gods and elemental forces), and monuments show their physical attributes (e.g. dress) [8; 24: 120–6, 346–58]. Local cults are less well documented, but a weather-god appeared in many cities, symbolized by a bull (*see* ART AND SYMBOLISM (ANCIENT NEAR EASTERN)), and the winged goddess Shauska was another prominent deity.

The Hittites [13:88] enlisted the aid of their gods as witnesses and guardians of contracts made on earth, and this included peace treaties drawn up with foreign powers such as Egypt (*c.*1250 BCE) [24: 201–6]. The law was enacted by men on the gods' behalf.

There were many places of worship, including open-air rock-sanctuaries and the temples at Boghazköy (*c.*1740–1460 BCE). The Hittites established a special holy place at Yazilikaya, where all the deities were represented; this symbolized centralized political power [13: 38]. In some cities, the TEMPLE was the centre of civil administration and had a large staff, whereas elsewhere it consisted of several small shrines. The temple was the god's home, and he was represented by either a statue or a cult-object such as a *huwasi* stone. His priests were servants who attended to his daily needs. The gods, invisible and immortal, had human failings which could result in human misfortune (EVIL). Divine will could be ascertained through extispicy or augury (DIVINATION), which the Hittites inherited from BABYLONIA. Also, MAGIC played an important role in society.

Burial customs (see AFTERLIFE (ANCIENT NEAR EASTERN)) included cremation and inhumation for both rulers and commoners from earliest times. Myths and legends (see ANCIENT NEAR EASTERN RELIGIONS) [24: 120–6] included only a few of Hittite origin; one myth – 'Slaying the Dragon' – dealt with the ritual combat between a divine hero and his opponent, and was performed at an annual festival to reinvigorate the earth and to confirm the victory of good over evil; a second dealt with the disappearance of the fertility god and the consequent loss of the land's abundance, which was only restored when the god returned.

Holocaust [XXII] The consequences of the anti-Jewish policies of Nazi Germany and its fascist allies from 1933 to 1945, culminating in genocide. It is estimated that close to 6 million people of Jewish origin died in the Nazi extermination programme, the 'Final Solution of the Jewish Problem', the most notorious part of which involved the mass gassing and cremation of victims in death camps like Auschwitz and Treblinka [50]. Most of the Jews killed by the Nazis came from Central and Eastern Europe (see EUROPEAN JEWRY). Polish Jewry, which before the war numbered more than 3 million, was almost completely destroyed. The basis of the policy behind the Holocaust was the racial theory of the Germans as a master race and the Jews as a subhuman group who corrupt pure Aryan peoples and have to be eliminated. These theories were put forward by 19th-century European racists, e.g. J. A. Gobineau and H. S. Chamberlain, but it was Hitler and his Nazi

propagandists who turned racist theory into an active social programme. Jews were discriminated against economically, made to wear a distinctive badge, the yellow star, were herded together into ghettoes, were used as slave labour, were experimented on by Nazi doctors, and were killed by mass shootings or gassings. [11; 17; 20; 25; 37: XXVII, XXVIII; 44; 52; 55: XXXI; 57: XX, XXI]

Holy see SACRED

Holy Experiment [XIII.B] The attempt by Quakers (see FRIENDS, RELIGIOUS SOCIETY OF), under the leadership of William Penn (1644–1718), to create a government run on Quaker principles in America (Pennsylvania). From its inception in 1681, the colony was noted for its good relations with Native Americans and for the enforcement of religious toleration. However, the lack of autonomy from the British Crown, the influx of other religious groups and 'the temptations to a non-religious life' [109: 533] which prosperity brought compromised Penn's original ideals, and Quaker influence and control gradually decreased. Finally, in 1756, nearly every Quaker resigned from the colony's Assembly over the Crown's demand for taxation for military purposes, marking an end to the Holy Experiment. [96: 220]

Holy Land [XXII] The biblical Canaan was, in Jewish belief, promised by God to Abraham and his 'seed' as an 'everlasting possession' (*Genesis* 17: 3), and again to the 'Children of Israel' while in slavery to the Egyptians (*Exodus* 6: 4) (see COVENANT; EXODUS). Its borders are variously described (*Genesis* 15: 18–21, *Deuteronomy* 1: 7–8, 11: 24, *Joshua* 1: 4, 13: 2–5), and Israelite settlement there reached its maximum during the reign of King David (see BIBLICAL HISTORY) [14 vol. 9: 112]. The name Palestine, derived from (country of) the Philistines, in common use for the past two millennia, was introduced by the Romans. From Mishnaic times (2nd century CE) it has been known among Jews as 'Eretz Yisrael'. Although there has been continuous Jewish settlement in the Holy Land since the time of the second TEMPLE, the majority of Jews have lived in the various countries of the diaspora from about the 3rd century CE. Traditional Jews have always taken the biblical account of the divine promise seriously, and Palestine is the Holy Land of JUDAISM [11; 26; 30: xx; 36: xvi; 44]

Holy Spirit (Biblical) [XIII.A] In the Hebrew BIBLE, GOD is described as exercising his power by his spirit ('breath') and speaks through prophets and sages. In the New Testament, JESUS is described as receiving the spirit at his baptism; after his death he is portrayed as appearing to his followers and passing on the same spirit to empower them. From New Testament times it has been generally accepted that Christians receive the spirit at BAPTISM. It may be interesting to note that the word for spirit has different genders in different early Christian languages. [9: 174–202; 11: III, 260–80]

Honmichi [XXVI] The significance that attaches to Honmichi, a Japanese new religion in the SHINTO tradition, is closely connected with its founder, its view of revelation and its attitude towards the government and the emperor. Onishi Aijiro (1881–1958), originally a TENRIKYO evangelist, came to believe that he had been divinely appointed the new embodiment of Tenrikyo teaching. He appealed to Tenrikyo to acknowledge his position, but was laid off instead. In 1925 he established the Tenri Kenkyukai (later Tenri Honmichi and now simply Honmichi). Two booklets prophesying the destruction of the nation if Japan engaged in war against other countries and denying the divinity of the emperor put Honmichi on a collision course with the government. A court finding of mental derangement saved Onishi from imprisonment for the 1928 booklet, but with the 1938 booklet he was sentenced to prison indefinitely. By government order Honmichi was prohibited and dissolved. Japan's defeat in the Second World War led to Onishi's release, and from that time until his death in 1958 he devoted himself to rebuilding Honmichi. Today it has over 300,000 members.

Unlike Tenrikyo, which maintains that revelation is essentially complete, Honmichi holds that revelation changes from age to age and is communicated in each age through a 'revealer'. Onishi himself was one such revealer. By implication, other revealers are also to appear. It is no surprise, then, that Honmichi has given rise to a considerable number of new religious groups.

Few Japanese religious groups have challenged the emperor system and the wartime policy of the government as outspokenly as Honmichi. Its object of worship is a non-traditional *kami*, Ten no Oya Kami-sama, or God the Heavenly Parent. [10: IX, 185–6]

Honmon Butsuryushu [XXVI] The chief significance of the Honmon Butsuryushu is that it was the first of the lay Japanese BUDDHIST associations to place special emphasis on the Lotus Sutra. Reiyukai, Rissho Koseikai and Soka Gakkai are its leading successors. [9: X, 208] Nagamatsu Nissen (1817–90), the founder, took the tonsure in the Nichiren school Honmon Hokke sect in 1848. Disappointed, however, with the stifling monastic life, he left the order and in 1857 formed the Honmon Butsuryuko, an association of lay believers affiliated with the Honmon Hokke sect. Continuing his criticisms of Buddhist clerics and their organizations, he devoted himself to building up a lay community of believers, using aggressive recruitment tactics and extolling the health benefits that would follow from drinking the water from their head temple. The Buddhist establishment and the medical establishment, thus challenged, responded by repeatedly bringing charges against Nissen and his group, who often spent time in police custody, but the association continued to attract new members. After Nissen's death, the Honmon Butsuryuko lost its character as a lay association and became an organization of Buddhist laypeople and clerics. As Honmon Butsuryushu, a sect rather than an association, it became independent in 1947. The head temple, Yuseiji, is in Kyoto. Honmon Butsuryushu has followers in Brazil, South Korea, China, Taiwan and North America. Adherents currently number about 550,000. [10: x, 208]

Honorifics, Titles and Styles of Address (Sikh) [xxxiii] Among the titles current in the SIKH PANTH the Arabic *Sahib* covers a particularly wide range. Used by the GURUS as a name of God it is now attached as an honorific postposition to personal names, the scripture, sanctified towns or villages, and important GURDWARAS. Other styles are prefixed and are more specific. NANAK, originally addressed as *Baba* (Father), is now (with his successors) generally known as Guru [25: 251–3]. *Bhagat* designates any poet (other than the Gurus) whose works appear in the ADI GRANTH (*see* BHAGAT BANI) [26: 60–1]. *Bhai* (Brother) is applied to male Sikhs of notable piety or religious learning, and is also used for a *granthi* (*gurdwara* custodian), *ragi* (*kirtan* singer) or *dhadi* (itinerant narrator of Sikh tradition). *Giani* designates a learned person; SANT a teacher of Sikh doctrine who attracts a following; and *Jathedar* the commander of a *jatha* (military or political unit). KES-DHARI Sikhs (those with uncut hair) are addressed as *Sardar* for men and *Sardarni* for women.

Hopi [v] The westernmost of the Pueblo Indians of North America, and members of the Uto-Aztecan linguistic group, the Hopi (from *hopituh shinu-mu*, literally 'the peaceful people') inhabit lands within the NAVAJO reservation. Their myths recount the gradual progression of the ancestors through four successive underground worlds before emerging and eventually settling in their present home on the Black Mesa of the Colorado plateau (*see* CREATION MYTHS) [26: i–v]. Central to Hopi religion is the concept of a dual division of both space and time between the upper and lower worlds, and a corresponding concern for cooperation between the two realms. Harmony between these realms is critical to the maintenance of health, food supply and social stability [2: iii]. The ceremonial cycle reflects both the cosmic pattern and the origin myth. Major divinities include Sotuqnangu (a type of sky-god), Masua (deity of earth and death), Tawa (father-sun), Kokyang Wuuti (spider-woman), and the twin war-gods (HERO TWINS). KACHINAS (spirits of the ancestors, vegetation and animal life) figure prominently in ceremonies held from June to December [3]. Other major festivals include Wuwuchim (new year and principal initiation rite), Soyal (winter-solstice ceremony) and Powamu (bean dance) which marks the appearance of the chief *kachinas*. Myths also relate the origin of clans and secret societies that play central roles in Hopi rituals.

Horoscope [x] In ASTROLOGY, an interpretation of an individual's (or group's, e.g. nation's) fate and character based on the positions of the heavenly bodies at a particular moment, usually birth. The horoscope has as its basic frame of reference (1) the zodiac, which is the circle of twelve 'signs' (Aries, Taurus, Gemini, Cancer, Leo, Virgo, Libra, Scorpio, Sagittarius, Capricorn, Aquarius, Pisces) traversed by the sun, moon and planets in periods of, approximately, 27 days (moon), one year (sun, Mercury, Venus), two years (Mars), 12 years (Jupiter), 30 years (Saturn), etc., and (2) a relatively fixed circle of 12 numbered 'houses', against which, as a result of the earth's daily rotation, the entire zodiac with the sun, moon, and planets appears to turn once every 24 hours. Casting a horoscope is thus like reading a number of pointers on a clock which itself turns quite rapidly against a second dial. A difference of an hour, even of a few minutes, can effect a considerable change; moreover, each horoscope is specific to a particular locality. Significant data are: (1) the positions of sun, moon and planets within the zodiac (e.g. sun in Aries); (2) the 'aspects', i.e. the angular distances, of the sun, moon and planets to each other (e.g. Venus in 'square' or 'quartile' aspect, i.e. at an angle of 90°, to Mars); (3) the positions of the sun, moon, planets and signs against the circle of houses and its four cardinal points (*see figure* 5), especially the 'ascendant' and 'midheaven' (i.e. what sign, etc., is rising in the east or culminating to the south at the given moment), e.g. moon in the seventh house, Scorpio rising. For interpreting horoscopes certain values have traditionally been assigned to the planets, signs, aspects and houses. The houses are each associated with particular areas of life or activity (e.g. the second with money-making, the eleventh with friends), the planets with activities and characters (e.g. Venus with love, 'mercurial' characters with Mercury), and the aspects with favourable or unfavourable situa-

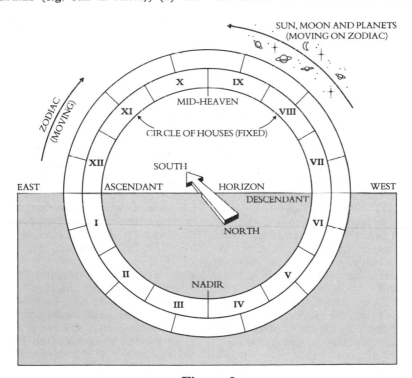

Figure 5
Elements in a horoscope

tions (e.g. planets in opposition or square/quartile aspect tend to have sinister implications). Casting and interpreting horoscopes has been for more than 2,000 years the focus of the 'science' of astrology. Though widely discredited, especially in the West, it is an exacting art demanding considerable expertise [techniques: 11: VIII; 12; 14].

Hsuan Hsueh [XII] 'Dark learning.' Sometimes referred to as neo-Taoism by modern scholars, an intellectual movement which developed in the 3rd and 4th centuries CE. The main exponents were Wang Pi (226–249 CE), Ho Yen (d. 249), and Kuo Hsiang (d. 312). Wang Pi was a former minister who wrote commentaries on the TAO TE CHING and the *I Ching* (Classic of Changes), emphasizing the ontological aspects of Taoist philosophy (TAO CHIA). According to Wang Pi, *wu* (Non-Being) is the source of all things and is equivalent to the *tao* of the *Tao Te Ching* and the *t'ai chi* (Supreme Ultimate) of the *I Ching*. *Wu* is the source and substance (*t'i*) of reality, but its function (*yung*) can only be manifested through *yu* (Being). Wang Pi's distinction between substance and function and his relating of it to the distinction between Being and Non-Being had an important influence on later Taoist thought, on NEO-CONFUCIANISM, and even on CHINESE BUDDHISM. Ironically, exponents of Hsuan Hsueh honoured CONFUCIUS as a greater sage than Lao Tzu because Confucius was at ease in the world of Being, and did not attempt the impossible by trying to speak of Non-Being. [7: XIX, 314–35; 35: V, 170–2]

Closely associated with Hsuan Hsueh was the movement known as Ch'ing T'an (Pure Conversation), which probably started in the Later Han dynasty (23–220 CE) but was adopted by the neo-Taoists for metaphysical discussion and speculation. The Seven Sages of the Bamboo Grove in the 3rd century CE were typical exponents. Eventually BUDDHIST concepts were introduced into the discussions. [15: III, 61–76; 73: 59–69; 115: 123–6]

Hsuan-tsang [XI] Chinese Buddhist pilgrim to India, translator and philosopher, the model for Tripitaka in the *Monkey* stories. Hsuan-tsang visited India in the 7th century and has left an important account. He studied at the great monastic university of Nalanda and his description has played a significant role in archaeological research. Hsuan-tsang also knew the great king Harsha. On his return to China Hsuan-tsang translated many texts from Sanskrit and established the Fa Hsiang Tsung school of Chinese YOGACARA. He was associated with the cult of MAITREYA, and vowed to be reborn in Tushita with Maitreya. Other famous monk-pilgrims were FA-HSIEN (5th century) and I-tsing (7th century). [11: 234–40]

Hsun Tzu [XII] (300–230 BCE) A naturalistic and rationalistic Confucian philosopher (*see* CONFUCIUS) who argued that human nature is basically evil and that goodness must be produced by moral training and, if necessary, formal constraints. He interpreted heaven (T'IEN) in purely naturalistic terms as the process of natural laws. He was sceptical about the existence of ghosts (KUEI) and spirits (SHEN), but defended the FUNERAL RITES and the ANCESTOR CULT in terms of their benefits for the living. [7: VI, 115–35; 26; 34: XII, 279–311; 111; 38: III, 235–67]

Hua Yen [XII] A scholastic and eclectic school of CHINESE BUDDHISM founded by Fa Tsang (643–712 CE) and based on the *Avatamsaka-Sutra* (*Hua Yen Ching*). In an attempt to elucidate the essential teachings of Hua Yen to the Empress Wu, Fa Tsang composed his *Treatise on the Golden Lion*, which remains one of the clearest expositions of Hua Yen teachings. Fa Tsang accepted the basic SAN LUN (SHUNYATAVADA or MADHYAMIKA) teaching on the EMPTINESS and consequent non-differentiation of DHARMAS and developed this into a doctrine of the mutual implication of *dharmas*, in which the coming into existence of any one *dharma* implies the simultaneous existence of all others. There are clear similarities between Hua Yen and the earlier T'IEN TAI teachings, the differences being largely matters of emphasis. Like the T'ien Tai school, Hua Yen classified Buddhist teachings according to their nature and the capacity of the BUDDHA's audience. The 'five doctrines' are also described in the *Treatise on the Golden Lion*. (*See* Kegon *in* NANTO ROKUSHU.) [7: xxv, 406–24; 12; 15: xi, 313–20; 18; 24: xiii, 328–33; 35: viii, 339–59]

Huehuetlatolli [xxv] The most formal and influential form of sacred instruction in Nahuatl culture (*see* MESOAMERICAN RELIGIONS) was the *huehuetlatolli*, 'ancient word' [8: iv]. These teachings consisted of polished rhetorical orations which transmitted the cultural traditions in a society where the writing system was not adequate for their verbal communications. *Huehuetlatolli* were delivered in the schools (*calmecac*), as prayers to the gods on ceremonial occasions, at the investiture of a king, for the departure and return of merchants and at ceremonies associated with the life-cycle. These ancient truths, which were delivered in an elegant, florid, intensely metaphorical style, aimed to instruct, inspire and illuminate the traditional values and meanings of the culture for the listeners.

Huitzilopochtli [xxv] One of the most important gods in MESOAMER-ICAN RELIGIONS was Huitzilopochtli (Humming-bird of the South), the tribal god of the wandering Mexicas who became the patron deity of the Aztec capital city, Tenochtitlan. The spectacular religious development that was founded on him is symbolized in two mythical episodes which were ritually celebrated by the Aztecs, one concerning the origin of the capital, the other telling of the birth of the ideal warrior, Huitzilopochtli, and the origin of massive HUMAN SACRIFICE. Aztec sacred history tells that Huitzilopochtli led his people, the Mexicas, from Chicomoztoc (the Place of Seven Caves), into the valley of Mexico, where he appeared in the form of a giant eagle landing on a cactus growing in the centre of Lake Texcoco (1325 CE). This event marked the foundation of the new community and a shrine was built on the spot to celebrate Huitzilopochtli's power and authority. This shrine, which became the TEM PLO MAYOR of the Aztec empire, and the ritual activity associated with it, were modelled after the myth of Huitzilopochtli's birth as a ferocious solar warrior at the cosmic mountain, Coatepec, and the slaughter of his 400 brothers and sisters [14: 42–6]. Huitzilopochtli's supreme power was commemorated at the festival of Panquetzalitzli (Raising of Banners), which involved special human sacrifices following the opening ritual called Ipaina Huitzilopochtli (the Swiftness of Huitzilopochtli) [7: 457–62]. In this ritual, a swift runner carried a dough image of the god through the lavishly decorated streets of the city, pursued by a multitude of revellers who never managed to catch the lead runner. This signified that the Aztec patron god was never captured in war, but was always triumphant over his enemies, whom he destroyed at the Templo Mayor. Historically, following the formation of the Aztec state in 1428 CE, the cult of Huitzilopochtli grew to include massive human sacrifices of captured warriors, women and children, which, it was thought, contributed to the consolidation of Aztec power, cosmic stability and Huitzilopochtli's dominance. [10: 156–72]

Hukam-nama [xxxiii] A SIKH term meaning 'letter of command'. From the time of GURU Hargobind (1606–44) such letters were sent to *sangats* (congregations) or individuals, giving instructions or requesting assistance. Today a *hukam-nama* is very rarely issued and always comes from one of the TAKHTS, normally from Akal Takht in Amritsar. It is believed to carry the authority of the PANTH as a whole and disobeying it is held to be a very serious offence. [7: 85–6]

Human Potential Movement (HPM) [xxviii] An umbrella term covering a wide range of groups whose beliefs and practices are designed to promote 'wholeness', 'self-awareness', 'self-development' or 'self-realization' for the enlightened individual. Some of the groups claim to help the individual discover 'the God within', giving rise to the term 'self-religions' [4: v]. While there is some overlap with the NEW AGE movement, the HPM is more concerned to look *inside* the self by using psychotherapy (in its very broadest sense) to develop people's potential. Individuals are 'guided' or encouraged to work things out for themselves, rather than being educated by an expert. Among the better-known methods, therapies and techniques are Bioenergetics, Biosynthesis, Co-counselling, Encounter groups, est (Erhard Seminar Training, now known as the Forum), Gestalt therapy, Guided Fantasy, Humanistic Psychology, LRT (Loving Relationship Training), Primal Therapy, Psychodrama, Rebirthing, Psychosynthesis and Transactional Analysis. The Esalen Institute in California is one of the most successful centres of the HPM, but there is no official organization uniting the different approaches, some of which can be very expensive [53: 45–68, 223–40].

Some of the techniques are used by Christian clergy, in prisons and hospitals and for training in a number of socially respectable institutions, with an increasing number of big business organizations paying for members of their managerial staff to attend one or another of the courses. Several of the groups have been attacked as quasi-religious, exploitative and/or psychologically harmful [5: 55–8; 57]. [General descriptions of the movement: 5: 182–3; 26: v; 36; 58; 59; 60; 73; 75: x; 76; guides with contact addresses: 8; 15; 18; 28]

Human Sacrifice (Aztec) [xxv] Human sacrifice, called *tlamictiliztli*, was a widespread MESOAMERICAN RELIGIOUS practice which proliferated during the expansion of Aztec power. Its stated purpose was the constant renovation of cosmic order and the nourishing of the gods, who were fed the blood and hearts of the *ixiptla*, or representative of the gods, in the form of the sacrificed victim. Aztec myths relate that the Fifth Sun (*see* TEZCATLIPOCA) was created through the sacrifice of the gods [12: 44–5], who subsequently created warfare among humans so that captured warriors could be ritually killed to feed the sun and other deities. Aztec warfare was carried out in part to supply the major temples with sacrificial victims.

The most highly valued sacrificial victims were captive warriors, who were treated with elaborate care and ceremony because they were considered the living representatives of the deities [2: ix]. Women, children and slaves paid as tribute from enemy provinces were also ritually sacrificed. The variety of sacrificial methods included shooting with arrows (*see figure 6*), beheading, immolation and, most commonly, heart extraction. In the latter case, the victim was killed with the *tecpatl*, a jewelled flint-knife wielded by the QUETZALCOATL priest or the TLATOANI (ruler). The victim was stretched over the *techcatl* (sacrificial

Figure 6

Aztec arrow and gladiatorial human sacrifice

stone), located at the top of the temple pyramid's steps (*see* TEMPLO MAYOR) so that the body could be rolled down and dismembered at the bottom following heart extraction. This action represented the descent of the sun into the underworld, now energized by the blood of the warrior (*see* CEMANAHUAC). Specific parts of the body, usually the thighs, were cut up into portions for sacrificial meals by the nobles, warriors and merchants into whom the divine energy passed. The skull was placed on the *tzompantli*, or skull-rack, in the ceremonial centre.

The intense political struggles of rival cities in late 15th- and early 16th-century CE central Mesoamerica resulted in the escalation of warfare, sacrifice and ritual CANNIBALISM [10: x]. In Tenochtitlan alone, major Aztec building renewals or inaugurations of kings were accompanied by the sacrifice of thousands of captured warriors to ensure the stability of the Aztec state and the motion of the cosmos. (*See* NEW FIRE CEREMONY.)

Humanism [XXXII] Since the 16th century the word 'humanist' has been used to distinguish students of subjects like poetry, history and moral philosophy from students of other kinds (e.g. of THEOLOGY). This remains one special use related to the word 'humanities'. More commonly, however, the word 'humanist' is used to mean a person with a set of entirely non-religious beliefs and values. MARXISM, UTILITARIANISM and other SECULAR ALTERNATIVES TO RELIGION can be regarded as forms of humanism. Marx himself accepted the label, although it is often repudiated by 20th-century Marxists because it is a label commonly claimed by non-Marxists.

The tradition of 'liberal' or 'ethical' humanism associated with the Ethical Societies founded in the late 19th century emphasizes what, from a Marxist point of view, is called 'bourgeois individualism'. There are no set doctrines attached to this form of humanism and, although humanists believe in the importance of political reforms, they are not committed to any particular political programme. They have been most active in defending the individual against imprisonment for political beliefs and in causes like abortion and euthanasia. Their position has been summed up as a belief in an 'open mind' and an 'open society' [5: 186] – a formulation due to the philosopher Karl Popper (1902–94) [20].

Liberal or ethical humanism can be distinguished in theory, if not always in practice, from scientific humanism. The emphasis of the former is on political reform, the latter on science, as the means of improving the human condition. The former emphasizes the freedom and dignity of the individual; the latter may deny, as does the well-known American psychologist B. F. Skinner (b. 1904) [24], that such terms have any place in a scientific view of man. It may be better to refer to an exclusive emphasis on science for the solution of all problems as 'scientism'. There are those, like Bertrand Russell (1872–1970) [23], who have attached importance to both science and social reform.

In the 19th century humanism took various church-like forms [28: 195], which gave it the character of a secular religion. These do not flourish in the same way today and the quasi-religious forms of humanism tend to be those which find a panacea for human ills in a particular theory of human nature such as Freudianism or existentialism. [*See* 25]

Humanity, Christian Doctrine of [XIII.B] Traditionally termed 'the doctrine of man'. Mainstream Christian teaching has portrayed humanity as composed of two elements, body and soul, the latter being purely spiritual. Together they constitute a complete human being. Christianity shares with other religions a belief in the immortality of the soul. It adds to this, however, the belief that the soul will ultimately be resurrected and 'clothed' in a spiritual 'body' (*see* AFTERLIFE). The main Christian tradition on the origin of the soul (following St Thomas Aquinas; *see* THOMISM) has held that each soul is created separately by God (Creationism); though some have seen it as transmitted by parents to children (Traducianism). Humanity is created in the 'image of God' (*imago Dei*), which was partly but not wholly destroyed by the fall and original sin (for the myth of Adam and the fall *see* SIN, CHRISTIANITY AND). For ROMAN CATHOLICISM and the EASTERN ORTHODOX CHURCH sufficient is left of the 'image' (including free will) to allow for receptiveness to God's grace (SALVATION). PROTESTANTISM originally saw the 'image' as completely destroyed. This has been greatly modified for many Protestants by the decline of CALVINISM and the rise of humanistic optimism since the 18th century. Developments in evolutionary theory, philosophy and psychology have greatly complicated and modified traditional Christian views of human nature, not always in an optimistic direction. Feminist theology has drastically challenged what is seen as the male-centred traditional views of God and humanity. (*See* GENDER.) [91; 114]

Humanity (in Judaism) [XXII] The biblical account of man being created in the image of God (*Genesis* 1: 27) was the basis of the Judaic understanding of human nature [10: III]. The medieval theologians were divided about whether or not humans' status was above that of ANGELS, but most agreed that humanity was the goal of creation. Kabbalists (*see* KABBALAH) saw humankind as a microcosm who played a central role in maintaining the harmonious function of all levels of reality. Humanity's task was to act with God as a partner in the continuing work of creation, and to bring about the Kingdom of God on earth by following the good inclination (*yetzer tov*) within and overcoming the evil inclination (*yetzer-ha-ra*) [30: XVII]. The prohibition on homicide is explained in terms of the 'image of God' within humanity, as are a number of other halakhic laws (*see* HALAKHAH). Human free will is a cornerstone of Jewish thought. [5; 14 vol. 11: 842; 27]

Hun-p'o [XII] The traditional Chinese theory of two souls, which developed early in the Chou dynasty (1027–402 BCE) has persisted, subject to some modifications, into modern Chinese popular religious belief. The *hun* soul is the higher spiritual element which is characterized as *yang* in nature (*see* YIN-YANG). After death this becomes *shen* (spirit). In the ancient belief the *shen* of the worthy and virtuous was thought to ascend to the Heavenly Palace of SHANG TI to reside indefinitely with the *shen* of other worthy and eminent beings. During the Han dynasty (206 BCE–220 CE), even the *shen* of ordinary people was believed to have the chance of temporary survival for four or five generations, while the dead person was honoured by their spirit tablet (*shen chu*) situated on the family altar.

The *p'o* soul is the gross or material aspect of the person which is equated with the *yin* quality. Originally this soul was thought to descend to the underworld or Yellow Springs, where it was controlled by the Lord of the Earth (Hou T'u). In another view the *p'o* soul was thought to remain with the body in the grave, where it was sustained by food offerings made by the family. If these were not provided or the body was improperly buried, then the *p'o* could become a dangerous ghost (*kuei*).

The considerably flexible Chinese popular religious beliefs about souls and survival were further modified by the popularity of BUDDHIST notions of KARMA, merit and rebirth. These clearly suggest that the functional and operational value of such beliefs in sustaining the Chinese ancestor and family system (*see* ANCESTOR CULT), and their supporting ethics, were more important than the precise metaphysical details of the souls and their nature. [72: 11, 103–10; 99: 1, 9–12; 45]

Hurrians [VIII] Hurrian peoples, who inhabited the mountainous regions south of the Caspian sea from *c.*2300 BCE, moved gradually southwards and westwards, forming important elements in several kingdoms including Mitanni, where they were dominated by a ruling caste of Indo-Aryans (INDO-EUROPEANS). They also contributed substanatially to the HITTITE empire, where their language and religion were important elements.

The theologians of the Hittite capital adopted Hurrian deities [13: 140–1], and some Mesopotamian gods were introduced to the Hittites in this way. The great rock-sanctuary of Yazilikaya, about 3 km from Boghazköy, was a state monument, carved in relief, showing not only deities of the Hittite kingdom (*see* ART AND SYMBOLISM (ANCIENT NEAR EASTERN)), but also some Hurrian deities that had been officially accepted into the Hittite pantheon.

In areas where Hurrians formed the main element in the population, Hurrian deities such as Teshub, the weather-god, and his consort, Hebat, were worshipped. They were prominent at Aleppo, Samuha and elsewhere. With increasing Hurrian influence on the state religion, Hebat was eventually identified with the sun-goddess of Arinna.

The most elaborate myths and legends in the Hittite archives were also drawn from the Hurrian religion, although many are only partly preserved [24: 120–6]. Two of the most important concerned the god Kumarbi, who was the father of the gods. One tells of the struggle for divine KINGSHIP and the creation (*see* COSMOLOGY (ANCIENT NEAR EASTERN)); it has been compared with the Theogony of Hesiod [1]. Kumarbi, originally a wise king, was impregnated by Anu, the great god, with three terrible gods, the weather-god, the Tigris and Tasmisu (a minion of the weather-god), whom he spat forth, impregnating the earth with them, and the earth in turn gave them birth.

The other – the 'Story of Ullikummi' – is fragmentary, but deals with the conspiracy by Kumarbi against Teshub. Kumarbi begat Ullikummi, who fought on earth against the gods; the conclusion (now missing) probably saw the restoration to power of Teshub and the defeat of Kumarbi and Ullikummi (*see* ANCIENT NEAR EASTERN RELIGIONS).

I

Icon [XIII.D] The word 'icon' simply means image. From an early period, however, it has come to refer specifically to the representational religious art of the Eastern churches, and most specifically to painted or mosaic panels depicting holy persons or sacred events usually executed in Byzantine or Russian style. In EASTERN ORTHODOX theology, however, the word 'icon' refers simply to such images of holy persons or sacred events as are fit and proper for religious use: it carries no stylistic implications. Many Orthodox churches contain icons painted in a Western style. Not every depiction of a holy person is an icon; a satirical painting of the Crucifixion is not an icon, nor is an erotic portrayal of the death of St Sebastian or a sentimental depiction of the weeping Magdalene. It is not only what a work depicts, but how it presents the religious content and significance of its subject matter that makes a work usable as an icon.

Orthodox and ROMAN CATHOLIC theology hold to the doctrine of the Second COUNCIL of Nicea that it is proper to venerate sacred images. Icons play an important role in Byzantine public worship. They are also seen both as a testimony to the reality of Christ's incarnation – he is truly human and can be portrayed, and truly God so that his image is to be worshipped – and also as offering a material vision of spiritual reality, testifying to the role of matter in salvation. In addition, icons are valued for their capacity to teach history, doctrine and morality. [22; 47; 64; 67; 75; 86]

Iconoclasm [XIII.D] In 726 CE the Byzantine Emperor Leo III ordered the removal of the image of Christ from the Chalke gate of the imperial palace, inaugurating a movement supported by many clergy and monks to end the cult of ICONS. The polemical writings of the iconophiles or iconodules who defended the veneration of icons made it clear that the controversy was not simply about the status of images; it raised fundamental questions of the reality of the Incarnation and the status of JESUS Christ as a human being, questions as to the nature of the EUCHARIST and the presence of Christ in the SACRAMENT, and parallel questions about the worship of relics and of the Cross. One useful fruit of the controversy was the sharpening of the distinction between different modes of worship: veneration or reverence (*proskynesis*) paid to holy persons, places and things, and adoration (*latreia*) owed to God alone.

It is the Iconoclast controversy that handed the term 'iconoclasm' into common use. There are, however, many other examples of religiously motivated image-breaking, from the Prophet MUHAMMAD's destruction of the idols in the KA'BA to the destruction of images in the REFORMATION. The term 'iconoclasm' is usually applied to such events either by those who venerate the images destroyed or by those who, like the classic iconoclasts, reject the cult of images as such. For those who accept the veneration of icons but approve, for example, the destruction of images and symbols of the Norse gods by Saints Boniface and Willibrod a second term, such as 'idol-breaking' is needed to make the distinction. [3; 34; 37; 47; 63; 68; 90; 99]

Iconography [XXXIV] The representation of objects or ideas through painting, drawing, sculpture, etc., or the study of such representations; derived from the Greek term *eikon* (image) and *graphia* (writing). While the term is generally used in the academic discipline of art history, it has particular reference to representations in a religious context. Religions depend a great deal on representations of gods, significant events or significant persons in the history of a religion. Artefacts used for ritual, ceremonial or meditative purposes are also included in the iconographical materials of a particular religion. Most religions manifest different aspects of their presentation iconically and the whole scene can be the research area of both art historians and students of religion. For the latter the subdiscipline of iconology, the study of the symbolic meanings and functions (*see* SYMBOL) of artistic and artefactual phenomena within the religious context, will be relevant. Iconicity in many circumstances can be held to partake in the depth of meaning of a particular religious expression. Even where it is claimed that certain visual representations are merely decorative, the behaviour of adherents points to the iconicity of these representations, i.e. to their acting as a medium of depth of meaning or religious signification. In some religious contexts, e.g. in much of ISLAM or certain forms of PROTESTANT CHRISTIANITY, the use of visual likenesses or representations is proscribed. These contexts would be described as aniconic. However, even where the strongest aniconic claims are made, buildings or some form of significant decoration, such as calligraphic decoration in Islamic buildings, can still be considered

iconic. In any ritual space, from a phenomenological perspective (*see* PHENOMENOLOGY OF RELIGION) the whole ethos, material and non-material, will function in an iconic manner for the adherents who frequent the space. Even the most aniconically conceived building in which ritualized activity takes place will, to a greater or lesser extent, function iconically for the adherent. The notion of iconicity can also be extended to the words, music and performance of religious functionaries, when the effects of such occurrences are taken into account. Iconicity may be transmitted through radio and television broadcasts of ritualized expressions of religion. [42; 121; 147; 16; 111; 124]

Iconography (Christian) [XIII.B] SS. Basil, John of Damascus and Thomas Aquinas (*c.* 1225–74 CE; *see* THOMISM) justified reverence to images, arguing that worship is directed to the reality represented. PROTESTANTISM, like ICONOCLASM in an earlier period, generally reacted violently against images, although Luther (*see* LUTHERANISM) allowed the crucifix (image of JESUS Christ on the cross). Anglo-Catholics (*see* ANGLICANISM) allow for the use of images. The EASTERN ORTHODOX CHURCH reverences ICONS. The chief Christian symbol is the cross, referring to the crucifixion of Jesus Christ, and to SALVATION. The early 'fish' symbol used of Christ and the EUCHARIST has recently been revived. (It supposedly refers to the Greek word for fish – *ichthus* – standing for the initials of 'Jesus Christ, Son of God, Saviour' in Greek [157: 514].) Other symbols have been drawn from animals, colours, numbers and objects connected with Christ, MARY and the SAINTS. People from Hebrew scripture (BIBLE) were used, as prefiguring Christ. Statues and other imagery proliferated in Western medieval churches (*see* ARCHITECTURE). Eastern images of Jesus, which since the 17th century have avoided symbolic representations, frequently show him in majesty (e.g. the *Pantocrator*) and are strongly influenced by the doctrine of his divinity. Western ones gradually shifted to realistic emphasis on his humanity. COUNTER-REFORMATION images reinforced devotions attacked by Protestantism. Modern Christian images reflect the variety of contemporary artistic styles, although applied to traditional subjects. [64; 146: VIII]

'Id [XIX] The general term in ISLAM for 'religious festival' (Turkish equivalent, *bayram*), used especially for the two great festivals. The first, the 'Id al-Adha ('of sacrifice') falls on 10 Dhu 'l-Hijja during the pilgrimage period (*see* HAJJ) and is traditionally associated with ABRAHAM's intended sacrifice of his son. The second, the 'Id al-Fitr ('of breaking the fast'), falls on 1 Shawwal, the end of Ramadan, the month of fasting (SAUM). Both are occasions for general rejoicing, the wearing of new clothes, etc., and the latter has become a major public holiday. The occasion of the Prophet's birthday (12 Rabi' I) or *maulid*, has over the centuries become a major festival, as have the birthdays of many local holy men (WALI) [77: XXIV–XXVII; 89]. Among the Shi'is (*see* SHI'ISM), the anniversary of al-Husain's killing (10 Muharram) releases a great outpouring of passion and emotion (*see* 'ALI, 'ALIDS *and* PASSION PLAY). Shi'is also celebrate the festival of Ghadir Khumm (18 Dhu 'l-Hijja), when, they hold, MUHAMMAD designated 'Ali as his divinely ordained successor. [38 s.v.; 48: 168–9; 130]

Ideology [XXXII] A system of beliefs shared by a group of people which affects the kinds of behaviour of which they approve and disapprove. In a broad sense a political party will commonly have an ideology which sets limits to the kind of policy it can be expected to pursue. But the word is also commonly used for sets of beliefs where particular importance is attached to profession and where the relation to practice may be obscure.

Marx (1818–83) (*see* MARXISM) and F. Engels (1820–95) regarded ideologies as impositions by the ruling class upon society as a whole of ideas which reflect and appear to confirm existing economic relationships. They are a kind of deception which, if successful, produces a 'false consciousness' among the people and a corresponding complacency about the established order of society. Religions, according to Marxism, are ideologies in this sense. [14; 15]

Marx's conception of ideology has proved very influential, and non-Marxists have adopted it in a modified form. The US sociologist Peter Berger, for example, follows Marx in reserving the word 'ideology' for cases where a particular idea serves a vested interest in society. [4: 130ff] The function of an ideology, as he sees it, is to preserve a vested interest by interpreting social reality so as to provide an appearance of justification for behaviour that would otherwise seem indefensible. Berger allows that ideologists may themselves be taken in by the deception which they practise on others. It is in this way that he thinks that religious persuasions can function as ideologies.

One example given by Berger is the role played by Protestant FUNDAMENTALISM (*see* AUTHORITY (CHRISTIAN)) in maintaining the racialist social system of the southern USA. Berger claims that REVIVALIST preachers, by identifying morality with private acts and public morality with the private acts of public persons, contribute to the maintenance of a social system whose central social arrangements are morally dubious. It is not that segregation is proclaimed as a God-given natural order but that attention is diverted from social evils which it would otherwise be difficult to ignore. In this way an ideology can help to preserve the existing social order without explicitly condoning it.

Iesu no Mitama Kyokai [xxvi] Known in English as the Spirit of Jesus Church, the Japanese Iesu no Mitama Kyokai traces its origin to a PENTECOSTAL experience at which church members spoke in tongues at a meeting in 1933 led by the Revd Murai Jun (1907–70). Convinced that they had recovered true Christianity and that other Christian organizations were on the wrong track, the group established itself under the leadership of Murai Jun. His successor is Murai Suwa, wife of the deceased founder. Like many pentecostal groups in North America, Iesu no Mitama Kyokai emphasizes speaking in tongues, anointing with oil for healing and blessing, dancing in the spirit and special revelations. Unlike such groups, however, it also practises vicarious baptism for the dead, a functional substitute for the traditional and widespread ancestral rites it rejects. Iesu no Mitama Kyokai also practises *godo irei sai*, a general memorial service for the spirits of the dead. Expressing the idea of reunion and fellowship with the dead, this rite parallels the BUDDHIST Bon festival held throughout Japan in July and August. Every year in March there is a special memorial service for Murai Jun and for pastors who have died during the preceding year. (The practice of holding annual memorial rites for the founder is widespread among religious organizations in Japan.) With its headquarters and a Bible school in Tokyo, Iesu no Mitama Kyokai claims an active membership of over 250,000 people and has overseas churches in South Korea, Taiwan and Brazil. [12: 356–7, 361–5]

Ifa [II] The chief YORUBA system of DIVINATION, and probably the most complex in Africa. Originating in the city of Ife, its use has spread to other west African societies (Benin, FON, and the Ewe of Togo and eastern Ghana) and also to Brazil and Cuba. Its characteristics are the precision of the system, its vast corpus of related verse and its religious foundation in the worship of the ORISHA, Ifa, or Orunmila. Orunmila is the divine patron of divination, the communicator to mankind of their destiny as decreed by Olodumare. Through Ifa one's destiny is revealed.

Ifa depends upon the manipulation of 16 palm-nuts or the toss of a chain from which – as in many systems of divination – 16 basic permutations are possible. Upon these depend 256 figures, for each of which Ifa provides a considerable number of verses. The diviner recites the relevant verses until the client chooses one. The verses constitute a vast corpus of unwritten scripture. Each provides guidance, including instructions to offer sacrifice, normally at the shrine of Eshu.

The Ifa diviner is called *babalawo* (father of secrets). Always a man, and a priest of Orunmila (Orisha), the *babalawo* has had years of apprenticeship and is required, especially, to memorize the verses. He may rise in honour through various initiations. The 16 diviners of the king of Ife, the Awoni, are the highest. [21; 23]

Igbo Religion [II] The Igbo, some 12 million in all, are a group of agricultural peoples living in southeastern Nigeria, linked by proximity of language and culture, but never politically. Their religion (or religions) appears to possess most of the characteristics common throughout Africa such as the veneration of ancestral spirits (*see* ANCESTOR VENERATION) and a range of nature deities, as well as a single overarching spirit, Chukwu or Chineke. It has, however, special characteristics as well as uncertainties. It needs to be noted that the Igbo have been in contact with CHRISTIANITY for over 150 years and are now among the most Christianized of African peoples. Moreover, relatively little was written about their religion until recently. There is, therefore, an understandable degree of divergence in interpretation of pre-Christian belief, a divergence which reflects two schools of thought within modern scholarship in regard to the degree to which African traditional religion may be described as 'monotheistic'.

Among special Igbo characteristics, though shared by some neighbouring peoples, two stand out. First, the place of the Earth Mother, Ala. Moral norms are related almost wholly to her, as is fertility, both human and agricultural. Ancestral spirits are seen as associated particularly with Ala. She appears as at least the equal of Chukwu, and may represent an earlier expression of monotheistic supremacy. A second special characteristic is the *Chi*, a mysterious and particular entity which gives every human a specific destiny. Again, the individual *Chi* may predate the universal Chineke.

The central issue of uncertainty remains the true nature of Chukwu and the history of this word. For many modern Igbo scholars such as Ikenga Metuh [42], Chukwu is the all-powerful creator, 'high' God of an essentially monotheistic tradition, to whom Ala and every *Chi* are created subjects. For others, notably Nwoga [44], there was no 'High God' in early Igbo tradition, only Ala and a multitude of *Chis*, each with an oracular character. Some oracular spirits were recognized as more effective than others. Most notable among these was the *Chi* of the Aro people which became known as Aro Chukwu, the leading Igbo oracle by the early 19th century, whose name was adopted by missionaries for the Christian Creator God. Whether Chukwu originally represents an expanded local oracle or a creator god of pre-Christian tradition, it has certainly become the name used in modern times by Christian and non-Christian alike for a supreme deity both transcendent and immanent.

Iglesia ni Cristo [xxvii] The largest independent church in the Philippines (*see* PHILIPPINES RELIGION), founded in 1914 by Felix Manalo (1886–1963) after experience in five mission churches. Manalo's son Eraño now presides over the movement, which is strongly anti-Catholic and well organized, with up to 1 million members. It is characterized by splendid and distinctive church buildings, a dogmatic UNITARIAN interpretation of the BIBLE and a fondness for public debate. The church, which used its block vote to support former President Marcos in return for administrative favours, has had several secessions. There are branches among Filipinos in many parts of the world. [6: 19–39; 8: 49–50]

Ijma' [xix] ('consensus') One of the bases of classical Islamic religious law for the Sunni mainstream (*see* SUNNA). Only the sectarian KHARIJITES rejected it, as did the Shi'is (*see* SHI'ISM), the latter substituting for it obedience to the authoritative IMAM. The consensus of the early Muslims, that of the Prophet MUHAMMAD's companions at the outset, which later broadened out to include that of all believers (or at least of all qualified ones), supplemented the QUR'AN and HADITH as sources of law when these two gave no clear guidance. It was founded on a tradition from the Prophet, 'My community will never agree upon error.' [38 'Idjmā'; 80: 178–9; 142: 33–9]

Illuminati [xxiv] A secret society devoted to anti-priestly and democratic ideals, founded in 1776 at Ingolstadt, Bavaria, by Adam Weishaupt (1748–1830). Initiates were trained in materialist philosophy under the guidance of the *Areopagus* (inner directorate). Having established the organization in Bavaria, Weishaupt decided in 1779 to infiltrate continental FREEMASONRY, both to recruit new members and to make use of the secrecy and discipline of Masonic lodges (particularly the defined grades of illumination) within his quasi-masonic association. Here the order spread rapidly until 1784, when internal quarrels led to publicity and it was suppressed by the Bavarian and other governments. [26: v]

Imam [XIX] Literally 'exemplar, model', hence 'leader'; denotes, first, the leader of the Muslim worship (*see* SALAT) in the MOSQUE. He may be any adult male Muslim of good character and standing in the community, and is not in any sense an ordained priest or minister, though larger mosques may employ a salaried IMAM. Second, it denotes the charismatic leaders of the Shi'a (*see* SHI'ISM), who hold that God has designated a line of the immaculate members of the family of 'ALI to act as the sources of spiritual and secular guidance for the community; hence knowledge of the Imam of the time is a prerequisite of all true believers. Since the disappearance of the 12th of the line in the later 9th century, there has been a period of occultation of the Imams; but the Shi'is now await the return (*raj'a*) of the expected Imam, who will re-establish a reign of justice and peace on earth (*see* MAHDI). Third, it can refer to the secular head of the community as a virtual equivalent of CALIPH. [20 s.v.; 38 'Imāma'; 69: XI]

Iman [XIX] 'Faith' in ISLAM, connected also with *mu'min* ('believer'). Most Islamic theologians agreed that faith involved the three elements of intention or conviction (*niyya*), external profession (*qaul*) and performance of works ('*amal*), but differed on their relative propor-

tions and/or importance. One school, the Ash'aris (*see* KALAM), laid greatest stress on conviction in the heart. Degrees of faith were recognized, with emphasis on essential articles of faith (as opposed to those without which a person does not necessarily cease to be a Muslim). All authorities agree that faith is required for salvation. (*See also* 'AQIDA, DIN, SHAHADA) [20 'Faith (Islam)'; 38 s.v.; 48: 47–8; 140: 111]

Imhotep [VI] The vizier of King Djoser (3rd dynasty, *c.*2800 BCE), Imhotep was the architect of the world's first major stone building – Djoser's step PYRAMID at Saqqara [7: II, 53]. He also achieved a reputation as a sage, and was deified and worshipped in the Late Period (*c.*600 BCE) as a god of healing. He was renowned among Egyptians and Greeks, who named his chapel at Saqqara, where people from all parts of Egypt sought miraculous cures, the Asklepieion.

Immortality of the Soul [XIV] The idea that some kind of spiritual component survives the death of the body is common to most of the world's religions. Few exclude a belief in a non-material aspect of the person surviving death, though the form varies considerably: some believe in rebirth, some in a chronologically linear perpetuation of spiritual identity, some in continuity with ancestors, or a link with one's descendants. In primal religions, as in the ancient Near East and Homeric Greece, that which goes on is seen as a shadowy survival, rather than a continuing person. Later Greek philosophy gives the soul more significance, and in different ways the traditions of Plato and Aristotle influenced subsequent Jewish, Christian and Islamic thought, with the Platonic stressing the superiority of soul over body and the Aristotelian their mutual interdependence. Each of the Abrahamic traditions taught that the soul was immortal, but that its independent existence was a temporary stage before the RESURRECTION of the total person. In HINDUISM the ATMAN is held to exist as an unchanging and undying entity passing from life to life, unaffected by the essentially unreal vicissitudes of the body. This Hindu concept was rejected by the Buddha in his doctrine of ANATTA, often translated as 'no-self', but it may be only partially correct to say that the Buddha rejected the soul, for he also denied extinction and affirmed rebirth. Some Buddhists affirm a continuing identity which can only be spoken of in negatives, but others give a more positive content to that which is reborn. The whole issue is a matter of considerable debate in contemporary as in earlier scholarship.

Within contemporary philosophy the concept of the soul has been much criticized and the 'biblical theology' movement of the 1960s and 1970s drew attention to similarities between modern materialism and the psychosomatic understanding of humankind in the Hebrew Bible. More recently, however, it has been appreciated that unless one holds to a totally literalistic view of resurrection some concept of the soul is a necessary condition for any reinterpreted understanding of what resurrection might mean. At a popular level many see NEAR-DEATH EXPERIENCES as supportive of belief in the soul's immortality, though the evidential character of these data is much disputed. [4; 5; 6; 13; 23; 37; 86; 88]

Implicit Religion [xxxiv] The shortest definition is 'commitment': an investment of a religious dimension in concerns which may not usually be called religious, such as communism, sport, consumerism, individualism and familism. Just as religious phenomena are accepted as having secular implications, so 'implicit religion' suggests that in some of what are considered to be secular commitments phenomena conventionally considered to be religious, or related to those often labelled religious, may be found. The term 'implicit' directs attention to areas of human behaviour usually seen as simply secular; 'religious' is applied here because it is holistic and exemplifies commitment. The concept of 'religion' here is seen as uniting the various levels of sociality (such as the individual, social and corporate) and of consciousness (subconscious, conscious and self-conscious); so the concept of implicit religion likewise reflects the symbiotic relationship between the sacred/profane and the secular.

Two drawbacks in the use of the term 'implicit religion' should be mentioned. On the one hand, the evidence for it may not be implicit: those practising an ideology, such as secularism, may for instance even describe their way of life as a sort of religion. Here it has the popular usage found in expressions such as 'reading the papers religiously', meaning carefully (i.e. regularly and diligently). In this case agreement between the actor and the observer on the use of the term is only to be expected. On the other hand, some may dispute that it is possible for an observer to describe behaviour as religious, whose actors themselves do not use that label. Presumably this reticence assumes that the term 'religion' attributes a value judgement, either positive or negative, or that 'implicit religion' is necessarily related to a particular religion such as Christianity. Just as 'religion' in general can be used neutrally, so 'implicit religion' is seen as neither leading to, nor stemming from, nor excluding, any specific named religion.

The identical expression was used [142: 36–38] to describe an approach within RELIGIOUS EDUCATION, influential in Britain in the 1960s and 1970s, and again in the 1990s, that concentrated on a 'personal quest for meaning in life in terms of [the pupil's own] actual experience'. It was however usually restricted to moments of transcendence experienced by individuals [73a] and became suspect as being 'woolly minded'. Dutch [27a] and Italian [125a] equivalents of the term however were also used (again quite independently of its earlier use in English) to refer in the first instance to more permanent and social commitments, as in this article.

Other related terms include 'invisible religion' [112], 'civil religion' [18a] and 'popular religion'. The concept of 'implicit religion' has sometimes been criticized on the grounds that 'if everything is religious, then the word becomes meaningless, and nothing is religious'. However, 'implicit religion' does not say 'everything is religious'; it says 'anything *may be* religious'. It is wider than religion through its concern with secularity, but narrower through its insistence on commitment. Its definition could then be seen as more focused and more consistent than the conventional use of 'religious'. [*See also* XIV 7; 9; 30; 44; 69; 76; 87]

Inari [XXI] Popularly called foxshrines, especially numerous in rural areas of Japan, *inari* have seated stone images of foxes at the entrance, the 'messengers' of the KAMI of agriculture, food and fertility [19: 504–10]. The SHINTO SHRINES are often dedicated to other *kami*, particularly Uga-no-mitama, the female *kami* of agriculture. The cult is very old and, among other explanations, was said in early times to appease foxes and prevent them damaging crops, or to neutralize foxpossession. The head shrine, Fushimi Inari in south-east Kyoto city, traditionally built in 711 CE, is noted for its thousands of votive *torii* (sacred gates) in long tunnels, covering the hill behind. The chief festival is Hatsu-uma, the 'first horse day' after the official first day of spring, welcoming back the agricultural *kami*.

India, Christianity in [XIII.B] Tradition claims that the APOSTLE Thomas reached India, and several churches survive from 4th-century CE Nestorian origins (*see* CHRISTOLOGY). They are the Malabarese and Malankarese Catholics, SYRIAN ORTHODOX, Jacobite and Nestorian (Mellusian) Churches, and the Mar Thoma church (*see* THOMAS CHRISTIANS). Western Christianity arrived with the Portuguese and notably the Jesuits (*see* MONASTICISM) St Francis Xavier (1506–52) and Robert de Nobili (1577–1656). De Nobili influenced high-CASTE Indians by acting like a Hindu GURU. The English East India Company was hostile to MISSIONS but the BAPTIST William Carey (1761–1834) landed in 1793. In 1813 the influence of the 'Clapham Sect' (*see* REVIVALISM) opened India to PROTESTANTISM. Alexander Duff (1806–78) initiated educational missions to the higher castes and, by the end of the 19th century, although all religions were tolerated by the government, American and European Protestant missions were numerous. Mass conversions occurred among the poorer castes. Political independence (1947) hastened the independence of local churches. Christianity in India, although more successful than in Pakistan, amounts to only 3% of the population. Westernization in India, however, has probably helped it to become more influential than in CHINA. The Church of South India (1947) incorporates ANGLICANISM, CONGREGATIONALISM, METHODISM and PRESBYTERIANISM. The Church of North India (1970) includes BAPTISTS too. [100: V, XVI; 121 vol. 3: XVII, vol. 5: XI; 122 vol. 3: VIII, vol. 6: III, vol. 7: XI; 150; 152; 153; 185]

Indian Shaker Church [xxvii] In 1881 a Squaxin Indian near Puget Sound (Washington), John Slocum, received a revelation during a coma. The next year a shaking paroxysm of his wife Mary was regarded as the spirit of God curing John of an illness. The Shaker Church they founded replaced SHAMAN healing by the new shaking and dancing rituals, along with Christian elements. In the 1970s over 20 congregations in the north-west USA embraced perhaps 2,000 adherents in this Indian Christian SYNCRETISM. [1; 12: 145–51; 26: 353–64]

Indo-Europeans [xxxvi] In c.5000 BCE there were groups of peoples living (probably) in eastern Europe which began to fragment, with groups migrating in different directions. Over two millennia or more, some travelled east and eventually settled in India (c.2000–1500 BCE), where they overpowered the civilization of the INDUS VALLEY. En route a few apparently settled in Iran, and a later 'wave' of these nomadic peoples colonized that country. They spoke of themselves as the 'Aryans', the noble ones. Scholars generally refer to the 'proto-Indo-Iranians' (the ancestors, on the south Russian steppes, of the Iranians) and the 'Indo-Aryans' (the Aryans who invaded India). These invaders brought with them a rich oral tradition, much of which is preserved in the HINDU Rig-VEDA and the AVESTA of ZOROASTRIANISM. Some Indo-Europeans, the Tocharians, travelled further east. Other Indo-Europeans travelled south, settling in Greece and Rome, while others migrated west and settled in various north European areas, e.g. Scandinavia. The existence of the parent groups of peoples can be established by the similarity of the respective descendent languages (e.g. Sanskrit, Greek and Latin). Certain rituals are similar in the religions of the countries in which the Indo-Europeans settled, which suggests an original common practice (e.g. the veneration of fire). The Indo-Europeans considered certain natural phenomena, such as the sun and sky, to be deities. G. Dumézil (b. 1898) (see TRIPARTITE IDEOLOGY) has attempted to reconstruct a common structure behind the various mythologies of the different religions which are of Indo-European descent. [8 vol. 1; 23: i]

Indus Valley [xvii] The site of an early Indian civilization dating from at least 2500 BCE, evidence of which began to be found from 1920 with the excavation of two sites, Harappa and Mohenjo-Daro. The findings from these sites suggest that many features of 'modern' HINDUISM are ultimately derived from this early period. The most notable examples are: the popularity of the cult of the mother-goddess; the ithyphallic deity, apparently meditating in a yogic posture, who strongly resembles SHIVA; the worship of the pipal-tree; the generally domestic-centred nature of popular cults; and the large part played by animals, especially the bull [12: 14–24; 80: 10–12], although not the COW. The archaeological evidence has been interpreted as an indication of the existence of great baths and possibly water rites. However, until the script of this civilization is interpreted, theories about its religious beliefs must remain largely speculation. [1]

Insan [xix] (Arabic 'man'). The doctrine of man in ISLAM. Islamic theology concentrated more on defining God and his attributes (ALLAH) than on man. The QUR'AN regards man as God's noble work, created from clay as his representation on earth and to serve and glorify him (see KHALQ). He is endowed with a soul (see RUH), which will return to God when the body perishes. The Qur'an is ambiguous about man's free will (see FATALISM (IN ISLAM)), but many traditions stress how man should act, in effect according him free will. While orthodoxy regards man as altogether different from the transcendent God, Sufi mystics (*see* SUFISM) have sought nevertheless to achieve closeness to, and even union with, God. (For women in Islam, *see* MAR'A.) [20 'Man (Islamic doctrine)'; 38 s.v.; 48: 32–3]

Institutions (Greek) [xvi] Greeks worshipped both as individuals and as members of a variety of groups. The most important worshipping group was the *polis*; others were (e.g. in Athens): the *oikos* (household), the *phratria* (allegedly a descent group, in reality probably originally a local subdivision of the *polis*), the *demos* (commune, borough), the *phyle* (tribe); some citizens also belonged to a *genos*, an aristocratic descent group which in democratic Athens had hereditary rights to one or more priesthoods. For certain rituals age, sex or occupation were the distinguishing criteria. There were also voluntary cult associations (*thiasoi, orgeones*) dedicated to particular cults. Institutions regulated inter-state activities. The most important was the *Amphictyoniai*, the Leagues responsible for inter-state sanctuaries. [2: 1.2; 4: 254–60; 18: 256; 31; 34; 35]

Intertestamental Literature [xiii.a] This refers to all the Jewish literature of the late second temple period, both Palestinian and non-Palestinian, which is not included in the Hebrew BIBLE. Because of their likely date of authorship, the 'apocrypha' (e.g. *Tobit, Judith, Wisdom of Ben Sira, 1 Maccabees*) of the SEPTUAGINT are often classed as inter-testamental literature, though many Christians would consider them canonical. Other texts include examples of many different genres: APOCALYPSES, histories, liturgical texts, narratives, poetry, rewritten versions of existing parts of the Bible, testaments, wisdom literature. Often a distinguished figure from the past,

like Enoch, Abraham, Jacob or Moses, is assigned the authorship of these works to give them authority; the term 'pseudepigrapha' is applied to such writings. The recovery of the DEAD SEA SCROLLS has provided contemporary manuscript evidence for many of these texts, which were previously known largely in translations passed on by Christians. The scrolls have also expanded the range of material, providing examples of biblical commentaries and paraphrases, rule books, targums, treatises and other genres. [22: III; 23]

Io [xxix] The supreme being in New Zealand Maori belief, barely traceable elsewhere in POLYNESIAN RELIGION. Io's identity was a secret known only to TOHUNGAS in a few Maori houses of learning (*whare wananga*). All life and power (MANA) comes ultimately from Io. He exists eternally in the highest of 12 heavens, acting through a hierarchy of gods and guardian spirits superior to the classic ATUA. No image of Io is known, and mention of his name in prayers and chants is rare. [6; 7; 16; 28]

Iroquois [v] A general designation for five North American Indian tribes (Mohawk, Seneca, Onondaga, Cayuga and Oneida) of Hokan–Siouan linguistic stock. Cosmogonic myths recount the birth of twin brothers, Ioskeha and Tawiscara (the principles of good and evil respectively) from the daughter of sky-woman (*see* CREATION MYTHS; HERO TWINS). Ioskeha, the CULTURE HERO, ultimately creates mankind, with divisions into moieties (or tribal subgroupings). A return of Ioskeha occasions the 'False Face' society; a group of medicine men, whose masks represent spirits benevolent to mankind, seek the prevention and cure of illness [24: XVII]. Aboriginal religion was transformed and renewed in the 18th century by the Seneca prophet HANDSOME LAKE.

Iruva [II] Iruva (with parallel forms of the word, Izuwa, Ilyuva, Lyuba, Luba, Loba, etc.) is one of the most widely spread names for God in Africa. It is mainly found in Tanzania (Chagga and Meru in the east; Kimbu, Nyamwezi and Sukuma in the west) and among neighbouring peoples; but it is also to be found in Congo (Brazzaville) and south-west Cameroon. The word means 'sun' in each language, though in some (Sukuma, for instance) there is now another secular word for sun too. These religions do not, however, identify God and the physical sun, but recognize a clear distinction. Iruva represents a basic, and certainly ancient, aspect of BANTU theology: God in the sky, symbolically male, life-giving. [34]

Ise Jingu [XXI] The grand shrines of Ise in Japan. These are two shrines, at Uji-Yamada and Ise in Mie prefecture (*see* SHINTO SHRINES) [19: 105–30; 32: 20–37; 34: 28–47]. They are 6 km apart, separated by the Isuzu river. The original shrine, the Naiku (inner shrine), was dedicated to AMATERASU-OMIKAMI, the sun-goddess, and according to tradition was founded in 4 BCE (perhaps actually in the 3rd century CE) after Emperor Suinin wanted to move the sacred mirror from his residence. The other shrine, Geku (outer shrine), was dedicated to Toyouke-omikami, the grain-goddess (KAMI), and is said to have been founded by Emperor Yuryaku in 475 CE (perhaps actually *c.*490). As a union of sky and earth deities, the site became the most revered spot in Japan, and pilgrimages and special imperial visits were made throughout the centuries. All persons nowadays hope to go once in a 60-year span. An imperial family daughter was for long dispatched as the chief priestess (*saigu*) at the shrines. At great expense and in an exceptionally elaborate ritual, the shrines are rebuilt on adjoining lots every 20 years. The *shintai* (or *go-shintai*: god

body) is transferred in the Sengushiki ceremony, and the old shrines are dismantled. The last rebuilding was in 1993–4.

Ishtadeva [XVII] 'Chosen god'; in HINDUISM, the deity principally worshipped by an individual or family. Although Hinduism is superficially polytheistic, in practice each Hindu tends to revere one god or goddess as fully embodying the nature of the supreme reality or BRAHMAN. For Shaivas this will be SHIVA or a member of his family, GANESHA or KARTTIKEYA; for Vaishnavas, VISHNU or one of his AVATARAS, such as RAMA or KRISHNA; for Shaktas some form of SHAKTI, the Goddess, such as DURGA or KALI. Other deities are not rejected, but regarded as representing aspects of the power of the chosen god. (*See* BHAKTI; PUJA.)

Ishvara [XVII] In Sanskrit 'the one who is able'; thus, a lord or king, and in Hindu tradition, the supreme god. Whereas specific names are used for the gods (e.g. SHIVA, VISHNU, etc.), this is the word which indicates 'God' in the general sense. In practice, however, it generally implies a Shaiva allegiance, Shiva being called, for example, Maheshvara (maha + ishvara), 'Great Lord'. Vaishnavas prefer Bhagavat, roughly 'Blessed One' (cf. BHAGAVADGITA).

Islam [XIX] The name of the faith means 'submission [to God]', the adherent or Muslim being therefore 'one who submits himself to God' (ALLAH), i.e. surrenders himself unconditionally to the divine will. Tradition regards Islam as the final unfolding of God's revelation to humankind, a complete system of faith and behaviour whose archetype is preserved in heaven with God, whereas earlier versions of the revelation, such as those given to the Jews and Christians, had been imperfect ones. The Prophet MUHAMMAD was only the channel for this revelation, hence it is misleading to speak of the faith as 'Muhammadanism'. Islamic theologians distinguished between the verbal profession of adherence to Islam (SHAHADA) and inner faith (IMAN), but connected them closely in that true intention in the heart leads inevitably to performance of the external duties of Islam (see PILLARS OF ISLAM) and overt profession of the faith. No distinction between the religious sphere and that of practical life is possible, and the all-embracing law of Islam (SHARI'A) covers all facets of human activity [38 s.v.; 48: IV; 136].

Islam spread rapidly from its birthplace in western Arabia (see HARAMAIN) in the early 7th century CE, so that, by 713, Arab believers stood on the Atlantic coast and the Indus river banks. Its actual penetration among the peoples of the intervening lands was naturally a slower process; in such regions as subSaharan Africa, Islamization is still proceeding. In some areas (e.g. the Arabian peninsula, north Africa), older faiths have been totally overlaid; in some (e.g. Egypt, Syria, Lebanon, Indonesia), significant non-Muslim minorities survive; in some (e.g. the Indo-Pakistan subcontinent, China), Islam is still a minority; and in some (e.g. Spain, the Balkans, South Russia), Islam has receded. Statistics for numbers of Muslims today are only approximate, in the absence of reliable censuses in many countries, but the total perhaps approaches 600 million. (See also AFRICA, ISLAM IN; CENTRAL ASIA AND KHAZAKSTAN, ISLAM IN; CHINA, ISLAM IN; DĪN; ISLAMIC DYNASTIES; SOUTH ASIA, ISLAM IN; SOUTH-EAST ASIA, ISLAM IN; WEST, ISLAM IN THE.)

Islamic Dynasties [XIX] In its early days, the Islamic community was directed by the CALIPHS of the 'Rightly guided' or 'Orthodox' line (632–61) of Medina; then by the Umayyad line (661–750) of Damascus; and then by the Abbasids in Baghdad (750–1258), latterly as puppet rulers only in Cairo (1261–1517). The central authority of the caliphate declined from the 9th century onwards, and various lines of provincial governors or local potentates, from Morocco to Central Asia, became autonomous and then virtually independent. In North Africa, Egypt and Syria a powerful rival caliphate, that of the Fatimids (909–1171), arose under Shi'i leadership (see SHI'ISM), and in Iraq and the Iranian world there arose the Sunni (see SUNNA) Turkish Seljuk dynasty of sultans or secular rulers (1038–1194). The reassertion of Sunni orthodoxy over political Shi-'ism led to the triumph in 1260 of the Turkish Mamelukes in Egypt and Syria as independent sultans. But their authority declined after the Ottoman Turkish conquest in 1517, as this latter dynasty (1342–1924) expanded across the Near East as far as the Persian Gulf and into Christian Europe as far as Hungary. The eastern Islamic world, however, suffered in 1217 and again in 1256 the cataclysmic invasions of the Mongols from inner Asia, and then likewise the ravages of the military conqueror Tamerlane (1336–1405). Eventually, new Turkish-directed empires arose in Muslim India, above all that of the Mughals (Moguls) of Delhi (1526–1858), and also in Persia, above all those of the Safavids of Isfahan (1501–1732) and the Qajars of Tehran (1779–1925). European economic and political encroachments, accentuated in the 19th century when Egypt broke away from Ottoman control, caused much of the Islamic world to fall under the domination of other empires, including those of Russia, Holland, Britain and France. Turkey and Persia alone preserved their independence, although the Ottoman empire was dismembered after the First World War and the Arab provinces formed into various, largely new, separate states. [19; 21; 64; 65]

Islamic Modernism [xix] Called into existence by the material and intellectual challenge of the West, and by the urgent need to adapt the faith to present conditions. Figures like Muhammad 'Abduh (1849–1905), rector of AL-AZHAR, sought to modernize traditional education, and his disciple Rashid Rida (1865–1935) and the Salafis (literally, 'those going back to the first Muslims') made the journal *al-Manar* a vehicle for a reformism which involved getting back to the original, pristine Islam, purged of accretions [8: II; 28: III; 78: XI; 123: 68–87]. Out of such trends sprang the Muslim Brotherhood of Hasan al-Banna' (1906–49), which emphasized social amelioration [28: VII; 94]; the increasing political activism of its adherents has made it suspect to several Islamic governments. [General surveys in 28: V–VII; 38 'Islāh'; 46; 52: X; 107: XII–XIII; for legal aspects, *see* 27: 149–225]

Island of Creation [VI] Various Egyptian myths explained the creation of the world, the gods, mankind and religion. Each myth incorporated the belief that an 'Island of Creation' had emerged from the primeval waters and had become the first god's home [6: I]. By the Old Kingdom (*c.*2600 BCE), the priests of Heliopolis, Memphis and Hermopolis promoted the most important of these, stressing their own deity's primal role in the creation. Later, the cosmogony of Thebes was added (*see* AMUN).

Isma'ilis [xix] A subsect of SHI-'ISM, which branched off from the main body in the later 8th century. Their adherents held that Isma'il, son of the sixth IMAM, should rightfully have been designated seventh Imam of the Shi'a (hence their alternative name of 'Seveners'). The Isma'ilis came to stress the internal, esoteric aspect of the QUR'AN and the teachings of ISLAM, by means of which they derived 'authoritative instruction' (*ta'lim*). This esoteric interpretation also involved a distinct cosmology, and the sect's followers made many valuable and subtle contributions to Islamic philosophy and theology [general survey in 38 'Ismā'īliyya']. With the establishment of the Fatimid dynasty in Egypt and Syria (*see* ISLAMIC DYNASTIES), whose Imams or CALIPHS claimed descent from Fatima, wife of 'ALI and daughter of the Prophet, the Isma'ilis achieved their greatest political success. Other groups in Syria and Persia became notorious in the 12th and 13th centuries as the 'Assassins', for their activism in politics and warfare [30; 78: V–VII; 81]. Isma'ilis survive today, substantially prosperous as a community and having shed their earlier radicalism, in the Khoja communities of India, Syria, Iran, and east Africa and the Bohoras of India. The Imams of the former group bear the title 'Agha Khan'. [2: II]

Israel, State of [xxii] The modern Jewish state founded in the ancient HOLY LAND of JUDAISM on 14 May 1948 [14 vol. 9: 301]. Mass Jewish return to Palestine began at the end of the 19th century under the influence of the ideals of ZIONISM [26; 40]. The Balfour Declaration of 1917, issued by the British government, promised the establishment of a Jewish national home in Palestine, which was then a British mandate territory. Nazi ANTI-SEMITISM gave a new impetus to Jewish nationalism, and to the immigration or *aliyah* to Palestine. The United Nations partition plan of 29 November 1947 envisaged two states in Palestine, one Arab and one Jewish. The Arab states refused to accept the idea of a separate Jewish state, and declared war on the fledgling Jewish state in 1948 [55: 448–68; 57: XXII, XXV]. An armistice was agreed in 1949, but a state of war continued between Israel and its neighbours, except for Egypt which signed a peace treaty at Camp David in the USA after President Sadat visited Jerusalem in November 1977, until a treaty with the Palestine Liberation Organization, sealed publicly on 13 September 1993, led to peace with Jordan in 1994 and negotiations with Syria. The state of Israel has a mixed legislature; most of its laws are dealt with in secular courts but issues of personal status come under the jurisdiction of religious courts. Jews, whether religious or secular, have to undergo MARRIAGE and divorce under the control of the Orthodox rabbinate (see RABBI). [25; 32; 44; 52]

Ittoen [xxvi] Like many organizations of religious character in Japan, Ittoen does not call itself a religion, or even a NEW RELIGIOUS MOVEMENT. Its religious orientation is so clear, however, that it frequently crops up in scholarly analyses of new religious movements in Japan. Ittoen is a utopian community of about 70 families in Kyoto. Under its present name it dates from 1913, the year of its founding by Nishida Tenko (1872–1968). Though it shows evidence of influence from both SHINTO and CHRISTIANITY, its primary orientation can be taken as BUDDHIST. Ittoen traces its origin to Nishida's experience of mystical enlightenment in 1905. After eight years of trying to resolve competing interests between tenant farmers and investors in a land reclamation project, Nishida withdrew and began to consider how people could live together without conflict. After three days and nights of fasting at a Shinto shrine, he awoke to hear a baby crying. This occasioned his insight that just as mother and baby, feeder and fed, take pleasure in each other and exist without conflict, so he should live 'naturally' in the presence of the Light (Ohikari), without worrying about himself, but simply performing humble tasks selflessly and receiving with gratitude whatever he was given. As he cleaned toilets and picked up trash, people

asked him why he did such things. Some followed him, and a 1913 gift of a building enabled him to form the Ittoen community. His bestseller, *The Life of Repentance* (1921), spread his ideas and increased his following. The current head of Ittoen is the founder's grandson, Nishida Takeshi. Today business corporations call on Ittoen to provide near-monthly training sessions in the Ittoen spirit, which emphasizes obedient service without thought of reward. [4: VI, 189–225]

Ius Divinum [xxxi] The sacred law of Rome, consisting essentially of traditional norms expounded by the priests (SACERDOTES) in the light of their written records of past incidents and the comments (responsa) of their predecessors. It was never codified, as were other areas of Roman law, but remained a priestly preserve; and it almost never gave rise to coercive legal action – coercion was left to the gods. The emperors, as members of all colleges, eventually inherited authority from the priests. [12: 195–200; 14; 19: 584–90]

Izumo Taisha [xxi] Izumo grand shrine; the chief shrine outside the official mythology of the Yamato tribe. It is located in Shimane prefecture on the Japan Sea side (see SHINTO SHRINES) [19: 326–53; 34: 6–7, 184–7]. It is dedicated to Okuninushi-no-mikoto, KAMI of fishing and sericulture, whose anti-Yamato hostility was mitigated by the gift of a palace and generous annual tribute, and who was traditionally given authority over the religious affairs of the country. Although rebuilt on a smaller scale after a sudden collapse in 1031, the shrine is still the largest in Japan. It has a high, raised floor, *taishazukuri* in style.

J

Jaguar (South America) [XXIII] Of all animal SYMBOLS in South American religions, the jaguar stands out as the most powerful and widely used. Supernatural jaguars are prominent in numerous CREATION MYTHS, COSMOLOGIES and eschatologies. Often in myth, a priomordial jaguar is got rid of in order to make way for the present world. Among Gê-speaking peoples, humanity obtains cooking fire from a primordial jaguar. Among numerous peoples of Central and South America the SHAMAN is associated with the jaguar, into whose powerful shape he may transform himself. [28]

Jahiliyya [XIX] 'Time of ignorance, barbarism'; the name given in post-Islamic times to the period of humankind preceding the Prophet MUHAMMAD's mission and the proclamation of the new faith of ISLAM. Hence in the QUR'AN the Jahiliyya is contrasted, as an age of violence, lawlessness and idolatry, with the enlightenment of Islam, the new ethical dispensation under the divine law and the worship of one God. [20 'Ethics (pre-Islamic)'; 38 Djahiliyya'; 54 vol. 1: 201–8; vol. 1: I]

Jain [XX] Follower of the spiritual conquerors (*jina*) and teachers who give the Jain religion its name [2; 4; 10; 12]. Jainism had emerged as a distinct soteriological path by the 6th century BCE, although the designation Jain does not itself appear until the early common era, perhaps in acknowledgement by the world-renouncing mendicant ascetics, around whom the religion had originally revolved, of the validity of the lay vocation.

Jainism teaches the means, envisaged as a combination of right faith, knowledge and conduct enacted through strict adherence to the requirements of a doctrine of non-violence (AHIMSA), by which human beings can escape the deleterious effects of the consequences of their previous actions (KARMA (JAIN DOCTRINE)), realize the innate potential of the soul (JIVA) and gain enlightenment, envisaged as full omniscience (KEVALIN), and final release from rebirth (MOKSHA (JAIN DOCTRINE)). While its earliest scriptural texts present a somewhat forbidding picture in their stress on the perils of unguarded action, the ontological solitude of each individual and the necessary practice of austerity, Jainism evolved over the centuries into a sophisticated intellectual worldview, built around a pluralist interpretation of the universe as consisting of myriads of embodied souls and modified substances, all characterized by the continual occurrence of permanence, change and decay, which in turn led to a relativistic approach to alternative philosophical viewpoints (ANEKANTAVADA), although in the last resort all non-Jain teachings are deemed to be essentially false. ATHEIST in its denial of the existence of a creator divinity overseeing human affairs, Jainism nonetheless acknowledges the divinity within its saving teachers (TIRTHANKARA) and elaborate patterns of worship, ritual and devotion have emerged in the course of the religion's history, similar to those found in HINDUISM but with a distinctively Jain gloss.

The principal structural feature of Jainism is its division into two main sects, the SHVETAMBARA and the DIGAMBARA, which in turn divided further during the medieval period into subsects based on the claims of various teacher lineages. Although there has never been any radical sectarian disagreement about the basics of Jain teaching, disputes over correct behaviour have been frequent and the most important factor in the historical development of the religion has been attempts to reform practice. Particularly noteworthy is the rejection of worship of images of the TIRTHANKARA advocated by some Shvetambara ascetic groups (STHANAKVASI; TERAPANTHI). However, unifying features transcend any regional and sectarian differences which might exist among the Jain community, the most significant of which is a universally followed vegetarianism. In recent years, Jain teachers such as Shrimad Rajacandra and Kanji Svami have strongly emphasized the more spiritual aspects of Jainism.

In medieval times Jainism was much patronized by royal and aristocratic families. Nowadays Jain laypeople are almost exclusively to be found among urban middle-class sections of society, being generally professionals, businesspeople and the like, often possessing great wealth, although there are also Jain agriculturalists to be found in parts of south India. According to the most recent census information, the Jains number approximately 3 million, with the largest concentrations being found in Gujarat, Karnataka, Madhya Pradesh, Maharashtra and Rajasthan. Of these only a relatively very small number are monks and nuns. The migration of Indians to east Africa and the subsequent displacement of many of them as a result of political upheaval has led to the presence of about 70,000 Jains in Britain and North America. There is also a small Jain community of south Asian origin in the Japanese city of Kobe, where a temple was built in 1985.

Jama'at-i-Islami [XIX] A political party formed in India in 1941 by Abu'l-A'la Mawdudi (1903–79). A self-taught Islamic scholar, Mawdudi was opposed to the setting up of a secular India, preaching the need for society to be fully based on the QUR'AN and the SUNNA. Originally opposed to the formation of Pakistan as a Muslim homeland, he nevertheless migrated there at the time of Partition in 1947. First as an opposition party, and then in collaboration with General Zia ul-Haq, the Jama'at-i-Islami has been active in the attempted Islamization of Pakistan. Within the subcontinent it remains a minority party that has never done well at the polls. Its supporters are generally drawn from the *muhajirs*, Urdu-speakers who migrated from India to Pakistan. Mawdudi was a prolific writer urging Islamic revival. This was to be achieved by Muslims, individually and collectively, fulfilling their duty of combining doctrinal correctness with moral purity. His books have been translated into several languages, finding particular success among university and college students. The Jama'at-i-Islami as a reform movement is represented by four organizations in Britain: the Islamic Foundation in Leicester, dealing with research and publishing; the Muslim Education Trust, formed in 1966 to cater for the needs of Muslim children in British schools; the UK Islamic Mission, a network of MOSQUES that has achieved considerable success in representing ISLAM to the wider British society; and Dawatul Islam, the Bangladeshi equivalent to the largely Pakistani UK Islamic Mission, a separation made necessary at the time of the civil war between East and West Pakistan in 1971. [35; 49; 99; 113]

Janam-Sakhis [XXXIII] Hagiographic accounts of the life of NANAK (see GURUS) [26: II]. Beginning with stories of Nanak's childhood, they take the reader through a narrative of early adulthood in the town of Sultanpur, extensive travels within and beyond India, and a final period of teaching back in the Punjab at Kartarpur. The characteristic form is the anecdote (*sakhi*), and most *janam-sakhis* comprise collections of anecdotes loosely organized in varying chronological patterns. These anecdotes follow earlier SUFI forms and it is evident that they circulated orally before being recorded. Some are simple borrowings from HINDU and Muslim sources. Others are the complex results of extended growth processes within the PANTH [25: v]. Wonder stories are prominent in all collections. Several manuscript *janam-sakhis* have survived from the mid-17th century onwards and these may be grouped as distinctive families or traditions [25: x]. The better-known are the *B40 Janam-sakhi*, the *Adi Sakhis* and the *janam-sakhis* of the Puratan and Bala traditions. A different style is followed by the *Miharban Janam-sakhi*. This uses the narrative structure of the *janam-sakhi* form, but concentrates on exegesis of Nanak's works [25: III]. The language of most *janam-sakhis* is Punjabi (see SIKH LANGUAGES). A late representative of the Bala tradition dominates the market in published *janam-sakhis*. [28: 95–8]

Jansenism [XIII.B] A movement in ROMAN CATHOLICISM named after Cornelius Jansen (1585–1638 CE), Bishop of Ypres, who promoted St Augustine's severe doctrines of God's grace (see AUGUSTINIANISM; SALVATION). Their severe MORAL THEOLOGY was opposed to Jesuit casuistry (see MONASTICISM), which was attacked by Blaise Pascal

(1623–62). Condemned by the PAPACY in 1653 [19: 269] and 1713, its influence continued in moral severity and resistance (sometimes political) to papal authority. The Jansenist-influenced diocese of Utrecht, Holland, became separated from the Papacy in the early 18th century and eventually supplied episcopal succession to the Old Catholic Church. [41; 53; 149]

Japan, Buddhism in [XXI] Japan adopted Buddhism and used it to complement the native SHINTO religion [general: 8: 44–8; 11; 14; 16; 21: 47–69, 191–213; 23; 26; 36]. The formal advent of Buddhism is recorded in the *Nihon Shoki* in 552 CE as the gift to Emperor Kimmei of some Buddhist objects from Paekche, the kingdom of south-west Korea [3: II, 65–7]. Other texts imply the year 538. The Soga family were willing to use the scriptures, banners and one or more images, but they did so in the face of strong opposition from other leading families, especially the Mononobe, the professional Shinto priests, and a plague was attributed to the anger of local gods. But since Buddhism was associated with literacy and other cultural advances, it proved irresistible. In a family power struggle the Soga destroyed the Mononobe in a battle of 587, securing the future of Buddhism. Emperor Yomei (r. 586–7) was the first ruler to profess Buddhism (see JAPANESE BUDDHAS AND BODHISATTVAS).

Major strides were made under Crown Prince SHOTOKU [3: II, 122–48; 25]. Architects, tile-makers, bronze-casters and sculptors were invited to build and decorate temples. Koreans taught the Japanese to read the Chinese *sutras* (scriptures) (see CHINESE BUDDHISM), making Chinese the basis for all Buddhist terminology, the Japanese using phonetic equivalents in most cases. The prince analysed the *sutras* and propagated their moralistic content.

As additional *sutras* were introduced, 'schools' of studies (NANTO ROKUSHU) formed, such as Jojitsu, Sanron and Kusha. By the 8th century, the Hosso, Kegon and Ritsu schools had assumed sectarian characteristics [11]. Archaeologists and historians have identified the existence of about 900 temples by the end of the 8th century, including the provincial temples ordered in the 66 provinces by Emperor SHOMU in 741, an edict which had the effect of making Buddhism the state religion. The temples of the Nara capital (710–84) accumulated such formidable wealth and power, dominating national policy, that the Emperor KAMMU moved the capital to another location, thereby greatly changing the course of Buddhist history.

Non-exclusiveness is typical of Japanese religion, the pluralistic nature of thought allowing borrowing, mixing and rationalization (*see* SYNCRETISM). Even today it is not clear whether some deities are Shinto or Buddhist. This was more and more apparent once the intellectualized, abstruse 9th-century esoteric sects were brought in, both TENDAI and SHINGON having much beyond the reach of the ordinary man or woman [17; 18; 38]. Tendai, however, proclaimed the Buddha-nature of the individual and had a versatile appeal, while Shingon joined forces with traditional Shinto holy spots (*see* RYOBU-SHINTO), introducing Buddhism to rural areas and rural people to additional mystical ceremonies [30; 31: 54–61]. An increasing overlap of Buddhist and Shinto ideas and practices indigenized Buddhism, without which it might never have been more than a religion of the educated and the upper classes. Buddhism became responsible for the affairs of the dead, and AMIDA WORSHIP in Tendai spread widely to dominate the 10th to 12th centuries, offering the Fujiwara aristocracy the 'Easy Path'. The Pure Land sect, with its teaching of an assured afterlife of eternal bliss, was popularized by writers and street preachers in the Kamakura period (1185–1333) [31: 61–7]. ZEN was acceptable to both the ruling class and the samurai (warriors) from the 13th century, the northern and southern Chinese versions represented in the Japanese Rinzai and Soto. Stressing sudden enlightenment and meditative discipline, they attracted upper and lower social levels [37]. The impact of Zen was far-reaching. It helped to produce a strong warrior class which based its principles on Zen discipline and Confucian concepts of loyalty (*see* CONFUCIUS) and abetted 200 years of civil war, finally resolved by the Tokugawa family ascendancy in the 17th century. These same principles were used to stratify the society as a device to enable the ruling elite to stay in power, while the shoguns supported selected temples and sects.

The most difficult period for Buddhism was early in the Meiji era (1868–1912), when the clergy was regarded as a deterrent to the modernizing process and Shinto was manipulated for nationalistic ends [19: 49–52]. Temples were destroyed and many priests forced out. Some priests voluntarily converted to become officials at Shinto shrines, as many were ordained in both religions. Relief came around 1877 with more even-handed treatment.

Despite extreme fragmentation today into sects and smaller associations, Buddhism and its temples now enjoy the affluence of the Japanese economy. Some thrive exclusively on the financial benefits of legislated Buddhist funerals. Those with historical treasures, where 'donations' are required at the entrance, have a new-found wealth and the political power which goes with it.

Japan, Christianity in [XXI] St Francis Xavier arrived in Kagoshima in 1549 and many converts were made to ROMAN CATHOLICISM before the missionaries were abruptly ordered out in 1587 [21: 71–87, 215–23; 28]. Persecutions started in 1597 and the exclusion policy almost succeeded in eliminating Christianity, the exception being the 'hidden' groups on Kyushu island. The first PROTESTANTS arrived in 1859, a few years after the country was opened again to Western contacts by Commodore Perry in 1854 [7; 12; 22]. Traditional Christian denominations were represented, and were noted especially for supporting many schools, universities and hospitals. Just prior to the Second World War, in order to centralize control, the government obliged more than 30 denominations to unite in an organization called the Nihon Kirisuto Kyodan (United Church of Christ in Japan). It still exists, but many denominations and groups do not belong to it. Christians in Japan tend to come from the educated classes. Less than 1% of the population is Christian. (*See also* EASTERN ORTHODOX MISSIONS.)

Japanese Buddhas and Bodhisattvas [XXI]

Japanese BUDDHIST terms were taken from Chinese or the original Sanskrit (Buddha = *butsu*; bodhisattva = *bosatsu*) [general: 8; 14; 16; 21: 47–69, 191–213; 26; 36]. Shakyamuni is the first recognized BUDDHA, the oldest Japanese image being one of 606 CE. THERAVADA JATAKA stories appeared only briefly before 650. By the 9th century the importance of Shaka had been eclipsed by esoteric introductions and TENDAI's interest in Yakushi (*Bhaishajya-guru-vaidurya-prabhasa*) and Amida (Amitabha) (*see* AMIDA WORSHIP), but Shaka worship was temporarily revived by NICHIREN [2] in the 13th century. Yakushi assumed early popularity as a healer and by the 8th century came to be the eastern earthly counterpart of the western,

distant Amida [36: 187–203]. The Hosso sect (*see* NANTO ROKUSHU) promoted the worship of four Buddhas: Shaka, Yakushi, Amida and Miroku (MAITREYA), the latter coming into Japan as a BODHISATTVA and identified with Prince SHOTOKU as a reincarnated Siddhartha. Yakushi almost disappeared from public interest after the 13th century under the growing impact of Amidism and ZEN. Except for some revived popularity around the time of Mappo in the 11th century, Miroku slipped into oblivion in later centuries. The monumental images in the large 8th-century temples are of Roshana (or Birushana; Sanskrit: *Vairocana*), the universal symbol of light, but this Buddha is better known in its more Japanized esoteric form as Dainichi Nyorai (The Great Illuminator Buddha). In SHINGON he is accompanied by a host of esoteric Buddhas and the Godaimyo-o (Five *Vidyarajas*, Great Kings), the chief of which is Fudo (*Acala*) [36: 148–81].

Sho Kannon, from the Chinese KUAN YIN (AVALOKITESHVARA), a bodhisattva of Amida, is known in eight fundamental forms, for instance, the Thousand-armed (*Senju*), Eleven-headed (*Juichimen*) and Horse-headed (*Bato*). Now referred to in English as the Goddess of Mercy, the feminization of Kannon is relatively modern in Japan. Classified with Kannon is Jizo (*Kshitigarbha*), represented as a monk with shaved head, often in a row of six (*Rokujizo*) for six classes of creation. He is still popular today as the patron saint of children, expectant mothers and travellers, and has become the deity of the souls of aborted foetuses (*see* JAPAN, BUDDHISM IN).

Japji [XXXIII]

A composition by NANAK which stands at the beginning of the ADI GRANTH. Unlike the remainder of the SIKH scripture it is not intended to be sung. Instead, devout Sikhs are expected to chant it early in the morning as a part of NIT-NEM. *Japji* (or *Japji Sahib*) consists of 38 stanzas with an epilogue, and expresses in words of particular beauty a long hymn of praise to God. It should be distinguished from GOBIND SINGH's *Jap Sahib*, which is also specified as a part of Nit-nem. [30: 86–93]

Jat [XXXIII] The dominant CASTE of rural Punjab and Haryana. In Pakistani Punjab the Jats are Muslim; in Indian Punjab, adjacent Haryana and northern Rajasthan they are SIKHS; and in the remainder of Haryana they are normally HINDUS. They are particularly prominent in the Sikh community (*see* CASTE (SIKH); PANTH), where they comprise more than 60% of all Sikhs. [26. 95–100]

Jataka [XI] A story of one of the previous 'births' (*jati*) of the BUDDHA. The *Jataka* collection constitutes one of the books of the SUTTA section of BUDDHIST scriptures (*see* TIPITAKA); the PALI version comprises 547 stories. From a traditional Buddhist perspective GOTAMA's attainment of enlightenment was the end result of the practice of 'perfections' (*see* PARAMITA) in countless lives spanning many aeons; during this period the Buddha-to-be (*see* BODHISATTVA) was born in many different realms – animal, human and divine (cf. CAKKAVALA) – and performed many selfless deeds, and it is these that are recounted in the *Jatakas*. Many *Jatakas* represent Buddhist versions of traditional folk tales adapted to illustrate Buddhist ethics in a simple but entertaining way. They have inspired great works of art from Arya Shura's (*c.*4th century CE) poetic masterpiece, *Jatakamala* [47], to the cave paintings of Ajanta in India and the reliefs of Borobudur in Java. They enjoy great popular appeal in Buddhist culture to the present day. [41; 15: 20–6]

Javanese Religion [XXIX] The religion of Java (an island of Indonesia) is officially ISLAM of the Sunni (*see* SUNNA), Shafi'ite school, but traces of the earlier HINDUISM and BUDDHISM are detectable, together with indigenous features relating to agriculture and local spirits. Solid reminders of the Indian era of Javanese religious history are the stone monuments of central Java (8th/9th century), notably Borobudur (a massive, multi-tiered STUPA, MAHAYANA Buddhist) and the group of three temples at Prambanan (dedicated to the Hindu triad of BRAHMA–VISHNU–SHIVA), on which are portrayed countless scenes from the life of the BUDDHA and the epic of RAMA (RAMAYANA) respectively [5]. Before Islam caused the fall of the Majapahit empire of Java in the 16th century, Shiva and the Buddha were worshipped side by side, or even jointly as Bhairava Buddha [26]. The Hindu deities LAKSHMI and Vishnu survive as Sri and Sadono in fertility ceremonies for rice cultivation [1]. Central to Javanese religion is a simple communal feast held on such occasions as birth, circumcision and marriage, known as the *slametan*. Its aim is community solidarity (*slamet*, from Arabic *salam*, 'peace'); there is Islamic prayer to ALLAH, but also the belief that the incense and the food aid in placating spirits. The *dukun* is a functionary practising healing, divination, and sorcery [13]. Mysticism is widespread, sometimes SUFI, sometimes Javanese (and owing much to the Hindu–Buddhist past). [26]

Jehovah's Witnesses [XIII.B] Charles Taze Russell (1852–1916 CE) of Pittsburgh, USA) founded this MILLENARIAN movement or SECT. He was succeeded by Joseph Franklin ('Judge') Rutherford (1869–1941). Witnesses tend to interpret the BIBLE literally, reject the TRINITY and understand JESUS CHRIST in ARIAN fashion. The millennium (see MILLENARIANISM) will begin after a final battle (Armageddon), following which the witnesses will rule with Christ. Other churches are rejected as ruled by Satan. Obedience to what is seen as divine law has led to clashes with governments, for example over refusal of military service and blood transfusions. Witnesses live plainly, refusing stimulants. They are active propagators of their faith, publishing the *Watchtower* magazine. [15; 62 vol. 7: 564–6; 133; 145: 341–7; 168; 182]

Jerusalem, Early Christianity at [XIII.A] Although JESUS gained many DISCIPLES in Galilee, the first Christian CHURCH was formed in Jerusalem shortly after his death. According to the *Acts of the Apostles* it grew speedily and met in several groups, some led by APOSTLES, others by Jesus' relatives, especially his brother James. Other groups, comprising Hellenists, renounced the TEMPLE order and, when forced to leave Jerusalem, promoted Christian advance in neighbouring provinces. The Jerusalem church became increasingly conservative. Demoralized by the execution of James in 62 CE, it left Jerusalem before the Roman siege eight years later. [5: 195–215, 349–72; 11: III, 757–68]

Jerusalem (in Islam) [XIX] To Muslims, this is the third most sacred city, after Mecca and Medina (see HARAMAIN). Occupied by the Arab armies in the time of the second CALIPH 'Umar (634–44), it was considered by the Muslims as holy because of the traditional interpretation of *sura* XVII, 1, in the QUR'AN, which speaks of the Prophet MUHAMMAD's night-journey (*mi'raj, isra'*), in the company of an angelic visitant, to 'the farthest place of prostration'. This became identified with the site of Solomon's temple in Jerusalem, certainly during the rule of the caliph 'Abd al-Malik (685–705), who in 691 built the Dome of the Rock on the site and

seems, perhaps for political reasons, to have encouraged pilgrimage (see HAJJ) to Jerusalem in addition to that to the Haramain. Muhammad probably followed Jewish practice in making Jerusalem the direction of prayer (*qibla*) in the first year or so after the migration from Mecca to Medina, before the Ka'ba at Mecca was made the devotional focus of the Islamic faith. Over the centuries Jerusalem has remained a place of veneration for Muslims, above all for those of the Syro-Palestinian region. [36; 38 'al-Kuds']

Jerusalem (in Judaism) [XXII] City in the Judaean hills and capital of the state of ISRAEL. Jerusalem became the centre of Israelite religion after its conquest from the Jebusites by King David (11th/10th centuries BCE) (see BIBLICAL HISTORY) and the building of the first TEMPLE there by his son Solomon. During the brief Babylonian captivity (6th century BCE) the holy city of Jerusalem was at the forefront of the captives' thoughts ('If I forget you, O Jerusalem . . .'; Psalm 137: 3–6). The revolt against Rome of 67–70 CE ended with the destruction of Jerusalem by the besieging Roman army [43: XXXII]. In the middle ages, under Christian and Muslim rule, the Jewish population of the city was small, but for the Jews of the diaspora it remained the holy city towards which all Jews turned in prayer (see HOLY LAND). After the war of 1948 the old city of Jerusalem was in Arab hands, the new and old sections only being united after the 1967 war. [11; 14 vol. 9: 1378]

Jesus [XIII.A] The GOSPEL narratives suggest Jesus was born in Bethlehem near JERUSALEM towards the end of the reign of Herod the Great (*c.*5 BCE). After describing his BAPTISM by JOHN THE BAPTIST, these narratives go on to focus on three aspects of Jesus' activity: his teaching, his miracles and his death. Jesus' teaching included PARABLES, some traditional forms of wisdom instruction (such as the Beatitudes, which urge a reversal of accepted values) and debates. The main topic of this teaching was the rule of GOD (*see* ESCHATOLOGY); the different gospel writers vary concerning whether he stressed such divine sovereignty could be experienced now or in the future and whether he taught that it was earthly or heavenly. His teaching shares most in common with what is known of some contemporary PHARISEE opinion, but there are also several parallels in the DEAD SEA SCROLLS. Jesus' miracles are usually understood as of two kinds. Few dispute that he had a ministry to the sick and marginalized, involving healings and exorcisms. Other miracles, such as the feeding of large crowds or walking on the water, are more difficult to understand, but were probably recounted because of what they said about Jesus' insight into and reflection of the activity of God. All four gospels describe the last week of Jesus' life in detail, but they cannot be harmonized into a single account. The titulus on the cross suggests that Jesus was sentenced to be crucified by Pontius Pilate, Roman governor of Judea, for political reasons. In drawing attention to the challenge of Jesus, various Jewish groups, especially the priests, seem to have brought religious charges against him. After his death his DISCIPLES claimed to experience his continuing presence among them, proclaiming that he had risen from the dead.

Little can be established with certainty about Jesus' self-understanding. It is far from clear that he intended to found a new religion, but his calling of 12 followers implies that he considered his activity to be a restoration of Israel. He seems to have accepted that his death was an inevitable part of this and that it would be of benefit to others in some way. Many roles have been used in order to make his activity more comprehensible: peasant, Galilean *Chasid* (pious man), rabbi, teacher of righteousness (*see* DEAD SEA SCROLLS), wandering Cynic preacher, zealot. The early Christians soon came to use a variety of titles of him in order to assert and define his messianic status and function. [4: 1316–28; 8; 10; 20; 26]

Jesus Fellowship [XXVIII] The Jesus Fellowship started in 1969 when members of the Bugbrooke Baptist Church, under the leadership of their Senior Pastor, Noel Stanton (1928?–), were 'filled with the Holy Spirit'. The Fellowship now has 70 'house families' throughout Britain in which married couples and single men and women, several of whom have committed themselves to a life of celibacy, live a community life. With the slogan 'Love, Power and Sacrifice' on their combat jackets, members of the Jesus Army (started in 1987) aggressively evangelize in towns and cities among the down-and-outs, saving drug addicts, criminals and lonely souls for JESUS. [5: 185–6; 19]

Jesus in Islam [XIX] In the QUR'AN, Jesus is called Isa and described as a *nabi* (prophet) and a *rasul* (messenger). He is the son of Maryam or Mary (who gives her name to a *sura* of the Qur'an and is venerated in popular Islam as an ideal of womanhood, along with the Prophet's daughter Fatima). The Qur'an treats at some length of his conception and birth to Mary, and regards his mission as confirming those of earlier prophets, as being attended by wondrous signs and miracles and as bringing his own sacred book, the *Injil* or Gospel, for his followers the Christians. His divine sonship is, however, specifically denied by the uncompromising unitarianism of Islam, as is his crucifixion; a gnostic interpretation here makes the person who died on the cross a substitute for Jesus. Jesus is also described as a *masih* (divinely anointed one), but the denial of his sonship to God means that he cannot be regarded as the promised Messiah in the Christian sense, even though a role is given to him, in Muslim eschatology, in connection with the MAHDI and with ANTI-CHRIST [101; 9; 38 s.v. 'Īsā; 86]

Jesus Movement [XXVIII] The Jesus Movement or 'Jesus Revolution' is an umbrella term used to describe the large number of conservative EVANGELICAL groups that emerged in the 1960s and spread throughout North America and Europe during the 1970s. The term 'Jesus freaks' was used to describe the members of these groups who, partly in reaction to the counter-culture of the 1960s, publicly displayed their 'rediscovery' of Jesus with Jesus posters, Jesus bumper stickers and 'Jesus Loves Me' T-shirts. Much of the movement was contained within the more evangelical or PENTECOSTAL branches of traditional Christianity, but several new groups (such as the Children of God, now known as THE FAMILY, the WAY INTERNATIONAL and the Christian World Liberation Front (CWLF) [26: VII–IX], which was militantly active in California) and communities (such as Shiloh [52]) were formed, some of these being viewed with utmost suspicion as dangerous heresies by some CULT-WATCHING GROUPS and more orthodox Christians. Also associated by some with the general trend were other movements such as the Catholic Charismatic Renewal movement and the Jews for Jesus, a movement which, through the Christianization of Jewish youth, has caused concern among orthodox Jewry [26: XII].

Jesus Prayer [XIII.D] A short prayer composed of phrases drawn from the New Testament. A common form of the prayer is: 'Lord Jesus Christ, Son of God, have mercy on me, a sinner.' The Jesus prayer can be used simply as a prayer. In EASTERN ORTHODOX monastic tradition it is normally repeated by each ordained monk a fixed number of times each day as a personally allocated measure. In HESYCHASM it is given a special role; the consciousness is carried inward with the breath to the region of the heart, and the Jesus prayer prayed there with intense attention. The prayer is at one and the same time a device for excluding thought and images and concentrating the attention, and an act of acknowledgement, orientation, worship, repentance and devotion, opening up the person who prays it to the transforming grace of Christ present in the depth of his or her own being. (*See also* MONASTICISM, CHRISTIAN; MYSTICISM, CHRISTIAN; STARETS). [13; 31; 32; 81; 82; 100]

Jihad [XIX] Literally, 'struggle': the term used in ISLAM for 'holy war', warfare against unbelievers, the underlying idea being that, since Islam is a universal religion, force may be used to expand its borders. *Jihad* ceases when DHIMMIS agree to accept the political authority of Islam, but continues against idolaters till they submit. It is a duty incumbent on all Muslims, hence usually considered as one of the PILLARS OF ISLAM. Increasingly, *jihad* has also been interpreted as warfare for the defence of Islam or else (especially in SUFISM) as a spiritual struggle against the evil in oneself. [20 s.v.; 38 'Djihād'; 104; 142: V]

Jingi-kan [XXI] The 'Office of Divine Affairs', first set up after the Taika Reform (646 CE), later defunct, and revived in 1871 by Emperor Meiji in order to control the SHINTO SHRINES and their property, which was then placed under national, prefectural or local jurisdiction [8: 27–32]. Priests were appointed as government officials; the emperor was the official head of the Shinto state (*see* KOKUTAI SHINTO). Short but violent suppression of BUDDHISM between 1868 and 1872 through a movement called Haibutsu Kishaku ('Throw out the Buddhas'), brought strong reaction, and resulted in a new bureau (1877) to accommodate both SHINTO and Buddhism. After the Second World War the Japanese constitution separated Shinto from the state and enforced the principle of religious freedom, a clause which was actually written into the constitution of 1889. [19: 48–52]

Jingu-ji [XXI] Japanese shrine-temples. Variously called *jingan-ji, jingo-ji, jinkyo-ji, jingu-in*, these were BUDDHIST temples, usually of either the TENDAI or the SHINGON sect, built to protect SHINTO SHRINES [19: 48–50; 35: 305] where Buddhist priests could chant *sutras* to enlighten the KAMI [21: 18]. They were often built within the precincts of the shrine itself. Their deities were mountain-spirits (*gongen*), their priests called *shaso* (shrine-priests). The oldest dated *jingu-ji* was built at Ise (*see* ISE JINGU) in 698, the home of Shinto. Once accepted there, hundreds were built elsewhere. By the 9th century they were ranked in importance just below the provincial temples for imperial favours. None is recorded as being built after 1627 and almost all were destroyed or renamed in the Meiji period (1868–1912) because it was thought that they disgraced the concept of the original *kami* of Japan.

Jinn (sing. *jinni*, English *genie*) [XIX] In Islam, spirit-beings originally created from fire. According to official doctrine, going back to the QUR'AN, they form an intermediate creation between mankind and the angels. They may be believers in Islam or unbelievers; the latter are therefore demons (*see* SATAN (IN ISLAM)). King Solomon is regarded as having commanded cohorts of *jinn* to build the Temple. Classical Islamic law defined the status of the *jinn* and even considered the question of intermarriage between humans and

jinn. In popular lore, they represent the untamed spirits of wild and desert places, normally invisible but capable of assuming corporeal form as men or animals, and are associated with the practice of magic and the service of talismanic formulae. [20 s.v.; 38 'Djinn'; 48: 50; 67 'Genii'; 77: x; 88; 116: 41–2]

Jiva [XX] JAIN term for the life-monad, most conventionally translated by 'soul' [4: 80–3; 10: 102–4]. All human beings, gods and those creatures living in the Jain hells possess a *jiva*, as do all forms of animal, plants, insects and even microscopic types of life. In essence, all *jivas* are alike, adapting themselves to the various karmically ordained bodies (*see* KARMA (JAIN DOCTRINE)) which house them through a process of expansion or contraction. Although their innate qualities of energy, bliss and omniscience, which for the non-liberated (*see* MOKSHA (JAIN DOCTRINE)) are occluded by karma, are the same, all *jivas* are differentiated from each other in liberation, and Jainism possesses no equivalent of the Hindu absolute (BRAHMAN).

Jnana Yoga [XVII] The way of knowledge: one of three or four alternative routes of spiritual development (YOGA) widely recognized in Indian thought. New ways of understanding human experience are intended to bring about some kind of transformation of fundamental motivation. Most of the HINDU DARSHANAS as well as the more wisdom-oriented forms of BUDDHISM would come into this category. Usually other forms of *yoga* would have an auxiliary role. [35: 101–4; 133: 143–5]

John the Baptist [XIII.A] Figuring in the New Testament (*see* BIBLE) as precursor of JESUS (whom he baptized), he was also a religious leader in his own right. A member of a Jewish priestly family, he preached in the Judaean wilderness. He called for national repentance and simple living because of the imminent arrival of the 'Coming One' who would execute divine judgement on Israel. Both in the New Testament and in the writings of JOSEPHUS he is described in prophetic terms; he urged his hearers to be baptized. His popularity (c.30 CE) excited the suspicion of Herod Antipas, tetrarch of Galilee and Peraea, who had him imprisoned and later put to death. His DISCIPLES survived as a distinct group for several decades, and MANDAEANS look back to him as their founder. [5: 145–54; 11: III, 887–99]

Jok [II] (*Juok*) The ancient NILOTIC name at once for God, for spirit and for spirits. Its use developed differently among the various Nilotic peoples. For some it has retained a monotheistic sense, as with the SHILLUK. With others, a basic monotheism has remained, but God is generally now known by another name: Nhialic (DINKA), Were or Nyasaye (southern Luo). *Jok* has in these cases retained rather its generic sense: spirit. The central Nilotic peoples (Acholi and Lango), conversely, continue to use the word *Jok*, but either lost or never had the strong monotheism characteristic of the NUER to the north and the Luo to the south. For them *Jok* refers only to a multiplicity of very limited and localized spirits, ancestral or otherwise, without any sense of unity or a pre-existing *Jok* (creator). Among the Nuer, Dinka and Padhola, too, evidence suggests a tendency away from the one creator towards 'spirits', though not comparably with Lango or Acholi. [6: 154–7; 13: 122–4; 45]

Jon Frum [xxvII] A diffused CARGO CULT on Tanna and adjacent islands in the New Hebrides (now Vanuatu), appearing intermittently since 1940. It focused on a mysterious Jon Frum, sometimes identified as the god of Tanna's highest moun-

tain, or (owing to contact with US troops) as the 'king of America', whence the cargo would come. The movement restored traditional customs, was anti-white and antimission (Presbyterian), in frequent conflict with the government, and was still active at independence in 1980. [12: 209–10; 26: 322–6; 27]

Jonang [xxxv] The Jonang tradition of Tibetan BUDDHISM was founded by Dolpopa Sherab Gyaltsen (1292–1361), a philosopher who propagated the controversial doctrine known as 'empty of any other' (Tibetan: *zhen tong*). Dolpopa was especially influenced by the notion of the 'BUDDHA-nature' (Sanskrit: *tatha-gatagarbha*; Tibetan: *desheg nyingpo*) inherent in all sentient beings, which is elaborated in the *Uttaratantrashastra*, a philosophical work attributed to MAITREYA. According to Dolpopa's theory, the *Prasangika* MADHYAMIKA view that the true nature of reality is itself empty (*rang tong*), being neither existent nor non-existent, is correct only at the level of relative truth. In ultimate truth the nature of reality is empty of anything apart from itself (*zhen tong*) and may therefore be described as ultimately existent [16].

The Jonang tradition was proscribed in the 17th century CE by the GELUG authorities, but their doctrines have been maintained by certain scholars of the KAGYU, SAKYA and NYINGMA schools.

Josephus [xxII] A 1st-century CE Jewish historian, Josephus Flavius was commander of the Jewish rebels in Galilee during the war against Rome, 67–70 CE. He defected to the Romans when he became disillusioned with Zealot ideology. He wrote a detailed account of the war in *The Jewish War*; an autobiographical sketch; a history of the Jews, *Jewish Antiquities*; and a work of Jewish apologetics, *Against Apion* [19: 52]. Josephus' writings were preserved by the Christian church. [14 vol. 10: 251]

Judaism [XXII] The religion of the Jewish people in the period following the destruction of the second TEMPLE in 70 CE, to be distinguished from the religion of the biblical and late second temple periods which centred on the sacrificial cult (*see* BIBLICAL HISTORY). The form which the religion of the Jews took in the era after 70 CE differed substantially in its ritual from that of the BIBLE. The basis of the new religious institutions developed by the councils of sages held first in Yavneh (70–132 CE) and then in Usha (post-140 CE) was the outlook of the PHARISEES [16: I–XII]. The shift in emphasis from temple cult to a religion of the home and SYNAGOGUE is characteristic of these councils. The role of the priest virtually disappeared and the religion became almost totally laicized, the RABBI being a teacher and authority on the HALAKHAH. The main ideas are of a teaching of divine origin, TORAH, contained in the Pentateúch and developed in the other books of the Hebrew BIBLE, which is accompanied by an oral teaching explaining the texts. This oral teaching is open to growth through biblical exegesis and MIDRASH. The commandments of God (MITZVAH) contained in Torah determine Jewish norms, and extend into every facet of the life of the individual and the community (KEHILLAH) [19: XI; 70: VIII–XII]. The belief in one god (THEISM) who will send a MESSIAH to usher in the redemption, who judges human actions, and who rewards and punishes humanity are integral themes of Jewish belief [14 vol. 10: 383]. In the 19th century reform movements sought to modify some of the beliefs and practices of traditional Judaism, which led to the setting up of REFORM and CONSERVATIVE Judaism as separate religious movements. [17; 38; 60]

Juggernaut [XVII] An anglicized form of Sanskrit *Jaggannatha*, 'Lord/Refuge of the World', an AVATARA of VISHNU, identified with KRISHNA, worshipped at Puri, Orissa. In an important annual festival, the image of Jagannatha is drawn through the streets in a huge temple-car (*see* MANDIRA). The idea that devotees formerly flung themselves to their deaths under the wheels of the 'Juggernaut car' dates back in the West to the 14th century, but there appears to be no Indian evidence for it.

Junrei [XXI] Medieval Japanese PILGRIMAGES. Pilgrimages from Kyoto to Nara, the 'southern capital' (*see* JAPAN, BUDDHISM IN), increased in popularity through the Mappo (End of the Law) period (1052 for Japan) and into the 13th century, as both SHINTO and Buddhist holy spots were visited, in particular the shrines at Kumano and the Nachi waterfalls and, later, Ise shrine (*see* ISE JINGU; SHINTO SHRINES). A contemporary writer said the roads were so thick with people they looked like ants. Internal peace in the Edo period (1615–1868) encouraged a revival of the practice, especially visits to the Kobo Daishi-related (*see* KUKAI) 88 temples of Shikoku, which required about two months, the 33 Kannon temples of the Kansai, and other routes. The physical effort was thought to induce communion with the BUDDHA, cures were sought, and even death on the trip was considered desirable for the aged. Buses and cars are used today.

K

Ka'ba [XIX] The approximately cube-shaped most holy shrine of ISLAM, regarded particularly as the House of God, and situated in the centre of Mecca within a sacred enclosure, the Haram, where special TABUS operate and from which unbelievers are excluded. It clearly existed before the coming of Islam, and Muslim tradition traces it back to the time of Abraham and Ishmael; it was cleansed of its idols by the Prophet MUHAMMAD and made the focal point of his new religion, Islam, one to which pilgrimage is required by the SHARI'A. In the eastern corner of the Ka'ba is set the Black Stone, a special object of veneration by pilgrims, who make a ritual circumambulation of the Ka'ba as part of the pilgrimage rites. The whole shrine is covered by a richly woven covering, the *kiswa*, traditionally provided by the ruling power in Egypt. In the courtyard of the Ka'ba is the well Zamzam, whose water has a special charisma for pilgrims. [38 s.v.; 47]

Kabbalah [XXII] The 'received tradition' of Jewish mysticism, particularly those forms of mystical teachings which were developed in the middle ages in south-west Europe, and later on in the Galilean city of Safed in Palestine [14 vol. 10: 489]. The main text of the Kabbalah is the ZOHAR, written down in 13th-century Spain [61: v]. Unlike exoteric Judaism the Kabbalah teaches that the creation of the world took place through a series of emanations from the Godhead or *Ein Sof* (*see* COSMOGONY. These emanatory structures, the 10 *sefirot* (*see* SEFIRAH, are the inner constitution of all reality as well as of the divine manifestation. They represent a finely balanced harmony enabling the flow of divine energy to sustain humanity and nature. Human sins affect this harmony, disturbing it and allowing the potential for evil within it to become active. The Kabbalah reinterprets all the main beliefs and rituals of JUDAISM in terms of its esoteric theology, which has pantheistic overtones. Its powerful images appealed to mystics and non-mystics alike. The most important development of Zoharic ideas was the Kabbalah of Isaac Luria (1534–72), which introduced a strong messianic (*see* MESSIAH) element, and led to messianic movements of a mystical type. (*See also* SITRA ACHRA.) [11; 61: VII, VIII; 62: 37; 70: VI]

Kachinas [V] Among PUEBLO Indians of the North American south-west, *kachinas* serve as the symbolic representations, often in human form, of the many powers and manifestations of nature and of the ancestors [3]. Myths relate that, in primordial times, humankind and the *kachinas* lived together, the latter freely bestowing their blessing of rain and general prosperity. Now, through the agency of human impersonators who dress and don masks to represent them, the *kachinas* return for part of the year to serve as intermediaries between man and the principal Pueblo deities [26: III]. The HOPI and the Zuni tribes have the greatest number of distant *kachinas*, who appear at specific annual celebrations.

Kadam [xxxv] The Kadam tradition of Tibetan BUDDHISM originated in the 11th century CE from the teachings of the Indian master Atisha (979–1053) and his Tibetan disciple Dromton (1005–64) [3]. During his residence in Tibet from 1040 till his death in 1053 Atisha emphasized the practice of *sutra* and TANTRA (2) doctrines in a 'graded path' (*lam rim*) and transmitted a series of instructions on *bodhicitta* ('thought of enlightenment') known as 'mind-training' (*lobjong*). Although the Kadam sect ceased to exist after the 14th century these teachings have been preserved within the GELUG and KAGYU schools.

Kagyu [xxxv] The Kagyu (more correctly, Dagpo Kagyu) tradition of Tibetan BUDDHISM was established in the 11th and 12th centuries CE by the three successive masters, Marpa the translator (1012–97), who studied TANTRA (2) in India; his student, Milarepa (1040–1123) [12]; and the latter's disciple Gampopa (1079–1153) who was heir both to Marpa and Milarepa's lineage and also the *sutra* teaching of the KADAM lineage. [17] After Gampopa's death the tradition split into four principal branches, Karmapa, Baram, Tshalpa and Phagmo Drupa, from the last of which eight sub-sects subsequently emerged. Under the leadership of the 17 incarnations of the Karmapa Lama, the Karma Kagyu branch has been the most extensive of the four chief lines. [21]

The most prized teaching of all the various Kagyu sects is the system of theory and meditation known as 'the great seal' (Sanskrit: *mahamudra*: Tibetan: *chag chen*) which Marpa received from his Indian GURUS Naropa and Maitripa. The term 'great seal' is derived from the Tantras and refers to the meditative realization that the world of appear-

ances and mind itself are inseparable and naturally empty. Thus all phenomena of SAMSARA and NIBBANA are 'sealed' with emptiness [2].

Although the Kagyu tradition is especially famed for its emphasis on devotion and meditation, it has also produced talented scholars such as the eighth Karmapa, Mikyo Dorje (1507–54), and Jamgon Kongtrul (1811–99), both of whom upheld the theory of 'the great middle' (Tibetan: *uma chenpo*), which represents a synthesis of the MADHYAMIKA and YOGACARA philosophies.

In recent years the Karma Kagyu sect, under the direction of the 16th Karmapa, Ranjung Rigpe Dorge, has established numerous centres in the UK, France and North America.

Kakon [xvi] (Greek: 'evil') Death is an inescapable evil, part of the human condition. But other evils, disease, painful old age, harsh toil, etc., it was thought, might have been avoided. One version of their origin tells of five successive 'races' of generally deteriorating merit and circumstances, the last one being 'our own'. In another version a quarrel between Zeus (*see* THEOI) and Prometheus (*see* THNETOI ANTHROPOI), who tried to cheat the gods on behalf of mankind, resulted in the estrangement between men and gods. The latter created the first woman, Pandora, who brought evil to men just by her presence; in another version she opened a jar and released diseases and banes upon the world. In Orphism (*see* ORPHEUS), mankind sprang from the Titans' (*see* COSMOS) ashes and carries the guilt of the Titans' murder of Dionysos-Zagreus, for which it must atone. [16: 43–56; 20: 131–43]

Kalam [xix] The medieval Islamic term for scholastic and apologetic theology, literally meaning 'discourse' but early acquiring the sense of 'disputation, controversy'. The defence of the faith by rational arguments, the stilling of believers' doubts and the strengthening of their belief were thus the aims of what became a highly sophisticated dialectical system employed, for example, against the Mu'tazilites (*fl.* later 8th–10th centuries), the conservative literalists and the Hellenizing philosophers. Two main schools of *kalam*, the Ash'ari and the Maturidi, emerged from the 10th century onwards [71: 375–515]. In recent times, its *raison d'être* has virtually disappeared, and Islamic modernists have tended to be practical people and reformers rather than apologetic theologians. [38 s.v.; 87: 153–242; 107: v]

Kali [XVII] ('Black') A Hindu goddess whose worship is perhaps one of the most misunderstood features of HINDUISM. Kali is said to have emanated from the beautiful goddess DURGA on the battlefield in order to conquer an army of demons (ASURAS), devouring them or drinking their blood. In art she is black or dark blue, with lolling tongue and dishevelled hair, garlanded with corpses and severed heads. Sometimes she dances on the lifeless body of her husband SHIVA, dramatizing the teaching that the male deity needs his female energy (SHAKTI) in order to function within creation [4: 219–20; 89: 54, 61–9]. Her most famous temple is at Kalighat in her city of Calcutta (*Kalikata*), where buffaloes are sacrificed to her, the practice being justified by the belief that beings who die in this way immediately obtain liberation (MOKSHA). Despite her terrifying appearance, Kali is loved as a mother by her worshippers (*see* BHAKTI), who included the 19th-century Bengali mystic and poet Ramakrishna [89: 77–9]. The devotional fervour with which she was worshipped at that time is vividly depicted by Satyajit Ray in his film *Devi*, 'The Goddess' (1960), in which a pious young woman comes to be seen as an incarnation of Kali.

The cult that forms round her leads to devastating psychological conflict, between traditional and westernized members of her family, but above all within the woman herself, who in her quiet humility cannot cope with the role that has been thrust upon her.

Kalpa Sutra [XX] Important SHVETAMBARA JAIN scripture [4: 57–9; 7: 217–311]. This text, which may date in part from about the 2nd century BCE, contains a biography of MAHAVIRA as well as historically important material about early ascetic lineages. It takes its name from its delineation of a variety of behavioural regulations (*kalpa*) for monks. The Kalpa Sutra's main significance for Shvetambara Jains lies in its recitation during the important annual festival of PARYUSHAN.

Kama [XVII] The name of the Hindu god of love [12: 317f], and also, together with ARTHA, DHARMA and MOKSHA, one of the four goals of life in Hindu tradition. Kama represents 'the pursuit of love of pleasure', both sensual and aesthetic. It relates closely to the way of life (ASHRAMA) of the married householder. Provision is therefore made 'for its regulated enjoyment rather than its suppression, and thus for the development of a well-rounded personality' [12: 258]. The texts in which the necessary guidance and techniques are set out are the *Kama-Shastra*, and *Kama-Sutra* of Vatsyayana, the latter written in the early centuries of the Christian era [12: 172]. These are represented as having been originally promulgated by the gods and sages, long ago, as part of a 'comprehensive code of conduct'. A close relationship between cosmic creation (envisaged in terms of the union of gods and goddesses) and human procreation is characteristic of Hindu religious ideas. The importance of sexual activity and erotic technique for the satisfaction of both husband

and wife is the basis of the classical texts.

Kami [XXI] SHINTO deities. Sacred objects, divine beings, natural phenomena or venerated symbols [14: 5–6; 19: 13–31; 32: 6–9], the *kami* are described as having a parent–child (*oya–ko*) relationship to people or, better, an ancestor–descendant relationship [21: 14–15]. Eighteenth-century writers were the first to attempt a definition: Motoori Norinaga (1730–1801) said that they were extraordinary, endowed with high virtuosity and inspired awe [21: 37–8]. While omnipresent in nature, associated in particular with specific mountains (*see* SACRED MOUNTAINS), rocks, waterfalls and other features, they are not all-powerful, nor are they all benign.

The *kami* have been classified as *amatsu-kami* and *kunitsu-kami*: celestial spirits which remain eternal and above, and terrestrial spirits which dispense benefactions to, or discipline, people on earth. They are variously said to have nomadic and agricultural sources, or Yamato tribal and Izumo tribal origins. But the classification copes with only the small number – traditionally, there are 8 million – which have been identified by name and with specific activities and human needs. The chief *kami* is AMATERASU-OMIKAMI, the sun-goddess, enshrined at ISE JINGU. Historical conditions continued to produce more *kami*, such as deified statesmen and military figures; and, since the Meiji period (1868–1912), all the soldiers killed in wars are now buried at Yasukuni shrine in Tokyo and referred to as *kami* [19: 441–59].

Kamma-tthana [XI] In THERAVADA BUDDHIST meditation practice (BHAVANA) *kamma-tthana*, originally an occupation such as trade or agriculture, may mean either the particular mental object which is the subject of practice or a given meditational path. In the first sense BUD-DHAGHOSA lists 40 *kamma-tthana* for SAMATHA meditation practice, classified according to their potential for development and their suitability for differing psychological types [15: 116–21; 96: 29–30]. Similar notions are found in north Indian Buddhist writings; the *Abhidharmakosha*, for example, recommends developing awareness of ugliness for the passionate, loving-kindness (*maitri*; Pali: *metta*) for the aggressive, and mindfulness of breath for the thought-ridden.

Kammu [XXI] The Emperor Kammu (736–806 CE) was Prince Yamabe, the first son of Emperor Konin, who ascended the Japanese throne in 781 and moved the capital to break the power of the Nara clergy (*see* JAPAN, BUDDHISM IN). As the last of the strong early emperors, he cut the income of the temples, defrocked and disciplined many priests and built new cities, first Nagaoka in 784, then Heian (Kyoto) in 794, obliging the temples to remain behind. Kammu was head of the Confucian academy (*see* CONFUCIUS) and supported the Buddhist temples of his choice, sending SAICHO and KUKAI to China. He successfully concluded the century-old war with the ancient, non-Japanese people, the Emishi (now called Ainu) in north Japan.

Kanjur [XXXV] The Tibetan canonical collection of the teachings of the BUDDHA, numbering 108 volumes and arranged and edited by the historian Buton (1290–1364). It contains the three *pitakas* of *sutra*, *abhidharma* (*see* ABHIDHAMMA) and VINAYA as well as various TANTRAS (2) revealed by the Buddha. The *sutra-pitaka* (SUTTA-PITAKA) includes both HINAYANA and MAHAYANA discourses.

The tantric collection preserved in the Kanjur includes only the 'new' Tantras diffused in Tibet from the 10th century onwards. The 'old' Tantras of the Nyingmapa

(NYINGMA) tradition are collected in the series known as *The One Hundred Thousand Tantras of the old Tradition*, edited by Jigme Lingpa (1729–97). The companion collection to the *Kanjur* is the *Tenjur*, a collection of 225 volumes of treatises and commentaries composed by various Indian masters.

Karah Prasad [XXXIII] The 'sacramental' food distributed in GURDWARAS and at the conclusion of important SIKH RITUALS. The food (*prasad*), which should be prepared in a large iron pan (*karah*), comprises equal parts of coarsely refined wheat-flour, sugar and ghee. The procedure to be followed in preparing it is detailed in *Sikh Rahit Maryada*, the current version of the KHALSA code (RAHIT-NAMA) [8: 173–4; 30: 80]. When distributed it must be offered to all, regardless of CASTE, creed or status. [26: 67–8, 86–7]

Karma [XVII] (Pali: *kamma*) 'deeds', 'work': an important concept in south Asian religions, shared by HINDUISM, BUDDHISM and JAINISM, though interpreted differently in detail. (For the Jain view, *see* KARMA (JAIN DOCTRINE).) *Karma* is specifically intentional action, carried out with some underlying attachment, and viewed as determining one's fortunes in the future, either in the same life or in a future one; and, on a deeper level, as binding one to SAMSARA, the round of death and rebirth.

Although Hindu texts such as the PURANAS seem to describe the law of *karma* in terms of strict cause and effect, with detailed descriptions of the evil rebirths consequent upon wrong action, in practice their views are less fatalistic, since they also prescribe powerful acts of merit, such as pilgrimages (TIRTHA-YATRA) or acts of worship (PUJA), designed to wipe out the effects of bad *karma*.

Buddhism, too, rejects a fatalistic view of *karma*. Certain good states of mind are believed to have a powerful effect in minimizing the effects of previous actions, and some of the ARAHATS, through the BUDDHA's teaching, are believed to have achieved Nirvana (*see* NIBBANA) despite previous bad *karma*. Both Hindus and Buddhists also accept the possibility of the transfer of merit (the result of good *karma*) from one being to another [93: 165–92].

The concept of *karma* has been adopted into Western NEW AGE philosophy, though sometimes with a degree of misunderstanding. The word is sometimes used in the sense of 'destiny', or the results of past actions, which are properly *karma-vipaka*, the maturing or working out of *karma*. Often, too, there is a belief that the incarnated being automatically makes progress towards liberation (MOKSHA) through learning the lessons of rebirth in different bodies. Indian thinkers either reject this idea, or regard such a process as impossibly slow: the way to liberation for them involves swimming upstream, against the current of *karma* [93: 1–37].

Karma (Jain Doctrine) [XX] Like HINDUISM and BUDDHISM, JAINISM teaches that action (*karman*) has consequences and that the parameters of existence of all creatures can be explained by their behaviour in past lives. In its very earliest phase, Jainism took a rigorous attitude towards *karma*, claiming that all actions of body, speech and mind, spontaneous or otherwise, set up negative consequences, with the task of the committed ascetic being to mute the physical and psychological behaviour as much as possible. However, this approach gradually became modified to take into account the influence of the intention lying behind any action. Uniquely, Jainism envisages *karma* as a material substance attracted to each soul (JIVA) through vibrations brought about by activity and then, somewhat mysteriously, clinging to it, thus impeding the soul's innate qualities.

Jain *karma* theory became highly complex by the medieval period. Its basic structure involves two varieties of *karma*, the 'harming' and the 'non-harming', each divided into four types. The former impedes the soul's perception, knowledge and energy respectively, and also brings about delusion, while the latter is responsible for the reborn soul's physical and mental circumstances, longevity, spiritual potential and experience of pleasant and unpleasant sensations. [4: 83–7; 5; 10: IV]

Karma Yoga [XVII] The way of action: one of three or four alternative routes of spiritual development (YOGA) widely recognized in Indian thought. The word *karma* means originally sacrificial or ritual action (cf. MIMAMSA), then performance of one's CASTE duties and worldly activities in general. *Karma yoga* is the path of development, either through perfect performance of religious activities or through the carrying out of affairs without concern for the fruits of action, i.e. motiveless and spontaneous undertaking of one's duties. [137: 16–20]

Karttikeya [XVII] 'Son of the *Krittika* (Pleiades)', or Skanda, 'the Leaper': a Hindu god of great importance, particularly in south India. Accounts of his birth differ, but he is generally now regarded as the son of SHIVA and PARVATI, born to conquer the demon (ASURA) Taraka as general of the army of the gods. He was nursed by the six goddesses of the Pleiades, and in art often has six heads and twelve hands: he rides a peacock (his VAHANA) and holds a spear. Sometimes he and his brother GANESHA appear as children in a family group with their parents. [4: 218, 223; 92: 104–15; 161–8; and cover: 109: 49]

Karuna [XI] Compassion; along with wisdom (PRAJNA), the two elements which are cultivated by the BODHISATTVA and attained in their highest degree by a BUDDHA (*see also* ANUKAMPA).

Various meditations are used in MAHAYANA Buddhism in order to develop first non-discrimination and then universal great compassion (*mahakaruna*). Common are: (1) The six causes and the one effect – in infinite rebirths all sentient beings must have been one's mother, the great kindness of mothers, all our 'mother sentient beings' are now suffering, great love for them, and great compassion, a realization of our duty and responsibility to help them, and finally the one effect – only by becoming a fully enlightened BUDDHA can one fully repay this debt to all beings; (2) Exchanging self and others – all sentient beings are alike in wanting happiness and the avoidance of suffering, the faults of cherishing oneself rather than others, the benefits of doing the reverse, and actually exchanging self and others – replacing spontaneous self-cherishing with cherishing others. Another common compassion meditation is 'taking and giving' – taking on the suffering of others with the in-breath, and breathing out happiness. [101: 197–204]

Kashrut [XXII] A general term for Jewish dietary requirements [14 vol. 6: 26]. JUDAISM considers the following categories as *kosher*, or fit to be eaten: (1) animals which chew the cud and have cloven hoofs e.g. cattle, sheep, goats, deer; (2) birds which are not birds of prey, and about which Jews have a tradition of their being eaten; (3) fish having fins and scales; (4) locusts of certain types. Before being eaten animals and birds have to be ritually slaughtered, examined to ensure they are not diseased, and animals have to have the sciatic nerve excised (*see* ANIMAL SLAUGHTER). Domesticated animals have the hindquarter fat removed. The blood must be removed from all meat by washing and salting, and meat cannot be cooked or eaten with milk [70: 201]. Indeed, different crockery and cutlery are used for meat and milk, and a time interval must elapse after eating meat before milk products can be eaten [23]. On PASSOVER (*see* CHAGIM) all food containing leaven is forbidden.

Kathina [XI] A BUDDHIST ceremony that takes place annually in October/November at the end of the rains retreat (*see* ASALHA). This ancient ceremony, prescribed by the SANGHA's monastic rule (VINAYA), centres on the formal offering of the *kathina* robe – a monk's robe specially prepared for the occasion – by laity to the Sangha in each local monastery (VIHARA). The offering of the *kathina* robe is an important expression of the laity's (*see* UPA-SAKA) commitment to supporting the Sangha, while the Sangha's acceptance of it is an acknowledgement of their responsibility to live as virtuous monks in accordance with the rules of Vinaya.

Katonda [II] This, the chief GANDA name for God, means 'creator'. Similar forms are widely used among other BANTU peoples as a secondary God-name, e.g. Matunda among Kimbu, Nyamwezi and Sukuma in Tanzania. Unlike some African God-names, whose meaning is lost or is strongly symbolical, Katonda has a high theological sense and goes with an absence of anthropomorphic myth. It represents one basic theme of Bantu theology, as IRUVA with its sun symbolism represents another.

Kehillah [XXII] The Jewish community, usually centring on a SYNA-GOGUE [1: III]. The lay leadership are elected to office by the members, and usually comprise a president, treasurer and wardens. In a traditional community only males are eligible for office. The RABBI of a *kehillah* is employed to teach,

preach, supervise ritual requirements and perform pastoral duties. The CANTOR will lead the prayers in the synagogue and officiate with the rabbi. The community might also employ a ritual slaughterer (*see* ANI-MAL SLAUGHTER; KASHRUT); a scribe to write and mend TORAH scrolls, and teachers for the religious school (*cheder*). Although the family is the most important unit of Judaism, much of the religion is dependent on communal life [14 vol. 5: 808]. All committed Jews would belong to a *kehillah* of one type or another, and traditional Jews will live within walking distance of fellow community members in order to be able to attend synagogue services on Sabbaths (SHABBAT) and festivals (CHAGIM). [58; 70: 207]

Kes-dhari [XXXIII] 'One who wears hair'. SIKHS are generally identified by uncut hair (*kes* or *kesh*). Not all Sikhs can be recognized in this way, however, for the KHALSA rule forbidding the cutting of hair is not accepted by every Sikh. There are five varieties of Sikh identity. Amrit-dhari Sikhs are initiated members of the Khalsa, having received *amrit* or the sanctified water of initiation. There is no way of accurately estimating the proportion of Sikhs who are Amrit-dhari, though 15% is sometimes hesitantly mentioned. Strictly speaking, only the Amrit-dhari Sikhs constitute the Khalsa, though in practice the second group is usually included. This comprises Kes-dhari Sikhs, those who observe some or all of the Khalsa RAHIT (always including the uncut hair) but do not take initiation. All Amrit-dhari Sikhs are also Kes-dhari, but only a minority of Kes-dharis are Amrit-dharis. The third group, the Sahaj-dhari Sikhs, cut their hair and do not observe the Rahit. The fourth group consists of those who belong to Khalsa families (bearing the name Singh for men or Kaur for women) but cut their hair. This group has no satisfactory name, although the term

Mona (shaven) Sikhs is sometimes used. Finally there are Patit (fallen) Sikhs, a term which strictly designates Amrit-dharis who have committed one of the four *kurahats* (serious lapses of the Rahit). It is however, loosely used to cover all Kes-dharis who cut their hair. [29: 110–15]

Kevalin [xx] In JAIN teaching, the individual who has achieved omniscience, the supreme and unique (*kevala*) knowledge which characterizes enlightenment. The most recent *kevalins* in this world era are the disciples of the 24th TIRTHANKARA MAHAVIRA. There was a dispute among the Jains as to the extent to which the *kevalin* functioned like unenlightened human beings, with the DIGAMBARA sect claiming that he did not need to consume food. [1: 49, 75–7]

Khalq [xix] Creation, in ISLAM. The orthodox, Qur'anic view is of a creation *ex nihilo* and in time by the pre-existing and eternal God (ALLAH), fashioning heaven and earth within six days. Authorities vary on what was the first thing created, whether the Pen, which set down the divine decree and all that could be brought into being, or the light and the darkness. Some later theologians put forward the idea of continuous creation, that God's sustaining power requires a fresh creative act at each moment of his creatures' existence. Others, influenced by NEOPLATONISM, regarded creation as an act of emanation from God, an epiphany of him, so that beings are mirrors of the divine essence. SHI'ISM introduced the idea of a pre-eternal creation of forms of light, whose temporal manifestations became the Prophet MUHAMMAD and the IMAMS. An important theological controversy of medieval times revolved round the question of the createdness or otherwise of the QUR'AN. The orthodox view, which came to prevail, was that it was

eternally pre-existent with God himself. [38 'Khalk'; 67 'Creation']

Khalsa [xxxiii] The SIKH order instituted by GURU GOBIND SINGH and inaugurated with an impressive ceremony held at Anandpur in 1699 (*see* GURUS) [14: vi; 15: vii]. The traditional reason given for the founding of the order has been the Guru's decision to provide his followers with a militant and highly visible identity, needed in order to nerve them for imminent trials. Although this explanation may still be valid it must be supplemented. Recent research has shown that although the word *khalsa* derives from the Arabic/Persian *khalisa*, 'pure', it relates to a secondary meaning, namely lands under direct crown control. The Guru's concern was to demolish the authority of the *masands*, deputies appointed by earlier Gurus to supervise an increasingly scattered flock of disciples. The *masands* had become corrupt, and it was to break their power that the Guru summoned all Sikhs to come under his direct personal control (*khalsa*) [11: 60–1; 14: 113–15]. Entry into the Khalsa is effected by an initiation rite (*amrit sanskar*) in which five devout Sikhs (*panj piare*) administer baptism using sweetened water stirred with a two-edged sword (*khande di pahul*). All who accept baptism must vow to live according to the RAHIT (the Khalsa code). Male initiates add 'Singh' to their given names and women add 'Kaur'. [30: 83–6]

Kharijites [xix] A sect which arose in early ISLAM, diverging after 657 from the Sunni majority (*see* SUNNA) over the question of politico-religious leadership in the community and such theological issues as the definition of the true believer and the relative importance of faith and works. A violent and radical force in the first centuries of the CALIPHATE, at times posing a threat to its stability, this activist aspect gradually subsided and left only an intellectual strand in Islamic thought [38 s.v; 78: II; 135: v]. However, some small groups stemming from the Kharijites have survived into modern times, notably the Ibadi communities of certain parts of north Africa, the east Asian coastlands and Oman. [8: XVI; 38 'Ibā-diyya']

Kimbanguist Church [XXVII] A movement known officially as L'Église de Jésus Christ par le Prophète Simon Kimbangu. It stems from the brief ministry of Simon Kimbangu (1889–1951), a Baptist catechist in the Lower Congo in 1921. He was wrongly sentenced to death for sedition (a punishment commuted to life imprisonment). Despite persecution for over 30 years, the movement is now the largest independent church in Africa, claiming 3 million members in Zaire and adjacent countries. One of Kimbangu's three sons, Diangienda Kuntima (1918–92), was spiritual head of the church for many years and encouraged theological training, assisted by the Swiss scholar, Marie-Louise Martin, and other expatriates. He was succeeded by the youngest son, Dialungana Kiangani, and the church embarked upon a national programme under the rubrics of 'Work and morality'. In 1970 it became a member of the World Council of Churches, and was later accorded privileged public status by the Mobutu government.

Kingship (Ancient Near East) [VIII] The kings of the ancient Near East ruled by divine consent; leaders in war, law and religion, their prime obligation was to serve the national god. The king, whose victory on earth merely reflected his god's success in heaven, was the god's high priest (see TEMPLES (ANCIENT NEAR EASTERN)), and in Babylon, in an annual ceremony (part of the New Year FESTIVAL), he had to 'grasp the hand of MARDUK', the national god,

in his temple, thus affirming his right to rule.

The king was the least static element in SUMERIAN society [23: 23–5] – the ruler of the most powerful city seized overall leadership until replaced by another – but Sargon of Agade (see ASSYRIANS) made provincial rulers accountable to him as overlord, establishing a centralized authority. Later, Hammurabi of Babylon (see HAMMURABI'S CODE) [7] drew up his code at the chief god's behest. In Elam (see ELAMITES) [15; 17], the kings were priests who held authority from the gods; descent passed through the female line and, if a king died, his brother usually inherited the throne and the royal widow. King and queen made daily donations at the temple. In-Shushinak was the royal god. Rival rulers of this period depended on omens (see DIVINATION (ANCIENT NEAR EASTERN)) in military action, the armies moving only under the leadership of a 'seer', who preceded them into battle.

The kings of Assyria, modelling their empire on Sargon's concept of centralized rule, were priests of Ashur. Seal impressions show the king receiving divine commands from the god [5], for it was believed that a ruler held power from the deity whose turn it was to rule the world. The kings had large harems, but one queen became chief consort, albeit any son could be chosen as heir. Several rulers built up libraries of religious and other texts [11].

The kings of Hattusas (c.1740–1460 BCE) welded together isolated city communities, creating the 'Land of Hatti', later to become the centre of the HITTITE empire [12]. Originally elective, the kingship was endowed with superhuman powers in the Empire period (c.1460–1190 BCE). Ancestral rulers received cults, but kings were not deified while alive. Queens had strong, independent roles, the queen mother retaining pre-eminence until her death [13: 63–6]. As chief priest, the king visited the main religious centres of his realm, and performed a royal ritual for the national god in his temple, preceded by a royal toilette.

Kingship, Sacral (Israelite and Early Christian) [XIII.A] The kings of Israel were sacral in the sense that they were anointed by Yahweh (GOD) through priestly or prophetic agency and were theoretically sacrosanct; but they were Yahweh's servants, subject to his law, not divine kings, like some ancient Near Eastern rulers (*see* KINGSHIP (ANCIENT NEAR EAST)). They originally exercised priestly privileges, but eventually lost these. The ideal of sacral kingship survived in Israel's expectation of the MESSIAH. JESUS claimed no royal status, but many of his followers later acknowledged him as the Davidic Messiah (Christ) and as a successor to Melchizedek, an early Jerusalemite priest-king. [10; 11: IV, 40–8; 22: II, 488–554]

Kitawala [XXVII] A widespread movement in central Africa under the influence of American JEHOVAH'S WITNESSES, or the Watch Tower (hence *tawala*) Bible and Tract Society. African versions arose in northern Nyasaland (now Malawi) under Elliott Kamwana from 1907 until he was deported in 1909, and in the then Northern Rhodesia (now Zambia) and Belgian Congo (now Zaire) under Nyirenda, who claimed to be Mwana Lesa (Son of God) and was executed in 1926. In spite of frequent persecution, the movement persists. [2: 57–8; 12: 37–9; 26: 83–4, 253–4]

Knights Templars [XXIV] A religious military order founded in 1119 at Jerusalem to protect Christian pilgrims against Muslim attack. Quartered originally near the site of the TEMPLE, they lived under monastic rule, but their activities were mainly military and administrative. Important in maintaining the Latin king-doms in the Holy Land, they also held property in Europe and acted as international bankers, conducting their internal affairs in strict secrecy. After the CRUSADES they lost their military importance and in 1312 Philip IV of France, jealous of the order's wealth and power, persuaded Pope Clement V to suppress it. The Grand Master Jacques de Molay and others were accused, probably falsely, of homosexuality, blasphemy and idolatry, and were executed in 1314 [1]. The mystery surrounding the Templars' beliefs and practices, and speculation aroused by their remarkable circular churches, have led to their being claimed as ancestors by several modern OCCULT and Masonic groups (*see* FREEMASONRY). The Knights of the Order of the Hospital of St John the Baptist was founded about the same time as the Templars by a monk named Gerard. The lives of these knights were devoted to the care and cure of sick pilgrims but, like the Templars, this religious order fell into disrepute. A surviving descendant today is the St John's Ambulance Brigade.

Kogi Religion [XXIII] The Kogi, together with the Ika and Sanha, are the contemporary descendants of the ancient Chibcha-speaking Tairona of the Sierra Nevada area of Colombia. The Kogi universe consists of nine different levels, from zenith to nadir, and is shaped like a spindle, centred on the all-important vertical axis. Like an immense whirling spindle, the universe weaves life from its male (the central shaft) and female (the whorl) elements, spinning the thread from which the universe's fabric is woven. The beam of light that, over the course of the year, is cast on to the floor of the temple is considered to be the pattern of life woven by the sun in the universe. A highly respected class of tribal priests, the *mama*, after some 18 years of training, learn the lore and practice necessary to maintain *yuluka*, harmony or balance, in the universe as the 'Law of the Mother'. The essence of their task is to turn back the sun when it threatens to burn the world, or to avert rain when it threatens to drown it. The cardinal directions of the universe are associated with colours, emotions, animals, mythical beings, the ideal village-plan, the structure of the ceremonial house with its four hearths, four principal clans, and so on. The centre of space is the place where the *mama* speak with God. [27]

Kokutai Shinto [XXI] (National Structure Shinto) Emperor-worship in Japan had its recognizable beginning in the claims made by the 8th-century writers for the divine origins of the earliest rulers, the Sun line [19: 389–425]. This ultimately led to veneration of the places where certain rulers lived, such as the Kashihara shrine (*see* SHINTO SHRINES) in Nara prefecture for 'emperor' Jimmu, and a few emperors became the object of particular cults, such as Emperor Ojin, known as HACHIMAN. By the 19th century all of the tombs identified with the royal family had come under the jurisdiction of the Imperial Household Agency and have since been treated as sacred. Westerners speak of Tennoism (*tenno* = emperor). Officially in Kokutai Shinto, the emperor, as the direct descendant of the sun-goddess AMATERASU-OMIKAMI, embodies the *kami* spirit as head of the SHINTO state and spoke with infallible authority. The concept has suffered historically through enfeeblement of the imperial system, but was revived by a rising nationalism among 17th-century writers, coming to a climax after Emperor Meiji took power from the Tokugawa in 1868, and was given moral validity in the Imperial Rescript on Education in 1890 [8: 108–10]. In 1945 the emperor publicly renounced his divinity.

Konkokyo [XXVI] At the time when Kawate Bunjiro (1814–83) was growing up, many people in what is now Okayama Prefecture, Japan, feared the *kami* Konjin. They held that Konjin moved about in accordance with times and seasons, and that humans who interfered with his movements would be chastised in one of two ways: by seven deaths in the family if the violation was unwitting, or by the elimination of the household if the violation was witting. When members of his family began to die one after the other, and when he himself became gravely ill, Kawate felt that he had somehow offended Konjin. In prayer he apologized for his errors and entrusted himself to this *kami*, whereupon Konjin showed himself to be not the malevolent being of popular belief but a deity of grace and love. Kawate announced that this *kami* was now to be addressed as Tenchi Kane no Kami or as Konko Daijin. In 1859 he declared that the *kami* had taken possession of him, and that he himself was henceforth to be known as Konko Daijin. From that time until his death in 1883, Konko Daijin opened his home to people wishing to consult about personal problems. He devoted his waking hours to *toritsugi*, the task of mediating between people and the *kami*. Konkokyo was formally organized as a religious body in 1885, and its head church is in Konkocho, a small town of religious character that faces the Inland Sea. *Toritsugi* remains the chief distinguishing feature of the sect. People with problems of any kind are welcome to receive *toritsugi* either at the head church or at any of the nearly 1,700 branch churches. Today Konkokyo has nearly 450,000 members and several overseas churches. Most overseas members are people who trace their ancestry to Japan. [10: IX, 182–3; 13: 133–50]

Korea, Christianity in [XIII.B] Christianity has experienced rapid growth in Korea in the 20th century, especially since 1960. The Christian population of South Korea in 1990 was between 10 million and 14 million, with 2 million ROMAN CATHOLICS and 8–12 million PROTESTANTS. Christianity is now the strongest single religion in South Korea, having overtaken BUDDHISM and Shamanism (*see* SHAMAN). The earliest Christian missionaries were Jesuits from China in 1785 (Pope John Paul II visited Seoul for the bicentenary in 1985), but for the next 100 years Catholicism grew very slowly. Meanwhile, sporadic Protestant attempts to enter Korea from Manchuria made little headway. However, in 1882 Japanese aggression forced 'the hermit kingdom' to forge an alliance with the USA. This signalled the beginning of a series of determined evangelistic campaigns by PRESBYTERIAN missionaries from North America. Consequently, the majority of Korean Christians today are Presbyterians, though schisms have led to the creation of more than 60 Presbyterian denominations, for example, the Koryo Presbyterian Church (conservative, 1946), and the Presbyterian Church of Korea Reunited Anti-Ecumenical (1951) and the Presbyterian Church in the Republic of Korea (liberal, 1954), many founded by indigenous leaders, for example, Pak T'ae-son, founder of the Olive Tree Church (1955), which has over a million adherents. Following the Korean War (1950–3) over a million Christians fled to South Korea from the North, where Christianity had been outlawed by the communist regime. The dramatic expansion of Protestant Christianity in South Korea since 1960 is American-inspired, with the churches modelled on a North American pattern. Nonetheless, certain peculiarly Korean features betray a residual Shamanist and Buddhist influence. Christianity is most popular in urban areas, with 7,000 churches in Seoul alone. Protestant Christianity's steadfast resist-

ance to Japanese occupation and to communism has earned political recognition. Syngman Rhee (President, 1948–60) was a Christian, as is Young Sam Kim, elected President in 1992. [20; 38; 175]

Krishna [XVII] ('Black') In HINDUISM, a divine hero and lover, regarded as an AVATARA of VISHNU, incarnate in order to overcome an evil king, Kamsa. A prominent figure in the MAHABHARATA, he gives the teachings of the BHAGAVADGITA while acting as his friend Arjuna's charioteer. In the arts, less attention is paid to his exploits as a king and hero than to his earlier life as a child brought up among cowherds, and as a lover of the cowherd women (*gopis*). In northern India he is often worshipped as Radha-Krishna, in the company of his mistress, the married *gopi* Radha, regarded here as an *avatara* of LAKSHMI. Their love is one of the great themes of painting, poetry and dance (*see* ART, HINDU). Through the phases of human passion, it symbolizes the mutual love (BHAKTI) of the deity and the human devotee, which overrides all earthly considerations. Krishna, like Vishnu and other *avataras*, is blue in colour and dressed in yellow: he wears peacock feathers in his crown. As Gopala, the cowherd, he plays his flute to charm the *gopis*, or dances with them in a circle, multiplying himself so that each girl has a Krishna to dance with [4: 207–12; 12: 303–6, 340–1, 428–9; 92: 204–231]. In south Indian temple art, by contrast, Krishna is generally represented with Rukmini and Satyabhama, the most senior of his sixteen thousand or so legal wives, identified with Vishnu's consorts Lakshmi and BHUDEVI [38: pl. 29; 120: pls 4a–b].

For some *bhakti* schools, including the HARE KRISHNA MOVEMENT, Krishna is not just an *avatara* like the rest but a full manifestation of Vishnu on earth, and Radha is the supreme SHAKTI.

Kshatriya [XVII] The name of one of the four VARNAS or classes in Hindu society, comprising the warriors and rulers. The original meaning is 'endowed with sovereignty' (or supremacy, or power), whether human or superhuman. The name, as well as other ancient evidence, raises the possibility that originally the rank-order of BRAHMAN and Kshatriya may have been Kshatriya first, rather than second to Brahman, the accepted order of later times. [12: 142f]

Kuan (Shih) Yin [XII] The Chinese term for AVALOKITESHVARA, the BODHISATTVA of compassion. *Kuan Shih Yin* means 'Hearer of the sounds (prayers) of the world'. In India Avalokiteshvara was represented as male, but in 8th-century China came to be represented as female [15: XII, 340]. Kuan Yin was adopted into the popular Chinese pantheon as the 'Goddess of Mercy', the protector of women and children and patroness of sailors. [4: VI, 180–200; 23: V, 47–57; 49: IX, 68–77]

Kukai [XXI] (774–835 CE) Posthumously known as Kobo Daishi, the priestly founder of the Japanese Buddhist SHINGON sect (*see* JAPAN, BUDDHISM IN). He was trained early in Kegon *sutras* (*see* NANTO ROKUSHU) at the Todai-ji in Nara (*see* NANTO SHICHIDAI-JI). His trilogy *Sankyoshiki*, describing his conversion as a result of a discussion between a Buddhist, a Taoist (*see* TAO CHIAO), and a Confucian (*see* CONFUCIUS), received imperial recognition and he was sent to China in 805. [18] He introduced esoteric doctrines on his return and, after being welcomed by the mountain-spirits (*see* SACRED MOUNTAINS), he built a Shingon temple on Mt Koya in Wakayama prefecture which grew into the Kongobu-ji and an immense complex of other esoteric temples. Through tireless activity and exposition of Shingon, he became the most

revered and mythologized saint after Prince SHOTOKU. Appointed to high posts by the court, he was given his posthumous title in 921, and is called 'the Daishi' (Great Master) in popular sentiment today. The Japanese have taken over the practice of CHINESE BUDDHISM of giving posthumous names to outstanding priests. Since it is the most reverent way of referring to them, most people call them today by their posthumous names.

Kumarajiva [XII] (344–413 CE) Probably the single most important figure in the history of CHINESE BUDDHISM. He was taken to China as a prisoner in 383 when Kucha in central Asia was raided by a Chinese expeditionary force. He spent 17 years as a captive in north China, during which time he mastered Chinese. In 401 he was taken to Ch'ang An, where he carried out his translation work and was honoured with the title 'National Teacher'. His major contribution was in the area of translation and the clarification of terms. He translated several important texts, including the 'Three Treatises' of the SAN LUN school, and the *Mahaprajnaparamita-shastra* (Great Perfection of Wisdom Treatise), the *Saddharmapundarika-sutra* (The Lotus of the True Dharma), the *Smaller Sukhavativyuha-sutra* (*see* CHING T'U TSUNG), the *Vimalakirti-nirdesha-sutra* and the *Shurangama-samadhi-sutra*. [15: III, 81–7; 85: III, 71–95]

Kurozumikyo [XXVI] One of the oldest of Japan's new religions, Kurozumikyo was founded by a SHINTO priest, Kurozumi Munetada (1780–1850). The sect traces its origin to Kurozumi's experience of religious conversion on 11 November 1814. Kurozumi, then critically ill, prayed to the sun-goddess AMATERASU-OMIKAMI and vowed to devote himself to her in absolute obedience. At that time he came to realize that KAMI and human beings are essentially one, and shortly afterwards began to preach this faith. He also healed a servant girl in the Kurozumi household by laying his hands on her and blowing on the affected part. Masses of people, hearing of his healing power, came to him for treatment. To assembled groups he preached in 'heavenly words', afterwards helping individuals with their physical problems. Some became believers, and many of those who accepted the new teaching came from the samurai class. After Kurozumi's death, his chief disciples carried on the work. By the end of the feudal period (1868), they had won about 100,000 adherents, including a number of court nobles. At the sect's meetings, however, distinctions of rank were not recognized. Within the group, all were of equal status – a radical departure for that day.

Government authorization for Kurozumikyo to exist as an independent Shinto sect was granted in 1876. Today Kurozumikyo adherents number approximately 300,000. The sect has its chief centre in the city of Okayama, about halfway between Kobe and Hiroshima. Since the death of the funder, sect leadership has fallen to successive generations of the Kurozumi family. Kurozumikyo reveres not only Amaterasu-omikami and the traditional *kami* pantheon but also the deified founder. A festival in honour of the founder is held each year in April. [8; 10: IX, 182]

Kusinara [XI] The Pali name (Sanskrit: *Kushinagara*) for modern Kasia in northern India, the site of the BUDDHA'S (*see* GOTAMA) death or PARINIBBANA. The event is frequently depicted in BUDDHIST art with the Buddha shown lying on his right side (the 'lion' posture) between two sal trees. Along with BODHGAYA, LUMBINI and SARNATH, it is one of four principal sacred sites to which Buddhists from many countries make pilgrimage. (*See also* VESAKHA.)

Kwakiutl [V] A Pacific north-west North American coastal group, along with the Bella Bella and Nootka, belonging to the Wakashan linguistic family. The group occupies both shores of Queen Charlotte Sound and the northern portion of Vancouver Island. The term *kwakiutl* (literally 'smoke of the world') is probably a reference to their mythic place of origin (*see* CREATION MYTHS). They were contacted early by Europeans, and trade with the latter gradually undermined their rigidly hierarchical society. Divided into clan groups (*numayma*) within villages, each clan traces its ancestry to a mythic animal ancestor who, in primordial times, became human. Priority among mythic forebears (e.g. the time of their transformation) yields a ranking of Kwakiutl clans. The primary religious concern is for humans to occupy their proper place in the cosmic scheme and thereby acquire the necessary supernatural power, *nawalak* (*see* COSMOLOGY). SHAMANS (*pexala*) acquire *nawalak* in excess of ordinary mortals, often through virtual identification with a granting spirit. Baxbakualanuxsiwae (the Great Man-Eater), chief among Kwakiutl deities, is central to the *hamatsa* cult (the principal secret society), whose dancers hold the highest rank in the winter ceremonial (*see* CALENDAR ROUND) [8: VIII]. Their ritual, performed at the time of year known as *tsetsaequa* ('full of secrets'), recreates for the initiate the death and reconstitution by the cannibal-god and is believed to facilitate the initiate's metamorphosis into full membership. The *potlatch* ('a giving') was a ceremonial distribution of wealth, probably linked originally to a death–rebirth motif present elsewhere in Kwakiutl practice. [7]

L

Lakshmi [xvɪɪ] '(Lucky) sign' in Sanskrit, or Shri, 'splendour': the Hindu goddess of good fortune, embodying love, beauty, fertility and wealth. Her representations in ART show her surrounded by lotuses (she is also *Kamala*, the lotus-goddess), dressed in the auspicious colour red, and adorned with the jewellery and make-up of a queen. Often she bestows money or other blessings on her worshippers. In one very ancient form of imagery, as *Gaja-Lakshmi* ('Elephant-Lakshmi'), she appears bathed by elephants, which symbolize the clouds of the rainy season. In myth she is the wife of VISHNU, and when he becomes incarnate on earth in an AVATARA, she accompanies him as his consort [4: 109, 116, 200; 58: 39, 41]. The motif of Gaja-Lakshmi occurs frequently in early Buddhist art, apparently symbolizing the conception or birth of the BUDDHA-to-be [58: 34].

Lam rim [xxxv] Tibetan for the 'graduated or graded path' to enlightenment. Associated in particular with the GELUG school, the *lam rim* organizes the path to Buddhahood in accordaɪce with three motivations for following the religious life: (1) the lowest, of those whose intended aim is something in SAMSARA (fame, wealth, a favourable rebirth, etc.); (2) the middling, for those with a strong sense of renunciation of *samsara* and wish for NIBBANA, associated with the ARAHATS; and (3) the highest motivation of those who see all suffering as equal to their own and wish for the MAHAYANA goal of perfect Buddha-

hood for the benefit of all. It is said that all Buddhists should progress gradually and sequentially through these stages, and all the practices of Buddhism can be fitted into this framework. The model of the three motivations appears to have originated with Atisha and the KADAM tradition. [31]

Land of Youth [vɪɪ] Tir na n-Og (Land of the Young) is one of several Irish names for a realm of bright beauty and fair women, free from death or suffering, which in Irish literature lies across the sea or within the *sid* (burial mound). Kings and heroes visit it to find LUG or Manannan ruling there [23: 314–25; 4: 181–3]. The Norse equivalent may be Odainsakr (Field of the Not-Dead) or Glasisvellir (Glittering Plains), ruled by the legendary King Gudmund, sometimes visited by men.

Langar [xxxɪɪɪ] The free refectory maintained by all Sikh GURDWARAS. The custom was introduced into the early PANTH from SUFI Muslim example, apparently as a means of encouraging everyone to ignore CASTE while attending a *gurdwara*. In the *langar* everyone must sit in straight lines (*pangat*) to avoid any suggestion of privilege. Although many Sikhs maintain their right to eat meat, only vegetarian meals are served in the *langar* to avoid controversy. People of any faith can eat in a *langar*. In large *gurdwaras* it is open daily, in the smaller ones less frequently. [7: 98–9; 9: 167–70; 10: 176–7]

Languages (Jewish) [xxii] The sacred language of JUDAISM is Hebrew, a North-West Semitic language. The Hebrew of the BIBLE is written in a consonantal form, the vowel system in general use today being the work of the Tiberian Masoretes of the 9th and 10th centuries, who formalized the traditional vocalization. Around the beginning of the Christian era Hebrew was replaced as a spoken language by Aramaic, and became a literary language. Aramaic is also of North-West Semitic origin, and some sections of the Bible, in the Books of *Daniel* and *Ezra*, are written in it. The Jerusalem and Babylonian TALMUDS, the TARGUM translation-commentaries on the Bible, parts of MIDRASHIC literature and the ZOHAR are all in Aramaic. In the middle ages Jews used Hebrew and Aramaic for composing religious texts, for correspondence with Jews in other countries and for prayer [4 vol. 7: xxx]. They usually spoke the native language of their host countries. As Jews were expelled from various European countries between the 13th and 15th centuries (*see* ANTI-SEMITISM: EUROPEAN JEWRY), they took with them these native languages, which they continued to speak as Jewish dialects. The most important of them are Yiddish, a medieval German dialect, and Ladino, a form of late medieval Spanish. [1: 359; 14 vol. 10: 66]

Lapps, Religion among the [ix] The Lapps are a nomadic people, herders of reindeer in northern Scandinavia, whose traditional religious outlook resembled that of the ESKIMO [6: 84–8; 7: 118–21]. Lapp beliefs were influenced by Nordic mythology (*see* ANCIENT EUROPE; *also* SYNCRETISM) and later by CHRISTIANITY. Correspondence between their deities and those of the EDDAS, and the fact that western Lapps have a more developed cosmogony than those of Finland, do not necessarily imply extensive bor-

rowing. Lapp gods represent elements and forces of the environment, such as the sun as cosmic primordial being, Pieve. This is a less clearly personified concept than those of the supporting gods (thunder, wind, moon). With the Eskimo Selna (Woman of the Sea) may be compared Væraldenolmai (Man of the World), associated with fertility, and, merged with him, Ratien-attje (ruling father for the Swedish Lapps). Many cult-sites (*seide, saivo, passe*) have been found, especially in Sweden, often associated with awe-inspiring natural features (trees, rocks). Large stones and platforms were used for SACRIFICE (e.g. of a white reindeer to Pieve). The role of the *noaide* (SHAMAN) is as significant for Lapps as for other Arctic cultures [6: 84–5; 7: 121–3], and their use of drumming to achieve a state of ecstasy is a salient feature. The drums were often decorated to represent gods or spirits [7: 120–4]. Lapp behaviour was ruled by TABUS, many of them governing the pursuit, slaughter and consumption of food animals. Those to do with the bear (the largest animal hunted) were of such importance that accounts of Lapp religion usually give prominence to what is called 'the bear cult' [6: 98–100]. The use of special 'bear language', rituals of capture and disposal, rules for the removal, placing and use of the skin, and, when all other parts had been eaten or ceremonially buried, a final festival of purification show how great was the Lapps' respect for the bear and its spirit. With similar behaviour towards other animals, this pattern of activity is evidence for a world-view in which no sharp distinction is made between humans and all that is living. Appreciation of this sense of unity and interaction with the whole visible environment and, through the shaman, with the world of spirits, is indispensable if one is to understand the place and function of the sacred among the Lapps.

Latin America, Christianity in
[XIII.B] Of the population of Latin
America, now well in excess of 300
million, over 90% acknowledge allegiance to the ROMAN CATHOLIC
Church. Consequently, over a third
of the world's Catholics inhabit the
'Latin' countries of South, Central
and North America. The conquest
of the Americas, initiated by Columbus in 1492, resulted in the forcible
conversion of the native population
and the attempted elimination of
their culture and religion. The
annexation of the continent to Rome
was further consolidated by extensive colonization from Spain and
Portugal. Notable exceptions to this
violation of the rights of the Indians
were Bartolome de las Casas
(1474–1566) and the Jesuits. The
various countries that make up Latin
America today won political independence during the 19th century.
The basic anticlericalism of the
republican movements led to a temporary alienation between church
and state, but the 20th century has
seen political powers seek to harness
the continuing popular influence of
the church in support of authoritarian regimes, including military
dictatorships. In the latter part of the
20th century, however, the rise of
LIBERATION THEOLOGY has challenged such close alliances between
church and state, with support for
social, political and economic
change coming from grassroots
Christian communities, members of
religious orders and radical priests.
By contrast, evangelical PROTES-
TANT groups, many of them sponsored by US agencies of right-wing
political sympathies, have been
actively proselytizing in recent years,
sometimes with the tacit support
of conservative regimes (e.g. in
Guatemala), and with some
success. Nonetheless, Roman
Catholicism retains its popular
appeal, even if in a syncretistic
form, incorporating elements of
pre-Christian beliefs and practices,
especially in some of the ceremonies
associated with the cult of the Virgin
MARY. [17; 24; 59]

Lenshina, Alice [XXVII] A Bemba
woman, born Alice Mulenga
Lubusha in a Church of Scotland
mission in northern Zambia, Alice
Lenshina experienced a mystic call
in 1953 and proclaimed a new way,
which elicited a mass response in
areas strong in PROTESTANTISM and
ROMAN CATHOLICISM. Her new
Lumpa ('best of all') Church, with
herself as Lenshina (i.e. 'Queen'),
lost some 600 lives in a clash with
the Kaunda government in 1964
due to refusal to give unconditional
support to the ruling political party,
following which the church was banned and she was detained. She died
in 1978. Her followers fled to neighbouring countries, but in the 1980s
the church was appearing again in
many parts of Zambia. [26:
94–100]

Leza [II] (or Lesa) The name for
God of a large number of African
peoples in Zambia and neighbouring
countries, among them the Bemba,
Ila and Lala. The etymological
meaning is uncertain. Leza is the
creator of the world, held immediately responsible for natural phenomena, especially when unusual,
and seen as a loving if somewhat
remote and incomprehensible father
of men. West of the Leza area the
major God-name is NZAMBI; in the
east MULUNGU or (in Malawi)
Chauta; and in the north IRUVA.
These together provide the core of
BANTU theological nomenclature,
but many tribes use other names,
despite an apparent tendency for
ones like Leza to spread from people
to people. The division between
names is not necessarily one
between theologies – equally the
same name may carry rather different connotations among different
peoples – yet Leza, Mulungu and
Nzambi all seem to speak of essentially the same belief in one God
(associated with the sky and with

thunder and lightning) quite unlike the ancestral spirits, creator of all things and ultimate source of morality, yet somewhat withdrawn and seldom the object of regular worship. [17; 25]

Lha–Dre [xxxv] The *lha* (gods) and *dre* (demons) are the supernatural beings of indigenous Tibetan folk-religion. According to Buddhist doctrinal classification they are 'deities of the world' (*jigten-pa*), distinct from the symbolic deities of BUDDHISM which embody the various qualities of enlightenment. By classifying the *lha* and *dre* in this manner and assigning them duties as 'oath-bound' protectors of religion, Buddhism in Tibet was able to assimilate their cults. The Tibetan religion is rich in such supernatural beings, both beneficent and malign. Especially significant are the deities who personify elemental and environmental forces, such as the *sa-dag* ('lords of the soil'), who are placated before any construction or farming is carried out, and the *lu*, spirits dwelling in watery environments, who also require placation. Alongside these and numerous other autochthonous deities Buddhism has brought to Tibet its own 'worldly gods', namely such Indian deities as SHIVA, VISHNU and BRAHMA, who now serve as oath-bound protectors of the Buddhist faith. [14; 24]

Li [xII] ('Rites of Propriety') The two components of the Chinese character *Li* mean 'spirit' and 'sacrifice', although in some contexts the term can be translated simply as 'religion' or 'morality' [17a: III, 51–61; 39: I, 11–18, 22–5]. Generally *Li* refers to formal rituals and sacrifices, which may be the rites of the official or state religion, communal and agricultural rites, or domestic rites such as FUNERAL RITES (*Sang Li*). *Li* also refers to the rules of proper conduct and the behaviour appropriate to specific circumstances. The detailed regulations of the

Li are found in the Classic of Rites (*Li Ching*) [69; 96]. Through most of Chinese history from Chou times (1027–402 BCE) the Ministry of Rites (*Li Pu*) was responsible for determining and regulating the sacrificial rites (*Chi Li*) of the official or state religion.

By the Ch'ing dynasty (1644–1911 CE) these were classified into three groups. The Great Sacrificial Rites were the offerings to heaven (T'IEN), Earth (*Ti*), the royal ancestors (*Tsu Tsang*) and the gods of the soil and grain (*She Chi*). The Medium Sacrificial Rites were the offerings to the sun and moon, representing the *yang* and *yin* principles (*see* YIN–YANG), the kings and emperors of former dynasties, the Sage Emperor Shen Nung and god of agriculture, and Lei Tsu the goddess of sericulture. The Great Rites were almost exclusively the concern of the emperor, who performed them on behalf of the people to ensure the perpetuation of the political and the natural order.

The Lesser Sacrificial Rites date mainly from after the end of the Han dynasty (221 CE) and were usually conducted not by the emperor but by local officials in state temples. They include offerings to the Sage Emperor Fu Hsi, the god of war (Kuan Ti), the god of literature Wen Chang and various local gods associated with the Ch'ing capital Beijing. [2; 4: III, 54–68; 20; 32; 99: V, 70–6]

Liberal Protestantism [xIII.c] A somewhat diverse movement in PROTESTANT theology which arose in the second half of the 19th century. Negatively, it is characterized by a rather critical attitude to naïve biblicism (e.g. to a simplistic affirmation of statements in the BIBLE) and to traditional dogmatic formulations of the Christian faith. Positively, it is concerned to present the spirit of the Christian GOSPEL in contemporary terms and to assert the importance of the individual's religious experience. Its early development was considerably influenced by Albrecht Ritschl (1822–89) and his followers. Ritschl insisted that religion is not reducible to other forms of experience, that religious knowledge is a matter of 'value judgements', that CHRISTOLOGY must take seriously the results of historical research into the life of JESUS, and that reconciliation with God must be expressed in moral activity in the world (see SALVATION). The classical expression of the liberal Protestant position was produced by Adolf Harnack (1851–1930). In *What is Christianity?* he expounded the Christian faith popularly in terms of a spirit expressing the parental reality of God, the community of humankind, the higher righteousness and the command of love. [22]

Liberation Theology [XIII.B] Liberation theology, according to its exponents, describes a way of doing theology which responds to the immediate demands of its context in the struggle to liberate the poor and oppressed. This approach to theology was popularized in Latin America in the late 1960s and early 1970s, though similar methodologies govern the approach of BLACK THEOLOGY and feminist theology, which are similarly concerned with the struggle to eliminate forms of oppression. Its geographical and historical context meant that liberation theology was initially mainly a ROMAN CATHOLIC phenomenon, and owed much to the impetus of the Second Vatican Council and the decision by the Latin American Episcopal Conference (CELAM) at Medellín in 1968 to opt for the model of liberation rather than development as the most appropriate response to the challenge of poverty and oppression in their continent: that is, the poor and oppressed must be encouraged to liberate themselves as opposed to continuing to be dependent on outside aid. Subsequently, this approach has been adopted by the World Council of Churches and many Christians in other Third World countries. The methodology owes much to MARXISM, with its emphasis on the cycle of praxis–reflection–praxis. Liberation theologians argue that theology must be committed to the cause of liberating the poor and oppressed, and that such commitment is true to the biblical witness, particularly as reflected in the Israelites' Exodus and in the life, death and resurrection of JESUS of Nazareth. In that sense this approach to theology is at odds with the academic, objective, rationalist approach which has dominated Western theology for the past two centuries. The seminal work is usually considered to be Gustavo Gutierrez's *A Theology of Liberation*, first published in 1971. [22; 23; 25; 81]

Lila [XVII] 'Joyful play': God's motivation for periodically creating the universe, in VEDANTA thought. It is sometimes mistakenly interpreted as capriciousness. A divine power free from all imperfection or defilement could not have motivated action based upon any need or partiality, otherwise it would be subject to the law of KARMA. So the act of creation is explained as joyful spontaneity or fun. [28: 117ff; 105: 361–3]

Linga [XVII] A symbol of the Hindu god SHIVA, and the main object of worship in most Shaiva temples. It is phallic in origin, consisting usually of a pillar representing the male organ resting in a pedestal representing the *yoni* or female organ, the whole therefore suggesting the completeness of Shiva joined with SHAKTI. Its symbolism is not, however, sexual in the erotic sense, as with MITHUNA/MAITHUNA imagery, but rather that of transforming power in its most primeval form. To Hindus, the *linga* is the most basic image of Shiva, alongside the many anthropomorphic forms, with which it may be combined in *lingas* with one or more faces of the god [4: 214–15].

Lingayata [xvII] A Hindu movement of somewhat puritanical character among the Shaivas (*see* SHIVA) of south India. Its members are strict vegetarians and abstain from alcohol. Their correct title is Virashaivas, 'Hero-Shaivas', their better-known name deriving from the fact that they avoid anthropomorphic images of the deity and worship him only in the form of the LINGA. Disregarding CASTE distinctions they do not accept the idea of the high status of BRAHMANS. The movement was founded in the 12th century by Basavanna, one of a group of Virashaiva poet–saints which also included the famous holy woman Mahadeviyakka. [108: 61–90, 111–42]

Literalism [xxxiv] A term with two meanings. (1) In the interpretation of sacred scripture, acceptance of statements at their face value or 'according to the letter', as opposed to interpreting them symbolically or metaphorically. (2) In theories of religion, a method of explanation which regards RITUALS and other religious actions as accounted for by beliefs about the world (for example, a DANCE occurs because the participants believe that SPIRITS can be induced by it to give rain), and as functioning as instruments of control of the conditions of life, rather than as symbols. [148: 11–12]

Liturgical Books, Christian [xIII.D] The various Christian churches make use of a wide variety of books containing text and sometimes the music used in services. In ROMAN CATHOLIC tradition the texts for daily public worship, the Divine Office, were collected together in the Breviary (*Breviarium*), the texts for the Mass in the Missal (*Missale*), those for the SACRAMENTS and other

services in the *Rituale* and those for services conducted by the bishop in the Pontifical (*Pontificale*). In earlier centuries the ritual for all the sacraments was contained in the Sacramentary (*Liber Sacramentorum*). The texts from the Breviary used during the daytime were frequently collected in Books of Hours, many splendidly illuminated. In the medieval period the Ordinal (*Ordinale*) contained directions for how the Divine Office should be read in the various periods of the ecclesiastical CALENDAR. Confusingly, the Anglican Ordinal is something completely different; it contains the rites for ordaining clergy. The music to be chanted during services was contained in the Antiphonary (*Antiphonarium*), containing music for the Divine Office; in the *Graduale*, containing music for the Mass; and in a composite book, containing both, the *Liber Usualis*. Rubrics, traditionally written or printed in red, give instructions on exactly how the rites are to be performed.

The Anglican *Book of Common Prayer* (*see* ANGLICANISM) contains texts for both sacraments and the daily office. More modern liturgical books sometimes contain the equivalent texts, sometimes a different selection.

In the EASTERN ORTHODOX Church, the *Euchologion* contains the priest's part of Matins (*Orthros*), Vespers (*Hesperinos*) and the MYSTERIES, as well as a range of blessings, prayers and other services. The Small *Euchologion* and the *Hagiasmatarion* contain a narrower selection of services. The *Horologion* contains the fixed parts of offices for the reader (*Anagnostes*) and the singers (*Psaltai*). Variable parts of services are contained in a number of different books: the *Menaia* contain the texts for each date, the *Triodion* gives texts for the 10-week period before Pascha (*see* CALENDAR, CHRISTIAN), including the texts for the services of Great Lent and Holy Week; the *Pentecostarion* covers the period from Pascha to All Saints. Texts for the cycle of the eight tones are contained in the *Oktoechos* or *Paraklitike*. The *Typikon* contains directions for putting together the texts and rituals for any particular day. The Book of Psalms (*Psalterion*), the book of gospel readings and the *Apostolos*, the book of readings from the Epistles and from the *Acts of the Apostles*, contain the biblical texts most frequently needed. The *Hieratikon* contains the priest's part for the divine liturgy and the *Diakonikon* the deacon's part.

PROTESTANT and Reformed churches have service books of their own, sometimes containing fixed forms for services, sometimes models and resource materials to assist in the construction of acts of worship.

Liturgical Dress, Christian [XIII.D] The vestments used by priests, deacons and other clergy when exercising their liturgical ministry derive from the formal dress of the Roman gentry of late antiquity. Traditional ROMAN CATHOLIC vestments include the chasuble (*casula*), used by the priest when celebrating Mass, and the cope (*paenula* or *pluviale*) for other solemn rituals. The EASTERN ORTHODOX *phelonion* corresponds to both of these vestments. Both garments derive from a full-circle cloak, cut open at the front (cope, *phelonion*) or at the sides (chasuble) to free the priest's arms. Copes are also used in certain solemn rituals by lower clergy. The Western deacon's typical vestment is the dalmatic, that of the sub-deacon the almost identical tunicle. Both priest and deacon wear a stole for sacramental rites, the priest's falling before him, the deacon's worn draped over one shoulder and across the body. The Eastern deacon and sub-deacon wear the *sticharion*, a long tunic with narrow sleeves, usually made of brocade (a similar garment is used by other lower clergy, ordained readers and altar servers); a deacon's stole (*orarion*) is

worn like that of a Western deacon, except during the central part of the liturgy when it is worn crossed over both shoulders and wound about the waist, the way a sub-deacon, reader or server wears it. A simpler silk *stikharion* is used by the priest in the same way as the Western alb (a long white tunic girdled with a cord). Eastern clergy also use a belt (*zone*) and cuffs (*epimanikia*) made of vestment material, and the priest wears a distinctive joined stole, the *epitrachelion*. A priest of high rank will also wear an *epigonation* or a *palitsa*, the one a diamond shape, the other a rectangle of stiffened and lined vestment material hanging at knee height from a cord. The mitre used by a Western bishop, or by an abbot or prelate privileged to wear one, is a tall, stiffened, double-tongue-shaped hat. It can be a simple mitre of cloth, a gold mitre or a precious mitre ornamented with real or paste gems. A similar mitre is used by Armenian bishops. The Eastern Orthodox mitre is crown-shaped. Earlier representations of Orthodox bishops usually show them wearing the *polystavrion*, a *phelonion* covered with an all-over pattern of crosses. Eastern bishops now use the *sakkos*, a dalmatic-like garment, and the *omophorion*, a stole-like garment corresponding to the Western *pallium* (a scarf-like garment of white wool worked with crosses given to senior archbishops by the Pope as a sign of authority. When attending services 'in choir', i.e. as participants but not officiating or celebrating, Roman Catholic clergy wear a cassock and surplice or *cotta*, Orthodox a deep-sleeved *rason*. The surplice and stole, or *rason* and *epitrachelion*, are also used when officiating at certain rites.

In both Eastern and Western traditions the colour of vestments has a symbolic meaning, though this varies in different places and periods. In both traditions white or gold vestments represent joyful celebrations; in the West red is the colour of martyrs and of the Holy Spirit, purple the colour of penitential seasons (saffron in the Sarum rite). In Orthodox tradition blue is associated with Theophany and red with feasts of the Blessed Virgin.

Liturgical Movement [XIII.B] A movement in ROMAN CATHOLICISM from the early 1900s to encourage congregational participation in the MASS, after a long period during which passivity or engagement in individual devotions had been customary. Results include: more frequent COMMUNION; simplified services; and translation of the Mass out of Latin, especially since the Second Vatican COUNCIL (1963) [1: 137–78]. Similar concerns have affected ANGLICANISM and other churches, and as a result the liturgies of the main Western churches now often share very similar patterns. Modern church plans show the movement's influence (*see* ARCHITECTURE). [48; 84; 117]

Liturgy (Jewish) [XXII] The thrice-daily recital of prayers in JUDAISM is modelled on the sacrificial ritual of the TEMPLE. The central part of the morning liturgy (*shacharit*) is the recitation of the SHEMA with its accompanying benedictions, followed by the AMIDAH, a prayer of 19 benedictions said standing and facing JERUSALEM. For certain parts of these prayers a quorum (*minyan*) of 10 adult males is necessary. Various benedictions, psalms and hymns have been added over the centuries. On Sabbaths (SHABBAT) and festivals an extra *amidah* (*musaf*) is said commemorating the extra sacrifice brought on those occasions in the Temple. The afternoon prayer (*minchah*) consists of a psalm, the *amidah* and a short concluding prayer. The evening service (*maariv*) consists of the *shema* and *amidah* with some short additional pieces [14 vol. 11: 392]. The traditional prayers are in Hebrew, although REFORM JUDAISM has introduced many vernacular

prayers since many modern congregations cannot understand the Hebrew LANGUAGE. [11; 29; 52; 56: VII, XII]

Logical Positivism [XXXII] A view hostile to metaphysics and much traditional theology, according to which there are only two classes of genuine statements. There are statements, like those of logic and mathematics, which are known to be true or false independently of experience (but which can, if true, be reduced by analysis to tautologies). The only other genuine statements, including those of natural science, are those which are verifiable by sense experience. Metaphysical or religious assertions which purport to make claims about the nature of the universe but which do not meet the criterion of verifiability are held to be strictly 'meaningless'. They might express feelings but they do not convey any information.

This view is associated with a group founded in the 1920s by Moritz Schlick. The group, consisting of mathematicians, scientists and philosophers, came to be known as 'the Vienna circle'. A forceful, though modified, version of logical positivism was introduced to the English-speaking world by A. J. Ayer (1910–89). [1] Ayer sought to reformulate the criterion of verifiability so that it would not, as had the stricter version of the Vienna circle, exclude important scientific statements as meaningless. Many following Karl Popper (1902–94) [19: I], take the view that falsifiability rather than verifiability is a more appropriate criterion for distinguishing scientific statements. This requirement is a more problematic one so far as religious affirmations are concerned. 'God is love', for example, would be verified by some kind of beatific vision in an afterlife. But it has been claimed, by A. G. N. Flew (b. 1923) [11: VI], that 'God is love' is not falsifiable and therefore is not a genuine statement. The critique of religious utterances as 'meaningless' has been questioned by P. G. Winch (b. 1926) and other philosophers influenced by the writings of Ludwig Wittgenstein (1889–1951) [e.g. 7: X–XII].

Lokayata [XVII] A system or movement in Indian thought which denied life after death and adopted a materialist standpoint. Classical Indian verse, drama and story refer not infrequently to materialist views of a popular kind; indeed, such notions are already present in the literature of the VEDA. More systematic materialist theories are first known from the period of the foundation of BUDDHISM and Jainism (*see* JAIN) (*c.*500 BCE). Eventually, a coherent philosophy of life with systematic expression and literature came into existence (by the 1st century CE, perhaps much earlier). Its foundation was mythologically attributed either to Brhaspati or to Carvaka. Little Lokayata literature survives, but the system appears to have held that sense experience is ultimately the only source of knowledge (*pramana*). Some sources portray it as recommending enjoyment of pleasure or advocating a hedonistic ethic. The Lokayata was strongly opposed to CASTE, the cult of deities and the support of religious professionals. [36: III, 512–50; 51: II, 215–26; 103: 27–35; 107: 227–49]

Loki [VII] Loki is found among the Scandinavian AESIR, sometimes accompanying ODIN and THOR on journeys. In the EDDAS he is represented as a TRICKSTER figure, expert at taking on bird or animal shapes, performing acts of mischief and getting in and out of dangerous and ridiculous situations. He helps the giants to steal the gods' treasures, and then uses his creative skills to win them back again [3: 176–82; 3a: 84–5]. In the poem *Lokasenna* [21: 90] he bitterly abuses all the Aesir and VANIR in turn, and is said to be responsible for BALDER's death and

to have been bound under rocks as a punishment. HEL, FENRISWOLF and the serpent encircling the world are all said to be the children of Loki. He and his sons fight against the gods at RAGNAROK. His relationship with the huge and sinister giant skilled in magical deceptions, Utgard-Loki ('Loki of the Outer Regions'), is not clear [3: 32–4, 182].

Lokuttara [XI] A technical term of the ABHIDHAMMA. The earliest BUDDHIST literature describes four grades of saint, collectively known ask 'nobles' (*ariya*; Sanskrit: *arya*): stream-enterer, once-returner, never-returner and ARAHAT. Having perfected the training in external morality (SILA), all are free from the danger of an unpleasant rebirth. All have seen the Buddhist goal and are as a result free from doubt and opinion (DITTHI). In *abhidhamma*, *lokuttara* (Sanskrit: *lokottara*) (literally 'supramundane', i.e. transcendent) refers to the type of consciousness, occurring initially as a momentary flash, which transforms the individual permanently into a 'noble'. It is the culmination of Buddhist meditation practice (BHAVANA), uniting in a harmonious balance the two aspects of calm and insight. *Lokuttara* mind involves a direct realization of the unconditioned and, being quite free of any trace of defilement, cannot give rise to any attachment and necessarily erodes unskilful tendencies (cf. SKILFUL MEANS). The four grades of saint are the result of different degrees of clarity in this realization. [5: 785ff]

Lotu [XXIX] A Tongan word for prayer or worship used by 19th-century Christian converts to refer to mission teachings and church services. When they in turn became missionaries to other Pacific islands the word was used generally for the Christian teaching. In modern Melanesian pidgin it can include any religion, Christian or otherwise.

Lovedu Religion [II] The religion of the Lovedu, who live in the Transvaal, is centred upon Mujaji, their divine queen, and ancestral spirits. They have no interest in cosmological myths, and belief in Khuzwane, the creator, is shadowy. They do not pray to him, nor do they see their ancestors as intermediaries. Both the control of nature, especially rain, and the whole life of society depend principally upon the queen, her physical health and emotional happiness. She herself depends not only upon her inner divine power, but also on special rain-medicines and the royal ancestor spirits. The queen's holiness requires seclusion and, finally, death at her own hands, but not a continuously ritualized life. Her death is followed by a period of natural and social confusion.

Throughout Lovedu society women are important. Many rituals are conducted by them and no ancestor spirit is more powerful than a mother's mother. Rain symbolizes the good life, coolness, fruitfulness, moderation, social reconciliation; heat symbolizes what is evil, sorcery, witchcraft, passion, fighting [6: 55–82; 37].

Lu Tsung [XII] The Chinese VINAYA School, founded by Tao Hsuan (596–667 CE). It was based on the 'Vinaya in Four Parts' (*Ssu Fen Lu*), which was translated in 412 CE. The school emphasized the rules of monastic discipline (PATI-MOKKHA: *see also* Ritsu *in* NANTO ROKUSHU.) [15: XI, 301]

Ludi [XXXI] Roman games, which included a wide range of public spectacles – racing, drama, displays of wild beasts, fighting, etc. – always presented in a religious context, preceded by rituals and processions and dedicated to a god or goddess. The great *ludi* (*plebeii* and *Romani*) seem to go back to the 6th century BCE, though there are ludic elements in older festivals, perhaps deriving from initiatory rites. Their frequency, popularity and extravagance increased as the empire grew. [8: 571–5; 22: 40–1, 183–6; 19: 597–8]

Lug [VII] The Irish Lug (Shining One), with the title 'Of the Long Arm', is thought to be related to the CELTIC deity equated with Mercury in Gaul [17: 27–9]. He appears in a medieval Welsh story in the *Mabinogion* as the hero Lleu Llaw Gyffes [16: 55–75]. Lug has much in common with the GERMANIC Wodan/ ODIN, since he is a god of many skills, including music and poetry, who brought wealth, was skilled in magic and warfare, carried a huge spear and was associated with the raven. He was said to have been fostered by Manannan Mac Lir, 'son of the sea' [17: 69–73]. He joined the TUATHA DE DANANN and led them to victory at the battle of Mag Tuired, when he slew his grandfather, Balor of the baleful eye, with his sling [23: 32–8]. He is represented as reigning as a king in the other world. His festival was Lughnasa, marking the beginning of harvest (*see* SAMHAIN), still remembered in popular tradition [18: I].

Lumbini [XI] The birthplace of the BUDDHA (*see* GOTAMA), situated just within the present-day southern Nepalese border. Tradition has it that his mother, Maya, gave birth to the BODHISATTVA in a grove of sal trees while standing up and holding on to a branch; this scene is frequently depicted in BUDDHIST art. The site is marked by a stone pillar set up by the emperor ASHOKA recording his own visit in the 3rd century BCE and is today one of four principal Buddhist pilgrimage centres (cf. BODHGAYA; KUSINARA; SARNATH) attracting pilgrims from all over the Buddhist world. (*See* VESAKHA.)

Lutheranism [XIII.B] Martin Luther (1483–1566) [11] was the father of the German REFORMATION.

His *Ninety-Five Theses* (1517) against 'Indulgences' [19: 182–91] (*see* PENANCE) provoked a general revolt against the PAPACY. His key doctrines [60] were that justification is by grace through faith alone, not by works (*see* SALVATION), and that the AUTHORITY of the BIBLE is supreme over CHURCH tradition. Lutherans [157: 848–50] came to dominate parts of northern Europe and there are substantial groups in the USA through German immigration.

European Lutheranism has commonly been organized in established churches with a tendency to Erastianism (*see* STATE, CHRISTIANITY AND THE). The Augsburg Confession (1530) [19: 210–12] is the chief Confession of Faith. A form of Lutheran 'SCHOLASTICISM' in the 17th century provoked PIETISM in reaction. Lutherans have been prominent in BIBLICAL CRITICISM and LIBERAL PROTESTANTISM, but in liturgy and eucharistic theology (*see* EUCHARIST) sometimes closer to ROMAN CATHOLICISM than other branches of PROTESTANTISM. [18; 62 vol. 9: 61–4]

M

Macedonian Orthodox [XIII.D]
After the Second World War the
Slav Macedonians achieved state-
hood within the Yugoslav federation
and almost immediately (1945) severed their ties with the Serbian
Orthodox Church and demanded
the restoration of the medieval Patriarchate of Ohrid. In 1958 this
church was unilaterally declared
autocephalous, with Metropolitan
Dositej as head. Since that date,
Ohrid has sought to assert Slav
Macedonian identity (centred on
Skopje) *vis-à-vis* the Greek Macedonian community (centred on
Thessaloniki) in the Balkans and
abroad. With the collapse of Yugoslavia friction has increased between
the two communities, the Slavs
looking back to the glories of the
West Bulgarian Empire and the
Greeks back to Byzantium – both
Skopje and Thessaloniki overlooking centuries of a common Orthodox heritage. That this dispute,
arising from controversy over
whether the Slav 'Macedonians'
actually have the right to claim this
title (the republic is on the fringes of
ancient Macedonia), should have
spilled over into the ecclesiastical
domain betrays a weakness in the
local or 'national' model that Orthodox Christianity has usually adopted. This example is by no means
unique as both the Bulgarian
Church and the Ukrainian Orthodox have been divided over related
issues. Like Ohrid, the smaller Turkish Orthodox Church is denied recognition (since the 1920s) among
the mainstream Orthodox. [38; 99]

Madhyamaka [XI] (Also known
sometimes as Madhyamika) One of
the major schools of MAHAYANA
Buddhist philosophy. Madhyamaka
appears to have been founded by
NAGARJUNA to demonstrate the
truth of the claim said to have been
made by the BUDDHA in the PRAJNA-
PARAMITA scriptures that *all* things
lack inherent existence. This applies
even to the Buddha or NIBBANA
(Nirvana). For Nagarjuna inherent
existence would mean unchanging
self-identity, and thus things could
not change. Moreover, if a thing had
inherent existence it would exist
from its own side, and could not
exist in causal dependence (for
example, in dependence upon mental activity such as conceptualization). Thus Nagarjuna sees a
contradiction between the idea of
inherent existence and that of
dependent arising (PATICCASAMUP-
PADA). Nagarjuna tried to demonstrate that all things are empty
(*shunya*) of inherent existence inasmuch as they originate in some form
of causal dependence. That quality
of EMPTINESS is called *shunyata*, and
the Madhyamaka perspective is
sometimes called SHUNYATAVADA.
Nagarjuna deconstructs any explicit
or implicit claim that something has
inherent existence by showing contradictions. Thus in the *Madhyamakakarika* (Verses on Madhyamaka)
Nagarjuna attempts to indicate the
contradictions involved in all concepts inasmuch as they entail inherent existence. He employs a rigorous
analysis for a critical purpose, and
the aim is insight into the emptiness
of inherent existence of all things.

This represents an extension of the Buddhist teaching of no-self (ANATTA) to all things. When applied in meditation such analysis can lead to insight (VIPASSANA), and a very deep form of letting-go which can be integrated into the project of the BODHISATTVA to help all sentient beings. Although things do not exist inherently, Nagarjuna does not teach that things do not exist at all. Thus the tradition is Madhyamaka ('Middling') inasmuch as it teaches the middle between inherent existence and complete non-existence. This middle is dependent arising, which seems to mean for Nagarjuna existence non-inherently.

After Nagarjuna and his disciple Aryadeva the Madhyamaka tradition in India appears to have split into a number of sub-schools, although it is not clear exactly how the schools were differentiated in India or how clear-cut these distinctions were. (*See also* NANTO ROKUSHU; SAN LUN TSUNG) [101: III; 78; 52; 63]

Madrasa [XIX] A higher institution of learning in traditional Islamic education. The MOSQUE was (and still is) a place of instruction and often the depository for a library. Children normally spent several years on the QUR'AN in a primary school attached to a mosque before joining the teaching circle of a prominent scholar for instruction in the Islamic sciences. *Madrasas*, or colleges, were founded, often with sectarian affiliations, from the 11th century onwards. The *madrasa* teacher, who was known as a *mudarris*, gave his students certificates of attendance and qualification to teach, in turn, the texts which had been studied [128: VI]. In the 20th century, these institutions have tended to be replaced by colleges and universities with curricula and teaching methods more nearly approximating to those of the West. (*See* AL-AZHAR *and* ISLAMIC MODERNISM.) [General surveys in 20: 'Education (Islam)'; 107: XI; 123; architecture: 93: I]

Madrasha [XIII.D] The fact that the words *madrasha* (Syriac), *midrash* (Hebrew) and *madrasa* (Arabic) share a common denominator, the concept of education, is a sign that the first is more than a hymn (the usual translation). Poetry was used by the Syrians from an early date to exercise the mind in spiritual abstraction; examples are the so-called *Hymn of the Soul* from the *Acts of the Apostle Judas Thomas*, the fragmentary verses of Bardaisan of Edessa and the compositions of Ephrem of Nisibis (d. 373). It was Ephrem who perfected the medium, using a variety of melodies with simple or complex syllabic patterns, which lent themselves to plain didacticism, to lyricism or to philosophical speculation. It may have been Ephrem who introduced the response, a single, unchanging line to be sung by the congregation after every verse of a *madrasha*.

Jerome tells (*On Famous Men*, 115) that Ephrem's works were often recited after the scriptural readings in the churches of Syria, and that some of them had already been translated into Greek with admirable success. Such translations called forth a great body of pseudo-Ephremic poetry in Greek; but it was not until the 6th century that the deacon Romanos, who came from the Syro-Greek milieu of Emesa, north of Damascus, perfected a truly Hellenic version of the Syriac *madrasha*, the *kontakion*. The *kontakion* is one of the few literary art-forms actually invented in the Christian empire of Byzantium. Recent research shows that the debt of *kontakion*-writers to Syriac models extends beyond the form to the content, including interpretations of Scripture, poetic techniques and literary motifs. The *madrashe* (pl.) of Ephrem of Nisibis remain the supreme expression of Christian faith in the form of didactic or meditative song. [106; 107]

Magen David [xxii] The six-pointed star of David, which has come to be identified as a typically Jewish symbol and appears on the flag of the state of ISRAEL. Its use as a uniquely Jewish symbol only dates back several centuries, prior to which it was used as a decorative motif by non-Jews as well [62: 257]. It is often found today on Jewish tombstones, and worn as an ornament round the neck by young Jews.

Magha Puja [xi] A BUDDHIST festival that takes place on the full-moon day (see UPOSATHA) of the month of Magha, the 11th month of the Indian calendar, corresponding to January/February. The festival commemorates the occasion when, according to tradition, the BUDDHA, in the first year after his enlightenment, summarized his teaching in three verses (DHAMMAPADA vv. 183–5) before an assembly of 1,250 ARAHATS. Today this festival is especially celebrated in Thailand.

Magi [xxxvi] A priestly tribe among the ancient Medes [22: 82–5]. They became the official priesthood of western Iran and thereby acted as the transmitters of ZOROASTRIANISM, even though ZOROASTER and his immediate followers were not part of the Magian tradition [8 vol. 1: 10f]. Zoroaster referred to himself as a *zaotar*, a fully qualified priest, and as a *manthran*, a composer of MANTHRAS [8 vol. 1: 183f]. In the AVESTA the general term for priest is *athaurvan*. But throughout the recorded history of western Zoroastrianism it is the *magi* who appear on official state records as the priests of the religion. Western (e.g. Greek and Roman) writers commented on their discipline, dress, study, worship, ethics, practices of divination and prophecy, and their purity laws. Although magic is named after them

there are no known practices of the Iranian clergy which really justify this. The *magi* were well educated, working as judges and scribes as well as royal advisers and 'chaplains'. In Sasanian times (3rd–7th centuries CE) a *mobadan mobad* (high priest of high priests) was appointed for the whole community.

Among PARSIS a high priest is called a *dastur*. Since the 16th century the senior *dastur* has been considered the *dastur* of the priestly city of Navsari. A *panthaki* has administrative responsibility over a specific region (*panthak*) and he employs *mobeds* (priests) to perform ceremonies within his area.

There is a two-stage initiation into the priesthood involving the rites of *navar* and *maratab* [47: viii]. The Zoroastrian priesthood is hereditary, but the lineage lapses if three successive generations fail to take at least *navar*. One who proceeds no further than this first initiation is known as *ervad*. The older term for priest was *herbad* and the text the *Herbedestan* provides an account of who can undertake religious studies, including women [39]. Women and lay persons (*behdin*) cannot be priests. Functionally, a Zoroastrian priest is a man of religious learning who can perform rites and who maintains the necessary ethical and ritual purity to do so; hence one term for a priest is a *yozdathrager*, the 'purifier'. As a man of spiritual power his actions, words and gaze can consecrate objects (*manthras*). Ritual power ('*amal*) can only be actualized in a clean place, i.e. free from the dirt associated with evil's weapons of decay and death (see ANGRA MAINYU), by a righteous priest who must recite with devotion and attention [38]. In ancient times the *magi* practised animal sacrifice; this is rare among modern Zoroastrians in Iran and has not been part of the Parsi practice for over 100 years. The liturgical dress of a priest is essentially ancient dress, long flowing robes in white (to symbolize purity), with a white cap. When praying before the fire the priest wears a white mask (*padan*) to prevent his impure breath defiling the sacred flame. The symbol of the priesthood is a *gurz*, or 'mace of MITHRA', a silver shaft with a bull's head at the end deriving either from the military maces (since the priest is a warrior against evil) of antiquity or indicative of the original sacrificial role of the priest. [Harper in 7; 28: 120–33; 30: 55–65]

Magic [XXIV] Ritual activity intended to produce results without using the recognized causal processes of the physical world. Present in all cultures and ranging from folk magic worked by simple traditional rules to sophisticated magical systems backed by complex metaphysics, magic generally depends upon a world-view in which things of one order are felt to correspond to things of another, so that operations performed symbolically in one realm will take practical effect elsewhere. The Azande sorcerer (*see* ZANDE RELIGION) depriving a popular man of his friends by the use of twigs from a tree which loses its leaves rapidly when cut [10], and the Renaissance courtier-magician seeking to compel a lady's love by a talisman (an object ritually constructed to bring special powers to its possessor; *see* AMULETS AND TALISMANS) of Venus, constructed of copper, at astrologically appropriate hours, both create a 'model' of a force which they seek to project.

Distinctions between magic operating 'mechanically' and magic inducing a spirit or god to act are not always useful. The man who ill-treats a lock of his enemy's hair to harm him probably expects automatic results; the Renaissance magician conjuring up a spirit to reveal celestial wisdom probably does not. But in medieval Europe holy water cured illness. Was virtue inherent in the consecrated substance, or were cures granted through faith and God's grace? Opinions differed [27].

Nor is magic altogether distinct from religious RITUAL, where symbolism helps evoke certain feelings and attitudes. It has been practised for the most exalted ends by deeply religious people (*see* WESTERN MAGICAL TRADITION). In the most general terms any repeated action performed with consciousness and intention is a magical ritual. The effectiveness of magical activity depends upon the integrity of the 'magician' and upon the precision and clarity of his or her action. In the West, magicians traditionally work in groups or 'lodges', the more formalized of these working within an 'order' which has a particular aim. Some examples of these are the 'HERMETIC ORDER OF THE GOLDEN DAWN' and the 'Order of Sentinels'. Inherent to the non-logical and creative functions of the human mind, magic shades off into religion, psychotherapy, art and technology, to all of which it has made fundamental contributions.

Magic (Ancient Egyptian) [VI] Important in daily life, Egyptian magic was based upon the 'sympathetic' principle, affirming that the spoken name or image of a living being or an object created the presence of the original. The magician could then control it, either by magical rites or by the recitation of formulae [17: x, 229]. It was used as a protection against hostile forces: illness (*see* MANSION OF THE GODS), ferocious animals and Egypt's enemies. Potsherds were inscribed with enemies' names, and then ceremonially smashed (the Execration Texts). [5]

Magic (Ancient Near Eastern) [VIII] Incantation priests (*see* TEMPLES (ANCIENT NEAR EASTERN)) recited spells as part of magical rituals which could drive out sickness, banish misfortune, curse enemies, protect property, or bring good luck and success. Illness was regarded as a demon (*see* EVIL) to be driven out with magic, assisted by medicine [23: 20–1]. Probably originating in Babylonia (*see* BABYLONIANS), although Elam (*see* ELAMITES) was regarded as a centre for witchcraft, magic was disseminated to northern Syria and the HITTITES, through the HURRIANS. In the Hittite empire, black magic was recognized in law as a crime [13: 161].

Mahabharata [XVII] 'The Great Epic of the Bharatas', containing 90,000 stanzas, is a compilation of ancient Indian epic material made probably between the 2nd century BCE and the end of the 1st century CE. The scene of the story is the upper Ganges plain, and its central concern is the battle between the Kauravas and the Pandavas, the other branch of the Bharatas, a people who claim to have descended from an eponymous ancestor, Bharata. In origin probably a 'martial ballad' [12: 409] the epic, preserved and transmitted by the Brahman class (*see* BRAHMANS), has probably had considerable didactic and religious material incorporated into it in the course of transmission. 'Warlike narratives . . . mingled with mythological scenes and moral discourses' [111: II] reveal the ethical values of ancient HINDU society and especially such matters as the duties of the individual. The central and best-known part of the epic is the discourse delivered by KRISHNA to the hero, Arjuna, known as the BHAGAVADGITA (Song of the Blessed One), that is, of Krishna as the AVATARA of the supreme God, VISHNU. The discourse concerns primarily the DHARMA of the KSHATRIYA or warrior class (VARNA). Another of the component parts is the *Shanti Parvan*, a discourse on ethics and government delivered by the dying Bhishma. Another is the story of Nala and Damayanti, told as a warning against the evils of gambling [12: 412–14].

Mahasanghika [XI] One of the divisions of the early Buddhist order which originated before the development of MAHAYANA and may well have exerted some influence on the development of Mahayana ideas. The name 'Mahasanghika' refers to those of the Great Assembly, which may originally have meant the majority in some monastic dispute. The common story that the Mahasanghikas originated in a group of morally lax monks who refused to accept their defeat at the Second Buddhist Council (*c.*4th century BCE) probably owes more to sectarian propaganda than to history. Mahasanghika sources know of this council and the resultant schism, but assert their orthodoxy. It is possible that the Mahasanghikas arose as an identifiable grouping some time soon after this (*see* THERAVADA).

The Mahasanghikas are known for the teaching of *lokottaravada*, the doctrine that the BUDDHA was in some sense supramundane. This involves the view that while the Buddha was in the world he was not tainted by it, and all his actions which might appear to involve some form of taint were done in order to conform to the ways of the world. Such teachings may well have influenced the development of Mahayana Buddhology, and it is possible that the Mahasanghikas were also involved in the development of the teaching of EMPTINESS. (*See also* MADHYAMAKA; SHUNYATAVADA.) [101: 16–20]

Mahavamsa [XI] The 'Great Chronicle' (in PALI) of the BUDDHIST history of Sri Lanka, a poetic work 'worthy the name of a true epic' [57: 141]. It covers the entire period from the lifetime of GOTAMA to the 4th century CE. It has been translated into English prose by W. Geiger and M. H. Bode. (*See also* CULAVAMSA; DIPAVAMSA.) [25; 57: 139–46]

Mahavastu [XI] The 'Great Event', that is, the life of GOTAMA, the BUDDHA, according to the Lokottaravada school of BUDDHISTS. The Sanskrit text was edited by E. Senart (Paris, 1882–97) and an English translation by J. J. Jones (London, Pali Text Society, 3 vols., 1949–56) is available. [40]

Mahavira [XX] Twenty-fourth TIRTHANKARA of the JAIN religion, traditionally regarded as having been born in 599 BCE. There is a dispute between the SHVETAMBARA and DIGAMBARA sects about the date of his birth, although they regard it as falling within the last quarter of the 6th century BCE. If the traditional dates of the BUDDHA are to be adjusted, as seems likely, then Mahavira's dates will also have to be moved.

The biography of Mahavira evolved gradually, with the very oldest Jain scriptures largely stressing the difficulties of his ascetic life prior to enlightenment. Early BUDDHIST texts offer virtually no useful data for him. The fully developed biography (the two main sects differ with regard to details) of Mahavira ('Great Hero') presents him as being taken in foetus form from heaven at the command of Indra, the king of the gods, and, after having first been erroneously placed in the womb of a Brahman woman (see BRAHMANS), then being deposited in the appropriate womb of a woman of the warrior (KSHATRIYA) class. His parents, depicted as being a king and queen, gave him the name Vardhamana ('Increasing') because of the prosperity which attended his birth. At the age of 30, Mahavira renounced the world and after $12\frac{1}{2}$ years of wandering mendicancy, part of which he spent with Makkhali Gosala, later to lead the Ajivika sect, he achieved omniscient enlightenment. The descriptions of his subsequent career do little more than describe his conversion of the 12 brahmans (GANADHARA) who were to form the basis of the Jain community, and his teaching of the doctrine of non-violence. After his death, his body was cremated and its relics taken to heaven by the gods.

It is customary to present Mahavira, one of India's most important religious teachers, as the adapter or reformer of a cosmography and ascetic law promulgated by PARSHVA, whom Jain tradition saw as his predecessor as *tirthankara*. Not unreasonably, Mahavira can be associated, at least from a historical point of view, with the central doctrinal tenets of Jainism: the world is full of souls; violence towards them, which can be caused by any sort of action, causes *karma* (see KARMA (JAIN DOCTRINE)) to cling to the soul, impeding its natural omniscience; and the means of destroying this *karma* in order to gain enlightenment and ensuing liberation (see MOKSHA (JAIN DOCTRINE)) is the practice of austerity and the cultivation of an attitude of friendship and non-violence towards one's fellow creatures. [4: I; 10: I]

Mahavrata [XX] The five 'great vows' ritually adopted by JAIN ascetics at the time of initiation as indicative of their renunciation of the world. They involve rejection of violence, lying, taking what has not been given, sexual activity and possessions. A variety of ancillary activities serves to amplify the great vows and bring out their full significance. [4: 135–8]

Mahayana [XI] (The Greater Vehicle) Mahayana is not a sect or school of BUDDHISM, nor was it the result of schism. Mahayana monks in India could be found in monasteries associated with non-Mahayana forms of Buddhism. Mahayana represents a particular vision of what the final goal of Buddhism should be, and the practices which are conducive to bringing about that goal. The goal is said to be complete Buddhahood, the perfection of wisdom (PRAJNA) and compassion (KARUNA), and is sought not as a personal liberation from suffering but rather in order to be able to help more effectively all sentient beings.

Our earliest sources for Mahayana ideas are MAHAYANA SUTRAS which may date from the 2nd century BCE (See PRAJNAPARAMITA). The BUDDHA is characterized by infinite compassion and through this compassion continues to help sentient beings (perhaps on another plane, a Pure Land; see BUDDHA, BODIES OF) even after his apparent death. To attain Buddhahood out of compassion for all sentient beings is thought to be immeasurably superior to attaining merely freedom from one's own suffering and rebirth (see NIBBANA; ARAHAT), and this Buddhahood should be the final goal of each practitioner. Those who aim for the goal of mere enlightenment are referred to derogatively as followers of a HINAYANA – an inferior vehicle. Thus Mahayana Buddhism is finally thought to be a matter of motivation for following the Buddhist path.

For Mahayana, since the Buddha remains after death out of compassion, in infinite time and space there must be infinite Buddhas all helping and capable of entering into relationship with sentient beings (see CHING T'U TSUNG; AMIDA WORSHIP; AMITABHA). Moreover, ultimately all beings should aim to obtain this supreme goal of Buddhahood for the benefit of others, that is, take the vow of the BODHISATTVA, and there are already infinite bodhisattvas well-advanced on the path to Buddhahood capable of engaging in compassionate acts for the benefit of beings (see AVALOKITESHVARA; MAITREYA; MANJUSHRI; TARA).

Mahayana Buddhism developed a number of philosophical schools although all took as their starting point the philosophy of EMPTINESS (see MADHYAMAKA; SHUNYATA-VADA), while at the same time offering interpretations which were quite diverse (see YOGACARA; TATHAGA-

TAGARBHA; JONANG). The philosophy of emptiness provided the basis for an essential equality and therefore equality of potential. All (including women such as Tara or laypeople) could in theory become fully enlightened Buddhas. Mahayana scriptures also developed the doctrine of SKILFUL MEANS (upaya-kaushalya), whereby the Buddha adapts his teaching to the level of his hearers. This helps explain the diversity of Buddhist teachings, which are each appropriate to a particular level of practice. This also supplies a basis for Mahayana ethics, which involves a bodhisattva adapting his or her conduct to the situation in the light of great wisdom and compassion, and therefore not always acting in the way which would be expected. It may be partly the adaptability of Mahayana which led to its predominance as a final aspiration for Buddhists in Tibet, China, Japan and east Asia (see CHINESE BUDDHISM; JAPAN, BUDDHISM IN). [101]

Mahayana Sutras [XI] The Sutras (Pali: SUTTA) of MAHAYANA claim to be the word of the BUDDHA himself, although the earliest surviving Mahayana sutras date from perhaps the 2nd century BCE. Sometimes the Buddha is said to have hidden the sutras until an appropriate time for their promulgation (See NAGARJUNA). Non-Mahayana traditions such as THERAVADA do not accept the Mahayana sutras as the word of the Buddha. There is evidence from the sutras themselves that some sutras may have been the result of visionary experience, and a view is found expressed that whatever is well said is the word of the Buddha. There is a large number of these sutras, and they vary in length. Some are extremely long, and there are also composite sutras. The sutras may not all have been composed in India, and sutras were certainly added to, both within and outside India, particularly in Central Asia. A feature of many Mahayana sutras is laudatory self-reference, the praising of the sutra itself and its miraculous effects, together with the penalties that come from its condemnation. Sutras often exhort their advocates to copy and enshrine them, worshipping them with incense, flowers, lamps and so on – the same form of offering traditionally made by Buddhists to STUPAS. Sometimes Mahayana sutras refer to themselves as the 'Dharma-body' (*dharmakaya*) of the Buddha, superior to his physical body as the doctrine (Dharma/DHAMMA) is superior to the Buddha's corporeal person. (*See also* BUDDHA, BODIES OF.) [101: I, II]

Mahdi [XIX] Literally 'divinely guided one': a term with millenarian and eschatological implications, used at various stages in Islamic history. It is the name given by mainstream Sunnis (*see* SUNNA) to the periodic revivers of the faith when it has grown weak or when the Muslim community has fallen into an oppressed and impotent state. It is also believed that towards the end of the world, before the Last Day (*see* QIYAMA), a Mahdi, often identified with the returned JESUS, will establish a reign of justice on earth. In SHI'ISM the Mahdi is a vital figure, identified with the Hidden IMAM who will reappear and rule by divine prescription. This idea of a messianic figure has often sustained Muslims through dark periods of their history, and religious leaders making such claims for themselves have frequently arisen; notable here is the Mahdi Muhammad Ahmad, who set up a theocratic state in the Sudan which endured from 1882 until 1898. [20 s.v.; 38 s.v.; 78: XI; 142: IV]

Mahikari Organizations [XXVI] The two major Mahikari (True Light) organizations are Sekai Mahikari Bunmei Kyodan and Sukyo Mahikari. The former claims about 75,000 members, the latter about

800,000. Both trace their origin to the Japanese teacher Okada Kotama (1901–74). In 1959 Okada had a revelatory experience. He was warned that the time had come for the world to change from material to spiritual civilization, but because people are too self-seeking to recognize the need for change, the KAMI would purge the world with fire. The *kami* also provided, however, a way of salvation: the action of light. Okada's mission was to allow the rays of the True Light to flow through the palm of his hand and thus purify people's souls and cleanse the world of impurity.

The *kami* that Mahikari adherents honour is Su-no-Okami. Their chief responsibility, following Okada's example, is to allow purifying light to flow from the palm of the hand into the soul of a suffering person. The action of light convinces people of the existence of the soul and of the *kami*, gives them strength to endure the baptism of fire and enables them to become 'seed-people' of the new and true civilization that is to come.

Sekai Mahikari Bunmei Kyodan was legally incorporated in 1963. One of the people who joined at that time was Sekiguchi Sakae (1909–), who rose to become a top leader and, when Okada Kotama died, claimed the right to be his successor. This claim was disputed by the founder's adopted daughter, Okada Keishu (1929–) The dispute finally resulted in a court case, and the court found in favour of Sekiguchi. He remains the *oshie nushi*, or doctrinal authority, of Sekai Mahikari Bunmei Kyodan. Those who broke away founded Sukyo Mahikari in 1978 and have installed Okada Keishu as the *oshie nushi* [3; 13: 243–85]

Maimonides, Moses [XXII] The greatest of medieval Jewish codifiers and theologians [14 vol. II: 754]. Maimonides was born in Córdoba (Spain) in 1135 CE but had to flee his native land to escape from a fanatical Islamic sect and eventually settled in Fostat (Egypt), where he died in 1204. For the later part of his life he was a physician at the court of the sultan. His fame rests on his two major works: the *Mishneh Torah*, a codification of all of rabbinical law and ritual; and *The Guide of the Perplexed* [42], which synthesizes Jewish and Aristotelian thought [24: 152; 28: xiii]. He also wrote an important commentary on the Mishnah, a survey of the 613 biblical commandments (Mitzvah) and medical treatises. Most of his writings, including his letters on legal and theological subjects to Jewish communities that had turned to him for advice, were originally in Arabic and were translated into Hebrew by others. Controversy surrounded many of his views. [31; 70: 60]

Maitatsine Movement [xxvii] This movement in northern Nigeria (nicknamed from a Hausa phrase often used in it) originated from a convert to Islam from northern Cameroun, a Muslim preacher named Mallam Muhammadu Marwa (b. 1920s), who claimed to supersede Muhammad, came to Kano in 1945 and became labelled as Mallam Maitatsine. After various conflicts with the Muslim authorities the movement exploded in a confrontation with the government in Kano in 1980. The founder was killed, some 4,000 lives were lost, and there have been intermittent subsequent disturbances. Unlike other new Islamic-related movements in west Africa there is no evidence that it represents interaction with African indigenous religions. It has been described as a form of 'closed Islam' with mahdist overtones, or as a Fundamentalist form of Islam, with Maitatsine, as the infallible interpreter of the Qur'an, rejecting all later Islamic sources. The supporters were mainly rural people threatened by modernizing changes brought about by centralized government, education and the social disturbances of the new oil wealth.

Maitreya [xi] All Buddhists agree that there have been many Buddhas in the past, and there will be many in the future. Maitreya (Pali: Metteyya) is the Bodhisattva accepted by all Buddhist traditions as the next Buddha in this world. He is at present residing in the Tushita heaven awaiting the appropriate time for his appearance. Descriptions of the world as it will be when Maitreya becomes a Buddha provide a form of Buddhist Millenarianism, and it is common for Buddhists to pray to be reborn in the world at that time in order to attain enlightenment under Maitreya's tutelage. Like all bodhisattvas, Maitreya in Mahayana Buddhism is actively participating in the world. Maitreya may have been associated with meditation practices developed in Kashmir involving visualizations, and there are stories of practitioners being carried up to Tushita and receiving a vision of Maitreya (*see* Asanga). A cult of Maitreya spread to Central Asia and China where it was particularly important at various times (*see* Hsuan-tsang). In art such as the Central Asian cave art Maitreya is often portrayed seated in 'Western' fashion teaching the doctrine. (*See* Japanese buddhas and bodhisattvas.) [101: 228–31]

Mala'ika [xix] Angels, in Islam. In Islamic cosmogony, these form a part of God's creation; sometimes described as made of light, they are considered by theologians, on the basis of the Qur'an, as superior to mankind in general but inferior to the 'messengers of mankind', i.e. prophets, who have to fight against the sinfulness of human nature. The Qur'an mentions by name Jibril (Gabriel), bearer of the revelation to Muhammad, and Mikha'il. Others are also cited, such as the angel who will sound the last trump before judgement (*see* Qiyama); those near to God's throne who hymn his praises; the angel of death; the keepers of heaven and hell; and the two recording and guardian angels over human individuals. Iblis, the rebel against God and tempter to evil of mankind, has an ambiguous position in Islamic lore; he behaves as a fallen angel, but is considered to be made from smokeless fire, like the JINN. (*See also* SATAN (IN ISLAM).) [20 'Angel(s) (Islam)'; 38 s.v.; 67 'Angels']

Male Cults (Melanesia) [xxix] Marking entry into adulthood in traditional Melanesian society are strenuous and painful rites (circumcision, blood-letting, tattooing) to purify young males from the weakening effect of contact with mothers and other women during childhood. Such public puberty rites are accompanied by secret initiations into male cults, during which tribal lore and ritual are gradually revealed. Novices are ceremonially washed, isolated from women and children, made to fast or eat special food, and teased and beaten by their elders [2]. All this takes place to gain the approval of ancestral spirits, who reside with the menfolk in the sacred cult house (HAUS TAMBARAN) and are invoked with chants and prayers, making themselves visible and audible through MASKS, flutes and drums, bullroarers and other sacred media. Male cult rites accompany births, initiations, marriages and funerals. Cult specialists arrange ceremonial exchanges of goods and wealth, like the Papuan *kula* and *hiri* cycles [20; 25] and the New Guinea Highlands pig-feasts and ritual dances (*see* SINGSING) [14; 23]. Besides cults common to all adult males, there have also been bachelor associations, sorcerers' cults and other secret societies. [9; 12; 29]

Mana [xxix] Power and authority in POLYNESIAN and MELANESIAN RELIGION. In Polynesia *mana* comes from kinship with gods (ATUA) and famous ancestors. Tribal chiefs embody the *mana* of their people and land. All who are strong, wise or skilful demonstrate *mana*. It is present in the orator's speech, the TOHUNGA's chant, the warrior's club and the craftsman's tool [16: 26–34]. Rules of *tapu* (TABU) preserve the potency and holiness of *mana*. A breach of *tapu* means a release of uncontrolled *mana*, dangerous to life and social order. The TOHUNGA uses water and cooked food to neutralize *mana* and restore right relations between sacred and profane things. Cooking and eating the bodies of slain enemies is the ultimate way to destroy their *mana* and that of their tribes [7: 400–2; 16: 267–70]. In Melanesia, possessing *mana* depends less on divine ancestry than on direct access to unseen powers, shown by success in warfare, ritual or sorcery, and by the fertility of wives, gardens and pigs. [9; 23; 28]

Mandaeans [xv] A small religious group of about 15,000 members who today inhabit southern Iraq and Khuzistan in Iran. A sizeable number also live in Baghdad, where some ply the traditional silversmithing skills [5]. They are the last living representatives of GNOSTICISM, which flourished throughout the Middle East during the first centuries CE. The modern communities term themselves *mandayye*, 'gnostics', or *nasorayye*, 'observants', while they are called *subbi*, 'baptizers' in Arabic. Their scriptures are written in the Mandaean language, belonging to the East Aramaic group and with a distinctive script that is connected to the Nabataean system of writing [25: 3]. The Ginza, 'Treasure', which they consider to be their holy book, was probably redacted in the 7th century CE from a miscellany of earlier sources to ensure the Mandaeans' inclusion by ISLAM among the 'Peoples of the Book'. The Ginza is divided into two parts: the Right Ginza consists of theological, mythological, cosmological and moral treatises that conclude with an apocalyptic 'history of the world'; the smaller Left Ginza, also called the 'Book of the Souls', contains hymns and songs on the fate of the soul [16]. The 'Book of John', sometimes called the 'Book of the Kings', comprises myths and legends about the teachings of John the Baptist. The Qolasta or 'Canonical Prayerbook' contains the liturgies used for ceremonies such as baptism and the ascension of the soul [4]. Other literature includes a marriage ritual, a rite for the consecration of priests and the 'Thousand and Twelve Questions', being ritual and moral instructions for priests [6], as well as an astrological code, 'The Book of the Zodiac' [3]. The journey of the soul to the celestial worlds is described and illustrated in the 'Scroll of Abatur'. Similar 'Cubist' drawings occur on inscribed pottery bowls which, together with lead tablets, comprise a genre of incantation literature that was written in the pre-Islamic period [35].

Their priestly hierarchy is divided into *tarmide*, 'disciples', and *ganzibre*, 'treasurers' or 'bishops'. There has been no *ris ama*, 'head of the people', for over a century. [25: 6]. The priests and the laity celebrate wearing the white ritual dress, called *rasta*, which is the symbol of the angels' heavenly garb. *Masbuta* or baptism, which is the most important and oldest of the Mandaean rituals, takes place every Sunday and on special occasions (marriage, after childbirth, at death) in the *mandi*-pool which is situated south of the *mandi*-hut, a cult-hut that is built near rivers or channels. Baptisms are always performed in running or 'living' water since these streams flow into the Lightworld, with its heavenly rivers called Jordans. The baptisand undergoes the following procedure: two triple-immersions, signature on the forehead and drinking of water, investiture with a tiny myrtle-wreath (symbol of spirit and life), anointing of the forehead with sesame, a holy meal of unleavened bread and water, recitatation of prayers as a 'sealing' against demons and finally the ceremonial handclasp called the *kusta*, 'truth' [29]. The *masqita* or ascension of the soul is the second most important ritual, being celebrated by at least four priests in the cult-hut on the third evening after death when the soul has begun its perilous journey lasting 45 days through the *matarata*, 'purgatories', to the Lightworld. The ceremony includes the preparation and consecration of loaves of unleavened wafers, probably representing the soul, which the priests eat since they impersonate Light-beings called *uthre* on earth. At all major rituals the *drafsa*, a banner which symbolizes light, and consists of a fringed silken strip, approximately 3 metres long, looped on a wooden cross-piece that is crowned by a myrtle wreath and has a gold thread securing seven myrtle twigs, is always present.

In the Mandaeans' dualistic cosmogony, the Lightworld vies against the world of dark, but no standard account occurs in the mythology [25: 13]. The Lightworld is headed by a supreme being variously called 'King of Light' (*malka dnhure*), 'Life' (*hayye*) and 'Great Mana' (*mana rbe*) who is surrounded by innumerable Light-beings. The King of Light has four emanations, the second, third and fourth being called Josamin, Abatur and Ptahil respectively. The world of darkness was originally a sea of chaos (the 'black waters') filled with demons including the *malake*, 'angels', the seven planets and the twelve signs of the zodiac. It is headed by the *malka dhsuke*, 'King of Darkness', otherwise called Ur, who is the son of Ruha, the fallen spirit of the cosmos and the female adversary of light. The creation of the world, which culminated in the moulding of Adam's body, resulted from the collaboration between the emanations and the world of darkness, and in particular from the efforts of Ptahil, who was condemned and not allowed to return to the Lightworld. Adam's body was animated by the soul which came, reluctantly, from the Lightworld. Adam received knowledge and redemption from the divine emissary and saviour Manda dHayye (Knowledge of Life), freeing his soul and spirit, an ambiguous component, from his body to return to the Lightworld. Together with his brother/son Hibil (Abel), Manda dHayye assisted the soul's ascension through the trials of purgatory and its weighing, on scales held by Abatur, against the pure soul of Sitil (Seth) at the threshold of the Lightworld.

The Mandaeans' religion shows, in its terminology and figurative language, clear connections with early CHRISTIANITY and the Jewish baptismal sects of the eastern Jordan region, where it probably arose [25: 4]. The Mandaeans have often been called the 'Christians of St John the Baptist', but this misidentification arose from the Portuguese missionaries in the 17th century CE. JOHN THE BAPTIST baptized both JESUS and Manda dHayye, but he was not a central figure in the Mandaean cult until, under pressure from ISLAM, he was accorded the status of a prophet. Jesus is utterly condemned and doomed to purgatory. There are also vehement anti-Jewish tendencies, including the classification of MOSES as a prophet of Ruha and the divine name Adonai as a demon.

Mandaean literature relates little about history, but the 'Scroll of the Divine Revelation' suggests that the community emigrated in the 2nd century CE from Jerusalem to northern Mesopotamia, as a result of persecutions by orthodox Jews. Later pressure from the Byzantine church resulted in their movement to southern Mesopotamia, the area with which they have become traditionally associated.

Mandala [XVII] (Sanskrit 'circle') A diagram used as a meditation aid, particularly in HINDUISM and MAHAYANA BUDDHISM. It is a form of *yantra* or meditation diagram, though in general the word *yantra* is used for the relatively simple forms, such as those associated with the *cakras* in TANTRA (1), while *mandala* is applied to the elaborate forms, designed to represent the entire cosmos. The aim of practice with a *yantra* or *mandala* is to integrate the consciousness and gain access to higher levels. In their painted form, *mandalas* generally combine the square, orientated to the directions, with the circle, representing totality. The deities believed to inhabit the *mandala* may or may not be explicitly shown. Sometimes the *mandala* may be made of perishable materials such as coloured sand, so that at the end of the process it can be dispersed, to overcome attachment [4: 121–3, 184; 57: 119–20, 266–7; XI 3: 87, 93, 181, 220–1, 237].

In a wider sense, the temple (MANDIRA) and the STUPA are *mandalas* and the supreme *mandala* is the human body (*see* TANTRA (1), (2)). Forms resembling the *mandala* seem to have arisen in many cultures, and it has been adopted into some Western psychological practice, notably by C. G. Jung.

Mandala (Buddhist) [XXXV] Originally probably a circle demarcating the sacred space into which an initiate enters (*see* TANTRA (2)). The initiate would visualize him- or herself – or the GURU conducting the initiation – as the central BUDDHA of the mandala, with the cosmos radiating out from his own being in the form of a Pure Land with its attendant BODHISATTVAS. Subsequently the mandala was elaborated into the Pure Land/cosmos as a mandala-palace, still based on a circular plan with doorways in each of the four directions. Mandalas employ a strict ICONOGRAPHY depending on the central Buddha.

In art mandalas can be portrayed in almost any size, but nowadays they are normally too small to be entered physically (*see figure 7*). Mandalas can be two-dimensional or three-dimensional, but in meditation they are visualized as three-dimensional. They can be inscribed by various means, such as painting on cloth, but Tibetans have also developed a way of drawing mandalas using coloured particles of sand. Mandalas can also be made by meditation, and the whole body of the practitioner can be visualized as a mandala. Tibetan Buddhism also has a 'mandala-offering' which involves visualizing the entire cosmos and offering it to the Buddhas, bodhisattvas or the teacher. [32]

Mandira [xvii] 'Dwelling place', the usual word among HINDUS for a temple. In some sense the god or goddess is regarded as living in it, embodied in the image or *murti*. Not all temples are elaborate buildings, or even built at all: the *murti* may be a numinous stone under a tree, and the *mandira* the small area of sacred space containing it. In a city, a *mandira* may be a roadside shrine, just large enough to contain an image of a deity, to which people will make offerings on their way to work. Each Hindu home normally contains a

Figure 7
A Nepalese mandala dedicated to the bodhisattva Manjushri

sacred area, whether a shrine room or just a corner containing a print of a favourite deity (ISHTADEVA). Moreover, a human being who acts as a medium for a deity may be regarded as a living shrine, and honoured as such. At the other extreme are the great temple-complexes, containing shrines to the main deity, such as VISHNU or SHIVA, and members of his or her family and entourage, such as LAKSHMI, PARVATI, GANESHA, the ALVARS or the NAYANNARS. They contain bathing places for the worshippers and halls for sacred music and dance. The spires (*shikhara*) of such temples often resemble the sacred mountain (*see* MERU, MOUNT), with different levels of sculptural decoration symbolizing the realms of animals, human beings and deities. The *murtis* of the main deities are housed in the *garbhagriha*, 'womb-house', a small room deep within the temple. Here the deities are treated like kings and queens of ancient India, symbolically awoken in the morning with music and prayers, bathed, dressed, fed, entertained and put to bed at night. Such temples have traditionally been among the most important patrons of the visual and performing arts.

Worship at a temple, large or small, is generally individual, not congregational, in nature, and is not confined to set times of day. The visitor goes alone or in a small group to make an offering (PUJA) and receive a sight (*darshana*) of the deity. He or she may receive a token of grace (*prasada*), such as food previously offered to the deity, or, in Shaiva temples, sweet-smelling ash on the forehead.

At festival times, the power of the deities is ritually transferred into portable counterparts of the main images, which are dressed, ornamented, placed in ceremonial cars (*ratha*) and taken out in procession. A famous example is that of Jagannatha at Puri (*see* JUGGERNAUT). Many of the famous south Indian bronzes were made as processional equivalents of the stone *murtis* in the *garbhagriha*. [4: 17–24; 88]

Mandylion [XIII.D] *Mandylion* (or *mandelion*) is a Greek word for one of the most important relics of Orthodox Christianity, the towel of Edessa, on which the Christ, the god–man, chose to leave the imprint of his uncapturable features. Its importance is twofold: it demonstrated Christ's support for those who pleaded the cause of images in the context of Christian worship; and it symbolized the blessing of immunity which Christian emperors promised to their subjects. This was made clear when the *mandylion* was brought from Edessa to Constantinople in 944; the Byzantine emperor portrayed himself as heir to the blessing given by JESUS to his contemporary and correspondent, King Abgar of Edessa. It was already implicit in the *Ecclesiastical History* of Eusebius, the first book of which studies the relationship between divine kingship and earthly kings, culminating with the story of King Abgar; Eusebius chose the year 313 in which to publish this Syriac legend in Greek, the year after Constantine the Great claimed the protection of the Cross for the Roman empire. Eusebius, however, mentions no *mandylion*, although by the 5th century the legend of King Abgar included both a promise of immunity to Edessa and a portrait of Jesus painted by the messenger of the King. At some date before 569 a miraculous portrait of Jesus on a cloth was discovered at Camulia in Cappadocia and placed under a lady's veil, which spontaneously took its imprint. The imprint went to Amasya, the cloth itself to the capital, Constantinople. This relic, the Camuliana, was to be borne before the armies of the Emperor Heraclius. It seems likely that it was to vie with the Camuliana that the portrait at Edessa was replaced with a similar relic; the painter, it was now related, had despaired of achieving a likeness and Christ had taken pity on him by imprinting his own features on a towel. Evagrius, recalling about 590 Edessa's finest hour, when it withstood a Persian siege in 544, disingenuously gave to the *mandylion* the credit for this and explained the promise of immunity as a prophetic fraud. When Edessa fell to the Persians, the promise of immunity was forgotten, until 'Edessa' was reinterpreted as Constantinople, as we have seen, in 944. Constantinople itself was not immune to siege, however; in 1204 it was plundered by European Christians and its relics, including the *mandylion*, went to enrich the cathedral treasuries of the West. At some date before 1287, St Peter's on the Vatican Hill acquired a rival *mandylion*; and, although this was shown to a Nestorian monk as the towel of Edessa and described as such in a beautifully illustrated Latin manuscript (Paris Latin 2688), a new legend grew up around this and similar relics in Europe, the legend of Veronica and her cloth. Edessa, by this time, was lost to Byzantium and to the Crusaders and had become a Turkish city with the name of Urfa; but the *mandylion* was not forgotten by the Muslim pilgrims who attribute the healing properties of a certain well at Urfa to the presence in its depths of a cloth (*mandil*) belonging to the Prophet Isa (Jesus). [3; 109]

Manichaean Teaching [xv] In common with many GNOSTIC systems, at the heart of MANICHAEISM is a DUALISM of body (entirely evil) and spirit (a part of divinity). To explain how the intermingling of good and evil took place in the created world, Mani developed an elaborate cosmogonic myth of a primeval invasion of the kingdom of light (the epitome of all that is good, beautiful and honourable) by the Prince of Darkness (the personification of greed, enmity and lust). To

defend the ill-equipped kingdom of light, its ruler, the Father of Greatness, has to evoke other deities and calls forth from within himself the Mother of Life, who in turn calls forth the PRIMAL MAN whom she arms with the five light elements, air, wind, light, water and fire. The Father thus comes to battle with darkness in the guise of the son, armed with his elements, which together with the Great Spirit comprise the Living Soul. In the initial encounter, the Primal Man, overwhelmed by the powers of darkness, is lulled into a death-like sleep and his armour of light elements partly devoured by the Archons of darkness. To the rescue of the Primal Man a new series of divinities is evoked, of whom the Living Spirit descends and calls out to him in a piercing voice. The Primal Man responds and is awakened, leading to a reunion of the Primal Man with the Father. There follows a complex process for the redemption of the light elements from the bodies of the Archons of darkness. Ten heavens and eight earths are created in whose lower sections the Archons of darkness are imprisoned, and a new evocation, the hermaphroditic (Third) Envoy, then seduces both male and female Archons with his/her good looks and induces them to ejaculate and abort the light-particles held captive in them. These fall on the earth and bring forth plant and animal life. An elaborate system involving the main planetary and stellar bodies is then set in motion to return the light-particles to their original abode.

Smarted by this apparent defeat, the Prince of Darkness creates a male and female demon; the former devours the offspring of the abortions, thereby ingesting their light-particles, and copulates with his partner who gives birth to the first man (Adam) and the first woman (Eve) who are microcosms of the universe (macrocosm), both possessing a mixture of light and matter.

Made blind and deaf by matter, Adam is forgetful of his distant divine origin: his soul, entrapped in the accursed body, has literally 'lost consciousness'. At that moment the transcendent JESUS whom the Manichaeans called 'Jesus-the-Splendour' comes to his aid. Jesus, who in Manichaeism and gnosticism generally plays a cosmic role, here appears as teacher and exorciser of demons. He shows Adam the Father in the heights and his own self cast down before the teeth of wild beasts, devoured by dogs, mingled with and imprisoned in all that exists, shackled in the corruption of darkness. Jesus also raises him and makes him eat of the tree of life, bringing him to full realization of the imprisonment of his divine soul by his sinful body. Manichaeism also offers a powerful image of the universal mixture of light and darkness and of the channels – sheltering light – separating off the darkness. To achieve the separation, the Third Envoy calls up the 'column of glory', up which the parts of light can climb. First they take their place in the moon, and when it wanes they are transported to the sun and thence to paradise. Eventually a new paradise is constructed for the light-gods. When the light-particles in the world have been purified sufficiently to come together in the Last Pillar, the end of the world starts: first a universal fire of 1468 years and finally the compression of darkness into a lump (Greek: *bolos*), in which certain sinful souls remain.

The long-term imprisonment of light by matter in the physical universe, seen by the Manichaeans as a form of crucifixion and personified by the 'suffering Jesus' (*Jesus patibilis*), means that those who have been illumined by Mani's *gnosis* must be instruments for its liberation. This requires both conscious effort for virtue and the avoidance of any action which might harm the light or prolong its captivity. Manichaeans are therefore enjoined to observe the 'five commandments' (fasting, alms-giving, no killing, no flesh-eating and poverty) and the 'three seals' i.e. those of 'mouth, hands and breast'. Since strict observance of these rules is possible only for a select few, the sect consists of a dyarchy of elect, who endeavour to keep all the laws, and hearers, who are allowed to marry and procreate and to generate wealth, so long as they serve the daily needs of the elect. [1; 12; 17; 20; 22; 30]

Manichaeism, History of [xv] Mani (216–c.226 CE), the founder of the religion which bears his name, grew up in a gnosticizing (*see* GNOSTICISM) Jewish–Christian community in BABYLONIA, but left it to inaugurate his highly evangelical religion which would later spread throughout the Sassanian empire as well as diffusing into the Roman empire through trade routes via Syria and the Red Sea and later into central Asia and China via the Silk Road. Augustine of Hippo (*see* AUGUSTINIANISM) was a Manichaean 'hearer' (*see* MANICHAEAN TEACHING) for nine years. While he was a student in Carthage, he was attracted to the sect by the DUALIST solution it offered to the problem of evil inherent in a monotheistic CHRISTIANITY. A collection of eight Manichaean codices in COPTIC was found by workmen in 1930 at Medinet Madi in upper Egypt, and vestiges of a major Manichaean community dating to the 4th century CE were found by archaeologists at the Dakhleh Oasis (Egypt) in 1990. The religion died out in central Asia in the 12th century but survived in south China until the 17th century, when it was extinguished by Confucian persecution (*see* CONFUCIUS) for being a secret religious sect with rebellious potential.

Mani drew his original ideas mainly from GNOSTIC and Jewish APOCALYPTIC writings. A zealous missionary at heart, his religion diffused within the Zoroastrian milieu

(*See* ZOROASTRIANISM) at an early stage and assimilated Zoroastrian deities into its pantheon. A more Judaeo-Christian version of his religion spread in the Roman empire and also into Parthia where it came under the influence of ZURVANISM and later of BUDDHISM. The two main streams (Judaeo-Christian and Zoroastrian) of Manichaeism later merged in central Asia, from where many Manichaean texts were recovered in the region of Turfan and in the Cave of Thousand Buddhas from Tun-huang. The lack of awareness by earlier scholars of the complex history of diffusion of the religion has led to its being seen either exclusively as a form of Zoroastrianism or as a Christian heresy. The Middle Iranian texts from Turfan came to prominence in the study of the HISTORY OF RELIGION (especially in the so-called *Religionsgeschichtliche Schule*) in the 1920s, when they were exploited by Reitzenstein to prove the existence of a pre-Christian Gnostic redeemer myth (*see* REDEEMED REDEEMER) in old Iranian religions regardless of the late date (7th–10th century CE) and provenance of these texts.

The Manichaean church in its most fully developed form in central Asia was arranged in dioceses and had as its head an *archegos* at Ctesiphon (near Baghdad) in Iraq until Islamic persecution in the 8th century CE forced the religion to shift its base entirely into central Asia where it became a major force in the development of MONASTICISM. Remains of well-executed wall paintings as well as thousands of fragments of manuscripts, many skilfully illuminated by Manichaean scribes, were found by German archaeologists in the Turfan area at the beginning of the 20th century. A Manichaean temple built in the 13th century, with a well-preserved statue of Mani, still stands near the modern city of Xuanzhou (the Zaitun of Marco Polo) in south China. [15; 17; 31; 32]

Manitou [V] An ALGONQUIN term roughly equivalent to 'mysterious' or 'supernatural', used as a noun to designate the supernatural world, and as an adjective to identify any manifestation thereof. In general, *manitou* may refer to: the supreme being; those spirits encountered in visions (*see* VISION QUEST); lesser spirits; or the various powers of nature or other cosmic features [8: 1]. Lesser entities exhibit or manifest the quality of *manitou*, as witness, for example, the Narragansett Indians, who used it to describe 'excellence' in men, women, birds, beasts, etc. The term suggests more the presence of a certain 'spirit' or 'disposition' rather than supernatural power, although the latter is frequently associated with a being that is *manitou*.

Manjushri [XI] Just as AVALOKITESHVARA serves in MAHAYANA BUDDHISM as the icon of great compassion (KARUNA), Manjushri is the BODHISATTVA who personifies great wisdom (PRAJNA). He is usually portrayed in art, particularly Tibetan art, wielding the Sword of Gnosis in his right hand with the stem of a lotus on which rests a PRAJNAPARAMITA scripture in his left. Often in East Asian art Manjushri is accompanied by a lion. Manjushri is ages old yet perpetually young, a 16-year-old youth described as 'the crown prince'. Texts frequently describe him as actually already a BUDDHA (as with Avalokiteshvara and particularly MAITREYA). Perhaps because of his role as wisdom incarnate, Manjushri often plays the role of interlocutor when philosophy is discussed in MAHAYANA SUTRAS. In Tibet Manjushri is particularly associated with the 'wisdom lineage' of MADHYAMAKA, and he is said to have appeared in a vision to Tsongkhapa in order to clear up his uncertainties about Madhyamaka interpretation (*see* GELUG). [101: 238–41]

Mansion of the Gods [VI] The term for TEMPLE in ANCIENT EGYPTIAN RELIGION. In the 'god's mansion' the priests performed regular rituals. Solar temples of the 5th dynasty, *c.*2480 BCE (*see* RE'), and those built for the Aten (18th dynasty, *c.*1360 BCE) (*see* ATENISM), developed from a different tradition, but the New Kingdom cult temples (for the god) and mortuary temples (for the dead – and deified – kings) developed from *c.*1500 BCE onwards from the primitive reed-shrines and symbolized the ISLAND OF CREATION [6; 9].

Interior walls, decorated with registers of scenes, showed the king performing rites for the god. Ritual sequences were privately enacted by the high priest. In the daily temple ritual, he cleansed, clothed, offered insignia to and fed the deity, while, in the ritual for the royal ancestors, the god's food was subsequently offered to the ancestral rulers of Egypt. Other rituals (*see* FESTIVALS (ANCIENT NEAR EASTERN)) took place periodically, amid public rejoicing, portraying special events in the god's life and mythology. The resurrection of Osiris was annually reenacted at Abydos and elsewhere. Statues of male deities were carried in procession to the neighbouring temples of their consorts for a period of several weeks. This reflected the belief in the gods in human terms, with a need for food, clothing and recreation.

Priests were involved in funerary and mortuary rites and in temple worship. The priesthood was hereditary in certain families [20: III, 60] and, although it sometimes entailed permanent, powerful appointments, it was usually a subsidiary profession held by lawyers, doctors or scribes, who spent three months annually in the local temple. As 'god's servants', they had no pastoral duties, but performed the rituals for the deity and instructed the young in the 'House of Life', an area of the temple used for education.

Mansion of the Ka [VI] The term for tombs in ANCIENT EGYPTIAN RELIGION. In pre-dynastic Egypt (*c.*3400 BCE), everyone was buried in simple pit-graves; then, brick-built mastaba-tombs ('bench-shaped') were introduced for royalty and the great nobles (*c.*3100). These became the standard noble tombs of the Old Kingdom (*c.*2700–2300 BCE), clustered around the royal PYRAMID and consisting of a superstructure and substructure (above and below ground), a *serdab* where a statue of the deceased stood and an offering chapel [7: I, 39].

With increasing democratization in funerary beliefs, provincial nobles built rock-cut tombs near their own capitals and, by the New Kingdom, royalty were themselves buried in deep tombs at Thebes (*c.*1570–1087 BCE), cut into the Valleys of the Kings and Queens, while their nobles' tombs were scattered throughout the same area. Whatever the design, the tomb – 'Mansion of the Ka' – was regarded as a 'house' for the deceased and, at the burial ceremony, the 'Opening of the Mouth' ritual was performed to bring alive the mummy (*see* MUMMIFICATION) and all the wall-scenes and contents of the tomb. [5]

Manthras [XXXVI] 'Sacred words', in ZOROASTRIANISM. Primarily these are the *Gathas* of ZOROASTER (*see also* AVESTA), but the term is also used to refer to all prayers. Zoroastrians should pray at the five religious divisions (*gahs*) of the day [8 vol. 1: 258–66]. Before praying, men and women – there is no difference in the duty of the sexes in this regard – should wash all exposed parts of the body: face, hands and feet. After untying the sacred cord (*kusti*) which all initiated Zoroastrians wear around the waist as a symbol of the religion after initiation (NAUJOTE), the worshipper faces the light and recites what are known as the '*kusti* prayers'. These involve the formal rejection of evil (ANGRA MAINYU) and the expression of allegiance to the good (AHURA MAZDA). There are a number of important traditional Zoroastrian prayers. The *Ahuna Vairya* (PAHLAVI: *Ahunvar*) is the first taught to any Zoroastrian child and was probably composed by Zoroaster himself. Others are the *Airyema isho, Yenghe hatam* and *Ashem Vohu* [10: III]. The *Fravarane* is a confessional giving assent to the key Zoroastrian teachings [8 vol. 1: 253–7]. All of these utterances are in Avesta, the sacred language. Zoroastrians believe that prayer in the language of revelation prevents thinking in merely human terms. Some PARSI reformists have called for vernacular translations to aid understanding, since few priests and virtually none of the laity understand Avesta. But the majority faithfully continue to use the language of their prophet, which is believed to create a unique spiritual aura. *Manthras* are thought to be words of power made effective through enactment, that is, through recitation. Unspoken, e.g. written, words, or those spoken by an unqualified person, e.g. a non-Zoroastrian (*juddin*), are dead *manthras*. Prayers to the heavenly beings (AMESHA SPENTAS, YAZATAS) effect their protective presence. [38]

Mantike [XVI] Greek divination. The aim of this was not so much to predict the future as to seek advice concerning a future action – at least until the appearance of Hellenistic astrological determinism (*see* ASTROLOGY). Inquirers were individuals or states. There were both skill-based and inspirational divination. The first involved the interpretation of omens (signs or events) by a *mantis* (diviner) or *exegetes* (official interpreter) chosen by Delphi. Its commonest forms were interpretation of sacrificial victims' entrails (*hieroskopia*) and of the flight of birds (*oionoskopeia*). In inspirational divination a god was thought to possess a person and speak through their mouth. This was the main divination

mode at Delphi (*see* TEMENOS). Apollo's *prophetis* (prophetess), who was called Pythia, gave oracular responses while divinely inspired. The Delphic oracle was the most important oracle (*manteion/chresterion*). It was consulted as a higher authority by Greeks and foreigners and it played an important advisory role both in religious matters and in civic and inter-state politics. Other forms of divination involved lots and the conjuration of ghosts at a *nekyomanteion* (oracle of the dead). Oracle-mongers peddled collections of oracles attributed to legendary seers. [2: I. 3; 4: 109–18; 11: 128–54; 26: 123–42; 27: 538–42; 28; 30: 298–326]

Mantra [XVII] In the Indian religions, any verse whose letters and sound are believed to contain power. The hymns of the VEDA, for example, are called *mantras*; but the word is often used specifically of short verses, which may or may not make sense as ordinary words, believed to embody the power of a deity, and chanted repetitively as an object of meditation, often with the aid of a set of beads (*mala*). The best known is the *mantra* of AVALOKITESHVARA, beloved of Tibetan BUDDHISTS: *Om mani padme hum.* [57: 117–20; XI 3: 87, 110, 244–5, 257]

Maori Movements [XXVII] Since interaction with Christianity the Maori people of New Zealand have produced some 60 identifiable independent religious movements. Among the earliest was that of a prophet-figure, Papahurihia, around 1833; it combined Christian worship and beliefs with traditional ways [7: 37–48]. Many such movements were small and short-lived, but five have had a significant place in New Zealand history. The Taranaki prophet Te Ua Haumene was schooled in a METHODIST mission and after a vision from the angel Gabriel developed his conciliatory Pai Marire ('good and peaceful') movement amid the tense situation of settler conflict over land in the 1860s. Worsening conflict was accompanied by the emergence from Pai Marire of a derivative nativistic, militant and millennial movement known as Hau Hau. This identified the Maori as the Jews chosen to inherit the land as their Canaan free from Europeans, and inspired fierce but unsuccessful fighting in the Anglo-Maori land wars of the 1860s [7: 191–209]. At the same time another Taranaki prophet, Te Whiti, retired to a new village, Parihaka, to study the BIBLE and from 1869, along with fellow prophet Tohu, developed a peaceful, prosperous, modernizing community of 'Israelites' expecting a millennium. Their organization of wide passive resistance to land encroachments led the government to detain the prophets without trial in 1882–3. Later dissension over funds divided the community between the prophets, who both died in 1907, leaving two small communities that survive, still divided [7: 238–53].

A larger movement is Ringatu ('upraised hand', from a Hau Hau ritual), founded by Te Kooti (*c.*1830–93) after his escape from unjust exile in the Chatham Islands in 1866, and developed while he eluded capture until pardoned in 1883. Israelite features included an oral liturgy and festivals drawing upon the Hebrew scriptures, and Saturday worship. A century later, with some 5,000 adherents, Ringatu is moving closer to the Christian churches. Its recent spiritual head, Monita Delamere (d. 1993), was knighted for public service in 1989 [7: 226–37].

The largest movement, the Ratana Church, with over 30,000 members, stems from Wiremu Ratana (1873–1939), a Methodist farmer who received a vision in 1918 and discovered healing powers in the world influenza epidemic later that year. Beginning as a faith healer

rejecting traditional Maori religion and tribalism, Ratana was welcomed by the churches, but by 1925 emphasis upon angels and Ratana as intermediaries led to formation of his own church, with its Ratana village. In 1931 a Ratana member was elected to one of the four Maori seats in parliament, later joined by two others who all allied with the Labour Party, thus giving the church considerable political influence. Under its president from 1967, Ratana's daughter Te Reo Hura (1904–91), the church also formed links with the National Maori Congress and with the Maori King movement by sharing presidency of the Congress with the Maori Queen. Maori morale owes much to this continuing indigenous church. [7: 377–87]

Mapuche Religion [XXIII] Ethnography has revealed two supreme beings: Pillán, an extraordinary, impersonal, formless and primal power who can assume forms and even make personal appearances as the god of thunder; and Ngeñechén, the head of the universe who resides on top of the cosmic mountain. Divine couples of the mythic age, responsible for the four cardinal points, continue to manifest their power in their historical descendants. Flood myths recount how a female SHAMAN-saviour, *machi*, saved humanity from destruction. The *machi* today preside over the all-important fertility rites, *Ngiyipún*; their song recalls entire genealogical litanies linking present lineages to supernatural beings. [22]

Mara [XI] In BUDDHIST mythology a tempter figure who is in certain respects analogous to Satan in JUDAISM, ISLAM and CHRISTIANITY. His name means 'bringer of death' and his most common epithet is 'Bad One' (*papimant*). Not exactly a personification of evil, Mara rather appears as the hold which the world – in particular the world of the senses – can have on the mind, and as the power of all kinds of experience to seduce and delude the unwary mind; seduced by Mara and his helpers one remains enchanted by SAMSARA and fails to find the path to the cessation of suffering. The BUDDHA's enlightenment is thus commonly conceived of as the defeat of Mara and his armies, which include desire, aversion, hunger and thirst, craving, tiredness and sleepiness, fear and doubt. The subject is a favourite of Buddhist art: in response to Mara's challenge the Buddha touches the ground with his right hand, calling on the earth to witness that he has perfected such qualities as generosity and wisdom over countless lifetimes (see PARAMITA). [55]

Mar'a [XIX] Arabic for 'woman'. Classical ISLAM regarded women as intellectually inferior to men and of subordinate legal status. Because of the development, at least in urban Islam, of female seclusion, women were virtually excluded from public life and had to exercise any influence from behind the scenes [77: XIII; 80: II]. The movement to open out women's lives and to give them greater rights is part of ISLAMIC MODERNISM, beginning with Qasim Amin (1865–1908), who both advocated a reinterpretation of the QUR'AN and tradition and also appealed to natural justice and individual freedom [66: VII]. In recent decades, secular legislation has in many Islamic countries been assisting this process, but much remains to be achieved at the local and internal family level (see MARRIAGE AND DIVORCE (IN ISLAM); VEILING (IN ISLAM); ZINA). [131]

Marae [XXIX] A sacred area in POLYNESIAN RELIGION containing a raised shrine (ahu) where priests (TOHUNGA) make offerings and recite chants (karakia). Gods and ancestors are sometimes represented by carved posts or stones. Maraes range from tiny paved clearings to massive stepped platforms (Society Islands) and walled enclosures (called heiau in Hawaii). [3] Among the New Zealand Maori, the marae was for communal gatherings, with the most tapu (TABU) activities of priests confined to small shrines (tuahu) elsewhere. [6: 272–8; 7: 477–84]

Marcionism [XIII.A] The teaching of Marcion, a Christian from Asia Minor, who settled in Rome c.144 CE. He maintained that Christianity was a completely new revelation, quite unrelated to the 'Old Testament' (see BIBLE) or to Jewish religion. He published the first known CANON of Christian scripture, edited in conformity with his beliefs.

Marduk [VIII] During the reign of Hammurabi (1792–1750 BC) (see BABYLONIANS; HAMMURABI'S CODE) [7], Marduk, the city deity of Babylon, emerged as supreme god of the pantheon. He was the last divine overlord and the custom of elevating to pre-eminence the deity of the paramount city-state now ceased [24: 23]. His significance was only finally eclipsed by Ashur, state-god of the ASSYRIANS [25: 39]. Marduk's powers included the ability to obtain medicines (see MAGIC) which expelled demons (see EVIL). The Epic of Creation, recited at Babylon, praised Marduk's victory over the dragon. (See ANCIENT NEAR EASTERN RELIGIONS.) [24: 60–71]

Marga [XI] A Sanskrit term (Pali: Magga), meaning the 'way' or 'path', and the term used in Indian religion generally and in BUDDHISM especially for the way of life which the adherent is to follow. Buddhism, because of its avoidance of the extremes of asceticism and hedonism, is called the Middle Way. The Buddhist life is set out in detail in the atthangika magga, the noble EIGHTFOLD PATH.

Maria Legio [XXVII] Known also as Legio Maria, the largest African independent church emerging from a background of ROMAN CATHOLICISM, founded in Kenya in 1963 by two Catholics of the Luo people, Simeon Ondeto and Gaudencia Aoko (b. 1943), and named after the Legion of Mary. Combining Catholic and PENTECOSTAL features with healing, exorcism, a strict ethic and strong African emphasis, it initially attracted upwards of 80,000 adherents, but has since declined and Gaudencia Aoko has left it.

Maronite [XIII.D] The Maronites are Christians obedient to Rome who maintain certain non-Roman customs, such as the marriage of priests, a different baptismal rite and the use of spoken and chanted Syriac in the liturgy. Their homeland is the Lebanon, where they form a significant political block with its guaranteed share in any government. Their obedience to Rome dates from the time of the crusades. Rome's need to minister to the Maronites explains the stimulation of Syriac scholarship in Europe in the 16th century and the collection of Syriac manuscripts by the Pope in the 17th century. It was a group of Maronite clerics, all of the Assemani family, which made Syriac literature widely accessible in Europe in the early 18th century.

Before the crusades the Maronites, who did not accept the theology of Maximus Confessor, were alienated from Byzantium by the COUNCIL of 680. They remained embittered opponents of the Syrian Orthodox.

It is wrong to portray the Maronites as a splinter-group. They formed the majority of Chalcedonians in Syria in the 8th century, when they were distinguished from the Imperial (or 'Melkite') Syrians loyal to Byzantium and acquired a PATRIARCH and a government charter of their own.

Their submission to Rome involved relinquishing their former opposition to the formulations of Maximus Confessor (e.g. 'two wills in the single person of Jesus Christ'); but by the time of the crusades there was division between East and West in the church at large and a common distrust of Byzantium counted for more than dogma.

The Maronites are named after a 5th-century monastic founder, John Maron, whose monastery near Apamea in Syria was to be a powerhouse of Chalcedonian polemics. [6; 111; 117; 120]

Maroon/Marronage [III] A Maroon is a runaway slave, or, nowadays, one born from runaway stock. Marronage refers to the varying states involved in flight and survival. The name comes from the Spanish *cimarron* and was originally used of the cattle which escaped into the hills of the island of Hispaniola. Later the meaning transferred to slaves who escaped into the interior of Hispaniola. The first of these runaways was recorded in 1502, when an African-American slave escaped successfully. The vicious system of slavery, based on coercion, saved its fiercest punishments for runaway slaves; these punishments, encapsulated in law, included castration and roasting alive. Such treatment varied from country to country. Slaves were not docile, defeated and resigned to a state of submissive obedience. They could co-operate, assimilating those features which they found profitable, or they could reject slavery; the Maroons belonged to this latter tradition of evasion or escape. This did not mean that they had no contact with majority religions, because they were never totally exclusive communities. For instance, they were always dependent for some goods, and trade brought them into direct contact with other islanders.

Maroon groups were found throughout plantation America, Brazil and the Caribbean, and occurred both in tiny bands and in great 'nations', as in Jamaica. They had responded directly to the pain of slavery. Their descendants persist, fiercely proud of their history and traditions of resistance. In the early 18th century planters wished to extend into the north-eastern part of the island of Jamaica, cutting off supply lines for the Maroons. The first Maroon War was precipitated, and Cudjoe emerged as a redoubtable leader. Among other leaders who gained fame at this time was Cuffee, and Nanny, the most legendary leader of them all. She maintained control over her troops as a great *obeahwoman* (*see* OBEAH). Peace was signed in 1739, and the Maroons were granted land rights. In return it was expected that the Maroons would help the colonial authorities to recapture runaway slaves, with a price of £3 a head. In 1795 these Jamaican Maroons went to war again and were eventually deported to Nova Scotia. Bitter weather there forced them to petition the British government, and in 1800 a group emigrated to the new country of Sierra Leone where they were eventually integrated into the Creole community.

Maroon religion is strongly African. The sacred and secular aspects of life are integrated and it is highly instrumental. Social relationships and institutions are regulated by proper ceremonies and reference to the ancestors and Guinea (Africa). It is strongly family-orientated in organization, and there are considerable Amerindian borrowings, especially in techniques for survival: in Cuba, Surinam, Brazil and Jamaica magical medicines were used in the past to render bullets harmless. Complex protection rites were used, and warriors wore protective AMULETS. There is a strong belief in OBEAH, and drummers from Maroon groups often act as specialist musicians in other African-Caribbean cults, for their art in calling down spirits is considered

very powerful (*see* ORISHAS (AFRO-CARIBBEAN)). A wide range of mediating spirits is recognized. Worship is characterized by dancing, possession and drumming. [2; 5; 55; 77]

Marrano [XXII] Word of Spanish origin meaning 'swine' and applied to those Jews in the Iberian peninsula who were forcibly converted to Christianity in the 14th and 15th centuries but maintained a secret Jewish life [54]. The expulsion of the Jews from Spain in 1492 was partly intended to prevent Marranos having contact with their old co-religionists (*see* EUROPEAN JEWRY). When Marranos were able to escape from Spanish-ruled territory and from the watchful eye of the Inquisition many of them reverted to JUDAISM. [14 vol. 12: 1022]

Marriage (Christian) [XIII.B] Christian marriage has always been characterized by the practice of monogamy (one current spouse only) and official resistance to divorce. Traditionally, marriage was justified primarily for producing children and avoiding fornication (*see* SEXUALITY), with partnership in the background. Modern Western Christians and Orthodox churches (*see* EASTERN ORTHODOX CHURCH), however, virtually reverse this order. ROMAN CATHOLICISM, the Orthodox Church and some in ANGLICANISM class marriage as a SACRAMENT. Condemnation of marriage has usually been regarded as an error, except by extreme ascetics. Christian distrust of sex, however, has been a factor in the value placed on celibacy as an aid towards high spiritual attainment (as in MONASTICISM). Roman Catholicism forbids marriage for all clergy. The Orthodox Church permits the ordination to the MINISTRY of married men as deacons or priests but not as bishops. An unmarried priest or deacon cannot marry and one widowed after ordination cannot remarry. Divorce is forbidden by church law for Roman Catholics and (officially) for Anglicans; but decrees of nullity (declaring that a true marriage never existed) can be obtained. In practice, the Eastern Orthodox and many churches in PROTESTANTISM accept divorce under secular law while upholding lifelong marriage as the ideal. (*See also* SEXUALITY, AND CHRISTIANITY.) [1: 249–58; 139: 206–7; 157: 889–90]

Marriage (in Judaism) [XXII] It is a positive duty for Jews to marry and have at least two children (one male, one female) in accordance with the commandment 'be fruitful and multiply' (*Genesis* 1: 22, 9: 1) [18: III]. The marriage ceremony takes place under a canopy (*chupah*) and consists in the groom giving the bride a ring in front of two witnesses and saying, 'Behold you are sanctified to me with this ring according to the law of MOSES and of ISRAEL' [64: 396]. This is preceded by a benediction over wine and over the ceremony. The marriage document (*ketubbah*) is read, followed by another blessing over wine and the seven marriage benedictions. The couple then retire to a room to be alone together (*yichud*), which completes the marriage ceremonies [16: 166]. For the marriage to be dissolved the couple need to undergo a religious divorce ceremony, in which the husband presents a specially written bill of divorce (*get*) to his wife. [70: IX; 5; 21; 27]

Marriage and Divorce (in Islam) [XIX] Muslim marriage is essentially a civil contract. The partners should be of equal social status, and the bride receives a dowry. Child betrothal is possible, but minimum marriage ages have now been laid down in many Islamic countries by the secular law (e.g. 18 for the bridegroom and 16 for the bride in the Egyptian code of 1931). However, marriage between minors remains valid in the eyes of the SHARI'A.

Polygamy retains its Qur'anic sanction, but is becoming exceptional and is discouraged by secular law codes. Unilateral divorce by the husband likewise remains valid according to the Shari'a; modern law has tried to mitigate this, but the woman is still comparatively disadvantaged. (*See* MAR'A.) [38 'Nikāh'; 48: 127–36; 67 s.vv.; 77: III, VI; 117: XXII]

Marxism [XXXII] A political creed derived from the work of Karl Marx (1818–83) which has been, since the 19th century, the dominant creed of communism. Communists generally believe in a society in which there is no private property. Marxists further believe, however, in the necessity and inevitability of a proletarian revolution to bring about a communist society. The underlying theoretical approach of Marxists is generally known as DIALECTICAL MATERIALISM.

Marxism is sometimes represented as a SECULAR ALTERNATIVE TO RELIGION. Marx himself held that the criticism of religion is the beginning of all social criticism. He saw religion as both an expression of human distress and a means of disguising its true causes. It is the 'opium of the people' because it offers them an illusory happiness. It is, in Marx's sense, IDEOLOGY. It helps to preserve the established order of society by encouraging the people to look to another world for their happiness. Revolution and religion were, for Marx, alternatives. To secure real human happiness it is necessary to abolish religion as their illusory happiness [15: 250].

Marxism has sometimes been seen as a kind of secular religion [28: 196ff]. The writings of Marx himself have tended to be treated more like a sacred text than a contribution to science. Scientists whose views seemed incompatible with dialectical materialism were once persecuted in the Soviet Union. More positively, perhaps, former Marxists sometimes use words like 'conversion' and 'faith' [28: 197] to describe what it was like for them to become a Marxist. These and other similarities with religions make it intelligible to describe Marxism as the major secular religion to have emerged in the last century. But such a description cannot be made without a good deal of qualification. Many would hold that it distorts religion, or Marxism – or both.

Mary, Virgin [xiii.a] The mother of Jesus. She figures prominently in the infancy narratives in the Gospels of Matthew and Luke, which stress the role of the Holy spirit in the conception of Jesus. According to the Gospel of John she was present at the crucifixion. Tradition suggests that John the Apostle took her to Ephesus. She is placed above the Saints for devotion in Roman Catholicism, in the Eastern orthodox church and among Anglo-Catholics. Special doctrines about her include the teaching that she is 'ever-virgin'; 'God-bearer' (Theotokos); and that her body was taken into heaven (the Assumption. The Immaculate Conception (that she was conceived without Sin) was defined dogmatically for Roman Catholics in 1854. This is generally rejected by the Orthodox Church. Popular claims for her as 'Co-Redemptress' with Christ have receded officially since the Second Vatican Council. Belief in the efficacy of her intercession with Christ has helped to encourage numerous special devotions and practices in her honour, such as the rosary cycle of prayers. The 'Sacred Heart' (iconographically represented as Christ opening his chest to reveal his heart as a symbol of his love for mankind) is an example of devotions to the person of Christ applied also to Mary. Pilgrimages are undertaken to places where there are famous images of Mary (e.g. Czestokova, Poland; Tinos, Greece; Guadalupe, Mexico) and where she has appeared in visions (e.g. Lourdes, France; Medjugorje, Croatia). Such visions have increased since the 19th century; they appear to be influenced by political or theological pressures and in general to reflect a reassertion of the supernatural aspects of Christianity in a secularizing world.

Eastern Christianity has a wide range of classic icon types; the Hodegetria, or 'Signpost icon', the prototype of which is attributed to St Luke, shows Mary holding the child Jesus in one arm, pointing to him with the other hand and looking out of the icon to draw the viewer to him; the Eleousa, the 'Virgin of tenderness', shows her holding the child close as they exchange loving glances; the 'Virgin sweetly kissing' shows the child's face turned up to her as his mother kisses him; the Galatrephousa, the Virgin giving milk to her son; the Platytera, 'She who is Wider than the Heavens', shows her enthroned with the child standing or sitting on her knee. In Eastern iconography the Virgin's maphorion, her outer veil, is almost always red, symbolizing her love of Christ; in Western art it is normally blue, the colour of Heaven.

In some countries, e.g. Italy and Latin America, her images and festivals appear to be coloured by pre-Christian cults (*see* Syncretism; Latin America, christianity in). Protestantism has generally rejected this theology and devotion, but some Protestants now express interest and sympathy. 'Mariolatry' is a Protestant term of abuse, implying idolatrous worship of Mary. Feminist theologians have significantly challenged the ideal of womanhood and sexuality implied by the traditional pictures of Mary. [196]

Masalai [xxix] A Papua New Guinea pidgin word covering a wide variety of animal and land spirits, demons and minor deities dwelling in caves, streams and forests. In Melanesian religion *masalai* are commonly feared and their haunts avoided, but they are not worshipped or venerated as are spirits of the recent dead or clan ancestors (TUMBUNA). *Masalai* may adopt animal or human forms to attack or deceive people. They enforce TABUS by inflicting accidents or sickness on those who trespass or infringe. [14: 179–82; 22; 23; 29]

Mashhad [XIX] A shrine in ISLAM, literally 'place of martyrdom, witness' (other frequent synonyms include *quba, turba* and, in the Persian world, *ziyaratgah*, 'place of pilgrimage'). The foremost shrine in Islam is, of course, the Prophet's tomb at Medina, usually visited after the Pilgrimage to Mecca (*see* HAJJ), but lesser shrines are scattered all over the Islamic world, with those of the earlier prophets, Muhammad's companions, and the early Muslims especially concentrated in Palestine, Syria and Iraq. The shrines of the Shi'i IMAMS and martyrs in Iraq and Iran (e.g. of 'ALI at Najaf, al-Husain at Karbala, 'Ali al-Rida at Mashhad in north-eastern Iran and his sister, Fatima at Qum) have been richly endowed by the Shi'i faithful (*see* SHI'ISM), and are goals of pilgrimage for them. They are jealously guarded against non-Muslims, and even Sunnis (*see* SUNNA) are unwelcome there. [24; 38 s.v.; 77: X; architecture: 93: I]

Masks (Melanesian) [XXIX] Masks are the most important artefacts in MELANESIAN RELIGION. From the intricate carvings and costumes of the Malangan and Dukduk cults of New Ireland and New Britain [9; 23: 45–53] to the towering Hevehe and fantastic Kovave constructions of the Papuan gulf, masks illustrate the high point of traditional art and ICONOGRAPHY [22; 29]. Central to MALE CULT rites, masks visibly dramatize the presence of powerful ancestors, gods and spirit-beings on whom society's security depends. Bullroarers, *garamuts* (slit-gongs or

drums made from hollowed logs) and bamboo flutes have a similar function, giving voices to the spirits. Housed in shrines, TABU to the uninitiated, these sacred objects are often destroyed after use, because of their dangerous MANA. Their ceremonial display is at times accompanied by elaborately rehearsed dancing, ritual fighting, fire dance, music and song, and vast communal feasts (SINGSING). [29]

Mass [XIII.B] (from the Latin *missa*, meaning dismissal, occurring at the end of the service.) A term used, mainly in ROMAN CATHOLICISM, for the EUCHARIST. PROTESTANTISM rejected it because of the association with the notion of eucharistic sacrifice, although Luther (*see* LUTHERANISM) constructed a 'German mass'. Anglo-Catholics have revived the term and the associated doctrines in ANGLICANISM. The 'canon of the mass' refers to the prayer consecrating the 'elements' (bread and wine). 'High mass' involves elaborate ceremonial, music and several assistants, by contrast with the more common 'low mass' – a distinction, however, which ended with the Second Vatican COUNCIL and the LITURGICAL MOVEMENT'S emphasis on congregational participation. 'Dry Mass' was a shortened form without the consecration of the bread and wine of the Eucharist, popular in the later middle ages. The Missal is a book containing the prayers and directives for celebrating mass throughout the year. 'Requiem masses' are for the dead at funerals and other occasions. These and other forms of mass have provided the occasion for much CHURCH MUSIC. [I: 137–78; 48: 254–6; 154 vol. 9: 413–28]

Mataco Religion [XXIII] Myths of a world-destroying cosmic fire are extremely important among the Mataco, Toba and Pilagá of the Gran Chaco Plain, Argentina. From the cosmic fire, two bird-beings,

Icanchu and Chuña, sought their homeland, which was indicated to them by Tokwaj, the TRICKSTER. There the Icanchu beat a drum producing the Firstborn Tree which bore all plants and species of the new world. Mataco ceremonies, especially the *Atj* festival, are performed to contact the powerful beings controlling the forces of the cosmos, preventing a repetition of the world-destruction. Religious specialists (*aiawu*), through cure and ritual combat with celestial beings, bear responsibility for the protection of humanity from harm. [33]

Matres [VII] The CELTIC *Matres*, the Divine Mothers, are often represented in Romanized form in groups of three in Gaul and Britain. They are accompanied by fertility symbols such as horns of plenty, fruit, loaves or children, and in Gaul by dogs, birds and trees. They may appear singly under local names, and many individual Celtic goddesses, such as Epona, the horse-goddess, had a maternal aspect [25: 205–13, 27: III]. They resemble the VANIR of Scandinavian tradition.

Matsuri [XXI] SHINTO ceremonies and festivals. Shinto as a religion is known primarily for its ceremonies and festivals, which invoke the presence of the KAMI and obtain their approval [general surveys: 19: 168–224]. Combining early shamanistic practices (*see* MIKO) with agricultural rituals, these marked seasonal changes, aided fertility and warded off plagues. The harvest festival (Niiname-sai) was traditionally the most important, thought of as the time when the male celestial *kami* descended to unite with the female terrestrial *kami*, terminating in a sacred feast. The national ceremonies (Kanname-sai and Niiname-sai) are today conducted by the emperor in private, since he has been formally deprived of his position as the public head of the Shinto state (*see* KOKUTAI SHINTO). Two of

the major festivals of Kyoto are anti-calamity parades. The first is the 15 May Aoi (popularly, hollyhock) festival, when leaves of *Asarum caulescens* (a wild ginger) are offered to the *kami* of the Shimogamo and Kamigamo shrines (*see* SHINTO SHRINES). This is said to have originated in the 6th century as an attempt to obtain relief from storms. The second is the July Gion festival, at the end of which large floats are washed and carried through the city; this traces back to a plague of 876. Some have fertility connotations, such as Tanabata, originally the seventh night of the seventh month of the lunar calendar, when two stars cross the sky to meet [9: 79–94]. Numerous festivals celebrate local events and invoke the neighbouring tutelary *kami*. These are accompanied by dancing and singing, the most popular being the *bonodori*, connected with the return of the souls from their short visit to earth, and rice-planting, growing and harvesting songs (*taue-uta*).

The order of ritual when conducted at a Shinto shrine in the presence of the *kami* follows a fixed pattern [32: 50–71]. It is done with great precision and deliberation. The priests purify (*See* HARAE) the participants who are requesting a special blessing; all make obeisances in the direction of the *shintai* (or *go-shintai*: the god body); the door of the inner sanctuary is opened and offerings of food or drink are proffered. Prayers are recited, music and dancing follow, and a branch of the evergreen *sakaki* tree is offered. The offerings are then removed, the door of the shrine closed, the last bows made, and the group enjoys feasting and drinking. At most Japanese marriage ceremonies today offerings are made and blessings are received at a Shinto shrine.

Maui [XXIX] A CULTURE HERO in POLYNESIAN RELIGION. It is believed that Maui was born to Taranga by miscarriage and thrown into the sea.

He was saved by the gods (ATUA), who taught him skills and magic. He became Maui-of-a-Thousand-Tricks, fishing up islands, slowing the sun, stealing fire and showing mankind the use of barbed hooks and spears. He died while trying to gain immortality for mortals from the goddess of death, Hine-nui-te-Po. [15; 22; 30]

Maya (1) [XI] The mother of GOTAMA, the BUDDHA, who, according to Buddhist tradition, possessed all the qualities required in the woman who was to bear a Buddha. She was not passionate, took no alcohol and observed the precepts of a lay Buddhist faithfully. According to tradition, on the day of her conception she had a dream in which the BODHISATTVA, in the form of a white elephant carrying a white lotus in his trunk, entered her right side; the scene is often depicted in murals in Buddhist temples. [56: 608f]

Maya (2) [XVII] An important concept in VEDANTA thought. *Maya* is originally the magical power of creating illusion or deceit, but in the ADVAITA VEDANTA it refers to the illusory existence of a world of multiplicity superimposed upon the single non-dual reality (BRAHMAN) by the power of ignorance (AVIDYA). *Maya* and ignorance may be identified, but, if distinguished, *maya* is the power of God (ISHVARA), which creates the illusion of a differentiated universe and conceals the divine unity behind appearances, while ignorance creates the seemingly separate self at the individual level. *Maya* is not hallucination. The world is seen under a false appearance like the snake on the path which is actually a rope; it is not purely imaginary. The power of *maya* is considered to be neither identical with *brahman* nor completely different. The term *maya* is sometimes used to refer to the SAMKHYA *prakrti* or the divine SHAKTI.

Mbona [II] One of the best-known territorial cults of central Africa. Its principal shrine is situated at Khulubvi by the Shire river in the far south of Malawi among the Mang'-anja people. Over 500 years old, its character has changed with altered political and social circumstances; its basic function was rainmaking, but to this was added its role as the official cult of the Lundu paramount chieftainship (although Mbona in the central later tradition was a martyr figure killed by a Lundu chief). If the shrine was effectively dependent upon the political power, it had also a certain spiritual and moral independence. The organization of the shrine, besides 'Mbona's wife', priests and medium, included representatives of many chieftainships and messengers bringing petitions from a wide area, including the Indian Ocean, far beyond Mang'-anja territory. Lesser Mbona shrines were set up elsewhere with a varying theology. Mbona illustrates both the historical depth and the inter-tribal spread of African religious institutions. [13: 73–94; 15: 147–86; 18: 219–40]

Medicine Bundles [V] In North America, within the context of the VISION QUEST, it was common for the visionary to receive a talisman (*see* AMULETS AND TALISMANS) as a tangible sign of the supernatural power conferred upon him by his GUARDIAN SPIRIT [8: VII]. The sacred bag or pouch might contain such objects representative and evocative of power as eagle feathers, shells, animal parts, tobacco, herbs or porcupine quills. Its conferment was often accompanied by instructions regarding its care and use, including certain prohibitions. A medicine song, often used in association with the medicine bundle, might also be added. The bundle thus served as an individual emblem, symbolizing the relationship between the visionary and his guardian spirit.

Medicine Man [v] General designation among Amerindians for a SHAMAN, diviner or healer [23: I]. Although details of election, initiation and role within the group vary, common elements may be observed. Among the Ogalala SIOUX, the *wicasa wakan* or *winyan wicasa* (literally 'man sacred', 'woman sacred') are distinguished from the *pejuta wicasa* (literally 'medicine man'), the latter being primarily concerned with conventional medicine [17: VI]. The general pattern for the former includes: some initial indication of spiritual election (e.g. childhood vision); additional omens; consultation with an established holy man (or woman); and, if so advised, embarkation on the VISION QUEST (*hanbleceya*, literally, 'crying for a vision') [23: III]. Those whose visions indicate a potential career undergo a period of apprenticeship wherein ritual and curing techniques are learned (*see* MIDEWIWIN). After his/her assumption of the role as visionary, healer, interpreter of dreams and intermediary with the supernaturals, the *wicasa wakan* or *winyan wicasa* renews his/her power. Loss of power, especially with the advance of years, occasions retirement and replacement by younger practitioners.

Meeting (Quaker) [XIII.B] The name given to (1) Quaker worship, (2) the body of worshippers and (3) units of Quaker organization. The intended meaning of the term is understood through the context in which it is used. Quakers (*see* FRIENDS, RELIGIOUS SOCIETY OF) conduct their business as worship, using a method of voteless decision-making to seek the will of God [82; 176]. The decentralized structure of Quaker organization, set up in the 1660s by George Fox [161: 85], was thus based on units of different kinds of meeting: preparative meeting, monthly meeting, quarterly meeting, yearly meeting. Different autonomous groups of Friends are divided by yearly meeting boundaries, e.g. Philadelphia Yearly Meeting, Australia Yearly Meeting.

The buildings early Friends used specifically for worship were called meeting houses, and this term is still used today among the more liberal branches. Some more evangelical Friends now use the term 'Friends' church' instead of, or in addition to, 'yearly meeting' and 'meeting house'.

Meher Baba [XXVIII] A relatively loose-knit movement of 'Baba-lovers' tries to follow the teachings of their Indian master, Meher Baba (1894–1969), who observed a silence from 1925 until his death. In 1924 Meher Baba established a colony, Meherabad, near Ahmednagar which offered shelter for the poor, a free school, hospital and dispensary. Western devotees are mainly to be found in the USA. Baba-lovers accept Meher Baba's claim to be the AVATARA of the age. His message was the metaphysical unity of all persons, and that the most direct path to self-realization is love and complete surrender to Baba. [39; 42: 895–6]

Melanesian Religion [XXIX] Melanesia comprises Irian Jaya, Papua New Guinea, the Solomon Islands, Vanuatu (formerly New Hebrides) and New Caledonia. Despite great regional diversity, general religious similarities exist and can be illustrated from Papua New Guinean examples. Oral traditions preserve stories and songs about the creators of local culture and bringers of knowledge and skills (DEMA DEITIES). More important, generally, are the tribal ancestors (TUMBUNA) and numerous land-spirits (MASA-LAI) inhabiting streams, trees or animals, who regulate spiritual power (MANA) within the tribal territory. Through dreams, possession, mediums and prophets the living keep in touch with their deities and ancestors, forming a continuing community. Right relationships, maintaining life and prosperity, are established through rituals. Central among these are MALE CULTS of initiation and purification, usually associated with shrines or spirit-houses (HAUS TAMBARAN). Birth, marriage and funeral rites also ensure peace and security. Elaborate festivals of ritual and dance (SING-SING) and complex trading exchanges renew bonds both with ancestor-spirits and with other social groups among the living. Birds, lizards, snakes, sharks and certain plants are recognized as totems in local custom and folklore, and serve to unite clan groups with their natural habitat. Secret techniques for healing, magic and sorcery (POISEN) are available for good or harmful use. Spiritual powers are believed to make themselves present on ritual occasions, in sacred MASKS, drums, flutes and other artefacts. After widespread missionary influence during the 20th century, traditional beliefs and practices have declined greatly. Yet they still lie beneath much Melanesian CHRISTIANITY, and reappear from time to time in prophetic movements and so-called CARGO CULTS. [2; 14; 20; 23; 25; 29]

Mencius [XII] Meng Tzu (371–289 BCE), the Confucian philosopher who comes closest to the thought of CONFUCIUS himself. He had an official post in the state of Ch'i for a time, but spent most of his life travelling from state to state, attempting to convert rulers to his teachings. He emphasized the Confucian values, goodness (*jen*) and righteousness (*i*), and believed knowledge of them to be innate in the human mind (*hsin*) [39: II, 123–32]. Although he argued for the innate goodness of human nature he also stressed the need for moral cultivation and moral reflection in order to recover the 'lost mind' [7: III, 51–83]. He regarded

such cultivation as conforming to the will of Heaven (*T'ien Ming*). Mencius insisted that rulers should govern in accordance with the Will of Heaven (T'IEN) and for the benefit of the people. He was on occasion quite critical of certain rulers, particularly King Hui of Liang. [19: V, 81–105; 34: VI, 106–31; 62; 84]

Mende Religion [II] The Mende of Sierra Leone and Liberia believe in Ngewo, creator of the universe and all spirits. The word's meaning is uncertain; an earlier name is Leve, 'the high-up one'. The earth is sometimes described as his wife. In emergency Ngewo is invoked directly, but normally through the ancestors: the near and known ones, the Kekeni, and through them the remote ones, the Ndebla. The Mende practise a complex ancestor-cult, including post-funeral grave-rites and further routine offerings, but especially sacrifices at times of misfortune (*see* ANCESTOR VENERATION). However, much of Mende religion is related to the major secret societies which control various areas of life: the Poro, male initiation and political advancement; the Sande, female initiation, childbirth and the maintenance of womanly virtue; the Humoi, the laws of marriage and sexual relationships. All have their own rituals, initiations and sacrifices. Mende religion is characterized by the balance of ancestor-cult and secret society, both subservient to Ngewo, remote but never absent [6: 111–37].

Mendelssohn, Moses [XXII] The first important Jewish thinker of the Enlightenment, Mendelssohn (1729–86) taught himself European languages and launched on a career as a German writer [14 vol. II: 1328]. He translated the BIBLE into German, printed in Hebrew characters to enable his co-religionists to learn that language, and advocated educational reforms and religious tolerance for Jews in his book *Jerusa-*

lem. He claimed that the beliefs of JUDAISM were not dogmas but the conclusions of a universal rational religion. [2; 44; 56: III; 70: 71]

Menstruation (in Judaism) [XXII] [5; 21; 27] The menstruant woman is considered ritually unclean in the BIBLE. In order to become ritually pure she bathes in a bath of living water (MIKVEH), usually spring or rain water. In post-TEMPLE times ritual impurity ceased to play a major role in Jewish religious life. The only surviving restrictions on the menstruant (*niddah*) relate to the prohibition on sexual relations with her husband until she takes a ritual bath a week after menstruation has ceased [14 vol. 12: 1141]. These laws are known as the laws of 'family purity' (*taharat ha-mishpachah*), and are strictly adhered to today by Orthodox Jews, though not by REFORM Jews. The RABBIS of the TALMUD explained the family purity laws not by reference to ritual impurity, but as necessary to prevent the husband taking his sexual relations with his wife for granted. When they resume their sex life together, after menstrual separation, they are like bride and groom once again. [70: 155]

Merkabah Mysticism [XXII] The mystical tradition of the early rabbinical period was known as Maaseh Merkabah, since the goal of this tradition was a vision of the divine throne or chariot (*merkabah*), depicted in the opening chapter of *Ezekiel* [22: III]. In order to attain to this vision the adept had to go into a state of mystical contemplation and then to pass through seven stages or 'halls' (*heikhalot*). Each hall is guarded by an ANGEL, who will not allow anyone through who does not know the correct mystical password. These passwords are meditational names made up of letter combinations of the Hebrew alphabet. The Merkabah tradition was an esoteric one which could only be passed on to a student who already had some mystical understanding, and could only be taught to one student at a time [70: 91]. The TALMUD tells how four sages went on a mystical journey to Paradise, and only one emerged unharmed [61: II]

Meru, Mount [XVII] In traditional HINDU, BUDDHIST (*see* CAKKAVALA) and JAIN cosmology, Meru is the legendary mountain at the centre of the world, round which the sun, moon and stars revolve. On the four sides of Meru are four continents, separated from each other by oceans and identified by the trees growing on them at the point adjacent to the mountain. Thus the southern continent, having a rose-apple (*jambu*) tree, was called the island (*dvipa*) of *jambu* (Jambudvipa). This contained the Himalaya mountains, and to its south was the land called Bharatavarsha (the land of the sons of Bharata – the eponymous ancestor of the people of India, to whom the name MAHABHARATA also refers). In another version of the cosmology found in the PURANAS, Jambudvipa encircles Meru, and is surrounded by an ocean and another continent, forming a concentric circle. In Tantric symbolism (*see* TANTRA (1)), Meru has the same function within the macrocosm as the spine within the microcosm, connecting the different realms or levels of consciousness. (*See also* MANDIRA.) [12: 490f]

Mesoamerican City (200–1521 CE) [XXV] Mesoamerican culture from the middle of the 2nd millennium BCE on was organized at ceremonial centres which developed, during the Classic period (200–900 CE), into impressive sacred cities [18: 225–35; 19: V]. The earliest example of the elaborate ceremonial centres at which incipient urban institutions were organized was the Olmec culture, whose priestly elites operating in scattered ceremonial precincts controlled long-distance trade, exquisite artistic traditions and widespread religious cults [10: 35–43]. Towards the end of the 1st millennium BCE new centres of culture developed in the central plateau of Mexico, the lowland Mayan region and the valley of Oaxaca [10: V]. While village farming communities and hunting and gathering peoples prospered within their spheres of influence, it was the city and city-state (*tlatocayotls*) which set the style for political organization, economic exchange and religious patterns. The major ceremonial cities like Teotihuacan, Tikal, CHOLOLLAN, Monte Albán, Tula, Xochicalco, Tajin, Chichen Itza and Tenochtitlan were characterized by hierarchically structured, functionally specialized social institutions which were the instruments for the creation of political, economic, social and sacred space [9: 11, III]. Directed by organized priesthoods and divine rulers, these sacred cities were marked by pyramid temples, palaces, ceremonial courtyards (*see figure 8*), market-places, terraces, BALL COURTS and platform mounds. Utilizing intellectual models from what could be termed cosmo-

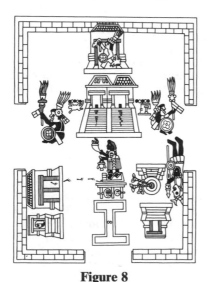

Figure 8
Aztec ceremonial centre (Great Temple of Huitzilopochtli, Tenochtitlan)

magical thought, which presupposed an intimate parallelism between the mathematically expressible regimes of the heavens and the biologically determined rhythms of life on earth [18: V], the sacerdotal elites organized their capitals around majestic shrines which linked the citizens to the supernatural world, tended to divide their kingdoms into four quarters conforming to the cosmological design and strove to achieve precise parallels between ritual, ritual architecture and cosmogonic dramas. Clear examples of this pattern were Teotihuacan, Tula Xicocotitlan, Chichen Itza and Tenochtitlan. Special variations of this pattern of organization were utilized in the Mixtec and Mayan regions. [5: VI; 10: 55–72]

Mesoamerican Religions [XXV] These include the religious traditions developed in central and southern Mexico, the Yucatan peninsula, El Salvador, Guatemala and parts of Honduras, Nicaragua and Costa Rica between 2300 BCE and 1521 CE. Civilizations like the Toltec, Mayan (*see* CLASSIC MAYA), Huastec, Mixtec and Aztec shared such cultural and religious features as: monumental ceremonial centres (*see* MESOAMERICAN CITY); complex ritual and solar calendars (*see* TONALPOHUALLI; CALENDAR STONE), which intermeshed to create 52-year cycles (*see* NEW FIRE CEREMONY); writing (*see* CODEX (MESOAMERICAN)); HUMAN SACRIFICE (AZTEC); and a cosmology designed in terms of four cardinal directions and the centre (CEMANAHUAC) inhabited by complex pantheons of gods (*see* HUITZILOPOCHTLI; OMETEOTL; QUETZALCOATL; TETEOINNAN; TEZCATLIPOCA; TLALOC). These religious traditions flourished in major cities like Teotihuacan, El Tajin, Tikal, Monte Alban, CHOLOLLAN, Tula (TOLLAN), Chichen Itza and Tenochtitlan, where organized priesthoods (TEOPIXQUE) and divine rulers (TLATOANI) organized community life around great ceremonial centres which connected the community to the supernatural realm and legitimated the authority of elite groups. Generally, these ceremonial centres consisted of pyramid temples, palaces, ceremonial courtyards, market-places, BALL COURTS and platform mounds. Elaborate calendrical rituals, often culminating in human sacrifices, of others or by self-immolation, were carried out within these ceremonial precincts.

Messiah (in Judaism) [xxII] From the Hebrew *mashiach*, or 'anointed one'. The Messiah is the appointed one of God who will come in some future time at the beginning of the messianic age [66: vi; 63: xxIx]. The Jewish EXILES will be gathered in to the HOLY LAND and there will be a resurrection of the dead and the judgement of mankind. Biblical references to the Messiah and the messianic age are couched in symbolic language, and were variously interpreted in rabbinical and medieval Jewish literature. The belief in the coming of the Messiah and the resurrection of the dead are two of MAIMONIDES' 13 principles of Jewish doctrine [31: xIII, xIV]. Throughout Jewish history the messianic hope has helped the Jews to survive suffering and persecution. It has also led to messianic movements which have at times generated a fever pitch of excitement among Jewish communities, and greatly enriched Jewish folklore with messianic legends and stories. [7; 11; 62: I]

Methodism [xIII.B] A section of the Evangelical Revival (*see* REVIVALISM) led by John Wesley (1703–91) [162] (*see* ARMINIANISM) [9] and George Whitefield (1714–70) (*see* CALVINISM). Wesley taught justification by faith and Christian perfection (*see* SALVATION), using lay preachers to develop a chain of fellowship societies. After separating from ANGLICANISM, English Methodism suffered many divisions, but it was largely reunited in 1932. Methodism is most numerous in the USA [31], pioneered there by Francis Asbury (1745–1816). The largest body is the United Methodist Church (1968), but black and other churches remain separate from this. CHURCH ORGANIZATION resembles that of PRESBYTERIANISM. WORSHIP combines formal and informal elements. Methodism does have a prayer book, historically derived from Anglicanism but recently revised under the influence of the LITURGICAL MOVEMENT. Its use is, however, not compulsory. Hymn singing is central and extemporary prayer customary. (*See also* CHRISTIAN FELLOWSHIP CHURCH, HARRIS MOVEMENT.) [50; 62 vol. 9: 434–5]

Mezuzah [xxII] Parchment roll on which the first two paragraphs of the SHEMA (*Deuteronomy* 6: 4–9, 11: 13–21) are handwritten [64: 41–2]. A *mezuzah* is attached to every doorpost in the traditional Jewish home, usually inside a decorated case [70: 199]. This is in fulfilment of a literal understanding of the commandment. 'You shall write them on the doorposts of your house' (*Deuteronomy* 6: 9, 11: 20). It is customary for Orthodox Jews to kiss the *mezuzah* on entering or leaving a house. [14 vol. 11: 1474]

Midewiwin [v] Literally, 'mystic doings', an occult-medicine society in North America, primarily found among the Ojibwa or Chippewa Indians. Members (*mide*) of the Midewiwin, having paid the requisite entrance fee and received instruction from an elder *mide*, may progress through initiatory rites into the society's four levels. Initiates, usually seeking secret healing rituals and powers for themselves, first acquire a knowledge of medicinal herbs and techniques, as well as of the mythic precedent. In the medicine-lodge (*midewigan*), the neophyte undergoes a ritual death and rebirth, having first been shot with *migis* (small white clam shells) and then revived through contact with the same MEDICINE BUNDLES. The initiate may then progress to the status of MEDICINE MAN, at the highest of the society's levels. [24: IX]

Midrash [XXII] Jewish tradition of biblical exegesis found in rabbinical (*see* RABBI) literature: the Palestinian and Babylonian TALMUDS, the Aramaic translations (TARGUM) of the BIBLE, and the various collections known by the name of Midrash. Midrash may be either Halakhic (*see* HALAKHAH), interpreting and applying the legal and ritual norms of the Bible, or Aggadic (*see* AGGADAH), expounding theological and ethical teachings on the basis of a biblical text [72: 18]. Midrashic exegesis does not, on the whole, seek the plain meaning of scripture but the relationship between a biblical idea or theme and the very different social and cultural context of rabbinical JUDAISM [63: 339; 67: 223; 68: xv]. One of the tasks of Midrash is reconciling texts which appear contradictory. It was the availability of Midrashic techniques which allowed Pharisaic Judaism (*see* PHARISEES) to survive the destruction of the second TEMPLE in 70 CE, and to reconstitute Judaism at the rabbinical councils of Yavneh and Usha in the 1st and 2nd centuries CE. [11]

Miko [XXI] Female shamans in SHINTO. Formally called *kamiko* and *ichiko*, these are the young women who are dedicated to the service of the KAMI and carry out duties at the SHINTO SHRINES [19: 137–9; 20: 187–215; 32: 43–6]. Traditionally selected from certain families, in a rigid regimen involving years of strict virginal life, the *kamiko* are trained to assist the Shinto priests and perform the sacred dances (*kagura*) (*see* MATSURI). They are seen at shrines wearing white blouses and red skirts, symbols of their vows. The *ichiko*, more properly

SHAMANS, evolved spontaneously as mediums, who may become possessed and be in contact with spirits not normally encountered through shrine activities. Many female shamans are identified in early SHINTO LITERATURE, especially as wives or daughters of emperors, or ruling alone, allowing the emperor to devote more time to politics. In medieval times, when official support for shrines and temples was reduced, the *miko* system broke down and mediums scattered and travelled, practising divination and exorcizing through incantations (*see* HARAE).

Mikveh [XXII] A pool or 'gathering' of natural water used for ritual purification in JUDAISM. It is usually constructed by allowing rain water to collect in a specially designed container; once the required minimum amount is present to constitute a *mikveh* a separate container of tap water is joined to the 'living water'. Ritual bathing takes place in the tap water which technically becomes an extension of the natural water, but can be changed by draining and refilling [70: 156]. The *mikveh* is used today by traditional Jews for a variety of purposes. Women bathe in it at the end of their period of menstrual separation (*see* MENSTRUATION) and after childbirth before resuming sexual relations with their husbands. Converts (*see* CONVERSION) to Judaism must immerse themselves (*tevilah*) in a *mikveh*, and vessels bought from GENTILES must be dipped in one before they can be used in the preparation of food. Pietistical Jews immerse themselves before prayers, or before the Sabbath (SHABBAT). [5; 14 vol. 11: 1534; 21; 27]

Milarepa [XXXV] Tibetan Buddhist hermit and meditator (1040–1123) who was instrumental in founding the KAGYU tradition. Through songs attributed to him, and his striking life story which is written in a racy colloquial style, Milarepa has become a revered example for Tibetan Buddhists. Initially a practitioner of black magic, Milarepa killed a number of enemies who had cheated and oppressed his family. He relented and became a pupil of Marpa, who made him perform various austere tasks in order to purify his previous misdeeds and test his motivation. After much hardship and an attempt to run away, Milarepa was given the teachings and retired to the mountains where he meditated and taught a teaching based directly on his own experience of the Buddhist path. Like Marpa, Milarepa never became a monk, although unlike Marpa he also never married. He represents a tradition going back to the Indian *siddhas* (*see* TANTRA (2)), but the story of Milarepa is less one of miracle than of the real human struggle to put the Buddhist teachings into practice. [12; 29]

Milinda [XI] Ancient Indo-Greek king, of the city of Sagala (identified with modern Sialkot) [56: 1090], whose 'questions' concerning BUDDHIST teaching and practice, addressed to the Buddhist *thera* (*see* THERAVADA), Nagasena, together with the latter's replies, constitute a PALI Buddhist classic, the *Milindapanha*, of which there was also a Sarvastivadin (*see* SARVASTIVADA) version [97: 330]. A Sinhalese translation was made in the 18th century [57: 284], and an English translation by I. B. Horner published in 1963. [37]

Millenarian and Prophetic Movements (South American) [XXIII] Throughout the South American continent, religious movements centring on prophets and the belief in the imminent end of the world and a promised paradise have been recorded among peoples of different languages and cultures. Prominent among them are the GUARANI of the south and western coast, TUKANO and ARAWAK of the north-west Amazon, Ticuna of the upper Solimoes, Cariban peoples of British Guiana and northern Brazil, Gê and Timbira peoples of north-east Brazil, TOBA and Moscovi of the Argentine Chaco and the Campa of eastern Peru. Beyond actual movements, the cosmogonies of numerous other peoples contain the seeds of millenarian expectations. The movements may then be the result not only of external pressures of the contact situation, but also of the internal dilemmas present in cosmological processes. Often, visions of the end embody critical theories of history, interpreting specific qualities of existence in time, foreseeing violent destruction as the necessary precondition to recreation.

Features that have been common to movements across the continent include: the incorporation of Christian symbolism in millenarian ideologies; political and economic displacement; the emergence of prophets; the expectation of an imminent catastrophe and the reinstallation of a paradisical state; the total suspension of normal routines; divestiture of foreign clothes, goods or foods; ceaseless dancing and unbroken festival performances as insignia of admission into the new age; dream and vision; miraculous abundance; the incarnation of gods in material or human form; the prominence of celestial powers; the reversion of the transformed earth to native control; arduous restrictions on believers; and the transformation of bodies in which believers become healthy, invulnerable or even immortal [33: 554; 30; 24; 42]

Millenarianism [XIII.B] The belief in a future 1,000-year period of JESUS Christ's rule on earth. Premillennialists believe it will follow the Second Coming of Christ; postmillennialists that it will prepare for that coming by spreading righteousness over the earth. Millenarianism has produced special 'Adventist'

SECTS, some specifically dating the 'End', such as the followers of William Miller (1782–1842) in the USA. Millenarianism tends to increase in times of political and social stress. [62 vol. 9: 521–32; 75; 157: 916; 174]

Mimamsa [XVII] 'Investigation': systematic HERMENEUTICS of the Vedic scriptures. This is very old, with origins in the period of the BRAHMANAS, but its surviving literature is much more recent. Two Mimamsas are distinguished, each of which is one of the six DARSHANAS or salvation-philosophies of classical HINDUISM: (1) *Purva-mimamsa* (investigation of the earlier portions of the Veda), also called *Karma-mimamsa* (investigation of ritual action) or just *Mimamsa*; and (2) *Uttara-mimamsa* (investigation of the later portions, i.e. the UPANISHADS), also called *Brahma-mimamsa* (investigation of BRAHMAN), but usually known as VEDANTA. The classic text of the *Purva-mimamsa* is the *Mimamsa-sutra*, attributed to Jaimini (*c*.2nd century BCE), with an authoritative commentary by Shabara (probably 6th century CE) [47: IX, 319]. The main concern was to expound the rules of interpretation of the VEDA, understood as eternal and authoritative. Vedic statements were explained as injunctions for the performance of sacrificial and other actions (KARMA) that would create a new potency capable of determining the individual's future after death. The Vedic gods were identified with the ritual words themselves.

More philosophically evolved Mimamsa systems were developed around the 8th century by Kumarila Bhatta and Prabhakara, drawing from NYAYA and BUDDHIST thought [47: IX, 324–5]. Distinctive views were set forth on the sources of knowledge (*pramana*), the nature of sound and the way in which things are known. The notions of a supreme deity (ISHVARA) and of a periodical creation and destruction of the universe were attacked. The influence of the KARMA-MIMAMSA has been very strong in ritual practice and some aspects of Hindu law. Its hermeneutics are central to the usual Hindu understanding of their scriptures as embodying eternal truths rather than historical accidents. [36: I, 367–405]

Ministry (Christian) [XIII.A, B] The organization and leadership of the early Christian communities was flexible and variable. There is no single norm for Christian ministry in the New Testament. According to the *Acts of the Apostles* the APOSTLES exercised leadership over the early communities from JERUSALEM, though this was resisted by some GENTILE churches. Later the apostles were replaced by a council of elders led by James. In many churches the leadership was charismatic. Even where there were elders on the Jewish model their authority might be overruled by itinerant prophets. In the church at CORINTH there was factional rivalry which PAUL tried to counter with a scheme of all-member ministry. In Philippi the church was administered by 'bishops' and 'deacons' (overseers and ministers). In the 1st century the institution of a single bishop in each church had scarcely emerged. Nor was there any idea of a sacrificing priesthood; as in Israel priesthood rested in the community as a whole. [A9: 103–23; A11: IV, 835–42; A12; A18: 254–71]

Later, in ROMAN CATHOLICISM, the EASTERN ORTHODOX CHURCH and ANGLICANISM priests were 'ordained' (consecrated) to administer SACRAMENTS (*see also* MARRIAGE (CHRISTIAN)). Priestly orders and confirmation (sacraments) are administered by bishops in Roman Catholicism and Anglicanism. Confirmation is administered together with baptism by Orthodox Church priests. The bishops' authority is thought to descend from JESUS' commission to the apostles (apostolic succession). PROTESTANTISM reacted against the sacrificial implications of 'priesthood' and the MASS, and against the special status of bishops. Protestants generally use the terms 'ministry' and 'minister'. When bishops were retained (in LUTHERANISM, American METHODISM and the MORAVIAN BRETHREN), they were seen mainly as useful traditional supervisory officials.

Some Protestants regarded other forms of ministry as of divine origin (see PRESBYTERIANISM) but many adapted ministry according to need. The deacon originally assisted the priest and administered charity. This continues in the Orthodox Church, and with varying functions in Protestantism. Roman Catholicism and Anglicanism retain the office as a stage to the priesthood. Various other offices are used in CHURCH ORGANIZATION and oversight which may be regarded broadly as 'ministries'.

Anticlericalism (hostility to the power and status of priests or ministers) has often occurred in Christian history [B173]. It was a factor in the REFORMATION which often reduced the status of the priesthood. Most churches now encourage a 'ministry' by lay people (i.e. those not ordained) [B200; B1: 56–65, 489–522]. The main Protestant denominations allow ordination of women; Roman Catholics and Orthodox do not allow the ordination of women to the priesthood, but an increasing number of churches in the Anglican communion now permit it. French Roman Catholics have experimented with 'worker-priests' [B177] engaged in secular occupations. [B1: 532–76; B120; B157: 1004]

Mirghanis [XIX] A major SUFI ORDER in the Sudan in the 19th and 20th centuries, where it is also referred to as the Khatmiyya. The order was founded by Muhammad 'Uthman al-Mirghani (1793–1852), a disciple of Ahmad b. Idris (1760–

1837) who was also the Sufi SHAIKH of Muhammad 'Ali al-Sanusi (see SANUSIS). The Mirghanis transformed themselves into a political party of considerable influence in the 20th century. [125]

Miri piri [XXXIII] At his accession the sixth Sikh GURU Hargobind (1606–44) is believed to have donned two swords, one representing the spiritual authority of his predecessors (piri) and the other his newly assumed temporal authority (miri). This belief, together with the creation of the KHALSA in 1699, justifies the Sikhs' fight for justice and (in extreme cases) the use of weapons. [7: 108; 23: 63; 28: 51–2]

Mishnah [XXII] The first text of rabbinical Judaism, edited from previous collections by RABBI Judah the Prince and his colleagues at the end of the 2nd century CE [12; 41: 83]. The Mishnah is divided into six sections: (1) agricultural laws and benedictions; (2) festivals (CHAGIM); (3) laws relating to women; (4) civil laws; (5) holy things; (6) ritual purity laws. The Mishnah deals primarily with halakhic (see HALAKHAH) issues and became the authoritative source for later Judaism. [67: V; 68: III, IV]

Missions, Western Christian [XIII B] Christianity eventually became a largely European religion after the conversion of the Roman empire and its 'barbarian' successors (but cf. ASIA, CHRISTIANITY IN; EASTERN ORTHODOX CHURCH). ISLAM soon barred access to the East (cf. CRUSADES). Subsequent missionary history is related to (without being wholly determined by) European trade and colonialism. Thus 16th-century Spanish, Portuguese and French expansion, as well as COUNTER-REFORMATION zeal, encouraged missions to the Americas and Asia. PROTESTANTISM, struggling for survival (and perhaps inhibited theologically by the doctrine of predestination (CALVIN-ISM)), lagged behind. The dramatic 19th-century development of Protestant missions relates to British colonial expansion, but even more to energies released by the Evangelical Revival (see REVIVALISM). The missions of ROMAN CATHOLICISM also revived. Missions made Christianity a world religion, while revealing its limitations. BUDDHISM, HINDUISM, Confucianism (see CONFUCIUS) and in particular ISLAM proved culturally and religiously resistant to it; AFRICAN RELIGIONS much less so. Missionaries (especially Protestants) were reluctant to accommodate to other religions, looked down on non-Western cultures and were slow to create churches independent of European control. Independence was accelerated by the shock of decolonization after 1945 and by communism in CHINA. The major churches now generally send missionaries to work overseas at the request and under the supervision of the local churches. Pioneer missionary work of the traditional kind is most often done by the more extreme EVANGELICAL churches and organizations.

It remains difficult to assess the missionary achievement, which may have been as much cultural and political as religious. Missionaries did important pioneering medical and educational works, although reforming zeal often damaged societies and their cultures (see ECUMENICAL MOVEMENT). Non-Western styles of Christianity are only slowly emerging (along with SYNCRETISTIC cults, perhaps in reaction against Westernization). But the future of Christianity may well lie outside Europe. [8: 385–437; 37 vol. 6; 52; 100; 121; 122; 147]

Mithraism [XVIII] Mithras was a god popular in the Roman empire from the 2nd to the 5th centuries CE. His cult was strongest in the frontier regions, notably along the Rhine and Danube, also in Rome and its port of Ostia. It was socially respectable, being popular among the military and officials. The cult claimed descent from ZOROASTER. Mithras was an Indo-Iranian deity (see INDO-EUROPEANS) and he is worshipped in both HINDUISM (as Mitra) and ZOROASTRIANISM (as Mithra) [XXXVI 25], but scholars are divided on whether the Roman cult of Mithras had any real continuity with these religions [18; 20; 24]. Some scholars believe that the Mithraic cult preserves ancient Iranian but non-Zoroastrian traditions [19; 27]. Among those who hold this view it is generally assumed that an important 'staging post' in the westwards migration of Mithraism was the kingdom of Commagene, a buffer state between the Iranian and Roman empires, where a 1st-century BCE relief shows a full-length portrait of Mithras who is referred to in a nearby inscription, but lacking most features of the Roman iconography [32]. Other scholars suggest that the Romans used the name and imagery of an Iranian figure to give an image of oriental mystery and wisdom to a Roman cult and believe that the new cult was created either in Anatolia or in the city of Rome [28; 21; 16; 29]. The Roman temples were made to look like caves, to imitate the universe, the cosmic cave, as the Romans perceived it. Mithras was spoken of as the creator and father of all; his worshippers also believed that he saved men. The focal point of temples was a relief showing Mithras slaying the bull (*tauroctony*), a scene interpreted in different ways by scholars, and probably by different Mithraists: as the act of creation, or of salvation, or as having esoteric astrological significance [15]. Other scenes which decorate many temples include a divine banquet shared by Mithras and Sol over the body of the bull, a myth scene which was re-enacted in the cult. Another common scene is of the birth of Mithras from a rock (he was known as *petrogenes*, rock-born, by contemporary authors), not as a baby but as a young man, often shown attended by the two torch-bearers who flank the other scenes, Cautes and Cautopates, and holding the dagger with which he will slay the bull and the orb symbolizing his sovereignty. There is little direct evidence to support the common assertion that his birth was celebrated on 25 December. One of the most difficult elements of Mithraic iconography to interpret is the 'lion-headed figure' or leontocephaline, a human figure with wings, a lion's head, encircled by a snake often shown holding keys and associated with fire. It has been seen as a type of Gnostic archontic power [25]. The Roman cult of Mithras may well have shared many aspects of belief with GNOSTICISM and have interacted with Roman magical thought as well as making extensive use of contemporary astrological belief. Temples were small and fellowship was a central emphasis of the cult (although women were excluded). There were seven grades of initiation, each of which stood under the protection of a planet: *Corvus* (Raven), protected by Mercury; *Nymphus* (Bride), protected by Venus; *Miles* (Soldier), protected by Mars; *Leo* (Lion), protected by Jupiter; *Perses* (Persian), protected by the moon; *Heliodromus* (Runner of the Sun), protected by the sun; and *Pator* (Father), protected by Saturn. Progression through the grades was believed to correspond to the ascent of the soul through the planetary spheres [16; 17]. The religious life was disciplined, ascetic and arduous. [19; 22; 23; 24; 26; 30; 31: xxxvi 55]

Mithuna/Maithuna [xvii] *Mithuna* in Sanskrit means '(male/female) couple', and *maithuna* means 'coupledness, that which is done by couples' – sexual intercourse. Both are used as technical terms in the study of Indian art: *mithuna* for any representation of a couple, who may be simply showing affection, or

engaging in any sexual activity from foreplay to full intercourse; *maithuna* for the more explicitly erotic themes, including elaborate postures derived from the Kamasutra (*see* KAMA) and those involving more than two participants. The latter seem to be restricted to Hindu iconography, though *mithunas* (generally just embracing) are also found in early BUDDHIST and JAIN art. Clearly, not all *mithuna/maithuna* images are of the same nature. Some seem to convey simple human happiness, alongside other images of delight such as music-making and dance, or mothers playing with their babies, designed to adorn the temple with all the pleasures of life. The more complicated *maithunas* have been thought by some to suggest the presence of orgiastic cults. Others seem to convey supreme bliss, suggesting symbolism like that of the Brihadaranyaka UPANISHAD, in which the bliss of the union of ATMAN and BRAHMAN is likened to that of lovers in embrace [106: 262–3] (*see* TANTRA (1); ART, HINDU) [39].

In the Buddhist art of Tibet, too, BUDDHAS and BODHISATTVAS are sometimes depicted in *yab-yum* ('father–mother') form, KARUNA, compassion (male) united with PRAJNA, wisdom (female) in the bliss of NIBBANA. (*See* TANTRA (2).)

Mitzvah [xxii] (literally 'commandment'; plural *mitzvot*) According to rabbinical tradition there are 613 *mitzvot* (248 positive, 365 negative) in the Pentateuch (BIBLE) [14 vol. 5: 760] which God commanded the Jewish people to obey, and seven Noachian *mitzvot* applicable to the sons of Noah, i.e. GENTILES. The best-known group of *mitzvot* is the ten commandments or Decalogue (*Exodus* 20: 2–14, *Deuteronomy* 5: 6–18) which is of central importance for JUDAISM. Care was taken, however, not to emphasize the Decalogue, to avoid creating the impression that only these ten *mitzvot* were divinely revealed. In the course of

time all halakhic norms (see HALA-
KHAH) built around the biblical
commandments came to be thought
of as *mitzvot*, since they drew their
ultimate authority from God. This is
based on the traditional Jewish exegesis of *Deuteronomy* 17: 9–11
('According to the TORAH which
they [i.e. the religious leaders] will
teach you' [45: 160, 668]), implying
that the rabbinical developments of
ritual have divine sanction. Certain
mitzvot play a major role in the life of
the Jew and are determinants of Jewish identity: CIRCUMCISION for the
male Jewish child; MARRIAGE and
laws of sexual relations; the duty of
Torah study; prayer; the dietary laws
(KASHRUT); the MEZUZAH parchment attached to the doorposts of
the Jewish home; contributions to
charity or *tzedakah*; the Sabbath
(SHABBAT) and festival (CHAGIM)
rituals. Modern Jews may not keep
all these commandments in quite the
traditional way, and REFORM JUDA-
ISM has modified many ritual details
[56: VII] to adjust Judaism to modern life, but the essentials of the
mitzvot still represent what is distinctive in Jewish religion. From the
medieval period until modern times
Jewish theologians have sought to
find reasons for the *mitzvot* (*ta'amei
hamitzvot*), and to explain their
value in psychological, ethical or
mystical terms. [5; 11]

Mizimu [II] The spirits of the dead
or ancestral spirits in many BANTU
languages (singular: *muzimu, mud-
zimu, mzimu*). Linguistically this is
one of the most widely extended
words in African religion (cf.
NGANGA); it is the normal word for
the dead from the SHONA in Zimbabwe, northward across Zambia,
Malawi and Tanzania to Rwanda,
and to the Banyoro and Baganda in
Uganda (see GANDA). It overlaps
with many God-names: LEZA,
Imana, MULUNGU, MWARI,
Ruhanga, KATONDA, but is nevertheless far from universal in Bantu
religions, seldom appearing in this
form in the west or south (*but see*
MODIMO). The *mizimu* can help or
harm the living, and receive regular
veneration (see ANCESTOR VENERA-
TION). The word itself indicates a
status and power not possessed by
living elders, and, significantly, is
not in the normal noun-class for
persons.

Mo Tzu [XII] (*c*.470–391 BCE) An
anti-Confucian, pragmatic philosopher who argued that the validity of
a theory, policy or action should be
determined by: (1) whether it was
employed by the sage-rulers in history; (2) whether there were contemporary testimonies to its validity;
and (3) whether it had any practical
outcome, in increasing the health,
wealth and general well-being of the
population [7: IX, 222–30]. His third
criterion was the most central to his
thought and he used it in condemning many Confucian values and
practices (see CONFUCIUS). He criticized the exclusive emphasis on filial
piety (*hsiao*) and differentiated love,
and condemned elaborate FUNERAL
RITES, rites (LI) generally and music
(*yo*). He emphasized the value of
Universal Love (*Chien Ai*) in terms
of the benefits it produces; and condemned offensive wars on similarly
utilitarian grounds. Mo Tzu found a
further sanction for his teaching on
Universal Love in his doctrine of the
Will of Heaven (*T'ien Ming*) [7: IX,
217–21; 39: 11].

Mo Tzu's advocacy of the policy
of 'Agreement with the Superior'
(*Shang T'ung*) on the political level
seems to have favoured a disciplined
and authoritarian theocratic state.
His condemnation of offensive wars
did not lead to pacifism but to the
organization of a disciplined military
force of loyal followers who were
trained to defend weaker states
against aggressors. [34: V, 81–105;
74: L, 257–9]

The later sections of the Mohist
texts, written after Mo Tzu's death,
are largely concerned with defensive
military tactics and the systematic

exposition of Mohist concepts [40]. As a movement Mohism flourished during the Later Warring States period (402–221 BCE), but it was practically extinct by the beginning of the Han dynasty (206 BCE). [7: IX, 211–31; 19: IV, 60–80; 34: V, 76–105; 74; 75]

Modernity [XXXIV] Religions are essentially conservative movements, usually organized to preserve traditions and the status quo. Historically, therefore, religions have always had to come to terms with changes in society and culture, and this has never been more true than in the 19th and 20th centuries, periods normally referred to as 'modern'. 'Modernity' and related terms such as 'modern', 'modernism' and 'modernization' have been important for religions as they have been for other aspects of human life. Modernism has been especially important in certain art forms, including painting, sculpture, architecture and literature, and has had its place also in certain forms of religion. Modernization has been important in certain technical contexts but not so much in religion. Modernity as a whole, as a way of expressing human responses to technical, scientific and intellectual progress, has sometimes taken a totally negative attitude towards religious beliefs and behaviour, and has continually manifested itself as a challenge to the traditional as expressed religiously. Religious responses to modernity have varied considerably from total disregard, to attempts to modernize religion, to completely adverse responses by reaffirming the traditional in a vigorous way, sometimes by so-called fundamentalist, reactionary behaviour, sometimes by the readoption of religious orientations which disappeared centuries ago, as in so-called NEW AGE religions or world-views. FUNDAMENTALISM, which originally referred to a form of extremely conservative American Christianity, with especial emphasis on the 'fundamentals' of this form of religion, including the inerrancy of scripture, has become a term which is used journalistically, and occasionally academically, also of certain forms of ISLAM, SIKHISM and HINDUISM. The participants of these forms of religion would claim to be reaffirming an earlier, pristine form of their religion, upholding traditions which are threatened by alleged westernized and secular values. In one religious context 'modernism' was the name given to the writings of a group of Roman Catholic scholars, most prominent among them Alfred Loisy (1857–1940) and George Tyrrell (1861–1909). The work of the modernists was condemned in the Papal Encyclical *Pascendi dominici gregis* in 1907. In 1962, however, Pope John XXIII (1881–1963), in his earlier years himself suspected of 'modernism', surprised his church and the world by inaugurating the Second Vatican COUNCIL. The aim of the Council, according to the Pope, was to create a 'new opening' (*aggiornamento*). By the end of the Second Vatican Council in 1965, during the pontificate of Pope Paul VI (1897–1978), many changes had occurred with regard to the relations between Rome and other churches and other religions. Internally, BIBLICAL CRITICISM was accepted and rituals were celebrated in the vernacular. In the Protestant and Anglican forms of religion the term normally associated with attempts to be modern is 'liberal'. The term liberal has historically referred to 19th-century Anglicans such as Frederick Denison Maurice (1805–72), the authors of *Essays and Reviews* (1860) who included Benjamin Jowett (1817–93) and Arthur Penrhyn Stanley (1815–81), one-time Dean of Westminster Abbey, and to 20th-century Anglicans such as W. R. Inge (1860–1954), Dean of St Paul's Cathedral, E. W. Barnes (1874–1953), Bishop of Birmingham, John A. T. Robinson

(1919–83), Bishop of Woolwich and author of *Honest to God* (1963) and David Jenkins (1925–), Bishop of Durham. The leading names among Protestant liberals were Friedrich Schleiermacher (1768–1834), Albrecht Ritschl (1822–89), Adolf von Harnack (1851–1930), Ernst Troeltsch (1865–1923), Paul Tillich (1886–1965) and Rudolph Bultmann (1884–1976), New Testament scholar and demythologizer. In ISLAM, modernism is associated with figures such as Jamal al-Din al-Afghani (1839–97) of Persia, Shaykh Muhammad 'Abduh (1849–1905) of Egypt, and Amir Ali (1849–1928) and Muhammad Iqbal (1877–1938) of India and Pakistan. Prominent among Muslim leaders who have tried to reaffirm traditional values was Ayatollah Khomeini (1902–89) in Iran. Among Hindus leading modernizers have included Ram Mohan Roy (1772–1833), Ramakrishna (1834–86) and his disciple Swami Vivekananda, Sri Aurobindo (1872–1950) and Mohandas Karamchand (Mahatma) Gandhi (1869–1948). A Hindu reformer who wished to counteract Western influence by reasserting tradition was Swami Dayananda, who founded the Arya Samaj. One of the main features of the effect of modernity upon religion is summed up in the way in which religions have become much more democratized, sometimes internally but extensively externally in that people feel themselves much freer to choose the religion of their choice [20]. This plurality, and the suggestion of the weakening of religious authority with the consequent relativizing of religious claims, is sometimes welcomed by religious leaders, at other times fiercely condemned and resisted. [22; 23]

Modimo [II] (sometimes Molimo, or Morimo) is the name for God among a number of southern African BANTU peoples: the Tswana, Sotho, Pedi, and others. The word is linked etymologically with *muzimu* (MIZIMU), the most common Bantu name for ancestral spirit. The ancestors are here called *Badimo*. This linguistic linkage between God and the ancestors has proved confusing to observers, but the deep distinction between the two remained clear enough in the minds of most users, even if this appears an area in which belief in the creator God had become more vague and ineffectual than elsewhere [17: 116–22].

Moksha [XVII] (or *mukti*) 'Setting free', 'liberation', generally seen as the goal of the spiritual life in the Indian religions: release from SAMSARA, the cycle of death and rebirth. Typically, though not invariably, *moksha* is the term favoured by HINDUS and JAINS, NIBBANA/NIRVANA by BUDDHISTS. All agree that it is possible for a human being to become liberated while still alive (*jivanmukta*). By Hindus, *moksha* is sometimes seen as the fourth and highest aim of human life, transcending DHARMA (duty), ARTHA (worldly success) and KAMA (love and pleasure).

Moksha (Jain Doctrine) [XX] Although JAINISM, like HINDUISM and BUDDHISM, views spiritual release as involving freedom from rebirth, it envisages the state of the liberated soul in an idiosyncratic fashion. The soul, once free of the occluding presence of *karma* which has impeded its innate qualities (*see* JIVA; KARMA (JAIN DOCTRINE)), leaves the final body which has housed it and rises in an instant to the top of the universe, envisaged in Jainism as a massive but finite tripartite structure, where is located the abode of the liberated, the 'Slightly Curving Place', which resembles a parasol in shape. There it stays eternally with the other liberated souls, innumerable in number, in a state of bliss and pure knowledge. Each liberated soul is envisaged as being ontologically isolated and distinct, and the Jains do not subscribe to a view of liberation as involving union with a world-soul. [4: 37–8, 88–90; 10: 268–71]

Monasticism, Christian [XIII.D]
The origin of Christian monasticism is unknown: tradition portrays St Antony the Great as the first monk and St Paul of Thebes as the first hermit, attributing the origin of the two forms of monasticism to Egypt in the 4th century, and this could well be correct. The word 'monk' comes from the Greek word *monachos*, which means 'solitary'; 'hermit' from *heremites*, a desert-dweller. The early monks and nuns were just that: men and women who fled the worldliness of urban life and the ethos of a church that was now an established institution of the Roman empire; they fled to the desert to repent and seek God by prayer, fasting and hard manual labour. In the desert they practised an ascetic lifestyle of great poverty and extreme simplicity (*see* ASCETICISM, CHRISTIAN). The DESERT FATHERS, the notable teachers and saints of the desert, became the reference point for all later Christian monastic spirituality. The earliest monks lived as hermits, or in small, loosely organized colonies around a teacher, or as clusters of solitaries, sometimes worshipping together. The COPTIC monk Pachomius gave a new shape to monastic life by establishing a large-scale monastic community organized on almost military lines.

Eastern Christian monasticism retains all the forms known from the desert period: some of the Coptic desert monasteries still survive from a very early period. Recluses living a strictly solitary life, mendicant monks living only on alms-food, tiny kellia of two or three monks living together, sketes of a handful of cottage-like cells gathered around a church and governed by a Dikaios all co-exist with highly organized cenobitic monasteries of various kinds. Apart from the Brotherhood

of the Holy Sepulchre, however, there is little in EASTERN ORTHODOX Christianity that resembles the Western religious orders with their different rules, lifestyles, habits and spiritualities. Nonetheless, Orthodox monasticism is very varied. The idiorhythmic life followed by many individuals and in many sketes on Mt Athos allows the individual to own property and to organize life with a minimum of communalization. The cenobitic life demands community of possessions and an ordered communal life under abbatial authority. Outside Mt Athos, many Orthodox monasteries have followed the advice of St Basil and developed a life of caring service to others, or have followed the Studite pattern, an urban monastic life, involved in the cares and problems of the whole community.

Acceptance into the monastic community is marked by the giving of the rason (cassock) of the house. The rasophore then lives the monastic life under the discipline of obedience, but not as an ordained monk or nun. There are two degrees of monastic ordination, to the Little Schema and to the Great Schema: both involve vows of permanent commitment, chastity and willing endurance. Each Orthodox monastery has its own *Typikon* which lays down its pattern of life. Detailed rules and constitutions, normal in the West, are comparatively rare. There are important Orthodox monasteries in America and a famous centre of religious life at Tolleshunt Knights in Britain founded by the late Archimandrite Sophrony, a disciple of the great HESYCHAST, St Silouan (*see* STARETS).

Western monasticism takes its distinctive form mainly from the monastic rule of St Benedict of Nursia; he lays down an ordered and disciplined life, with a strong emphasis on the singing of the divine office, under the authority of an abbot who is to be at once spiritual father and ruler of the house. Celtic monasticism represented an older tradition closer to the monks of the desert, strongly ascetic and more varied in lifestyle. The Cluniac reform of St Benedict of Aniane introduced much longer hours of prayer, relieved the choir monks of most manual work and created a hierarchically structured family of monasteries almost all under the direct authority of the Abbot of Cluny, individual houses having a prior governing in his name. The Cluniacs gained a reputation for magnificent liturgy, ordered scholarly life and splendid churches. The Cistercians, the White Monks, represented a return to what they thought was the primitive rule: hard work, poverty, simplicity of life, rejection of privacy, austerity in church architecture and furnishings. If the Benedictines in general kept learning alive in the early medieval period, the Cistercians drained the marshes and transformed agriculture. The medieval period also saw the introduction of bearded monks or lay brothers, free from choir duties and devoted to manual work: the distinction between choir monks and lay brothers has faded since the Second Vatican Council. St Benedict's rule envisaged the monastery as a self-sufficient totality. It became common, however, for similar houses to band together into congregations with a degree of collective organization. The English Congregation is the oldest, and is marked by the unusual institution of temporary abbots.

Hermit monasticism has always existed in unorganized forms; under St Bruno, founder of the Carthusians, and St Romuald, founder of the Camaldolese, eremitical monasticism took on an ordered and structured form; in the case of Camaldoli, cenobitic, eremitic and recluse lifestyles coexisted in the one order. In the period of the CRUSADES the military orders, the KNIGHTS TEMPLARS and the Hospitallers, combined a version of the monastic life, inspired by Cîteaux, with a military vocation.

Monasticism is essentially a life of repentance dedicated to God. From early times, a similar but pastorally orientated form of life existed inspired by St Augustine: that of the canons regular, clerics living a monastic life with an abbot, but essentially pastoral in outlook. The medieval orders of friars extended the pastoral and missionary life by rejecting the rule of stability that bound a monk or canon to the house in which he took his vows. While monks or canons did in fact travel and change houses, this was by way of exception. The friars belonged to the order, not the house, and could be moved wherever needed. Significantly, the original female counterpart orders to the friars are orders of nuns living in stability and under enclosure. The Beguines, Beghards and the Third Orders represent varying degrees of lay acceptance of a monastic lifestyle: the Third Orders began as lay religious societies living under a rule suited to lay life and under the direction of the friars, but also developed 'regular' versions who live in community under vows.

The Fourth Lateran Council took steps to halt the burgeoning variety of religious orders, but in the long run it failed. The COUNTER-REFORMATION saw a new form of religious life, that of the clerks regular, such as the Jesuits: clerics living in community and under vows, but without the obligation to sing the divine office in choir which the friars had retained. Orders of brothers and sisters devoted to teaching or nursing grew also. The Second Vatican Council led to a widespread reform and modernization of monastic and other religious orders.

The REFORMATION had put an end to the monastic life where it triumphed, but the 19th century saw the return of monasticism to the ANGLICAN Communion. Orders of religious sisters devoted to works of mercy paved the way, avoiding the PROTESTANT dislike of religious vows and the suspicion of the enclosed contemplative life. Soon groups parallel to the Roman Catholic monks, friars, clerks regular and contemplative nuns were once more established and continue to play an important role in the life of the church. With the foundation of Taizé, Protestant monasticism at last came into being, and that monastery plays a unique ecumenical role. [33; 69; 74; 78; 99]

Monism [XXXIV] As a world-view, belief that reality is of one kind (as against DUALISM and pluralism). A monist may hold that all is SPIRIT (one meaning of idealism) or matter (materialism). As a view of man, monism rejects any dualism of body and mind, or of flesh and spirit. Neutral monism holds that the material and the spiritual, the physical and the mental, are aspects of one being or substance. Some PANTHEISM is explicitly monist. [43: 133–4]

Monotheism [XXXIV] Belief that there is one, but only one, divine being [121a: 1] (cf. GODS; HENOTHEISM; THEISM) [41: 4]. The term is often used more specifically for belief in the supreme personal creator-God of JUDAISM, CHRISTIANITY and ISLAM [36: 76 7], although the Christian doctrine of the TRINITY is monotheism modified (or more than this, as e.g. some Jews and Muslims see it). Theories of religious evolution, which saw monotheism as emerging from POLYTHEISM [145: 19, 52], were countered by arguments that it was original or primordial [110: 98–9; 145: 63–4, 183–4], or that it arose historically by revelation through PROPHECY in the context of protests against idolatry [110: 103–4].

Moral Majority [IV] One among many movements that arose in American PROTESTANT FUNDAMENTALISM, EVANGELICALISM and PENTECOSTALISM around the time of the election of President Ronald Reagan in 1980. This particular expression of what came to be called the 'new Christian right' was invented by the best known fundamentalist of his day, the Reverend Jerry Falwell of Lynchburg, Virginia. Falwell was pastor of the burgeoning Thomas Road Baptist Church, and founder of a college that became Liberty University. He was also extremely successful as a preacher and fundraiser on television. While fundamentalists in the main had eschewed political action in the previous generation, usually being critical of moderate and liberal church participation in the public forum, Falwell and his associates turned this approach on its head and called their colleagues and constituencies to give public and explicit expression to their involvements.

Although the Moral Majority professed to welcome ROMAN CATHOLICS, Jews and unbelievers as well as Protestants into its coalition, one fed by television preaching and supported through mass mailings and generous donations, its real strength came from the Protestant right. The Moral Majority gained its greatest support with its opposition to legal abortion, a cause which attracted the energies of many Catholics and other non-fundamentalists. Falwell and his colleagues enlarged this moral mission, however, to include opposition to pornography and obscenity in public media and support for a large national defence and free enterprise economics.

The Moral Majority showed considerable favour to, and was favoured by, President Reagan and made its way into the corridors of power. However, a backlash developed and many politicians shied away from it, seeing it as extremist. Opposition groups formed, and the Moral Majoritarians gradually put their energy into other kinds of organizations. When in 1989 Falwell dissolved the movement, he claimed it was unnecessary because it had known victories; and opponents said that it was a spent force. [10]

Moral Re-Armament [XIII.B] Movement founded by the American LUTHERAN Frank N.D. Buchman (1878–1961) in the 1920s which from 1929 called itself the 'Oxford Group'. Concentrating on the affluent and influential, it operated through small groups cultivating the 'Four Absolutes' (honesty, purity, unselfishness, love). As 'Moral Re-Armament' (MRA) its interest expanded to political and social regeneration from 1938. During the Cold War period following the Second World War, MRA claimed influence at high levels of political and industrial life, with an anti-communist orientation, but has had less publicity in recent years. [39]

Moral Theology [XIII.B] Love for God and humankind may be said to be the root principle of Christian morality. It came to be regarded as the chief 'theological virtue' (with faith and hope) as contrasted with the 'cardinal (i.e. fundamental) virtues' (prudence, temperance, fortitude and justice) derived from classical ethics. Moral distinctions and precepts were elaborated in the medieval period, still influenced by classical thought but also by the development of PENANCE. By the 17th century an elaborate casuistry (the science of cases of conscience) had evolved. The Jesuits developed 'probabilism', a system emphasizing freedom of conscience, and therefore seen by some as favouring leniency to sinners, which was opposed by JANSENISM, and notably by Blaise Pascal (1623–62) in his *Provincial Letters* (1656–7). Early PROTESTANTISM reacted against such complexities. They regarded them as promoting SALVATION by 'works' (i.e. salvation achieved through man's own actions), and

thus as 'Law' rather than GOSPEL. But they generally resisted antinomianism (the rejection of a moral law). ANGLICANISM and PURITANISM developed a casuistry based on their own doctrines. Modern Christians have been influenced by the complexities of contemporary society; by concern for SOCIAL MORALITY; and by non-Christian moral reflection. Some simply apply the general 'law of love', liberally adapted to circumstances ('situation ethics') [67]. Others make fresh attempts to develop detailed guidelines between general principles and individual cases. In the USA especially, much use has been made of psychologically influenced 'pastoral counselling'. (*See also* SEXUALITY, AND CHRISTIANITY.) [139]

Morality [XIV] The concept of morality stands in a problematic relation to religious thought. The term *rita*, for example, plays a significant role in the VEDAS; it designates the fixed order of the cosmos, the order of the rituals which image and sustain it and, at a personal and social level, the network of duties and responsibilities, breach of which invites punishment by Varuna, the divine defender of oaths and vows. In later Hindu writings the term DHARMA is the focal term expressing the social order as it is divinely ordained, the balance of CASTES and life-stages that marks the perfect society (e.g. in the description of the City of Ayodhya in the Valmiki RAMAYANA) and the caste-, gender- and life-stage-based system of duties and responsibilities that shapes the life of each individual. The lawbooks, the Dharma Shastras, express the social reality of *dharma* in terms of a code of laws with appropriate sanctions against transgressors. Neither *rita* nor *dharma* corresponds precisely to the concept of morality. *Rita* is the fixed order of things, violation of which invites the god who guards that order to use his magical powers to bind the transgressor: the concept is both wider and narrower than morality. *Dharma*, as expounded in the law-books, differs from the modern concept of morality in that it defines duties and responsibilities in terms of caste status and life-stage, not in terms of personal responsibility as such. Moreover, certain provisions of the law codes would strike a philosopher as morally bizarre; the Brihaspati Smriti, for example, prescribes (XXIII, 13–14) punishments for a woman who is a rape victim.

Parallel difficulties would face anyone seeking a precise counterpart of the concept of morality in other religions. The body of commandments Jewish tradition finds in the TORAH are not generally of universal application: most apply only to adult Jews, and several do not bind women. They do not, therefore, constitute a morality in the common understanding of the term, though they have an important role in moral guidance and the solution of moral problems. A much narrower set of commandments, the seven commandments of the Covenant with Noah (*Genesis* 8–9), are believed by traditional JUDAISM to bind all humanity. The scriptural text, however, includes among the injunctions imposed on Noah and his sons abstinence from meat with blood in it (*Genesis* 9: 4), a proscription which, though reiterated in *Acts* 15: 20, would strike most philosophers as having a ritual or religious rather than a moral significance. In BUDDHIST thought, the term *dharma* has a rather different use from its use in HINDUISM; it refers more usually to the truth the BUDDHA preached rather than to the pattern of life inculcated. The term SILA tends to replace it in that context; but *sila* equally is not simply identifiable with morality, since *sila* means rather discipline or self-training. This narrows the concept too much for it to map precisely on to the concept of morality.

The concept of morality has been shaped by centuries of philosophical, theological and more recently sociological debate. It is a concept with firm roots in West European intellectual history, being grounded in the discussions of ethics by the Greek philosophers and in the mediation of Stoic, Cynic, Aristotelian and to some extent Platonic ethics through the thought of the early Christian writers, of the SCHOLASTICS and of the later moral theologians as well as in the investigations of secular philosophers of more recent times. Consequently, it would be odd to expect any exactly parallel concept to have emerged within religious traditions which do not draw on these intellectual roots. In recent years there has been considerable public debate of a range of moral issues: the justification of euthanasia and abortion; the nature and extent of environmental responsibility; the ideal of global social justice; the limits of individual liberty; the function and role of legal punishment; the existence and nature of human rights, animal rights, children's rights; the justification of trade in human organs; the principles of just distribution of scarce resources (e.g. costly medical treatments). In all such cases, many religions have an articulate viewpoint to bring to the debate, or the theoretical resources to construct one. Evidence of this is contained in the resolutions of the 1993 World Parliament of Religions aiming towards a global ethic. One of the emerging features of inter-religious encounter is precisely this: the entry of a wide variety of religious groups into the field of public moral debate with the intention of pursuing consensus rather than simply defending a local ideal of human conduct.

Moravian Brethren [XIII.B] The Bohemian Brethren (cf. HERESY (MEDIEVAL CHRISTIAN)) were 'renewed' by the Lutheran Count Zinzendorf in Germany (1722) under PIETIST influence and later became an independent church for which apostolic succession (see MINISTRY, CHRISTIAN) has been claimed. Early Moravians developed economically self-sufficient communities (later dissolved); missions overseas; and devotional methods which influenced METHODISM. Their piety centres on special devotion to the humanity of JESUS. [62 vol. 10: 106–8; 124; 157: 938]

Mormons [XIII.B] 'The Church of Jesus Christ of Latter-Day Saints.' The Mormons' visionary founder Joseph Smith (1805–44) in the USA claimed to translate the revealed *Book of Mormon*, which supplements the BIBLE. Brigham Young (1805–77) led the sect to Salt Lake City (1847). Early violence and polygamy (later abandoned) brought clashes with the government. There were also secessions from the main church, the most important being the Reorganized Church of Jesus Christ of Latter-Day Saints (1852). Mormonism is a highly American form of MILLENARIANISM. JESUS Christ was, it teaches, revealed to early immigrants in America, and will found a new Jerusalem there. The church is ruled by an elaborate hierarchy. Baptism and marriage can be contracted vicariously for the dead to 'seal' them in the faith. Mormons avoid stimulants and give two years' free service to the church. [2: 501–9; 4; 30; 62 vol. 10: 108–12; 86; 145: 348–54; 156]

Moses (in Judaism) [XXII] Moses (*c.*13th century BCE) is the central figure from the BIBLE for rabbinical JUDAISM, and is referred to as 'Moses, our RABBI'. According to MAIMONIDES' seventh principle of Jewish doctrine, Moses was the greatest of the prophets [31: VIII], and the Pentateuch, which was revealed to him by God, is a unique, unchanging revelation [31: IX, X]. The oral traditions of Judaism are also thought to originate with Moses, who spent 40 days being instructed by God at Sinai. [14 vol. 12: 371; 16: 15]

Mosque [XIX] (Arabic *masjid*, 'place of prostration', or *jami'* '(place of) congregating together', used especially for larger mosques), the building in which Muslims can worship congregationally, often also used for educational and teaching purposes (*see* MADRASA). Although the daily worship (SALAT) can be performed anywhere, it is especially meritorious when done in a mosque as an expression of solidarity with other believers, and must be so performed on a FRIDAY morning, when a sermon (*khutba*) is usually preached. Originally a place of public assembly, the mosque acquired more and more an atmosphere of sanctity, like a Christian church, so that a state of ritual purity (TAHARA) became necessary for all entrants, and the admission of women (MAR'A) was allowed only to a limited extent and reluctantly [20 s.v.; 48: 76–80; 67 'Masjid']. Mosques vary from simple, roofless constructions of palm trunks in Africa to the architectural splendours of the great mosques of Cairo, Istanbul or Isfahan. Notable features include the provision of a fountain or cistern in the courtyard, for the performance of preparatory ablutions; an apsidal niche (*mihrab*) oriented towards Mecca (the *qibla* direction; *see* HARAMAIN), which the believers face in rows under the leadership of the IMAM or prayer-leader; in larger mosques, a minaret, which the *muezzin* ascended (in pre-electrical-recording days) to give the call to prayer (*adhan*); a pulpit (*minbar*), from which the sermon is delivered; in larger mosques, again, a platform (*dakka*), used as a seat for the *muezzin*; and a stand (*kursi*) or lectern for the QUR'AN, used here liturgically [82: II; 93: I]. The floor of the mosque is often covered in carpets, and the walls may be decorated with Qur'anic texts in fine calligraphy and vegetal or abstract patterns (*see* ART (IN ISLAM)). [74]

Mourides [xxvII] The Mouridiyya Brotherhood is the largest new religious movement among Muslim peoples of west Africa, founded among his own Wolof people in Senegal by a saintly marabout of the Qadiriyya order in the SUFI tradition, Amadu Bamba (*c.*1850–1927), after his visionary call in 1886 to renew ISLAM. In the same year an aristocratic Wolof, Ibra Fall (1858–1930) introduced new features into Islam by making a total personal submission to Amadu Bamba and organizing young men as aspirants ('mourides'), not for study but for manual work on the marabout's land. This captive labour force led to the founding of prosperous agricultural villages with emphasis on the new crop of groundnuts and to the foundation of Touba, a new holy city as a place for the annual Magal pilgrimage for the hundreds of thousands of members acquired in the 20th century. Amadu Bamba was succeeded in turn by three sons; the third, Abdu Lahette, from 1968 introduced many reforms to counter laxity and corruption in the movement. As an Africanized form of Islam producing Senegal's major crop, the Mourides have wielded considerable economic and political power, but its authoritarian structure, unsatisfactory farming methods, and elementary and unorthodox understanding of Islam throw doubt upon its long-term future and suggest its value may have been as an agent of transition. Ibra Fall, who had originally set the new style, moved away from the rural movement and developed a distinct branch known as the Bay Fall, with urban commercial as well as farming activities, and lived in luxury in St Louis from 1912. In the 1970s there were estimated to be some 50,000 followers under marabouts from the Fall family, emphasizing their Wolof origins, and

regarded as heretics by the main body. [14]

Mudra [xvII] Gesture, significant in south Asian religion, dance and visual arts. In Hindu, Buddhist and Jain ART, the *mudras* formed by deities are as significant as the attributes they may hold in identifying them and expressing their characters. Commonly found in all these religions are *abhaya-mudra*, the hand held palm out with the fingers upwards, granting freedom from fear, and *varada-mudra*, the hand held palm out with fingers downward, granting favour (*see figure 9*). For example DURGA, whose numerous other hands hold weapons for the battle against demons, may form *abhaya-* and *varada-mudras* with her foremost pair of hands, showing her kindness to her devotees. Other *mudras* have more specific reference, for example *dharmacakrapravartana-mudra*, the gesture of setting in motion the wheel of the dharma (*See* DHAMMA), associated with the BUDDHA at the time of his first teaching, and with associated figures such as the goddess personifying the Perfection of Wisdom, PRAJNAPARAMITA. The gestures could naturally be used in ritual to invoke the deities with whom they were associated, an important practice in TANTRA.

Muhammad [xIx] The prophet of ISLAM. Traditionally regarded as having been born *c.*570 in the west Arabian trading town of Mecca (*see* HARAMAIN), Muhammad spent his early life as a merchant. In middle life an interior conviction dawned on him that he was the prophet chosen by God (ALLAH) to convey the eternal message to his people the Arabs, just as MOSES had brought it to the Jews and JESUS to the Christians. The divine revelations to him continued from around 610 until his death in 632, and form the QUR'AN. Their original message, probably to the Arabs only in the first place, was eventually broadened out into a

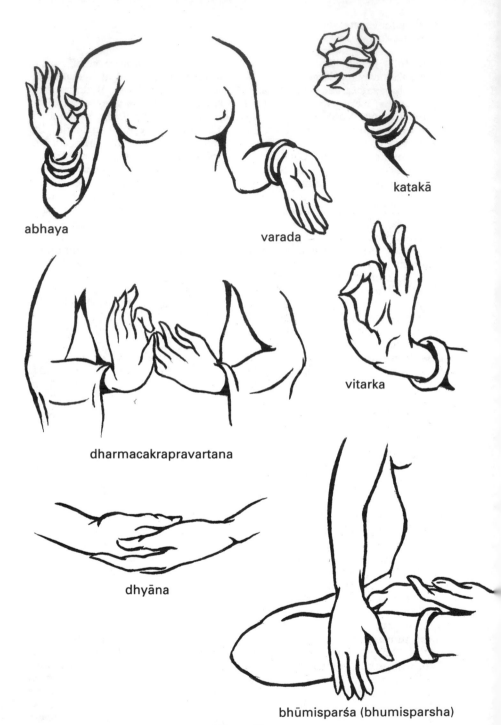

abhaya

kaṭakā

varada

dharmacakrapravartana

vitarka

dhyāna

bhūmisparśa (bhumisparsha)

Figure 9
Mudras

universal one, so that Muhammad becomes the prophet for all mankind, with a divine message superseding all previous ones (*see* NABI). The progress of his apostleship in Mecca was impeded by the hostility of his pagan fellow-townsmen, with their attachment to the ancient gods, so that in 622 he and his followers migrated to the town of Yathrib, now renamed Medina. This departure (*hijra*) came to mark the beginning of the Muslim era (*see* CALENDAR (IN ISLAM)). At Medina, Muhammad organized his Meccan followers plus the Medinan converts or 'Helpers' into a dynamic religiopolitical group, whose authority was by his death extended over much of the Arabian peninsula, providing the basis for the future military expansion of Islam [20 s.v.; 32; 65 vol. 1: II; 67 s.v.; 71. 283–336; 85; 114; 132]. Although Muhammad always protested that he was only a man, the channel chosen for God's revelation but not himself an angel or divine being, later generations of the faithful erected him into a miracle-working figure and into the archetype of humanity, the Perfect Man. [6; 120]

Muhpatti [xx] Cloth mouth-shield worn by SHVETAMBARA JAIN ascetics to diminish the possibility of destroying minuscule life forms in the air through breathing and thus signifying their religion's commitment to non-violence. Although all Shvetambara Jain ascetics possess *muhpattis* and laypeople will often wear them during ritual to avoid polluting sacred objects, it is only ascetics of two sects, the STHANAKVASI and the TERAPANTH, who wear them permanently. [4: 216–17]

Mulungu [II] Mulungu (or a related word: Mlungu, Murungu, Mluku; in Swahili, Mungu, Milunga) is one of the most widely used names for God in eastern Africa, from the Zambezi in the south to Kenya and peoples like the Kamba and Gikuyu in the

north. This is the effect partly of Swahili influence on the hinterland, partly of the preference of Muslims and Christian missionaries for using Swahili. Yet the use of the word by many inland peoples certainly precedes this: it was noted on the middle Zambezi by Portuguese in the 17th century. The meaning and etymology are unclear. Among a few peoples (e.g. the Kinga) there may be a plural, *milungu*, meaning ancestral spirits, but in most languages Mulungu is emphatically singular, supreme and non-ancestral. [17; 25]

Mummification [VI] A chemical method used by the Egyptians, from the Old Kingdom to the Christian era (*c.*2600 BCE–*c.*400 CE), to preserve the human corpse. Herodotus (*c.*484–430 BCE) [14: 160] distinguished three grades of mummification. The most expensive method, available at first only for royalty but gradually adopted by all wealthy persons, involved removal of the viscera, dehydration of the tissues by means of natron, and subsequent anointing and bandaging of the body; amulets were inserted between the layers of bandages. [3; 4] It was believed to be important to preserve the body so that the soul, which left at death, might return to take food offerings. (*See also* ANIMAL CULTS.)

Music (in Islam) [XIX] Music has not been used liturgically as extensively in ISLAM as in certain other faiths, although its use is by no means lacking. Islamic theologians disagreed over the lawfulness of listening to music (*sama'*), and traditions exist supporting both sides; but it is true that in many pious quarters the use of music was frowned on as frivolous. However, elegant cantillation of the QUR'AN (*tajwid*) existed from an early time, and the call to prayer in the MOSQUE (*adhan*) was in effect chanted musically. Dancing, instrumental music and the chanting of poems or hymns in vernacular tongues became characteristic, above all, of much Sufi ritual and *dhikr* sessions (*see* SUFI INSTITUTIONS), being viewed as inducements to ecstasy and an approach to the godhead. [77: XVIII–XIX; 82: VI]

Music (Jewish) [XXII] In JUDAISM sound takes precedence over ICONOGRAPHY as the main form of religious expression. Ancient Hebrew song is referred to on numerous occasions in the BIBLE, and in the TEMPLE the Levites were singers in the sacrificial cult [4 vol. 1: 123]. Percussion and stringed instruments are also mentioned. Music was used to induce the ecstatic trances of the prophets (*see* PROPHECY), and David played for King Saul to soothe his troubled spirit (*see* BIBLICAL HISTORY). Many of the biblical Psalms are preceded by instructions indicating their melodies. With the destruction of the second temple, Jewish music underwent a complete change. As a sign of mourning instrumental music was forbidden in the SYNAGOGUE liturgy. The Pentateuch and other biblical books were chanted according to traditional melodies, some of which have been preserved down to modern times. The synagogue CANTOR, whose original role was simply as prayer leader, has in the course of time become a musical performer with a distinctive style. Cantorial music has been influenced by European operatic traditions, folk-songs and Israeli popular tunes, as well as by Chasidic melodies which CHASIDISM developed for the purpose of serving God through the joy of song and dance [49: XX]. Instrumental music is played at Jewish weddings, and on Sabbaths (SHABBAT) and festivals (CHAGIM) hymns are sung by the Jewish family at meals. [11; 14 vol. 12: 554; 29: I–III; 36: V]

Mwari [II] The name for the High God among the SHONA of Zim-

babwe and the Venda of the Transvaal. Among BANTU theologies that of Mwari seems to possess a special, even ambiguous, character. For the Venda, Mwari (or Mwali) was originally, it appears, a hero king. For the Shona he (or perhaps she, for Mwari has some strongly feminine attributes including the title Mbuya – Grandmother) is above all the giver of rain and fertility, whose greatest praise-name is Dzivaguru (Great Pool). The cult of Mwari seems to have been brought into Shonaland at some uncertain date, probably little by little replacing in name an earlier High God. Since the early 19th century at the latest it has centred on cave-shrines in the Matopo hills, the principal shrine being now at Matonjeni. The cult is significantly inter-tribal: when the Ndebele conquered western Shonaland in the 19th century they quickly adopted Mwari, and Venda lineages continue to be influential among the priests, but the chief area of influence is undoubtedly southern Shonaland. The cult organization includes priests, mediums, dancers and messengers, who link the shrine with different parts of the country and bring offerings and petitions for rain.

Across several centuries and political changes the Mwari cult has retained a widely extended religious and political influence through an institutional, oracular and ritual pattern notably different from that associated with the recognition of the one God among most other Bantu peoples. [15: 287–313; 18: 179–218; 26]

Myalism [III] A dynamic present-world-orientated tradition which rejects negative and tragic life experiences, blaming them on witchcraft and sorcery, OBEAH, in the Caribbean. It emerged in the later 18th century in Jamaica and Myal was a significant feature in the last Jamaican slave rebellion (1831–2). Immediately thereafter its members were persecuted. Their response was to become even more active and to try to gain converts, thus challenging missionary religion. Action by the Jamaican government was taken to attempt to control its expression, but it is characteristic of such a movement that this only appeared to increase the fervour of the members.

Myalism is a classic African-Caribbean mode of religious expression, in that it syncretizes African belief systems and behaviour, and borrows from observed Christian worship (see SYNCRETISM). By the end of the 19th century Christian elements were apparent, such as the use of hymns from the Sankey Hymnal. Certainly Myal allowed disparate groups of slaves to come together and create some sort of African solidarity in the face of slavemaster brutality. Characteristic features included charismatic leadership and a belief in the prevalence of the power of good; the quest to eradicate evil may have led to hunts for witches/obeahmen. The movement developed beyond the original groups, and it is through these extended groups that new relationships and roles were developed: initiates learned to co-operate with each other in social and political matters as well as inspirational affairs. Additional power came from the fact that Europeans played no part in its ceremonies. In fact the initiation to Myal included a dance which brought protection against Europeans.

The Black Baptist Church (see NATIVE/BLACK BAPTISTS) was developing concurrently in Jamaica, and there seemed room for sympathetic possibilities, but further co-operation, or even fusion, was inhibited by what the Black Baptists saw as less and less orthodox and controllable Myal behaviour. In Myalism prophetic visions and possession were characteristic of conversion and acceptance. Myalists claimed power and inspiration from baptism by immersion and the power of St JOHN THE BAPTIST, often calling their church after him. Black BAPTISTS meantime shared the importance of total immersion at baptism, but for them JESUS remained the central figure.

By the mid-19th century three grades of membership had emerged: Archangels, Angels and Ministering Angels. Archangels specialized in divination, and were the ritual experts. Angels spoke of their visions, and they concentrated on searching out obeah. The third group, in bands of about 20, worked at the practical side of things. They tried hard to get converts, and dug up obeah medicines and charms. All grades could be male or female. They led well-ordered lives. In the mid-19th century the Myalists had the characteristics of a prophetic and millennial cult. Although their teaching did not come from the BIBLE, they insisted on God's authority for them to clear the way for the coming of Jesus Christ.

Myalists disliked both planters and missionaries, and there were work stoppages on the plantations when the Africans insisted that they had to do God's work in obeah eradication. The planters called the police (1941–2), and missionaries denounced them, accusing them of madness. Myalists responded that they were not mad, but 'had the spirit'. Myalists came into direct competition with the missionaries by trying to gain occupation of the meeting houses built by some missionaries on plantations. Although in the following years there was heavy suppression of Myalism, when the REVIVAL came in the 1960s it became obvious that Myal elements of dancing, drumming and possession had been kept alive. It could be argued that revival in Jamaica had more in common with Myalism than with Christianity. It seems that these same elements, together with visions and prophecies, occur and reoccur in the island, for instance in the language and predictions of BED-WARDISM and in the religious counter-culture of RASTAFARIANISM. [17; 59; 67; 74; 83; 86]

Mysteria [XVI] Greek cults accessible only after initiation undergone by personal choice, often apparently involving closer contact with the divinity. They began as community agrarian rites, then acquired initiatory aspects and soteriological functions, promising a blissful afterlife. Most important were the Eleusinian Mysteries, intimately connected with the Athenian *polis* cult (*see* GREEK RELIGION), honouring primarily Demeter and Kore (= Persephone). (*See* AFTERLIFE (GREEK); MYTHOS; ORPHEUS; THEOI.) In Hellenistic times Mystery-cults multiplied. *Mysteria* became attached to the cults of certain oriental gods. These, like the Bacchic/Dionysiac Mysteries (*see* ORPHEUS), were not tied to a particular locality. [4: 276–304; 5; 17: 792–80]

Mysteries (Eastern Orthodox) [XIII.D] The EASTERN ORTHODOX CHURCH recognizes seven principal mysteries (SACRAMENTS): baptism, chrismation, confession, EUCHARIST, MARRIAGE, *euchelaion* and ordination. Baptism is by triple immersion in the name of the TRINITY. Chrismation, the 'seal of the Spirit', corresponds to confirmation. It is given by anointing with chrism (sanctified perfumed oil), usually at baptism. Marriages are consecrated by prayers and blessings, by the crowning of bride and groom, and by their sharing a common cup of wine. *Euchelaion* corresponds to the sacrament of extreme unction. It includes seven Epistle (*see* BIBLE) and GOSPEL readings and seven blessings of oil which is used to anoint the sick or, on Wednesday in Holy Week, the whole congregation.

Monastic profession (*see* MONASTICISM) is often accounted a mystery, as are: the blessing of water at

Epiphany (*see* LITURGICAL YEAR) and of grapes at the festival of the Transfiguration; funeral and memorial services; and the *artoklasia*, a blessing of bread, wine and oil usually celebrated at vespers (*hesperinos*). All these rites are in the *Euchologion* (*see* LITURGICAL BOOKS).

The rite of the eucharist begins with a service of preparation (*prothesis, proskomide*) of the bread (*artos, prosphoron*) and wine. The 'Liturgy of the Catechumens' includes a long litany, the singing of antiphons (in the Russian use, psalm verses; in Greek use, short verses addressed to the Blessed Virgin MARY and JESUS Christ), the hymns of the day (*apolytikia troparia*) and the 'Kontakion', the refrain from a verse-sermon once sung at this point. The Trisagion ('Holy God, Holy and Mighty, Holy and Immortal, have mercy on us') is sung before readings of the *Apostolos* and Gospel (*see* LITURGICAL BOOKS).

The 'Liturgy of the Faithful' begins with further litanies, the 'Cherubic Hymn' and the great entrance of the clergy carrying the bread and wine. The Nicene CREED precedes the Anaphora, the prayer of offering and consecration which begins with the exhortation 'Lift up your hearts', a preface, and hymn 'Holy, holy, holy'. After the commemoration of the Last Supper the bread and wine are consecrated by the invocation (*epiklesis*) of the HOLY SPIRIT. After the communion and the dismissal prayers, *antidoron*, blessed but not consecrated *prosphoron*, is distributed to all.

For most of the liturgy the priest, as emissary of the people before the throne of God, stands at the holy table behind the *iconostasis*. The ICON-screen represents the Communion of the Saints; the altar behind it joins heaven to earth when the Holy Spirit descends to change the bread and wine into the body and blood of Christ. [5; 15; 83; 89]

Mystery-Cult [xxxiv] Devotion, often to a single god or goddess, in which secret RITUALS and doctrines have a place. Examples abound in the ancient Mediterranean world of religious societies, outside the 'civic' or official religion, which imparted their secrets only to initiates (Greek: *mustae*). Initiation often involved purification ritual, instruction and a revelation of the god, usually in a sacred drama. Of major importance among the Greek mysteries were the Dionysian (later Orphic) and Eleusinian (MYSTERIA); in the early Roman empire, MITHRAISM; from Egypt, those of Isis and Osiris (*see* MYSTERY-CULTS (ROMAN); and further east, those of Attis, Cybele and Sabazius.

Similar cults are found down to our own times (e.g. FREEMASONRY, ROSICRUCIANISM), many of them exemplifying SYNCRETISM. Their rituals and related myths played and probably still play an important role in personal religion, especially when offficial and established religions fail to satisfy individual needs. Such cults have no necessary connection with MYSTICISM, but many could be classified as SALVATION-religions of a sacramental kind (*see* SACRAMENTS).

Mystery-Cults (Roman) [xxxi] Mystery-cults in the Roman world were always perceived as introductions from the east, but were in fact Greek, or Graeco-oriental, in origin [6: 1–11]. The earliest was the cult of Bacchus, which spread widely through Italy in the 3rd/2nd centuries BCE, until brutally persecuted by the authorities in 186 BCE [10: 53–8]. Mystery-cults presented new problems to authorities accustomed only to dealing with groups (*collegia*) providing for banqueting and the funerals of members; but the persecution was sporadic and short-lived. The most important cults (of Bacchus from Greece, Isis from Egypt, Attis from Asia Minor; *see also* MITHRAISM) had structural similarities; all constituted themselves as groups with some system of authority, based on initiation into membership; and all claimed to offer secret knowledge and, through different rites and myths, created structures based on the reversal of received ideas on reality, morality, life and death [6; 10: 222–8; 17: v–ix]. Mysteries, however, in general fitted unproblematically into the pagan world – their innovativeness and interest in the afterlife have been exaggerated in many modern studies by anxiety to find anticipations of Christianity. But they did pioneer, at least for the west, the possibility of groups based on individual choice, and hence led to an intensification of commitment and religious experience. [6; 13: 220–3; 18: xxxviii, xlvii]

Mysticism [xiv] In theistic traditions often described as a fundamentally unitive experience of love and communion with God, in non-theistic traditions as a intuitive, contemplative approach to ultimate reality. In each case it is understood as an experience beyond ordinary human experience and reason, but not antagonistic to them. The study of mysticism is undertaken from the perspectives of theology, philosophy and psychology and touches on questions about the nature and interpretation of religious experience [89].

Examples of mystical experience can be found throughout the world's religions. For most people mystical experience is only indirectly accessible through mystical literature which exists in many different genres. Common to them is the insistence on an experience of fundamental unity or oneness transcending the diversity of everyday life. Some maintain that mysticism is the 'heart' of all religion (*see* SPIRITUALITY) and the key to a unity of all religions. Many religions prescribe techniques of contemplation and meditation, and a variety of spiritual disciplines and ascetic practices as a means to reach mystical experience. Mystics maintain that their experience is fundamentally ineffable, i.e. it cannot be adequately expressed; yet this claim does not preclude the describability of such experiences to which the mystical literature in all religions bears witness.

The comparative study of mysticism is mainly a 20th-century phenomenon. Classical works on mysticism are largely descriptive and often assume that mystical experience is always the same, wherever it occurs. A more differentiated position takes the experience to be the same, but sees its interpretation as varying dependent on different religious and cultural backgrounds. A third position maintains that there are a small number of different types of mystical experience. Work on typologies of mysticism was pioneered by Stace [84], who distinguished introvertive and extrovertive types, and Zaehner [90], who identified a panenhenic mysticism of oneness with nature; an impersonal, monistic mysticism of the soul's interior unity; and a mysticism of the soul's loving union with a personal God, which he judged to be the highest type. These theories have been much debated by others [1: II, IV]; the study has now shifted to a much more philosophical analysis of mysticism and a pluralistic approach to the different mystical phenomena in world religions [28; 46; 47; 48]. While philosophers debate the nature of mystical language, literature and experience, and their inherent truth-claims, psychologists are interested in the analysis of 'peak' experiences and the expansion of consciousness, especially in relation to drugs. Others pay attention to GENDER differences and examine the specific characteristics of women's mystical writings, particularly numerous in the Christian tradition.

Mysticism is not only a historical phenomenon, but of great contemporary interest for the transformation of religious awareness and spiritual practice in modern society. The varieties of mysticism provide a focal point for the comparative study of world religions today, and the wealth of mystical literature both ancient and modern is a living proof of the persistence of the human quest for unity, transcendence, holiness and perfection.

Mysticism, Christian [XIII.D] The Christian mystic seeks the most total union possible with God. Through prayer and self-discipline the mystic seeks to go beyond the concepts and images of theology and come to God himself. Whether it is possible to attain direct, unmediated knowledge of God is a matter of controversy. Diadochus of Photike presents the spiritual life as a path of continual transformation under the influence of the fire of God's love, but one which can never result in the direct cognition of God. St Gregory Palamas speaks of seeing the Uncreated Light that transfigured Christ on Mt Tabor, the immediate experience of God in his energies. For St Gregory of Nyssa the mystic is led beyond the illuminating knowledge of God to an 'unknowing' of him in darkness, just as Moses encountered God first in the burning bush, then in the cloud, and then (*Exodus* 33) in thick darkness. St Bernard of Clairvaux, St Teresa of Avila and St John of the Cross use images of sexual love and spiritual marriage to express the reality of union with God.

The origins of Christian mysticism are to be sought in the New Testament, in the experience of JESUS himself, in the theology of St John's Gospel, in the visionary experience recorded in *Revelation* and in the teachings of St Paul. The forms of Christian mystical practice owe much to the impact of philosophical and Egyptian ASCETICISM and Platonic philosophy. It is at least probable that there were mystics in the early church who practised something similar to the MERKABAH MYSTICISM of the early rabbinic period; several texts normally read as APOCALYPTIC give a clear impression of belonging to such a tradition. It is perhaps partly in reaction to the dangers of such practices that Evagrius of Pontus taught a spirituality based on an austere version of Middle Platonism, and on the introjection into the life of the individual of the cosmic battle between the angels and the demons. He teaches the practice of wordless, imageless prayer, and the purification of the mind until it attains the sapphirine clarity of the sky. Evagrius refers to the ultimate self as *nous*, mind or intellect: Middle Platonism conceived of God as *nous*, so that this language expresses the nature of the image of God in humanity. Later Byzantine mystics sometimes retain this language, but more often speak of the heart as the place of pure prayer. The heart image is drawn from the more body-rooted thought forms of the Jewish BIBLE, but it signifies little real difference in understanding of the human person.

Western Christian mysticism drew on the DESERT FATHERS and on Cappadocians, but was also shaped by St Augustine of Hippo and Pope St Gregory the Great. The elaborate sacramental mysticism of the 5th-century teacher who wrote under the pseudonym 'Dionysius the Areopagite' had great influence in the West through a translation by the philosopher Erigena; pseudo-Dionysius is an important figure in the East also, but less influential in mystical theology.

The medieval period saw a great flowering of mysticism in Western Europe. The cultural renewal instituted by the reign of Charlemagne, the transformation effected from the 12th century onwards by the new universities, by the development of the mendicant orders and by knowledge of Greek and Arabic thought mediated through contact with Jewish scholars in southern Spain, the influence of the asceticism of the CATHARS and the simplicity and poverty of the Poor Men of Lyons and similar groups, the shift in cultural and religious horizons effected by the CRUSADES and the devastating impact of the Black Death all contributed to the growth of a great variety of styles of spirituality. The SCHOLASTIC theologians drew on the resources of Greek philosophy to explore the nature of the spiritual life and of the knowledge of God. New and reformed religious orders – Cluniacs, Carmelites, Cistercians, Carthusians, Franciscans, Augustinian friars, Dominicans, Servites – developed their own distinctive styles of spirituality, varying from the mixture of personal contemplative prayer and long, elaborate offices typical of Cluny to the austerity, simplicity and silence of the Cistercians to which St Bernard welded the love-centred mysticism with a strong devotion to the humanity of Jesus which the Cistercians bequeathed to the military orders, and which the latter combined with the warrior zeal of the crusader (*see* MONASTICISM, CHRISTIAN). The Franciscans brought the devotion to Jesus in his humanity into popular religion, and focused it especially on the figure of the baby in the crib, and on the sufferings and death of Christ. The whole period is marked by an extraordinary variety of approaches. Different models of human nature were embattled: the Augustinian emphasis on the will and on free choice stood opposed to the Aristotelian emphasis on the intellect and on knowledge, understanding and practical reasoning. The cataphatic way of doctrine, devotion, worship and sacrament, morality and study was in tension with the apophatic way that seeks God in a darkness beyond words, concepts or images. The anonymous *Cloud of Unknowing* is a masterpiece of the apophatic way.

The medieval period was rich in women mystics: the writings of the abbess Hildegard of Bingen show a subtle and complex intellect at work in harmony with an intuitive and visionary spirit, a combination found in the very different, and clearly mystical *Revelations* of Julian of Norwich. Many women mystics belonged to the lay societies of Beguines, some living at home, some in ordered communities. They, their male counterparts the Beghards, and the Brethren and Sisters of the Common Life were a focus for the development of the *Devotio Moderna*, devout, contemplative, devotional and practical; its most famous product is the *Imitation of Christ* of Thomas à Kempis. The mediaeval East saw the growth of HESYCHASM side by side with the intensely personal mysticism of St Simeon the New and the mysteric and sacramental spirituality evidenced in St Nicolas Cabasilas' *The Life in Christ*. The Jacobite Maphrian, Gregory Bar Hebraeus, provides the rare example of a self-taught mystic who draws on classic Christian sources, but also on Muslim writers such as Al-Ghazzali.

Renaissance humanism brought a renewed interest in the mystical aspects of Pythagorean and NEOPLATONIST philosophy and also in the Tree-of-Life mysticism of the KABBALAH, and produced Christian versions of kabbalistic mysticism which mix meditative and ritual practice with the study of ASTROLOGY, NUMEROLOGY and a complex angelology (*see* ANGELS). This tradition survived and in the 19th and 20th centuries drew many adherents among students of the OCCULT.

The magisterial REFORMATION was generally cold to mysticism, but the spiritual tradition of the radical Reformation offered an intimacy with God, a direct illumination by the Spirit and a discovery of Christ in the heart of the believer that could easily open to mystical development. The silent centring down of Quaker prayer (*see* FRIENDS, RELIGIOUS SOCIETY OF) and the ecstatic dancing and giving of spiritual gifts of the SHAKERS show two later counterparts of this tendency.

COUNTER-REFORMATION spirituality developed complex methods of prayer, beginning with reflective, discursive meditation on the doctrines of the faith and the life of Christ, and making use of detailed visualizations to move the practitioner to repentance, commitment and devotion. These practices were aligned with the purgative way (*see* THREE WAYS); the illuminative way was often thought of as a subsequent stage where simple affective prayer could take over, leading to the prayer of quiet of the unitive way, what might happen thereafter being left to the grace of God. The most famous product of this tradition is the SPIRITUAL EXERCISES of St Ignatius Loyola. The controversy over Quietism led to an emphasis among ROMAN CATHOLICS on active methods.

The Oxford Movement, while centrally concerned with the doctrinal and liturgical tradition of the ANGLICAN Church, roused new interest in the spiritual heritage of the church in England, the medieval church, the Eastern church and in contemporary Roman Catholic spiritual life.

The impact of contact with Asian religions in the 19th and 20th centuries, and the wider availability of EASTERN ORTHODOX, SUFI and hasidic spiritual texts has led to a more open and investigative approach. The writings of Thomas Merton, William Johnston, Bede Griffiths, John Main and Raimundo Panikkar are all evidence of this. In some cases, the outward forms and spiritual practices of Asian religions have been taken on by Christian spiritual teachers. A very wide range of mystical texts has now become available in translation, and renewed interest has arisen in the writings of Meister Eckhardt, in Hildegard of Bingen and other notable women mystics and visionaries, and in the English mystics.

The academic study of mysticism has generated important discussions on the psychological status of mystical states, on the nature of spiritual 'technique', on the sociology of spirituality and on the relation between mystical experience and drug-induced experiences on the one hand and psychopathological states on the other. In a literate age this has opened up the possibility of involvement in the study and practice of mysticism to a very wide audience. [1; 11; 13; 15; 20; 49; 81; 82; 91; 93]

Mythology [xxxiv] Derived from the Greek word *mythos*, such related terms as mythic, mythology and mythological are commonly used in the study of religion(s) in a technical sense which is absent from the vernacular use of the terms. Adherents of religions are frequently distressed to see the term used of something important in their religion. However, the terms are not used to refer to erroneous or false reporting, as in general use. Rather, they are used to refer to the use of stories and the interpretation of stories and events as employed in religions to convey truth or truths that vernacular forms of speech cannot always convey. Plato used the term 'myth' to refer to stories of the gods in contrast to descriptions of historical events. Myths are believed to 'make up a body of "assumed knowledge" about the universe, the natural and supernatural worlds, and man's place in the totality. At best, the term "myth" is a weak one, for it implies a uniform, sacred explanatory power for etiological narratives everywhere. The disadvantages inherent in this assumption are obvious.' [108: 168] Myths are stories which are intended to convey important meanings relating to the origin of the world, the origin of the tribe, the meaning of death or the way of salvation or liberation. Myths are often described in terms of symbolic language, often related to rituals, used to give explanations or provide didactic support to the practices and beliefs of a religious group. In recent studies of mythology various theories have been advanced concerning the ways myths operate in different religious contexts. Theories vary between religious [53; 56], psychological [95] and structural interpretations [108: 185–97]. No single theory, hitherto, has sufficed to satisfy scholars and gain universal acceptance. One of the problems is that myths work in different ways in different religious and cultural contexts. For instance, there may be occasions when a myth is the explanation of a ritual already existing; on other occasions, the ritual is a way of enacting an already existing myth [108: 66–78]. There is no religious context which does not provide evidence of the existence of myths, ahistorical in origin and significance, or mythological interpretations of historical, including legendary, events. An example of the former is the Creation narratives in the first book of the Hebrew scripture. An example of the latter is the difference between the reporting of the crucifixion of Jesus of Nazareth, a historical event, and the mythological interpretation of the event as a divine act of salvation. [149: 139]

Mythos (peri *Theon*) [xvi] Myths concerning the Gods in Greek religion. The early history of the gods is the early history of the Cosmos. There are myths concerning individual gods, mostly describing their births, acquisition of functions, and, as with Heroes, actions leading to the foundation of a cult or ritual. Thus, central to the Eleusinian Mysteria is the myth of Persephone's abduction by the Underworld god Hades. Her grieving mother Demeter (*see* Theoi), who was responsible for agriculture, caused famine, and it was eventually arranged that Persephone would spend some months each year in Hades and some with Demeter. [1; 2: ii. 1; 12; 16; 20: 119–31, 249–52; 6: 69–77]

N

Nabi [XIX] One of the Islamic terms for 'prophet', together with *rasul*, literally 'messenger'. The latter is sometimes considered to be the higher rank, as sent from God to a people with a specific version of scripture, and MUHAMMAD is often termed 'the messenger of God'; but in practice the terms are often interchangeable. Tradition mentions former prophets as numbering over 100,000, and the QUR'AN includes many prophets and patriarchs from the Hebrew scriptures and New Testament (*see* BIBLE), such as like JOHN THE BAPTIST and JESUS, in addition to certain native Arabian figures. All were forerunners of Muhammad, who is the culmination of the line, and all the scriptures which they brought are believed to confirm the final and fullest revelation, the Qur'an [20 'Prophet(s) (Islam)'; 48: 50–1; 67 'Prophet'; 70]. Hence later religious leaders in Islam whose claims have seemed to rank them with the prophets, such as Baha'ullah (*see* BAHA'IS) and Mirza Ghulam Ahmad (*see* AHMADIS), have been placed outside the pale of Islam by the orthodox.

Nag Hammadi [XIII.A] A town in Upper Egypt, on the west bank of the Nile, near which was discovered in 1945 a jar containing 13 leather-bound papyrus codices, comprising some 52 COPTIC documents of the 4th century CE, nearly all Gnostic in character (*see* GNOSTICISM). Many were translations of earlier Greek originals and are pseudepigraphic. In them the teachings of various Gnostic schools, previously known for the most part through the writings of their critics, are now directly accessible. Of particular note are the Apocryphon of John (2nd century CE), which provides the earliest example of a complete Gnostic myth, and the Gospel of Thomas, which contains 114 sayings of JESUS, some of which are to be found in the canonical GOSPELS but in a slightly different form. [11: IV, 982–93; 14; 17; 19]

Nagarjuna [XI] According to Tibetan legend the Indian MAHA-YANA Buddhist thinker Nagarjuna lived for 600 years and during that time performed many miracles as well as establishing the MADHYA-MAKA school of philosophy. He is supposed to have discovered the PRAJNAPARAMITA scriptures among the *nagas*, underwater serpents, where they had been deposited by the BUDDHA until the time was ripe for their dissemination. Nagarjuna attained a high level of BODHI-SATTVA practice, and after death was reborn in Sukhavati (AMITABHA).

Modern scholars speak of at least two Nagarjunas. The first was the Madhyamaka philosopher (*c*.2nd century CE) who may have come from the south of India. Many works have been attributed to him, and his most famous authentic work is the *Madhyamakakarika* (Verses on Madhyamaka). The second Nagarjuna was a Tantric (*see* TANTRA (2)) alchemist and yogin who lived much later (*c*.7th or 8th century). The eventual figure of Nagarjuna is a composite of legend rather than history.

Nalanda [XI] A town in Bihar (India), scene of some of the BUDDHA'S DISCOURSES (see GOTAMA), and later one of the major centres of Buddhist learning, following the rise of MAHAYANA, attaining great prestige between the 8th and 12th centuries CE.

Nam [XXXIII] The concept of *nam* or the 'divine name' is widespread in Indian devotional belief. For NANAK, and so for the SIKHS, it is absolutely fundamental. Sometimes the word appears in the ADI GRANTH as *hari-nam* or *ram-nam*, 'the Name of God', although usually the simple form *nam* is used. It serves as a summary expression for the nature of AKAL PURAKH or God. Anything which may be affirmed concerning God is an aspect of the *nam*. God is, for example, all-powerful and all-knowing and it therefore follows that omnipotence and omniscience are features of the *nam*. Men and women must strive to overcome transmigration by bringing their lives into harmony with the *nam*. For this reason the regular disciplined practice of NAM SIMARAN is enjoined. [27: 195–6; 28: 50–1; 30: 38–42]

Nam Simaran [XXXIII] Sikh meditation technique. GURMAT affirms that liberation (*mukti*) is attained primarily through the discipline called *nam simaran* or *nam japan*, 'remembering' or 'repeating' the divine name. NAM signifies all that constitutes the being and nature of God (AKAL PURAKH) [27: 195–6]. For NANAK (see GURUS), *nam simaran* meant regular disciplined meditation on the manifold *nam*. The essence of *nam* is harmony, and they who sustain the discipline will progressively merge with the divine harmony, ultimately passing beyond the transmigratory round into the ineffable bliss (*sahaj*) which for Nanak is final liberation (see SACHKHAND). With this sophisticated technique there also continues literal

nam japan, the practice of uttering a word, syllable or MANTRA of particular religious import (e.g. *satnam*, VAHIGURU), either as a pious ejaculation or in extended repetition. For the latter procedure a *simarani* (rosary) is commonly used [25: 263]. A third method practised by SIKHS is the singing or chanting of *gurbani* (compositions from the sacred scripture). Daily NIT-NEM is thus a form of *nam simaran*.

Nanak, Guru [XXXIII] Nanak, acknowledged by SIKHS as the first GURU and the founder of their faith, was born in the Punjabi village of Talvandi Rai Bhoi (now Nankana Sahib) in 1469. The hagiographic JANAM-SAKHIS give much detail about his life, but are not trustworthy. It seems that after a childhood spent in his village he was sent by his father Kalu to work in Sultanpur Lodhi. There he had a vision which summoned him to renounce everything and venture out to preach the NAM. For several years Nanak travelled extensively within India and possibly beyond. Although the *janam-sakhis* are replete with anecdotes about these travels, none of them can be accepted. Eventually he settled down in Kartarpur on the Ravi river and there continued to receive his followers and those in search of enlightenment. He died there in 1538 or 1539, having bestowed the leadership of his PANTH on a loyal disciple who became Guru Angad. [1: IV–VI; 27: IV]

Nanto Rokushu [XXI] These are the Six Sects (Jojitsu, Sanron, Kusha, Hosso, Kegon, Ritsu) of the Southern Capital, the term given by later writers to the religious distinctions of the Heijo (Nara) capital (see JAPAN, BUDDHISM IN) [11]. The term 'sects' implies distinct beliefs and practices, but these were more philosophical schools, often more than one being studied at any one time [36: 105–33]. Jojitsu (*Satyasiddhi-*

shastra, Chinese *Ch'eng-shih*, Treatise on the Completion of the Truth) and Sanroń (MADHYAMAKA, Chinese SAN LUN, the Middle Path) are both attributed to a Korean priest, Ekan, who arrived in about 625 CE. Kusha (*Abhidharmakosha* VAIBHA-SHIKA; Chinese *Chu-she*, Treasury of Analyses of the Law) came in with a priest called Chitsu in 658. Kusha was absorbed by Hosso in the 8th century and Jojitsu and Sanron have also disappeared. The other three became sectarian and still have a substantial number of temples and adherents. Hosso was based on the *Yogacara-bhumishastra* (YOGACARA school, Chinese FA HSIANG, Treatise on Yoga; or *Vijnaptimatra*, Japanese *Yuishiki*, Consciousness-only). Like Sanron, it was the Middle Path, with the Eightfold Negation. For the Japanese it was based on the Chinese sect founded by Tzu-en. Several priests venerating MAITREYA (Japanese *Miroku*) (*see* JAPANESE BUDDHAS AND BODHISATTVAS) returned with variations from China, particularly Dosho in 654 and Gembo in 735. Many important early temples belonged to Hosso, which by the 8th century venerated four Buddhas: Shaka, AMIDA, Yakushi and Miroku. Kegon (*Avatamsaka*, Chinese HUA YEN, Garland) has confused beginnings, but perhaps was propagated from around 736 in Japan by a Chinese priest called Dogen, who had settled at the imperially supported Todai-ji. Ritsu (*Vinaya*, Chinese *Lu*, Rules) was brought by the Chinese priest known in Japan as Ganjin, who had been invited to ordain novitiates. He survived several shipwrecks and performed the ceremony at the Todai-ji in 754 (*see* NANTO SHICHIDAI-JI), later building the Toshodai-ji. Like Jojitsu and Sanron inasmuch as it embodies both MAHAYANA and THERAVADA elements, Ritsu stresses prescribed rules and discipline. (*See also* SHUNYATAVADA.)

Nanto Shichidai-ji [XXI] These are the Seven Great Temples of the Southern Capital (*see* JAPAN, BUDDHISM IN), the chief temples of the old Nara capital which remained throughout Japanese history as the most popular pilgrimage from the Kyoto capital (*see* JUNREI). They dominated 8th-century politics and were the cause of Emperor KAMMU moving the capital farther north. In 796 they were listed in the following order, believed to have been that of their relative importance [26: 55–148]: Todai-ji, built by Emperor SHOMU, finished about 752, the main hall containing the Great Buddha; Kofuku-ji, the Fujiwara family temple; Ganko-ji, the old Asuka-dera or Hoko-ji; Daian-ji, the old Daikandai-ji; Yakushi-ji, finished around 690; Saidai-ji, built by Empress Shotoku around 765 and rivalling Emperor Shomu's Todai-ji in splendour and size; and the Horyu-ji, built by Prince SHOTOKU in 607, but rebuilt after a fire in the late 7th century, the only one outside the old city of Nara. Most of them have been reduced by frequent fires, but some are still major attractions for both pilgrims and tourists today.

Nastika [XVII] 'A denier': a term of opprobrium in Indian thought; in orthodox HINDUISM one who denies the authority of the revelation of the VEDA or (later) the existence of God, e.g. a follower of BUDDHISM or Jainism (*see* JAIN). The latter understood it as meaning a denier of the law of KARMA and life after death, e.g. an adherent of the LOKAYATA, who in turn interpreted it as denying the authority of sense experience.

Nath Tradition [XXXIII] The ascetic Nath or Kanphat tradition of India comprises a cluster of yogic sects (*see* YOGA), all claiming descent from the semi-legendary Gorakhnath and all teaching the efficacy of HATHA YOGA as the means of spiritual liberation. Nath beliefs derive from esoteric Tantrism (*see* TANTRA (2)) [27: 243–4]. The tradition figured prominently in early SIKH development for two reasons. First, the Sant movement (of which NANAK was a conspicuous representative – *see* GURUS) was significantly affected by Nath ideals (SANT TRADITION OF NORTHERN INDIA). Nath doctrine affirms that the rigorous application of *hatha yoga* induces a psychophysical process whereby the spirit ascends to mystical bliss [27: 191–2]. The Sants rejected the physical features of *hatha yoga* in favour of meditation technique, but accepted the concept of a spiritual ascent to ultimate bliss [27: 151–3]. Second, the Naths were also important to the early PANTH in that they clearly provided powerful competition. JANAM-SAKHI anecdotes give considerable prominence to debates between Nath masters (called Siddhs) and Guru Nanak [11: IV; 25: 66–70, 144–57]. The tradition, though greatly weakened, still survives.

Nation of Islam [III] There were several forerunners of the Nation of Islam (Black Muslims) in the USA. These sects had sought to come to terms with the negative oppression of the black experience, some by means of displacement: such was their shame at the negative connotations of blackness and Africa that they appropriated the Middle East or Asia as their continent of origin. They repudiated such terms as 'negro', 'coloured' and 'black', and they denied that their God was Christian. The Moorish Science Temple was the most prominent of these groups. It was founded in Newark, New Jersey, by the Noble (Timothy) Drew Ali about 1913. The Christian names of converts were changed in order to reject the slavemasters' religion, food prohibitions and general asceticism were practised, but above all was the rejection of Christianity. Later the Temple split up, but many of the members were converted to the Nation of Islam.

In Detroit in 1933–4 a man called Wallace Fard (*c.*1877–?1934) announced that he was the incarnation of ALLAH, the 'Supreme Ruler of the Universe'. He exalted all Africans and Asiatics. One of his earliest converts was to succeed him as leader: this was Elijah Poole (1897–1975), who became Elijah Muhammad. Born in rural Georgia, he became 'Prophet' of the Nation in 1934, soon after Fard had disappeared. Muhammad developed the theology of the Nation in a fortnightly newspaper, *Muhammad Speaks*. In the issue of 2 May 1959 he wrote: 'You have made yourselves the most foolish people on earth by loving and following after the ways of the Slavemasters, whom Allah has revealed to me to be none other than real devils, and their so-called Christianity is not the religion of Jesus or any other prophet of Allah.' The Mahdi, or Saviour, is black, and black men originally inhabited the moon. The first people to inhabit the earth were black people, members of the tribe of Shabbaz. Blacks in the USA are the chosen people, and whites are inferior to them both physically and mentally. The Resurrection means only that the time has come for the black man to get justice. After the final judgement, blacks will inherit the earth, and have power over it.

Initially strongly separatist, the Nation demanded a land for its people. The black man was to observe the clever but devilish white man and learn to succeed by applying his white strategies. The Nation had, and still has, a striking conversion history, missioners being 'fishers of men'. Converts were usually from the lower classes and originally a high proportion came from penitentiaries. The significance of the cult was that it was thought by converts and adherents to achieve a rebirth. A new name was given in rejection of the 'foreign', imposed

Christian one, and the regenerated convert became a dignified and proud member of the Temple. Blacks who had felt rejected by the majority community in turn placed great distance between themselves and white people. The Nation offered an integrated self-sufficiency to its members, together with a sense of importance that arose from the secrecy of the Nation. Written records were kept to a minimum, and when attempts were made to try to infiltrate communists into the Nation in 1932 to discredit it, they were unsuccessful.

Since economic self-sufficiency lay at the heart of the Nation's practice, in order that its members should be served and supported as Temples spread throughout the USA so hotels and co-operative stores were set up, the only failure being in agriculture. Boys and girls were educated in separate schools, with a very limited curriculum drawn from Black Muslim teachings. In every issue of *Muhammad Speaks* the tenets of the Nation were reiterated. Freedom and justice were demanded by black people, as was equality of opportunity. They wanted to establish a separate state, where all Black Muslims could live in peace – including those currently in gaol, who would all be released, thus acknowledging the injustice to black men of the American penal code. Brutality against the Nation was to cease, and equal rights were demanded immediately. Until there was equality under the law, no taxes would be paid. Separate but equal education was to be provided. Interracial marriages were forbidden, while their version of ISLAM was to be taught without impediment. There was always a stringent moral code with strong food TABUS. Tobacco and alcohol were forbidden. Prayers took place five times a day, and Temple meetings were compulsory. A convert's main business was the regeneration of criminals. The member had to live to

benefit society and be self-reliant.

The most famous convert was Malcolm Little, 'Malcolm X' (1925–65), who was assassinated on 21 February 1965 in Harlem, New York, at the age of 39. It was suspected that his killers came from within the Nation, since Elijah Muhammad had disapproved of him for some time, but proof was never discovered. In 1964 Malcolm had left the Nation to found the Muslim Mosque Inc. He developed an interest in orthodox Islam, and made his HAJJ in 1964, afterwards taking the name El-Hajj Malik El-Shabbaz. This pilgrimage convinced him of the wrongness of racial exclusivity, leading him to found the Organization of Afro-American Unity, which would deal with the non-religious affairs of the Muslim Mosque Inc. and which would accept support from all races. He visited Nigeria, Ghana and Algeria before returning home.

The Nation has continued to grow in strength, although no one knows its total membership figure. It has normalized its relations with other religious groups, and has co-operated with conventional Muslims. In the latter 1960s the Nation spread far into the diaspora, and has continued to have a powerful impact in personally politicizing members. Because much of the Nation's history and organization remains in the oral tradition, it has been able to retain a high level of secrecy. There has been fission and heresy. The *Jamaat-al-Musilmen* in Trinidad were responsible for the attempted coup in 1990, while other Black Muslim groups disassociated themselves from such violent action. In some countries, including the USA and UK, Black Muslims have converted to conventional Islam. [18; 35; 38; 61; 66; 72; 94; 97]

Native American Church [xxvii]
This church includes some 100,000 adherents from over 50 North American Indian tribes (*see* AMER-

ICAN INDIANS (NORTH) AND ESKI-
MOS: NEW RELIGIOUS MOVEMENTS)
loosely united through sacramental
ingestion of the non-narcotic hallucinogenic buds of the peyote plant
(PEYOTISM) in Saturday all-night
rites, round an earthen altar and
sacred fire in a peyote house or *tipi*,
followed by a communal breakfast
on Sunday morning. Peyote beings
peace and healing, is an antidote
against alcoholism and gives visions
of the Peyote Spirit, often understood as JESUS. Erroneous identification of peyote as a narcotic led to its
being banned by tribal councils,
missionaries and government, but
better understanding has enabled
the church to win a good deal of
religious freedom for a religion that
claims to be an Indian Christianity.
[12: II; 17; 22; 26: XIII]

Native/Black Baptists [III] In
Jamaica slave instruction in Christianity began modestly in 1754,
given by Moravians (*see* MORAVIAN
BRETHREN). In 1783 about 400 families and 4,000–5,000 of their slaves
fled to Jamaica to escape the new
republican government in the USA.
With them came black free men,
including George Liele (Lisle) and
Moses Baker, who were BAPTISTS.
They began to preach, drawing large
crowds, although they would only
accept slave converts with the permission of their owners and they
taught obedience to those masters.
They may well have held views different from mainstream Baptists.
George Lewis had been born in
Africa, and he certainly rejected
white Christianity in favour of his
black version, which was characterized by the demand for black
empowerment. Baptist groups proliferated which were independent of
the established Baptist church, conversion only being confirmed after a
dream establishing spiritual possession. For these Native/Black Baptists baptism became the central
ritual, the power of the water coming
from the the African belief-system,

and JESUS becoming secondary to
JOHN THE BAPTIST. MYALISTS
strongly identified with the Baptists.

While conventional Baptists
attracted slaves because they
preached equal rights and emancipation, Native Baptists were far more
outspoken, and attracted more
slaves and freed blacks. Lisle was
persecuted and accused of inciting
slave rebellion, and repeated legislation attempted to oppress the free
worship of Black Baptists. The language of the Hebrew BIBLE was very
attractive to all the Baptists, especially the ideas of a chosen people
and of exile. Worship offered far
more freedom for individual expression. Over the years the churches
tended to move along the African–
European continuum (*see* CREOLE/
CREOLIZATION) towards the African
end. Despite oppression, the churches continued to grow in number,
and after independence from British
rule on 5 August 1962 the status of
the churches rose, their members
taking great pride in their 'Jamaican'
character. [2; 10; 31; 50; 67; 69;
86]

Natural Religion [XXXIV] A spontaneous and unargued religious
response to the world, or religious-
ness which develops in human
experience untaught [145: 39; 153:
40–3, 217–18, 226]. As such, it is
contrasted with 'the positive religions' [153: 45] as specific traditions, or systems claiming authority
for their doctrines. In 18th-century
Europe, natural religion (as e.g. in
David Hume's *Dialogues* thereon)
denoted those beliefs supposedly
common to all mankind, or at least
attainable by human reason (one
form of DEISM), a meaning for
which NATURAL THEOLOGY is now
the widely accepted term. [24:
32–4]

Natural Theology [XIII.C] The
understanding of the nature and
existence of GOD and of the duty,
freedom and immortality of human

beings, which is held in Western thought to be obtainable through rational reflection on the world, taking account of human thought and experience. It is usually contrasted with revelation, i.e. that theological understanding which is held to have been given to humankind by God, either through some quasi-verbal communication or through events discerned as disclosing God's nature. Some theologians (e.g. Barth; see NEO-ORTHODOXY) hold that the only authentic knowledge of God is by divine self-revelation. Others (e.g. Aquinas; see THOMISM) hold that some valid conclusions may be reached by reason but that revelation provides the norms of correct understanding. Especially since John Locke (1632–1704), other theologians have seen natural theology as the only acceptable foundation of theological understanding. 'Apologetics' is the use of the arguments of natural theology to defend the reasonableness of religious beliefs. [3; 3a; 6a; 15; 17; 18b; 18c]

Naujote [xxxvi] The PARSI term for the rite of initiation in ZOROAS-TRIANISM. (By Irani Zoroastrians it is called *sedrepushan*.) The term is understood by most Parsis as meaning 'new birth'. The rite traditionally takes place at the age of puberty, but nowadays among Parsis usually at nine or eleven (even numbers are considered inauspicious). Essentially it consists of the donning, for the first time, of the sacred shirt (*sudreh*) and cord (*kusti*) [47: VII]. These are the traditional 'badges' of the religion, said to symbolize the 'armour of the faith' for the believer in the war against evil. The *sudreh* is a white cotton garment, worn next to the skin with a token purse at the v of the neck to symbolize the duty of storing up righteousness. The *kusti* is a length of plaited lamb's wool, tied three times round the waist to the accompaniment of prayers several times a day (see MAN-THRAS). Before initiation a child is

thought not to be morally responsible for its actions, but thereafter its thoughts, words and deeds are stored up for judgement (see CHIN-VAT BRIDGE; FRASHOKERETI). Initiation and the wearing of *sudreh* and *kusti* are the duties of all Zoroastrians, men and women. There are disputes among Zoroastrians concerning who may undergo the *naujote*. Iranian Zoroastrians and some young Zoroastrians born in the West argue that anyone who believes in the religion may be initiated. The traditional Parsi position is that only those born of Zoroastrian parents may be initiated. A judge in the Bombay High Court in 1906 ruled that only the offspring of a Parsi male can be considered to be a Parsi, but typically orthodox priests require that both parents are Parsis. The position is justified by arguing that every person is born into the religion which AHURA MAZDA considers appropriate for their spiritual development and that people should be religious in the tradition into which they were born into and by which they are conditioned. *Juddins* (non-Zoroastrians) are not necessarily seen as inferior, but rather as different. [9: 236–40; 29, pt III: 42–4; 30: 41–4; 31; 46: 70–4]

Navajo [v] Members of the Athapascan linguistic group, the Navajo migrated from the west of what is now Canada to the North American south-west prior to 1300 CE, gradually replacing a hunting economy with sheep-raising and agriculture [19]. Navajo myths recount the emergence of humankind into this, the fifth world, through four previous subterranean realms. The present world is inhabited by two classes of beings, the Yeis (or 'holy people') and the Earth-Surface People (humans). Begochiddy began the creative process in the first world and guided the Yeis through the successive worlds to this one. In the fifth world, the Navajo have been especially blessed by Changing-

Woman, a holy person of miraculous birth, who acts kindly towards mankind. The Yeis are neither all-powerful nor supreme. Instead, each has responsibility for some aspect of this world (e.g. control of weather, movements of heavenly bodies, care of animals). Humans, too, have specific responsibilities and together, through moral and ceremonial behaviour, they and the Yeis preserve the harmony of existence [13: v–vii]. Myths relate that when the work of creation was complete, Begochiddy saw that it was 'beautiful', i.e. its parts were all in harmony. The central concern of Navajo religion is therefore to preserve 'beauty' at all levels, as witness the common refrain of prayers, 'May I always walk with beauty all around me.' [2: 1] (see SAND-PAINTINGS.)

Nayannar [xvii] 'Leader', the title of certain Shaiva (see SHIVA) saints, thought to have lived between 500 and 1000 CE. There are 63 Nayannars, 60 men and three women, revered in south India for their devotion (BHAKTI) to Shiva. Their bronze images have their own shrine in the large Shaiva temples (MANDIRA) of Tamil Nadu. Like the ALVARS, their Vaishnava (see VISHNU) counterparts, the Nayannars come from all levels of society, and are identified by their own special attributes and gestures (MUDRA). Particularly striking are the images of the boy-saint Sambandar and the fierce, emaciated figure of Karaikkal Ammai, playing the cymbals as she raptly watches the dance of Shiva [38: 1–86, 129–81].

Nazarite Church [xxvii] A large independent church, ama-Nazaretha, named from the biblical Nazarites and founded by Isaiah Shembe (1870–1935) among the Zulu in Natal in 1911. The great festivals of Tabernacles in July and New Year in January centre upon the holy centre of Ekuphakameni

near Durban and the holy mountain, Nhlangakazi. After the death in 1976 of J. G. Shembe, who had succeeded his father, a leadership dispute arose between J. G. Shembe's son Londa and his elder brother Amos which led to litigation, violence and division of the church. [12: 46–7; 18: 110–11, 194–6, 227–32, 281–94, 328–30]

Ncwala [ii] The name of the great annual festival of renewal of the Swazi king (*nkosi*), one of the more striking surviving expressions of sacred monarchy in Africa. It takes place immediately following the summer solstice. Its complex series of rites, with their stress on the king's liminal weakness and the popular chanting of songs of execration, provide a symbolic death followed by revitalization of the *nkosi* and so too of his people. The unity of the nation, despite the recalled divisions of past and present, is strengthened and symbolized by the ritual renewal of its king [38: 197–225].

Near-Death Experiences [xiv] This term is used to describe a pattern of experience which tends to be reported by approximately 35% of people resuscitated from apparent death. Research shows that the experience has been reported in almost all cultures and traditions and across the centuries. However, the increasing ability of modern medicine to resuscitate has led to a recent upsurge in the number of cases. The experiences include reports of 'leaving the body', 'looking down on the resuscitation attempts', 'feeling a sense of life-review', 'meeting deceased relatives and friends' and enjoying a series of religious experiences of a mystical type including 'encounters' with a bright light sometimes perceived in personal terms and identified with a figure from the percipient's own religious traditions. The pattern of experiencing appears to be common across religious traditions, cultures and world-views, though naturally the terminology used in the religious descriptions is culture-specific. The mode of the experience is clearly hallucinatory in form, though its status is harder to evaluate. Many researchers insist that the experience is entirely natural and the product of features such as cerebral anoxia, psychological stress or other natural causes associated with the universal human experience of dying. Others see the experiences as evidential of consciousness preparing for the survival of death and suggest that the experiences as a whole be treated as veridical. All agree that reported 'observations' of the dying in this state are remarkably accurate, and the fact of having the experience tends to have a profound impact on the percipient's subsequent beliefs and values.

Similarities can be seen between near-death experiences and mystical experiences from several traditions. Parallels may particularly be seen with descriptions of the dying process in the Bardo Thodol (The Tibetan Book of the Dead) and with such Jodo Shinshu (Pure Land Buddhist) texts as the Amitayur-dhyana and Sukhavativyuha sutras, where the Buddha of Infinite Light is seen as appearing at the moment of death to welcome the dying into Buddha's Pure Land – a land pictured in imagery very reminiscent of contemporary Western near-death visions. [6; 10; 72a; 75; 83]

Neo-Confucianism [XII] A Confucian (see CONFUCIUS) response to teaching of Taoism (TAO CHIA) and BUDDHISM that emerged as an identifiable movement during the Sung dynasty (960–1126 CE). Chou Tun I (1017–73) was an early contributor to the movement and his theories provide the basis for all later Neo-Confucian metaphysical and cosmological speculation. His influential *Explanation of the Diagram of the Supreme Ultimate* explains the generation of the YIN–YANG forces, the

Five Elements (WU HSING) and all phenomena, including human intelligence and moral principles, from the *T'ai Chi* (Supreme Ultimate) or *Wu Chi* (Ultimate Non-Being). He states that by acting in accordance with these principles the sage can achieve tranquillity. [7: XXVIII, 460–80].

Eventually, two traditions of Neo-Confucian thought developed: the School of Principle (*Li Hsueh*), systematized by Chu Hsi (1130–1200), and the School of Mind (*Hsin Hsueh*), best represented by Lu Chiu Yuan (1139–93) and later by Wang Yang Ming (1472–1529).

Chu Hsi's literary output was immense. He argued that all existence is composed of varying combinations of Principle (LI), which is unchanging and derives from the Supreme Ultimate; and Substance (*Chi*), which determines the change and differentiation of phenomena. He maintained that moral cultivation and the purification of *Chi* required detailed investigation into the nature of phenomena [5; 6; 7: XXXIV, 588–653; 10].

The School of Mind was more monistic and idealistic in character, reducing all reality to the single Principle (*Li*), which is identical with the mind (*hsin*). Therefore *Li* was discovered by investigation of the mind, through meditation and moral reflection. Wang Yang Ming developed this view, suggesting that the mind is essentially pure and has innate knowledge of moral principles, such that if the mind is penetrated through meditation, good conduct is inevitable. [7: XXXV, 654–91; 8; 10; 17; 35: x–xv]

Neo-Orthodoxy [XIII.C] A widely influential school of theology in PROTESTANTISM which shares the fundamental insights of Karl Barth (1886–1968). It is so called because it seeks to re-express the classical Protestant orthodoxy of the REFORMATION period. It is also known as 'kerygmatic theology' (since it sees theology as the proclamation – Greek *kerygma* – of GOD's saving and revelatory activity in Christ (*see* CHRISTOLOGY: SALVATION)), 'dialectical theology' (since it holds that God so surpasses human understanding that descriptions of the divine inescapably involve paradoxical expressions), and 'crisis theology' (since it stresses the divine Word as a judgement – Greek *krisis* – on the world). Barth rejected attempts to derive a knowledge of God from nature and human experience (NATURAL THEOLOGY) on the grounds that human reason has been hopelessly corrupted by the Fall (*see* SIN). God, as the utterly transcendent and sovereignly free, is only to be known through divine self-revelation to humankind, a revelation uniquely given in the 'Word of God' manifested in JESUS CHRIST and made known through the BIBLE. [3; 14]

Neo-Paganism [XXVIII] has mushroomed since the 1960s and now has hundreds of thousands of adherents in the West. Neo-Pagan groups differ with regard to tradition, scope, structure, ritual and the names by which they call their deities [1]. Goddess worship is prevalent among Neo-Pagans. There are few Neo-Pagan temples; meetings may be held in sacred places (such as Glastonbury), in woods or in houses. Paganism, which may be POLYTHEISTIC, PANTHEISTIC and/or ANIMISTIC, is essentially a religion of nature. Through establishing a 'right relationship' with the cosmos, RITUAL is seen as a tool to counter the alienation brought about by humanity's 'advancement' and separation from nature. According to definitions, there may be some overlap between Neo-Paganism, the NEW AGE, Ritual Magick [42: 817–851], Wicca or WITCHCRAFT. [1: 4; 5: 195–200; 8; 10; 14; 15; 18; 36; 38; 40; 41: IV/R; 42: 827–51; 43]

Neoplatonism [XXIV] A version of the Platonic philosophy inaugurated

by Plotinus (204–70 CE), who developed a mystical interpretation of Plato's teaching (*see* PHILOSOPHIA). Starting from the Platonic doctrine of the soul's ability to ascend by a purified love to contemplation of the 'forms' – perfect archetypes of which the sensible world is merely a flawed reflection – Plotinus postulated three 'hypostases' or levels of true reality beyond the material world. These were the soul (*psyche*), the intellect (*nous*) and the One or the Good; they could be viewed as metaphysical entities or as states which the philosopher might experience in contemplation. The soul corresponded to mind in the individual: it was the agent of thought, memory and sensory perception. It survived death, and if insufficiently purified from worldly desires would be reincarnated in a new body. The intellect was the timeless repository of the 'forms': ascending to this level, man might perceive truth intuitively, without discursive thought. The One was God, the ultimate reality and hence indescribable. Union of the individual with the One was the goal of the philosophic life and was to be attained by the practice of virtue and contemplation [29].

Plotinus's successors – Porphyry (*c.*232–305 CE), Proclus (*c.*412–85), Iamblichus (*c.*250–350) and others – elaborated the hypostases into a complex hierarchy, some levels of which were identified with the Greek gods (THEOI), and advocated *theurgy*, a system of ritual magic, as a means of purifying the soul. Neoplatonism was prominent in the Near East until the 6th century, offering a coherent alternative to CHRISTIANITY, on which it had a lasting influence, notably through the 6th-century Platonic school at Alexandria and the writings (*c.*500 CE) attributed to Dionysius the Areopagite.

New Age [XXVIII] is an umbrella term applied to a vast network of more or less overlapping individuals and groups with a wide range of beliefs and orientations. There is no agreement about the boundaries of the New Age, which may merge with complementary medicine, the HUMAN POTENTIAL movement, NEO-PAGANISM, New Thought, OCCULTISM, SHAMANISM and/or Wicca or WITCHCRAFT. Some New Age ideas can be traced to pre-Christian times, others may be bound up with some versions of Christianity, but they more commonly incorporate aspects of Buddhist, Hindu and other religions and/or philosophies from the East – thus, reincarnation is a popular belief among New Agers. Ideas from Alice Bailey, Helena Blavatsky and GURDJIEFF may exist side by side with ecologically aware philosophies advocating alternative technology, holism and the importance of the feminine (and, perhaps, the Goddess [56: xvii–xx]). Some New Agers focus on astrology, believing that the Age of Aquarius heralds a new consciousness; some have a faith in the power of crystals, other natural products, or artefacts that can harness energies. Others (or some of the same individuals) turn to 'channellers', who transmit messages from 'Ascended Masters' or other spiritual beings which may have existed thousands of years ago on this or another planet [56: xiv]. Just as the concept of New Age has no clear boundaries, groups termed New Age may themselves be amorphous, with their members belonging to a number of different organizations. [1; 5: 188–92; 8; 14; 15; 18; 28; 36; 40; 41: iii; 42: 161; 43; 57; 58; 59; 60; 73; 76]

New Church [xxiv] The 'Church of the New Jerusalem'; followers of Emanuel Swedenborg (1688–1772), a Swedish scientist who began in 1743 to experience visions and converse with angels. Swedenborg turned to theology, teaching that there is a 'correspondence' between the external universe and spiritual realities (the sun's heat and light, for example, correspond to the love and wisdom of God) and that the BIBLE has an 'inner' spiritual sense to be read in the light of such correspondences. The revelation of this inner sense is the second coming of JESUS CHRIST as the Word and inaugurates a new church upon earth. Humanity must strive to open its 'interiors' to heaven by repentance, virtue and love of God. Evil states of mind are 'hells'; after death those accustomed to them gravitate there permanently. Others rise to heaven, forming 'societies' of ANGELS ranked according to their degrees of love and faith. [28] Members of Swedenborgian churches today are few in number: some 3,000 in Great Britain and 7,000 in the USA. The main American groups are the General Church of the New Jerusalem and the General Convention of the New Jerusalem in the USA.

New Fire Ceremony [xxv] The greatest renewal ceremony in Aztec religion (see MESOAMERICAN RELIGIONS) was the New Fire Ceremony, called Toxiuhmolpilia, the Binding of the Years [2: 21–7]. It took place at the completion of a 52-year cycle called Xiuhmolpilli, and initiated another CALENDAR ROUND depicted in codex and stone as a tied bundle of 52 reeds (see CALENDAR STONE; TONALPOHUALLI). The Toxiuhmolpilia took place at midnight on the Hill of the Star at the outskirts of Tenochtitlan, following the ritual extinguishing of all domestic and temple fires, the breaking of pots and the sweeping of all homes in the realm. A distinguished war captive was ritually sacrificed and a fire was started in his chest after his heart was offered to the absent sun (see HUMAN SACRIFICE). The fire was taken to all temples and towns in the Aztec empire, signifying the revitalization of the society and the heavens.

New Jerusalems or Holy Villages (Tribal Peoples) [xxvii] New tribal movements have created many 'holy cities' or villages, often with biblical names: Salem in Fiji, also in Nigeria (God's Kingdom Society); Paradise in the Solomon Islands (*see* CHRISTIAN FELLOWSHIP CHURCH); Guta ra Jehova ('City of Jehovah') in Zimbabwe (Mai Chaza's church); Sione ('Zion') of ALICE LENSHINA: and Nineveh of the African Israel Church Nineveh in Kenya. Other notable examples include Aiyetoro ('happy city') of the Holy Apostles' Community in Nigeria; Nkamba in Zaire (*see* KIMBANGUIST CHURCH); Ekuphakemeni of the NAZARITE CHURCH; and Amakokopai of the Hallelujah Religion in Guyana. There are also many in the PHILIPPINES. There may be administrative, economic, educational and healing aspects to the religious activities in these cities or villages. Members come long distances on pilgrimages to major festivals; for example 100,000 or more gather ever Easter at Zion City Moriah of the Zion Christian Church in northern Transvaal to share in the blessings of the new community as an outpost of heaven. [2: 174, 273; 18: 152–4]

New Martyrs [xiii.d] EASTERN ORTHODOX saints martyred after the fall of Constantinople (1453). The Ottomans never systematically persecuted their Christian subjects, but all apostates from Islam (including those reverting to Christianity) and non-Muslims who were considered to have insulted the Islamic faith faced the death penalty. Some Orthodox zealots, like John of Ioannina (d. 1526), invited martyrdom by preaching in public, while 'Ethnomartyrs', like the Ecumenical PATRIARCH Gregory V (d. 1821), were executed for failing to uphold Islamic hegemony. Mainly Christians of the Near East by origin, this group also includes Turks, such as Ahmet (d. 1582) and Hasan (d.

1814), Pomaks, such as Boris (d. 1913) and even a Briton, Sir Henry Abbot (d. 1876).

A general assault on religion accompanied the 1917 revolution in Russia. A priest from Chicago, John Kochurov, and Metropolitan Vladimir Bogoyavlensky of Kiev were among the first clergy to be killed by militant atheists. The execution of Metropolitan Benjamin Kazansky of Petrograd (1922) inaugurated a state campaign against the Orthodox that was to continue for decades. In 1981 the RUSSIAN ORTHODOX CHURCH ABROAD canonized these Russian New Martyrs, including Tsar Nicholas II and his family. Numerous Serbian clergy, the Czech Archbishop Gorazd Pavlik, Maria Skobtsova and others martyred by the Nazis or their supporters during the Second World War are similarly revered. [4; 30; 48; 57; 66; 70] (*See also* ANARGYROI; SALOI)

New Religious Movements (American Christian) [iv] Each generation has its own 'new religious movements', but the term came to be applied particularly to those that developed in a period of cultural ferment in the 1960s and 1970s. At mid-century Americans were pictured as seeking religious conformity, as being content with Protestant, Catholic and Jewish as their spiritual contexts. In the years of the John F. Kennedy and early Lyndon B. Johnson presidencies, the national mood was characterized by a passion for practical politics and some measure of progressivism, usually in a secular setting. Then, suddenly, reaction set in and in the course of the late 1960s and then through the 1970s any number of new religious movements took shape (*see* NEW RELIGIOUS MOVEMENTS IN THE WEST). Many of these elaborated on themes from ancient and OCCULT wisdom, for example from Egypt in the period of the PYRAMIDS. More was imported and transformed in passage from HINDU and

BUDDHIST or other Asian sources. There were also importations and revivals of African spirituality; or from Caribbean and South American religions other than Christianity.

However, numbers of particularly intense movements drew also on Christian sources. The best known was the UNIFICATION CHURCH, a blend of Korean Christianity, SHAMANISM and the personal vision of Dr Sun Myung Moon, introduced in 1972. The most notorious was the People's Church (PEOPLE'S TEMPLE), a group formed under the influence of the Reverend Jim Jones, originally a Christian (Disciples of Christ) minister, who led hundreds of his followers to a commune in Guyana where in 1978 he led 914 people to mass suicide. (After this event the term 'cult' was associated with the place of the death, 'Jonestown', and was used only pejoratively) (see CULT-WATCHING GROUPS). The Children of God also emerged from Christian roots, led by David ('Mo') Berg, and achieved notoriety for its overt interest in sexual expression, including seduction to lure new converts.

The catalogue of such movements easily grows into listings of hundreds, most of them ephemeral. Some are self-enclosed FUNDAMENTALIST, PENTECOSTAL or charismatic movements which either disappear or moderate. But America is always a promising territory for a new New Religious Movement. [6; 14; 18; 19]

New Religious Movements in Primal Societies [xxvii] For several centuries, but increasingly in the 20th, the tribal peoples of the Americas, Asia, Africa and the Pacific have produced a wide range of new religious movements through interaction with more sophisticated and powerful cultures and religions – especially with CHRISTIANITY, less often with HINDUISM and BUDDHISM, and only occasionally with

ISLAM. Since these movements show differences from the traditions upon which they draw they are commonly rejected by adherents of the contributing religions. Their variety is indicated by the range of names used for different movements: nativistic, revitalization, millennial, messianic, syncretist, separatist, adjustment, prophetic or healing movements, independent churches or sects [26: 484–92]. There may be well over 10,000 such movements identifiable in the last 100 years, with 12 million or more adherents.

The movements commonly arise among confused, powerless or disintegrating peoples whose needs are not met by either their traditional religion or the new invasive faith. The founders are often charismatic figures who claim to have had a mystic experience of communication with the spirit world and to have been charged with bringing the new religion to their people; even in cultures dominated by senior men, founders may be young men or women. There is often a dramatic rejection of some traditional ways, especially of reliance on the ancestors, SHAMANS, the medicine bags (MEDICINE BUNDLES) or magic objects, and traditional rituals and divinities. Other traditional elements, especially reliance upon dreams as a means of revelation and polygamous marriage, are often retained. The new divinity is usually one supreme personal god who demands a reformed way of life with insistence on peace and love, sexual discipline, industry, and avoidance of alcohol and tobacco. This strict ethic is sustained by new rituals and songs, often with drumming or dancing, new symbolisms and forms of worship of considerable creativity.

A very pragmatic religious blessing is offered, with healing, revelations and power from the spirit world, protection from evil forces, the promise of a new order of freedom and prosperity, and a new community in place of the disrupted social order. The new hope, self-respect, and dignity contribute to the survival of a tribal people faced with the invasive and dominant society, and so may assist long-term accommodation to modernization and development. In so far as the hopes may be unrealistic and the ecstatic worship an escape from action, the new movements may be of no more than temporary benefit or even be deleterious. In either case they are authentic new religious forms of considerable extent and importance across the world of tribal cultures. [12; 20; 22; 26]

New Religious Movements in the West [xxviii] The current wave of new religious movements (NRMs) in the West became publicly visible in the mid-1960s, largely as part of the 'counter-culture'. During the 1970s the movements spread throughout the Western world, especially America (they have been particularly visible in California: see NEW RELIGIOUS MOVEMENTS (AMERICAN CHRISTIAN)), Australia, New Zealand and Western Europe (especially England, Germany and Austria); then, after 1989, they started evangelizing in Eastern Europe and the erstwhile Soviet Republics (especially Russia). The number of NRMs in the West depends very much on the definition used [5: 145–8], but it has been estimated that there are somewhere between 1,000 and 2,000 distinguishable movements. Counting the membership depends again on definitions, but few have had more than a thousand fully committed members at any one time (the turnover rate in most of the best-known movements has been very high), many having only a few hundred or less [5: 148–9].

A variety of theories have been offered as explanations for the rise of the current NRMs: it is said that they exemplify a reaction to and/or a reflection of contemporary (secular-

izing, materialistic and/or pluralistic) society [55]; that they meet the psychological, emotional, social and/or spiritual needs of 'seekers' and/or inadequate people; that they achieve what success they do only through 'brainwashing' or mind control techniques [3; 5; 6; 12; 22; 29; 44]; or, in a more cosmic vein, that they herald the dawn of a NEW AGE: the Age of Aquarius [58].

Useful comparisons can be made with contemporary Japan, India and Africa and with other periods in history which have seen a proliferation of NRMs – such as Rome in the 1st and 2nd centuries CE, North and Central Europe in the 1530s, England from 1620 to 1650 and, in North America, the Great Awakening of the 1730s, which was followed by the Second Great Awakening of 1820 60 (see GREAT AWAKENINGS). The present NRMs are, however, somewhat distinct in that they tend to attract followers disproportionately from the prosperous and educated sections of society and they draw not only from the Christian tradition (e.g. THE FAMILY, PEOPLE'S TEMPLE, UNIFICATION CHURCH), but from a wide variety of other religions and philosophies, such as HINDUISM (e.g. ANANDA MARGA, BRAHMA KUMARIS, HARE KRISHNA, SAHAJA YOGA, SRI CHINMOY), BUDDHISM (e.g. SOKA GAKKAI), NEO-PAGANISM – and, indeed, from other sources such as psychoanalysis (e.g. HUMAN POTENTIAL MOVEMENT), science fiction (CHURCH OF SCIENTOLOGY) and some esoteric and/or OCCULT TRADITIONS (e.g. CHURCH UNIVERSAL AND TRIUMPHANT, ECKANKAR, EMIN, TOPY, WHITE EAGLE).

Lumped together in popular parlance under the pejorative label of 'cults', NRMs have been attacked in the mass media and by anti-cultists (see CULT-WATCHING GROUPS). However, the only generalization that can be made about the movements is that any generalization would almost certainly be refuted by one of their number. They differ not only in their theologies, but also in their practices, their authority structures and organizations, their lifestyles and their attitudes towards sex, women, food and the 'host' society in which they find themselves. However, the very fact that they are *new* religions means that converts are likely to have more idealist expectations (of the millennium, utopia or self-perfection) and, at least initially, greater commitment than those who have been born into their religion. This, and the fact that converts have tended to be young adults with few responsibilities, has given rise to characteristics that differ from those of more established religions [5: 1]. That said, however, nothing new remains new for ever, and most of the NRMs now have a middle-aged membership, with responsibility for second- and even third-generation dependants. Furthermore, while many NRMs were founded by a charismatic, sometimes a messianic, leader, several of the leaders have now died and this has led to further changes in the movements. [4; 5; 6; 11; 13; 25; 26; 28; 35; 36; 41; 42; 44; 53; 55; 56; 59; 60; 66; 72; 73; 76; 78; *see also individual movements for specific reading*]

Nganga [II] Probably the most widely extended of all African religious terms, found in societies all across BANTU Africa from the Bakongo in the west to the Swahili in the east and ZULU (*inyanga*) in the south. The *nganga* is the common religious expert, the doctor who can control evil forces. His or her character and powers, however, vary considerably. Everywhere the *nganga* is someone who uses medicines – herbs or fetishes (NKISI). Probably the *nganga* is also a medium and a diviner, although in Kongo (the Bakongo language) there is a distinction between the *nganga*, the doctor-ritualist, and the *ngunza*, the medium and seer; and

among the Tanzanian Segeju the *nganga* is a herbalist but not a diviner. In Swahili a distinction is made between the mere herbalist (*nganga wa majani*), the witch-doctor (*nganga wa kuagua*), who has special powers to recognize and deal with witchcraft (*uchawi*), and the 'sorcerer', who can curse or counter-curse (*nganga wa litegu*). If the greatest force of evil is usually seen to be witchcraft, then the *nganga* is above all the anti-witchcraft expert. In general the *nganga* detects the cause of an evil through DIVINATION by oracles or SPIRIT-POSSESSION, and then endeavours to remove it through medicines and ritual.

Nibbana [XI] (Sanskrit: *nirvana*) In BUDDHISM and other religions of Indian origin *nibbana* is the highest possible happiness. The *Oxford English Dictionary*'s preferred explanation – 'In Buddhist theology, the extinction of individual existence and absorption into the supreme spirit . . .' – is both misleading and incorrect. Buddhism does not recognize a supreme spirit and rejects annihilation as a goal. Although Buddhist tradition explains *nibbana* as meaning 'without craving', it originally meant 'blowing out' – the quenching of the fires of greed, hate and delusion. Psychologically this is a state of great inner freedom and spontaneity, in which the mind has supreme tranquillity, purity and stability. This is the achievement of the Buddhist saints (*see* ARAHAT; LOKUTTARA) and the goal of their followers.

Early Buddhist works actively and intentionally avoid resolving questions concerning the ontological status of *nibbana* or the post-mortem condition of the saint. Such issues were seen as liable to distract from the task in hand, necessarily productive of one-sided views (DITTHI) and even perhaps as unanswerable, given the limitations of ordinary language. Subsequent ABHIDHAMMA analysis distinguishes between the transcendent (*lokuttara*) state of mind and an unconditioned element, later referred to as *nibbana*. Here *nibbana* is in effect the unchanging and uncharacterizable component of the enlightened state. Outside the context of *abhidhamma* psychology this can appear a rather static and rigid conception. So MAHAYANA Buddhist writings often criticize it as inadequate and too limiting a view of truth. (*See* EMPTINESS; SHUNYATAVADA.) [16: 69ff; European interpretation: 99; traditional: 80: 165ff; 96: 469ff]

Nichiren [xxi] (1222–82) The founder of the Japanese sect bearing his name, sometimes called Hokkeshu (Lotus sect) [2; 36: 228–37]. Nichiren, who was born Zennichimaru in Chiba prefecture, took the vows in a local temple in 1237 and studied TENDAI on Mt Hiei from 1242 (*see* SACRED MOUNTAINS; SAICHO). His adherents date the initiation of Japan's first native sect to 1253, when Nichiren termed the mantra *Namu-myoho-rengekyo* (Homage to the Lotus of the Good Law) a summation of the *Lotus Sutra* and his followers adopted the incantation. He preached virulently in Kamakura, attacking social evils, other sects and the authorities. For this and his writing he was banished to the Izu peninsula, but within three years was back in Kamakura intensifying his criticisms. His doctrines centred on the Three Great Secrets, *honzon*, *daimoku* and *kaidan* – by implication, the adoration of Shaka, the wonderful truth in the *Lotus Sutra* and the importance of the moral law [36: 235–7]. Deviating from Tendai theory, he saw himself as a disciple of the living Shaka (*see* JAPANESE BUDDHAS AND BODHISATTVAS); indeed, his followers call him an incarnation of Bosatsu Jogyo, an early disciple of the BUDDHA. Exiled again in 1271 and sentenced to death on Sado island, he is said to have miraculously survived, and he retired two years later in a temple in Yamanashi prefecture called Kuonji, where he is buried. There are almost 40 sub-sects today, the chief of which is Nichiren Shoshu, with its head temple, Daiseki-ji, in Shizuoka prefecture [21: 205–12].

Nihang [xxxiii] The Nihangs, originally called AKALIS, are a group of militant SIKHS distinguished by their dark-blue garments and impressive array of steel weapons. During the 18th century they commanded formidable respect as fierce warriors, a tradition which they still endeavour to keep alive as they rove the Punjab on horseback. The Nihangs are militarily organized as an 'army' (the Budha Dal). Their daily discipline includes lengthy *kirtan* hymn-singing and ritual consumption of an infusion of *bhang* (cannabis). [30: 132]

Nikaya [xi] A BUDDHIST term meaning 'collection' or 'group' which is commonly used with reference to the classification of scriptures. Ancient versions of the SUTTA-*pitaka* (*see* TIPITAKA) arranged the discourses of the BUDDHA into four or five collections according in the first place to their length. The *digha* (Pali; Sanskrit: *dirgha*) collection comprised the long discourses [55; 76], while the *majjhima* (Sanskrit: *madhyama*) comprised those of medium length [59]. The shorter discourses were divided into two collections: the *samyutta* (Sanskrit: *samyukta*), which arranged discourses by topic, and the *anguttara* (Sanskrit: *ekottara*), which arranged them according to the number of items listed in the discourse. Finally there was a miscellaneous *khuddaka* (Sanskrit: *kshudraka*) collection. The use of the term *nikaya* in this context is characteristic of the PALI Tipitaka of the THERAVADA school. An alternative and probably later term is *agama*. This latter term is now used primarily with reference to the Chinese

Agamas, which are translations of the same basic material contained in the Pali Nikayas, but from versions handed down by other ancient Indian schools of Buddhism. The term *nikaya* is also used with reference to a particular ordination lineage of the Buddhist SANGHA (cf. BHIKKHU). [65: 30–95; 29: 111–12]

Nilotic Religion [II] The Nilotic group of peoples stretches from the SHILLUK in the north, NUER, DINKA and Anuak also in the Sudan, through the Acholi, Lango and Padhola in Uganda, to the Luo in western Kenya. This relatively small group of peoples has a closely connected history, but their religions show some striking contrasts. The common root may lie in a strong pastoral and democratic monotheism, reminiscent of ancient Israel, perhaps best represented by the Nuer, yet the Acholi present one of the clearest African examples of an apparently godless religion (*see* JOK), while the divine kingship of the Shilluk strikingly contrasts with the non-hierarchical character of Nuer religion. Nearest in type to the Nuer may be the most remote in distance – the Kenyan Luo with their strongly monotheistic worship of Nyasaye, creator and protector. [6: 138–63; 13: 122–35; 28; 39; 45]

Nit-Nem [XXXIII] Every SIKH is expected to repeat appointed selections from the scriptures (ADI GRANTH) thrice daily. This is called *nit-nem*, the 'daily rule'. The first selection is recited during *amrit vela*, the period of calm before sunrise. Having risen and bathed before daybreak, the devout Sikh repeats GURU NANAK's JAPJI and two works by GURU GOBIND SINGH (the *Jap Sahib* and *Ten Savayyas*) (*see* GURUS). At sunset *Sodar Rahiras*, the evening liturgy, is chanted or sung. This comprises a selection of nine hymns grouped near the beginning of the Adi Granth, plus two extracts from the DASAM GRANTH, a portion of

Guru Amar Das's hymn *Anand*, and two brief compositions by Guru Arjan. Finally, *Kirtan Sohila* is chanted or sung immediately before sleeping. This short selection of five hymns is also included in the Sikh funeral order. All the daily liturgies except *Kirtan Sohila* conclude with a recitation of ARDAS, the Sikh prayer. [30: 86–105]

Nkisi [II] (plural: *minkisi*) Bakongo name for the material object with spiritual power in it, encountered very widely in Africa and generally known to Europeans as a 'fetish'. It is known to the AKAN as *suman*, to the MENDE as *hale*, to the NUER as *kulangni*, to the GANDA as *mayembe*, etc. The meaning of such terms may also be 'medicine'. It is essentially an unimportant element in African religion, to be clearly distinguished from divinities (ORISHA) or ancestor-spirits (*see* ANCESTOR VENERATION). The *nkisi* is a physical object or bundle of objects made by its owner from certain TABU or symbolic materials in which a spirit is thought to reside, but so that it has no named existence apart from this singular object. Even there it may be nameless. The fetish is at the service of its owner, who may as a NGANGA gain his reputation thereby; it is used to promote private ends, defensive or offensive, and is often much feared. Its power may be vaguely held to drive from some original act of God, but its character lies in its materiality, particularity and potential dangerousness. In some societies its role is very marginal, in others – Bakongo especially – it may come almost to dominate life for a time, until in reaction there is a cleansing destruction of *minkisi* and a return to more elevated religion. [3: IV; 29: 99–105; 46: 9–24]

Nomos [XVI] Law. Greek laws were man-made but they were considered to be divinely sanctioned. Unwritten laws and customs were given by the gods in the past, and Zeus (*see*

THEOI) was thought to watch over law and justice. Written law codes (the earliest dating from the mid-seventh century BCE) were often sent to Delphi or another oracle (*see* MANTIKE) for divine approval. Impiety (*asebeia*) was an offence punishable in law. In a famous Athenian impiety trial in 399 BCE the philosopher Socrates was condemned to death and executed. [10: 251, 255–7; 9: 189–92; 11: 207–18; 15: 136–51]

North America, Jews in [XXII] The first Jewish settlers in the North American continent were SEFARDI MARRANOS, of Iberian origin, who moved to New Amsterdam (later New York) in 1654, having originally settled in South America. German and East European Jewish migrants subsequently joined the original Sefardi settlers, the Jewish population rising substantially with the influx of refugees from persecution in Russia and Poland in the late 19th century. The North American Jewish population today is over 6 million, with about 300,000 in Canada and close to 3 million in New York State. The USA has the largest Jewish population in the world. Religious life in North America is divided into three main streams, Orthodox, CONSERVATIVE and REFORM. Orthodoxy consists of a variety of independent congregations as well as a large, organized community of Modern Orthodox Jews whose main educational institution is Yeshiva University (founded 1897) in New York. Conservatism, the largest organizational SYNAGOGUE group, has its rabbinical seminary, the Jewish Theological Seminary (1887), also in New York. Reform Judaism, which is more radical than its counterparts in the rest of the English-speaking world and has Americanized its JUDAISM, runs the Hebrew Union College (1875) in Cincinnati. [3; 7; 13; 19: 274, 407; 25; 32; 36: XIV; 44; 56: XII–XV; 57: VIII, XV, XVI]

Nubian Christianity [XIII.D] CHRISTIANITY was first brought to Nubia by traders and refugees from religious persecution in Egypt. In 540 Julian headed a mission to the Nubian peoples and after 580 Longinos extended this to include Alodia (Alwa). Within decades the three kingdoms of Nobatia, Alodia and Makuria (dominating most of present-day Sudan) had adopted Christianity. Closely linked to the Copts of Egypt, the Nubians adapted the Greek script for their language and developed a distinctive religious art. With the Arab invasion of Egypt (641) the Nubian Christians became increasingly isolated, their lands open to Bedouin settlement from the 13th century. Nobatia was largely under Muslim control by the 10th century, but Makuria held out to 1317 and Alodia was only occupied by the Muslim Funj in 1504. Arab tribes settled across the Sudan, creating a new Islamic culture that eventually totally eclipsed Christianity. [6; 7; 99] (*See also* AFRICAN ORTHODOX; COPTIC CHRISTIANITY; ETHIOPIAN CHRISTIANITY; ISLAM.)

Nuer Religion [II] The Nuer are a pastoral NILOTIC people living in the southern Sudan. They lack any structured political hierarchy. Their wealth and joy lie in their cattle. Nuer religion is preoccupied with Kwoth (God, or Spirit). Kwoth is believed to have created all things; he is far yet near, an all-powerful father, the base and guardian of morality. Formerly, it seems, the Nuer believed only in Kwoth and Colwic spirits (people killed by lightning and taken by Kwoth), but more recently other spirits, such as Deng and Buk (Abuk among the DINKA), entered Nuer life via the Dinka. These and the totemic spirits remain essentially refractions of the one Kwoth, who is invoked both in all sacrifices and frequently in private life by brief intercessions.

The central Nuer religious act is the sacrifice of an ox to Kwoth, either on social occasions or for the expiation of sin (but not to affect the processes of nature: the Nuer have no interest in rain-making). If no ox is available, a cucumber may be substituted, with the tacit approval of Kwoth. Everyone is his own priest and no special time or place is required for the act. The ox, mystically representing humanity, is consecrated, Kwoth is invoked at length and the beast is then immolated with a spear thrust. The Nuer are proud individualists, cherishing equality, but before Kwoth they are 'as ants', humble and accepting [28].

Numa (Calendar of) [xxxi] Numa (*c*.700 BCE, according to tradition) was the second king of Rome (after the founder Romulus, traditionally dated 754 BCE). All Roman religious institutions were attributed to him, many anachronistically, and the relatively sophisticated Roman calendar must have reached the form we know at least a century after Numa's time. The earliest copies we have date from the 1st century BCE, when the system was entirely solar, although showing survivals from a solar/lunar phase. Each day was given a character determining its religious, legal and political nature [16; 22: 38–49]. Most significantly for our knowledge of early religion, copies of the Calendar always include certain festivals in capital letters; these include the oldest fixed festivals and it is this set which goes back to an early date and provides the only solid information about early Roman religion [19: 574–7]. The character of many of these early festivals was a matter for conjecture to the earliest writers now extant, but progress (partly by comparative methods) has been made towards understanding at least the general pattern of the year [introduction: 19: 604–9; 22]. Thus, February was a month of purifications (including probably the Lupercalia, in which naked priests ran through the city striking bystanders with strips from the hide of a sacrificed goat) [8: 348–50; 10: 28–30; 22: 76–8]; March opened the season of war (the arms of Mars, the war-god, were paraded by the dancing priests, the *Salii*, in the dress of archaic soldiers) [12: 114–16; 22: 85–6]; April has rituals of growth (including the sacrifice of cows in calf at the Fordicidia) [8: 37–8; 22: 102]. The festivals of high summer concern the preservation of the water supply and the stored food from the harvest. The most famous single festival is perhaps the Saturnalia, the classical predecessor of Christmas, at which in historical times there was feasting, present-giving and exchange of roles [22: 205–7].

Numen [xxxi] The power of a Roman deity, the force of the word *numen* being 'nod'. It is commonly used in the classical period (1st century BCE/1st century CE) in cases where the presence of deity, for instance in a grove, is suspected but undetermined; also in combination with the emperor's name (*Augusti numen*) to avoid specifically calling him a god (*see* EMPEROR-WORSHIP). According to one line of evolutionary theory, *numen* represents an earlier state of development than 'god' (*see* DI DEAEQUE).

Numerology [xxiv] The attribution of mystical or symbolic meaning to numbers, probably universal in religion. Small numbers can suggest groupings and patternings; multiplication by hundreds of thousands can preserve these qualities while suggesting changes of scale, degrees of sacredness, etc. Western numerology is derived from Pythagoras (6th century BCE), who thought number the basic principle of the cosmos and assigned qualities to numbers according to their mathematical properties. The other main source is the BIBLE, all of whose numbers were regarded as significant by most commentators up to the 18th century. St Augustine (354–430 CE) was keenly interested in numerology (*see* AUGUSTINIANISM). Jewish students of KABBALAH had their own numerological system, *gematria*. Biblical number symbolism parallels BABYLONIAN and Egyptian traditions possibly ASTROLOGICAL in origin [15]. A system of numerology similar to that of Pythagoras was current in China by the 1st century CE, and Hindu and Buddhist teachings embody many number-patterns. Numerology is important in many forms of MAGIC, DIVINATION and religious art [5]. Popular usage of numerology derives significance from the 'numerical value' of the birth date or name of the person.

Nurcus [XIX] The followers, within Turkey and then in the Turkish migrant workers' diaspora in Germany, the Netherlands, etc., of Shaykh Sa'id Nursi (*c*.1876–1960), an Islamic Kurdish dervish and scholar, who nevertheless denied that his disciples constituted a Sufi order of the traditional type (*see* SUFISM, SUFI ORDERS). His teachings emphasized *nur*, 'light' (whence the name of his movement, 'illuminationists') as a spiritual inner light, to be equated with faith, with divine illumination attainable through study of the QUR'AN, and his ideas are particularly expressed in his *Risale-i Nur*, 'Epistle of Light', containing his commentaries on the Qur'an. The Nurcus can be classed as a modern Islamic revivalist movement, with a strong religious basis in the Qur'an and SUNNA, yet accepting scientific and technological progress and, within Turkey, basically endorsing the political and social status quo. [38, art. 'Nurculuk'; 91]

Nyabingi [III] Originally an anti-white cult in Kenya; the term was appropriated by RASTAFARIANS for their large celebratory gatherings. While the first Nyabingis, held in the late 1960s, were Jamaican in membership, as the faith spread across the black diaspora membership has become international, although the largest Nyabingis are still held in Jamaica. [6; 39; 40; 70; 73; 88; 100]

Nyau [II] Powerful dance societies traditional among the Chewa and Mang'anja of Malawi. These peoples are matrilineal and uxorilocal (i.e. legal descent is through women and a man lives in his wife's village after marriage). The Nyau balance this appearance of female domination with a strongly male organization. Membership of the societies is wholly male; they possess a secret vocabulary; and their dances are characterized by masks, which are thought to represent the animals of the wild and the spirits of the dead. Nyau rituals are chiefly related to rites of passage, being performed especially at burials, commemorations of the dead, and female initiation rites. Nyau religion is communal and populist rather than orientated to kingship, kinship or a shrine with its religious professionals. It appears to represent an ancient stratum of Malawian history prior to the arrival of the Phiri invaders of the 14th century. Comparable societies are found in many parts of Africa [13: 252–73].

Nyaya [XVII] One of the six DARSHANAS or salvation-philosophies of classical HINDUISM. The *Nyaya* or 'Method' school emerged from the VAISHESHIKA during the first two centuries CE with the *Nyaya-sutra* (attributed to Akshapada Gautama), but the standard commentary of Vatsyayana dates from the late 5th century. In origin the *Nyaya* was a school of rhetoric, but it early developed a careful analysis of the authoritative sources of knowledge (*pramana*) and the forms of syllogistic argument, leading eventually to very detailed studies of logic. The *Nyaya-sutra* taught 16 categories (*padartha*); correct knowledge of these brought about by systematic discussion would lead to liberation (MOKSHA), although YOGA practice was recommended as an auxiliary. The influential *Udayana* (late 11th century) formulated the Hindu proofs for the existence of God (ISHVARA) and initiated developments in logic which culminated in the formation of a new school. The later *Nyaya* was given its authoritative presentation by Gangesha (early 14th century). The *Vaisheshika* was incorporated into a single system, which remains an influential school of realism in Hindu thought into recent times. [53: VI, 2, 76–112; 101: II, 1–110; 103: 165–90; in translation: 101: II, 211–716; 107: 356–85]

Nyingma [XXXV] The Nyingma tradition represents the oldest elements in Tibetan BUDDHISM, having its origins in the missionary work of the 8th-century Indian masters. Padmasambhava and Shantirakshita [4]. However, the Nyingma finally became a distinct tradition by the 14th century through the organizing efforts of figures such as the 'omniscient' Longchen Rabjampa (1308–63), the systematizer of the doctrine of 'great perfection'.

The Nyingma school consists of both ordained practitioners and lay yogins (*ngak pa*), who follow the unbroken oral-transmission lineage teachings of the Nyingma patriarchs and the teachings of the *terma* ('rediscovered treasures'), works composed and concealed most usually by Padmasambhava and subsequently rediscovered and propagated by a predicted *terton* ('treasure finder') [22].

The principal teaching of the tradition is the 'great perfection' (*dzog chen*), which was introduced into Tibet in the 8th century by Vimalamitra and Padmasambhava. This teaching represents the pinnacle of TANTRA (2) and the highest of the nine *yanas* ('vehicles') distinguished by the Nyingmas. The term 'great perfection' denotes the unsurpassable nature of liberation attained through the realization of the primordial purity of awareness [10].

The Nyingma have maintained a decentralized organization with six major branches, each with its own special codification and transmissions of the shared doctrine. In exile in India the head of the Nyingma tradition is at present Padma Norbu Rinpoche from the Palyul branch.

Nzambi [II] This is one of the most widely used African names for God, appearing in some form (Nyame, Ndjambi, etc.) all across west central Africa from among the Herero in Namibia and Lozi in Zambia to many peoples in Zaire and Cameroon. It may or may not be one with the AKAN Nyame. The etymological meaning is uncertain. Nzambi was certainly in use by the Bakongo (adjective Kongo) in the 16th century and appears in the earliest dictionary of a BANTU language, the Kongo dictionary of Georges de Gheel (d. 1652), but the theory that it was introduced by European missionaries is unlikely. Myths suggest that Nzambi, who is creator and master of the world, withdrew from earth on account of the crimes of men. [17; 25]

O

Obeah [III] The word is said to be derived from the Akan of West Africa, meaning literally 'he who takes a child', and would seem to have been associated with the initiation rites of a west African sorcerer. *Obeah* was recognized early in the slave history of Jamaica, though similar systems occur throughout the black diaspora. The practitioners of *obeah* are *obeahmen*, although women may well be involved. Initially it was connected with the African religion of the 'Koromontynes'. While Akan/Koromontyne religion took a 'conservative' path to the MAROONS, it also encountered Christianity. In the earlier case, African elements remained dominant, and the African religious and social pattern was continued as much as possible (though with Christian additions); *obeah* is part of this process. In the latter case, remembered items from Africa were combined with behaviour and beliefs as observed by the Africans of things European and Christian. The slave society which fostered *obeah* had an absolute belief in witchcraft, and where the slaveowners drove underground any overt mechanisms for handling the oppression of slavery, *obeah* flourished. *Obeah* thus became a system of alternative health maintenance, both spiritual and physical, and a system of sorcery which was used initially against the slaveowner class as enemy, and later against anyone else in the community. Because it was hidden from the dominant society, its very secrecy gave it power because it used covert mechanisms.

In Jamaica, MYALISM developed to counteract the malign influence of *obeah*.

The craft of *obeah* is based on the belief that a man's DUPPY/JUMBIE/ZOMBIE is vulnerable, especially so at times of danger and illness, and at death. The *obeahman*'s power comes from his ability to 'catch' a duppy and prevent it from being properly incorporated in the world of the ancestors. The *obeahman* could use the power of the duppy to 'work' for him: a duppy might labour in the fields; the winning of duppies would increase an *obeahman*'s status, and therefore his capacity to earn more through private consultations. The function of the Myal men was to protect society against these anti-social practitioners. However, not all *obeah* activity was malign, for the slaves often found that they relied heavily on *obeahmen*'s wisdom in the local pharmacopaeia. One of the *obeahman*'s functions was to work with benign alternative, protective, magical and actual medicine.

Europeans were quick to dismiss *obeah* as superstition, but they ignored the fact that the Africans had brought with them a healthy fear of charms and incantations, and were used to the notion of preventative medicine and local 'doctors'/spiritual healers. Although the initial impetus in *obeah* had come from slaves of Akan origin, it attracted those of other ethnic origins who shared the same attitudes to spiritual and physical health. *Obeah* was revitalized, too, by the waves of slaves arriving from Africa who kept alive the fragmented but dynamic African religious system. The power of *obeah* spread throughout the Caribbean and in areas of further population dispersal, particularly in the Americas.

The rejection in so many African–Caribbean churches of allopathic medical intervention arises in part from a doubt as to the virtue of medical materials, which may be associated with witchcraft. For some who reject *obeah* completely, the corollary is that faith alone within a church suffices as healing power. [2; 10; 67; 86]

Occult [xxiv] Literally 'hidden', but applied loosely to any matter supposed to be supernatural (or concerned with the supernatural) not clearly falling within the province of the major religions. Occultism encompasses various methods of developing hidden or latent magical or Psychic powers through extensive training (intellectual, emotional and physical) to discipline the will. Often there is the implication that such knowledge is available only to an initiated few. Those known as occultists may be students of the Western magical tradition or members of the Theosophical society or practitioners of Hermetism, Witchcraft or Kabbalah. Other topics often regarded as occult include Tarot or Divination, Magic and Psychic powers. [8]

Odin [vii] One of the main cults in Scandinavia in the Viking age was that of Odin, leader of the Aesir. He was known as Wodan (Old English Woden) to the Germanic peoples. The Romans equated him with Mercury, and he bears resemblances to the Celtic Lug. Odin was associated with magic, poetry, ecstasy, the gaining of wealth, possibly with healing [26: ii, 155], and the dead. He was worshipped by kings and warriors. His spear decided victory in battle, and the Berserks, fighting in wild fury, were his dedicated followers [3: 66–9; 4: 78–82]. The Valkyries did his bidding, conducting dead warriors to his hall, Valhalla. He was represented as a riding warrior with a spear, attended by raven, eagle and wolf. His eight-legged horse Sleipnir carried him through the sky, followed, in later folklore, by a wild troop of the dead. He also appeared as an old, one-eyed man in a cloak, wandering in disguise to cause strife. Important myths associated with Odin were the regaining of the mead of inspiration, the sacrifice of an eye to gain knowledge, and the acquisition of runic lore (*see* Runes) by hanging in torment on Yggdrasil [3: 9; 3a: 76–9]. He was doomed to be devoured by Fenriswolf at Ragnarok.

Olam Ha-Ba [xxii] 'The World to Come', the most general Jewish term for the hereafter [14 vol. 12: 1355]. Originally referring to the post-Resurrection era of the Messianic age (*see* Messiah), it later also signified the condition of the soul in the world to come after the death of the body. The classical statement of the Talmud [10: 365], that in Olam Ha-Ba there is 'no eating, no drinking, no procreation, no business dealings, no jealousy, no hate and no competition. But the righteous sit with crowns on their heads deriving pleasure from the radiance of the Divine Presence [Shekhinah]', was understood by commentators as referring to either of these two conditions [31: 401]. Since Jewish theology worked with a rather fluid doctrinal frame of reference the belief in the resurrected body-cum-soul coexisted with the belief in the immortality of the soul. Different teachers and schools stressed different aspects of the doctrine of Olam Ha-Ba. (*See also* Reincarnation.) [70: 31]

Old Believers [xiii.d] A revision of the Liturgical books of the Russian Orthodox church carried out in

1666 under the authority of the PATRIARCH Nikon brought Russian services into line with contemporary Greek practice. Nikon was opposed by zealous believers who saw his reforms as a fundamental betrayal of true Orthodoxy. In particular they objected to the sign of the Cross made with three fingers in the Greek style, claiming the traditional Russian custom of using two fingers expressed the dual nature of the Crucified. While Nikon seems to have been prepared to allow opponents to use the old rites under certain conditions, he reacted vigorously to their total opposition to his reforms: rapidly they became a separate church led by the Archpriest Avvakum. A terrible and long-lasting persecution of Old Believers or Old Ritualists (*Staroobradtsy*) ensued. St Avvakum was burned and huge numbers put to death. Whole communities also died in acts of voluntary self-immolation.

A shortage of clergy, and in particular of bishops to ordain them, caused the Old Believers serious problems. Some were prepared to accept priests seceding from the patriarchal church; other groups decided to live without priests altogether. In 1846 the first full Old Believer hierarchy was established at a synod held at the Balkan Belokrinitsa monastery, which elected an archbishop. The Old Believer Church of the Belokrinitsa Hierarchy was officially recognized by the Russian Orthodox Church in 1971. A second priestist (*popovtsy*) church was organized in 1923, the Old Believer Church of Ancient Orthodox Christians. Several groups of priestless (*bespopovtsy*) Old Believers exist. They have no ordained clergy; spiritual leadership is provided by lineages of teachers. The Pomortsy Old Believers have a significant strength outside Russia, in Latvia, Lithuania, Estonia and Belarus. The Pomortsy were the first priestless Old Believers to include prayer for the Tsar in their worship; more

intransigent groups such as the Fedoseevtsy resisted this. More radical *bespopovtsy* groups have serious problems with the status of matrimony as a MYSTERY and are divided on this issue.

Both Orthodox and EASTERN CATHOLIC 'uniate' Old Believers exist; the Orthodox Edinovertsy date back to the 18th century, but are now in the main fully assimilated. (*See* EASTERN ORTHODOX CHURCH; RUSSIAN SECTS.) [9; 45; 50; 56; 99]

Old Calendar Movement [XIII.D]
From the 1920s traditionalist Orthodox Christians have set up alternative groupings (True Orthodox Churches) in protest at the adoption of the Gregorian calendar by certain Orthodox churches. In Greece a lay movement was joined by dissenting bishops in 1935. In that year Metropolitan Chrysostomos of Florina assumed leadership of the traditionalists and sought to hold together the various factions. Originally a million strong, the Greek Old Calendarists weathered a series of severe state-sponsored persecutions but internal unity proved elusive. In 1937 Bishop Matthew of Vrestheni separated from those who refused to dissociate themselves totally from the 'State' churches – which still contained many 'Zealot' sympathizers. This issue led to further fragmentation after 1979.

In Romania the hieromonk Glicherie Tanase rallied opposition to the reforming PATRIARCH Miron after 1924. The Romanian traditionalists (numbering over 2 million) were also persecuted and they were only joined by a bishop, Galaction Cordun, in 1955. The Old Calendarists have maintained tenuous links with both the RUSSIAN ORTHODOX CHURCH ABROAD and with the Patriarchate of Jerusalem. Since the fall of communism connections have also been developed with the CATACOMB CHURCH of Russia. The Balkans remain the centre of the movement but affiliated communities can be found through out the Orthodox diaspora and also in Italy, Portugal and east Africa. [14; 17; 59]

Omer, Counting of [xxii] On the second day of PASSOVER an *omer* measure of barley from the new barley harvest was offered up in the Jerusalem TEMPLE. Each of the next 49 days was then counted till the wheat harvest at the festival of PENTECOST, a festival for which no fixed CALENDAR date is assigned.in the BIBLE [59: 87]. This ritual is known as the Counting of the Omer, and continues today although there has been no offering of barley since the destruction of the temple in the 1st century CE. In the middle ages the Omer period became one of semimourning for Jews. This was based on a Talmudic precedent (*see* TALMUD), the pupils of Rabbi Akiva having died during this period in the 2nd century CE, but it was mainly a response to the CRUSADES and to periodic Easter pogroms. During the Omer mourning period no weddings are held, and Orthodox Jews do not listen to music or have their hair cut. The mourning is interrupted on the 33rd day of the Omer (*lag b'omer*) which is the anniversary of the death of the mystic R. Simeon bar Yochai, the death of a saint being regarded by Kabbalists (*see* KABBALAH) as a wedding of the soul with God [69: 116; 70: 191]. Pilgrimage takes place on that day to Simeon's tomb in Meron, in the Galilee.

Ometeotl [xxv] The primordial creator, the fundamental divine power in central MESOAMERICAN RELIGION [12: 80–103]. The creation myth pictured Ometeotl dwelling in the highest level of heaven, called Omeyocan, from which the universe was generated through the actions of four divine children, each considered a major aspect of the high god. Ometeotl was a sexually dualistic deity personified in a number of forms, of which the most outstanding were Ometecuhtli–Omecihuatl, Tonactecuhtli–Tonacacihuatl, In Tloque Nahuaque and Ipalnemoani. The male half was usually merged with solar deities, which personified the celestial force *par excellence*, and the female half merged with the maternal earth fertility goddesses [17: 408–11]. Although there was no cult dedicated to Ometeotl, he was considered to be present in all things and beings. He generated human life through the souls which dropped from heaven into the wombs of women. His unceasing activity was expressed in the actions of all deities but especially TEZCATLIPOCA (the Smoking Mirror) and QUETZALCOATL (the Feathered Serpent).

Omoto [xxvi] In 1892 in Japan Deguchi Nao (1836–1918), normally a quiet woman, suddenly began to speak as a medium for the KAMI Konjin. Her family, thinking her deranged, temporarily confined her in a room, but using a nail, she scratched messages from the *kami* into a pillar. Thus began the writing of the *Ofudesaki*, which Nao, though unlettered, continued to write as a *kami* medium the rest of her life.

Deguchi Onisaburo (1871–1948), born Ueda Kisaburo, was adopted into the Deguchi family when he married Nao's youngest daughter Sumi. A spiritualist himself, he rewrote the crudely written *Ofudesaki* in literate Japanese under the title *Omoto Shinyu* (Omoto *kami* counsels). He also gave oral accounts of the spirit-world on the basis of his own experiences. Omoto scribes took down his messages and published them in an 81-volume book, the *Reikai Monogatari* (story of the spirit-world). These works are the Omoto scriptures.

Omoto teaches that messages from the spirit-world make it imperative to reform the visible world. This teaching led to clashes with the pre-war government. In 1921 its leaders were arrested, but were freed in the general amnesty declared when Emperor Showa acceded to the throne in 1926. In 1935 the government arrested Omoto leaders, destroyed its buildings, dissolved the organization and confiscated its property. People belonging to or influenced by Omoto, claiming to have received new messages from the spirit-world, have often started their own movements; notable among these are ANANAIKYO, BYAKKO SHINKOKAI, SEICHO NO IE and SEKAI KYUSEIKYO.

Because of Onisaburo's writings, his spiritualism, his skill as an organizer and his systematization of doctrine, Omoto drew members from many ranks of society. Today there are over 180,000 adherents. The Omoto headquarters is in Kameoka, near Kyoto. Succession has regularly fallen to women in the Deguchi line. [10: IX, 184–5]

Oracle Bones (Chinese) [XII] Over 100,000 DIVINATION or oracle bones dating from the Shang period (1523–1027 BCE) have been unearthed in Honan province. In Shang times heated bronze rods were applied to the bones to produce cracks, which were then interpreted. The later Shang bones bear inscriptions using 5,000 different characters, usually addressed to the Shang royal ancestors concerning ritual, military, agricultural and domestic matters. They provide valuable information about Shang religion and civilization and about the development of the Chinese language. [14: 31–42; 82: II, 55–66; 101; 114: IV, 55–60]

Oracles [XXIV] The connotations of these messages of the gods (Latin: *oracula*) are largely determined by their importance in ancient Greece and are distinct from those of 'prophecy', which is more associated with divine revelation through human mediums in ancient Israel and in EARLY CHRISTIANITY. The terms are however often inter-

changed indiscriminately. The world 'oracle' refers both to divine pronouncements (Latin: *orare*, to speak, to request) and responses concerning the future or the unknown, as well as the place where such pronouncements are given. The questioner delivers a specific or a general question on future events and receives a verbal response (unlike other forms of divination) that may be both literal and symbolic (but not always comprehensible). A further usage of 'oracle' designates the human medium through which prophetic declarations of oracular sayings are given: a presiding priestess (the Pythia) performed this function in the Delphic oracles and was considered to be the medium for the voice of Apollo [12: 20, 95–7]. Emphasis was placed on certain sacred places, often near pools, springs or other natural features considered of particular potency; at each site a specific deity had dominion: Apollo at Delphi, Zeus at Olympia, the Egyptian god Amun at Karnak.

An oracle can be a vision or revelatory dream or can be inspired by a particular god; it was traditionally often experienced in a state of trance or *ekstasis*. At Delphi, for instance, the ecstatic utterances of the priestess were sometimes translated by a priest. All consultations were preceded by elaborate preliminary ritual requirements on the part of both the questioner and the interpreter, and strict rules accompanied the deliverance of the oracular statements. In ancient Greece the enigmatic precision and ingenuity of these oracles were famous.

ORACLE BONES, from which prognostications by spirits were read, were among the earliest features of Chinese religion; heat was applied to the bones of animals, and the response of the spirit was given in the cracks which subsequently appeared. Oracles who speak in the words of bystanding spirits are a common feature of popular religion in China, where they give guidance in matters of justice and public concern. Other descriptions of oracular possessions include those where acts of self-injury are committed by the supplicant without feeling any pain.

Origin of Religion [xxxiv] (1) The manner in which religious beliefs and practices first arose in human history or prehistory.

(2) The root or source of religion in the experience and development of an individual or group.

In both senses, origin was a major concern of theorists in the earlier period of work in the SCIENCES OF RELIGION [145: ii, iii; 158: ii]. Many anthropologists [118; 166] made conjectures about (1), but often sought support for their theories in psychological or sociological hypotheses concerned with (2) [117: 27–41, 45–80, 104–44; 171: 217–33]. It now seems doubtful that good empirical evidence for (1) can be found. As to (2), the question of what factors cause, promote or preserve religious credence or commitment must be clearly distinguished from the question of the truth of specific beliefs or the efficacy of actual practices. To show how religion must have originated if it is an illusion is not to have proved that all religion is in fact illusory. [75: iii; 110: 165–72]

Orisha [ii] The many divinities of YORUBA RELIGION, partly comparable with the Vodu of FON, the Abosum of AKAN, the Lubaale of GANDA, the Cwezi of Nyoro or even the Mhondoro of SHONA religion. Probably the most complex pantheon in Africa, their number is asserted to be hundreds, but the chief figures are relatively few. In mythology the *orisha* are children and ministers of the one supreme God, Olodumare; in modern devotional practice individual *orisha* are treated as almost independent deities, each with its own cult centres, praise songs (*oriki*) and prayers.

In general *orisha* are characterized both as nature spirits and as historical figures, the myths describing them highly anthropomorphically. Among the most important are Obatala (Orisha-nla), originally deputed to create the natural world and, in some accounts, father of all other *orisha*; Orunmila, patron of IFA DIVINATION; Eshu, the unpredictable TRICKSTER, dangerous or evil and therefore important to conciliate; Ogun, patron of iron and steel work; Shango, author of thunder and lightning but also ancestor of the kings of Oyo. There is almost endless variety in *orisha* mythology and devotion; it would be mistaken to reduce it to a single unchanging system, where place and time produce such major differences. [40]

Orishas (Afro-Caribbean) [iii] These deities of the YORUBA religion appear widely where SYNCRETISM occurs between Christianity and African religion. Very often individual *orisha* are associated with spirits in an African religion like VOODOO. In Haitian Voodoo the *orishas* have become *loas*. Many *loas* have *orisha* names although some qualities and personal characteristics may differ. Many additional ones may be added from contact cultures, such as Carib or Amerindian. In Trinidad there is a specific cult called *Orisha*, and although members of other churches may consider it to have low prestige, some adherents have dual affiliation with a more mainstream church (*see* SANGO). [8; 10; 23; 86]

Oro [xxix] A war-god, first worshipped as the son of Ta'aroa (TANGAROA) at Ra'iatea in the Society Islands (Tahiti). Oro became the supreme god, largely displacing Ta'aroa and TANE, the ancient Polynesian ATUA. (*See* POLYNESIAN RELIGION.) Oro was patron god of the ARIOI cult, whose travelling dancers spread his name to islands further away. [16; 22; 30]

Orpheus, Orphism [XVI] Orpheus was a legendary Thracian singer, credited, from the 6th century BCE, with poems containing theogonic, cosmogonic and eschatological teachings. Orphism is the broad multifarious current of sectarian thinking they contain. One strand originated with Pythagoras, a Samian sage and 'miracle worker' who founded a sect in south Italy. He expounded the theory of reincarnation (*metempsychosis*), the kernel of Orpheo-Pythagoreanism. The Pythagoreans governed Kroton for a time. They studied music and mathematics. Their way of life (*bios*) involved rigid rules with many ritual TABUS. They sought to purify their soul, atone for the Titans' crime (*see* KAKON), and escape the cycle of reincarnation. Individuals were initiated into the sect and followed a vegetarian Orphic *bios* to earn a happy afterlife. From the late 5th century BCE onwards gold leaves inscribed with texts giving instructions about what one should do and say in the Underworld in order to achieve heroization or deification were placed in some graves in different parts of the Greek world. The most important divinity in them is Persephone; in a recently discovered pair of gold leaves from Thessaly as in three (also recently discovered) bone tablets from Olbia, Dionysos is very important. The Bacchic/Dionysiac MYSTERIA, whose doctrine was Orpheo-Pythagorean, promised atonement, escape from reincarnation, and happy afterlife through initiation, ritual rules and ecstatic rites. The Orphic/Eleusinian strand (*see* MYSTERIA) (if it is right that the Eleusinian doctrine was related to Orphism) omits *metempsychosis*. Both strands contain a trend offering salvation by ritual means and an ethical trend (*see* ETHIKE). Orphic literature bloomed in Hellenistic times – much of it learned, some connected with local cults –

and continued to be associated with the Pythagorean sect, revived in the 1st century BCE (Neo-Pythagoreans) after a decline. [3; 5; 38]

Orthodox Church *see* EASTERN ORTHODOX CHURCH

Osirian Triad (Osiris, Isis, Horus) [VI] Osiris, a mythical Egyptian human king and the bringer of civilization, was murdered by his brother SETH [12; 13]. His dismembered body was reassembled by his wife, Isis, who then posthumously conceived their son, Horus. As Osiris' avenger, Horus fought Seth [23]. The divine judges found in his favour, and he became king of Egypt, while Osiris, resurrected as divine judge of the dead in the underworld, became the symbol of immortality. His worshippers sought individual resurrection through righteous lives. The cult gained popular support from the Middle Kingdom period on, *c*.1900 BCE.

Owner of the Animals [V] Among North American Indian hunting-tribes, particularly those in the north, the notion is widespread that animal species are governed by a supernatural owner. This prototypical figure, often mentioned in myth, may also be arranged in a hierarchical order with other owners of other animal species. A close parallel usually exists between the social structures in such hunting groups and those believed to be present in the animal world [11]. Over all other owners a universal ruler may be placed (e.g. Sedna among the ESKIMO). Success in hunting is frequently based upon achieving a favourable relationship with the 'owner', either through collective rituals (including abstinence from eating the flesh of the species), or perhaps on an individual level in those cases where the owner is identified with a person's GUARDIAN SPIRIT.

P

Paccekabuddha [XI] (Pali; Sanskrit: *pratyekabuddha*) A BUDDHIST term for an 'individual' or 'solitary' BUDDHA who becomes enlightened, not like the 'disciples' (*see* ARAHAT) by first hearing and then following the teachings of a perfectly and fully awakened Buddha, but by discovering by himself (or herself) the eternal truth of the way things are. Unlike fully awakened Buddhas, *paccekabuddhas* lack the capability to teach the DHAMMA and so do not establish a Buddhist dispensation (*sasana*). [50]

Pacific Religions [XXIX] Ancient religions of Oceania and island south-east Asia. Over 30,000 years ago, by gradual migration, the ancestors of today's Melanesians (Australoid) came from south Asia through the Malay peninsula and Indonesia to New Guinea and Australia. Mongoloid peoples from northern China later moved southwards, largely replacing the Australoids in mainland south-east Asia and Indonesia. More recent were the migrations by sea of Mongoloid (and Caucasoid?) peoples from coastal south China. Travelling via the Philippines and skirting Melanesia they settled in the Tongan and Samoan islands in about 1500 BCE. From there, further voyages radiated outwards to the Society and Marquesas islands, Hawaii, New Zealand and elsewhere, spreading a common language, culture and religion throughout Polynesia [3; 22; 28].

Early in the common era Indonesian rulers, impressed by Indian and Chinese trade and civilization, adopted HINDUISM and BUDDHISM. Absorbing much from local religion, these faiths flourished in the great empires of medieval Java and Sumatra. From the 13th century ISLAM spread through south-east Asia, again without displacing the ancient local religions. The introduction of CHRISTIANITY into the Pacific began with the Europeans who arrived in the 16th century to chart and lay claim to the 'South Sea' (named 'Pacific' by Magellan in 1520); 19th- and early 20th-century colonization was accompanied by extensive missionary activity. PROTESTANTISM, ROMAN CATHOLICISM and sectarian churches have proliferated. Like the Indian religions and Islam in Indonesia, Christianity in the Pacific is itself being modified as indigenous converts seek to make it a faith of their own. (*See also* AUSTRALIAN, BALINESE, BATAK, DAYAK, FIJIAN, JAVANESE, MELANESIAN, PHILIPPINES and POLYNESIAN RELIGIONS.)

Pahlavi [XXXVI] This term refers to two subjects: (1) a dynasty which ruled in Iran from 1925 to 1979; (2) the language of Iran from about the 3rd to the 9th century CE. (The dynasty was named after the culture and language of this period.) The term is synonymous with 'Middle Persian' (Middle as opposed to the Old of the inscriptions and the New of recent times). Because Pahlavi was the language of Iran during the period when most ZOROASTRIAN texts came to be written down, it is the language in which most texts of that faith survive. The final redactions of many of the religious texts were made in the 9th century, when Zoroastrian priests (MAGI) were active in defence of their faith, making or re-editing translations and compiling summaries of the AVESTA. Large sections of the Pahlavi books preserve ancient beliefs [55: 31–66]. Chief among the collections of ancient materials is perhaps the BUNDAHISHN [translation: 4], other apocalyptic works [5] and the *Dinkard*, which also contains some expository material [44; 53; 56; 57]. Important expositions of the faith include *Menog i Khrad* [59], *Shkandgumanig Vizar* [63: 59–66] and *Dadestan i denig* [58; 60]. One of the most popular religious texts among Zoroastrians is *Arda Viraz Namag* (The Book of the Righteous Viraz), a vision of heaven and hell [24a]. Modern studies of Zoroastrianism have the Pahlavi texts as one of their main sources, and recent studies have emphasized the diversity of traditions in these texts [53a].

Pali [XI] The language of the THERAVADA Buddhist scriptures. Pali means, literally, scriptural text, as opposed to commentary. The language was called Magadhi, i.e. the language of ancient Magadha, said to have been spoken by GOTAMA himself. Pali differs to some extent from the related Middle Indian dialect known as Magadhi to the later Sanskrit grammarians, although it was doubtless one of the dialects of the later enlarged kingdom of Magadha. The orally preserved discourses attributed to the BUDDHA and his disciples were probably current in a number of dialects from the beginning. When they were written down in Ceylon in the 1st century BCE, a more uniform Pali language naturally arose. In north India the greater prestige of Sanskrit led to the gradual displacement of Middle Indian. The work of commentators such as BUDDHAGHOSA made Pali the language of Theravada Buddhism, with a considerable literature down to modern times. [26]

Pancanamaskara [XX] The 'five homages': the most important ritual formula of the JAIN religion, both employed during ritual occasions and also generally believed to bring about protection from misfortune. Composed in Prakrit perhaps at the beginning of the common era, although held by Jains to be eternal, it consists of a series of invocations to the five exemplary figures of Jainism: 'Homage to the omniscient ones, homage to the liberated souls, homage to the teachers, homage to the preceptors, homage to all monks in the world.' There is also a further explanatory portion: 'This is the five homages which destroys all evil. It is the best auspicious statement of all auspicious statements.' [4: 70–2]

Pan-Islamism [XIX] The idea that the common religious bond of ISLAM should have a political manifestation. This was publicized by the polemicist Jamal al-Din al-Afghani (1838–97) and taken up by the Ottoman Sultan 'Abd al-Hamid II (1876–1909),who pictured himself as protector of all Muslims [38 s.v.]. The concept had a particular attraction for communities on the periphery of Islam threatened by Western domination, e.g. Africa, the Caucasus, Central Asia and India [1: IV], but the proliferation of nation-states across the Islamic world in the post-1920 years has impeded material realization of the ideal. [20 s.v.]

Panth [XXXIII] The Sanskrit word *panth* (literally 'path' or 'road') is used to designate groups in India following particular teachers or doctrines. The early SIKH community was thus known as the Nanak-panth or 'followers of NANAK' (*see* GURUS) [11: VI]. Later generations increasingly dropped the prefix, with the result that the community came to be known as, simply, 'the Panth'. This remains the preferred title today, in English usage as in Hindi or Punjabi. [26: I; 28: 51–5]

Pantheism [xxxiv] Belief that the whole of reality is divine [43: 132]. Pantheism may be cosmic (world-affirming), equating God and nature, or acosmic (world-denying), holding sense-experience to be illusory and only the divine to be real. The former is similar to panentheism (as e.g. in PROCESS THEOLOGY), for which God includes and permeates, but is not exhausted by, all that is known in sense-experience.

Papa [xxix] An earth-mother who, with RANGI the sky-father, gave birth to the gods (ATUA) in the creation myths of POLYNESIAN RELIGION. Their son TANE made himself a wife (the first human being) out of earth from Papa's body. To ease Papa's grief at her enforced separation from Rangi, the gods turned her face towards the underworld. All creatures live on her broad, kindly back. [7; 15; 16; 22]

Papacy [xiii.b] 'Pope' (father) is now normally used of the bishop of Rome as head of ROMAN CATHOLICISM, and 'Vicar of Christ' on earth (though it is also a title of the PATRIARCH of Alexandria). His authority is held to descend from JESUS Christ through the APOSTLE PETER as first bishop of Rome. Orthodox theologians, however, interpret the biblical Petrine texts to refer to the episcopal office rather than the papacy. Roman authority in the West over doctrine and jurisdiction developed early, and some medieval Popes claimed wide powers over secular rulers. The Vatican City still gives the Pope status as an independent ruler. Challenges to papal authority like Gallicanism (see STATE, CHRISTIANITY AND THE) and the CONCILIAR MOVEMENT receded in the 19th century with the rise of Ultramontanism (appeal 'beyond the mountains' – the Alps – to Rome). The First Vatican COUNCIL (1870) defined as 'dogma' (see AUTHORITY) the infallibility of the Pope when pronouncing with full formality (ex cathedra) on faith and morals, even apart from a General Council of the Church [19: 273]. Other important papal pronouncements are published in 'bulls' (from the Latin for the seal attached to them) and in circular letters ('encyclicals') to churches. The 'Old Catholics' after 1870 (with an earlier schism in Utrecht) rejected papal infallibility and various Roman customs [149]. The relationship between the authority of Popes, bishops and councils has been reconsidered since the Second Vatican Council (1962–5) but papal claims remain a major problem for the ECUMENICAL MOVEMENT. The EASTERN ORTHODOX CHURCH rejects them in favour of autocephaly, though allowing Rome a primacy of honour. Papal authority is also rejected by Old Catholics, PROTESTANTISM and ANGLICANISM, although some Anglo-Catholics accept it with limitations. [1: 37–56; 118; 190; 192]

Parables [xiii.a] Stories, similes or metaphors, usually drawn from ordinary life, illustrating some religious or ethical principle. They are found in the Hebrew BIBLE and the New Testament as well as in rabbinic traditions. The story attributed to Nathan of the poor man's ewe lamb brought home to King David the wrong he had done by taking Uriah's wife. JESUS' parables (such as those of the sower, the good Samaritan, the prodigal son) are particularly well known: each illustrates an aspect of his message about GOD's rule, his dealings with human beings and human mutual responsibility. [11: v, 146–52; 18: 136–41]

Paramita [xi] (Pali: *parami*) 'Perfection', referring in MAHAYANA BUDDHISM to a mental quality developed to the degree characteristic of a BODHISATTVA. Most common is a list of six: giving (DANA), morality (SILA), acceptance, strength, meditation (*dhyana*) and wisdom (PRAJNA). Giving which is developed to the highest (*parama*) extent is the 'perfection of giving', but it is often traditionally explained, as 'gone to the far shore' (*para*), i.e. transcendent. The lists of *paramita* ultimately derive from the earlier BODHI-PAKKHIYA-DHAMMA, but outline the *bodhisattva* path and the necessary transformation in motivation [21: 165–269]. A special place is often given to the perfection of wisdom (PRAJNAPARAMITA) with the remaining five equated to SKILFUL MEANS. A list of ten *parami* appears in some of the latest works of the PALI scriptures, but they play a more important role in the later THERAVADA writings, e.g. DHAMMAPALA [4: 254–331]. They are understood as equally necessary for the path of the ARAHAT and viewed as underlying tendencies accumulated over many lives.

Parinibbana [XI] (Pali; Sanskrit: *parinirvana*) In early BUDDHIST texts this term is sometimes used as a simple alternative to NIBBANA but can also refer specifically to the death or 'final passing away' of a BUDDHA or ARAHAT. By the extinguishing of all defilements (*kilesa-nibbana*) at the moment of enlightenment the process of rebirth (*see* SAMSARA) is deprived of its fuel and the being who has accomplished this is no longer reborn; the subsequent death of such a being is thus no ordinary death and is referred to as *parinibbana* (i.e. full or final *nibbana*) or *khandha-nibbana*, since the mental and physical 'aggregates' (*see* ANATTA) that constitute a living being do not manifest again after death to form the basis of another life. However, attempts to categorize the exact ontological status of the Buddha or *arahant* after death are strongly resisted by Buddhist writings: it should not be said that he or she exists, does not exist, both exists and does not exist, neither exists nor does not exist; in short he or she is untraceable or unfathomable (*ana-nuvejja*).

Parshva [XX] Twenty-third TIR-THANKARA of the JAIN religion. Parshva must be regarded as a historical figure who, if Jain dating be accepted, lived some time in the 9th century BCE. The 24th *tirthankara*, MAHAVIRA, may have adapted some of Parshva's views on ascetic law and cosmography. Parshva is traditionally regarded by Jains as a saviour figure and is the object of much devotional activity. The story of his rescue of a snake from a Hindu fire sacrifice and the snake's subsequent protection of Parshva from demonic attack is universally known within Jainism. [1; 4: 26–9]

Parsi Religious Reforms [XXXVI] The first major reform movement began in 1746 and was concerned with the calendar. It was realized that there was a discrepancy of a month between the calendars followed by the Parsis and the Zoroastrians in Iran (owing to a difference of practice in intercalation in the 365-day year). A group of Parsis in Surat adopted the Irani calendar and called it the *qadimi* or 'ancient' one. Their 'Kadmi' movement provoked a reaction by others, defending the traditional Parsi calendar, who called themselves Shen-shais (the meaning is disputed, possibly 'of the city', i.e. of Surat), later interpreted as Shahanshai, i.e. 'royalists'. This caused bitter, even violent, divisions. In 1906 a third calendar was introduced called *Fasli* ('seasonal'), which was based on the Gregorian calendar used in the West. These divisions involve few ritual and practically no doctrinal differences and nowadays there is little animosity between the groups. In numerical terms the most powerful group are the Shahanshai. [10: 189f, 212]

In 1818 a Parsi priest, Mulla Firoze, published a book brought by his father from Iran, the *Desatir* (Ordinances). This was followed in 1843 by the English translation of a similar work known as the *Dabistan*.

Both claimed to contain secret mystical teachings of ZOROASTER. For a period they caused a flurry of excitement, before it became clear that they were modern writings of a Persian SUFI sect [10: 197f].

After about 1870 Western education resulted in increasing Christian (almost wholly Protestant) influence on the educated liberals. This was apparent mainly in calls for the use of the vernacular (rather than the AVESTA) in prayers (MANTHRAS); in appeals for the abandonment both of the purity laws and of *nirang* (consecrated bull's urine traditionally used for physical and spiritual purification); and also in some doctrinal changes, notably the abandonment of traditional myths (BUNDAHISHN; FRASHOKERETI) and belief in a devil (ANGRA MAINYU). Such reforms, inevitably, produced an orthodox reaction. This was often expressed in language and ideas derived from the THEOSOPHICAL SOCIETY, a movement which encouraged all Indians to reject Western 'materialism' and preserve their Eastern 'spirituality', because the latter was allegedly in tune with occult forces. Behramshah Shroff (1858–1927) founded a specifically Parsi Theosophical/occultist movement, Ilm-i Kshnoom (interpreted as meaning 'Science of (Spiritual) Satisfaction'), claiming to have received an esoteric teaching not from masters in Tibet (as in THEOSOPHY) but from a secret race of giants hidden in mountain caves in Iran. Rebirth, asceticism and vegetarianism are three features of these two movements which diverge from traditional Zoroastrian teaching. Parsis influenced by either movement are orthodox in that they faithfully preserve traditional prayers and rites [32].

The above reforms are those reported in English-language publications. In Gujarati there are emotive debates on more 'internal' matters, mainly ritual concerns such as detailed funeral practices. In both languages there is a debate over the possibility of accepting converts. The term 'Parsi' is understood in terms of race or caste, hence conversion is generally considered to be impossible. A vocal minority, especially in communities outside Bombay, is canvassing for the acceptance of converts, partly in order to counter the decline in numbers. In Delhi it was agreed in 1992 that the children of mixed marriages could become members of the association (*anjuman*) and the following year the World Zoroastrian Organization, based in London, decided that the non-Zoroastrian spouse in a mixed marriage could become a full member. In America further developments have occurred with the initiation of a 'white' American in 1983 and at the end of the decade a controversial teacher in California began active proselytism, a step traditional Zoroastrians continue to reject vigorously [31]. The orthodox reaction is that intermarriage and proselytism would inevitably result in such a tiny minority (representing 0.016% of India's population) being swamped, thus destroying their identity and heritage. In such circumstances religious issues and community survival are inseparable subjects [29: pt III].

Parsis [XXXVI] 'The Persians', the descendants of a small group of Zoroastrians who left their Iranian homeland to escape from Islamic oppression and seek a land of religious freedom. They settled in north-west India (Gujarat) in 936 CE (the precise date has been disputed). Their early history is written in the *Tale of Sanjan (Qissa-i Sanjan)* [10: 166–8]. They generally lived in peace with the Hindus, but Muslim invasions of the region in 1297 and 1465 caused bloodshed and aroused deep fears of a return to the conditions in Islamic Iran. In the 15th century the first of a series of letters, or *Rivayets* [10: 173], was sent from Iranian co-religionists in answer to Parsi questions relating to religious practice. Under European, especially British, rule from the 17th century onwards the Parsis moved in increasing numbers to the new port and growing commercial capital of western India, Bombay. There are numerous travellers' accounts of the Parsis from this region in this period which provide invaluable information on their history, beliefs and practices [21]. In the 19th century they acquired wealth and power out of all proportion to their numbers. By 1947 and Indian independence they numbered approximately 112,000 in India, with about 61% in the one city of Bombay. By the 1980s census data show that numbers were declining at the rate of 20% per decade, with an increasing proportion in Bombay and over 90% of the population living in urban areas. The Parsi community in India is now, in numerical terms, the main centre of ZOROASTRIANISM. Trading opportunities in the British empire led the Parsis to travel and settle in different countries, so there are now small communities in Australia (Sydney and Melbourne), Singapore, Hong Kong, Pakistan (Karachi), England (London), Canada (Toronto, Montreal and Vancouver), and the USA (in some 17 cities especially New York, Chicago and Los Angeles). The communities in Aden and east Africa were forced to leave in the 1960s and 1970s, although very small groups remain in Nairobi, Mombasa and in Durban in South Africa.

Most of the Parsi migrants have been well-educated professionals. The increasing numbers in the diaspora and the social standing of these members have resulted in increasing influence of local leaders in social and religious reform. Typically they argue that the beliefs and practices of the 'old country' are not necessarily appropriate in the 'new world'. There are two main diaspora bodies, apart from numerous local groups, namely the World Zoroastrian Organization (WZO), founded

in London in 1980, and the Federation of Zoroastrians of North America (FEZANA), formally constituted at a conference in Toronto in 1988. The latter is concerned, among other things, to evolve a teaching and liturgical practice that are meaningful to the youth brought up in a Western, largely Protestant, environment. [10: XI–XIV; 29: pt III; 30; 32; 34; 37; 41]

Parvati [XVII] 'Daughter of the Mountain'; the wife of SHIVA, and for many HINDUS the Goddess (*Devi* or SHAKTI) *par excellence*. She is said to have been the goddess SATI, reborn after her self-immolation as the child of the god of the Himalayas. After falling in love with Shiva, who was practising asceticism (TAPAS) in the mountains, she herself undertook severe ascetic practices in order to win him as her husband. He eventually agreed to her desire, on condition that she would accompany him in both sides of his life, as a wife while he was a family man and as a fellow-ascetic while he was a yogi. In art and literature they are portrayed as deeply in love, though sometimes quarrelling, either over their children, GANESHA and KARTTIKEYA, or when he makes her jealous (cf. GANGA). Like him, she has many names and forms: in his company she is gentle, appearing as a beautiful, queenly woman, holding a lotus, whether as dark Parvati, golden Uma or white Gauri: worshipped alone she may be formidable, as DURGA or KALI. [4: 213, 217–18; 92: 154–73, 261–9]

Paryushan [XX] Important SHVE-TAMBARA JAIN festival [4: 185]. 'Abiding' is the period of eight days falling in late August or early September which forms the climax of the four-month rain retreat when Shvetambara ascetics reside in the midst of the lay community. Among the various rituals which take place at this time is the recitation of the

KALPA SUTRA. The last day of Paryushan is 'Annual' (*Samvatsari*),
when Shvetambaras ask each other
for forgiveness.

Passion Play (in Islam) [XIX] The
ta'ziya (literally 'consolation, com-
miseration') constitutes one of the
few approaches in pre-modern Islamic literature to the Western-type
drama. Essentially a phenomenon of
SHI'ISM, these plays provide a focus
for the intense feelings of ordinary
believers concerning the martyr-
doms of early Shi'ism, in particular
the death in battle of 'Ali's son al-
Husain (*see* 'ALI, 'ALIDS). They are
accordingly staged around the anniversary of this event, ten Muharram
(*see* 'ID), among the Shi'i communities of Iran, the Indo-Pakistan subcontinent and certain emirates of the
western shores of the Persian Gulf.
In the forms at present known, the
actual texts of the plays do not seem
to date beyond the 18th century. [37
'Ta'ziya'; 102]

Passover [XXII] (Hebrew: *Pesach*)
Jewish festival (CHAGIM) commemorating the liberation of the Israelites
from slavery in Egypt [14 vol. 13:
163; 69: 154]. Passover, PENTECOST
and TABERNACLES were pilgrimage
festivals, when Jews would go up by
foot to the TEMPLE in Jerusalem,
and on Passover a Pascal lamb was
brought as a sacrifice, to be eaten by
extended family groups during the
first night of the festival. Passover is
also a harvest festival, the lunar CAL-
ENDAR being intercalated to ensure it
always falls in spring, and an *omer*
(*see* OMER, COUNTING OF) measure
of the new barley crop was offered
up on the second day. Today no
sacrifices are brought but a ritual
family meal, accompanied by a
retelling of the EXODUS story from a
Haggadah text (*see* AGGADAH), takes
place on the first night of Passover
(and also on the second night in the
diaspora). This night is called *seder*
('order') night. The youngest child
asks four questions (*mah nishtanah*)

about the meal, and four cups of
wine, each one symbolizing a dimension of divine redemption, are
drunk. Bitter herbs (*maror*), usually
lettuce or horseradish, are eaten to
symbolize suffering, and unleavened
bread (*matzah*), the diet of the poor
and of slaves, is used during the
whole festival. No leaven is consumed or kept at home and the
Jewish kitchen has to undergo a rigorous cleaning [59: 38; 70: 188].
Although many modern Jews do not
keep Passover strictly, even highly
assimilated Jews continue the tradition of the family *seder* meal.

Path [XXXIII] For SIKHS *path* means
a reading of any portion of the
sacred scriptures. Particular merit
attaches to a complete reading of the
ADI GRANTH. This may be done
intermittently (*sadharan path*, 'ordinary reading') or within a specified
period. For special purposes an
akhand path, or 'unbroken reading',
is performed. This requires a continuous relay of readers and is completed within 48 hours. [8: 134–5;
26: 68] If this is not practicable the
reading may be spread over seven
days (*saptahik path*). [8: 172–3; 30:
80]

Paticcasamuppada [XI] This BUD-
DHIST term literally means 'arising
together in dependence upon' and
refers to the way in which the basic
phenomena of existence (DHAMMA)
are understood to exist. According
to the principle of *paticcasamuppada*
(Pali; Sanskrit: *pratityasamutpada*)
or 'dependent arising' phenomena
do not exist independently by virtue
of their own inherent power, but
rather occur in dependence upon
and conditioned by one another; the
only exception to this rule is the
'unconditioned' (Pali: *asamkhata*;
Sanskrit: *asamskrita*) or NIBBANA.
This understanding is of fundamental importance to Buddhist philosophy and psychology.
Paticcasamuppada is classically
expounded by way of a formula

detailing a cycle of 12 links or stages (*nidana*). This formula begins with 'ignorance' (Pali: *avijja*; Sanskrit: *avidya*) which is a fundamentally distorted perception of the way things are; ignorance has given rise to inappropriate actions (link 2) which in turn have resulted in our present circumstances (links 3–7); we tend to respond to these circumstances with 'craving' (Pali: *tanha*; Sanskrit: *trishna*) (link 8), liking and identifying with some experiences and rejecting others; such responses set up mental habits and patterns of behaviour that tend to perpetuate themselves in the form of 'grasping' (*upadana*) and 'becoming' (*bhava*) (links 9–10); these will eventually determine future circumstances (links 11–12). However, the chain can be cut at certain points, leading to a cycle that ends in the cessation of suffering (DUKKHA). In the ABHIDHAMMA the twelvefold formula is understood on different scales as descriptive either of the stages involved in birth, death and rebirth, or of the processes of thought from moment to moment.

Paticcasamuppada is the key to the Buddhist understanding of the nature of KARMA, causality, change and free will. Our actions are not seen as absolutely determined by the past, but neither are they entirely free from it. This outlook is presented as 'the middle way' between 'annihilationism' (the view that cause and effect are absolutely different) and 'eternalism' (the view that cause and effect are the same) (cf. DITTHI), and is a corollary of the theory of 'no-self' (ANATTA). It is regarded as the fundamental law of things and equivalent to the Buddha's Dhamma itself since it explains both why beings continue to suffer in SAMSARA (the second of the FOUR NOBLE TRUTHS) and how it is possible for them to change their circumstances and attain freedom (the fourth Truth). Consequently much of Buddhist thought is concerned with drawing out and stating

the proper understanding of *paticcasamuppada* (*see* ABHIDHAMMA; SHUNYATAVADA; MADHYAMAKA). [34: 54–60]

Patimokkha [XI] (Pali; Sanskrit: *pratimoksha*) The BUDDHIST monastic code to which fully ordained members of the SANGHA must adhere. The individual rules that comprise the code are fully analysed in the VINAYA; their number varies from tradition to tradition. In THERAVADA tradition there are 227 rules for monks (BHIKKHU) and 311 for nuns (BHIKKUNI); in the eastern tradition (of China, Korea and Japan) 250 for monks and 348 for nuns; and in Tibetan tradition 258 for monks and 366 for nuns. Despite the variations there is a common core of some 150 major rules accepted by all. For the most part these rules merely detail in a particular way what is involved in keeping the ten precepts (*see* SILA) of the novice. The rules are divided into categories depending on the seriousness attached to their being breached. Four fundamental rules prohibit sexual intercourse, theft, the intentional killing of a human being and deceiving the laity (*see* TISARANA, UPASAKA) by knowingly laying false claim to spiritual attainments. Failure to comply with these rules involves 'defeat' and the individual in question is permanently barred from the Sangha. Traditionally all members of the Sangha in a given locality gather on the fortnightly UPOSATHA days to recite the *patimokkha* and confess any breaches. [34: 225–7]

Patit [XXXIII] If a SIKH commits a serious breach of the RAHIT (the KHALSA code) he should be declared *patit* ('fallen') and expelled from the Khalsa. Serious breaches include cutting one's hair and smoking. To secure readmission a *patit* must confess his sin and undergo a second initiation. Although the actual discipline is seldom invoked, the word *patit* is commonly used with reference to conspicuous offenders. Strictly, it applies only to those who have previously received Khalsa initiation. (*See also* KES-DHARI.) [7: 126; 29: 33, 114–15]

Patriarch [XIII.D] As Christianity spread through the Roman empire, the bishops of the major regional capital cities, ROME, ALEXANDRIA and ANTIOCH, and later those of JERUSALEM and Constantinople, came to be recognized as holding positions of particular honour and authority, especially in the matter of hearing appeals against decisions of local bishops and settling disputes among them. By the decision of the COUNCIL of Chalcedon (451) the sees of Rome and Constantinople held pre-eminent jurisdiction in West and East respectively, as bishops of the Roman empire's two capital cities. The Roman Popes resisted this decision and actively pursued recognition of their claims to universal jurisdiction over the entire church.

The hierarchs of these five ancient sees came to be known as patriarchs, though the Patriarch of the West, the bishop of Rome, and the Patriarch of Alexandria both use also the title 'Pope'. As the autocephaly (independence) of other major national churches was recognized, the chief hierarchs of several (Russia, Romania, Bulgaria and Serbia) were also designated patriarch. Not all heads of autocephalous churches use the title, however; the Church of Cyprus and the Church of Sinai are both headed by archbishops and the chief bishops in the Georgian Orthodox Church use the title 'Catholicos' or 'Catholicos-Patriarch'. The heads of the Oriental Orthodox churches also make use of the titles 'Patriarch' and 'Catholicos', as do heads of some of the Oriental and EASTERN CATHOLIC churches. Certain Roman Catholic hierarchs bear the courtesy title 'Patriarch', for example the Patriarch of Venice, and for a long time Latin patriarchs of sees taken over by Roman Catholics in the period of the CRUSADES were appointed, though apart from the Latin Patriarch of Jerusalem they held the title as an honorific dignity. In many cases several patriarchs of different traditions hold the same title; for example, there are Greek Orthodox, Latin Catholic and Armenian Patriarchs of Jerusalem. The Eastern Orthodox have sometimes opposed the model of the five ancient patriarchates acting independently but in fraternal communion (the Pentarchy) to the Roman model of the monarchical PAPACY to explain the organization of the church in the early centuries. Sometimes the patriarchal jurisdiction cannot easily be exercised in a given area; in such a case, a senior bishop is appointed as Exarch to act on the patriarch's behalf. After the spread of ISLAM many exarchs were appointed to rule churches no longer in the Roman empire. [37; 55; 99]

Paul [XIII.A] Also known by his Jewish name, Saul, he was born into a Jewish family of Tarsus in Cilicia, a family sufficiently distinguished to have acquired Roman citizenship. He was educated under Gamaliel I in JERUSALEM. At first he vehemently opposed the early CHURCH, but was called (*c.*33 CE) to become one of its leading exponents, especially among non-Palestinian Jews and GENTILES. He is suitably regarded as the founder of Gentile Christianity.

After a brief attempt to evangelize the Nabataean Arabs immediately after his conversion, he evangelized in Syria and Cilicia, then (with Barnabas) in Cyprus and Galatia (central Asia Minor), then (with Silvanus and Timothy) in Macedonia and Greece and then (*c.*52–55 CE) in EPHESUS and the province of Asia. In the principal cities of those provinces he established churches, comprising mainly Gentile converts with a smaller proportion of Jewish converts. He preached that JESUS the

Christ should be acclaimed as Lord, that the benefits of his death could be participated in through BAPTISM, and that through faith the believer could appropriate God's gracious justification of humanity. He insisted that religious and social barriers between Jews and Gentiles had been abolished. This required a reappraisal of the Jewish law, a process which created tension between Paul and conservative Jewish Christians. He punctuated his missionary work with visits to the Jerusalem church.

According to the *Acts of the Apostles*, on his last visit to Jerusalem Paul was arrested and prosecuted on a charge of violating the sanctity of the TEMPLE. As a Roman citizen he appealed to have his case transferred to the imperial tribunal in Rome and was sent there in 59 CE. He spent two years there under house arrest waiting for his appearance before Caesar. Tradition says that he was executed on the Ostian Way near Rome.

The New Testament (*see* BIBLE) includes 13 letters bearing his name; most of them are generally considered authentic, but it is impossible to construct a systematic view of Paul's theology from them, since nearly all are framed around the particular problems of his addressees. [4: 1329–37; 5; 11: v, 186–201; 13: ii, 97–145; 16: 127–205]

Pelagianism [xiii.c] The theological doctrine in CHRISTIANITY that each person has responsibility for ensuring his or her own SALVATION. Its name is derived from Pelagius, a British monk who was active early in the 5th century and who attacked Augustine's view that moral goodness is possible only through an act of divine grace (*see* AUGUSTINIANISM). Pelagius maintained that every person has free will, that a person's sinful state is not inherited and that grace is an aid to (rather than the sole source of) human righteousness (*see* SIN). He denied that GOD has predestined each person to heaven or hell. Pelagianism was eventually condemned as heretical. [6; 10]

Penance (Christian) [xiii.b] The SACRAMENT for the forgiveness of sins. In early centuries it was elaborate, severe and public, and allowed only once in a lifetime. The medieval system involved private confession to a priest (from 1215 at least once a year for Western Christians). The priest then formally pronounced the penitent forgiven (absolution) and ordered 'penances' to be done. This system continues today. 'Penances' are an earthly punishment for SIN and an aid in controlling it. Originally they could be very severe; later they were commuted to simple prayers or even cash payments. Papal 'indulgences' were then developed during the middle ages to channel aid from the 'treasury of merits' available in the virtues of JESUS Christ and the SAINTS. They could be substituted for penances (though not for confession). Abuses of this system (such as the sales of indulgences by 'pardoners') provoked Luther's *Ninety-Five Theses*, which precipitated the REFORMATION. Indulgences were reformed (though not abolished) in 1567. [114: 216–22; 436–40; 154 vol. ii: 72–84]

Pentecost [xxii] (Hebrew: *Shavuot*) Jewish festival (CHAGIM) occurring 50 days after PASSOVER, this period of seven weeks being known as the *omer* (*see* OMER, COUNTING OF). The English name of the festival derives from the Greek for 50 and its Hebrew name means 'weeks'. Pentecost is a festival of the wheat harvest and also commemorates the giving of the ten commandments to Moses on Mt Sinai – divine revelation being viewed as 'spiritual bread from heaven' [59: 88]. SYNAGOGUES are decorated with shrubs and flowers in honour of the harvest and also because the desert mountain is said to have been covered in flowers at the moment of revelation.

Some Jews stay awake the night before Pentecost studying the TORAH (*tikkun leil shavuot*), to signify that they are keen to accept the Torah all over again [70: 193]. During the morning service of Pentecost the Book of Ruth is read because it too is set at harvest time, it tells of a Gentile woman's acceptance of the Torah, paralleling the acceptance of it by the Israelites at Mt Sinai, and because Pentecost is the traditional day of birth and death of King David, a descendant of the biblical Ruth [69: 180].

Pentecostalism [XIII.B] Alluding to the descent of the HOLY SPIRIT (*see* TRINITY) on the APOSTLES at Pentecost (Whitsun), the term is applied to a movement beginning in Los Angeles, USA (1906 CE). It spread to AFRICA, EUROPE and LATIN AMERICA. It has been characterized by spiritual healing and by ecstatic speaking in 'tongues' (*glossolalia*), either unintelligible or apparently echoing existing languages not consciously known to the speaker. Its churches include the Elim Foursquare Gospel [205], the Assemblies of God and many others, a number being black churches. Since the 1960s 'charismatic' movements resembling Pentecostalism have appeared in ANGLICANISM, PROTESTANTISM and ROMAN CATHOLICISM. [62 vol. 11: 229–31; 92]

People's Temple [XXVIII] Led by the Reverend Jim Jones (1931–78), an ordained minister of the Disciples of Christ, who first attracted attention as a social reformer and healer in California in the late 1960s. Following complaints about mistreatment of his followers, Jones moved to 'Jonestown' in the Guyana jungle. In November 1978, Congressman Leo Ryan was shot after an investigative visit to Jonestown and over 900 bodies were discovered in the colony. Many had committed suicide by drinking Kool-Aid laced with cyanide, but tape-recordings and reports from the few survivors and those who examined the bodies revealed that many, perhaps the majority, had been murdered. [25: VII; 27; 42; 76]

Peter [XIII.A] One of the original 12 APOSTLES called by JESUS. After leading the JERUSALEM church for some 20 years after Jesus' death, he embarked on a wider ministry in the eastern Mediterranean, working with both Jewish and GENTILE Christian communities. He finally went to ROME, where he was martyred under the Roman emperor Nero (54–68 CE). The Roman PAPACY claims descent from him as the first bishop of Rome. Two letters in the New Testament bear his name; some have questioned their authenticity. [11: V, 251–63]

Peyotism [V] An indigenous religious movement, with pre-Columbian antecedents, that emerged as a distinct form among Amerindian tribes of the southern plains of North America in the 19th century. It is based on the use of mescal (obtained from peyote cactus, *Lophophora williamsii*), which has a hallucinogenic effect [14]. The drug was originally used for medicinal purposes (and occasionally, during warfare, for divination). Peyotism spread rapidly among the disfranchised and oppressed, culminating in 1918 in the formation of the NATIVE AMERICAN CHURCH [8: X]. This syncretistic cult combines such indigenous elements as drumming, singing, visions and the use of the sacred pipe with Christian practices of healing, prayer and sacramentalism. [23: VI]

Pharaoh [VI] A title derived from the Egyptian word for 'palace'. Pharaoh was the king of Egypt, an absolute, divine monarch, and the myth that he was begotten by the chief state-god and born to the principal queen underlined the chasm which existed between pharaoh and his subjects. As divine heir, he was responsible for the founding and upkeep of the temples (MANSIONS OF THE GODS), the performance of the rituals and the efficacy of the FUNERARY PRACTICES [11: II, 46]. In return, he received the kingship, military supremacy and peaceful prosperity for Egypt and its inhabitants, whom he owned. However, he was subject to *ma'at*, the principle of divine order throughout the universe, and at his coronation was imbued with the necessary regal powers, which were periodically renewed at his jubilee-festivals [17: VI, 113].

After the unification of the Two Lands, c.3100 BCE, the king symbolized the union of north and south. The living king was Horus incarnate; at death, he became Osiris (*see* OSIRIAN TRIAD).

Pharisees [XXII, XIII.A] Members of a Jewish movement flourishing before the Christian era in Palestine, whose spiritual descendants fashioned rabbinical JUDAISM. Three main sources provide information about the Pharisees: (1) rabbinical literature composed after the demise of the movement by Jews who saw themselves as the heirs of Pharisaism (*see* RABBI); (2) New Testament literature (*see* BIBLE), which associates the Pharisees with their opponents the SADDUCEES, and is consistently hostile in its descriptions of Pharisaic religion; (3) JOSEPHUS, the 1st-century CE Jewish historian, who was writing in part for a non-Jewish readership and describes the various movements with Judaism in terms of Greek philosophical schools [XXII 63: XXVI]. Because of the different bias of these sources there is some disagreement about when Pharisaism began and about the exact nature of its tenets and practices [XXII 48; 51]. The traditional view is that they represent those Jews who subscribed to the oral traditions of biblical interpretation, as opposed to the Sadducees, who were inclined to

a literalist understanding of the Bible text. The movement is thought to have begun some time after the Maccabean revolt against the Hellenizing policies of the Seleucid rulers of Palestine in the 2nd century BCE, when they split away from the religio-political establishment (*see* BIBLICAL HISTORY) (Pharisee means 'separatist'). They formed brotherhoods (*haburot*) whose members encouraged one another in devotion to the law. Their interpretation of the law adapted it to changing conditions: they were the only religious party in Israel capable of surviving the catastrophe of 70 CE. JESUS agreed with them on RESURRECTION, ANGELS and DEMONS, but his association with 'sinners', and some of his interpretations of the law generally, incurred their disapproval. Several Pharisees joined the early JERUSALEM CHURCH. [XIII.A 21: 380–451; XIII.A 22: II, 388–403]

Phenomenology of Religion [XXXIV] A sub-discipline of RELIGIONSWISSENSCHAFT, or more precisely *systematische Religionswissenschaft*, that part of the STUDY OF RELIGION(S) which is mainly concerned with systematizing the wide range of data collected by the HISTORY OF RELIGION(S). Though its roots go back to modern philosophy (Kant, Hegel and Husserl) it established itself as a separate branch within *Religionswissenschaft* in the 20th century through the works of Gerardus van der Leeuw, Friedrich Heiler, Kurt Goldammer, Geo Widengren and, to some extent, MIRCEA ELIADE. Its aim was to systematize religious manifestations, found in religious traditions, in the form of a general religious morphology applicable to all of them independently of their cultural backgrounds and settings. It was hoped that thus, through the comparative morphology of religious manifestations, the essence of religion would be reached and expressed. But, as van der Leeuw said: 'This phenomenology of religion consisted not merely in making an inventory and classification of phenomena as they appear in history, but also a psychological description which necessitated not only a meticulous observation of the religious reality, but also a systematic introspection; not only the description of what is visible from outside, but above all the experience born of what can only become reality after it has been admitted into the life of the observer himself' [145: 231; 24: III].

The method used is that of *epoché*, an attempt to avoid both inadequately judging the religious phenomena of another religious tradition from the evaluative perspective of one's own and enthusiastically embracing the foreign tradition by taking an objective approach to the real essence of these religious manifestations, excluding subjective evaluations. This noble project, however, was soon exposed to harsh criticism on the grounds of introspection. Opponents argued that such an approach was not neutral at all but on the contrary relied on personal, i.e. subjective evaluations, going beyond the limits of an open-ended presentation which neither rejects nor asserts the real existence of what religious manifestations stand for. Also, according to phenomenologists, it ultimately sets up an empathetic experience as the necessary source of knowledge, as musicality is required for a proper understanding of music. The question, consequently, was and is whether the study of religion should, as concerns its results, rather be paralleled with that of music or with that of, for instance, illnesses, where medical research work is not based on the presumption that the researcher has personal experience of the illness under study. The discussion on introspection has totally blocked further development of the phenomenology of religion since 1970. Yet it would have been worth

attempting the direct application of its morphology to the great world religions in order to discuss the value of these categories for appropriate description of religious phenomena. The only attempt in this direction made so far has been that of Peter McKenzie, who followed Heiler's categories in his description of Christians [115]. Heiler's morphology of religious manifestations is divided into three parts: (1) the world of religious manifestations; (2) the world of religious thought; and (3) the world of religious experience. All three parts are further subdivided into numerous aspects, for example, for (1) religious objects (natural, such as stones, trees, stars, sun and moon; manufactured, such as arms, flags, rings, liturgical dress); for (2) the concept of God, gods and goddesses, the concept of men and women, their destinies and afterlife as well as ideas concerning the invisible world of angels, spirits, souls, etc.; and for (3) the main manifestations of personal and collective religious experience, such as awe, fear, joy, piety, etc., and extraordinary forms of religious experience such as inspirations, visions, auditions and ecstasy [76].

It is noteworthy that van der Leeuw was mainly interested in 'primitive religions' on the presumption that the pure essence of religion is obvious there, while later religious periods, though rich in religious systematizations, were further removed from the original religious inspiration of humankind [107]. Against this preference for indigenous religions, Geo Widengren made use of the data recorded in the writings of the great religious traditions of humankind [176]. Widengren was thus opposed to van der Leeuw's implicit decadence theory, which maintains that humankind was religious in its beginnings, then became metaphysical and finally became non-religious, as suggested by Comte's positivism and repeated in many modern writings. Eliade, too, had this decadence theory in mind when he tried to show that hierophany is found in ancient times and has to be brought back if humankind wants really to become human again. [24: IX; 49; 59a, vol. 3: 578–80; 98a; 133a]

Philippine Independent Church [xxvII] This church, once claiming several million members but now stabilized at about a million adherents, emerged after the revolution against Spain when Gregorio Aglipay (1860–1940), a Filipino Catholic priest, became its Supreme Bishop in 1902. Religious practice remains Catholic and the main concern is independent responsibility. A drift into UNITARIANISM produced splits in the 1940s, but a return to orthodoxy led to alliance with the Philippine Episcopal Church (American Protestant Episcopal Church in origin) for consecration of bishops and joint ministerial training. More recent developments include a desire for a more Filipino ethos and form of ministry. [24]

Philippines Religion [xxIx] The Philippines are the only Christian nation in south-east Asia, with a Muslim minority in the south and tribal peoples in the hills. Filipinos are ROMAN CATHOLICS for the most part, Christianized by the Spanish after 1570, when Manila was taken from the Muslims. As in Indonesia, Indian religions had preceded ISLAM and, although their penetration was not as deep as in Java or Bali, Sanskrit loan words remain in the national language, Tagalog. Thus the term *diwata* (Sanskrit *devata*, 'divine beings', 'divinity') is found in many dialects, including that spoken by the Tasaday, a small group of 'stone age' people allegedly 'discovered' in southern Mindanao in 1971, who seem to have a very simple religion and culture. The Ifugao of northern Luzon, by contrast, divide the cosmos into five regions and people it with hundreds of gods

or spirit beings, each one of whom has a department (e.g. wind, rain, war, fishing, weaving), and all of whose names must be learned by the priests. [26]

Philistines [vIII] The horde known to the Egyptians as the 'Sea Peoples' first threatened Egypt *c.*1232 BCE, but was repulsed. The Egyptian records give the name of one group of these people as the Peleset, and they have been identified as the later biblical Philistines [21]. The overthrow of the HITTITE empire in *c.*1200 BCE enabled the Sea Peoples to push down through Syria–Palestine and again they were only stopped at Egypt's boundary. Although some of the Peleset and their associates may have settled there before *c.*1200 BCE, it was their repulsion by Ramesses III of Egypt in 1183 BCE which forced them to make their homeland in the coastal plain known since as Palestine.

They had connections with Anatolia, the Mycenaean Greeks (*see* GREEK RELIGION) and Crete, but little is known of their early religion. The gods later associated with them – Dagon, 'Ashtoreth and Ba'alzebub – were adopted from existing Canaanite cults [2: 15–21]. It is possible that their sky-cult and the allusions to bees and flies in their cults reflect a link with the Greek world. Their burial customs included both cremations (at 'Azor) and burial chambers (at Tell Far'ah) which recall the Mycenaean type.

Philosophia [xvI] In so far as it seeks an ultimate explanation of the COSMOS, much Greek philosophy can be seen as philosophy of religion, constructing physical/metaphysical counterparts to religious beliefs (e.g. Milesians, 6th century BCE and Plato, 428/7–348/7 BCE). Some thinkers (e.g. Heraclitus, *fl.* *c.*500 BCE) associated natural or metaphysical entities with traditional divinities. Stoicism (*c.*300 BCE to *c.*260 CE) defended traditional beliefs, reinterpreting gods as natural phenomena. Later Stoicism achieved a synthesis with popular beliefs (including ASTROLOGY), a mystical development which had wider influence. A strand critical of traditional religion began with Xenophanes (b. *c.*570 BCE). Another critical wave began in the mid-5th century (Sophists; Democritos b. *c.*460 BCE). In earlier Hellenistic times such criticisms are common (e.g. the Epicureans, Cynics and Sceptics). Most philosophers of religion practised and recommended civic cults. [7: VI; 11: 191–218; 21: 81–3, 130–4; 22: 41–50, 100–1, 144–65, 211–34; 27: 121–71, 854–69; 37: 216–63]

Philosophy (Jewish) [XXII] The BIBLE and rabbinical literature (*see* RABBI) discuss theological issues through stories and PARABLES, rather than in abstract terms. It was only in Islamic countries in the middle ages that a tradition of philosophical theology emerged within JUDAISM [24; 28]. The first important philosopher was the Babylonian sage Saadiah Gaon (882–942 CE), whose *Book of Beliefs and Opinions* advocates rational reflection on religious truth as a valid alternative to revelation. The next major figure was the Spanish poet–theologian Judah Halevi (d. 1141), who sought to show the limitations of philosophy in his *Kuzari*, and claimed that revelatory truth began where philosophical investigation left off. Moses MAIMONIDES (1135–1204) was the greatest of these medieval philosopher–theologians, and his controversial work *The Guide of the Perplexed* attempts a synthesis of Jewish and Aristotelian thought [42]. There was a new flowering of Jewish philosophy during the 18th-century ENLIGHTENMENT in Europe. The first important figure of modern Jewish philosophy was Moses MENDELSSOHN (1729–86). [2; 7; 11; 17; 38; 42; 52; 56: III; 70: IV, V]

Philosophy of Religion [XXXII, XXXIV] Critical reflection on the concepts and beliefs involved in religion. Philosophy of religion in the Western tradition includes natural THEOLOGY and to that extent is concerned with what can be established in religion by reason alone. Central to the traditional agenda of philosophy of religion have been the various ARGUMENTS FOR THE EXISTENCE OF GOD. Philosophers of different religious faiths or none have sought to justify or question the acceptance of THEISM or to prove or question the immortality of the soul [XXXII, 7: 257ff].

Philosophy of religion has been an integral part of the Western tradition of metaphysics at least since Plato. Philosophies such as STOICISM or PANTHEISM have frequently served for their adherents as substitutes for the socially dominant religion. In the Western tradition there has always been some degree of tension between religion and philosophy. There have been attempts, in ancient and modern times, to harmonize particular philosophies with particular religions. Some philosophies, such as Epicureanism, have mostly been thought inconsistent with religious belief while others, like Platonism, have seemed on the face of it congenial. THOMISM is a harmonization, effected by Thomas Aquinas, between CHRISTIANITY and Aristotelian philosophy which has been and remains very influential, especially for ROMAN CATHOLICS. The project of producing such a harmonization is the project of a Christian philosophy. (*See also* PHILOSOPHY (JEWISH).) Harmonizations have also been made with more recent philosophies such as EXISTENTIALISM and EMPIRICISM. Though only a believer is likely to be motivated to produce such harmonizations, they do not presuppose faith but are concerned to demonstrate consistency, or at least a high degree of consistency, between acceptance of religious belief and a particular philosophy.

Philosophers of religion have also been concerned with internal consistency within a set of religious beliefs. It has often been claimed that it is impossible to believe in a God who is omnipotent and infinitely caring at the same time as accepting the reality of EVIL. Here, and elsewhere, in modern times, philosophers have often played a critical role. Some 20th-century philosophical movements (e.g. LOGICAL POSITIVISM, MARXISM, scientific HUMANISM) have been overtly hostile to religion. Philosophies have been among the modern SECULAR ALTERNATIVES TO RELIGION. Partly as a result of the challenge of Logical Positivism, there has been, within the analytical tradition of philosophy, a concern with the question whether or not it is possible to make meaningful statements in religion [XXXII 11: 96ff]. This has resulted in harmonizations of religious belief with empiricism that largely reduced Christianity to its ethical content [XXXII, 6]. There has been a reaction, particularly influenced by the later writings of Ludwig Wittgenstein (1889–1951) to such REDUCTIONISM and in general to the SCIENTISM it involves. Followers of Wittgenstein have called in question the project of justifying religious belief and shifted attention to the need for a better understanding of the nature of religious belief and of the way in which religious language actually works. Wittgenstein himself suggested that an expression of religious belief was not like an expression of opinion about a matter of fact and that religious belief was misunderstood if it was thought of as a matter of evidence. His followers have developed this suggestion in a number of ways. Norman Malcolm, for instance, defended the view that at the bottom of any system of beliefs are 'groundless beliefs' [XXXII 7; 143ff]. D. Z. Phillips has argued that the role of the philosopher in

religion was to describe it and not to sit in judgement on the rationality of religious beliefs. He has rejected, accordingly, such apologetic projects as THEODICY [XXXIV 80; XXXII 7: 103ff]. He has also insisted that the criteria of intelligibility of discourse cannot be found outside religion and are given 'by religious discourse itself' [XXXIV 131: 68]. Critics have branded this position as a new kind of FIDEISM and other philosophers have continued to investigate the rationality of religious belief, recognizing the centrality of scientific rationality [XXXIV 122].

Nonetheless, philosophers have become more concerned with the actual workings of religious language and with arriving at a better understanding of religion [XXXIV 131: 9ff, 155ff, 199ff]. They have written books on topics such as the nature of faith [XXXIV 77; 97] and RELIGION [XXXIV 151] as well as the meaning of life [XXXIV 73]. In doing so they have recognized that what they write will be well wide of the mark unless it is based upon a careful consideration of what religious believers actually do and say.

Phoenicians   [VIII]   Little was known of the mythology and religious beliefs of the peoples of Syria–Palestine in early times, until the excavations of a large area of the Syrian coastal town of Ras Shamra (Ugarit) were undertaken, when a wealth of documentary evidence was discovered [4: 19–31]. Cuneiform texts in Ugaritic [24: 129–49] contained mythological and liturgical information, and threw light on other less well attested sources on Phoenician religion (see ANCIENT NEAR EASTERN RELIGIONS), such as the *Phoenikike Historia*, attributed to the priest Sanchuniathon, whose dates are disputed but who was reputed to have lived before the Trojan war. His writings were preserved in Greek in the works of Philo of Byblos (1st century CE) and survive in an abridged version of Eusebius, writing some 300 years later. In addition to other Phoenician literary sources, further evidence was provided by Hebrew scriptures (see BIBLE) and archaeology.

The TEMPLES were obviously important, although of a simpler design than Egyptian or Mesopotamian examples; some shrines had *massebot* (standing stones). The deities had characteristics variously attributable to Egypt, Mesopotamia or Anatolia. Resheph, the war-god, 'Anath, Lady of Heaven, and Horon, god of the underworld, were widely worshipped; however, BA'AL, a war-god, was one of the most important deities and the leading god at Ugarit. The chief god of the Ugaritic pantheon was El, an old man, who was sometimes called Father of Ba'al.

Various rites, including those of animal sacrifice, occur in both Hebrew scriptures and the Ras Shamra texts, and the Jews may have adopted most offering rituals and perhaps some FESTIVALS from these people. It seems that there was a priestly hierarchy at Ugarit, and that BABYLONIAN DIVINATION and magico-medical texts (see MAGIC) had been absorbed into the religion.

The mythology included an important legend, found in several ancient Near Eastern religions, which sought to explain the annual death and revival of the vegetation [4: 27], but there is no literary indication that survival after death was part of their belief (see AFTERLIFE). However, most graves were supplied with goods and the family vaults below the houses at Ugarit were furnished and provisioned by relatives. They poured libations down a clay pipe, which ran vertically from ground level to a receptacle below, to which the dead had access through a window cut in the vault [4: 22].

It is uncertain whether features claimed to be part of the later religious tradition – sacred prostitution and infant sacrifice – were already practised as early as *c.*1300 BCE.

Pietism [XIII.B] A movement in LUTHERANISM led by P. J. Spener (1635–1705) and A. H. Francke (1663–1705). It stressed practical and inward religion rather than dogmatic theology, and was liable to narrow moral attitudes. Most Pietists remained within the church, using private meetings and education; others founded SECTS. Pietism influenced the MORAVIAN BRETHREN and the Evangelical Revival (see REVIVALISM). [181]

Pilgrimage [XXXIV] The journey taken by a pilgrim, from the Latin *peregrinus* (foreigner) extended to mean one who travels in foreign countries. Pilgrimage is a journey of some significance for the person doing the travelling, whether in common parlance, or in a 'secular' guise, as in visits to the shrines of national heroes or famous artists or composers (some would argue that modern tourism is a form of surrogate pilgrimage), or in its stricter religious context. In the latter case it is a ritual journey over a geographical area from one's domiciliary environment to a place of religious significance, undertaken for one or more of a variety of religious purposes. Such purposes include religious duty, devotional exercise, profession of faith, penitential examination, expiation of sins committed, self-discovery, the quest of a miracle, search for healing or advice and as an act of spiritual renewal. Pilgrimage is a term also used for the interior journey of the individual soul or spirit in a search for the ultimate goal of one's religious aspirations, as in the English classic *The Pilgrim's Progress* by John Bunyan (1628–88). The physical journey is a feature of many religions with centres of attraction. There are the traditionally international centres of JERUSALEM (Jewish, Christian), Mecca

(Islamic), Santiago de Compostela (Christian) [160], SARNATH (Buddhist) and the more recently international Lourdes (Christian). Varanasi (or Benares; Hindu) and Amritsar (Sikh) have exercised an attraction for Hindus and Sikhs within India for a number of centuries, as have Badrinath and Madurai for Hindus in the north and south respectively. In addition there are more localized centres such as Pandharpur (Maharashtra, India), a centre for the cult of Khandoba, an incarnation of VISHNU [123], and various sites in India and Pakistan which enshrine the relics of a Muslim saint, for example Nasrapur, near Pune. Covadonga (Asturias, Spain), is the legendary site of the first successful battle of the Christians against the Moors, and it is rapidly becoming a national shrine. In most religions pilgrimage is an optional activity, undertaken in order to accumulate merit above the normal. In ISLAM, however, pilgrimage to Mecca (HAJJ) is counted as one of the five obligations of a Muslim's religious life. The choice of a place of pilgrimage is dependent on a number of different motivations. Sometimes a place will be associated with the life of a founder of religion. Examples include Jerusalem, the place associated with the death of JESUS, Mecca, the site of a pre-Islamic cult and deliberately chosen by the founder, MUHAMMAD, while still alive; and Sarnath, believed to be the location of the BUDDHA's first sermon and today a place of pilgrimage for, among others, Japanese Buddhists. In other cases extraordinary events, such as apparitions of a departed significant person, may lead to pilgrimage status. An example of this is Lourdes, where a vision of the Blessed Virgin MARY, mother of JESUS Christ, is claimed to have taken place. Lourdes is now a point of pilgrimage specifically for the purposes of miraculous healing. In other instances sites of pilgrimage which are held to house the relics of a

significant person have become centres of international pilgrimage. One of the best known is Rome, where the main basilica is built over what is believed to be the tomb of St Peter. Santiago de Compostela, where it is claimed that the relics of St James, one of the disciples of Jesus, lie, has also been important throughout many centuries [96]. Santiago is significant for the status of the route across northern Spain (*el camino*) which leads to the city. Pilgrims to this day carry a passport which is stamped at certain locations along the way. The Temple of the Buddha's Tooth in Kandy, Sri Lanka, enjoys similar eminence, as does the Hazrat Bal mosque in Srinagar, Kashmir, which houses a hair of the Prophet Muhammad's beard. Pilgrimage is very much a popular religious phenomenon, that is, dictated by the ordinary religious adherent rather than the organizational hierarchy, which often later acknowledges the power of attraction of a pilgrimage site and institutionalizes it. The motivation to be a pilgrim is complex but one of its features must be that the devotee sees in it something of the successful achievement of the whole of life including the successful arrival at one's final goal. (*See also* PILGRIMAGES, CHRISTIAN; TIRTHA-YATRA.)

Pilgrimages, Christian [XIII.B] Journeys for devotion, penance, thanksgiving or the fulfilment of a vow. Divine grace (*see* SALVATION) is felt to be especially potent in places visited by JESUS Christ or SAINTS or MARY; where they have appeared in visions; or where their relics are kept (*see* TURIN SHROUD). Abuses of pilgrimage (both commercial and spiritual) were criticized by reformers, and pilgrimages (seen as salvation by 'works') were abolished in PROTESTANTISM. They remain popular in ROMAN CATHOLICISM and the EASTERN ORTHODOX CHURCH, especially to holy ICONS and monasteries. Major pilgrimage centres include

JERUSALEM; Rome (where SS. PETER and PAUL were martyred); Lourdes (where visions of the Virgin Mary were claimed in 1858 and where healing is thought to occur); and Walsingham in England (which from the 12th century to the REFORMATION had a replica of the Virgin Mary's house and was revived as a pilgrimage centre in the 1920s; for recent developments *see under* MARY, VIRGIN). [154 vol. II: 362–74; 183]

Pillars of Islam [XIX] The basic institutions of the Islamic law or SHARI'A, incumbent upon every sane male believer from the age of responsibility for actions, normally at puberty or at about 15 years of age. The majority community of the Sunnis (*see* SUNNA) came to number these 'pillars' as five: the profession of faith (SHAHADA); worship (SALAT); alms-giving (ZAKAT); pilgrimage (HAJJ); and fasting (SAUM). To these some added holy warfare (JIHAD). The minority community of SHI'ISM regard recognition of the IMAM as a basic principle of Islam. [77: III; 140: II]

Pleroma [XV] Although used in Greek New Testament writings meaning 'fullness' (of God) or 'fulfilment' (of the law), pleroma is primordially a technical term in the Gnostic documents (*see* GNOSTICISM), especially the writings of the Valentinian school (*see* VALENTINIANISM). The fall of Sophia from the pleroma, the divine fullness and order – implying therefore the necessary deficiency and status of chaotic disorder of the created world – is a major theme in these speculations, where the redemptive GNOSIS thus obtains a status of complete revealed knowledge in opposition to ignorance or agnostic unawareness of the self, namely the darkened status of oblivion, of unconsciousness of the true roots and origins which lay in the light world. The perfectness of the pleroma is often rendered by the use of number symbolism in these writings. [7;13;18;24a]

PL Kyodan [XXVI] Perfect Liberty Kyodan, commonly abbreviated to PL Kyodan, was formally inaugurated in Japan in 1946 by Miki Tokuchika (1900–83). Its first and central teaching is that 'life is art' (*jinsei wa geijutsu de aru*). Each person has individual, KAMI-given talents. The purpose of human life is to develop these endowments, to live selflessly, creatively and happily. When this happens, a person is at one with the *kami* (*shinjin goitsu*). This is perfect liberty. The 'arts' one may develop are limitless. This person may have a talent for singing, that one for library work, still another for golf. The important thing is to cultivate one's talents, remembering to be grateful to all who have gone before and to do what will make a contribution to the world. PL Kyodan teaches *migawari*, meaning that a member struck by sudden grief or suffering may commit it to the head of the organization, who will accept it vicariously as his own. There is also an incantation, *oya shikiri*, the utterance of which is said to give a person *kami*-like power and thus release from present problems. Members may also carry a protective AMULET. The organization is known for its computerized health records on all members.

PL Kyodan has a close historical and doctrinal connection with an earlier organization, Tokumitsukyo. It considers Kanada Tokumitsu (1863–1919) as its founding father and Miki Tokuharu (1871–1938), Tokuchika's father, as its first-generation founder. Tokuchika himself is called the second-generation founder, and the third is his son Takahito (1957–), the current leader.

With its chief centre in Osaka Prefecture, PL Kyodan claims well over 1 million members in Japan, and nearly as many in its overseas branches. [10: XII, 228–9; 13: 213–42]

Plymouth Brethren [XIII.B] A Christian (Protestant) body that originated in England through the work, in particular, of J. N. Darby (1800–82), a former priest in ANGLICANISM. The original teaching of the Brethren was strongly biblical, and influenced by CALVINISM and sometimes MILLENARIANISM. They have no separated MINISTRY, and worship centres on the 'Breaking of Bread', a simple rite intended as a memorial of JESUS Christ's Last Supper (cf. EUCHARIST). The chief types of Brethren are the 'Open' and 'Exclusive'. The Exclusives' severe standards lead them to reject many aspects of modern life and to restrict social contacts with non-Brethren, even members of their own families. [40]

Pocomania/Pukumina [III] Found in Jamaica. The second spelling is now preferred, since the translation of Poco-Mania as 'little madness' does not appear apposite. Pukumina appears in the REVIVAL continuum of Jamaican African-Caribbean cults. It is generally disapproved of by most Jamaicans. In some ways it inverts the positive values of KUMINA, and from the perspective of good citizens is seen to be deviant since its adherents use rum and smoke ganga/cannabis. They create disturbances, and disrupt the peace. There is little emphasis on the BIBLE, but much on singing and dancing. Pukumina may well use more extreme forms of healing than Kumina. Ceremonies may take place away from the villages and *obeahmen* (*see* OBEAH) may be associated with it, so that members may get access to their magical power. It has a similar pantheon of spirits to Kumina and possession by these spirits is the aim of the cult. [2; 10; 67; 86]

Poisen [XXIX] A Melanesian pidgin term for sorcery or black MAGIC directed against a chosen victim, intended to cause illness or death. A common method is to recite spells while pointing an arrow or fingernail, or to burn or destroy something belonging to the victim. Many more elaborate techniques are recorded [12]. A sorcerer, it is believed, can draw power from spirits and gods enabling him to fly, become invisible or change into animal form. He may use snakes or crocodiles to attack his victims. Serious and persistent illnesses are commonly attributed to the effects of *poisen*. Traditional healing methods include divination or mediumship intended to detect sorcerers or witches and overcome their influence. Victims may be expected to confess misdeeds (theft, adultery, etc.), so as to help identify enemies likely to be using *poisen* against them. The widely held belief in *poisen* thus helps sanction communal morality [8; 23: 137–60; 25; 29]. Accusations of sorcery have, however, been a common cause of feuds and warfare. Sorcerers are regarded as dangerous nonconformists and social outcasts, yet their ritual skills are constantly in demand for healing, rain-making, warding off evil influences, and in the form of charms and spells to ensure success in courting, gardening and hunting.

Politike [XVI] (Greek: 'politics') The *polis*, which provided the framework for the articulation and practice of religion (*see* GREEK RELIGION), was in its turn articulated by, its subdivisions given identity and ideological cohesion through, cult (*see* INSTITUTIONS (GREEK)). *Polis* religion, with its monumental temples and important festivals, became the focus of polis ideology, patriotism and propaganda which in their turn affected the religion through which they were expressed. Myth and cult, for example, were deployed in the service of 'political' needs. Panhellenic sanctuaries became involved in inter-state rivalries for their control. The Delphic oracle gave political advice (*see* MANTIKE). In the Hellenistic period a ruler cult was established, in which monarchs were honoured through divine rituals. This cult, which was a focus of ideological cohesion between Greeks and non-Greeks, expressed power relations – including gratitude and loyalty. [15; 26; 27: 834–9, 843–4; 31; 32: 23–77; 34; 35]

Polynesian Religion [XXIX] The traditional beliefs of the Polynesians (*see* PACIFIC RELIGIONS). Their myths tell how the cosmos came into being from an original emptiness (*kore*). Primal darkness (*po*) gradually gave place to sun, moon and stars. Gods (ATUA), nature and humankind emerged, each sharing in the creation drama. The uncreated source (*tumu*) is left undescribed, or personified as a great creator-god TANGAROA. (In New Zealand Maori religion, the supreme being is IO.) Foremost in creation are the primal parents RANGI (or *Atea* – sky) and PAPA (earth), their son the god TANE, who formed the first human being, and the culture hero MAUI. (Variants of these names are found among different island groups.) Other *atua* include gods with distinct activities (Tu, god of war; Rongo, god of food-cultivation; Whiro, god of the underworld). Minor gods and spirits, good and bad, feature in local stories and customs [6; 7; 15].

Best-known gods may represent renowned ancestors, chiefs who led early migrations through the Pacific and settled in the major island groups. Spiritual power and authority (MANA) flows from the gods through tribal ancestors to living chiefs and people. Themselves highly revered, chiefs have the services of priests (TOHUNGA) and prophets skilled in healing and divination, and possessors of secret knowledge of rites and incantations for controlling the powerful spiritual forces. Commoners are protected from the dangerous effects of *mana* by strict systems of *tapu* (TABU). Prayers and sacrifices take place at sacred temples and gathering-places (MARAE). Gods and spirits, involved with most affairs in life, are offered the first fruits of harvest, fishing or battle, invoked with chants on important occasions (e.g. childbirth, warfare, canoe-building, treefelling) and honoured at feasts and *kava*-drinking ceremonies. Funeral rites send the deceased's spirit (Maori: *wairua*) on its journey to Reinga, gateway to the underworld, and thence to HAWAIKI, the legendary homeland. [7; 16; 21; 22; 28; 30]

Polytheism [XXXIV] Belief in, or worship of, many GODS [43: 132; 124: 58–96], a term sometimes used pejoratively (e.g. by THEISTS, or in missionary literature). Some comparative studies erred in this way, but to evaluate what is labelled polytheism as inferior or evil is not appropriate in RELIGIONSWISSENSCHAFT or phenomenological work (*see* PHENOMENOLOGY OF RELIGION). Practices and beliefs formerly called idolatry [110: III, IV] are open to interpretation, functionally or symbolically (*see* FUNCTIONALISM; SYMBOL), as significant expressions of the human response to the complexity of the world and whatever superhuman power(s) may lie behind it. [36: 72–4; 41, especially I; 121a]

Popular Religion [XXXIV] There is no single definition of what constitutes 'Popular Religion'. Some scholars have defined it as rural in contrast to urban forms of religion, the religion of the peasant in contrast to that of the ruling classes; or, in a variation of this definition, the religion of the masses as contrasted with that of the intellectual or sophisticated classes. If, however, popular religion is seen in contrast to 'official' religion, the latter defined as religion founded on authoritative documents and propagated and maintained by religious specialists, priests or hierarchy, then the term 'popular' can apply to any layperson, whether peasant or ruling-class, who adopts beliefs and practices which may be at odds with the religious specialist's views. The term has been extended in some contexts to describe 'civil religion', by which is meant the general religious and cultural ethos generated by the elites or governing classes whereby loyalty to the state (and, conversely, disloyalty) is defined by certain moral and attitudinal norms. Popular religion can also mean the religion of ethnic or minority groups located in a context of a major and dominant religion. The term can also be applied to esoteric beliefs and practices, some of which may be only marginally identified as religious, for instance the practice of and belief in ASTROLOGY or other such pseudo-scientific practices. The term is employed sometimes as an analogue of FOLKLORE or 'folk religion' [28]. Although the concept of popular religion has been around for some time, interest in the study of religious attitudes which might be described as popular is fairly recent. From the 19th century onwards scholars, adopting a Western approach to the systematic study of religions or the study of religions as systems of beliefs and practices, would concentrate their studies on religious documents, including scriptures, dogmas and liturgies. If they acknowledged the existence of any religious behaviour parallel to these 'core' or 'mainstream' elements in a specific religious context, they might report the parallel behaviour; but they would usually refer to it in derogatory fashion, using terms such as 'superstition' or 'fetish'. The STUDY OF RELIGIONS was essentially defined in terms of the religious specialists. Thus, in referring to HINDU-ISM in the late 19th century, a writer could refer to popular religion in northern India as 'popular superstitions and usages' in contrast to 'the official creed' of 'Brahmanism ... the official religion of the Hindus', in spite of the fact that there has never been any 'official' hierarchy or organization in India which could really act in such a cohesive manner. Even a more recent scholar refers to the religion of Hindus settled in Britain as 'one of popular Hinduism, not its intellectual counterpart' [101]. A major change in more recent writing is that this writer and others do treat the religious traditions so described as having their own integrity and justification without treating them as aberrations or departures from the 'norms' as laid down by the religious specialists. Important studies have taken place with regard to British and European religious behaviour which is an alternative to that of the religious specialist [78; 38; 140; 102]. The current attitude within the study of religions has been summed up thus: 'The term "popular religion", as with its close relative "popular culture", is easier to use than to define. It is not merely the antithesis of "official religion", nor is it a systematic and unified alternative to it. Moreover, the traditional polarities used by historians and sociologists to get to the essence of popular religion – Christian and pagan, traditional and modern, rational and irrational, religious and irreligious, internal and external – have proved to be insufficiently flexible to cope with the sheer diversity of popular belief and practice' [78: 181–2]. One response to this dilemma would be to acknowledge that what has stood for the study of religions for so long, the study of 'great tradition', to the total neglect of 'little tradition' [133a] should be transformed so that the study of religions rejects false dichotomies based on the biases of those who determined what the study of religions should be from their elitist or class background and adopts a holistic approach based on the actual forms of religions as they exist [167]. (*See also* IMPLICIT RELIGION.)

Positivism [XXXII] A loosely used word commonly associated with the doctrine that the only real knowledge of the world is that provided by the methods of natural science. The phrase 'positive philosophy' was coined by Auguste Comte in the 19th century. Comte distinguished three stages in the development of the human mind. In the first stage – the 'theological' – all phenomena are supposed to be brought about by the immediate action of supernatural beings. In the second ('metaphysical') stage these beings are replaced by abstract forces. The final ('positive') state is reached when people abandon such metaphysical abstractions in favour of an empirical approach to the causes of phenomena. Comte's historical analysis into three stages is no longer considered to be sound. But other forms of positivism (e.g. LOGICAL POSITIVISM) are independent of it. An attempt to identify and account for positivism as a historical phenomenon has been made by Leszek Kolakowski. [13]

Possession (in African-Caribbean Religions) [III] Possession by the HOLY SPIRIT or by other spirits is common in Afro-Caribbean religions. In SYNCRETIC churches an indicator of their conventionality or not is whether possession is by the Holy Spirit, or by others, maybe ancestors or from a syncretic pantheon (*see* VOODOO, SANGO). In all such groups possession is culturally learned, complex and a normal part of the worship experience. Certain techniques may be used to facilitate possession. They may include rhythmic hand-clapping, dancing and hyperventilation. In some religions, like Voodoo, there may be a careful preparation of the person to be possessed. A pole may be at the centre of the dancing area of the yard or hall down which a spirit will descend. The pole may be decorated in a particular way in order to indicate which spirit is requested. Additionally, specific patterns may be drawn on the floor so the spirit can see them.

The state of possession is potentially dangerous in these churches because the devotees allow their own spirit to be displaced, so becoming vulnerable. When in a possession state the subject may well behave in an extraordinary way, defying rationality. The subject rarely retains any memory of the possession experience. [15; 56]

Prajna [XI] (Pali: *panna*) Usually translated as 'wisdom', prajna is in BUDDHISM a mental event commonly associated with insight into the true nature of things (*see* VIPASSANA), and is classed with SILA and SAMADHI as the third of the three constituents of the Buddhist path. Prajna is also the most important of the six perfections (PARAMITA) attained by the BODHISATTVA on the path to Buddhahood. Often prajna is thought to result initially from conceptual investigation into how things are, which leads eventually in meditation to direct experiential and non-conceptual understanding of the true way of things, the final ultimate truth. In ABHIDHAMMA prajna is said to be accurate and direct discernment of the flow of mental events and their objects (*dhammas*). In the PRAJNAPARAMITA literature this is said to be not the 'perfection of wisdom' (*prajnaparamita*), which is to discern the EMPTINESS of all things without exception (*see also* MADHYAMAKA) and is finally a state of consciousness which is direct non-conceptual insight into emptiness itself. In YOGACARA prajna is the flow of non-conceptual, non-dual consciousness, which is in Yogacara thought itself the ultimate reality or Thusness (*tathata*). Thus 'prajna' for each tradition of Buddhism refers to that state of mind which discerns whatever is held to be the ultimate truth, and this discernment is said finally to be not merely intellectual but a direct experiential understanding and awareness. [101: 42–5]

Prajnaparamita [XI] The 'perfection of wisdom', a term used in BUDDHISM primarily to refer to a class of MAHAYANA SUTRAS. The oldest scriptures of MAHAYANA appear to be of the perfection of wisdom type, although these scriptures continued to be produced for some centuries. Some are very long, but they include the short and popular *Heart Sutra* and *Diamond Sutra*. The scriptures contain two principal messages: (1) The EMPTINESS of all things without exception, even including the BUDDHA, NIBBANA and emptiness itself (*see also* MADHYAMAKA). Insight (VIPASSANA) into the final nature of all things, which is their emptiness, leads to the perfection of PRAJNA, wisdom. (2) The supremacy of the BODHISATTVA and his or her great compassion (KARUNA) which aims for perfect Buddhahood for the benefit of all sentient beings. This is said to leave far behind the enlightenment – personal freedom from suffering and rebirth – aimed at by the ARAHAT. The bodhisattva strives to save all sentient beings, yet this salvific activity is to be embedded in the perfection of wisdom which sees all sentient beings as empty. It was NAGARJUNA who set out to show in rational terms what this means. The perfection of wisdom is often referred to as the sixth in the list of perfections (PARAMITA) attained by the bodhisattva on his or her path to Buddhahood. It is said to be like the eyes which guide the other perfections and give them the quality of perfection. [18; 101: II]

Prakriti [XVII] In SAMKHYA philosophy, something which produces other things from itself, especially the 'original producer' or ground which gives rise to the experienced realm of mind and matter. *Samkhya* holds that the effect is inherent in the cause; so *prakriti* is also seen as the intrinsic nature of the manifest world. This is single and all-pervading, composed of the three GUNAS (modalities) in equilibrium. It transforms into the various levels of experience; these are manifold, differentiated, and specifically located, composed of varying relationships between the *gunas* in disequilibrium. *Prakriti* is related to the VEDANTA notions of BRAHMAN and MAYA (2), but it is not illusory and is sharply distinguished from the spiritual core of man (*purusha*). Man has mistakenly identified with the forms of *prakriti* but is intrinsically conscious, free, and apart from the vicissitudes of body, sense and mind. The world of multiplicity is formed by *prakriti* purely to enable man to enjoy the senses and obtain liberation by knowing himself. Just as a dancing-girl dances for the amusement of the spectator, not for herself, so the creative dance of *prakriti* is for the benefit of the onlooking spirit.

Prehistoric Religion [XXX] Those practices of *Homo sapiens* and earlier hominids (*Homo erectus*) from before recorded history which evidence from cultural remains suggests were religious, with the conjectured associated beliefs [6: LX]. Since there is, by definition, no written record of prehistory, theories about the behaviour and thought of early man must be based on reconstruction and inference from fossils, bones and artefacts. Use of the method of historical–cultural comparison [5; 9] requires caution [3: 17; 5; 10]. Most theories about beliefs assume 'the psychic unity of all mankind'.

Fragments of skulls, jaws and split bones from the earliest period (lower palaeolithic: *Homo erectus* from sites such as Ternifine in Algeria, Mauer near Heidelberg, the Trinil beds in

Java and Choukoutien near Beijing) suggest a 'cult of skulls', some concern or reverence for the dead and perhaps RITUAL cannibalism [6: I; 9: I]. Remains of human burials by *Homo sapiens* from the middle and late palaeolithic (Neanderthal in the Rhineland and similar fossils from Ehringsdorf, Saccopastore and sites in north Africa, the Middle East, Uzbekistan, Zimbabwe and Java) again give indications of ritual by the position and posture of skeletons, provision of grave goods and the use of red ochre on the corpse [1: II; 10].

The second main phase begins with hunting peoples using more specialized flint tools (from *c.*40,000 to 35,000 years ago) [1: III, IV; 2: III]. The artistic activity of the first humans of the modern type (e.g. cave paintings of the Gravettian, Solutrean and Magdalenian cultures, at sites in northern Spain and south-west France such as Altamira, Lascaux, Mas d'Azil and Niaux, but also in Italy, Sicily and the Urals) may be the key to European religion in the last Ice Age [6: VI, VIII; 8: V; 9: 46–50 & pl. 1–25; 11] as centred on human and animal fertility, although other interpretations are possible [2: 6!]. Much controversy also surrounds the significance of the so-called 'Venus figurines' in ivory, stone or clay found from the Pyrenees to the southern USSR [2: 54–8; 5; 6: VI; 8: LV; 9: 108–14 & pl. 26–33, 55–6].

With the economic revolution of the warmer Holocene (neolithic period in Europe) and especially the advent of farming [1: V], the fertility theme gains in prominence (e.g. human, mainly female, figurines and animal statuettes from the Danube region). Settlement is marked by the use of fixed shrines and temples (as in Malta and Gozo) [9: 52–9] and the megalithic tombs and monuments scattered across Europe [2: 139–44; 9: 159–88]. From the same period (i.e. before 1500 BCE), the rock-art and animal-head tools and weapons of hunting and fishing peoples of north Eurasia suggest the development of SHAMANISM in the circumpolar region [2: 144–7; 9: 135–42].

A growing and world-wide body of archaeological evidence from Africa, India, China, the Far East, Australia, the Pacific and the New World [2: VIII–XII; 3: X–XII; 7] has made it impossible to imagine that there was a single system of beliefs and practices which could properly be thought of as 'palaeolithic religion' or 'neolithic religion', still less something called 'prehistoric religion' [8; 10; 12].

Presbyterianism [XIII.B] The English-speaking version of 'Reformed Churches', deriving from the doctrine and church organization of CALVINISM. The Presbyterian hierarchy of church courts (local, regional and national) is staffed with ministers (*see* MINISTRY) and 'elders'. The Westminster Confession (*see* CREEDS) is the classic standard of faith [19: 244–7]. The EUCHARIST has traditionally been celebrated rather infrequently, but with searching preparatory services. Presbyterianism is the established church in Scotland [33] and is strong in Northern Ireland. Migrants from these two countries carried it to the USA [2], where it is now a major group of churches. Divisions within Presbyterianism have usually arisen out of disagreements over issues characteristic in Calvinistic teaching, e.g. predestination, moral and church discipline, and the proper relationship between church and STATE. The United Reformed Church combined English Presbyterians and most of CONGREGATIONALISM in 1972. [62 vol 11: 522–6; 137; 157: 1120]

Primal Man [XV] As a fundamental concept, the Primal Man is attested in several variants in connection with the 'Urmensch–Adam' speculations and the Anthropos-myth in the quite divergent Gnostic systems (*see* GNOSIS; GNOSTICISM) [13; 24a]. These doctrines of the God 'Man' are in essence the results of gnostic interpretations of the Old Testament Adam and of other mythological narratives of the Ancient East [11]. As a result of the fall of a heavenly being, there is a need to liberate the divine light-substance imprisoned in the created world. The Primal Man is consubstantial with the Highest God, and he therefore forms the divine substance (pneuma) as a kind of 'inner man' within visible man. Thus the Gnostic Primal Man, Adam, became the prototype of every man destined to be redeemed through divine knowledge, which implies awareness of his true heavenly (original) nature. Similar speculations, which are also found in the MANDAEAN evidence, were elaborated in an extremely detailed way in MANICHAEISM [33]. As divine emanation of the first creation, the Primal Man, harnessed with the elements (the sum of which constitute the higher worldly divine light-soul), takes up the struggle with the powers of darkness which are attacking the realm of light. Defeated by the forces of darkness, he falls temporarily into oblivion of his true nature. By means of the gods belonging to the second emanation, however, the Primal Man will be the first to be redeemed through an act of awareness of his real nature. This recollection of his true origins is the basic concept of the divine redemptive gnosis. Because of the mixture of light and darkness caused by the initial defeat, cosmos and man were created as salvational instruments for the imprisoned light-soul, split up as light particles. Thus the Primal Man becomes an ideal for the Gnostic believer as he is the first redeemed. It is noteworthy that the Primal Man was identified with the Zoroastrian Ohrmazd (an adaptation of AHURA MAZDA; *see* ZOROASTRIANISM) in the Eastern Manichaean documents.

The figure of the Primal Man (attested in later Islamic Gnostic doctrines, in classical or medieval hermetic writings and medieval and Renaissance esoteric writings as well) played a crucial role in the concepts of the German *Religionsgeschichtliche Schule*. (*See also* REDEEMED REDEEMER). [2; 23]

Process Theology [XIII.C] A form of theological understanding that has developed, particularly in relation to Christian belief, under the influence of the metaphysical insights of A. N. Whitehead (1861–1947) and Charles Hartshorne (b. 1897). Among its basic tenets are that to be real is to be in process (e.g. to be continually responding to the environment) and so to have a temporal dimension; that reality consists of a plurality of entities which are significantly self-creating and intimately related to each other; and that GOD is the chief exemplification of and not an exception to the ultimate metaphysical principles. Whereas Whitehead's fundamental work (*Process and Reality*, 1929) is a cosmological treatise which develops a unified understanding of reality through reflection on its constituent parts, Hartshorne has paid more attention to *a priori* arguments as a way to establish the nature and reality of God. Although there are important differences among process theologians, they generally agree that God has a temporal aspect, and that God both is maximally affected by all other entities and influences them in ways that are compatible with their freedom. In contrast to the THEISM which asserts the distinction between the world and a timeless, impassible God and the PANTHEISM which identifies God and the world, process theology advocates a panentheism in which God embraces the world and lovingly seeks to lure all things towards their maximum aesthetic satisfaction. [3a; 4; 6a; 18b; 18c]

Prodigia [xxxi] Signs received by the Romans that the normal order between gods and men (*pax deorum*, 'peace of the gods') had been disturbed. The signs took the form of events contrary to the Romans' perception of the normal – not necessarily supernatural events by modern standards. They included natural disasters, buildings struck by lightning, abnormal births, wild animals penetrating cities, the rain of blood, milk and stones, or animals speaking [10: 32–4]. Lists survive from the republican period (509–3 BCE) of such prodigies, reported year by year to the authorities so that the priests could identify the god or goddess offended and recommend appropriate measures (*remedia*) to restore the balance [8: 600–10; 15]. The evil threatened was thus to be avoided. The lists provide for us a valuable index of Roman categories of the natural and supernatural. They were no longer kept under the empire (after 31 BCE), when prodigies ceased to be part of the state's routine, and were attached rather to the lives of individuals or to great catastrophes. [13: 159–66]

Projection Theories of Religion [xiii.c] This term refers to various arguments in Western thought which maintain that 'God' is not a reality, independent of human beings, on whom the world depends for its continued existence, but a product of the human mind whose reality is only that appropriate to a mental construction, even though an unconscious invention. David Hume (1711–76) followed Thomas Hobbes (1588–1679) in suggesting in *The Natural History of Religion* (1757) that belief in gods arose when primitive people personified the unknown forces controlling nature and offered worship to them in an attempt to placate them. L. A. Feuerbach (1804–72) argued that 'God' is an illusory reality which represents to humans the qualities which they regard as ideal. His the-ory had an important influence on the hostile views of religion advanced by Karl Marx (1818–83) and Friedrich Nietzsche (1844–1900). Émile Durkheim (1858–1917), an early sociologist, saw religion as providing a mythological representation of social structures, affirming thereby the values and rules of society in a quasi-objective form. Sigmund Freud (1856–1939) treated religion as an 'illusion' and suggested that the idea of God is basically a magnified version of the image of the human parent, unconsciously produced by people in an infantile desire for protection against the harsher aspects of the real world. [11; 25]

Prophecy (Jewish and Christian) [xxii, xiii.a] Biblical revelation is based on the idea of GOD communicating to certain chosen individuals through prophetic inspiration. The content of the prophet's message and the style in which it is couched differ from prophet to prophet (*see* BIBLE). The TALMUD recognizes that the divine word interacted with the personality of the individual prophet. 'No two prophets prophesy in the same fashion' [xxii 15 Nezikin vol. iii: 593]. The Jewish tradition distinguishes between the prophetic message of MOSES and that of the other prophets. The Bible itself depicts God as speaking to Moses 'face to face and not in riddles' (*Numbers* 12: 8). The RABBIS see God as revealing himself to Moses through a clear glass, but to the other prophets through a cloudy glass. Only one of the functions of prophecy was that of foretelling the future, although this is the notion primarily associated with prophecy today. A more important prophetic role was that of a religious teacher, someone who would stand up against the corruption of the ruling class in the name of the COVE-NANT with God. Talmudic Judaism considers the age of prophecy to have come to an end with the post-exilic prophets Haggai, Zechariah and Malachi. The rabbinical sage has since superseded the prophet. [xxII 11; 14 vol. 13: 1151; 31: VII, VIII; 36: 59]

In the early CHURCH, JOHN THE BAPTIST and JESUS are variously recognized as eschatological prophets, and in general Christian prophets played a prominent part. They were recognized as mouthpieces of the HOLY SPIRIT. Some travelled from place to place. Responsible teachers insisted that the validity of the prophets' claims should be tested by the content of their utterances. The chief literary product of New Testament prophecy is the *Revelation* of John. [xIII.A 1; 11: v, 495–502]

Protestantism [xIII.B] Forms of Christianity originating in the REFORMATION. The term derives from the 'protestation' of the German princes (1529) against ROMAN CATHOLICISM. Protestants stressed the authority of the BIBLE and justification by faith (*see* SALVATION) against what they felt to be the errors of Rome. Numerous different types developed such as LUTHERANISM, CALVINISM, and many later forms. ANGLICANISM may be regarded as containing Protestant and 'reformed Catholic' elements which are not 'Roman'. Although often defined in terms of its origins (especially in Lutheranism and Calvinism), it is really necessary to characterize Protestantism in terms of its whole development. Compared with Roman Catholicism, it has generally been less sacramental (*see* SACRAMENTS) and ceremonial in WORSHIP; less subject to priesthood and more open to lay activity (*see* MINISTRY). Modern Protestantism has been exceptionally open (and vulnerable) to secular thought; and has emphasized life within the world. It nevertheless includes extremes of religious outlook, from conservative 'FUNDAMENTALISM' to extreme 'liberalism' in theology (*see* AUTHORITY). Organization varies from relatively central-

ized PRESBYTERIANISM and METHODISM to the localized churches of CONGREGATIONALISM and the BAPTISTS. Social attitudes have ranged from the conservatism of much REVIVALISM to the American SOCIAL GOSPEL. [55; 62 vol. 12: 23–38; 208: 101–33]

Providence Industrial Mission [xxVII] The first independent ETHIOPIAN-type church founded (in 1900) in Nyasaland (now Malawi), assisted by the black National Baptist Convention. John Chilembwe, its founder, was educated in the USA. He died leading the 1915 rising. His impressive 'New Jerusalem' church at the Chiradzulu headquarters was dynamited and the movement banned: it was revived in 1925 under Dr Malekebu. The larger section of the now divided church belongs to the Malawi Christian Council and Chilembwe is a national martyr. [26: 252–6]

Psychic Powers [xxIV] Special abilities ascribed to holy persons of most religions and sometimes to other exceptional individuals. They include levitation (raising the body from the ground without perceptible means of support), psychokinesis (moving objects without physical contact), precognition (knowledge of future events), telepathy (knowledge of others' thoughts), clairvoyance, and clairaudience ('seeing' and 'hearing' beyond the range of sensory perception). The last four are often classified as 'extrasensory perception' (ESP). BUDDHIST texts list powers, such as levitation, clairaudience, invisibility, and telepathy, available to those skilled in meditation. Similar powers have been attributed to Muslim and Hindu mystics, and levitation is ascribed to several Christian mystics. St Teresa of Avila (1518–82 CE), for example, describes 'raptures' in which (to her embarrassment) her body was lifted from the ground (*see* MYSTICISM (CHRISTIAN)). Current opinions on the genuineness of these phenomena vary. Laboratory tests indicate at least a slight incidence of ESP (other powers have proved harder to test), but its mechanism remains unknown. [4]

Psychology of Religion [xxxiv] The psychology of religion applies the theories and methods of psychology to the study of religious phenomena. The discipline of psychology embraces a number of different activities concerned with the behaviour, beliefs, attitudes, emotions, well-being and functioning of humans studied either as individuals or in social groups. Different branches of psychology may be concerned primarily with healing, understanding or modifying aspects of mental life. Distinctions are generally made between such fields as educational, social, occupational, counselling, depth and clinical psychology. The subject matter studied by the psychology of religion, the methods of study applied and the theories generated vary greatly according to the psychological perspective adopted. There is nothing intrinsic in the methods of psychology which is either inimical to religion or supportive of it. The task of assessing the truth claims of religion belongs to theology or philosophy, not to psychology.

Some early theories in the psychology of religion were shaped by depth psychology. In a study entitled *The Future of an Illusion* Sigmund Freud (1856–1939) saw the origins of religion in the neurotic individual's longing for a protective father figure [66; 181: vi]. Carl Gustav Jung (1875–1961) took a much more positive view of the role of religion in promoting human development and psychological well-being in his study *Modern Man in Search of a Soul* [95; 181: ix]. Two other early strands in the psychology of religion are exemplified by William James (1842–1910) [94; 181: x] and Edwin Starbuck (1866–

1947) [181: xi] James set out to describe the varieties of religious experience through the qualitative organization of personal documents. Starbuck concentrated on understanding religious conversion through the quantitative analysis of questionnaire data. Contemporary interests in the psychology of religion include the following areas of study: attitudes towards religion, conversion, faith development, gender differences in religion, personality and religion, personality and spirituality, religious experience, religious judgement, religious orientations and religious thinking.

Attitudes Studies in attitudes towards religion apply theories and methods developed by social psychology. Social psychology defines an attitude as a relatively stable underlying predisposition to respond favourably towards or negatively against something. Attitude measurement techniques are able to locate individuals on continua from most favourable to most unfavourable [90: 391–6]. For example, considerable research has concentrated on the development of attitudes towards Christianity during childhood and adolescence. Studies using a scale developed by Leslie J. Francis (b. 1947) have demonstrated the contributory influence of such factors as age, sex, personality, social class, home background, parental example, church, school and peer pressure. Attitudes to Christianity have also been shown to be related during childhood and adolescence to higher levels of personal well-being [90: viii].

Conversion Conversion generally refers to the dramatic change in religious attitudes, beliefs and behaviours following religious experience. Psychology of religion has been interested in the phenomena of conversion from the early studies of Starbuck and James. Modern studies of conversion distinguish five stages [19: iii]: (1) a period of growing awareness; (2) a period of realization; (3) a period of consideration; (4) a point of encounter; and (5) a period of incorporation. There is no clear evidence to suggest that some types of people are more susceptible to conversion than others. [90: 182–93]

Faith development James W. Fowler proposed a theory of faith development, concerned with the way in which individuals make meaning and give significance to their lives. [65; 66]. Faith is understood as a verb, as an active process. The theory is said to be empirically grounded on the basis of 'faith development' interviews during which individuals are invited to tell their life story and the story is probed by the interviewer. The theory proposes a hierarchical series of seven differentiated stages. Fowler describes these stages as follows: stage 0, infancy and undifferentiated faith; stage 1, intuitive–projective faith; stage 2, mythical–literal faith; stage 3, synthetic–conventional faith; stage 4, individuative–reflective faith; stage 5, conjunctive faith; stage 6, universalizing faith. Stage 0 is characterized by the prelanguage stage of infancy; stage 6 is characterized by such exemplars as Gandhi, Martin Luther King Jr and Mother Teresa of Calcutta. Each of Fowler's stages is characterized by a distinctive location on seven developmental 'aspects' of faith. Fowler describes these seven aspects as (1) form of logic, based on Jean Piaget; (2) perspective-taking, based on Robert Selman; (3) form of moral judgement, based on Lawrence Kohlberg; (4) bounds of social awareness; (5) locus of authority; (6) form of world coherence; and (7) symbolic function.

Gender differences Considerable evidence exists in Western Christian culture that girls and women display more signs of religiosity than boys and men [8: v] (*see* GENDER). Females are more likely to believe in God, to attend public worship and to engage in personal prayer. This finding has been variously explained in terms of differences in developmental needs and in social conditioning. More recently psychological theories have concentrated on gender differences as a personality variable. Such theories recognize that feminine and masculine characteristics are present in varying degrees in both men and women and suggest that *femininity*, rather than being female, is fundamental to religiosity.

Personality Different psychological models of personality lead to different interpretations of religion. The dimensional model of personality propounded by Hans J. Eysenck's (b. 1916) provides a good example [62]. Eysenck proposes three major dimensions of personality which can be assessed by a 90-item instrument, the 'Eysenck Personality Questionnaire'. The first dimension is extraversion–introversion: the extravert is sociable and impulsive, while the introvert is more withdrawn and reflective. The second dimension is neuroticism–stability: the neurotic is anxious and tends to worry a great deal. The third dimension is psychoticism/toughmindedness–tendermindedness: the psychotic is cold and tough. Many empirical studies have now shown that religion is unrelated both to neuroticism–stability and to extraversion–introversion. Psychoticism is the personality dimension fundamental to religiosity. There is a clear inverse relationship between psychoticism and religiosity. Eysenck's theory explains this relationship in terms of conditionability. Those who score high on psychoticism condition less easily into tenderminded social attitudes, within the domain of which religion is located [30: xii; 143: xi].

Spirituality The personality theory most exploited to interpret individual differences in spirituality is the Myers–Briggs Type Indicator (MBTI), named after Katherine C. Briggs (1875–1968) and Isabelle Briggs Myers (1897–1980). Based on the theory of Carl Jung, the MBTI is a self-completion questionnaire which sets out to assess four basic differences in personality type [125]. The first difference concerns the source of psychological energy: introverts are energized by the inner world of ideas, while extraverts are energized by the outer world of people. Introverts prefer meditation and personal prayer; extraverts prefer social worship. The second difference concerns the way we take in information: sensing people prefer data and allow the eye to inform the mind, while intuitive people prefer ideas and allow the mind to inform the eye. Sensing people may be inspired by the detailed exegesis of scripture, while intuitive people may be inspired by abstract association of ideas. The third difference concerns the way we make decisions: thinking people prefer objective logic, while feeling people prefer subjective values. Thinking people may be inspired by theological reflection, while feeling people may be inspired by social action. The fourth difference concerns the way we relate to the outer world: perceiving people prefer a flexible, spontaneous approach, while judging people prefer an ordered and planned approach. Perceiving people may prefer spontaneous worship, while judging people may prefer ordered liturgy [47].

Religious experience After William James's pioneering work in *The Varieties of Religious Experience* [94], renewed interest in the field was stimulated when Alister Hardy (1896–1985) established the Religious Experience Research Unit in Oxford. Much of the work of the centre under the directorship of Edward Robinson [137; 138] concentrated on describing and classifying reports of religious experience, elicited through the question: 'Have you ever been aware of or been influenced by a presence or a power, whether you call it God or not, which is different from your every-

day self?' Employing the same question among a random sample of the adult population in Nottingham, David Hay reported that 62% of people said they had had this type of experience at least once or twice in their lives [74]. The survey conducted by Andrew Greeley in the USA in 1973 found that 35% of American adults claimed to have had a religious experience [74].

Religious judgement Fritz K. Oser proposed a developmental theory of religious judgement, concerned with the way in which individuals make decisions which involve religious dimensions [126; 65]. The theory is based on a series of semi-clinical interviews which explored the responses of individuals to 'religious dilemma' stories, narratives prompting decisions which involve religious issues. The theory proposes five stages. Each stage is qualitatively different. Individuals develop from one stage to the next. At stage one God interferes actively and unmediated in the world. At stage two God remains external but can be influenced. At stage three God is pushed out of the world. At stage four subjects surrender again to God's salvation plan. At stage five subjects still adopt a religious standpoint but no longer feel the need to be grounded in a salvation plan. The universality of these stages has yet to be established.

Religious orientations Attempts have been made to characterize and measure different ways of being religious. Gordon W. Allport (1897–1967) developed measures to distinguish between extrinsic and intrinsic ways of being religious [181: v]. The extrinsic orientation was religion as a means to self-serving ends, while the intrinsic orientation values religion for itself. Bernard Spilka uses the terms consensual and committed religion to make a similar distinction. C. Daniel Batson adds a third orientation which he characterizes 'religion as a quest', which is open-ended and questioning [15]. Scales measuring these orientations continue to make an important contribution to the empirical psychology of religion.

Religious thinking Ronald Goldman proposed a developmental theory of religious thinking, building on the developmental psychology of Jean Piaget [69; 65]. Piaget suggests that the individual's ability to think logically develops through a hierarchical sequence of stages from intuitive through concrete to abstract. Goldman interviewed 200 children between the ages of six and fifteen. The interviews were stimulated by three Bible stories and three 'projective' pictures. Projective techniques encourage the children to project their own feelings and ideas on to the characters in the pictures. On the basis of these interviews Goldman describes five stages of religious thinking which he characterizes as: (1) intuitive religious thinking; (2) intermediate between intuitive and concrete religious thinking; (3) concrete religious thinking; (4) intermediate concrete–abstract religious thinking; and (5) abstract religious thinking. Subsequently John H. Peatling attempted to translate Goldman's theory into a questionnaire test to enable testing of much larger samples of children than could be tested through individual interviews [157: III].

Pudgalavada [XI] The view of certain ancient BUDDHIST schools that the 'person' (Pali: *puggala*; Sanskrit: *pudgala*) has ultimate ontological status. The view was characteristic of the Vatsiputriya-Sammatiyas, who split from the Sthaviras (*see* MAHASANGHIKA; THERAVADA) in *c.*3rd century BCE, but was rejected by all other non-Mahayana and Mahayana schools as drastically compromising the fundamental Buddhist teaching of 'no self' (ANATTA). According to the Pudgalavadins, an enduring 'person' was necessary to explain, among other things, the mechanism of KARMA

and rebirth. This mysterious 'ineffable' (*avaktavya*) person was said to be neither the same as nor different from the five aggregates. The writings of the Pudgalavadins themselves do not survive and our understanding of their position is based on the refutations of it by other Buddhist schools. Although *pudgalavada* must be regarded as uncharacteristic of mainstream Buddhist thought, according to HUSAN-TSANG over a quarter of the Buddhist monks in India in the 7th century belonged to the Sammatiya school. [16: 122–34]

Pueblo Religions [v] A term generally used to designate a large group of Amerindians, primarily agriculturists, of various linguistic families, living in the south-western USA and inhabiting characteristic communal dwellings of adobe (unburnt, sun-dried brick). The group includes Tamoan, Keresan, Zunian and HOPI peoples. Central religious features include an emergence-type cosmogonic myth (*see* CREATION MYTHS), in which Spider Grandmother (or a similar figure) leads the primal people out to the earth's surface and, through various wanderings, to their new home. Maintenance of a fragile agricultural economy requires sustained cooperation between supernaturals (Sky-Father, Earth-Mother, Mother-Corn, the KACHINAS) and humankind. The religio-agricultural calendar (CALENDAR ROUND) prescribes the performance of specific dances, especially the corn and snake dances, to ensure fertility and collective well-being, with secret societies usually taking important roles [24]. Conception of the AFTERLIFE is often vague; the SOUL is believed to linger briefly in this world after death and then to return through the place of emergence to the underworld. [16]

Puja [XVII] (worship) Worship in HINDUISM is mainly of three kinds:

temple worship, domestic worship and various forms of communal worship. A temple is the home of a deity who has been installed in the inner sanctum by an act of consecration. The consort of the deity and other associated deities will usually also be represented somewhere within the temple. VISHNU and his AVATARAS, most commonly RAMA and KRISHNA, are usually represented by images (*murti*), as is the Goddess in her various forms, but SHIVA is in most cases represented by a LINGA, a black stone in the shape of the male organ, set often in a *yoni* which takes the form of the female organ. The deities are served by priests (*pujari*) – not necessarily Brahmans – who carry out a programme of worship at set times of the day beginning before dawn. The deity will be woken, bathed and fed; hold court and have a rest; and finally be returned to bed, all this to the accompaniment of ceremonies such as *ar(a)ti* (a service of light), the ringing of bells and the sounding of a conch, religious music, hymns, prayers and offerings of various kinds. The individual worshipper's act of worship is private: he will offer obeisance to the deity (*pranama*), say prayers and make an offering, usually receiving back *prasada*, a piece of food consecrated by the deity, which is considered a great blessing. The worshipper comes to the temple primarily to obtain a *darshana* (sight, experience) of the deity and to pay homage, but there may also be a specific petition or request relating to worldly matters that the worshipper hopes the deity will grant. Domestic worship is a feature of most households, where there is usually an area set aside and maintained in a state of ritual purity. There, an image of the household's ISHTADEVA, or chosen deity, is often kept, to whom prayers are said and offerings made, sometimes together with an *ar(a)ti* ceremony. There is a wide variety of domestic worship, depending on the status and religious affiliations of the household: a well-to-do family might have a Brahmin priest conduct a domestic ritual involving a fire-oblation (*homa* or *havana*), or a family might create geometrical designs on the ground with different coloured powders (*yantra*) to symbolize their *ishtadeva*. Pious individuals within the household may have their own private patterns of worship, starting the day with ritual ablutions and reciting prayers, for example. Communal worship in the form of hymn-singing (*kirtana*) is the characteristic form of BHAKTI devotion and is widely practised, especially in sectarian gatherings where it is usually accompanied by an *ar(a)ti* ceremony and the distribution of *prasada*. Another form of communal worship is the sponsored *katha*, recitation of a religious text, for which priests are hired to recite and the audience is invited. The sponsoring of such recitations is meritorious, but usually the texts themselves state what specific benefits can be expected both for its hearers and for the sponsors. Finally, a quite different style of worship is found in villages with regard to the *gram devatas*, the village gods, where it is common to find a priest, rarely of a high CASTE, becoming possessed by a deity and acting as the medium through which the deity speaks to the villagers, usually about remedies for their specific problems and illnesses, and what the deity expects from them in return for such help. Possession sometimes also occurs to particularly susceptible devotees during *kirtana*, communal hymn-singing. [5: II; 132]

Punna [XI] (Pali; Sanskrit: *punya*) In BUDDHISM the word *punna* refers to those actions and deeds performed by an individual which are regarded as auspicious, skilful and meritorious, and will bear good results, creating opportunities to further the practice of the BUDDHA's teaching (DHAMMA) both in the present and in the future. Meritorious acts include making devotional offerings of flowers, incense and candles, giving alms to members of the SANGHA (*see* DANA), taking the precepts (*see* SILA), going for refuge (*see* TISARANA) and practising meditation (BHAVANA). Often making merit is seen as a particular focus of lay Buddhist practice; the attainment of final enlightenment is commonly thought of as beyond the reach of the ordinary layperson who thus hopes by the performance of meritorious actions to bring about conditions favourable to the gaining of enlightenment in some future rebirth. But actions performed out of calculated self-interest are precisely not meritorious, and all Buddhist traditions emphasize the efficacy of 'the transference of merit' which is achieved by dedicating the merit of one's actions to benefit all beings. [34: 42–4]

Puranas [XVII] In Indian tradition, a class of sacred compositions dealing with ancient (*purana*) times and events. There are 18 principal Puranas, which date from the Gupta period (beginning of the 4th century CE) onwards. These, it has been said, form part of the real scriptures of the HINDUS, in the sense that they have been available to and known by low-CASTE people, whereas the VEDA texts were the preserve of the BRAHMANS [12: 301]. The Puranas are arranged in three divisions: (1) those which exalt the god BRAHMA; (2) those which exalt VISHNU; and (3) those which exalt SHIVA. Among the more important are, in the first division, the *Bhavishya Purana*; in the second, the *Vishnu* and the *Bhagavata Puranas*; and in the third, the *Agni Purana* (or the *Vayu Purana* which sometimes takes its place). Although in their received form they date from the Gupta period, they embody much legendary material of a greater age [12: 302] and are an important source of background

data for the study of popular HINDU-ISM. [92: 15–18]

Puritanism [XIII.B] Originally an English 16th-century movement to 'purify' the Church of England. At first Puritans attacked vestments (*see* LITURGICAL DRESS) and ceremonies. Some, however, adopted PRESBYTERIANISM and hoped to alter the English church to this system. Others accepted bishops and the Book of Common Prayer, with modifications. Puritanism was an element in the English Civil Wars (1642–8) but after the restoration of the Church of England (*see* ANGLICANISM) in 1660–2 many Puritans were expelled from the church and persecuted until they achieved toleration in 1689 (*see* BRITAIN, CHRISTIANITY IN). Puritans were among the pioneers of the North American colonies [2: VIII–X; 144], and have had lasting effects on US religion and society. 'Puritan' is also loosely used for severe and narrow moral views on e.g. SEXUALITY. [62 vol.12: 102–6; 157: 1146; 172; 178]

Purohita [XVII] An important religious office among the ancient Aryans (*see* INDO-EUROPEANS), that of chief priest, whose function was to perform the sacrifices which maintained well-being and secured victory in battle. He was also the 'chaplain' to the royal court, who might on occasions be required to advise the king. [12: 34, 91, 101]

Purva [XX] The 'Previous' (*purva*) texts are a body of literature accepted by all sects of the JAIN religion as forming the basis of their scriptural tradition. Only the names of these texts survive and their contents are universally regarded as lost. From a philological point of view, it is questionable whether the *Purvas* existed in the form claimed for them. [4: 59–60]

Pyramids [VI] Our term 'pyramid' is derived from the Greek name *pyr* *amis*; the Egyptian word, however, was *mer*, perhaps meaning 'place of ascension' [7: VII, 284]. The pyramids (the most famous are at Gizeh) were royal tombs, built for most rulers of the Old (*c.* 2700–2200 BCE) and Middle Kingdoms (1980–1786 BCE). Each was part of a complex which also included a valley building, causeway and mortuary temple where the king's burial rites and subsequent mortuary rites were performed. Developed from the step pyramid (*see* IMHOTEP), the true pyramid probably symbolized a 'ramp' to facilitate the deceased king's ascent to heaven [7: VII, 290]. Associated with the solar cult (*see* RE'), the pyramid remained exclusively a royal burial-place, and magical texts (*see* FUNERARY PRACTICES) [10] were inscribed inside later pyramids to provide assistance for the king's victory over death (*see* MAGIC (ANCIENT EGYPTIAN)). The construction of such complexes exhausted economic resources but promoted a strong political and religious unity.

Q

Qadi (Cadi) [XIX] The judge in
ISLAM, functioning in the SHARI'A
courts and theoretically acting as
judicial representative of the CAL-
IPH. Normally he was a Muslim male
of good character and recognized
learning. Although his jurisdiction
embraced both civil and criminal
law, in practice the state took over
most of the latter sphere. In modern
times, the possibility of appeal from
the qadi's judgements has been
introduced in most Islamic countries. The competence of his court
has been generally reduced to first-
instance adjudication, and some
countries have abolished the Shari'a
courts altogether. [20 s.v.; 38
'Kāḍī'; 48: 148–54; 80: 339–50;
142: 141–5]

Qadiris [XIX] A SUFI ORDER which
traces its origins to 'Abd al-Qadir al-
Jilani in 12th-century Baghdad and
which spread throughout the Muslim world. It was through the Qadiri
SHAIKH Sidi al-Mukhtar al-Kunti
(1729–1811) that organized Sufism
penetrated into west Africa and led
to the establishment of many sub-
branches. The JIHAD leader, 'Uthman dan Fodio (1754–1817), was a
Qadiri, as were many of his followers
(*see* AFRICA, ISLAM IN). The Murids
of Senegal, founded by Amadu
Bamba (d. 1927), are a branch of
the Qadiris, whose international network of *zawiyas* now extends to
many of the major cities of Europe
and America, where Murids engage
in petty trade and commerce. [63;
90; 125]

Qiyama [XIX] Resurrection in
ISLAM, followed by the last judgement. Islamic eschatology posits a
last hour, with the end of the world
preceded by disturbances on earth
such as the appearance of ANTI-
CHRIST. People will be physically
raised from the grave by the angel
Israfil, rounded up, and judged by
God; their good and bad deeds will
be weighed in a balance. Only the
Prophet MUHAMMAD, it is generally
recognized, may intercede for
human souls, although the QUR'AN
is rather vague about this. Later,
however, popular Islam allowed the
intercession of a host of local saints
and holy men (WALI). The judged
souls must pass across the narrow
bridge which spans hell; sinners will
fall into the depths, but the saved
will enter paradise (*see* AKHIRA).
Some authorities admit also an earlier, limited judgement of humankind in the tombs, with the
possibility of punishment or bliss
there, before the resurrection and
judgement proper. [38 'Kiyāma';
48: 51–3; 71: 197–250]

Quakerism (History of) [XIII.B]
Quakerism grew from its origins in
Britain in the 1650s (*see* FRIENDS,
RELIGIOUS SOCIETY OF) through the
period of restoration Quakerism,
benefiting from the Act of Toleration in 1689. By the beginning of the
18th century, the early leaders were
dead and Robert Barclay (1648–90)
had systematized Quaker theology in
his influential 'Apology'. Barclay differed from earlier Quaker thinking in
at least one important respect: he
claimed that people were only given

one opportunity to 'turn to the Light' and experience regeneration [73: 82]. In contrast to the first generations of Friends, this quietist period was one of withdrawal from the world and disciplined waiting [161: 121]. Numbers fell, a trend exacerbated by the strict enforcement of rules – Friends were disowned for marrying non-Quakers or for owning a piano, for example.

Victorian Quakerism saw a variety of changes [98: I]. In the first half of the 19th century, Friends became increasingly worldly. Denied university places and renowned for their honesty, many had become successful industrialists, and were influenced by the EVANGELICALISM of their ANGLICAN counterparts. The Quaker 'peculiarities' (endogamy, standardized dress, and the use of 'thee' and 'thou' as modes of address) were optional by 1860. Some Friends began to question the doctrine of the inward Light as unscriptural.

By the end of the 19th century, however, Quakers in Britain had adopted a liberal theology which accommodated BIBLICAL CRITICISM and which celebrated reinterpretations of Fox's teachings and the concept of the inward Light [98: 32–43]. In the 20th century, this liberalism has become increasingly open and individualized. In some MEETINGS the influence of the BIBLE is small, and some have described British Quakerism as pluralistic and 'post-Christian'. The idea of 'that of God within everyone' is used to define British Quaker belief, although its interpretation is individual. The unprogrammed meeting has been retained. Membership numbers are stable at around 18,000 in 500 local meetings, with the vast majority entering the group as adults [62 vol. 12: 129–33].

In America, following the early concentration of FRIENDS' efforts in the HOLY EXPERIMENT in Pennsylvania and elsewhere on the eastern seaboard, the Revolution marked the end of Quaker political and demographic influence. The expansion of settlements across North America brought with it an expansion of Quaker traditions [161: 153].

The first major schism was in 1827 in the Philadelphia Yearly MEETING, between the mystical interpretation of Quakerism, epitomized by the views of Elias Hicks (1748–1830), and the more Bible-centered views of Joseph John Gurney (1788–1847) [97]. Other Yearly Meetings also divided along these 'Hicksite' and 'Orthodox' lines [108: XII]. In 1843, John Wilbur (1774–1856) clashed with Gurney over the move of the Orthodox group away from quietist principles to more evangelical ones [108: XIII]. Wilburite Yearly Meetings were joined by other 'Conservative Friends' in the 1870s, when many Orthodox Yearly Meetings adopted 'programmed' meetings and a pastoral system and began to push for toleration of the outward sacraments [83: 130–7]. The small number of Conservative Meetings are still part of the unprogrammed tradition. Most of the remaining Orthodox Yearly meetings adopted the Richmond Declaration of Faith in 1887 [83: 137–9]. This group of Yearly Meetings went on to form an umbrella association called Five Years Meeting, later Friends United Meeting (FUM) [74]. Some of these meetings are programmed, most are not. The old Hicksite Yearly Meetings, unprogrammed and generally liberal, are mainly affiliated to the umbrella organization of Friends General Conference (FGC), while some, as part of reunited Hicksite/Orthodox Yearly Meetings, are jointly affiliated with FUM and FGC. Other Yearly Meetings have together formed Evangelical Friends International (EFI). There are also unaffiliated Yearly Meetings of both liberal and evangelical dispositions. The total number of Friends in North America is around 120,000, of whom half are in FUM-affiliated Meetings [74].

The pattern of Quakerism outside Britain and North America is largely the result of incidental or explicit mission work, or the result of expatriate Friends forming local Meetings. Quakerism in the rest of Europe is numerically small at around 2,000. The Ireland Yearly Meeting began in the 17th century, but continental Quakerism is generally more recent. There are also unprogrammed Yearly Meetings in Australia and New Zealand. Mission work by FUM and EFI and their predecessor bodies, together with missionaries from British Quakerism's evangelical period, has resulted in meetings in various parts of the Middle East and Asia, and very large constituencies in Africa and in Central and Southern America. A few of these meetings are unprogrammed, but most are part of the pastoral and programmed tradition. With 45,000 Friends in Africa, and some 25,000 in Central and Southern America, the unprogrammed tradition of Friends is, worldwide, numerically the smaller of the two. [74]

Quechua Religion [xxiii] The Quechua of southern Peru divide the universe into three great estates: Hanaqpacha, the upper world, in which are found Christian deities, the saints and spirits of the dead; Kaypacha, this world, in which the entire gamut of spirits and supernatural beings are located; and Ukhupacha, the inner world, inhabited by little people. Three mythological eras are distinguished: a dark era of the spirits, lit only by the moon; a rebellious era of the *ñawpa*, who are blinded and dried by the newly risen sun; and the era of man, which provides a range of vacillating lights.

Quechua worship is directed to the spirits inhabiting the mountains and earth, whose existence is independent of their material habitats.

The system in general is structured around the two great deities – Roal, the creator spirit who occupies the top of the hierarchy, and Pachamama, who permeates the system from top to bottom, being linked with femininity and the fertility of the earth. Quechua gods are intimately related to everyday activities and intervene directly in determining the success or failure of such activities in accord with individual conduct and the quality of relationships to the gods. [13; 22]

Quest of the Historical Jesus [xiii.c] A phrase used to describe attempts to determine the actual character of the teaching, faith and events of the life of JESUS. The phrase comes from the title of the English translation of the highly influential treatment of the history of the quest from H. S. Reimarus (1694–1768) to W. Wrede (1859–1906) by Albert Schweitzer (1875–1965), which first appeared in 1906. After criticizing the unsatisfactoriness of previous attempts to delineate the historical understanding of Jesus, Schweitzer offered his own interpretation of Jesus' thought as dominated by the expectation of the imminent arrival of God's kingdom. This, however, was controversial: and the main significance of his study was to highlight the manner in which interpreters moulded their pictures of Jesus according to their own convictions. The 'quest', nevertheless, has continued with some vigour in spite of the increasing appreciation of the relative paucity of the source materials and the fact that they have been recorded to support some theological conviction about the significance of Jesus. [7; 18a; 30]

Quetzalcoatl [xxv] The feathered serpent, one of the most powerful and complex gods in MESOAMERICAN RELIGIONS. Called Kukulcan in the post-CLASSIC MAYAN culture, he appears both as a major celestial

creator god and as intimately identified with a historical priest-king,
Topiltzin Ce Acatl Quetzalcoatl (*see*
TOPILTZIN QUETZALCOATL) [I: VII].
In the clearly mythical traditions
Quetzalcoatl, one of the four children of the divine pair, OMETEOTL,
arranges the original universe and
participates in the creation and
destruction of several of the world
ages (*see* CEMANAHUAC). In a number of sources, he is depicted as the
victim of his brother Tezcatlipoca,
the smoking mirror (*see figure 10*). As
the creation of the cosmos unfolds,
Quetzalcoatl invents agriculture and
the calendar, and restores human
life through a cosmic descent into
the underworld where he outwits the
lord of the dead, Mictlantecuhtli [2:
v; 14: 38–40]. This great creative
force also took the form of Ehecatl,
the wind god [19: 107], and Tla-
huizcalpantecuhtli, the morning star
(Venus). Sculpted and painted
images of Quetzalcoatl appear in a
number of ceremonial cities, including Teotihuacan [16: 21–8], Tula,
Xochicalco, Cholula, Tenochtitlan
and Chichen Itza, where he is
usually associated with the central
shrine (*see* MESOAMERICAN CITY).
Historically, Quetzalcoatl was the
patron of the Toltecs and he
inspired Topiltzin Ce Acatl Quetzalcoatl in his priestly rituals and cultural inventions. Quetzalcoatl
became the patron deity of CHOL-
OLLAN and the patron god of the
Aztec schools of higher learning, the
Calmecacs. Quetzalcoatl's cult was
taken by the Toltecs into the Yucatan Maya area during the 10th century and revitalized in the cities of
Chichen Itza and Mayapan. [4: VI]

Qumran [XIII.A] A site on the
north–western shore of the Dead
Sea which was occupied from *c.*130
BCE to 68 CE. The remains of communal buildings there, especially a
number of large MIKVEH, suggest
that the occupants were particularly
concerned with ritual purity. Minor
industrial facilities within the communal compound together with
agricultural installations nearby suggest the community may have been
nearly self-sufficient. The north–
south alignment of the graves
implies a particular eschatological
hope found in the BIBLE that final
salvation would come from the
north. In 11 caves nearby, some of
which were immediately adjacent to
the site, the remains of over 850
manuscripts have been found (*see*
DEAD SEA SCROLLS). These seem to
have been either brought to the site
by those who joined the community
there or written at the site itself. The
occupants of the site are commonly
identified with the ESSENES. [11: v,
590–4]

Qur'an (Koran) [XIX] The sacred
book of ISLAM. Islamic dogma holds
that the Qur'an is the uncreated
word of God, hence pre-existent to
the world and to man, whose archetype is laid up in heaven. This was
released to the Arabs, in the Arabic
language, through the transmission
of the Prophet MUHAMMAD (*see*
NABI), in a series of revelations,
eventually regarded as a message for
all mankind and replacing imperfect
and corrupt previous versions of the
heavenly scripture. But the message
is God's alone, without any human
interference [70]. The Qur'an text is
sacred in itself, and a good Muslim
should be ritually pure (TAHARA)

Figure 10
Ehecatl-Quetzalcoatl and Tezcatlipoca

before touching a copy. In its present, canonical form, the Qur'an seems to date from the collection of materials made in the CALIPHATE of 'Uthman (644–56). In form, it is about the length of the New Testament (*see* BIBLE), and is conventionally divided into *suras* or chapters revealed at Mecca or at Medina, although in fact many *suras* are composite and contain elements from both periods. The earlier *suras* proclaim the basic message of the unity of God (ALLAH); of the thanksgiving and obedience due to him from mankind; of the working of God in history from the creation (KHALQ) to the last days; and of judgement (QIYAMA) and the afterlife (AKHIRA). The later, Medinan *suras* contain a considerable number of divine prescriptions on legal and social topics, all of these embodied in the law of Islam or SHARI'A [summary: 67 s.v.; selected translations: 71: 17–75]. Much of the Qur'an is assonantal in style and language, and is recited for liturgical or devotional purposes in a particular manner of cantillation (*tajwid: see* MUSIC (IN ISLAM)). The question whether the Qur'an, being God's literal word and specifically revealed in Arabic, could be translated much exercised Muslim scholars in the past. Gradually, interlinear translations of other Islamic languages were allowed, and now independent translations exist in all the major languages of the world. [General surveys: 29; 38 'Kur'an'; 48: 61–5; 67 s.v.; 107: II; 108; 137; on exegesis: 12; 46].

R

Rabbi [xxii] Originally this was the title of an ordained Palestinian sage in the early rabbinical period, meaning 'My Master' [63: 325]. In later JUDAISM it became the general term for a halakhic (see HALAKHAH) authority or teacher of the oral TORAH [14 vol. 13: 1445]. The present ordination of rabbis involves an examination on selected topics of Jewish law by an ordained rabbi, who may then ordain the successful candidate (semikhah). This ordination differs from that practised in the first few centuries CE, which was thought to go back in an unbroken chain to MOSES. The chain has, in fact, been broken and so ordination today does not confer the special status on its recipients that attaches to the older type of ordination. The rabbi in Judaism is not a priest, but primarily a teacher and spiritual guide. [11; 70: 207]

Radhasoami Satsang [xvii] (The Radhasoami True Fellowship) A NEW RELIGIOUS MOVEMENT that has spread from northern India to the USA, UK, South Africa and elsewhere, garnering over $1\frac{1}{2}$ million adherents worldwide. It was founded in Agra in 1861 by Swami Shiv Dayal Singh, who propounded a new form of spiritual practice, SURAT SABD YOGA, that could be adopted by modern businessmen, housewives and administrators. The term *Radhasoami* literally means the Lord (*svami*, or *soami*) of Radha, the consort of the HINDU god KRISHNA, but since the movement does not believe in a God with anthropomorphic characteristics, the term

Radhasoami is construed to mean the master of spiritual energy. In some branches of the movement *Radhasoami* is regarded as the name of God and the name of the highest level of consciousness, and the very uttering of the word conveys spiritual power.

Based on the teachings of the medieval Hindu SANT TRADITION, Radhasoami and other modern SANT movements (collectively known as SANT MAT) are organized around several central concepts: GURU, the notion that ultimate reality and absolute authority are located in a person with whom one can have a redemptive relationship; *bhajan* (literally 'music'), the idea that the self can be transformed into its ethereal essence, a divine harmony, through love and meditation practices; SATSANG ('the true fellowship'), the concept of communal organization that provides an alternative to Hindu and Western forms of social structure; *seva*, or service, an understanding of social responsibility and ethics based on obedience to the guru; and *bhandara*, the idea that time and space are centred in great communal gatherings held at the headquarters of each branch of the movement. New groups emerge when the death of a guru produces more than one successor.

Today there are some 20 branches of the movement, each of them consisting of a residential community, led by a guru, and a large network of affiliated members, many of whom have constructed their own neighbourhood worship centre (a *satsang ghar*). The largest – the Beas branch

– has built a spiritual city near Amritsar in Punjab. Led by Maharaj Gurinder Singh, nephew of the previous master, Charan Singh, it also has large followings in Delhi, Bombay and abroad. One of the most significant offshoots of the Beas branch, the Ruhani Satsang ('Spiritual Fellowship') was founded in Delhi by Kirpal Singh in 1948 and is currently led by his grandson, Sant Rajinder Singh. It does not, however, refer to itself as Radhasoami nor use the word in its religious terminology. The oldest branch of the movement, Soamibagh, is located at the site of the founding guru's meditation garden near Agra, where a colossal cathedral-like marble tomb in honour of the founding guru has been under construction for most of the 20th century. Since 1949 Soamibagh has had no single acknowledged spiritual leader. Across the road from Soamibagh is its rival community, Dayalbagh, led by Master M. B. Lal, former head of Lucknow University. During the 1930s and 1940s Dayalbagh's prosperity grew through an enormous complex of industries, shops and model farms and dairies developed through a kind of spiritual socialism. In recent years Dayalbagh has established several colleges and a university supported by India's central government. Smaller branches of Radhasoami are located at Huzuri Bhavan in Agra, in honour of the second guru at Agra, Rai Saligram; the Dhara Sindhu Pratap Ashram in Gwalior, founded by Swami Shiv Dayal Singh's brother; the Manavta Mandir in Hoshiarpur, led for years by a guru, Faqir Chand, who renounced the power of guruship; and Radhasoami Bagh in Benares, which reveres the third guru at Agra, Brahm Sankar Misra, the only Radhasoami master to come from the priestly CASTE.

The leaders of the various branches of the Radhasoami Satsang tend to be, like its founder, urban office-workers and administrators from India's traditional merchant castes and classes (*khatri* and *arora* in Delhi and the Punjab; *bania* and *sindhi* in the area near Bombay). Other leaders have been businessmen, professors and military officers. Many of the followers (especially in the Beas branch) are urban workers and villagers from *chamar* and other lower castes. Increasingly the followers in the UK, USA and elsewhere in the West include immigrants who find in the Radhasoami fellowship a more accessible and modern form of spirituality than is provided by traditional Hindu rituals and customs. [6; 52; 60; 65; 67; 115; 134]

Raëlians [xxvɪɪɪ] An 'atheistic religion' founded in 1974 by a French racing-car journalist born as Claude Vorilhon (1946–), renamed Raël, after an extraterrestrial had appeared to him and invited him into his craft to explain about the Elohim, 'our fathers from space', who wanted him to pass on messages and build an embassy where they (the Elohim) could meet human political leaders. Around 20,000 believers (mainly in France, Quebec and Japan) are expected to practise Sensual Meditation daily. It is claimed that Rael's mother was inseminated by the Elohim in a UFO (Unidentified Flying Object). [5: 200–1; 42: 734–5; 71]

Ragnarok [vɪɪ] The Icelandic account of Ragnarok, meaning the 'doom (or twilight) of the powers', comes in the Prose EDDA [28: 52–8] based largely on one poem, *Voluspa*, in the Poetic EDDA [21: 1–13]. First comes a season of terrible cold, when men forsake old loyalties and the rule of law; then Heimdall's horn warns of a host of giants and monsters approaching, led by the treacherous LOKI, along with FENRISWOLF and the World-Serpent. ODIN and his army from VALHALLA come out with the AESIR to do battle, but neither side is victorious; the wolf devours Odin, to be killed in turn by

Odin's son Vidar; THOR and the Serpent slay one another, as do Heimdall and LOKI. A fire-giant, Surt, sets the world ablaze, and it finally sinks beneath the sea. This story may be based on vague folk-beliefs about the world's ending, influenced by an ancient tradition of a battle between gods and giants, experience of volcanic eruptions and Christian teaching concerning the last judgement [3: 202–10; 4: 188–95]. According to the unknown poet, earth rises again cleansed and green from the sea, while the tree YGGDRASIL survives, a shelter for the sons of the gods and one human pair, who begin a new age.

Rahit [XXXIII] The SIKH Rahit is the code of discipline which all who enter the KHALSA order must vow to observe. According to tradition the Rahit was promulgated by GURU GOBIND SINGH when he inaugurated the Khalsa in 1699 (*see* GURUS). The first RAHIT-NAMA or recorded code appears almost half a century later. Others followed during the period 1750–1850, all claiming to reproduce the Guru's actual words. The *rahit-namas* must surely incorporate a nucleus which derives directly from the 10th Guru, but amid the varying *rahit-nama* versions it is difficult to identify this nucleus with assurance [11: 59–60]. It is clear that much of the Rahit evolved during the course of the 18th century, reflecting such features of the PANTH's life as its predominantly JAT (*see* CASTE) constituency and its conflicts with Muslim enemies [26: 50–3]. An authorized version was eventually issued in 1950 by the Shiromani Gurdwara Parbandhak Committee under the title *Sikh Rahit Maryada*. This document specifies correct GURDWARA procedure, supplies approved RITUALS, and defines personal observances in careful detail [30: 79–86]. The latter include an obligation to bear the 'FIVE Ks' (uncut hair, dagger or sword, breeches, comb and iron

bangle) and to avoid four particular sins (cutting one's hair, eating meat killed in the Muslim manner, adultery and smoking) [19: IV; 35: IV]. Anyone who infringes the Rahit is called a *tanakhahia* and may be required to make amends by fine or penance. If the breach is serious the offender is branded a PATIT (apostate). [29: 30–4, 114–15]

Rahit-nama [XXXIII] A *rahit-nama* is a manual which records any version of the SIKH Rahit (the KHALSA code of conduct) [29: 30–40]. The original Rahit is attributed to GURU GOBIND SINGH (1675–1708) (*see* GURUS) and the early *rahit-namas* all claim to reproduce his actual words. Although there is considerable uncertainty concerning sequence and dates it seems that the earliest formal *rahit-namas* emerged during the mid-18th century. These were prose collections of miscellaneous injunctions attributed to Chaupa Singh and Nand Lal. Subsequently there appeared at least two more in prose (the *Prem Sumarag* and the *Sau Sakhian*) and five shorter *rahit-namas* in verse. [11: XII] From these and other sources Singh Sabha scholars attempted to distil the original Rahit, and in 1915 they published their reformist views as an entirely new *rahit-nama* (*see* TAT KHALSA). This manual, the *Gurmat Prakas Bhag Sanskar*, failed to win acceptance. Not until *Sikh Rahit Maryada* was issued in 1950 did an authoritative *rahit-nama* finally appear. [30: 79–86]

Rain-Making (African) [II] Rain is a central religious theme in many African religious systems, particularly in the drier east and south. The power to make rain may be a basic attribute of kingship, as among the ZULU, LOVEDU and SHILLUK, or the granting (or withholding) of rain may be related rather to a major territorial cult, such as that of MWARI or MBONA. Elsewhere particular clans, lineages or simply individuals may be credited with such powers. On the wet west coast, however, rain-stopping is seen as beneficial while rain-making may be malevolent; but in general the activities of rain experts here are more individualistic and marginal to both religion and society. Rain-makers and rain-stoppers work not only by innate personal power but also through the use of certain medicines and rituals, including public dances. The source of their ability may be understood as a matter of inherited (or acquired) esoteric knowledge, the collaboration of the ancestors or the direct gift of God. For some peoples, e.g. the NUER, such concerns are unknown.

Rajneeshism [xxviii] Bhagwan Shree Rajneesh (1931–90) 'realized his enlightenment' at the age of 21. In 1974 he founded an ashram at Puna to which thousands of visitors flocked to hear him talk and take part in his meditations, some of which, such as Rajneesh Dynamic Meditation and chaotic breathing techniques, involve considerable physical exertion. His teachings are frequently radically antinomian; drawing from both Western and Eastern traditions, they embody a vision of 'Zorba the Buddha', rejecting asceticism but embodying internal awareness. In 1981, Bhagwan moved to 'Rajneeshpuram', a 64,000-acre estate in Oregon where thousands of his 'sannyasins', wearing sunset-coloured clothes and a mala with his picture, engaged in the 'worship' of building a vast community complex. By 1985, however, Bhagwan's secretary, Sheela, and others were accused of a number of criminal activities, including murder [23: v], and Bhagwan returned to India, where he took on the name Osho. Since his death, Osho's 'sannyas movement', based at Puna, has continued throughout the world. [5: 200–1; 41: IV/L; 42: 952–3; 51; 53: 241–70; 68]

Rama [xvii] An incarnation (AVATARA) of the Hindu deity VISHNU. Rama's life and exploits are recounted in the great epic RAMAYANA. Probably in origin a folk hero around whom a cult developed in his native region of India, Ayodhya (Oudh, now in eastern Uttar Pradesh state), Rama gradually came to be regarded as an avatara of Vishnu. He is regarded by Vaishnavas as the ideal of manhood and model for human conduct, and his wife Sita (meaning 'furrow' – she sprang from the ploughed soil) is held up as the ideal of Hindu womanhood: chaste, faithful and devout. Perhaps in origin an agricultural goddess, she is regarded as an avatara of LAKSHMI, or (in south India) of Vishnu's other wife BHUDEVI, the Earth Goddess. The cult of Rama is strongest in the Hindi-speaking area of northern India and adjacent states such as Gujarat, where the BHAKTI movement flourished between the 13th and 18th centuries CE. In recent years the putative birthplace of Rama has become a focus for nationalists attempting to create a 'Hindu FUNDAMENTALISM', who in 1992 demolished a MOSQUE on the site, causing widespread unrest.

In art (see ART (HINDU)) Rama is blue in colour, like Vishnu himself, and holds a bow and arrow. In temple imagery and devotional prints he is accompanied by Sita, his half-brother Lakshmana and the monkey-god HANUMAN. Miniature paintings depict events from the Ramayana, particularly the battle of Rama and Lakshmana against the 10-headed, 20-armed demon Ravana.

Ramanuja [xvii] The most influential thinker of the VAISHNAVA VEDANTA and leading authority in the Shri Vaishnava sect of HINDUISM, traditionally dated 1017–1137 CE (but in fact probably d. 1157). Ramanuja strongly criticized the ADVAITA VEDANTA of SHANKARA for its monism and its doctrine of MAYA

(2). In Ramanuja's system, known as Particularized Non-dualism (*Vishishtadvaita*), God's relationship to the universe is that of the soul to the body; just as the soul is in intimate union with the body yet distinct in particular respects, so God and the universe are united but particularized. God is the substance of all particularized things, substance and particular being inherently united. He is equally the cause of all created things (the cause being of the same nature as the effect) and the ruler of the universe as the soul is the ruler of the body. Ramanuja is greatly concerned to emphasize the perfection and supremacy of God, his positive qualities and his identity with VISHNU. Like other Vaishnavas he affirms that Vishnu has a transcendent celestial form, consort, retinue and abode, all of which are eternal and flawlessly beautiful. He also stresses the grace of God, his accessibility to the devotee, his generosity and his affectionate, forgiving nature. [Philosophy: 36: III, 165–398; life: 28: 24–48; theology: 28: 65–198; translation: 107: 543–55]

Ramayana [XVII] The epic story of RAMA, a Sanskrit composition in 24,000 stanzas attributed to the ancient Indian sage and poet Valmiki. Basically the story of the life of Rama, the prince of Ayodhya, capital of the kingdom of Kosala, and of his devout and noble wife Sita, the epic also includes much of ancient Indian folklore and moral values. Its main effect is to hold up the ideal types of Hindu manhood and womanhood; it has been said that the *Ramayana* makes its hero, Rama, DHARMA itself in flesh and blood. Contemporary literature of the period (? 8th or 7th century BCE) makes no mention of Rama. The life and exploits of a relatively minor ruler were probably elaborated by local bards only later, before the time (*c*. 1st century BCE or CE) when the epic was put together into what became the received Sanskrit text.

The theological point of view it conveys is that VISHNU, who incarnates (*see* AVATARA) himself from time to time when evil threatens to overcome the world, did so on this occasion in order that, as Rama, he should put an end to the wickedness of the demon Ravana, who in the story carries off Sita. In this he was aided by the monkey-god HANUMAN [12: 305, 414–17]. A lyrical version entitled the *Ramacaritmanas* (Sacred Lake of the Acts of Rama) was rendered into Hindi from the Sanskrit original by the poet Tulsidas (1532–1623), in a work which has justly been described as 'the great bible of the Hindi-speaking peoples' [138: 141–3]. Although the majority of the people of rural India are unable to read, this is a major source of their religious ideas, known as it is to them through public recitations and readings, and dramatizations at the great festival times, especially at the autumn festival of Dusserah (*see* FESTIVALS (HINDU)). [4: 204–6]

Ramgarhia [XXXIII] A distinctive Sikh CASTE formed entirely of those from an artisan background (notably the Tarkhan or carpenter caste) who became SIKHS. Tarkhans were joined by much smaller groups, such as some from the Raj (mason) and Lohar (blacksmith) castes. Many Ramgarhias were taken to east Africa by the British for railway construction; most of these have since migrated to Britain and North America. In these migrant situations they commonly protect their distinctive identity by such features as exclusive Ramgarhia GURDWARAS. [26: 102–3]

Rangi [XXIX] A sky-father in New Zealand Maori religion, known as Atea in other Pacific creation stories. In the Maori version, Rangi and the earth-mother PAPA, who lie embracing, are forced apart by their children the gods (ATUA), led by TANE. Rangi's tears of grief continue to fall as rain. In Tahiti, Tonga and

Samoa, Rangi's role as creator of gods and men is played by TAN-GAROA. [7; 16; 22]

Rastafarians [xxvii] A variety of dynamic movements in Jamaica and Dominica since the 1930s among poor landless men, inspired by Marcus Garvey's BACK TO AFRICA MOVEMENT and the accession of Ras Tafari (hence the name) as Emperor of Ethiopia. The latter is still regarded as the Messiah of the black race who, it is believed, are the true Jews, about to be redeemed. White culture and CHRISTIANITY are repudiated by BIBLE selections retained. A puritan ethic sustains personal dignity, and *ganja* (marijuana) smoking is a peaceful, mystical experience. After earlier repression by the colonial government, the movement has become accepted and politically influential, even as a reconciling force, in Jamaica, and has spread to other parts of the Caribbean, to the eastern USA, England, and further afield, especially in one of the main forms, The Twelve Tribes of Israel. The Jamaican singer and band leader Bob Marley did much to spread the movement with his reggae music and was given a Jamaican state funeral when he died in 1981. His touring band brought the movement to New Zealand in 1979 and the appeal to Maori youth led to an authentic community in Auckland, but also to adoption without understanding by a criminally active gang around Ruatoria that smeared the image in public, as has also happened elsewhere. A small token settlement in Ethiopia on land at Sheshamane gifted by Haile Selassie in 1955 has survived, but the millennial back-to-Africa motif has been transposed for most into a search for cultural identity wherever they are, assisted by efforts to remain distinct from the 'Babylon' of white culture while playing a more positive part in that same culture. [12: 63–9; 16: 124–30; 25; 26: 135–7]

Rationalism [xxxii] A rather ambiguous word, sometimes used to characterize an emphasis on reason as opposed to experience (and thus contrasted with EMPIRICISM) and at other times to characterize an emphasis on reason as opposed to the emotions. It appears to have been in this latter sense that HUMANIST groups have claimed the title 'rationalist' (e.g. the Rationalist Press Association). Rationalists, in this sense, maintain that religion has no basis in reason.

Re', Cult of [vi] The worship of Re', the sun-god, centred on Heliopolis, reached its zenith in the Old Kingdom (*c*.2480 BCE), when the king's father, Re', became royal patron. This cult influenced temple liturgy (*see* MANSIONS OF THE GODS) and FUNERARY PRACTICES (*see* PYRAMIDS) [7]. Even when the Old Kingdom collapsed and Re' lost his royal supremacy, solar beliefs continued to permeate religion (*see* AMUN). In the solar hereafter (*see* AFTERLIFE), originally reserved for royalty, the king (PHAROAH) joined the gods, crossing the heavens in the celestial barque.

Redeemed Redeemer [xv] A basic concept formulated by the German *Religionsgeschichtliche Schule* [23] which found its classical expression in the writings of Richard Reitzenstein. Based upon mythological elements which might be retraced to the Indo-Iranian, Zurvanite world [11] or Mesopotamian beliefs [34], the Redeemed Redeemer, the *salvator salvandus*, connotes the redeemer who is in need of salvation himself, a concept which is rooted in the complex Gnostic (*see* GNOSTICISM) and MANICHAEAN relational patterns between PRIMAL MAN, redeemer gods and divine messengers. Although present in the Gnostic writings, its clearest definition is found in the Manichaean texts (both the Oriental and Western sources). Here the Primal Man is not only a redeemer, but is also in need of redemption himself. Indeed, after the mixture of good and evil, namely light and darkness, the light elements are imprisoned in the material, evil world. These divine particles are omnipresent in plants, trees, animals and men, and all together they form the divine world-soul, the living soul or the divine essence which itself is God, suffering in this world. This living soul is identified with JESUS as the Jesus Patibilis, distinct of course from the historical Jesus. The passion and redemption of the Jesus Patibilis, the omnipresent crucified Jesus, or the Living Soul, is therefore a major theme in the Manichaean documents. The Primal Man has to rescue his self, i.e. his soul (pneuma), which is incarcerated. The creation (depicted in the cosmogonical texts) is a kind of salvational machinery in order to accomplish this epuration. The eschatological dimension is quite clear: men and cosmos serve the distillation of light and contribute to the restoration of the primordial equilibrium. Therefore Gnosticism and related systems use a tripartite time concept, which according to some scholars is related to Indo-Iranian beliefs. This 'three-time' doctrine, in addition to the knowledge of the two principles, is the nucleus, the basic element, of the redemptive GNOSIS for the adherents of the aforementioned beliefs.

Reductionism [xxxii] There are two sides to reductionism. To begin with the negative, it requires an account of the conditions which need to be met if a claim is to be meaningful or worth considering. Reductionist accounts presuppose that these conditions are not met by e.g. Christianity as it is traditionally presented, or by statements of religious belief generally. Such accounts are, however, not merely negative. On the contrary, a reductionist proposes to save the day by analysing or translating the unacceptable material in, or into, terms which satisfy the conditions stated. This is the positive side of reductionism.

A common form of reductionism rejects the metaphysical dimension of a religion, retaining only its ethical content. L. A. Feuerbach (1804–72) (see PROJECTION THEORIES OF RELIGION) claimed that Christian theology was fraught with contradictions and that, once these were eliminated, it would be clear that statements about God were really only disguised statements about humanity [10]. R. B. Braithwaite (b. 1900), in the spirit of 20th-century EMPIRICISM, has maintained that to have a religious belief is to intend to behave in a particular way, a way which is associated with certain traditional stories [6].

Exponents often do not style themselves reductionists as such and the label commonly implies, by way of criticism, that something crucial has been left out by the process of 'reduction'. The label may thus be a controversial one, to the extent that there is disagreement as to what is crucial. This kind of controversy has surrounded the programme of DEMYTHOLOGIZING in Christian theology.

Reform Judaism [xxii] A movement which began in response to the gradual dissolution of medieval Jewish society in the late 18th century. Early reformers, who were influenced by the educational ideas of Moses MENDELSSOHN and by the general atmosphere of the ENLIGHTENMENT, sought to update the service and liturgy of the SYNAGOGUE. Ideological changes began in a more formal way with the rabbinical conferences of the 1840s in Germany, which brought modernist RABBIS together to agree on a common platform [6; 56: vii]. From its inception Reform Judaism has been divided between moderates and radicals. Abraham Geiger (1810–74), an early moderate, wanted far-reaching changes but, as a source for updating JUDAISM, only those which depended on the Jewish tradition. Radical reformers, like Samuel Holdheim (1806–60), believed that Judaism should jettison its antiquated rituals while preserving the core of its ethical monotheism. Many of these radical ideas were transplanted to North America, where Reform developed in the mid-19th century under Rabbi I. M. Wise (1819–1900), and were formulated in the Pittsburgh Platform of 1885 (see NORTH AMERICA, JEWS IN). In Britain, by contrast, Reform Judaism has remained tradition-orientated, and more thoroughgoing changes were only introduced with the founding of Liberal Judaism in London (1902). [7; 11; 44; 70: 215]

Reformation (Protestant) [XIII.B] A movement for theological and moral reform in the Western Christian Church during the 16th and 17th centuries CE. Theologically, it was an attempt to recover what was considered to be the teaching of the BIBLE and early Christianity. Biblical AUTHORITY was asserted over that of tradition and the PAPACY. SALVATION was alleged to be by 'faith' rather than 'works'. SACRAMENTS and WORSHIP were simplified. MONASTICISM and priestly views of MINISTRY were attacked and lay status elevated. Martin Luther's *Theses* (see LUTHERANISM) triggered the German Reformation in 1517. The more radical Huldreich Zwingli (1484–1531) reformed the church in Zürich at about the same time. In the next generation John Calvin in Geneva initiated another major Reformation tradition (see CALVINISM). In Britain the Reformation was slower and more conservative (see BRITAIN, CHRISTIANITY IN). The religious changes of the Reformation were accompanied by social and political upheavals which led to a permanent split in Western Christianity. PROTESTANTISM produced

established churches in parts of Germany, Scandinavia, Holland, and Britain (see STATE, CHRISTIANITY AND THE). Smaller reforming groups of the 16th-century 'Radical Reformation' in various parts of Europe [203] included early forms of UNITARIANISM, 'Spirituals' (akin to later QUAKERS; see FRIENDS, RELIGIOUS SOCIETY OF) and ANABAPTISTS, who rejected established (state) churches. ROMAN CATHOLICISM was, however, reformed and reinforced by the work of the COUNTER-REFORMATION. [19: 182–212; 34; 37 vol. 3; 46: 311–99; 55: I–IV; 62 vol. 12: 244–54]

Reincarnation (Jewish) [XXII] In Hebrew *gilgul*, meaning (the) 'turning' (of the wheel) [14 vol. 7: 573]. The belief in reincarnation was central to KABBALAH teaching about the destiny of the soul, although it was rejected by some non-mystics as a sectarian belief alien to Jewish thought [70: 95]. The Kabbalists continued to believe in the resurrection of the dead in a future age (see OLAM HA-BA) but saw humans as having to undergo a variety of rebirths before then in order to fulfil their tasks on earth. [61: 281]

Reiyukai [XXVI] Reiyukai teachings may be understood as a fusion of two ideas: the importance of regular performance of ancestral rites and reliance on the Lotus Sutra. A Japanese new religion in the NICHIREN BUDDHISM tradition, Reiyukai traces its origin to Kubo Kakutaro (1892–1944) and his sister-in-law Kotani Kimi (1901–71). He was the organizer and systematizer, she the SHAMAN-like medium and healer. In accordance with their division of labour, Reiyukai has incorporated a similar division into its organization. Among couples of executive rank, the wife serves as the medium linking believers and the spirits, the husband as the realistic organizer. Together, they are called 'parents' and those they persuade to become members are their 'children'. As its name suggests, Reiyukai, 'the society of friends of the spirits', attaches great importance to harmonious relationships between living people and the spirits, especially ancestral spirits. The belief is that ancestral spirits are aware of their descendants and bestow good fortune on them, but that if their achievement of enlightenment is hindered by the failure of their descendants to perform the proper rites, they send misfortune on them to remind them of their duty. The prime responsibility of the Reiyukai member, therefore, is to assemble in a home altar the mortuary tablets of all ancestors, both paternal and maternal, and morning and evening to make offerings of food and drink and to read aloud the *Aokyokan*, or 'Blue Sutra', a simplified version of the Lotus Sutra.

After Kubo died and Kotani was left as the sole head, friction occasionally led 'parents' to break away, taking their 'children' with them. Reiyukai has given rise to about 30 such groups. The best known is probably Rissho koseikai. Reiyukai claims about 3,200,000 members. [9; 10: x, 208–9]

Religion [xxxiv] A general term used in most modern European languages to designate all concepts concerning the belief in God(s) and Goddess(es) as well as other spiritual beings or transcendental ultimate concerns. It is also the common denominator for the institutions/bodies representative of these concepts and/or concerned with their propaganda, including typical ways of human behaviour as an experience or a consequence of this belief. Thus, Christianity is labelled as a religion in this modern sense and, by extension, the term is also applied to other religious traditions of humankind such as Islam, Hinduism and Buddhism. The implicit presumption of this labelling is that there is something in common in all cultural traditions of all times which justifies speaking of them in terms of religion(s). The presumption is, in fact, threefold: it supposes that the term is not limited to modern times only but can also be used for former times of Europe's religious history; it suggests that it might be applicable to non-European traditions as well; and it suggests a common reference system for all of them.

Concerning Europe's religious history, it is noteworthy that there are different etymological explanations of the term from the beginning and that these differences are due to the peculiarities of the religions which the authors had in mind. Cicero, for instance, saw the roots of the word in *relegere*, referring thus to repetitive veneration practices typical of his Roman religion. The 4th-century Christian author Lactantius declared it to be derived from *religare*, indicating, by doing so, that there is a close tie between God and humankind. Etymology, consequently, is not helpful in understanding the modern meaning of religion as a technical term applicable to all the religious traditions of Europe. It is not even so in Christianity alone. Feil has proved that in ancient and medieval times Christians spoke of their religion in terms of *fides* (belief), *secta* (line to be followed) or *lex* (law) rather than of *religio* which has become the general term used to designate Christianity only in more recent times, after the Reformation period [62a]. The extension of the term to earlier periods of Europe's religious history is thus questionable and acceptable only in so far as it is a matter of common usage to call all these religious traditions religions. That is why we speak of Roman, Greek, Celtic, Germanic, Baltic, Slavonic religions etc.

In respect of non-European traditions the use of the term religion is even more problematic. It has been shown that the various self-denominations of the great religious traditions of humankind are very much related to the concepts these religions stand for, so that the characteristics of each of these terms are not interchangeable with those of others [3; 39a]. An additive, all-aspects-embracing description of what is meant by religion in different cultures [76: 2–4] denies these cultural differences by simply juxtaposing them without saying that there is no common base for all of them. Consequently, the question must be asked whether or not the use of the term can be generally admitted in spite of obvious differences.

The use of religion as a technical term in an academic discipline poses the problem of the selection of subjects to be dealt with. In fact, the STUDY OF RELIGION(S), RELIGIONS-WISSENSCHAFT, aims to cover all cultural trends of thought excluding European philosophy, modern sciences and contemporary ideologies, leaving a range of heterogeneous material that is then said to be the world of religion(s). Generations of researchers have hoped and thought that a common reference system could be found precise enough to embrace all these heterogeneous traditions and helpful in eliminating all others. This attempt, however, has failed. The alternatives are either to favour a precise definition or to take the term as operational without an implicit definition. In the first case, the proposed definitions may be wider or narrower: for instance, one might say that religion is the belief in gods, thereby excluding, as subjects of study, those religious traditions that have no such belief; or one might declare all ultimate concerns to be religious, with the result that phenomena such as patriotism are included. In the second case, particular religious traditions are studied and compared with others in certain aspects without asking why these traditions belong to the world of religion(s). Such a way of approaching the subject seems to be justified by the fact that people know what an author who speaks of religion(s) has in mind even if no definition of the subject is given. The term is thus used as in everyday language, without the pretension of an academic definition to start with. Research work in this operational sense consists in providing, besides historical data, a frame to structure the material through systematization and typologies which need no other justification than to be appropriate to the data, without claiming that such a structuration reveals the intrinsic nature of the material itself [5; 21; 40a; 131a; 153].

However, it would be wrong to conclude on this note and ignore the fact that many observers of religion have attempted to provide a definition which would be as inclusive or as exclusive as they themselves considered religion to be. The following are a few of the best-known definitions of religion: 'The essence of religion consists in the feeling of an absolute dependence' (Friedrich Schleiermacher); 'A religion is a unified system of beliefs and practices relative to sacred things . . .' (Émile Durkheim); 'Religion is that which grows out of, and gives expression to, experience of the holy in its various aspects' (Rudolf Otto); 'Religion is what an individual does with his solitariness' (Alfred North Whitehead); 'Religion is the sigh of the oppressed creature . . . It is the opium of the people' (Karl Marx); 'Religion is the state of being grasped by an ultimate concern' (Paul Tillich). Max Weber began his important work entitled in translation *The Sociology of Religion* with these words: 'To define "religion", to say what it *is*, is not possible at the start of a presentation such as this. Definition can be attempted, if at all, only at the conclusion of the study' [173: 1]. Unfortunately, the work, according to manuscript notes, remains unfinished, so we never did get Weber's definition. It is in the nature of the topic that even if the work had been completed we would, perhaps, still not have got a definition from him.

Religionswissenschaft [XXXIV] A German technical term for the academic STUDY OF RELIGIONS, apart from THEOLOGY. Originally introduced by Friedrich Max Müller (1823–1900), it established itself as an academic discipline in German universities by the end of the 19th century and at the beginning of the 20th. The English translation of the word was always under debate because the term *Wissenschaft* refers to both sciences and humanities. Max Müller himself used the English form 'science of religion' but was not followed in this; later, translations such as 'comparative religion' or HISTORY OF RELIGION(S) had more success. Germans, however, are rather unhappy with these more current translations because of their selectivity. Each of these is for them typical of one or another sub-discipline of *Religionswissenschaft*, which itself covers all of them. It is therefore common in German universities to subdivide *Religionswissenschaft* into two main branches, one, *Religionsgeschichte* (history of religions), dealing with history, the development and the doctrines of different religions in the past and present, while the other, usually called *systematische Religionswissenschaft*, is more concerned with systematizing and theorizing religious data. To this second branch belong sub-disciplines such as 'ethnology of religions', 'geography of religions', PHENOMENOLOGY OF RELIGION, PSYCHOLOGY OF RELIGION, SOCIOLOGY OF RELIGION and 'TYPOLOGY of religion'. As concerns PHILOSOPHY OF RELIGION, most German scholars of *Religionswissenschaft* see it as a sub-discipline of philosophy and argue that it cannot be a sub-discipline of *Religionswissenschaft* because of its speculative methods and its interests in truth-claims expressed by religions.

Religionswissenschaft is based on philological, historical and socio-empirical methods only. Unlike theology, which looks at religion(s) from a believer's perspective, *Religionswissenschaft* is an intentionally neutral enterprise, providing and checking religious data and consequently free from judgements on particular religions and religious practices. All phenomena are dealt with in a similar descriptive way. This, however, has not been and still is not always done successfully. Judgements reflecting prejudices are sometimes found in the vocabulary in the use of terms such as 'superstition' or 'heresy', or even 'orthodox'. Such terms have meaning only within the framework of a given dogmatic system, and if there is no such system, as in *Religionswissenschaft*, they are better avoided and replaced with others of no implicit evaluation. What is true of vocabulary applies even more strongly to descriptions of particular religions, where often mainstream perspectives prevail and thus follow 'insider' positions, instead of showing the wide range of historical reality including winners and losers alike.

As regards methodology, *Religionswissenschaft* is clearly defined and hence again distinct from theology. In practice, however, the distinction between them is often less methodological than practical, determined by their respective subjects of concern. The division of labour is difficult to maintain because the study of Christianity in Europe has for a long time been – and still is – the exclusive domain of theologians, and theologians have also been working in the field of *Religionswissenschaft*. In consequence, the methodology used in both disciplines is not questioned as such, so that theology and *Religionswissenschaft* are separated more by their fields of research than by their respective methodologies, and the theoretical distinction in work seems obsolete to many academics outside the field. This situation is changing at present in Germany because, on the one side, more and more of Christianity will be included in the curriculum of *Religionswissenschaft* and thus constitute a field of research while, on the other side, in the interest of Christian dialogue with other religions, those religions become part of the curriculum of Christian theology. Thus in both cases the question arises: which type of research is that of *Religionswissenschaft* in contrast with that of theology? Similar observations can also be made for other religions which show a growing interest in historical study of their own tradition as well as a concern with wider knowledge of other religions. It is, therefore, too simple to say that *Religionswissenschaft* is the outsider's view of a religion while theology is the insider's thinking in it.

Adequate description of a religion in *Religionswissenschaft* requires the retracing of religious thinking as if the scholar were a believer, so that the insider is able to recognize it as his or her own. This task may sometimes even go beyond the systematization found in religious traditions themselves: so, for instance, in studies of Native American religions or of new religious movements, *Religionswissenschaft* has systematized the teaching data to the extent that it has developed a systematic presentation of the teachings of the respective religions which later on was and still is being used as a doctrinal reference by insiders. Moreover, by comparison with other religious traditions, *Religionswissenschaft* puts forward systematizations of religious data which are rejected by the insiders. This applies in particular to general categories such as those of PHENOMENOLOGY OF RELIGION where particular aspects of religious traditions are interrelated with phenomena which, in the eyes of the followers, may have nothing in common with the main concern of the respective religions as understood and interpreted by their adherents. [6; 7; 99; 103; 168; 175a]

Religio-Political Movements among Tribal Peoples [xxvii] Contact with powerful, sophisticated societies disturbs the tribal order, especially in colonial situations or through the ferment of new ideas introduced by Christian MISSIONS. A violent reaction of protest or rebellion has often arisen intertwined with NEW RELIGIOUS MOVEMENTS, particularly in the earlier periods of contact and before alternative channels for action, such as nationalist political parties and trades unions, have developed. In the 20th century, tribal or peasant revolts with religious dimensions have occurred in Peru, Indonesia, the Colorums of the PHILIPPINES, and in risings such as the messianic Govindgiri movement among the Bhils of India in 1912 [9: 240–3]. In east Africa there was the Maji-Maji ('water') movement 1905–6 in Tanganyika, and a series of nativistic cults in Kenya in intermittent clashes with government [26: 240–5, 259–68]. The PROVIDENCE INDUSTRIAL MISSION, ALICE LENSHINA'S Lumpa Church, and the Israelites of South Africa [26: 61–3] were involved in political or military clashes, as were the RASTAFARIANS in the Caribbean and the CARGO CULTS of Melanesia, where a revolt in the Baliem valley of Irian Jaya in 1977 and the attempted secession of Jimmy Steven's Nagriamel movement in Vanuatu in 1980 had religious dimensions. In the long run these movements tend to become more religious and less political. [26: viii]

Religious Education (in Schools) [xxxiv] There was a marked increase during the 1970s in the study of religions in schools in Western countries, most noticeably in those with statutory provision for religious education. In the UK the comparative study of religion (RELI-

GIONSWISSENSCHAFT) had previously been included in many religious education syllabuses, but it was confined to the 16–18 age group and seen as peripheral to the main task of sharing the Christian faith with the pupils (*see* CHRISTIANITY). Three factors contributed to the inclusion of religions in their own right: (1) awareness of the growing numbers of adherents of non-Christian religions living in Britain; (2) the challenge from philosophers of education to justify the school curriculum as appropriate for all pupils; and (3) the development of religious studies departments in universities and colleges of education. A widely accepted aim for religious education is that the pupils should be helped to understand the nature of RELIGION. This involves a thematic approach in the earlier years (festivals, sacred places, sacred writings, symbols, growing up in a religion, etc.), with a study of individual religions in the upper years of secondary schooling [1; 84]. An influential book in this development was *Secular Education and the Logic of Religion* [150] by Ninian Smart, who later became director of Schools Council projects on religious education in secondary and primary schools, based at Lancaster University. Shap, a working party founded in 1969 to promote the study of religions in schools [82], has provided in-service support for teachers, including a handbook [29] and an annual calendar of religious festivals. Conferences have also been run by the Standing Conference for Inter-Faith Dialogue in Education (SCIFDE), a movement linked with the World Congress of Faiths. The study of religions is an option in public examinations at 16-plus and 18-plus [83]. The 1988 Education Reform Act stipulated, for the first time, that religious education must take account of the beliefs and practices of the major religions represented in Britain.

In some Scandinavian countries (which also have statutory provision for religious education) pupils have the possibility of studying religions. Sweden has long had a religious studies approach to the subject, and world religions may be taught in any section of the school system. In the early 1990s Denmark allowed the merging of two formerly separate subjects, 'Non-Christian religions and other life stances' and 'Christian knowledge'. In several countries where religious education has no official place in the curriculum some study of religions may take place within such subjects as social studies or liberal studies. In New Zealand, for example, learning about the culture of the peoples of the Pacific Islands is encouraged by the education authorities, although there are also attempts to develop an examination syllabus on religions for older pupils. In Australia, the state of Victoria has developed units which include some study of religions for senior pupils; South Australia has had for some time a PHENOMENOLOGY OF RELIGION approach to religious education.

In the USA the Supreme Court Schempp decision (1963) expressly allowed 'teaching about religion' in public schools [129]. However, because this comment of the judge is less widely known than the decision forbidding prayer and devotional reading of the BIBLE, only a minority of schools include the study of religions. A number of attempts have been made to change this situation, through teacher education programmes, the production of curriculum materials, etc., by, for instance, the former Public Education Religion Study Center (PERSC) at Wright State University, Dayton, Ohio; the World Religions Curriculum Development Center, Minneapolis, Minnesota; and Argus Communications.

Dramatic changes within a society have caused some countries to rethink their approach to religious education. In South Africa, for example, greater acceptance of a multi-cultural society has led to an awareness of the need for multi-faith religious education. In Poland the 'science of religion' was introduced into a number of secondary schools in 1986; however, the church hierarchy opposed this and exerted pressure for only Christian (ROMAN CATHOLIC) teaching to be given in schools.

In many countries it is still assumed that the role of religious education is to nurture pupils in the dominant faith of the country, whether it be Christian, Muslim or Jewish. Sri Lanka, however, provides religious education in each pupil's own religion, and in Singapore's short-lived experiment in the 1980s with a Religious Knowledge O-level examination most pupils chose their own faith from among the six options available. A growing awareness of the number of pupils of other faiths, particularly Muslims, within their schools has led some countries, for example Germany, Austria and Belgium, to provide Islamic education for these pupils as an alternative to the normal confessional Christian teaching. In the Netherlands, on the other hand, the recognition of ethnic minority groups within the country has led to an expansion of non-confessional multi-faith religious education. [92; 159]

Religious Pluralism [XIV] The primary use of this term is to refer to the increasingly common experience of living in communities in which several faiths coexist [32: 1]. It is also used to describe theological responses within Christianity to the issues raised by such experience. Such responses are frequently classified in three ways. 'Exclusivism', championed by such thinkers as Karl Barth and Hendrik Kraemer [54; 55], stresses the radical uniqueness of Christianity. 'Inclusivism', taught by thinkers like Hans Küng [56] and taken up both by the Second Vatican

Council and by Pope John Paul II, gives primacy to Christianity, but also sees Christ's saving work as at least partially present in other traditions which have many spiritual values. 'Pluralism' sees each of the great traditions as comparable in value and of probable equal performance [42: VII–VIII]. The last position has been so vigorously developed and defended by John Hick in recent decades that it has acquired almost a technical reference to his theological position and hence this latter response to global religion is the one which will now be described.

The central difficulty in the way of global understanding of religion is how one can do justice to what appear to be common themes in the reported religious experience of the human race, while at the same time facing up to the tremendous diversity of the world's religions. People of many religions believe themselves to be responding to transcendent reality. Yet perceptions of that reality differ profoundly, not only between religions but within them. Hick's solution to this dilemma is to draw attention to the way in which each of the world's religions has drawn a distinction between God in him/her self (or the real as such) and that reality as perceived by us. God (or transcendent reality) lies beyond our comprehension, but not beyond our experience. Kant's distinction between things in themselves, and things as we perceive them might provide a useful analogy for this. Hick believes that all of the world's religions are responses to a single divine reality, and that differences in describing that which they claim to encounter are culturally conditioned human projections. Each 'name' of God represents a different *persona* of the divine reality as responded to in human history. This also applies to traditions which reject personal concepts of the divine and appear instead to speak of the absolute, or the real; for people in such traditions seem as much concerned for the transcendent as those who prefer more personal images to describe that reality. The experiential claims of each of the major religions should be treated on a par, because each is capable of bringing about human transformation, experience of SALVATION/liberation and a sense of cosmic optimism and well-being. Each teaches, in different ways, the importance of dying to self and the moral ideals of goodwill, love and compassion. From the perspective of a human observer the mixed record of each of the world religions should make us pause in seeking to do any such 'grading of religion' ourselves. John Hick's hypothesis has attracted a great deal of comment, including detailed criticism by such scholars as Kenneth Surin [32: VIII; 42: 204–6] and Gavin D'Costa [32: IX; 25: II]. The theory provides a focus for contemporary debate on the appropriate relationships between world faiths and is a central issue in the study of the contemporary HISTORY OF RELIGIONS. [20; 24; 25; 32; 36; 38; 39; 40; 41; 42; 53; 54; 55; 56; 71; 79; 85]

Religious Studies in Higher Education [XXXIV] The evolution of the modern university in the second half of the 19th century provided the milieu for modern studies in religion. There were various roots of such RELIGIONSWISSENSCHAFT: the comparative study of religion, various area studies and philological enterprises, such as the famous *Sacred Books of the East* series edited by Max Mueller (1823–1900), the evolution of anthropology and sociology, the independent development of PHILOSOPHY OF RELIGION, and new historical studies, beyond older models of Church history and the like. Phenomenology also began to supply a way of looking at religions differing from the older theological and seminary models (*see* PHENOMENOLOGY OF RELIGION). These varying strands came together

most conspicuously, as far as university education is concerned, in the 1960s, when religious studies, defined in that context as the cross-cultural, multidisciplinary, empathetic and theoretical study of religion and religions, began to take its place in the anglophone universities of the world, and to an extent elsewhere. There had been precursors: in the USA, for example, in the departments in Iowa and Princeton (the former having a kind of 'menagerie' theory, with adherents of differing faiths professing them in a scholarly way, jointly; the latter beginning to break well beyond the bounds of the Christian religion), while in Chicago a powerful school of history of religions was attached to the Divinity School, with such notable teachers as Joachim Wach (1898–1955) and Mircea Eliade (1907–86). In Britain, there were chairs of comparative religion and similar institutions at Leeds, Manchester, Oxford and London. In continental Europe there were various chairs of the history and phenomenology of religion, notably in Uppsala, Lund, Leipzig, Paris and Leiden. Religious studies as a new multidisciplinary subject incorporating history of religions, cross-cultural topics, social scientific approaches and ethical and philosophical reflections, however, came to prominence chiefly in the 1960s and early 1970s, with two major trends: first, the foundation of departments in some major public universities in the USA and analogous developments in Canada and Britain; and second, the broadening of the scope of studies in religion offered at private institutions of higher education. The new interest among students and others in non-Western religions, dissatisfaction with the relatively austere approach on offer in philosophy departments and a growth in questing and questioning fuelled the popularity of the subject. In Canada a number of Catholic and other denominational universities developed religious studies rather than theology under the influence of the public financing of programmes. In Britain the foundation of a major department at Lancaster had a general effect on the system; some former purely theological departments added religious studies to their remit, and notably expanded opportunities for study were created at London, at the University of Wales, Lampeter, in Scotland at Edinburgh and Stirling, and elsewhere. Departments were set up in the 1960s and 1970s in Cape Town and Pietermaritzburg and elsewhere in South Africa, in Australia in Brisbane, Sydney and elsewhere, in New Zealand in Christchurch, Dunedin, Wellington and Massey University, among others. Religious studies also became a not uncommon offering in anglophone universities in Africa. Since the collapse of the Soviet empire it is re-emerging in the whole area previously under Soviet domination. It exists here and there in mainland Asia, and strongly in Japan. In the USA major graduate programmes evolved at Harvard (with its Center for the Study of World Religions), Chicago, Princeton, the University of California at Santa Barbara, Virginia and Iowa; and in Canada, at McMaster, Toronto and elsewhere. These exist in parallel to courses offered in divinity schools and programmes in Jewish Studies, Buddhist Studies and other more specialized and sometimes 'committed' studies.

Since the inception of religious studies in its modern form, various forces have changed its intellectual character somewhat. Notable has been the emergence of women's studies and its new insights on religions (*see* GENDER). Also, the growth of interest in HERMENEUTICS has influenced textual and other studies. A certain drawing together of political science and religious studies has been influenced by the work of scholars such as Michel Foucault (1926–84), together with the emergence of unmistakably important phenomena such as the Iranian revolution. A further influential recent development is the drawing together of studies of religions as traditionally defined and of 'secular' world-views, including varieties of nationalism. Other related fields waiting to be similarly developed concern music, the arts, economic theory and practice, religious diasporas and public policy including law and ethics.

There are probably up to 2,000 departments of religious studies across the world. The subject has come to flourish, but it is still somewhat new in conception, with its commitment to explore religions in our closely interacting global civilization. Interest in it is undeniable in a world where religions interact, as do secular ideologies with religion, and where diaspora communities are now a commonplace. In all cultures there are increasing numbers of religious individualists who are not constrained by tradition, while backlashes against the whole flock of modernist tendencies help to consolidate new and challenging FUNDAMENTALISMS and other revivals. Also, religious studies in higher education have helped to promote new kinds of religious education or studies in religion in schools (*see* RELIGIOUS EDUCATION (IN SCHOOLS)). Religious studies is in one sense a branch of social science but has also begun to play a vital role in the humanities, both because of its cross-cultural commitments and because of its serious consideration of diversity of human world-views. [59a vol. 11: 243–6, vol. 12: 231–41, vol. 14: 64–92; 99; 131b; 145; 149; 175]

Resurrection [XIV] A belief common to JUDAISM, CHRISTIANITY and ISLAM that at the end of time God will reassemble human corpses. The belief is not present in the earliest forms of the Hebrew religion, but became prevalent during the persecution of Antiochus Epiphanes in the 2nd century BCE, when it seemed that only hope of a life beyond could vindicate continuing trust in God. Some scholars suggest that the idea originated in early ZOROASTRIANISM and entered Judaism from that source (though subsequently fading from Zoroastrianism). Belief in bodily resurrection was common in intertestamental Judaism, and in Rabbinic Judaism became so normative that MAIMONIDES saw it as a defining element of Jewish identity. In Christianity belief in the physical resurrection of JESUS made the resurrection hope a central tenet. In the QUR'AN it is repeatedly taught as integral to belief in the creative and sustaining power of God.

In recent centuries belief in a literal understanding of resurrection has declined and reinterpretations of the concept are now common. The rise of modern cosmology called into question belief in a localized heaven in the sky to which the bodies of the saved could ascend, and it became bizarre to continue to see volcanoes as vent-holes of a hell beneath the earth. In popular Christianity and Judaism belief in the immortality of the soul, which was formerly integrated to belief in the resurrection of the body, became separated from it. Among theologians the meaning of resurrection has been changed so that there is no longer an expectation that we will get our old bodies back, but rather that we will be given 'spiritual bodies' suited for a life in heaven beyond our comprehension. More radical reinterpretations use the word resurrection to mean that we live on in God's memory, or even that the concept be understood wholly in existential terms as referring to a change of lifestyle in the present. [3a; 4; 6; 13; 15; 21; 22; 23]

Revitalization Movements (Amerindian) [v] Relatively recent attempts on the part of previously acculturated Amerindian groups to regain and reaffirm earlier religious traditions. Often syncretistic (see SYNCRETISM) in doctrine and ceremonial, drawing both encouragement and inspiration from the pan-Indian movement, tribes that include the Wampanoag, Narragansett, and other North American eastern groups are reasserting the value of such forms as the SWEAT LODGE, VISION QUEST, traditional healing techniques, dances, and use of the sacred pipe. Revitalization efforts are often not endorsed by all the Indians and frequently occasion the scepticism of scholars. [5: XIV]

Revival [III] In African-Caribbean religion, part of a worldwide feature of religious revival within Christianity and the response to it. BEDARD-ISM, KUMINA and Pukumina (see POCO-MANIA/PUKUMINA) have developed from the Revival movement. Bedward is said to be the father of 20th-century Jamaican Revival. MYALISM shares some characteristics with Revival, in style, in dress, in asceticism, in a sense of mission to search out and destroy OBEAH. It is useful to think of these churches as being on a continuum of SYNCRETISM between Christianity and African religion. The Revival Church and the Revival Zion Church are notable examples of Revival churches in Jamaica. The Revival Zion Church claims to be the national church of Jamaica, although its membership does not warrant this claim.

In 1860 in Jamaica people who wished to enhance their social status, and who were literate, joined the missionary churches, both Anglican and Nonconformist. Because the organization of these churches was autocratic and formal, relating to the parent churches in Europe, black members could play no part in leadership or decision-making. When the US Great Religious Revival of 1860–1 (see REVIVALISM) spread to

Jamaica its 'new' mission created many converts. Membership of missionary churches fell, and independent black-led churches developed which countenanced a style of worship which allowed for more ardent and exuberant behaviour. POSSESSION (IN AFRO-CARIBBEAN RELIGION), glossalalia, healing, prophecy and divination were encouraged, and remain central. Large numbers of Jamaicans who would be excluded from other churches because they were living together but not married, could join.

The new leaders were uneducated formally, and were 'appointed' by the HOLY SPIRIT, their adherents recognizing their charisma. They called themselves 'shepherds' and led their 'flocks'. Since the BIBLE was the source of their literacy they made heavy reference to its language. Meetings were held in the yard/garden of the leader. The groups stressed the value of social responsibility and sharing.

In 1929 PENTECOSTALISM arrived from the USA, and effected a new alignment. While membership of missionary churches decreased sharply, that of all other groups soared. Many who had remained at the African end of the Revival continuum joined the Pentecostals, and others felt that their style of worship was endorsed by the Pentecostals. Orthodox Christians thought that many of the Revivalists were not Christian, but Revivalists believed that as long as possession was by the Holy Spirit, or his agents, then they were Christian. Revivalists agreed that members of cults which were possessed by their African ancestors were not Christian, although cult members themselves believed that this experience did not invalidate their 'Christian' status.

In the Revival yard the consecrated area is the 'seal'. Revivalists believe in many supernatural beings. The Holy Spirit attends services, as do some Old Testament prophets, as well as the dead, especially the souls of departed leaders. Dreams and visions are crucial. Principal ritual objects are Bibles, candles, a bell and crosses, which have been adopted from mainstream churches, and therapeutic herbs and flowers, water, swords and sometimes stones which are said to hold 'power'. Worship includes drumming, clapping, groaning, loud prayer, preaching, possession, healing and spiritual dancing. Participants dance round and round inside a group of onlookers. There are three kinds of meetings: rituals for special occasions, which may last for days and involve elaborate ceremonies called 'tables'; prayer meetings; and street meetings held for gaining converts. Tremendous effort is put into all these. Prayer is referred to as 'workings'. Elements of African ancestor beliefs are strong, particularly about death. It is believed that everyone has a DUPPY, which is particularly vulnerable to *obeah*. Baptism is usually by total immersion. [2; 26; 37; 50; 67; 84; 87]

Revivalism, History of [XIII.B] Outbreaks of intense, often mass religious excitement, originally in the international 'Evangelical Revival' which began in the 1720s. This included German MORAVIANS and English METHODISM, ANGLICANISM and EVANGELICALS. In the American 'GREAT AWAKENING' the outstanding theologian Jonathan Edwards (1705–58) combined CALVINISM with the philosophy of John Locke (*see* NATURAL THEOLOGY) to explain the process of religious 'conversion', i.e. of turning the person from a life of sin to one dedicated to JESUS Christ. This revival emphasized 'inward religion'; justification by faith (*see* SALVATION) experienced in a 'new birth'; lay preaching; and groups for religious fellowship. It represented a reaction against Western materialism and rationalism, recalling older religious patterns such as PURITANISM. Although often affecting artisan groups in England, it included the upper-class 'Clapham sect' led by William Wilberforce (1759–1833), the anti-slavery campaigner. Spontaneous 18th-century revivalism was succeeded in the 19th century by the work of Americans such as Charles Finney (1792–1875), who cultivated techniques for engineering revivals. Later campaigners included Dwight L. Moody (1837–99) and his musical colleague Ira D. Sankey (1840–1908); Billy Sunday (1862–1935); and Billy Graham (b. 1918) [70]. Perfection ('Holiness') Revivalism developed in America [54] and in the SALVATION ARMY. Revivalism has been common in the USA, with claims to be a significant influence on social reform [179], although it has often been politically conservative. In Britain it has been less influential, partly because ANGLICANISM has not been very responsive to it. [2: xviii–xx, xxvi, xxvii; 135; 148: xvii; 194]

Revivalism (US) [iv] While the concept of 'revival' is as old as the ancient scriptures of many religions, the modern coinage 'revivalism' was historically closely identified with certain PROTESTANT and especially American Protestant movements. Revivalism was the force that characterized the GREAT AWAKENINGS in America, drew upon the talents of rhetorically gifted ministers and demanded constant adaptation through various cultural shifts. Ordinarily it has been associated with great revivalist preachers – Charles Grandison Finney, Dwight L. Moody, Billy Sunday and Billy Graham are prime examples – but revivalism has also been associated with intensified preaching missions by less well known ministers in local churches and tents [20: iv, vii, xi].

The assumptions behind revivalism tended to lead to some changes in the doctrine of God, either overtly recognized or quietly assumed. If one believes that God is absolutely foreknowing and predestining even as he is inscrutable, it would be easy to develop a fateful sense: God will save whom God will save, and no preacher need stir emotions and no individual need become responsible. But the revivalist tends to assume and to spread the assumption that individuals can make choices and should be forced to take decisions, and that a loving God welcomes positive response. The to-be-revived individual is a sinner whose will turns from God or who is blind and deaf in the spiritual sense.

The revivalist asks for the whole being of the participants: mind, body, spirit, soul, will – however the components are described, all come into play; what critics call 'emotionalism' is also welcomed. One makes a decision, but the turning to salvation and the peace of God are finally credited not to human achievement but to the grace of a loving God. Revivalism appeared and appears in contrast to overly rational and 'cool' preaching and counters apathy, passiveness or wilful resistance. The revived often build new religious communities – congregations, denominations or movements – and have frequently carried their revived faith into efforts at moral reform. [17]

Rimé [xxxv] The 19th-century Rimé or 'ecumenical' movement of Tibet developed as a response to the sectarian strife that had periodically plagued BUDDHISM. The movement, which began in eastern Tibet, initiated a renaissance of culture and spirituality throughout the country. It was led by a number of prominent teachers from various traditions such as the Kagyupa (KAGYU) master Jamgon Kongtrul (1811–99) [21], the Sakyapa (SAKYA) scholar Khyentse Wangpo (1819–92) [4] and the Nyingmapa (NYINGMA) Chogyur Dechen Lingpa (1829–70) [4]. The movement was an attempt not to form a new sect but rather to establish a climate in which the spiritual wealth of each particular religious tradition could be available to all. In furtherance of this aim Jamgon Kongtrul collected the doctrines and instructions of all the Tibetan traditions in his famous *Five Treasures*, which comprise over 100 volumes.

Rissho Koseikai [XXVI] With over 6 million members, one of the most prominent of the new religious movements in Japan. It began in 1938 when Naganuma Myoko (1889–1957), a REIYUKAI medium, and Niwano Nikkyo (1906–) a Reiyukai unit leader, found themselves unable to accept Kotani Kimi's downgrading of the Lotus Sutra and left Reiyukai with some 30 followers to start their own organization. As in several other new religions, Naganuma was the female SHAMAN-like figure who counselled people with problems, Niwano the male organizer and systematizer. Initially, Naganuma played the major role. With few exceptions, the guidance she gave as coming from the KAMI and BUDDHAS was binding on all, including Niwano. When she died, however, Niwano shortly declared that the first 20 years of Rissho Koseikai existence had been a period of accommodation (*hoben jidai*) and that it was now entering a period of manifest truth (*shinjitsu kengen jidai*). Whereas the first period emphasized the spiritualistic medium and divine messages, the second emphasizes the teacher-organizer and the rational, objective articulation of doctrine for the purpose of making the organization fit to serve the modern age.

People who become members are expected to perform the ancestral rituals before the mortuary tablets in the home every morning and evening. At least once a month they are also to go to the local meeting place and participate in a *hoza* group at which people sitting in a circle (*za*) present their problems and receive guidance from the group leader in light of the Buddhist law (*ho*). Ris-

sho Koseikai has members in several countries, and has played an active role for many years in helping refugees, initiating agricultural projects and working for world peace. [2]

Rites (Greek) [XVI] Sacrifice was the central rite of Greek religion. It involved the ritual slaughter of animals, followed by the division of the carcass between men and gods and feasting. The slaughter was preceded by a procession to the altar, music, song, ritual handwashing, sprinkling of the victim, the throwing of barley groats on to the victim and the altar, prayers and libations. It was followed by burnt offerings to the gods. Recipient and occasion determined the type of victim. Sacrifices were basically of two main types, one for celestial and one for chthonic cult. Heroic cults (*see* HEROES) involved mostly chthonic rites, as did most, but not all, cults for chthonic deities (*see* CHTHONIAN RELIGION); but Olympian gods also received chthonic sacrifices in certain cults. Usually, though not invariably, the celestial sacrifice, called *thysia*, took place on a raised altar (*bomos*) (*see* TEMENOS); the chthonic sacrifice called *enagisma* took place at a low or sunken altar (*eschara*) or pit (*bothros*). The victim's blood flowed on or into the altar. Usually the victim's flesh was eaten by the participants; the gods' share (fat and bones, sometimes with pieces of meat) was burnt. In some sacrifices the victim was burnt whole. Not all chthonic sacrifices were holocausts, though many were, and not all holocaust sacrifices were chthonic; the ritual markers of chthonic sacrifices included the type of altar, the type of libations and the way the animal's head was held during the sacrifice. Libations (offerings of wine, milk, honey, water, oil) poured on the ground or altar, were performed on many occasions. Certain deities received the first fruits (*aparchai*) of the crops. Processions and dances were ubiquitous in divine cult. Rites for special occasions included purification rites and rites of passage, such as birth and the incorporation of the child into the *oikos* (*see* INSTITUTIONS (GREEK)) through the ceremony *Amphidromia*; the presentation of children to a divinity and the *phratria* (*see* INSTITUTIONS (GREEK)); marriage; death. In historical times transformed initiation rituals were integrated in divine cults, some as rites involving only a representative number of participants (e.g. the Athenian *arrhephoroi*), others in 'educational' institutions involving civic and military training as well as ritual roles (e.g. the Spartan *agoge* and the Athenian *ephebeia*). Certain cults, especially that of Dionysos, involved ecstatic dances. [4: 54–109; 8; 14: 21–37, 104–20; 29; 31: 255–9; 2: I.1, 2; 37: 1–151]

Rites (South American) [XXIII] Everywhere in South America, passages in the life-cycle (birth, naming, male and female initiation, marriage and death) are marked by ritual celebration in which human growth and change become intimately linked to the creative powers of mythic beings (*see* CREATION MYTHS). In many cases, subsistence activities, such as hunting, gathering, fishing and agriculture, as well as crafts (canoemaking, blowgun manufacture, pottery) are likewise given ritual meaning through their connection to mythic modes of being. Four examples illustrate the variety of ritual forms in South America:

The *Turé* festival is found among ethnically mixed and historically reconstituted native peoples of north-eastern Brazil, the Guianas and parts of the Amazon. A form of spiritual renewal, it consists of a celebration of supernatural beings (called *Os Encantados*) which are invoked by SHAMANS to come to participate in the sacred space of the dance festival. Among these beings, the anaconda, or *Cobra Grande*, is prominent, as are the spirits of deceased shamans.

The so-called *Yurupary* complex of the north-west Amazon, based on an extensive mythic tradition, involves an all-male puberty ritual with the use of sacred flutes and trumpets which are kept secret from women; a fruit-gathering and exchange ritual, usually of palm fruits; and periodic social/ritual gatherings of two or more groups, the purpose of which is to reaffirm alliances and exchange marriage partners.

The *Kwarup* festival, the principal cycle of all Indians of the upper Xingu (central Brazil) is the great rite of passage celebrated in coordination with death, usually at least a year after the death of someone of chiefly status or lineage. During the *Kwarup*, marriages take place, pubescent girls emerge from their initiatory seclusion, relatives of the dead come out of mourning, the community concludes its mourning and the fate of the dead is settled. As it marks a transition, it renews individual, social and cosmic being.

While the spectacle of the 'Dance of the Conquest' among Andean native peoples is one of drama, not ritual, it is still a symbolic re-enactment of the historical death of the Inca on a par with the mythic disappearance of primordial beings, marking the appearance of eschatological time that the tragic event created. The drama re-enacts a reality, but one which is ultimately questionable and susceptible to critical reappraisal. [37: I; 14; 1]

Rites of Passage [XXXIV] This common English expression is a translation of the French expression *rites de passage* coined by the Flemish anthropologist Arnold van Gennep in his seminal work published in 1909. Van Gennep used the term to categorize those rites or rituals which mark the transition of humans from one stage of life to another. An alternative English term increasingly used for these transitions is 'life-cycle rites'. Different cultures have a variety of such rituals. Estimates of the number of such rites in HINDU-ISM vary from 16 to 40. Rites are related to both physiological and social stages in life; these do not necessarily coincide. Hinduism recognizes four stages in life: the youth, the householder, the hermit and the final renouncer; the last stage is a preparation for death. Although van Gennep and others list a whole variety of rites related to the individual life and to group and national life, throughout most cultures there are four events in life which universally provide occasion for rites: birth, puberty, marriage and death. Van Gennep called the rites ones of 'passage' on the analogy of geographical transitions and the rites associated with crossing territorial boundaries [67: 1]. Under the category of rites of passage van Gennep also identified three sub-categories: rites of separation, transition rites and rites of incorporation. There are various theories which aim to explain the 'why?' of rites of passage. Generally they are seen as aids to assist the movement from one set of responsibilities to another, or to assist the group, family or tribe to come to terms with the transition or separation of one of its members and the anxiety such a transition may cause. This is especially the case with rites associated with death, whether that of a family member or of a national hero. Van Gennep's explanation is that these are 'actions and reactions to be regulated and guarded so that society as a whole will suffer no discomfort or injury' [67: 3]. It is sometimes argued that in certain modern societies the disappearance of such rites has led to the disorientation of individuals and societies and may be the cause of social disruption.

Ritual [XXXIV] Originally a term for the language of religious ceremonial, as in 'reading the last rites'. For at least a century the term has been used for formalized religious activity, to include both the language and the ceremonial. Clerics who introduced Roman Catholic ceremonial into the Church of England in the 19th century were dubbed 'ritualists'. In more recent times the term has been applied loosely to any activity of a repeated kind, as in biology for the mating activity of various species of the animal kingdom. '[E]ven among those who have specialized in this field there is the widest possible disagreement as to how the word ritual should be used and how the performance of ritual should be understood' [106: 526]. So general has the use of the term become that it has been suggested that the term be used for 'culturally defined sets of behaviour' denoting the 'communicative aspect of behaviour', whether of a religious kind or not. '[N]o useful distinction may be made between ritual acts and customary acts but that in discussing ritual we are concerned with aspects of behaviour that are expressive (aesthetic) rather than instrumental (technical)' [106: 525]. 'As a social animal, man is a ritual animal . . . Social rituals create a reality which would be nothing without them. It is not too much to say that ritual is more to society than words are to thought' [46: 62]. However, there is still good reason to restrict the use of the term to the religious realm, that aspect of repetitive behaviour sometimes referred to as 'magico-religious', [67: vii] while acknowledging that in certain situations it is not easy, sometimes impossible, to separate the specifically religious from the generally cultural in areas of human behaviour. For Durkheim, 'rites are the rules of conduct which prescribe how a man should comport himself in the presence of . . . sacred objects' [48: 41]. Ritual in its derived sense of including words and actions is present in every religious environment, even in religious contexts where there is an affirmation of antiritualism, such as Christian PROTESTANTISM and mystical expressions of various religions, such as SUFI ISLAM or ZEN BUDDHISM. Even in Christian Quakerism (*see* FRIENDS, RELIGIOUS SOCIETY OF) the silence of the gathered congregation can be seen as 'ritual silence'. Occasionally religion itself is referred to as ritual: 'we have got to the position in which Ritual replaces Religion in anthropologists' writing' [46: 65]. Whereas in some treatments of religion reference is made to sacred space, sacred person, other writers will refer to ritual space and ritual person. There is a clear relation between ritual and myth, but no agreement as to whether myth gives rise to ritual or vice versa. Robertson Smith thought that rites explained myths and that ritual was the key to so-called primitive religion [61: 53]. In many instances the performance of a ritual is a dramatization of a myth. This is one way of describing the action of the EUCHARIST or MASS in the Christian religion. The eucharist is the ritualization of the event of the passion and death of Jesus understood mythologically in terms of human SALVATION. It has been argued that the meaning and value of human acts, other than 'pure automatism' 'are not connected with their crude physical datum but with their property of reproducing a primordial act, of repeating a mythical example', so that even the act of eating, it is argued, is not for the purpose of nutrition but to renew a communion with the divine [56: 4]. 'Rituals and significant profane gestures acquire the meaning attributed to them, and materialize that meaning, only because they deliberately repeat such and such acts posited *ab origine* by gods, heroes, or ancestors' [56: 5–6]. ELIADE's assertions, in some instances, have been severely challenged, on the grounds both that his sources have not always been of the best and that his interpretations go beyond what the sources allow, basing, as he did, his 'insights' into one civilization on observations of a completely distinct and incomparable civilization [156: 1–10, 14–17]. Furthermore, Smith argues that ritual is not explicitly linked to some event before time, as Eliade asserts, but can be demonstrated, time and again, to arise out of purely local, temporal, even accidental occurrences. Smith suggests that 'ritual is an exercise in the strategy of choice. What to include? What to hear as message? What to see as a sign? What to perceive as a *double entendre*? What to exclude? What to allow to remain as background noise? What to understand as simple "happening"? . . . It requires us to perceive ritual as a human labor, struggling with matters of incongruity. It requires us to question theories which emphasize the "fit" of ritual with some other human system' [155: 116]. In many cultures there are a set number of rituals which relate to different stages of human life (*see* RITES OF PASSAGE).

Rituals (Roman) [XXXI] The essential ritual, establishing contact between men and gods, was animal sacrifice, mostly of cattle, sheep and pigs. The programme included rites of preparation, prayer to the recipient and the 'immolation' of the victim by the sprinkling on its head of corn-meal and wine. Then, after the killing (carried out by lower-class specialists – *victimarii* – on the officiant's behalf), the entrails (*exta*) were assessed by *haruspices*, through whom the gods accepted or rejected the sacrifice. The victim was cooked and finally the *exta* returned to the god; the rest (*profanum*) was consumed by the human participants. If the victim was rejected, the whole procedure was repeated until an acceptable sacrifice was found (*perlitatio*) [8: 558–9; 12: 386–92; 19: 594–5]. Many other rituals included this programme; in lustration, the area to be purified was walked around by the procession of victims and participants [10: 4–8, 36–7]; in the triumph, the victorious general was accompanied in procession through the city by his army, his prisoners and the victims for sacrifice to Jupiter [23]. In these and many other rituals, great importance was attached to the meticulous preservation and re-creation of traditional utterance and action; this was also the interest of the antiquarian writers whose descriptions we have. We have no liturgy or coherent explanation of the meaning of rituals, and know of few if any myths associated with them, if such there ever were. It is an exaggeration to say that the Romans had no mythology; but what survives either concerns the founders of the city or has been transformed into narratives about kings and heroes, or tales about specific places in the city. Roman myth, in other words, has been detached from ritual and grounded in time or space (4; 8: 47–78].

Rituals (Sikh) [xxxiii] The principal Sikh rituals are a cluster associated with routine GURDWARA worship and five which mark important rites of passage. All require the presence of the ADI GRANTH. A copy of the sacred volume is installed in every *gurdwara* and there treated with great reverence. When closed it is wrapped in an elegant cloth (*rumala*). It is opened only under a canopy and is then symbolically protected by waving a whisk over it. Those who come to a *gurdwara* for *darshan* ('audience') first remove their shoes and cover their heads. Each bows to the floor before the scripture, makes an offering and, if *kirtan* (the singing of scriptural selections) is in progress, sits in the *gurdwara*, always at a level below the scripture. At the conclusion of *kirtan* the congregation recites ARDAS, and KARAH PRASAD is distributed [20: v, vi; 30: 80]. The five individual ceremonies mark the birth of a child (*janam sanskar*), the bestowing of its

name (*nam sanskar*), initiation into the KHALSA (*amrit sanskar*), marriage (the *Anand* wedding service), and death (*miratak sanskar*) [8: 112–29; 10: vi; 20: iii; 30: 81–3; 34: 106–10]. For *amrit sanskar*, sweetened water is stirred with a two-edged sword and administered by five devout Sikhs [30: 83–6]. Ritual forms are also followed for such procedures as transporting the scripture and conducting an *akhand* PATH.

Rizalistas [xxvii] Several hundred thousand members of a complex of rurally orientated religious movements in the PHILIPPINES take this generic name from José Rizal y Mercado (1861–96), an intellectual leader martyred in the revolution against Spain, and now a national hero. Rizalistas regard him as divine or a messiah who will return to remove poverty and exploitation. The larger movements are Bathalismo (from Bathala, 'God'), Banner of the Race Church (Watawat ng Lahi), resembling Catholicism, Sacred Church of the Race (Iglesia Sagrada ng Lahi) with its own ancient secret 'Bible', and the Adarnistas (after 'Mother Adarna', the founder) for whom Rizal never died but lives as true God and man. Forms of worship range from simple house prayer meetings to Catholic rituals. [6: 40–56]

Roman Catholicism [xiii.b] Western Christians in communion with the PAPACY; also termed 'CATHOLICS'. It is the largest church of Western Christianity, spread elsewhere by European colonization and MISSIONS. Some ancient EASTERN CATHOLIC churches are in communion with Roman Catholicism but follow their own form of worship and customs, e.g. married clergy [157: 1407]. The term Roman Catholic is sometimes applied to the whole of this communion. CHURCH ORGANIZATION is by an authoritative hierarchy under the papacy. WORSHIP is markedly SACRAMENTAL, centred on the MASS. Doctrine is drawn from scripture and tradition, and defined infallibly as 'dogma' through COUNCILS and the papacy (*see* AUTHORITY). The church has a rich tradition of spirituality and MYSTICISM, especially through MONASTICISM. Roman Catholicism has favoured close relationships between the STATE AND CHRISTIANITY, which has often led to conflict. It has a marked capacity for incorporating diverse Christian traditions and (especially at the popular level) pre-Christian elements. Accommodation to the modern world has proved more difficult. Nineteenth-century Liberal Catholicism and the more extreme Modernist movement (a minority of intellectuals, mainly in late 19th-century France, condemned in 1907) [126; 163] attempted theological adjustment to modern science and history. Social Catholicism in 19th-century France and Germany was concerned with democracy and social reform [19: 387–95; 191]. Since the Second Vatican Council (1962–5) [1] there has been a ferment of change in most areas of Roman Catholic life, including worship (*see* LITURGICAL MOVEMENT), church relations (*see* ECUMENICAL MOVEMENT), and social reform (*see* SOCIAL MORALITY), but also corresponding conservative reaction. [8; 32; 62 vol. 12: 129–45; 121 vol. 4: I–IX; 90; 208: 134–65]

Roman Religion [XXXI] The religion of the ancient Romans derived elements – at least the worship of gods – from its INDO-EUROPEAN inheritance. However, apart from some evidently very ancient rituals, the earliest religion of which we have any understanding is that of the 6th-century BCE monarchic period (754–509 BCE) (*see* NUMA, CALENDAR OF), when the native tradition was already undergoing modification through contacts with Etruscans, with Greeks from south Italy and with Carthaginians [19:

578–81]. The republican period (509–31 BCE) saw a wide, ever-increasing range of deities (DI DEAEQUE), their worship being maintained either by the state or by clans, families and other groups, both types being under the supervision of the priests (SACERDOTES). An elaborate system of ritual and rules penetrated all transactions, so the gods had their place in all aspects of life (*see* AUSPICIA; PRODIGIA) [8: 89–133; 12: VIII; 19: 590–8]. The later republican period saw important changes: first, cults emerged, based on voluntary membership, with their own authority structure and offering personal religious experience; second, the ambitions of competing aristocratic leaders led them to claim special divine patronage (*felicitas*) and honours tending towards deification [8: 526–50; 13: I; 25]. In creating the new regime of the empire, Augustus (31 BCE), under the guise of reviving ancient forgotten cults, transformed many institutions to the service of the new monarchy, while the first steps were taken towards the establishment of EMPEROR-WORSHIP [2: VIII; 13: II; 20: 53–62]. The cult of the emperor in all provinces and of Roman gods in the Latin-speaking provinces (*see* SYNCRETISM) characterized the period of the empire [2: IX; 20]; and paganism displayed continuing vigour into the late empire, as the evolution of new systems shows (*see* MITHRAS; MYSTERY-CULTS) [11: III–V]. The decline of dedications and temple-building in the 3rd century CE is part of the transformation of city life rather than evidence of specifically religious change [12: 28–53; 13: 230–5]. Competition with CHRISTIANITY, rather than internal deterioration, led to the eventual marginalization of pagan practice.

Rome, Early Christianity at [XIII.A] Roman Christianity apparently originated in the large Jewish community of the city. Disturbances caused by the introduction of Christianity led to the expulsion of Jews from Rome by Claudius in 49 CE. But in a few years they were back. In c.57 CE Paul's letter to the Roman Christians indicates that the CHURCH of the capital, while founded on a Jewish base, now included a majority of GENTILE members. PAUL spent two years in Rome under house arrest between c.60 and 62; PETER visited the city shortly afterwards. In 65 the church of Rome survived a murderous attack by Nero. A generation later, as the first letter of Clement shows, it was acquiring a position of moral leadership among Gentile churches. [5: 279–83, 373–93; 11: v, 830–9]

Rosary, Christian [XIII.D] Either a chaplet of beads or knots for counting prayers, or the set of prayers said with its use. Rosaries can be used to count many repetitions of the same prayer or mantram or fixed sequences of prayers or formulae. A variety of Hindu, Buddhist, Muslim and Christian prayer-ropes exists. The principal Christian forms of prayer rope are the komboschini or chotki used by Orthodox Christians to count repetitions of the JESUS PRAYER and the chaplet of five or fifteen decades of beads (actually of ten + one) with a tail of one + three + one + a crucifix used to recite the Rosary of the Blessed Virgin MARY, a sequence of meditations on events in the lives of Christ and his mother measured by the recitation of the CREED, the Lord's Prayer, the Hail Mary and the Short Doxology. A wide variety of other less known Catholic rosaries exists, including the rosary of the Incarnation, the rosary of the seven sorrows of Mary, and the rosary of the seven joys. [20]

Rosh Ha-shanah [XXII] ('New Year'; literally 'head of the year') Two-day Jewish new year festival (CHAGIM). The Jewish year begins in the autumn, before the onset of the rainy season. Rosh Ha-shanah is a

time of judgement when God, 'the king of all creation', sits on His heavenly throne of justice and judges humankind for their deeds in the past year. It begins the 10 days of repentance which culminate in the YOM KIPPUR fast. The ram's horn (*shofar*) is sounded 100 times during the morning LITURGY of the festival to awaken people to repentance. On the afternoon of the first day people go to a stream and, in a ritual known as *tashlikh* ('casting'), they symbolically cast their sins away into the water [69: 196]. Although Rosh Hashanah and Yom Kippur are known as days of awe, the former is also a festive day celebrated with fine clothes and good food and drink, because Jews trust in God's mercy and forgiveness. Foods are eaten which are positive symbols for the year ahead, thus bread is dipped in honey rather than in salt to signify a sweet year [70: 174]. People greet each other with the words: 'May you be written down [in the heavenly book] of those who will have a good year.'

Rosicrucianism [XXIV] A mystical brotherhood described in two anonymous manifestos published at Kassel, Germany, in 1614/15. [33] Proclaiming a revival of learning and piety, the documents recounted the life of one Christian Rosenkreutz (supposedly 1378–1484), who had brought scientific and alchemical (*see* ALCHEMY) knowledge from the East, founding the Order of the Rosy Cross, which men of goodwill and learning were now invited to join. The documents depict the initiatory aspects of Rosicrucianism rendered in the alchemical metaphors of the 'Chymical Marriage', initiation as a Red Cross knight, and death and rebirth as elemental transmutation. The Rosy Cross also had Christian associations as the rose of the Virgin MARY and the cross of JESUS Christ. The manifestos aroused intense excitement but the Rosicrucians could not be found. Probably they were fictitious, and the allegories in the manifestos may have been intended to stimulate non-sectarian cooperation in scientific and magical studies in a Europe torn by religious conflict. Their influence however persisted and a revival of interest took place in the late 19th century with the formation of the Societas Rosicruciana in Anglia, highly influential in the founding of the GOLDEN DAWN [16: II]. Since then numerous OCCULT organizations have claimed Rosicrucian origins, a contemporary example being the Ancient and Mystical Order Rosae Crucis (AMORC), based at San Jose, California, which instructs its members in esoteric doctrines by correspondence course.

Ruh [XIX] The Islamic term for 'spirit', in usage difficult to separate from *nafs*, 'soul, self, the permanent individuality of man' [37 'Nafs']. The soul is immortal and will survive the last day and judgement (QIYAMA) and return to God. Among Sufi mystics (*see* SUFISM), the idea of the pre-existence of the soul (e.g. MUHAMMAD'S) appears. The spirit is conceived as the vital spark which God blows into a person but which departs at death. The term *ruh* is also used of angels (MALA'IKA) and, in the QUR'AN, of 'the spirit' sent by God to man, which in revelatory contexts is equated with Gabriel. [20 'Soul (Islam)'; 67 s.v.]

Runes [VII] Runic symbols, representing sounds, each with a special name, were arranged in sets of eight to form a *futhark* or alphabet. Unlike the Ogam symbols used in Ireland, they were not based on the Latin alphabet. Runes were used by the GERMANIC and Scandinavian peoples from the 2nd century CE until after the VIKING age, sometimes for straightforward messages, recorded verses or inscriptions, but often for magical purposes [7: V, VI]. ODIN

was said to have taught men runic lore.

Russia and the North Caucasus, Islam in [XIX] According to the 1989 census returns of the former Soviet Union there are almost 20 million Muslims in Russia and the north Caucasus. However, these do not form a single, homogeneous group, but exhibit wide geographical, ethnic and linguistic diversity. The term 'Tatar', which was used loosely in Russian to cover all the Turkic-speaking peoples found in European Russia and Siberia, implies stronger ethnic and cultural links than these peoples actually possess. The use of the term 'Tatar' was further confused by the creation in 1920 of the Tatar Autonomous Republic within the Russian Federation, making 'Tatar' serve also as the official designation of the inhabitants of that Republic. The largest concentrations of Muslims in the present-day Russian Republic are found in the Volga–Ural region (Tatar, Bashkir and Chuvash Autonomous Republics), in the north Caucasus (Daghestan, Chechen–Ingush and Kabarda Autonomous Republics) and among the half million Turkic-speaking peoples of Siberia. Almost all Muslims found in Russia are Sunni (*see* SUNNA) and, with the exception of those living in Daghestan, adhere to the Hanafi legal school. The Muslim peoples of Daghestan adhere to the Shafi'i legal school. Muslims first came under Russian rule in large numbers in the mid-16th century after the fall of Kazan in 1552 and of Astrakhan in 1556 to Ivan IV ('the Terrible'). While many of the Tatars in Russia are descendants of the Tatars who conquered Russia in the 13th century, not all of them are, and the Muslims of Daghestan (implausibly) trace their acceptance of Islam back to the Arab conquest of their territory in the 8th century, although full conversion of these peoples to Islam only took place in the 16th century.

Two groups of historically important Muslims who once were found within the territory of the present Russian Republic (the Circassians and the Crimean Tatars) have, as a result of Russia's repressive policies (which may fairly be called genocide) well-nigh disappeared from present-day Russia. In the 19th century one million Circassians from the north–west Caucasus emigrated to Turkey. Daghestan was fought over by Timur and Toqtamish of the Golden Horde in the late 14th century, invaded by the Ottomans in the second half of the 16th century, invaded again by the Persians in the 18th century and annexed by Russia early in the 19th century, an event which marked Daghestan's transition from an alignment with the south to one with the north, although the sense of belonging to the Islamic world continued to generate religiously inspired revolts well into the 20th century – the most famous of these being that associated with Shamil in the mid-19th century. This furiously puritanical movement, which can be regarded as a precursor of later resurgence movements in the Islamic world, and which stressed the importance of the SHARI'A and the outward observances of Islam, sprang from a SUFI revival which had begun in Shrivan towards the close of the 18th century and which was spread to Daghestan in the 1820s by leaders of the Naqshbandi SUFI ORDER. Followers of this movement (*murids*) proclaimed a holy war (JIHAD) against invaders and sought to rid their land of alien and anti-Islamic elements, both indigenous and foreign. The Murid movement (as it became known) was finally crushed by the Russians in 1859. The other important movement associated with Islam in Russia was the *Jadid* (modernist) movement, which began in the mid-19th century among the affluent Volga–Ural Tatars, whose MADRASAS – in the cities of Kazan, Ufa, Orenburg and

Troitsk – were beginning to gain a worldwide reputation. Building on the thought of the liberal Bukharan thinker Abu Nasr Kursavi (1783–1814), Shihabeddin Marjani (1818–89), Rizaedin Fahreddin-oglu (1859–1936), 'Abd ul-Qayyum Nasiri (1825–1902) and Ismail Bey Gasprali (1851–1914) sought to rid Islam of the dogmaticism of traditional theology and to prove that Islam was compatible with progress and science. Condemning *taqlid* (blind obedience to tradition), and advocating a renewal of *ijtihad*, these thinkers asserted the right of every believer to find his own interpretation of religious, cultural and social questions in the QUR'AN and the HADITH. The *Jadid* movement has been called 'the Tatar Renaissance of the nineteenth century'. Gasprali was also conscious of the potential might of Islam and urged (against the radical pan-Turkism of Jamal al-Din al-Afghani) a liberal pan-Turkism which he believed could become an equal partner with Russia within a unified empire and which would eventually conquer the world. His influence on the wider Islamic world, particularly through his newspaper *Terjuman* ('The Interpreter'), which was published from Baghchesaray in the Crimea from 1883 to 1914, was considerable [15: 78–9, 90–1]. Gasprali's ideas are not without support in Russia and in Central Asia today.

Russian Orthodox Church Abroad [XIII.D] Also known as the Synodical Church, this is now (since 1950) based in the USA and is no longer an exclusively Russian concern. First set up as the 'Higher Church Administration' in Stavropol during the Russian Civil War, the hierarchs followed the defeated White armies into exile but managed to maintain close links with the CATACOMB CHURCH in the Soviet Union. Metropolitan Antony Khrapovitsky led the Synod first to Constantinople (1920) and then to Yugoslavia

(1921). The Synod was originally endorsed by PATRIARCH Tikhon Belavin (d. 1925) but it refused to recognize Sergei Starogorodsky as his successor and cut all links with Moscow when the latter demanded loyalty to the Soviet authorities. Since 1927 the ROCA has not been in communion with the Moscow Patriarchate and its staunchly traditionalist stance has increasingly isolated it from most other Orthodox churches. However, the ROCA has sponsored missions in many countries and is represented in Russia by the Free Russian Orthodox Church.

Only briefly uniting the Russian diaspora, the ROCA itself has now dwindled to 150,000 faithful but continues to exert influence over the Orthodox worldwide. This has been sustained through many monasteries, including Jordanville in the USA and Brookwood in England; renowned elders, like Seraphim Rose (d. 1982) (*see* STARETS); and a plethora of publications in many languages. Above all, charismatic bishops like John Maximovitch (d. 1966) have won the admiration of Orthodox of all jurisdictions. In particular, John Maximovitch carried Orthodoxy across the world, working among Orthodox and non-Orthodox alike in Shanghai (from 1934), in the Philippines, in America and then in Europe (after 1951), ending his life as Archbishop of San Francisco. This outstanding missionary was finally canonized in 1994. [2; 13; 74; 76; 99; 102] (*See also* CATACOMB CHURCH; EASTERN ORTHODOX MISSIONS; NEW MARTYRS; OLD CALENDAR MOVEMENT.)

Russian Sects [XIII.D] A group of religious movements, the oldest of which, the Khlysty or Khristovoverie, originates in the 17th century. The Khlysts sought Christ's spirit in the depths of their own soul, not in the rituals of the state church. They rejected the doctrine, the traditions and the authority of the Orthodox Church and followed leaders of their own they called 'Christs', but unlike later sects still maintained some contact with the church and occasionally attended services. Their own services used singing and dancing to attain a state of ecstatic exaltation called *radenie* in which they were inspired by the Spirit. They fasted and practised asceticism to prepare for *radenie*.

A particularly austere and authoritarian group, the Postniki (Fasters) became a distinct sect under the Christ Kopylov in the mid-18th century; a century later (*c.*1840) it split to produce the Old Israel and then about 1885 the New Israel, each following a different Christ. The New Israel practised the re-enactment of events in sacred history, sometimes in great numbers of participants. Many Postniki emigrated to Uruguay in 1911–12. The Skoptsy (the Castrators) emerged from the Khlysts in the late 18th century. Led by the Christ Selivanov, who introduced a 'baptism by fire', they practised castration of males that many women paralleled by cutting away their breasts. The Doukhobors (Spirit-wrestlers), founded in the late 18th century, replaced Khlyst asceticism with a sternly upright morality and an emphasis on pacifism, mutual help and rejection of state authority. Just before 1900 many Doukhobors emigrated to Canada. The Molokans (Milk-drinkers or Spiritual Christians) emerged from the Doukhobors in the first decades of the sect's origins under the leadership of Simon Uklein. The Molokans are strongly democratic, see God as indwelling in human reason and seek the Kingdom of God in an egalitarian, fraternal society. All the sects were oppressed and frequently actively persecuted throughout both the tsarist and the communist periods. [45] (*See also* CATACOMB CHURCH; OLD BELIEVERS.)

Ryobu-Shinto [XXI] Dual-aspect Shinto. Ryobu-Shinto (or Honchi-suijaku) is the convergence of SHINTO and BUDDHIST deities (*shinbutsu shugo*) (*see* JAPANESE BUDDHAS AND BODHISATTVAS), often attributed to the philosophy of the priest Gyogi (670–749). It began in the 8th century with such practices as the conducting of each other's ceremonies by Shinto and Buddhist priests [14: 72–6; 21: 18; 30; 35: 304–6]. 'Honchi' means 'actual Buddha'; 'suijaku' is the same as *gongen* (*see* JINGU-JI), the mountain KAMI, which are said to be transitional forms of the BUDDHA, in transit to Japan from their origin in India.

This Buddhist–Shinto SYNCRETISM was fostered by the spread of Buddhist temples into remote areas of Japan, which required an accommodation with the local *kami* and so entailed their worship. The emperor (*see* KOKUTAI SHINTO) could be both the embodiment of the Shinto sungoddess, AMATERASU-OMIKAMI, and the Buddha Dainichi. Formally called Ryobu-Shinto, the cult was officially proscribed in the Meiji period (1868–1912) as degrading Shinto, but the belief it embodied is still current.

S

Sacerdotes [XXXI] Roman priests belonged to a number of different colleges, each with its own defined sphere of religious action. The senior college, that of the *pontifices*, was unique in including different types (the *rex*, the survivor of the one-time king, and *flamines*, each devoted to a different deity, as well as the *pontifices* themselves); one from among these was chosen (from the 3rd century BCE, elected) as *pontifex maximus* and acted as the college's public representative. The *pontifices* were responsible for most matters of cult, such as sacrifices (*see* RITUALS), temples (TEMPLA), festivals and the calendar (*see* NUMA); the *augurs* for the AUSPICIA; and the *fetiales* for the rituals of declaring war and making treaties [2: 1; 8: 76–93; 12: 394–414; 21: 36–57]. All these priests came from leading families and all except the *rex* and *flamines* continued to play leading parts in political and military life, in no sense forming a separate estate. Each college had its own body of law and kept its own books and records; typically, the priests acted as expert advisers (to the Senate or to individuals) on problems of the sacred law (IUS DIVINUM). Since the political and religious spheres were in no way separate, their decisions very frequently had great political importance [13: 1]. It is not surprising, therefore, that the emperors became members of all the important colleges and tended increasingly to act on their behalf [2: 191–8; 13: 63–5; 21: 66–74].

Sach-khand [XXXIII] For GURU NANAK and his successors, *mukti* ('release') corresponds to the condition of ineffable bliss (*sahaj*) awaiting all who persevere in NAM SIMARAN. The practice of *nam simaran* demands both disciplined meditation and a pattern of virtuous living applied in the midst of the everyday world. Those who faithfully pursue *nam simaran* will progressively ascend to ever-increasing heights of spiritual attainment. Ultimately, passing beyond the transmigratory round of death and rebirth, they enter *sach-khand*, the 'Realm of Truth' where *sahaj* reigns and all disharmony is stilled [27: 219–26]. *Mukti* for Nanak was thus the mystical climax of a spiritual ascent. Orthodox GURMAT continues to affirm this belief. It is, however, a doctrine and a discipline which must elude all but the spiritually awakened. For many, *sach-khand* is conceived as a 'heavenly abode', a place to which one's spirit goes at physical death rather than a mystical condition transcending death.

Sacraments (Christian) [XIII.B] Material signs believed by Christians to have been ordained by JESUS Christ to symbolize and convey spiritual gifts (e.g. the bread and wine in the EUCHARIST convey the presence and power of Christ). To be valid, a sacrament should have the correct 'matter' (material sign), 'form' (formula of administration) and 'intention' (to do what the church intends). This guarantees that grace (*see* SALVATION) is conveyed, whatever the personal character of the priest (see MINISTRY). Effective reception, however, depends on the condition of the recipient. Christian tradition came to recognize seven sacraments, above all baptism and the eucharist. Baptism is generally administered to infants (except for BAPTISTS). It brings incorporation into the CHURCH. Confirmation, when the recipient personally reaffirms promises made at baptism on his/her behalf, conveys a further measure of grace. PENANCE deals with sin after baptism. Extreme unction is a preparation for death. Matrimony sanctifies MARRIAGE. Priestly ordination ('orders') conveys grace for various grades of ministry. At the REFORMATION, PROTESTANTISM retained only baptism and the eucharist as genuine sacraments, though some modern forms of ANGLICANISM have allowed a sacramental quality to the rest. The two main Christian groups to reject the use of sacraments are the Quakers (see FRIENDS, RELIGIOUS SOCIETY OF) and SALVATION ARMY. Protestant use of sacraments is marked by great variety of interpretation and practice. (See also MYSTERIES (EASTERN ORTHODOX)) [114: VIII, XVI; 157: 1218–19; 123].

Sacred (the) [XXXIV] (The Holy) The terms 'sacred' and 'holy' are coterminous, even synonymous, and are different only in that they derive from different linguistic backgrounds. 'Sacred' derives from the Latin sacer, meaning 'consecrated to a divinity'; 'holy' derives from north European languages, with its roots in terms which stand for 'health' or 'wholeness'. Thus etymologically the terms differ considerably in their meanings; but in English usage they are to all intents and purposes synonymous. The term 'sacred' has been used in English writing on religion for many centuries, whereas in English translations of the Hebrew and Greek scriptural texts it is the word 'holy' that is used. In the Bible 'holy' stands for qadosh in Hebrew

and hagios in Greek. In other European languages these terms are rendered with derived forms of the word sanctus, itself derived from the word sacer. The Hebrew term stands for a state in which someone, something or some place is considered to be 'consecrated', 'set apart', 'dedicated' to the divinity. Latin and Greek renderings aim to reflect these basic meanings. If there is a difference in emphasis in the use of the terms 'holy' and 'sacred' in English, then 'holy' has appeared often as reflecting more of a moral state within a religious context, while the 'sacred' has been used of the distinctively religious state which is significantly differentiated from another state, usually referred to as 'the secular' or more traditionally as 'the profane'. It is more usual to speak of 'the sacred and the profane', reflecting something of the original context of the use of these terms in the Hebrew/Christian religious environment. The sacred, in the Roman, Latin context is related to the sanctum, the space inside the temple. The profane is the space outside the sanctum, in the forecourt or 'in front of' the temple, pro fanum. Émile Durkheim (1858–1917) defined religion in terms of the all-encompassing nature of the relationship between the sacred and the profane, and the complete, the absolute, differentiation between them. 'In all the history of human thought there exists no other example of two categories of things so profoundly differentiated or so radically opposed to one another' [48: 38]. Durkheim arrives at a definition of religion conceived purely in terms of the sacred: 'A religion is a unified system of beliefs and practices relative to sacred things, that is to say, things set apart and forbidden – beliefs and practices which unite into one single moral community . . . all those who adhere to them' [48: 47]. Durkheim's thesis about the absolute polarity of the sacred and the profane in all religions has been criticized. There are instances in which things sacred can be used for non-sacred purposes in certain religious contexts [161: 137–8]. Rudolf Otto (1869–1937) based his most important study [127] on his objections to the use of the term 'holy' 'in an entirely derivative sense' in which it meant merely 'completely good' [127: 5]. This work set the foundation of the use of the terms 'sacred' and 'holy' for the next 70 years. Otto stressed the root of the meaning of the holy in the Hebrew and Christian contexts that have already been identified. In addition, he tried to emphasize the 'extra' meaning of holy 'above and beyond the meaning of goodness' by claiming to coin a word which would express this extra dimension. The word he offered was 'the numinous', from the Latin *numen* which expresses among other meanings 'the might of a deity'. (Otto might have genuinely thought he was coining a new term, but the word 'numen' was used in English in the 19th century as a synonym for 'sacred'.) Otto analysed the 'holy' in terms of *mysterium tremendum atque fascinans*, seeing it as having the power to create awe and 'creature feeling', and as having the power both to attract and to repel. The holy represented something 'wholly other', not to be compared or referred to except by analogy to anything else in the universe. Furthermore: 'There is no religion in which [the numinous] does not live as the real innermost core, and without it no religion would be worthy of the name' [127: 6]. Here, Otto would appear here to agree with Durkheim. Other scholars have followed Otto in maintaining that 'the sacred is . . . what gives birth to religion', that 'it functions as the essence, the focus, the all-important element in religion.' Whereas previous to Otto scholars might have recognized that the sacred or the holy was a category which described certain aspects of some religions, after Otto many

scholars came to define religion in terms of the sacred or the holy. Otto's work proved to be of seminal importance and influenced later scholars such as Paul Tillich [162 vol. 1, 215–18; 163: 11], Friedrich Heiler [115] and Mircea Eliade [53: 123–4; 54: I]. Eliade believed that religion is to be defined in terms of the experience of the sacred, that the sacred was 'an element in the structure of [human] consciousness'; thus to be human 'or, rather, to become' human means to be 'religious'. He described experiences of the sacred which occurred throughout the history of religion as 'hierophanies' [57: preface]. However, it is not at all proved that the sacred is as pervasive in all religions as some scholars would claim, nor that all instances of differentiated and symbolized things, beings and places should be categorized as sacred. In order to maintain the universality of the concept of the sacred the original sense of the term has to be stretched to unacceptable levels of application; but even more importantly it is impossible, except on an intuitive basis [10: 2–5] as opposed to an empirical basis, to classify together such diverse human activities as are reported when universality is claimed.

Sacred Mountains [XXI] In Japan some mountains, mostly volcanic and cone-shaped, have been identified by ascetics as having local spirits (KAMI), called *gongen* (*see* RYOBU-SHINTO). They have, therefore, attracted groups of climbers who desire spiritual invigoration, especially *yamabushi* (*see* SHUGENDO) [4: 79–81; 20: 141–79; 31: 58–61]. Mt Fuji (altitude 3,776 m), climbed since the 17th century (last eruption 1707), was especially revered by the Fuso-kyo, a SHINTO sect worshiping Sengen Daishin (the Great Deity of Mt Fuji), but it now offers chiefly seasonal recreation. Mt Ontake (3,036 m, first recorded eruption 1980), which straddles

Gifu and Nagano prefectures, is the second most sacred. It is revered by Ontake-kyo, a sect worshipping Ontake Okami (the Great Deity of Ontake). Near Mt Haguro in Yamagata [15], a local cult taught that salvation was achieved by self-mummification through starvation and dehydration. Other sacred mountains include the numerous Zao Gongen peaks with their shrines, headed by Kimbusen in Nara prefecture (and the variations Kinbusan, Kinposan, Kimpusen, and Mitake mountains in other prefectures), Tateyama in Toyama prefecture and Hakusan on the border of Ishikawa and Gifu prefectures.

Sacred Substances (South America) [XXIII] South American cultures, perhaps more than those in any other region of the world, make religious use of plants that spark luminous visions. Prominent among these are hallucinogenic snuffs (*Piptadenia*) and plant infusions (*Banisteriopsis*). SHAMANS particularly use hallucinogenic snuffs to divine the future, ajudicate quarrels, perform sorcery, identify hunting and fishing areas and heal illness. Plant infusions (*yajé*, *ayahuasca*) are common in both tribal and urban contexts. In addition, tobacco, fermented beverages and a number of plant stimulants (capsicum pepper, coca, *guaraná*) and narcotics (*datura*) are central to religious rituals. [10]

Sacrifice [XXXIV] (From the Latin, 'to make holy') The action of 'offering' (an alternative term to sacrifice) something within a ritual action. The something sacrificed has to represent value or purity rather than the casual use of a surplus item. The sacrificer has to be seen to be making a 'sacrifice', to be losing something of value, for the action to be efficacious. The offering of an object is very common in many religious contexts [24: 37–9]. [For examples of religions and the types of sacrifices made in living religions see 'sacrifice' in the Index of Subjects in 26: *Historia Religionum*, II.] When something is offered it may be animate or inanimate. The former may be an animal owned by the sacrificer or by the group doing the sacrifice. In extreme cases there have been occurrences of human beings being sacrificed. Generally speaking, however, the usual subjects of animate sacrifice were (sometimes are) domestic animals, including fowls, sheep, goats and oxen. Among the inanimate subjects of offerings are rice, grain, milk and water. Such offerings are linked especially to the first fruits of harvest. The purpose of the sacrifice may be to propitiate a divinity, to seek a boon or some favoured result such as success in war or the success of a harvest, the removal of some pestilence or sickness, or an act of thanksgiving. The action of the sacrifice, if an animate subject is used, is first to slaughter the animal and then offer the animal's blood ritually at an altar; sometimes the main aim of slaughtering the animal is that the group making the offering may share in the eating of the cooked flesh of the animal. There is no agreement as to whether the sacrificial action is centred on the slaughter, i.e. on the spilling of the lifeblood, or in the offering of the blood by sprinkling or pouring on the altar. The argument against the action being centred on the slaughter is that in certain instances the slaughtering is not done by the main performer of the ritual, whether priest or clan chieftain or some other recognized person, but by a layperson, with the sacrificer, the recognized person, then taking the blood or the carcase and performing the ritual proper. In the offering of inanimate materials the sacrifice may be by burning, as in the case of grain, or by libation, as in the pouring of milk at many Hindu shrines, whether on horned altars or on the abstract *linga* as in Shaivite ritual. The sacrificer, as has already been suggested, may be a specialist by vocation and training, selected by a group or through hereditary connection; a priest; or it could be some other person holding state or group authority. One of the clearest group of sacrificers were, and in some cases are, the (hereditary) Brahman CASTE in HINDUISM (*see* BRAHMANS).

There has been a tendency in the history of religions to transform the sacrifice of things from animate to substitutionary objects, sometimes, as in certain Hindu sacrifices, through the breaking of terracotta models of the animal traditionally slaughtered. Sometimes the action has been transformed, as in the burning of incense instead of the flesh of animals or grain. Sometimes the transformation has been to mental or oral expressions of sacrifice. Even before the destruction of the second temple in Jerusalem in CE 70 and the effective end of ritual sacrifices in JUDAISM a cult of liturgy and prayer had grown up alongside the altar. Following the destruction of the temple the synagogue emerged as the centre of Jewish ritual with an already existing liturgy of the sacrifice of prayer and praise. In similar fashion BUDDHISM and JAINISM, and much later BHAKTI sects, emerged partly in reaction to the perceived cruelty of brahminical sacrifice in Hinduism. Whether the sacrifice is actual or substitutionary, the basic assumption of the voluntary suffering of loss for the sake of the goal to be achieved is constant. [11; 26; 43; 49; 93; 110; 176].

Saddha [XI] A PALI term (Sanskrit: *shradda*) meaning 'faith' (or trust), which is present, according to BUDDHIST traditions [67: 141], in any 'wholesome' consciousness. Until wisdom is achieved, the Buddhist acknowledges that faith is necessary. Somewhat subordinate in the THERAVADA tradition, faith is regarded in the MAHAYANA as ranking equal with wisdom [13: 144f], for faith is one of the five cardinal virtues (with

vigour, mindfulness, concentration and wisdom), and the 'seed' without which, it is held, spiritual growth cannot begin [16: 47].

Sadducees [XIII.A] A religious party in JUDAISM between 150 BCE and 70 CE. The origin of the designation is uncertain. The Sadducees were theologically conservative, rejecting post-exilic views on ANGELS and DEMONS and the belief in the bodily resurrection; views on purity akin to theirs may survive in some of the DEAD SEA SCROLLS. Socially they were aristocrats; they supported the Hasmonean priest-kings and the leading priestly families of the Herodian and Roman periods. They seem to have opposed JESUS because of his stance towards the TEMPLE and they were against the Jerusalem CHURCH, not least because of its emphasis on resurrection. [21: 317–40; 22: II, 404–14].

Sadhu [XVII] A virtuous, worthy, or honourable person, literally 'one who is straight', or without defect; in Hindu tradition a saint. Usually he – more rarely she – is one who has renounced ordinary life, but unlike the *swami*, who belongs to an order, the *sadhu* remains independent.

Sahaja Yoga [XXVIII] Her Holiness Mataji Nirmala Devi (1923–), who is said to have been born self-realized, began teaching her techniques of Sahaja Yoga in 1970, offering self-realization to others throughout the world. Self-realization is seen by Sahaja Yogis as both a physiological process and a spiritual transformation in which the Kundalini (*see* TANTRA (1)) is awakened within and passes up the spinal cord through six *cakras*. A cool breeze may be sensed, some people reporting extreme happiness or deep peace and improved mental and emotional health. The movement is experienced as an extended family over which 'Mother' exerts a powerful influence. [5: 207–9; 31; 42: 931–2]

Sahajayana [XI] One of the later schools of MAHAYANA BUDDHISM, which emphasized the practice of what was 'innate' or 'natural' (*sahaja*) to humans [42: 354]. This is a form of TANTRA (2), and the characteristic teaching of this school is found in the early Bengali collections of poems known as *caryapada*, which originated in eastern India in about the 8th century CE (or later), and are associated with Krishnacarya and others [97: 515]. The poet's name indicates the affinity of this Buddhist tantric school with (Hindu) Vaishnavism (*see* VISHNU/VAISHNAVA VEDANTA).

Sai Baba [XXVIII] Sathya Sai Baba (1926) is one of India's best-known gurus, his followers in the West being mainly, but not exclusively, among the immigrant Asian population. At the age of 13 he was unconscious for several days; three months later, he announced that he was a reincarnation of Sai Baba of Shirdi. Baba's fame is largely due to miracles to which many testify, but which Baba himself says are merely to persuade people of his real aim which is the teaching and spread of DHARMA. His ashram near Puttaparthi is a place of pilgrimage with lodging for several thousand resident followers. [42: 931; 47]

Saicho [XXI] (767–822), posthumously known as Dengyo Daishi, was the priestly founder of the TENDAI sect. [23: 258–9] He was born into the Miura family in Shiga prefecture. He entered the cloister at the age of 12, later built a small place of worship on Mt Hiei overlooking Lake Biwa, and took the vows in 786. Selected by the emperor to go to China, he went in the mission of 804, and travelled and studied on Mt T'IEN-T'AI. Returning to Japan the following year, he preached Tendai doctrines which, through his

Kegon training (*see* NANTO ROKUSHU), were designed to introduce the BUDDHA-nature to the ordinary man. His efforts to strengthen the Mt Hiei temple were thwarted by the Nara clergy, but it received the name of Enryaku-ji and the right to perform ordinations after his death. He was given his posthumous name in 866. [17]

Saints, Christian [XIII.B] At an early stage holy persons, after their death, began to be invoked in prayer by Christians to win God's favour. They included martyrs who had died for the faith; 'confessors' who had suffered for it; and holy virgins. Much use was made of the stories of saints' lives (including much legendary matter) in the middle ages for public and private devotion; and PILGRIMAGES were made to their relics. PROTESTANTISM rejected devotion to saints, but Anglo-Catholics (*see* ANGLICANISM) have allowed it. Early recognition of saints was often localized and informal. During the 12th century the PAPACY took over formal declaration of a saint's status (canonization) for the whole church. Beatification is for more restricted devotion (in one area) as well as being a stage in the long process of canonization. In the EASTERN ORTHODOX CHURCH canonization is usually by a synod of bishops for an autocephalous church. Canonizations have continued and even increased in recent years, and have included both Roman Catholics and Orthodox in the USA. [7; 63]

Sakya [XXXV] The Sakya tradition of Tibetan BUDDHISM takes its name from the monastery founded at Sakya in south-western Tibet in 1073 by Konchog Gyalpo of the Khon clan, an influential family that had previously been NYINGMA in affiliation. Konchog Gyalpo studied the 'new TANTRAS' with the translator Drokmi Lotsa. The most important of the teachings which he received from his GURU was the unified *sutra* and TANTRA (2) doctrine known as 'The Path and its Fruit' (Tibetan; *lam dre*), developed by the 9th-century yogin Virupa. According to this teaching SAMSARA and NIBBANA are just the expression of the clear brilliance (Tibetan: *gsal*) and EMPTINESS (Tibetan: *stong*) of mind itself. Thus the yogin, who perceives the true nature of his own mind by following the practice of 'The Path and its Fruit', realizes the fundamental inseparability of *samsara* and *nibbana* [24].

The Sakya sect was given definite shape by the work of 'the five masters': Sachen Kunga Nyingpo (1092–1158); Sonam Tsemo (1142–82); Dragpa Gyaltsen (1147–1216); Sakya Pandita (1182–1251); and Chogyal Phagpa (1135–80). Since that time the tradition and its two sub-sects, Ngor and Tshar, have been adorned by many eminent scholars and yogins [1].

The head of the Sakya sect is always drawn from the male line of the Khon family. The present head, Ngawang Kunga, is the 41st to hold the office. [1]

Salat [xix] (Persian and Turkish: *namaz*) The sequence of utterances and actions making up the Muslim worship (better than 'prayers'), accounted one of the PILLARS OF ISLAM. Its performance at five points of the day, from dawn till evening, is prescribed for all able-bodied adult believers. It may be performed alone, but congregational worship, e.g. in a MOSQUE, is more meritorious and is obligatory on FRIDAYS. [38 s.v.; 48: 70–81; 67 'Prayer'; 71: 537–49; 80: 155–9]

Sallekhana [xx] The religious suicide traditionally regarded as the ideal mode of death for pious members of the JAIN religion, although hardly ever practised in modern times. As envisaged in classical Jain literature, the ascetic practice of 'scouring out' (*sallekhana*) negative

factors involved monastic reinitiation and the gradual withdrawal from food and water in a lucid state of meditation. Inscriptional evidence suggests *sallekhana* was practised by lay Jains in the medieval period. [4: 155–6]

Saloi [xiii.d] 'Fools for Christ' (Russian: *iurodivye*). These individuals, revered by Eastern Christians, deliberately adopted a crazed style of behaviour, a feigned lunacy that was intended to challenge current social values. Among the earliest holy fools recognized by the church were Isidora of Tabennisi (d. 369) and Symeon of Edessa (d. 590). Popular devotion to Andrew the Scythian (9th century) made this form of asceticism popular in Russia from the 11th century. The Russian tradition of 'foolishness for the sake of Christ' reached its peak with Basil of Mangazeia (d. 1552), to whom the famous cathedral in Moscow's Red Square is dedicated. Xenia of St Petersburg (d. 1796), Theofil (d. 1853), Pelagia (d. 1884) and Pasha of Sarov (d. 1915) continued to use 'foolishness' to rebuke and teach the Russian faithful in the modern era. The priest Panagis Basias (d. 1888) is one of the few examples of a Greek holy fool in the post-Byzantine period. [46; 77; 98; 104] (*See also* ANARGYROI; NEW MARTYRS.)

Salutations (Sikh) [xxxiii] The common Sikh salutation is 'Sat Sri Akal' ('True is the Immortal One'). This is also used as a triumphal cry in Sikh assemblies. A leader calls 'Jo bole so nihal' ('Blessed is he who cries . . .') and the gathering responds with 'Sat Sri Akal!' A more formal greeting is 'Vahiguruji ka Khalsa, Siri Vahiguruji ki fateh' ('Hail to the Guru's KHALSA, hail the GURU's victory'). The latter portion may be used as a response.

Salvation [xxxiv] A term which originates in the Judaeo-Christian traditions but which is indiscriminately, and misleadingly, applied to other religious traditions in some approaches to the comparative study of religions. The English term has its root in the Latin terms for 'health' or 'deliverance'. Scripturally the English has been a translation of Hebrew terms which have a basic meaning of 'safety' or 'deliverance' and of Greek terms which have the basic meaning of 'safety' or 'soundness'. Thus salvation properly refers to a state wherein a person is removed from peril or threat into a haven of protection. Some scholars argue that salvation is the goal of every religion, that the practice of religion is directed away from life as it is towards life and afterlife as it ought to be. Salvation in these terms means deliverance, rescue from unfortunate existence, from alienation, sin, evil and the consequences of these negative forces. To speak thus of salvation may be correct as it applies to the family of religions deriving from JUDAISM. Indeed, in some manifestations of this family of religions and their sub-families salvation and the achieving of salvation often appears to be an all-consuming, almost pathological obsession. In many smaller religious manifestations, tribal or pre-literate, the notion of salvation is not by any means so clearly defined. Often the nearest the adherent comes to the notion of salvation is merely to seek to avoid negative influences in life, simply to survive physically against the hidden powers. Among many Asian religions the scene is different again. Within HINDUISM there are many different aspects to the living of life and expectations for the future. A fairly common feature is the belief in the law of consequences of deeds performed in one life which appear in a subsequent life. This is known as the operation of KARMA/SAMSARA. A person's present state is not so much to do with the notion of sin as with ignorance, a lack of wisdom to perceive what is the real state of the human being. Such lack of wisdom entails being wrapped up in present existence, failing to realize that present existence is unreal, illusory (see MAYA). The goal in such a situation is to understand, to perceive; through meditation, through good works, through the loving power of the divine, either as alternative strategies or engaging in all together, to improve one's standing in the spiral of existence, thereby achieving a better rebirth and taking a step nearer the final solution which is release from current existence and entry into Nirvana. The ultimate goal as expressed here is the same in BUDDHISM except that here the realization of what one's present existence consists of is somewhat different. It is the realization of DUKKHA, of the unsatisfactoriness of existence, sometimes rather heavily translated as 'suffering'; having realized what existence consists of, the aim is to take steps through a stratified series of stages of awareness and activity until, again, one enters Nirvana (see NIBBANA). In SIKHISM there is yet a different awareness of existence operating which largely centres on awareness of the ego, of self-centredness. The goal in this instance is to achieve GURU-centredness, where Guru stands for God, to deliver oneself into the grace of the Guru/God, who will transport the faithful disciple across the ocean of existence to the shore of bliss, where stands the court of the divine, to be yoked with the divine and never to have to return and return in successive births. To bundle such diverse notions of human existence and of remedies for human existence under the one term 'salvation' is extremely misleading, forcing, as it does, the rich diversity of different religious solutions to the problems of existence into one undifferentiated and inaccurate scenario.

Salvation, Christian Doctrine of
[XIII.B] Salvation for Christians depends upon 'grace'. This is divine favour and supernatural power freely

given by God, shown above all in the 'Atonement' (reconciliation, or at-one-ment, between humanity and God) wrought by JESUS Christ. Human beings' SIN prevents them from approaching God; reconciliation is made through Christ's sacrificial death (see CHRISTOLOGY). There have been many theories about atonement (none officially defined as 'dogma'; see AUTHORITY). Early theories about Christ's death as a 'ransom' paid to Satan are no longer generally accepted. For St ANSELM, only Christ could completely 'satisfy' God's just punishment of sin. More persistent is the view that Christ's taking human form (Incarnation) made it possible for human beings also to become divine. PROTESTANTISM has often emphasized 'penal substitution' – that Christ bore the punishment due to sinful humanity. Peter Abelard (1079–1142) thought that the love of Christ shown by his death moves humans to love God. This 'moral influence' theory has been popular in modern times. By 'justification', ROMAN CATHOLICISM has meant the conveying of grace to make people holy. Protestantism has seen it rather as God forgiving people and treating them as though righteous because of Christ's atonement. Protestants have emphasized 'justification by faith', 'faith' being understood as a response to God inspired by divine grace and as faith in the person and work of Jesus Christ. For Protestantism salvation is 'by grace through faith' in Jesus Christ to avoid the idea of PELAGIANISM, namely salvation by human effort ('works'). (REVIVALISM has emphasized a sudden 'conversion' experience as the beginning of 'real' Christianity.) Roman Catholicism allows that 'merits' (rewards for human works assisted by God's grace) can contribute to salvation. It also emphasized the crucial role of SACRAMENTS. St Augustine (see AUGUSTINIANISM), CALVINISM and JANSENISM taught 'predestination': that the saved (some add, the damned) are chosen from all eternity (contrast ARMINIANISM). The process of making Christians holy ('sanctification') has typically been differently conceived in Roman Catholicism and Protestantism. The former emphasizes the human potential for holiness (aided by divine grace), whereas the latter (e.g. LUTHERANISM, BAPTISTS and PRESBYTERIANISM) has been more pessimistic about the possibility of human holiness on earth. METHODISM and some forms of revivalism have taught a special gift of 'Perfection' in this life. In recent years Roman Catholic and Protestant understandings of salvation and of the respective roles of grace and human effort have tended to move closer to each other. The tradition of salvation of the EASTERN ORTHODOX CHURCH is less legalistic that that of the West. The aim and purpose of salvation is seen rather as *theosis* ('deification'). [54; 56; 68; 72; 114: VII, XIV; 195]

Salvation Army [XIII.B] A 19th-century Christian movement. The Army had its origins in REVIVALISM, being founded by William Booth (1829–1912), a former METHODIST, in 1878. It adopted military uniforms, bands, ranks and metaphors for its organization and activities. From 1890 social work was given a larger place but popular evangelism has continued to be characteristic of the army. The SACRAMENTS and ordained MINISTRY are rejected. The army's headquarters is in London but it works extensively in the USA and overseas MISSIONS [43: 198]

Samadhi [XI] A term used in BUDDHISM and other Indian religions in the context of the practice of YOGA and meditation (see BHAVANA; DHYANA YOGA; SAMATHA). An approximate translation is 'concentration'. In Indian accounts of the workings of the mind *samadhi* refers to the mind's general capacity to rest undisturbed on an object of perception. When this capacity is developed in meditation practice it is understood as resulting in the attainment of various ecstatic altered states of consciousness where the mind becomes completely absorbed in the object of contemplation. Such states themselves may be termed *samadhi*, though the usual term in Buddhist sources is 'absorption' or 'meditation' (Pali: *jhana*; Sanskrit: *dhyana*). Buddhist texts most commonly talk in terms of four or eight such attainments, conceived of as forming a hierarchy of higher states of consciousness; non-Buddhist sources such as the *Yoga-Sutras* have different but to some extent parallel arrangements. While such states of consciousness are regarded as the basis for the gaining of higher knowledge, it is also emphasized that they can lead to self-delusion of various kinds, and Buddhist texts continually speak of the need for mindfulness (Pali: *sati*; Sanskrit: *smriti*) and clear understanding (cf. PRAJNA), together with the parallel development of good conduct (SILA), when developing *samadhi*. [48: 41–81]

Samaritans [XIII.A] Israelites of central Palestine, descended from subjects of the northern kingdom and settlers planted there by ASSYRIAN kings. They were rebuffed by the returning Jewish exiles when they offered to cooperate in rebuilding the TEMPLE; later they were permitted by the Persians to build a temple on Mount Gerizim (*see* BIBLICAL HISTORY). This temple was destroyed by the Hasmoneans at the end of the 2nd century BCE, but the Samaritans continue to worship on Gerizim to this day. Their Hebrew BIBLE is confined to the five books of the law; the authenticity and antiquity of most of its text have been verified from similar forms of the books among the DEAD SEA SCROLLS. [11: V, 932–47; 22: II, 16–20]

Samatha [XI] One of the two main types of BUDDHIST meditation practice (BHAVANA). *Samatha* (Sanskrit: *shamatha*) is a state of calm or inner peace, brought about as a result of overcoming undisciplined activity of body and mind, especially the five 'hindrances': greediness for sense objects, angriness, sloth and drowsiness, excitement and guilt, timorous doubt. Training in alertness and joyful contentment is emphasized. *Samatha* practice aims to develop the four meditations (Pali: *jhana*; Sanskrit: *dhyana*), involving a type of altered state of consciousness bringing great joy, purity and inner tranquillity [59: 325–32]. Psychic sensitivities (*iddhi*) such as clairvoyance are often described as ensuing and still higher levels of consciousness are mentioned. Since all of these states are vulnerable to loss, they are generally considered as a desirable/optional/essential preliminary (according to the school of instruction) to insight (VIPASSANA) meditation which gives more permanent results. Numerous methods of training in calm meditation are described (*see* KAMMA-TTHANA). [34: 246–53; 46a; 96]

Samhain [VII] The CELTIC quarterly feasts were Samhain, 1 November; Imbolg, 1 February; Beltene, 1 May; and Lughnasa, 1 August [24: 197–201]. Samhain marked the beginning of winter, when the way to the 'other world' lay open, as at Yule (the winter solstice) in Scandinavia. Men might be visited by supernatural powers or the dead, and might enter the *sid* (burial mounds). Irish literature has many tales of strange happenings and deaths of heroes taking place at Samhain [17: 126; 23: 89–94].

Samkhya [XVII] One of the six DARSHANAS or salvation-philosophies of classical HINDUISM. The system is attributed to the sage Kapila, but the earliest surviving complete account is that of the *Samkhya-karika* of

Ishvara-krsna (?4th century CE) [translations: 77: 257–82; 107: 424–52]. *Samkhya* evidently developed in yogic circles responsible for parts of the post-Buddhist UPANISH-ADS (VEDA) and of the MAHABHA-RATA [51: 217–320; 77: 77–165]. The word *samkhya* means a collection of numbered lists, i.e. pre-literate systematic theory as opposed to YOGA 'work practice'. Probably what is intended is not so much conceptual analysis as a type of salvific knowledge produced by investigation (cf. JNANA YOGA). *Samkhya* envisages a hierarchic universe of mind and matter emanating from a cosmic ground (PRAKRITI) owing to imbalances in the three constituent modalities (GUNA). Humanity (*purusha*), i.e. the spiritual or conscious element, has mistakenly identified with successively grosser levels of existence, being unaware of its essential freedom and independence. *Prakriti* mechanically performs action without consciousness; *purusha* is a conscious witness 'who neither acts nor refrains from action'. To attain liberation the individual must understand the difference between him or herself and *prakriti*. When seen, *prakriti*, 'like a shy maiden', appears no more. *Samkhya* posits an ultimate difference between spirit and the stuff of which mind and matter are made and a plurality of individual persons. It does not accept a supreme deity and regards the universe as eternal and real, but cyclic. Declining after the 1st millennium CE, *Samkhya* revived from about the 14th century, ultimately taking a more theistic form. Through the medium of yoga (and later VEDANTA) it has exercised a pervasive influence on Indian thought. [28; 36: I; 53: VI; 77; 103: 114–32]

Samsara [XVII] Literally, 'wandering': a term used in religions of Indian origin to signify the continuing process of birth and death for life after life in many differing forms and conditions of existence. This is usually seen as involving not only lives as a human being but also periods of time (sometimes very long) either in various pleasant states as a deity (*deva*) in some kind of heaven or in unpleasant states as an animal, spirit or inhabitant of a hell-realm. All such births are the result of previous actions (KARMA) and conform to a law of similarity between action and result. All of this is sometimes viewed psychologically, especially in modern interpretations, and explained as referring to changing states of mind in ordinary life. Existence in *samsara* is thought to involve suffering and to be unsatisfactory compared with the ultimate spiritual goal (MOKSHA; NIBBANA).

Samskara [XVII] These are the traditional Hindu life-cycle rites that constitute both a social and a religious validation of the major transitions of a Hindu's life. *Samskara* is often, loosely, translated as 'sacrament' but the primary meaning is 'refinement'. The traditional texts enumerate some 16 *samskaras*, but these have been much reduced in contemporary practice. Three prenatal rites have barely survived into modern usage, so the first *samskara* observed in a Hindu's life are the rituals surrounding birth (*jata-karma*). Although there is great diversity of custom, the various rituals have two main purposes: to protect the new-born child and its mother from evil spirits, and to contain the pollution released by birth (*sutaka*). The mother is isolated during the birth, usually looked after by a lower-CASTE midwife, and, being ritually polluted, remains in isolation afterwards until a ceremony on the sixth day after the birth when she has her first bath and solid food and the house is purified. After another ceremony on the 12th day her touch ceases to be polluting but it requires another rite after five weeks before she can resume cooking. Various precautions are taken to protect the child, such as the use of AMULETS or charms, or giving the child an opprobrious name, all designed to ward off harmful influences, especially the evil eye (*nazar*). The name-giving ceremony (*namakarana*) is considered a separate *samskara*. The next *samskara*, which is optional but very common, is *cudakarana* or *mundana*, ritual tonsure. This can happen in any of the early years and often is done at a religious fair or at a temple on some festive occasion. Traditionally of great importance but now of a more ambivalent significance is *upanayana*, initiation or confirmation within the Aryan fold. It is the rite by which the three higher VARNAS attain their twice-born status by being invested with the sacred thread and receiving a MANTRA from their GURU. It has to be performed before marriage and always by a Brahmin, and marks the point at which an individual becomes personally responsible for maintaining the CASTE rules for purity. There is quite a lot of laxness with regard to the *upanayana* in modern usage. The next *samskara* is *vivaha*, marriage, which represents the high point of ritual purity for a Hindu, being the mid-point between the pollution of birth and the greater pollution of death. There is enormous diversity of practice throughout the subcontinent in the celebration of marriage, which can sometimes take several days. Common to most weddings are a highly complex system of gift-exchange and present-giving, the tying of the bride's and bridegroom's clothes together, the joining of their hands, the actual or symbolic circumambulation of the sacred fire or marriage pavilion several times (*phera*), numerous acts of worship and the utterance of Sanskrit *mantras*, and great festivity and ribaldry. Finally there is the *antyesti samskara*, the funeral ceremonies. Death presents a double danger: the massive pollution released which affects relatives proportionately to the degree of their

relatedness, and the risk that the spirit of the deceased (*preta*) might not move on to become an ancestor (*pitri*) but remain as a ghost (*bhuta*) to trouble the living. Although there is considerable variation in practice, all funeral rites have the purpose of containing this twofold danger. The corpse is usually cremated, preferably on a funeral pyre lit by the deceased's eldest son. The relatives remain in ritual isolation for a period of 10 or 11 days, after which a ritual called *shraddha* is performed in which offerings of milk and balls of rice or barley (*pinda*) are made to enable the departed to acquire a spiritual body for its future journey. The *shraddha* is repeated annually.

These short descriptions of the *samskaras* as they are observed today show how at each major transition in a Hindu's life rites are performed to establish new relationships or reinforce old ones on both the social and the religious plane, the degree of elaboration with which they are performed depending on the standing and status of the family concerned. [5: III; 98]

San Lun Tsung [XII] Three Treatises school. The Chinese MADHYAMIKA school (*see also* SHUNYATAVADA) was founded by KUMARAJIVA (344–413 CE) and developed by Seng Chao (384–414) and Chi T'sang (549–623). The three texts were 'The Middle Stanzas' (*Madhyamika-Karika*) and the 'Treatise on Twelve Gates' (*Dvadashanikaya*), both by Nagarjuna, and the 'Hundred Treatises' (*Shata-Shastra*) of Aryadeva. All three texts were translated by Kumarajiva. In his essays Seng Chao makes considerable progress in interpreting basic *Madhyamika* ideas in authentically Chinese terms, and his choice of language frequently reflects his own neo-Taoist interests [7: XXI, 343–56; 35: VII, 258–69; 70]. Chi T'sang's writings 'The Two Levels of Truth' (*Er Ti Chang*) and 'The Deep Meaning of the Three Treatises' (*San Lun Hsuan I*) reflect a much more traditional and Indian approach to *Madhyamika*. (*See also* NANTO ROKUSHU.) [7: XXII, 357–69; 35: VIII, 293–9; 85]

Sanatan Sikhism [XXXIII] Sanatan is the term which describes Sikhism in general prior to the influence of the Singh Sabha being brought to bear on it late in the 19th century. Sanatan Sikhism assumed an inclusive view of the Sikh faith, accepting beliefs drawn from a wide range of HINDU and Muslim tradition (beliefs in the VEDAS, Hindu epics, idolatry, SUFI *pirs*, etc.). With the rise of the Singh Sabha the Sanatan Sikhs were arrayed as a conservative group within it against the reformist TAT KHALSA group, the latter insisting upon an exclusive definition of Sikhism. According to the Tat Khalsa view SIKHS were neither Muslim nor Hindu. They were wholly independent of both. Gradually the Tat Khalsa won the battle for the right to define Sikh belief and to lay down the rules for its observance. Ever since the early 20th century Sikhism has been interpreted according to the principles promulgated by the Tat Khalsa. (*See also* SIKH REFORM MOVEMENTS.) [29: V–VI]

Sand-Paintings [V] By those North American Indians who use them (south-western tribes particularly), sand-paintings are not primarily intended as works of art, but rather as powerful tools in the service of ceremonial medicine. According to NAVAJO myths, the first sandpaintings were made by the Yeis on the shifting clouds of the sky. The technique was given to mankind. Sand-paintings (or more properly, 'dry-paintings') are made during ceremonies called *sings*, which are given to restore individual and/or cosmic harmony [13: VI]. These ceremonies have two dimensions, one to cure a specific disease or to acquire holiness, the other to exorcize evil. Each type has its own myth, ritual and set of sandpaintings. For the Navajo, a sandpainting correctly executed within the context of a *sing* becomes a kind of 'sacrament', in the sense that it does what it symbolizes. Thus the figures depicted in the sand-painting do truly represent the Yeis, and when the sick person is brought into contact with their images, she or he is brought into contact with their healing power. [19]

Sangha [XI] The community of BUDDHIST monks (BHIKKHU) and nuns (BHIKKHUNI) whose way of life is governed by the monastic code set out in the VINAYA. It has sometimes been suggested that the BUDDHA's (*see* GOTAMA) original intention was to found only a monastic movement and that the involvement of non-religious represents something of a compromise; such a view is difficult to maintain in the light of the fact that the Vinaya seems deliberately to set out to make the Sangha entirely dependent on lay support for its material needs. The reciprocal relationship that exists between the Sangha and lay followers (UPASAKA) is much valued in traditional Buddhist societies. Lay supporters provide the monks' requisites (food, lodging, clothing and medicine; *see* DANA) as a way of acquiring 'merit' (PUNNA), while the Sangha gives the gift of DHAMMA which involves both formal teaching and being available to respond to the lay community's spiritual needs. The Sangha exists today as three major ordination lineages: the Theravadin (*see* THERAVADA), the 'northern' (Tibetan) and the 'eastern' (Sino-Japanese and Korean); the Theravadin Sangha tends to be the most traditionalist in its approach to the monastic way of life and the Vinaya. The Vinaya makes no provision for such an office as 'head of the Sangha'; authority is formally a matter of the relative seniority (measured from the time of ordination) of a monk, although in the course of the Sangha's history formal offices of authority over local and national Sanghas have been instituted.

As one of 'the three jewels' to which the Buddhist goes for 'refuge' (*see* TISARANA) the Sangha is usually understood not in terms of the community of monks, but in terms of the 'noble community' (*ariya-sangha*) – the community of Buddhist 'saints' who have realized the teaching, be it as monk or nun, layman or laywoman (*see* ARAHAT). [29: 87–117; 100]

Sangiti [XI] A BUDDHIST 'council'. *Sangiti* refers to the 'communal recitation' of Buddhist scriptures (*see* TIPITAKA) by members of the Buddhist order (SANGHA) for the purpose of agreeing an authentic received form. According to Buddhist tradition, the first such council consisted of an assembly of 500 ARAHATS and took place at Rajagaha (Sanskrit: Rajagriha) soon after the BUDDHA's PARINIBBANA. Some 100 years later a second council was held at Vesali (Sanskrit: Vaishali) in order to settle a dispute about ten points of VINAYA. Most accounts suggest that this council ended in concord; certainly all extant *Vinayas* suggest that the ten points were unanimously rejected. However, from this point on the accounts of different Buddhist traditions and schools diverge. Soon after the council of Vesali it seems that the first split occurred in the Sangha, between the *Theras* (Pali; Sanskrit: *Sthaviras*) and the MAHASANGHIKAS, leading eventually to the division of the Sangha into the 18 ancient schools (cf. HINAYANA).

According to Sinhalese THERAVADA sources their lineage is to be traced back to a third Buddhist council which took place in *c*.250 BCE at Pataliputta during the reign of ASHOKA, but their account of this council is not corroborated by northern Buddhist sources. A fourth council is reckoned to have taken place in Sri Lanka in *c*.25 BCE when the Pali canon was finally committed to writing, while the fifth and sixth councils were held in Burma in 1871 and 1954–6 (the latter coinciding with the 2500th anniversary of the Buddha's death according to the traditional reckoning).

Turning to Buddhist traditions other than the Theravada, the council held in Kashmir under the auspices of the emperor Kanishka (*c*.100 CE) established the authentic VAIBHASHIKA tradition, while the Lhasa council of 792–4, where the Indian Kamalashila debated various points with the Chinese Ho-shang, was of great significance in the history of Tibetan Buddhism. [97: 201ff]

Sango/Shango [III] The original ancestor of all the YORUBA, and the god of thunder. The cult in Trinidad originated in the 19th century among Africans of Yoruba origin and sympathy. It is a SYNCRETISM of African and Roman Catholic beliefs, and many members have dual affiliation with Shango and the SPIRITUAL BAPTISTS. It has been held in generally low esteem until recently, when a level of rehabilitation has occurred. Individual groups may vary considerably in size, but annual meetings are held which may draw a thousand people, some of whom, including ardent Roman Catholics, may come for healing or CONJURE purposes. A Shango 'chapelle' may be found in a rural yard, or in an otherwise abandoned town house. Several stones/altars accommodate the spirits; there is a cult house; a tent provides space for private consultations or mournings. The chapelle may have the same ritual objects as in a VOODOO 'tonelle', but African objects are further integrated. Particularly important are the 'stones'. These hold the spirits' power. Shango is the god of thunder, and these stones represent the messages sent by Shango from the sky.

Yoruba gods are elided with Roman Catholic SAINTS; for example, Obatala fuses with St Benedict. Shango demands a variety of animal sacrifices. The colours that represent him are red and white, and when his spirit dances it uses a whip and fire as accoutrements. Shangoists believe in the double soul, or rather the soul and the spirit, the duppy (see DUPPY/JUMBIE; ZOMBIE). The language used is CREOLE with additional African words, although there were areas where Yoruba words persisted till recently. Drumming, ritual dancing and possession may continue for hours and climax in sacrifices of chickens or goats. Prophecy, CONJURE, healing and medicine for spiritual, social and physical illness are central procedures.

The same cult occurs in Grenada. Trinidadian Shango must be strongly affected by Grenada, since migration has resulted in more Grenadaians living now in Trinidad than in Grenada itself. In Grenada Shangoists co-operate more openly with Spiritual Baptists. Additionally in Grenada there is the African Feast Cult, founded by Norman Paul after a series of visions in 1948. Although it is denied by its adherents, there are strong similarities between the cult and Shango. [23a; 86]

Sanguma [xxix] Melanesian pidgin for killing a victim by sorcery. Unlike the gradual effects of POISEN, *sanguma* involves a sudden attack by one or more supernaturally empowered assailants on a lone victim, who is tormented into insanity, ritually disembowelled or stabbed with poisoned bones and thorns and allowed to return home believing his recovery to be impossible. Like *poisen, sanguma* is invoked to explain madness or sudden death and relate them to infringements within the moral order. [8; 14; 29]

Sanhedrin [xiii.A] (From Greek *synedrion*, 'council') The supreme court of the Jewish nation, first mentioned in 198 BCE and mentioned again by JOSEPHUS, in the New Testament and in rabbinic literature, though there is disparity between the descriptions of its role and functions in the various sources. Under the Hasmoneans (see BIBLICAL HISTORY) it was the ruler's advisory council. Its authority was minimal under Herod (37–4 BCE). During the Roman administration it controlled Jewish internal affairs, subject to the governor's overriding authority. It comprised 71 members, the high priest being president. Of these, SADDUCEES constituted the majority; PHARISEES formed an influential minority. Its members met in the Chamber of Hewn Stone in the TEMPLE (see JERUSALEM). It came to an end in 66–70 CE. [11: v, 975–80; 22: ii, 199–226]

Sant [xxxiii] Although the succession of Sikh GURUS ended early in the 18th century, the ancient master/disciple tradition survived within the PANTH. Many SIKHS continued to attach themselves to individual preceptors, men who disavowed the status of GURU but acquired reputations as teachers or exemplars. These preceptors eventually acquired the title of Sant, previously applied in the SANT TRADITION to any ordinary devotee. They continue to flourish within the Panth, some of them commanding substantial influence. [28: 55–6]

Sant Mat [xvii] (The way of the saints) A term that refers to religious movements in modern India that are led by gurus descending from the medieval HINDU SANT TRADITION. Prominent among these movements are the RADHASOAMI SATSANG and one of its offshoots, the Ruhani Satsang ('Spiritual Fellowship'). When Sawan Singh, the 'Great Master' of the Beas Branch of Radhasoami, died in 1948, one of his leading disciples, Kirpal Singh, left Beas to establish the Ruhani Satsang at Sawan Ashram in New Delhi. He initiated 80,000 persons into Sant Mat, many of whom were Europeans and Americans attracted to the fellowship when Kirpal Singh went on world tours in the 1960s and early 1970s. When he died in 1974, he was succeeded by his son, Darshan Singh, and by several other contenders to the Ruhani Satsang throne, including Ajaib Singh and Thakar Singh, each of whom formed his own organization. One of Kirpal Singh's American initiates, Paul Twitchell, utilized Sant Mat ideas in forming the ECKANKAR movement (*eckankar*, the first term in the morning prayer of GURU NANAK, literally means 'one Om') [xxviii 34; 69]. Other spiritual leaders who have adopted Sant Mat concepts and practices include Anukul Thakur, Maharaj-ji – the so-called 'boy guru' who led the DIVINE LIGHT MISSION – and John-Roger Hinkins, who led a spiritual movement in Southern California. Their popularity in the West peaked during the 1970s and 1980s. The phrase *sant mat* originated in the poetry of the 16th-century Kabir, a great SANT of medieval India. [6; 52; 60; 65; 67; 115; 134]

Sant-sipahi [xxxiii] The ideal SIKH. Spiritual qualities are summed up in the first word. A Sikh should be pious and humble like a *sant*, devoted to the NAM and willing to be the dust under everyone's feet. Yet a Sikh should also possess the martial qualities of a *sipahi* (soldier), inflexibly courageous and prepared to fight gallantly for justice even to the point of death. [28: 55–6]

Sant Tradition of Northern India [xxxiii] The SANT tradition of northern India is commonly confused with Vaishnava (*see* VISHNU) BHAKTI. It is, however, a distinct movement, one which draws heavily on Bhakti antecedents but also has other roots. Two major sources can be identified. Vaishnava Bhakti is one of these, and for most Sants is clearly the dominant source. To it must be added the NATH TRADITION, a source which is particularly evident in the works of Kabir (probably *c*.1440–1518). SUFI influence may also have contributed to the development of Sant ideals. Like Bhakti adherents, the Sants stress devotion as essential to *mukti* (*see* SACH-KHAND). They differ in their insistence that God is *nirguna* (without form or 'qualities') and can be neither incarnated nor represented iconically (*saguna*). To the Naths they evidently owe their stress on interior religion. God, immanently revealed, is contemplated inwardly and all exterior forms are spurned. The two most prominent representatives of the tradition are NANAK and Kabir. [27: 151–8; 28: 23–31]

Santeria [III] (from Spanish: 'the saints') The generic term for a group of African gods in Cuba, and their devotion in a syncretic cult which elides African and Roman Catholic elements (*see* CREOLE/CREOLIZATION). Many YORUBA ORISHAS are identified with Catholic SAINTS. Shopana, the Yoruba god of smallpox, is associated with Lazarus and all skin diseases. All the spirits in Santeria have very distinctive appearances, characters and tastes. Shopana enjoys maize; he wears clothes made of jute; he needs to use crutches. Shango (*see* SANGO) wears red-and-white beads, likes to eat ram and is associated with St Barbara. In order to encourage a spirit to possess a devotee, the animal appropriate to that spirit is sacrificed. This is called 'feeding the gods'. Other African-derived elements are drumming, dancing and singing.

The system of divination strongly resembles the Yoruba IFA system, although the *orishas* may differ from those in Africa in character and qualities. The Abakwa Society of Santeria is directly related to the Egbo Society of Calabar and is a mutual aid society for young men, markedly African in language and dance. After the Cuban revolution of 1958, President Fidel Castro suppressed Santeria as he did the Roman Catholic church, but as Cuban refugees from his regime dispersed, especially to the USA, they took Santeria with them. [7; 71; 86]

Sanusis [XIX] A SUFI ORDER, strong in north Africa and the eastern Sahara, founded by Muhammad al-Sanusi (1791–1855). It emphasized a simple, purified form of ISLAM and established *zawiyas* (*see* SUFI INSTITUTIONS) across the Sahara as centres of evangelism, education and agricultural activity among the superficially Islamized peoples there. After 1911, it was the spearhead of resistance to the Italians in Libya, and after the Second World War its leader Sayyid Idris became King of Libya, reigning until 1970. [78: IX; 125: 118–20; 145]

Saramakas/Saramaccas [III] A MAROON group found in Surinam, one of the six clans of the so-called 'bush negroes'. This term distinguishes the bush negroes from the 'town' African slaves who did not run away from their owners. The territory in which the Saramakkas found themselves in the 18th century was very inhospitable. This made pursuit of them difficult, but it also made their own lives very hazardous, and there was great suffering: even the river near which they settled was contaminated, calling for the performance of powerful rituals in the name of a great oracle-deity to purify the water. They protected their villages as carefully as they conserved their African beliefs. They believed in the power of their ancestors, and their ancestors' OBEAH. They believed that protective AMULETS rendered them safe against bullets. As their communities developed and stabilized, so the somewhat fractured institutions and kinship networks of their early settlements appear to have developed less

coercive and less centralized institutions. The possibility of supernatural punishment replaced that of harsh guerrilla leaders. By the 19th century it appears that highly individual cults had given way to more communally expressed religious observations.

In the 20th century 'town' negroes had spirits which were of African origin and were called *winti*. Leba is of the greatest significance: he is the guardian of the crossroads, whose origin is the god/TRICKSTER of West African religion (*see* VOODOO). In the region midway between the coastal towns and the Saramakkan villages, the people are of African and African/Dutch origins, and the structure of their religion has both European and African elements. The spirits of earth, the forest and the water live in a highly stratified order which parallels the earthly social order. Most of the *winti* are considered to be fallen angels. There is a belief in the significance of dreams, and their interpretation; in the idea of the werewolf; in the mirror used by the *bonu-man* in diagnosing spiritual or psychic ill-health; in the story of the fall of angels; and in holy water.

The inland Saramakkas have a Supreme God, although he has no special priests. Lower gods may be malevolent or benign, though their attitude may depend on how they are being treated. Minor gods may appear for consultation, by possessing initiates. The cause of misfortune may be revealed and treated. The treatment for harmful magic is *wisi*, the witch a *wisiman*, and their power is opposed by the *obiamen* (*see* OBEAH) who are healers. The chief priests have considerable status, and may act in a civil role when important decisions have to be implemented. At the core of Saramakka culture lie their stories, *kointu*, which are told at burial times in order that the deceased be properly incorporated into the world of the ancestors.

The language of the Saramakkas is said to be the oldest African-American CREOLE. Some of the negative attitudes to the language have previously influenced the way in which the whole culture has been viewed. [46; 54; 76; 77; 78; 86]

Sarasvati [XVII] For most Hindus Sarasvati, the goddess of arts and learning, is the consort of BRAHMA, showing his creative power in action in the human world. A river goddess in the VEDA (*see* GANGA), she became identified with Vac, goddess of speech, and hence of inspiration: she is invoked for blessings, second only to GANESHA, at the beginning of any poetic composition. In art she generally appears dressed in white, holding a *vina*, a deep-toned stringed instrument, and attended by her animal (VAHANA), the sacred goose (*hamsa*), or in modern versions by peacocks or swans. In eastern India she is sometimes portrayed as one of the wives of VISHNU (her rivalry with LAKSHMI, goddess of fortune, providing a playful explanation of why good artists and poets are seldom rich).

In keeping with the non-sectarian nature of the arts (*see* ART (HINDU)), Sarasvati is revered in the other south Asian religions, particularly JAINISM, which is popular among craftworkers. In Tibetan BUDDHIST iconography she appears as a consort of the BODHISATTVA of wisdom, MANJUSHRI.

Sarnath [XI] The place outside Benares (Varanasi) where the BUDDHA (*see* GOTAMA) gave his first discourse. This first discourse constitutes the 'turning of the wheel of DHAMMA' and is said to have been delivered in a deer park two months after the Buddha's enlightenment, when he taught the noble EIGHT-FOLD PATH to five wandering ascetics who had been his companions during the period he practised severe austerities. A characteristic pose of the BUDDHA IMAGE with the hands held in front of the chest indicates the first discourse. The site at Sarnath has been venerated from at least the time of ASHOKA, although the Dhamekh STUPA which marks the exact location of the first teaching is basically a 5th-century structure. Sarnath is one of four principal BUDDHIST pilgrimage centres (cf. BODHGAYA; KUSINARA; LUMBINI) attracting pilgrims from all over the Buddhist world. (*See also* ASALHA.)

Sarvastivada [XI] The view that 'all exists' (*sarvam asti*) and the name of the non-MAHAYANA BUDDHIST school that propounded this view. The view does not belong to the earliest phase of Buddhist thought, but becomes a matter of dispute among Buddhist ABHIDHAMMA schools from the 3rd century BCE. The view is rejected by the early THERAVADA in the *Kathavatthu* and by the SAUTRANTIKAS. It addresses in part a basic problem that arises when the theory of KARMA is combined with the Buddhist understanding of phenomena (DHAMMA) as impermanent (ANICCA): how can something that no longer exists (an action performed long in the past) have a present result? The answer proffered by the followers of *sarvastivada* is to suggest that to designate phenomena as past or future is not actually to say that they do not exist, but rather that they exist in a particular way, namely in the past or the future; thus all phenomena are said to exist in the three times of past, present and future. Quite how this view of time should be understood was a matter of some discussion among Sarvastivadins; VASUBAND-HU's *Abhidharmakosha* records the views of four teachers: Dharmatrata, Ghoshaka, Vasumitra and Buddha-deva. The standard systematization of the Sarvastivadin Abhidharma as a whole is that of the VAIBHASHIKAS. As a philosophical school the Sarvastivada no longer survives, but as a lineage of the SANGHA it is today represented by Tibetan monastic

Buddhism which follows the VINAYA of a later sub-school, the Mulasarvastivada. [16: 138–41; 89: 64–80; 51: 601–3]

Satan (in Islam) [XIX] The Devil is termed Iblis (from the Greek *diabolos*, via Judaeo-Christian intermediation) and al-Shaitan (Satan). In the QUR'AN Iblis is the angel who disobeyed God (ALLAH) by refusing to acknowledge God's creature Adam as his superior. He was expelled from paradise and secured the fall from grace of Adam and Eve (*see* MALA'IKA). Al-Shaitan has the dual signification of Satan specifically, who perpetually seeks to lead mankind astray by his insidious suggestions, and of devils or evil spirits in general, corresponding here to the unbelieving JINN. However, on the day of judgement (QIYAMA), Iblis/Satan and his hosts will be consigned to hell-fire. In Islamic lore, Satan is often given the epithet *al-Rajim* 'the one who should be stoned', from one of the practices traditional in the pilgrimage to Mecca (*see* HAJJ). [37 'Shaitan'; 48: 88]

Satanism [XXIV] The worship of Satan or other central figures from Christian demonology. Satanism, essentially a reaction against Christianity, has historically been a rare occurrence. From the late middle ages witches were accused of devil-worship (*see* WITCHCRAFT), but there is almost no reliable evidence that it took place. The distinctive rite of Satanism is supposedly the 'black mass' – a blasphemous parody of the MASS, celebrated by an unfrocked priest, with black candles and inverted crucifix, involving defilement of the consecrated host (EUCHARIST), sexual indulgence and sometimes animal or even human sacrifice. But no description of it exists from before the later 19th century. Medieval heretics (*see* HERESY) were accused of perverting the mass, and in 17th-century France distorted versions were occasionally celebrated for magical purposes, but Satanism was not involved. Modern Satanism dates from the 19th-century 'OCCULT revival', which included a synthetic 'revival' of Satanism in imitation of practices attributed in previous centuries to witches and sorcerers. Satanism continues to lead a fitful existence among those who find excitement in doing things they believe to be wicked, and is sustained partly by popular fiction and cinema and partly by occasional ecclesiastical denunciations, which have always tended to stimulate interest in it. [25]

Sati [XVII] A term used by Hindus meaning, literally, 'a virtuous woman'. The word carried the special meaning of a woman whose virtue leads her to immolate herself with her dead husband on his funeral pyre. It is also the name of a goddess, the first wife of SHIVA, who immolated herself in shame at her father's mistreatment of her husband, and was later reborn as PARVATI. It has been suggested that the origin of the custom was the practice of providing a dead man, at his funeral, with all that he would need in the other world: his horses, his possessions and his widow [12: 188]. It has been regarded in Hindu society as in theory voluntary, but social pressure was strong enough to keep the practice in force as late as the 19th century, in some cases even where it was not voluntary. In 1839 it was forbidden by Lord William Bentinck, following a campaign against it by some reformist Hindus, notably Ram Mohan Roy (1774–1833). The custom, normally practised only by the higher VARNAS (especially the KSHATRIYAS), never met with universal approval, and was rejected by the LINGAYATAS and many Tantric groups (*see* TANTRA (1)). Occasional instances are still reported. From *sati* comes the Anglo-Indian word 'suttee' generally misapplied to the ritual rather than the woman carrying it out. [80: 366]

Satsang [XVII] (True fellowship) The form of worship and communal organization common to India's SANT MAT movements, including the RADHASOAMI SATSANG. The term originates in the medieval SANT TRADITION, where it referred to the fellowship of saints. In the SIKH tradition it connotes a communal gathering featuring chanting and worship. In Radhasoami and related movements it is a central concept: like the word 'church', it carries the multivalent meanings of institution, community and worship. The most intimate form of *satsang* is between an individual and the GURU; this *satsang* can take place in a spiritual form during meditation, which is called SURAT SABD YOGA. One also meets the guru spiritually during *satsang* events. These spiritual gatherings may indeed feature a living master seated on a raised platform, bestowing on his followers the blessing of his *darshan* (sight). The worship consists of chanted readings of the poetry of medieval Sants such as Kabir and GURU NANAK, and the writings of masters in the Radhasoami tradition. This is followed by a homily delivered by a leader of the movement or by the master himself, and ends with the distribution of *prasad*, sacred food made from wheat paste. The entire Radhasoami organization is itself designated as *satsang*, implying that the communal fellowship of the movement is the organization's defining characteristic. The merchant-CASTE leadership of the movement places few restrictions along caste or gender lines, and the Radhasoami *satsang* tends to be a more egalitarian community than the society at large. [67]

Saum [XIX] Fasting, accounted one of the PILLARS OF ISLAM. Fasting during the daylight hours of the month of Ramadan is obligatory on all healthy adults, and is still strictly observed in most of the Islamic world. The end of the fast is celebrated by a festival of rejoicing, the 'Id al-Fitr (*see* 'ID). There are other voluntary fast days in the Islamic calendar, e.g. on 'Ashura day, 10 Muharram. [38 'Sawm'; 48: 102–4; 67 'Fasting'; 80: 160–1]

Sautrantika [XI] An important non-MAHAYANA BUDDHIST philosophical school that flourished from *c.*1st century CE. The Sautrantikas adhered to the *sutranta* (Pali: SUTTANTA) method in their interpretation of the *Sutras* (*see* TIPITAKA). Sautrantikas did not accept the authority of the ABHIDHAMMA texts and were especially critical of certain VAIBHASHIKA positions (*see* SARVASTIVADA). Sautrantika views are known principally from VASUBANDHU's *Abhidharmakosha* which expounds Vaibhashika Abhidharma with comments from an essentially Sautrantika perspective. Among the characteristic teachings of the Sautrantika school were an understanding of phenomena as radically momentary (*see* ANICCA) and the theory of 'seeds' (*bija*). The theory of seeds was intended to show, among other things, how past actions (KARMA) can have present results: actions sow seeds in the mental continuum of a being, modifying it until such time as the fruit is born; Sautrantikas also taught that the minds of all beings are capable of enlightenment by virtue of their possessing certain wholesome seeds. The theory adumbrates certain features of the YOGACARA 'store consciousness' (ALAYA-VIJNANA). [16: 134, 141–4]

Sayyid, Sharif [XIX] Originally meaning in Arabic 'tribal leader' and 'noble', these words have come in the Islamic world to designate those claiming descent from the Prophet MUHAMMAD through his daughter Fatima and son-in-law 'ALI. Becoming over the course of centuries extremely numerous, and now found as far afield as India and Indonesia, these descendants have formed something like a spiritual aristocracy in Islam, and often a social one also, in that they frequently enjoyed financial and other privileges; certain families of them have achieved political power, such as the Sayyid kings of Delhi, the Sharifs of Mecca and the present-day ruling dynasty of Morocco, the 'Alawis. [37 s.vv.]

Scepticism [xxxii] A religious sceptic is one who denies that there are any grounds for reasonable belief in religious matters. Scepticism is a legacy of Greek philosophy in the Western world. Often, as in the writings of the 18th-century philosopher David Hume [12], it tries to distinguish between the kind of knowledge human beings can achieve (that of natural science) and kinds of knowledge that are not possible (metaphysical and religious). But thorough sceptics, Hume included, have frequently found themselves obliged to deny that there are grounds for quite ordinary beliefs about the world. There has, for this reason, been a tradition of scepticism – particularly strong in 16th-century France – in which it is an ally of religion [18]. Michel de Montaigne, for instance, held that no real knowledge could be acquired by human reason and that, therefore, it could only be acquired through faith and revelation. Nowadays, however, the world 'sceptic' is more commonly applied to someone – Bertrand Russell (1872–1970), for example – who is unsympathetic to religion.

Schleiermacher, Friedrich Daniel Ernst [xiii.c] (1768–1834) After education in colleges of the Herrnhüter Brethren, Schleiermacher went to university at Halle in 1787, where in 1804 he was appointed professor, moving later (1807) to Berlin. In *On Religion: Speeches to its Cultured Despisers* (1799) and *The Christian Faith* (1821), he defended religion against the rationalism of the ENLIGHTENMENT by asserting that its essence lies in the 'feeling' of absolute dependence and that the concept of God is to be understood as derived from this feeling. [14; 19; 29]

Scholasticism [xiii.c] The Christian theological method used primarily by medieval scholars to draw out the implications of revealed truths expressed by the scriptures (BIBLE) and the Fathers of the church, to establish their mutual consistency, and to reconcile apparent contradictions between them and natural understanding (see AUTHORITY). Although the basic principles (of the primary authority of revealed truth and of the use of logic) had long been enunciated, the method flourished, especially in the 12th and 13th centuries, with the development of dialectical methods of reasoning, the use of subtle distinctions and the incorporation of Aristotelian thought. Among the foremost scholastics are Albert the Great (c.1200–1280), Aquinas (see THOMISM), Bonaventura (1221–74) and Duns Scotus (c.1264–1308). One basic dispute within medieval scholasticism was between realists (cf. William of Champeaux, c.1070–1121), who maintained that concepts ('universals') have a mode of existence of their own, and nominalists (cf. Abelard, 1079–1142, and William of Occam, c.1300–c.1349), who maintained that only actual individuals exist and that universals are abstractions from them made by the understanding. [6; 12]

Scientism [xxxii] The tendency to invoke the authority of science in matters commonly thought to be outside its province [8] or to elevate science to the level of a panacea for all human ills. 'Scientism' is a term of abuse with no fixed meaning. It is sometimes used by writers in MARX-ISM to refer to an IDEOLOGY shared by scientists [22]. It is also used to mean POSITIVISM or scientific HUMANISM.

Scriptures [I] From the Latin *scriptura* ('a writing'), a term often used loosely to denote particular holy books of diverse religions. Commonly the authority of such writings is seen as deriving from the gods (HAMMURABI'S CODE); established by some holy person by, for example, being seen in a revelation (QUR'AN); by attribution to legendary persons (CONFUCIAN CANON); by the believed spiritual potency of its words (FUNERAL PRACTICES (ANCIENT EGYPTIAN)); by its use in RITUAL (e.g. ADI GRANTH; AVESTA; VEDAS); or by a combination of such factors (BIBLE). Because revelations, however authoritative, are thought to occur in a specific time and place, the interpretations, adaptations or supplements to such revelations can also acquire considerable authority (e.g. HADITH, TORAH). The relevant weighting of scripture and the official bodies which interpret it can vary within a religion (*see* AUTHORITY (CHRISTIAN)), as can the officially listed texts which comprise a CANON of scripture (*see* TIPITAKA). Such official works are not necessarily the books most widely read or understood by adherents. The written scripture is generally the product of a lengthy oral holy tradition wherein the material often has a verse or musical form to aid memorizing [XIV 82a]. The interpretation of scripture is commonly the task of a professional class of priests or scholars (*see* HERMENEUTICS; RABBI). [2]

Sects (Christian) [XIII.B] The term 'sect' may be used pejoratively of bodies regarded as heretical (*see* HERESY, ORTHODOXY, SCHISM). As a neutral technical term in sociological analysis of Christianity, however, a 'sect' denotes a body with certain characteristics, such as extreme emphasis on some aspects or doctrines of the Christian tradition at the expense of others; personal conversion as a condition of membership; and condemnation of the values and institutions of ordinary society. This is contrasted with the 'church' type of Christianity, which is characterized by a comprehensive or balanced range of teaching; membership including whole nations or requiring only minimal qualifications; and a high degree of accommodation to the values and institutions of society at large. 'Denomination' is used of bodies which are more broadly based and open to ordinary society than sects, while less comprehensive and socially tolerant than 'churches'. In this classification ANGLICANISM, the EASTERN ORTHODOX CHURCH and ROMAN CATHOLICISM would be 'churches' and METHODISM and PRESBYTERIANISM (for example) 'denominations'. (Outside sociological discussion, however, 'church' and 'denomination' are usually used simply as synonymous terms for any organized Christian body. For specialized theological uses cf. CHURCH (CHRISTIAN).) Sects often originate in a 'charismatic' leader; and a number emphasize MILLENARIANISM. The connection often made with the socially deprived is not invariably correct. In some cases, time brings a more balanced doctrinal system and erodes separation from society (e.g. PENTECOSTALISM) [204; 205]. A large number of sects have developed in the USA [27; 141] notably CHRISTIAN SCIENCE, JEHOVAH'S WITNESSES and MORMONS. Extreme deviations from the mainstream of Christianity and the introduction of extensive extra-Christian elements may be held to qualify some sects as 'cults' rather than as Christian sects (*see* AFRICA, NEW RELIGIOUS MOVEMENTS IN).

Sects and Societies (Chinese) [XII] Sects and societies with political and religious ideologies have frequently arisen in China during periods of disunity. The Yellow Turbans, who rebelled against the Han government in 184 CE, are an early example. Many later sects were syncretistic in nature, often reflecting a BUDDHIST influence, focusing upon MAITREYA BODHISATTVA. One famous example was the White Lotus Society, founded in the 12th century CE, which rebelled in 1351 and helped to overthrow the Yuan (Mongol) rulers in 1368. [46; 80; 122: IX, 218–43]

Secular Alternatives to Religion [XXXII] Discussion of alternatives to religion needs a perspective on the nature of religion. Secular alternatives are not themselves religions but must share enough in common with religions to present themselves as options which exclude religious adherence. Someone who adopted a theoretical standpoint which, for that individual, excluded religious belief (as, for example, SCEPTICISM and DIALECTICAL MATERIALISM commonly do) need not accept any alternative to religion. There need not be anything which plays a role in his or her life analogous to that of religion in the life of a believer. But there are those whose theoretical standpoint is secular but for whom certain commitments perform the same function as does adherence to a religion.

J. M. Yinger (b. 1916) [28: 190f] has offered a 'functional definition' of a religion as 'a system of beliefs and practices by means of which a group of people struggles with the ultimate problems of human life'. He suggests that POSITIVISM, with its faith in science, MARXISM, with its faith in revolution, and Freudianism, with its faith in psychoanalysis, have all served as secular alternatives to religion. UTILITARIANISM seems to have functioned as such an alternative for J. S. Mill and his 'sect'. [16: 69f] So has HUMANISM, with church-like institutions such as the South Place Ethical Society in London.

Yinger himself takes the view that such alternatives can be no more than partial since they do not really come to terms with the ultimate problems of human life. In doing so he begs the question, from the point of view of those who adhere to these alternatives, as to what the ultimate problems of human life are. He implies that humans have needs which only a 'proper' religion could satisfy. Marxists and many humanists would deny such a claim and insist, on the contrary, that religion diverts people from their true needs. This indeed is part of Marx's point in characterizing religion as IDEOLOGY. Marx himself, following Ludwig Feuerbach (1804–72) to some extent, approached religion in a spirit of REDUCTIONISM, seeing as a merely human phenomenon what its practitioners see as involving rather more. What Yinger refers to as the 'partial' nature of Marxism as a secular religion is the other side of the same coin.

Secularization [XXXIV] Secularization has primarily been discussed in SOCIOLOGY OF RELIGION, but in history, theology and in other disciplines too. It deals with the social functions of religion and with the problem of personal existence in society. The revival of interest in secularization in the 1960s in part signalled a dissatisfaction with narrowly positivistic assumptions and methods then extant.

The term secularization, used in several different contexts, together with the cognates 'secular', 'secularist', 'secularism', 'secularity', has provoked many-sided analysis mainly directed to scrutiny about the way in which modernization brings it about that 'religious institutions, actions and consciousness lose their social significance'. This impact of modernization may be understood under three heads: social differentiation (see 'laicization' below); societalization, i.e. life in modern societies is less favourable to religion than life in small-scale communities; and rationalization, in which we come to think about things in terms of a rational system of ideas, rather than e.g. appeal to magic (Wallis and Bruce in 32: 8ff). Dobbelaere distinguishes between laicization of societal institutions, decline in church involvement, and religious change [44: 5ff]. Shiner presents six types of secularization: decline of religion; conformity with 'this world'; disengagement of society from religion; transposition of religious beliefs and institutions; desacralization of the world; and social change [146]. Martin has called for nuanced interpretation which respects the subtlety of the subject matter and avoids the danger of generalization. Problems have arisen, for instance, from supposing 'that the American and European cases represent two variations on the same underlying theme of global secularization'.

It is not surprising that the meaning of 'secularization' is elusive when the meanings of RELIGION are so problematic. The distinction between functional definitions (what a religion does) and substantive definitions (what a religion is) leaves many puzzles unresolved. Opposition to mainstream theories of secularization have come from Greeley [70], who claims that the persistence of religion is based on the human need for an ultimate interpretative scheme, and from Stark and Bainbridge, whose thesis concludes that secularization is self-limiting.

Secularization, understood as laicization, goes back in its concrete meaning to the negotiations leading to the Treaty of Westphalia in 1648 and was proposed by Longueville to describe the ambiguous making over of ecclesiastical territories to Brandenburg. Secularization also came to refer, in canon law, to permission given to a religious to live henceforth outside their religious house. Used in a broader sense of laicization,

secularization is a neutral term referring to processes in society whereby parts of, or the whole of, society cease to be determined by religion, e.g. the transfer of secular control of activities – such as law, education and social welfare – formerly undertaken by religious agents.

In judging the cogency of an appeal to secularization, does much rest on the predication of an appropriate historical base-line, i.e. an age of faith after which decline sets in? Sorokin starts from what he claims to be medieval Catholicism. But it is a very selective and optimistic reading.

The neutral meaning of the cognate 'secularity' refers to the outcome of secularization, namely human autonomy. But secularization can also refer to a process whose outcome is 'secularism' based on a socio-political programme or ideology. A classic instance of this use is G. J. Holyoake's *Secularism: the Practical Philosophy of the People* (1854) [85]. Holyoake's secularism had socialist, rationalist, anticlerical and agnostic elements; it was a 'system of ethical principles'. He was a social reformer, especially advocating cooperation. His memoirs are entitled *Sixty Years of an Agitator's Life* (1892). Holyoake's 'successor' was Charles Bradlaugh, who stood for a more explicitly secularist anti-Christian propaganda. In France, the term 'secularization' itself was associated with positivism and materialism.

Keller [*Sacramentum Mundi*, VI, 64ff] periodizes the history of Christianity to bring out the motif of secularization. In the New Testament message neither the worldly nor the Christian realm preponderates. The second stage, running from patristic to modern times, is marked by the dominance of religious over secular, even the absorption of the latter by the former. Facing objections from the start, this religious view gave way to secularization in the modern era. Scientific truth called into question the unity of the one truth. The church progressively lost its political influence over the state. In spirituality, detachment from the world is called into question. The bodily and material spheres were accorded a real value of their own. What is to be the Christian attitude to this process? Crudely put, the world is to be subordinated to religion *or* the holy is realized in the profane, i.e. the religious task is the worldly one.

Some theologians, influenced by Karl Barth who set 'faith' over against 'religion', welcomed secularization, but in a negative sense. More positively, however, the PROTESTANT Gogarten and the ROMAN CATHOLIC Metz treat secularization, as distinct from secularism, as a necessary and proper consequence of Christian faith. The most remarkable figure apparently to hold such views is the German martyr-theologian Dietrich Bonhoeffer. Bonhoeffer's theological views changed more than once and his mature position is not altogether clear. The term 'secular Christianity' is sometimes used for a group of theologians in the 1960s including also Cox, van Buren and R. G. Smith, drawing upon Bonhoeffer and other sources [27; 40].

It is important to observe the kind of world in which the concept of secularization flourished among sociologists of religion and 'radical' theologians in the 1960s and after. The end of the Cold War, the increase in wealth, the acceleration of technological development and the decline in formal religious observance in *some* parts of the world led to an increased anthropocentric optimism in many quarters. However, the recent renewed impact of major religions in the political arena should give fresh food for thought about the connections between secularization, religion and social systems. Will advantages accrue from looking at the secularization thesis from religious standpoints other than Christianity? [32; 34; 35; 68; 119; 139; 177; 178; 179]

Sefardim [XXII] Jews of Spanish or Portuguese origin who left the Iberian peninsula at the end of the 15th century when the Jews were expelled (*see* EUROPEAN JEWRY), and settled in north Africa, the Levant, the Far East and northern Europe [36: VI]. Spanish Jewish culture was highly developed and the Sefardi refugees tended to dominate the Jewish communities in the areas of their new settlement. This explains why Jews in Islamic countries have come to be known as Sefardim, although many of them are not originally of Spanish origin. Some descendants of the Sefardi refugees still put the suffix 'Sefardi Tahor' ('Pure Sefardi') after their names. Sefardi Jews differ from their ASHKENAZI co-religionists in a number of ritual and cultural ways, some of which are explicable by the differences between the Christian and Islamic host cultures in which they lived [70: 211]. More than half the population of modern ISRAEL consists of Sefardi-oriental Jews. [52; 73]

Sefirah [XXII] (plural *sefirot*) One of the 10 stages in the process of divine emanation central to kabbalistic thought (*see* KABBALAH) [14 vol. 14: 1104]. First mentioned in the *Sefer Yetzirah* (3rd century), the concept is more fully developed in the ZOHAR, where the *sefirot* are depicted as manifestations of different aspects of the Godhead, *Ein Sof*, in the structuring of reality [70: 95]. The images used for the *sefirot* in kabbalistic literature are highly personalized, but the mystics themselves emphasize the divine unity behind them (*see also* SITRA ACHRA). [61: 208]

Seicho no Ie [XXVI] One of the best known of the new religious movements in Japan, Seicho no Ie, the 'house of growth', owes its origin to the work of Taniguchi Masaharu

(1893–1985). With its headquarters in Tokyo, the organization claims a membership of nearly 2 million, including overseas adherents. Taniguchi was a cultured man who sought religious truth for many years. Once, during meditation, he heard a voice saying, 'The material world is nothing. True reality is everything. True reality is KAMI.' He then had a vision of the *kami* and of his own true self. Filled with joy, he wanted to share this enlightenment with others. In December 1929 he heard the voice say, 'Now arise' (*ima tate*), and beginning in March 1930 he began to publish the journal *Seicho no Ie*. Taniguchi, unlike many leaders of new religious movements, had a gift for clear, logical expression. He attracted many by his writings. The current leader is his adoptive son-in-law, Taniguchi Seicho (1919–).

Seicho no Ie teachings may be divided into 'vertical truth' and 'horizontal truth'. Vertical truth means that human beings are in principle the highest expression of the self-manifestation of the *kami*. The truth about humans is that they are filled with inexhaustible wisdom, love, life and virtue. Horizontal truth means that in this phenomenal world the human heart holds the key as to whether one will be rich or poor, happy or unhappy, healthy or unhealthy, etc. To know the truth of the basic perfection of human life is to be free of all unhappiness and disease. The way to this knowledge is to read Seicho no Ie writings daily and to meditate in accordance with Seicho no Ie precepts so as to drive evil feelings from the heart, open it up to its innate goodness and thenceforth live a life of gratitude. [10: xII, 226–7; 11; 13: 107–8, 110, 112, 119, 121–3; 14; 18]

Sekai Kyuseikyo [xxvI] Known in the West as the Church of World Messianity, Sekai Kyuseikyo traces its origin to the founding of the Dainihon Kannon Kai, or 'Great Japan Avalokitesvara Society', by Okada Mokichi (1882–1955) in Tokyo in 1935. Okada, himself prone to illness, joined OMOTO in 1920. He devoted himself to mastering its theory and practice of spiritual healing and eventually became a leader. Criticized for his independent healing techniques, however, Okada, with a handful of followers, quit Omoto in 1934 and the following year started what later became Sekai Kyuseikyo. Its headquarters are located in Atami, Shizuoka Prefecture, and the current leader is the founder's daughter, Okada Itsuki (1927–). Members are said to number about 860,000.

Sekai Kyuseikyo seeks to rid the world of war, poverty and disease by building an ideal world, 'paradise on earth', characterized by truth, goodness, beauty and constant peace. Like many new religions, it considers itself as transcending the category of 'religion'. Two activities for which it is best known are *jorei* and *shizen noho*. *Jorei* is a faith-healing technique. The idea is that the healing power of divine light flows from the palm of a believer into the body of one needing help. Originally only the founder exercised this technique, but now it is possible to all who have received light. The divinity from which this healing light flows is variously spoken of as Su, Kannon, etc. *Shizen noho*, a food-growing technique, is 'natural agriculture'. From the idea that plants are weakened by artificial and animal fertilizers, Sekai Kyuseikyo calls for organic farming. Holding that beauty is essential to paradise, Sekai Kyuseikyo has gathered many *objets d'art* and displays them in its two museums. [10: x, 227–8, 11; 13: 151–88; 14; 18].

Septuagint [xIII.A] The Greek translation of the Hebrew BIBLE, begun at Alexandria in the 3rd century BCE for the benefit of the Greek-speaking Jewish community in that city. The Pentateuch (the first five books) was translated first; according to tradition its translators were 70 or 72 elders of Israel (hence the title of the version, from Latin *septuaginta*, 70). Copies of some biblical books in Greek have been found among the DEAD SEA SCROLLS. Since the 1st century CE the Septuagint has been the standard version of the Hebrew Bible for Greek-speaking Christians; it also contains some books (apocrypha) which are not part of the Hebrew Bible, but which are authoritative for many Christians. [7: I, 141–9, 159–79; 11: V, 1093–1104]

Seth [VI] The Egyptian figure of Seth, represented as a mythical, pig-like animal (*see* ANIMAL CULTS), and identified with Typhon by the Greeks, was originally an important pre-dynastic deity whose supporters fought the 'Followers of Horus' (*see* OSIRIAN TRIAD). In Plutarch's Myth of Osiris (*c*.100 CE) [13], Seth, as the embodiment of evil, murders Osiris. The Hyksos (who ruled in Egypt *c*.1600 BCE) identified him with their god BA'AL and he achieved some support in the 19th dynasty (*c*.1300 BCE). The success of the Osiris cult ensured the eventual destruction of most Sethian representations [23].

Seva [XXXIII] In the early Sikh PANTH *seva* meant service rendered to GURU and *sangat* (the gathered community). When the line of personal Gurus ended, this obligation shifted to the abode of the eternal Guru, the GURDWARA. *Seva* was thus directed to *sangat* and *gurdwara*, which in practice meant such activities as maintaining the premises or serving in the LANGAR. This remains the dominant concept [34: 111], although the modern ideal also embraces humanitarian service in a broad sense. [10: 176–9; 30: 83]

Sexuality [XIV] An individual's sexuality is a significant element of her or his identity, constructed on the basis of personally appropriated and socially ascribed gender, preferred category of sexual partner, preferred and actual modes of sexual behaviour, and modes of erotic experience. Access to a range of concepts and models to support the individual's construction of a sexual identity and to enable that identity to be lived socially is a relatively modern phenomenon. Religious prescriptions and proscriptions as to sexual roles and sexual conduct usually exist embedded in a normative mythical, theological or metaphysical mapping of human identity and destiny and of the world in general. In a modern Western society, there is a virtual market-place in which varieties of such mappings are offered for adoption side by side with non-religious psychological, sociological, political and philosophical alternatives. Specific problems arise when a modern Western understanding of sexuality is brought into the critique of traditional religious sexual norms, especially when those norms are expressed in texts believed to be of divine origin or authority. A historian or sociologist may well be tempted to see the prohibition against a man 'having intercourse with a man as with a woman' in *Leviticus* 20: 13 as functioning socially to sustain male supremacy and proscribe any act compromising a male's gender status. For a religious believer who ascribes divine authority to the scriptures, such an interpretation, which reads the text as reflecting the values and customs of the society in which it was written, is insolent REDUCTIONISM.

The *Vinaya-Pitaka* of the Buddhist scriptural canon shows how sophisticated ancient religious texts can be. In prescribing the code of behaviour expected of the monastic SANGHA, the text carefully distinguishes sexual conduct which is to be punished as a violation of monastic discipline from conduct so gravely pathological as to require treatment not punishment.

Interpreting codes of religious and especially monastic behaviour raises the serious problem that specific gestures or modes of physical contact do not carry an objective, cross-cultural, transhistorical meaning. ROMAN CATHOLIC missionary priests in Japan found the traditional kissing of the altar as a gesture of respect in tension with the explicitly sexual meaning of kissing in traditional Japanese culture. A Muslim family from north India would take it for granted that their son might marry his cousin: a Hindu family of the same ethnic origin would react with shocked dismay should their son seek to do the same.

Just as feminist scholars have challenged history or theology grounded on unexamined male assumptions, and have sought to retrieve and represent women's religious experience and activity within a female framework of interpretation, a parallel challenge faces gay and lesbian scholars, to recover a range of gay and lesbian religious experience, activity, identity and meaning even more shrouded from immediate view by moral (see MORALITY) and religious prohibition. The investigation of gay or lesbian religious history is even more problematic. A major question exists as to the period at which homosexual or lesbian sexualities were recognized at all; there is plenty of religious literature concerned with the regulation of sexual acts among persons of the same gender, but most such writing in no way recognizes the existence of a homosexual or lesbian sexual identity, still less that of, for example, a transsexual identity. The problem is complicated because homosexual identities are constructed in quite different ways in different cultures.

Sexuality,   and   Christianity [XIII.B] Traditional Christian teaching sharply differentiates the sexes and their roles. Women have been subordinated to men, commonly excluded from the MINISTRY (see WOMEN (IN EARLY CHRISTIANITY)), and suspected by some ascetics as sources of temptation. At the same time the place of the Virgin MARY and of female SAINTS is prominent in Catholic devotion (see ROMAN CATHOLICISM). Sexuality was closely connected with SIN (especially following St Augustine (see AUGUSTINIANISM)) and MARRIAGE regarded as a remedy for it. Pursuit of holiness in MONASTICISM involved a vow of chastity (abstention from sex and marriage); and virginity was highly valued. Homosexuality [42], abortion and contraception, as well as fornication (sex between unmarried persons) and adultery (sex between persons married to other partners), have all traditionally been regarded as serious sins. Roman Catholicism and some SECTS in PROTESTANTISM have been particularly severe. But in recent years many Christians have taken a much more positive view of sexuality as good if rightly used. Artificial contraception is widely practised, even among Roman Catholics (despite condemnation by the PAPACY, in 1968). Many Christians now accept abortion, though others (especially Roman Catholics) strongly oppose it. Divorce is widely accepted although Roman Catholicism officially allows only decrees of nullity (i.e. rulings that a marriage has been, for various reasons, found to be invalid). Anglicans officially forbid the remarriage of divorced persons in church, but this ban is not always observed. Homosexuality, though condemned by many, is increasingly tolerated, though the admission of homosexuals to the MINISTRY has become highly controversial. Nevertheless, associations and even churches of gay Christians have been formed, especially in the USA (e.g. the Metropolitan Community Church). In general, many Christians have greatly relaxed earlier severe attitudes on sexuality and sexual morality. Recognition of women's rights and their role in the church has been improved under feminist influence. (*See also* GENDER; SOCIAL MORALITY.) [139: 316–18, 360–2]

Shabad [XXXIII] *Shabad* (*shabda*, 'word') has two related meanings in SIKH usage. For GURU NANAK it designated the divine revelation, the 'Word' which mystically communicates the message of NAM (GURMAT). [5: 297; 27: 191–4]. As Nanak himself came to be regarded as the inspired communicator of the *shabad* his hymns were treated as its actual expression. This belief was necessarily extended to all who succeeded him as Guru, and *shabad* thus became the generic term for any hymn recorded in the ADI GRANTH. [25: 240–1, 288]

Shabbat [XXII] Saturday, the Jewish Sabbath, is a day of complete rest for the traditional Jew, as its Hebrew name *Shabbat* ('Rest') indicates. It celebrates the creation of the world by God and its total dependence on him (*Genesis* 2: 1–3, *Exodus* 20: 8–11). It also commemorates the redemption of the Israelites from slavery in Egypt (*see* EXODUS) (*Deuteronomy* 5: 12–15). In some degree it has been incorporated into traditional Christian practice, although JESUS was criticized for his apparent laxity regarding Sabbath laws. Rabbinical literature sees in the *Shabbat* and its rituals one of the most distinctive aspects of Israel's COVENANT relationship with God [70: 169]. The TALMUD sets out the 39 main categories of work prohibited on the sabbath [10: 154]. The *Shabbat* rituals include the lighting of at least two candles by the woman of the household before sundown on Friday evening when *Shabbat* begins; *kiddush* (sanctification of the day), recited over wine on Friday evening and at Saturday lunchtime; and a ceremony of separation (HAVDALAH) on Saturday night when *Shabbat* terminates. [14 vol. 14: 557]

Shah [XXXVI] 'King', of Iran. In ZOROASTRIAN Iran it was believed that the good king was chosen by AHURA MAZDA because of his righteous support for truth and his opposition to evil. In royal art the king was depicted as having superhuman size and strength, with which he overcame human and cosmic forces of chaos. His presence was veiled from ordinary mortals. Legends surround the birth of many of these monarchs, and honorifics such as 'brother of the sun and moon' were applied to them, but they were not thought of as divine (as a PHAROAH was). Divine grace (*khvarenah*; Pahlavi: *khwarr*) was given to the righteous king but this could be withdrawn if he sinned. A classic example of this was the mythical king Yima (Jamshid in later texts). His reign established the ideal kingdom, which all monarchs should seek to emulate, one where justice, order and bounteousness abounded. But then he committed the sin of pride and falsehood, and the *khvarenah* left him. Religion and politics were intertwined in Zoroastrianism. ZOROASTER himself had sought and obtained a royal patron and throughout the history of Zoroastrian Iran kings and priests worked together. Kings were often shown in art in a priestly posture and Pahlavi writers stressed the unity of religion and kingship; as one (Tansar, 3rd century CE) put it, they are 'brothers, born of one womb, never to be separated' [28: 98–109; 64: XIV].

Shahada [XIX] The profession of faith, considered to be one of the PILLARS OF ISLAM: 'There is no God but God, and Muhammad is His messenger.' It is an essential element of the Muslim worship (SALAT) and the formula by which one professes Islam. [48: 70]

Shahname [XXXVI] 'The Book of Kings', composed in Persian by a poet under the pseudonym of Firdausi, 'the Paradisal', in the 11th century CE. Firdausi gave final shape to an ancient heroic and epic tradition, using in particular a Persian translation of the PAHLAVI *Khwaday Namag*, a text written by four ZOROASTRIAN priests which is unfortunately no longer extant. The *Shahname* surveys the history of Iran from the time of creation until the Muslim invasion, transforming myth into legend for the earlier period. The narrative is characterized more by a love of Iran than of ISLAM and displays an element of fatalism typical of its genre. [42; 52]

Shaikh [XIX] Originally Arabic for 'elder', *shaikh* is widely used in both Islamic religious and secular contexts for 'leader, person accorded respect', e.g. in a tribe or other social grouping. One particular usage was in the title 'Shaikh al-Islam' for the supremely recognized scholar or legal expert in a region or state; this office persisted in Ottoman Turkey until 1924 [37 'Shaikh al-Islam']. Among the SUFI ORDERS, the shaikh (Persian *pir*, Turkish *baba*) was the head of the community, often with a spiritual pedigree going back to the founder, and his postulants were known as *murids*, i.e. 'seekers (after spiritual enlightenment)'. [125 glossary]

Shakers [XIII.B] A SECT originating with Ann Lee of Manchester, England, who emigrated to the USA with a few followers in 1774 and died in 1784. 'Mother Ann' came to be regarded as an expression of the female principle in GOD and as an agent of SALVATION. In the USA the Shakers developed a complex community life for men and women, based on the belief that celibacy is a way to a holy life. The principle of 'simplicity' was followed in many areas of life and exemplified in their furniture, now greatly prized for aesthetic reasons. 'Shaking' developed from involuntary spirit-possession into formal ritual dancing, though this is no longer practised. From a possible maximum of 6,000 members in the 1840s, Shakers have declined to one tiny community today. [3; 62 vol. 8: 200–1; 180]

Shakti [XVII] Of all the major religions, HINDUISM probably gives the greatest importance to the feminine side of deity, called *Shakti*, 'Power', or *Devi*, 'Goddess'. For Hindus, both male and female are necessary and complementary on the cosmic scale, just as they are in nature and society. In order to fulfil his role in the creation, preservation and destruction of the cosmos (*see* TRIMURTI), each of the great male deities needs the complementary energy of his Shakti, generally personified as his wife.

There is already evidence of devotion to goddesses in the INDUS VALLEY civilization, for example in what appear to be cult-scenes on seals. In contrast, the hymns of the VEDA are predominantly addressed to male deities, though reverence is also paid to such female beings as Aditi, 'Infinity', goddess of space and mother of many of the gods, and Ushas, the goddess of the dawn (cf. Greek Eos, Roman Aurora). It is likely, however, that goddess-worship continued to flourish at the popular level, for by the Epic period (*see* MAHABHARATA, RAMAYANA) goddesses had once again a powerful place in Hindu worship, both as consorts of gods and in their own right. The PURANAS recount many myths, still popular today, of the exploits of goddesses, especially the wife of SHIVA in her many forms, such as SATI, PARVATI, DURGA and KALI [92: 238–69]. No doubt many local goddesses came to be seen as aspects of her [12: 311–12].

For Shaktas, devotees of Shakti, the Goddess represents the highest conceivable form of divinity, just as VISHNU does for Vaishnavas and Shiva for Shaivas, and is the subject of profound devotion (BHAKTI).

They identify her with the supreme BRAHMAN, or Absolute, and regard BRAHMA, Vishnu and Shiva as emanating from her [26: 10, 68].

TANTRA (1), with its emphasis on the role of the female, gave a great impetus to goddess-worship. Only united with his Shakti, say the Shaktas, can Shiva exert his powers [26: 48]. Without her he is *shava*, a corpse: hence the many representations of Kali standing, dancing, or seated in sexual intercourse, on the corpse-like form of her husband [89: 60–3, 70, 83]. (For other goddesses, see BHUDEVI; GANGA; LAKSHMI; SARASVATI.)

Paradoxically, this emphasis on the power of the female may have been partly responsible for the restricted lives led by the majority of women in Hindu society. The energy of a woman, and particularly her sexual desire, are thought to be so strong as to threaten family and society if not controlled by the authority of a man: hence the tradition of early marriage, and the fear of the widow. In the same way, Shakti normally takes on a peaceful form when in the company of her husband, but a fierce or formidable one when alone.

The term Shakti is sometimes used by analogy for consorts of BUDDHAS and BODHISATTVAS in MAHAYANA BUDDHISM, though they are more correctly called PRAJNA, 'Wisdom': see TANTRA (2). [69]

Shaman [XIV] 'Shaman' is the name given by the Tungus of Siberia to ritual practitioners who are considered to act as intermediaries with the spirit world. In an ecstatic state, the shaman journeys to the realm of the spirits, seeking help as a healer or seer and conducting the soul of a newly deceased person. The journey is experienced as a flight or as possession. The shaman additionally binds society together by the ritual enshrining of an account of historical origins. 'Shamanism' labels the practices of such practitioners, and

is used by extension for similar activities among Arctic and Ural-Altaic groups. As a result of diffusion and cultural survival shamans are found among the LAPPS, Inuit (see ESKIMO-ALEUT), American Indians, the Ainu in Japan, the Koreans, in many parts of south-east Asia such as Vietnam, Thailand and Indonesia, and elsewhere. The term 'shaman' is also employed in the sciences of religion, where the provenance would include Africa, ancient Israel, the Pacific and parts of Europe.

The Finnish folklorist Ake Hultkrantz defines a shaman as an intermediary who exhibits behaviour which supports the belief that he or she is inspired by spirits [26]. To Mircea Eliade [27], ecstasy is itself the defining force in what he labels an archaic technique. Eliade thus excludes or differentiates non-ecstatic sorcerers and priests, as do many other accounts. However, it is now noted that in many societies practitioners who go into trance coexist with non-ecstatic hereditary specialists. To Vincent Crapanzano, Gannath Obeyesekere and other scholars – and implicit in Levi-Strauss' analysis of Franze Boas' 1930 account of the Kwakiutl Indian Quesalid from Vancouver – ecstasy is the expression of a social idiom. Shamans must remain aware of their surroundings to communicate effectively, hence a loss of consciousness is neither definitive nor constant. Shamans are not so much possessed by spirits but rather control them [57]. Nonetheless, shamans claim direct contact with spirits, whether those of people, plants, animals or other natural objects, with 'master spirits' who inhabit mountains and rivers, and with 'helping spirits' who guide individual shamans or may initiate the call to practice. The protection offered by spirits provides illustration of their power: a shaman in trance becomes capable of remarkable feats such as climbing a ladder of swords, walking on coals, dancing on knives, swallowing hot embers and self-stabbing without wounding.

Ethnographic accounts have tended to localize shamanic behaviour and to interpret shamanic practices in a wider social context. As a consequence, a marked divergence in practice and canon between different social groups has been noted. This has tended to have the effect of marginalizing shamanism in anthropological literature. Theories of diffusion, popularized particularly by those working in Eurasia, have accordingly been displaced. As a topic in religion, in contrast, a greater focus is now put on potentially universal human proclivities that allow a practitioner to move into particular psychological states.

Many early accounts identified shamans with hysteria, psychological illness and mental disorder; trance was interpreted as an expressive outlet. Interpretations of trance now vary, and describe the effects of a plethora of hyperventilation and bodily disorientation exercises. Trance, Gilbert Rouget tells us [73], may often be induced by music and dance, with or without repetitive actions. There is a growing awareness that 'ecstasy' and 'trance' are Euroamerican concepts. Parallel to this, behavioural scientists have begun to seek a more rational basis for a shaman's 'altered states of consciousness' or 'non-ordinary realities'. Some explanations, detailed by Atkinson [3] and Ruth-Inge Heinze [35] and in Hoppál and Howard [43], frame shamanic ecstasy as a particular form of an altered state of consciousness. Some, such as Michael Harner [33], see a specific unitary 'shamanic state of consciousness', while others find a single state common to shamans, magicians and witch doctors.

Along with much of the world's folklore, the practices associated with shamanism are on the wane. In Europe and America, however, participants in the 1960s drug culture imbibed hallucinogens used among American Indians to 'jump-start' consciousness [3]. Jungian psychotherapy has combined with this usage to arouse NEW AGE interest in the subject; developing in part from the popular accounts of Carlos Castaneda into the explorations of Michael Harner and Richard Schechner, neo-shamanism replaces the intermediary function of the Siberian shaman with an enhancement of personal experience for discovery, communication, performance and healing. [27; 31; 43; 82].

Shamans and Religious Specialists (South American) [xxiii] In Amazonia at least, the different manifestations of shamanism can be roughly divided between two ideal types, 'vertical' and 'horizontal'. Though all forms of shamanism combine authoritative knowledge (based on the experience of possession, ecstasy or the mastery of a canon) with inspiration, in vertical shamanism the component of secret, esoteric knowledge transmitted within a small elite predominates, while in horizontal shamanism, the emphasis is more democratic, depends less on 'saying' than on 'doing' and involve the more classic shamanistic features of trance and possession. Horizontal shamanism appears to be associated with the more egalitarian, less complex and forest-based societies with an ideological emphasis on warfare and hunting. There, secular power is separate from sacred power; shamans are both morally ambiguous and have relatively low status and prestige. Shamanism is individualistic, open to all men, often involves widespread use of hallucinogenic substances and is only peripherally involved in life-crisis RITES. Vertical shamanism appears to be associated with more complex, ranked societies with less emphasis on warfare and hunting. Here secular and ritual powers are often merged and limited to a few powerful men who are morally unambiguous, enjoy high prestige and status and play a key role in social reproduction through elaborate ancestor-oriented life-crisis rituals. Their knowledge is relatively closed and is founded on a mythology developed into an elaborate dogmatic canon. The relationship between the two types may be one of complementarity, or it may contain elements of contradiction and political tension interwoven with more complementary, abstract cosmological principles. [4; 11; 16; 28]

Shambhala [xxxv] In Tibetan Buddhist mythology, Shambhala, a land held to be situated to the north of Tibet, is the mystic kingdom ruled by the lineage holders of the Kalachakra TANTRA (2) (Wheel of Time Tantra). It is said that king Sucandra of Shambhala received this tantra from the BUDDHA in the latter's 80th year and entrusted it to his successors [13], the last of whom, Rigden Pema Karpo, is expected to return and establish Shambhala as a universal kingdom.

Shang Ti [xii] 'Lord on High.' Originally the main deity of the Chinese Shang period (1523–1027 BCE). He was not seen as the creator of the world, but controlled the orderly progress of the seasons. He was also a warrior-god responsible for defending the Shang population. After the overthrow of the Shang by the Chou dynasty in 1027 BCE the functions and identity of Shang Ti gradually merged with the more abstract T'IEN (Heaven), supreme being of the Chou. [94: ii, 12–15; 99: i, 4–5]

Shankara [xvii] An influential Indian religious philosopher (probably 8th century CE). Shankara developed the ideas of Gaudapada and established the authoritative form of ADVAITA VEDANTA. Many of the works attributed to him are probably not authentic, but important commentaries on the BRAHMA-

SUTRA and various UPANISHADS (VEDA) are certainly the work of Shankara. He may also have been the author of a number of devotional hymns. Shankara appears to have been responsible for the organization of orders of Hindu mendicants (*sannyasins*) and the foundation of four major centres, at Shringeri and elsewhere. The heads of these institutions, called *Shankaracaryas*, exercise considerable influence over Smarta and many Shaiva (*see* SHIVA) Hindus. Shankara himself is widely recognized as an emanation of Shiva.

Shari'a [xix] Literally 'clear path', the term for the canon law of ISLAM, the totality of God's prescriptions for mankind, hence considered of divine origin and not the result of human legislation. It is essentially concerned with man's outward conformity to the laws of Islam. As a consequence many authorities assert that these external observances must be supplemented by good intentions and inner faith (IMAN), and the Sufis (SUFISM) regard the Shari'a as only the minimal starting-point for the adept embarking on the Sufi path of self-enlightenment. The Shari'a includes the so-called PILLARS OF ISLAM, binding on all adult male believers. Its prescriptions have been classified on a scale of desirability as: obligatory, recommended, legally indifferent, disapproved or prohibited. The Sunni mainstream (*see* SUNNA) bases the Shari'a on the QUR'AN; the traditions of the Prophet MUHAMMAD and early Muslims; the consensus of the community (IJMA'); and analogical reasoning (*qiyas*), where the previous three factors provide no explicit guidance [20 s.v.; 37 s.v.; 52: vi; 80: vi; 107: vi]. SHI'ISM stresses the Qur'an, the body of traditions from 'ALI and his family, and the consensus of the Shi'i scholars or *mujtahids*. Even in the early centuries of Islam, a secular law (*qanun*) existed alongside the Shari'a, and in many parts of the Islamic world local custom ('*ada*) had remained influential (*see for example* SOUTH-EAST ASIA, ISLAM IN). In modern times, with the introduction of Western-type codes in most west Asian countries, the Shari'a has tended to shrink; in this process one of the most resistant spheres has been that of personal law, including marriage and inheritance. [27: XI–XIV; 117: XIII–XV]

Shay [VI] In ancient Egypt fate was personified as a goddess, Shay, whose name meant 'that which is decreed' [17: 269]. Associated with the creator-god Khnum, Shay was present at birth and, after death, at the 'day of judgement' (*see* AFTERLIFE). The Egyptian view of fate or destiny encompassed the individual's life-span, appointed at birth, and the manner of the person's death. Less frequently, it meant the content of his or her life – favourable events and misfortune.

Shekhinah [XXII] The 'Divine Presence', the most general Jewish term for the immanence of God in the world (*see* THEISM). Among the many names or descriptions of God in rabbinical literature (*see* RABBI) the *Shekhinah* represents the closeness of God to humankind, and God's loving concern for humanity [30: 61]. The TALMUD pictures the *Shekhinah* as having gone into EXILE with the exile of the Jewish people from the HOLY LAND. There are no implications of DUALISM or POLYTHEISM in the aggadic (*see* AGGADAH) imagery of the *Shekhinah* [10: 42]. For the kabbalists (*see* KABBALAH) the *Shekhinah* is the 10th SEFIRAH, the most distinctly female element within the divine structure [61: 226]. Through the *Shekhinah* the flow of divine energy comes down to earth. Human sins enable the powers of evil to gain control of the *Shekhinah* and disrupt this flow, causing disharmony and catastrophe for the world. The TEMPLE and the Tabernacle (*Mishkan*) erected in the

wilderness after the EXODUS from Egypt were thought of as representing the indwelling of God. [14 vol. 14: 1349]

Shema [XXII] Biblical passages affirming the unity of God, the complete love with which he must be served and the acceptance of his commandments, which are recited twice daily in the Jewish liturgy [19: 94]. The three paragraphs of the *Shema* are *Deuteronomy* 6: 4–9 and 11: 13–21 and *Numbers* 15: 37–41, the last of which contains a reference to God's redeeming acts in history as exemplified in the EXODUS from Egypt. The *Shema* is also recited by the believer before retiring at night, and by the dying man. [64: 41–2]

Shemini Atzeret [XXII] ('Eighth Day of Assembly') Jewish festival (CHAGIM), lasting one day in Israel and two in the diaspora, at the end of TABERNACLES. The festival LITURGY includes prayers for rain, signifying the onset of the Palestinian rainy season, chanted by the CANTOR dressed in white garments. A celebration is held in the SYNAGOGUE as the yearly Pentateuchal reading is completed, and the TORAH is begun all over again with the story of the Creation. This celebration is known as *simchat torah*, and all the Torah scrolls are paraded round the synagogue seven times with singing and dancing. Each congregation appoints a 'Bridegroom of the Torah', who makes a blessing over the end of *Deuteronomy*, and a 'Bridegroom of Bereshit', who makes a blessing over the beginning of *Genesis* (*bereshit* in Hebrew). Children in the synagogue gather on to the central *bimah* platform and a large prayer shawl (*tallit*) is lifted above their heads while a blessing over the Torah is made on their behalf [59: 196; 70: 182]. After the service sweets are distributed to the children and a party is held for the whole community.

Shichi Fukujin [xxi] Seven gods of good luck in Japan. Along with various household and travellers' guardians, these seven gods, combined from sources as distant as India, function as a group. They travel together on the *Takarabune* ('Treasure Ship') [19: 511–14], and are often seen around the home as small images. They are: Bishamonten, connoting riches; Benten, the only female, which connotes good luck and music; Ebisu, good fortune; Daikoku, the father of Ebisu and identified with Okuninushi-no-mikoto, wealth (*see* Izumo taisha); Fukurokuju, long life; Hotei, prosperity; and Jurojin, longevity.

Shi'ism [xix] One of the two great forms (the other being Sunnism – *see* Sunna) of Islam. Originally referring to the 'partisans (*shi'a*) of 'Ali', this group developed over the centuries its own body of law (differing only in certain minor directions, e.g. inheritance and the status of women, from that of the majority Sunnis) and theology. It also proved fissiparous, one of the most significant offshoots from the main body of Imami or 'Twelver' Shi'ism being the Isma'ilis. Shi'i tenets involve the recognition of 'Ali and his descendants as the true Imams [general surveys: 20 'Sht'a'; 33; 37 'Shī'a'; 48: 37–42; 61; 69; 95]. Although numerically a minority within Islam, various Shi'i dynasties achieved political and military power in medieval Islam (*see for example* Caliph, caliphate). An especially important event was the conversion of Persia in the 16th century from Sunnism to Shi'ism by the Safavid dynasty (*see* Islamic dynasties) [78: ii–vi, x]. Today, Shi'is are significant above all in Iran, Iraq and the Indo-Pakistan subcontinent, but there are also communities in Turkey, Syria, Lebanon, east Africa and eastern Arabia. The Iranian Revolution of 1978–9 has reawakened Shi'i consciousness in parts of the Islamic world adjoining Iran (*see also* Ayatullah).

Shilluk Religion [ii] The Shilluk, a small sedentary Nilotic people living on the west bank of the Nile around Fashoda, have provided a famous example of Divine kingship. Juok (Jok), creator of the world and of all peoples, is occasionally invoked, but the central figure of Shilluk religion is Nyikang, the hero who led them in migration to their present home and founded the Shilluk kingdom and its customs. Although descended from Juok, Nyikang was a man, while his mother, Nyakaya, was a river creature, like a crocodile. The doer of many marvellous deeds, Nyikang led his people across the river, fought with the sun, never died, and is closely linked with Juok. He lives on in each *reth*, the sacred king upon whom the order and prosperity of the Shilluk depend.

There are shrines for Nyikang all over Shillukland. In his solemn installation the *reth* is captured by the image of Nyikang in a mock battle and then possessed by his spirit. He is the chief priest for rain and victory in war, and all national misfortune is blamed upon him. Traditionally, if his powers waned, he could be suffocated by his wives or killed by a rival, so that Nyikang might possess a fitter reincarnation. The moral qualities associated with the *reth* and prized by the Shilluk are those of courage, military success, cleverness and passion [6: 138–63; 27: iv].

Shingon [xxi] Shingon (= Chinese Chen yen), the True Word, a tantric Buddhist sect (*see* Tantra (2)), was introduced to Japan by the priest Kukai, who had been sent to China in 804 ce [14: 49–58; 18; 36: 148–84]. Ten years after his return in 806 he built a modest meditation place on Mt Koya in Wakayama prefecture, which later became the Kongobu-ji, the centre of Shingon Buddhism, where he is also buried.

His *Juju Shinron* of 822 is a 10-volume exposition of spiritual attainment, later abbreviated to three volumes entitled *Hizoboyaku* (The Jewel Key to the Store of Mysteries). To demonstrate the supremacy of Shingon, he graded the doctrines in 10 steps, from subhuman desires, through moralism, undemanding mysticism, two levels of THERAVADA, MAHAYANA, Hosso (*see* NANTO ROKUSHU), TENDAI and Kegon to, finally, the esoteric Shingon. Kukai brought painted MANDALAS from China, magical diagrams symbolizing the Kongokai, the Diamond or permanent cycle (*Vajradhatu*), and the Taizokai, the Womb or material cycle (*Garbhadhatu*). Central to Shingon beliefs is Dainichi (*Mahavairocana*), Buddha of Infinite Light. Dainichi is the source of all existence, absolute and permanent, through whom Buddhahood is attained in this life. Dainichi is an expanded concept of Roshana Buddha of the Kegon and Ritsu sects (*see* NANTO ROKUSHU). Called *mikkyo*, secret teachings of Dainichi Nyorai (esoteric sects refer to Buddhas as Nyorai, not Butsu), including a large pantheon, were revealed only to the initiated. Sculpture and painting were thought to serve as mediums in transmitting divinity to believers, particularly images of the five Buddhas of the Kongokai – Ashuku, Hosho, AMIDA, Fukujoju and Dainichi – and of the Taizo-kai – Dainichi, Hodo, Kaifuke, Muryoju and Tenkuraion [24: 77]. The chief of the Godai myo-o (Five *Vidyarajas*) is Fudo (*Acala*), who is the most frequently represented Shingon bodhisattva (*see* JAPANESE BUDDHAS AND BODHISATTVAS). Shingon today has about 45 sects and subsects called *shu* (16 listed) and *ha* (22 listed), and by other organizational names [21: 194–8]. The To-ji in Kyoto is the chief temple for esoteric practices.

Shinnyoen [XXVI] A Japanese new religion that stands in the esoteric BUDDHIST tradition and relies heavily on spiritualism as well, Shinnyoen owes its origin to Ito Shinjo (1906–89) and Ito Tomoji (1912–67). It currently claims about 680,000 adherents and has branches in France, the USA, Taiwan and elsewhere.

Ito Shinjo was an aeronautical engineer with an interest in divination and fortune-telling. On 4 February 1936 his wife, Tomoji, tutored by her aunt, Yui Tamae, received the power to serve as a spirit medium. Shinnyoen traces its origin to this date, for it was from this time that Shinjo, influenced by his wife and her aunt, determined to follow the path of religion, forming in the same year an organization that met in their home. In 1948 he established Makoto Kyodan, which in 1951 was renamed Shinnyoen.

At its chief centre in Tachikawa, Shinnyoen has in a place of honour a large statue of the BUDDHA experiencing enlightenment. It attaches special importance to the *Daihatsu Nehangyo*, or Sutra of the Great Demise, said to contain the last sermon of the Buddha. Shinnyoen teaches that the power to be a medium is potential in all possessors of the buddha-nature, i.e., all people, and only needs to be brought out through Shinnyoen ascetic practices. To become a medium is the highest goal of the Shinnyoen believer, for the medium has not only 'polished' his or her buddha-nature but is also in touch with the world of the ancestral spirits. In *sesshin shugyo*, the practice of focusing the heart, a medium serves as a mirror in which one sees into one's own heart by means of the words the medium utters while in a state of trance.

Two of Ito Shinjo and Tomoji's daughters, Ito Shinso and Ito Shinrei, serve together as the current leaders of Shinnyoen.

Shinto [XXI] The religion indigenous to Japan. It was so named (from the Chinese *shin tao*, 'way of the gods') in the 8th century, after BUDDHISM was introduced, to distinguish the two religions. In Japanese it was probably then called *kami-no-michi* [general surveys: 8: 98–147; 19; 21: 29–45; 32; 34]. As a set of prehistoric agricultural ceremonies, it was never endowed with a supporting body of philosophical or moralistic literature (*see* SHINTO LITERATURE). Early shamans (MIKO) performed the ceremonies; eventually those of the Yamato tribe did so on behalf of the other tribes and their chieftain assumed duties that led to headship of the Shinto state. Shinto became political by the 8th century when Yamato writers ascribed divine origins to the imperial family and so claimed legitimacy for rule (*see* KOKUTAI SHINTO).

Shinto ceremonies are designed to appeal to the KAMI, the powers of nature, for benevolent treatment and protection, and consist of abstinence (*imi*), offerings, prayers and purification (HARAE (MATSURI)). Community ceremonies take place at fixed times during the year, and visits to SHINTO SHRINES are made at stages marking life's progress. The *kami* are the mysterious forces of nature associated primarily with permanent topographical features, in particular unusual mountains (SACRED MOUNTAINS), rocky cliffs, caves, springs, trees and stones. Hosts of folk tales have evolved around these holy spots. The tales often refer to animal possession, chiefly involving foxes, racoon-dogs, badgers, dogs and cats bewitching people, more often women than men. Celestial bodies play only incidental roles as Shinto *kami*.

Shinto stresses the importance of purity, and since death and a variety of other pollutions are to be avoided, Shinto is concerned primarily with life and the benefits of this world, which are seen as divine gifts. Ethically, what is good for the group is morally proper. Devotion and sincerity are expected. Aberrations can be erased by purification. Purification procedures make worshippers presentable, and therefore their pleas acceptable to the *kami*. Traditionally, the village (*ujiko*) head maintains the shrine for the tribal deity (*ujigami*) (*see* SHINTO SHRINES).

A 1339 treatise on Shinto, politics and history, *Jinno Shotoki*, was used as a guide to the above practices and administrative procedures until the early Meiji period (1868–1912). The religion was then divided into Shrine Shinto (*Jinja*) and Sectarian Shinto (*Kyoha*). An Imperial Rescript on Education made it the formal foundation of the state, taking as its authority the work of the Mito school, that is, the *Dai Nippon-shi*, the large history of Japan written by Tokugawa Mitsukuni (1628–1700), *daimyo* (lord) of Mito (now Ibaragi prefecture). The divinity of the emperor was stressed (*see* KOKUTAI SHINTO), based on Confucian concepts of loyalty to the emperor and the state (*see* CONFUCIUS). After the Second World War Shinto lost its status as an official religion, shrine membership was not required and contributions became voluntary. The 'nationalization' of Yasukuni shrine, home of the remains of the war dead, is a current issue.

Shinto Literature [XXI] SHINTO has no philosophical literature in which the religious beliefs are explained and the nature of divinity is rationalized, but a written SHINTO MYTHOLOGY exists. There is also literature on the laws governing the indigenous religion, the procedures for SHINTO SHRINE ceremonies, and the administrative structure controlling shrines and ceremonies. By the 7th century a family of professional priests, Nakatomi, the ancestors of the later Fujiwara, the ruling family of the 10th–12th centuries, with divine descent, were qualified to transmit the practices orally and in writing. The first texts are the earliest books of the *Rokkokushi* (Six National Histories), namely the *Kojiki* (Records of Ancient Matters), presented to the court in 712 CE, and the *Nihongi* or *Nihon Shoki* (Chronicles of Japan), completed in 720 [translations: 3; 10]. The former concludes with the year 628, but the final century is dealt with exclusively by genealogical lists. The latter is much fuller, and terminates with the reign of Empress Jito in 696. Both contain the myths, transition from KAMI to human rule, accounts of reigns and many references to the building of Shinto shrines and BUDDHIST temples, and to cyclical and special worship ceremonies (MATSURI). These two books formed the basis of the literal beliefs accepted by the Japanese in their most nationalistic periods, in particular the phase leading to the Second World War. Following these are the *Shoku Nihongi* (Continuing Chronicles of Japan), completed in 797 and covering the period up to 791, and three others with content up to 853, after which official recording was terminated, albeit lectures on the *Nihon Shoki* were delivered at the Heian (Kyoto) court for about another century. The literature on the laws is a substantial body of 50 books known as *Engishiki*, named after the Engi era (901–22), completed in 927 [6]. The first 10 volumes are directions for executing the *Jingi-ryo*, the laws dealing with Shinto and shrine ceremonies, as well as the administrative organization and duties of the JINGI-KAN, the bureau of *kami* affairs. Book 8 contains most of the official prayers and liturgies known as *norito*. [33]

Shinto Mythology [XXI] The mythology of Japan is embodied in the early sections of the 8th-century books *Kojiki* and *Nihon Shoki* (*see* SHINTO LITERATURE), where the course of events is described by Yamato court scholars to validate divine imperial origins [translations and general surveys: 3, 1: 1–108; 10: 15–164; 19: 227–388]. A less significant cycle for the Izumo area (*see* IZUMO TAISHA) is preserved in the 8th-century *Izumo Fudoki*. Much cosmology is taken from Chinese sources. The cosmos, resembling an egg in shape, separated. The place above, *Takamahara*, the High Plain of Heaven, was presided over by Takamimusubi (*musubi-no-kami* = KAMI of the mysterious generative spirit [21: 14]), and exists only to propagate the land below. After seven generations, Izanagi and Izanami created the Eight-Island Country (Oyashimaguni) of brine drops from a spear-tip. Further creations climaxed with AMATERASU-OMIKAMI, (the sun-goddess). Evil was represented in the person of her brother Susano-o. Below the High Plain of Heaven is *Nakatsu-kuni*, Middle Land, identifiable with the Eight-Island Country, and then a lesser-known *Tokoyo-no-kuni* (originally a distant land across the sea), a spirit world which is good but not better than this world since many would like to return here. Finally, there is *Yomi-no-kuni*, a cavernous underground space which, although populated by hideous creatures charged with blocking the exit of the newly arrived dead, is not thought of as a place of punishment. Death and purification (HARAE) were introduced when Izanami died on the birth of the Fire God and went to *Yomi-no-kuni*. After trying and failing to extricate her, Izanagi went off to purify himself in a river. The sun-goddess eventually dispatched her grandson Ninigi-no-mikoto to rule the land after being assured of ultimate success, and he and his followers fought their way from south Japan to the Yamato plain with divine help. Ancient writers terminated the so-called Age of the Gods with the first 'emperor', but exceptionally long reigns with little content continue through the first nine rulers until Sujin (*c*.3rd century CE) [3.1: 109–49; 10: 164–212], who may be the first historical personality of the Yamato tribe.

Shinto Shrines [XXI] Shrines of all sizes, in groves of trees, are noticeable features of the Japanese landscape [19: 92–131; 34: 145–504]. The first were probably SHAMANS' houses (*see* MIKO), set apart and distinguished by being placed on a raised floor like the earliest storehouses, unpainted types being known as *shinme* (at ISE JINGU) and *taisha* (at IZUMO TAISHA). Shrine architecture has distinctive features. All shrines have sacred gates (*torii*), but other features depend on the size and purpose of the shrine. Larger ones have an offering-building like a gate (*heiden*), beyond which worshippers normally do not go, an oratory (*haiden*) and main hall (*honden*) [32: 26–39]. Within the main hall is the *goshintai* (god-body) or *mitamashiro* (spirit-substance), often a mirror, but more often nothing. Sacred areas are marked off by straw ropes (*shimenawa*), and evergreen *sakaki* trees (*Cleyera ochnacea* or *Cleyera japonica*) grow in prominent places. Shinto architecture often includes BUDDHIST temple characteristics, but roofs in particular remain distinctive, with *chigi* and *katsuogi*, the V-shaped gable extensions and ridge logs for weights. Several styles are recognized from the Heian period (794–1185). The Kasuga, Nagara and HACHIMAN types are generally distinguished by their roof shapes and porches, the Hachiman by a pair of buildings under a single roof. Most are painted in red and white. Shrines often have a pair of stone 'lions', borrowed from Chinese and Buddhist sources. Many shrines have special KAMI, such as INARI, fox shrines [19: 504–10], *shinme*, horse shrines [19: 101–2] and *okami*, wolf shrines [19: 103]. Ise and Isonokami have live, long-tailed cocks as symbols of the sun-goddess AMATERASU-OMIKAMI, as the crowing of the rooster helped to lure her out of the cave in which she had hidden and restored the light. *Mikoshi* are the portable shrines carried in processions (*see* IZUMO TAISHA; TOSHOGU SHRINE.

Ship-Funeral [VII] The ship had been a funeral symbol in Scandinavia in the Bronze Age, but in the 7th century CE it began to be used in burials and cremations on an elaborate scale. The most famous ship-burials are those of SUTTON HOO in Suffolk in England (7th century), Oseberg and Gokstad in Norway (9th century), and in the Vendel and Valsgarde cemeteries in Sweden. Ship-graves are also found in areas of Viking settlement, including Russia. The dead were laid in richly equipped ships, with ritual objects, weapons, personal possessions and often several horses, as well as cattle, dogs and birds. Women as well as men were granted ship-funerals, and the practice may have been associated with the cult of the VANIR, the deities of fertility who had the ship as a symbol. Boats, or parts of boats, were used in humbler graves, and the practice was known in pre-Christian East Anglia (England) as well as in Scandinavia. [5: 111–20; 3a: 18–20]

Shipibo Religion [XXIII] In Shipibo (eastern Peru) mythology, animals establish the movement of cosmic history by stealing fire. In an epoch before the present age, people did not possess fire and the sun stood still. This first age is construed as selfish and unique, a time when the 'bad Inca' Yoashico (the moon) kept everything to himself. Birds stole coals of his fire, causing a new age of periodicity. The main Shipibo festivals are the 'Big Drinks' (*Ani Shrêati*), girls' initiation ceremonies involving great consumption of fermented brew, ritual cutting of the girl's clitoris and blood sacrifice of animals. [29]

Shiva [XVII] One of the most important gods of HINDUISM, as destroyer

(*Hara*) completing a triad (TRI-MURTI) with BRAHMA the creator and VISHNU the preserver of the world. The equivalent deity in the VEDA is Rudra, 'the Howler', who is occasionally called *shiva*, 'gracious', 'auspicious', as a (perhaps euphemistic) title. As ever with destructive aspects of deities, it is important to remember that for Hindus, destruction is not equated with evil. The stages of creation, existence and destruction of the universe, followed by a period of non-existence before it is created again, are seen as natural stages, like day and night, out-breath and in-breath, life and death. Like Vishnu, Shiva is a BHAKTI deity, loved by his worshippers, who are called Shaivas [108].

Whereas Brahma is the archetypal priest, and Vishnu the king, Shiva is the archetypal *yogi* or renouncer, practising asceticism in the Himalayas (*see* TAPAS). But as sexual and spiritual energy are believed to come from the same source, he is represented as the passionate lover of his wife, PARVATI, the Mother of the World (*Jagadamba*), whose gentle and destructive aspects mirror his own (*See* DURGA; KALI; SHAKTI). They are frequently represented with their children, GANESHA and KARTTIKEYA. As well as his anthropomorphic forms, he is worshipped as the LINGA or phallus, and in early artistic representations (up to about 600 CE) he is generally shown with an erect phallus [59: pl. 53–4]. Shiva and Parvati are the principal deities of Hindu Tantra (TANTRA (1)), from whom its teachings are believed to have come [91].

In art, Shiva is often represented nearly naked, or wearing just a loincloth, like a wandering SADHU. He is generally white in colour, though in fierce forms he may be black or red, and in some modern prints he is blue, like Vishnu. He has three eyes, the third, which is vertical, in the middle of his forehead, being the eye of wisdom, but also capable of dealing destruction. Instead of a crown, he has an ascetic's piled-up hair, in which rest a crescent moon and, often, the tiny form of the goddess GANGA. His ornaments are skulls and snakes, and the beautiful but narcotic datura flower. His distinctive attribute, in most parts of India, is the *trishula* or trident, though in south India it may be replaced by an axe. His animal (VAHANA) is Nandin, the bull.

Best known of Shiva's many forms is that of Nataraja, the King of Dancers, whose steps and gestures (*see* MUDRA) express the creation, preservation and destruction of the universe, and the possibility of liberation from it (MOKSHA). [4: 225–6; 58: 307–10; 120: pl. 24, 27b]

Shomu [XXI] The Emperor Shomu (699–756 CE). Born Prince Obito, son of Emperor Mommu, he succeeded his aunt Empress Gensho in 727 and was responsible for spreading BUDDHISM in Japan. He ordered all the 66 province headquarters to have *sutras* read, make Yakushi BUDDHA IMAGES (*see* JAPANESE BUDDHAS AND BODHISATTVAS), build seven-storeyed pagodas (buildings usually housing relics of the Buddha) (740), and then complete monasteries and nunneries (741), called *kokubun-ji* and *kokubunni-ji*. These were to have a healing effect, following a smallpox plague in 737. No original buildings of these provincial temples remain, but some operate today as minor temples and others exist as protected archaeological sites. Shomu erected the Todai-ji, the immense temple in Nara with its enormous bronze Roshana Buddha, dedicated in 752 (*see* NANTO SHICHIDAI-JI) [26: 118–48]. He was the first male ruler to abdicate, which he did in 749 in order to devote more time to his Buddhist interests. His collection of hundreds of fine decorated objects of every sort is preserved in the Shosoin, a wooden storehouse in the compound of the Todai-ji in Nara (*see* JAPAN, BUDDHISM IN).

Shona Religion [II] The Shona of Zimbabwe consist of a number of related peoples, and their traditional religion was neither identical nor unchanging. In the 17th century, according to a Portuguese observer, the Mutapa Shona believed in one God, named MULUNGU or Umbe, and in ancestor spirits, *midzimu* (*see* MIZIMU), especially the (more powerful) spirits of dead kings. The modern pattern is not dissimilar. God is now named MWARI (of unsure origin). His cult is far more prominent in the south, around the central shrine-cave at Matonjeni, than in the north. The prayers of ordinary Shona are normally directed to their dead ancestors, the *midzimu*, who may pass them on, probably via the tribal spirits (*mhondoro*), to God. The *mhondoro* (literally 'lion') is perhaps the most characteristic feature of Shona religion, especially in the north. There is a hierarchy of the most powerful ancestor spirits, those of dead kings and chiefs (the highest being Chaminuka and Dzivaguru), each of which has its own territorial area, special cult and medium. The name of the spirit is taken by the medium, so that the two become almost identified in popular tradition. They are rainmakers, linked each with a sacred pool, and closest to Mwari, whose characteristics they largely share. Thus *Dzivaguru* (great pool) is both Mwari's most favoured praise-name at Matonjeni and the leading *mhondoro* in the north-east.

Other aspects of Shona religion include belief in witchcraft, in various evil or dangerous spirits (called *shavi* and *ngozi*) and in the ministrations of the NGANGA. [2: 104–27; 11: 341–50; 15: 235–55; 26]

Shotoku [XXI] Prince Shotoku, BUDDHISM's most sainted personality in Japan, was born the son of Emperor Yomei, named Toyosato Yatsumimi [25: 371–462]. He was appointed crown prince (*Taishi*) and regent by his aunt Empress Suiko in 594 and received the title of *Jogu* (Upper Palace). He welcomed Korean priests, studied the *sutras*, built temples, most notably the Shitenno-ji and Horyu-ji, and is credited with the so-called Seventeen-Article Constitution, a brief series of Confucian moralistic guides (*see* CONFUCIUS), only one of which has Buddhistic content: respect for the BUDDHA. He was already a legendary figure by the 8th century when the *Nihon Shoki* was written (*see* SHINTO LITERATURE) [3, II: 122–48]. His birth was sudden and painless, and it was said that he could then communicate fluently. He had a prodigious memory and his prognostications were accurate. He died after a one-month illness and was buried at Shinaga, now Taishi-cho, Osaka. The Taishi cult was fully developed when Fujiwara Kanesuke wrote the *Shotoku Taishi Denryaku* (Biography of Crown Prince Shotoku) in 917. Numerous feats, miracles and predictions were attributed to him and he was described as a reincarnated Buddha whose life had similarities to that of Siddhartha (GOTAMA). All later sects, including ZEN, gained wider acceptance by claiming inspiration from the teachings of the prince.

Shruti [XVII] In Hindu tradition, 'that which is heard directly', that is, by a sage or *rishi* (an inspired poet or sage, one who sings); hence directly revealed scripture, as distinct from *smriti*, which is 'memorized tradition' and secondary to direct revelation. The VEDA, BRAHMANAS, Aranyakas and UPANISHADS are regarded as *shruti*, while other Hindu literature, for example the PURANAS, is *smriti*.

Shugendo [XXI] The formal Japanese practices of *yamabushi*, mountain ascetics, who climb SACRED MOUNTAINS to become spirit-possessed, exorcize evil spirits (*see* HARAE) and transmit the will of the KAMI to local villagers [4: 165–6,

198–201; 14: 57–8; 15]. Organized into *ko*, groups, they are closely connected with the esoteric BUDDHIST sects of SHINGON and TENDAI. En-no-Gyoja (En-no-Ozunu or En-no-Shokaku) of the late 6th century is revered as the first *yamabushi*, having acquired this status after visiting Mt Mino in Osaka. Shugendo was spread widely in the 9th century by a priest, Shobo. It was officially banned in 1872 as corrupted SHINTO, but *yamabushi* are still active today.

Shulchan Arukh [XXII] The most authoritative code of Jewish law, composed by the SEFARDI sage RABBI Joseph Caro in the late 16th century with glosses by Rabbi Moses Isserles, who included ASHKENAZI HALAKHAH and customs [14 vol. 14: 1475]. The name means 'prepared table', and it was intended to present the *halakhah* in a brief and easily accessible form [18: 13]. Its four sections, which deal with different aspects of Jewish ritual life, are called 'Orach Chayim', 'Yoreh Deah', 'Even Ha-Ezer', and 'Choshen Mishpat'. [70: 124]

Shunyatavada [XI] One of the two main forms of systematic MAHAYANA BUDDHIST thought, also known as MADHYAMAKA. Although preceded by a more inspired *sutra* literature, Mahayana treatises (*shastra*) written in classical Sanskrit appear to have begun with the writings of Nagarjuna (*c.*2nd century CE). In the influential *Madhyamaka-karika* he applied the methodology of the Mahayana *sutras* as a higher-order critique of philosophical insights, especially those of the VAIBHASHIKA *abhidharma* [translation: 90: 183–220]. Many other works are attributed to Nagarjuna, probably incorrectly, but he was certainly the author of one or two further treatises. Others were the work of his disciple Aryadeva. A considerable commentarial literature followed [60: 87–103]. Two distinct schools arose: the Prasangika of Buddhapa-

lita (*c.*400–450 CE), and the Svatantrika of Bhavaviveka (*c.*490–570 CE), differing on the question of the viability of positive statements of the Madhyamaka position. The Prasangika Candrakirti (7th century) commented on the *Madhyamaka-karika* [translation: 87]. The Shunyatavada (Doctrine of Emptiness) became a sect in the Far East (SAN LUN TSUNG; *and see* NANTO ROKUSHU) and plays a central part in the Tibetan monastic curriculum (TIBETAN RELIGIONS).

The Madhyamaka method is intended to bring about an experiential understanding of EMPTINESS, in order to dissolve rigid views (DITTHI). It should be seen as the theoretical component of insight (VIPASSANA) meditation, intended to facilitate the breakthrough to the transcendent (LOKUTTARA) understanding. Nagarjuna distinguishes truth in the highest sense (*paramartha-satya*) from conventional truth (*samvrti-satya*), following *abhidharma* (*see* ABHIDHAMMA) usage in which conventional truth is the commonsense view and the highest truth is the understanding of the FOUR NOBLE TRUTHS, whether ordinary (insight) or transcendent (*lokuttara*). For Nagarjuna, however, only the deepest understanding could be the 'highest' truth and any insight differentiating into independent entities would be conventional. [69: 76–96; 78; 90; 101]

Shvetambara [XX] One of the two main sects of the JAIN religion. The name Shvetambara means 'white-robed' and signifies the most conspicuous way in which the monks of this sect can be distinguished from their counterparts in the DIGAMBARA sect, whose male ascetics are naked. The earliest Jain scriptures envisage nudity as the normal state for a monk, exemplified most clearly by MAHAVIRA and his disciples (GANADHARA). However, options allowing for the possibility of ascetic attire gradually appeared, explained partly with reference to the decline in attainments during the corrupt world age, and a fully self-aware sect of white-robed monks which formally differentiated itself from those monks who chose to reject clothes was probably in existence by the 5th century CE. By the 11th century, the Shvetambara sect had split into a variety of sub-sects (see GACCHA) based on the claims of rival teacher lineages. There are also in existence today two Shvetambara lineages, the STHANAKVASI and the TERAPANTH, who reject the practice of image worship.

Unlike the Digambaras, the Shvetambaras accept the possibility of spiritual liberation for women, and there always seem to have been almost three times as many nuns as monks within the sect. In addition, the Shvetambaras argue that the fully enlightened person (KEVALIN) is sufficiently human to require food; they also accept the validity of the scriptural tradition composed in ARDHAMAGADHI. Many of the most eminent Jain teachers have been Shvetambaras, and figures such as Haribhadra (8th century?), Hemacandra (12th century) and Yashovijaya (17th century) provided authoritative and powerful elaborations of Jain doctrine. There are approximately 2 million Shvetambara Jains in India today, around 2,000 of whom are monks and 6,000 nuns. They are found in the greatest numbers in Gujarat, Madhya Pradesh and Rajasthan. [2; 4; 7; 8; 9; 10; 12]

Sibylline Books [XXXI] Oracular books attributed to one of a number of sibyls, prophetesses associated with many different centres all over the ancient Mediterranean world. The Roman books were attributed to the sibyl of Cumae in Campania and were certainly written in Greek hexameters [8: 604–5; 19: 617–18]. They seem to have contained little if any prophecy, only ritual prescriptions to be used after disaster or foul

PRODIGIA. They were kept by a special college of priests (SACERDOTES) and consulted on the instructions of the Senate [2: 22–5]. They were especially influential in recommending the introduction of new cults and rituals from the Greek world, down to the time of Augustus (c.31 BCE–14 CE), when they were associated with the Secular Games, designed to usher in the new age of imperial rule [10: 176–84; 13: 82–90]. Many other books attributed to sibyls circulated in antiquity, from various dates, some as early as the 1st century BCE, of which one collection still survives: its oracles, dating from various periods, are prophetic in character and at least partly Jewish in origin [13: 267].

Siddha Yoga [XXVIII] Swami Muktananda Paramahamsa (1908–82), a disciple of Bhagwan Nityananda of Ganeshpuri (d. 1961), spread Siddha meditation throughout India and the West, establishing the Siddha Yoga Dham Associates Foundation in 1975. Before his death, Muktananda appointed the present leader, Gurumayi Chidvilasananda, as his successor; he also appointed her brother, Subash Shetty (then known as Swami Nityananda), but after some bitter controversies the latter left the movement in 1985 and established Shanti Mandir Seminars. Siddha yoga is said to take place spontaneously within a disciple whose kundalini (see TANTRA (1)) has been awakened by a Siddha Guru [46: 200], *shaktipat* being the name given to the initiation involving this transmission of spiritual power (SHAKTI) [46: 199]. The practice of the yoga includes chanting (especially the MANTRA *Om Namah Shivaya*), mediation, service and devotion to the guru; disciples also attend courses organized by the Syda Foundation at Shree Muktananda Ashram in South Fallsburg, New York and elsewhere around the world. [42: 935–6; 46]

Siddur [xxii] The 'order' of Jewish prayers, the term used for the week-day and Sabbath prayer-book [14 vol. 13: 985]. A separate collection of festival prayers is called the *Machzor*. The first *siddurim* were composed in Babylonia in the post-Talmudic period (*see* TALMUD) [29: introduction]. In different communities differing orders of prayers are used, and over the last 1,000 years many prayer-books have been written representing the various rites. The main divisions today are between the ASHKENAZI and the SEFARDI prayer-books. [64]

Sigalovada [xi] Name of a famous discourse of GOTAMA, the BUDDHA, addressed to a young BRAHMAN householder of Rajagaha, which sets out the ethical and social duties entailed in the common human rela tionships: parent/child; teachers/pupils; husband/wife; friend/friend; employer/workpeople; laypeople/*bhikkhu*. The discourse, known as the *Sigalovada Sutta*, is widely known in Sir Lanka, Burma and Thailand to Buddhist laypeople. [53: 135-7]

Sikh [xxxiii] (pronounced very nearly as in English 'sick': the pronunciation 'seek' is incorrect) A Sikh (=learner) is a follower of GURU NANAK and his successors (GURUS). The authoritative *Sikh Rahit Maryada* defines a Sikh as one who believes in AKAL PURAKH, the 10 Gurus and their teachings, the ADI GRANTH, and the initiation (*amrit*) instituted by the 10th Guru [30: 79]. It adds that he should believe in no other religion (RAHIT-NAMA). This is a rigorous definition, for it seems to affirm that only the *amrit-dhari* (those who have received the KHALSA initiation) are to be recognized as Sikhs. In practice KES-DHARI Sikhs (those who do not receive initiation but keep their hair uncut) are also accepted as Sikhs. The *sahaj-dhari* Sikhs (those who cut their hair and do not observe the

RAHIT) occupy, however, an uncertain position. [28: v; 29: vii]

Sikh Dharma of the Western Hemisphere [xxxiii] Founded in the USA in 1971 by Harbhajan Singh Khalsa Yogiji, commonly called Yogi Bhajan, the movement is best known through its educational branch called 3HO (Healthy Happy Holy Organization). It now claims more than 5,000 Western adherents scattered over 17 countries. Within the wider Sikh community its members are distinguished by their white apparel (including turbans for women as well as for men) and by a rigorous discipline of yoga and med-itation. The movement is also distinctive in that it possesses an ordained ministry. Its followers practise kundalini YOGA and medi-tation. [29: 118-19]

Sikh Diaspora [xxxiii] Until the late 19th century migrant SIKHS were chiefly traders, who settled elsewhere in India or neighbouring lands to the west. This range was substantially enlarged by the British army. Sikh soldiers stationed in Sin-gapore and Hong Kong began the Punjabi migration to both territo-ries, a small flow which soon exten-ded down to Australia, New Zealand and Fiji. Most were male JAT Sikhs (*see* CASTE (SIKH)), virtually all of them seeking temporary unskilled employment. Others meanwhile had discovered opportunities along the west coast of North America and semi-skilled artisans found employ-ment laying east African railways. Early in the 20th century these doors were closed. When the Punjabi flow recommenced after the Second World War it issued from both India and Pakistan, with most of its mem-bers migrating to England but sig-nificant numbers again going to North America. As before, a sub-stantial majority of those from India were Sikhs from districts bordering the upper Satluj. By 1978 there were approximately 250,000 Sikhs in

Britain. In the early 1990s the figure was approaching half a million. There are also large communities of well over 200,000 each in the USA and Canada. [8: 161–5; 28: 102–9]

Sikh Festivals [XXXIII] Apart from anniversaries associated with the GURUS (known as GURPURABS) the SIKHS also celebrate three important festivals each year. These have HINDU antecedents, but all three have distinctly Sikh associations. The date of each is fixed according to the native calendar of India. Baisakhi falls in April, Divali in October/November and Hola Mohalla in February/March. Baisakhi, the New Year festival, marks the harvesting of the spring crop and is also the anniversary of the founding of the KHALSA. Divali or the Festival of Lights has obvious Hindu origins, but in its Sikh form commemorates the laying of the foundation of HARI-MANDIR SAHIB. Hola Mohalla is held on the day after the Hindu Holi festival and was evidently intended to turn Sikhs' attention away from the practices associated with Holi. The festival centres on Anandpur, scene of the founding of the Khalsa, and focuses devotion on GURU GOBIND SINGH. Maghi (the first day of the month of Magh which falls in January) is also a popular Sikh festival. [8: 129–32; 10: VII]

Sikh History [XXXIII] Sikh history begins with GURU NANAK (b. 1469). In the Punjab during the 16th century the growing community of his followers (the PANTH) remained inconspicuous, but Mughal (Mogul) hostility (*see* ISLAMIC DYNASTIES) developed early in the 17th century and eventually issued in open warfare at the beginning of the 18th century (*see* GURUS). Following the death of the last Guru in 1708 many Sikhs rallied to the rebellion raised by Banda, one of his disciples. Banda was executed in 1716 and Mughal forces continued to harry the Sikhs for many years, but

towards the middle of the century fortunes changed as Mughal authority disintegrated. Sikh guerrilla bands called *misls* emerged, hastening the Mughal collapse and obstructing Afghan invasions (1747–69). Success led to internecine strife, until eventually the Shukerchakia *misl* emerged triumphant at the end of the century. Its leader, Ranjit Singh, became Maharaja of the Punjab and ruled unchallenged until his death in 1839. Military activity had powerfully encouraged the growth of militant traditions in the Panth, particularly within the KHALSA and among its dominant JAT constituency (*see* CASTE (SIKH)). Political success was, however, accompanied by a weakening of the earlier religious traditions and after the British annexation of the Punjab in 1849 many foresaw the ultimate extinction of the Panth. Revival came later in the century with the rise of the influential Singh Sabha movement (*see* SIKH REFORM MOVEMENTS), preaching a return to old Khalsa values and buttressing its appeal with a range of social and intellectual activities [4: XXIII–XXXIV].

During the 20th century interest has moved more to political action. Early in the century this was directed to securing panthic control of the GURDWARAS. From this campaign in the early 1920s the AKALI Dal emerged as the strongest Sikh political party, a strength it has retained until recent years. At independence in 1947 the Sikhs found the line of demarcation between India and Pakistan ran through the Punjab. Those in Pakistan all migrated to India where the Panth began a series of agitations leading to a demand for Khalistan (independent Punjab), an issue which remains unsettled (*see* SIKH POLITICS). As a result of recent disturbances the Akali Dal has fragmented and no longer commands the strength it once had. (*See also* SIKH POLITICS; SIKH REFORM MOVE-

MENTS; TAT KHALSA.) [General histories: 13; 18; 19]

Sikh Languages [XXXIII] Sikhs attach a deeply affectionate importance to the Punjabi language and its Gurmukhi script. Although most of the JANAM-SAKHIS are recorded in Punjabi the language of the ADI GRANTH is more complex. In a general sense it can be called *Sant bhasha* ('SANT language'). This designates a simple language based on Khari Boli, the Hindi of the Delhi region, which was widely used for popular religious poetry. There are, however, significant variants, with the early GURUS tending strongly towards Punjabi and Guru Arjan more to western Hindi [26: 69–70]. Under GURU GOBIND SINGH the emphasis shifted to Braj, language of the Mathura region and the KRISHNA cycle (*see* DASAM GRANTH). In the late 18th century it swung strongly and permanently back to Punjabi.

Sikh Martyrs [XXXIII] Unyielding courage is one of two key principles invoked in the defence of the Sikh faith; the other is martyrdom. Martyrs are held up as objects of intense admiration by devout Sikhs, their deaths seen as total obedience to the GURU and as shining examples to all who follow after. Two of the Gurus, Arjan and Tegh Bahadur, are regarded as martyrs, as are the two younger sons of GOBIND SINGH who were bricked up alive. The death of Dip Singh during the 18th century is seen as supreme martyrdom. In recent years the killing of Jarnail Singh Bhindranwale in the Indian army's 1984 assault on the Golden Temple (*see* HARIMANDIR SAHIB) is viewed in the same light. (*See also* SIKH HISTORY; SIKH POLITICS.) [17: VIII; 28: 116]

Sikh Politics [XXXIII] In 1947, when their homeland was divided between India and Pakistan, the Sikhs in Pakistan all migrated to Indian Punjab. There an agitation was begun for their own state within the Indian union (Punjabi Suba). This was granted in 1966, but proved to be inadequate. In 1973 the Sikh political party, the AKALI Dal, passed the Anandpur Resolution demanding greater autonomy for the Punjab. Relations with the Indian government deteriorated and in June 1984 the Indian army assaulted the Golden Temple (HARIMANDIR SAHIB) where a group of radical Sikhs were entrenched, killing their leader Jarnail Singh Bhindranwale. In retaliation the Indian Prime Minister, Mrs Gandhi, was assassinated. Since then the demand for Khalistan (independent Punjab) has steadily grown and most Sikhs are now disillusioned with government policy. If, however, a greater autonomy were granted it seems that they would be content for the Punjab to remain within India. [28: 109–19]

Sikh Reform Movements [XXXIII] Defeat in 1849 confronted the Sikh PANTH with a threatening future (*see* SIKH HISTORY). Although the victorious British subsequently enlisted many Sikh soldiers, the question of Sikh identity and even survival became critical. The eventual response was the Singh Sabha (Singh Association) movement. In 1873 a Singh Sabha was formed in Amritsar and another in Lahore six years later. Others followed in areas populated by Sikhs, all supporting a generally reformist policy with strong emphasis on the recovery of distinctive Sikh values. This policy was applied through literature, education, religious assemblies, preaching and public controversy. A split soon appeared, however, between Amritsar and Lahore, each supported by its group of smaller *sabhas*. Although temporary unity was achieved in 1902 by the formation of the Chief Khalsa Diwan, as an umbrella organization, this proved too cautious for the so-called TAT KHALSA or 'neo-Sikhs' [4: XXIII–XXXIV].

Ardent Sikh opinion turned increasingly against the government and found a specific cause in opposition to control of GURDWARAS by hereditary supervisors (*mahants*). This produced the AKALI movement and a period of vigorous agitation, beginning in 1920. The government eventually gave way and in 1925 transferred control of the principal *gurdwaras* to an elective board, the Shiromani Gurdwara Parbandhak Committee or SGPC. (*See also* SANATAN SIKHISM; TAT KHALSA). [13: VII–VIII; 23: XIII]

Sikh Sects [XXXIII] Although it is sometimes claimed that there are no Sikh sects [34: VI], there are distinctive groups claiming to represent the true GURMAT which are commonly regarded as heretical. The earliest of these is the ascetic order of Udasi *sadhus*, followers of NANAK's son Siri Chand (*see* GURUS) and evidently a Sikh extension of the NATH TRADITION [34: 58–66]. The Nirmala order is usually traced from five Sikhs whom Guru GOBIND SINGH is said to have sent to Banaras to acquire Sanskrit learning. Widely respected for their contribution to traditional Sikh scholarship, they are unorthodox in their Vedantic leanings and their celibacy [7: 121]. Nineteenth-century uncertainties produced the Nirankari movement, initiated in Peshawar by Baba Dayal (1783–1855) and stressing return to the pristine teachings of Nanak [23: 123–5]. The movement must be distinguished from a group with a similar name, the Sant Nirankari Mandal. This group, which has more recent beginnings, has been in violent confrontation with orthodox Sikhs over the troubles which led to the storming of the Golden Temple (*see* HARIMANDIR SAHIB) by government forces in June 1984 [29: 119]. The Nirankaris are regarded as heretical principally because they accept a continuing line of living Gurus. This also applies to the Namdhari or Kuka movement, fol-

lowers of Balak Singh (1797–1862) and of his more famous millenarian successor Ram Singh (1816–85). Namdhari Sikhs preach a rigorous doctrine of the KHALSA and are distinguished by wearing white clothes of homespun cotton with the turban tied horizontally across the forehead [23: 127–35]. Another group noted for its strictness comprises the followers of Randhir Singh (1878–1961), known as the Bhai Randhir Singh da Jatha. Features of their discipline include the *keski* (under-turban) as one of the FIVE Ks instead of the *kes*. In recent years of trouble with the Indian government some have formed themselves into the Akhand Kirtani Jatha [7: 35–6]. One rapidly growing sect, particularly among overseas Sikhs, is the Nanaksar movement, disciples of a line of SANTS based in Kaleran (near Ludhiana) [7: 118]. Many Sikhs also belong to the RADHASOAMI SATSANG of Beas. This too can be regarded as a Sikh sect, although many Hindus are also its followers [29: 115–19]. (*See also* SIKH DHARMA OF THE WESTERN HEMISPHERE.)

Sila [XI] (Pali; Sanskrit: *shila*) A BUDDHIST term meaning 'wholesome/ethical conduct'. *Sila* is seen as the basis of the Buddhist path. Unwholesome actions motivated by attachment, aversion and delusion are seen both as intrinsically disturbing and as leading to unpleasant results (*see* KARMA), bringing future suffering to oneself and others. Their avoidance fosters both happiness and the conditions conducive to the practice of meditation (BHAVANA). Perfect conduct, however, is not seen as achieved by mere adherence to a set of moral rules; it is itself an expression of an inner transformation brought about by following the Buddhist path. The aspiration to wholesome conduct is most commonly realized by undertaking the five precepts or 'bases of training' (*sikkhapada*): refraining from (1) harming living creatures, (2) taking what is not given, (3) sexual misconduct, (4) false speech, (5) intoxicants that lead to heedlessness. Together with 'going for refuge' (*see* TISARANA), taking these precepts represents the essential act of becoming a Buddhist. Committed lay followers (UPASAKA) may on occasion (*see* UPOSATHA) take eight precepts, replacing refraining from sexual misconduct with complete sexual abstinence and adding refraining from (6) eating after midday, (7) attending entertainments and using perfumes, etc. and (8) using luxurious beds. Novice members of the Buddhist order (SANGHA) and occasionally lay followers take ten precepts which are the same as the eight except that the seventh is considered as two and refraining from handling money is added as the tenth. [34: 196–216]

Sin, Christianity and [XIII.B] For Christians sin is essentially disobedience to the will of God. Moral failure is the result of a sinful condition. All humanity is in a sinful state ('original sin') as a result of Adam's 'fall'. In Christian mythology Adam was the first man, who, tempted by his wife Eve, lost his superior nature by disobedience to God and so 'fell' from grace (*see* SALVATION). This fall story has been challenged in the light of science and history, but the basic belief has been maintained in the human bias to sin as a falling short of God's purpose for humanity. This is now sustained by reference to history and contemporary observation. In the light of this view of human nature the Christian doctrine of salvation was developed, together with remedies such as the SACRAMENTS, especially PENANCE. Debate on original sin and its effects on free will has led to much controversy (*see* e.g. AUGUSTINIANISM; JANSENISM; PELAGIANISM). Early PROTESTANTISM took a more pessimistic view than that general in ROMAN CATHOLICISM (except for Jansenism). Since the 18th century many Protestants have developed more optimistic (perhaps less theological) views of human moral capacity. Twentieth-century experience has tended to revive earlier pessimism, especially after the HOLOCAUST. However, strictly theological views of sin as disobedience to the will of God have tended to become more generalized condemnation of moral failures. In Roman Catholicism (and sometimes Protestantism) MORAL THEOLOGY has been characterized by elaborate distinctions between sins as an aid to spiritual guidance ('casuistry'). 'Mortal' sins are gross, deliberate and knowing, entailing loss of grace and damnation. 'Venial' sins are less serious and do not entail loss of all grace. Both forms of sin, it is believed, are forgiven by God if real regret and true resolve to lead a new life are shown ('contrition') [91; 114: XIII]

Singsing [XXIX] Festival of dance and ritual feast found universally in MELANESIAN RELIGION. *Singsings* accompany many MALE CULT rites. Whole communities share in preparations, clearing ceremonial dance grounds, rebuilding shrines and HAUS TAMBARAN, preparing sacred MASKS and gathering food supplies. Through dance and drama, spirits of the dead (TUMBUNA) are welcomed, and obliged (by generous offerings of food and valuables, and especially the ritual slaughter of pigs) to continue their favour and the spiritual power (MANA) they make available. Renewed relationships with ancestors and gods bring the hope of harmony among the living, and fertility in nature. Major *singsings* may occur seasonally (at harvest or New Year) or after much longer intervals. Complex trading exchanges may be entered into, to obtain the hundreds of surplus pigs required. Though greatly modified by Christian influence, *singsings* continue in the form of pig-feasts, notably in the New Guinea highlands. [23; 29]

Sinhalese Buddhism [XI] By about the 12th century THERAVADA BUDDHISM had recovered its former dominant position among the Sinhala-speaking population of the island of Ceylon. Despite the medieval immigration of Tamil-speaking Hindus and later political domination by various missionizing European nations, Buddhism remains the religion of the Sinhala majority in the modern state of Sri Lanka, with about 13 million adherents. Traditional Sinhalese Buddhism was closely associated with Sinhalese nationalism and monarchy and existed in a complex relationship with various *deva* cults at the local level. The last century has seen the rise under European secularist and Theosophical influence (*see* THEOSOPHY) of a Buddhist modernism. Deva cults and traditional ritual practices were seen as corruptions of the original pure Buddhism. A strong reformist tendency emerged, with a rather rationalistic interpretation based partly on the work of late 19th-century scholarship, notably that of T. W. Rhys Davids (1843–1922) and the Pali Text Society (founded 1881). The reasonable and 'scientific' nature of Buddhism was stressed. This led to some revival of Buddhist missionary activity and influenced modernizing tendencies in other Buddhist countries. Traditional attitudes remain dominant in village Buddhism, with modernizing tendencies widespread among the Western-educated; there are many intermediate positions. [28; 29; 30]

Sioux [V] (or Dakota) The dominant group of the Hokam–Siouan Amerindian linguistic stock, in North America, the western division of which includes the well-known Ogalala Sioux. Religious conceptions have undergone considerable transformation with European contact. Among major elements is a belief in an all-powerful and invisible being, Wakonda (or Wakantanka), who is both the original source of all power and the cosmic governor. There are also intermediary beings (manifestations of *wakan* – literally 'sacred' – power, including the sun, earth, moon, thunder-beings and the elements) and more localized spirits-of-the-place (e.g. water spirits, spirits of the lodge, etc.; *see* COSMOLOGY) [17: V–VIII]. Contact with the supernatural world was possible through individual VISION QUESTS, which involved personal austerities (such as the SWEAT LODGE rite), contact with, and even acquisition of, GUARDIAN SPIRITS, and a possible career as a *wicasa wakan* (literally 'man sacred') [23: XIII]. The best-known ceremonial, the SUN DANCE, probably of relatively late origin, was often an annual event and usually performed in the summer. Central features included the construction of the lodge, dances based on cosmological motifs, individual self-mutilation and sun-gazing. The decline of traditional culture somewhat isolated major religious features (notably the vision quest, use of the sacred pipe, the calumet, and the sun dance). The GHOST DANCE flourished briefly among the Sioux.

Sitra Achra [XXII] A term used in KABBALAH for the powers of evil, meaning literally 'other side'. Evil is part of the divinely emanated structure underlying all reality, made up of the 10 *sefirot* (*see* SEFIRAH) [14 vol. 10: 585]. The *Sefirah* of Din (Judgement) plays an important role in providing limitation in the cosmos, and a by-product of this limitation is the Sefiriotic substructure of the Sitra Achra – the world of evil often described as the shell (*kelippah*) surrounding the light of holiness [61: 239]. Evil has no life of its own, and must derive life-giving energy as a parasite on holiness. The sins of men allow the Sitra Achra to gain temporary dominance over the SHEKHINAH, the lowest of the *sefirot*, thereby unleashing evil on humankind. In the Kabbalah evil is not seen as a force independent of God, but as a potential within creation which sin beings on to the plane of actuality. [70: 101]

Skilful Means [XI] The most frequent translation of the Buddhist term *upaya-kaushalya* (Pali: *upaya-kosalla*). An *upaya* is an expedient device or cunning stratagem, while *kaushalya* has both the sense of skilfulness and that of moral wholesomeness. *Upaya-kaushalya* is the clever ability of the BUDDHA or BODHISATTVA (motivated by compassion) to make use of tricks in a spiritually completely wholesome way in order to assist progress in the teaching. This notion, which in the earlier Buddhist literature is often exemplified but rarely explicitly formulated, comes into prominence later. The MAHAYANA especially tends to view the whole teaching of the Buddha as consisting of many skilful means. [70]. It is taken into the later THERAVADA, especially by DHAMMAPALA. [4: index]

Slavery (in Islam) [XIX] ISLAM took over this universal west Asian institution, with masters having sexual rights over female slaves. The QUR'AN nonetheless enjoins kindness and provides for the manumission of slaves. In medieval Islam, slave soldiers were able to rise to high positions of power, as among the Egyptian Mamelukes and the Ottoman Turkish janissaries (troops recruited in boyhood from the Christian peoples of the Balkans). In modern times, it has virtually disappeared from the Islamic world. [38 "Abd'; 48: 136–8; 67 s.v.; 77: III, VI]

Slavs [VII] The Slav peoples, speaking one language until the 9th century CE, expanded from a homeland in central Europe or the Ukraine over an area extending from the Oder to the Urals and into the Balkan peninsula. Some western Slavs were not converted to CHRISTIANITY until the 12th century, but information about beliefs comes from unreliable sources, such as 11th- and 12th-century chroniclers and early missionaries [13: 1025]. Something, however, may be learned from oath formulas, archaeological evidence and a rich folk tradition [11: VIII]. The Slavs worshipped a thundergod, Perun ('Striker'), associated with the oak; Svarog, father of the sun, linked with fire and battle; Volos/Veles, god of flocks; and an earth-goddess Mokosh ('moist'). They had many local deities like Svantevit, god of war and harvest, whose temple at Arcona on the isle of Rugen was destroyed in 1168; some of these had sacred horses used for divination. The religion had strong shamanic elements (*see* SHAMAN), human sacrifice and a tendency towards dualism. Comparative philologists have established links between names of Slav deities and those of Iran and India (*see* INDO-EUROPEANS) [13: 1026]. Stone figures of gods, some with three or four faces, holding drinking-horns, have been found, and there is evidence for simple temples [11: VIII, 151–9].

Social Gospel [IV] One of numerous American movements advocating social change in the name of Christian faith which prospered early in the 20th century. Others were related to Anglo-American Christian Socialism and various ROMAN CATHOLIC reform movements.

The PROTESTANT Social Gospel rose partly in reaction to social Darwinist messages of individualism and competition, which the Social Gospel leaders thought denied the communal and corporate character of Christian life and of institutions influenced by Christian faith. Positively, they shared in the ethos of secular progressivism, a set of rather optimistic assessments of what could occur to humanize the economic, political and social orders if people of good will undertook careful planning. Similarly, they were advocates of liberal theology; this meant that they stressed the immanence or nearness of God, the divine involvement in human affairs. They wanted to be responsive to the judgement called forth by the Hebrew prophets; to the Kingdom of God – their favourite metaphor in the teaching of JESUS; and to reformist impulses. Under BAPTIST professor Walter Rauschenbusch, CONGREGATIONAL-IST minister Washington Gladden and other academic and clerical leaders, the Social Gospel advocated the 'Christianizing' of the social order and the advancement of the Kingdom of God. The change of climate against progressivism that came in the aftermath of the First World War led to a decline in the Social Gospel, but it has repeatedly inspired subsequent leaders of social movements, including the Reverend Martin Luther King Jr. [1: XLVII; 26]

Social   Morality   (Christian) [XIII.B] Early Christian social concern was largely evinced in individual charitable work. This has never ceased to be practised, but links between church and state (*see* STATE, CHRISTIANITY AND THE) brought wider responsibilities, and complications. Thus the medieval church tried to curb and civilize warfare by the concepts of God's Peace and God's Truce. But it fostered the CRUSADES, and pacifism has always been a minority Christian view [65: VII]. Slavery [165] was originally tolerated and even justified theologically (except by minorities), although eventually attacked under Christian influence. Established churches have tended to endorse the existing social and political order, especially where favourable to the church. This has coexisted with relief of suffering and moralizing campaigns (especially by PROTES-TANTISM) against limited problems like alcohol and Sunday work. Traditional theology placed a high value

on work and regarded private property as divinely ordained. ROMAN CATHOLICISM has traditionally regarded poverty as a source of virtue, but Protestantism sometimes saw it as a sign of moral failure. In modern times most churches have come to approve of collective and state action for social welfare [19: 275–9; 35]. This has been given theological expression in the American Protestant SOCIAL GOSPEL [93]; Social Catholicism [191]; and, most radically, in Christian Socialism [107] and recent LIBERATION THEOLOGY [140]. In the USA and Britain in the 1980s there was a political trend towards stress on individual self-help to reduce reliance on state welfare. In addition, some extreme EVANGELICAL groups in the USA, such as the self-styled MORAL MAJORITY, backed restrictive attitudes on social and sexual morality, especially through the Republican Party. Some also taught that prosperity and the acquisition of wealth are both the product and evidence of Christian achievement. In England, however, there has been much opposition from the mainstream Christian bodies to such views and the 1990s may see a partial return to an emphasis on community responsibility for social welfare. (*See also* SEXUALITY, AND CHRISTIANITY.)

Sociology of Religion [XXXIV] The sociology of religion is concerned not with the truth of the beliefs that people hold, but with empirical questions such as what kinds of people hold what kinds of beliefs under what kinds of conditions, and what are the consequences both for themselves and for the wider society of their holding such beliefs [114: 1]. The range of areas of study in the sociology of religion is considerable, covering not only investigations into particular religious groupings, such as Southern BAPTISTS [2], ROMAN CATHOLICISM [87], EVANGELICAL-ISM [88], BUDDHISM [13: V], ISLAM

[136: IX; 165] and AFRICAN RELI-
GIONS [13: VI], and comparisons
between religions [173], but also the
nature and extent of relations
between religious institutions and
beliefs and other areas of society,
such as the economy [172], the family [114: III], politics [136], the
media [71] or aesthetics and sexual
practices [173: XIV]. Sociologists of
religion are also interested in assessing the conditions under which religions may lead to conflict,
disintegration, cohesion and/or solidarity within a society; and relat-
edly, in a number of processes such
as conversion, defection, proselytization [114: III], adaptation, SEC-
ULARIZATION and rationalization
[13], and in comparing different
kinds of religious organization and
authority [173; 182] – the role of the
charismatic leader being but one
example [13: X, XI].

Sociological studies of religion can
be dated from around the time of
August Comte (1798–1857), but
perhaps the best-known classics are
to be found among the works of
Émile Durkheim (1858–1917) and
Max Weber (1864–1920). In *The
Elementary Forms of the Religious Life*
[48], Durkheim sought to demonstrate that religion played a role in
the life of a society by providing a
moral authority which was greater
than any individual but which actually mirrored and reinforced the
structure and culture of the society
in which it was practised. Weber's
The Sociology of Religion [173] is
arguably still one of the best introductions to the subject, although he
is possibly better known for *The
Protestant Ethic and the Spirit of Capitalism* [172], in which he questioned
the Marxist belief that the economy
is the basic determinant in society,
and sought to show how beliefs
(such as particular forms of PROTES-
TANTISM) could contribute to economic changes (such as the rise of
modern capitalism).

During the latter half of the 20th
century, there have been a number

of key issues attracting the attention
of sociologists of religion. One of
these has been the secularization
thesis, with Bryan Wilson's definition of the process as one 'whereby
religious thinking, practice and institutions lose social significance' [178:
14] having set the agenda for a
fierce, continuing debate about the
extent to which, and the ways in
which, religion continues to be of
importance to individuals and to
society [13; 17; 21; 63; 112; 136;
182]. Closely allied to this topic
have been studies of the growth of
FUNDAMENTALISM (variously defined to include not only Protestantism, but also Islamic and other
varieties of resolute beliefs and practices), the development of NEW
RELIGIOUS MOVEMENTS and the
beliefs and practices of non-
institutionalized religion, be this
'privatized', 'invisible' [112], 'folk',
'common', 'customary' [87: 90–3]
or 'IMPLICIT' RELIGION [71; 114: IV].
Other areas of growing interest have
been relations between religion and
identity, gender, immigration and
multiculturalism, and globalization
[136]; perceptions of the body
[165]; and studies on clergy and
congregations, on age, sex, GENDER,
class and generational differences,
and on types of religious and/or spiritual experiences.

Although many sociologists have
written about religion, it was not
really until after the Second World
War that the subject became widely
established as a sub-discipline, with
practitioners referring to themselves
primarily as sociologists of religion.
The various national and international social science associations
usually have a section for those specializing in religion and a number of
independent professional organizations, some with their own journals,
now exist to further communication
between those interested in studying
religious behaviour. Among the
most prominent are the Society for
the Scientific Study of Religion,
founded in 1949, which now has

well over 1,500 members and publishes the *Journal for the Scientific Study of Religion*; the Association for the Sociology of Religion (originally founded in 1938 as the American Catholic Sociological Association), which now has 650 members – its journal *Sociological Analysis* changed its name to *Sociology of Religion* in 1993; the Religious Research Association, which publishes the *Review of Religious Research*, and has about 450 members; and the Société Internationale de Sociologie des Religions, now associated with *Social Compass*, with a membership of around 400.

The methods employed by sociologists of religion include surveys, questionnaires, interviewing and participant observation. Occasionally a covert approach has been adopted, with the researcher feigning a personal interest in being a believer in order to have access which might otherwise be denied. Such practices are the subject of considerable debate on both ethical and methodological grounds. Sometimes the investigators are genuinely members of the religion under investigation – sociological research into Roman Catholicism has, for example, been undertaken by Catholic priests, nuns and laypersons, by members of other religions and by agnostics and atheists. In theory at least, the findings of such researchers ought not to differ because of their beliefs, as the sociology of religion espouses a methodological agnosticism – that is, it does not address questions about the nature of God or the meaning of the Virgin Birth, nor can it draw upon non-empirical entities such as the Holy Spirit to explain such happenings as a conversion or miracles. [59a, vol. 13: 393–401]

Soka Gakkai [XXI] A lay BUDDHIST association, an offshoot of NICHIREN Shoshu, which has become prominent in Japan because of its entry into politics (through Komeito, the Clean Government Party) [21: 207–8]. Its beginnings are dated to 1930, when it was founded by Tsunesaburo Makiguchi and Josei Toda. Both were imprisoned during the Second World War, Makiguchi dying in prison. It was built up rapidly after 1947, with particular strength in the large cities, and by 1970 it claimed more than 16 million adherents. They work diligently to gain new members and contribute liberally towards the final supremacy of the Nichiren beliefs [2]. Happiness is seen by its worldly oriented members as achievable through profit, goodness and beauty [14: 114–18].

Songs and Chanting (South American) [XXIII] Recent research on the relations between narrative and music in South America shows that the distinction between spoken and sung speech is by no means clear-cut. Often, the musicality of speech is conceptually and pragmatically integrated within genres of spoken speech, such as narratives and ceremonial dialogues. It has been suggested, moreover, that the formalized speech varieties of myth, magic and ritual carry the propositional force of articulate speech to its outermost limits through the use of semantic principles that differ qualitatively from those used in everyday speech. Specialized ritual languages are seen as metaphorical processes of connecting the known, experienced world of natural, social beings with an unknown or partially known universe of mythic meanings. The mythic powers evoked in such languages are seen as emergent properties, or a sort of hidden dimension, of the world of everyday things and life experiences.

Ritual chanting and song imbue human bodily processes and everyday activities of production, exchange and consumption with mythic powers of creation, destruction and regeneration. The power of ritual specialists (*see* SHAMANS AND

RELIGIOUS SPECIALISTS) derives in part from their unique abilities to employ naming processes in chants as a way of converting their potentially life-taking powers into life-giving powers. Parallel to this transformation of negative into positive emotions, ritual chanting converts mythic images of bodily and cosmic destruction into symbols of growth and regeneration through controlled contact with mythic powers. [3; 32]

Soul (Amerindian) [v] In North America, most Amerindian tribes, with the exception of the southwestern groups, affirm the existence in each person of two souls, a 'free' soul and a 'life' or 'breath' soul [8: XI, 131–4]. The former, usually identified with the personality, is able to leave the body during dream or vision states (*see* VISION QUEST), often travelling to distant places and, on rare occasions, even visiting the land of the dead. Disease, disability, loss of memory, etc., are regarded as indicators of the free soul's absence. In the SHAMAN, such ecstatic experiences are brought under control, enabling him voluntarily to frequent spirit realms either to seek out and bring back the wandering or stolen souls of sick persons, or to serve as guide for souls of the deceased to the land of the dead. Soul wandering, especially in the case of youth, was interpreted by the SIOUX as an indication that one should undertake a vision quest, possibly even that one was marked for a career as a holy man [17: VI]. With the permanent departure of the free soul came death and the consequent 'evaporation' of the life or breath soul. Although belief in the soul's preexistence was generally affirmed, conceptions were usually vague. After death, the free soul might travel considerable distances, perhaps along the Milky Way, and experience tests or ordeals before passing into the land of the dead. [10]

Souls (South American) [XXIII] Sullivan [33: v] has distinguished two systematic tendencies in Native South American soul beliefs: (1) physiological, which affirms that the soul is a spiritual element situated in specific body parts, coterminous with the functioning of bodily organs and defined by 'animal' appetites (food, sex); often, such souls extend to animals, who are the doubles of human soul-elements; (2) epistemological, in which spiritual elements are associated with specific human faculties (thought, memory). Here, the human being is affirmed as a self-contained and autonomous being set apart from the object of its perceptions.

In some cultures, souls are linked in a network extending back to the primordium; in others, the soul is associated with ceremonial groups based on names, residence or types of ritual performance. Frequently, multiple souls gained throughout a lifetime comprise the person, each of which is transformed at the moment of death. Dream-souls and dream interpretation are particularly important in numerous cultures. Sonic imagery – in naming ceremonies, sacred music and song – is everywhere constitutive of the person. Articulated to the notion of the person is a rich symbolism of corporality through which South American cultures express fundamental values used to understand spaces constitutive of human life. [2]

South American Indian Religions [XXIII] The South American continent is notable for its enormous linguistic diversity (estimated at some 1,500 different languages, present or extinct), the antiquity of its occupation and the tremendous range of its socio-cultural formations (from small-scale hunter–gatherer societies in Amazonia to imperial states in the Andes). Similarly, the religious lives of South American Indians have displayed an enormous variety of forms. Following five centuries of contact with Europeans, this panorama has been greatly reduced or modified and, given the relative lack of detailed, comparative and historical studies of religion, it is exceedingly difficult to give a composite picture of the whole today. Nevertheless, certain themes emerge from contemporary accounts.

CREATION MYTHS affirm the divine origin of the universe *ex nihilo*, through transformation or, most importantly, through multiple epochs. Elaborate cosmological structures (*see* COSMOLOGY), coupled with frequently found beliefs in multiple souls and a rich symbolism of the human body, integrate humankind into a system of spatial and temporal orders through which life unfolds. Humanity's relationship to the divine, often through priests and/or SHAMANS, ranges from worship and supplication to mystical union with divinities, ritual combat or celebration of divinely instituted festivals. Ritual life (calendric feasts, war rituals, rites of passage) in some cases renews links with primordial creative powers; in others, is a way of producing the future (*see* RITES). Ritual music, songs and chants are the great symbols of culture, expressing change, reproduction through time and acts of creation. Enormous importance is given to the mystery and power of death as integral to human existence. For many cultures, mortality initiates a life-condition of constant transition and metamorphosis. MILLENARIAN AND PROPHETIC MOVEMENTS frequently express this dilemma, inherited from primordial times, and the utopic quest for immortality. While Christianity has struck deep roots throughout the continent, quite frequently it has been reshaped by native peoples and incorporated into pre-existing structures.

South Asia, Islam in [xix] ISLAM is numerically and politically very important in this region: in Afghanistan, Muslims comprise 100% of the population (1994 estimate, 20 million); in Pakistan 97% (1992 projection, 113 million); in Bangladesh 80% (1991 census, 88 million); and in the Indian Union 11% (1991 census, 92 million).

Arab raiders reached Sind in 711, but Islam was not extensively planted in northern India until the 13th century and after, setting down strong roots also in south India. Until the tightening of British control by the mid-19th century, the dominant military and ruling class over much of India was Muslim, although large concentrations of peasants in the Indus valley and lower Ganges valley had also found in Islam an escape from the rigours of the Hindu CASTE system. British rule curtailed the power of the Muslim landed classes, causing a crisis of confidence in the community during the late 19th and early 20th centuries, only now being restored since the establishment of the officially Muslim state of Pakistan (1947) and that of Bangladesh (1971). In the Indian Union, Muslims are especially numerous in Uttar Pradesh, Bihar and West Bengal. Mainly medium and small peasants and craftsmen, they consider that they are underrepresented in government and other public services [general surveys in: 8: VI; 65: II, 1–119].

Islam in the subcontinent has long been characterized by a strong strain of Sufi mysticism (SUFISM), some of whose adepts explored the common ground of religious experience with their Hindu counterparts (*see* BHAKTI), while fairly rigorously orthodox SUFI ORDERS like the Naqshbandis have also been strong. The tendency towards syncretism was further seen in the attempt of the 16th-century Mughal (Mogul) emperor Akbar (1556–1605) at a monotheistic synthesis, the 'divine faith'. Such trends have always evoked fierce reaction from the defenders of Islamic orthodoxy, fearful of a blurring of Islam's distinctiveness [1: IV–IX; 2: IV–V].

Hence the recurring features of puritanical reform movements and nostalgia for the simplicity and justice of earliest Islam (attitudes similar to those of the Arabian WAHHABIS), recently also in reaction against Western-type modernism. Such feelings have been strong in determining the political and religious ethos of Pakistan and the ideal of achieving there an 'Islamic republic' [1: IX; 28: IV, VII–VIII, X]. Also noteworthy is the persistence of a strain of SHI'ISM, which has recently produced some notable leaders for Islam in the subcontinent [2: II].

South-East Asia, Buddhism in
[XI] THERAVADA Buddhism is the religion of about 110 million people, the great majority of the population, in an area including the states of Burma, Cambodia, Laos and Thailand and extending into parts of Bangladesh and Assam in the west and areas of Vietnam to the east. Buddhism was traditionally introduced to the area by emissaries of the Emperor ASHOKA (3rd century BCE), but archaeological investigation has not as yet detected unambiguous signs of Buddhism before the early centuries CE. By the latter part of the 1st millennium various forms of both HINDUISM and Buddhism were probably scattered over the whole area, with local concentrations patronized more exclusively by particular dynasties. Theravada was already important in the Pyu state of Shri Kshetra and the Mon territory of Dvaravati, perhaps in a form influenced by the Theravada centres in south India. In the early 11th century new influences from Ceylon (Sri Lanka) were felt in the Mon territory of Ramanna and soon led to their energetic adoption by the newly formed Burmese kingdom, in close contact with Ceylon (see SIN-HALESE BUDDHISM). During the first half of the 2nd millennium this form of Theravada established itself as the principal religion of the area, leaving only residual reminders of other forms of Buddhism and Hinduism. It was similarly adopted by the incoming Thais and the previously Mahayanist and Hindu Khmers of Cambodia.

Although institutionally affected by the ending of the Burmese monarchy, the Burmese SANGHA has remained very conservative, specializing in ABHIDHAMMA studies. An active and partly lay movement for the revival of insight (VIPASSANA) meditation has emerged [48]. In Thailand, in the absence of colonial rule, the close connection with the state has continued. Interest has focused especially on very strict forms of monastic practice, with a strong reform movement based upon VINAYA traditions. Buddhist modernism in Sri Lanka and even JAPAN has had some influence and calm (SAMATHA) meditation remains important. [86; 92; 93; 93a]

South-East Asia, Hinduism in
[XVII] Hindu religion, in its various forms, was an important component of the cultures of south-east Asia until at least the 13th century, and still maintains a recognizable presence in certain places; elsewhere, although not recognizable, it has affected cultural development. The process of Hinduization can be traced to at least the 1st century CE, with the introduction of the Hindu style of kingship, which necessitated Brahmanical consecration and support. Moreover, the spread eastwards from India of the cults of VISHNU and SHIVA and the associated art-forms and styles of architecture (see ART (HINDU)) was a continuation of the process of geographical spreading which had been going on within India from at least the beginning of the 1st millennium BCE. In this way what are now called Burma, Thailand, Laos, Kampuchea, Sumatra and Java were all areas in which Hindu religion was prominent. Cambodia, formerly the Khmer kingdom, was an important centre of Hindu culture until the

13th century, when BUDDHISM became dominant. Thailand still maintains a small community of BRAHMANS in the capital, Bangkok, for the necessary ceremonial and cultic duties associated with Thai kingship. In Indonesia Hindu religion survives most notably in the island of Bali. [81]

South-East Asia, Islam in [XIX] ISLAM is numerically strong in the peninsula and archipelago parts of this region: in Indonesia, Muslims comprise an estimated 90% of the population (1990 estimate 164 million) and in Malaysia 65% (1993 estimate, 12.3 million), with sizeable minorities in Burma, Thailand and the Philippines (10% or slightly more of the population in each country). The faith was carried to the region by Muslim merchants and traders *en route* for China (*see* CHINA, ISLAM IN), and by the 15th century there were Muslim principalities in Malacca, Java, Sumatra, Kalimantan (Borneo), Sulawesi (Celebes), the Moluccas and the Philippines. In certain areas, the work of SUFI ORDERS has been significant, with Java in particular evolving its own variety of mysticism. Official Islam in Indonesia has been strongly orthodox in tone, with, for example, great stress on the pilgrimage (HAJJ). Against tendencies towards SYNCRETISM with the old pagan or Hindu–Buddhist strains, whose modern representatives are the esoteric *kebatinan* groups, it was above all opposed to the religious and social pressures of Dutch colonial rule and Christianity. Hence Islam was the uniting force behind indigenous organizations with political and economic aims, like the Sarakat Islam (1911), the more traditionalist and academic Nahdat-ul-Islam (1926), etc., which became spearheads of nationalist feeling against the Dutch, and the post-war fundamentalist Dar-ul-Islam movement. In the post-1949 independence period, Islam has remained a major element of the national identity and ideology. Yet in many ways Indonesian Islam retains an appreciable amount of the pre-Muslim social heritage, seen in the persistence side by side with the orthodox SHARI'A system of *adat* or customary law, with very different marriage and inheritance practices, some even in flat contradiction to the Shari'a. [General surveys in: 20 'Islam (in Indonesia'; 38 'Indochina', 'Indonesia'; 65 vol. 2: 121–207]

Southcottians [XIII.B] Christian SECT founded by Joanna Southcott (1750–1814) who claimed to have revelations from God as the 'woman clothed with the sun' and expected to give birth to a new MESSIAH (the 'Shiloh') in 1814. (This refers to *Revelation*, 12: 1 and *Genesis*, 49: 10 in the King James (1611) version of the BIBLE). Her followers split under several leaders after her death and the sect is now extinct. However, the Panacea Society still advertises that a box of her prophecies should be opened by the ANGLICAN bishops to benefit the nation. [12; 94]

Spirit [XXXIV] (1) The most general term (a spirit, spirits) for any superhuman (usually invisible) being. Most cultures, past and present, have accepted the existence of spirits, of a more or less personal kind, able to affect human life in some way. The individual human may be held to possess one or more spirits, separable from the physical body. As surviving bodily death, spirits may be the objects of a cult (*see* ANCESTOR-WORSHIP). Events in the physical environment or in human consciousness may be attributed to spirits (*see* ANIMISM; SHAMAN). Superior, named and well-characterized spirits are GODS.

(2) The singular concept defies definition. Denoting the form of being which has no distinctively material properties, 'spirit' (derived like its equivalents in many langua-

ges from words for breath or wind, as invisible, yet powerful and life-giving), connotes life, consciousness, self-activity. RELIGION is often regarded as having to do with 'the things of the spirit', what is spiritual [127: 193–6]. To elucidate such language is a major task for RELIGIONS-WISSENSCHAFT and the PHILOSOPHY OF RELIGION.

Spirit-Possession [II] An important element in most African religious systems. Innumerable cults have at their ritual centre the medium through whom the deity or ancestral spirit speaks. In the more established cults possession tends to be formalized, even assumed, predictable and confirmatory of the given order. In new and socially marginal cults possession may be more violent, revelatory and innovating. The one-to-one relationship between a powerful spirit and its principal medium may create an almost symbiotic unity to give the medium a truly prophetic character, sense of mission and public role. In many societies DIVINATION depends largely on spirit-possession: in possession the NGANGA detects witchcraft or the causality behind other misfortunes. In particular, through possession he can cope with the possessed. For spirit-possession is at once the privilege of the religious specialist and the affliction of countless common people. If someone is possessed unexpectedly by a spirit (possibly, but not necessarily, malevolent) the medium can interrogate that spirit, discover the cause, and resolve it: a well-known spirit may have felt neglected and require a sacrifice; an ancestor may have intervened to stir the conscience over parental neglect; or some new spirit may be simply announcing its existence in this way. One possessed may discover in consequence a vocation to mediumship. ZULU ancestral spirits, for example, first 'brood' over a person called to be an *inyanga* (Zulu form of *Nganga*). Possession is

distinct from mediumship, being initially a disorder rather than a public role, but it easily leads to the latter.

Thus spirit mediumship may be mainly ritualistic, revelatory or therapeutic. It may be conservative or radical, institutionalized or marginal to society. It is a means of expression, proof of the proximity of the spiritual world, but capable of many messages. [2; 24: 136–96]

Spiritual Baptists (Shouters) [III] Mainly found in Trinidad. There is much migration in the Caribbean, and it is thought that the church came from St Vincent, maybe at the beginning of the 20th century. It was only in 1951 that the Spiritual Baptists were allowed to worship openly; until then they were oppressed by an Ordinance of the British colonial authorities which claimed that they disturbed the peace when they 'shouted'. This Ordinance of 1917 'rendered illegal indulgence in the practice of the Bodies known as the Shouters'. This 'shouting' occurred when worshippers were possessed by the Holy Spirit. The Shouters saw themselves as a persecuted people. Others thought them to be a fundamentalist cult, drawn from lower-class people, with little structure or theology, although it is clear that by the 1980s, while the status of the church remained low, its incorporation as the International Spiritual Baptist Ministerial Council of Trinidad and Tobago, together with its affiliation with the Christian Council of Trinidad and Tobago and the Caribbean Conference of Churches, indicated that it was accepted by the wider community as a valid church.

The Spiritual Baptist church has an altar dominated by flowers, crucifixes, texts and 'holy' pictures influenced by ROMAN CATHOLICISM, which is the dominant Trinidadian church. The main part of the Spiritual Baptist church will be left open for dancing, in the typical wheeling/circular pattern. At the centre of this area there may be a decorated post.

The HOLY SPIRIT will 'descend' into the church at this point to possess the members. The leader of the group will have been selected by the Holy Spirit. He will be charismatic, and the group will acknowledge his power of leadership and his inspirational influence. Members wear long white gowns with headties and sashes for full services; and the colours of these may indicate their status in the church, for there are many officers, some of whom have practical tasks such as administration of the building, others of whom bear titles such as Prophet, Healer, Diviner and Interpreter. Baptism is the central ritual of the church and members are prepared most rigorously for this. It takes place in the nearest river or on the seashore, and places of veneration, or where a particular ceremony has been held, are marked by ritual flags. Services include hymn-singing and clapping, but no drumming, and well-known prayers, like the Lord's Prayer. There are also long original prayers, BIBLE reading, and one or more sermons. Street meetings are held to gain converts. Individual prophets, carrying the bell, book (Bible) and light, may preach on the streets. Members set up temporary shrines on town streets. They do not associate with Shango people (*see* SANGO), because none of their spirits emanates from Africa, and they consider themselves a conventional Christian church. It is true that they are fission-prone, but what has emerged is a church which expresses the needs and national feelings of many people. [62; 86; 89]

Spiritual Exercises [XIII.D] A system of meditations designed by St Ignatius Loyola, divided into four 'weeks' – not exact lengths of time, but major divisions each requiring several days to complete. The discursive meditations and contemplative visualizations (imaginative mental representations of sacred events and mysteries of the faith)

draw the exercitant, the person making the Exercises, to see all things as either means to the service of God or obstacles, and to discern the will of God and choose a way of living that flows from his will. [20]

Spiritualism [XXIV] A modern (mainly Christian) faith centring on communication with spirits of the dead, who it is believed retain their personalities and are accessible through a 'medium' (a person gifted and trained in such communication). There is no fixed form for the service or 'seance', which may be held in a private home or at a Spiritualist church. There are usually prayers and hymns before (normally in darkness or dim light) the medium attempts to contact a 'guide' (spirit helper who assists other spirits in communicating). Greetings and personal messages from dead relatives and friends are relayed to the congregation, and there may be 'physical phenomena': objects manipulated without visible agency (*see* PSYCHIC POWERS) or brought mysteriously from afar ('apports'), or the 'materialization' of a spirit in a tangible body formed of 'ectoplasm' (a diaphanous substance said to be exuded from the medium's body). Some mediums also practise healing by spirit aid.

Spiritualism originated in Hydeville, New York State, in 1848, when the Fox sisters accidentally discovered their mediumistic powers. It spread rapidly, attracting widespread interest as promising tangible evidence of an afterlife. But its claims have remained controversial and it survives today as a minor religious movement in most Western countries. It has similarities to traditions of SPIRIT-POSSESSION in many non-Christian religions. [23]

Spirituality [XIV] Difficult to define as the word is used in many different contexts. Its roots are in the Christian tradition where it has a long history in theology and religious practice [60; 81]. The spiritual as an inward quest has often been contrasted with the material, physical and external. Some understand the 'spiritual' as more diffuse and less institutionalized than the 'religious'. Others, on the contrary, take spirituality as the very centre and heart of religion, encountered particularly through religious and mystical experience (see MYSTICISM). The subject matter of spirituality is a perennial human concern, but the critical, comparative reflection on spirituality in a global context is a recent phenomenon. Many religions have no precise word for 'spirituality'; yet today the notion of spirituality has become universalized and is now used inside and outside religions, and also in an inter-faith and secular context. The modern interest in spirituality goes together with an emphasis on the individual subject, self-development and a more differentiated understanding of human psychology. Spirituality has now become a universal code word to indicate the search for direction and meaning. In modern secular society spirituality is being 'rediscovered' as a lost or at least hidden dimension in a largely materialistic world.

Spirituality has been described as an attempt to grow in sensitivity – to self, to others, to non-human creation and to God; or as an exploration into what is involved in becoming human, a quest for full humanity. The way in which spirituality finds concrete expression varies greatly from culture to culture, and from one religion to another. Each religious tradition knows many different schools of spirituality, and past and present spirituality are not necessarily the same, not even in the same religion. From a historical point of view different spiritualities are different cultural forms or the expression of different religious ideals. From the point of view of a person of faith, spirituality forms part of the breakthrough of the spirit into history, a

piercing through and behind history (see SPIRIT). Spirituality, not as an idea or concept, but as praxis found throughout human history, is resonant with the longings of the human heart for the permanent, eternal, everlasting – for wholeness, peace, joy and bliss – which have haunted human beings through the ages, and for which many persons on our planet are searching today.

Three distinct but interdependent levels are to be distinguished in the contemporary understanding of spirituality: (1) spirituality as lived experience or praxis; in a religious context this can be seen as a faith's wisdom to live that faith; (2) spirituality as a teaching that grows out of this praxis and guides it in turn, i.e. the spiritual disciplines and counsels of perfection found in different religions; (3) the systematic, comparative and critical study of spiritual experiences and teachings which has developed in our own time in quite a new way [Cousins' introduction to 19; 45; 77: 15–37; 81]. Such critical study has produced the series Classics of Western Spirituality [70] and another on World Spirituality: An Encyclopedic History of the Religious Quest [19].

In the past, much of spirituality as lived and taught was developed by a social, cultural and intellectual elite which alone had the necessary leisure for cultivating mind and spirit. In the different schools of spirituality two main models can be found: (1) an ascetic/monastic model of renunciation spirituality; (2) a model of 'householder spirituality', where asceticism is less dominant. In the Christian tradition the predominant locus of sanctification, of living a spiritual ideal, was the cloister, an alternative parallel community separated from mainstream society. With the rise of PROTESTANTISM the locus of sanctification shifted from the cloister to ordinary life in society with its day-to-day relationships and responsibilities. A new 'spirituality-of-being-in-the-world' developed, not without precedents in earlier Christian teaching. Both models are also found in most Indian religions, but SIKHISM, and also ISLAM and JUDAISM, promote the householder rather than the ascetic/monastic model of spirituality. However, across the religious traditions one is struck by the discovery that what appears at first as gender-neutral spiritual advice to apparently asexual spiritual seekers in practice often turns out to be the advice of male spiritual mentors to their male disciples, so that spiritual writings throughout world religious literature contain many sexist, anti-women passages which now come in for a good deal of criticism (*see* GENDER).

Contemporary understandings of spirituality are sometimes too imitative, static and anchored in the past, thereby failing to capture the dynamic, transformative quality of spirituality as lived experience, as the great adventure of the human mind and soul in seeking its own transcendence by crossing boundaries of emotion, intellect and imagination. Creative new developments in the contemporary understanding of spirituality are linked to a new enquiry into human spiritual energy resources and the importance of our global spiritual heritage for the future of humankind [19; 51; 67]; the dialogue across different spiritual traditions and the importance of inter-faith dialogue for newly emerging spiritualities [2; 66]; and the many new developments in women's spirituality [52]. Spirituality now also features as a topic in contemporary education; for example the British Education Reform Act (1988) requires schools to promote the spiritual development of pupils across the whole curriculum (*see* RELIGIOUS EDUCATION (IN SCHOOLS)) and some institutions of higher education in the UK and USA already run certificate courses or even degree programmes on spirituality (*see* RELIGIOUS STUDIES IN HIGHER EDUCATION).

Sri Chinmoy [XXVIII] Sri Chinmoy Kumar Ghose (1931–) entered the Sri Aurobindo Ashram at the age of 12. In 1964, he left India for the USA 'to offer his spiritual wealth at the feet of truly aspiring seekers' [42: 938]. In initiation (*siksha*) the guru gives the disciple a portion of his life-soul. Disciples promise to serve the master and are expected to meditate for 15 minutes twice a day and to refrain from drugs, alcohol, tobacco and meat. Physical fitness is promoted through a number of organized athletic activities, and 'Peace Concerts' have been held around the world. [5: 209–10; 16]

Starets [XIII.D] The EASTERN ORTHODOX starets (or *gerontas*) is usually a monk or a priest popularly recognized as being a 'spiritual elder', counselling the faithful in all matters. Although this tradition of eldership (*starchestvo*) ultimately goes back to the Desert Fathers of late antiquity it truly became a focus for the wider Christian community after the reforms of Tsar Peter the Great. With the gradual subjection of the Russian and Balkan churches to the state, monks, nuns and even lay elders came to inherit much of the spiritual authority hitherto associated with the episcopate.

Based in Romania, Paissy Velichkovsky (d. 1794) revitalized the role of the monastery in society, but it was Seraphim of Sarov (d. 1833) who inaugurated the era of the starets in Russia. After years as a hermit he began to receive a steady stream of visitors from every walk of life, all seeking advice. His mantle was inherited by the Optina elders (including Leonid, d. 1841; Makary, d. 1860; Amvrosy, d. 1891; Joseph, d. 1911; and Varsonofy, d. 1913)) and by John of Kronstadt (d. 1908). Porphyrios of Oropos (d. 1991) is but the latest of a long line of Greek elders. Sophrony Zakharov (d. 1993) brought the Athonite traditions of his elder Silouan (d. 1938) to Tolleshunt Knights in England. Maria Gysi of Whitby (d. 1977) and Seraphim Rose of Platina (d. 1982) have also contributed to the revival of this tradition in the West, while monks like Matthew the Poor of Egypt have kept it alive in the deserts of the ancient elders. [13; 19; 21; 26; 31; 39; 40; 52; 53; 81; 82; 88; 89; 91; 103] (*See also* HESYCHASM; JESUS PRAYER.)

Star-Worship (Astrolatry, Sabaism) [x] The sun, moon, planets and stars have been worshipped as gods in a number of cultures. Star-worship evolves from the awe felt at the beauty, regularity, mystery and power of the heavenly bodies (especially of the sun) and in response to their effect, real or imagined, on terrestrial and human life. The sun and moon, in particular, are perceived as the givers of time (time being measures by their motions) and the sun as the regulator of the cycle of the seasons. Star-worship usually accompanies, indeed triggers, the early development of astronomy and calendrics and sanctions the parallel growth of ASTROLOGY. This was certainly so in Mesopotamia in the last two millennia BCE [10: I–III] and in Central America among the Maya [9: V]. Star-worship probably underlies the prehistoric megalithic astronomical sites of northern Europe [9: II–III; e.g. Stonehenge] and similar sites in North America [9: IV; e.g. the Big Horn medicine wheel]. From Mesopotamia star-worship passed into Graeco-Roman culture [6]. Sun-worship became, in the 3rd century CE, something of an official religion in the Roman empire, contemporary ideology seeing in the divine emperor (EMPEROR-WORSHIP) a terrestrial counterpart of the sun as sovereign of the universe. At the same time Mithras was worshipped as a solar god (*see* MITHRAISM) and his mysteries incorporated much arcane astral lore.

State, Christianity and the [XIII.B] Christianity has had a great variety of relationships with the state. Under the Roman empire from the time of Constantine (d. 337) the church became increasingly privileged and eventually dominant. It then persecuted paganism and HERESY [79]. The 'Gelasian theory' (Pope Gelasius, d. 496) expressed the supremacy of the church over the state. Views of this kind during the middle ages inflamed many conflicts between Popes and princes [19: 97–115]. Ideally, Western 'Christendom' (the Christian world) was felt to be ruled by God through the Holy Roman Emperor and other princes for secular affairs, and by the PAPACY and CHURCH in spiritual matters. Some Popes and emperors, however, aspired to ultimate control of both sides of human existence. 'Theocracy' has been used to describe church claims of this kind, and the term 'Cesaropapism' to describe the control of the church and theology exercised by Eastern emperors. The REFORMATION typically initiated 'established churches' in PROTESTANTISM This meant a single state-supported church for all citizens. 'Erastianism' is the term applied to complete state control of church jurisdiction in such churches. In Catholic France (*see* ROMAN CATHOLICISM), 'Gallicanism' largely subjected the church to the monarchy [19: 270; 149; 157: 548]. In Geneva, CALVINISM approximated to a theocracy. The claims of Christianity (or of any religion) to exclusive truth have often led to persecution of religious deviation (heresy and schism). This was reinforced when states with established churches regarded heresy as treasonable. Political and intellectual changes during and after the 17th century encouraged the development of toleration, although initially deviants did not enjoy full civil rights. Attitudes in ROMAN CATHOLICISM hardened under Pius IX (1846–78) and later against the modernists; but toleration was affirmed by the Second Vatican COUNCIL. Growth in religious toleration seemed to be promised as communist rule collapsed in Eastern Europe in the 1990s, but political divisions and civil strife resulting from this have in some cases been sharpened by religious divisions (notable in the former Yugoslavia between Orthodox, Roman Catholics and Muslims). Since the early 19th century there has been a general tendency to 'disestablishment', or at least to reduce the privileges of established churches. Many states have become religiously neutral. But even without establishment, Christianity may act as a source of national identity, as could be seen in e.g. Poland under communist rule. [61]

Sthanakvasi [xx] SHVETAMBARA JAIN sect which rejects image worship and advocates the permanent wearing of the mouth-shield (MUHPATTI) by its ascetics. Taking some óf their inspiration from an iconoclastic 15th-century teacher called Lonka, the Sthankavasis regard their founding teachers as being the 17th-century monks, Lavaji and Dharmasimha. The name Sthanakvasi means 'living in lodging halls', a label used by the sect to distinguish itself from its image-worshipping opponents who lived in buildings attached to temples. The Sthanakvasis, of whom there are several hundred monks and nuns, remain a significant component of Jainism in India. [4: 211–18]

Stoicism (Roman) [xxxi] Stoicism reached Rome in the 2nd century BCE and the leaders of the school (Panaetius, c.185–109 BCE, and Posidonius, c.135–c.50 BCE), exercised much influence over the ideas of Roman nobles on morality and the ruling of the empire. It offered them a means of combining their polytheistic tradition with the conception of a universe guided and structured by reason (*logos*), which

was seen as divine and as including the other gods, as aspects of the *logos*. [10: III; 13: 35–9, 140–55, 207–15]

Store-front Churches [III] Found wherever small African-American diaspora sects are establishing themselves, or where there has been fission in a church and a group of members has split off. This is typical of some black churches, and the store-front churches are typically black and of lower-class membership (*see* BLACK CHURCHES IN AMERICA). They are often found in the northern ghettos. Both in the Caribbean and in Britain it is common to find modest churches based in the homes of their leaders, in a room dominated by a sympathizer, or in business accommodation out of hours. This is quite the reverse of the house church movement, for storefront churches would like nothing better than to be able to afford to establish themselves in permanent buildings. This is why the storefront space is sometimes a temporary strategy. Some of the churches offer worship, healing and private consultations. Most of them are charismatic and evangelical, and tend to be 'spiritual'. [4; 51; 81]

Structuralism [xxxiv] In the study of literature, a search for underlying (hidden) configurations which will offer an explanation of the more obvious (visible) patterns and may reveal how e.g. what is written or told simplifies and organizes the diversity of experience of those who use (write, tell, read, hear, even live by) what is so analysed. Such methods have been applied to the study of sacred scripture, including the BIBLE; and especially to mythical and totemic thought, notably by anthropologists. [12: 24; 105; 158: 48–9]

Study of Religion(s) [xxxiv] The study of religion(s) has always posed problems of methodology since the modern discipline developed rather haphazardly out of more traditional ways of studying religion and religions. Discussion about the methodology of the study of religion(s) has become virtually a sub-discipline of the whole. It is necessary to refer to the study of religion and of religions in the singular and the plural because some scholars attempt to describe religion in terms of broad categories common to more than one religion whereas others concentrate on the content of a single religion on the grounds that each religion and its components are unique to itself. Whatever the emphasis, the study of religion or of religions is an activity that has been carried on for many centuries. The practice occurred among the ancient Greeks. It has also occurred among the practitioners of religions, Western and Eastern, especially those who played a leadership role in those religions, over many centuries. For the most part, they studied the religions they themselves practised, though exceptionally some figures might study the religion of others. Such studies were sometimes called theology, sometimes philosophy. In many senses, therefore, the study of religions is an ancient practice.

In a very important sense, however, the study of religion(s), as a distinctive intellectual, academic attitude towards the study of the world's religions, is a very modern practice which did not exist until after the European, specifically German, ENLIGHTENMENT. [128: 3] Religion during the Enlightenment, when it was not being condemned as the domain of priests and the realm of superstition, came to be seen as a part of human history and cultural development and an object of study, rather than as the subject of the way life should be ordered. Even before the period of the Enlightenment global exploration was bringing awareness of the diverse cultures of the world to the attention of an ever wider audience. This increased tre-

mendously during the 19th century, which is when the academic study of religion(s) really began to take off. It did not come to anything like full flower, however, until the middle of the 20th century (*see* RELIGIOUS STUDIES IN HIGHER EDUCATION).

The description 'the study of religion(s)' (a more accurate description than 'religious studies' since the activity itself is not religious) is designed to divide this activity off from those studies which are undertaken to enable religious practitioners to reflect on the truths of their respective religions. If theology is concerned with the object of religion, such as God, gods or eternal life, philosophy with the meaning of the object of religion, then the study of religion(s) is concerned with the origin, function and meaning of religion as such. [144: 21] The study of religion(s) is not the study of, for instance, what God is, but of what people believe God to be. Theology, it is said, is confessional, the study of religion(s) non-confessional, even humanistic. The study of religions or of religious phenomena is intended to be neutral, empirical, objective and judgementally value-free. There is considerable debate and intellectual conflict over whether those who practise the study of religion(s) should be, on the one hand, or can be, on the other, totally neutral in the way in which they treat their academic subject. The debate is, at one level, a futile exercise, since no one can claim to be ultimately without bias, whether a religious practitioner in affiliation or orientation or of no religious persuasion. There are those who have argued that religion cannot be studied in a neutral, non-evaluative way, since religion, though a phenomenon which is a part of the total human experience, is an irreducible phenomenon and inexplicable in other than *sui generis* religious terms. Any other kind of approach is bound to be reductionist [170: 9; 54: xi]. Some scholars would not necessarily agree with this judgement, though they would nevertheless say that any study of religion(s), especially the study of religious phenomena outside the scholar's own experience, should be done with 'empathy' [149: 211]. Others [144: 1] argue that since religion is a form of human activity, the way for religion(s) to be studied is by empirical, social scientific methods, on the grounds that the object of the study of religion(s) is religion itself, not the truth of religious claims. Closely related to this debate is the question of whether religion(s) can only be studied successfully, however success might be judged, by religious practitioners. If religion can only be understood in *sui generis* religious terms then it follows that religion(s) cannot be studied successfully by one who is not a religious practitioner. The counter-argument is again based on the fact that religion is a specifically human activity and can, therefore, be studied as such by those who have no religious affiliation or orientation. There is also the issue of whether scholars can or ought to remain neutral in the face of facts about a particular phenomenon which the scholar or a particular culture would consider reprehensible [134]. This major issue is exemplified by the awareness of the different approaches of 'insiders' and 'outsiders' to the study of religion(s). The term 'outsider' refers to scholars working on religions and religious phenomena that are not part of their personal experience. This applies to the scholar whether or not he or she is a practitioner in any religion or no religion. Some would argue that a scholar who is a religious practitioner is better able to empathize with an alien tradition than someone who has no religious affiliation at all. However, the issue is not as simple as it may seem [144: 1]. The question needs to be put: why does the academic study of religions demand an empathy which other areas of academic study apparently do not?

Not only does the study of geography apparently not need empathy, the question never seems to have been raised.

One of the problems in discussing the study of religions, especially as it applies to academic study, is that it involves a number of different disciplines or methods. The overall study has been described as polymethodic [152: 22]. There is some question as to whether the study of religion(s) can be referred to as a discipline at all [91]. This issue is reflected in the fact that what is described here as the study of religion(s) has borne a number of different names: science of religion, comparative religion(s), HISTORY OF RELIGION(s), PHENOMENOLOGY OF RELIGION(s) in the English language, and RELIGIONSWISSENSCHAFT or *Religionsgeschichte* in German. The study also employs a number of different methods, including linguistics, philology, history, sociology, anthropology and psychology. Thus we have specialists in SOCIOLOGY OF RELIGION and PSYCHOLOGY OF RELIGION [4]. Among other areas of study it may include the study of SCRIPTURES, communities, RITUAL, ethics, FOUNDERS OF RELIGIONS and functionaries of religions. The study of religion(s) also includes the study of arts and artefacts and culture in general. In the latter case the study is often approached from the standpoint that religions and religious phenomena are always contextualized in particular cultures and cultural expressions. It could be argued, especially in relation to cultures in which what is generally regarded in the West as 'religious' is indistinguishable from the rest of human expressions, that the study of religion(s) is properly the study of aspects of culture. This approach marks off the study of religion(s) from the older and more traditional ways of studying religions. [59a, vol. 11: 243–6, vol. 12: 231–41, vol. 14: 64–92; 124a; 128; 159a; 175a]

Stupa [XI] (Sanskrit; Pali: *thupa*) A monumental burial mound enshrining the relics of a BUDDHA or Buddhist saint. The Buddhist tradition of *stupa* building begins with the story of GOTAMA's relics being divided and enshrined in eight *stupas*; subsequently *stupas* were constructed all over India, especially under the patronage of the emperor ASHOKA; as BUDDHISM spread beyond India so did the tradition of *stupa* building. The styles and sizes of *stupas* vary enormously, from the hemispherical *stupas* of Sanchi (*c*.1st century BCE/CE) in central India to the tiered pagoda of Horyuji (7th century) in Japan, from a few feet to hundreds of feet in height and diameter. The *stupa* commonly consists of three parts: the base in the form of a raised platform providing a path for ritual circumambulation (*pradakshina*), the main dome, and the summit formed by a cuboid structure topped with a spire; the whole structure is orientated to the cardinal directions by four gates. The architecture of the *stupa* has a developed symbolism: essentially the *stupa* is at once a representation of the cosmos (*see* CAKKAVALA; cf. MANDALA) and of the stages of the Buddhist path. The *stupa* was and continues to be a great focus of devotional Buddhist practice. Other terms for *stupa* include *cetiya*/*caitya*, *dagaba* (Sinhalese) and *chorten* (Tibetan). [31; 19]

Subud [XXVIII] Founded in Indonesia by Muhammad Subuh Sumohadiwidjojo (1901–87) or 'Bapak' in the 1930s, Subud came to the West in the 1950s. 'SUsila BUdhi Dharma means to follow the Will of God, with the help of the Divine Power that works both within us and without.' Of central importance is a spiritual exercise known as the 'latihan', which is practised in single-sex groups for about 30 minutes twice a week; individuals may feel an inner vibration directing them to move, laugh, cry, sing, dance or pray. An individual's initial experience of the latihan is known as 'the opening'. [42: 886–7; 67]

Sufi Institutions [XIX] Sufis or dervishes (*see* SUFISM) early congregated in houses or convents, variously called *ribats*, *khanaqahs* and *zawiyas*, as foci for living communally, for fulfilling the duty of JIHAD against unbelievers and as centres for educational activity and evangelism among un-Islamized or imperfectly Islamized peoples (*see for example* SANUSIS). These were often established as charitable foundations (WAQF) by the gifts of the pious [38 'Khānkāh']. Within Sufi circles, a special liturgical ritual (*dhikr*, literally 'remembrance (of God)') was often practised, which might include repeated chanting of the names of God (ALLAH), often with the aid of a rosary, controlled breathing exercises, dancing (especially among the Mevlevis – *see* SUFI ORDERS) to the accompaniment of music, etc. [77: X]. In certain frontier regions like Anatolia, the practices of some orders, e.g. the Bektashis, showed a distinct SYNCRETISM with Christian practices [18: IV–VI].

Sufi Orders [XIX] By the 12th century, SUFIS began to coalesce into groups (*tariqas*, literally 'ways') under the leadership of Sufis with outstanding spiritual gifts (*see* SHAIKH), and with full adherents (not however necessarily celibate) and the equivalents of Christian 'lay brethren' or 'tertiaries'. These orders became very numerous as subdivisions developed, and spread all over the Islamic world. On the peripheries, such as west Africa, the Sudan, the Indo-Pakistan subcontinent and central Asia, they have played a leading role in Muslim evangelism and remain especially influential there today. In their heyday in the pre-modern period, the orders supplied in the Sunni world (*see* SUNNA) a focus for the emotional aspect of believers' religious needs, analogous to devotion to the IMAMS in the Shi'i one (*see* SHI'-ISM), and acted as a cohesive social force in the community, especially, though not exclusively, among the lower classes. Prominent orders include the QADIRIS, of Iraqi origin but later active in India; the Naqshbandis, especially active among Turkish peoples; the Shadhilis, characteristically north African; the Ahmadis, centred on Lower Egypt; the recently established TIJANIS, active in north and west Africa [90]; the SANUSIS; etc. In Ottoman Turkey, the Bektashis were connected with the elite military force of the Janissaries (*see* SLAVERY) and have survived in recent times, in Albania especially [18]; while the Mevlevis (also called the 'whirling dervishes') were particularly connected with the ruling classes and were famed for their use of music and gyratory dancing (recently revived, but essentially as a tourist attraction). In the past, extravagances such as firewalking, snake-handling, riding over adherents on horseback, etc., were practised. (For Sufi doctrines *see* SUFISM; for their ceremonies and meeting-places *see* SUFI INSTITUTIONS.) [General surveys: 37 'Tarīka'; 52: IX; 67 'Faqīr'; 125; 13]

Sufism, Sufis [XIX] The Sufis ('wearers of wool', i.e. the coarse garments of the ascetic), also dervishes ('poor men') and, in north Africa, marabouts, are the mystics of ISLAM. At the outset they were influenced by the ascetics of the Eastern Christian churches, but later they developed mainly within the framework of orthodox Islam, except for an extravagant, antinomian wing of the movement in eastern Persia that may have been influenced by religious currents from the Indian world. Within these latter Sufis, pantheistic and monist ideas, revolving round 'the unity of all existence', are discernible, as in the ideas of the great Spanish Muslim mystic Ibn al-'Arabi (1165–1240) [71: 640–66].

The majority of Sufis remained, however, within the bounds of orthodoxy, regarding the 'Sufi path', progress through the 'stations' of worldly renunciation, etc., and the 'states' of spiritual gifts conferred by God such as nearness to him, etc., as the means to real communion-with and knowledge (*ma'rifa*) of God. In this way such ideals as self-annihilation (*fana'*), self-perpetuation with God (*baqa'*) and even infusion or indwelling of the Divine Being (*hulul*) could be achieved. These could only uneasily be reconciled with orthodox theology and the external observances of the SHARI'A. Sufis were often at odds with the ULEMA, and the celebrated al-Hallaj paid with his life in 922 for his views [78: V]. The achievement of a *modus vivendi* between these two great aspects of Islam was realized by the theologian and Sufi al-Ghazali (1058–1111). Sufism later evolved into distinct orders (SUFI ORDERS), and these had their own places of congregation and rituals (SUFI INSTITUTIONS). Sufism has been a great stimulus to, and a persistent strain in, Islamic literature, seen for instance in the work of the great Persian poets Rumi (1207–73) and Hafiz (*c*.1325–*c*.1390). [General surveys: 7; 8: XIII; 82: IV; 84; 107: VIII–XI; 142: VI]

Sumerians [VIII] Sumer, the earliest Mesopotamian civilization (*see* ANCIENT NEAR EASTERN RELIGIONS), consisted of city-states, separated from each other by the desert; they had diverse but well-organized societies. The period of Sumerian supremacy, the Jemdet Nasr period, was *c*.3000–2550 BCE [20; 23: 18–20; 26]. Not a true theocracy, in which the whole state is owned and administered by the TEMPLES, Sumerian organization was functionally secular: individuals owned land and property and the cities traded their agricultural produce and technological skills. Nevertheless, the temple was the focus of each city, embodying its identity, and the collective skills of the community were directed towards the god and his temple. Although administration of the city was secular, the men executing these duties were also often temple administrators. The temple, in receipt of an income from its estates and from gifts supplied by the community, fulfilled an obligation to the people by funding secular and trading ventures through loans from its funds.

Each city had its chief deity, accompanied by spouse, children and lesser deities. Each pantheon was at first independent, although myths and ritual visits provided a link between the gods. As cities were absorbed into larger units, some gods were eliminated and others, belonging to subject cities, had temples at the capital. A loose federation of city-states emerged, accepting a regular change in leadership and the pre-eminence of one city. Local cults continued, but seven major deities [16: 130] and their consorts were finally recognized throughout Mesopotamia, and their characteristics lost something of their purely local significance. Nippur, Ur, Uruk and Sippar became important religious centres.

All deities had priests, who served their temples, attending to their daily needs. The prime obligation of the king (see KINGSHIP (ANCIENT NEAR EASTERN)) was to serve his god, and royal military victories were regarded as a reflection of the god's success in heaven. Priestesses also played an important role in some cults.

Literature included the first COSMOLOGY and cosmogony, wisdom texts, and the 'Flood' story [24: 72–9], namely the EPIC OF GILGAMESH.

Only the gods were immortal; humans, created to serve the gods, descended to a dark and dreary netherworld after death (see AFTERLIFE). Nevertheless, some funerary preparations were elaborate, such as the fine equipment provided in the Royal Tombs at Ur (c.2500 BCE). [26: 74–81]

Sun and Moon [xxiii] In numerous cultures of South America, the primordial figures of Sun and Moon (or their transformations) have a prominent place in creation stories. They are variously related as siblings, husband and wife or formal friends. They are frequently responsible for, or associated with, themes of life and death, periodic order and dynamic principles in culture and the cosmos. Among the Campa, Moon created manioc and engendered the Sun, the Great Transformer and source of life; ironically, the Sun is the author of death. Among the Gê, relationships of ritual companionship or formal friendship are modelled on the dialectical collaboration of Sun and Moon who created the world. [33]

Sun Dance [v] Probably the best known and most dramatic of North American Indian ceremonies is the Sun Dance of the Plains [7: viii]. Known among the Oglala SIOUX as *Wi wanyang wacipi* ('sun-gazing dance'), its characteristic feature was the participant's fixed gaze upon the sun while dancing, which thus produced a trance. Although early cosmological elements are present (see COSMOLOGY), the dance as it is now most commonly known is probably of relatively recent origin. It was usually performed annually (over a period of from two to five days) when the tribal groups assembled. A 'pledger', one who had as a result of a dream or vision vowed to perform the dance, usually acted as sponsor, although there might be lesser sponsors. Central features of the dance included (with regional variations) building the sun-dance lodge (often cosmological in design), preliminary dances, use of the sacred pipe (calumet), and the actual sun dance itself. Participants either danced while gazing at the sun and blowing whistles, or, in the case of those resolved to do so beforehand, attached themselves to the sacred pole by thongs and skewers through the chest muscles and then pulled outwards until the muscles were torn free. Performance of the dance not only satisfied the pledger's vow, thereby demonstrating personal resolve and leading to the acquisition of individual power, it also helped to achieve cosmic regeneration and tribal well-being. [4]

Sunna [xix] 'Custom, code of behaviour'; in Islam, means in particular the Prophet Muhammad's example, by explicit precept or implicit approval, as embodied in the Hadith or tradition literature. The Sunna therefore complements and often confirms or explains the Qur'an, and is one of the basic sources (*usul*) of the divine law or Shari'a recognized by the majority of Muslims. Its followers are therefore called the 'people of the Sunna and the community', hence Sunnis or Sunnites, as opposed to the minority group of Shi'is or Shi'ites (*see* Shi'ism), who substitute for the democratic consensus of the community the authority of the Shi'i doctors and the infallible Imam. [37 s.v.; 48: 67–8; 54 vol. II: I]

Surat Sabd Yoga [xvii] (The yoga of spirit and word) A form of Yoga available to both householders and ascetics, developed in 1861 in north India by Swami Shiv Dayal Singh, the founder of Radhasoami Satsang. The initiate concentrates on an internal image of the Guru, undertakes a chant (*simran*) of the sacred names given at the time of initiation and listens for ethereal sounds. Through a process likened to music (*bhajan*), the soul during meditation departs the body through the highest centre (*chakra*, literally 'wheel') of spiritual energy in the body – the inner eye located behind the forehead. With the mystical form of the guru as its guide, the soul begins its ascent through increasingly rarefied regions of consciousness. According to Radhasoami cosmology, the world was created through something akin to the 'big bang'; but the only pure form of existence – a rarefied state of light and sound – that remains on earth is the soul or spirit (*surat*). The aim of Surat Sabd Yoga is to liberate the soul from earthly captivity, propel it through space and reunite it with the eternal sound current (*sabd*) reverberating throughout the universe. Some of these physiological concepts may be found in the Nath tradition, and the idea of the guru as intercessor may be found in Vaishnava (*see* Vishnu) Bhakti. Early forms of the yoga were advocated in 17th- and 18th-century esoteric teachings based on Kabir and other exponents of India's medieval Sant tradition. [67]

Sutta [xi] (Pali; Sanskrit: *sutra*) The term for a discourse of the Buddha. *Suttas* constitute the collection of Buddhist scriptures known as the *Sutta-pitaka* (*see* Tipitaka), which arranges *suttas* in four or five sections (Nikaya). A *sutta* always opens with the formula 'Thus I have heard. Once the Blessed One was staying at . . .' An introduction then sets the scene which forms the background to the subsequent instruction given by the Buddha. The form of this instruction may be a dialogue between the Buddha and interlocutor or simply a long disquisition by the Buddha. Not all *suttas* are presented as delivered by the Buddha; some are attributed to certain of his chief monks (Bhikkhu) and nuns (Bhikkhuni). The subject matter of the *suttas* is varied, embracing technical instruction in meditation (*see* Bhavana; Samatha; Vipassana), story and myth, social comment and philosophical analysis. Although most often addressed to the Sangha, *suttas* may also be addressed to ordinary householders, Brahmans, kings and even gods and demons.

(*See also* MAHAYANA SUTRAS; SUT-
TANTA.) [65: 30ff]

Suttanta [XI] The discourses
(SUTTA) of the BUDDHA contained
in the *sutta-pitaka* are referred to in
PALI as *suttantas* (Sanskrit: *sutranta*),
especially if fairly long. A *suttantika*
(Sanskrit: *sautrantika*) monk was
originally one who specialized in
memorizing the discourses, as
opposed to the disciplinary rules.
Suttanta teaching was later contrasted with ABHIDHAMMA teaching.
Suttanta was held to be the Buddha's teaching in specific situations
to meet particular individual needs;
further exposition or qualification
might be necessary for completeness. *Abhidhamma*, by contrast, provides a full and exact account, not
tailored to any particular situation.
Suttanta teaching is often concerned
with describing or mapping processes over a period of time as sequences, whereas *abhidhamma* uses the
same categories to analyse specific events as distinct moments
(*see* BODHI-PAKKHIYA-DHAMMA). Although the *abhidhamma* method
acquired great prestige and tended
at times to supersede *suttanta*, the
suttanta method has retained considerable practical importance in
THERAVADA Buddhism. In north
India it influenced the rise of the
SAUTRANTIKA school, reacting
against the VAIBHASHIKA *abhidharma*.

Sutton Hoo [VII] In 1939 a ship-
burial of the early 7th century CE was
excavated at Sutton Hoo near
Woodbridge in Suffolk. It held a
king's treasure, including some
superb ceremonial objects [8].
Whether the grave was a cenotaph or
originally held a coffin or cremated
remains is still under discussion.
This discovery provides important
evidence for religious symbolism at
the close of the pre-Christian period
in Anglo-Saxon England. It estab-
lishes elaborate SHIP-FUNERALS as
an East Anglian practice [8; 19: IV]

Sweat Lodge [V] An Amerindian
rite of purification, practised widely
in North America, but especially
among central and south-western
tribes, to revivify individuals spiritually and/or physically. It also often
served as preparation for contact
with the supernaturals [17: VIII].

Following construction of the
sweat lodge (usually fashioned from
willow saplings bound with thongs
and covered with blankets or skins,
and often modelled after a pattern
revealed in the CREATION MYTH),
the participants under the supervision of a leader, enter and arrange
themselves around a pile of heated
stones. To the accompaniment of
prayers and songs, the leader pours
water over the stones as well as
lighting and sharing the sacred pipe
(calumet). The presence within the
lodge of the gods or spirits prompts
individual and collective prayers [1:
III]. The rite, with minor variations,
is widely used among Amerindian
groups today.

Symbol [XXXIV] The term 'symbol'
is derived from a Greek root suggesting the joint impact of two separate
entities, as for instance in the
divided halves of a token or coin
which when brought together signify
the completion of a contract. By
derivation the Greek word *symbolon*
suggests the meaning of 'a sign or
token by which one infers a thing'.
The term 'symbol' thus attains the
meaning of something which stands
for something else. Words in a language operate like symbols. We
might take four letters of an alphabet
– a, e, k, l – which in that order, in
English, stand for nothing. If we
rearrange them thus: l-a-k-e, they
become a word, 'lake', and in English this word stands for a geographical phenomenon with all kinds of
mental and physical associations.
Within religions words operate in a
similar way, but go beyond the mere
signification of something else.
While in English it is possible for
images to be conjured by the word

'lake', perhaps even powerful emotions, romantic emotions for instance, the word is not conceived as 'having power' in the way that words have 'symbolic power' in religious contexts. In the religious context words do not simply signify something, they are often seen as signifying and operating the power of that which they signify. On a more elementary level it can be argued that within a religion words can only operate as symbols of that which they symbolize. In a religious context, the only way to use words in describing what must be described is the symbolic way. Religions and religious expressions can only be transmitted by the symbolic use of language. The words may be ordinary in their usual provenance but attain a symbolic status which is quite outwith ordinary discourse when applied to the supernatural which they purport to express. This symbolic significance extends, in a religious context, beyond words to movements, artefacts, material substances and geographical locations. Religions are symbolic systems or sets of symbolic systems. 'A religious symbol uses the material of ordinary experience in speaking of God, but in such a way that the ordinary meaning of the material used is both affirmed and denied. Every religious symbol negates itself in its literal meaning, but it affirms itself in its self-transcending meaning. It is not a sign pointing to something with which it has no inner relationship. It represents the power and meaning of what is symbolised through participation' [162 vol. 2: 9]. Tillich's statement can be applied to more than the notion of God. It can be applied to any and every religious form of expression that demands the transmission of meaning and power. Signs, when compared with symbols, are often arbitrarily chosen, as for instance in the use of road traffic signs on an international scale. Religious symbols tend to be generated in a non-selfconscious way, by group creation and transmission, and to be peculiar to a particular religious context, although the peculiarity may be carried by a religion world-wide with the expansion of the particular religion. Frequently, however, religious expressions even of a very strong character can be translated symbolically to another cultural environment only with great difficulty, and often the attempt meets with failure. Symbols or symbolic materials often signify different meanings in different cultural settings, but also within the same cultural setting symbols may manifest different levels or aspects of meaning. This property of symbols has been described as 'multi-vocality'. The term 'symbol' is used exclusively in the Christian religion for the credal statements, formularies and confessions which are the basis, according to some Christian traditions, of doctrinal orthodoxy (see CREEDS (CHRISTIAN)). This use of 'symbol' has given rise to the study named 'Symbolics'. [148]

Synagogue [XXII] The main public institution of JUDAISM, thought to have begun during the Babylonian captivity in the 6th century BCE (see BIBLICAL HISTORY) [29: III; 72: VI]. After the Jerusalem TEMPLE had been destroyed, in 587 BCE, early synagogues were necessary for the exiles (see EXILE) to carry on religious activities. When the Israelites returned and rebuilt the temple, about 70 years later, they still used synagogues, but the latter had a minor role until the 1st century CE. With the destruction of the second temple in 70 CE the synagogue became the main locus of worship and of study, filling the gap left by the absence of a single religious centre and of the sacrificial ritual. The traditional synagogue has an ark, or cupboard, in the Jerusalem-facing wall, where the handwritten scrolls of the Pentateuch (see BIBLE) are kept. At the centre of the synagogue is a *bimah*, a raised platform from which the Pentateuch is read and where in many congregations the CANTOR stands to lead the prayers. Women sit separately from men in Orthodox synagogues, but in Conservative and Reform temples (as they are called in North America – see REFORM JUDAISM) the sexes sit together. The synagogue is led by a group of laymen who are elected to office, and is a totally lay institution with no priestly roles. [14 vol. 15: 579; 63: 423]

Synanon Church [xxvIII] The Synanon Foundation, originally founded in California by Charles Dederich as a therapeutic group for alcoholics and drug addicts, became formally known as the Synanon Church in 1980 [42: 665]. Theological beliefs are derived from BUDDHISM and Taoism and thinkers such as Ralph Waldo Emerson and Aldous Huxley. The Synanon Game, described as the central sacrament, involves a small group exchanging confessions, repentance and absolution as equals. Synanon has been the subject of several bitter controversies; it achieved considerable publicity when a rattlesnake was put through the letter-box of a lawyer representing someone suing the group. Synanon closed in the early 1990s. [26: vi; 42: 665–6; 45]

Syncretism [xxxIV] The term used for the mixing together of diverse historical elements in a single whole. In the religious context it is often used in a pejorative sense, since it is regarded as a process which causes impurity in what is claimed to be an otherwise pure form of religion based on an impeccable revelation. This is the way the term is often used in Christian theology. Claims have been made that CHRISTIANITY and ISLAM are 'un- and anti-syncretistic' [xiv 55: 406]. However, in the objective STUDY OF RELIGIONS syncretism appears as a common feature of all observed religions and the process of delineating this study has been described as moving 'from

a theological term of reproach to a concept in the science of religion' [132: 5]. So universal is the occurrence of syncretism in the history of religions that it has been argued that it is useless to employ it as a category in the historical study of religions [10: 146]. It is true that the term is used with no agreed meaning in most studies, but attempts have been made to bring some order into the study. Pye catalogues some of the most important attempts and himself offers a systematic basis for studying syncretism, both theoretically and in the context of a particular Japanese example. Syncretism is sometimes viewed as a completed process, sometimes as a continuing, dynamic state. It is argued, however, that the completed process should be termed 'synthesis' and that syncretism is always a dynamic process, which can lead to 'assimilation', whereby the disparate elements break apart, or synthesis, which is sometimes identified as a 'new religion'. [132: 9]

Syncretism (Roman) [xxxI] In the ancient world, the formation of new cults by the merging of elements from different traditions, characteristically in the circumstances of political or cultural dominance/subjection. The Romans had long adopted Greek or Etruscan gods, or modified their own by the introduction of rituals, myths and iconography (see DI DEAEQUE). They also took from the Greeks the belief that different peoples worship the same gods, though under different names. The process in reverse began when the Romans administered areas culturally inferior (as they saw it) to themselves. The Roman gods, or at least their names, were widely used throughout the Western empire. It is hard to distinguish cases of simple importation of Roman deities from cases where local deities survived disguised under a Roman name – and both these cases from those of genuine syncretism [12: 356–7]. In north Africa, for instance, the wide dispersion of Saturn, a god little remembered at home in Italy, implies the adoption of his name for the local Ba'al-Hamon. Sometimes the merging led to the use of both local and Roman names, as in Sulis Minerva at Bath (England). The Roman empire also created the context for a different process, whereby such deities as Isis (from Egypt) or Sol Invictus (the unconquered sun; *see* MITHRAISM) were identified with many local gods, so moving towards wider claims to supremacy. [11: 34–5; 13: 280–7; 17: 150–3]

Syrian Orthodox Church [XIII.D] Closely allied to the COPTIC Church, with which it shares, as do other oriental Orthodox, a history of opposition to the imperial Church of Byzantium, the Syrian Orthodox Church remains loyal to Severus, a PATRIARCH of ANTIOCH who was deposed and exiled after the death, in 518, of his patron, the Emperor Anastasius. This theologian evolved a CHRISTOLOGY opposed to that of the imperially sponsored COUNCIL of Chalcedon (451), summed up in the description 'one person *out of* [not *in*] two natures', first formulated before Chalcedon by Cyril of ALEXANDRIA. It was the Emperor Justinian's campaign against the party of Severus, combined with his consort Theodora's support for the Severan Jacob Baradaeus (after whom the Syrian Orthodox are also called 'Jacobites'), that legitimized an alternative, so-called 'Monophysite', structure of spiritual authority acknowledged by the majority of Christians in the Middle East, though not by the CHURCH OF THE EAST. A century later the Oriental Orthodox Churches came under Arab rule, which confirmed by its political frontiers their alienation from Byzantium. Liberated by the crusaders around 1100 from both Byzantium and the Arabs, the Syrian Orthodox were well on the way towards union with the ROMAN CATHOLICS, or Latins, when the process was broken off by the failure of the crusades. Most of the Syrian Orthodox Patriarchs of Antioch have resided in north Mesopotamian monasteries (e.g. Qenneshre on the Euphrates and, later, the Saffron Monastery near Mardin), not at Antioch itself. Ataturk expelled the patriarchate from the Republic of Turkey. The present incumbent, Zakka I, presides, from his residence in Bab Tooma, Damascus, over a church no longer confined to the Middle East, but scattered as far abroad as Australia and the USA, with important concentrations in the lands of the Teutons and in southwest India. In this diaspora the name 'Assyrian', properly attached to the Church of the East, has made some inroads on Syrian Orthodox identity, with the pretension to stand for a national identity of indigenous Mesopotamians transcending ecclesiastical divisions, though not including Aramaic-speaking Jews from Iraq. The villagers of Tur 'Abdin speak Aramaic (Turoyo) but this last remaining rural enclave of Syrian Orthodoxy is being rapidly depleted by migration due to the insecurity of life in south-east Turkey. Syriac, the old Aramaic dialect of Edessa, still has an important place in Syrian Orthodox culture and religion. [6; 112; 113; 114; 119; 120]

T

Tabernacles [XXII] (Hebrew: *Sukkot*) Seven-day Jewish autumn festival (CHAGIM) during which traditional Jews dwell in a tabernacle (*sukkah*), thus giving the festival its name, to remember the desert booths in which the Israelites lived after the EXODUS from Egypt. They also take four agricultural species: a palm branch (*lulav*), a citrus fruit (*etrog*), three myrtle and two willow branches, and shake them each day to symbolize the end of the agricultural year and the beginning of the rainy season. The four species are waved during morning prayers in SYNAGOGUE, except on the Sabbath (SHABBAT), and are carried round the synagogue *bimah* platform while *hoshana* ('hosanna') prayers are chanted [59; xx; 69: 191; 70: 180]. On the seventh day of Tabernacles, *hoshana rabba*, seven such circumambulations take place. The eighth day of Tabernacles is a separate festival called SHEMINI ATZERET.

Tablighi-Jama'at [XIX] A group founded by Muhammad Ilyas (1885–1944) with the intention of inspiring Muslims through preaching (*tabligh*). Starting from a DEOBANDI position, Ilyas aimed to revive ISLAM by increasing individual piety. His main requirements were: understanding the significance of *tauhid* (unity of God); the proper observance of SALAT (prayer); acquiring religious knowledge; the giving of due respect to Muslims; sparing time for joining a *tabligh* group; remaining sincere and self-appraising. Through teaching and example, Muslims were exhorted to lead an Islamic lifestyle. They were then invited to commit themselves to a specific amount of time, from a few weeks to several months, as itinerant preachers. Though originating in India, this popular movement has spread throughout the Islamic world, gaining adherents from many different nationalities. The Arabic form of the name is Jama'at at-Tabligh. Under the leadership of Muhammad Ilyas' son Yusuf (d. 1965) the group expanded its vision to become a mission to non-Muslims as well. It spread to Europe and America with migration: in France it is known as Foi et pratique, having been introduced by Algerian Muslims, and in Germany it is the Teblig movement, organized by Turkish migrant workers. Though without a distinct organizational structure, the movement is represented in Britain both in the form of local MOSQUES with a *tablighi* emphasis and centrally by its establishment in Dewsbury. Following a period of residence at the centre, volunteers then visit mosques of all persuasions to preach, or will undertake door-to-door visitation in areas of predominantly Muslim population. [49; 99; 113]

Tabu (Taboo, Tapu) [XXIX] A restriction or ban on potent and sacred things. In POLYNESIAN RELIGION anything possessing great MANA is *tapu* (*kapu* in Hawaii). Chiefs and their families are surrounded with restrictions to protect the *mana* of their divine ancestry from being lost through contact with common things. The chief's person, especially his head, is sacrosanct, as are his house, food and utensils, clothing and possessions. Also highly *tapu* are tombs of chiefs; shrines and sacred stones; first-fruits and offerings for the gods; chants, genealogies and sacred lore; and groves or springs of water for ceremonial use. *Tapus* govern agriculture, fishing, building and carving, since all such work requires the help and protection of patron gods (ATUA) [7; 16; 30].

A danger to *mana*, and thus also *tapu*, are bloodstained warriors, women menstruating or in childbirth, the sick and dying, and corpses or bones of the dead. *Tapu*-removal is the reason for many religious rites. Using incantations, water, cooked food and other neutralizing things, the TOHUNGA lifts *tapus*, purifying people and objects from the potentially harmful effects of misplaced *mana*. Children are freed from the *tapu* of birth by ceremonies of purification and name-giving. Newly made buildings, war canoes, weapons and tools are freed of *tapu* and consecrated to endow them with fresh *mana*. *Tapus* are enforced by spirits and gods, who send sickness or death, or withdraw their protection allowing accident or defeat to punish *tapu*-breakers. *Tapu* is known in MELANESIAN RELIGION as *tambu*. [23; 28]

Tahara [XIX] Ritual purity in ISLAM, a state required before participation in the SALAT, touching the QUR'AN and other ritual acts. A major purification (*ghusl*), after e.g. coitus or menstruation, is distinguished from a minor one (*wudu'*), performed before the *salat* or worship. Sand may be used if water is lacking. [37 s.v.; 67 'Purification']

T'ai Shan [XII] Mount T'ai in Shantung province has been the focus of a popular cult since the Shang period (1523–1027 BCE). It was the site of imperial sacrifices between 110 BCE and 1008 CE. The

god of T'ai Shan, the 'Great Divine Ruler of the Eastern Peak' (*Tung Yueh Ta Ti*), is the grandson of the Jade Emperor (*Yu Huang*) in the popular CHINESE PANTHEON. He can determine a person's life-span and is one of the judges of the dead, hence some of the courts of hell were traditionally sited at T'ai Shan. [4: IV, 476–90; 49: XIX, 113–22; 98: XXIII, 178–85]

Takht [XXXIII] The *takht* ('throne') signifies for Sikhs a seat of temporal authority within the PANTH. The first of these institutions was established in Amritsar by Guru Hargobind early in the 17th century (*see* GURUS). Temporal involvement had become unavoidable and Akal Takht, symbolically sited beside HARIMANDIR SAHIB, was to serve as its focus (*see* GURDWARAS (HISTORIC LOCATIONS)). Three other places, all associated with GURU GOBIND SINGH, were subsequently declared to be *takhts* (Anandpur, Patna and Nanded) [19: VII]. Akal Takht has, however, retained its pre-eminence. During the political campaigns of the 20th century, as in the 18th-century struggles, it has been the place for debate and for promulgating major decisions (*gurmatta*). The role of the other three *takhts* has been less explicit and attempts to invoke their uncertain authority have seldom been made. In 1966 the Shiromani Gurdwara Parbandhak Committee (*see* SIKH REFORM MOVEMENTS) designated Damdama Sahib near Bhatinda a fifth *takht*. [9: 176–9]

Talmud [XXII] The main text of rabbinical JUDAISM, a wide-ranging commentary on the MISHNAH [70: 121]. The Palestinian (or Jerusalem) Talmud was edited towards the end of the 4th century CE, and the Babylonian Talmud, more authoritative for later Judaism than the Palestinian version, was edited at the end of the 5th century. Both Talmuds are in Aramaic (*see* LANGUAGES

(JEWISH)). The extant Talmudic commentary does not cover all of the six orders of the Mishnah. The Palestinian Talmud comments on 39 of the Mishnah's 63 tractates, and the Babylonian on 37. The Babylonian Talmud is, however, much longer and its discussion of issues more wide-ranging than the Palestinian Talmud. In general, Talmudic material may be divided into HALAKHAH, legal and ritual matters, and AGGADAH, theological, ethical and folklorist matters. The Halakhah of the Babylonian Talmud is binding on all traditional Jews, and the Aggadah, while not binding, is central to later Jewish theology. [10; 11; 15; 45; 67; 68]

Tane [xxix] The most active god (ATUA) in POLYNESIAN RELIGION. Forcing apart his parents RANGI and PAPA (heaven and earth), Tane brought life-giving sunlight to the world. Forests are his children, birds and insects his messengers. Woodcarvers and canoe-builders honour him with food offerings. In Maori myth, Tane brought to life a woman modelled from earth, making her mother of the human race. Wood or stone male figures (called *tiki*) represent Tane's procreative power. [7; 16; 22; 28]

Tangaroa [xxix] The god of the ocean, known throughout Polynesia (*see* POLYNESIAN RELIGION). Seafarers and fishermen invoke his blessing, throwing back as an offering the first fish caught. In Samoa and Tonga (as Tangaloa) and in Tahiti (as Ta'aroa), Tangaroa was worshipped as supreme being, uncreated father of gods (ATUA) and of mankind. Whether that was Tangaroa's ancient role or a late development is uncertain. [7; 16; 22; 30]

Tantra (1) [xvii] Literally, 'weaving', 'thread'; refers to a group of Hindu and Buddhist texts and hence the esoteric teachings contained within them. In itself non-sectarian,

it has influenced most south Asian religious traditions, especially HINDUISM and MAHAYANA BUDDHISM, in India and beyond. As a way of spiritual development, it aims to find release (MOKSHA, NIBBANA/ Nirvana) through working with and transforming, not rejecting, the whole of the body, mind and emotions. It views every being as a microcosm, mirroring the universe or macrocosm, so bearing some resemblance to the WESTERN MAGICAL TRADITION [57: 117–27: for Buddhist Tantra, *see* TANTRA (2)].

Hindu Tantra regards the cosmos as having emanated from the supreme, unmanifest reality (BRAHMAN) in progressively grosser forms, from top to bottom: mind, space, air, fire, water, earth. These same levels are also found in every human being, their energies concentrated at different centres (*cakras*, 'wheels') within the body. The main *cakras* are those of earth, at the base of the spine; water, in the sexual area; fire, at the navel; air, in the heart; space, in the throat; and mind, in the forehead, between the brows. Each *cakra* has its own name and meditative diagram or *yantra* (*see* MANDALA), set in a lotus of a different number of petals. The male and female aspects of deity, visualized as different forms of SHIVA and SHAKTI, live together in each of these *cakras*. The unmanifest is represented by the *sahasrara* ('thousand-spoked') *cakra*, seen as a thousand-petalled lotus just above the top of the head, in which Shiva and Shakti are blissfully united. It will be seen that though the *cakras* may bear some relation to glands or other physical organs, the Tantric system is essentially concerned with the body as experienced through meditation and YOGA, rather than through physiology.

The *cakras* are linked by a system of three channels or *nadis*: Sushumna in the centre of the spine, which corresponds to MOUNT MERU in the cosmos, and the solar and lunar channels, Ida and Pingala, at each side. Liberation for the Tantrika (practitioner of Tantra) consists of the rising of an energy called Kundalini, visualized as a Shakti in the form of a snake. In the unenlightened, Kundalini is asleep in the lowest *cakra*, coiled round Shiva in the form of a LINGA. The task of the Tantrika is to awaken Kundalini so that she will rise through Sushumna, eventually passing through the fontanelle into the *sahasrara cakra*. This is considered to be a particularly fast and direct method of spiritual practice, but a dangerous one, not to be undertaken without the guidance of a GURU [26: 6–24].

Tantra characteristically uses powerful and poetic imagery, centered on the basic human concerns of sexuality and death, to shake preconceptions about the nature of the world. It has gained a lurid reputation in the West through its use, under strictly controlled circumstances, of sexual intercourse as a meditative technique. In traditional India it shocked through its social attitudes: Tantrikas rejected, at least within the ritual context, all inequalities of CASTE and sex, and, because every woman is a form of the Goddess, declared the burning of widows (*see* SATI) a grave sin [95: 130–7].

Tantra has had a profound influence on the art of India and related cultures (*see* ART (HINDU)), its reverence for the body as true to one aspect of Indian life as the asceticism of the renouncer is to another.

Tantra (2) [xxxv] In the BUDDHIST tradition, the term *tantra* (also known as the *vajrayana*, 'indestructible vehicle', or *mantrayana*, 'mantra-vehicle') refers to a series of ritual texts originally delivered as discourses by the BUDDHA in human or divinized form. The Tantras deal with the invocation of deities, the acquisition of magical power and the attainment of enlightenment by means of meditation, MANTRA, *mudra* and YOGA [26]. According to tradition they were transmitted in relative secrecy until the 4th or 5th century CE, after which time they were propagated widely in India, especially by the famed group of Tantric saints known as the '84 perfect ones' (Sanskrit: *siddha*; Tibetan: *drupthop*), who included such figures as Saraha, Krishnacharya and Naropa.

Tantric theory and practice is essentially a development within MAHAYANA Buddhism, sharing the latter's ethical and philosophical basis. It expresses the Mahayana doctrine of the inseparability of *samsara* and *nirvana* (NIBBANA) in the notion of 'simultaneously arising' (Sanskrit: *sahaja*; Tibetan: *lhan-chik kye-pa*). According to this precept, as all phenomena are fundamentally empty (*shunya*) they are intrinsically pure. Thus *samsara* and *nirvana* arise simultaneously from the same basis. Recognition of this simultaneously arising nature or underlying purity transforms moral defilements (Sanskrit: *klesha*; Tibetan: *nyonmong*) into PRAJNA and the psychophysical constituents (*skandhas*) into BUDDHAS. [8; 19]

This practice of Tantra depends upon the receipt of instruction from a GURU (Tibetan: *lama*) who stands in the unbroken succession of masters of the teaching. The Tantric master gives teaching in three main ways: first, through 'empowerment' (Sanskrit: *abhisheka*; Tibetan: *wangkur*), in which he empowers the student to meditate on a deity; second, by 'textual transmission' (Sanskrit: *agama*; Tibetan: *lung*), in which he bestows the blessing of the relevant text; and third, by 'instruction' (Sanskrit: *upadesha*; Tibetan: *khrid*), in which he explains the method of practising the particular teaching. (*See also* CHEN YEN; SHINGON) [13; 23]

Tao Chia [xii] Taoist school. The term is commonly used in recent times to refer to Taoist philosophy as represented in texts such as the TAO TE CHING, the CHUANG TZU, the *Lieh Tzu* and the *Huai Nan Tzu*; and in the tradition of philosophical reflection upon these works that includes the neo-Taoist exponents of the Dark Learning (HSUAN HSUEH) such as Wang Pi (226–49 CE), Ho Yen (d. 249 CE) and Kuo Hsiang (d. 312 CE). In the above sense it is distinguished from TAO CHIAO (Taoist sect). [21; 55; 115: 163]

Tao Chiao [XII] Taoist sect or religious Taoism. The term literally means 'Teachings of the Way'. It is now used to refer to established sects and movements that seek access to the *Tao* as the supreme reality, and consequent immortality, through meditational, liturgical and alchemical means (*see* ALCHEMY (CHINESE)). Religious Taoism incorporates ideas and images from philosophical Taoist texts, especially the TAO TE CHING, as well as the theory of YIN-YANG, the quest for immortality (*hsien*), mental and physical discipline, interior hygiene, internal alchemy (*nei tan*), healing and exorcism, pantheons of gods and spirits, and ideals of theocratic states [17a: V, 85–6; 55: V, 107–48; 73: III, 85–147; 88: 1–7; 115: 88–123].

Religious Taoism emerged in the form of distinct movements towards the end of the Later Han dynasty (23–220 CE). The most important was the Heavenly Master (*t'ien tsun*) or Five Pecks of Rice sect, founded by Chang Tao Ling (34–156) in Szechuan. Chang is said to have achieved immortality by gaining mastery over hundreds of spirits whose names and functions he identified and preserved for his disciples in the *Auspicious Alliance Canonical Registers*. At the head of this pantheon are the 'Three Pure Ones' (*san ch'ing*), the Lords of Heaven, Earth and Man. Knowledge of this and similar registers determines the rank of the orthodox priest in the established Taoist sects. Chang founded a

successful church state in Szechuan. (*see* TAO TSANG.) [17a: VI, 103–5]

The Sacred Jewel (*ling pao*) sect was a peaceful movement which developed early in the 4th century CE. Its adherents developed important Taoist rituals such as the rite of cosmic renewal and ritual method of controlling spirits. These rituals were adopted by the Heavenly Master sect in the 5th century and later by all sects which claimed to be orthodox. The Highest Pure (*shang ch'ing*) or Mao Shan sect which emerged early in the 4th century emphasized methods of controlling the spirits through meditation rather than ritual. Many sects of varying degrees of orthodoxy emerged during the T'ang and Sung dynasties (618–1126). Described collectively as Spirit Cloud (*shen hsiao*) Taoists, they constitute the majority of Taoist priests in modern Taiwan, where they are called 'Masters of Methods' (*fa shih*) or Red-headed Taoists and are distinguished from the more orthodox 'Tao Masters' (*tao shih*) or Black-headed Taoists. [21; 73; 88: V, 84–105; 89; 90; 116]

Tao Te Ching [XII] The most famous and influential Taoist text (*see* TAO CHIAO), traditionally attributed to Lao Tzu, supposedly a contemporary of CONFUCIUS (551–479 BCE) [34: VIII, 170–91]. It is, however, impossible to identify accurately the author or the date of this obscure and aphoristic text. The fact that it criticizes established Confucian values [63 or 104: XVIII, XIX, XXXIII] and is not mentioned by MENCIUS (371–289 BCE) but is discussed by HSUN TZU (300–230 BCE) suggests that it existed in some form between 350 and 300 BCE.

According to the *Tao Te Ching*, the nameless unchanging essence and source of heaven and earth may be called the *Tao*. Although the *Tao* produces and sustains all things, it does so without volitional or purposeful action (*wu wei*) [63 or 104: XXXVII]. The passive and the productive aspects of the *Tao* are described as non-Being (*wu*) and Being (*yu*) respectively [63 or 104: II, V, XI]. To accord with the *Tao*, the sage-ruler must be without desires, intentions or volitional actions. If he truly achieves this state of non-doing then he will achieve tranquillity and is fit to rule the empire. [7: VII, 136–76; 19: VI, 106–26; 21; 38: III, 215–35; 55; 63; 104; 115: I, II, 1–83]

Tao Tsang [XII] The Taoist (*see* TAO CHIAO) canon, which achieved its present form of 1,120 volumes in 1436 CE. An earlier form of the canon was even longer, but many volumes were destroyed, and its order was disrupted when Kublai Khan had it burned in 1281 CE. The classification of the *Tao Tsang* into the *San Tung* (Three Vaults) and the *Ssu Fu* (Four Supplements) dates from at least the early 4th and early 5th centuries CE respectively. This form of classification has been applied to the subsequent versions of the *Tao Tsang*, although the precise contents of these categories have been subject to some variations.

The first of the *San Tung*, the *Tung Chen* (True Vault) contains mainly the meditation and ritual texts of the Yu Ching (Jade Capital) or Shang Ch'ing (Highest Pure) sect of Mao Shan. The second is the *Tung Hsuan* (Mysterious Vault), largely devoted to the *Ling Pao* (Sacred Jewel) texts, and gives details of many rituals and talismans. The third section is the *Tung Shen* (Spirits Vault), which initially contained the *San Huang Wen* (Three Emperors Writ) and the *Meng Wei Ching Lu* (Auspicious Alliance Canonical Registers), the 24 registers of the names and functions of spirits discovered by Chang Tao Ling (34–156 CE) of the Heavenly Master (*t'ien tsun*) sect.

The *Ssu Fu* (Four Supplements) contain many important texts, some of which are earlier than those in the *San Tung*. The *T'ai Hsuan* (Great

Mystery) section contains the TAO TE CHING. The central text of the *T'ai Ping* (Great Peace) section is the *T'ai Ping Ching* (Classic of Great Peace). The *T'ai Ch'ing* (Great Purity) section contains works on ALCHEMY and philosophical Taoism (TAO CHIA). The *Cheng I* (Orthodox One) section is based upon the canonical works of the Heavenly Master sect. [17a: VI, 111–12; 89: 31–61; 116: VIII, 253–67]

Tapas [XVII] Literally 'heat' or 'fire'; in Hindu tradition, particularly, the heat generated by an ascetic through austerities. In the *Rig-veda* (*see* VEDA) it is tentatively suggested that the world was generated through some primeval *tapas* [12: 251]. There is also a tendency to regard *tapas* as a magical power, not necessarily used for moral ends (DHARMA). In Puranic myth (*see* PURANAS), demons such as ASURAS use ascetic *tapas* to force boons from the gods which can be used against them, though naturally there is always some condition to the boon which eventually brings about the demon's downfall (as with the Buffalo Demon slain by DURGA).

Tara [XXXV] The Buddhist cult of the female BODHISATTVA Tara developed in India, but it has become particularly important in Tibetan BUDDHISM where it was introduced by the Indian missionary Atisha (11th century; *see* KADAM). Tara incarnates the dynamic saving energy of all the Buddhas, and she is closely connected with AVALOKITESHVARA, appearing in art with him from the 6th century CE. According to a Tibetan story Tara was born from one of Avalokiteshvara's tears at seeing the suffering of sentient beings. Another story has it that she was previously a princess whose spiritual development was such that she was urged to transform into male form in order finally to achieve Buddhahood. In response she said she would work 'until SAMSARA is empty' in a female form. Tibetans frequently speak of Tara as already a fully enlightened female Buddha. Like MANJUSHRI she is said to be age-old yet perpetually 16. In Tibetan art Tara has two principal forms: (1) the Green Tara, seated with left leg drawn up and the right on a lotus 'footstool', often holding the stem of a blue lotus in each hand; and (2) the White Tara, associated with long-life practices, seated in lotus posture with an eye in each hand and foot, holding the stem of a white lotus in the left hand. [XI 101: 236–8; 27; 34]

Targum [XXII] An Aramaic translation–commentary to the BIBLE. At the end of the second TEMPLE period Jews adopted Aramaic as their mother tongue and could not understand the Hebrew text of the Bible (see LANGUAGES (JEWISH)) [70: 46]. During public readings the Bible would be accompanied by a paraphrastic translation in Aramaic [16: 164; 63: 20]. In the course of time these were edited into official versions. The best known is *Targum Onkelos* on the Pentateuch, which avoids the use of anthropomorphisms in its translation. [14 vol. 15: 811]

Tarot [XXIV] A pack of 78 cards used originally for games, now increasingly for DIVINATION. Fifty-six cards form four suits of 14 cards each, called the Lesser, or Minor Arcana (Latin *arcanus*: secret or mysterious) while 21 unsuited 'trumps', with designs of a powerfully symbolic nature (the Wheel of Fortune, the Tower, Love, Fortitude, and so on), along with the card of the Fool or Wanderer, form the Greater/Major Arcana. The cards appeared in about 1440 in northern Italy, where playing-cards were already known. The trump designs were perhaps drawn from one of the visual memory-systems [31] common at the time: they were originally unnumbered and players had to remember their sequence. In 1781 Antoine Court de Gébelin (1719–84) proposed an Egyptian hermetic source (see HERMETISM) for the cards, and a certain Alliette ('Etteilla') (d. 1791) began their use in divination. 'Eliphas Lévi' (see WESTERN MAGICAL TRADITION) later proposed a Kabbalistic interpretation, on which modern divinatory use is based, viewing the trumps as emblems of the 22 'paths' connecting the *sefirot* of the 'Tree of Life' (see KABBALAH). [9]

Tat Khalsa [XXXIII] Originally, Tat ('pure') Khalsa was the name given to a section of the PANTH which opposed the SIKH leader Banda in the early 18th century. Since the late 19th century, however, the name describes the radical group within the Singh Sabha which pressed to have its exclusivist interpretation of the Sikh faith accepted by the Panth. Within the Singh Sabha it was opposed by the conservative SANATAN SIKHS who believed that Sikhism was merely one of the many varieties of Hindu tradition. The Tat Khalsa vigorously contested this, maintaining that Sikhism was an entirely separate religion. Eventually it defeated the Sanatan Sikhs and ever since the early 20th century its interpretation has been accepted as orthodox. Prominent members of the Tat Khalsa included the poet and theologican Vir Singh [31: v] and the encyclopedist Kahn Singh Nabha. (*see also* SIKH HISTORY; SIKH REFORM MOVEMENTS.) [29: V–VI]

Tathagatagarbha [XI] The 'essence of the Buddha' (*tathagata*), or 'womb of the Buddha' a term commonly used in MAHAYANA BUDDHISM to refer to the Buddha-nature, that which because it is possessed by sentient beings enables them to become fully enlightened Buddhas. The idea of the tathagatagarbha was put forward in a number of Indian Buddhist sutras, and expounded particularly in a treatise said to have been revealed by the BODHISATTVA MAITREYA, the *Ratnagotravibhaga* (also known as the *Uttaratantrashastra*). In China Fatsang (7th century CE) saw the tathagatagarbha teaching as a further and final revelation beyond MADHYAMAKA and YOGACARA. Texts treating the tathagatagarbha frequently refer to it as having 'the perfection of self', and particular problems were caused by the suggestion that some element in each sentient being which enables one to become enlightened could be referred to as a 'self' (*see* ANATTA). Commonly it is stated that the name 'tathagatagarbha' is given to the ultimate truth (*dharmakaya*; *see* BUDDHA, BODIES OF) when it is obscured by defilements in the unenlightened person. There is a tendency for each Mahayana tradition to say that the tathagatagarbha is whatever that tradition considers to be the ultimate way of things – EMPTINESS for MADHYAMAKA, the non-dual stream of consciousness for YOGACARA. Thus this could only be a 'self' in a metaphoric sense. It is said to be beyond all conceptions of self. In Tibet there was a debate between those like the JONANG tradition which took quite literally the statements made in Indian tathagatagarbha sources that the tathagatagarbha is itself an ultimate reality, always enlightened and radiant even in those who appear to be unenlightened, in some sense the *true* self, identifiable perhaps with non-dual radiant consciousness, and those like the GELUG who held that this is tantamount to a non-Buddhist doctrine of self and that the tathagatagarbha is ultimately empty of inherent existence on the MADHYAMAKA model, like all things, and it is absurd to say that sentient beings have really been enlightened all along. In East Asian Buddhism the Buddha-nature teachings became extremely influential and widespread, interpreted quite literally as the true self, the absolute nature of all things, non-dual mind. Thus all things become in reality

mind, and sometimes the conclusion was drawn that in seeking to save all sentient beings the BODHISATTVA must also save even blades of grass. (*see also* T'IEN-T'AI; SAICHO; JAPAN, BUDDHISM IN) [101: v; 35]

Tattvartha Sutra [xx] Collection of short statements, composed in Sanskrit probably around the 4th or 5th centuries CE by Umasvati, which summarize the doctrine and practice of the JAIN religion. Accepted as authoritative by both the DIGAMBARA and SHVETAMBARA sects, its ten chapters about the 'meaning of the fundamental entities' (*tattvartha*) have a serious of important commentaries on them, the most important of which are by medieval Digambara writers. [4: 74–5, 185–6]

Tefillin [xxii] The two black leather boxes worn on the left arm and head by adult male Jews during weekday morning services. *Tefillin* are known in English as 'phylacteries'. They contain the four passages in the BIBLE (*Exodus* 13: 1–10, 11–16; *Deuteronomy* 6: 4–9, 11: 13–21) which command the Jew to put, or bind, the words of God as a sign on his hand and between his eyes. The hand *tefillah* has these passages on one parchment, and the head *tefillah* on four separate parchments. [19: 502]

Temenos [xvi] A *temenos* (sanctuary) was dedicated to one or more deities and served a *polis* (*see* GREEK RELIGION), a smaller community, all the Greeks (for example the Panhellenic sanctuaries of Delphi and Olympia), or a section of them. A wall, or boundary markers, separated it from secular space. Sanctuaries varied in shape, size and splendour and in the number and size of their buildings. Unlike the altar (*bomos, eschara* (*see* RITES)), the temple (*naos*) was not an essential religious part of the Greek sanctuary; some sanctuaries are earlier than their temples and some never acquired a temple. Some sanctuaries contained a sacred tree, stone or spring. Some were grove sanctuaries or cave sanctuaries. Votive offerings (*anathemata*) were dedicated, gifts to the gods to be used in cult or simply to be, and adorn the sanctuary; some of these (e.g. statues) stood in the open. Buildings included store rooms, dining rooms, porticoes; some sanctuaries had areas for games and dramatic performances. The primary function of most temples was to house the cult statue of the deity, to which worshippers addressed prayers and made offerings which they placed on offering tables (*trapezai*); the main ritual activity, sacrifice, took place on the altar outside. In some temples important cult activities took place inside. In the temple of Apollo at Delphi (*see* MANTIKE; POLITIKE) sacrifices took place inside (as well as outside) the temple, as did the oracular consultation. Temples varied in size and magnificence; some were richly decorated with mythological sculptures. The cult statue was in the *cella*, the indispensable part of a Greek temple; the *prodomos* or *pronaos* housed the more impressive *anathemata*; the *opisthodomos* housed offerings and functioned as a treasury. Some temples had an *adyton* at the back of the cella; *adyton* means a place not to be entered (by ordinary worshippers, that is); it was the inner sanctum. Altars were not only situated in sanctuaries but also in houses, in the streets, in civic buildings. [2: I. 1; 11: 67–97, 155–90; 24; 36]

Templa [XXXI] Originally, Roman *templa* were rectangular areas either in the sky or on the earth, so defined by the augurs (SACERDOTES) as to provide the basis for interpreting signs either from lightning or from the flight of birds (AUSPICIA). The terrestrial ones were said to be *loci effati*, freed from evil forces, and thereby inaugurated. Temples in our

sense (properly *aedes sacrae*) were usually, but not necessarily, *templa* [8: 314–19; 10: 12–14; 14: 2256–96]. The worship of the gods was initially carried out at open-air altars (*arae*) and these remained outside the temple, as the essential context for sacrifices (*see* RITUALS). The building was added to house the god's image and to store the paraphernalia of the cult and the dedications made by individuals as the result of private vows to the god. Eventually they became storehouses of art-treasures from conquered Greece. Some functions were proper to *templa* in the strict sense; only in them, for instance, could meetings of the Senate take place. [8: 316]

Temple (Jerusalem) [XIII.A, XXII] (Hebrew, *Bet Ha-Mikdash*) The first Israelite temple in Jerusalem was built by Solomon (*c.*950 BCE). Phoenician architects constructed it on a common Near Eastern plan: from east to west one proceeded through the courtyard, vestibule and nave ('holy place') to the inner sanctuary ('holy of holies') where stood the ark, the symbol of Yahweh's presence (*see* GOD). In 587 BCE it was destroyed by the Babylonians. The site lay derelict for 70 years, until a new temple (Zerubbabel's), of modest proportions, was built by permission of the Persian king (*see* BIBLICAL HISTORY). This temple was profaned by Antiochus IV (167 BCE); its rededication under Judas Maccabeus three years later is celebrated in the minor festival of Hannukah. Under Herod (from 19 BCE) it was greatly enlarged and beautified. In its outer court JESUS taught when he visited Jerusalem. It was destroyed by the Romans in 70 CE [XIII.A 11: VI, 350–69; 22: II, 237–313; XXII 14 vol. 15: 942]. Traditional Jews believe that a third temple will be built in the age of the MESSIAH. [XXII 63: 535]

Temples (Ancient Near Eastern) [VIII] Originally created by the secular community in Sumer (see SUMERIANS) [23: 17–20], temples acquired land and possessions. As the god's home, tended by divine servants, some temples also had a social duty (see HAMMURABI'S CODE) to make capital available to worshippers, and to provide accommodation for orphans, the offspring of religious prostitution and children dedicated in times of famine. Temples were renewed and restored by successive rulers (see KINGSHIP (ANCIENT NEAR EASTERN)), and varied considerably in size and style during different periods [13: 145–9; 25: 40]

Most societies acknowledged the king as high priest of the chief god. At every temple (the 'god's dwelling'), the priests acted as divine servants [13: 149–55]; they performed rituals, obtained oracular prophecies (see ASTROLOGY) and administered the god's lands. Organized as hierarchies, priesthoods were passed down in families; ritual purity was demanded for performance of the rites. Some establishments had priestesses whose duties included sacred prostitution. At Ur, and Larsa, the high priestess acted as the 'god's wife', while others enjoyed special business and inheritance concessions [23: 17–20]. In the temples, priests attended to the deity's supposed bodily needs through ritual enactment, and propitiatory offerings were brought by those seeking healing. These included first-fruits and animal sacrifices (see HITTITES; PHOENICIANS; SUMERIANS), and occasional examples occur of human sacrifice (see HITTITES), following a military defeat [13: 151]. At FESTIVALS special rites were enacted in which the rules took part [13: 151–6; 17: 39]. The main non-temple rites were those concerning burials (see AFTERLIFE).

Templo Mayor [xxv] The most powerful and monumental Aztec shrine was what the Spanish called the Templo Mayor (1325–1521 CE),

located in the centre of the capital, Tenochtitlan. It was a huge pyramid temple, called Coatepec (see HUITZILOPOCHTLI), meaning Snake Mountain, supporting the great shrines to Huitzilopochtli, the sun and war god, and TLALOC, the rain and agricultural god, to whom massive HUMAN SACRIFICES of warriors, women and children were made. The shape, iconography and ritual actions at the Templo Mayor commemorated the myth of Huitzilopochtli's birth at the cosmic mountain, his dismemberment of the goddess Coyolxauhqui representing the moon, and his destruction of the *centzon huitznahua*, the 400 gods of the south representing the stars.

Tendai [xxi] Named after the mountain and the sect in Chekiang province, China, T'IEN-T'AI. The priest SAICHO introduced Tendai concepts to his monastery Ichijoshikan-in on Mt Hiei, northeast of Kyoto, on his return in 805 [14: 49–58; 21: 55–7, 191–3; 36: 134–48]. His *Kenkai-ron* was a treatise explaining the MAHAYANA injunctions leading to initiation. Tendai's philosophical base is the Lotus Sutra (*Hokkekyo*) as used by the Kegon sect (see NANTO ROKUSHU), and Yakushi Buddha is the chief deity (see JAPANESE BUD-

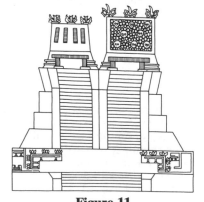

Figure 11

The Great Temple of Huitzilopochtli and Tlaloc, Texcoco

DHAS AND BODHISATTVAS). Saicho built the first Lotus Sutra meditation hall in 812, and the formal adoption of the *nembutsu* practice in 851 opened the way for major developments in AMIDA WORSHIP. Tendai became distinctly esoteric when ENNIN introduced the tantric (*see* TANTRA (2)) use of mandalas and accompanying rituals about 25 years after Saicho's death. Simple ZEN-style meditation was practised. Despite imperial support, the lack of sectarian exclusiveness alienated the Nara clergy (*see* JAPAN, BUDDHISM IN) and Saicho failed during his lifetime to get a formal name for his temple and to break the grip of the Nara clergy (*see* NANTO SHICHIDAI-JI) on ordinations. Both were later approved, the temple becoming the Enryaku-ji in 823 (era name: 782–806). All of the Kamakura schools of BUDDHISM owed their origins to monks trained in Tendai: Pure Land [36: 194–203], ZEN [37] and NICHIREN [2]. The temple took on a strong political colouring by medieval times, its warrior-monks feuding violently with other temples and shrines, terrorizing the city of Kyoto at night. Eventually Oda Nobunaga (1534–82) burned the Enryaku-ji in 1571, killed most of the priests and dispersed many of its possessions. Some later rebuilding was ordered by Toyotomi Hideyoshi (1536–98) and Tokugawa Ieyasu (1542–1616), and the Enryaku-ji now consists of three separated sub-temples.

A major doctrinal contribution by Tendai has been in attributing the BUDDHA-nature to the ordinary person, affirming that enlightenment is aided by moralistic ways and rigorous meditation [36: 139–42]. The monks indulge in strict disciplinary training, reading *sutras* rather than commentaries, and studying the Triple Truth of Tendai: the Void (*see* EMPTINESS), the Temporary (*see* ANICCA) and the Middle Path. (*See also* T'IEN-T'AI).

Tenrikyo [XXI] A Japanese faith-healing sect tracing its founding to a female shaman (MIKO) Nakayama Miki (1798–1887), with headquarters at Tenri in Nara prefecture [21: 225–6]. It was made sectarian by the man now regarded as a spiritual co-founder, Iburi Izo [21: 98–100]. The adherents revere both a creator deity, Tenri-O-no-mikoto, and the spot where creation took place. Happiness and prosperity are achieved by mastering human frailties and failures. Work and service in harmony are believed to lead towards reincarnation in a more virtuous state. The sect heads are all descendants of Nakayama Miki. All holders of formal offices connected with the widespread, strongly mission-oriented organization are adherents.

Teopixque [XXV] The priests, of various levels, who directed all facets of ceremonial and educational life in late pre-Hispanic central Mexico (1325–1521 CE) [19: 78–90, 147–50]. Most temples had full-time resident priests and the larger temples had both male and female religious specialists or *cihuateopixque*, who acted as the primary intermediaries between the society and the gods.

One of the principal responsibilities of the *teopixque* was the transmission of the historical and religious traditions in oral form (*see* HUE-HUETLATOLLI) [12: 177–83] and pictorial books called *amoxtlacuilolli*. They also directed the elaborate ritual schedules for the temples, the construction and renovation of ceremonial buildings, the fabrication of statues, the sacrifice of animals and humans (*see* HUMAN SACRIFICE) and the education of the nobles. Controlling the priestly hierarchy were the dual high priests called *quequetzalcao* (*see* TOPILTZIN QUETZAL-COATL), who also directed the activities of part-time rotational priests and votive penitent priests. The latter usually came from the upper classes and their temporary service in the temples gained them divine favour and prestige. All priests painted themselves black, practised sexual abstinence, performed a rigorous schedule of offerings and carried out penitential exercises, especially blood-letting from special parts of the body. On special ceremonial occasions, the TLATOANIS took the roles of priests, to lead ceremonial dances and perform human sacrifices.

Terapanth [XX] SHVETAMBARA JAIN sect which rejects image-worship and advocates the permanent wearing of the mouth-shield (MUHPATTI) by its ascetics. The Terapanth was formed in the 18th century CE by Acarya Bhiksu, who left the STHANAKVASI sect because of its supposed laxity in order to promulgate his own brand of Jainism which he claimed was directly based on the scriptures in respect to matters such as nonviolence. Differing interpretations of the name Terapanth are found, according to which the 'path' (*panth*) of 'thirteen' (*tera*) is taken as referring to either the 13 main precepts of Jainism or an original 13 adherents. Eight teachers have succeeded Acarya Bhiksu, each of whom has assumed a dominant position, so that the sect has remained virtually immune to fission. Today, the sect is strongest in Rajasthan, its place of origin. [4: 218–24]

Terma [XXXV] Tibetan, referring to 'hidden treasures', usually texts, teachings or sometimes sacred objects held to be miraculous and thought to have been hidden until the time is ripe for their revelation or promulgation. Normally they are said to have been hidden by the legendary *siddha* (*see* TANTRA (2)) and missionary to Tibet Padmasambhava, or one of his consorts, in the 8th century CE and rediscovered by 'treasure revealers' (*tertons*) many centuries later. Often the termas are just fragments of text, or said to be written in secret scripts, and the revealer is required to go deep into the mind to uncover their actual form. The model for termas as hidden texts may be found in Indian BUDDHISM in some of the early MAHAYANA SUTRAS such as PRAJNAPARAMITA. [33]

Teteoinnan [XXV] MESOAMERICAN RELIGIONS had a rich array of mother-earth goddesses, which were forms of Teteoinnan, Mother of the Gods [2: VII]. These goddesses were representatives of the distinct but sometimes combined qualities of terror and beauty, regeneration and destruction. The goddesses were worshipped in earth-mother cults especially developed in the Huaxteca culture on the gulf coast and among the Aztecs in central Mexico. These cults were generally concerned with the abundant powers of the earth, women and fertility. Among the most prominent goddesses were Tlazolteotl, Xochiquetzal, and Coatlicue (*see* HUITZILOPOCHTLI). Tlazolteotl was the earth-mother concerned with sexual powers, passions and the pardoning of sexual transgressions [17: 420–2]. Conceived in quadruple or quintuple forms as the *lxcuiname*, her powers sometimes merged with the malevolent death forces associated with the earth, crossroads and dangerous places. The youthful dimension of the earth-mother was Xochiquetzal, the goddess of love and sexual desire [7: XVI]. Pictured as an attractive nubile maiden associated with flowers, feasting, and pleasure, she was also the goddess of pregnancy, childbirth and the feminine arts, like weaving. A ferocious goddess, Coatlicue, the Serpent Skirt, represented the cosmic mountain which conceived all stellar beings and devoured all beings into her repulsive, lethal and fascinating form. Her statue (*see* AZTEC SCULPTURE) is studded with sacrificed hearts (*see* HUMAN SACRIFICE), skulls, hands, ferocious claws and giant-snake heads. [12: 89]

Tezcatlipoca [xxv] Tezcatlipoca, the Smoking Mirror, was one of the four great creator-gods of MESOA-MERICAN RELIGIONS, who arranged the universe and set the cosmic ages in motion through periodic celestial battles which resulted in periods of stability called 'Suns' (see CEMANA-HUAC) [2: 80–101]. Tezcatlipoca was sometimes cast as the supernatural antagonist of QUETZAL-COATL, the deity associated with cultural creativity, urban order and wisdom. Yet Tezcatlipoca has the most overwhelming power and protean personality of any Mesoamerican deity. His many forms reflect the omnipotent character of the numinous forces of central Mesoamerican religion. Among his aspects were Itztli, a calendar god; Tepeyollotl, an ancient jaguar–earth god; Ixquimilli–Itztlacoliuhqui, a god of punishment; and Omacatl, the spirit of revelry. The Smoking Mirror stood for the contradictory forces of youthful vitality and ferocious darkness. According to the Toltec tradition (see TOLLAN), Tezcatlipoca drew his uncanny powers from his major accoutrement, an obsidian mirror which cast a magical spell over the Toltec king TOPILTZIN QUETZALCOATL, resulting in the downfall of the kingdom and the reintroduction of HUMAN SACRIFICE into ceremonial practices. [6: 371–92]

Theism [xxxiv] (1) Belief in a single divine being ('God' rather than a GOD) as personal, actively related to but distinct from the divinely created reality which includes the human race. Thus, theism holds to both the immanence (the presence within and interaction with the world) and the transcendence (the 'otherness', independence and separation from the world) of God. In this, it is contrasted with PANTHEISM on the one side and, on the other, with that DEISM which holds God to be the creator but not active in what he created.

(2) More specifically, the worldview which is the putative conclusion of classical ARGUMENTS FOR THE EXISTENCE OF GOD, the self-existent perfect Spirit upon whom the world depends for its existence, continuance, meaning and purpose. [37: VI; 75: 80–4]

Theism (Jewish) [xxII] The belief in one God who has created heaven and earth is at the very centre of faith in JUDAISM (see GOD (IN HEBREW AND CHRISTIAN SCRIPTURES)). The unity of God, and the need for humans to relate to him in love, are expressed in the first verses of the SHEMA, the central affirmation of Jewish belief repeated twice daily in the liturgy: 'Hear O Israel, the Lord is our God, the Lord is one. You shall love the Lord your God with all your heart, with all your soul, and with all your might' (*Deuteronomy* 6: 4–5). MAIMONIDES, the great medieval theologian, states in his formulation of the essential principles of Judaism [31: II–VI; 64: 93] that the Jew must believe in the existence of one unique, perfect, incorporeal God who has created and sustains all that is, who is pre-existent, cannot be compared to any created being, and on whom all creatures are dependent. The Jewish mystics (see KABBALAH), while accepting the basic unity of God, were unhappy about the philosophical and somewhat abstract slant of Maimonides' formulation. They developed a THE-OSOPHICAL system in which different aspects of the divine activity are personified and related to human experience, the world itself having emanated from God. [14 vol. 7: 641; 52]

Theodicy [xiii.B] That branch of NATURAL THEOLOGY which attempts to defend the goodness and omnipotence of GOD (see CHRISTIAN CONCEPT OF) against objections arising from the presence of evil in the world. The term was coined by G. W. Leibniz (1646–1716), but the problem was present from the beginning in Christianity and within Judaism before it. (*See also* EVIL, CHRISTIAN DOCTRINE OF.)

Theoi [XVI] Gods. Greek deities were anthropomorphic, possessing immortality, extensive powers, knowledge, happiness and beauty. They were not omnipresent. They protected morality (ETHIKE), though they themselves sometimes cheated and committed adultery. Each had a MYTHOS, a cult corpus, certain functions, and embodied certain concepts (e.g. Apollo order). Divine personalities developed over time and varied between cities and again in the Panhellenic facet of GREEK RELIGION, which influenced local conceptions. Deities helped but did not generally have affection for humans (except for their own children), but they occasionally showed compassion. Worshippers did not generally feel affection for or intimacy with the gods, except in certain cults, especially MYSTERIA and healing cults. Human relations with the gods focused on paying the honour due to them through sacrifices, other cult observances, and abstention from divinely disapproved behaviour. No god was entirely negative, but each had a dangerous side. Greatest were the 12 *Olympioi*, residing on Mount Olympos, a divine family headed by Zeus (*see* COSMOS) which included Hera, Poseidon, Apollon, Artemis, Athena, Aphrodite, Ares, Hermes, Hephaistos, Demeter and Hestia (or Dionysos). Hades, Persephone and other Underworld deities are *Chthonioi* (*chthon* = earth); but the distinction is not absolute: deities in each category have sides and cults belonging to the other. There are many minor divinities (e.g. Pan, *Nymphai* (Nymphs), *Mousai* (Muses), river gods) and personifications (e.g. *Nemesis* (*see* ETHIKE)). Hellenistic Greeks craved divine protection and personal contact, hence the popularity of deities that

lent themselves to this, like Dionysos, Asklepios, and the newly introduced Oriental gods, especially Isis and Sarapis. [2: II. 1–3; 4: 119–89, 216–25; 6: 35–48; 10: 75–80; 15; 17; 31: 248–55]

Theosophical Society [XXIV] An organization founded in 1875 in New York by the Russian clairvoyant (*see* PSYCHIC POWERS) Helena Petrovna Blavatsky (1831–91) and Col. H. S. Olcott (1832–1907) to promote universal brotherhood, the study of comparative religion and the investigation of 'unexplained laws of nature and the powers latent in man'. It propagates doctrines based on Blavatsky's eclectic, visionary writings [3], which draw on HINDUISM and BUDDHISM. All religions are viewed as versions of the one 'esoteric' truth, 'THEOSOPHY'. The individual's spiritual development, it is believed, is supervised by a secret brotherhood of Masters or *Mahatmas*, believed to reside in Tibet. The universe consists of seven interpenetrating 'planes'; each of us, accordingly, has seven bodies (divine, spiritual, intuitional, mental, emotional, etheric, physical), the first three comprising the 'ego' or 'overself', which reincarnates countless times, experiencing KARMA (happiness and suffering as results of good and evil actions) and evolving towards full 'selfhood' in conscious cooperation with the divine purpose. The cosmos itself evolves over vast periods, planets forming 'planetary chains' of seven successive similar planets: our earth, which is the fourth earth, will be followed by three more in future. Study of such complexities plays an important part in theosophy. Members are encouraged to practise meditation but no particular religious practice is enjoined.

The founders moved their headquarters to India in 1877. After Olcott's death leadership passed to the social reformer Annie Besant (1847–1923), who in 1911 proclaimed J. Krishnamurti (b. 1895) the coming 'World Teacher', a role he later repudiated. The Society's influence has diminished since the 1930s, but it is still active in 60 countries, and is still prominent in India, today appealing chiefly to eclectic Hindus. Its international headquarters are at Adyar, Madras. Offshoots include Theosophical Society International in Pasadena, California (led by William Q. Judge, one of the original founders of the Theosophical Society); the United Lodge of Theosophists (founded in the USA in 1909); and the Anthroposophical Society (*see* ANTHROPOSOPHY).

Theosophy [XXIV] (Wisdom of God) Refers to any system of thought concerned with divine revelation as its basis and whose central experience is of an inward illumination by the spirit of God. The wisdom takes God as its principle and seeks to apprehend the universe, in all its aspects as they are in God. It claims to embody those truths as belonging to all religions, but many manifestations of theosophy fall short of this ideal – the Theosophical Society's emphasis on HINDU teachings illustrates this. The word sometimes refers to secret knowledge transmitted throughout the ages as an esoteric philosophy known as 'the ancient wisdom' or theosophy. It can describe any articulate mystical system; it has been applied especially to KABBALAH, NEOPLATONISM and the system of JAKOB BOEHME. It now most often refers to the teachings of the THEOSOPHICAL SOCIETY.

Theotokos [XIII.D] 'The one who gave birth to God': a title of MARY the mother of JESUS. Nestorius, PATRIARCH of Constantinople (from 428 to 431) supported one of his subordinates, Anastasius, who opposed the use of the title; he warned that this title could easily be misunderstood and, while he did not absolutely forbid its use, recommen-

ded rather the title 'Christotokos', 'the one who gave birth to Christ'. Cyril, Pope of ALEXANDRIA, attacked Nestorius as a heretic and in 431 he was condemned and deposed at the COUNCIL of Ephesus.

Orthodox Christians have a great devotion to the Theotokos, and a wealth of poetry and iconography celebrates her role in salvation. The Hodigitria (the Signpost) is an ICON-type whose origin legend attributes it to St Luke; it shows Mary, robed in the red of love, gazing out of the icon as she points to the child Jesus whom she holds in her arm. As the Eleousa Mary (the Mother of Mercy) she holds the infant Jesus who gazes at her as she gazes tenderly at him. The Amolyntos (the Virgin Most Afflicted) wears sombre dark red robes and gazes in compassion at the child in her arms as angels in the skies above her reverently carry the instruments of the Passion.

In Orthodox worship Mary is venerated as ever-virgin and as sinless, as the fervent intercessor for humanity, and as the Queen of Heaven, 'more honoured than the Cherubim, more glorious than the Seraphim'. If Jesus Christ represents the ultimate descent of God into human life, Mary is the supreme moment in the ascent of humanity to meet God. The conception and birth of Christ is the fruit of her free decision, her humble submission to God's will. The title 'Theotokos' has remained a symbol of christological orthodoxy among Eastern Christians, and is one of the most common titles of Mary in Eastern worship; in the West, the corresponding titles 'Deipara' and 'Dei Genetrix' are less used and the title 'Mater Dei' (Mother of God) is far more common. [99]

Theravada [XI] The most usual name for the BUDDHISM of Ceylon (Sri Lanka) and south-east Asia. Theravada (Sanskrit: *Sthaviravada*), 'doctrine of the elders', was upheld by one party in the first Buddhist schism (4th century BCE). Although some scholars believe the MAHAYANA to originate ultimately from the opposing MAHASANGHI-KAS, all extant branches of the Buddhist order (SANGHA) derive from these original elders. The term is applied to one particular branch, a variety of Vibhajjavada (Sanskrit: *Vibhajyavada*), 'doctrine of analysis', which claimed to preserve the authentic teachings of the original elders. This school was strong in ancient Ceylon; in fact the early history of the Theravada outside the island is not well known. In the 5th century CE it was widely distributed in southern India and south-east Asia, but the most authoritative centre was the Mahavihara at Anuradhapura in Ceylon.

The Theravada closed its scriptural canon (TIPITAKA) in the 1st century BCE, preserving the use of a Middle Indian language (PALI). A more archaic scriptural tradition strengthened its claim to be a more authentic preserver of the teaching. The classical form of Theravada doctrine was established between the 5th and 10th centuries CE by a series of Pali commentators, notably BUDDHAGHOSA and DHAMMAPALA, from the mainland as well as from Ceylon. A later school flourished in the 12th and 13th centuries. By this time standard Pali verses and chants had been established for many ritual and devotional purposes, following an earlier tradition of chants (*paritta*) for healing and exorcism. The combination of Mahavihara doctrinal orthodoxy with new devotional forms replacing brahmanic ritual (*see* BRAHMANS) and MAHAYANA ceremonial proved effective both in SIN-HALESE BUDDHISM and in SOUTH-EAST ASIA (*see* BUDDHISM IN).

Classical Theravada recognizes the three alternative goals of ARAHAT, PACCEKABUDDHA and fully awakened BUDDHA. It is usually the path of the disciple (*savaka*; San-skrit: *shravaka*) to Arahatship which is set forth, but a *bodhisatta* (Sanskrit: BODHISATTVA) path to Buddhahood is recognized (*see* PARAMITA). Theravada differs from the Mahayana in rejecting the suitability of the *bodhisatta* role for all and not accepting the authority of the Mahayana scriptures. The path of Arahatship is not considered selfish, but as 'beneficial for both self and others'.

Thnetoi Anthropoi [XVI] Mortal men, mortals (*brotoi*). There was no consistent myth of human creation, only different tales about the following: the origin of woman and of earlier divinely created superior races (*see* KAKON); a flood, after which the sole survivors, Deukalion and Pyrrha (parents of Hellen, the Greeks' eponymous ancestor), turned stones into people; and the minor god Prometheus, humankind's champion and benefactor, who created men from clay. Humans' position in the universe (COSMOS) was considered to be humble, and an unbridgeable gap separated them from gods (THEOI). Another tendency, that became predominant in Hellenistic times, blurred the limits, so that, for example, (to begin with some exceptional) men were believed to become HEROES after death and monarchs were deified (*see* POLITIKE). Orphism (*see* ORPHEUS) ascribed a divine spark to mortals: they sprang from the ashes of the Titans who had devoured Dionysos-Zagreus (*see* COSMOS). Gods were thought to intervene in men's life; Zeus and fate somehow determined events, but humans were thought to have free will – a paradox challenged by Hellenistic astrological (*see* ASTROLOGY) and Stoic (*see* PHILOSOPHIA) determinism. [9: 155–6; 10: 74–83; 20: 131–4; 27: 144–52]

Thomas Christians [XIII.D] India, according to the apocryphal *Acts of the Apostle Judas Thomas* (*c*.200 CE), was the field of mission of Thomas, one of the twelve; accordingly, the Christians of the Malabar coast (Kerala State in south-west India) regard him as their founder and honour his tomb at Maylapur, near Madras. Kosmas Indikopleustes found Christians in this area in the 6th century and there is nothing improbable about the suggestion that Christianity spread quickly in the wake of the Jewish traders in southern Asia. The Thomas Christians originally belonged to the CHURCH OF THE EAST; for this reason Syriac, the Aramaic dialect of Mesopotamian Edessa, was their liturgical language. The majority of them now use Malayalam. Syriac liturgy and theology (both poetical and literalist) are still studied in the seminaries of Kerala, especially at the Ecumenical Research Institute, SEERI, which organizes international conferences in the subject. The Indian Christians who are reunited at such conferences are divided in their ecclesiastical allegiance, some 'Nestorian', others 'Jacobite', others ROMAN CATHOLIC and others independent, with further subdivisions; for example, the 'Jacobites' are divided into those obedient to the SYRIAN ORTHODOX PATRIARCH of Antioch and those who insist on regional autonomy. The bone of contention between these latter two groups is alleged to be the gift, by Victoria of England, of £800 to the said Patriarch for use in India; the rightful administrator of this sum has yet to be determined by the courts of justice. Further division is caused by the CASTE-like differentiation between northerners and southerners, who maintain a separate group-loyalty. The Portuguese, who once administered this coast, at first accepted and later rejected the particularity of the Thomas Christians' traditions; the Vatican had sometimes been reluctant to admit local customs and languages (Malayalam and Syriac), but with the Second Vatican Council came a change of heart. There are said to be as many as 3 million people in all the churches which are known collectively as those of the Thomas Christians, more than 2 million of them in COMMUNION with Rome; the 'Mar Tuma Church' belongs to the ANGLICAN Communion. [6; 108; 116; 120]

Thomism [XIII.C] The theological school which basically follows the teaching developed by Thomas Aquinas (c.1225–74) and which has, until recently, enjoyed officially a dominant position in Roman Catholic theological instruction (see ROMAN CATHOLICISM). Aquinas was a Dominican philosopher and theologian, whose many works culminated in the *Summa contra Gentiles* (a missionary textbook in which he defends NATURAL THEOLOGY) and the unfinished *Summa theologica*. In these he used the recently rediscovered works of Aristotle to produce a systematic presentation of Christian theology. According to Aquinas, certain truths about the existence and nature of GOD can be determined by natural reason although they are also normatively revealed (see ARGUMENTS FOR THE EXISTENCE OF GOD). Other truths, however, lie beyond reason's competence (although they are not contrary to it) and are knowable only through revelation. The influence of Aristotle is particularly seen in Aquinas' treatment of the attributes of God. His doctrines of God as unmoved, impassible and simple may follow from Aristotelian principles but lie uneasily with Christian views of God as a loving agent. [5: 12]

Thor [VII] The cult of Thor was very popular in the VIKING age, particularly in western Scandinavia, and many people and places were named after him. Like the GERMANIC Donar (Anglo-Saxon Thunor), he was a sky-god, controlling winds and storms, and was associated with the oak. Thursday was his day. His hammer represented lightning and he guarded the Aesir from attack. He protected his worshippers, and presided over the Law Assembly; oaths were sworn on his sacred ring. He was pictured as a red-bearded figure with fiery eyes and a huge appetite, drawn by goats in a wagon which rattled across the sky, causing thunder [3: III]. Small hammers were worn as Amulets in the late Viking age, and hammer and swastika were carved on memorial stones as his symbols. Many tales, serious and comic, were told of his encounters with Frost-giants and his fishing for the World-Serpent [3a: 79–84]. He was to perish when he slew the serpent at Ragnarok.

Three Ways [XIII.D] Traditional Christian spiritual theology distinguishes three ways of progress to perfection: the purgative, the illuminative and the unitive. These are sometimes thought of as three successive stages, sometimes as three aspects of a single process. (*See* Mysticism, christian.) [20]

Thunderbird [v] A widely recurring figure of Amerindian mythology, cult and art. An intermediary, celestial spirit (occasionally pitted against chthonian beings), the thunderbird is usually conceived of as an eagle or great bird that produces thunder by flapping its wings and lightning by opening and closing its eyes. In eastern North America, thunderbirds are often four in number, one for each of the cosmic quarters. [8: IV]

Tibetan Astrology [xxxv] Three different Buddhist astrological systems were practised in Tibet. One, *kar tsi*, was derived from the system of the Kalachakra Tantra (2), which entered Tibet from the mystic kingdom of Shambhala, via India. Calculations in this system are based on 9 planets, 12 residences (zodiacal signs) and 27 constellations. The second system, *jung tsi*, was originated by the Bodhisattva Manjushri, and introduced from China. Here calculations are based on the five elements of wood, fire, earth, metal and water; it has a 12-year cycle, with each year corresponding to an animal and the eight trigrams of divination of the *I Ching* (Book of Changes; *see* Confucian canon). The third system, *wang char*, was originally thought to have been set out by Shiva, and was introduced to Tibet from India. It relates to a type of Numerology, and uses circular diagrams which have a talismanic value (*see* Astrology; Astrology (indian)). [14]

Tibetan Religions [xxxv] Two principal religious traditions have appeared in recorded Tibetan history: Bon and Buddhism. Although the Bon tradition represents the oldest forms of Tibetan religion, it has in the course of time been severely modified, to the point where it now resembles a Buddhist sect. The introduction of Buddhism was gradual, occurring over four centuries (from the 7th to the 11th centuries CE), largely through the agency of Indian masters such as Padmasambhava and Atisha and Tibetan scholars such as Marpa Lotsava. Thus in general terms Tibetan Buddhism, despite a certain influence from China and Central Asia, represents Buddhist theory and practice as it had developed in India over the first 1,500 years of its existence.

Four major sects have dominated Buddhism in Tibet: Kagyu, Sakya, Nyingma and Gelug. Each sect possesses its own particular lineages of ritual, meditational and philosophical teachings and monastic organization. However, all share the triple division of doctrine and practice into the three *yanas* ('vehicles'; Tibetan: *theg-pa*) of Hinayana, Mahayana and *tantrayana* (*see* Tantra (2)). [24]

T'ien [XII] This Chinese term, usually translated as Heaven, refers to the absolute principle or supreme being controlling the universe. *T'ien* was worshipped by Chinese rulers from the beginning of the Chou dynasty (1027 BCE) onwards (*see* SHANG TI). As an anthropomorphic popular deity *T'ien* is worshipped as the Jade Emperor (*Yu Huang*) (*see* CHINESE PANTHEON). *T'ien* is also used in a more abstract sense as fate, destiny or the operation of purely natural forces (*see* HSUN TZU). [7: VI, 116–23; 34: III, 30–32; 39: I, 15–18; 94: II, 12–31; 99: I, 4–5]

T'ien-T'ai [XII] A scholastic and eclectic school of CHINESE BUD-DHISM, founded by Hui Ssu (515–77 CE) and Chih I (Chih K'ai) (538–97), based principally upon the Lotus Sutra (*Saddharmapundarika*) and on Chih I's two commentaries on it, and upon Hui Ssu's 'Method of Concentration and Insight in the Mahayana' (*Ta Ch'eng Chih Kuan Fa Men*). The basic doctrine is that of the Threefold Truth, which asserts that *dharmas* (*see* DHAMMA) are: (1) empty (*see* EMP-TINESS), because they are without self or being of their own; (2) existing temporarily by depending on causes and conditions; and (3) inter-mediate, because they are empty and exist at the same time. Hence things are both distinct and also part of a unified organic whole. This idea was developed into the teaching of the '3,000 realms in one thought moment'. In the 10 levels of exist-ence (of BUDDHAS, BODHISATTVAS, PRATYEKABUDDHAS, ARAHATS, gods, demons, humans, hungry ghosts, animals, beings in HELLS), each level shares the characteristics of the other levels, giving 100 realms. Each of these has 10 charac-teristics of suchness (*tathata*), giving 1,000 realms. Each 1,000 is divided into living beings, elements (*skand-has*) and space, giving 3,000. All these 3,000 realms of existence interpenetrate and entail each other,

and in every single thought-moment each of these realms is immanent. According to Hui Ssu the imma-nence of the 'real suchness' (*Bhuta-tathata*) and the 'womb of the Buddhas' (*Tathagata-garbha*) in all realms, *dharmas* and beings, can be experienced by the method of con-centration and insight [7: XXIV, 396–405; 24: XIII, 309–28; 35: IX, 360–83]. According to Chih I, all the different doctrines and methods contained in the Buddhist *sutras* were taught by the BUDDHA at dif-ferent periods of his career for beings at different levels of understanding, hence all the *sutras* could be regar-ded as the authentic word of the Buddha. This view was systematized into the theory of the five periods and the eight teachings. (*see* TEN-DAI). [15: XI, 305–13]

Tijanis [XIX] A SUFI ORDER of con-siderable influence in northern and western Africa, founded in the Maghreb by Ahmad al-Tijani (1737–1815). Al-Tijani claimed that he received permission to found his order directly from the Prophet MUHAMMAD in a vision and that he was the last or 'seal' of the saints (*see* WALI). Unlike other Sufis, Tijanis are forbidden to affiliate with other orders. The JIHAD leader, 'Umar b. Sa'id al-Futi (1794–1864), was a major proselytizer of the Tijani order in 19th-century west Africa (*see* AFRICA, ISLAM IN). Subsequent sub-branches have been important, such as the Hamallists, founded by Ahmad Hamallah (1883–1943), and the Niass Tijanis, founded by Ibra-him Niass (1902–76). The Niass branch of the order is based in Sen-egal but has significant followings throughout Africa, especially in Ghana, Nigeria and Sudan; from the 1980s, it began to establish *zawiyas* (*see* SUFI INSTITUTIONS) in the USA among Afro-American Muslims. [63; 90; 125]

Tillich, Paul [XIII.c] (1886–1965) Theologian; studied at Berlin,

Tübingen and Halle. After teaching theology at Marburg, Dresden and Frankfurt, he had to leave Germany in 1933 because of his religious socialism. He became professor of Philosophical Theology at Union Theological Seminary, New York. His theology, which was considerably influenced by the ideas of F. W. J. Schelling (1775–1854) and by EXISTENTIALISM, attempted to correlate faith and culture. He maintained that God is being-itself, not one being among others, and that all other statements about God are essentially symbolic. [3; 20]

Tipitaka [XI] (Pali; Sanskrit: *Tripitaka*) The name for the canonical collection of those BUDDHIST scriptures which are regarded as 'the word of the BUDDHA' (*buddhavacana*). For several centuries after the death of the Buddha (*see* GOTAMA) the Tipitaka was largely preserved by oral transmission and memorization (cf. SANGITI) by monks who specialized in particular sections. A number of different recensions existed in ancient times, but only one version survives complete in an ancient Indian language, namely the PALI Tipitaka of the THERAVADA school; this comprises some 29 separate works, amounting to over 50 volumes in printed editions. Large sections of other recensions do survive, however, in Chinese and Tibetan translation. The term *tipitaka* means 'three baskets', which refers to the classification of texts according to the three divisions of 'monastic discipline' (VINAYA), 'discourses' (SUTTA) and 'further teaching' (ABHIDHAMMA). There is substantial agreement among the ancient schools over the content of the Vinaya-pitaka and Sutta-pitaka but rather less agreement over the content of the Abhidhamma-pitaka. This suggests that the two former collections are generally older and represent the teachings of Gotama Buddha more directly than the Abhidhamma. With the rise of the MAHAYANA further 'discourses of the Buddha' were produced (*see* MAHAYANA SUTRAS, PRAJNAPARAMITA) which the non-Mahayana schools declined to acknowledge as authentic 'words of the Buddha' and thus excluded from their Tripitakas. These *sutras* do, however, come to form a significant part of the later Chinese Tripitaka and Tibetan KANJUR. [51: 141–91]

Tirthankara [XX] 'Maker of the ford': designation of each of the chain of 24 saving teachers which, according to the JAIN religion, appears in the course of every world age and forms the ford (*tirtha*), the community of monks and nuns, laymen and laywomen, which enables human beings to gain liberation. Each *tirthankara* attains his lofty status as a result of a very rare form of *karma* (*see* KARMA (JAIN DOCTRINE)) which is in turn brought about by 16 types of assiduously practised religious actions. *Tirthankaras* are distinguished from the ordinary enlightened person (KEVALIN) by the miraculous phenomena which attend them. According to Jain tradition, all *tirthankaras* are human beings, members of the warrior class who renounce the world through being awakened to their destiny by the gods. After a period of austerity, at the end of which and without the aid of a teacher they attain omniscient enlightenment, they reactivate the eternal doctrine of non-violence, found a community and then die, achieving liberation and freedom from rebirth (*see* MOKSHA (JAIN DOCTRINE)).

The names of the *tirthankaras* of this world era are Rishabha, Ajita, Sambhava, Abhinandana, Sumati, Padmaprabha, Suparshva, Candraprabha, Suvidhi or Pushpadanta, Shitala, Shreyamsa, Vasupujya, Vimala, Ananta, Dharma, Shanti, Kunthu, Ari, Malli (according to the SHVETAMBARA sect, a woman), Munisuvrata, Nami, Nemi, PARSHVA and MAHAVIRA. Each of them has a distinguishing mark by which icons can be identified. [4: 1; 10: 1; 14: VIII]

Tirtha-yatra [XVII] 'Fording a crossing to the divine': pilgrimage, an activity highly meritorious in HINDUISM; although not enjoined for salvation, it has become one of its most basic activities. Throughout the Indian subcontinent pilgrimages are constantly taking place on every scale, whether to local, regional or to all-India sacred sites like Kashi (Banaras), Prayag (Allahabad), Hardvar, Mathura, Ayodhya, Dvaraka in Gujarat or Conjeevaram in the south. *Tirtha* means a fording-place (and *yatra* a journey) but the term now includes all sacred sites, although the majority of major sites are associated with rivers. Each major site has its own particular speciality, usually described in texts and manuals relating to it which enumerate the particular benefits that derive from performing particular rituals at particular spots on the site at particular times. Almost invariably the pilgrim will perform a *pradakshina* (circumambulation) of the sacred object in a clockwise direction, and will be guided in what to do by one of the priests or other functionaries who serve the pilgrims. Some sites are particularly beneficial for removing sins, some for performing obsequies for the dead (*shraddhas*), some for achieving *darshana*, an experience of a deity; some, especially more regional or local sites, are famous for curing blindness or infertility or for the attainment of some other kind of worldly end. There are many thousands of sites throughout the subcontinent to which some form of pilgrimage is made. At many sites, at auspicious dates, there are religious fairs, *melas*, the most famous of which are the huge *kumbha melas*, four of which take place every 12 years, one at each of Prayag, Hardvar, Ujjain, where it is called Simhastha, and Nasik in Maharashtra. To these *melas* come

millions of Hindus; prominent among them are the *sadhus*, the monks of the various ascetic orders, to be with whom is to attain additional blessings. Pilgrimage not only provides the pilgrim with a variety of religious and spiritual benefits, it defines the sacred geography of the subcontinent and has a very strong integrative effect within Hinduism. [16; 17]

Tisarana [XI] (Pali: Sanskrit: *trisharana*). A BUDDHIST term meaning 'the three refuges'. These are 'the three jewels' (Pali: *tiratana*, Sanskrit: *triratna*) of BUDDHA, DHAMMA and SANGHA. Going to the three jewels for refuge constitutes the essential act of becoming a Buddhist and is realized by the recitation of a three-fold formula ('I go for refuge to the Buddha . . . to the Dhamma . . . to the Sangha') which is itself repeated three times. Although the act of going for refuge does not constitute a once and for all initiation into Buddhism, it is nevertheless a significant ritual and devotional expression of faith and trust in the three jewels. The refuges and precepts (*see* SILA) may be formally and publicly requested from a member of the Buddhist order or they may be recited privately. [80: 53–85; 9]

Tjurunga [XXIX] The Aranda term for a type of cult object, in AUSTRALIAN RELIGION. The term also encompasses the sacred conceptions, traditions and actions associated with each particular object. Usually an elongated board with rounded or pointed ends, it is sometimes a stone slab, or a shell, or even a tuber (such as a yam). The name *tjurunga* indicates a connection with a spirit being, and when a sacred board is used as a bullroarer the voice of the indwelling spirit is heard. The term can also be applied to the small implement used in sorcery for causing death from a distance ('pointing the bone'; *see also*

Melanesian POISEN). [21: 140–59; 27: 612–13; 28]

Tlaloc [xxv] The most popular and widespread deity in Mesoamerican culture was Tlaloc (Chac in Mayan culture), the fertilizing rain-god. Tlaloc was often conceived in quadruple and quintuple forms called the *tlaloques*, each assigned to one of the sacred directions and given a sacred colour. This pattern usually involved a pre-eminent Tlaloc, with dwarfish *tlaloques* named, for instance, Opochtli, Nappatecuhtli, Yauhqueme, Tomiauhtecuhtli [17: 414–16]. The *tlaloques* were believed to dwell in the prominent peaks, where rain clouds emerged from caves to fertilize the land through rain, rivers, pools and storms. Tlaloc's power was also manifested in the thunder, lightning, snow and cold sicknesses which threatened the community. One mountain, called Mount Tlaloc in Spanish colonial times (after 1521), was believed to be the original source of the water and vegetation which nurtured human beings. The supreme importance of this deity is reflected in the fact that his shrine was placed alongside HUITZILOPOCHTLI's at the TEMPLO MAYOR in the centre of Tenochtitlan. At the same time, Tlaloc was the god of the masses, who worshipped him in every agricultural community in the land [7: VIII].

Two other major gods were intimately associated with Tlaloc: Chalchiuhtlicue, the goddess of waters, and Ehecatl, the wind-god [2: 108]. Chalchiuhtlicue was usually identified with the maize-earth gods while Ehecatl, an aspect of the great god QUETZALCOATL, was known as *in tlachpancauh in tlaloque*, 'the roadsweeper of the rain-gods', meaning that Ehecatl's forceful presence announced the coming of the fertilizing rains. Tlaloc's supreme importance for fertility is reflected in the murals of Tlalocan, the rain-god's paradise where sea animals, spirits, butterflies and moisture mingle together in a realm of abundance [19: 83–8]. This abundance demanded valuable HUMAN SACRIFICES, in the form of children, at the various feasts of Tlaloc, which took place in different towns and cities. In one major festival the rulers of the Aztec empire solemnly participated in a special ceremony to sanctify the waters for the coming agricultural year. [7: 158]

Tlamatinime [xxv] 'Knowers of things', the teachers and philosophers who transmitted the revered ancient teachings of Nahuatl culture in the Calmecacs of the Aztec empire (1425–1520 CE) (*see* MESOAMERICAN RELIGIONS). They were responsible for composing, painting and articulating the moral teachings, sacred histories, calendric lore and esoteric wisdom which had been inherited from the Toltecs of the Classic period (*see* TOLLAN) [17: XVII]. They were considered the embodiment of knowledge, which they taught in didactic oral presentations called HUEHUETLATOLLI and pictorial forms to the future nobles and rules of towns and cities. They used refined metaphorical forms called 'flower and song' to reflect upon the transitory nature of human existence, the true nature of god, the destiny of human life and the precise character of cosmological order. One group of *tlamatinime* is reputed to have criticized in sophisticated poetic forms the mystico-militaristic attitudes of the Aztec state.

Tlatoani [xxv] 'Chief speakers', the supreme rulers of Nahuatl-speaking groups in Mesoamerica. They controlled civil, military, fiscal and religious affairs in towns and cities. The Aztec Tlaotani [10: 192–3, 236–42; 17: 351–5] was responsible for ensuring the stability and renewal of cosmic order and was considered the living representative of HUITZILOPOCHTLI, the Aztec patron deity. Among his ritual functions was the redistribution of warriors' uniforms and arms to nobles, for whom he held lavish military banquets. In special festivals, as at the periodic inauguration of the TEMPLO MAYOR, the Tlatoani acted as a high priest to initiate massive HUMAN SACRIFICES of captive warriors (*see* TEOPIXQUE).

Toba Religion [xxIII] Traditional mythology of the Toba (Argentina and Bolivia) stressed cosmic cataclysms by water, fire, darkness or snowfall. Supernatural beings, classified into land, sky, earth and water beings, were both potentially dangerous and potentially helpful to humans. Since they significantly influenced human existence, it was important to maintain a proper relationship with them, through the celebration of the great algaroba fruit festivals and through the curing powers of SHAMANS. Dreams and visions were an important means of access to the spirit-world. Since the beginning of this century, Toba have engaged in MILLENARIAN AND PROPHETIC MOVEMENTS and rebellions. PENTECOSTALISM, to which many Toba now adhere, has supported mythological concerns with imminent world catastrophe and the curing power of religious specialists. [41]

Tohunga [xxIX] A specialist of the sacred, in POLYNESIAN RELIGION. The *tohunga* is priest, medium, exorcist, healer and prophet. He officiates at birth, initiation and death rites, and leads worship at the MARAE. He protects his people from the effects of violated *tapu* (TABU) and from sorcery or evil curses (*makutu*). Tribal lore and sacred knowledge (brought from the highest heaven by TANE in three baskets) was revealed by *tohungas* to initiates in houses of sacred learning (Maori: *whare wananga*). [6; 7; 16]

Tollan [xxv] The ideal city-state of Mesoamerica's golden age, ruled by TOPILTZIN QUETZALCOATL and the creator-god QUETZALCOATL [16:

80–4]. In myth and sacred history, Tollan was pictured as the place where the concepts and institutions associated with great cities were crystallized. In Tollan, the calendar, ceremonial architecture, medicine, astrology, wisdom, art and rituals were developed to an exquisite degree. This sense of excellence is reflected in the related terms, *toltecatl*, meaning 'skilled artist', and *toltecayotl*, signifying artistic creativity of a superior quality [6: 24–47]. Historically, Tollan has been identified with the city of Tollan Xicocotitlan (also called Tula), which prospered between the 9th and 11th centuries CE [10: 121–6]. Tollan literally means 'place of reeds', but the term came to signify a place of abundance, a congregation of people, a metropolis. The prestige that was attached to this symbolic meaning is reflected in the number of cities, including Tollan Teotihuacan, Tollan Cholollan (*see* CHOLOLLAN), Tollan Tenochtitlan and Tollan Chalco, that derived part of their authority from an association with the Toltec traditions of the great mythical and historical Tollan.

Tonalpohualli [xxv] The 'count of days' or ritual calendar, which guided many of the lavish religious events in Mesoamerican ceremonial centres (*see* MESOAMERICAN CITY). It was also used for astronomical computations, the casting of horoscopes and the determination of lucky and unlucky days. It was consulted in *tonalamatls* (books of days) for every important event in family, political, religious and imperial matters. The *tonalamatls* recorded, in elaborate pictorial form, 260 named days, each designated by a number and a sign taken from a revolving system of 20 day signs and 13 numbers. The ritual year consisted of 20 13-day weeks in which each day was assigned a sacred colour, cardinal direction, a Lord of the Day, a Lord of the Night and a sacred bird. The *tonalpohualli* system shows that, for

Mesoamerican people, time exuded supernatural character and influence. A specialist, the *tonalpohuaque*, functioned mainly to determine the lucky and unlucky days, through careful examination of the five special characteristics associated with each day. This calendar system intermeshed with the solar calendar, *xihuitl* ('grass'), which consisted of 18 months of 20 days, each completed by five unnamed days to make a 365-day year. The new year's day of these two calendars coincided once every 52 years (*see* NEW FIRE CEREMONY), which constituted an Aztec century, *xiumolpilli*, and the critical period of cosmic renewal. [2: 16–22; 17: XIII]

Topiltzin Quetzalcoatl [xxv] One of the most widely taught histories in Mesoamerican culture (*see* MESOA-MERICAN CITY) narrated the career of the Toltec priest-king Topiltzin Quetzalcoatl, 'Our Young Prince the Feathered Serpent', also known as Ce Acatl (One Reed), Naxcitl (Four-Footed) and Tepeuhqui (Mighty One), who ruled in a golden age in TOLLAN, where ceremonial order, agricultural abundance, social harmony and artistic excellence constituted the archetypal sacred city [14: 40–2]. Topiltzin Quetzalcoatl, who was revered as a semi-divine priest-king, refounded the 10th-century capital of Tollan on a new religious system based on an esoteric theology and an intense ritual system excluding HUMAN SACRIFICE. He was credited in Toltec oral and pictorial traditions with the invention of the calendar, jewel-working and all artistic excellence [7: I]. The combined sources paint a marvellous picture of his kingdom and sacred career. His ceremonial centre had four jewelled temples associated with four cosmic regions (*see* CEMA-NAHUAC). He made ritual sacrifices on four sacred mountains near the city and in one ecstatic vision communicated directly with the Lord of Duality (OMETEOTL), who dwelt in the highest heaven. He was a law-giver who dispensed his authority from a sacred mountain to all regions of his kingdom. Into this paradisal city came an enemy sorcerer, Tezcatlipoca, whose magical mirror and tricks enticed Topiltzin Quetzalcoatl into breaking his priestly vows and betraying his royal authority. After burying his treasures, Topiltzin Quetzalcoatl fled to Tlapallan, the sacred shore where, in alternate versions, he sacrificed himself on a funeral pyre and became the Morning Star (*Tlahuizcalpante-cuhtli*), or disappeared across the sea on a raft of serpents promising to return one day and restore his ideal kingdom. This tradition had immense influence on the Aztecs, whose high priests were called QUETZALCOATL and who initially identified the Spanish invader Cortes (1485–1547) as the returning Toltec king who would restore the wonders of Tollan. [10: 324–5]

TOPY [xxviii] Thee Temple Ov Psychic Youth originated in England in the early 1980s around the time that the pop musician Genesis P Orridge left 'Throbbing Gristle' to start his own group, 'Psychic TV'. The writings of Aleister Crowley and William Burroughs are among the main inspirations for TOPY beliefs, but other influences include paganism, the Church of Satan, surrealism, and strands of anarchism, BUDDHISM and any ideas that are anti-dogma, anti-bureaucracy or anti-absolute-truth. Individualism and individual responsibility for all aspects of one's life are stressed, and MAGIC, including 'ritual sex magick', is seen as a tool for liberating an individual's energy. TOPY had effectively ceased to exist by the mid-1990s. [5: 212–13]

Torah [xxii] Literally, 'teaching'; the most general term in JUDAISM for the divine teaching. In its narrow sense it refers to the Pentateuch, or the first five books of the Hebrew

BIBLE: *Genesis, Exodus, Leviticus, Numbers* and *Deuteronomy*. Torah is also used to refer to the whole of the Hebrew Bible, to the oral teachings of Judaism, or – in its widest sense – to the whole of traditional Jewish law and lore. The common English translation of Torah as 'Law' misrepresents the concept, giving a narrow legal connotation to the much broader Jewish idea of revelation. Torah is part of an open-ended system; as such it requires study, and new insights into the world of God must be sought so that it can be applied to a variety of differing circumstances. The Torah is seen by Judaism as the product of the COVENANT by God with Israel, God who, as one of the benedictions of the liturgy puts it, 'has chosen us from amongst all the nations and given us His Torah' [64:5]. It was revealed to the Israelites during their wanderings in the wilderness through the agency of MOSES. It is of a twofold nature: the written Torah of the Hebrew Bible and the oral Torah [72: IV], which was eventually written down in rabbinical literature (*see* RABBI) [46: III]. The scroll of the Pentateuch read publicly in the SYNAGOGUE is called a *sefer Torah*, or Book of the Torah. Orthodox Judaism, while applying traditional teachings to novel situations created by modern technology, takes a very conservative stance on Torah: the divine teaching is sacrosanct, and cannot simply be changed or abandoned at will. It can, however, be reinterpreted by competent authorities, who bring the Torah insights of the past to bear on the present. [11; 38; 70: VII]

Toshogu Shrine [XXI] (Japan) The burial site of the early Tokugawa family shoguns (generals), in a heavily forested part of Tochigi prefecture at Nikko, situated below the SACRED MOUNTAIN Nantai, Lake Chuzenji and Kegon waterfalls [32: 70, 101; 35: 262–87]. In a form of ancestor-worship, construction of

elaborate buildings was started in 1634 by Kyoto craftsmen, on the orders of Tokugawa Iemitsu (1603–51) for his grandfather Ieyasu (1542–1616). Expenses were unlimited; the finest workmen were used. The largest BUDDHIST temple at Nikko is of the TENDAI sect and is associated with mountain worship. The original shrine (*see* SHINTO SHRINES) is called Futaarasan (meaning Mt Nantai). Ritual climbing and the burial of *sutras* (*Kyozuka*) for religious benefits were popular in the Edo period (1615–1868).

Totem [XXXIV] An animal or plant species, or other natural phenomenon, regarded as specifically related to the origin, welfare and/or organization of a human (usually descent) group [43: 58–60, 199]. The Ojibwa (ALGONQUIN tribe, North America) word provides the technical term 'totemism' for a belief system involving, e.g., TABU and increase rites, and some idea of descent from a mythical totemic ancestor (e.g. among Australian tribes) [58: 85–6]. Among the many theories of totemism [158: 48; 183: 113–14], its symbolic function in social cohesion was stressed by Durkheim [48; 58: 231; 158: 30; 183: 55–6]. In contrast, STRUCTURALISTS like Lévi-Strauss [105; 109; 158: 48] emphasize the role of distinctive and ambivalent totem-concepts in the communication of meaning.

Transcendental Meditation (TM) [XXVIII] After graduating in physics, Maharishi Mahesh Yogi (1911/18–) studied for 13 years with Swami Brahmananda Saraswati Maharaj (1869–1953), who rediscovered the technique known as transcendental meditation. In 1957, Maharishi launched a 'spiritual regeneration' movement to teach TM around the world. The movement gathered momentum in the West after the Beatles and other celebrities began meditating in the late 1960s; the World Plan (to spread the teachings of the Science of Creative Intelligence) was announced in 1972; an advanced SIDDHA YOGA programme (including special training in levitation) was introduced in the late 1970s, and the Ayurvedic Medical Programme in the 1980s. The Maharishi International University in Iowa offers Bachelor's and Master's degrees. By the early 1990s, over a million individuals are said to have taken the basic TM course. Many claims and counter-claims have been made by its practitioners and its critics about the effectiveness of TM for both meditators and the surrounding society. [5: 213–14; 24; 25: 65–71; 41: IV/N; 42: 945–7; 53: 163–84; 62]

Trickster [V] In North American Indian mythology, the trickster often presents a light-hearted variant of the CULTURE HERO. Typically a type of demiurge who continues, rather than initiates, the task of creation (see CREATION MYTHS), this curious figure portrays a mixture of conflicting character traits, alternately sly, cunning, constructive and generally well disposed to mankind, as well as amoral, frivolous, a prankster and highly sexed [18]. The trickster (also 'trickster-transformer') may be theriomorphic (common forms include coyote, blue jay, mink, hare and raven) or may display human features, although the latter are often exaggerated or ill-defined. Occasionally thought to be of divine origin (e.g. Algonquian Glooscap), the trickster is often referred to in myth as 'Old One', but this is indicative less of advanced years than of his timelessness. Albeit his techniques may include deceit, stupidity and laziness, the trickster often unwittingly achieves results that benefit humankind (e.g. regulation of the seasons, domestication of animals) or provides instruction necessary for human existence (e.g. the use of fire, the art of agriculture, the practice of

medicine). The trickster's presence in myth and ritual often provides a comic relief which eases the solemnity of such settings. [8: III]

Trimurti [XVII] 'Triple form'; the three Hindu gods BRAHMA, VISHNU and SHIVA viewed as a triad, embodying the three cosmic forces of creation, preservation and destruction. Although the grouping was originally perhaps an artificial one, designed, like the figure of HARIHARA, to overcome sectarian conflict, it is now a living part of Hindu worship. The three consorts, SARASVATI, LAKSHMI and PARVATI, are regarded as embodying the female aspects (see SHAKTI) of these cosmic forces. In practice the Hindu will offer devotion (BHAKTI) to one deity in particular (cf. ISHTADEVA), while revering the others as manifestations of the same supreme reality (BRAHMAN). Composite forms such as *trimurti* are probably more popular among Shaivas than among Vaishnavas [but see 4: 198–9].

Trinity [XIII.B] Although rooted in Jewish MONOTHEISM, Christian belief in the divinity of JESUS Christ and the HOLY SPIRIT led to the development of the doctrine of the Trinity. This states that one God reveals himself in the three 'persons' of Father, Son (Jesus Christ) and Holy Spirit [119]. These three persons are nevertheless regarded as a unity, sharing one 'substance'. The doctrine was eventually defined by early COUNCILS and theologians as 'three persons in one substance' (*homoousion*). This was an attempt to assert a real distinction between the persons (denied by e.g. Sabellius, *fl.* 3rd century CE) while maintaining their unity, equality and eternity (e.g. against ARIANISM, 4th century CE). For the Western Church the Holy Spirit proceeds from the Father 'and the Son' (the *'filioque'* clause added to the Nicene CREED). This is rejected by the EASTERN ORTHODOX CHURCH, which sees the 'procession' of the Spirit as being from the Father through the Son. The development of these doctrines has been constantly influenced by current philosophy, and in modern times the views described here have often been challenged (e.g. by PROCESS THEOLOGY). Even the DEATH OF GOD was proclaimed by some in the 1960s. There has also been a recurring Christian tradition of UNITARIANISM. (Cf. GOD, CHRISTIAN CONCEPT OF.) [69; 114: IV, V, X; 157: 575–7]

Tripartite Ideology [XXXVI] The theory of Georges Dumézil (1898–) and his followers that the earliest INDO-EUROPEANS had a hierarchically ordered tripartite (threefold) society which was precisely paralleled in the myths and epics of the world of the gods. In both society and myth the first, or priestly, sector was magico-religious, concerned with justice and sovereignty. The second, that of the warriors, was concerned with physical prowess or force; and the third was that of the productive workers who provided nourishment for the living world. Dumézil argues that because this social and mythical structure was inherent in the early Indo-European tradition its ideas are preserved in its daughter cultures, e.g. Greece, India, Iran, Rome and Scandinavia. The way in which Dumézil has applied this theory to his analysis of the respective religions has caused considerable scholarly debate. His critics consider that he has forced the evidence, for example in the way he has categorized deities. [43]

Tuatha de Danann [VII] The Irish name for a group of gods, 'Peoples of the goddess Danu'. Danu was confused with Anu, a beneficent goddess associated with the Irish province of Munster, both possibly derived from an early CELTIC mother-goddess (see MATRES). The group included LUG, the DAGDA, Nuadu 'of the Silver Arm', Gobniu

the Smith and Dian Cecht the Healer [27: 38, 52; 17: 57–61]. They overcame various enemies, but after the coming of CHRISTIANITY were said to retreat into the sid, the ancient burial mounds of Ireland. [17: 65]

Tukano Religion [XXIII] Tukano-speaking peoples inhabit the northwest Amazon and the eastern Colombian rainforest. Divided into numerous linguistic groups, they nevertheless express common religious concerns. Religious life revolves around the central importance of the sacred flutes and trumpets, representing the first ancestors, which are fundamental to initiation rituals and festivals of the ripening of fruits. Cosmology expresses a predominant concern with the themes of mortality and immortality, death and rebirth, and the conjunction of male and female principles in the creation and reproduction of culture. Lengthy narratives recount the journeys of Anaconda-canoes which brought the first ancestors to Tukanoan lands. SHAMANS and chanters are the principal specialists. MILLENARIAN traditions and missions have considerably altered religious life since the 19th century. [14; 26]

Tulku [XXXV] Tibetan for a teacher who has been identified as the reincarnation of a specific named previous teacher. In origin the term corresponds to the Sanskrit nairmanikakaya – 'transformation body' (see BUDDHA, BODIES OF). Such teachers reincarnate usually under their own control in fulfilment of their BODHISATTVA vow to help sentient beings. Often after their identification tulkus are taken to the monastery or location of their previous incarnation and trained to readopt their old position. The first identified tulku in Tibetan history was probably the Third Karmapa in the late 13th century, head of the Karma KAGYU school. Tulkus form an elite in Tibetan religious life, and the abbots and religious leaders are frequently (but not invariably) chosen from among the tulkus. The most famous example of a tulku is the DALAI LAMA. [28]

Tumbuna [xxix] A collective term in Melanesian pidgin for clan ancestors who, while they dwell in a spiritland, are constantly in touch with their living descendants. Spirits of the recently dead are honoured by funeral rites to ensure their continued support for the living. Ancestral spirits are invoked in the HAUS TAMBARAN and MALE CULT rituals and SINGSINGS, where they receive offerings of food and wealth. They make themselves present through dreams, mediums and diviners, and in sacred stones, MASKS and other objects. Obligations to ancestral spirits are the highest religious duties. They are believed to pass on from the creative gods and goddesses the power (MANA) which makes tribal rites and customs effective, bringing health, social harmony and material well-being (SALVATION, in religious terms). Neglect of the spirits invites disease, death and failure of crops [2; 14; 23; 29]. Prophet-led renewal movements (sometimes called CARGO CULTS) may involve attempts to placate ancestor-spirits believed to be withholding power and blessings or bestowing them on others.

Tun-Huang [xxxv] The *Tun-Huang* collection of Tibetan and Chinese manuscripts, discovered in the early years of the 20th century near the oasis of Tun-Huang in Chinese Turkestan, is important for the light it sheds on the early development of BUDDHISM in Tibet. It is likely that the Tibetan manuscripts, largely religious in content, are the debris of a clerical centre which flourished during the years of Tibetan occupation of the area between *c.*780 and 850 CE. Certain manuscripts include reference to the vital part played by the two Tibetan kings, Srongsten Gampo and Trisong Detsun, in the establishment of Buddhism, and also to the Indian Tantric master Padmasambhava, and are particularly important in constituting contemporary evidence of the latter's missionary role. Evidence is also provided as to the nature of the Buddhism being introduced: mention is made of both *sutra* and TANTRA (2) doctrines and of the cycle of the meditational deity Dorje Phurba and BARDO doctrine, both of which became prized teachings of the NYINGMA tradition. [15]

Tupian Religion [xxiii] Variability among Tupian cosmologies defies any attempt at generalization. Some groups have relatively undeveloped cosmologies; others, true theologies. All, however, have at least one characteristic in common: ambivalence (of the SHAMAN, of human society, of the gods), a principle which constitutes their culture. In the tripartite series of Tupian cosmology (animal–human–divinity, or nature–culture–supernatural), culture is thought of as an intercalated moment, a precarious space between the other two terms, a constant motion of transformation, or becoming other (animal or divine).

For the Araweté of north-eastern Brazil (one of the best-described of contemporary Tupian peoples), humans were 'abandoned' by the gods at the beginning of time when a cataclysm separated the different levels of the universe. Divinity is understood in the specific sense of these gods (*Maï*) who originally separated from humanity, but also in the wider sense of subject/transcendental cause. The gods are known especially through their song, vocalized by SHAMANS who bring the gods to earth in nightly rituals. The Araweté believe that the souls of the recently deceased are devoured by the gods and ultimately transformed into them; it is the destiny of humans, then, to be consumed and transformed into gods. [20; 36]

Turin Shroud [XIII.B] A cloth marked by the apparent image of a crucified man, claimed to be that of JESUS Christ. It was first recorded in France in the 1360s, but has been in Turin since 1578. Since relics of this kind were often faked in the middle ages to create or publicize PILGRIMAGE centres, the shroud would normally be explained in this way. Recent interest has been stimulated by scientific tests to determine its date and source, which resulted (1988) in apparently proving its medieval origin. The means by which the image was produced, however, are not explained.

Even if the image were proved to have been made by the body of Jesus Christ, its religious significance would remain debatable. In ROMAN CATHOLICISM relics of this kind are considered vehicles of divine grace (*see* SALVATION); but in PROTESTANTISM they are often thought of as an obstacle to direct communion with God. [206]

Typology [XXXIV] (1) A method of interpretation of sacred literature, in which characters or events from an earlier period (e.g. the Hebrew scriptures) are seen as prefiguring or foreshadowing others described or occurring later (e.g. the MESSIAH, or JESUS Christ in the New Testament (BIBLE)).

(2) In the study of religions, the method of analysis and classification according to type, in which Heinrich Frick (1893–1952) was a pioneer. Thus, 'founded' religions may be contrasted with those that 'developed'; religions may be grouped as tribal (primal) or national, or as 'world religions'; or as prophetic and mystical. These are 'ideal types' (in the sense in which Max Weber (1864–1920) used that term). [43: 12–14; 75: 25–9]

Tzitzit [XXII] Fringes worn at the corners of four-cornered garments by Jews, as commanded in the BIBLE (*Numbers* 15: 37–41), to remind them of God's commandments. Since four-cornered garments are not part of normal Jewish dress any more, a special four-cornered fringed prayer shawl (*tallit*) is worn for morning prayers. A smaller four-cornered fringed garment (*tallit katan*) is worn by traditional Jews as an undervest throughout the day. Women do not have to wear *tzitzit*. [14 vol. 15: 743, vol. 16: 1187]

U

Ulema, 'Ulama' [xix] 'Learned men', the body of religious and legal scholars in ISLAM. Members of this class have always been recruited by study under other recognized scholars in such institutions as AL-AZHAR in Cairo (*see also* MADRASA) [128: II–III, v], and cannot really be considered as a priestly caste. The *ulema* have nevertheless been generally recognized in Sunni Islam (*see* SUNNA) as custodians and interpreters of the corpus of sacred knowledge, often defending it against secular encroachments, even though they might at times be in receipt of official salaries [20 s.v.; 37 s.v.]. A parallel body in SHI'ISM is that of the *mujtahids* (*see* AYATULLAH).

Umbanda/Spiritism [III/XXVII] This is a comprehensive term for a syncretistic 'spiritist' complex characteristic of urban Brazil but expanding into Latin America. It features communication with spirits through mediums who are possessed in séances, in order to provide knowledge or power to deal with the personal problems brought by clients, who may then become regular cult members. The spirits are drawn eclectically from African ancestors or deities, from legendary figures among the African ex-slave population, from notable Amerindian leaders, from nature spirits in Brazilian tribal religions, from the Virgin MARY or the saints of Portuguese folk Catholicism, and from OCCULT powers and spirits that feature in Alan Kardec's (1804–69) French philosophic form of SPIRITUALISM that has been highly influential in

Brazil. The latter explains the appeal to the educated and upper classes; the spirits, who become equivalent to local Catholic patron saints, appeal to the masses. In Brazil members of Umbanda and Spiritism, which parallel elements in the same movement, generally have dual affiliation with the Roman Catholic church, in part because the Catholics offer status, and neither Umbanda nor Spiritism is given official status. Adherents do not see anything problematic in this dual affiliation. There are millions of Spiritists in Brazil, probably more than 4,000 centres in Sao Paulo alone.

Spiritualism had penetrated deep into Brazil by 1870. Originally it attracted intellectuals, then the white lower class, followed by those of mixed race and the blacks, who were admitted as long as they agreed to be in touch only with the white dead, not with their own forebears. Next the spirits of blacks and Amerindians were allowed to participate after they had been 'cleansed' during special Umbanda ceremonies. The black and mixed-race community in Brazil had great problems in acknowledging their origins in Africa, so negative an image had been accepted, so that their attitude to possession by African spirits was ambivalent. Often they re-routed the origins of their spirits to Egypt or India. From the 1950s Umbanda has become a religion of wide appeal, because since 1953 a *modus vivendi* has been achieved with the Roman Catholic Church. The Catholic elements of Umbanda have been emphasized, and the African elements are not so conspicuous. Because of this its membership has been widened, although it remains predominantly black.

Caboclo spirits are dead Brazilians; *preto velho* are African–Brazilian slave spirits; *crianca* are the spirits of dead children; *exu* are female spirits. All the spirits are potentially malign, except the *exu* who may develop enough spirituality to counteract the evil of the other categories. The final type of spirit in Umbanda merges YORUBA ORISHAS with Catholic SAINTS. This is typical of an African/Roman Catholic SYNCRETISM (*see also* VOODOO, SANGO). Spirit mediumship is central to Umbanda. It functions to help the individual to relate to the community of the 'other' world. While in SANTERIA possession is by Orishas, lesser spirits effect possession in Umbanda.

It is believed that all illnesses are spiritual in origin. Some may be caused by malign spirits, but *quimbanda* (sorcery) is the most likely cause. Spirit mediums can help counteract malign influence during trance with advice, often of a practical nature. Umbanda is not a revivalist cult (*see* REVIVAL). Umbanda has proved a powerful fusion of Africa, South America and Europe. [III 9; III 32; III 86; III 90; XXVII 4]

Unification Church [XXVIII] The Holy Spirit Association for the Unification of World Christianity was founded in Korea in 1954 by the Reverend Sun Myung Moon (1920–), but it did not have much success in the West until the early 1970s when Moon moved to America. The main tenets of Unification theology are to be found in the Divine Principle, which offers a special interpretation of the BIBLE with additional revelations from Moon. The Fall is said to be the result of sexual misconduct by Eve and Adam, and history is seen as a struggle to restore the Kingdom of Heaven on earth. Jesus should have

married, but he was murdered before he could complete his mission; he was thus able to offer only spiritual salvation to the world. Moon, the Lord of the Second Advent, claims to have laid the foundation for the restoration of God's kingdom through his marriage to his present wife in 1960. Members take part in a weekly 'Pledge', but the most important Unification ritual is the 'Blessing' – a mass wedding in which couples 'matched' by Moon are married.

The Unification Church is connected with numerous organizations which own many valuable properties and businesses. Associated ventures include the International Religious Foundation, the Council for World's Religions, the Confederation of the Associations for the Unification of the Societies of the Americas (CAUSA), the Collegiate Association for the Research of Principles (CARP), the Professors' World Peace Academy and the *Washington Times*. It has its own seminary in New York state, and a school and university in Korea. Unificationists (popularly known as 'Moonies') have typically joined in their early 20s and are disproportionately well educated and from the middle classes. From the early 1970s, most members in the West lived in Unification centres and worked long hours for the movement, frequently fundraising and/or 'witnessing' to potential converts. By the early 1990s, however, Unificationists were typically married and living with young children on a more independent basis.

The movement has been the subject of considerable hostility from parents, the media and the anti-cult movement (*see* CULT-WATCHING GROUPS), with accusations including brainwashing, deception, splitting up families, political involvement with the Korean KCIA, and exploitation of the membership. Moon served a sentence for tax evasion in the mid-1980s after which he returned to live mainly in Korea. The movement itself claims victimization, particularly when its members are illegally kidnapped and 'deprogrammed'. [3; 5: 214–16; 6: 42–51, v; 10; 11: vii, x, xii; 25: iii, xiii; 41: iv/o; 42: 753–5; 53: 305–64]

Unitarianism [xiii.b] Christians (although some deny them the title) rejecting (as inimical to the unity of God) the doctrines of the TRINITY and divinity of JESUS CHRIST (*see* CHRISTOLOGY; GOD, CHRISTIAN CONCEPT OF), together with the Fall (*see* SIN), Atonement (*see* SALVATION) and eternal punishment. 'Socinians' (from Fausto Sozzini, 1539–1604) and 18th-century 'Arians' (*see* ARIANISM) were strongly biblical and allowed a special status to Christ. Later, more philosophical Unitarians in England and the USA eroded this. Modern Unitarianism is diverse and difficult to classify, except as 'liberal' religion. [157: 1408–9; 199; 202]

Upanishads [xvii] Texts in the Vedic tradition (*see* VEDA), influential in the development of Hindu thought. *Upanishad* means 'a sitting down close to' a GURU, hence an esoteric teaching. Like the BRAHMANAS, to which they were attached, they are explanations of Vedic teaching, but on a mystical rather than a ritual level. The earliest Upanishads, such as the Brihadaranyaka and Chandogya, seem to come from the same period of philosophical questioning as BUDDHISM and JAINISM, and address the same questions about the nature of reality. They are closely linked with another group of texts, the Aranyakas or Forest Teachings, with which they overlap in terms of content: the Brihadaranyaka Upanishad – the Upanishad of the Great Forest Teaching – can be seen as belonging to both [95: 2, 34–9].

The Upanishads postulate an essential self, the ATMAN, within all living beings, constantly reincarnated in accordance with KARMA, but itself pure and untouched. This self is ultimately of the same nature as the BRAHMAN, the self of the universe, and can achieve liberation from rebirth (MOKSHA) by union with it. Some later Upanishads see reality in more theistic terms, identifying the Brahman with SHIVA or VISHNU. The BHAGAVADGITA is a Vaishnava Upanishad of this type. (*See also* VEDANTA.) [106]

Upasaka [xi] A Buddhist lay follower. The term implies not just any Buddhist layperson who takes 'the three refuges' (TISARANA), but one who is committed to supporting the SANGHA and to a certain degree of religious practice. Laymen (*upasaka*) and women (*upasika*), who usually wear white clothing in the THERAVADA tradition, take on the eight precepts (*see* SILA), particularly on observance days (UPOSATHA) but also on other occasions and for longer periods such as the three months of the rains (*see* ASALHA). [100: 164–80]

Uposatha [xi] A BUDDHIST observance day. Such days coincide with the quarter phases of the moon. In practice the days of the new and particularly the full moon are more significant than the other two days. Important Buddhist festivals generally fall on full-moon days (*see* ASALHA; VESAKHA; MAGHA PUJA). On the days of the new and full moon the SANGHA traditionally convenes to recite the monastic rule (PATIMOKKHA), while for lay followers (UPASAKA) these are occasions for visiting monasteries (VIHARA) and increased religious practice. [34: 191–5]

USA *see* AMERICA/AMERICAN/NORTH AMERICA

Utilitarianism [xxxii] A secular moral philosophy according to which the only considerations that are relevant to deciding what is good and bad, or right and wrong, in any particular course of action have to do with its effects on the total sum of human happiness. In a broad form this point of view found acceptance among a number of 'enlightened' 18th-century philosophers, especially in France (C. A. Helvétius, 1715–71) and Britain (D. Hume, 1711–76, and J. Bentham, 1748–1832). The label 'utilitarian' was first used, in the 19th century, as a term of abuse, but it was adopted by John Stuart Mill (1806–73). Mill's 1863 essay on Utilitarianism [16] provided a classical statement of this position. Much attention has since been given by moral philosophers to criticizing and amending Mill's account.

Although it is now widely rejected, utilitarian thinking has permeated thought about moral matters in many countries, especially Britain. Many would agree with the utilitarian view that the only justifications there could be for punishing someone are that doing so might deter him or her from repeating certain actions or that doing so might deter others from committing those actions. They would agree, that is to say, in rejecting punishment as retribution or punishment for punishment's sake. The idea of an eye for an eye, or a tooth for a tooth, has no place in utilitarian thought. This is one among many moral issues where utilitarians have stood against what has been taught in the name of Christianity.

V

Vahanas [XVII] 'Vehicles': the animal symbols of the Hindu gods and goddesses. The deities may ride on or be accompanied by their *vahanas*, who also embody aspects of their characters. For example, BRAHMA and his consort SARASVATI both have as their *vahana* the *hamsa* or goose, often mistranslated as a swan (a bird not indigenous to India). The goose, because of its beauty and the power of its flight, is in the UPANISHADS a symbol of the ATMAN or self, soaring up to find union with the supreme reality or BRAHMAN: hence perhaps its connection with the god and goddess of creation. VISHNU rides the mythical bird Garuda, depicted as either all bird or part-bird, part-human. The bird element generally resembles an eagle or a vulture, as befits a solar being. However, when at rest between world-cycles Vishnu lies on the waters on the serpent Ananta, 'Endless', suggesting that he unites in himself the powers of the Garudas and the Nagas (deified snakes), which in myth are seen as implacable foes. Vishnu's main consorts, LAKSHMI and BHUDEVI, are both attended by elephants. SHIVA rides the bull, Nandin, who clearly expresses the virile character of the god, while his consort PARVATI generally has as her *vahana* a lion or tiger, though this varies with her different forms. River goddesses naturally tend to ride aquatic creatures: GANGA (Ganges) has a *makara*, a mythical crocodile-like beast, while Yamuna (Jumna) has a turtle. Each divine being has his or her own *vahana*, but those of the great gods have myths and charac-

ters of their own, and Garuda or Nandin may have his own shrine within a temple complex (*see* MANDIRA).

In Jainism and BUDDHISM too, enlightened beings and deities may be accompanied by their *vahanas*. For example, the JAIN TIRTHANKARA Rishabhanatha is identified by a bull, while the BODHISATTVA MANJUSHRI may be depicted riding a lion.

Vahiguru [XXXIII] The term *vah guru* first appears in the Sikh JANAMSAKHIS, where it means 'Praise to the GURU' and is used to signal the conclusion of a *sakhi* or anecdote. At this early stage it was also used as an appropriate MANTRA for NAM SIMARAN. The two words gradually coalesced to form one of the characteristic names of God and today it is the most popular of all such names for Sikhs [28: 49]. The term occurs at only two places in the ADI GRANTH, both of them in panegyrics by Guru Arjan's bards. (*See also* AKAL PURAKH.)

Vaibhashika [XI] One of the principal schools of BUDDHIST *abhidharma* (Pali: ABHIDHAMMA), developed in the SARVASTIVADA sect in north India. The Sarvastivadins had their own *abhidharma-pitaka*, now extánt only in Chinese and Tibetan translations, developed during the 3rd to 1st centuries BCE. A *vibhasha* is a commentary setting out various opinions and the school is named after the *Mahavibhasha* or 'Great Commentary', composed in Kashmir in the 2nd century CE. This

Kashmir interpretation became very influential. A series of manuals following the Vaibhashika viewpoint were composed over the next five centuries, although other schools of Sarvastivadin *abhidharma* also existed. One group, appealing to the authority of *sutranta* (Pali: SUT-TANTA), the earlier form of Buddhist scripture, were known as SAUTRAN-TIKAS. They criticized Vaibhashika doctrines not supported by the *sutras* (Pali: SUTTA) and set forth new explanations of their own. The consequent controversy was summarized in a masterly compendium – the *Abhidharmakosha* of VASU-BANDHU (4th or 5th century). Partly owing to the identification of its author with the influential YOGA-CARA writer, this work eclipsed all rivals and was itself the basis of a considerable literature. In the Far East it became the basis for a sect (Chu She; *see* NANTO ROKUSHU), while it still remains part of the Tibetan monastic curriculum (*see* TIBETAN RELIGIONS).

The Vaibhashika *abhidharma*, although formed from a common background in early *abhidhamma*, differs on many points of detail from the THERAVADA *abhidhamma*, but the fundamental aim and methodology are similar. The later Vaibhashikas develop a very systematic and detailed account, mapping out the stages of the Buddhist path at length. Their viewpoint tends to underlie MAHAYANA Buddhist writings and is often criticized as the HINAYANA position. [General account: 89; the path: 33: 215ff]

Vaisheshika [XVII] One of the six DARSHANAS or salvation-philosophies of classical HINDUISM, founded by Kanada in perhaps the 2nd century BCE. Kanada's fundamental text, the *Vaisheshika-sutra*, was largely superseded by the later manual of Prashastapada (early 6th century CE) [translation: 107: 386–423]. A series of commentaries and manuals based upon this were produced down to the 12th century [53: VI, 2, 53–75]. Thereafter the system merged almost completely with the later NYAYA. Kanada claimed that spiritual development and liberation (MOKSHA) were to be achieved by fully understanding how the world of experience is constructed from six fundamental categories (*padartha*): substance, quality, activity, commonness, particularity (*vishesha*) and unity (or inherence). The pluralistic and realistic system of the *Vaisheshika* included much detail based upon observation of the natural world and its laws. Especially well known is the *Vaisheshika* concept of indivisible 'atoms' without magnitude, from which larger entities are constructed. Mind, which is minute in size, is distinguished from spirit, which is infinite; both are eternal. Although Kanada was probably not a theist, Prashastapada and his successors gave a definite although limited role to the will of God (ISH-VARA). [51: 3–180; 103: 146–64]

Vaishnava Vedanta [XVII] A series of influential HINDU Vaishnava (*see* VISHNU) theologians created a number of VEDANTA schools during the medieval period, both developing and reacting against the ADVAITA VEDANTA of SHANKARA. Vaishnava sectarian writings and saints influenced all of these, but individuals were variously affected by later NYAYA and SAMKHYA thought, even to some extent by ISLAM. The principal forerunner of the Vaishnava Vedanta was Bhaskara (9th or 10th century CE). Bhaskara attacked Shankara as a crypto-BUDDHIST and claimed to represent a more authentic tradition. The most influential figure was RAMANUJA (12th century); also important were Nimbarka and Madhva (both 13th century), Vallabha (1479–1531) and certain of the followers of Caitanya (1485–1533). Most of these are authoritative for particular Vaishnava sectarian traditions (*sampradaya*). [36: III, IV; 105: 39–102]

The various systems differ considerably, but all emphasize the positive nature of God (BRAHMAN = VISHNU), stress the importance of BHAKTI as the most effective spiritual practice and deny that the individual soul can ever be so wholly merged into the divine as to lose its identity completely. The role of divine grace is stressed. They are generally inclusivist: competing systems are not so much denied as incorporated and subordinated in a hierarchy of knowledge. Generally a knowledge of the highest brahman superior to the experience of an undifferentiated absolute is claimed. God is in principle held to be both the efficient and the material cause of the universe, but in practice care is taken to avoid a simplistic pantheism. The system of Madhva goes rather further in emphasizing distinctions between God, the universe and the individual soul. Several Vaishnava thinkers deny the possibility of liberation in this life (*jivanmikti*) and most assert that God has a particular form (i.e. that of Vishnu).

Valentinianism [xv] Valentinus, an Egyptian of the Phrebonitic nome who lived in Rome 136–165 CE, was arguably the most important and influential Gnostic thinker (*see* GNOSTICISM) of the 2nd century. His teaching drew more criticism from the Christian church than any other Gnostic, and also exercised a deep influence on modern thinkers like Rudolf Steiner and Carl Jung.

According to one version of his teaching, the heavenly world, the PLEROMA, consists of twenty-eight AEONS (worlds) which are arranged in Syzygies (pairs). They are the hypostasized attributes of the Monad, or Father, and emanated from him because he did not love solitude and had the power of generation. The youngest of these emanations, Sophia (wisdom), discovering that the Father could generate without a partner, desired to imitate him; however, begotten and born after many others, she did not have the power of the unbegotten one and brought forth that of which she was capable, an abortion, without form and void. This caused great consternation among the other Aeons of the Pleroma, and the Father, paying heed to their entreaty, sent them to her aid. Two new Aeons, Christos and the Holy Spirit, were brought forth by the Syzygia, Nous (intelligence) and Aletheia (truth) and separated the abortion of Sophia from the Aeons, thus removing the cause of the alarm. They drew her with them within the Pleroma, which was thereupon closed by the emanation from the Father of yet another Aeon, the Cross, marking the limit of the Aeons (also called Boundary). Outside this boundary remained Sophia's abortion, fashioned by Christos and the Holy Spirit into an Aeon as perfect as any within the Pleroma. She is also called Sophia but is generally distinguished from her mother as the Sophia Without the Pleroma. On completing their tasks, Christos and the Holy Spirit returned to the Syzygia of their origin, Aletheia and Nous. The thirty Aeons of the Pleroma now determined to present a common progeny to the Father as proof of their unity, agreement and peace. This 'common fruit of the Pleroma' was JESUS.

Distressed by the departure of the Aeons who had formed her, the Sophia Without turned to fervent pleading with the one who had left her. Christos, now inside the Pleroma, and the other Aeons took pity on her and sent forth the 'common fruit of the Pleroma', Jesus, who entered into a partnership with her and relieved her of the four main passions which were besetting her, namely fear, grief, perplexity and entreaty, turning them into hypostases. The fear he made into a psychic essence, the grief into a material (hylic) one, perplexity into a demonic, while entreaty and the supplication for ascent were made into repentance and the power of the psychic substance, which is called 'the right'.

From the psychic substance came the demiurge or creator who presided over the psychic sphere; below this is the cosmos and, lowest of all, the chaos of unformed matter. The souls of men proceed from the demiurge, who is controlled, unwillingly, by his mother Sophia Without the Pleroma. As a result of this twofold influence certain souls are 'pneumatic' (spiritual), others 'psychic', and the rest, given wholly to the element of matter and the devilish essence in which they are incarnated, are 'hylic'. The law and the prophets likewise came from the demiurge. The 'psychic' soul has 'a veil upon his heart' (*2 Cor.* 3: 15) blinding it to the higher world of the spirits. For the redemption of souls and rectifying of creation, Jesus, the 'new man', was born through MARY the Virgin. He cured the suffering of the souls just as Christos had healed the Sophia Without the Pleroma. The 'pneumatic' souls, belonging to the higher sphere, require only the influence of the esoteric knowledge (GNOSIS) imparted by Jesus. Once ascended to the Pleroma they will unite with angelic beings. 'Psychic' souls, i.e. the majority of the church, have to make good, with Jesus' aid, their deficiencies by faith and good works, and they will be raised to the Middle Sphere, the heaven of the Sophia Without the Pleroma. Thus, in each of three worlds, Pleroma, Middle Sphere and Cosmos, a saviour was required. Sophia is saved by Christ, her offspring by Jesus and the souls which stem from the demiurge by Jesus, the son of Mary. On completion of the process of perfecting the 'psychic' souls, the fire hidden in the world will blaze and burn; after consuming all matter it will be consumed with it and pass into non-existence.

The Valentinians were the most distinctive of all the Egyptian Gnostic sects because they possessed a hierarchical ecclesiastical organization. Identifiable cells were still found in the 4th and early 5th century when they became the victims first of sectarian strife within Christianity and later of the anti-heretical laws of the Christian emperors. [7; 9; 24; 27]

Valhalla [VII] The Scandinavian Valhalla ('Hall of the Slain') was the place to which kings and outstanding warriors were conducted after death by the VALKYRIES, if they had died in battle or been sacrificed to ODIN. Here Odin presided over a life of fighting and feasting, and warriors who fell each day were raised again to take part in a banquet, with unending supplies of roasted pork and mead. Odin collected the finest champions in order to have these support in the last great conflict at RAGNAROK [3: 149–53]. Poems and memorial stones of the VIKING age represent the dead warrior on horseback arriving at Valhalla, welcomed by a woman with a drinking-horn [5: 124–9]. Valhalla appears to be an image developed by artists and poets to glorify those who died in battle; it was not, like HEL, a universal realm of the dead, but reserved for privileged heroes who were Odin's worshippers.

Valkyries [VII] The early GERMANIC conception of Valkyries was that of fierce battle-spirits devouring the slain, and the CELTIC war-goddesses Morrigan and Badb show similar characteristics. All are associated with crows and ravens on the battlefield [4: 92–100]. In Norse literature Valkyries appear as supernatural brides of heroes (*see* FYLGJA), helping them in battle and welcoming them after death. Sometimes they are represented as dignified women on horseback, escorting dead kings to VALHALLA and offering them horns of mead.

Vanir [VII] These were the Scandinavian fertility deities, sometimes
represented as fair giants dwelling in
earth or sea, who provided wives for
the AESIR. They were linked with
land-spirits of mountains or lakes,
and with dead ancestors in the earth
to whom offerings were made. Freyr
('Lord'), whose phallic statue was at
Uppsala, was the male fertility-god,
and thought of as the founder of the
Swedish royal dynasty. His sister
Freyja had many names, and may
probably be identified with the
giantesses Gerd and Gefion, and
ODIN's wife Frigg, as well as Germanic Frija, who gave Friday its
name [3: IV]. Njord, god of ships,
sea and lakes, was their father [3:
132–8]. The fertility deity might be
taken in a wagon to bless the farms.
Women with prophetic gifts, who
visited homes, practised divination
and foretold children's destinies
(VOLVA), were probably linked with
the Vanir. These deities had a ship
and a golden boar as their symbols.

Varna [XVII] Four 'classes', or
broad divisions, existed in ancient
Hindu society, according to the classical texts. The highest class was that
of the BRAHMANS; next came the
warrior class (KSHATRIYA); and then
the merchant class (Vaishya). These
three constituted the 'twice-born'
(*dvija*) classes [12: 139, 163] who
were invested with the sacred thread
at their *upanayana*, or initiation into
society (their 'second' birth). Below
these three were the workers, or serfs
(*Shudras*), who suffered from many
social disabilities. Some modern
scholars interpret the difference
between *Shudras* and the twice-born
classes as having been one of colour,
the literal meaning of *varna*, the
latter perhaps having descended
from lighter-skinned Aryan (INDO-
EUROPEAN) immigrants into India
[12: 138; 138: 24, 49]. According to
one of the hymns of the *Rig-veda* (*see*
VEDA), the 'Purushasukta', the four
classes were constituted at the creation of the world: a primeval being
called Purusha (Man) was sacrificed, and from his mouth the Brahman class were created, from his
arms the Kshatriyas, from his thighs
the Vaishyas and from his feet the
Shudras [139: 10]. This idealistic
doctrine of the Brahmans, that all
humanity is divided into four classes, is purely scriptural. It should not
be confused with existing social divisions, known as *jati*, or 'birth-
groups', which entail recognition of
group identity, endogamy, commen-
sality, occupational privileges and
other distinctions. The dominant *jati*
in any particular area (in real terms)
is not necessarily the Brahman. The
European use of the word CASTE
largely led to confusion of the two,
especially in the British period, since
the latter relied very largely on Brahman informants. Those who fell outside the fourfold division were
traditionally considered 'Untouch-
able'. Gandhi's name for them,
Harijan, often translated as 'Children of God' (Hari = VISHNU), is
not favoured by the people themselves, who prefer such terms as
Dalit, 'Oppressed'.

Vassa [XI] The Buddhist 'Lent',
which occurs annually (as the word
vassa signifies, etymologically) during the monsoon season (which also
is signified by the word *vassa*). The
practice (by ascetics) of forming
small groups that live in a sheltered
place for the period of the rains
appears to have started early in the
history of BUDDHISM and to have
been subsequently adopted by other,
non-Buddhist groups in India. [23:
54–7]

Vasubandhu [XI] Buddhist thinker,
said to have been the brother of
ASANGA and converted by him to
MAHAYANA. According to tradition,
prior to adopting Mahayana, Vasubandhu had written the great compendium of ABHIDHAMMA known as
the *Abhidharmakosha* (*see* VAIBHA-
SHIKA). Having become a follower of
Mahayana, Vasubandhu, like his

brother, developed the YOGACARA school, and wrote some important summaries such as the *Vimshatika* (Twenty Verses) and *Trimshika* (Thirty Verses) as well as a number of commentaries.

Modern scholars are inclined towards the view that there were two Vasubandhus; Vasubandhu the Older, who was a follower of Mahayana and lived perhaps during the 4th century CE, and the Abhidhamma commentator Vasubandhu the Younger, who possibly lived during the 5th century. (*See also* FA HSIANG TSUNG.)

Veda [XVII] Literally, 'knowledge', a body of literature regarded as the source of HINDUISM, directly 'heard' (SHRUTI) at the beginning of the world-cycle by *rishis* or inspired sages. In historical terms, it consists of four collections (*samhita*) of ritual verses called MANTRAS, probably composed over several centuries from around 1000 BCE, though containing earlier material, and not put into writing for several centuries after. Most ancient is the *Rig-veda*, the Veda of Hymns, of which the *Yajur-veda*, the Veda of Prayers, and the *Sama-veda*, the Veda of Chants, are to a great extent adaptations for use by specific types of priests (BRAHMANS). Latest is the ATHARVA-VEDA, the Veda of the Atharvans or Magician Priests, whose contents are largely concerned with private, rather than state, rituals.

The language of the Veda is an early form of Sanskrit, an INDO-EUROPEAN tongue closely related to the ancient Iranian language of the AVESTA, and certain names and concepts are common to Vedic religion and ZOROASTRIANISM. The god Mitra, protector of the cosmic and moral order *rita* (*see* DHARMA) and of friendship is the counterpart of Mithras (*see* MITHRAISM). In other cases, ZOROASTER's reforms have meant that certain names are applied to benevolent beings in one

system and malevolent ones in the other (*see* AHURA MAZDA; ASURA).

There are differences between the practices and beliefs described in the Veda and those now current in Hinduism. Central to Vedic religion is the sacrifice (*yajna*), in which food is offered to the gods in the sacred fire. Such sacrifices involved the ritual slaughter of animals and the preparation of a hallucinogenic drink called Soma, both of which have fallen into disuse with the growing emphasis placed on non-violence (AHIMSA) and the rejection of the use of intoxicants among Hindus. Moreover, many of the deities more prominent in the Veda have since fallen into obscurity, while others, little mentioned or unknown there, are now the main foci of Hindu worship. Important in the Veda are Indra, a warrior king and demon-slayer associated with storm and rain; Agni, the fire-god, mediator between gods and human beings in the sacrifice; and Varuna, a god of the sky and the waters, invoked, often jointly with Mitra, as a guardian of *rita*. Although still known, these gods now have a relatively small and specialized role, for example as guardians of the directions. In contrast, the principal gods of later Hinduism either have a lesser place, like VISHNU and SHIVA, or, like BRAHMA, are not mentioned at all. Especially striking, in comparison with their later importance, is the rather small role played by goddesses (*see* SHAKTI) [12: 232–41].

The teachings of the Vedas were traditionally restricted to members of the upper three VARNAS, and in practice mainly to men of the Brahman class. The main developments of later Hinduism, such as the BHAKTI and TANTRA (1) movements, were not confined to this elite.

The Veda was vital to the development of Hindu philosophy. In allusive and often paradoxical language, it asked questions about the nature of the universe and the origins and destiny of human beings. The BRAH-MANAS, Aranyakas and UPANISHADS attempted to explain the ideas contained within its symbolism. (*see* JNANA YOGA; DARSHANA; VEDANTA.) Other sciences, too, were developed as adjuncts to the Veda, for example *iyotisha-shastra*, astronomy/astrology, to ensure that the sacrifices were carried out at the proper times (*see* ASTROLOGY (INDIAN)); and grammar, necessary to ensure that the Veda was correctly preserved and understood as the vernacular languages changed [95: 1–4; 12: 247–9, 321–8, 387–8, 489–91].

However, the Veda is not just of historical interest, but a living part of Hinduism. The mantras are still chanted by Brahman priests, in temple ceremonies (*see* MANDIRA) and as part of domestic ritual (*see* PUJA, SAMSKARAS). Its power is still revered even when the language is not understood. Acceptance of the authority of the Veda is what distinguishes Hindus of every persuasion from, for example, BUDDHISTS or JAINS. [94]

Vedanta [XVII] One of the six orthodox DARSHANAS or salvation-philosophies of classical HINDUISM. 'Vedanta' means 'culmination of the VEDAS' and refers to the UPANISHADS as the final and climactic portion of the Vedic revelation. In practice Vedanta means the branch of scriptural exegesis (MIMAMSA) concerned with the Upanishads and the system developed therefrom. The fundamental Vedanta text is the BRAHMA-SUTRA, but the Upanishads themselves and also the BHAGAVADGITA are obviously important. In origin the Vedanta is simply theology, its main concern being with knowledge of the divine power (BRAHMAN). In practice it has expanded to incorporate elements from the other *darshanas*, which have tended to become mere ancillaries to the Vedanta. The early history of Vedanta is obscure; it seems to have competed for a long period

with a rival SAMKHYA interpretation of the Upanishads. It did not form a fully elaborated system until the 7th and 8th centuries CE when the ADVAITA VEDANTA developed, partly influenced by MADHYAMAKA BUDDHISM. In the medieval period a number of VAISHNAVA VEDANTA schools arose.

Veiling (in Islam) [XIX] Veiling apparently originated for the protection of the Prophet's wives, and was later extended to all free Muslim women. Its adoption marks the transition from childhood to puberty [77: VI]. It was never, however, very practicable for peasant and working women, and ISLAMIC MODERNISM has often attacked it as a symbol of women's subjection; but with the recent resurgence of Islamic fundamentalism, there has been pressure on women to retain it. (*See* MAR'A.) [38 'Hidjāb']

Vesakha [XI] The festival that celebrates the birth, enlightenment and death (*see* PARINIBBANA) of the BUDDHA (*see* GOTAMA). This festival falls on the full-moon day (*see* UPOSATHA) of the month of Vesakha (Pali; Sanskrit: *Vaishakha*), the second month of the Indian calendar corresponding to April/May. In many BUDDHIST countries this is a 'festival of lights': temple compounds and shrines are decorated with candles or simple oil lamps; in Sri Lanka paper lanterns are made and then burnt at the close of the festival. [34: 192–3]

Vestal Virgins [XXXI] Six priestesses who served in Vesta's temple in Rome (*aedes Vestae*); the *pontifex maximus* (*see* SACERDOTES) chose them, when very young, by *captio* ('taking'), to remain in service for 30 years, caring for the temple and maintaining the sacred fire on the goddess's hearth. They had to preserve their virginity on pain of being buried alive. Their sexual status, however, symbolically combined that of virgin with elements of matron, bride and even man. Any failure in the fulfilment of their duties threatened the safety of the state (*salus publica*). [1; 8: 585–8; 12: 108–11; 19: 607–9]

Vihara [XI] A PALI and Sanskrit term for a BUDDHIST monastery; the term is still current in the THERAVADA tradition. In addition to accommodation for monks (BHIKKHU), the typical *vihara* comprises a shrine hall housing a BUDDHA IMAGE, a preaching hall used on UPOSATHA days, a hall for the performance of communal acts of the SANGHA such as the recitation of the PATIMOKKHA and ordination, and finally a STUPA and *bodhi* tree (*see* BODHGAYA). Many village *viharas* house just two or three monks, but important centres may accommodate hundreds. The *vihara* is not simply a monastery; it also functions as an important focus of lay religious activity (*see* UPASAKA; PUNNA). [28: 89–92]

Vikings [VII] The Scandinavian Viking age lasted from the late 8th to the 11th century CE. Skills in shipbuilding and navigation enabled searaiders (Vikings) from Norway, Sweden and Denmark to attack many European kingdoms. Scandinavians also won wealth through trading voyages and service as mercenaries, while settlements were made in Iceland, Greenland and parts of the British Isles [14]. CHRISTIANITY was not established in Scandinavia until the close of the Viking age, and much of our knowledge of pre-Christian northern religion comes from Icelandic medieval literature [3: 9–16] (*see* EDDA). The chief gods were ODIN and THOR, and there was a rich store of myths and legends about supernatural beings and realms. Archaeological finds have revealed elaborate funeral customs, including SHIP-FUNERAL, and sacrificial rites (*see* VOTIVE OFFERINGS). [5: VI]

Vinaya [XI] The BUDDHIST monastic rule, the subject of the first section of Buddhist scriptures (TIPITAKA). A number of different versions of the 'basket of discipline' (*vinaya-pitaka*) survive in Pali, Sanskrit, and in Chinese and Tibetan translation, but only three are in current use: THERAVADA tradition uses a version in PALI; the eastern tradition (of China, Korea and Japan) uses one inherited from the Dharmaguptakas, an ancient subschool of the *Sthaviras* (*see* SANGITI); Tibetan tradition uses one inherited from the Mulasarvastivadins (*see* SARVASTIVADA). The *Vinaya* falls into two basic parts. The first is a detailed analysis (*vibhanga*) of the rules that comprise the PATIMOKKHA and govern the life of the individual monk (BHIKKHU) or nun (BHIKKHUNI). The second comprises 20 'sections' (Pali: *khandhaka*; Sanskrit: *skandhaka*) which set out the proper procedures for conducting the various communal acts of the SANGHA, such as ordination and the recitation of the *patimokkha* on UPOSATHA days. In general the *Vinaya* seeks to establish a lifestyle that avoids the extremes of sensual indulgence and excessive asceticism, and is conducive to a certain mindfulness as the basis for the practice of meditation (BHAVANA). How strictly contemporary Buddhist monks follow the details of *Vinaya* varies considerably from tradition to tradition and from monastery to monastery; the Theravada tends to be more conservative in its approach to the *Vinaya* than other traditions. [34a; 65: 18–29; 100]

Vipassana [XI] One of the two main types of Buddhist meditation practice (BHAVANA). *Vipassana* (Sanskrit: *vipashyana*) is direct experiential insight into reality, brought about by the practice of constant awareness, especially mindfulness of the four foundations: body, feelings, state of mind and mental processes [66: 7–115]. Guidance from those who have already developed insight and careful attentiveness is necessary. Previous calm (SAMATHA) meditation practice is usual, although in some modern schools, especially from Burma, this is considered a distraction. Eventually various degrees of direct insight will arise. Understanding of the specific nature and interconnectedness of mental and material phenomena will lead the meditator eventually to experience the three general characteristics: impermanence (ANICCA), unsatisfactoriness (DUKKHA) and insubstantiality (ANATTA). The ensuing detachment gives rise to strongly positive emotions with a consequent danger of premature satisfaction. If this is avoided, a stronger level of insight is reached, accompanied by the experience of the various states of the Buddhist path (BODHI-PAKKHIYA-DHAMMA). The culmination would be a permanent breakthrough to the transcendent (LOKUTTARA). [33: 191–247; 48; 96: 341–406]

Vishnu [XVII] One of the most important Hindu gods, the second of the principal triad (TRIMURTI), embodying the power of preservation. In the VEDA he is a relatively minor figure with sky and solar connections, noted chiefly for the three paces in which he covered the universe (earth, air and heaven), but in the epics (MAHABHARATA and RAMAYANA) and PURANAS he has become (along with SHIVA and SHAKTI) one of the main foci of BHAKTI devotion. His followers are called Vaishnavas. Whereas BRAHMA is the archetypal priest and Shiva the *yogi*, Vishnu is the king, whose function is to protect his land and its people. He preserves the world by becoming incarnate in AVATARAS, in order to conquer ASURAS (demons) and other powers of evil. Two of the *avataras*, RAMA and KRISHNA, are the centres of important *bhakti* cults. Like an ancient Indian monarch, Vishnu has many wives, among

them personifications of victory, prosperity and the sacred *tulasi* plant, but his main consort is LAKSHMI, the goddess of good fortune. In south India he is generally represented with two consorts, Shridevi (Lakshmi) on his right (seen from his point of view) and BHUDEVI, the Earth Goddess, on his left [120: pl. 42a, 95a]. In art (*see* ART (HINDU)) Vishnu is blue in colour, and his principal attribute is the *cakra*, a flaming discus or wheel, both perhaps suggesting his connections with sky and sun. His animal symbol (VAHANA) is Garuda, the king of the birds [4: 196–212; 92: 175–237]. In one distinctive form of imagery, Vishnu sleeps on the coils of the serpent Ananta, 'Endless', who in turn rests on the waters of the cosmic ocean. The duration of each universe is said to be Vishnu's day, and the period of non-existence between universes his night. At the beginning of a new cycle, he awakes, and a lotus grows on a long stalk from his navel. From the lotus Brahma appears to create the universe anew. [58: 113–14, 468–9; 59: pl. 103]

Vision Quest [V] Probably the most characteristic feature of North American Indian religion, the vision quest is susceptible of many interpretations and variations [8]. Among the Algonquian (*see* ALGONQUIN) and Plains Indians, where the vision quest has received fullest elaboration, the practice is generally associated with a rite of passage as well as with the acquisition of a GUARDIAN SPIRIT. Classically, an individual (usually a young male), prompted beforehand by some omen or encouraged by the elders, sets out to acquire spiritual power by means of a vision of a supernatural being. Ascetic practices (including fasting, thirsting, use of the SWEAT LODGE, enemas, etc.) are first undertaken as preparation; the individual then retires to a remote place to pray and beg for a vision. At length, often after additional mortifications, the youth is granted a dream or a vision of a spirit (usually appearing in animal guise). This guardian spirit teaches the young person a 'spirit song', grants special powers and frequently bestows a MEDICINE BUNDLE or other symbol of newly acquired powers. If indicated in the vision, the individual may embark upon a career as MEDICINE MAN or SHAMAN. Renewal of power might be achieved by occasional repetition of the initial experience. [17: VIII, 59–63, 91–3]

Visions, Christian [XIII.D] Visions are common phenomena in religious history. Sometimes the vision is a shared experience (e.g. the dancing suns of Fatima, and the apparitions of MARY on the roof of her church in Old Cairo); sometimes it occurs in public, but remains private to an individual or group (e.g. the visions of Bernadette at Lourdes); sometimes the vision is in private (e.g. the revelatory visions of Julian of Norwich). St Teresa of Avila distinguishes between the kind of vision in which the visionary experiences herself as actually seeing something, and the intellectual vision where the act of perception is entirely mental. Frequently the visionary claims to have received revelations by means of visions; notable cases include Hildegarde of Bingen, Julian of Norwich, St Gertrude, St Margaret Mary Alacoque and the visionaries of Lourdes and Fatima. Traditional spiritual theology advises the greatest caution and prudence when dealing with visions. Closely related phenomena are auditions – the auditory counterpart of visions – and revelatory dreams. The writings of Bar-Hebraeus contain an interesting collection of insights he claims to have received as auditions.

Volva [VII] The Icelandic sagas contain accounts of a divination ceremony known as *seid*, over which a *volva* or female seer presides. She sits on a high platform, and apparently gains hidden knowledge in a state of trance, like SHAMANS in north-eastern Europe and Asia in later times [3: IV, 117–23]. It seems probable that *seid* took place in Norway rather than Iceland, although the most famous account is set in Greenland in the Saga of Erik the Red. The *volva* predicted the coming season as well as individual futures, and seems to be associated with the VANIR. ODIN had the powers of a seer [3: VI, 141–9], but in the Poetic EDDA he too consults a *volva* for knowledge of past or future [21: 117–19]; and certain poems are presented as the revelations of a *volva* [21: I, 137]. In Roman times certain female seers were held in great esteem by the Germans, and are mentioned by Tacitus (1st century BCE) and other writers.

Voodoo/Voudou/Vaudou/Vodun
[III] The term comes from the FON of west Africa, where it is the term for lesser divinities. Central to the concepts inherited from Africa are notions of death and resurrection. Voodoo is the name of a specific social and ritual dance and also of a total world-view with a full 'folk theology', the most significant religion to the majority of Haitians who will also be Roman Catholics. It is the pre-eminent CREOLE syncretic Caribbean religion. Some 115 African ethnicities fuse into the Haitian identity, together with European influences, especially from Roman Catholicism; it has also incorporated Indian and North American elements, and continues to modernize and adapt. Between 1730 and 1790 Voodoo established itself on the island as increasing numbers of slaves were imported. Between 1790 and 1800 the Africans from many ethnic groups used Voodoo to invoke the gods to try to free themselves. Greatly fearing its power, the black leaders then tried to suppress it. Despite these attempts, the period up to 1850 saw it widely

diffused and highly developed, and very much in its modern form.

In Voodoo, God rules with JESUS, the SAINTS and the HOLY SPIRIT. God is all-powerful, and has power that the *loas* do not. The *loas* come from Africa and are ORISHAS, known as 'powers'. Saints and mysteries/ *loas* are inherited by succeeding generations of Haitians, and they concern themselves with the everyday affairs of their devotees. God concerns himself with matters of the soul. The dead, and twins, influence everyday life, and are reverenced in specific cults, as are the *loas*. Since Voodoo is widely spread through the island, ritual details and worship vary from group to group.

There are two rites. *Rada* is the more benign and earlier: its *loas* are nearer Guinea/Africa, and include Legba, the go-between, who protects doors and gateways; Damballa, the supreme god, whose symbol is the snake; Guede, who handles matters of both birth and death; and Erzulie, the female *loa*. In the Petro cult the *loas* are malign, or warlike, and are clearly SYNCRETISMS, as illustrated by their dress and behaviour when they possess an initiate. Mait' Calfour, for instance, is the Petro Master of the Crossroads, and likes to dress sharply, wear sunglasses and smoke a cigar. Principal symbols in Voodoo are doors, crosses and crossroads. The cross and crossroads represent in two planes the relation between the spiritual and the physical worlds, between Guinea/Africa and the ancestors and the 'real' world. Just as in YORUBA religion, the actual and the spirit world mirror each other in the way that they are structured. The saints and the *loas* are arranged in a strict hierarchy, and they are thought to project characteristics and qualities of the devotees' own society.

A *houngan* (priest) takes many years in training: his female counterpart is the *mamba*. The whole purpose of worship is to be possessed by a *loa*. Worship takes place in a *tonelle*, at one end of which is a pole. This helps to focus the energy of the rites which call down possession, and represents the point of entry of the *loa* which must possess the initiate. The person possessed is said to be 'ridden' by the *loa*, as if the *loa* 'mounted' the initiate, like a rider on a horse. The ceremonies start with a sacrifice, maybe of a chicken or a goat. The *loas* have particular preferences in the animal of sacrifice, food, colours and behaviour. A *vevers* is traced on the floor, to indicate to the *loas* above which one is being called. Since possession is the central intention of Voodoo, initiates learn the pattern of behaviour that goes with each *loa*. The initial possession may be by a *bossu*, a wild spirit which has not been properly incorporated into the other world, but as the initiate gains experience, a *loa* of a high order will descend. The group will recognize the *loa* from the role the possessed acts out.

The negative side of Voodoo is expressed through the *bocor*, the sorcerer. He uses the power that he accesses for his own ends. He upsets the social and religious equilibrium because his behaviour contradicts the values of Voodoo; he frightens people, and yet offers them his services. By using the local pharmacopaeia, he is said to be able to *zombify* people, that is, he can seize their bodies and their ZOMBIES and get them to work for him. While the idea of zombification appeared untenable to outsiders until fairly recently, it now appears that by using certain drugs the *bocor* can suspend animation and then reanimate a person. American scientists are currently studying possibilities, because the application of this ability in modern medicine has great potential. It is the activities which surround the *bocor*, together with sensational films, which have given Voodoo such a negative status. For its adherents it provides a coherent and integrated world-view, which has been taken into the wider world by the many Haitians fleeing oppression at home. [3; 16; 20; 33; 34; 47; 58; 68]

Votive Offerings (Ancient European) [VII] Both CELTIC and GERMANIC peoples left offerings in sacred places or dropped them into water. In Denmark in the Roman period much war booty, often deliberately damaged, was abandoned at Vimose, Nydam and other sites, presumably as offerings for victory. Other deposits of a less warlike character, such as gold rings, pottery, wooden farm objects, textiles and animals, were probably offered to the fertility powers, as at Thorsbjerg in Denmark [5: 66–79]. Ritual treasures like the great metal cauldron found at Gundestrup in Denmark were dismantled and abandoned in the same way [12: 141–8]. The Celts left votive offerings near springs and threw them into lakes, as at the famous site of La Tène (5th century BCE), or down ritual shafts, a number of which have been excavated in Britain [12: 132–5; 25: 24–8]. At the sanctuary of Sequana, at the source of the Seine, many carved wooden figures were found, left by pilgrims who went there for healing [17: 14–19].

Vrata [XVII] In Hindu tradition, a vow taken upon oneself, or an austerity undertaken, such as continence or fasting. Initiation into the vow (and completion of it) are marked in some special way, by an act of devotion, or by bathing.

W

Wahhabis [XIX] A puritanical Islamic reform movement begun in Arabia by Muhammad b. 'Abd al-Wahhab (1703–92), reviving the conservative Hanbali tradition (*see* FIQH) and aiming at the eradication of idolatrous accretions in popular religion like saint-worship (*see* WALI). It became the driving force behind the military expansionism of the Saudi family, spreading over most of the Arabian peninsula by the early 20th century, and also securing a certain influence in Indian Islam. It remains today the official ideology of the Saudi Arabian kingdom. [8: XIV; 20 s.v.; 37 'Wahhābīya'; 78: XI]

Wali [XIX] Saint or holy man in ISLAM, literally 'friend, person near to God'. Popular Islam has come to recognize a hierarchy of saints, whose overt qualifications are the performance of miracles and the exercise of charisma or saintliness (*baraka*) [77: X; 88: VI–VII]. To the ordinary Muslim, a local saint is often a more potent and real figure than the distant prophets (NABI). Hence the healing power and intercession of the saint is sought for the living and dead alike. Pilgrimage (*ziyara*) is made to his tomb; and the anniversary of his death may be celebrated as a festival (*maulid*; *see also* 'ID) [24; 89]. The devotion shown to many Sufi leaders often led to the formation of specific SUFI ORDERS, crystallizing round their residences or tombs. In certain areas, e.g. north Africa and the Indo-Pakistan subcontinent, the cult of saints and holy men has been especially widespread.

[20 'Saints (Islam)'; 37 s.v.; 48: 56–8; 142: VI]

Waqf [XIX] 'Pious endowment'; in ISLAM a gift of, for example, property or money placed in trust so that the income can be used for a charitable or educational purpose such as the upkeep of a MOSQUE, hospital, SUFI convent, etc. It has also been possible to establish a *waqf* for one's own family. *Waqf* lands have become extensive, and modern Islamic governments have discouraged family *waqf*s and have placed charitable ones under various degrees of central government control. [37 'Wakf'; 48: 143–6]

Warao Religion [XXIII] The Winikina-Warao, or Boat People, of the Orinoco Delta express the view of all life as a gradual process of dying, of returning to the *wa*, the dugout canoe-coffin which is the vagina of Dauarani, Mother of the Forest. Human life first arrived in this canoe and life is a process of returning to the womb. Warao life is orchestrated to ensure the SOUL's existence in a mythical abode; to that end, human beings and supernatural beings mutually provide for one another's needs. Religious specialists include three classes of SHAMANS (priest-shamans; dark shamans, who mediate with the land of the dead; and light shamans, with the land of light) and artisans (especially canoe-makers, basket-makers). [39]

Way International [XXVIII] The Way International describes itself as a non-denominational biblical research, teaching and fellowship ministry. The movement grew out of the teachings of Dr Victor Paul Wierwille (1916–85), whose 'Power for Abundant Living' (PFAL) classes, originally started in the USA in 1953, attracted members of the JESUS MOVEMENT in the late 1960s; it is claimed that 100,000 had participated in them by 1983. The movement offers a number of other courses in Wierwille's theology, which rejects conventional understandings of the TRINITY, accepting that JESUS is the son of God, but not God the Son. [22: VI; 41: IV/Q; 42: 555–6; 77]

West, Hinduism in the [XVII] Indian Hindus and Indians of other religions migrated to Western countries from the mid-19th century in response to colonial labour requirements [125; 130]. They went first to Mauritius, British Guiana (Guyana), Trinidad, Natal (South Africa) and Dutch Guiana (Surinam) as indentured labourers, then to east Africa to work in British administration and as construction workers [30; 125; 130; 15]. After the Second World War, a small number of semi-skilled Hindus went to Britain, and these were followed in the 1960s and early 1970s by migrants direct from Asia and Asian refugees from the newly independent countries of Tanzania, Malawi, Kenya and Uganda [27; 71]. Surinamese Hindus moved in the same period to the Netherlands [128; 127], and Indian professionals emigrated to the USA and Canada [134; 136]. In the 1980s groups settled also in Australia and New Zealand. There are about 4 million people of Indian origin now living in these countries [30; 130; 27; 136], including Hindus, SIKHS, JAINS and a small number of people of other religions. Their ethnic and linguistic backgrounds differ according to their region of origin, though English is now widely spoken.

Hindus who settled outside India crossed *kala pani*, the 'black waters', transgressing Hindu teachings on ritual purity and leaving the sacred land of *Bharat*, India. Most Hindus responded to this separation from home by reproducing similar religious institutions and practices. In east Africa and Britain, where a 'chain migration' of related families has occurred, this extended to CASTE matters [15; 27; 71; 116; 8]. Endogamous marriages and the establishment of caste associations have been the principal features. In all countries, the role of the brahman (*see* BRAHMANS) has remained important for temple PUJA, worship, and SAMSKARA, life-cycle rites. In Surinam and the Caribbean, however, an early brahminization of Hindu beliefs and practices occurred, with brahmans influential in many aspects of religious life [130; 128; 127]. In other countries, the majority of religious organizations, including the management committees of temples, have been led by enthusiastic and skilled laypersons. They have organized temple building projects, worship programmes, ecumenical ventures, sectarian meetings, youth and women's groups, fund-raising activities, visits of spiritual leaders and the employment of brahmans. Brahmans have been brought from India to serve in temples for limited periods (they have also operated as household priests). In the USA, links with pilgrim institutions in India have led to the employment of brahmins from Tirupati, Madurai and Varanasi [136].

The style of MANDIRAS, Hindu temples, has varied considerably. In some countries, existing buildings such as schools and churches have been converted [27; 71]. In others, local styles have been adapted for new temples: Christian church architecture has been influential in Trinidad [130]. In the USA, temples in the traditional styles of north and south India have been constructed using imported materials and expertise [134; 136]. *Murtis*, stone images of deities such as RAMA, KRISHNA, GANESHA and DURGA, have been installed. Devotees visit temples to take DARSHANA, particularly during festivals. These occasions vary according to the nature of the local Hindu population, its ethnic mix and size. Gujarati Hindus in eastern and southern Africa, Britain and the USA gather for *Navaratri*, nine nights of folk dancing to the goddess Ambamata, whereas south Indians keep *Pongal*, a winter solstice festival, and Bengalis celebrate *Durga puja*, the annual worship and procession for the great goddess [15; 27; 71; 136; 123]. *Divali*, the festival of lights, *Shivaratri*, *Ramanavmi* and *Janamashtami*, anniversaries of Shiva, Rama and Krishna respectively, are universally popular. Other important large-scale rituals include *yagna* or *havan*, a sacrificial rite [130; 71], and *Satyanarayan katha*, a programme of worship and scripture-reading sponsored by families [136; 123]. The latter occurs generally in people's homes. This arena, rather than the temple, is the place of daily *puja*, generally organized by women (also the principal agents in fasts and VRATA or vows) [27; 63]. Children's knowledge of Hindu concepts, myths, ethics and practices is attained primarily though conversation, story-telling and the imitation of social and religious behaviour and ritual in the home [63].

Hindu organizations are widespread. The two principal types are sectarian bodies and 'ecumenical' associations [136]. Of the former, the Swaminarayan movement has been important in areas where Gujaratis have settled (east Africa, Britain, the USA). A devotional movement founded by Sahajananda Swami (later known as Swaminarayan) in the early 19th century, it stresses worship of Swaminarayan as the supreme person. The Akshar Purushottam Sanstha, a branch of the movement, has grown quickly in the West, offering an ascetic path for young men and opportunities for education and service for both laywomen and laymen through the mediums of both English and Gujarati [27; 136; 63; 134; 135]. The *Arya Samaj* has been influential throughout the Hindu diaspora. It has sent leaders to Hindu communities worldwide and has preached Hindu ethics and the abandonment of deity worship [130; 15; 27; 71; 63; 123]. As in India, at times, it has opposed the *sanatani* movement of popular Hindu belief and ritual commonly referred to as *sanatana dharma*, eternal tradition [71; 136]. Other important sects include the Ramakrishna Mission (in Britain and South Africa, and, known as the Vedanta Society, in the USA), founded in the late 19th century by Swami Vivekananda [27; 123; 33]; the Divine Life Society, formed in 1937 by Swami Sivananda and active in eastern and southern African Hindu communities [15; 123]; the International Society for Krishna Consciousness (ISKCON), the HARE KRISHNA MOVEMENT, which has attracted considerable support among Indian Hindus in South Africa, Britain and the USA [27; 136; 63; 123; 72]; and the SAI BABA movement, followers of the south Indian charismatic leader, Sathya Sai Baba, which has grown in popularity among Indian Hindus in Trinidad and Britain [130; 27; 71; 63; 21]. (*See also* NEW RELIGIOUS MOVEMENTS IN THE WEST.)

Ecumenical organizations, those which have sought to bring together Hindu communities either countrywide or on a global basis, have focused on issues such as Hindu education, temple building, fundraising, links with India, community representation and inter-faith participation. *Maha sabhas*, Hindu societies, have grown up in the Caribbean and in eastern and southern Africa, and have sought to unite local Hindus. In Trinidad, the *Maha sabha* produced a Hindu 'creed', established schools, trained priests and represented Hindu interests in national politics [130]. The National Council of Hindu Temples has sought to act as an overarching organization for Hindus in Britain [71; 63]. Undoubtedly the most widely influential body, however, has been the Vishwa Hindu Parishad, founded in India in the 1960s to promote the interests of Hindu DHARMA globally [71; 136]. Its presentation of Hinduism emphasizes common beliefs and practices rather than regional differences. In an international conference in Denmark in 1985, it stressed the importance of identity and mission or representation, the inward and outward concerns of diaspora Hindus [136]. Generally, it encourages members to be active as emissaries of a Hindu India as well as in representing Hinduism nationally and locally.

A further link between India and the diaspora Hindu communities has been the *swamis*, SADHUS and SANTS, holy men (and occasionally women) who have travelled to teach, to open temples, to initiate disciples and to care for their followers. Some of these figures have impressed not only Indian Hindus but also Westerners with their messages of India's spiritual heritage. Swami Vivekananda, who visited America in 1893 and inspired many with his speech at the World Parliament of Religions in Chicago, Bhaktivedanta Swami, who arrived there in the mid-1960s and later founded ISKCON, and Maharishi Mahesh Yogi, famous for his association with the Beatles, are among the most well known and influential of these. The Vedanta Society (the American version of the Ramakrishna Mission), the Hare Krishna Movement (ISKCON) and TRANSCENDENTAL MEDITATION were the formal products of their preaching, and these became popular not only in the USA but throughout Europe and in Africa

[71; 123; 33; 72; 110; 23; 112]. Young people, especially, were attracted to them, and, like other NEW RELIGIOUS MOVEMENTS, they were viewed critically by government agencies, churches, anti-cult bodies (*see* CULT-WATCHING GROUPS) and the media [24; 13; 9]. Other neo-Hindu groups with Western memberships have included the BRAHMA KUMARIS, SIDDHA YOGA, ANANDA MARGA Yoga, the Divine Light Mission (now ELAN VITAL) and the neo-Sannyas movement of Rajneesh (*see* RAJNEESHISM) [71; 9; 87]. (*See also* HINDUISM (MODERN DEVELOPMENTS).)

West Indies, Christianity in the [XIII.B] Early Christian influence was through Spanish colonization and missions to slaves. METHODISM since 1760 has had considerable success; it was followed in the 19th century by BAPTISTS and ANGLICANISM. ROMAN CATHOLICISM has mainly been active in former French and Spanish colonies. Hostility by slave owners hindered some missions until after emancipation (1833). Evangelical REVIVALISM has attracted West Indians who have also produced many Pentecostalist sects (*see* PENTECOSTALISM) of their own, often transmitted by immigrants in Britain since 1945 (notably RASTAFARIANS; *see also* AFRO-AMERICANS). [92: 187–90; 121 vol. 3: XI, vol. 5: IV; 122 vol. 5: IV, vol. 7: VII]

Western Buddhism [XI] Some interest in Buddhism developed in Europe during the 19th century, derived in part from colonial and missionary efforts, in part from intellectual and academic tendencies. Hindu and Buddhist ideas were also introduced by the Theosophical movement (*see* THEOSOPHY). The early 20th century brought a Buddhist movement on a very small scale in Europe, especially in the UK. This was associated with the THERAVADA Buddhist modernism developed in Ceylon (SINHALESE BUDDHISM), which emphasized the rational and practical nature of Buddhism. After declining in the inter-war period this tendency recovered some ground and continues to exercise influence. An interest in ZEN was aroused by the writings of D. T. Suzuki and the work of Japanese missionaries, resulting in the 1950s in a short-lived vogue in the USA connected with the beatnik movement. A small core of committed long-term practitioners remained. Beginning in the 1960s Tibetan refugees succeeded in establishing Buddhist centres in a number of Western countries; these benefited considerably from interest in meditation and mysticism during the 1970s. Theravada missionary activity, begun from Ceylon (Sri Lanka) by the Maha Bodhi Society, was now taken up also from Thailand and a number of small monasteries were established in Europe and the English-speaking countries. The 1970s and 1980s saw a considerable increase in the number of small Buddhist groups in the Western world. Some are eclectic or mixed, but many concentrate on some particular branch of Theravada, Tibetan Buddhism (see TIBETAN RELIGIONS), NICHIREN or Zen (Shin and SHINGON occur only rarely, except among immigrants). The increased presence of Asian leadership and of Westerners trained in Asia or by Asians is noticeable. Because of their concentration among the more highly educated, members exercise an influence disproportionate to their numbers.

Western Magical Tradition [XXIV] European magical practices originating in the Renaissance, when older magical traditions (see MAGIC) were integrated with HERMETISM, KABBALAH and NEOPLATONISM. These provided systems of symbolic correspondences whereby through RITUAL the magician could attune himself, as microcosm, to the great universe, or macrocosm, and thence to celestial and divine powers. Although such techniques also lent themselves to worldly uses, the central concern was to purify the adept spiritually and fit him to 'act as a conscious channel for the work of God in His creation' [19], any practice tending to increase pride or egotism being condemned as 'black' magic. Beginning with Pico della Mirandola (1463–94) and Marsilio Ficino (1433–99), the tradition grew by experiment and speculation, important innovators (representing a tiny proportion of the total) including the cryptographer Trithemius (1462–1516), the chemist Paracelsus (1462–1516) and the mathematician John Dee (1527–1608). Obscure groups carried the tradition through the later 17th and 18th centuries. An 'OCCULT revival' of popular interest began in the mid-19th century, and the tradition was restated and developed by 'Eliphas Lévi' (A. L. Constant, 1810–75) (see TAROT) [21], by 'MacGregor' Mathers (see GOLDEN DAWN) and by E. A. 'Aleister' Crowley (1875–1947), whose flamboyantly aggressive behaviour earned notoriety. The tradition is still practised, inconspicuously, by organizations throughout the Western world. [18]

Western Orthodox Christianity [XIII.D] The expression 'Western Orthodox' is ambiguous: it can refer to Orthodox Christians who use a Western Rite in their services, or to diaspora communities of EASTERN ORTHODOX settled in the West, or to the distinctive theological approaches and religious culture that have emerged in Western Europe and North America. In addition, Celtic Christianity and sometimes more generally Western Christianity before the Great Schism of 1054 are occasionally referred to as Western Orthodoxy by Eastern Orthodox writers. There exist Roman Rite and Anglican Rite communities under various Orthodox jurisdictions, most notably the Patriarchate of Antioch. There exist also small communities, Orthodox in faith but Western in rite, which are not currently recognized by any major Eastern Orthodox communion. Other groups, like the Orthodox Church of the British Isles, have successfully established links with the COPTIC Patriarchate of Alexandria. The dominant tradition of Orthodox worship in Western countries, however, remains the Byzantine Rite. [99]

White Eagle Lodge [XXVIII] Began in the 1920s as an English centre offering the spiritualist teachings of a Native American, White Eagle – 'a very wise soul who has guided the Lodge from the Spirit world for many years'. White Eagle communicated through the mediumship of Grace Cooke (d. 1979), to whom he gave the name Minesta. He taught communion with God through meditation and offered 'a way of life which is gentle and in harmony with the laws of life' – life being governed by five cosmic laws: reincarnation, cause and effect, opportunity, correspondence and equilibrium or balance. The philosophy also embraces ASTROLOGY and healing. [37; 42: 712–13]

Windigo [V] An Ojibwa (north-west woodlands) North American term referring to a cannibalistic figure prominent in Algonquian (*see* ALGONQUIN) mythology. Stories attribute the origin of the *windigo* to a lost hunter, forced by impending starvation to eat human flesh, thereafter becoming a forest-dwelling monster preying on unsuspecting human beings. Occasionally the SHAMAN, in his trance state, may have a vision of a *windigo*, less frequently gaining one as his spirit helper. [24: IX]

Wine-Drinking (in Islam) [XIX] The QUR'AN came to condemn wine-drinking and drunkenness, and it was later accounted a grave sin (*kabira*) (*see* DHANB). Later jurists

had to define wine – was non-grape wine unlawful? – and widened the prohibition to include spirits and narcotic drugs. Nevertheless, wine-drinking has been popular among hedonistic elements, and forms a widespread motif of Sufi mystical and other poetry in Arabic, Persian and Turkish (*see* SUFISM). [38 'Khamr'; 48: 156–7]

Wisdom Literature (Ancient Egyptian) [VI] Presented as advice given by a father or sage, the Egyptian Wisdom Texts [8: 54–84, 234–42] embodied traditions and practical morality intended to assist well-to-do young men to progress in society. Preserved in schoolboy copies, the earliest works are of Ptahhotep (*c.*2400 BCE), for Kagemni (*c.*2400 BCE) (Old Kingdom) and Merikere (*c.*2200 BCE). Royal propaganda was stressed in Middle Kingdom examples, and later texts of the New Kingdom (*c.*1290 BCE) included the Maxims of Ani (*c.*1550 BCE but written *c.*900 BCE) and the Teachings of Amenemope (*c.*1290 BCE) [8: 214–34].

Witchcraft (Western) [XXIV] Contemporary witchcraft (Old English: *wiccecraeft*, lit. wise craft) bears little resemblance to that described in the literature of the witchcraft trials that gripped Europe in the 16th and 17th centuries. During this time witches were accused of making 'pacts' with Satan (*see* SATANISM) which were considered to have rendered their often harmful magic effective. An elaborate belief-system grew up: witches bore a 'witch's mark' (blemish) on the body, attended a *sabbat* (devil-worshipping orgy) at night, to which they ran in animal form or flew, and kept a 'familiar' (personal devil in animal form). The 1484 papal bull (*see* PAPACY) sanctioned the exercise by the church of inquisitorial powers on a mixture of local religions, including forms of pagan worship (Latin: *paganus*, lit. country-dweller). Before 1700 at least 200,000 people were executed, mainly in continental Europe, although the craze took hold in Britain and there was an outbreak at Salem, Massachussetts [27]. This meaning of the term as conscious harming by magical or 'psychic' means (*see* MAGIC; PSYCHIC POWERS) is distinct from its anthropological usage, largely derived from African cultures, where it means a maleficent power innate in certain people who can mysteriously harm others: traditionally a witch cannot help being one and may not know that he or she is [10]. Modern Western witchcraft, however, was inspired by the theories of anthropologist Margaret Murray (1863–1963), who saw European witchcraft as a survival of a benign pre-Christian fertility religion [11]. This form of witchcraft is polytheistic, finding its pantheon in various European pre-Christian and pre-Celtic nature religions (termed 'the old religion'). The prime deities are 'the Goddess' – manifest as the triple goddess of maiden, mother and crone – and the Horned God, a symbol of creativity. Considerable emphasis is placed in modern witchcraft on natural magic, and ritual work with herbs, trees, and flowers for benign purposes. The basic organization of witches is in covens operating under one of six ancient 'houses'. Traditional 'craft' was family-based, with the lineage passing from mother to daughter. Recounting the lineage of a coven traditionally takes place on All Hallows Eve (31 October – the celebration of SAMHAIN which was adopted by the Christian faith as the Feast of All Souls). Other pagan festivals traditionally celebrated by witches are the solstices: Beltane, the spring festival, is associated with maypole and morris dancing, and the summer solstice (in England) with celebrations at Stonehenge and Glastonbury. It must be stressed that modern practitioners of witchcraft are anxious to dissociate it from its earlier maleficent reputation.

Witchcraft Eradication (African) [II]

The chief explanation of unexpected sickness, death and misfortune in many African religious systems is witchcraft and sorcery. In some societies, while the fear of witchcraft did exist, it was seldom focused firmly upon individuals. In many others witchcraft was regularly countered through a witch-doctor (*see* NGANGA), but notorious witches were detected and killed, often through the poison or drowning ordeal.

In modern times governments have forbidden such ordeals, simply denying all reality to witchcraft, but belief in it has hardly lessened, inevitably stimulating new ways of witchcraft control. Sudden waves of village-to-village witch-cleansing organized by itinerant experts have arisen, particularly in central Africa. Among the best known of these movements is the Mcape cult, which spread in the 1930s from Malawi to all the neighbouring countries and has had many successors. Such movements claim to cleanse everyone once for all, provided evil medicines are destroyed and the cult's own medicine taken, which will kill anyone who should return subsequently to witchcraft. They provide a sort of instant millennium, inevitably followed by disillusionment when the old troubles still recur. [5: 103–40; 10: 123–41]

Women (in Early Christianity) [XIII.A]

Although women were not included among the 12 APOSTLES, many of JESUS' closest DISCIPLES were women, outstandingly Mary Magdalene. According to the GOSPELS, women (including MARY) were the most faithful as Jesus was crucified and were the first to witness to the resurrection of Jesus. They played an important part in the spread of CHRISTIANITY. PAUL taught that BAPTISM nullified all distinctions of gender, race and status. He refers gratefully to women who collaborated in his mission. Restrictions on women's role in the church are post-apostolic. The authorship of passages which represent Paul as imposing such restrictions is doubtful. [11: vi, 957–61]

Women (in Judaism) [xxii] Woman is described in the BIBLE story of the creation of the first human couple, Adam and Eve, as a 'helpmeet opposite' man. This seems to summarize her role in JUDAISM, where public religion, e.g. SYNAGOGUE worship, the office of RABBI and TORAH study, is essentially a male preserve [69: 205; 70: 133]. Woman's role is primarily as a wife and mother, who is not bound to keep all the commandments as the male is [14 vol. 16: 623]. REFORM JUDAISM has given women a more public role. [5; 11; 21; 27; 37: xxiv–xxvi]

Wondjina [xxix] In the northern Kimberley region of Western Australia the name *wondjina* (or *wandjina*) is given to the ancestral spirit beings of the so-called Dreaming (here named *ungud*; see ALTJIRANGA). They are depicted in famous cave paintings (noted by George Grey in 1838), and are believed to have each imprinted their own image in these pictures and to continue their existence through them. Each has a nose and eyes but no mouth or sexual characteristics. Rituals for the increase of natural species are connected with them as totemic ancestors (*see* AUSTRALIAN RELIGION). [21: 219–23; 22: 120; 28]

Worldwide Church of God [xxviii] The Radio Church of God, which was founded by Herbert W. Armstrong (1892–1986) in the USA in 1933, changed its name to the Worldwide Church of God in 1968. The Church's theology is non-Trinitarian, with the BIBLE

being accepted as the infallible word of God and the theory of evolution being rejected. Christmas and Easter are denounced as pagan festivals; the Sabbath is kept on Saturdays [41: 154–5]. It is claimed that the Church has nearly 100,000 members in 122 countries [42: 578]. Among the periodicals published by the Church is *The Plain Truth*, offered free in newsagents and to listeners of 'The World Tomorrow' radio and television shows. The Church has been the subject of considerable controversy, partly as a result of sexual scandals surrounding both Armstrong and his son, Garner Ted, who left to set up the Church of God International in 1978 [41: 151–9]. The Church offers a Christian education and training for ministers on its two Ambassador College campuses. A critical quarterly, *Ambassador Report*, is published by ex-members. [32; 41: ii/N; 42: 576–8]

Worship (Biblical and Christian) [xiii.A, B] There is no systematic description of early Christian worship, but all the evidence suggests that it was modelled on the non-sacrificial worship of the Jewish SYNAGOGUE. The focus of such worship was the reading and exposition of the BIBLE. To this might be added hymns, psalms and prayers, some of which survive in the New Testament. To begin with no priestly class was appointed to conduct the worship, nor (in GENTILE CHRISTIANITY) was any special day of worship prescribed. [A.9: 124–49; A.11: vi, 973–89; A.18: 237–44]. The distinctive feature of Christian worship was the EUCHARIST, originally central to the main service (and taken in the course of a communal meal) but later frequently celebrated by itself at a separate gathering. It became one of the seven SACRAMENTS. 'Liturgy' denotes all the fixed services of the church, or specifically the Eucharist, which for the EASTERN ORTHODOX CHURCH joins heaven to earth [B.195: 269–72]. The divine office is the daily public prayer of the Western church, which priests are obliged to recite. The *Breviary* contains material for this, including the canonical hours, from Matins in the early hours of the morning through Lauds, Prime, Terce, Sext, None and Vespers to Compline at night. Recitation of scripture, especially psalms (*see* CHURCH MUSIC), has always been central to these services, but over the centuries much legendary matter from lives of SAINTS was included. The *Breviary* was revised in the 16th century and much simplified in 1971. ANGLICANISM drastically simplified fixed services in its *Book of Common Prayer* (1662). PROTESTANTISM greatly reduced the scope of fixed forms. The Westminster Directory of 1645 (*see* PRESBYTERIANISM) was largely an outline and directions rather than fixed prayers. Much Protestant worship still emphasizes preaching, 'free' prayer and hymns, although there has been some increase in formal liturgical and especially sacramental worship in the main Protestant churches. (*See also* LITURGICAL MOVEMENT.) [B.1: 137–78; B.47; B.48]

Wu Hsing [XII] The Five Phases or Elements in early Chinese metaphysics were systematically developed into a theory of the regulating of nature, heaven and human society by the philosopher Tsou Yen (305–240 BCE). Each phase is represented by a natural element. These are: earth, wood, metal, fire, water. These characterize the quality and function of all phenomena as they change and interrelate. The emphasis in Five Phases theory is always upon the tendency of these qualities to change into another state.

X

Xango [III] Occurs in Recife, Brazil. Its members are lower-class. YORUBA Oshala, Oshagun and Oshalufan are the three major deities, who form a 'Trinity'. *Oshala* is often associated with JESUS, as is the *orisha* Shango/Xango (*see* SANGO/SHANGO). Eshu, the TRICKSTER, wrongly associated with Satan, is the messenger, and 'Master of the Crossroads' between life and death. IFA, the system of Yoruba divination, has gradually atrophied. The most important members of the cult are the mediums, because for a brief time during possession the god is made incarnate. [86; 90]

Y

Yanomami Religion [XXIII] The Yanomami comprise four linguistic sub-groups inhabiting the mountainous rainforest of northern Brazil/ southern Venezuela. While mythic accounts vary considerably among these groups, a common theme found widely holds that after the destruction of the primordial world by a cosmic flood, humans originated from the blood of the moon (*see* CREATION MYTHS; SUN AND MOON). The souls of dead Yanomami, whose bone-ashes are consumed by their kin, are incorporated into the blood-lakes of the moon, where they are regenerated and later reincarnated, through falling rain, to a new existence on earth. Thus human metamorphosis is manifest in cosmic structures whose mythic history is known. Multiple soul elements comprise a complex relational system intimately connected to cosmic processes. [2; 17]

Yasna [XXXVI] Literally 'worship', in ZOROASTRIANISM. As Zoroastrians believe that AHURA MAZDA created the world, so life and work in that world is part of religious duty and can be considered a part of worship [63: VI, VII; 64: XIII]. Temple worship was a late entry into the religion (*see* FIRE). In ancient times prayers were offered close to Mazda's creations – i.e. at the household fire, on mountain tops or near waters. But it is considered essential in Zoroastrianism that worship is offered in total purity, free from the defilement of ANGRA MAINYU. This is difficult to maintain and so increasingly worship has been offered in temples, especially among PARSIS with the growing urbanization of Bombay in the 19th and 20th centuries (*see* MANTHRAS). Zoroastrians who have migrated to the West do not have the resources to consecrate a totally pure temple but in Britain, America, Canada and Australia they have purchased or built their own meeting-places with a prayer-room, generally referred to in America as 'Darbe Mehrs', a misunderstanding of the ancient name *dar-i Mihrs* [10: 33].

Yasna also refers to a specific, highly complex rite, one deriving from Indo-Iranian times (*see* INDO-EUROPEANS) [47: XII]. Originally it involved animal sacrifice, but this is no longer the case among Parsis. The rite consists of the consecration of various items, e.g. water, 'barsom twigs' (now metal strips, replacing the traditional plants which symbolize the plant world), milk, clarified butter (*goshudo*) and sacred bread (*darun*), and especially, the juice from the haoma (later *hom*) plant (*soma* in HINDUISM). This latter is pounded in a mortar and strained through the *varas* ring, which is made from the hairs of a sacred bull. After the preparatory *paragna* rite follows the *yasna* proper [38], the recital of the 72 chapters of the *yasna* text (AVESTA). The rite is performed by an officiating priest (*zaotar, zot*) with an assistant (*raspi*) who tends the sacred fire [8 vol. 1: 159–60; 228; 20: 56–9].

The *yasna* (and all temple rites except the feeding of the fire, the *boy* ceremony) is not performed in the main prayer-room of a temple, but in a separate room called the *yazishngah* or *urvisgah* where the area of purity is marked off by channels (*pavis*). Laity may attend these rites but rarely do so, as congregational worship is not a feature of Zoroastrianism. Essentially the layperson offers his worship to Mazda in private. The purpose of the priestly rites, such as the *yasna*, is to give pleasure and strength to the spiritual beings (AMESHA SPENTAS; YAZATAS); to re-consecrate and benefit the material world of which man is a part; and to bring the spiritual and material worlds together. In the disaspora communities the lack of the pure temple makes the celebration of the *yasna* impossible. The most popular rite has therefore become the *jashan*, a traditional ritual which with the exchange of certain prayers can be used as an act of thanksgiving, or as a celebration or blessing, or to honour the dead. While it can be performed in the temple, it is often used in the home or in more public places. The *jashan*, therefore, already had a flexible use outside temple precincts. In the diaspora it acts as a focal point at which members of scattered groups can congregate. It shares with other Zoroastrian rites the intention of honouring the creator and his creation [46: 66–9]. The word *jashan* also refers to specific days in the Zoroastrian calendar. Each month is named after a heavenly being and one day in the month is also dedicated to each of them. When the day and month dedications coincide these are celebrated by a *jashan* and are known as *jashan* days; thus the Mihr *Jashan* is the day of Mihr (= Mithra) in the month of Mihr [12: 253–5].

Yazatas [XXXVI] 'Beings worthy of worship', in ZOROASTRIANISM (PAHLAVI: *yazad*). AHURA MAZDA and AMESHA SPENTAS are worthy of worship, and therefore can be considered *yazatas*, but the term usually refers to a class of heavenly beings who are often compared to ANGELS in JUDAISM, CHRISTIANITY and ISLAM (scholars believe that Zoroastrianism may have influenced the other religions in this respect [29: pt II]). They are mostly the 'gods' of the ancient Iranians, who have been incorporated into Zoroastrianism by making them the created heavenly helpers of Mazda. One of the most popular is Mithra; another is Verethraghna (later Bahram), the *yazata* of victory to whom the highest grades of FIRE temples are dedicated. An important female *yazata* is Anahita (later Anahid). *Yashts* (AVESTA) days (*roz*) of the month, and the months (*mah*) are named after, or dedicated to, the most popular *yazatas* [8 vol. 1: index; 10: index].

Yeshivah [XXII] The main educational institution of traditional JUDAISM, with an all-male student body usually ranging in age from early teens to mid-20s. The *yeshivah* curriculum concentrates on certain tractates of the Babylonian TALMUD and its many commentaries [70: 113]. The method of study involves the preparation of a text by two, or sometimes three, students (*chavruta*) together who will discuss the implications of a particular subject (*sugya*) and argue the pros and cons of various interpretations. A lecture is then delivered by a RABBI on the *yeshivah* staff, and students raise objections and questions to his exposition. After the lecture a further session of *chavruta* study will go over (*chazarah*) the rabbi's lecture (*shiur*) [19: 182; 67: XXX]. The narrow curriculum and the casuistical method of study (*pilpul*) of some *yeshivot* have been severely criticized by Jewish educationists, but they nevertheless remain characteristic of the *yeshivah* system. [39; 69: 206]

Yezidism [XVIII] A Kurdish sect, originating with the Muslim mystic Shaikh Adi ibn Musafir (d. 1162 CE) [4; 8]. Shaikh Adi's followers formed an order which became influential in many parts of the Islamic world [8: 101f] (*see* SUFI ORDERS). A rift occurred in this movement, one group staying within the pale of ISLAM while another claimed that obedience to the outer requirements of Islam (PILLARS OF ISLAM) was unnecessary. The latter tendency became dominant in Kurdistan, which had remained an important centre of the movement; there, moreover, local myths and traditions of ancient Iranian origin came to form part of the beliefs of the group. This offended orthodox Muslims, who branded the movement as heretical [4: 90]. In the 14th and 15th centuries the Kurdish Yezidi tribes were large and influential, but their power and numbers declined from the 16th century onwards. Since the 15th century the Yezidis have been the object of persecutions and intense hostility on the part of their neighbours, who came to regard them as devil-worshippers. In the 1980s almost the entire Yezidi population of Turkey was forced to migrate to Germany because of Muslim ill-will. There are now *c*.200,000 Yezidis in northern Iraq, *c*.40,000 in Armenia, Azerbaijan and Georgia, and *c*.5,000 in Syria.

Until recently all that was known of the Yezidi sacred tradition were two short works, known as the Sacred Books, and a few texts of lesser importance [5: 199–206]. A substantial body of sacred hymns (*qewl*) has now come to light. SUFI imagery plays a role in this tradition, but the myth of the cosmogony shows an unmistakably ancient Iranian structure. God first created a pearl, and later evoked a heptad consisting of the peacock angel (Malak Tawus), who is its leader, and six other angels [5: 202]. The world was then created from the pearl, and the heptad was entrusted with the responsibility for it [5: 203]. Malak Tawus is the originator of both good and evil in the world, and has sometimes been identified with the devil. The Yezidis, however, think of him as a wholly venerable being, claiming that evil has no objective existence.

Yezidi mythology shows a tendency to make historical phenomena fit a preconceived pattern [1: 49]. Some of Shaikh Adi's successors are described as his contemporaries; together they are regarded as incarnations of the heptad, and as the founders of the lineages of SHAIKHS (religious leaders) [1: 5f, 31]. Every Yezidi must recognize the authority of a Shaikh and a *pir* (i.e. a descendant of companions of Shaikh Adi who were not members of his family) [1: 34], who are nominally responsible for his spiritual welfare. They must also choose a 'brother (or sister) of the hereafter' from a family of Shaikhs, who will help the soul after death [1: 40f].

Theology does not play a major role in Yezidism; obedience to the authorities of the faith and observance of customs and rituals are central elements. Feasts are a significant part of religious life; the most important is the Festival of the Assembly, an autumn festival held at Lalish which culminates in a bull sacrifice [1: I]. The Valley of Lalish is the centre of the religious universe of Yezidism. It houses the great sanctuary, the shrine of Shaikh Adi, and a number of lesser shrines.

Yggdrasil [VII] The World Ash, the guardian tree of the AESIR in pre-Christian Scandinavia. It was thought to mark the centre of the nine worlds of gods, men, giants, the dead, and other supernatural beings. A drink from Mimir's spring, at the foot of Yggdrasil, gives wisdom [3: 190–6; 4: 170–1]. The name Yggdrasil probably means 'horse of Ygg', i.e. ODIN, who once hung upon it. The tree is to survive RAGNAROK, sheltering those destined to repeople the world in the new age.

Yin–Yang [XII] The ancient Chinese theory of the two opposite and complementary forces in nature. The Yin force is associated with the feminine, the earth, darkness, cold, the night, the moon and passivity. The Yang force is associated with the masculine, the heavens, light, heat, the day, the sun and activity. According to Yin–Yang theory the seasonal cycle and the whole of the natural order are explained in terms of the progression and alteration of the balance of the two forces. The great Han Confucian Tung Chung Shu (176–104 BCE) combined Yin–Yang and the Five Elements (WU HSING) theories and applied them to interpreting historical, social and political processes, as well as the natural order. [7: XI, 244–50; 34: III, 32; 35: II, 7–132; 88: I, 8–16]

Yoga [XVII] The word *yoga* is related to the English 'yoke'; its primary meaning is probably 'work', i.e. spiritual practice, but the alternative sense of 'union', i.e. with the divine, is widely used. In fact the word is used in several different ways. It may indicate one of the (three or four) spiritual approaches of Indian religion: ritual (KARMA YOGA), devotional (BHAKTI YOGA), intellectual (JNANA YOGA) or meditational (DHYANA YOGA), especially the last. Sometimes it means 'practice' as opposed to 'theory'. It may refer to a particular technique or method: HATHA YOGA, emphasizing the physical; *raja yoga*, the mental; *kundalini yoga*, arousing vital energy; *mantra yoga*, utilizing particular sounds; *laya yoga*, sinking into the divine; *asparsha yoga*, detaching from contact; *taraka yoga*, employing eidetic-visual phenomena; *nada yoga*, based upon similar noise phenomena; and so on.

Yoga can also refer to sectarian spiritual approaches – SHIVA-*yoga*, *Jaina yoga* (*see* JAIN), etc. – but in isolation often refers to the *yoga* school of Patanjali (*see* YOGA-DARSHANA), a type of *dhyana yoga* and the prestigious royal yoga (*raja yoga*) *par excellence*. In its widest use

yoga is a collective term for all of the above; in this sense it is a universal phenomenon. In the somewhat narrower sense of 'Indian magico-spirituality' its ultimate origins are very old. Some scholars believe it can already be identified in illustrations from the INDUS VALLEY civilization (*c.*2000 BCE). Others have preferred to see an INDO-EUROPEAN origin in the Vedic *vratya* movement. No doubt spontaneous mystical tendencies and a shamanistic background (*see* SHAMAN) also played a part. [General: 35: 1–109; 45: 123–56; 133: 93–150]

Yogacara [XI] One of the two main forms of systematic MAHAYANA BUDDHIST thought. The Yogacara (*see* YOGA) school emphasized the importance of calm (SAMATHA) meditation as a prerequisite to the development of wisdom. MAHAYANA SUTRAS containing many of the ideas later taken up by Yogacara writers were in existence by the 3rd century CE, but Yogacara systematic (*shastra*) literature probably dates from the 4th or 5th century CE. The fundamental works of the school are attributed to MAITREYA and ASANGA, but there is debate as to whether this Maitreya is a historical teacher of Asanga or the BODHI-SATTVA Maitreya inspiring certain of Asanga's writings. Important works are also attributed to Asanga's brother VASUBANDHU, traditionally the author of the *Abhidharmakosha* (*see* VAIBHASHIKA), converted to Mahayana in old age.

Using both Mahayana and *abhidharma* (ABHIDHAMMA) sources, the Yogacarins created a vast synthesis, mapping the stages of the path in great detail and constructing a Mahayana *abhidharma*. Notable developments were the eight consciousnesses (*see* ALAYA-VIJNANA) and an elaborated understanding of the nature of a BUDDHA. [32a] The Yogacarins claimed a middle way between the realist SARVASTIVADA and the nihilist SHUNYATAVADA, affirming that although self and separate entities are non-existent, thusness (*tathata*), i.e. ultimate truth and consciousness itself, are not non-existent. The school is as a consequence known as the Vijnanavada ('Consciousness doctrine'). Owing to its denial of the independent reality of matter, it is sometimes referred to as the Idealist school.

Yogacara has influenced most later Mahayana traditions. In Tibetan Buddhism (*see* TIBETAN RELIGIONS) it is especially influential among the older sects, while in the Far East it was the basis of one school (FA HSIANG TSUNG; *see also* NANTO ROKUSHU) and important for several others. A branch of the Yogacara specializing in logic and epistemology was formed by Vasubandhu's pupil Dinnaga, making use of methods developed by the Hindu NYAYA school. The tradition of Dinnaga and later Dharmakirti (7th century) is of considerable philosophical importance and exercised a significant influence upon later Hindu and Buddhist logic. [Translations 72: 328–37; logic 88; general 10; 101]

Yoga-darshana [XVII] One of the six DARSHANAS or salvation-philosophies of classical HINDUISM. The yoga school is concerned with the description of the stages of the spiritual path, of methods of practice and of the forms of contemplative experience. Closely related to the SAMKHYA, it emerges from the same Upanishadic milieu. The most authoritative text is the *Yoga-sutra* attributed to the grammarian Patanjali (2nd century BCE) but almost certainly compiled around the 4th century CE [translation: 107: 453–86]. The principal commentator is 'Vyasa' (perhaps 6th century), but a number of later commentaries exist, including many modern ones [history: 51: 217–354]. The classical yoga accepts the same world view as the Samkhya, differing mainly in its subject matter but also in accepting a limited role for a supreme deity (ISHVARA).

The great success of the *Yoga-sutra* is due to a skilful synthesis of two distinct approaches to *yoga*, perhaps originally from different sources. One emphasizes cessation (*nirodha*) of all mental activities; yogic practice and detachment will remove all tendency to identify with those activities and bring about a return to innate independence and purity. The other is a more positive account in terms of an Eightfold Path: (1) restraints (*yama*) or external moral precepts; (2) observances (*niyama*), i.e. internal moral purification; control of (3) posture (*asana*) and (4) breath (*pranayama*); (5) and (6) control of attention (both steps); (7) *dhyana* and (8) *samadhi*, states of meditative absorption which lead to the arousing of yogic knowledge and eventually liberation (MOKSHA). Such a mixture of moral, physical and meditational training is typical of DHYANA YOGA. [45: 9–122; 49: 1–20; 133: 130–40]

Yom Kippur [XXII] ('Day of Atonement') Twenty-five hour fast-day which is the culmination of the 10 days of repentance beginning with the New Year (ROSH HA-SHANAH). Before the FAST begins it is customary, in many traditional communities, to perform a ceremony of atonement (*kapparot*) which involves a person waving a chicken over his head and declaring that its death should substitute for any punishment due to him. Some people prefer to perform this ceremony with money instead of a chicken, the money being given to charity [59: 149]. Pietists undergo a symbolic flogging before the onset of the fast as an added atonement. The day begins at sundown with *Kol Nidrei*, a service of annulment of religious vows [70: 179], and the fast ends the next day when three stars appear, at which point the *shofar* (ram's horn) is blown in the SYNAGOGUE. On Yom Kippur there is no eating or drinking, no washing, sexual relations or wearing leather shoes. People dress in white, to signify the forgiveness of sins, and the Book of Jonah, with its message of repentance, is read. In biblical times the High Priest used to enter the Holy of Holies of the Jerusalem TEMPLE on this day to offer up incense, and a goat was sent off into the wilderness carrying away the sins of the people of Israel [69: 31].

Yoruba Religion [π] The Yoruba, a people of some 10 million in western Nigeria, have a religion which varies considerably with city and province. It might well be described as many religions. What is common is the underlying, anthropomorphically expressed belief in one supreme God, Olorun (Lord of Heaven) or Olodumare (meaning unclear). His primacy in myth, proverb and occasional personal prayer is clear; nevertheless, modern Yoruba religion is characterized less by Olodumare than by the multitudes of ORISHA, with their mass of shrines, priests, festivals and sacrifices. There is now almost no public worship of Olodumare, nor mention of him in the *oriki* of *orisha* worship, so that Yoruba religion appears as polytheism, although each *orisha* is treated in worship almost monotheistically. The complex system of IFA DIVINATION, an effectively unifying factor across the cults, is very important.

Yoruba religion is among those thriving most in Africa today. Its *orisha* cults, divination and secret societies have been fully adapted to urban, industrial society; noteworthy are Ogun's patronage of mechanics and bus-drivers, and the popularity of the shrines and festivals at Oshogbo, renewed by Susanne Wenger, a convert to the *orisha* in the 1970s [22; 35; 40].

Z

Zakat [XIX] The religious alms tax (near-synonym *sadaqa*) accounted one of the PILLARS OF ISLAM. It is levied on various categories of possessions, according to fixed rates, and used for charitable purposes as laid down in the QUR'AN. In the present Islamic world, in which Western-type fiscal systems have often been adopted, this tax on incomes is largely voluntary. [37 s.v.; 48: 105–7; 67 s.v.; 80: 159–60]

Zande Religion [II] The Azande (= the people; adjective: Zande) live in north-east Zaire and south-west Sudan, and are a highly secular but traditional society, valuing courtesy, good judgement, humour, hospitality and scepticism. Its kings were greatly respected, but not for religious reasons. The existence of Mbori, the supreme being, maker of all things and thought to reside at the head of streams, may be unquestioned, but arouses little interest, no regular cult and few personal prayers. Nor is there great interest in, or ritual devoted to, other spiritual beings.

Zande explanation of misfortune and especially death is in terms of witchcraft (*mangu*) and bad magic, i.e. sorcery (*gbegbere ngua*). The theory of these is partly moral (the ill will of evil men), partly materialist; it is not a matter of the agency of spiritual beings, but of certain mysterious physical powers at work in people and things. Thus the witch has an identifiable substance in his body which provides his power. His action can be detected through DIV-INATION, either through the use of oracles (*soroka*) – of which the most reliable is the poison oracle (the administration of a substance called *benge* to fowls) – or through the mediumistic activities of witch-doctors (*abinza*). The initiation of the latter again chiefly consists in learning what trees and herbs provide the right medicine with which to detect witchcraft.

The oracle's power lies in the *benge* itself, not in any spiritual agent behind it; it may be administered by anyone. The sorcerer's power lies in the use of offensive medicines, which may be countered by other good magic. Magic (*ngua*) is physically the same, whether good or bad: the differentiation derives from the human moral purpose utilizing it. *Mangu, ngua* and *soroka* appear as theories of science rather than religion, powerful in a secularized society in which religious belief and ritual are minimal. [27: 162–203; 29]

Zen [XXI] Meditation (*dhyana*; Chinese: CH'AN; Japanese: *zen*) [8: 87–92; 13; 36: 203–28, 240–1, 250–3; 37]. Meditating in the way of the historic BUDDHA (GOTAMA) first appeared as a formal practice in Japan in the 9th century, but made no headway until the priest Eisai (1141–1215) returned in 1191 from his second trip to China (*see* JAPAN, BUDDHISM IN). After trying to settle in Kyushu he was identified with an unpopular Kyoto Zen priest and ordered to cease. Eisai preached Lin-chi (Japanese: Rinzai) in Kyoto, then in Kamakura where he gained the support of the military ruler, moving into the Kennin-ji in Kyoto in 1202 and teaching a mixed form of esoteric TENDAI and Zen. His Jufuku-ji temple in Kamakura was pure Zen. He stressed *koan* (paradoxical questions), tea-drinking and sudden enlightenment. Rinzai has appealed chiefly to the aristocracy. Soto Zen has become more popular, spread by the priest Dogen (1200–53), who had once studied under Eisai [29]. He introduced Ts'ao-tung (Japanese: Soto) in 1227 after a trip to China, and lived in Kyoto where he wrote *Fukan Zazengi* (General Teaching for Seated Meditation), an exposition of meditation practices free of other sectarian rituals. Tendai monks forced him to move and he settled in the Daibutsu-ji, a temple in Fukui prefecture, in 1244. The temple was renamed Eihei-ji and shares headquarters responsibilities with the Soji-ji, which was moved to Yokohama in 1898 [21: 203–4]. His *Shobo Genzo*, written in Japanese rather than in the customary Chinese, stresses discipline, work, practice and philosophical questions to find one's Buddha-nature in the 'realization of self'. Soto appealed to the peasants and the lower-level samurai (warriors) for its value in teaching self-control. Priests were cultural advisers to shoguns (generals), involved in commerce and sponsored allied arts, such as garden design, tea ceremony and calligraphy. The painting of subjects integral to Zen questions was a religious exercise, but traditional painting and sculpture were distractions to be avoided.

A somewhat less important sect is Obaku, the Chinese Huang-po, brought by the priest Yin-yuan (1594–1673) and called Ingen in Japan, with headquarters at the large Chinese-style Mampuku-ji (Obakusan) near Uji. Much Chinese ritual is still retained there along with *nembutsu* (*see* AMIDA WORSHIP). Rinzai has 14 current schools (*ha*) or sub-sects, and there are several relatively independent schools. Besides the unmistakable influence Zen has had on Japanese life and thought as a whole, Soto has broadened its acceptance by including extensive Pure Land funerary beliefs and practices [21: 202–5].

Ziggurat [VIII] The stepped temple tower, built of mud brick, was a notable feature of Mesopotamian cities; the most imposing survival is at Ur (*c*.2113 BCE) [20]. An artificial mountain re-creating the mountains on which the SUMERIANS had worshipped in their northern homelands, the ziggurat sometimes incorporated a shrine on the summit, and was always associated with the city-god's cult. The ELAMITES [17: 17–22] adopted the ziggurat, and at Susa it followed the pattern at Nippur, Babylon and elsewhere, while at Choga-Zanbil it differed from the Mesopotamian examples in both planning and construction.

At Ashur (*see* ASSYRIANS) the god's TEMPLE, rebuilt in the 13th century BCE, combined the temple and ziggurat in a single complex.

Zina [XIX] A term which in ISLAM denotes illicit sexual relations and covers the concepts of both adultery and fornication; sexual relations are thus condemned when occurring outside marriage or concubinage. The prescribed penalties are flogging or stoning (with variations in the legal schools and according to the legal status of the two parties), but guilt can only be proved on the evidence of four eyewitnesses. In practice, women considered as erring have often been disposed of by their relatives without recourse to formal law. Sodomy and bestiality are also strongly reprehended. [37 s.v.; 77: III]

Zionism [XXII] A Jewish nationalist movement, the aim of which was the setting-up of a Jewish state in the HOLY LAND as a homeland for the

Jewish people [14 vol. 16: 1031]. The first Zionist congress was held in Basel in 1897 on the initiative of Theodor Herzl (1860–1904), the father of political Zionism. Herzl brought together the various groups of Zionists who had come to recognize the necessity of Jewish self-determination in their own country [40]. The World Zionist Organization (1897) became the umbrella body of the movement, although individual groups representing socialist, religious, cultural and revisionist forms of Zionism have maintained their separate identities [26]. With the founding of the STATE OF ISRAEL in 1948 the Zionist movement achieved its main political objective, and since then has concentrated on providing financial aid to Israel, supporting Jewish immigrants who have gone there (*aliyah*) from all over the world, and educating diaspora Jews. [11; 25; 44; 52; 58: 197; 70: 79]

Zionist Movements (African) [xxvii] A general term used in southern Africa for new movements, or for the less orthodox, more PENTECOSTAL types, distinguished from ETHIOPIAN CHURCHES. Zionists correspond to the ALADURAS of Nigeria and the 'spiritual churches' of Ghana, and to the general 'prophet-healing' type which since about the 1920s has been more common. They are more African in worship and polity, sometimes more SYNCRETISTIC in beliefs, and emphasize the power of the HOLY SPIRIT. [12: 43–7; 18: 53–5, 95–9, 315–19: 26: 58–9]

Zohar [xxii] The main text of the KABBALAH. It appeared in mysterious circumstances in Spain towards the end of the 13th century. The Kabbalist Moses de Leon (*c.*1240–1305) started circulating manuscripts purporting to be the teachings of a circle of mystics living in Palestine in the 2nd and 3rd centuries. Despite doubts expressed by individual kabbalists, including contemporaries of de Leon, about the authenticity of de Leon's claim, the kabbalistic tradition has come to accept that the *Zohar* is a genuinely ancient text [70: 99]. It is thought to preserve the mystical teachings of RABBI Simeon bar Yochai and his disciples, although exactly how the original manuscript reached Spain is unclear. Modern scholarship views the Zoharic literature as a series of pseudepigraphic texts composed by Moses de Leon and other unknown Kabbalists in the late 13th and early 14th centuries [61: v]. The *Zohar* is in the form of a MIDRASH on the BIBLE. [14 vol. 16: 1193]. Its main teaching concerns the 10 emanations (SEFIRAH) through which the world came into being, and which underlie all reality.

Zombi/Zombie In KUMINA the highest sky deity is Oto, King Zombi. Ancestral spirits are collectively referred to as zombies, derived from the Kikongo *dzambi*, 'god'. Trindadian 'jumbie', Jamaican 'duppy', Monserratian 'jumbee' and Brazilian 'zumbie' share the same derivation. All zombies in Kumina are invoked by drumming, dance and singing. *Obeahmen* (*see* OBEAH) are generally associated with such ceremonies. The primary function of these ceremonies is to invoke zombies for the purpose of personal possession. In Haitian VOODOO, a zombi is a soulless body. The soul has been interred, and raised again; the body is then used for slave labour in gardens and plantations, for housework and house building. The zombies are the slaves of Voodoo practioners, generally *bocors*. A *houngan* may be a *bocor*. Zombis constitute a reality in Haitian culture. Zombification is the process by which such enslavement is effected. In Haiti the legal and ethical implications are rarely alluded to. Zombification is caused by the use of drugs produced from a plant and a small fish. The result, after the individual had been certified dead, buried, exhumed and revived, is that the personality of the zombi is severely diminished. Haitians therefore fear becoming zombies. [2; 33; 34; 34a; 50a; 68; 69a; 86; 90a]

Zoroaster [xxxvi] Greek form of the Iranian name Zarathushtra (later Zardusht) of the prophet, who was of the Spitama family. Most scholars believe that he lived in eastern Iran but there is less agreement over his dates. Recent PARSI tradition dates him around 6000 BCE, but this date is not accepted by any Western academic. Instead, a date of around the 6th century BCE has been preferred [26: III; 64: 33], although recent research suggests an earlier date of approximately 1200 BCE as more likely [8 vol. 2: 1–3; 10: 18; 25]. On this dating he is one of the first prophets in the HISTORY OF RELIGIONS. His teaching is preserved in 17 hymns, known as the *Gathas*, which constitute a central portion of the liturgy of the YASNA and are contained in the Zoroastrian holy book, the AVESTA [translations: 11: 34–45; 19; 35; 48: 344–90; 54].

Zoroaster believed that he had seen God, AHURA MAZDA, in visions and that he had been set apart for his priestly and prophetic mission from the beginning. Ahura Mazda, he taught, was the creator of all that is good and is alone worthy of absolute worship. The prophet has, therefore, been termed the first monotheist. Opposed to Ahura Mazda, he taught, is the opposing 'twin spirit', the malign source of violence, evil and death, ANGRA MAINYU. Man has freedom to choose between these two powers. The righteous will oppose evil, spread the Good Religion of Zoroaster, care for the Good Creation (plants, animals and fellow humans) and worship Mazda in purity. Zoroaster vigorously rejected the *daevas*, the gods of the Indo-Iranians (*see* INDO-EUROPEANS) such as Indra (*see* VEDA), because of their violent and amoral nature. This he saw epitomized in the destruction wrought by the invaders who were threatening the stability of his settled farming community. Humanity's eternal destiny, he taught, would be decided by the use each person made of their free will, at the individual judgement after death (*see* CHINVAT BRIDGE) and at the universal judgement after the resurrection (*see* FRASHOKERETI). The righteous, he believed, would go to heaven and the wicked to hell – a dark abyss of misery, bad food and woe. Zoroaster was, then, the first prophet to teach a belief in the two judgements, heaven, hell and the resurrection of the body. [8 pt 1, VII–IX; 10: II–III]

Passages in the Avesta and the later PAHLAVI literature narrate various legends concerning his life. According to them his birth had been foretold to men of ancient times and was marked by miracles. The forces of evil tried to destroy the young child, but he was divinely protected. He was a priest given to solitary meditation. His first vision came at the age of 30. At first his message was rejected and he was violently attacked, but he persevered and converted the king Vishtaspa (later Gushtasp) by miraculously curing his favourite horse when all other remedies had failed. Thereafter Zoroaster's teaching became the official religion of the realm. According to tradition he was murdered at the age of 77 while praying at the altar. In modern Parsi belief he is thought of by some of the orthodox as representing the presence of God on earth, that is, as being more than an ordinary man. For Zoroastrians in Iran he is simply the prophet of God. Two of the most popular of all Parsi festivals are Khordad-Sal (commemorating Zoroaster's birth) and Zarthusht-no Diso (commemorating his death) [12: 253, 255]. [8 vol. 1: XI; 28: 92–7]

Zoroastrian pseudepigrapha [xviii] The Greeks of the Hellenistic age (3rd century BCE and later) held in high repute the sages, real and imagined, of alien cultures [14]. Among these were the Persian MAGI in general and ZOROASTER in particular. Consequently, much literature came into circulation attributed to these figures [11; 10]. The actual authors are unknown. It used to be supposed that this corpus was ultimately the product of Hellenized magi of the Iranian diaspora in Asia Minor, the so-called Magusaeans [11; on actual Zoroastrianism of that period and region, 12: VIII–XI]. With the likely exception of the *Oracles of Hystaspes* and of some material preserved in Dio Chrysostom (see below), this view is now untenable, since it has been demonstrated that apart from a few trace elements the bulk of the Zoroastrian pseudepigrapha transmits not the teachings of ZOROASTRIANISM, but the miscellaneous encyclopedic information of Hellenistic learning [10]. Its authors used the names and authority of Zoroaster and the magi for legitimation, not to deceive but under the sincere misapprehension that they were transmitting the wisdom of the sages of long ago and far away.

Except for the recently recovered *Zostrianos*, the pseudepigrapha are extant only in quoted fragments and references. The material falls generally into one of two classes, astrology or magic. Most of the astrology was attributed to Zoroaster himself [10: 521–39], in part because of a fanciful Greek etymology for his name (Zo-ro-aster = influence of the living star). The magic, however, was mostly attributed to Ostanes [10: 553–64], supposedly one of the magi who accompanied Xerxes on his invasion of Greece (479 BCE) and later met and taught the philosopher Democritus of Abdera. There may be a historical reality behind the story. What is not historically true is that Ostanes was the originator of the magic (and alchemy) that passed under his (and Democritus') name. Like the astrology it is the product of

Hellenistic Greek 'science', based on the theory of 'universal sympathy', the doctrine that the world is an interconnected whole and that all parts can be accessed and manipulated provided one discovers the arcane links that bind them. It was not inappropriate that this magic should be associated with a famous Persian magus. 'Magic' (*mageia*) is etymologically derived from 'magus', and for the Greeks it was peculiarly, if mistakenly, the activity of the magi [10: 511–21].

Three other items of pseudepigrapha should be mentioned. (1) The *Oracles of Hystaspes* are a collection of eschatological prophecies, falsely attributed to Zoroaster's royal patron, Vishtaspa. They belong, however, within the actual Zoroastrian tradition and reflect, though with many distortions, that religion's reaction first to Macedonian, then to Roman, domination [12: 376–81; 13]. (2) Two cosmological and eschatological myths are reported by the 1st–2nd century CE Greek author Dio Chrysostom (*Oration* 36.39–end) as hymns sung by the magi. It is impossible to tell, finally, whether they are Dio's invention or actual liturgical hymns of contemporary Magusaeans, much transformed and allegorized [10: 539–48]. (3) The tractate *Zostrianos*, no. VIII, 1 from the NAG HAMMADI Coptic Gnostic Library, is a typical piece of GNOSTIC spiritual ascent literature. It purports to be the 'teachings of Zoroaster'. It is not. Rather, it is a perfect example of the borrowing of the great magus' name to validate the wisdom of an entirely different tradition [10: 550–3].

Zoroastrianism [XXXVI] The religion of the followers of the Iranian prophet ZOROASTER (*c*.1200 BCE). The history of the religion prior to the 6th century BCE is largely unknown. Thereafter it became the state religion of three successive Iranian empires: the Achaemenids (*c*.549–331 BCE); the Parthians (2nd century BCE to 224 CE); and the Sasanians (224–642 CE), the boundaries of whose territories extended into what is now Afghanistan and Pakistan and westwards into what is now Iraq, and at times into Palestine and what is now Turkey. Zoroastrian Iran was finally defeated by the expansion of ISLAM, but for over 1,000 years Zoroastrianism was the official religion of three major world empires, making it, perhaps, the most powerful world religion of the time. The last Zoroastrian monarch was Yazdegird (d. 652 CE). The modern Zoroastrian calendar begins with his coronation and the designation *anno Yazdegird* (AY) is used.

Since the end of the Zoroastrian state the religion has been persistently and harshly persecuted by Muslims in Iran, so that the faithful few have been forced to retreat into remote villages, especially near the desert cities of Yazd and Kerman, where they have generally lived in abject poverty. Greater freedom was granted under the PAHLAVI dynasty, and the new Islamic Republic has promised to preserve the rights of minorities. It is a considerable tribute to the strength of the faith that even a small group has survived the millennium of oppression. They are often referred to as the 'Zardushti', or as *gabr* (*gaur/gor/guebre*), meaning 'infidel'. They themselves sometimes use the term 'Mazda yasnians' (worshippers (YASNA) of Mazda (AHURA MAZDA)).

In the 10th century CE some Zoroastrians left Iran to seek a new land of religious freedom and settled in north-west India, where they are known as PARSIS (= Persians). The main centres of Zoroastrianism nowadays are India (mainly Bombay), 72,000; Iran, 30,000 plus; Pakistan, 2,000; Britain, 5,000; and North America (USA and Canada), 6,000 (all figures are approximate).

Traditional Zoroastrian teachings are found in the holy book, the AVESTA, and the PAHLAVI literature. An essential feature of all worship (YASNA), centred on FIRE, is physical and moral purity (*see* DAXMA; MAGI; MANTHRAS). Zoroastrianism is often described as a DUALISM because of its teaching on a wholly good God, AHURA MAZDA, who is opposed by the evil ANGRA MAINYU. It is, however, a central part of this optimistic religion that evil will be defeated (*see* FRASHOKERETI). There is no idea of a spirit/flesh dualism because both the spiritual and the material worlds are the creation (BUNDAHISHN) of God. Humans therefore, have a religious duty to care for both the material and the spiritual aspects of their existence. It is a religion which inculcates the highest moral ideals. Once the believer has been initiated (NAUJOTE) he or she (there is little difference in the religious duties of the sexes) should fight evil in all its forms.

Zoroastrianism has considerable historical importance because of its geographical position astride the routes between East and West, and also because of its profound influence on JUDAISM, CHRISTIANITY and ISLAM, especially in regard to beliefs on heaven, hell, resurrection of the dead and the final judgement (*see* FRASHOKERETI). It is also thought that it inspired a belief in a saviour to come in HINDUISM (Kalkin; *see* AVATARA) and BUDDHISM (the BUDDHA to come – *see* MAITREYA). [1; 2; 3; 10; 11; 23; 41; 50]

Zulu Religion [II] The Zulus have been exposed to Christianity for so long (*see* AFRICA, CHRISTIANITY IN) and their royal political system was so severely damaged in the 19th century that it is now particularly difficult to describe their traditional religion as a whole. Many 19th-century observers denied that Zulus believed in one creator God. The argument centred on the word *Unkulunkulu*, meaning the aged or first or most revered one. It is certainly a praise-name for God but is at least as much used for the ancestors. The principal specific titles for God are *iNkosi yaphezulu*, Lord-of-the-sky, and *uMvelingqangi*. The latter means 'first to appear' but with the implicit suggestion of twins, the twin of sky being earth. *UMvelingqangi* is male, earth female; together they bring forth the human world.

Unkulunkulu the God is not *Unkulunkulu* the ancestors, who are beneath the earth rather than in the sky. Thunder and lightning are acts of God, whereas sickness and other troubles in life may be caused by the ancestors, the *idlozi* or *abaphansi* (those under the earth). The ancestors protect the living, ask for 'food', are pleased with ritual and sacrifice, punish neglect and take possession of diviners (*inyanga*). Most *inyanga* are women. The diviner reveals the mind of the ancestors, fights witchcraft, and – very often – acts as a herbalist, but the former is her principal role. [24]

Zurvan [XXXVI] 'Time', made into the first cause in the major heresy within ZOROASTRIANISM, Zurvanism. The origins of the heresy are unknown. It was perhaps the dominant tradition at the court of the Sasanians (224–642 CE) and lasted into Islamic times, but then withered away. Speculation on Time as the source and controller of all things may well have been due to BABYLONIAN influence on Zoroastrianism. Zurvan was thought of as the father of the 'twin spirits', AHURA MAZDA and ANGRA MAINYU, and therefore, by implication, beyond the distinctions of good and evil. This led to some un-Zoroastrian teachings, for example that if Time controls all things then it follows that man has no free will, an idea alien to the prophet ZOROASTER. Also, with Zurvan as father of the twin spirits, Ahura Mazda is no longer the sole creator and alone worthy of absolute worship. It also suggests that good and evil are not absolute opposites as they are traditionally conceived in Zoroastrianism. There is no evidence to show that Zurvanism ever involved a separate ritual and it may be doubted if it ever formed a separate cult; it was rather perhaps an aberrant movement within Zoroastrianism [10: 67–70, 112–13, 118–23; 53a; 62; 64: VIII–IX].

Bibliography

Edited by N. K. Firby

Editorial Note

The following subject lists have been compiled separately by the contributors of articles in the *Dictionary* and inevitably there are some instances of overlap and inconsistency. The subject scope of each list reflects the specialities of the contributor. When there are a number of compilers, they are listed alphabetically, unless one compiler is primarily responsible for this section of the bibliography.

The editions listed are not exhaustive: the first is that to which any page references are made. A later edition or reprint date may follow, but this does not indicate that the work is in print and 'new edn' does not necessarily indicate revised text: often it is a paperback edition. Two publishers noted before one date indicates a joint English/United States publication, with the same pagination. Earlier editions are noted when the date is significant.

N.K.F.

[I]   General Books on Religions

Compiled by John R. Hinnells

1   BRANDON, S. G. F., *A Dictionary of Comparative Religion*, London, Weidenfeld/New York, Scribner, 1970
1a BROWN, A. (ed.), *Festivals in World Religions*, ed. on behalf of the Shap Working Party on World Religions in Education, London, New York, Longman, 1986
2   BRUCE, F. F., and RUPP, E. G. (eds), *Holy Book and Holy Tradition*, Manchester, Manchester University Press/Grand Rapids, Mich., Eerdmans, 1968
3   ELIADE, M. (ed.), *From Primitives to Zen: A Thematic Sourcebook of the History of Religions*, London, Collins/New York, Harper & Row, 1967; new edn London, Fount Books, 1978
4   ELIADE, M. (ed.), *The Encyclopedia of Religions*, 16 vols, London, Collier Macmillan/New York, Macmillan, 1987
5   ELIADE, M., *Patterns in Comparative Religion* (tr. Rosemary Sheed), London/New York, Sheed & Ward, 1958; new edn 1979
6   FOY, W. (ed.), *Man's Religious Quest*, London, Croom Helm/New York, St Martin's, 1978
7   HASTINGS, J., *Encyclopaedia of Religion and Ethics*, 13 vols, Edinburgh, T. & T. Clark, 1908–26 repr.; 12 vols, New York, Scribner, 1961
8   HINNELLS, J. R. (ed.), *A Handbook of Living Religions*, Harmondsworth/New York, Penguin Books, 1984; new edn, 1991
9   HINNELLS, J. R. (ed.), *Who's Who of World Religions*, London, Macmillan, 1991; Penguin, 1996
10 LING, T., *A History of Religion East and West*, London, Macmillan/New York, St Martin's, 1968; New York, Harper Colophon, 1970

11   MOORE, A. C., *Iconography of Religions: An Introduction*, London, SCM/ Philadelphia, Pa, Fortress, 1977
12   NOSS, J. B., *Man's Religions*, 6th edn, New York, Macmillan, 1980
13   PARRINDER, E. G., *A Dictionary of Non-Christian Religions*, Amersham, Hulton Educational, 1971; Philadelphia, Pa., Westminster, 1973
14   PARRINDER, E. G., *Man and His Gods*, Feltham, Hamlyn, 1971; repr. 1973
15   PYE, E. M. (ed.), *Macmillan Dictionary of Religions*, London, Macmillan, 1993
16   SMART, N., *The Religious Experience of Mankind*, New York, Scribner, 1969; London, Fontana, 1971; repr. Fount 1977
17   SMART, N. (ed.), *The World's Religions*, Cambridge, Cambridge University Press, 1989, 1992
18   SMITH, HUSTAN, *The Religions of Man*, New York, Harper & Row, 1965 (© 1958)
19   SMITH, WILFRED CANTWELL, *The Faith of Other Men*, New York, Harper & Row, 1972
20   STRENG, F., et al., *Ways of Being Religious: Readings for a New Approach to Religion*, Englewood Cliffs, NJ, Prentice-Hall, 1973
21   SUTHERLAND, S. (ed.), *The World's Religions*, London, Routledge, 1988
22   WHALING, F. (ed.), *Religion in Today's World*, Edinburgh, T. & T. Clark, 1987
23   ZAEHNER, R. C. (ed.), *A Concise Encyclopedia of Living Faiths*, 3rd edn, London, Hutchinson/Boston, Mass., Beacon Press, 1977; 1st edn, New York, Hawthorn Books, 1959; 4th rev. edn publ. as *Encyclopedia of Living Faiths*, London, Hutchinson, 1988

Three series of books have been published on religion around the world with wide-ranging coverage. Nos 24 and 25 are designed to provide reliable and authoritative introductions to the various religions. No. 26 consists of compendia of new translations of important texts from the different religions.

24   STRENG, F. (ed.), *The Religious Life of Man*, Encino, Cal., Dickenson Publishing Co.
25   HINNELLS, J. R., and SMART, N. (eds), *The Library of Religious Beliefs and Practices*, London/Boston, Mass., Routledge
26   HINNELLS, J. R., and DONIGER, W. (eds), *Textual Sources for the Study of Religion*, Chicago, Ill., Chicago University Press

[II]   *African Religions*

Compiled by Adrian Hastings

(a)   General and Thematic Surveys

1   ARENS, W., and KARP, I. (eds), *Creativity of Power: Essays on Cosmology and Action in African Societies*, Washington, DC, Smithsonian Institution Press, 1989
2   BEATTIE, J., and MIDDLETON, J. (eds), *Spirit Mediumship and Society in Africa*, London, Routledge/New York, Holmes & Meier, 1969
3   BOOTH, N. W. (ed.), *African Religions: A Symposium*, New York, NOK, 1977

4 DE HEUSCH, L., *Sacrifice in Africa: A Structuralist Approach*, Manchester, Manchester University Press, 1985
5 DOUGLAS, M. (ed.), *Witchcraft, Confessions and Accusations*, London, Tavistock Publications, 1970
6 FORDE, D. (ed.), *African Worlds: Studies in the Cosmological Ideas and Social Values of African Peoples*, London/New York, International African Institute/Oxford University Press, 1954, 1963
7 FORTES, M., and DIETERLEN, G. (eds), *African Systems of Thought*, London, International African Institute/Oxford University Press, 1965
8 MBITI, J. S., *African Religions and Philosophy*, London, Heinemann Educational/New York, Praeger, 1969
9 MBITI, J. S., *Concepts of God in Africa*, London, SPCK, 1970, 1975; New York, Praeger, 1970
10 MIDDLETON, J., and WINTER, E. H. (eds), *Witchcraft and Sorcery in East Africa*, London, Routledge/New York, Praeger, 1963
11 PARRINDER, E. G., *African Traditional Religion*, 3rd edn, London, Sheldon, 1974
12 P'BITEK, O., *African Religions in Western Scholarship*, Nairobi, East African Publishing House, 1970; Nairobi, East African Literature Bureau, 1971
13 RANGER, T. O., and KIMAMBO, I., *The Historical Study of African Religion*, London, Heinemann, 1972; Berkeley, Cal., University of California Press, 1972, repr. 1976
14 RAY, B. C., *African Religions: Symbol, Ritual and Community*, Englewood Cliffs, NJ, Prentice-Hall, 1976
15 SCHOFFELEERS, J. M. (ed.), *Guardians of the Land: Essays on Central African Territorial Cults*, Gwelo, Mambo Press, 1978
16 SHORTER, A., *Prayer in the Religious Traditions of Africa*, Nairobi, Oxford University Press, 1975; new edn Oxford University Press (East Africa), 1979
17 SMITH, EDWIN W. (ed.), *African Ideas of God: A Symposium*, 2nd edn, London, Edinburgh House, 1961
18 WERBNER, R. P. (ed.), *Regional Cults*, London, Academic Press, 1977
19 ZAHAN, D., *The Religion, Spirituality and Thought of Traditional Africa*, Chicago, Ill., University of Chicago Press, 1979
20 ZUESSE, E. M., *Ritual Cosmos: The Sanctification of Life in African Religions*, Athens, Ohio, Ohio University Press, 1979

(b) Monographs

21 ABIMBOLA, W., *Ifa Divination Poetry*, New York, NOK, 1977
22 AWOLALU, J. O., *Yoruba Beliefs and Sacrificial Rites*, London, Longman, 1979
23 BASCOM, W., *Ifa Divination: Communication Between Gods and Men in West Africa*, Bloomington, Ind./London, Indiana University Press, 1969
24 BERGLUND, A.-I., *Zulu Thought-Patterns and Symbolism*, London, C. Hurst/New York, Holmes & Meier, 1976
25 DAMMANN, E., 'A Tentative Philological Typology of Some African High Deities', *Journal of Religion in Africa* (Leiden), vol. 2, 1969, pp. 81–95
26 DANEEL, M. L., *The God of the Matopo Hills: An Essay on the Mwari Cult in Rhodesia*, Leiden, Afrika-Studiecentrum, 1969; The Hague, Mouton, 1970
27 EVANS-PRITCHARD, E. E., *Essays in Social Anthropology*, London,

Faber, 1969 (prev. publ. Faber, 1962); New York, Free Press of Glencoe, 1963

28 EVANS-PRITCHARD, E. E., *Nuer Religion*, London, Oxford University Press, 1956, 1971

29 EVANS-PRITCHARD, E. E., *Witchcraft, Oracles and Magic Among the Azande*, new edn, abr. Eva Gillies, Oxford, Clarendon Press, 1976

30 FORTES, M., *Oedipus and Job in West African Religion*, Cambridge University Press, 1959; repr. with an essay by R. Horton 1983

31 GABA, C. R. (ed.), *Scriptures of an African People*, New York, NOK, 1977

32 GOODY, J., *The Myth of the Bagre*, Oxford, Clarendon Press, 1972

33 GRIAULE, M., *Conversations with Ogotemmêli*, London, Oxford University Press/International African Institute, 1965, 1975; New York, Oxford University Press, 1976

34 HARJULA, R., *God and the Sun in Meru Thought*, Helsinki, Lutheran Theological College of Makumira/Finnish Society for Missiology and Ecumenics, 1969

35 IDOWU, E. B., *Olódùmarè: God in Yoruba Belief*, London, Longman, 1962, 1966

36 JAMES, W., *The Listening Ebony: Moral Knowledge, Religion and Power among the Uduk of Sudan*, Oxford, Clarendon Press, 1988

37 KRIGE, E. J. and J. D., *The Realm of a Rain-Queen: A Study of the Pattern of Lovedu Society*, London/New York, Oxford University Press, 1943; repr. New York, AMS, 1976

38 KUPER, H., *An African Aristocracy; Rank Among the Swazi of Bechuanaland*, London/New York, Oxford University Press/International African Institute, 1947; repr. of 1965 edn New York, Holmes & Meier, 1980

39 LIENHARDT, G., *Divinity and Experience: The Religion of the Dinka*, Oxford, Clarendon Press, 1961; new edn Oxford University Press, 1987

40 MCKENZIE, P. R., 'Yoruba Orisa Cults', *Journal of Religion in Africa*, vol. 8, 1976, pp. 189–207

41 MCNAUGHTON, P., *The Mande Blacksmiths: Knowledge, Power and Art in West Africa*, Bloomington and Indianapolis, Indiana University Press, 1988

42 METUH, E. I., *God and Man in African Religion: A Case Study of the Igbo of Nigeria*, London, Geoffrey Chapman, 1981

43 MIDDLETON, J., *Lugbara Religion: Ritual and Authority Among an East African People*, London/New York, Oxford University Press/ International African Institute, 1960; new edn Washington, DC, Smithsonian Institution Press, 1987

44 NWOGA, D., *The Supreme God as Stranger in Igbo Religious Thought*, Ekwereazu, Ahiazu Mbaise, Hawk Press, 1984

45 P'BITEK, O., *Religion of the Central Luo*, Nairobi, East African Literature Bureau, 1971, 1977

46 RATTRAY, R. S., *Religion and Art in Ashanti*, Oxford, Clarendon Press, 1927; repr. of 1970 edn Oxford University Press, 1980; repr. of 1927 edn New York, AMS, 1977

47 RICHARDS, A. I., *Chisungu: A Girls' Initiation Ceremony among the Bemba of Northern Rhodesia*, London, Faber, 1956

48 ROSCOE, J., *The Baganda*, 2nd edn, London, Cass, 1965; New York, Barnes & Noble, 1966

49 TURNER, V. W., *The Drums of Affliction: A Study of Religious Processes Among the Ndembu of Zambia*, Oxford, Clarendon Press/London, International African Institute, 1968

50 WILSON, M., *Rituals of Kinship Among the Nyakyusa*, London, Oxford University Press/International African Institute, 1957; repr. 1970
51 WILSON, M., *Communal Rituals of the Nyakyusa*, London/New York, Oxford University Press/International African Institute, 1959, repr. 1970

(*See also* III, 52, 54; XIII(B), 87, 88; XIII(D), 10; XIX, 63, 106, 124, 127; XXVII, 2, 5, 10, 13, 14, 15, 18, 21)

[III]   *Afro-Caribbean Religions*

Compiled by Kathy Williams

1 ABRAHAMS, R., and SWED, J. E. (eds), *After Africa*, New Haven, Conn., Yale University Press, 1983
2 ALLEYNE, M., *The Roots of Jamaican Culture*, Bridgetown/London, Pluto Press, 1988
3 ARISTIDE, J.-B., *In the Parish of the Poor: Writings from Haiti*, tr. from the French, Maryknoll, NY, Orbis Books, 1990
4 BAER, H. A., *The Black Spiritual Movement*, Knoxville, Tenn., University of Tennessee Press, 1984
5 BARRETT, L., 'Africa in the Americas: The Islands Inbetween', in BOOTH, N. S., JR (ed.), *African Religions*, London, NOK, 1977; New York, NOK, 1979
6 BARRETT, L., *The Rastafarians: The Dreadlocks of Jamaica*, London, Heinemann, 1977
7 BASCOM, W. R., 'The Focus of Cuban Santeria', *Southwestern Journal of Anthropology*, vol. 6, 1960, pp. 64–8
8 BASTIDE, R., *African Civilisations in the New World*, New York, Harper & Row, 1971
9 BASTIDE, R., *Les Religions Africaines au Brésil: Vers Une Sociologie des Interpénétrations des Civilisations*, Paris, Presses Universitaires de France, 1960
10 BECKWITH, M., *Black Roadways: A Study of Jamaican Folk Life*, Chapel Hill, NC, University of North Carolina Press, 1929
11 BERNAL, M., *Black Athena: The Afro-Asian Roots of Classical Civilisation*, London, Free Association Books, 1987
12 BISNAUTH, D., *A History of Religions in the Caribbean*, Kingston, Kingston Publishers, 1989
13 BOESAK, A., *A Farewell to Innocence*, Maryknoll, NY, Orbis Books, 1977; Johannesburg, Ravan Press, 1977 (© 1976)
14 BOOTH, N. S., JR (ed.), *African Religions*, London, NOK, 1977; New York, NOK 1979
15 BOURGUIGNON, E., *Culture and Varieties of Consciousness*, Menlo Park, Cal., Cummings Publishing Co., 1973
16 BOURGUIGNON, E., *Religion, Altered States of Consciousness and Social Change*, Columbus, Ohio, Ohio State University Press, 1973
17 BRATHWAITE, E. K., *The Folk Culture of the Slaves in Jamaica*, rev. edn, London, New Beacon Books, 1981; prev. edn 1970
18 BREITMAN, G. (ed.), *By Any Means Necessary: Speeches . . . by Malcolm X*, New York, Pathfinder Press, 1970
19 BRERETON, B., *A History of Modern Trinidad: 1783–1962*, Kingston, Jamaica/London, Heinemann Educational Books, 1981

20   BROWN, K., *Madame Lola: A Voodoo Priestess in Brooklyn*, Berkeley, Cal., University of California Press, 1991

21   BRUCE, C. E., and JONES, W. R. (eds), *Black Theology II: Essays on Formation and Outreach of Contemporary Black Theology*, Lewisburg, Bucknell University Press, 1987

22   BURKETT, R. K., *Garveyism as a Religious Movement*, Metuchen, NJ, Scarecrow Press, 1978

23   CARR, A., *A Rada Community in Trinidad*, Port of Spain, Paria, 1989

23a CARR, A., *A Rada Cult in Trinidad*, Port of Spain, Paria, 1989

24   CARTER, H. A., *The Prayer Tradition of Black People*, Valley Forge, Pa, Judson Press, 1976

25   CHESNUTT, C. W., and SHEPARD, R. A., *Conjure Tales*, London, Collins, 1975; New York, Dutton, 1973

26   CHEVANNES, B., 'Revival and Black Struggle', *Savacou*, vol. 5, 1971, pp. 27–40

27   CLEAGE, A. J., JR, *The Black Messiah*, New York, Sheed & Ward, 1969

28   COOPER, N.-L., and MITCHELL, H. H. *Soul Theology: The Heart of American Black Culture*, Nashville, Tenn., Abington Press, 1992

29   CRANHAM, M., and KNIGHT, F. W. (eds), *Africa and the Caribbean*, Baltimore, Md, Johns Hopkins University Press, 1979

30   CRONON, E. D., *Black Moses: . . . Marcus Garvey and the Universal Negro Improvement Association*, Madison, Wisc., University of Wisconsin Press, 1955, 1969

31   CURTIN, P., *Two Jamaicas: . . . a Tropical Colony, 1830–1865*, New York, Greenwood Press, 1968 (© 1955); Cambridge, Mass., Harvard University Press, 1955

32   DE FREITAS, B. T. and W. C., *Os Orixas e a Lei de Umbanda*, Rio de Janeiro, Editora Eco, n.d., pp. 77–118

33   DEREN, M., *Divine Horsemen; The Living Gods of Haiti*, New York, Delta Publishing Co., 1974; London, Thames & Hudson, 1953

34   DESMANGLES, L. G., *The Faces of the Gods: Voodoo and Roman Catholicism in Haiti*, Chapel Hill, NC, University of North Carolina Press, 1992

34a DOBBIN, J. D., *The Jombee Dance of Montserrat*, Columbus, Ohio, University of Ohio Press, 1986

35   DRAPER, T., *The Rediscovery of Black Nationalism*, New York, Viking Press, 1970

36   DUNDES, A., *Mother Wit from the Laughing Barrell: Readings in the Interpenetration of Afro-American Folklore*, New York, Garland, 1973, 1981; Englewood Cliffs, NJ, Prentice-Hall, 1972 (© 1973)

37   ERSKINE, N. L., *Decolonising Theology: A Caribbean Perspective*, Maryknoll, NY, Orbis Books, 1981

38   ESSIEN-UDOM, E. U., *Black Nationalism*, Chicago, Ill., University of Chicago Press, 1962

39   FARISTZADDI, M., *Itations of Jamaica and I*, Miami, Judah Anbesa Ihntahnahshinahi, 1986

40   FRISCHAUER, K., *Nyabingi*, London, Grove Press, 1987

41   GARDINER, J. J., and ROBERTS, J. D. (eds), *Quest for a Black Theology*, Philadelphia, Pa., United Church Press, n.d., [Pilgrim Press, 1971]

42   GARVEY, A. J., *Garvey and Garveyism*, New York, Collier Books, 1970

43   GARVEY, A. J. (ed.), *Philosophy and Opinions of Marcus Garvey*, vol. 1, New York, Atheneum Press, 1974; prev. publ. New York, Universal

Publishing House, 1923–5; New York, Arno, 1968–9; London, Cass, 1967

44 HAMID, I., *In Search of New Perspectives*, Bridgetown, Caribbean Ecumenical Consultation for Development, 1971

45 HASKINS, J., *Voodoo and Hoodoo: The Craft as Revealed by Traditional Practitioners*, Chelsea, Scarborough House, 1990

46 HERSKOVITS, M. J., and F., *Surinam Folklore*, New York, Columbia University Press, 1936

47 HERSKOVITS, M., *Life in a Haitian Valley*, New York, Doubleday, 1974; prev. publ. New York/London, Knopf, 1937

48 HILL, R. (ed.), *The Marcus Garvey Papers*, Los Angeles, University of California Press, 1983

49 HILL, R. A., and BAIR, B. (eds), *Marcus Garvey: Life and Lessons*, Los Angeles, University of California Press, 1987

50 HOGG, D., 'Jamaican Religion: A Study in Variation', PhD dissertation, New Haven, Conn., Yale University, 1964

50a HURBON, L., *Dieu dans le Vaudou Haitien*, Paris, Payot, 1972

51 HURSTON, Z. N., *The Sanctified Church*, Berkeley, Cal., Turtle Island, 1983

52 JACOBS, S. H. (ed.), *Black Americans and the Missionary Movement in Africa*, London, Greenwood Press, 1982

53 JAMES, C. L. R., *The Black Jacobins*, New York, Random House, 1965

54 JANZEN, J. M., *Lemba, 1650–1930: A Drum of Affliction in Africa and the New World*, New York, Garland, 1982

55 KNIGHT, F. W., *The Caribbean: The Genesis of a Fragmented Nationalism*, New York, Oxford University Press, 1978

56 KIEV, A. (ed.), *Magic, Faith and Healing*, New York, Free Press, 1964

57 LA GUERRE, J., *Calcutta to Caroni: The East Indians of Trinidad*, London, Longman Caribbean, 1974

58 LAGUERRE, M., *Voodoo and Politics in Haiti*, New York, St Martin's, 1989

59 LEWIS, G. K., *The Growth of the Modern West Indies*, New York Monthly Review Press, 1968

60 LINCOLN, C. E. (ed.), *The Black Experience in Religion*, New York, Schocken Books, 1974

61 LINCOLN, C. E., *The Black Muslims in America*, New York, Beacon Press, 1961; 3rd rev. edn Grand Rapids, Mich., Eerdmans, 1994

62 LOVELACE, E., *The Wine of Astonishment*, London, Heinemann Educational/Deutsch, 1982

63 MARTIN, TONY, *The Pan-African Connection: From Slavery to Garvey and Beyond*, Dover, Wellesley, The Majority Press, 1983

64 MARTIN, TONY, *Race First*, Westport, Conn., Greenwood Press, 1979

65 MARX, G. T., *Protest and Prejudice*, New York, Harper & Row, 1967

65a MITCHELL, H., and SCHULLER, R. H., *Black Belief*, New York, Harper & Row, 1975

66 MITCHELL, H., and SCHULLER, R. H., *Self-Esteem: The New Reformation*, New York, Vantage Press, 1982

67 MOORE, J. G., 'Religion of Jamaican Negroes: A Study of Afro-Jamaican Acculturation', Ann Arbor, Mich., University Microfilms, Doctoral Series, Publication 7053, 1954 (1953)

68 MULRAIN, G., *Theology in Folk Culture: The Theological Significance of Haitian Folk Religion*, Frankfurt am Main, Verlag Peter Lang, 1984

584   Bibliography

69   NETTLEFORD, R., *Caribbean Cultural Identity: The Case of Jamaica*, Kingston, Institute of Jamaica, 1978

69a NICHOLLS, D., *From Dessalines to Duvalier: Race, Colour and National Independence in Haiti*, Cambridge, Cambridge University Press, 1979

70   NORWOOD, M., *I am a Rastafarian*, London, Franklin Watts, 1986

71   ORTIZ, F., *Los Bailes y el Teatro de los Negros en al Folklore de Cuba*, Havana, Ediciones Cardenas y Cia, 1951

72   OSOFSKY, G., *Harlem, the Making of a Ghetto*, London, Longman/ New York, Harper & Row, 1966

73   OWENS, J. V., *Dread*, Kingston, Sangsters, 1976

74   PATTERSON, O., *The Sociology of Slavery*, Jamaica, Sangsters in association with Granada, 1973

75   PORTER, A. T., *Creoledom: A Study of the Development of Freetown Society*, London, Oxford University Press, 1963; repr. with corrections 1966

76   PRICE, R., *Alabi's World*, Baltimore, Md, Johns Hopkins University Press, 1990

77   PRICE, R. (ed.), *Maroon Societies*, Baltimore, Md, Johns Hopkins University Press, 1973

77a PRICE, R. (ed.), *Maroon Societies: Rebel Slave Communities in the Americas*, Baltimore, Md, Johns Hopkins University Press, 1979

78   PRICE, S., *Co-Wives and Calabashes*, Ann Arbor, Mich., University of Michigan Press, 1984

79   RAMDIN, R., *From Chattel Slave to Wage Earner, A History of Trade Unionism in Trinidad and Tobago*, London, Martin Brian & O'Keefe, 1982

80   REDKEY, E. S. (ed.), *Black Exodus: Black Nationalist and Back-to-Africa Movements, 1890–1910*, New Haven, Conn., Yale University Press, 1969

81   ROSENBERG, B. A., *The Art of the American Folk Preacher*, New York, Oxford University Press, 1970

82   SALLEY, C., and BEHM, R., *Your Church is Too White*, London, Lion Publishing, 1973

83   SCHULER, M., 'Myalism and the African Religious Tradition in Jamaica', in CRANHAM, M. E., and KNIGHT, F. W. (eds), *Africa and the Caribbean*, Baltimore, Md, Johns Hopkins University Press, 1979

84   SEAGA, E., *Pocomania: Revival Cults in Jamaica*, Kingston, Institute of Jamaica, 1982

85   SENIOR, O., *The A–Z of Jamaican Heritage*, London, Heinemann Educational, 1983

86   SIMPSON, G. E., *Black Religions in the New World*, New York, Columbia University Press, 1978

87   SIMPSON, G. E., *Religious Cults of the Caribbean, Trinidad, Jamaica and Haiti*, Puerto Rico, Institute of Caribbean Studies, 1970

88   SMITH, M. G., AUGIER, R., and NETTLEFORD, R., *The Rastafari Movement in Jamaica*, Kingston, University of the West Indies Press, 1966

89   STAPLETON, ARCHBISHOP A. L., *The Birth and Growth of the Baptist Church in Trinidad and Tobago and the Caribbean*, Siparia, International Spiritual Baptist Ministerial Council, 1983

90   STURM, F. G., 'Afro-Brazilian Cults', in BOOTH, N. S., Jr, *African Religions*, London, NOK, 1977; New York, NOK, 1979

90a THOMPSON, I., *Bonjour Blanc: A Journey Through Haiti*, London, Hutchinson, 1992

91   UYA, O. E., *Black Brotherhood*, Lexington, Ky, Heath Press, 1971

92 VERTOVEC, S., *Hindu Trinidad: Religion, Ethnicity and Socio-Economic Change*, Basingstoke (distrib.), Macmillan Caribbean, 1992 (Warwick University Caribbean Studies)

93 VINCENT, T., *Black Power and the Garvey Movement*, Berkeley, Cal., Ramparts Press, 1971

94 WASHINGTON, J. R., *Black and White Power Subjection*, New York, Beacon Press, 1971

95 WASHINGTON, J. R., *Black Sects and Cults*, Garden City, NY, Doubleday Anchor, 1973; new edn Lanham, Md, University Press of America, 1984

96 WEST, R., *Back to Africa: A History of Sierra Leone and Liberia*, London, Jonathan Cape, 1970

97 WILMORE, G., *Black Religion and Black Nationalism*, New York, Doubleday, 1972

98 WILMORE, G. S., *Black Religion and Black Radicalism: An Interpretation of the Religious Experience of Afro-American People*, Maryknoll, NY, Orbis Books, 1983; 2nd rev. edn 1989

99 WILMORE, G. S., and CONE, J. H., *Black Theology: A Documentary History, 1966–1979*, Maryknoll, NY, Orbis Books, 1979; vol. 1, new edn, 1966–79; vol. 2, 1980–92, 1993

100 YOCHANAN, J. B., *The Black Man's Religion*, New York, Alkebu-Lan Associates, 1974

(*See also* XXVII, 3, 25)

[IV]   *American Religions*

Compiled by Martin E. Marty

1 AHLSTROM, S. E., *A Religious History of the American People*, New Haven, Conn., Yale University Press, 1972, new edn 1974; Garden City, NY, Doubleday, 2 vols, 1975

2 ALBANESE, C. L., *America: Religion and Religions*, 2nd edn, Belmont, Cal., Wadsworth, 1992

3 BOWDEN, H. W., *American Indians and Christian Missions: Studies in Cultural Conflict*, Chicago, Ill., University of Chicago Press, 1981; new edn 1985

4 DOLAN, J. P., *The American Catholic Experience*, Garden City, NY, Doubleday, 1985

5 CARROLL, J. W., JOHNSON, D. W., and MARTY, M. E., *Religion in America: 1950 to the Present*, San Francisco, Cal., Harper & Row, 1979

6 ELLWOOD, R. S., and PARTIN, H. B., *Religious and Spiritual Groups in Modern America*, 2nd edn, Englewood Cliffs, NJ, Prentice-Hall, 1988

7 GAUSTAD, E. S., *Historical Atlas of Religion in America*, rev. edn, New York, Harper & Row, 1976

8 HANDY, R. T., *A History of the Churches in the United States and Canada*, Oxford/New York, Oxford University Press, 1977

9 HENNESEY, J., *American Catholics: A History of the Roman Catholic Community in the United States*, New York, Oxford University Press, 1981; new edn 1983

10 HILL, S. S., and OWEN, D. E., *The New Religious Political Right in America*, Nashville, Tenn., Abingdon, 1982

11 HUTCHISON, W. R., *Errand to the World: American Protestant Thought and Foreign Missions*, Chicago, Ill., University of Chicago Press, 1987

12 JACQUET, C. H., JR (ed.), *Yearbook of American and Canadian Churches:
1990*, Nashville, Tenn., Abingdon, 1990

13 LINCOLN, C. E., and MAMIYA, L., *The Black Church in the African–
American Experience*, Durham, NC, Duke University Press, 1990

14 LIPPY, C. H., and WILLIAMS, P. W. (eds), *Encyclopedia of American
Religious Experience: Studies of Traditions and Movements*, 3 vols, New
York, Schribner's, 1988

15 MARSDEN, G. M., *Fundamentalism in American Culture: The Shaping of
Twentieth-Century Evangelicalism, 1870–1925*, New York, Oxford University Press, 1980, 1981; new edn 1983

16 MARTY, M. E., *Pilgrims in their Own Land: Five Hundred Years of Religion
in America*, Boston, Mass., Little, Brown, 1984

17 MCLOUGHLIN, W. G., *Revivals, Awakenings, and Reform*, Chicago, Ill.,
University of Chicago Press, 1978; new edn 1980

18 MELTON, J. G., *The Encyclopedia of American Religions*, 3rd edn, 2 vols,
Detroit, Mich., Gale Research, 1989, 1991

19 MOORE, R. L., *Religious Outsiders and the Making of Americans*, New
York, Oxford University Press, 1986; new edn 1988

20 NOLL, M. A., *A History of Christianity in the United States and Canada*,
Grand Rapids, Mich., Eerdmans, 1992; London, SPCK, 1993

21 NUMBERS, R. L., and BUTLER, J. M., *The Disappointed: Millerism and
Millenarianism in the Nineteenth Century*, Bloomington, Ind., Indiana
University Press, 1987

22 REID, G. G., et al. (eds), *Dictionary of Christianity in America*, Downers
Grove, Ill., Inter-Varsity, 1990

23 ROOF, W. C., and MCKINNEY, W., *American Mainline Religion: Its
Changing Shape and Future*, New Brunswick, NJ, Rutgers, 1987

24 SHIPPS, J., *Mormonism: The Story of a New Religious Tradition*, Urbana,
Ill., Illinois University Press, 1985

25 SWEET, L. I., (ed.), *The Evangelical Tradition in America*, Macon, Ga,
Mercer, 1984

26 WHITE, R. C., and HOPKINS, C. H., *The Social Gospel: Religion and
Reform in Changing America*, Philadelphia, Pa, Temple, 1976

27 WUTHNOW, R., *The Restructuring of American Religion: Society and Faith
since World War II*, Princeton, NJ, Princeton University Press, 1988

[V]   *Amerindian Religions*

Compiled by Stephen J. Reno

1 BROWN, J. E., *The Sacred Pipe: Black Elk's Account of the Seven Rites of the
Oglala Sioux*, Baltimore, Md, 1971, Harmondsworth, Penguin, 1972;
University of Oklahoma Press, 1975; first publ. 1953

2 CAPPS, W. H., *Seeing with a Native Eye*, New York, Harper & Row,
1976

3 COLTON, H. S., *Hopi Kachina Dolls, with a Key to Their Identification*, rev.
edn, Sante Fé, NM, University of New Mexico Press, 1959, 1971

4 DELORIA, E., 'The Sun Dance of the Oglala Sioux', *Journal of American
Folklore*, vol. 42, 1929, pp. 354–413

5 DELORIA, V., *God is Red*, New York, Grosset & Dunlap, 1973; New
York, Dell, 1975

6 DUBOIS, C., *The 1870 Ghost Dance*, Berkeley, Cal., University of
California Press, 1939

7 GOLDMAN, I., *The Mouth of Heaven: An Introduction to Kwakiutl*

Religious Thought, New York, Wiley, 1975; repr. New York, Krieger, 1980

8 HULTKRANTZ, A., *The Religions of the American Indians*, Berkeley, Cal., University of California Press, 1979; new edn 1981

9 HULTKRANTZ, A., 'The Structure of Theistic Beliefs among North American Indians', *Temenos*, vol. 7, 1971, pp. 66–74

10 HULTKRANTZ, A., *Conceptions of the Soul Among North American Indians*, Stockholm, Ethnographical Museum of Sweden, 1953

11 HULTKRANTZ, A., 'The Owner of the Animals in the Religion of the North American Indians', in A. Hultkrantz (ed.), *Supernatural Owners of Nature*, Stockholm, Acta Universitae Stockholmiensis, 1961

12 HULTKRANTZ, A., *Prairie and Plains Indians*, Leiden, Brill, 1973

13 KLUCKHOHN, C., and LEIGHTON, D., *The Navajo*, rev. edn, Cambridge, Mass., Harvard University Press, 1974

14 LABARRE, W., *The Peyote Cult*, 4th edn, New York, Schocken, 1975, 1976; Hamden, Conn., Shoe String Press, 1975

15 MARSH, G. H., 'A Comparative Survey of Eskimo–Aleut Religion', *Anthropological Papers of the University of Alaska*, vol. 3, 1954, pp. 21–36

16 PARSONS, E. C., *Pueblo Indian Religion*, Chicago, Ill., University of Chicago Press, 1939

17 POWERS, W. K., *Oglala Religion*, Lincoln, Nebr., University of Nebraska Press, 1977

18 RADIN, P., *The Trickster: A Study in American Indian Mythology*, New York, Philosophical Library, 1956; repr. Westport, Conn., Greenwood/ New York, Schocken, 1972

19 REICHARD, G., *Navaho Religion: A Study in Symbolism*, 2 vols, New York, Pantheon, 1950; 2nd edn Princeton University Press, 1963

20 ROOTH, A. B., 'The Creation Myths of the North American Indians', *Anthropos*, vol. 52, 1957, pp. 497–501

21 SLOTKIN, J. S., *The Peyote Religion: A Study in Indian–White Relations*, Glencoe, Free Press, 1956; repr. New York, Octagon, 1975

22 STURTEVANT, W. C., (gen. ed.), *Handbook of North American Indians*, vol. 15, *Northeast*, ed. B. G. Trigger, Washington, DC, Smithsonian Institution, 1978

23 TEDLOCK, D. and B., *Teachings from the American Earth*, New York, Liveright, 1975; rev. edn, New York, W. W. Norton, 1992

24 UNDERHILL, R. M., *Red Man's Religion*, Chicago, Ill., University of Chicago Press, 1965; new edn 1972

25 WALLACE, A. F. C., 'Revitalization Movements', *American Anthropologist*, vol. 58, 1956, pp. 264–81

26 WATERS, F., *Book of the Hopi*, New York, Ballantine, 1971, 1974; Penguin Books (US), 1977; prev. publ. New York, Viking, 1963

(*See also* XXVII, 1, 23)

[VI]   *Ancient Egyptian Religions*

Compiled by A. Rosalie David

1 ALLEN, T. G. (ed.), *The Egyptian Book of the Dead: Documents in the Oriental Institute Museum at the University of Chicago*, Chicago, Ill., University of Chicago Press, 1960, repr. Ann Arbor, Mich., University Microfilms, 1971; and, *The Book of The Dead; or, Going Forth By Day . . .* (tr. T. G. Allen), Chicago, Ill., Chicago Oriental Institute/University of Chicago Press, 1974; London, 1975

588 Bibliography

2 BONNET, H., *Reallexikon der ägyptischen Religionsgeschichte*, Berlin, De Gruyter, 1952

3 DAVID, A. R., *Mysteries of the Mummies: The Story of the Manchester University Investigation*, London, Cassell, 1978; New York, Scribner, 1979

4 DAVID, A. R. (ed.), *The Manchester Museum Mummy Project*, Manchester, Manchester Museum/Manchester University Press, 1979

5 DAVID, A. R., *The Ancient Egyptians: Religious Beliefs and Practices*, London, Routledge, 1981

6 DAVID, A. R., *A Guide to Religious Ritual at Abydos*, Warminster, Aris & Phillips, 1981

7 EDWARDS, I. E. S., *The Pyramids of Egypt*, new edn, Harmondsworth/Baltimore, Md, Penguin, 1972, 1975, new edn, 1991; London, Ebury & Joseph/New York, Viking, 1972
ELLIOT SMITH, SIR GRAFTON *see* no. 21, SMITH

8 ERMAN, A. (ed.), *The Ancient Egyptians: A Source Book of their Writings*, New York, Harper Torchbooks, 1966; Magnolia, Mass., Peter Smith; German edn, *Die Literatur der Ägypter*, Leipzig, 1923, first tr. as *The Literature of the Ancient Egyptians*, London, Methuen, 1927, repr. New York, Arno, 1976

9 FAIRMAN, H. W., 'The Kingship Rituals of Egypt', in S. H. Hooke (ed.), *Myth, Ritual and Kingship*, Oxford, Clarendon Press, 1958

10 FAULKNER, R. O., *The Ancient Egyptian Pyramid Texts*, Oxford, Clarendon Press, 1969; Warminster, Aris & Phillips, 1985

11 FRANKFORT, H., *Ancient Egyptian Religion*, New York, Columbia University Press, 1948; New York, Harper & Row, 1961; Magnolia, Mass., Peter Smith

12 GRIFFITHS, J. G., *The Conflict of Horus and Seth*, Liverpool, Liverpool University Press, 1960

13 GRIFFITHS, J. G., *The Origins of Osiris and His Cult*, Leiden, Numen, 1980 (Supplement 40)

14 HERODOTUS, *The Histories* (tr. A. de Selincourt, rev. A. R. Burn), Harmondsworth/Baltimore, Md, Penguin, 1972

15 KEES, H., *Der Götterglaube im alten Ägypten*, 2nd edn, Berlin, Akademie-Verlag, 1956

16 KEES, H., *Totenglauben und Jenseitsvorstellungen der alten Ägypter*, 2nd edn, Berlin, Akademie-Verlag, 1956

17 MORENZ, S., *Egyptian Religion*, London, Methuen/Ithaca, NY, Cornell University Press, 1973; German edn *Ägyptische Religion*, Stuttgart, Kohlhammer, 1960

18 PORTER, B., and MOSS, R., *Topographical Bibliography of Ancient Egyptian Hieroglyphic Texts, Reliefs and Paintings*, Oxford, Clarendon Press, 1927–; Oxford University Press/Griffith Institute, 1970–

19 PRITCHARD, J. B. (ed.), *Ancient Near Eastern Texts Relating to the Old Testament*, 2nd edn, Princeton, NJ, Princeton University Press, 1955; 3rd (de luxe) edn, with *Supplement*, 1969 (refs in text are to 2nd edn)

20 SAUNERON, S., *The Priests of Ancient Egypt*, New York/London, Evergreen Books, 1960; New York, Grove, 1980; French edn *Les Prêtres de l'ancienne Égypte*, Paris, Seuil, 1957

21 SMITH, SIR GRAFTON ELLIOT, and DAWSON, W. R., *Egyptian Mummies*, London, Kegan Paul International, 1991; first publ. 1924

22 SMITH, RAY W., and REDFORD, D. B., *The Akhenaten Temple Project*, vol. 1, Warminster, Aris & Phillips, 1976

23 VELDE, H. TE, *Seth, God of Confusion*, Leiden, Brill, 1967

[VII] *Ancient European Religions*

Compiled by Hilda Ellis Davidson

1 BALYS, J., 'Lithuanian Mythology', in *Funk and Wagnalls Standard Dictionary of Folklore, Mythology and Legend*, 2 vols, New York, Funk & Wagnalls, 1949–50; repr. 1970

2 CAESAR, JULIUS, *The Conquest of Gaul* (tr. S. A. Handford), Harmondsworth, Penguin, 1951, 1970

3 DAVIDSON, H. R. E., *Gods and Myths of Northern Europe*, Harmondsworth/Baltimore, Md, Penguin, 1964, new edn 1990; Santa Fé, NM, Gannon, n.d.; repr. as *Gods and Myths of the Viking Age*, New York, Bell, 1981

3a DAVIDSON, H. R. E., *The Lost Beliefs of Northern Europe*, London/New York, Routledge, 1993

4 DAVIDSON, H. R. E., *Myths and Symbols in Pagan Europe*, Manchester, Manchester University Press, 1988; new edn 1989

5 DAVIDSON, H. R. E., *Pagan Scandinavia*, London, Thames & Hudson/New York, Praeger, 1967

6 DUMÉZIL, G., *Gods of the Ancient Northmen* (tr. E. Haugen), Berkeley, Cal./London, University of California Press, 1973, 1974, 1978

7 ELLIOTT, R. W. V., *Runes: An Introduction*, Manchester, Manchester University Press/New York, Philosophical Library, 1959

8 EVANS, A. C., *The Sutton Hoo Ship Burial*, London, British Museum, 1968; 2nd edn by R. Bruce-Mitford, 1972

9 GELLING, P., and DAVIDSON, H. R. E., *The Chariot of the Sun*, London, Dent/New York, Praeger, 1969

10 GIMBUTAS, M., *The Balts*, London, Thames & Hudson/New York, Praeger, 1963

11 GIMBUTAS, M., *The Slavs*, London, Thames & Hudson/New York, Praeger, 1971

12 GREEN, M., *The Gods of the Celts*, Gloucester, Alan Sutton/Totowa, NJ, Barnes & Noble, 1986; new edn Alan Sutton, 1993

13 JAKOBSON, R., 'Slavic Mythology', in *Funk and Wagnalls Standard Dictionary of Folklore, Mythology and Legend*, 2 vols, New York, Funk & Wagnalls, 1949–50; repr. 1970

14 JONES, G., *A History of the Vikings*, London/New York/Toronto, Oxford University Press, 1968

15 KENDRICK, SIR THOMAS D., *The Druids: A Study in Keltic Prehistory*, London, Methuen, 1927; repr. New York, Barnes & Noble, 1966; 2nd edn, 1928, repr. London, Cass, 1966; facsimile of 1927 edn, Brodick, Banton Press, 1991

16 *The Mabinogion* (tr. G. and T. Jones), London, Dent/New York, Dutton, 1949

17 MACCANA, P., *Celtic Mythology*, London, Hamlyn, 1970; London, Newnes, 1983

18 MACNEILL, M., *The Festival of Lughnasa*, London, Oxford University Press, 1962

19 OWEN, G. R., *Rites and Religions of the Anglo-Saxons*, Newton Abbot, David & Charles/Totowa, NJ, Barnes & Noble, 1981

20 PIGGOTT, S., *The Druids*, Harmondsworth, Penguin, 1974; London, Thames & Hudson/New York, Praeger, 1968; 2nd edn, London, Thames & Hudson, 1975, new edn 1985

21   *The Poetic Edda (Edda Saemundar)* (tr. L. M. Hollander), 2nd edn, Austin, Tex., University of Texas Press, 1962; repr. 1964

22   POWELL, T. G. E., *The Celts*, London, Thames & Hudson, 1958, 1980; New York, Praeger, 1958

23   REES, A. and B., *Celtic Heritage*, London, Thames & Hudson, 1961, new edn 1973, (US) 1977; New York, Grove Press, 1961

24   ROSS, A., *Everyday Life of the Pagan Celts*, London, Batsford/New York, Putnam, 1970

25   ROSS, A., *Pagan Celtic Britain*, London, Routledge/New York, Columbia University Press, 1967

26   SAXO GRAMMATICUS, *History of the Danes*, I–IX, vol. 1 (tr. P. Fisher), vol. 2 (commentary by H. R. E. Davidson), London, Brewer/Totowa, NJ, Rowman, 1979–80

27   SJOESTEDT, M. L., *Gods and Heroes of the Celts* (tr. M. Dillon), London, Methuen, 1949; New York, Gordon Press, 1976

28   *Snorri Sturluson: Edda* (tr. A. Faulkes), London/Melbourne, Dent, Everyman Classics, 1987

29   TACITUS, *The Agricola and the Germania* (tr. H. Mattingly, rev. S. A. Handford), Harmondsworth, Penguin, 1970, (US) 1971

30   TIERNEY, J. J., 'The Celtic Ethnography of Posidonius', in *Proceedings of the Irish Royal Academy*, vol. 60, 1959, pp. 189ff

31   TODD, M., *The Northern Barbarians, 100 BC to AD 300*, London, Hutchinson, 1975

32   TURVILLE-PETRE, E. O. G., *Myth and Religion of the North*, London, Weidenfeld/New York, Holt, Rinehart, 1964; repr. Westport, Conn., Greenwood, 1975

[VIII]   *Ancient Near Eastern Religions*

Compiled by A. Rosalie David

1   BARNETT, R. D., 'The Epic of Kumarbi and the Theogony of Hesiod', *Journal of Hellenic Studies*, vol. 45, 1945, pp. 100–1

2   BARNETT, R. D., 'The Sea Peoples', *Cambridge Ancient History*, rev. edn, vol. 2, ch. 28, Cambridge, Cambridge University Press, 1969; 3rd edn, vol. 2, pt 2, 1975

3   DRIVER, SIR GODFREY R., *Canaanite Myths and Legends (from Ras Shamra)*, Edinburgh, T. & T. Clark, 1956, 1971; 2nd edn 1978

4   DROWER, M. S., 'Ugarit', *Cambridge Ancient History*, rev. edn, vol. 2, ch. 21(b), Cambridge, Cambridge University Press, 1968; 3rd edn, vol. 2, pt 2, 1975

5   FRANKFORT, H., *Cylinder Seals: A Documentary Essay on the Art and Religion of the Ancient Near East*, London, Macmillan, 1939

6   FRANKFORT, H., *The Art and Architecture of the Ancient Orient*, Harmondsworth, 1954, 1970, Baltimore, Md, 1955, 1978, Penguin; New York, Viking, 1969

7   GADD, C. J., 'Hammurabi and the End of His Dynasty', *Cambridge Ancient History*, rev. edn, vol. 2, ch. 5, Cambridge, Cambridge University Press, 1965; 3rd edn, vol. 2, pt 1, 1973

8   GELB, I. J., *Hittite Hieroglyphic Monuments*, Chicago, Ill., University of Chicago Press, 1939

9   GELB, I. J., *Hurrians and Subarians*, Chicago, Ill., University of Chicago Press, 1944

10 GRAY, J., *Near Eastern Mythology: Mesopotamia, Syria, Palestine*, London, Hamlyn, 1969

11 GRAYSON, A. K., *Assyrian Royal Inscriptions*, Wiesbaden, Harrassowitz, 1972–6 (Records of the Ancient Near East, vols 1 and 2)

12 GURNEY, O. R., 'Hittite Kingship', in HOOKE, S. H. (ed.), *Myth, Ritual and Kingship*, Oxford, Clarendon Press, 1958

13 GURNEY, O. R., *The Hittites*, Harmondsworth/Baltimore, Md, Penguin, 1964 (© 1952); new edn London, Allen Lane, 1975; rev. edn Penguin, 1990

14 HINZ, W., 'Persia, *c.*2400–1800 BC', *Cambridge Ancient History*, rev. edn, vol. 1, ch. 23, Cambridge, Cambridge University Press, 1963; 3rd edn, vol. 1, pt 2, 1971

15 HINZ, W., *The Lost World of Elam*, London, Sidgwick & Jackson/New York, New York University Press, 1972

16 KRAMER, S. N., *History Begins at Sumer*, London, Thames & Hudson, 1958, 2nd edn, 1961; Garden City, NY, Doubleday, 1959; new edn, Philadelphia, Pa, University of Pennsylvania Press, 1988; first publ. as *From the Tablets of Sumer*, Indian Hills, Colo, Falcon's Wing, 1956

17 LABAT, R., 'Elam, *c.*1600–1200 BC', *Cambridge Ancient History*, rev. edn, vol. 2, ch. 29, Cambridge, Cambridge University Press, 1963; 3rd edn, vol. 2, pt 2, 1975

18 LAESSØE, J., *People of Ancient Assyria* (tr. from the Danish *Frå Assyriens Arkiver* by F. S. Leigh-Browne), London, Routledge/New York, Barnes & Noble, 1963

19 LANGHE, R. DE, 'Myth, Ritual and Kingship in the Ras Shamra Tablets', in HOOKE, S. H. (ed.), *Myth, Ritual and Kingship*, Oxford, Clarendon Press, 1958

20 LLOYD, S., *Foundations in the Dust: A Story of Mesopotamian Exploration*, Harmondsworth/Baltimore, Md, Penguin, 1955; rev. edn London, Thames & Hudson, 1980; London, Oxford University Press, 1947, repr. New York, AMS, 1977

21 MACALISTER, R. A. S., *The Philistines, Their History and Civilisation*, 3rd (1st US) edn, Chicago, Ill., Argonaut, 1965; prev. publ. London, Oxford University Press, 1913

22 NEUGEBAUER, O., *The Exact Sciences in Antiquity*, New York, Harper Torchbooks, 1962; 2nd edn Providence, RI, Brown University Press, 1957, repr. 1970; New York, Dover, 1969

23 POSTGATE, N., *The First Empires*, Oxford, Elsevier/Phaidon, 1977

24 PRITCHARD, J. B. (ed.), *Ancient Near Eastern Texts Relating to the Old Testament*, 2nd edn, Princeton, NJ, Princeton University Press, 1955; 3rd (de luxe) edn, with Supplement, 1969 (refs in text are to the 2nd edn)

25 WISEMAN, D. J., 'Assyria and Babylonia *c.*1200–1000 BC', *Cambridge Ancient History*, rev. edn, vol. 2, ch. 31, Cambridge, Cambridge University Press, 1965; 3rd edn, vol. 2, pt 2, 1975

26 WOOLLEY, SIR CHARLES L., *The Development of Sumerian Art*, London, Faber/New York, Scribner, 1935; repr. Westport, Conn., Greenwood

[IX] *Arctic People's Religions*

Compiled by Eric H. Pyle

1 BIRKET-SMITH, K., *The Eskimos* (tr. W. E. Calvert, rev. C. Daryll Forde), new edn London, Methuen, 1959

2 DIÓSZEGI, V., *Tracing Shamans in Siberia* (tr. from the Hungarian by A. R. Babó), New York, Humanities, for Oosterhout, Netherlands, Anthropological Publications, 1968

3 DIÓSZEGI, V. (ed.), *Popular Beliefs and Folklore Tradition in Siberia*, The Hague, Mouton, 1968

4 HERBERT, W., *Eskimos*, London, Collins, 1976, new edn 1978; New York, Franklin Watts, 1976

5 MURDOCK, G. P., *Our Primitive Contemporaries*, New York, Macmillan, 1934

6 SPENCER, A., *The Lapps*, Newton Abbot, David & Charles/New York, Crane-Russak, 1978

7 VORREN, Ø., and MANKER, E., *Lapp Life and Customs* (tr. from the Norwegian by K. MacFarlane), London/New York, Oxford University Press, 1962

8 WEYER, E. M., *The Eskimos*, New Haven, Conn., Yale University Press/London, Oxford University Press, 1932; repr. Hamden, Conn., Shoe String Press, 1962

(*See also* V, 15; XII, 107; XIII(D), 30, 62, 80; XIV (Shamanism), 27, 33, 35, 43, 57, 73, 82; XXI, 4)

[X]   *Astrology*

Compiled by Roger Beck

1 ALLEN, D. C., *The Star-Crossed Renaissance*, New York, Octagon, 1966, repr. of Durham, NC, Duke University Press, 1941; London, Cass, 1967

2 BOLL, F., BEZOLD, C., and GUNDEL, W., *Sternglaube und Sterndeutung: die Geschichte und das Wesen der Astrologie*, 6th edn (rev. H. G. Gundel), Stuttgart, Teubner, 1974

3 BOUCHÉ-LECLERQ, A., *L'Astrologie grecque*, Paris, 1899 edn, repr. Brussels, Culture et Civilisation, 1963

4 CRAMER, F. H., *Astrology in Roman Law and Politics*, Philadelphia, Pa, American Philosophical Society, 1954 (*Memoirs of the American Philosophical Society*, 37)

5 CULVER, R. B., and IANNA, P. A., 'Astrology and the Scientific Method', *Astronomy Quarterly*, vol. 1, 1977, pp. 85–110, 147–72

6 CUMONT, F., *Astrology and Religion among the Greeks and Romans*, New York, Dover, 1960, repr. of 1912 edn, New York/London, Putnam; Magnolia, Mass., Peter Smith

7 EISLER, R., *The Royal Art of Astrology*, London, Herbert Joseph, 1946

8 GAUQUELIN, M., *The Cosmic Clocks: From Astrology to a Modern Science*, Chicago, Ill., Regnery, 1967; London, Peter Owen, 1969; St Albans, Paladin, 1973; rev. edn San Diego, Cal., ACS Publications, 1982

9 KRUPP, E. G. (ed.), *In Search of Ancient Astronomies*, Garden City, NY, Doubleday, 1978; New York, McGraw-Hill, 1979; London, Chatto, 1980

10 LINDSAY, J., *Origins of Astrology*, London, Muller/New York, Barnes & Noble, 1971

11 MACNEICE, L., *Astrology*, London, Aldus/Garden City, NY, Doubleday, 1964

12 MAYO, J., *Teach Yourself Astrology*, London, English Universities Press, 1964, repr. 1968; New York, Mckay, 1980

13 NEUGEBAUER, O., and VAN HOESEN, H. B., *Greek Horoscopes*, Philadelphia, Pa, American Philosophical Society, 1959 (*Memoirs of the American Philosophical Society*, 48); Ann Arbor, Mich., University Microfilms, 1978

14 PARKER, D., and PARKER, J., *The Compleat Astrologer*, New York, McGraw-Hill, 1971; London, Mitchell Beazley, 1971, 1979; New York, Bantam, 1975

15 PINGREE, D. E., 'Astrology', *Encyclopaedia Britannica: Macropaedia*, 15th edn, vol. 2, 1974, pp. 219–23

16 WEST, J. A., and TOONDER, J. G., *The Case for Astrology*, New York, Coward, McCann/London, Macdonald, 1970; Penguin, 1973

[XI] *Buddhism*

Compiled by Rupert Gethin, L. S. Cousins, Trevor Ling
and Paul Williams

1 ARONSON, H. B., *Love and Sympathy in Theravāda Buddhism*, Delhi, Motilal Banarsidass, 1986 (first publ. 1980 as *Love, Compassion, Sympathetic Joy and Equanimity in Theravāda Buddhism*, Ann Arbor, Mich., University Microfilms, 1980; PhD dissertation, University of Wisconsin, 1975)

2 AUNG, S. Z. (tr.), ANURUDDHA, *Compendium of Philosophy* (ed. Mrs C. Rhys Davids), London, Pali Text Society, 1910; repr. 1979

3 BECHERT, H., and GOMBRICH, R. F. (eds), *World of Buddhism: Buddhist Monks and Nuns in Society and Culture*, new edn London, Thames & Hudson, 1991

4 BODHI (tr.), *The Discourse on the All-Embracing Net of Views*, Kandy, Buddhist Publication Society, 1978

5 BUDDHAGHOSA, *Path of Purification* (tr. Ñānamoli), 2nd edn, Colombo, Semage, 1964; repr. 2 vols., Berkeley, Cal., Shambhala, 1976

6 CARRITHERS, M., *The Buddha*, Oxford, Oxford University Press, 1983

7 CARRITHERS, M., *The Forest Monks of Sri Lanka: An Anthropological and Historical Study*, Delhi, Oxford University Press (India), 1983

8 CARTER, J. R., *Dhamma: Western Academic and Sinhalese Buddhist Interpretations: A Study of a Religious Concept*, Tokyo, Hokuseido Press, 1978

9 CARTER, J. R., *The Threefold Refuge in Theravāda Buddhist Tradition*, Chambersburg, Pa, Anima Books, 1982

10 CHATTERJEE, A. K., *The Yogācāra Idealism*, 2nd rev. edn, Delhi, Motilal Banarsidass, 1975; Livingston, NJ, Orient Book Distributors, 1976

11 CH'EN, K. K. S., *Buddhism in China: A Historical Survey*, Princeton, NJ, Princeton University Press, 1964; repr. 1972

12 COLLINS, S., *Selfless Persons: Imagery and Thought in Theravāda Buddhism*, Cambridge, Cambridge University Press, 1982; pb edn 1990

13 CONZE, E., *Buddhism: Its Essence and Development*, Oxford, Cassirer, 1951, 3rd edn, 1960, 1974; Magnolia, Mass., Peter Smith; New York, Harper & Row, 1959

14 CONZE, E., *Buddhist Meditation*, London, Allen & Unwin, 1956, 1972

15 CONZE, E., *Buddhist Scriptures*, Harmondsworth/Baltimore, Md, Penguin, 1959; repr. 1979

16 CONZE, E., *Buddhist Thought in India*, London, Allen & Unwin, 1962; Ann Arbor, Mich., University of Michigan Press, 1967

17 CONZE, E., *A Short History of Buddhism*, London, Allen & Unwin, 1979

18 CONZE, E. (tr.), *The Short Prajñāpāramitā Texts*, London, Luzac, 1973; Totowa, NJ, Rowman, 1974

19 DALLAPICCOLA, A. L., *The Stupa: Its Religious, Historical and Archaeological Significance*, Wiesbaden, Franz Steiner Verlag, 1980

20 DASGUPTA, S. N., *A History of Indian Philosophy*, vol. 1, Cambridge, Cambridge University Press, 1922, repr. Delhi, Motilal Banarsidass, 1975; Livingston, NJ, Orient Book Distributors, 1975; Atlantic Highlands, NJ, Humanities, 1975

21 DAYAL, H., *The Bodhisattva Doctrine in Buddhist Sanskrit Literature*, London, Kegan Paul, Trench, Trubner, 1932, repr. Delhi, Motilal Banarsidass, 1970; Livingston, NJ, Orient Book Distributors, 1975

22 DUTT, S., *The Buddha and Five After-Centuries*, London, Luzac, 1957

23 DUTT, S., *Buddhist Monks and Monasteries of India*, London, Allen & Unwin, 1962

24 DUTT, N., *Buddhist Sects in India*, Calcutta, Mukhopadhyay, 1970; Delhi, Motilal Banarsidass; Livingston, NJ, Orient Book Distributors

24a EMMERICK, R. E., 'Buddhism among Iranians', *Cambridge History of Iran*, ed. A. J. Arberry, vols. 1–7, 1968–91, vol. 3(2), pp. 949–64

25 GEIGER, W., *The Dīpavaṃsa and Mahāvaṃsa* (tr. E. M. Coomaraswamy), Colombo, Cottle, 1908

26 GEIGER, W., *Pali Literature and Language*, 2nd edn, Calcutta, Calcutta University Press, 1956; new edn rev. and ed. K. R. Norman, Oxford, Pali Text Society, 1994

27 GETHIN, R. M. L., *The Buddhist Path to Awakening: A Study of the Bodhi-Pakkhiyā Dhammā*, Leiden, Brill, 1992

28 GOMBRICH, R. F., *Precept and Practice: Traditional Buddhism in the Rural Highlands of Ceylon*, Oxford, Clarendon Press, 1971

29 GOMBRICH, R. F., *Theravāda Buddhism: A Social History from Ancient Benares to Modern Colombo*, London, Routledge, 1988

30 GOMBRICH, R., and OBEYESEKERE, G., *Buddhism Transformed: Religious Change in Sri Lanka*, Princeton, NJ, Princeton University Press, 1988

31 GOVINDA, L. A., *The Psycho-Cosmic Symbolism of the Buddhist Stūpa*, Emeryville, Dharma Press, 1976

32 GRIFFITHS, P. J., *On Being Mindless: Buddhist Meditation and the Mind–Body Problem*, La Salle, Ill., Open Court, 1986

32a GRIFFITHS, P. J., *On Being Buddha: The Classical Doctrine of Buddhahood*, Albany, State University of New York Press, 1994 (Towards a Comparative Philosophy of Religions series, eds Frank E. Reynolds and David Tracy)

33 GUENTHER, H. V., *Philosophy and Psychology in the Abhidharma*, new edn, Berkeley, Cal., Shambhala, 1976; Delhi, Motilal Banarsidass, 1974

34 HARVEY, P., *An Introduction to Buddhism: Teachings, History and Practices*, Cambridge, Cambridge University Press, 1990

34a HOLT, J. C., *Discipline: The Canonical Buddhism of the Vinaya-pitaka*, Delhi, Motilal Banarsidass, 1981

35 HOOKHAM, S., *The Buddha Within*, Albany, NY, State University of New York Press, 1991

36 HORNER, I. B., *The Book of the Discipline*, vols 1–3 (English tr. of *Bhikkhu-Vibhanga*, or *Suttavibhanga*), London, Oxford University Press, 1938, 1942; repr. Oxford, Pali Text Society, 1992–3

37 HORNER, I. B., *Milinda's Questions* (English tr. of *Milinda-Pañha*), 2 vols, London, Pali Text Society, 1963–4; repr. 1990

38 JAYATILLEKE, K. N., *Early Buddhist Theory of Knowledge*, London, Allen & Unwin, 1963

39 JAYAWICKRAMA, N. A., *The Story of Gotama Buddha*, Oxford, Pali Text Society, 1990

40 JONES, J. J., *Mahāvastu* (tr. from the Buddhist Sanskrit), 3 vols, London, Luzac, 1949, 1952, 1956; repr. London, Pali Text Society, 1973–8

41 JONES, J. G., *Tales and Teaching of the Buddha*, London, Allen & Unwin, 1979

42 JOSHI, L., *Studies in the Buddhistic Culture of India*, Delhi, Motilal Banarsidass, 1967, 1977; Mystic, Conn., Verry, 1977

43 KALUPAHANA, D. J., *Buddhist Philosophy: A Historical Analysis*, Honolulu, University Press of Hawaii, 1976

44 KAWAMURA, L. S. (ed.), *The Bodhisattva Doctrine in Buddhism*, Waterloo, Ont., Wilfrid Laurier University Press, 1981 (Canadian Corporation for Studies in Religion Supplements, 10)

45 KEOWN, D., *The Nature of Buddhist Ethics*, London, Macmillan, 1992

46 KERN, H., *Saddharmapundarika [Sutra]* (English tr.), Oxford, Clarendon Press, 1884, 1909 (Sacred Books of the East, vol. 21); repr. New York, Krishna; Magnolia, Mass., Peter Smith

46a KHANTIPALO, B., *Calm and Insight: A Buddhist Manual for Meditators*, London, Curzon Press, 1981

47 KHOROCHE, P., *Once the Buddha Was a Monkey: Ārya Śūra's Jātaka-māla*, Chicago, Ill., University of Chicago Press, 1989

48 KING, W. L., *Theravada Meditation*, [University Park, Pa], Pensylvania State University Press, 1980

49 KLOETZLI, R., *Buddhist Cosmology: From Single World System to Pure Land*, Delhi, Motilal Banarsidass, 1983

50 KLOPPENBORG, R. *The Paccekabuddha: A Buddhist Ascetic*, Leiden, Brill, 1974

51 LAMOTTE, É., *History of Indian Buddhism: From the Origins to the Śaka Era*, Louvain, Institut Orientaliste, 1988

52 LINDTNER, CHR., *Nagarjuniana: Studies in the Writings and Philosophy of Nāgārjuna*, Copenhagen, Akademisk Forlag, 1982 (Indiske Studier IV)

53 LING, T., *The Buddha: Buddhist Civilization in India and Ceylon*, London, M. T. Smith/New York, Scribner, 1973

54 LING, T., *The Buddha's Philosophy of Man: Early Indian Buddhist Dialogues*, London, Dent, 1981

55 LING, T., *Buddhism and the Mythology of Evil*, London, Allen & Unwin, 1962

56 MALALASEKERA, G. P., *Dictionary of Pāli Proper Names*, 2 vols, London, Luzac, 1960, first publ. 1937–8; repr. London, Pali Text Society, 1974

57 MALALASEKERA, G. P., *The Pāli Literature of Ceylon*, Colombo, Gunasena, 1928; London, Royal Asiatic Society, 1928; New York, International Publications Service, 1958

58   MARASINGHE, M. M. J., *Gods in Early Buddhism*, Vidyalankara, University of Sri Lanka (Ceylon), 1974

59   *Middle Length Sayings* (Majjhima-Nikāya), vol. 1 (tr. I. B. Horner), London, Pali Text Society, 1954; repr. Oxford, Pali Text Society, 1993

60   MURTI, T. R. V., *The Central Philosophy of Buddhism*, London, Allen & Unwin, 1955, 1980

61   NAGAO, G. M., *Mādhyamika and Yogācāra* (tr. Leslie S. Kawamura), Albany, NY, State University of New York Press, 1991

62   ÑĀNAMOLI, *The Life of the Buddha According to the Pali Canon*, Kandy, Buddhist Publication Society, 1992

63   NAPPER, E., *Dependent Origination and Emptiness*, Boston, London/ Sydney, Wisdom Publications, 1989

64   NORMAN, K. R. (tr.), *Elders' Verses II (Therīgāthā)*, London, Pali Text Society, 1971; repr. Oxford, Pali Text Society, 1992

65   NORMAN, K. R., *Pāli Literature, Including the Canonical Literature in Prakrit and Sanskrit of all the Hīnayāna Schools of Buddhism*, Wiesbaden, Otto Harrassowitz, 1983

66   NYANAPONIKA, *The Heart of Buddhist Meditation*, London, Rider, 1962

67   NYANATILOKA, M., *Buddhist Dictionary*, 2nd rev. edn, Colombo, Frewin, 1956; 1950 edn repr. New York, AMS, 1977; San Francisco, Cal., Chinese Materials Center, 1977

68   PANDE, G. C., *Studies in the Origins of Buddhism*, 2nd edn, Delhi, Motilal Banarsidass, 1974; Livingston, NJ, Orient Book Distributors/ Mystic, Conn., Verry, 1974

69   PREBISH, C. S., *Buddhism*, [University Park, Pa], Pennsylvania State University Press, 1975

70   PYE, M., *Skilful Means: A Concept in Mahayana Buddhism*, London, Duckworth, 1978

71   RADHAKRISHNAN, S., *The Dhammapada* (Pāli text, English tr. and notes), London/New York, Oxford University Press, 1950; Bombay, 1969

72   RADHAKRISHNAN, SIR SARVEPALLI, and MOORE, C. A. (eds), *A Source-Book in Indian Philosophy*, Princeton, NJ, Princeton University Press, 1957; repr. 1973

73   RAHULA, WALPOLA, *History of Buddhism in Ceylon*, Colombo, Gunasena, 1956; New Delhi, Orient Longman, 1969

74   RAHULA, WALPOLA, *What the Buddha Taught*, London, Gordon Fraser, 1967; new edn London, Wisdom Books, 1990

75   RHYS DAVIDS, T. W., *Buddhist India*, 1st edn, London/New York, 1903; 8th edn Calcutta, Gupta, 1959; Delhi, Indological Book House, 1970

76   RHYS DAVIDS, T. W., and C. A. F., *Dialogues of the Buddha*, pts 1–3, London, Oxford University Press, 1899–1921, repr. London, Luzac, 1956–65; repr. London, Pali Text Society, 1977

77   ROBINSON, R. H., *Early Mādhyamika in India and China*, Madison, Wisc./London, University of Wisconsin Press, 1967, repr. Livingston, NJ, Orient Book Distributors, 1976; Mystic, Conn., Verry, 1977

78   RUEGG, D. S., *The Literature of the Madhyamaka School of Philosophy in India*, Wiesbaden, Otto Harrassowitz, 1981 (A History of Indian Literature, VII:I, ed. J. Gonda)

79   SADDHATISSA, H., *The Buddha's Way*, London, Allen & Unwin, 1971; New York, Braziller, 1972

80 SADDHATISSA, H., *Buddhist Ethics*, London, Allen & Unwin, 1970; New York, Braziller, 1971

80a SCHMITHAUSEN, L., *Ālayavijñāna: On the Origin and the Early Development of a Central Concept of Yogācāra Philosophy*, Tokyo, International Institute for Buddhist Studies, 1987 (Studia Philologica Buddhica, Monograph Series IVa–b)

81 SCHUMANN, H. W., *The Historical Buddha: The Times, Life and Teachings of the Historical Founder of Buddhism*, London, Arkana/ Penguin, 1989

82 SECKEL, D., *The Art of Buddhism*, London, Methuen/New York, Crown, 1964

83 SGAM-PO-PA, *Jewel Ornament of Liberation* (tr. H. V. Guenther), London, Rider, 1959, 1970; Berkeley, Cal., Shambhala, 1971

84 SILVA, P. DE, *An Introduction to Buddhist Psychology*, London, Macmillan, 1979

85 SNELLGROVE, D. L., *The Image of the Buddha*, London, Serindia/ Paris, Unesco, 1978; New York, Kodansha, 1978

86 SPIRO, M. E., *Buddhism and Society*, London, Allen & Unwin, 1971; New York, Harper & Row (© 1970)

87 SPRUNG, M., *Lucid Exposition of the Middle Way: The Essential Chapters from the Prasannapadā of Candrakīrti*, London, Routledge, 1979; Boulder, Colo, Prajna, 1980

88 STCHERBATSKY, T., *Buddhist Logic*, 1930 (Bibl. Buddhica, XXVI, pts I and II), repr. 2 vols, Dover, 1962; repr. of 1932 edn, The Hague, Mouton, 1958

89 STCHERBATSKY, T., *The Central Conception of Buddhism*, 2nd edn, Calcutta, Gupta, 1956; 3rd edn 1961, repr. Mystic, Conn., Verry; Livingston, NJ, Orient Book Distributors, 1979

90 STRENG, F. J., *Emptiness: A Study in Religious Meaning*, New York, Abingdon, 1967

91 STRONG, J. S., *The legend of King Aśoka (Aśokāvadāna)*, Princeton, NJ, Princeton University Press, 1983

92 TAMBIAH, S. J., *The Buddhist Saints of the Forest and the Cult of Amulets*, Cambridge, Cambridge University Press, 1984

93 TAMBIAH, S. J., *World Conqueror and World Renouncer: A Study of Buddhism and Polity in Thailand against a Historical Background*, Cambridge, Cambridge University Press, 1976

93a TAYLOR, J. L., *Forest Monks and the Nation-State: An Anthropological and Historical Study in Northeastern Thailand*, Singapore, Institute of Southeast Asian Studies, 1993

94 THAPAR, R., *Aśoka and the Decline of the Mauryas*, London, Oxford University Press, 1961; 2nd rev. edn London, OUP, 1974, Bombay, 1973

95 THOMAS, E. J., *The Life of the Buddha: As Legend and History*, 3rd edn, London, Routledge, 1949; repr. 1969, 1975

96 VAJIRAÑĀNA, P., *Buddhist Meditation in Theory and Practice*, Colombo, Gunasena, 1962

97 WARDER, A. K., *Indian Buddhism*, Delhi, Motilal Banarsidass, 1970

98 WEERARATNE, W. H., *Individual and Society in Buddhism*, Colombo, World Fellowship of Buddhists, 1977

99 WELBON, G. R., *Buddhist Nirvana and Its Western Interpreters*, Chicago, Ill., University of Chicago Press, 1968

100 WIJAYARATNA, M., *Buddhist Monastic Life According to the Texts of the Theravāda Tradition*, Cambridge, Cambridge University Press, 1990

101 WILLIAMS, P., *Mahayāna Buddhism: The Doctrinal Foundations*, London/New York, Routledge, 1989

(*See also* XII; XXI; XXXV)

[XII]   *Chinese Religions*

Compiled by Stewart McFarlane

1   AHERN, E., *The Cult of the Dead in a Chinese Village*, Stanford, Cal., Stanford University Press, 1973
2   BILSKY, L. J., *The State Religion of Ancient China*, 2 vols, Taipei, Chinese Association of Folklore/South Pasadena, Cal., Langstaff, 1975
3   BODDE, D., *Festivals in Classical China*, Princeton, NJ, Princeton University Press, 1975
4   BREDON, J., and MITROPHANOW, I., *The Moon Year: A Record of Chinese Customs and Festivals*, Shanghai, Kelly & Walsh, 1927; repr. Taipei, Ch'eng Wen/San Francisco, Cal., Chinese Materials Center, 1972
5   BRUCE, J. P., *Chu Hsi and His Masters*, London, Probsthain, 1923; repr. New York, AMS; New York, Krishna
6   BRUCE, J. P. (tr.), CHU HSI, *The Philosophy of Human Nature*, London, Probsthain, 1922; repr. New York, AMS
6a BUSH, R. C., *Religion in Communist China*, New York, Abingdon, 1970
7   CHAN, W. T., *A Source Book in Chinese Philosophy*, Princeton, NJ, Princeton University Press, 1963, 1969
8   CHAN, W. T. (tr.), WANG YANG-MING, *Instructions for Practical Living and Other Neo-Confucian Writings*, New York, Columbia University Press, 1963
9   CHAN, W. T. (tr.), HUI NÊNG, *The Platform Scripture*, New York, St John's University Press, 1963
10 CHANG, C., *The Development of Neo-Confucian Thought*, vol. 1, New York, Bookman Associates, 1957; London, Vision, 1958; New Haven, Conn., College and University Press, 1957; Westport, Conn., Greenwood, 1977
11 CHANG, C. Y., (tr.), TAO-YÜAN, S., *Original Teachings of Ch'an Buddhism*, New York, Pantheon, 1969
12 CHANG, G. C. C., *The Buddhist Teaching of Totality*, [University Park, Pa], Pennsylvania State University, 1971; London, Allen & Unwin, 1972
13 CHANG, K. C., *The Archaeology of Ancient China*, 3rd rev. edn, New Haven, Conn., Yale University Press, 1977
14 CHANG, K. C., *Shang Civilization*, New Haven, Conn., Yale University Press, 1980
15 CH'EN, K., *Buddhism in China*, Princeton, NJ, Princeton University Press, 1964, 1974
16 CH'EN, K., *The Chinese Transformation of Buddhism*, Princeton, NJ, Princeton University Press, 1973
17 CHING, J., *To Acquire Wisdom: The Way of Wang Yang Ming*, New York, Columbia University Press, 1976
17a CHING, J., *Chinese Religions*, London, Macmillan, 1993

18   COOK, F. H., *Hua Yen Buddhism*, [University Park, Pa], Pennsylvania State University Press, 1977

19   CREEL, H. G., *Chinese Thought from Confucius to Mao Tse Tung*, Chicago, Ill., University of Chicago Press, 1953; London, Eyre & Spottiswoode, 1954; London, Methuen, 1962

20   CREEL, H. G., *Confucius, the Man and the Myth*, London, Routledge, 1951; New York, J. Day, 1949, repr. Westport, Conn., Greenwood, 1973

21   CREEL, H. G., *What is Taoism?*, Chicago, Ill., University of Chicago Press, 1970, 1977

22   DAY, C. B., *Chinese Peasant Cults*, Shanghai, Kelly & Walsh, 1940; 2nd edn Taipei, Ch'eng Wen, 1969; repr. San Francisco, Cal., Chinese Materials Center, 1974

23   DAY, C. B., *Popular Religion in Pre-Communist China*, San Francisco, Cal., Chinese Materials Center, 1975

24   DE BARY, W. T., et al. (eds), *Sources of Chinese Tradition*, New York, Columbia University Press, 1960

25   DORÉ, H., *Researches into Chinese Superstitions*, vols 6–10, Shanghai, T'u Se Wei, 1920; repr. Taipei, Ch'eng Wen, 1966

26   DUBS, H. (tr.), HSÜN TZE, *Works*, London, Probsthain, 1928, repr. Taipei, Ch'eng Wen, 1966; San Francisco, Cal., Chinese Materials Center, 1973

27   DUMOULIN, H., *A History of Zen Buddhism*, New York, Pantheon, 1963; Boston, Mass., Beacon Press, 1969

28   DUMOULIN, H., *Zen Buddhism: A History*, vol. 1, *India and China*, New York, Macmillan, 1988

29   DUMOULIN, H., *Zen Buddhism: A History*, vol. 2, *Japan*, New York, Macmillan, 1990

30   EBERHARD, W., *A History of China*, 4th rev. edn, London, Routledge/ Berkeley, Cal., University of California Press, 1977

31   EITEL, E. J., *Feng-Shui*, London, Trübner, 1873; repr. Bristol, Pentacle Books, 1979

32   FEHL, N. E., *Li: Rites and Propriety in Literature and Life*, New York, International Publications Service/Chinese University of Hong Kong, 1971

33   FEUCHTWANG, S., *The Imperial Metaphor: Popular Religion in China*, London, Routledge, 1992

34   FUNG, Y. L., *A History of Chinese Philosophy*, vol. 1, Princeton, NJ, Princeton University Press, 1952; first publ. Peiping, Vetch, 1937

35   FUNG, Y. L., *A History of Chinese Philosophy*, vol. 2, Princeton, NJ, Princeton University Press/Leiden, Brill, 1953

36   GILES, L., *Descriptive Catalogue of the Chinese Manuscripts from Tun Huang in the British Museum*, London, British Museum, 1957

37   GRAHAM, A. C. (tr.), *The Book of Lieh Tzu*, London, Murray, 1960; 2nd rev. edn London, Mandala, 1991

38   GRAHAM, A. C. (tr.), CHUANG TZU, *The Inner Chapters*, London, Allen & Unwin, 1981; new edn London, Mandala, 1986

39   GRAHAM, A. C., *Disputes of the Tao*, La Salle, Ill., Open Court, 1989

40   GRAHAM, A. C., *Later Mohist Logic, Ethics and Science*, Hong Kong, Chinese University Press/London, School of Oriental and African Studies, 1978

41   GRANET, M., *The Religion of the Chinese People*, Oxford, Blackwell, 1975; New York, Harper & Row, 1975, 1977

42   GRANET, M., *Festivals and Songs of Ancient China*, New York, Dutton, 1932, repr. New York, Gordon Press, 1975; New York, Krishna

43   GREGORY, P. N. (ed.), *Sudden and Gradual Approaches to Enlightenment in Chinese Thought*, Honolulu, University of Hawaii, 1987

44   GROOT, J. J. M. DE, *The Religious System of China*, vols 1–3, *Disposal of the Dead*, Leiden, Brill, 1892; repr. Taipei, Ch'eng Wen, 1976

45   GROOT, J. J. M. DE, *The Religious System of China*, vols 4–6, *On the Soul and Ancestral Worship*, Leiden, Brill, 1892, repr. Taipei, Ch'eng Wen, 1976

46   GROOT, J. J. M. DE, *Sectarianism and Religious Persecution in China*, 2 vols, Amsterdam, Müller, 1903–4, repr. Shannon, Irish University Press, 1973; New York, Barnes & Noble, 1974

47   HAMILTON, C. H. (tr.), VASUBANDHU, *Wei Shih Er Shih Lun; or, The Treatise . . . on Representation-Only*, New Haven, Conn., American Oriental Society, 1938

48   HENRICKS, R. G. (tr.), LAO-TZU, *Te-Tao Ching*, London, Bodley Head, 1990

49   HODOUS, L., *Folkways in China*, London, Probsthain, 1929; repr. Taipei, Ch'eng Wen, 1974

50   HSU, F. L. K., *Under the Ancestors' Shadow*, Stanford, Cal., Stanford University Press, 1967

51   HUGHES, E. R. (tr.), TA HSÜEH, *The Great Learning, and The Mean-in-Action*, London, Dent, 1942; New York, Dutton, 1943

52   HUGHES, E. R., *Chinese Philosophy in Classical Times*, London, Dent/New York, Dutton, 1942 and repr.; New York, Gordon Press, 1977

53   JORDAN, D. K., *Gods, Ghosts and Ancestors: The Folk Religion of a Taiwanese Village*, Berkeley, Cal., University of California Press, 1972

54   JORDAN, D. K., and OVERMYER, D. L. (eds), *The Flying Phoenix: Aspects of Sectarianism in Taiwan*, Princeton, NJ, Princeton University Press, 1986

55   KALTENMARK, M., *Lao Tzu and Taoism*, rev. edn, Stanford, Cal., Stanford University Press, 1969

56   KARLGREN, B., *The Book of Documents*, Stockholm, Museum of Far Eastern Antiquities, 1950

57   KARLGREN, B. (tr.), *The Book of Odes*, Stockholm, Museum of Far Eastern Antiquities, 1950; repr. London, Kegan Paul, 1950

58   LAMOTTE, E. (tr.), ASAṄGA, *La Somme du Grande Véhicule*, Louvain, Bureaux du Muséon, 1938

59   LA VALLÉE POUSSIN, L. DE (tr.), VASUBANDHU, *L'Abhidharmakośa*, 6 vols, Paris, Geuthner, 1923–31; new edn Brussels, Institut Belge des Hautes Études Chinoises, 1971

60   LA VALLÉE POUSSIN, L. DE (tr.), HIUEN TSANG, *Vijñaptimātratā siddhi, La Siddhi de Hiuen Tsang*, Paris, Geuthner, 1928–9

61   LAU, D. C. (tr.), CONFUCIUS, *The Analects*, Harmondsworth, Penguin, 1979

62   LAU, D. C. (tr.), *Mencius*, Harmondsworth, Penguin, 1970

63   LAU, D. C. (tr.), LAO TZU, *Tao Te Ching*, Harmondsworth/Baltimore, Md, Penguin, 1963

64   LEGGE, J., *The Chinese Classics*, vol. 1, *The Confucian Analects, The Great Learning, and The Doctrine of The Mean*, London, Trübner, 1861–72; 2nd edn Oxford, Clarendon Press, 1893–5, repr. 1935; New York, Krishna

65   LEGGE, J., *The Chinese Classics*, vol. 2, *The Works of Mencius*: as no. 64

66   LEGGE, J., *The Chinese Classics*, vol. 3, *The Shoo Ching*: as no. 64

67   LEGGE, J., *The Chinese Classics*, vol. 4, *The She Ching*: as no. 64

68 LEGGE, J., *The Chinese Classics*, vol. 5, *The Ch'un Ts'ew with the Tso Chuan*: as no. 64

69 LEGGE, J. (tr.), *Li Ki*, Oxford, Clarendon Press, 1885 (*Sacred Books of the East*, ed. F. M. Müller, vols 27, 28: *The Sacred Books of China*), repr. Delhi, Motilal Banarsidass, 1966; Mystic, Conn., Verry

70 LIEBENTHAL, W. (tr.), *Chao Lun: The Treatises of Seng Chao*, 2nd rev. edn, Hong Kong, Hong Kong University Press, 1968

71 LIU, K. C. (ed.), *Orthodoxy in Imperial China*, Berkeley, Cal., University of California Press, 1990

72 MASPERO, H., *China in Antiquity*, Folkstone, W. Dawson, 1978; Amherst, Mass., University of Massachusetts Press, 1979

73 MASPERO, H., *Mélanges posthumes sur les religions et l'histoire de la Chine*, vol. 2, *Le Taoisme*, Paris, Publications du Musée Guimet, 1950; Paris, Presses Universitaires de France, 1967

74 MEI, Y. P., *Motse: The Ethical and Political Works*, London, Probsthain, 1929, repr. Westport, Conn., Hyperion Press, 1973; Taipei, Ch'eng Wen, 1974

75 MEI, Y. P., *Motse, the Neglected Rival of Confucius*, London, Probsthain, 1934; repr. Westport, Conn., Hyperion Press, 1973

76 MÜLLER, F. M. (ed.), *Buddhist Mahāyāna Texts*, Oxford, Clarendon Press, 1894 (*Sacred Books of the East*, vol. 49), repr. Delhi, Motilal Banarsidass, 1965, new edn of 1894 edn 1985; Mystic, Conn., Verry

77 MUNRO, D. (ed.), *Individualism and Holism: Studies in Confucian and Taoist Values*, Ann Arbor, Mich., University of Michigan Press, 1985

78 NEEDHAM, J., *Science and Civilisation in China*, Cambridge, Cambridge University Press, vol. 2, 1956; repr. 1962

79 NEEDHAM, J., *Science and Civilisation in China*, Cambridge, Cambridge University Press, vol. 5, pt 3, 1976

80 OVERMYER, D., *Folk Buddhist Religion*, Cambridge, Mass., Harvard University Press, 1976

81 OVERMYER, D. L., *The Religions of China*, New York, Harper & Row, 1986

82 RAWSON, J., *Ancient China*, London, Book Club Associates, 1980; London, British Museum/New York, Harper & Row, 1980

83 REICHELT, K. L., *Truth and Tradition in Chinese Buddhism*, Shanghai, Commercial Press, 1927; repr. of 1934 edn New York, Paragon, 1969

84 RICHARDS, I. A., *Mencius on the Mind*, London, Kegan Paul, Trench, Trubner/New York, Harcourt, Brace, 1932, repr. London, Routledge, 1964; Westport, Conn., Hyperion Press, 1980

85 ROBINSON, R. H., *Early Madhyamika in India and China*, Madison, Wisc., University of Wisconsin Press, 1967; repr. Livingston, NJ, Orient Book Distributors, 1976; Mystic, Conn., Verry, 1977

86 SANGREN, S., *History and Magical Power in a Chinese Community*, Stanford, Cal., Stanford University Press, 1987

87 SASO, M. R., *Blue Dragon, White Tiger: Taoist Rites of Passage*, Hawaii, University of Hawaii Press, 1990

88 SASO, M., *Taoism and the Rite of Cosmic Renewal*, Pullman, Wash., Washington State University Press, 1972

89 SASO, M., *The Teachings of Taoist Master Chuang*, New Haven, Conn., Yale University Press, 1978

90 SASO, M., and CHAPPELL, D. W., (eds), *Buddhist and Taoist Studies*, vol. 1, Honolulu, University Press of Hawaii, 1977

91 SEKIDA, K., *Two Zen Classics: Mumonkan and Hekiganroku*, New York, Weatherhill, 1977

92   SHRYOCK, J. K., *The Origin and Development of the State Cult of Confucius*, New York/London, American Historical Association, Century Co., 1932; repr. New York, Paragon, 1966

93   SIVIN, N., *Chinese Alchemy: Preliminary Studies*, Cambridge, Mass., Harvard University Press, 1968

94   SMITH, D. H., *Chinese Religions*, London, Weidenfeld/New York, Holt, Rinehart, 1968

95   SMITH, D. H., *Confucius*, St Albans, Paladin, 1974; New York, Scribner/London, Temple Smith, 1973

96   STEELE, J. (tr.), *The I Li; or, Book of Etiquette and Ceremonial*, London, Probsthain, 1917

97   SUZUKI, D. T., *Essays in Zen Buddhism*, ser. 1, London, Rider, 1949, 1970; New York, Grove Press, 1961; Taipei, Ch'eng Wen/San Francisco, Cal., Chinese Materials Center, 1971; prev. publ. London, Luzac, 1927

98   THOMPSON, L. G., *The Chinese Way in Religion*, Encino, Cal., Dickenson, 1973

99   THOMPSON, L. G., *Chinese Religion: An Introduction*, 2nd edn, Encino, Cal., Dickenson, 1975; 4th rev. edn Belmont, Cal., Wadsworth, 1989

100 TSUKAMOTO, Z., *A History of Early Chinese Buddhism*, tr. L. Hurvitz, 2 vols, Tokyo/New York, Kodansha, 1985

101 TUNG, T. P., *Fifty Years of Studies in Oracle Bone Inscriptions*, Tokyo, Centre for East Asian Cultural Studies, 1964

102 VINCENT, I. V., *The Sacred Oasis: Caves of the Thousand Buddhas, Tun Huang*, Chicago, Ill., University of Chicago Press/London, Faber, 1953

103 WALEY, A. (tr.), *The Book of Songs*, London, Allen & Unwin, 1937; New York, Grove Press, 1960

104 WALEY, A. (tr.), LAO-TZU, *The Way and Its Power*, London, Allen & Unwin, 1934, 1977; New York, Grove Press, 1958

105 WALEY, A. (tr.), CONFUCIUS, *The Analects*, London, Allen & Unwin, 1938; New York, Random House, 1966

106 WALEY, A., *Three Ways of Thought in Ancient China*, London, Allen & Unwin/New York, Barnes, 1939; Garden City, NY, Doubleday, 1956

107 WALEY, A. (ed. and tr.), CH'Ü YÜAN, *The Nine Songs: A Study of Shamanism in Ancient China*, London, Allen & Unwin, 1955

108 WALEY, A. (ed.), *Ballads and Stories from Tun-Huang*, London, Allen & Unwin/New York, Macmillan, 1960

109 WARE, J. R. (tr.), KO HUNG, *Alchemy, Medicine and Religion in the China of AD 320*, Cambridge, Mass., MIT Press, 1966

110 WATSON, B. (tr.), CHUANG TZU, *The Complete Works*, New York/London, Columbia University Press, 1968

111 WATSON, B. (tr.), HSÜN TZU, *Basic Writings*, New York, Columbia University Press, 1963

112 WATSON, B. (tr.), MO TZU, *Basic Writings*, New York, Columbia University Press, 1963

113 WATSON, J. L., and RAWSKI, E. S. (eds), *Death Ritual in Late Imperial and Modern China*, Berkeley, Cal., London, University of California Press, 1988

114 WATSON, W., *Early Civilizations in China*, London, Thames & Hudson/New York, McGraw-Hill, 1966

115 WELCH, H., *Taoism: The Parting of the Way*, Boston, Mass., Beacon Press, 1957, 1966; London, Methuen, 1958

116 WELCH, H., and SEIDEL, A. (eds), *Facets of Taoism: Essays in Chinese Religion*, New Haven, Conn., Yale University Press, 1979; new edn 1981

117 WERNER, E. T. C., *A Dictionary of Chinese Mythology*, Shanghai, Kelly & Walsh, 1932; repr. Boston, Mass., Longwood Press, 1977

118 WILHELM, R. (tr.), *The I Ching; or Book of Changes. The Richard Wilhelm Translation Rendered into English by C. F. Baynes*, London, Routledge, 1951; New York, Pantheon, 1950

119 WRIGHT, A. F., *Buddhism in Chinese History*, London, Oxford University Press/Stanford, Cal., Stanford University Press, 1959; new edn Stanford University Press, 1970

120 WRIGHT, A. F., *Studies in Chinese Buddhism*, ed. R. M. Somers, New Haven, Conn., Yale University Press, 1990

121 WU, K. M. (tr.), *The Butterfly as Companion: Meditations on the First Three Chapters of the Chuang Tzu*, Albany, NY, State University of New York Press, 1990

122 YANG, C. K., *Religion in Chinese Society*, Berkeley, Cal., University of California Press, 1961

123 ZURCHER, E., *The Buddhist Conquest of China*, 2 vols, Leiden, Brill, 1959

(*See also* XI, 77; XIII(B), 106; XIX, 68)

[XIII]   *Christianity: (A) Bible and Early Church*

Compiled by George J. Brooke

1 AUNE, D. E., *Prophecy in Early Christianity and the Ancient Mediterranean World*, Grand Rapids, Mich., Eerdmans, 1983

2 BARTON, J., *Reading the Old Testament: Method in Biblical Study*, London, Darton, Longman & Todd, 1984

3 BECKWITH, R. T., *The Old Testament Canon of the New Testament Church and its Background in Early Judaism*, London, SPCK, 1985; new edn Grand Rapids, Mich., Eerdmans, 1986

4 BROWN, R. E., FITZMYER, J. A., and MURPHY, R. E., *The New Jerome Biblical Commentary*, London, Chapman, 1989; student edn of 2nd rev. edn 1993

5 BRUCE, F. F., *New Testament History*, rev. edn, London, Pickering and Inglis, 1982; first US edn Garden City, NY, Doubleday, 1971

6 BRUCE, F. F., *Paul: Apostle of the Free Spirit*, Exeter, Paternoster, 1977, 1981; publ. in US as *Paul: Apostle of the Heart Set Free*, Grand Rapids, Mich., Eerdmans, 1977

7 *Cambridge History of the Bible*, vol. 1, eds P. R. Ackroyd and C. F. Evans, *From the Beginnings to Jerome*; vol. 2, ed. G. W. H. Lampe, *The West from the Fathers to the Reformation*; vol. 3, ed. S. L. Greenslade, *The West from the Reformation to the Present Day*, Cambridge, Cambridge University Press, 1963–70, 1975–6; new edn, 3 vols, 1988

8 CROSSAN, J. D., *The Historical Jesus*, Edinburgh, T. & T. Clark, 1991; new edn 1993

9 DUNN, J. D. G., *Unity and Diversity in the New Testament*, London, SCM/ Philadelphia, Pa, 1977; 2nd rev. edn London, SCM, 1990

10 DUNN, J. D. G., *Christology in the Making*, London, SCM/Philadelphia, Pa, Westminster, 1980; 2nd rev. edn London, SCM, 1989

11 FREEDMAN, D. N. (ed.), *The Anchor Bible Dictionary*, 6 vols, Garden City, NY, Doubleday, 1992

12 HANSON, R. P. C., *Christian Priesthood Examined*, Guildford, Lutterworth, 1979

13 KOESTER, H., *Introduction to the New Testament*, 2 vols, Philadelphia, Pa, Fortress/Berlin, de Gruyter, 1982

14 LAYTON, B., *The Gnostic Scriptures*, London, SCM, 1987

15 MEEKS, W. A., *The First Urban Christians*, London/New Haven, Conn., Yale University Press, 1983; new edn 1984

16 PERRIN, N. and DULING, D. C., *The New Testament: An Introduction*, 2nd edn, New York/London, Harcourt, Brace, Jovanovich, 1982; 3rd edn publ. as *New Testament: Proclamation and Parenesis, Myth and History*, 1993

17 ROBINSON, J. M. (ed.), *The Nag Hammadi Library in English*, Leiden, Brill, 1977, 2nd edn 1988: San Francisco, Cal., Harper & Row, 1978, 2nd edn 1988

18 ROWLAND, C., *Christian Origins*, London, SPCK, 1985

19 RUDOLPH, K., *Gnosis*, Edinburgh, T.& T. Clark, 1983

20 SANDERS, E. P., *Jesus and Judaism*, London, SCM/Philadelphia, Pa, Fortress, 1985

21 SANDERS, E. P., *Judaism: Practice and Belief 63 BCE–66 CE*, London, SCM/Philadelphia, Pa, Trinity Press International, 1992

22 SCHÜRER, E., *The History of the Jewish People in the Age of Jesus Christ* (new English version, rev. and ed. G. Vermes, F. Millar, M. Black, M. Goodman), vols 1–3, Edinburgh, T. & T. Clark, 1973–87

23 STONE, M. E. (ed.), *Jewish Writings of the Second Temple Period*, Assen, Van Gorcum/Philadelphia, Pa, Fortress, 1984

24 TUCKETT, C. M., *Reading the New Testament: Methods of Interpretation*, London, SPCK, 1987

25 VERMES, G., *The Dead Sea Scrolls in English*, Harmondsworth/Baltimore, Md, Penguin, 3rd edn 1987; 4th edn 1995

26 VERMES, G., *Jesus the Jew*, London, Collins, 1973; New York, Macmillan, 1974; new edn London, SCM, 1983

[XIII]   *Christianity: (B) History and Doctrine*

Compiled by Henry D. Rack, D. P. Davies and Ben Pink Dandelion

1 ABBOTT, W. M. (ed.), *The Documents of Vatican II in a New and Definitive Translation*, London/Dublin, G. Chapman, 1966; New York, Herder, 1966; New York, Association Press, 1966, 1974

2 AHLSTROM, S. E., *A Religious History of the American People*, New Haven, Conn., London, Yale University Press, 1972, new edn 1974; Garden City, NY, Doubleday, 2 vols, 1975

3 ANDREWS, E. D., *The People Called Shakers*, New York, Oxford University Press, 1953; rev. edn London, Dover, 1963

4 ARRINGTON, L. T., *The Mormon Experience*, London, Allen & Unwin, 1979

5 ASHE, G., *The Virgin*, London, Routledge, 1976; new edn Harmondsworth, Arkana/Penguin, 1991

6 ATA, A. T. WADE (ed.), *Religion and Ethnic Identity: An Australian Study*, 2 vols, Richmond, Vic., Spectrum, 1988, 1989

7 ATTWATER, D. (ed.), *The Penguin Dictionary of Saints*,

Harmondsworth/Baltimore, Md, Penguin, 1965, repr. 1979; 2nd edn, rev. C. R. John, 1983

8   AUBERT, R. (ed.), *The Church in a Secularised Society* (*The Christian Centuries*, vol. 5), London, Darton/New York, Paulist Press, 1978

9   AYLING, S., *John Wesley*, London, Collins, 1979; repr. 1981

10 BACON, M. H., *The Quiet Rebels: The Story of the Quakers in America*, New York, Basic Books, 1969

11 BAINTON, R. H., *Here I Stand: A Life of Martin Luther*, London, Hodder, 1951; Nashville, Tenn., Abingdon, 1950; New York, Mentor, 1955; 2nd rev. edn Oxford, Lion Publishing, 1987

12 BALLEINE, G. R., *Past Finding Out: The Tragic Story of Joanna Southcott and her Successors*, London, SPCK, 1956

13 BARRETT, D. R., *World Christian Encyclopedia*, Nairobi/New York, Oxford University Press, 1992

14 BEBBINGTON, D., *Evangelicalism in Modern Britain: A History from the 1730s to the 1980s*, London, Unwin Hyman, 1987

15 BECKFORD, J. A., *The Trumpet of Prophecy: A Sociological Study of Jehovah's Witnesses*, Oxford, Blackwell, 1975

16 BEESON, T., *Discretion and Valour: Religious Conditions in Russia and Eastern Europe*, London, Collins, 1974; New York, Fount, 1976

17 BEESON, T., and PEARCE, J., *A Vision of Hope: The Churches and Change in Latin America*, London, Collins, 1984

18 BERGENDOFF, C., *The Church of the Lutheran Reformation: A Historical Survey of Lutheranism*, St Louis, Mo, Concordia, 1967

19 BETTENSON, H. (ed.), *Documents of the Christian Church*, 2nd edn, London, Oxford University Press, 1963; repr. 1967, 1977, etc.

20 BIERNOTZAI, W. E., et al., *Korean Catholicism in the 70s*, Maryknoll, NY, Orbis, 1975

21 BOCIURKIW, B. R., and STRONG, J. W. (eds), *Religion and Atheism in the USSR and Eastern Europe*, London/New York, Macmillan, 1975; Toronto, University of Toronto Press, 1975

22 BOFF, L., *Jesus Christ Liberator: A Critical Christology for our Time*, London, SPCK, 1980; Maryknoll, NY, Orbis, 1978

23 BOFF, L. and C., *Introducing Liberation Theology*, London, Burns & Oates, 1987

24 BOFF, L., and ELIZONDO, V., *1492–1992, The Voice of the Victims*, London, SCM, 1990

25 BONINO, J. M., *Doing Theology in a Revolutionary Situation*, Philadelphia, Pa, Fortress, 1975

26 BOUWSMA, W. J., *John Calvin: A Sixteenth Century Portrait*, New York, Oxford University Press, 1988; new edn 1989

27 BRADEN, C. S., *These Also Believe: A Study of Modern American Cults and Minority Religious Movements*, New York, Macmillan, 1949; repr. 1957

28 BRAITHWAITE, W. C., *The Beginnings of Quakerism*, London, Macmillan, 1912, repr. York, Sessions, 1981; 2nd edn, rev. H. J. Cadbury, Cambridge, Cambridge University Press, 1955

29 BRAITHWAITE, W. C., *The Second Period of Quakerism*, London, Macmillan, 1919, repr. York, Sessions, 1979; 2nd edn, rev. H. J. Cadbury, Cambridge, Cambridge University Press, 1961

30 BRODIE, F. M., *No Man Knows My History: The Life of Joseph Smith, the Mormon Prophet*, 2nd edn, New York, Knopf, 1971

31 BUCKE, E. S. (ed.), *The History of American Methodism*, 3 vols, Nashville, Tenn., Abingdon, 1964

32 BULLOUGH, S., *Roman Catholicism*, Harmondsworth/Baltimore, Md, Penguin, 1963

33 BURLEIGH, J. H. S., *A Church History of Scotland*, London, Oxford University Press, 1960; repr. 1963

34 CAMERON, E., *The European Reformation*, Oxford, Clarendon Press, 1991

35 CAMP, R. L., *The Papal Ideology of Social Reform, 1878–1967*, Leiden, Brill, 1969

36 CHADWICK, W. O., *From Bossuet to Newman*, Cambridge, Cambridge University Press, 1957

37 CHADWICK, W. O. (ed.), *Pelican History of the Church*, 6 vols, Harmondsworth/Baltimore, Md, Penguin, 1960–71 and repr.; London, Hodder, 1962–72: vol. 1, CHADWICK, H., *The Early Church*; vol. 2, SOUTHERN, R. W., *The Western Church in the Middle Ages*; vol. 3, CHADWICK, W. O., *The Reformation*; vol. 4, CRAGG, G. R., *The Church and the Age of Reason*; vol. 5, VIDLER, A. R., *The Church in an Age of Revolution*; vol. 6, NEILL, S., *A History of Christian Missions*

38 CLARK, A. D., *A History of the Church in Korea*, Seoul, Christian Literature Society of Korea, 1971

39 CLARK, W. H., *The Oxford Group: Its History and Significance*, New York, Brookman Associates, 1951

40 COAD, F. R., *A History of the Brethren Movement*, Exeter, Paternoster/ Grand Rapids, Mich., Eerdmans, 1968; 2nd edn Paternoster, 1976; Stony Point, SC, Attic, 1976

41 COGNET, L., *Le Jansenisme*, 3rd edn, Paris, Presses Universitaires de France, 1968

42 COLEMAN, P., *Christian Attitudes to Homosexuality*, London, SPCK, 1980

43 COLLIER, R., *The General Next to God: The Story of William Booth*, New York, Dutton, 1965; London, Collins, 1965, Fontana, 1968, 1976; new edn Fount, 1975

44 CONE, J. H., *Black Theology and Black Power*, New York, Seabury, 1969

45 CROWDER, C. M. D., *Unity, Heresy and Reform, 1378–1460: The Conciliar Response to the Great Schism*, London, Arnold/New York, St Martin's, 1977

46 CUNLIFFE-JONES, H., and DREWERY, B. (eds), *A History of Christian Doctrine*, Edinburgh, T. & T. Clark, 1978; Philadelphia, Pa, Fortress, 1980

47 DAVIES, H., *Worship and Theology in England*, 5 vols, Princeton, NJ, Princeton University Press/London, New York, Oxford University Press, 1961–75

48 DAVIES, J. G. (ed.), *A Dictionary of Liturgy and Worship*, London, SCM, 1972, repr. 1978; New York, Macmillan, 1972; as *Westminster Dictionary of Worship*, Philadelphia, Pa, Westminster, repr. 1979

49 DAVIES, J. G., *The Secular Use of Church Buildings*, London, SCM/ New York, Seabury, 1968

50 DAVIES, R. E., *Methodism*, Harmondsworth, Penguin, 1963; new edn London, Epworth, 1976

51 DAVIES, R. E., *Religious Authority in an Age of Doubt*, London, Epworth, 1968; Geneva, Ala., Allenson, 1968

52 DELACROIX, S. (ed.), *Histoire universelle des missions catholiques*, 4 vols, Paris, Grund, 1956–9

53 DELUMEAU, J., *Catholicism between Luther and Voltaire*, London, Burns & Oates/Philadelphia, Pa, Westminster, 1977

54 DIETER, M. E., *The Holiness Revival of the Nineteenth Century*, Metuchen, NJ/London, Scarecrow Press, 1980

55 DILLENBERGER, J., and WELCH, C., *Protestant Christianity Interpreted through its Development*, New York, Scribner, 1954

56 DILLISTONE, F. W., *The Christian Understanding of Atonement*, London, Nisbet/Philadelphia, Pa, Westminster, 1968

57 DOWLEY, T. (ed.), *The History of Christianity*, Berkhamsted, Lion Publishing, 1977; publ. in US as *Eerdmans Handbook to the History of Christianity*, Grand Rapids, Mich., Eerdmans, 1977

58 DRUMMOND, R. H., *A History of Christianity in Japan*, Grand Rapids, Mich., Eerdmans, 1971

59 DUSSEL, E., *A History of the Church in Latin America: Colonialism to Liberation (1492–1979)*, Grand Rapids, Mich., Eerdmans, 1981; *A History . . . (1492–1992)*, London, Burns & Oates, 1992

60 EBELING, G., *Luther: An Introduction to His Thought*, London, Collins, 1970, repr. 1972; Philadelphia, Pa, Fortress, 1970

61 EHLER, S. Z., and MORRALL, J. R. (eds), *Church and State Through the Centuries: A Collection of Historic Documents with Commentaries*, London, Burns & Oates, 1954; New York, Biblo & Tannen, 1967

62 ELIADE, M. (ed.), *Encyclopedia of Religion*, 16 vols, New York/London, Macmillan, 1987

63 FARMER, D. H., *Oxford Book of Saints*, Oxford, Clarendon Press, 1978; Oxford University Press, 1982, 3rd rev. edn 1992

64 FERGUSON, G., *Signs and Symbols in Christian Art*, London/New York, Galaxy/Oxford University Press, 1966, repr. 1979; new edn 1977

65 FERGUSON, J., *War and Peace in the World's Religions*, London, Sheldon, 1977, repr. 1980; New York, Oxford University Press, 1978

66 FINDLAY, J. F., *Dwight L. Moody, American Evangelist, 1837–99*, Chicago, Ill., University of Chicago Press, 1969

67 FLETCHER, J. F., *Situation Ethics: The New Morality*, Philadelphia, Pa, Westminster, 1966; London, SCM, 1966, repr. 1974

68 FLEW, R. N., *The Idea of Perfection in Christian Theology*, London, Oxford University Press, 1934, repr. 1968; Atlantic Highlands, NJ, Humanities, repr. 1968

69 FORTMAN, E. J., *The Triune God: A Historical Study of the Doctrine of the Trinity*, London, Hutchinson, 1971; Philadelphia, Pa, Westminster, 1972

70 FRADY, M., *Billy Graham: A Parable of American Righteousness*, London, Hodder/Boston, Mass., Little, Brown, 1979

71 FRANKL, P., *Gothic Architecture*, Harmondsworth/Baltimore, Md, Penguin, 1962 (Pelican History of Art)

72 FRANKS, R. S., *The Work of Christ: A Historical Study of Christian Doctrine*, London, 1934; repr. London/New York, Nelson, 1962

73 FREIDAY, D. (ed.), *Barclay's Apology in Modern English*, Newberg, Oregon, Barclay Press, 1991; prev. publ. privately, Elberon, NJ, 1967

74 FRIENDS WORLD COMMITTEE FOR CONSULTATION (FWCC), *Quakers Around the World*, London, FWCC, 1994

75 FROOM, LEROY E., *The Prophetic Faith of Our Fathers*, 4 vols, Washington, DC, Review and Herald, 1946–54

76 GOTTSCHALK, S., *The Emergence of Christian Science in American Religious Life*, Berkeley, Cal., University of California Press, 1973, 1979

77   GRAEF, H. C., *Mary: a History of Doctrine and Devotion*, 2 vols, New York/London, Sheed & Ward, 1963–5; 2nd rev. edn 1985

78   GRANT, R. M., *A Short History of the Interpretation of the Bible*, rev. edn, London, Black, 1965; publ. in US as *The Bible in the Church*, New York, Macmillan, 1948

79   GREENSLADE, S. L., *Church and State from Constantine to Theodosius*, London, SCM, 1954; new edn London, Greenwood, 1981

80   GREENSLADE, S. L., *Schism in the Early Church*, London, SCM/New York, Harper & Row, 1953

81   GUTIERREZ, G., *A Theology of Liberation*, rev. edn, London, SCM, 1988

81a HABEL, N. C., *Religion and Multiculturalism in Australia*, Adelaide, 1992

82   HALLIDAY, R., *Mind the Oneness: The Foundation of Good Quaker Business Method*, London, Quaker Home Service, 1991

83   HAMM, T. D., *The Transformation of American Quakerism: Orthodox Friends, 1800–1907*, Bloomington, Ind., Indiana University Press, 1988

84   HAMMOND, P., *Liturgy and Architecture*, London, Barrie & Rockliff, 1960; New York, Columbia University Press, 1961

85   HANDY, R. T., *A History of the Churches in the United States and Canada*, Oxford/New York, Clarendon Press, 1976, 1979 (Oxford History of the Christian Church)

86   HANSEN, K. J., *Mormonism and the American Experience*, Chicago, Ill., University of Chicago Press, 1981; repr. 1983

87   HASTINGS, A., *The Church in Africa, 1450–1950*, Oxford, Oxford University Press, 1994

88   HASTINGS, A., *A History of African Christianity, 1950–1975*, Cambridge/New York, Cambridge University Press, 1979

89   HASTINGS, A., *History of English Christianity, 1920–86*, London, Collins, 1986; *History . . . 1920–90*, London, SCM, 1991

90   HASTINGS, A. (ed.), *Modern Catholicism: Vatican II and After*, London, SPCK, 1986, 1991

91   HICK, J., *Evil and the God of Love*, new edn, London, Fontana/Collins, 1968, repr. 1970; 2nd edn London, Macmillan, 1977; New York, Harper & Row, 1977; new edn of 2nd edn London, Macmillan, 1985

92   HOLLENWEGER, W. J., *The Pentecostals*, London, SCM, 1972, 1976; Minneapolis, Minn., Augsburg Publishing, 1972, 1977

93   HOPKINS, C. H., *The Rise of the Social Gospel in American Protestantism, 1865–1915*, New Haven, Conn., Yale University Press, 1940; repr. 1967

94   HOPKINS, J. K., *A Woman to Deliver Her People: Joanna Southcott and English Millenarianism*, Austin, Tex., University of Texas Press, 1982

95   HUBBARD, G., *Quaker by Convincement*, Harmondsworth, Penguin, 1974, repr. 1976; new edn London, Quaker Home Service, 1985

96   ILLICK, J. E., *Colonial Pennsylvania: A History*, in KLEIN, M. M., and COOKE, J. E. (eds), *A History of the American Colonies in Thirteen Volumes*, New York, Scribner's, 1976

97   INGLE, L., *Quakers in Conflict: The Hicksite Reformation*, Knoxville, Tenn., University of Tennessee Press, 1986

98   ISICHEI, E., *Victorian Quakers*, Oxford, Oxford University Press, 1970

99   JANELLE, P., *The Catholic Reformation*, Milwaukee, Wisc., Bruce, 1949, repr. 1975; London, Collier-Macmillan, 1971

100 JARRETT-KERR, M., *Patterns of Christian Acceptance: Individual*

Response to the Missionary Impact, 1550–1950, London/New York, Oxford University Press, 1972

101 JAY, E. G., *The Church: Its Changing Image through Twenty Centuries*, 2 vols, London, SPCK, 1977–8; Atlanta, Ga, John Knox, 1980

102 JEDIN, H., *Ecumenical Councils of the Catholic Church: An Historical Outline*, New York, Freiburg/Edinburgh, Herder, 1960

103 JEDIN, H., and DOLAN, J. P. (eds), *A History of the Church*, 10 vols, London, Burns & Oates, 1980–1; prev. publ. as *A Handbook of Church History*, Freiburg, Herder, 1965

104 JOHN, DEWITT, *The Christian Science Way of Life*, Englewood Cliffs, NS, Prentice-Hall, 1962; 2nd rev. edn Christian Science Publishing Society, 1971

105 JOHNSON, P., *A History of Christianity*, London, Weidenfeld/New York, Atheneum, 1976; new edn Harmondsworth, Penguin, 1990

106 JONES, F. P., *The Church in Communist China: A Protestant Appraisal*, New York, Friendship Press, 1962

107 JONES, P. D'A., *The Christian Socialist Revival, 1877–1914*, Princeton, NJ, Princeton University Press, 1968

108 JONES, R. M., *The Later Periods of Quakerism*, 2 vols, London, Macmillan, 1921

109 JONES, R. M., with SHARPLES, I., and GUMMERE, A. M., *The Quakers in the American Colonies*, London, Macmillan, 1911, 1923

110 JONES, R. T., *Congregationalism in England, 1662 1962*, London, Independent Press, 1962

111 JULIAN, J., *A Dictionary of Hymnology*, New York, Dover, 1957; New York, Gordon Press, 1977; prev. publ. London, Murray, 1892

112 KAMEN, H., *The Rise of Toleration*, London, Weidenfeld/New York, McGraw-Hill, 1967

113 KAMEN, H., *The Spanish Inquisition*, London, Weidenfeld, 1965: New York, New American Library, 1966, 1977

114 KELLY, J. N. D., *Early Christian Doctrines*, 5th rev. edn, London, Black, 1977, 1985; New York, Harper & Row, 1978

115 KING, R. H., *George Fox and the Light Within, 1650–1660*, Philadelphia, Pa, Philadelphia Yearly Meeting, Friends Book Store, 1940; Ann Arbor, Mich., University Microfilms, 1965 (MF of typescript)

116 KNOWLES, D., *Christian Monasticism*, London, Weidenfeld/New York, McGraw-Hill, 1969

117 KOENKER, E. B., *The Liturgical Renaissance in the Roman Catholic Church*, Chicago, Ill., University of Chicago Press/Cambridge, Cambridge University Press, 1954; 2nd edn St Louis, Mo, Concordia, 1966

118 KUNG, H., *Infallible? An Inquiry* (tr. Eric Mosbacher), London, Collins, 1971, 1972; (tr. E. Quinn) Garden City, NY, Doubleday, 1971

119 LAMPE, G. W. H., *God as Spirit*, Oxford, Clarendon Press, 1977

120 LASH, N., and RHYMER, J., *The Christian Priesthood*, London, Darton, 1970

121 LATOURETTE, K. S., *Christianity in a Revolutionary Age*, 5 vols, Westport, Conn., Greenwood, repr. 1973 (© 1958–62); London, Paternoster, 1971

122 LATOURETTE, K. S., *A History of the Expansion of Christianity*, 7 vols, London, Eyre & Spottiswoode/New York, Harper, 1939–47; London, Paternoster, 1971; Grand Rapids, Mich., Zondervan

123 LEEMING, B., *Principles of Sacramental Theology*, new edn, London, Longman, 1960, repr. 1962; Westminster, Md, Newman, 1960

124   LEWIS, A. J., *Zinzendorf, the Ecumenical Pioneer*, London, SCM/ Philadelphia, Pa, Westminster, 1962

125   LIPPY, C. H., *The Christadelphians in North America*, Lewiston, NY, Edwin Mellen Press, 1989

126   LOOME, T. M., *Liberal Catholicism, Reform Catholicism, Modernism*, Mainz, Mathias-Grünewald, 1979

127   LOOMIS, R. S., *The Grail: From Celtic Myth to Christian Symbol*, Cardiff, University of Wales Press, 1963

128   MCAVOY, T. T., *A History of the Catholic Church in the United States*, Notre Dame, Ind./London, University of Notre Dame Press, 1969

129   MCDANNELL, C., and LANG, B., *Heaven: A History*, New Haven, Conn., Yale University Press, 1988

130   MCDONALD, H. D., *Ideas of Revelation . . . A.D. 1700–1860*, London, Macmillan/New York, St Martin's, 1959

131   MCGRATH, A. E., *A Life of John Calvin: A Study in the Shaping of Western Culture*, Oxford, Blackwell, 1990; new edn 1993

132   MACKEY, J. P., *The Modern Theology of Tradition*, London, Darton/ New York, Herder, 1963

133   MCKINNEY, G. D., *The Theology of Jehovah's Witnesses*, London, Marshall, Morgan & Scott, 1963

134   MCLEOD, H., *Religion and the People of Western Europe*, Oxford, Oxford University Press, 1981

135   MCLOUGHLIN, W. G., *Modern Revivalism: Charles Grandison Finney to Billy Graham*, New York, Ronald Press, 1959

136   MCMANNERS, J. (ed.), *Oxford Illustrated History of the Church*, Oxford, Oxford University Press, 1990; new edn 1992

137   MCNEILL, J. T., *The Celtic Churches: A History, AD 200 to 1200*, Chicago, Ill., University of Chicago Press, 1974

138   MCNEILL, J. T., *The History and Character of Calvinism*, New York, Oxford University Press, 1954, 1967

139   MACQUARRIE, J. (ed.), *A Dictionary of Christian Ethics*, London, SCM/Philadelphia, Pa, Westminster, 1967; as *New Dictionary of Christian Ethics*, ed. J. MacQuarrie and J. F. Childress, new edn, London, SCM, 1990

140   MECHAM, J. L., *Church and State in Latin America*, rev. edn, Chapel Hill, NC, University of North Carolina Press, 1966

141   MELTON, J. G., *The Encyclopedia of American Religion*, 2 vols, 3rd rev. edn, Detroit, Mich., Gale Research Company, 1988, 1991

142   MIEGGE, G., *The Virgin Mary*, London, Lutterworth/Philadelphia, Pa, Westminster, 1955

143   MILLER, P., *Jonathan Edwards*, New York, Meridian, 1959; Westport, Conn., Greenwood; first publ. New York, Sloane, 1949; new edn, Greenwood, 1973

144   MILLER, P., and JOHNSON, T. H. (eds), *The Puritans: A Source Book of their Writings*, 2 vols, rev. edn, New York, Harper & Row, 1963; Magnolia, Mass., Peter Smith

145   MOLLAND, E., *Christendom*, London, Mowbray, 1959, repr. 1961; New York, Philosophical Library, 1959

146   MOORE, A. C., *The Iconography of Religions*, London, SCM/ Philadelphia, Pa, Fortress, 1977

147   MOORHOUSE, G., *The Missionaries*, London, Eyre Methuen/ Philadelphia, Pa, Lippincott, 1973

148   MOORMAN, J. R. H., *A History of the Church in England*, 3rd edn, London, Black, 1973, repr. 1980; New York, Morehouse, 1973

149   MOSS, C. B., *The Old Catholic Movement*, London, SPCK, 1948

150   MUSADADAN, A. M., *History of Christianity in India*, vol. 1: *To the mid-16th Century*, Bangalore, Christian Theological Publishing in India, 1984

151   NEILL, S., *Anglicanism*, Harmondsworth, Penguin, 1958, repr. 1960; 2nd edn London, Mowbray, 1978; 4th edn New York, Oxford University Press, 1978

152   NEILL, S., *History of Christianity in India: Beginnings to 1707*, Cambridge, Cambridge University Press, 1985; *History of Christianity in India, 1707–1858*, Cambridge, Cambridge University Press, 1985

153   NEILL, S., *The Story of the Christian Church in India and Pakistan*, Grand Rapids, Mich., Eerdmans, 1970

154   *New Catholic Encyclopedia*, 15 vols, McGraw-Hill, 1967; 17 vols, Washington, DC, Catholic University of America

155   *New Harvard Dictionary of Music*, ed. Don Randel: article on 'Psalmody, Latin', Cambridge, Mass., Belknap Press/Harvard University Press, 1986

156   O'DEA, T., *The Mormons*, Chicago, Ill., University of Chicago Press, 1957, 1964

157   *The Oxford Dictionary of the Christian Church*, 2nd edn (ed. F. L. Cross and E. A. Livingstone), London/New York, Oxford University Press, 1974

158   PEEL, R., *Christian Science: Its Encounter with American Culture*, New York, Henry Holt, 1959; Sommer, 1979

159   PEVSNER, SIR NIKOLAUS, *An Outline of European Architecture*, 7th edn, Harmondsworth/Baltimore, Md, Penguin, 1963, 1975; new edn 1990

160   POWERS, J. M., *Eucharistic Theology*, London, Burns & Oates, 1968; New York, Herder, 1967; New York, Seabury, 1972

160a PROZESKY, M., *A New Guide to the Debate about God*, London, SCM, 1992

161   PUNSHON, J., *Portrait in Grey: A Short History of the Quakers*, rev. edn, London, Quaker Home Service, 1986

162   RACK, H. D., *Reasonable Enthusiast: John Wesley and the Rise of Methodism*, London, Epworth Press, 1989; 2nd edn 1992; New York, Trinity Press, 1989

163   REARDON, B. M. G. (ed.), *Roman Catholic Modernism*, London, Black/Stanford, Cal., Stanford University Press, 1970

164   REAY, B., *Quakers and the English Revolution*, London, Temple Smith, 1985

165   RICE, C. D., *The Rise and Fall of Black Slavery*, London, Macmillan/New York, Harper & Row, 1975, 1976

166   RILEY-SMITH, J., *What were the Crusades?*, London, Macmillan/Totowa, NJ, Rowman & Littlefield, 1977

167   ROBERTSON, A., and STEVENS, D., *The Pelican History of Music*, 3 vols, Harmondsworth/Baltimore, Md, Penguin, 1960–8; repr. 1978

168   ROGERSON, A., *Millions Now Living Will Never Die: A Study of the Jehovah's Witnesses*, London, Constable, 1969

169   ROUSE, R., NEILL, S., and FREY, H. (eds), *A History of the Ecumenical Movement*, 2 vols (vol. 1, 2nd edn), London, SPCK/Philadelphia, Pa, Westminster, 1967–70; 3rd rev. edn London, World Council of Churches, 1986

170   ROWELL, G., *Hell and the Victorians*, Oxford, Clarendon Press, 1974

171   RUNCIMAN, SIR STEVEN, *A History of the Crusades*, 3 vols, Cambridge, Cambridge University Press, 1951–4, repr. 1966–8; Harmondsworth, Penguin, 1965

172   RUTMAN, D. B., *American Puritanism: Faith and Practice*, Philadelphia, Pa, Lippincott, 1970; New York, Norton, 1977

173   SANCHEZ, J. M., *Anticlericalism: A Brief History*, Notre Dame, Ind., University of Notre Dame Press, 1972

174   SANDEEN, E. R., *The Roots of Fundamentalism*, Chicago, Ill., Chicago University Press, 1970; Grand Rapids, Mich., Baker Books, 1978

175   SHEARER, R. E., *Wildlife: Church Growth in Korea*, Grand Rapids, Mich., Eerdmans, 1962

176   SHEERAN, M. J., *Beyond Majority Rule: Voteless Decisions in the Society of Friends*, Philadelphia, Pa, Philadelphia Yearly Meeting, 1983

177   SIEFER, G.,*The Church and Industrial Society*, London, Darton, 1964

178   SIMPSON, A., *Puritanism in Old and New England*, Chicago, Ill., University of Chicago Press, 1955

179   SMITH, TIMOTHY L., *Revivalism and Social Reform in mid-Nineteenth Century America*, Nashville, Tenn., Abingdon, 1957; Magnolia, Mass., Peter Smith; Baltimore, Md, Johns Hopkins University Press, 1980

180   STEIN, S. J., *The Shaker Experience in America*, New Haven, Conn., Yale University Press, 1992; new edn 1994

181   STOEFFLER, F. E., *The Rise of Evangelical Pietism*, Leiden, Brill, 1965, and *German Pietism during the Eighteenth Century*, Leiden, Brill, 1973

182   STROUP, H. H., *The Jehovah's Witnesses*, New York, Columbia University Press, 1945; repr. New York, Russell & Russell, 1967

183   SUMPTION, J., *Pilgrimage: An Image of Mediaeval Religion*, London, Faber/Totowa, NJ, Rowman, 1975

184   SYKES, S. W., and CLAYTON, J. P., *Christ, Faith and History*, Cambridge, Cambridge University Press, 1972; new edn 1978

185   THEKKADETH, J., *History of Christianity in India*, vol. 2: *16th to 17th Centuries*, Bangalore, Christian Theological Publishing in India, 1982

186   THOMAS, K., *Religion and the Decline of Magic*, Harmondsworth, Penguin, 1973, new edn 1991; New York, Scribner, 1971; London, Weidenfeld, 1971

187   THOMAS, T. (ed.), *The British, their Religious Beliefs and Practices, 1800–1986*, London, Routledge, 1988

188   TODD, J. M. (ed.), *Problems of Authority*, London, Darton, 1962, 1964; Baltimore, Md, Helicon, repr. 1964

189   TORBET, R. G., *A History of the Baptists*, Philadelphia, Pa, Judson, 1950; repr. Valley Forge, Pa, Judson, 1963, rev. edn 1973

190   ULLMANN, W., *A Short History of the Papacy in the Middle Ages*, London, Methuen, 1972, 1974

191   VIDLER, A. R., *A Century of Social Catholicism, 1820–1920*, London, SPCK, 1964

192   VON ARETIN, K. O., *The Papacy and the Modern World*, London, Weidenfeld/New York, McGraw-Hill, 1970

193   WAKEFIELD, W. L., and EVANS, A. P. (eds), *Heresies of the High Middle Ages: Selected Sources*, New York, Columbia University Press, 1969; new edn 1991

194   WARD, W. R., *The Protestant Evangelical Awakening*, Cambridge, Cambridge University Press, 1992

195   WARE, T. (KALLISTOS), *The Orthodox Church*, Harmondsworth/ Baltimore, Md, Penguin, 1963, 1969, 1980; 2nd rev. edn 1993

196   WARNER, M., *Alone of Her Sex: The Myth and Cult of the Virgin Mary*, London, Weidenfeld, 1976; new edn London, Picador, 1985, 1990

197   WASHINGTON, J. R., *Black Religion: The Negro and Christianity in the United States*, Boston, Mass., Beacon Press, 1964; new edn Lanham, Md, University Press of America, 1984

198 WATSON, B., *A Hundred Years' War: The Salvation Army, 1865–1965*, London, Hodder, 1965

199 WATTS, M., *The Dissenters*, vol. 1, *From the Reformation to the French Revolution*, Oxford, Clarendon Press, 1978

200 WEBER, H. R., and NEILL, S., *The Layman in Christian History*, London, SCM/Philadelphia, Pa, Westminster, 1963

201 WENDEL, F., *Calvin*, London, Collins, 1963, Fontana, 1978; New York, Harper & Row, 1963

202 WILBUR, E. M., *A History of Unitarianism*, 2 vols, Cambridge, Mass., Harvard University Press, 1946–52

203 WILLIAMS, G. H., *The Radical Reformation*, Philadelphia, Pa, Westminster/London, Weidenfeld, 1962

204 WILSON, B. R., *Religious Sects*, London, Weidenfeld/New York, McGraw-Hill, 1970

205 WILSON, B. R., *Sects and Society*, London, Heinemann/Berkeley, Cal., University of California Press, 1961; Westport, Conn./London, Greenwood, new edn, 1978

206 WILSON, I., *The Turin Shroud*, London, Gollancz, 1978; Harmondsworth, Penguin, 1979 (US edn *The Shroud of Turin*, Garden City, NY, Doubleday, 1978)

207 WITTKOWER, R., *Architectural Principles in the Age of Humanism*, London, Academy edn, repr. 1973; Tiranti, 1962; New York, Norton, 1975 (© 1971)

208 ZAEHNER, R. C. (ed.), *A Concise Encyclopedia of Living Faiths*, new edn, London, Hutchinson, 1977; first publ. Boston, Mass., Beacon Press, 1959; 4th rev. edn as *Encyclopedia of Living Faiths*, London, Hutchinson, 1988

(*See also* XXI, 8, 22, 28; XIV; XXVI, 1)

[XIII] Christianity: (C) Philosophy, Theology

Compiled by David A. Pailin

1 ALTIZER, T. J., and HAMILTON, W., *Radical Theology and the Death of God*, Harmondsworth, Penguin, 1968; first publ. Indianapolis, Ind., Bobbs-Merrill, 1966

2 BULTMANN, R., *Jesus Christ and Mythology*, New York, Scribner's, 1958; London, SCM, 1960; new edn New York, Scribner's/Edinburgh, T. & T. Clark, 1980

2a CLARKE, P. B., and BYME, P., *Religion Defined and Explained*, Basingstoke, Macmillan, 1993

3 COBB, J. B., *Living Options in Protestant Theology: A Survey of Methods*, Philadelphia, Pa, Westminster, 1962; new edn University Press of America, 1986

3a COBB, J. B., *A Christian Natural Theology*, Philadelphia, Pa, Westminster, 1965

4 COBB, J. B., and GRIFFIN, D. R., *Process Theology: An Introductory Exposition*, Belfast, Christian Journals, 1977; first publ. Philadelphia, Pa, Westminster, John Knox Press, 1976

5 COPLESTON, F. C., *Aquinas*, Harmondsworth, Penguin, 1955; Baltimore, Md, Penguin, 1956; rev. edn *Thomas Aquinas*, London, Search Press, 1976

5a FORD, D. F., *Modern Theologians: Introduction to Christian Theology in the 20th Century*, 2 vols, Oxford, Blackwell, 1989

6 HARNACK, A., *History of Dogma*, 7 vols in 4, New York, Dover, 1961

6a HARTSHORNE, C., *A Natural Theology for Our Time*, La Salle, Ill., Open Court, 1967

7 HARVEY, V. A., *The Historian and the Believer*, New York, Macmillan, 1966; London, SCM, 1967

8 HICK, J., *The Existence of God*, New York, Macmillan/London, Collier-Macmillan 1964

9 KEE, A. (ed.), *A Reader in Political Theology*, London, SCM, 1974; Philadelphia, Pa, Westminster, 1975

10 KELLY, J. N. D., *Early Christian Doctrines*, London, Black, 1958; 5th edn 1977, repr. 1985; rev. edn New York, Harper & Row, 1978

11 KÜNG, H., *Does God Exist? An Answer for Today*, London, Collins/Garden City, NY, Doubleday, 1980; new edn London, SCM, 1991; first publ. as *Existiert Gott?*, Munich, Piper, 1978

12 LEFF, G., *Mediaeval Thought: Saint Augustine to Ockham*, Harmondsworth/Baltimore, Md, Penguin, 1958; Harmondsworth, Penguin, 1970; London, Merlin Press, 1959; Atlantic Highlands, NJ, Humanities, 1958

12a MCGRATH, A. E. (ed.), *Blackwell Encyclopaedia of Modern Christian Thought*, Oxford, Blackwell, 1993

13 MACINTYRE, A., 'The Logical Status of Religious Belief', in TOULMIN, S. E., HEPBURN, R. W. and MACINTYRE, A., *Metaphysical Beliefs*, pp. 167–211, London, SCM, 1957

14 MACKINTOSH, H. R., *Types of Modern Theology: Schleiermacher to Barth*, London, Nisbet/New York, Scribner, 1937

15 MACQUARRIE, J., *Principles of Christian Theology*, London, SCM, 1966, rev. edn 1979; New York, Scribner, 1966, 2nd edn 1977

16 MIGUEZ BONINO, J., *Revolutionary Theology Comes of Age*, London, SPCK, 1975; publ. in US as *Doing Theology in a Revolutionary Situation*, Philadelphia, Pa, Fortress, 1975

17 MITCHELL, B., *The Justification of Religious Belief*, London/New York, Macmillan, 1973; New York, Seabury, 1974

18 MURCHLAND, B. (ed.), *The Meaning of the Death of God: Protestant, Jewish and Catholic Scholars Explore Atheistic Theology*, New York, Random House, 1967

18a OGDEN, S. M., *The Point of Christology*, London SCM, 1982

18b PAILIN, D. A., *God and the Processes of Reality*, London, Routledge, 1989

18c PAILIN, D. A., *Probing the Foundations*, Kampen, Netherlands, Kok Pharos, 1994

19 PALMER, R. E., *Hermeneutics: Interpretation Theory in Schleiermacher, Dilthey, Heidegger and Gadamer*, Evanston, Ill., Northwestern University Press, 1969

20 PAUCK, W. and M., *Paul Tillich, His Life and Thought* (2 vols), vol. 1, London, Collins, 1977; New York, Harper & Row, 1976

21 PHILLIPS, D. Z., *The Concept of Prayer*, London, Routledge, 1965; New York, Schocken, 1966

22 REARDON, B. M. G., *Liberal Protestantism*, London, Black/Stanford, Cal., Stanford University Press, 1968

23 ROBERTS, D. E., *Existentialism and Religious Belief*, New York, Oxford University Press, 1957

24 RUSSELL, L. M., *Human Liberation in a Feminist Perspective: A Theology*, Philadelphia, Pa, Westminster, 1974, 1983

25 SHAW, D. W. D., *The Dissuaders: Three Explorations of Religion*, London, SCM, 1978

26 SOUTHERN, R. W., *Saint Anselm and his Biographer*, Cambridge, Cambridge University Press, 1963; new edn 1992

27 STEPHEN, SIR LESLIE, *History of English Thought in the Eighteenth Century*, 2 vols, London, Smith, Elder, 1876, repr. New York, Harcourt, Brace/London, Hart-Davis (© 1962); Magnolia, Mass., Peter Smith; facsimile of 1902 edn, Bristol, Thoemmes Press, 1991

28 STROMBERG, R. N., *Religious Liberalism in Eighteenth Century England*, London, Oxford University Press, 1954

29 WILLIAMS, R. R., *Schleiermacher the Theologian*, Philadelphia, Pa, Fortress, 1978

30 ZAHRNT, H., *The Historical Jesus*, London, Collins/New York, Harper & Row, 1963

[XIII]   *Christianity: (D) Eastern*

Part 1: Compiled by David J. Melling and Dimitri Brady

1 *Christian Spirituality*, volumes in the series 'World Spirituality', New York, Crossroad Publishing Company/London, SCM, 1989–

2 *Declaration of the Hierarchs of the Russian Orthodox Church Outside Russia*, *Orthodox Life*, vol. 43(3), Jordanville, 1993

3 *The Oxford Dictionary of Byzantium*, New York/London, Oxford University Press, 1991

4 *Two English Orthodox New Martyrs*, *The Shepherd*, vol. 12(3), Brookwood, Monastery of St Edward, 1991

4a ALBERT, M., et al., *Christianismes Orientaux*, Paris, Centre National de la Recherche Scientifique, 1993

5 ARSENIEV, N., *Mysticism and the Eastern Church*, tr. from the German by A. Chambers, Crestwood, NY, St Vladimir's Seminary Press, 1979, 1984

6 ATIYA, A. S., *A History of Eastern Christianity*, Millwood, Kraus Repr., 1980; first publ. London, Methuen, 1968

7 ATIYA, A. S. (ed.), *The Coptic Encyclopaedia*, 8 vols, New York, 1991

8 ATTWATER, D., *The Christian Churches of the East*, 2 vols, Milwaukee, Wisc., Bruce, 1948, 1961: new edn Leominster, Thomas More Books, vol. 1, 1961, vol. 2, 1962; prev. publ. as *Catholic Eastern Churches*, Milwaukee, Bruce, 1935

9 AVVAKUM, *His Life, Written by Himself*, Ann Arbor, Mich., Slavic Publications, 1979

10 BAYEGO, N., *Father Kyrillos Pasha Kasule of Uganda*, *Sourozh*, no. 45, London, 1991

11 BOLSHAKOFF, S., *Russian Mystics*, Kalamazoo, Mich., Cistercian Publications, 1980; new edn 1984

12 BRADY, D., 'The Holy Physicians in Greek Orthodox Tradition', in *Sophia*, vol. 2, Manchester, Manchester Metropolitan University, 1993

13 CHRISTENSEN, D., *Not of This World: The Life and Teachings of Seraphim Rose*, Platina, Cal., St Herman Press, 1993

14 CHRYSOSTOMOS, ARCHIMANDRITE, *The Old Calendar Orthodox Church of Greece*, Etna, Cal., CTOS, 1986

15 CLEMENT, O., *The Roots of Christian Mysticism*, London, New City, 1993

16   COLLIANDER, T., *The Way of the Ascetics: The Ancient Tradition of Discipline and Inner Growth*, Crestwood, NY, St Vladimir's Seminary Press; reissue 1992; new edn 1989
CONSTANTELOS, D. *see* no. 44 KONSTANTELOS

17   CYPRIAN, BISHOP OF OROPOS AND PHYLE, *The True Orthodox Christians of Romania*, Orthodox Word, no. 102, Platina, Cal., 1982
CONSTANTELOS, D. *see* no. 44 KONSTANTELOS

18   *Damaskin, The Last Years of Metropolitan Pyotr Polyansky of Krutitsy and Kolomna, Journal of the Moscow Patriarchate*, vol. 2, Moscow, 1993

19   DE BEAUSOBRE, I., *Russian Letters of Direction, 1834–1860, Marcarius, Starets of Optino*, Crestwood, NY, St Vladimir's Seminary Press, 1975

20   DOWNEY, M. (ed.), *The New Dictionary of Catholic Spirituality*, Collegeville, Liturgical Press, 1993

21   DUNLOP, J. B., *Staretz Amvrosy*, London, Mowbrays, 1972

22   EVDOKIMOV, P., *The Art of the Ikon*, tr. S. Bigham, Redondo Beach, Cal., Oakwood, 1990; new edn 1991

23   FLETCHER, W. C., *The Russian Orthodox Church Underground, 1917–1970*, London, Oxford University Press, 1971

24   FLORENSKY, ST PAUL, *Salt of the Earth*, Platina, Cal., St Herman Press, 1987

25   GARRETT, P. D., *St Innocent, Apostle to America*, Crestwood, NY, St Vladimir's Press, 1979, 1980

26   GERASIM ELIEL, *Father Gerasim of New Valaam*, Platina, Cal., St Herman Press, 1989

27   GEROSTERGIOS, ASTERIOS, *St Photios the Great*, Belmont, Cal., Institute for Byzantine and Modern Greek Studies, 1980

28   GILLES, P., *The Antiquities of Constantinople*, 2nd edn, New York, Italica Press, 1988; first publ. privately, London, 1729

29   GOLDER, F. A., *Father Herman, Alaska's Saint*, Platina, Cal., St Herman Press, 1968

30   HACKEL, S., *Pearl of Great Price: The Life of Mother Maria Skobtsova, 1891–1945*, Crestwood, NY, St Vladimir's Seminary Press, 1981

31   HAUSHERR, I., *Spiritual Direction in the Early Christian East*, Kalamazoo, Mich., Cistercian Studies, 1990

32   HAUSHERR, I., *The Name of Jesus*, Kalamazoo, Mich., Cistercian Studies, 1978

33   HEPPELL, M., *The Paterik of the Kiev Caves Monastery*, Cambridge, Mass., Harvard University Press, 1989

34   HERRIN, J., *The Formation of Christendom*, Oxford, Blackwell, 1987; new edn Fontana, 1989

35   HILL, H. (ed.), *Light from the East*, Toronto, Anglican Book Centre, 1988

36   HUNT, E. D., *Holy Land Pilgrimage in the Later Roman Empire*, Oxford, Clarendon Press, 1984

37   HUSSEY, J. M., *The Orthodox Church in the Byzantine Empire*, Oxford, Clarendon Press, 1986; new edn in *Oxford History of the Christian Church*, Oxford University Press, 1990

38   ILIEVSKI, D., *The Macedonian Orthodox Church*, Skopje, Macedonian Review Editions, 1973

39   JARDINE GRISBROOK, W., *The Spiritual Counsels of Father John of Kronstadt*, Crestwood, NY, St Vladimir's Seminary Press, 1981; new edn Cambridge, J. Clarke, 1982

40 JOHN ALEKSEYEV, *Christ Is In Our Midst*, London, Darton, Longman & Todd, 1979

41 KHOLMOGOROV, ST SYMEON, *One of the Ancients*, Platina, Cal., St Herman Press, 1988

42 KNOWLES, D., *Christian Monasticism*, London, Weidenfeld, 1969

43 KNOWLES, D., *From Pachomius to Ignatius*, Oxford, Clarendon Press, 1966 (Sarum Lectures, 1964–5)

44 KONSTANTELOS, D. J., *Byzantine Philanthropy and Social Welfare*, Athens, Phos, 1986 (repr.)

45 LANE, C., *Christian Religion in the Soviet Union*, London, Allen & Unwin, 1978; new edn 1979

46 LAZAR, PUHALO, and NOVAKSHONOFF, V., *God's Fools*, Montreal, Synaxis Press, 1990

47 LIMOURIS, G., *Icons, Windows on Eternity: Theology and Spirituality in Colour*, Geneva, World Council of Churches, 1990

48 LIZARDOS, G., and PAPADOPOULOS, L. J., *New Martyrs of the Turkish Yoke*, Seattle, St Nektarios Press, 1985

49 LOUTH, A., *The Origins of Christian Mystical Tradition: From Plato to Denys*, Oxford, Oxford University Press, 1981, 1983

50 LUPININ, N., *Religious Revolt in the XVIIth Century: The Schism of the Russian Church*, Princeton, NJ, Kingston Press, 1984

51 MAINSTONE, R. J., *Hagia Sophia*, London, Thames & Hudson, 1988

52 MARTIIA, *Papa Nicolas Planas*, Booton, Holy Transfiguration Press, 1981

53 METROPHANES, *St Paisius Velichkovsky*, Platina, Cal., St Herman Press, 1976

54 MEYENDORFF, J., *St Gregory Palamas and Orthodox Spirituality*, Crestwood, NY, St Vladimir's Seminary Press, 1974, 1980

55 MEYENDORFF, J., *The Byzantine Legacy in the Orthodox Church*, pp. 235ff, Crestwood, NY, St Vladimir's Seminary Press, 1982

56 MEYENDORFF, P., *Russia, Ritual and Reform*, Crestwood, NY, St Vladimir's Seminary Press, 1991

57 MILLAR, L., *Grand Duchess Elisabeth of Russia*, Redding, Nikodemos Press, 1991

58 MORRIS, R. (ed.), *Church and People in Byzantium*, Birmingham, Centre for Byzantine, Ottoman and Modern Greek Studies, University of Birmingham, 1990

59 MOSS, V., *The Struggle of the True Orthodox Christians of Greece*, Woking, True Orthodox Publications, 1992

60 NIKODEMOS OF THE HOLY MOUNTAIN, *A Handbook of Spiritual Counsel*, tr. P. A. Chambers, New York, Paulist Press, 1989

61 OBOLENSKY, D., *The Byzantine Commonwealth*, London, Weidenfeld, 1971

62 OLEKSA, M., *Orthodox Alaska: A Theology of Mission*, Crestwood, NY, St Vladimir's Seminary Press, 1992

63 OSTROGORSKY, G., *History of the Byzantine State*, 2nd edn, Oxford, Blackwell, 1968

64 OUSPENSKY, L. (tr. A. Gythiel, selections tr. E. Meyendorff), *Theology of the Icon*, Crestwood, NY, St Vladimir's Seminary Press, vol. 1, 1990, vol. 2, 1992; new edn 2 vols, 1991

65 PALMER, G. E. H., SHERRARD, P., and WARE, K. (tr. and ed.), *The Philokalia* [5 vols], London, Faber, 1979, 1981–, comp. St Nikodemos of the Holy Mountain and St Makarios of Corinth; new edn vol. 1, 1983, vol. 2, 1990

66 PARIS, E., *Convert or Die: Catholic Persecution in Yugoslavia During*

World War II (tr. from the French by L. Perkins), Chino, Chick Press, 1990

67   PARRY, K., 'The Role of the Icon in the Eastern Orthodox Tradition', in *Sophia*, vol. 1, Manchester, Manchester Metropolitan University, 1992

68   PELIKAN, J., *The Christian Tradition*, vol. 2, *The Spirit of Eastern Christendom (600–1700)*, Chicago, Ill., University of Chicago Press, 1974, new edn, 1977

69   PENNINGTON, M. B., *Monastic Life*, Petersham, St Bede's Publications, 1989

70   POLSKY, M., *The New Martyrs of Russia*, Montreal, 1979, 1972; Munich, Brotherhood of St Job of Pochaev

71   RUNCIMAN, S., *The Fall of Constantinople*, Cambridge, Cambridge University Press, 1965

72   RUNCIMAN, S., *The Great Church in Captivity*, Cambridge, Cambridge University Press, 1968; new edn 1985

73   RUSSELL, N. (tr.), WARD, B. (ed.), *The Lives of the Desert Fathers*, London, Mowbray, 1981

74   SEIDE, G., *Monasteries and Convents of the Russian Orthodox Church Abroad*, Munich, Monastery of St Job of Ponchaev, 1990

75   SENDLER, E., *The Icon, Image of the Invisible* (tr. S. Bigham), Redondo Beach, Cal., Oakwood Publications, 1988

76   SERAPHIM ROSE, *Blessed John the Wonder Worker*, Platina, Cal., St Herman Press, 1987

77   *Seraphim's Seraphim*, Boston, Mass., Holy Transfiguration Press, 1979

78   SHERRARD, P., *Athos the Holy Mountain*, London, Sidgwick & Jackson, 1982

79   SMIRNOFF, E., *Russian Orthodox Missions*, Welshpool, Stylite, 1986

80   SMITH, B. S., *Orthodoxy and Native Americans: The Alaskan Mission*, Syosset/New York, St Vladimir's Seminary Press, 1980

81   SOPHRONY, ARCHIMANDRITE, *The Monk of Athos: Staretz Silouan*, Crestwood, NY, St Vladimir's Seminary Press, 1975 (1973), new edn 1983; rev. edn, with additional material of *The Undistorted Image* (London, Faith Press, 1958), London, Mowbray, 1973

82   SOPHRONY, ARCHIMANDRITE (ed.), SILOUAN, STARETZ, *Wisdom from Mount Athos: Writings* (tr. from the Russian by R. Edmonds), Crestwood, NY, St Vladimir's Seminary Press, 1975; new edn 1983; rev. edn, originally pt. 2 of *The Undistorted Image* (London, Faith Press, 1958), London, Mowbray, 1974

83   SPIDLIK, T., *The Spirituality of the Christian East* (tr. from the French by A. P. Gythiel), Kalamazoo, Mich., Cistercian Publications, 1986

84   STAMOULIS, J. J., *Eastern Orthodox Mission Theology Today*, Maryknoll, NY, Orbis, 1986

85   STRATOUDAKI WHITE, D., and BERRIGAN, J. R., *The Patriarch and the Prince*, Brookline, Mass., Holy Cross Orthodox Press, 1982

86   STUART, J., *Ikons*, London, Faber, 1975

87   SULLIVAN, D. F., *The Life of St Nikon*, Brookline, Hellenic College Press, 1987

88   THAISIA, *Letters to a Beginner*, Wildwood, Cal., St Xenia Press, 1993

89   THEKLA, *Mother Maria: Her Life in Letters*, London, Darton, Longman & Todd, 1979

90   TRAVIS, J., *In Defense of the Faith*, Brookline, Mass., Hellenic College Press, 1984

91 TURNER, H. J. M., *St Symeon the New Theologian and Spiritual Fatherhood*, Leiden, 1990

92 VELIMIROVIC, ST NICOLAS, *The Life of St Sava*, Crestwood, NY, St Vladimir's Seminary Press, 1989

93 VLACHOS, HIEROTHEOS, *A Night in the Desert of the Holy Mountain*, Levadia, Nativity of the Theotokos Press, 1991

94 WADDELL, H. (ed.), *The Desert Fathers*, Bury St Edmunds, St Edmundsbury Press, 1987; new edn London, Constable, 1987

95 WARD, B., *Harlots of the Desert: . . . Repentance in Early Monastic Sources*, Oxford, Mowbray, 1987

96 WARD, B., *The Wisdom of the Desert Fathers*, Oxford, Fairacres Press, 1986

97 WARD, B., *The Sayings of the Desert Fathers*, Oxford, Mowbray, 1981

98 WARE, KALLISTOS T., *The Fool in Christ as Prophet and Apostle*, *Sobornost*, vol. 6(2), 1984

99 WARE, KALLISTOS T., *The Orthodox Church*, new (2nd rev.) edn, Harmondsworth/New York, Penguin, 1993

100 WARE, KALLISTOS, T., *The Power of the Name*, Oxford, Fairacres Publications (2nd rev. edn, S. L. G. Press), 1986

101 WELCH, J., *When Gods Die: Introduction to John of the Cross*, New York, Paulist Press, 1990

102 YOUNG, A., *The Russian Orthodox Church Outside Russia*, St Bernardino, St Willibrord Press, 1993

103 ZANDER, V., *St Seraphim of Sarov*, London, SPCK, 1975; new edn, Crestwood, NY, St Vladimir's Seminary Press, 1985

104 ZNOSKO, V., *Hieroschemamonk Feofil*, Jordanville, Holy Trinity Press, 1987

Part 2: Compiled by Andrew Palmer and David J. Melling

105 ABRAMOWSKI, L., and GOODMAN, A., *A Nestorian Collection of Christological Texts*, 2 vols, Cambridge, Cambridge University Press, 1972

106 BROCK, S., *The Luminous Eye*, Kalamazoo, Mich., Cistercian Studies, 1992

107 BROCK, S., *St Ephrem the Syrian: Hymns on Paradise*, New York, 1990; 2nd edn Kalamazoo, Mich., Cistercian Studies, 1992

108 BROWN, L. W., *The Indian Christians of St Thomas*, Cambridge, Cambridge University Press, 1982

109 CAMERON, A., *The History of the Image of Edessa: The Telling of a Story*, *Okeanos*, 80–94

110 COAKLEY, J. F., *The Church of the East and the Church of England*, Oxford, Oxford University Press, 1992

111 DIB, P. (tr. BEGGIANI, S.), *History of the Maronite Church*, Detroit, Maronite Apostolic Exarchate, 1971

112 FIEY, J. M., *Communautés Syriaques en Iran et Irak des Origines à 1552*, Aldershot, Variorum, 1979

113 FIEY, J. M., *Jalons pour une Histoire de l'Église en Iraq*, Louvain, CSCO Subsidia, T36, 1970

114 HADDAD, R. M., *Syrian Christians in Muslim Society*, Princeton, NJ, Princeton University Press, 1970; new edn London, Greenwood Press, 1981

115 JOSEPH, J., *The Nestorians and their Muslim Neighbours*, Princeton, NJ, Princeton University Press, 1961

116   KOLLAPARAMBIL, J., *The Babylonian Origin of the St Thomas Christians*, Rome, Pont. Inst. Stud. Or., 1992
117   MOOSA, M., *The Maronites in History*, New York, Syracuse University Press, 1986
118   MOULE, A. C., *Christians in China before the Year 1550*, London, SPCK, 1930
119   PALMER, A., *Monk and Mason on the Tigris Frontier*, Cambridge, Cambridge University Press, 1990
120   SPULER, B., *Die Morgenlandischen Kircher*, Leiden, Brill, 1964
121   VOOBUS, A., *History of the School of Nisibis*, Louvain, CSCO Subsidia, 1965

[XIV]   Cross-Cultural Studies

Compiled by Edward Bailey, Paul Badham, Keith Howard, Ursula King, Martin E. Marty and David J. Melling

1   ALMOND, P. C., *Mystical Experience and Religious Doctrine: An Investigation of the Study of Mysticism in World Religions*, Berlin, Mouton, 1982
2   ARAI, T., and ARIARAJAH, W., (eds), *Spirituality in Interfaith Dialogue*, Geneva, World Council of Churches, WCC Publications, 1989
3   ATKINSON, J. M., 'Shamanisms Today', *Annual Review of Anthropology*, vol. 21, 1992, pp. 307–30
3a   AVIS, P., *The Resurrection of Jesus Christ*, London, Darton, Longman & Todd, 1993
4   BADHAM, P., *Christian Beliefs About Life After Death*, Basingstoke, Macmillan, 1976; New York, Barnes and Noble, 1977; London, SPCK, 1978
5   BADHAM, P. and L. (eds), *Death and Immortality in the Religions of the World*, New York, Paragon House, 1987
6   BADHAM, P. and L., *Immortality or Extinction?*, London, Macmillan/New York, Barnes & Noble, 1982; 2nd edn London, SPCK, 1984
7   BAILEY, E. I., 'The Implicit Religion of Contemporary Society: Some Studies and Reflections' and 'Implicit Religion: A Bibliographical Introduction', *Social Compass*, no. 37, 4 Dec. 1990
8   BELLAH, R. N., 'Civil Religion in America', *Daedalus: Journal of the American Academy of Arts and Sciences*, vol. 96(1), Winter 1967; repr. with commentaries and response in CUTLER, D. R. (ed.), *The World Year Book of Religion*, London, Evans Bros, 1969
9   BERGER, P. L., *A Rumour of Angels: Modern Society and the Rediscovery of the Supernatural*, Harmondsworth, Penguin, 1971; New York, Doubleday, 1969
10   BLACKMORE, S., *Dying to Live: Science and the Near-Death Experience*, London, Grafton, 1993
11   BLUM, F., *The Ethics of Industrial Man: An Empirical Study of Religious Awareness and the Experience of Society*, London, Routledge, 1970
12   BORG, M. B. TER, *Een Uitgewaairde Eeuwigheid: bet Mensetijk Tekort in de Moderne Cultuur*, The Hague, Baarn, 1991
13   BOWKER, J., *The Meanings of Death*, Cambridge, Cambridge University Press, 1991
14   BUCHANAN, C. H., 'Women's Studies', in ELIADE, M. (ed.), *The Encyclopedia of Religion*, vol. 15, pp. 433–40, New York, Collier Macmillan/London, Macmillan, 1987

15 CARNLEY, P., *The Structure of Resurrection Belief*, Oxford, Clarendon Press, 1987; new edn Oxford University Press, 1993

16 CARR, A., *Transforming Grace: Christian Tradition and Women's Experience*, San Francisco, Harper & Row, 1990, 1992

17 CHRIST, C., and PLASKOW, J. (eds), *Womanspirit Rising: A Feminist Reader in Religion*, New York/San Francisco, Harper & Row, 1979; repr. 1992

18 COOEY, P. M., EAKIN, W. R., and MCDANIEL, J. B., *After Patriarchy: Feminist Transformations of the World Religions*, Maryknoll, NY, Orbis Books, 1991; Paulist Press, 1991

19 COUSINS, E. (gen. ed.), *World Spirituality: An Encyclopedic History of the Religious Quest*, 25 vols, New York, Crossroad Publishing Company, 1985–; London, Routledge/SCM, 1986–

20 COWARD, H., *Indian Attitudes to Religious Pluralism*, Albany, NY, State University of New York Press, 1987

21 DAHL, M. E., *The Resurrection of the Body*, London, SCM, 1962

22 DALEY, B. E., *The Hope of the Early Church: Handbook of Patristic Eschatology*, Cambridge, Cambridge University Press, 1991

23 DAVIS, S. T., *Death and Afterlife*, Basingstoke, Macmillan, 1989

24 DAWE, D. G., and CARMAN, J. B., *Christian Faith in a Religiously Plural World*, Maryknoll, NY, Orbis Books, 1978

25 D'COSTA, G., *Theology and Religious Pluralism*, Oxford/New York, Blackwell, 1986

26 DIÓSZEGI, VILMOS, and HOPPÁL, MIHÁLY (eds), *Shamanism in Siberia*, Budapest, Akadémiai Kiadó, 1978

27 ELIADE, M., *Shamanism: Archaic Techniques of Ecstasy*, Princeton, NJ, Princeton University Press, 1964, 1972; new edn Harmondsworth, Arkana/Penguin, 1989

28 FORMAN, R. K. C., (ed.), *The Problem of Pure Consciousness: Mysticism and Philosophy*, New York/Oxford, Oxford University Press, 1990

29 GROSS, R. M., *Buddhism after Patriarchy: A Feminist History, Analysis and Reconstruction of Buddhism*, Albany, NY, State University of New York Press, 1993

30 HALMOS, P., *The Faith of the Counsellors*, London, Constable, 1965; New York, Schocken Books, 1966

31 HAMAYON, R., *La chasse à l'âme: Esquisse d'une théorie du chamanisme sibérien*, Nanterre, Société d'Ethnologie, 1990

32 HAMNETT, I. (ed.), *Religious Pluralism and Unbelief: Studies Critical and Comparative*, London/New York, Routledge, 1990

33 HARNER, M., *The Way of the Shaman*, San Francisco, Harper & Row, 1980

34 HAY, D., *Exploring Inner Space: Scientists and Religious Experience*, Harmondsworth, Penguin, 1982

35 HEINZE, R-I., *Shamans of the Twentieth Century*, New York, Irvington Publishers, 1991

36 HEWITT, H. (ed.), *Problems in the Philosophy of Religion: Critical Studies in the Work of John Hick*, London, Macmillan, 1991

37 HICK, J., *Death and Eternal Life*, Basingstoke, Macmillan Press, 1989, 1971

38 HICK, J., *God and the Universe of Faiths: Essays in the Philosophy of Religions*, London, Macmillan, 1973; New York, St Martin's, 1974; London, Fount/Collins, 1977; new edn Basingstoke, Macmillan, 1988

39 HICK, J., *An Interpretation of Religion: Humanity's Varied Response to the Transcendent*, Basingstoke, Macmillan/New Haven, Yale University Press, 1989

40   HICK, J., *A John Hick Reader*, ed. P. Badham, Basingstoke, Macmillan, 1990

41   HICK, J., *Problems of Religious Pluralism*, London/Basingstoke, Macmillan/New York, St Martin's, 1985

42   HICK, J., and KNITTER, P. F., *The Myth of Christian Uniqueness: Towards a Pluralistic Theology of Religions*, Maryknoll, NY, Orbis Books, 1987

43   HOPPÁL, MIHÁLY, and HOWARD, K. (eds), *Shamans and Cultures*, Budapest, Akadémiai Kiadó/Los Angeles, International Society for Trans-Oceanic Research, 1993

44   HORI, I., *Folk Religion in Japan: Continuity and Change*, Chicago/London, University of Chicago Press, 1969, 1968

45   JONES, C., WAINWRIGHT, G., and YARNOLD, E. (eds), *The Study of Spirituality*, London, SPCK, 1983, 1986

46   KATZ, S., (ed.) *Mysticism and Philosophical Analysis*, London, Sheldon Press, 1978, New York, Oxford University Press, 1978

47   KATZ, S., (ed.), *Mysticism and Religious Traditions*, Oxford/New York, Oxford University Press, 1983, 1984

48   KATZ, S., (ed.), *Mysticism and Language*, New York, Oxford University Press, 1992

49   KING, U., (ed.), *Feminist Theology from the Third World: A Reader*, London, SPCK; Maryknoll, NY, Orbis, 1994

50   KING, U., (ed.), *New Perspectives on Religion and Gender*, Oxford, Blackwell, 1995

51   KING, U., *The Spirit of One Earth: Reflections on Teilhard de Chardin and Global Spirituality*, New York, Paragon House, 1989

52   KING, U., *Women and Spirituality: Voices of Protest and Promise*, 2nd edn, London, Macmillan/University Park, Pa, Pennsylvania State University Press, 1993

53   KNITTER, P., *No Other Name?*, London, SCM, 1985; Maryknoll, NY, Orbis Books, 1985

54   KRAEMER, H., *The Christian Message in a Non-Christian World*, New York, Harper & Row/London, Edinburgh House Press, 1938

55   KRAEMER, H., *Religion and the Christian Faith*, London, Lutterworth Press, 1956

56   KÜNG, H., *Christianity and the World Religions: Paths of Dialogue with Islam, Hinduism and Buddhism*, tr. from the German by P. Heidegg, London, Collins, 1987; SCM, 1993

57   LEWIS, I. M., *Ecstatic Religion: A Study of Shamanism and Spirit Possession*, 2nd edn, London, Routledge, 1989

58   LOADES, A. (ed.), *Feminist Theology: A Reader*, London, SPCK/Louisville, Ky, Westminster/John Knox Press, 1990

59   LUCKMANN, T., *The Invisible Religion: The Problem of Religion in Modern Society*, London/New York, Macmillan, 1967

60   MAGILL, F. N., and MCGREAL, I. P. (eds), *Christian Spirituality: The Essential Guide to the Most Influential Spiritual Writings of the Christian Tradition*, San Francisco, Harper & Row, 1988

61   MARSDEN, G., *Fundamentalism and American Culture: The Shaping of Twentieth Century Evangelicalism, 1870–1925*, Oxford, Oxford University Press, 1980; new edn New York, Oxford University Press, 1983

62   MARTY, M. E., and APPLEBY, R. SCOTT (ed.), *Fundamentalisms and Society: Reclaiming the Sciences, the Family and Education*, Chicago/London, University of Chicago Press, 1993

63 MARTY, M. E., and APPLEBY, R. SCOTT (eds), *Fundamentalisms and the State*, Chicago/London, University of Chicago Press, 1993

64 MARTY, M. E., and APPLEBY, R. SCOTT (eds), *Fundamentalisms Observed*, Chicago, University of Chicago Press, 1991

65 MARTIN, M. E., and APPLEBY, R. SCOTT, *The Glory and the Power: The Rapid Rise of Fundamentalism in the 1990s*, Boston, Mass., Beacon Press, 1993

66 MITCHELL, D. W., *Spirituality and Emptiness: The Dynamics of Spiritual Life in Buddhism and Christianity*, New York/Mahwah, NJ, Paulist Press, 1991

67 MULLER, R., *New Genesis: Shaping a Global Spirituality*, New York, Doubleday, 1982

68 NESTI, A., *Il Religioso Implicito*, Roma, Ianua, 1985

69 PANIKKAR, R., *Worship and Secular Man*, London, Darton, Longman and Todd, 1973; Maryknoll, NY, Orbis Books, 1973

70 PAYNE, R. J. (ed.-in-chief), *The Classics of Western Spirituality*, New York, Paulist Press, 1980; London, SPCK, 1978–

71 PHAN, P. C. (ed.), *Christianity and the Wider Ecumenism*, New York, Paragon House, 1990

72 PLASKOW, J., and CHRIST, C. P. (eds), *Weaving the Visions: New Patterns in Feminist Spirituality*, San Francisco, Harper & Row, 1989; repr. 1992

72a RING, K., *Life at Death: A Scientific Investigation of the Near-Death Experience*, New York, Coward, McCann & Geohagen, 1980

73 ROUGET, G., *La musique et la transe: Esquisse d'une théorie générale des relations de la musique et la possession*, Paris, Éditions Gallimard, 1980

74 RUETHER, R. R., 'Androcentrism', in ELIADE, M. (ed.), *The Encyclopedia of Religion*, vol. 1, pp. 272–6, New York, Collier Macmillan/London, Macmillan, 1987

75 SABOM, M., *Recollections of Death*, London, Corgi, 1982; New York/London, Harper & Row, © 1982

76 SADLER, A. L., *Cha-No-Yu: The Japanese Tea Ceremony*, Rutland, Vt, C. E. Tuttle, 1982, 1963; first publ. London, Kegan Paul, Trench Trubner, 1934

77 SCHNEIDERS, S. M., 'Spirituality in the Academy', in HANSON, B. C. (ed.), *Modern Christian Spirituality: Methodological and Historical Essays*, pp. 15–37, Atlanta, Ga, Scholars Press, 1990

78 SCHOOLS COUNCIL, *Working Paper 36: Religious Education in Secondary Schools*, London, Evans, 1971

79 SHARMA, A. (ed.), *God, Truth and Reality: Essays in Honour of John Hick*, London, Macmillan, 1993

80 SHARMA, A. (ed.), *Women in World Religions*, Albany, NY, State University of New York Press, 1987

81 SHELDRAKE, P., *Spirituality and History: Questions of Interpretation and Method*, New York, Crossroad, 1992; London, SPCK, 1991

82 SIIKALA, A-L., and HOPPÁL, MIHÁLY, *Studies on Shamanism, Ethnologica Uralica*, 2, Budapest, Akadémiai Kiadó/Helsinki, Finnish Anthropological Society/Atlantic Highlands, NJ, Humanities, 1992

82a SMITH, W. C., *What is Scripture? A Comparativist Approach*, Minneapolis, Fortress Press, 1993

83 SOGYAL RIMPOCHE, *The Tibetan Book of Living and Dying*, London, Random House, 1992

84 STACE, W. T., *Mysticism and Philosophy*, London, Macmillan, 1961; Philadelphia, Pa, Lippincott, 1960

85 SULLIVAN, F., *Salvation Outside the Church? Tracing the History of the Catholic Response*, London, Chapman, 1992
86 SWINBURNE, R., *The Evolution of the Soul*, Oxford, Clarendon Press, 1986
87 TOWLER, R., *Homo Religiosus: Sociological Problems in the Study of Religion*, London, Constable/New York, St Martin's, 1974
88 WARD, K., *The Battle for the Soul*, London, Hodder, 1985
89 WOODS, R., (ed.), *Understanding Mysticism*, Garden City, NY, Doubleday, 1980; London, Athlone Press, 1981
90 ZAEHNER, R. C., *Mysticism Sacred and Profane: An Inquiry into Some Varieties of Praeternatural Experience*, London/New York, Oxford University Press, 1961, repr. 1978; Oxford, Clarendon Press, 1957

[XV] *Gnostics, Mandaeans, Manichaeism*

Compiled by Erica C. D. Hunter, Samuel N. C. Lieu and A. Van Tongerloo

1 ASMUSSEN, J. P., and BÖHLIG, A., *Gnosis III. Der Manichäismus*, Zurich/Munich, 1980
2 COLPE, C., *Die Religionsgeschichtliche Schule*, Göttingen, Vandenhoeck & Ruprecht, 1961
3 DROWER, E., *The Book of the Zodiac (Sfar Malwašia)*, London, Royal Asiatic Society, 1949
4 DROWER, E. (tr.), *The Canonical Prayer Book of the Mandaeans*, Leiden, Brill, 1959
5 DROWER, E., *The Mandaeans of Iraq and Iran*, Oxford, Clarendon Press, 1937; repr. Leiden, 1962
6 DROWER, E., *The Thousand and Twelve Questions (Alf Trisar Šualia)*, Berlin, Akademie Verlag, 1960
7 FIROLAMO, G., *A History of Gnosticism* (tr. A. Alcock), Oxford/Cambridge, Mass., Blackwell, 1990, 1992
8 FOERSTER, W. (ed.), *Gnosis: A Selection of Gnostic Texts* (tr. R. McL. Wilson), vol. 2, *Coptic and Mandaean Sources*, Oxford, Clarendon Press, 1974
9 FOERSTER, W. (ed.), *Gnosis I. Patristic Evidence* (English tr. ed. R. McL. Wilson), Oxford, Clarendon Press, 1972
10 FOERSTER, W., 'Das System der Basilides', *New Testament Studies*, vol. 9, 1963, pp. 233–55
11 HARTMAN, S., Gayômart: *Étude sur le syncrétisme dans l'ancien Iran*, Uppsala, Ahnqvist & Wicksell, 1953
12 HUTTER, M., 'Das Erlösungsgeschehen im manichäisch-iranischen Mythos, Motiv- und traditionsgeschichtliche Analysen' in WOSCHITZ, K. M., HUTTER, M., and PRENNER, K., *Das manichäische Urdrama des Lichtes*, Graz, 1989
13 JONAS, H., *The Gnostic Religion*, 3rd edn, New York, 1970; London, Routledge, 1992; Boston, Mass., Beacon Press, 1963
14 JUNKER, H., 'Über iranische Quellen der hellenistischen Aionvorstellung', in *Vorträge der Bibliothek Warburg, 1921/1922*, 1923, pp. 123–78
15 KLIMKEIT, H-J., *Manichaean Art and Calligraphy*, Leiden, Brill, 1982 (*Iconography of Religions*, 20)
16 LIDZBARSKI, M., *Ginză. Der Schatz oder, Das grosse Buch der Mandäer*, Göttingen/Leipzig, 1925

17 LIEU, S. N. C., *Manichaeism in the Later Roman Empire and Medieval China*, 2nd edn, Tübingen, 1992

18 MACDERMOT, V., 'The Concept of Pleroma in Gnosticism', in KRAUSE, M., *Gnosis and Gnosticism*, Leiden, Brill, 1981, pp. 76–81 (Nag Hammadi Studies, 17)

19 PALLIS, S., *Mandaean Studies*, 2nd rev. edn, London, H. Milford/ Copenhagen, Branner 1926 (1927), repr. Amsterdam, Philo Press, 1974; London, H. Milford/Oxford University Press, 1982; Berkeley Cal., University of California Press, 1927 repr.

20 PUECH, H-CH., 'The Concept of Redemption in Manichaeism', in CAMPBELL, J. (ed.), *The Mystic Vision*, New Jersey, 1968, pp. 247–314

21 PUECH, H-CH., *Le Manicheisme, Son fondateur – sa doctrine*, Paris, Musée Guimet, 1949

22 REEVES, J. C., *Jewish Lore in Manichaean Cosmogony: Studies in the 'Book of the Giants'*, Cincinnati, 1991 (Hebrew Union College Monographs)

23 REITZENSTEIN, R., *Das iranische Erlösungsmysterium*, Bonn, Marcus & Weber, 1921

24 RUDOLPH, K., *Gnosis: The Nature and History of an Ancient Religion* (English tr. ed. R. McL. Wilson), Edinburgh, 1977; San Francisco, Harper & Row, 1983

24a RUDOLPH, K., *Gnosis: The Nature* Edinburgh, T. & T. Clark, 1983

25 RUDOLPH, K., *Mandaeism*, Leiden, Brill, 1978 (Iconography of Religions, 21)

26 RUDOLPH, K., *Die Mandaer*, 2 vols, Göttingen, 1961 (Forschungen zur Religion und Literatur des Alten und Neuer Testaments, Neue Folge, 56)

27 SAGNARD, F. M. M., *La Gnose valentinienne et le témoinage de saint Irénée*, Paris, 1947 (Études de philosophie médiévale, 36)

28 SASSE, H., 'Aion', in *RAC*, vol. 1, (1950), pp. 194–204

29 SEGELBERG, E., *Masbūtā. Studies in the Ritual of Mandaean Baptism* (a thesis), Uppsala, 1958

30 SUNDERMANN, W., 'Cosmogony and Cosmology III (in Manichaeism)', *Encyclopaedia Iranica*, vol. 6(3), Costa Mesa, 1993, pp. 310–15

31 SUNDERMANN, W., 'Studien zur kirchengeschichtlichen Literatur der iranischen Manichäer I–III' *Altorientalische Forschungen*, vol. 13(1), Berlin, 1986, pp. 40–92; vol. 13(2), 1986, pp. 239–317; vol. 14(1), 1987, pp. 41–107

32 TARDIEU, M., *Le Manichéisme, Que sais-je?*, no. 140, Paris, 1981

33 WIDENGREN, G., *Mani and Manichaeism*, London, Weidenfeld, 1965

34 WIDENGREN, G., *Mesopotamian Elements in Manichaeism*, Uppsala, Lundequist; Leipzig/Wiesbaden, Harrassowitz, 1946, King and Saviour, Studies in Manichaean, Mandean and Syrian-Gnostic Religion, pt 2

35 YAMAUCHI, E., *Mandaic Incantation Texts*, New Haven, Conn., American Oriental Society, 1967 (American Oriental Series, vol. 49)

(*See also* XIII(A), 14)

[XVI]   *Greek Religion*

Compiled by Christiane Sourvinou-Inwood

1 BREMMER, J. (ed.), *Interpretations of Greek Mythology*, London/Sydney, Croom Helm, 1987
2 BRUIT ZAIDMAN, L., and SCHMITT PANTEL, P. *Religion in the Ancient Greek City*, Cambridge, Cambridge University Press, 1992
3 BURKERT, W., *Lore and Science in Ancient Pythagoreanism*, Cambridge, Mass., Harvard University Press, 1972
4 BURKERT, W., *Greek Religion: Archaic and Classical*, Oxford, Blackwell, 1985
5 BURKERT, W., *Ancient Mystery Cults*, Cambridge, Mass./London, Harvard University Press, 1987
6 CARPENTER, T. H., *Art and Myth in Ancient Greece*, London/New York, Thames & Hudson, 1991
7 CUMONT, F., *Astrology and Religion among the Greeks and Romans*, London/New York, Constable, 1912; repr. New York, Dover 1960; Magnolia, Mass., Peter Smith
8 DETIENNE, M., and VERNANT, J-P., *The Cuisine of Sacrifice among the Greeks*, Chicago/London, University of Chicago Press, 1989
9 DODDS, E. R., *The Greeks and the Irrational*, Berkeley/Los Angeles/London, University of California Press, 1951
10 DOVER, K. J., *Greek Popular Morality in the time of Plato and Aristotle*, Oxford, Blackwell, 1974; Berkeley, Cal., University of California Press, 1975
11 EASTERLING, P. E., and MUIR, J. V., *Greek Religion and Society*, Cambridge, Cambridge University Press, 1985
12 EDMUNDS, L. (ed.), *Approaches to Greek Myth*, Baltimore/London, Johns Hopkins University Press, 1990
13 FARAONE, C. A., and OBBINK, D. (eds), *Magika Hiera: Ancient Greek Magic and Religion*, New York/Oxford, Oxford University Press, 1991
14 GARLAND, R., *The Greek Way of Death*, London, Duckworth, 1985
15 GARLAND, R., *Introducing New Gods: The Politics of Athenian Religion*, London, Duckworth, 1992
16 GORDON, R. L. (ed.), *Myth, Religion and Society* (Cambridge, Cambridge University Press, 1981)
17 GUTHRIE, W. K. C., *The Greeks and their Gods*, London, Methuen, 1950; Boston, Mass., Beacon Press, 1951
18 HUMPHREYS, S. C., *Anthropology and the Greeks*, London/Henley/Boston, Mass., Routledge, 1978
19 KEARNS, E., *The Heroes of Attica*, London, 1989 (*Bulletin of the Institute of Classical Studies* Supplement 57)
20 KIRK, G. S., *The Nature of Greek Myths*, Harmondsworth, Penguin, 1974; New York, Overlook Press, 1975
21 LLOYD-JONES, H., *The Justice of Zeus*, Berkeley/Los Angeles/London, University of California Press, 1971; 2nd edn/1983
22 LONG, A. A., *Hellenistic Philosophy: Stoics, Epicureans, Sceptics*, London, Duckworth/New York, Scribner, 1974
23 LUCK, G., *Arcana Mundi: Magic and the Occult in the Greek and Roman Worlds*, Baltimore/London, Johns Hopkins University Press, 1985
24 MARINATOS, N., and HAGG, R. (eds), *Greek Sanctuaries: New Approaches*, London, Routledge, 1993
25 NILSSON, M. P., *A History of Greek Religion*, Oxford, Clarendon Press,

1925, 2nd edn 1949; repr. New York, Norton, 1964, Westport, Conn., Greenwood, 1980

26 NILSSON, M. P., *Cults, Myths, Oracles and Politics in Ancient Greece*, Lund, Gleerup, (Acta Inst. Athen. Sueciae, 1), repr. New York, Cooper Square, 1972

27 NOCK, A. D., *Essays on Religion and the Ancient World* (sel. and ed. Z. Stewart), 2 vols, Oxford, Clarendon Press/Cambridge Mass., Harvard University Press, 1972

28 PARKE, H. W., *Greek Oracles*, London, Hutchinson, 1967

29 PARKER, R., *Miasma: Pollution and Purification in Early Greek Religion*, Oxford, Clarendon Press, 1983; new edn Oxford University Press, 1990

30 PARKER, R., 'Greek States and Greek Oracles', in CARTLEDGE, P., and HARVEY, F. D. (eds), *Crux*, Exeter, Imprint Academic, 1985, pp. 298–326

31 PARKER, R., 'Greek Religion', in *Greece and the Hellenistic World: The Oxford History of the Classical World*, Oxford, Oxford University Press, 1986, pp. 248–68

32 PRICE, S. R. F., *Rituals and Power: The Roman Imperial Cult in Asia Minor*, Cambridge, Cambridge University Press, 1984

33 SIMON, E., *Festivals of Attica: An Archaeological Commentary*, Madison, Wisc., University of Wisconsin Press, 1983

34 SOURVINOU INWOOD, C., 'What is Polis Religion?', in MURRAY, O., and PRICE, S. (eds), *The Greek City from Homer to Alexander*, Oxford, Clarendon Press, 1990, pp. 295–322

35 SOURVINOU-INWOOD, C., 'Further Aspects of Polis Religion', in *Archeologia e storia antica Annali. Istituto Universitario Orientale. Napoli, Dipartmento del mondo classico e del mediterraneo antico*, 10, 1988 [1990], Naples, Istituto Universitario Orientale, 1990, pp. 259–74

36 TOMLINSON, R. A., *Greek Sanctuaries*, London, Elek/New York, St Martin's, 1976

37 VERSNEL, H. S., *Faith, Hope and Worship: Aspects of Religious Mentality in the Ancient World*, Leiden, Brill, 1981

38 WEST, M. L., *The Orphic Poems*, Oxford, Clarendon Press, 1983

(*See also* X, 3, 13; XXXIV, 69a)

[XVII]   *Hinduism*

Compiled by L. S. Cousins, Mark Juergensmeyer, Kim Knott, Trevor Ling, Valerie J. Roebuck and Simon Weightman

1 ALLCHIN, B., and F. R., *The Birth of Indian Civilization: India and Pakistan before 500 AD*, Harmondsworth, Penguin, 1968

2 AMAR CHITRA KATHA, A series of over 200 children's books in cartoon-strip format published by the India Book House Education Trust, Bombay, gives a remarkable picture of Hindu (and other) myth as it is seen in India today: see, e.g. no. 164, *Tales of Shiva*; no. 160, *Tales of Vishnu*; no. 176, *Tales of Durga*; and no. 89, *Ganesha*

3 ANDERSON, W., *The Brotherhood in Saffron*, New Delhi, Penguin, 1988

4 ARTS COUNCIL OF GREAT BRITAIN, *In the Image of Man*, London, Arts Council, 1982

5   BABB, L. A., *The Divine Hierarchy: Popular Hinduism in Central India,* New York, Columbia University Press, 1975

6   BABB, L., *Redemptive Encounters: Three Styles in the Hindu Tradition,* Berkeley, Cal., University of California Press, 1987; Delhi, Oxford University Press

7   BAILEY, G., *The Mythology of Brahmā,* Oxford, Oxford University Press, 1983

7a   BAIRD, R. D. (ed.), *Religion in Modern India* [Papers, some of which were presented at a Conference on Religion in Modern India, University of Iowa, 1980], New Delhi, Manohar, 1981

8   BALLARD, R. (ed.), *Desh Pardesh: The South Asian Experience in Britain,* London, Hurst, 1994

9   BARKER, E., *New Religious Movements: A Practical Introduction,* London, HMSO, 1989

10   BASHAM, A. L., *History and Doctrines of the Ājīvikas,* London, Luzac, 1951; new edn Delhi, Motilal Banarsidass, 1983

11   BASHAM, A. L., *The Origins of Development of Classical Hinduism,* ed. and ann. K. G. Zysk, Boston, Mass., Beacon Press, 1989; Delhi Motilal Banarsidass, 1990

12   BASHAM, A. L., *The Wonder That Was India,* 3rd edn, London, Sidwick, 1967, Fontana, 1971; New York, Taplinger, 1968

13   BECKFORD, J., *Cult Controversies: The Societal Response to the New Religious Movements,* London, Tavistock, 1985

14   BÉTEILLE, A., *Castes: Old and New,* London/Bombay/New York, Asia Publishing House, 1969

15   BHARATI, A., *The Asians in East Africa,* Chicago, Ill., Nelson-Hall, 1972

16   BHARATI, A., 'Pilgrimage in the Indian Tradition', *History of Religions,* vol. 3, no. 1, 1963

17   BHARDWAJ, S. M., *Hindu Places of Pilgrimage in India,* Berkeley, Cal., University of California Press, 1973; new edn, 1984

18   BHATTACHARJI, S., *The Indian Theogony: A Comparative Study of Indian Mythology from the Vedas to the Purāṇas,* Cambridge, Cambridge University Press, 1970; repr. Columbia, Mo, South Asia Books, 1978

19   BILIMORIA, P., *Hinduism in Australia: Mandala for the Gods,* Geelong, Vic., Spectrum/Deakin University Press, 1988

20   BORTHWICK, M., *Keshub Chandra Sen: A Search for Cultural Synthesis,* Calcutta, Minerva, 1977

21   BOWEN, D., *The Sathya Sai Baba Community in Bradford: Its Origin and Development, Religious Beliefs and Practices,* Leeds, University of Leeds, 1988 (Community Relations Project Monograph Series)

22   BROCKINGTON, J. L., *The Sacred Thread: Hinduism in its Continuity and Diversity,* Edinburgh, Edinburgh University Press, 1958, 1981

23   BROMLEY, D. G., and SHINN, L. D. (eds), *Krishna Consciousness in the West,* Lewisburg, Bucknell University Press, 1989

24   BROMLEY, D. G., and SHUPE, A. D., *Strange Gods: The Great American Cult Scare,* Boston, Mass., Beacon Press, 1981

25   BROWN, J. M., *Men and Gods in a Changing World: Some Themes in the Religious Experiences of Twentieth-Century Hindus and Christians,* London, SCM, 1980

26   BROWN, W. N. (ed. and tr.), *The Saundaryalaharī, or Flood of Beauty,* traditionally ascribed by Śaṅkarācārya, Cambridge, Mass., Harvard University Press, 1958

27 BURGHART, R. (ed.), *Hinduism in Great Britain: The Perpetutation of Religion in an Alien Cultural Milieu*, London, Tavistock, 1987

28 CARMAN, J. B., *The Theology of Rāmānuja*, New Haven, Conn., Yale University Press, 1974

29 CARTMAN, J., *Hinduism in Ceylon*, Colombo, Gunasena, 1957

30 CLARKE, C., PEACH, C., and VERTOVEC, S. (eds), *South Asians Overseas: Migration and Ethnicity*, Cambridge, Cambridge University Press, 1990

31 COLLET, D., *The Life and Letters of Ram Mohan Roy*, Calcutta, Sadharan Brahmo Samaj, 1962

32 DAMEN, F. L., *Crisis and Renewal in the Brahmo Samaj*, Catholic University of Louvain, 1983

33 DAMRELL, J. D., *Seeking Spiritual Meaning: The World of Vedanta*, London, Sage, 1977

34 DANIÉLOU, A., *Hindu Polytheism*, London, Routledge/Princeton, NJ, Princeton University Press, 1964

35 DANIÉLOU, A., *Yoga: The Method of Re-Integration*, New York, University Books, 1955; London, Johnson, 1949, new edn 1973

36 DASGUPTA, S. N., *A History of Indian Philosophy*, 5 vols, Cambridge, Cambridge University Press, 1922–55, repr. Delhi, Motilal Banarsidass, 1975; Livingston, NJ, Orient Book Distributors; Atlantic Highlands, NJ, Humanities, 1975

37 DE BARY, W. T., et al., *Sources of Indian Tradition*, New York/London, Columbia University Press, 1958; new edn Delhi, Motilal Banarsidass, 1988

38 DEHEJIA, V., *Slaves of the Lord: The Path of the Tamil Saints*, New Delhi, Munshiram Manoharlal, 1988

39 DESAI, D., *Erotic Sculpture of India: A Socio-Cultural Study*, New Delhi, Tata/McGraw-Hill, 1975

40 DEUTSCH, E., and BUITENEN, J. A. B. VAN, *A Source Book of Advaita Vedānta*, Honolulu, University Press of Hawaii, 1971

41 DHAR, S. N., *A Comprehensive Biography of Swami Vivekananda*, 2 vols, Madras, Vivekananda Prakashan Kendra, 1975–6

42 DHAVAMONY, M., *The Love of God According to Śaiva Siddhānta: A Study in the Mysticism and Theology of Śaivism*, Oxford, Clarendon Press, 1971

43 DONIGER, W., and SMITH, B. K., *The Laws of Manu*, Harmondsworth, Penguin, 1991

44 DUTT, R. C., *The Ramayana, and the Mahabharata, Condensed into English Verse*, London, Dent/New York, Dutton, 1910, repr.

45 ELIADE, M., *Patanjali and Yoga*, New York, Schocken, 1975, repr. 1976; prev. publ. New York, Funk & Wagnalls, 1969

46 EMBREE, A. T. (ed.), *Sources of Indian Tradition*, vol. 1, *From the Beginning to 1800*, 2nd edn, New York, Columbia University Press, 1988

47 *Encyclopaedia Britannica: Macropaedia*, 15th edn, 19 vols (© 1975–8) (refs in text to vol. and p.)

48 FARQUHAR, J. N., *Modern Religious Movements in India*, New York, Macmillan, 1915; repr. New Delhi, Munshiram Manoharlal, 1967

49 FEUERSTEIN, G., *The Philosophy of Classical Yoga*, Manchester, Manchester University Press, 1980

50 FISCHER, L., *The Life of Mahatma Gandhi*, London, Granada, 1982

51 FRAUWALLNER, E., *History of Indian Philosophy* (tr. V. M. Bedekar), 2 vols, Delhi, Motilal Banarsidass; Livingston, NJ, Orient Book Distributors, 1973; New York, Humanities, 1974

52   GOLD, D., *The Lord as Guru: Hindi Sants in the Northern Indian Tradition*, New York/Oxford, Oxford University Press, 1988 (1987)

53   GONDA, J., *A History of Indian Literature*, Wiesbaden, Harrassowitz, 1973– (refs in text to vol. and fascicule)

54   GONDA, J., *Viṣṇuism and Śivaism: A Comparison*, London, School of Oriental and African Studies/Athlone Press, 1970; New Delhi, Munshiram Manoharlal, 1976; Oriental Books, 1976

55   GRAHAM, B., *Hindu Nationalism in Indian Politics*, Cambridge, Cambridge University Press, 1990

56   GRAY, B. (ed.), *The Arts of India*, Oxford, Phaidon, 1981

57   HARDY, F. (ed.), *The World's Religions: The Religions of Asia*, London, Routledge, 1988, 1990

58   HARLE, J. C., *The Art and Architecture of India*, Harmondsworth, Penguin, 1986

59   HARLE, J. C., *Gupta Sculpture: Indian Sculpture of the Fourth to the Sixth Centuries AD*, Oxford, Clarendon Press, 1974

60   HAWLEY, J., and JUERGENSMEYER, M., *Songs of the Saints of India*, New York/Oxford, Oxford University Press, 1988

61   HAY, S., *Sources of Indian Tradition*, vol. 2: *Modern India and Pakistan*, New York, Columbia University Press, 1988

62   HOPKINS, T. J., *The Hindu Religious Tradition*, Belmont, Cal., Wadsworth, 1971

63   JACKSON, R., and NESBITT, E., *Hindu Children in Britain*, London, Trentham Books, 1993

64   JASH, P., *History of Śivism*, Calcutta, Roy & Chowdhury, 1974

65   JONES, K., *Socio-Religious Reform Movements in British India, The New Cambridge History of India*, vol. 3(1), Cambridge, Cambridge University Press, 1989

66   JORDENS, J. T. F., *Dayānanda Saraswatī, His Life and Ideas*, Delhi, Oxford University Press, 1978

67   JUERGENSMEYER, M., *Radhasoami Reality: The Logic of a Modern Faith*, Princeton, NJ, Princeton University Press, 1991

68   KING, U., 'Iconographic Reflections on the Religious and Secular Importance of the Bhagavadgītā within the Image World of Modern Hinduism', *Journal of Studies in the Bhagavadgītā*, vols 5–7, 1985–7, pp. 161–88

69   KINSLEY, D. R., *Hindu Goddesses: Visions of the Divine Feminine in the Hindu Religious Tradition*, Berkeley, Cal., University of California Press, 1986

70   KINSLEY, D. R., *Hinduism: A Cultural Perspective*, Englewood Cliffs, NJ, Prentice-Hall, 1982; 2nd rev. edn 1993

71   KNOTT, K., *Hinduism in Leeds: Religious Practice in the Indian Hindu Community and in Hindu-Related Groups*, Leeds, University of Leeds, 1986 (Community Religions Project Monograph Series)

72   KNOTT, K., *My Sweet Lord: The Hare Krishna Movement*, Wellingborough, Aquarian Press, 1986

73   KOPF, D., *The Brahmo Samaj and the Shaping of the Modern Indian Mind*, Princeton, NJ, Princeton University Press, 1978

74   KOSAMBI, D. D., *The Culture and Civilisation of Ancient India*, London, Routledge, 1965; Delhi, Vikas, 1975

75   KRISHNANANDA, SWAMI, *The Divine Life Society*, Sivanandanagar, Yoga Vedanta Forest Academy Press, 1967

76   LANNOY, R., *The Speaking Tree: A Study of Indian Culture and Society*, London/New York, Oxford University Press, 1971, 1974; Bombay, 1968

77   LARSON, G. J., *Classical Sāmkhya*, Delhi, Motilal Banarsidass, 1969
78   LIEBERT, G., *Iconographic Dictionary of the Indian Religions: Hinduism – Buddhism – Jainism*, Leiden, Brill, 1976; new edn Delhi, Sri Satguru Publications, 1990
79   *The Life of Sri Ramakrishna, Compiled from Various Authentic Sources*, Calcutta, Advaita Ashrama, 1928
80   LING, T. O., *A History of Religion East and West*, London, Macmillan, 1968, 1969; New York, St Martin's, 1968
81   LING, T. O., 'Hinduism: Introduction into South-East Asia', in BRANDON, S. G. F., *A Dictionary of Comparative Religion*, London, Weidenfeld/New York, Scribner, 1970, pp. 171–3, 331–3, 595–6, 608–9
82   LIPNER, J., *Hindus, Their Religious Beliefs and Practices*, London, Routledge, 1994 (Library of Religious Beliefs and Practices)
83   LUTGENDORF, P., *The Life of a Text*, Berkeley, Cal., University of California Press, 1991
84   MCDERMOTT, R. A., *Radhakrishnan: Selected Writings on Philosophy, Religion and Culture*, New York, E. P. Dutton, 1970
85   MAHARISHI MAHESH YOGI, *The Science of Being and the Art of Living*, London, SRM, 1967
86   MATHUR, A. P., *Radhasoami Faith: A Historical Study*, Delhi, Vikas, 1974
87   MELTON, J. G. (ed.), *The Encyclopedia of American Religions*, 3rd edn, Detroit, Mich., Gale, 1989, 1991
88   MICHELL, G., *The Hindu Temple: An Introduction to its Meaning and Form*, London, Elek, 1977; New York, Harper & Row, 1978
89   MOOKERJEE, A., *Kali: The Feminine Force*, London, Thames & Hudson, 1988
90   NANDDAS, *The Round Dance of Krishna and Uddhav's Message*, (ed. and tr. S. McGregor), London, Luzac, 1973
91   O'FLAHERTY, W. D., *Asceticism and Eroticism in the Mythology of Śiva*, London/New York, Oxford University Press, 1973
92   O'FLAHERTY, W. D. (ed.), *Hindu Myths: A Sourcebook* (tr. from the Sanskrit), Harmondsworth, Penguin, 1975
93   O'FLAHERTY, W. D. (ed.), *Karma and Rebirth in Classical Indian Traditions*, Berkeley/Los Angeles/London, University of California Press, 1980
94   O'FLAHERTY, W. D. (ed. and tr.), *The Rig Veda*, Harmondsworth, Penguin, 1981
95   O'FLAHERTY, W. D. (ed. and tr.), *Textual Sources for the Study of Hinduism*, Manchester, Manchester University Press, 1988, new edn Chicago University Press
96   O'MALLEY, L. S. S., *Indian Caste Customs*, Cambridge, Cambridge University Press, 1932, repr. 1974; Totowa, NJ, Rowman/London, Curzon/New Delhi, Vikas
97   OSBORNE, A., *The Incredible Sathya Saibaba*, London, Rider, 1958; new edn London, Sangam Books, 1985
98   PANDEY, R. B., *Hindu Samskaras: Socio-Religious Study of the Hindu Sacraments*, 2nd rev. edn, Delhi, Motilal Barnarsidass, 1969, repr. Mystic, Conn., Verry; Livingston, NJ, Orient Book Distributors, 1976; Banarsidass, 1987
99   PINGREE, D., *Jyotiḥśāstra: Astra and Mathematical Literature*, Wiesbaden, Otto Harrassowitz, 1981: vol. 6, fascicle 4 of GONDA, J., *A History of Indian Literature*, Wiesbaden, Harrassowitz, 1973–
100 POCOCK, D. F., *Mind, Body and Wealth: A Study of Belief and Practice*

in an Indian Village, Oxford, Blackwell/Totowa, NJ, Rowman & Littlefield, 1973

101   POTTER, K. H., *Encyclopaedia of Indian Philosophies*, vol. 2, *Indian Metaphysics and Epistemology*, Delhi, Motilal Banarsidass, 1977; Princeton, NJ, Princeton University Press (© 1977); New York, International Publications Service, 1977

102   PRABHUPADA, A. C. B., *The Science of Self Realization*, London, International Society for Krishna Consciousness, 1977

103   PULIGANDLA, R., *Fundamentals of Indian Philosophy*, New York, Abingdon, 1975

104   PURANI, A. B., *Life of Sri Aurobindo*, Pondicherry, Sri Aurobindo Ashram, 1964

105   RADHAKRISHNAN, SIR SARVEPALLI (tr.), BĀDARĀYANA, *The Brahma Sutra*, London, Allen & Unwin, 1960

106   RADHAKRISHNAN, SIR SARVEPALLI (ed. and tr.), *The Principal Upaniṣads*, London, Allen & Unwin, 1953

107   RADHAKRISHNAN, SIR SARVEPALLI, and MOORE, C. A. (eds), *A Source-Book in Indian Philosophy*, Princeton, NJ, Princeton University Press, 1957; repr. 1973

108   RAMANUJAN, A. K. (tr.), *Speaking of Śiva*, Harmondsworth, Penguin, 1973

109   RAWSON, P., *Indian Sculpture*, London, Dutton, 1966

110   RAYAPATI, J. P. R., *Early American Interest in Vedanta*, London, Asia Publishing House, 1973

111   RENOU, L. (ed.), *Hinduism*, London/New York, Braziller, 1963; Bombay, Taraporevala, 1969

112   ROCHFORD, E. B., *Hare Krishna in America*, New Brunswick, NJ, Rutgers University Press, 1985

113   ROEBUCK, V. J., *The Circle of Stars: An Introduction to Indian Astrology*, Shaftesbury, Dorset/Rockport, Mass., Element Books, 1992

114   SASTRI, K. A. N., *Development of Religion in South India*, New Delhi, Orient Longman, 1963

115   SCHOMER, K., and MCLEOD, W. (eds), *The Sants: Studies in a Devotional Tradition of India*, Berkeley, Cal., Berkeley Religious Studies Series; Delhi, Motilal Banarsidass, 1987

116   SCHWARTZ, B., *Caste in Overseas Indian Communities*, San Francisco, Cal., Chandler, 1967

117   SHARMA, D. S., *The Renaissance of Hinduism*, Benares, 1944

118   SINGER, M. (ed.), *Krishna: Myths, Rites and Attitudes*, Honolulu, East–West Center, 1966; Chicago, Ill., University of Chicago Press, 1969

119   SIVAPRIYANANDA, S., *Astrology and Religion in Indian Art*, New Delhi, Abhinav Publications, 1990

120   SIVARAMAMURTI, C., *South Indian Bronzes*, New Delhi, Lalit Kala Akademi, 1963

121   SMART, N., *Doctrine and Argument in Indian Philosophy*, London, Allen & Unwin/Atlantic Highlands, NJ, Humanities, 1964; new edn Brighton, Harvester, 1977

122   SMITHSONIAN INSTITUTION, *Aditi: The Living Arts of India*, Washington, DC, Smithsonian Institution, 1985

123   SOOKLAL, A., *A Socio-Religious Study of the Hare Krishna Movement in South Africa*, Westville/Durban, Research Unit for the Study of New Religions, 1985

124   SRINIVAS, M. N., *Caste in Modern India*, London/Bombay/New York, Asia Publishing House, 1962; Bombay, 1977; London, J. K. Publishing, 1979

125 TINKER, H., *The Banyan Tree: Overseas Emigrants from India, Pakistan and Bangladesh*, Oxford, Oxford University Press, 1977

126 UNDERHILL, M. M., *The Hindu Religious Year*, Oxford, Oxford University Press/Calcutta, Association Press, 1921

127 VAN DEN BURG, C. J. G., 'The Structural Conditioning of Identity Formation: Surinamese Hindus and Religious Policy in the Netherlands', in SHADID, W. A. R., and VAN KONINGSVELD, P. S. (eds), *The Integration of Islam and Hindus in Western Europe*, Kampen, Kok Pharos, 1991

128 VAN DER VEER, P., 'Religious Therapies and their Valuation among Surinamese Hindustanis in the Netherlands', in VERTOVEC, S. (ed.), *Oxford University Papers on India*, vol. 2, part 2, *Aspects of the South Asian Diaspora*, Delhi, Oxford University Press, 1991

129 VARĀHAMIHIRA, *Bṛhajjātaka*, in SASTRI, V. SUBRAHMANYA (ed. and tr.), *Varahamihira's Brihat Jataka*, Bangalore, 1929; repr. 1971

130 VERTOVEC, S., *Hindu Trinidad: Religion, Ethnicity and Socio-Economic Change*, London, Macmillan Caribbean, 1992 (Warwick University Caribbean Studies, 5)

131 WALKER, B., *Hindu World: An Encyclopaedic Survey of Hinduism*, 2 vols, London, Allen & Unwin, 1968

132 WEIGHTMAN, S. C. R., *Hinduism in the Village Setting*, Milton Keynes, Open University Press, 1978

133 WERNER, K., *Yoga and Indian Philosophy*, Delhi, Motilal Banarsidass, 1977; Columbia, Mo, South Asia Books, 1979

134 WILLIAMS, R. (ed.), *A Sacred Thread: Modern Transmission of Hindu Traditions in India and Abroad*, Chambersburg, Penn., Anima Publications, 1992

135 WILLIAMS, R. B., *A New Face of Hinduism: The Swāmīnārāyan Religion*, Cambridge, Cambridge University Press, 1984

136 WILLIAMS, R. B., *Religions of Immigrants from India and Pakistan: New Threads in the American Tapestry*, Cambridge, Cambridge University Press, 1988

137 ZAEHNER, R. C., *The Bhagavad-Gītā*, Oxford, Clarendon Press, 1969; New York, Oxford University Press, 1973

138 ZAEHNER, R. C., *Hinduism*, London/New York, Oxford University Press, 1962; new edn 1966

139 ZAEHNER, R. C., *Hindu Scriptures*, London, Dent/New York, Dutton, 1966; new edn Everyman, Dent, 1992

140 ZIMMER, H. R., *Myths and Symbols in Indian Art and Civilization*, Princeton, NJ, Princeton University Press/New York, Pantheon, 1946; Princeton University Press, 1971

[XVIII] Iranian Religions (Excluding Zoroastrianism)

Part 1: Compiled by P. Kreyenbroek

1 EDMONDS, C. J., *A Pilgrimage to Lalish*, London, Royal Asiatic Society, 1967

2 ELAHI, B., *The Path of Perfection: The Spiritual Teachings of Master Nur Ali*, London, Century, 1987; 2nd rev. edn Shaftesbury, Dorset, Element Books, 1993

3 EMPSON, R. H. W., *The Cult of the Peacock Angel*, London, Witherby, 1928

4   FRANK, R., *Scheich 'Adî, der grosse Heilige der Jezîdîs*, Berlin, Mayer & Muller, 1911
5   GUEST, J. S., *The Yezidis: A Study in Survival*, London/New York, KPI, 1987
6   HAMZEH'EE, M. R., *The Yaresan: A Sociological, Historical and Religio-Historical Study of a Kurdish Community*, Berlin, Klaus Schwarz, 1990
7   IVANOW, W., *The Truth-Worshippers of Kurdistan: Ahl-i Haqq Texts*, Leiden, Brill, 1953
8   LESCOT, R., *Enquête sur les Yezidis de Syrie et du Djebel Sindjar*, Beirut, Institut Français du Damas, 1938
9   MOKRI, M. (ed.), *Shah-Nama-ye Haqiqa, Le Livre des Rois de Vérité: Histoire Traditionalle des Ahl-e Haqq*, Paris, H. Maisonneuve, 1966

Part 2: Compiled by Roger Beck

9a   BARTON, T., *Ancient Astrology*, London/New York, Routledge, 1994
10   BECK, R., 'Excursus, "Thus Spake Not Zarathustra": Zoroastrian Pseudepigrapha of the Greco-Roman World', in BOYCE, M., and GRENET, F., *A History of Zoroastrianism*, vol. 3, *Zoroastrianism under Macedonian and Roman Rule*, Leiden, Brill, 1991
11   BIDET, J., and CUMONT, F., *Les Mages hellénisés: Zoroastre, Ostanès et Hystaspe d'après la tradition grèque*, 2 vols, Paris, Les Belles Lettres, 1938; repr. 1973
12   BOYCE, M., and GRENET, F., with a contribution by BECK, R., *A History of Zoroastrianism*, vol. 3, *Zoroastrianism under Macedonian and Roman Rule*, Leiden, Brill, 1991 (*see also* XXXVI, 8)
13   FLUSSER, D., 'Hystaspes and John of Patmos', in SHAKED, S. (ed.), *Irano-Judaica*, Jerusalem, Hebrew University, 1982, pp. 12–73
14   MOMIGLIANO, A., *Alien Wisdom: The Limits of Hellenization*, Cambridge, Cambridge University Press, 1975
14a   TESTER, S. J., *A History of Western Astrology*, Woodbridge, Suffolk/Wolfeboro, NH, Boydell Press, 1987

Part 3: Compiled by John R. Hinnells

15   BECK, R., 'Mithraism since Franz Cumont', in TEMPORINI, H., and HAASE, W. (eds), *Aufstieg und Niedergang der Römischen Welt: Geschichte und Kultur Roms im Spiegel der neuren Forschung*, vol. 17, part 2(4), Herausg. von W. Haase, Berlin/New York, Gruyter, 1984
16   BECK, R., 'In Place of the Lion: Mithras in the Tauroctony', in HINNELLS, J. R., *Studies* (no. 24 below), pp. 29–50
17   BECK, R., *Planetary Gods and Planetary Orders in the Mysteries of Mithras*, Leiden/New York/Copenhagen/Cologne, Brill, 1988
18   BIANCHI, U., *Mysteria Mithrae*, Leiden, Brill, 1979 (*Études préliminaires aux religions orientales dans l'empire romain*, ed. M. J. Vermaseren, 80)
19   CUMONT, F., *The Mysteries of Mithra* (tr. T. J. McCormack), new edn, New York, Dover, 1956; this tr. prev. publ. 1903; 1911, repr. Magnolia, Mass., Peter Smith.
20   FRANCIS, E. D., *Études mithraiques*, Leiden, Brill, 1978 (*Acta Iranica*, ed. J. Duchesne-Guillemin, 17)
21   GORDON, R. L., 'Mystery, Metaphor and Doctrine in the Mysteries of Mithras', in HINNELLS, J. R., *Studies* (no. 24 below), pp. 103–124
22   HINNELLS, J. R., (ed.), *Mithraic Studies*, 2 vols, Manchester, Manchester University Press, 1975

23 HINNELLS, J. R., *Persian Mythology*, 2nd expanded and rev. edn, Feltham, Middlesex, 1985; 1st edn New York, London, Hamlyn, 1973

24 HINNELLS, J. R., (ed.), *Studies in Mithraism: Papers Associated with the Mithraic Panel Organized on the Occasion of the XVIth Congress for the History of Religions*, Rome, 1990, (Storia delle religioni, 9), Rome, "L'Erma" di Bretschneider, © 1994

25 JACKSON, H. M., 'The Meaning and Function of the Leontocephaline in Roman Mithraism', *Numen*, vol. 32, 1985, pp. 17–45

26 *Journal of Mithraic Studies*, vols 1–3, London, Routledge, 1976–80

27 KREYENBROEK, P. G., 'Mithra and Ahreman in Iranian Cosmogonies', in HINNELLS, J. R., *Studies* (no. 24 above), pp. 173–82

28 LIEBESCHUETZ, W., 'The Expansion of Mithraism among the Religious Cults of the Second Century', in HINNELLS, J. R., *Studies* (no. 24 above), pp. 195–216

29 ULANSEY, D., *The Origins of the Mithraic Mysteries: Cosmology and Salvation in the Ancient World*, New York, Oxford University Press, 1989; new edn 1991

30 VERMASEREN, M. J., *Corpus inscriptionum et monumentum religionis mithriacae*, 2 vols, The Hague, Nijhoff, 1956–60

31 VERMASEREN, M. J., *Mithras the Secret God* (tr. T. and V. Megaw), London, Chatto and Windus/Toronto, Clarke, Irwin, 1963

32 WALDMAN, H., 'Mithras Tauroctonus', in HINNELLS, J. R., *Studies* (no. 24 above), pp. 265–77

[XIX] Islam

Compiled by Edmund Bosworth, Louis Brenner, A. Rippin, Elizabeth Scantlebury and James Thrower

1 AHMAD, A., *Studies in Islamic Culture in the Indian environment*, Oxford, Clarendon Press, 1964

2 AHMAD, A., *An Intellectual History of Islam in India*, Edinburgh, Edinburgh University Press, 1969

3 AHSANI, S. A. H., and KASULE, O. H., 'Muslims in Latin America: A Survey. Parts I and II', *Journal of the Institute of Muslim Minority Affairs*, vol. 5, 1984, pp. 454–67

4 AKINER, S., *Islamic Peoples of the Soviet Union: A Historical and Statistical Handbook*, 2nd edn, London, Kegan Paul International, 1986

5 ALI, MUHAMMAD, *A Manual of Hadith*, 2nd edn, London and Dublin, Curzon Press/Atlantic Highlands, NJ, Humanities, 1978 (repr. of Lahore, 1951 edn with additional preface)

6 ANDRAE, T., *Die Person Muhammeds in Lehre und Glauben seiner Gemeinde*, Stockholm, Norstedt, 1918

7 ARBERRY, A. J., *Sufism: An Account of the Mystics of Islam*, London, Allen & Unwin, 1950, 1979

8 ARBERRY, A. J. (ed.), *Religion in the Middle East: Three Religions in Concord and Conflict*, vol. 2, *Islam*, Cambridge, Cambridge University Press, 1969

9 ARNALDEZ, R., *Jésus: fils de Marie, prophète de l'Islam*, Paris, Desclée de Brouwer, 1980

10 ARNOLD, SIR THOMAS W., *Painting in Islam: A Study of the Place of*

Pictorial Art in Muslim Culture, New York, Dover, 1965 (republ., with new introduction, of 1st 1928 edn); Magnolia, Mass., Peter Smith

11 ARNOLD, SIR THOMAS W., *The Caliphate*, London, Routledge, 1965, repr. 1967; New York, Barnes & Noble; first publ. Oxford, Clarendon Press, 1924

12 AYOUB, MAHMOUD, *The Qur'an and its Interpreters*, Albany, NY, State University of New York Press, 1984

13 BALDICK, J., *Mystical Islam: An Introduction to Sufism*, London, I. B. Tauris, 1989

14 BARTOL'D, V. V., *Four Studies in the History of Central Asia*, 3 vols (tr. V. and T. Minorsky), Leiden, Brill, 1956–63

15 BENNIGSEN, A., and BROXUP, M., *The Islamic Threat to the Soviet State*, London, Croom Helm, 1983

16 BENNIGSEN, A., and LEMERCIER-QUELQUEJAY, C., *The Evolution of the Muslim Nationalities of the USSR*, Oxford, Oxford University Press, 1961

17 BENNIGSEN, A., and LEMERCIER-QUELQUEJAY, C., *Islam in the Soviet Union*, London, Pall Mall Press, 1967

18 BIRGE, J. K., *The Bektashi Order of Dervishes*, London, Luzac/Hartford, Conn., Hartford Seminary Press, 1937; repr. New York, AMS, 1982

19 BOSWORTH, C. E., *Islamic Dynasties: A Chronological and Genealogical Handbook*, Edinburgh, Edinburgh University Press/New York, Columbia University Press, 1967; 2nd edn Edinburgh University Press, 1980

20 BRANDON, S. G. F. (ed.), *A Dictionary of Comparative Religion*, London, Weidenfeld/New York, Scribner, 1970

21 BROCKELMANN, C., *History of the Islamic Peoples* (tr. J. Carmichael and M. Perlmann), London, Routledge, 1952; New York, Capricorn, 1960; tr. prev. publ. New York, Putnam, 1947/ London, Routledge, 1949

22 BROWNE, E. G. (ed.), *Materials for the Study of the Bábí Religion*, Cambridge, Cambridge University Press, 1918

23 BURRELL, R. M., (ed.), *Islamic Fundamentalism*, London, Royal Asiatic Society, 1989

24 CANAAN, T., *Mohammedan Saints and Sanctuaries in Palestine*, London, Luzac, 1927

25 CHITTICK, W. C. (ed. and tr.), *A Shi'ite Anthology*, London, Muhammadi Trust, 1980; rev. edn A. Tabatabai, London, Kegan Paul International, 1985, 1987

26 CHOUEIRI, Y. M., *Islamic Fundamentalism, 1749–Present Day*, London, Pinter/Boston, Twayne, 1990

27 COULSON, N. J., *A History of Islamic Law*, Edinburgh, Edinburgh University Press, 1964, 1979

28 CRAGG, K., *Counsels in Contemporary Islam*, Edinburgh, Edinburgh University Press, 1965

29 CRAGG, K., *The Mind of the Qur'ān: Chapters in Reflection*, London, Allen & Unwin, 1973

30 DAFTARY, F., *The Ismā'īlīs: Their History and Doctrines*, Cambridge, Cambridge University Press, 1990; new edn 1992

31 DANIEL, N. A., *Islam and the West: The Making of an Image*, Edinburgh, Edinburgh University Press, 1960; 2nd rev. edn Oxford, Oneworld Publications, 1993

32 DASHTI, 'ALI (tr. BAGLEY, F. R. C.), *Twenty Three Years: A Study of the Prophetic Career of Mohammad*, London, Allen & Unwin, 1985

33 DONALDSON, D. M., *The Shi'ite Religion: A History of Islam in Persia and Irak*, London, Luzac, 1933; New York, Gordon Press, 1976

34 DONALDSON, D. M., *Studies in Muslim Ethics*, London, SPCK, 1953
35 DONNAN, H., and WERBNER, P. (eds), *Economy and Culture in Pakistan: Migrants and Cities in a Muslim Society*, London, Macmillan, 1991
36 DUNCAN, A., *The Noble Sanctuary: Portrait of a Holy Place in Arab Jerusalem*, London, Longman, 1972
37 *Encyclopaedia of Islam*, 5 vols, Leiden, Brill/London, Luzac, 1913–38; repr. 1987
38 *Encyclopaedia of Islam*, new edn, Leiden, Brill/London, Luzac, 1960–; New York, Humanities
39 ESIN, E., *Mecca the Blessed, Madinah the Radiant*, London, Elek/New York, Crown Publishing, 1963
40 ESSLEMONT, J. E., *Bahá'u'lláh and the New Era*, 3rd rev. edn, Wilmette, Ill., Bahá'í Publications Trust, 1970; 4th edn 1980; rev. edn Oakham, Leics., BPT, 1974
41 ETTINGHAUSEN, R., *Arab Painting*, Lausanne, Skira, 1962; London, Macmillan, 1977; New York, Rizzoli, 1977
42 FARMER, H. G., *A History of Arabian Music to the XIIIth Century*, London, Luzac, 1929; repr. 1973
43 AL-FARUQI, ISMA'IL, 'On the Nature of Islamic da'wah', *International Review of Missions*, vol. 65, 1976, pp. 391–409
44 FORSYTH, J., *A History of the Peoples of Siberia*, Cambridge, Cambridge University Press, 1992
45 FREEMAN-GRENVILLE, G. S. P., *The Muslim and Christian Calendars, Being Tables for the Conversion of Muslim and Christian Dates from the Hijra to the Year AD2000*, London, New York, Oxford University Press, 1963; 2nd edn London, R. Collings/Totowa, NJ, Rowman, 1977
46 GÄTJE, H., *The Qur'ān and Its Exegesis: Selected Texts, with Classical and Modern Muslim Interpretations* (tr. and ed. by A. T. Welch), London, Routledge/Berkeley, Cal., University of California Press, 1976
47 GAUDEFROY-DEMOMBYNES, M., *La Pélerinage à la Mekke: Étude d'histoire religieuse*, Paris, Geuthner, 1923; Philadelphia, Pa, Porcupine Press, 1977 (issued also as thesis, University of Paris, under title, 'Contribution a l'étude du pélerinage de la Mekke . . .', 1923)
48 GAUDEFROY-DEMOMBYNES, M., *Muslim Institutions*, London, Allen & Unwin, 1950
49 GERHOLM, T., and LITHMAN, Y. G. (eds), *The New Islamic Presence in Western Europe*, London, Mansell, 1988
50 GIBB, H. A. R., *The Arab Conquest of Central Asia*, London, Royal Asiatic Society, 1923
51 GIBB, SIR HAMILTON A. R., *Modern Trends in Islam*, Chicago, Ill., University of Chicago Press, 1947, repr. New York, Octagon, 1971
52 GIBB, SIR HAMILTON A. R., *Islam: A Historical Survey*, 2nd edn, [London], Oxford University Press, 1975; as *Muhammedanism: An Historical Survey*, 2nd edn, OUP, repr. 1969
53 GLASSÉ, C., *The Concise Encyclopaedia of Islam* (ed. Peter Hobson), London, Stacey International, 1989, new edn, 1991
54 GOLDZIHER, I., *Muslim Studies* (ed. S. M. Stern), 2 vols, London, Allen & Unwin, 1967–71; Albany, NY, State University of New York, 1967–72
55 GRABAR, O., *The Formation of Islamic Art*, New Haven, Conn./London, Yale University Press, 1973
56 GRAHAM, W. A., *Beyond the Written Word: Oral Aspects of Scripture in the History of Religion*, Cambridge, Cambridge University Press, 1987 (1988); new edn 1993

57 GRAY, B., *Persian Painting*, Geneva, Skira, 1961; London, Macmillan, 1977; New York, Rizzoli, 1977

58 GUILLAUME, A., *The Traditions of Islam: An Introduction to the Study of Hadith Literature*, Oxford, Clarendon Press, 1924, repr. New York, Arno, 1980; new edn Richmond, Surrey, Curzon Press, 1993

59 GUILLAUME, A., *Islam*, Harmondsworth, Penguin, 1954, 1969

60 HADDAD, Y. Y. (ed.), *The Muslims of America*, New York, Oxford University Press, 1991; new edn 1994

61 HALM, H., *Shiism*, Edinburgh, Edinburgh University Press, 1991; new edn 1994

62 HAMBLY, G., et al., *Central Asia*, London, Weidenfeld, 1969

63 HISKETT, M., *The Development of Islam in West Africa*, London, Longman, 1984

64 HITTI, P. K., *History of the Arabs from the Earliest Times to the Present*, 10th edn, London, Macmillan/New York, St Martin's, 1970

65 HOLT, P. M., LAMBTON, A. K. S., and LEWIS, B. (eds), *The Cambridge History of Islam*, vol. 1, *The Central Islamic Lands*, vol. 2, *The Further Islamic Lands, Islamic Society and Civilization*, Cambridge, Cambridge University Press, 1970; new edn in 4 vols, 1977

66 HOURANI, A., *Arabic Thought in the Liberal Age, 1798–1939*, London/New York, Oxford University Press, 1962

67 HUGHES, T. P., *A Dictionary of Islam*, London, W. H. Allen/New York, Scribner, 1885, repr. Allen, 1935; London, Luzac, 1966; New York, Gordon Press, 1980; new edn Sittingbourne, Kent, Asia Publishing House, 1988

68 ISRAELI, R., *Muslims in China: A Study in Cultural Confrontation*, London, Curzon, 1980; Atlantic Highlands, NJ, Humanities, 1979

69 JAFRI, S. H. M., *Origins and Early Development of Shi'a Islam*, London, Longman/Beirut, Librairie du Liban, 1979

70 JEFFREY, A., *The Qur'an as Scripture*, New York, Moore, 1952; New York, Arno, 1980

71 JEFFREY, A., *A Reader on Islam: Passages from Standard Arabic Writings Illustrative of the Beliefs and Practices of Muslims*, The Hague, Mouton, 1962; New York, Arno, 1980

72 KASULE, OMAR HASAN, 'Muslims in Trinidad and Tobago', *Journal of the Institute of Muslim Minority Affairs*, vol. 7, 1986, pp. 195–213

73 KETTANI, M. A., *Muslim Minorities in the World Today*, London, Mansell, 1986

74 KHATIBI, A., and SIJELMASSI, M., *The Splendour of Islamic Calligraphy*, London, Thames & Hudson, 1976; New York, Rizzoli, 1977

75 KOZLOV, V. I., *The Peoples of the Soviet Union*, London, Hutchinson, 1988

76 KRAEDLER, L., *Peoples of Central Asia*, Uralic and Altai Series, vol. 26, Bloomington, Ind., Bloomington University Press, 1966

77 LANE, E. W., *An Account of the Manners and Customs of the Modern Egyptians*, London, Knight, 1836, often republ.; London, East–West Publications (UK), 1978; Magnolia, Mass., Peter Smith

78 LAOUST, H., *Les Schismes dans l'Islam: introduction à une étude de la religion musulmane*, Paris, Payot, 1965

79 LAWRENCE, B. B., *Defenders of God: The Fundamentalist Revolt Against the Modern Age*, San Francisco, Harper & Row, 1989

80 LEVY, R., *The Social Structure of Islam*, Cambridge, Cambridge University Press, 1957, 1969; 2nd edn of *The Sociology of Islam*

81 LEWIS, B., *The Assassins: A Radical Sect in Islam*, London, Weidenfeld, 1967; New York, Basic Books, 1968; repr. New York, Octagon, 1980

82 LEWIS, B. (ed.), *The World of Islam: Faith, People, Culture*, London, Thames & Hudson, 1976; US edn, *Islam and the Arab World*, Knopf, 1976; new edn London, Thames & Hudson, 1992

83 LINCOLN, C. E., *The Black Muslims in America*, new edn, Boston, Mass., Beacon Press, 1973

84 LINGS, M., *What is Sufism?*, London, Allen & Unwin, 1975; Berkeley, Cal., University of California Press, 1977; new edn Cambridge, Islamic Texts Society, 1993

85 LINGS, M., *Muhammad: His Life Based on the Earliest Sources*, London, Allen & Unwin, 1983; 2nd edn Cambridge, Islamic Texts Society, 1992

86 MCAULIFFE, J. D., *Qur'ānic Christians: An Analysis of Classical and Modern Exegesis*, Cambridge, Cambridge University Press, 1991

87 MACDONALD, D. B., *The Development of Muslim Theology, Jurisprudence and Constitutional Theory*, Karachi, 1960; London, Routledge, 1903, repr. New York, Russell, 1965

88 MACDONALD, D. B., *The Religious Attitude and Life in Islam*, Chicago, Ill., University of Chicago Press, 1909, repr. Beirut, Khayats, 1965; New York, AMS; new edn London, Darf Publications, 1985

89 MCPHERSON, J. W., *The Moulids of Egypt*, Cairo, NM Press, 1941; repr. New York, AMS, 1977

90 MARTIN, B. G., *Muslim Brotherhoods in Nineteenth Century Africa*, Cambridge, Cambridge University Press, 1976

91 MERMER, ALI, 'Aspects of Religious Identity: The Nurcu Movement in Turkey Today', PhD dissertation, Durham University, 1985

92 METCALF, B. D., *Islamic Revival in British India: Deoband, 1860–1900*, Princeton, NJ Princeton University Press, 1982

93 MITCHELL, G. (ed.), *Architecture of the Islamic World: Its History and Social Meaning*, London, Thames & Hudson/New York, Morrow, 1978

94 MITCHELL, R. P., *The Society of the Muslim Brothers*, London, Oxford University Press, 1969; new edn New York, Oxford University Press, 1993

95 MOMEN, MOOJAN, *An Introduction to Shi'i Islam: The History and Doctrines of Twelver Shi'ism*, New Haven, Conn./London, Yale University Press, 1985; new edn 1987

96 MOTTAHEDEH, R., *The Mantle of the Prophet: Learning and Power in Modern Iran*, London, Chatto & Windus, 1986

97 NETTON, I. R., *A Popular Dictionary of Islam*, London, Curzon/Atlantic Highlands, NJ, Humanities, 1992

98 NICHOLSON, R. A., *Studies in Islamic Mysticism*, Cambridge, Cambridge University Press, 1921, repr. 1967, 1979; new edn London, Curzon, 1994

99 NIELSEN, J., *Muslims in Western Europe*, Edinburgh, Edinburgh University Press, 1992

100 PADWICK, C. E., *Muslim Devotions: A Study of Prayer Manuals in Common Use*, London, SPCK, 1960

101 PARRINDER, G., *Jesus in the Qur'an*, London, Faber/New York, Barnes & Noble, 1965

102 PELLY, SIR LEWIS, *The Miracle Play of Hasan and Husain, Collected from Oral Tradition*, London, W. H. Allen, 1879; repr. Farnborough, Gregg, 1970

103 PERKINS, M., and HAINSWORTH, P., *The Bahá'í Faith*, London, Ward Lock Educational, 1980; new edn 1989

104 PETERS, R. (ed. and tr.), *Jihād in Mediaeval and Modern Islam: The*

Chapter on Jihād from Averroes' Legal Handbook . . ., Leiden, Brill, 1977

105 POSTON, L., *Islamic Da'wah in the West: Missionary Muslim Missionary Activity and the Dynamics of Conversion to Islam*, New York, Oxford University Press, 1992

106 POUWELS, R. L., *Horn and Crescent: Cultural Change and Traditional Islam on the East African Coast, 800–1900*, Cambridge, Cambridge University Press, 1987

107 RAHMAN, F., *Islam*, London, Weidenfeld/New York, Holt, Rinehart (© 1966); 2nd edn, Chicago, Ill., University of Chicago Press, 1979

108 RAHMAN, F., *Major Themes of the Qur'ān*, Minneapolis/Chicago, Bibliotheca Islamica, 1980

109 RINGGREN, H., *Studies in Arabian Fatalism*, Uppsala, Lundeqvist/ Wiesbaden, Harrassowitz, 1955

110 RIPPIN, A., *Muslims, Their Religious Beliefs and Practices*, vol. 1, *The Formative Period*, London/New York, Routledge, 1990 (Library of Religious Beliefs and Practices)

111 RIPPIN, A., *Muslims, Their Religious Beliefs and Practices*, vol. 2, *The Contemporary Period*, London, Routledge, 1993 (Library of Religious Beliefs and Practices)

112 RIPPIN, A., and KNAPPERT, J. (ed. and tr.), *Textual Sources for the Study of Islam*, Manchester, Manchester University Press, 1986; new edn Chicago University Press

113 ROBINSON, F., *Varieties of South Asian Islam*, Research Paper No. 8, Centre for Research in Ethnic Relations, Coventry, University of Warwick, 1988

114 RODINSON, M., *Mohammed*, London, Allen Lane/Penguin, 1971, new edn Harmondsworth, Penguin, 1991; New York, Pantheon, 1980

115 AL-SAID, LABIB, *The Recited Koran*, Princeton, NJ, Darwin Press, 1975

116 SAVORY, R. M. (ed.), *Introduction to Islamic Civilization*, Cambridge/ New York, Cambridge University Press, 1976

117 SCHACHT, J., *An Introduction to Islamic Law*, Oxford, Clarendon Press, 1964

118 SCHACHT, J., and BOSWORTH, C. E. (eds), *The Legacy of Islam*, 2nd edn, Oxford, Clarendon Press, 1974; repr. Oxford University Press

119 SCHIMMEL, A., *Islamic Calligraphy*, Leiden, Brill, 1970; New York, Adler

120 SCHIMMEL, A., *And Muhammad is His Messenger: The Veneration of the Prophet in Islamic Piety*, Chapel Hill, NC/London, University of North Carolina Press, 1985

121 SIVAN, E., *Radical Islam: Medieval Theology and Modern Politics*, New Haven, Conn., Yale University Press, 1985; 2nd edn 1990

122 THACKSTON, W. M., JR, *The Tales of the Prophets of al-Kisa'i*, Boston, Twayne, 1978

123 TIBAWI, A. L., *Islamic Education: Its Traditions and Modernization into the Arab National Systems*, London, Luzac, 1972; 2nd edn 1979

124 TRIMINGHAM, J. S., *A History of Islam in West Africa*, Oxford, Oxford University Press, 1962 (first publ. 1959); new edn 1970

125 TRIMINGHAM, J. S., *The Sufi Orders in Islam*, Oxford, Clarendon Press, 1971; Oxford University Press, 1973

126 TRIMINGHAM, J. S., *Christianity Among the Arabs in Pre-Islamic Times*, London, Longman/Beirut, Librairie du Liban, 1979

127 TRIMINGHAM, J. S., *The Influence of Islam upon Africa*, 2nd edn, London, Longman/Beirut, Librairie du Liban, 1980

128 TRITTON, A. S., *Materials on Muslim Education in the Middle Ages*, London, Luzac, 1957

129 TRITTON, A. S., *The Caliphs and their Non-Muslim Subjects: A Critical Study of the Covenant of 'Umar*, London, 1930; repr. London, Cass, 1970

130 VON GRUNEBAUM, G. E., *Muhammadan Festivals*, repr. London, Curzon Press, 1976; New York, Humanities, 1976; prev. publ. New York, Schuman, 1951; London, Abelard Schuman, 1958

131 WADDY, C., *Women in Muslim History*, London, Longman/Beirut, Librairie du Liban, 1980

132 WATT, W. M., *Muhammad, Prophet and Statesman*, London, Oxford University Press, 1961; new edn New York, Oxford University Press, 1974

133 WATT, W. M., *Islamic Philosophy and Theology*, Edinburgh, Edinburgh University Press, 1962; new edn 1979; 2nd rev. edn repr. 1987

134 WATT, W. M., *A History of Islamic Spain*, Edinburgh, Edinburgh University Press, 1965, 1978

135 WATT, W. M., *Islamic Political Thought: The Basic Concepts*, Edinburgh, Edinburgh University Press, 1968

136 WATT, W. M., *What is Islam?*, London, Longman/Beirut, Librairie du Liban, 1968; 2nd edn Longman, 1979; New York, Praeger, 1968

137 WATT, W. M., *Bell's Introduction to the Qur'ān Completely Revised and Enlarged*, Edinburgh, Edinburgh University Press, 1970, 1970

138 WATT, W. M., *The Formative Period of Islamic Thought*, Edinburgh, Edinburgh University Press, 1973

139 WAUGH, E. H., BAHA ABU-LABAN, R. B. QURESHI (eds), *The Muslim Community in North America*, Edmonton, Alberta, University of Alberta Press, 1983

140 WENSICKER, A. J., *The Muslim Creed: Its Genesis and Historical Development*, Cambridge, Cambridge University Press, 1932, London, Cass, 1965

141 WHEELER, G., *The Peoples of Soviet Central Asia*, London, Bodley Head, 1966

142 WILLIAMS, J. A., *Themes of Islamic Civilization*, Berkeley, Cal./London, University of California Press, 1971

143 WINNER, T. G., *The Oral Art and Literature of the Kazakhs of Russian Central Asia*, Durham, NC, Duke University Press, 1980, repr. of 1958 edn

144 ZENKOVSKY, S. A., *Pan-Turkism and Islam in Russia*, Cambridge, Mass., Harvard University Press, 1960

145 ZIADEH, N. A., *Sanūsıyah: A Study of a Revivalist Movement in Islam*, Leiden, Brill, 1958

[XX] *Jainism*

Compiled by Paul Dundas

1 BLOOMFIELD, M., *The Life and Stories of the Jaina Savior Pārśvanātha*, Baltimore, Md, Johns Hopkins University Press, 1919; New York, Arno Press, 1979

2 CARRITHERS, M., and HUMPHREY, C. (eds), *The Assembly of Listeners: Jains in Society*, Cambridge, Cambridge University Press, 1991

3 DELEU, J., *Viyāhapannatti (Bhagavaī): The Fifth Aṅga of the Jaina Canon*, Brugge, Rijksuniversiteit te Gent, 1970

4 DUNDAS, P., *The Jains*, London/New York, Routledge, 1992 (Library of Religious Beliefs and Practices)

5 GLASENAPP, H. VON, *The Doctrine of Karma in Jain Philosophy*, Bombay, Bai Vijibai Jivanlal Panalal Charity Fund, 1942

6 HINUBER, O. VON, *Das Ältere Mittelindisch im Überblick*, Vienna, Österreichischen Akademie der Wissenschaften, 1986

7 JACOBI, H. (tr.), *Jaina Sutras: Part One* (*Sacred Books of the East*, vol. 26), New York, Dover, repr. 1968; Delhi, Motilal Banarsidass, 1989; first publ. Oxford, Clarendon Press, 1884

8 JACOBI, H. (tr.), *Jaina Sutras: Part Two* (*Sacred Books of the East*, vol. 45), New York, Dover, repr. 1968; new edn of 1881 edn Delhi, Motilal Banarsidass; first publ. Oxford, Clarendon Press, 1895

9 JAINI, P. S., *Gender and Salvation: Jaina Debates on the Spiritual Liberation of Women*, Berkeley, Cal., Los Angeles/Oxford, University of California Press, 1991

10 JAINI, P. S. *The Jaina Path of Purification*, Berkeley, Cal., University of California Press, 1979; Indian edn Delhi, Motilal Banarsidass, 1979

11 MATILAL, B. K., *The Central Philosophy of Jainism (Anekānta-Vāda)*, Ahmedabad, L. D. Institute of Indology, 1981

12 SCHUBRING, W., *The Doctrine of the Jainas*, Delhi, Motilal Banarsidass, 1962; English tr. by W. Beurlen of *Die Lehre der Jainas*, Berlin, de Gruyter, 1935

13 SCHUBRING, W., *Kleine Schriften*, Wiesbaden, Steiner, 1977

14 SHAH, U. P., *Jaina-Rūpa-Maṇḍana* (Jaina Iconography), New Delhi, Abhinar Publications, 1987

[XXI]   *Japanese Religions*

Compiled by J. Edward Kidder

1 ANDREWS, A. A., *The Teachings Essential for Rebirth*, Tokyo, Sophia University Press, 1973

2 ANESAKI, M., *Nichiren the Buddhist Prophet*, Cambridge, Mass., Harvard University Press/London, Oxford University Press, 1916; Magnolia, Mass., Peter Smith

3 ASTON, W. G. (tr.), NIHONGI, *Chronicles of Japan from the Earliest Times to AD 697*, 2 vols, London, Allen & Unwin, 1956, prev. publ. London, Kegan Paul, 1896; Rutland, Vt, Tuttle, 1971, 1972

4 BLACKER, C., *The Catalpa Bow: A Study of Shamanistic Practices in Japan*, London, Allen & Unwin/Totowa, NJ, Rowman, 1975

5 BLOOM, A., *Shinran's Gospel of Pure Grace*, Tucson, University of Arizona Press, 1965

6 BOCK, F. (tr.), ENGI-SHIKI, *Procedures of the Engi Era* (bks I–V), Tokyo, Sophia University Press, 1970

7 BOXER, C. R., *The Christian Century in Japan, 1549–1650*, Berkeley, Cal., University of California Press, 1967 (© 1951), 1974

8 BUNCE, W. K. (ed.), *Religions in Japan: Buddhism, Shinto, Christianity*, 3rd edn, Rutland, Vt/Tokyo, Tuttle, 1959; London, Greenwood, 1978

9 CASAL, U. A., *The Five Sacred Festivals of Ancient Japan: Their Symbolism and Historical Development*, Tokyo, Sophia University/Rutland, Vt, Tuttle, 1967

10 CHAMBERLAIN, B. H. (tr.), *Kojiki; or, Records of Ancient Matters. Transactions of the Asiatic Society of Japan*, vol. 10, Supplement, Tokyo, 1882

11 DE VISSER, M. W., *Ancient Buddhism in Japan: Sutras and Ceremonies in Use in the Seventh and Eighth Centuries AD, and their History in Later Times*, 2 vols, Leiden, Brill, 1935

12 DRUMMOND, R. H., *A History of Christianity in Japan*, Grand Rapids, Mich., Eerdmans, 1971

13 DUMOULIN, H., *A History of Zen Buddhism*, New York, Random House, 1963 (*see also* XII, 29)

14 EARHART, H. B., *Japanese Religion: Unity and Diversity*, 2nd edn, Encino, Cal., Dickenson, 1974; 3rd rev. edn, Belmont, Cal., Wadsworth, 1982

15 EARHART, H. B., *A Religious Study of the Mount Haguro Sect of Shugendō: An Example of Japanese Mountain Religion*, Tokyo, Sophia University, 1970; New York, International Publications Service, 1970

16 ELIOT, SIR CHARLES, *Japanese Buddhism*, London, Routledge/New York, Barnes & Noble, 1959; prev. publ. London, Arnold, 1935; new edn (ed. Sir George Sansom) Richmond, Surrey, Curzon Press, 1993

17 GRONER, P., *Saichō: The Establishment of the Japanese Tendai School*, Berkeley, Cal., University of California Press, 1984

18 HAKEDA, Y. S. (tr.) *Kūkai: Major Works*, New York, Columbia University Press, 1972

19 HERBERT, J., *Shinto: At The Fountainhead of Japan*, New York, Stein & Day/London, Allen & Unwin, 1967

20 HORI, I., *Folk Religion in Japan: Continuity and Change*, Chicago, Ill., University of Chicago Press/Tokyo, University of Tokyo Press, 1968; University of Chicago Press, 1974

21 HORI, I., et al. (eds), *Japanese Religion: A Survey by the Agency for Cultural Affairs*, 2nd edn, Tokyo/Palo Alto, Cal., Kodansha International, 1974

22 IGLEHART, C. W., *A Century of Protestant Christianity in Japan*, Rutland, Vt/Tokyo, Tuttle, 1959

23 INAGAKI, H., *A Dictionary of Japanese Buddhist Terms*, 2nd edn, Kyoto, Nagata Bunshodo, 1985

24 *Japanese–English Buddhist Dictionary*, Tokyo, Daitō Shuppansha, 1965

25 KAMSTRA, J. H., *Encounter or Syncretism: The Initial Growth of Japanese Buddhism*, Leiden, Brill, 1967

26 KIDDER, J. E., *Japanese Temples: Sculpture, Paintings, Gardens and Architecture*, Tokyo, Bijutsu Shuppansha/Amsterdam, Abrams/London, Thames & Hudson, 1964

27 KITAWAGA, J. M., *Religion in Japanese History*, New York, Columbia University Press, 1966

28 LAURES, J., *The Catholic Church in Japan: A Short History*, Rutland, Vt/Tokyo, Tuttle, 1954; repr. Westport, Conn./London, Greenwood

29 MASUNAGA, R., *The Sōtō Approach to Zen*, Tokyo, Layman Buddhist Society, 1958

30 MATSUNAGA, A., *The Buddhist Philosophy of Assimilation: The Historical Development of the Honji-Suijaku Theory*, Rutland, Vt, Tuttle/Tokyo, Sophia University Press, 1969

31 NAKAMURA, H., HORI, I., and NOMA, S., *Japan and Buddhism*, Tokyo, Association of the Buddhist Jayanti, 1959

32 ONO, S., *Shinto: The Kami Way*, Rutland, Vt/Tokyo, Bridgeway Press (Tuttle), 1962; prev. publ. as *The Kami Way: An Introduction to Shrine Shinto*, 1960

33 PHILIPPI, D. L. (tr.), *Norito: A New Translation of the Ancient Japanese Ritual Prayers*, Tokyo, Institute for Japanese Culture and Classics, Kokugakuin University, 1959

34 PONSONBY-FANE, R. A. B., *Studies in Shinto and Shrines*, Kyoto, Ponsonby-Fane Memorial Society, 1953; prev. publ. 1943; publ. as vol. 1 of *Collected Works*, New York, International Publications Service, 1954

35 PONSONBY-FANE, R. A. B., *The Vicissitudes of Shinto*, Kyoto, Ponsonby-Fane Memorial Society, 1963; publ. as vol. 5 of *Collected Works*, New York, International Publications Service, 1963

36 SAUNDERS, E. D., *Buddhism in Japan, with an Outline of Its Origins in India*, Philadelphia, Pa, University of Pennsylvania Press, 1964; repr. London/Westport, Conn., Greenwood, 1977; Berkeley, Cal., University of California Press, 1964

37 SUZUKI, D. T., *Zen and Japanese Culture*, New York, Pantheon, 1959; London, Routledge/Princeton, NJ, Princeton University Press, 1959, new edn 1992; rev. and enlarged edn of *Zen Buddhism and Its Influence on Japanese Culture*, 1938

38 TAJIMA, R., *Les Deux Grands Mandalas et la doctrine de l'ésotérisme Shingon*, Paris/Tokyo, Presses Universitaires de France, Maison Franco-Japonaise, 1959

(*See also* XXVI, NEW RELIGIOUS MOVEMENTS IN JAPAN)

[XXII]   *Judaism*

Compiled by Alan Unterman

1 ABRAHAMS, I., *Jewish Life in the Middle Ages*, New York, Atheneum, 1969, repr. 1975; first publ. 1896, repr. by arrangement with the Jewish Publication Society of America

2 ALTMANN, A., *Moses Mendelssohn: A Biographical Study*, Philadelphia, Pa, Jewish Publication Society of America/[Tuscaloosa, Ala], University of Alabama Press/London, Routledge, 1973

3 AUERBACH, J. S., *Rabbis and Lawyers: The Journey from Torah to Constitution*, Bloomington, Ind., Indiana University Press, 1990

4 BARON, S. W., *A Social and Religious History of the Jews*, 2nd edn, 17 vols, Philadelphia, Pa, Jewish Publication Society of America; New York/London, Columbia University Press, 1952–76; vol. 18, Index, 1983

5 BIALE, R., *Women and Jewish Law: An Exploration of Women's Issues in Halakhic Sources*, New York, Schocken, 1984, 1986

6 BLAU, J. L. (ed.), *Reform Judaism: A Historical Perspective*, New York, Ktav, 1973

7 BOROWITZ, E. B., *Reviewing the Covenant: A Theology for the Post Modern Jew*, Philadelphia, Pa, Jewish Publication Society, 1991

8 BUBER, M., *Early Masters*, vol. 1 of *Tales of the Hasidim*, 2 vols, New York, Schocken, 1961, repr. 1968–9, new edn 1970; new edn in 1 vol 1991; prev. publ. London, Thames & Hudson, 1956

9 BUBER, M., *Later Masters*, vol. 2 of *Tales of the Hasidism* (no. 8 above)

10 COHEN, A., *Everyman's Talmud*, London, Dent/New York, Dutton, 1949; New York, Schocken, 1975, new edn 1978; prev. publ. London, Dent, 1932

11 COHEN, A. A., and MENDES-FLOHR, P., *Contemporary Jewish Religious Thought: Original Essays on Critical Concepts, Movements, and Beliefs*, New York, Free Press, 1988; Collier-Macmillan, 1988

12 DANBY, H. (tr.), *The Mishnah*, London, Oxford University Press, 1954; first publ. 1933

13 DERSHOWITZ, A. M., *Chutzpah*, Boston, Mass., Little, Brown, 1991
14 *Encyclopaedia Judaica*, 16 vols and yearbooks, Jerusalem, Keter, 1971–2; New York, Macmillan
15 EPSTEIN, I. (ed.), *The Babylonian Talmud*, 18 vols, London, Soncino, 1961; 35 vols, London, Haarlem, 1935–52
16 EPSTEIN, I., *Judaism*, Harmondsworth, Penguin, 1959, repr. 1968; new edn 1990
17 FACKENHEIM, E. L., *To Mend the World: Foundations of Future Jewish Thought*, New York, Schocken, 1982
18 FELDMAN, D. M., *Marital Relations: Birth Control and Abortion in Jewish Law*, New York, Schocken, 1974; new edn publ. as *Birth Control in Jewish Law: Marital Relations, Contraception and Abortion*, London, Greenwood, 1980
19 FINKELSTEIN, L., *The Jews*, vol. 2, *Their Religion and Culture*, new edn, New York, Schocken, 1971
20 FRIEDLANDER, A. H., *Out of the Whirlwind: A Reader of Holocaust Literature*, New York, Schocken, 1976, repr. 1978; New York, Union of American Hebrew Congregations, 1968
21 GOLD, M., *Does God Belong in the Bedroom?*, Philadelphia, Pa, Jewish Publication Society, 1992
22 GRUENWALD, I., *Apocalyptic and Merkavah Mysticism*, Leiden, Brill, 1980
23 GRUNFELD, I., *The Jewish Dietary Laws*, 2 vols, London/New York, Socino, 1972
24 GUTTMANN, J., *Philosophies of Judaism: The History of Jewish Philosophy from Biblical Times to Franz Rosenzweig*, New York, Holt, Rinehart/ London, Routledge, 1964; New York, Schocken, 1974
25 HERTZBERG, A., *Jewish Polemics*, New York, Columbia University Press, 1992
26 HERTZBERG, A. (ed.), *The Zionist Idea: A Historical Analysis and Reader*, New York, Atheneum, repr. 1971; repr. of 1959 edn Westport, Conn., Greenwood, 1970
27 HESCHEL, S. (ed.), *On Being A Jewish Feminist: A Reader*, New York, Schocken, 1983
28 HUSIK, I., *A History of Mediaeval Jewish Philosophy*, New York, Meridian/Philadelphia, Pa, Jewish Publication Society, 1960; New York, Atheneum, 1969; prev. publ. New York, Macmillan, 1916
29 IDELSOHN, A. Z., *Jewish Liturgy and its Development*, New York, Schocken, 1967; prev. publ. New York, Holt, Rinehart, 1932
30 JACOBS, L., *A Jewish Theology*, London, Darton, 1973; New York, Behrman, 1973
31 JACOBS, L., *Principles of Jewish Faith: An Analytic Study*, London, Vallentine, Mitchell/New York, Basic Books, 1964; new edn Northvale, NJ, Aronson/London, Kuperard, 1989
32 JACOBSON, H., *Roots Schmoots: Journeys among Jews*, New York, Penguin, 1993
33 JAKOBOVITS, I., *Jewish Medical Ethics*, New York, Bloch, 1967; rev. edn 1975
34 KANIEL, M., *Judaism*, Poole, Dorset, Blandford, 1979 (The Art of World Religions)
35 KATZ, J., *Exclusiveness and Tolerance: Jewish–Gentile Relations in Medieval and Modern Times*, New York, Schocken, 1962; repr. of 1961 edn Westport, Conn./London, Greenwood, 1980
36 KEDOURIE, E. (ed.), *The Jewish World*, London, Thames & Hudson, 1979; New York, Abrams, 1979

37 KELLNER, M. M. (ed.), *Contemporary Jewish Ethics*, New York, Sanhedrin, 1978

38 LAMM, N., *Torah Umadda: The Encounter of Religious Learning and Worldly Knowledge in the Jewish Tradition*, Northvale, NJ, Aronson, 1990

39 LANDAU, D., *Piety and Power: The World of Jewish Fundamentalism*, London, Secker & Warburg, 1993

40 LAQUEUR, W., *A History of Zionism*, New York, Holt, Rinehart, 1972; New York, Schocken, 1976; new edn 1989

41 LIEBERMAN, S., *Hellenism in Jewish Palestine: Studies in the Literacy Transmission, Beliefs and Manners of Palestine in the I Century BCE – IV century CE*, 2nd edn, New York, Jewish Theological Seminary of America, 1962

42 MAIMONIDES, i.e. MOSES, BEN MAIMON, *The Guide of the Perplexed* (tr. S. Pines), Chicago, Ill., University of Chicago Press, 1974, 1963; new edn in 2 vols 1975

43 MARGOLIS, M. L., and MARX, A., *A History of the Jewish People*, New York, Harper Torchbooks, 1965: New York, Atheneum, 1969; prev. publ. Philadelphia, Pa, Jewish Publication Society, 1927

44 MENDES-FLOHR, P., and REINHARZ, J., *The Jew in the Modern World: A Documentary History*, New York, Oxford University Press, 1980

45 MONTEFIORE, C. G., and LOEWE, H. (eds), *A Rabbinic Anthology*, New York, Schocken, 1974, repr. of 1968 Macmillan edn with new prolegomena

46 MOORE, G. F., *Judaism in the First Centuries of the Christian Era*, 3 vols, Cambridge, Mass., Harvard University Press, 1927; repr. 1966

47 NAMENYI, E., *The Essence of Jewish Art*, New York/London, Yoseloff, 1960

48 NEUSNER, J., *The Rabbinic Traditions about the Pharisees before 70*, Leiden, Brill, 1971

49 RABINOWICZ, H., *The World of Hasidism*, London, Vallentine, Mitchell/Hartford, Conn., Hartmore, 1970

50 REITLINGER, G., *The Final Solution: The Attempt to Exterminate the Jews in Europe, 1939–1945*, new rev. edn, New York, Yoseloff/London, Vallentine Mitchell, 1968; San Diego, Cal., A. S. Barnes, 1961

51 RIVKIN, E., *A Hidden Revolution: The Pharisees' Search for the Kingdom Within*, Nashville, Tenn., Abingdon, 1978; London, SPCK, 1979

52 ROSENBERG, B. H., and HEUMAN, F. (eds), *Theological and Halakhic Reflections on the Holocaust*, Hoboken, NJ, Ktav, 1992

53 ROTH, C., *A History of the Jews in England*, 3rd edn, Oxford, Clarendon Press, 1979

54 ROTH, C., *A History of the Marranos*, rev. edn, Philadelphia, Pa, Jewish Publication Society, 1947; New York, Schocken, 1974; repr. of 1932 edn New York, Arno, 1975

55 ROTH, C., *A Short History of the Jewish People*, rev. and enlarged edn, London, East and West Library, 1969; repr. Hartmore, Conn., Hartmore, 1970; New York, Hebrew Publications, 1978

56 RUDAVSKY, D., *Modern Jewish Religious Movements: A History of Emancipation and Adjustment*, New York, Behrman, 1967; 3rd rev. edn 1979; first publ. as *Emancipation and Adjustment: Contemporary Jewish Religious Movements*, New York, Diplomatic Press/London, Living Books, 1967

57 SACHAR, H. M., *The Course of Modern Jewish History*, New York, Delta, Dell, 1958, rev. edn 1977; Cleveland, World Publishing Co./London, Weidenfeld, 1958

58 SACKS, J., *One People? Tradition, Modernity, and Jewish Unity*, London, Littman Library of Jewish Civilization, 1993

59 SCHAUSS, H., *Guide to Jewish Holy Days*, New York, Schocken, repr. 1970

60 SCHIFFMAN, L. H., *Who Was A Jew? Rabbinic and Halakhic Perspectives on the Jewish–Christian Schism*, Hoboken, NJ Ktav, 1985

61 SCHOLEM, G. G., *Major Trends in Jewish Mysticism*, 3rd edn, repr. New York, Schocken, 1961; prev. publ. Schocken, 1954; London, Thames & Hudson, 1955; 3rd edn Schocken, 1976

62 SCHOLEM, G. G., *The Messianic Idea in Judaism and other Essays on Jewish Spirituality*, New York, Schocken/London, Allen & Unwin, 1971

63 SCHURER, E., *The History of the Jewish People in the Age of Jesus Christ*, vol. 2 (rev. and ed. G. Vermes, F. Millar and M. Black), Edinburgh, T. & T. Clark, 1979

64 SINGER, S. (tr.), *The Authorized Daily Prayer Book*, 2nd rev. edn, London, Eyre & Spottiswoode, 1968

65 SKLARE, M., *Conservative Judaism: An American Religious Movement*, new, augmented edn, New York, Schocken, 1972; new edn University Press of America, 1985

66 SOLOMON, N., *Judaism and World Religion*, London, Macmillan, 1991

67 STEINSALTZ, A., *The Essential Talmud* (tr. from the Hebrew by Chaya Galai), New York/London, Bantam, 1977

68 STRACK, H. L., *Introduction to the Talmud and Midrash*, New York, Meridian/Philadelphia, Pa, Jewish Publication Society, 1959; New York, Atheneum, 1969; publ. as *Introduction to the Talmud and Midrash* by H. L. Strack and G. Stemberger, Edinburgh, T. & T. Clark, 1991

69 UNTERMAN, A., *Dictionary of Jewish Lore and Legend*, London, Thames & Hudson, 1991

70 UNTERMAN, A., *Jews: Their Religious Beliefs and Practices*, London/Boston, Mass., Routledge, 1981; new edn 1991

71 UNTERMAN, A., *Judaism*, London, Ward Lock Educational, 1981

72 WEINGREEN, J., *From Bible to Mishna*, Manchester, Manchester University Press/New York, Holmes & Meier, 1976

73 ZIMMELS, H. J., *Askenazim and Sephardim*, London, Oxford University Press, 1958

[XXIII]   Latin American Religions

Compiled by Robin M. Wright

1 AGOSTINHO, P., *Kwarip: Mito e Ritual no Alto Xingu*, São Paulo, Editora Pedagógica e Universitária/Universidade de São Paulo, 1974

2 BARANDIARAN, D. DE, 'Vida y Muerte entre los Indios Sanema–Yanoama', *Antropológica* (Caracas), vol. 21, Dec. 1967, pp. 3–65

3 BASSO, E. B., *A Musical View of the Universe: Kalapalo Myth and Ritual Performances*, Philadelphia, Pa, University of Pennsylvania Press, 1985

4 BROWMAN, D. L., and SCHWARZ, R. A. (eds), *Spirits, Shamans, and Stars: Perspectives from South America*, The Hague, Mouton, 1979

5 BUTT, A. J., 'The Birth of a Religion', *Journal of the Royal Anthropological Institute of Great Britain and Ireland*, vol. 90, 1960, pp. 66–106

6 CADOGAN, L., *Ayvu Rapyta. Textos Miticos de los Mbyá–Guarani del Guairá*, Boletin no. 227, São Paulo, Universidade de São Paulo, 1959 (Anthropology Series, no. 5)

7 CARNEIRO DA CUNHA, M., *Os Mortos e os Outros: Uma Análise do Sistema*

Funerário e da Noção de Pessoa entre os Indios Krahó, São Paulo, Hucitec, 1978

8 CIVRIEUX, M. DE, *Religion y Magia Kar'ña*, Caracas, Universidad Católica 'Andrés Bello', Instituto de Investigaciones Historicas, 1974

9 CIVRIEUX, M. DE, *Watunna: An Orinoco Creation Cycle* (ed. and tr. D. M. Guss), San Francisco, North Point Press, 1980

10 COOPER, J., 'Stimulants and Narcotics', in STEWARD, J. H. (ed.), *Handbook of South American Indians*, Washington, DC, USGPO, vol. 5, 1948, pp. 1525–58

11 CROCKER, J. C., *Vital Souls: Bororo Cosmology, Natural Symbolism, and Shamanism*, Tucson, University of Arizona Press, 1985

12 FOCK, N., *Waiwai: Religion and Society of an Amazonian Tribe*, Copenhagen, National Museum, 1963 (Nationalmuseets Skrifter, Ethnografisk Raekke vol. 8)

13 GOW, R., and CONDORI, B., *Kay Pacha*, Cuzco, Centro de Estudios Rurales Andinos 'Bartolomé de las Casas', 1976

14 HUGH-JONES, S., *The Palm and the Pleiades: Initiation and Cosmology in North-West Amazonia*, Cambridge/New York, Cambridge University Press, 1979

15 KENSINGER, K. M. (ed.), *Marriage Practices in Lowland South America*, Urbana, University of Illinois Press, 1984 (Illinois Studies in Anthropology 14)

16 LANGDON, E. J., and BAER, G. (eds), *Portals of Power: Shamanism in South America*, Albuquerque, University of New Mexico Press, 1992

17 LIZOT, J., *Le Cercle des Feux: Fais et Dits des Indiens Yanomani*, Paris, Seuil, 1976

18 LYON, P. J. (ed.), *Native South Americans: Ethnology of the Least Known Continent*, Boston, Mass., Little, Brown, 1974

19 MAYBURY-LEWIS, D. (ed.), *Dialectical Societies*, Cambridge, Mass., Harvard University Press, 1979

20 MÉTRAUX, A., *Religions et Magies Indiennes d'Amérique de Sud*, Paris, Gallimard, 1967

21 NIMUENDAJÚ, C., *Mitos de Creación y de Destruición del Mundo como Fundamentos de la Religión de los Apapokuva-Guarani*, Lima, Centro de Antropologia y Aplicación Prática, 1978

22 NUÑEZ DEL PRADO, J. V., 'The Supernatural World of the Quechua of Southern Peru as Seen from the Community of Qotobamba,' in LYON, P. J. (ed.), *Native South Americans: Ethnology of the Least Known Continent*, Boston, Mass., Little, Brown, 1974

23 OLIVERA, M. A., 'Mapuche Religion', in M. Eliade, ed., *Encyclopedia of Religions*, New York/London, Macmillan, 1987, vol. 9, pp. 185–7

24 OSSIO, A., and JUAN, M., *Ideologia Messiánica del Mundo Andina*, Lima, Ignacio Prado Pastor, 1973

25 PERRIN, M., *The Way of Dead Indians: Myths and Symbols among the Goajiro*, Austin, Texas, University of Texas Press, 1987

26 REICHEL-DOLMATOFF, G., *Amazonian Cosmos: The Sexual and Religious Symbolism of the Tukano Indians*, Chicago, Ill., University of Chicago Press, 1971

27 REICHEL-DOLMATOFF, G., 'Funerary Customs and Religious Symbolism among the Kogi', in LYON, P. J. (ed.), *Native South Americans: Ethnology of the Least Known Continent*, Boston, Mass., Little, Brown, 1974

28 REICHEL-DOLMATOFF, G., *The Shaman and the Jaguar: A Study of Narcotic Drugs Among the Indians of Colombia*, Philadelphia, Pa, Temple University Press, 1975

29 ROE, P. G., *The Cosmic Zygote: Cosmology in the Amazon Basin*, New Brunswick, NJ, Rutgers University Press, 1982

30 SCHADEN, E., 'Le Messianisme en Amérique de Sud', in PEUCH, H-C. (ed.), *Histoire des Religions*, vol. 3, Paris, Gallimard, 1976

31 SCHADEN, E., 'Les Religions Indigènes en Amérique du Sud', in PEUCH, H-C. (ed.), *Histoire des Religions*, vol. 3, Paris, Gallimard, 1976

32 SCHERZER, J., and URBAN, G. (eds), *Native South American Discourse*, Amsterdam, Mouton de Gruyter, 1986

33 SULLIVAN, L. E., *Icanchu's Drums: An Orientation to Meaning in South American Religions*, New York, Macmillan, 1988

34 URTON, G. (ed.), *Animal Myths and Metaphors in South America*, Salt Lake City, Utah, University of Utah Press, 1985

35 URTON, G., *At the Crossroads of the Earth and Sky: An Andean Cosmology*, Austin, Tex., University of Texas Press, 1981

36 VIVEIROS DE CASTRO, E. B., *Araweté: os Deuses Canibais*, Rio de Janeiro, Zahar Editores/ANPOCS, 1986

37 WACHTEL, N., *The Vision of the Vanquished: The Spanish Conquest of Peru through Indian Eyes, 1530–1570*, New York, Barnes & Noble, 1977

38 WEISS, G., *The World of a Forest Tribe in South America*, New York, American Museum of Natural History, 1975 (Anthropological Papers of the American Museum of Natural History, vol. 52, part 5)

39 WILBERT, J., *Folk Literature of the Warao Indians: Narrative Material and Motif Content*, Los Angeles, UCLA Latin American Center, 1970

40 WILBERT, J., and SIMONEAU, K. (eds), *Folk Literature of the Mataco Indians*, Los Angeles, UCLA Latin American Center, 1987

41 WRIGHT, P., 'Dream, Shamanism and Power among the Toba of Formosa Province', in LANGDON, E. J., and BAER, G. (eds), *Portals of Power: Shamanism in South America*, pp. 149–74, Albuquerque, University of New Mexico Press, 1992

42 WRIGHT, R. M., 'Guardians of the Cosmos: Baniwa Shamans and Prophets', Parts I and II, *History of Religions* (University of Chicago), August/November 1992, pp. 32–58, 126–45

[XXIV]   *Magic and the Occult*

Compiled by Grevel Lindop and Keith Munnings

1 BARBER, M., *The Trial of the Templars*, Cambridge/New York, Cambridge University Press, 1991, 1978; new edn 1993

2 BLAU, J. L., *The Christian Interpretation of the Cabala in the Renaissance*, Port Washington, NY, Kennicat, 1965, repr. of 1944 edn, New York, Columbia University Press

3 BLAVATSKY, H. P., *An Abridgement of The Secret Doctrine* (ed. E. Preston and C. Humphreys), London, Theosophical Publishing House, 1971, 1966

4 BOWLES, N., and HYNDS, F., *Psi Search: The Comprehensive Guide to Psychic Phenomena*, New York, Harper & Row, 1978/London, 1979

5 BUTLER, C., *Number Symbolism*, London, Routledge/New York, Barnes & Noble, 1970

6 COUDERT, A., *Alchemy: The Philosopher's Stone*, Boulder, Colo, Shambhala, 1980

7 DEWAR, J., *The Unlocked Secret: Freemasonry Examined*, London, Corgi, 1990; Kimber, 1966, repr. 1972

8 DRURY, N., and TILLETT, G., *The Occult Experience*, London/Boston, Mass., Routledge, 1978; London, Hale, 1991

9 DUMMETT, M., *The Game of Tarot*, London, Duckworth, 1980

10 EVANS-PRITCHARD, SIR EDWARD E., *Witchcraft, Oracles and Magic among the Azande*, Oxford, Clarendon Press, 1937, repr. 1951; abridged edn, Oxford University Press, 1976

11 GARDNER, G. B., *Witchcraft Today*, London, Rider, 1954; Secaucus, NJ, Citadel Press, 1955, 1970

12 GILCHRIST, C., *Divination – The Search for Meaning*, London, Dryad Press, 1987

13 HARTMANN, F., *The Life and Doctrines of Jacob Boehme*, London, Kegan Paul, Trench, Trubner, 1891; facsimile of 1929 edn, Hastings, Society of Metaphysicians, 1986

14 HEMLEBEN, J., *Rudolf Steiner: A Documentary Biography*, East Grinstead, Goulden, 1975

15 HOPPER, V. F., *Medieval Number Symbolism*, New York, Columbia University Press, 1938; Folcroft, Pa, Folcroft Library, 1938

16 HOWE, E., *The Magicians of the Golden Dawn: A Documentary History of a Magical Order*, London, Routledge, 1972; New York, Weiser, 1978

17 JUNG, C. G., *Psychology and Alchemy* (tr. R. F. C. Hull), London, Routledge, 1992 (1953); Princeton, NJ, Princeton University Press, 1980; publ. as vol. 12 of *Collected Works*, New York, Pantheon, 1953, 2nd edn 1966

18 KING, F., *Ritual Magic in England, 1887 to the Present Day*, London, Spearman, 1970; US edn publ. as *The Rites of Modern Occult Magic*, New York, Macmillan, 1971

19 KNIGHT, G., *The Practice of Ritual Magic*, 3rd edn, Wellingborough, Aquarian Press, 1979; New York, Weiser

20 LAGUERRE, M., *Voodoo Heritage*, Beverley Hills, Cal./London, Sage, 1980

21 'LEVI, ELIPHAS' (CONSTANT, A. L.), *The History of Magic* (tr. A. E. Waite), London, Rider, 1969; New York, Gordon Press

22 LEWINSOHN, R., *Prophecy and Prediction*, London, Secker, 1961

23 NELSON, G. K., *Spiritualism and Society*, London, Routledge/New York, Schocken, 1969

24 OUSPENSKY, P. D., *In Search of the Miraculous*, Harmondsworth, Penguin, 1992

25 RHODES, H. T. F., *The Satanic Mass*, New York/London, Rider, 1954; Secaucus, NJ, Citadel Press, 1955, 1974, 1975; New York, Wehman

26 ROBERTS, J. M., *The Mythology of the Secret Societies*, London, Secker/New York, Scribner, 1972

27 THOMAS, K., *Religion and the Decline of Magic*, London, Weidenfeld/New York, Scribner, 1971; Harmondsworth, Penguin, 1991, 1973

28 TOKSVIG, S., *Emanuel Swedenborg, Scientist and Mystic*, New Haven, Conn., Yale University Press, 1948; London, Faber, 1949

29 WALLIS, R. T., *Neoplatonism*, London, Duckworth, 1972

30 WEBB, J., *The Harmonious Circle*, London, Thames & Hudson/New York, Putnam, 1980

31 YATES, F. A., *The Art of Memory*, London, Routledge/Chicago, Ill., University of Chicago Press, 1966; rev. edn Harmondsworth, Penguin, 1970

32 YATES, F. A., *Giordano Bruno and the Hermetic Tradition*, Chicago, Ill., University of Chicago Press, 1991; London, Routledge, 1964, 1978; New York, Random House, 1969

33 YATES, F. A., *The Rosicrucian Enlightenment*, London, Routledge, 1972;

St Albans, Paladin, 1975; Boulder, Colo, Shambhala, 1978, London, Arkana/Penguin 1986

(*See also* II, 2, 5, 10; XII, 109; XXVII, 26; XXVIII, 1, 38, 40; XXIX, 12)

[XXV]   *Mesoamerican Religions*

Compiled by David Carrasco

1 BERNAL, I., *Mexico Before Cortez*, rev. edn, Garden City, NY, Anchor Books, Doubleday, 1975
2 BRUNDAGE, B., *The Fifth Sun*, Austin, Tex., University of Texas Press, 1979
3 CASO, A., *The Aztecs, People of the Sun*, Norman, Okla, University of Oklahoma Press, 1958, repr. 1970
4 COE, M., *The Maya*, New York, Praeger, 1973, prev. publ. New York. Praeger/London, Thames & Hudson, 1966, 5th rev. edn 1987; Harmondsworth, Penguin, 1971
5 CULBERT, T. P., *The Lost Civilization: The Story of the Classic Maya*, New York, Harper & Row, 1974
6 DAVIES, N., *The Toltecs, until the Fall of Tula*, Norman, Okla, University of Oklahoma Press, 1977
7 DURAN, D., *Book of the Gods and Rites and the Ancient Calendar* (tr. and ed. F. Horcasitas and D. Heyden), Norman, Okla, University of Oklahoma Press, 1975; first publ. 1971
8 EDMONSON, M., *Sixteenth-Century Mexico: The Work of Sahagun*, Albuquerque, University of New Mexico Press, 1974
9 HARDOY, J., *Pre-Columbian Cities*, New York, Walker/London, Allen & Unwin, 1973
10 KATZ, F., *The Ancient American Civilizations*, New York, Praeger/London, Weidenfeld, 1972
11 KUBLER, G., *The Art and Architecture of Ancient America*, 2nd edn, Harmondsworth, Baltimore, Md, Penguin, 1975; New York, Viking, 1976
12 LEON PORTILLA, M., *Aztec Thought and Culture*, Norman, Okla, University of Oklahoma Press, 1978, 1982; first publ. 1963
13 LEON PORTILLA, M., *Time and Reality in the Thought of the Maya*, Boston, Mass., Beacon Press, 1973; 2nd edn Norman, Okla, University of Oklahoma Press, 1990
14 LEON PORTILLA, M., *Pre Columbian Literatures of Mexico*, Norman, Okla, University of Oklahoma Press, 1969
15 ROBERTSON, D., *Mexican Manuscript Painting of the Early Colonial Period: The Metropolitan Schools*, New Haven, Conn., Yale University Press, 1959
16 SEJOURNE, L., *Burning Water: Thought and Religion in Ancient Mexico*, Berkeley, Cal., Shambhala, 1976; London, Thames & Hudson, 1978
17 WAUCHOPE, R. (gen. ed.), *Handbook of Middle American Indians*, vol. 10, *Archaeology of Northern Mesoamerica*, Austin, Tex., University of Texas Press, 1971
18 WHEATLEY, P., *The Pivot of the Four Quarters*, Chicago, Ill., Aldine, 1971
19 WOLF, E., *Sons of the Shaking Earth*, Chicago, Ill., University of Chicago Press, 1959, 1962

(*See also* XXVII, 3, 25)

[XXVI] *New Religious Movements in Japan*

Compiled by David Reid

1 CALDAROLA, C., *Christianity: The Japanese Way*, Leiden, Brill, 1979
2 DALE, K. J., and AKAHOSHI, S., *Circle of Harmony*, Pasadena, Cal., William Carey Library/Tokyo, Seibunsha, 1975
3 DAVIS, W., *Dojo: Magic and Exorcism in Contemporary Japan*, Stanford, Cal., Stanford University Press, 1980
4 DAVIS, W., *Japanese Religion and Society: Paradigms of Structure and Change*, Albany, NY, State University of New York Press, 1992
5 EARHART, H. B., *Gedatsu-kai and Religion in Contemporary Japan: Returning to the Center*, Bloomington, Ind./Indianapolis, Ind., Indiana University Press, 1989
6 EARHART, H. B., *The New Religions of Japan: A Bibliography of Western-Language Materials*, 2nd edn, Ann Arbor, Mich., University of Michigan Center for Japanese Studies, 1983
7 ELLWOOD, R. S., *The Eagle and the Rising Sun: Americans and the New Religions of Japan*, Philadelphia, Pa, Westminster, 1974
8 HARDACRE, H., *Kurozumikyō and the New Religions of Japan*, Princeton, NJ, Princeton University Press, 1986
9 HARDACRE, H., *Lay Buddhism in Contemporary Japan: Reiyūkai Kyōdan*, Princeton, NJ, Princeton University Press, 1984
10 HORI, I., et al. (eds), *Japanese Religion: A Survey by the Agency for Cultural Affairs* (tr. Abe Yoshiya and David Reid), Tokyo/Palo Alto, Cal., Kodansha International Ltd, 1972; 2nd edn 1974
11 MCFARLAND, H. N., *The Rush Hour of the Gods*, London/New York, Macmillan, 1967
12 MULLINS, M., 'Japanese Pentecostalism and the World of the Dead: a Study of Cultural Adaptation in Iesu no Mitama Kyōkai, *Japanese Journal of Religious Studies*, vol. 17, 1990, pp. 353–74
13 MULLINS, M., and YOUNG, R., (guest eds), *Japanese New Religions Abroad*, special issue of *Japanese Journal of Religious Studies*, vol. 18, 1991
14 OFFNER, C. B., and VAN STRAELEN, H., *Modern Japanese Religions: With Special Emphasis upon Their Doctrines of Healing*, Leiden, Brill/Tokyo, Enderle), 1963
15 PYE, M., 'National and International Identity in a Japanese Religion (Byakkō Shinkōkai)', in HAYES, V. (ed.), *Identity Issues and World Religions: Selected Proceedings of the XVth Congress of the International Association for the History of Religions*, South Australia, Australian Association for the Study of Religion, 1986
16 READER, I., *Religion in Contemporary Japan*, Basingstoke/London, Macmillan Academic and Professional Ltd/Honolulu, University of Hawaii Press, 1991
17 REID, D., *New Wine: The Cultural Shaping of Japanese Christianity*, Berkeley, Cal., Asian Humanities Press, 1991
18 THOMSEN, H., *The New Religions of Japan*, Tokyo, Tuttle, 1963; new edn London, Greenwood, 1978

(*See also* [XXI] JAPANESE RELIGIONS)

[XXVII]   New Religious Movements in Primal Societies

Compiled by Harold W. Turner

1 BARNETT, H. G., *Indian Shakers*, Carbondale, Ill., Southern Illinois University Press, 1957, 1972

2 BARRETT, D. B., *Schism and Renewal in Africa*, Nairobi, Oxford University Press, 1968

3 BARRETT, L. E., *The Rastafarians: The Dreadlocks of Jamaica*, Kingston, Jamaica, Sangsters/London, Heinemann Educational, 1977

4 BRUMANA, F. G., and MARTINEZ, E. G., *Spirits from the Margin: Umbanda in São Paulo*, 'Uppsala, Acta Universitatis Upsaliensis, Almqvist & Wiksell, 1990

5 DANEEL, M. L., *Quest for Belonging*, Gweru, Zimbabwe, Mambo Press, 1987

6 ELESTERIO, F. G., *Three Essays on Philippine Religious Culture*, Manila, De La Salle University Press, 1989

7 ELSMORE, B., *Mana from Heaven*, Tauranga, New Zealand, Moana Press, 1989

8 ELWOOD, D. J., *Churches and Sects in the Philippines*, Dumaguete City, Silliman University, 1968

9 FUCHS, S., *Rebellious Prophets: A Study of Messianic Movements in Indian Religions*, London/New York, Asia Publishing House, 1965

10 HALIBURTON, G. M., *The Prophet Harris*, London, Longman, 1971; New York, Oxford University Press, 1973

11 KAMMA, F., *Koreri: Messianic Movements in the Biak–Numfor Culture Area*, The Hague, Nijhoff, 1972

12 LANTERNARI, V., *Religious of the Oppressed*, New York, Knopf/London, Macgibbon & Kee, 1963; New York, Mentor, 1965

13 MARTIN, M.-L., *Kimbangu: An African Prophet and his Church*, Oxford, Blackwell, 1975; Grand Rapids, Mich., Eerdmans, 1976

14 O'BRIEN, D. B. C., *The Mourides of Senegal*, Oxford, Clarendon Press, 1971

15 PEEL, J. D. Y., *Aladura: A Religious Movement Among the Yoruba*, London, Oxford University Press, 1968

16 SIMPSON, G. E., *Black Religions in the New World*, New York, Columbia University Press, 1978

17 STEWART, O. C., *Peyote Religion: A History*, Norman, Okla, University of Oklahoma Press, 1987; new edn 1993

18 SUNDKLER, B. G. M., *Bantu Prophets in South Africa*, 2nd edn, London, Oxford University Press, 1961

19 TROMPF, G. W. (ed.), *Cargo Cults and Millenarian Movements*, Berlin/New York, Mouton de Gruyter, 1990

20 TURNER, H. W., *Bibliography of New Religious Movements in Primal Societies*, 6 vols, Boston, Mass., G. K. Hall, 1977–92

21 TURNER, H. W., *Religious Innovation in Africa*, Boston, Mass., G. K. Hall, 1979

22 TURNER, H. W., 'Tribal Religious Movements, New', in *Encyclopaedia Britannica*, 15th edn, *Macropaedia*, vol. 18, (© 1976), pp. 697–705

23 WALLACE, A. F. C., *Death and Rebirth of the Seneca*, New York, Knopf, 1970; New York, Random House; New York, Vintage, 1973

24 WHITTEMORE, L. B., *Struggle for Freedom: History of the Philippine Independent Church*, London, SPCK, 1961

25 WILLIAMS, K. M., *The Rastafarians*, London, Ward, Lock Educational, 1981

26 WILSON, B. R., *Magic and the Millennium*, London, Heinemann/New York, Harper & Row, 1973; New York, Beekman, 1978

26 WORSLEY, P., *The Trumpet Shall Sound*, 2nd edn, New York, Schocken/ London, MacGibbon & Kee, 1968

(*See also* XIII(B), 27)

[XXVIII]   *New Religious Movements in the West*

Compiled by Eileen Barker

1 ADLER, M., *Drawing Down the Moon; Witches, Druids, Goddess-Worshippers, and Other Pagans in America Today*, 2nd edn, Boston, Beacon Press, 1979; rev. edn 1986

2 ARMIN, R., *The Poem of the Church of Emin Coils*, London, Regal Print Company, 1978

AVERY, K. Q. *see* no. 33 below

3 BARKER, E., *The Making of a Moonie: Brainwashing or Choice?*, Oxford, Blackwell; repr. Aldershot, Gregg Revivals, 1993, 1984

4 BARKER, E. (ed.), *New Religious Movements: A Perspective for Understanding Society*, New York, Edwin Mellen Press, 1982

5 BARKER, E., *New Religious Movements: A Practical Introduction*, London, HMSO, 1989

6 BECKFORD, J., *Cult Controversies: The Societal Response to the New Religious Movements*, London, Tavistock, 1985

7 BEIT-HALLAHMI, B., *Despair and Deliverance*, Albany, NY, State University of New York, 1992

8 BRADY, K., and CONSIDINE, M., *The London Guide to Mind Body & Spirit*, London, Brainwave, 1988

9 BROCKWAY, A. R., and RAJASHEKAR, J. P. (eds), *New Religious Movements and the Churches: Report and Papers of a Consultation Sponsored by the Lutheran World Federation and the World Council Churches*, Geneva, WCC Publications, 1987

10 BROMLEY, D. G., and SHUPE, A., *'Moonies' in America: Cult, Church and Crusade*, Beverly Hills, Cal., Sage, 1979

11 BROMLEY, D. G., and HAMMOND, P. E. (eds), *The Future of New Religious Movements*, Macon, Ga, Mercer University Press, 1987

12 BROMLEY, D. G., and RICHARDSON, J. T. (eds), *The Brainwashing/ Deprogramming Controversy: Sociological, Psychological, Legal and Historical Perspectives*, New York, Edwin Mellen Press, 1983, vol. 5, p. 367

13 BROMLEY, D. G., and SHUPE, A. D., *Strange Gods: The Great American Cult Scare*, Boston, Mass., Beacon Press, 1981

14 BURNETT, D., *Dawning of the Pagan Moon: An Investigation into the Rise of Western Paganism*, Eastbourne, Marc, 1991

15 BUTTON, J., and BLOOM, W. (eds), *The Seeker's Guide: A New Age Resource Book*, London, Aquarian, 1992

16 CHINMOY, SRI, *A Sri Chinmoy Primer*, Forest Hills, NY, Vishma Press, 1974

17 CHURCH OF SCIENTOLOGY, *What is Scientology?*, Copenhagen, New Era, 1992

18 CONSIDINE, M. (ed.), *The Whole Person Catalogue: The Ultimate Source Book for the New Age Seeker*, London, Brainwave, 1992

19 COOPER, S., and FARRANT, M., *Fire in our Heart: The Story of the Jesus Fellowship*, Eastbourne, Kingsway Publications, 1991

20 DOWNTON, J. V., *Sacred Journeys: The Conversion of Young Americans to Divine Light Mission*, New York, Columbia University Press, 1979

21 ENROTH, R., *Evangelising the Cults*, 2nd rev. edn, Milton Keynes, Word Publishing, 1991

22 ENROTH, R., *Youth, Brainwashing, and the Extremist Cults*, Grand Rapids, Mich., Zondervan, 1977

23 FITZGERALD, F., *Cities on a Hill: A Journey through Contemporary American Cultures*, New York, Simon & Schuster, 1981

24 FOREM, J., *Transcendental Meditation*, New York, Dutton, 1974

25 GALANTER, M., *Cults: Faith, Healing, and Coercion*, New York/Oxford, Oxford University Press, 1989

26 GLOCK, G. Y., and BELLAH, R. N. (eds), *The New Religious Consciousness*, Berkeley, Cal., University of California Press, 1976

27 HALL, J. H., *Gone from the Promised Land: Jonestown in American Cultural History*, New Brunswick, NJ, Transaction, 1987

28 HARVEY, D. (cd.), *Thorsons Complete Guide to Alternative Living*, Wellingborough/New York, Thorsons, 1986

29 HASSAN, S., *Combatting Cult Mind Control: Protection, Rescue and Recovery from Destructive Cults*, Wellingborough, Aquarian Press, 1988

30 HUBBARD, L. R., *Dianetics:The Modern Science of Mental Health*, Copenhagen, New Era, 1950

31 KALBERMATTEN, G. DE., *The Advent*, Bombay, The Life Eternal Trust Publishers, 1979

32 KELLY, R., and DITZEL, P. *The Millennium and Beyond*, Pasadena, Cal., Worldwide Church of God, 1990

33 KING, G., and AVERY, K. Q., *The Age of Aetherius*, Los Angeles, Aetherius Society, 1975; rev. edn, 1982

34 LANE, D. C., *The Making of a Spiritual Movement: The Untold Story of Paul Twitchell and Eckankar*, Del Mar, Cal., Del Mar Press, 1983

35 LEVINE, S., *Radical Departures: Desperate Detours to Growing Up*, San Diego/London, Harcourt Brace Jovanovich, 1984

36 LEWIS, J. R., and MELTON, J. G. (eds), *Perspectives on the New Age*, Albany, NY, State University of New York Press, 1992

37 LIND, I., *The White Eagle Inheritance: The Spiritual Teachings of White Eagle and their Applications in Daily Life*, Wellingborough, Turnstone Press, 1984

38 LUHRMANN, T. M., *Persuasions of the Witch's Craft: Ritual Magic in Contemporary England*, Cambridge, Mass., Harvard University Press, 1989

39 MEHER BABA, *Discourses*, 3 vols, Walnut Creek, Cal., Sufism Reoriented, 1967; Sheria Press, 1988

40 MELTON, J. G., *Magic, Witchcraft and Paganism in America*, 2nd edn, New York, Garland, 1991

41 MELTON, J. G., *Encyclopedic Handbook of Cults in America*, New York/London, Garland, 1992

42 MELTON, J. G., *The Encyclopedia of American Religions*, 4th edn, Detroit, Gale, 1993

43 MELTON, J. G., CLARK, J., and KELLY, A. A., *New Age Almanac*, Detroit, Visible Ink Press, 1991

44 MELTON, J. G., and MOORE, R. L., *The Cult Experience: Responding to the New Religious Pluralism*, New York, Pilgrim Press, 1982

45 MITCHELL, D., MITCHELL, C., and OFSHE, R., *The Light on Synanon*, New York, Seaview Books, 1980

46 MUKTANANDA, SWAMI, *The Perfect Relationship: The Guru and the Disciple* (tr. Swami Chidvilasananda), South Fallsburg, NY, SYDA Foundation, 1980

47 MURPHET, H., *Sai Baba: Man of Miracles*, London, Vrindavanum Books, 1971; new edn Molecroft, Chingford, Sawbridge Enterprises, 1985

48 PATRICK, T., and DULACK, T., *Let Our Children Go*, New York, Ballantine, 1976

49 PRABHUPADA, HIS DIVINE GRACE A. C. B., *Bhagavad-Gita As It Is*, Los Angeles/London, Bhaktivedanta Book Trust, 1983

50 PROPHET, E. C., *The Lost Years of Jesus: Documentary Evidence of Jesus' 17-Year Journey to the East*, Livingston, Mont., Summit University Press, 1984

51 RAJNEESH, B. SHREE, *The Orange Book: The Meditation Techniques of Bhagwan Shree Rajneesh*, Rajneeshpuram, Or., Rajneesh Foundation International, 1983; prev. publ., Antelope, Or., Man Anand Rajneesh Puram Sannyas International Commune, 1981

52 RICHARDSON, J. T., STEWART, M., and SIMMONDS, R. B., *Organised Miracles: A Study of a Contemporary, Youth, Communal, Fundamentalist Organisation*, New Brunswick, NJ, Transaction, 1979

53 RICHARDSON, J. T. (ed.), *Money and Power in the New Religions*, Lewiston, NY, Edwin Mellen Press, 1988

54 RICHARDSON, J. T., BEST, J., and BROMLEY, D. G., *The Satanism Scare*, New York, Aldine de Gruyter, 1991

55 ROBBINS, T., *Cults, Converts and Charisma*, Newbury Park, Cal., Sage, 1988

56 ROBBINS, T., and ANTHONY, D. (eds), *In Gods We Trust: New Patterns of Religious Pluralism in America*, New Brunswick, NJ, Transaction, 1990

57 ROSEN, R. D., *Psychobabble: Fast Talk and Quick Cure in the Era of Feeling*, New York, Atheneum, 1977

58 ROSZAK, T., *Unfinished Animal: The Aquarian Frontier and the Evolution of Consciousness*, London, Faber, 1976

59 SALIBA, J. A., *Psychiatry and the Cults: An Annotated Bibliography*, New York, Garland, 1987

60 SALIBA, J. A., *Social Science and the Cults: An Annotated Bibliography*, New York/London, Garland, 1990

61 SARKAR, P. R., *Baba's Grace: Discourses of Shrii Shrii Anandamurti*, Los Altos Hills, Cal., Ananda Marga, 1973

62 SCOTT, R. D., *Transcendental Misconceptions*, San Diego, Cal., Beta Books, 1978

63 SHINN, L. D., *The Dark Lord: Cult Images and the Hare Krishnas in America*, Philadelphia, Pa, Westminster, 1987

64 SHUPE, A. D., and BROMLEY, D. G., *The New Vigilantes: Deprogrammers, Anti-Cultists, and the New Religions*, Beverly Hills, Cal., Sage, 1980

65 SHUPE, A. D., BROMLEY, D. G., and OLIVER, D. L., *The Anti-Cult Movement in America: A Bibliography and Historical Survey*, New York, Garland, 1984

66 STARK, R., and BAINBRIDGE, W. B., *The Future of Religion: Secularization, Revival and Cult Formation*, Berkeley/Los Angeles/London, University of California Press, 1985

67 SULLIVAN, M. B., *Living Religion in Subud*, London, Subud Publications International, 1990

68 THOMPSON, J., and HEELAS, P., *The Way of the Heart: The Rajneesh Movement*, Wellingborough, Aquarian Press, 1986

69 TWITCHELL, P., *ECKANKAR*, New York, Lancer Books, 1969

70 VAN ZANDT, D. E., *Living in the Children of God*, Princeton, NJ, Princeton University Press, 1991

71 VORILHON, C. 'R.', *Sensual Meditation: Awakening the Mind by Awakening the Body*, Tokyo, AOM Corporation, 1986

72 WALLIS, R., *Salvation and Protest: Studies of Social and Religious Movements*, London, Pinter, 1979

73 WALLIS, R., *The Elementary Forms of the New Religious Life*, London, Routledge, 1984

74 WALLIS, R., *The Road to Total Freedom: A Sociological Analysis of Scientology*, London, Heinemann, 1976

75 WALLIS, R. (ed.), *Sectarianism: Analyses of Religious and Non-Religious Sects*, London, Peter Owen, 1975

76 WESTLEY, F., *The Complex Forms of the Religious Life*, Chico, Cal., Scholars, 1983

77 WIERWILLE, V. P., *Jesus Christ is not God*, New Knoxville, Ohio, American Christian Press, 1975

78 WILSON, B. R., *The Social Dimensions of Sectarianism: Sects and New Religious Movements in Contemporary Society*, Oxford, Clarendon Press, 1990

(*See also* XIII(B), 27)

[XXIX]   *Pacific Religions*

Compiled by Brian E. Colless and Peter Donovan

1 AKKEREN, P. VAN, *Sri and Christ: A Study of the Indigenous Church in East Java*, London, Lutterworth, 1970

2 ALLEN, M. R., *Male Cults and Secret Initiations in Melanesia*, Melbourne, Melbourne University Press/London, New York, Cambridge University Press, 1967

3 BELLWOOD, P., *Man's Conquest of the Pacific*, Auckland, Collins, 1978, London, 1979; New York, Oxford University Press, 1979

4 BERNDT, R. M. and C. H., *The World of the First Australians*, 2nd edn, Sydney, Ure Smith, 1977

5 BERNET KEMPERS, A. J., *Ageless Borobudur*, Servire Wassenaar, 1976, Pomona, Cal., Hunter House

6 BEST, E., *Maori Religion and Mythology*, Wellington, 1924, repr. Government Printer, Wellington, 1976 (*Dominion Museum Bulletin*, no. 10); New York, AMS, 1976

7 BUCK, SIR PETER (Te Rangi Hiroa), *The Coming of the Maori*, Wellington, Maori Purposes Fund Board/Whitcombe & Tombs, 1949; 2nd edn, 1950 (distr. London, Whitcoulls)

8 BURRIDGE, K., *Tangu Traditions*, Oxford, Clarendon Press, 1969

9 CODRINGTON, R. H., *The Melanesians*, Oxford, Clarendon Press, 1891; repr. New York, Dover, 1972

10 ELIADE, M., *Australian Religions: An Introduction*, Ithaca, NY/London, Cornell University Press, 1973

11 ELKIN, A. P., *Aboriginal Men of High Degree*, 2nd edn, St Lucia, University of Queensland Press, 1977; New York, St Martin's, 1978

12 FORTUNE, R. F., *Sorcerers of Dobu*, London, Routledge, 1932; rev. edn London, Routledge & Kegan Paul, 1963; 1932 edn repr. Darby, Pa, Arden, 1979

13 GEERTZ, C., *The Religion of Java*, Glencoe, Ill., Free Press, 1960; Chicago, Ill., University of Chicago Press, 1976

14 *Gods, Ghosts, and Men in Melanesia* (ed. P. Lawrence and M. J. Meggitt), Melbourne/London/New York, Oxford University Press, 1965

15 GREY, G., *Polynesian Mythology*, London, Murray, 1855, repr. Christchurch, Whitcombe & Tombs, 1956; repr. of 1906 edn New York, AMS, 1976

16 HANDY, E. S. C., *Polynesian Religion*, Honolulu, 1927 (*Bernice P. Bishop Museum Bulletin*, 34); repr. New York, Kraus, 1971

17 HOOYKAAS, C., *Religion in Bali*, Leiden, Brill, 1973

18 JENSEN, E., *The Iban and Their Religion*, Oxford, Clarendon Press, 1974, 1975

19 LOEB, E., *Sumatra: Its History and People*, Vienna, 1935; repr. Kuala Lumpur, Oxford University Press, 1972, London, 1973; new edn of 1935 edn, Oxford University Press (East Asia), 1990

20 MALINOWSKI, B., *Argonauts of the Western Pacific*, London, Routledge, 1922, 1978, new edn 1992; New York, Dutton, 1922, 1961

21 NEVERMANN, H., WORMS, E. A., and PETRI, H., *Die Religionen der Südsee und Australiens*, Stuttgart, Kohlhammer, 1968

22 POIGNANT, R., *Oceanic Mythology: The Myths of Polynesia, Micronesia, Melanesia, Australia*, London, Hamlyn, 1967

23 *Powers, Plumes and Piglets* (ed. N. C. Habel), Bedford Park, South Australia, Australian Association for the Study of Religions, 1979

24 SCHÄRER, H., *Ngaju Religion: The Conception of God among a South Borneo People*, The Hague, Nijhoff, 1963; tr. of *Die Gottesidee der Ngadju– Dajak in Süd-Borneo*, Leiden, Brill, 1946

25 SELIGMANN, C. G., *The Melanesians of British New Guinea*, Cambridge, Cambridge University Press, 1910; repr. New York, AMS, 1976

26 STÖHR, W., and ZOETMULDER, P., *Die Religionen Indonesiens*, Stuttgart, Kohlhammer, 1965

27 STREHLOW, T. G. H., 'Australia', in BLEEKER, C. J., and WIDENGREN, G. (eds), *Historia Religionum: Handbook for the History of Religions*, Leiden, Brill, vol. 2, 1971, pp. 609–28

28 SWAIN, T., and TROMPF, G. *The Religions of Oceania*, London, Routledge, 1995

29 TROMPF, G. W., *Melanesian Religion*, Cambridge, Cambridge University Press, 1991

30 WILLIAMSON, R. W., *Religion and Social Organization in Central Polynesia*, Cambridge, Cambridge University Press, 1937; repr. New York, AMS, 1977

(See also XXVII, 6, 7, 8, 19, 24)

[XXX]   *Prehistoric Religions*

Compiled by Eric H. Pyle

1 CLARK, G., *The Stone Age Hunters*, London, Thames & Hudson, 1967; New York, McGraw-Hill, 1967

2 CLARK, G., *World Prehistory*, 2nd edn, Cambridge, Cambridge University Press, 1969; 3rd edn 1977

3 CRAWFORD, O. G. S., *The Eye Goddess*, London, Phoenix House, 1957; New York, Macmillan, 1958, Washington, DC, Delphi Press, 1993

4 DANIEL, G. E., *The Megalith Builders of Western Europe*, London,

Hutchinson, 1958, 1963; New York, Praeger, 1959; London/Baltimore, Md, Penguin, 1963

5 FLEMING, A., 'The Myth of the Mother Goddess', *World Archaeology*, vol. 1, 1969, pp. 247–61

6 JAMES, E. O., *Prehistoric Religion*, London, Thames & Hudson/New York, Praeger, 1957; New York, Barnes & Noble, 1961

7 JENNINGS, J. D., and NORBECK, E. (eds), *Prehistoric Man in the New World*, Chicago, Ill., University of Chicago Press, 1964, 1971

8 LEROI-GOURHAN, A. G. L., *The Art of Prehistoric Man in Western Europe*, London, Thames & Hudson, 1968

9 MARINGER, J., *The Gods of Prehistoric Man*, London, Weidenfeld/New York, Knopf, 1960

10 NARR, K. J., 'Approaches to the Religion of Early Palaeolithic Man', *History of Religions*, vol. 4, 1964, pp. 1–22

11 SIEVEKING, A., *The Cave Artists*, London, Thames & Hudson, 1979

12 UCKO, P. J., and ROSENFELD, A., *Palaeolithic Cave Art*, London, Weidenfeld (World University Library); New York, McGraw-Hill, 1967

[XXXI] *Roman Religion*

Compiled by John A. North

1 BEARD, M., 'The Sexual Status of Vestal Virgins', *Journal of Roman Studies*, vol. 70, 1980, pp. 12–27

2 BEARD, M., and NORTH, J. (eds), *Pagan Priests*, London, Duckworth, 1990

3 BEARD, M., NORTH, J. A., and PRICE, S. R. F., *History of Roman Religion*, 2 vols, Cambridge, Cambridge University Press, 1984

4 BREMMER, J. N., and HORSFALL, N. M., *Roman Myth and Mythography*, London, Institute of Classical Studies, 1987 (BICS Supplement 52)

5 BROWN, P. R. L., *The Making of Late Antiquity*, Cambridge, Mass./London, Harvard University Press, 1979

6 BURKERT, W., *Ancient Mystery Cults*, Cambridge, Mass./London, Harvard University Press, 1987; new edn 1989

7 DODDS, E. R., *Pagan and Christian in an Age of Anxiety*, Cambridge/New York, Cambridge University Press, 1965; New York, Norton, 1979

8 DUMÉZIL, G., *Archaic Roman Religion*, 2 vols, Chicago, Ill./London, University of Chicago Press, 1970, 1971 (Eng. tr. from 1st edn, 1966); 2nd edn, *La Religion romaine archaïque*, Paris, Payot, 1974 (not avail. in Eng. tr.)

9 FONDATION HARDT, *Entretiens*, vol. 19, Geneva, 1973 (*Le Culte des souverains dans l'empire romain*)

10 GRANT, F. C., *Ancient Roman Religion*, New York, Liberal Arts Press, 1957; Indianapolis, Ind., Bobbs-Merrill, 1957

11 LANE FOX, R., *Pagans and Christians*, London, Viking, 1987; new edn Harmondsworth, Penguin, 1988

12 LATTE, K., *Römische Religionsgeschichte*, Munich, Beck, 1960 (*Handbuch der Altertumswissenschaft*, vol. 5, part 4)

13 LIEBESCHUETZ, J. H. W. G., *Continuity and Change in Roman Religion*, Oxford, Clarendon Press/New York, Oxford University Press, 1979; Oxford, Oxford University Press, 1989

14 LINDERSKI, J., 'The Augural Law', *Aufstieg und Niedergang der Römischen Welt*, vol. 2, part 16/3, pp. 2146–2312, Berlin/New York, 1986

15 MCBAIN, B., *Prodigy and Expiation*, Brussels, 1982 (Collection Latomus 177)

16 MICHELS, A. K., *The Calendar of the Roman Republic*, Princeton, NJ, Princeton University Press, 1967; repr. Westport, Conn./London, Greenwood, 1978

17 NOCK, A. D., *Conversion: The Old and the New in Religion from Alexander the Great to Augustine of Hippo*, London/New York, Oxford University Press, 1933; repr. 1952, pb 1961; new edn University Press of America 1988

18 NOCK, A. D., *Essays on Religion and the Ancient World* (ed. Z. Stewart), Oxford, Clarendon Press/Cambridge, Mass., Harvard University Press, 1972

19 NORTH, J. A., 'Religion in Republican Rome', *Cambridge Ancient History*, vol. 7, part 2, pp. 573–624; 2nd edn 1989

20 PRICE, S. R. F., *Rituals and Power: The Roman Imperial Cult in Asia Minor*, Cambridge, Cambridge University Press, 1984

21 SCHEID, J., *Religion et piété à Rome*, Paris, Éditions la Découverte, 1985

22 SCULLARD, H. H., *Festivals and Ceremonies of the Roman Republic*, London, Thames & Hudson, 1981

23 VERSNEL, H. S., *Triumphus: An Inquiry into the Origin, Development and Meaning of the Roman Triumph*, Leiden, Brill, 1970

24 WARDMAN, A., *Religion and Statecraft among the Romans*, London, Granada, 1972

25 WEINSTOCK, S., *Divus Julius*, Oxford, Clarendon Press, 1971

[XXXII]   *Secular Alternatives to Religion*

Compiled by Stuart Brown

1 AYER, A. J., *Language, Truth and Logic*, London, Gollancz, 1936, 2nd edn 1946; Harmondsworth, Penguin, 1971, new edn 1990; Magnolia, Mass., Peter Smith

2 BAIER, A., 'Secular Faith', *Canadian Journal of Philosophy*, vol. 10, 1990, pp. 131–48

3 BEATTIE, P., 'The Religion of Secular Humanism' and 'A Response to My Critics', *Free Inquiry*, vol. 6, 1985/6, pp. 12–17, 52–3

4 BERGER, P. L., *Invitation to Sociology: A Humanistic Perspective*, ch. 5, Garden City, NY, Doubleday, 1963; Harmondsworth, Penguin, 1966, 1970; New York, Overlook 1973

5 BLACKHAM, H. J., *Humanism*, 2nd edn, Brighton, Harvester/New York, International Publications Service, 1976

6 BRAITHWAITE, R. B., *An Empiricist's View of the Nature of Religious Belief*, Cambridge, Cambridge University Press, 1955, repr. in HICK, J. (ed.), *The Existence of God*, New York, Macmillan/London, Collier-Macmillan, 1964; with author's *Theory of Games*, Bristol, Thoemmes Press, 1994

7 BROWN, S. C. (ed.), *Reason and Religion*, Ithaca, NY/London, Cornell University Press, 1977

8 CAMERON, I., and EDGE, D., *Scientific Images and their Social Uses: An Introduction to the Concept of Scientism*, London/Boston, Mass., Butterworth, 1979

9 CHARLTON, D. G., *Secular Religions in France 1815–1870*, London, Oxford University Press, 1963

10 FEUERBACH, L. A., *The Essence of Christianity* (tr. George Eliot, 1841), New York, Harper & Row, 1957, 1991; Magnolia, Mass., Peter Smith

11 FLEW, A., and MACINTYRE, A. (eds), *New Essays in Philosophical Theology*, London, SCM, 1955; New York, Macmillan, 1955, 1964

12 HUME, DAVID, *Dialogues Concerning Natural Religion* (1779) (ed. N. Kemp Smith), Oxford, Clarendon Press, 1935; 2nd edn Indianapolis, Ind., Bobbs-Merrill [1947]

13 KOLAKOWSKI, L., *Positivist Philosophy from Hume to the Vienna Circle*, Harmondsworth, Penguin, 1972

14 MARX, KARL, *Selected Writings in Sociology and Social Philosophy* (ed. T. B. Bottomore and M. Rubel), Harmondsworth, Penguin, 1963, new edn 1970, 1990; New York, McGraw-Hill, 1963; first publ. London, Watts, 1956

15 MARX, KARL, *Writings of the Young Marx on Philosophy and Society* (ed. and tr. L. D. Easton and K. H. Guddat), Garden City, NY, Anchor Books/Doubleday, 1967

16 MILL, J. S., *Essential Works* (ed. M. Lerner), New York, Bantam, 1961

17 OWEN, D. R. G., *Scientism, Man and Religion*, Philadelphia, Pa, Westminster, 1952

18 POPKIN, R. H., *The History of Scepticism from Erasmus to Descartes*, rev edn, New York/London, Harper & Row, 1968; Atlantic Highlands, NJ, Humanities, 1964; publ. as *The History of Scepticism from Erasmus to Spinoza*, Berkeley, Cal., University of California Press, 1979, London, 1980

19 POPPER, K. R., *The Logic of Scientific Discovery*, London, Hutchinson, 1959, rev. edn 1972, 1974; New York, Harper & Row, n.d.; New York, Basic Books, 1959; rev. edn London, Routledge, 1992

20 POPPER, K. R., *The Open Society and Its Enemies*, vol. 2, *The High Tide of Prophecy: Hegel, Marx and the Aftermath*, London, Routledge, 1945, 4th edn 1962; 5th edn London, Routledge/Princeton, NJ, Princeton University Press, 1966, 1968

21 RAMSEY, P., 'Religious Aspects of Marxism', *Canadian Journal of Philosophy*, vol. 5, pp. 143–55

22 ROSE, H. and S. (eds), *The Radicalisation of Science*, ch. 2, London, Macmillan, 1976

23 RUSSELL, BERTRAND (3RD EARL RUSSELL), *Human Society in Ethics and Politics*, London, Allen & Unwin, 1954; New York, Simon & Schuster, 1955

24 SKINNER, B. F., *Beyond Freedom and Dignity*, Harmondsworth/Penguin, 1973; New York, Knopf, 1971; New York, Bantam, 1972

25 STEVENSON, L., *Seven Theories of Human Nature*, London, Oxford University Press, 1974; 2nd edn New York, Oxford University Press, 1990

26 TENNANT, F. R., *Philosophical Theology*, 2 vols, Cambridge, Cambridge University Press, 1928–30; lib. edn Cambridge University Press, 1969

27 WILSON, E. O., 'Scientific Humanism and Religion', *Free Inquiry*, 1991

28 YINGER, J. M., *The Scientific Study of Religion*, New York, Macmillan/London, Collier-Macmillan, 1970

[XXXIII] *Sikhism*

Compiled by Hew McLeod

1 BANERJEE, A. C., *Guru Nanak and His Times*, Patiala, Punjabi University, 1971

2 BANERJEE, A. C., *Guru Nanak to Guru Gobind Singh*, New Delhi, Rajesh Publications, 1978

3 BANERJEE, A. C., *The Sikh Gurus and the Sikh Religion*, New Delhi, Munshiram Manoharlal, 1983

4 BARRIER, N. G., *The Sikhs and Their Literature*, Delhi, Manohar Book Service, 1970

5 BASHAM, A. L. (ed.), *A Cultural History of India*, Oxford, Clarendon Press, 1975

6 COLE, W. O., *Sikhism and its Indian Context, 1469–1708*, London, Darton Longman and Todd, 1984

7 COLE, W. O., and PIARA SINGH SAMBHI, *A Popular Dictionary of Sikhism*, London, Curzon Press and Glenn Dale, Riverdale Company, 1990

8 COLE, W. O., and PIARA SINGH SAMBHI, *The Sikhs: Their Religious Beliefs and Practices*, London/Boston, Mass., Routledge, 1978

9 GOBIND SINGH MANSUKHANI, *Aspects of Sikhism*, New Delhi, Punjabi Writers, 1982

10 GOBIND SINGH MANSUKHANI, *A Book of Sikh Studies*, Delhi, National Book Shop, 1989

11 GREWAL, J. S., *From Guru Nanak to Maharaja Ranjit Singh: Essays in Sikh History*, Amritsar, Guru Nanak Dev University, 1972

12 GREWAL, J. S., *Guru Nanak in History*, Chandigarh, Panjab University, 1969

13 GREWAL, J. S., *The Sikhs of the Punjab*, vol. 2(3) in *The New Cambridge History of India*, Cambridge, Cambridge University Press, 1990

14 GREWAL, J. S., and BAL, S. S., *Guru Gobind Singh: A Biographical Study*, Chandigarh, Panjab University, 1978 (prev. publ. 1967)

15 HARBANS SINGH, *Guru Gobind Singh*, 2nd rev. edn, New Delhi, Sterling Publishers, 1979; Livingston, NJ, Orient Book Distributors, 1979

16 HARBANS SINGH, *Guru Nanak and the Origins of the Sikh Faith*, Bombay/New York, Asia Publishing House, 1969

17 HARBANS SINGH, *The Heritage of the Sikhs*, 2nd rev. edn, New Delhi, Manohar, 1983

18 HARBANS SINGH, and BARRIER, N. G. (eds), *Punjab Past and Present: Essays in Honour of Dr Ganda Singh*, Patiala, Punjabi University, 1976

19 JOHAR, S. S., *Handbook on Sikhism*, Delhi, Vivek, 1977; Columbia, Mo, South Asia Books; Mystic, Conn., Verry, 1978

20 JOHAR, S. S., *The Sikh Gurus and Their Shrines*, Delhi, Vivek, 1976; Mystic, Conn., Verry, 1977

21 JUERGENSMEYER, M., and BARRIER, N. G. (eds), *Sikh Studies: Comparative Perspectives on a Changing Tradition*, Berkeley, Cal., Graduate Theological Union/Lancaster-Miller, 1979

22 KHUSHWANT SINGH, *A History of the Sikhs*, vol. 1, Delhi, Oxford University Press, 1991

23 KHUSHWANT SINGH, *A History of the Sikhs*, vol. 2, 2nd edn, Delhi, Oxford University Press, 1991

24 MACAULIFFE, M. A., *The Sikh Religion: Its Gurus, Sacred Writings and Authors*, 6 vols in 3, repr. Delhi, Chand, 1963, 1970; first publ. Oxford, Clarendon Press, 1909; new edn New Delhi, Chand, 1986, 6 vols

25 MCLEOD, W. H., *Early Sikh Tradition: A Study of the Janam-Sakhis*, Oxford, Clarendon Press, 1980

26 MCLEOD, W. H., *The Evolution of the Sikh Community*, Oxford, Clarendon Press, 1976

27 MCLEOD, W. H., *Guru Nanak and the Sikh Religion*, Delhi, Oxford University Press, 1976

28 MCLEOD, W. H., *The Sikhs: History, Religion and Society*, New York, Columbia University Press, 1989

29 MCLEOD, W. H., *Who is a Sikh? The Problem of Sikh Identity*, Oxford, Clarendon Press, 1989

30 MCLEOD, W. H. (tr. and ed.), *Textual Sources for the Study of Sikhism*, Chicago, Ill., University of Chicago Press, 1991

31 NRIPINDER SINGH, *The Sikh Moral Tradition: Ethical Perceptions of the Sikhs in the Late Nineteenth Century*, Columbia, Mo, South Asia Books, 1990

32 O'CONNELL, J. D., et al. (eds), *Sikh History and Religion in the Twentieth Century*, Toronto, University of Toronto Centre for South Asian Studies, 1988

33 TALIB, G. S. (tr.), *Sri Guru Granth Sahib*, 4 vols, Patiala Punjabi University, 1984–92

34 TEJA SINGH, *Sikhism: Its Ideals and Institutions*, rev. edn, Bombay, Orient Longmans, 1951; repr. Amritsar, Khalsa Bros, 1970

35 *Sikhism* (Essays by Fauja Singh, Trilochan Singh, Gurbachan Singh Talib, J. P. Singh Uberoi and Sohan Singh), Patiala, Punjabi University, 1969

[XXXIV] The Study of Religions

Compiled by Terence Thomas, P. Antes, Edward Bailey, Eileen Barker, Stuart Brown, A. Dyson, Gavin Flood, Leslie J. Francis, Jean Holm, David J. Melling, Eric H. Pyle and Ninian Smart

1 *A Framework for Religious Education in Cambridgeshire: Agreed Syllabus of Religious Education*, Ely Resources and Technology Centre, 1982

2 AMMERMAN, N. T., *Baptist Battles: Social Change and Religious Conflict in the Southern Baptist Convention*, New Brunswick/London, 1990

3 ANTES, P., 'Religion, dīn et dharma dans la perspective d'une recherche comparative' in Ugo Bianchi with Fabio Mora and Lorenzo Biachi (eds), *The Notion of 'Religion' in Comparative Research: Selected Proceedings of the XVI Congress of the International Association for the History of Religions, Rome, 3–8 September 1990*, Rome, 'L'ERMA' di Bretschneider, 1994, pp. 763 8

4 ANTES, P., *How to Study Religious Experience in the Traditions*, British Association for the Study of Religions/Occasional Papers, Cardiff, BASF, 1992

5 ANTES, P., ' "Religion" einmal anders', in *Temenos*, vol. 14, 1978, pp. 184–97

6 ANTES, P., 'Religion in den Theorien der Religionswissenschaft', in KERN, W., POTTMEYER, H. J., and SECKLER, M. (eds), *Handbuch der Fundamentaltheologie*, vol. 1: *Traktat Religion*, Freiburg-Basel-Wien, Herder, 1985, pp. 34–56

7 ANTES, P., 'Systematische Religionswissenschaft – zwei unversöhnliche Forschungsrichtungen?', in *Humanitas religiosa: Festschrift für Haralds Biezais zu seinem 70 Geburtstag*, Stockholm, Almqvist & Wiksell, 1979, pp. 213–21

8 ARGYLE, M., and BEIT-HALLAHMI, B., *The Social Psychology of Religion*, London, Routledge, 1975

9 ASTLEY, J., and FRANCIS, L. J. (eds), *Christian Perspectives on Faith Development: A Reader*, Leominster, Gracewing, 1992

10   BAIRD, ROBERT D., *Category Formation and the History of Religions*, The Hague/Paris, Mouton, 1971; 2nd rev. edn, 1991

11   BANTON, M. (ed.), *Anthropological Approaches to the Study of Religion*, London, Tavistock, 1966, 1968; New York, Methuen, 1968

12   BARBOUR, I. G., *Myths, Models and Paradigms: A Comparative Study in Science and Religion*, London, SCM, 1974; New York, Harper & Row, 1974, 1976; new edn Harper/Edinburgh, T. & T. Clark, 1990

13   BARKER, E. V., BECKFORD, J. A., and DOBBELAERE, K. (eds), *Secularization, Rationalism and Sectarianism*, Oxford, Clarendon Press, 1993

14   BARNHART, J. E., *The Study of Religion and its Meaning*, The Hague/Paris/New York, Mouton, 1977

15   BATSON, C. D., and VENTIS, W. L., *The Religious Experience: A Social Psychological Perspective*, New York, Oxford University Press, 1982

16   BECHERT, H. B., and GOMBRICH, R., *The World of Buddhism*, London, Thames & Hudson, 1984

16a BEIT-HALLAMI, B., *Prolegomena to the Psychological Study of Religion*, Lewisburg, Bucknell University Press, 1989

17   BELLAH, R. N., MADSEN, R., SULLIVAN, W. M., SWIDLER, A., and TIPTON, S. M. (eds), *Habits of the Heart: Individualism and Commitment in American Life*, Berkeley, Cal., Tata/McGraw-Hill, 1985

18   BELLAH, R. N., 'Religious Evolution', in ROBERTSON, R. (ed.), *Sociology of Religion*, Harmondsworth, Penguin, 1971, pp. 262–92

18a BELLAH, R. N., 'Civil Religion in America', *Daedalus: Journal of the American Academy of Arts and Sciences*, vol. 96(1), Winter 1967; repr. with commentaries and response in CUTLER, D. R. (ed.), *The World Year Book of Religion*, vol. 1, London, Evans Bros, 1969

19   BENNER, D. G., *Psychology and Religion*, Grand Rapids, Mich., Baker Book House, 1988

20   BERGER, P. L., *Facing up to Modernity*, Harmondsworth, Penguin, 1979; first publ. New York, Basic Books, 1977

21   BERGER, P. L., *The Social Reality of Religion*, London, Faber, 1969; Harmondsworth, Penguin, 1973; publ. in US as *The Sacred Canopy*, 1967

22   BERGER, P. L., *The Heretical Imperative*, London, Collins, 1980

23   BERGER, P. L., BERGER, B., and KELLNER, H., *The Homeless Mind*, Harmondsworth, Penguin, 1973

24   BETTIS, J. D. (ed.), *Phenomenology of Religion*, London, SCM/New York, Harper & Row, 1969

25   BIANCHI, UGO, *The History of Religions*, Leiden, Brill, 1975

26   BLEEKER, C. J., and WIDENGREN, G., *Historia Religionum: Handbook for the History of Religions*, vol. 2, *Religions of the Present*, Leiden, Brill, 1971

27   BONHOEFFER, D., *Letters and Papers from Prison*, 7th. imp., London, Collins Fontana, 1965; new edn London, SCM Press, 1971; prev. publ. London, SCM 1953

27a BORG, M. B. TER, *Een Uitgewaairde Eeuwigheid: bet mensetijk tekort in de moderne cultuur*, The Hague, Baarn, 1991

28   BOWMAN, M., *Phenomenology, Fieldwork and Folk Religion*, British Association for the Study of Religions Occasional Papers, Cardiff, BASR, 1992

29   BROWN, A., (ed.), *The Shap Handbook on World Religions in Education*, 5th edn, London, Commission for Racial Equality, 1987

30   BROWN, L. B., *Advances in the Psychology of Religion*, Oxford, Pergamon, 1985

31 BROWN, L. B., *The Psychology of Religion: An Introduction*, London, SPCK, 1988

31a BROWN, L. B., *The Psychology of Religious Belief*, London, Academic Press, 1987

32 BRUCE, S., (ed.), *Religion and Modernization: Sociologists and Historians Debate the Secularization Thesis*, Oxford, Clarendon Press, 1992

33 BUDD, S., *Sociologists and Religion*, New York, Macmillan, 1971; London, Collier-Macmillan, 1973

34 BUDD, S., *Varieties of Unbelief: Atheists and Agnostics in English Society 1850–1960*, London, Heinemann, 1977

35 CALLAHAN, D. (ed.), *The Secular City Debate*, London, Collier-Macmillan, 1966

36 CASSIRER, E., *Language and Myth* (tr. S. K. Langer), New York, Dover, 1946, repr. 1953; New York/London, Harper & Row, 1946; repr. Magnolia, Mass., Peter Smith

37 CHRISTIAN, W. A., *Oppositions of Religious Doctrines*, London, Macmillan/New York, Herder, 1972

38 CHRISTIAN, JR, W. A., *Person and God in a Spanish Valley*, Princeton, NJ, Princeton University Press, 1972

39 CHRYSSIDES, G. D., *The Advent of Sun Myung Moon*, Basingstoke, Macmillan, 1991

39a 'Comment une religion de définit elle-même', in BALADIER, CHARLES (ed.), *Le Grand Atlas des Religions*, réalisé par *Encyclopaedia Universalis*, Paris, Encyclopaedia Universalis France, 1988, pp. 34–43

40 COX, H., *The Secular City: Secularization and Urbanization in Theological Perspective*, London, SCM, 1969

40a CUMPSTY, J. S., *Religion as Belonging: A General Theory of Religion*, Lanham, Md/New York/London, University Press of America 1991

41 DANIÉLOU, A., *Hindu Polytheism*, London, Routledge/New York, Pantheon (Bollingen Foundation)/Princeton, NJ, Princeton University Press, 1964

42 DAVIES, J. G., *Temples, Churches and Mosques*, New York, Pilgrim; Oxford, Blackwell, 1982

43 DHAVAMONY, M., *Phenomenology of Religion*, Rome, Gregorian University Press, 1973

44 DOBBELAERE, K., 'Secularization: A Multi-Dimensional Concept', *Current Sociology*, vol. 29, 1981, pp. 5ff

45 DOBBELAERE, K., *Secularization: A Multi-Dimensional Concept*, London, 1981

46 DOUGLAS, M., *Purity and Danger*, London, Routledge, 1978; repr. with corrections 1969

47 DUNCAN, B., *Pray Your Way: Your Personality and God*, London, Darton, Longman & Todd, 1993

48 DURKHEIM, E., *The Elementary Forms of the Religious Life* (tr. J. W. Swain), 2nd edn, London/Boston, Mass., Allen & Unwin, 1976

49 ELIADE, M., *A History of Religious Ideas* (tr. W. R. Trask), 3 vols, Chicago/London, University of Chicago Press, 1978–1985; new edn vol. 2 1985, French edn vol. 3 1988; publ. in French as *Histoire des croyances et des idées religieuses*, 1976–1983

50 ELIADE, M., *Autobiography*, 2 vols, Chicago/London, University of Chicago Press, 1990

51 ELIADE, M., *From Primitives to Zen*, London, Collins, 1977; repr. in *Essential Sacred Writings from Around the World*, New York/San Francisco, Harper, 1991

52   ELIADE, M., *Journal*, 4 vols, Chicago/London, University of Chicago Press, 1989–90

53   ELIADE, M., *Myths, Dreams and Mysteries*, Glasgow, Collins, Fontana, 6th imp. 1977; first publ. in French as *Mythes, Rêves et Mystères*, Paris, Gallimard, 1957

54   ELIADE, M., *Patterns in Comparative Religion* (tr. Rosemary Sheed), London/New York, Sheed & Ward, 1958, new edn 1979; first publ. in French as *Traité d'histoire des Religions*, Paris, Payot, 1948

55   ELIADE, M., *Shamanism: Archaic Techniques of Ecstasy* (tr. W. R. Task), New York, Pantheon, 1964; London, Routledge, 1988; London/New York, Arkana/Penguin, 1989; first publ. in French as *Le Chamanisme et les techniques archaïques de l'extase*, Paris, Payot, 1951

56   ELIADE, M., *The Myth of the Eternal Return* (tr. W. R. Task), London/New York, Arkana/Penguin, 1989; first publ. in French as *Le Mythe de l'éternal retour: archétypes et répétition*, Paris, Gallimard, 1949)

57   ELIADE, M., *The Quest: History and Meaning in Religion*, Chicago/London, University of Chicago Press, 1969

58   ELIADE, M., *The Sacred and the Profane* (tr. W. R. Trask), New York, Harcourt, Brace, 1968

59   ELIADE, M., *Yoga, Immortality and Freedom*, Princeton, NJ, Princeton University Press, 1973

59a   ELIADE, M. (ed.), *The Encyclopedia of Religion*, 16 vols, London, Collier, Macmillan/New York, Macmillan, 1987

60   ELIADE, M., and KITAGAWA, J. M., *The History of Religions: Essays in Methodology*, Chicago/London, University of Chicago Press, 1959, 6th edn, 1973

61   EVANS-PRITCHARD, E. E., *Theories of Primitive Religion*, London, Oxford University Press, 1965; new edn London, Greenwood, 1986

62   EYSENCK, H. J., and EYSENCK, M. W., *Personality and Individual Differences: A Natural Science Approach*, New York, Plenum, 1985

62a   FEIL, E., *Religio: Die Geschichte eines neuzeitlichen Grurdbegriffs vom Frühchristentum bis zur Reformation*, Göttingen, Vandenhoeck & Ruprecht, 1986 (Forschungen zur Kitchen- und Dogmengeschichte, 36)

63   FINKE, R., and STARK, R., *The Churching of America, 1776–1990: Winners and Losers in our Religious Economy*, New Brunswick, NJ, Rutgers University Press, 1992

64   FOWLER, J. W., *Stages of Faith: The Psychology of Human Development and the Quest for Meaning*, San Francisco, Harper & Row, 1981

65   FOWLER, J. W., NIPKOW, K. E., and SCHWEITZER, F., *Stages of Faith and Religious Development: Implications for Church, Education and Society*, London, SCM, 1992

66   FREUD, S., *The Future of an Illusion*, New Haven, Conn., Yale University Press, 1950

67   GENNEP, A. VAN, *The Rites of Passage*, London, Routledge, 1977; first publ. in French, 1909

68   GILBERT, A. D., *The Making of Post-Christian Britain: A History of the Secularization of Modern Society*, London, Longman, 1980

68a   GLOCK, C. Y., and HAMMOND, P. E. (eds), *Beyond the Classics? Essays in the Scientific Study of Religion*, New York, Harper & Row, 1973

69   GOLDMAN, R., *Religious Thinking from Childhood to Adolescence*, London, Routledge, 1964

69a   GRANT, F. C. (ed.), *Hellenistic Religions: The Age of Syncretism*, Indianapolis, Ind., Bobbs-Merrill/New York, Liberal Arts, 1953

70   GREELEY, A. M., *The Persistence of Religion*, London, SCM, 1973

71 HADDEN, J. K., and SHUPE, A., *Televangelism: Power and Politics on God's Frontier*, New York, Holt, 1988

72 HALL, T. W. (ed.), *Introduction to the Study of Religion*, San Francisco, Harper & Row, 1978; London, 1979

73 HANFLING, O., *The Quest for Meaning*, Oxford, Blackwell, 1989

73a HAY, D., *Exploring Inner Space: Scientists and Religious Experience*, Harmondsworth, Penguin, 1982

74 HAY, D., *Religious Experience Today: Studying the Facts*, London, Mowbray, 1990

75 HEBBLETHWAITE, B. L., *The Problems of Theology*, Cambridge, Cambridge University Press, 1980

76 HEILER, F., *Erscheinungsformen und Wesen der Religion*, Stuttgart, Kohlhammer, 1961

77 HELM, P., *The Varieties of Belief*, London, Allen & Unwin, 1973

78 HEMPTON, D., ' "Popular Religion" 1800–1986', in THOMAS, T. (ed.), *The British: Their Religious Beliefs and Practices*, London/New York, Routledge, 1988

79 HEWITT, H., *Problems in the Philosophy of Religion: Critical Studies in the Work of John Hick*, London, Macmillan, 1991

80 HICK, J., *Evil and the God of Love*, London, Macmillan, 1966; new edn of 2nd rev. edn 1985

81 HICK, J., and ASKARI, H., *The Experience of Religious Diversity*, Aldershot/Brookfield, Vt, Gower, 1985

82 HINNELLS, J. R. (ed.), *Comparative Religion in Education*, London, Oriel, 1970

83 HOLM, J. L., *The Study of Religions*, London, Sheldon/New York, Seabury, 1977

84 HOLM, J. L., *Teaching Religion in School*, Oxford, Oxford University Press, 1975

85 HOLYOAKE, G. J., *Secularism: The Practical Philosophy of the People*, London, G. J. Holyoake & Co., 1854

86 HOLYOAKE, G. J., 'The Trial of George Jacob Holyoake, 1842', in *Religion in Victorian Britain*, vol. 3, *Sources*, Manchester/New York, Manchester University Press in association with The Open University Press, 1988, pp. 340–52

87 HORNSBY-SMITH, M. P., *Roman Catholic Beliefs in England: Customary Catholicism and Transformations of Religious Authority*, Cambridge, Cambridge University Press, 1991

88 HUNTER, J. D., *Evangelicalism: The Coming Generation*, Chicago, University of Chicago Press, 1987

89 HURTADO, L. (ed.), *Goddesses in Religions and Modern Debate*, Atlanta, Scholars, 1990 (University of Manitoba Studies in Religion)

90 HYDE, K. E., *Religion in Childhood and Adolescence: A Comprehensive Review of the Research*, Birmingham, Ala, Religious Education Press, 1990

91 ISICHEI, E., 'Some Ambiguities in the Academic Study of Religion', in *Religion*, vol. 23(4), October 1993, pp. 379–90

92 JACKSON, R. (ed.), *Approaching World Religions*, London, Murray, 1981

93 JAMES, E. O., *Sacrifice and Sacrament*, London, Thames & Hudson, 1962

94 JAMES, W., *The Varieties of Religious Experience*, New York, Longman, 1902; London/Glasgow, Collins/Fontana, 1960–8; new edn Penguin, 1983

95 JUNG, C. G., *Modern Man in Search of a Soul*, London, Routledge, 1933
96 KENDRICK, T. D., *St James in Spain*, London, Methuen, 1960
97 KENNY, A., *What is Faith?*, Oxford, Oxford University Press, 1992
98 KEYES, C. F., *Charisma: From Social Life to Sacred Biography*, in WILLIAMS, M. A. (ed.), *Charisma and Sacred Biography*, Journal of the American Academy of Religion Series, vol. 48(3, 4), American Academy of Religion, 1982, pp. 1–22
98a KING, U., 'Historical and Phenomenological Approaches to the Study of Religion', in WHALING, F. (ed.), *Contemporary Approaches to the Study of Religion*, vol. 1, pp. 29–164, Berlin/New York/Amsterdam, Mouton, 1984
99 KING, U., *Turning Points in Religious Studies*, Edinburgh, T. & T. Clark, 1990
100 KITAGAWA, J. M. (ed.), *The History of Religions: Retrospect and Prospect*, New York, Macmillan, 1985
101 KNOTT, K., *Hinduism in Leeds*, Department of Theology and Religious Studies, University of Leeds, 1986
102 LADURIE, E. LE ROY, *Montaillou: Catholics and Cathars in a French Village, 1294–1324*, London, Scolar, 1978/9; first publ. in French as *Montaillou: village occitan de 1294–1324*, Paris, Gallimard, 1975
103 LANCZKOWSKI, GÜNTER, *Einführung in die Religionswissenschaft*, Darmstadt, Wissenschaftliche Buchgesellschaft, 1980
104 LANCZKOWSKI, GÜNTER, *Einführung in die Religionsgeschichte*, Darmstadt, Wissenschaftliche Buchgesellschaft, 1983
105 LEACH, E. A. (ed.), *The Structural Study of Myth and Totemism*, London, Tavistock, 1967, 1968; New York, Methuen, 1968
106 LEACH, E. R., 'Ritual', in D. L. Sills (ed.), *International Encyclopaedia of the Social Sciences*, vol. 13, New York, Free Press, 1968
107 LEEUW, G. VAN DER, *Religion in Essence and Manifestation*, London, Allen & Unwin, 1938; New York, Harper & Row, 1963; publ. in German as *Phänomenologie der Religion*, Tübingen, Mohr, 1933, 4th edn 1977
108 LESSA, W. A., and VOGT, E. Z. (eds), *Reader in Comparative Religion: An Anthropological Approach*, 4th edn, New York/London, Harper & Row, 1979
109 LÉVI-STRAUSS, C., *Totemism* (tr. R. Needham), new edn with introduction by R. C. Poole, Harmondsworth, Penguin, 1969; publ. in French as *Le Totémisme aujourd'hui*, Paris, Presses Universitaires de France, 1962
110 LEWIS, H. D., *Our Experience of God*, London, Fontana, 1970; Allen & Unwin, 1959; New York, Macmillan, 1960
111 LIMOURIS, G., (comp.), *Icons: Windows on Eternity*, Geneva, World Council of Churches Publications, 1990
112 LUCKMANN, T., *The Invisible Religion: The Problem of Religion in Modern Society*, London/New York, Macmillan, 1967, 1978
113 LURKER, M., *Dictionary of Gods and Goddesses, Devils and Demons* (tr. G. L. Campbell), London/New York, Routledge, 1987; repr. 1988
114 MCGUIRE, M. B., *Religion: The Social Context*, 3rd rev. edn, Belmont, Cal., Wadsworth, 1992
115 MCKENZIE, P., *The Christians: Their Practices and Beliefs*, London, SPCK, 1988
116 MCMANNERS, J., 'Enlightenment: Secular and Christian (1600–1800)', in MCMANNERS, J. (ed.), *The Oxford History of Christianity*, ch. 8, Oxford, Oxford University Press, 1993

117   MALEFIJT, A. DE WAAL, *Religion and Culture*, London, Collier-Macmillan, 1968, repr. 1970; New York, Macmillan, 1968

117a MALONY, N. H. (ed.), *Psychology of Religion: Personalities, Problems and Possibilities*, Grand Rapids, Mich., Baker Book House, 1991

118   MARETT, R. R., *The Threshold of Religion*, New York, AMS, 1977, repr. of 1900 edn, London, Methuen

119   MARTIN, D., *A General Theory of Secularization*, Oxford, Blackwell, 1978

120   MAYBAUM, I., *Trialogue between Jew, Christian and Muslim*, London, Routledge, 1973

121   MICHELL, G., *The Hindu Temple: An Introduction to its Meaning and Forms*, Chicago/London, University of Chicago Press, 1988; first publ. New York, Harper & Row, 1977

121a MILLER, D. L., *The New Polytheism: Rebirth of the Gods and Goddesses*, New York, Harper & Row, 1974

122   MITCHELL, B., *The Justification of Religious Belief*, London, Macmillan, 1973

123   MOKASHI, D. B., *Palkhi: An Indian Pilgrimage* (tr. P. C. Enghlom), Albany, NY, State University of New York Press, 1987

124   MOORE, A. C., *Iconography of Religions*, London, SCM/Philadelphia, Pa, Fortress, 1977

124a MORRIS, B., *Anthropological Studies of Religion: An Introduction*, Cambridge, Cambridge University Press, 1987

125   MYERS, I. B., and MCCAULLEY, M. H., *Manual: A Guide to the Development of the Myers/Briggs Type Indicator*, Palo Alto, Cal., Consulting Psychologists Press

125a NESTI, A., *Il Religioso Implicito*, Rome, Ianua, 1985

126   OSER, F., and GMÜNDER, P., *Religious Judgement: A Developmental Approach*, Birmingham, Ala, Religious Education Press, 1991

127   OTTO, R., *The Idea of the Holy* (tr. J. W. Harvey), London/New York/Toronto, Oxford University Press, 1939; 2nd edn Oxford University Press, repr. 1968; this edn prev. publ. New York 1950, 1958

128   PAILIN, D. A., *Attitudes to Other Religions: Comparative Religion in Seventeenth- and Eighteenth-Century Britain*, Manchester University Press, 1984

128a PALOUTZIAN, R. F., *Invitation to the Psychology of Religion*, Glenview, Ill., Scott, Foresman and Co., 1983

129   PANOCH, J. V., and BARR, D. L., *Religion Goes to School*, New York, Harper & Row, 1968

130   PEACOCKE, A. R., *Creation and the World of Science*, Oxford, Clarendon Press, 1979

131   PHILLIPS, D. Z. (ed.), *Religion and Understanding*, Oxford, Blackwell, 1967

131a PROZESKY, M., *Religion and Ultimate Well-Being: An Explanatory Theory*, London, Macmillan/New York, St Martin's, 1984

131b PYE, M. (ed.), *Marburg Revisited*, Marburg, 1989

132   PYE, M., *Syncretism versus Synthesis*, British Association for the Study of Religions Occasional Papers, Cardiff, 1993

133   RADHAKRISHNAN, S., *Eastern Religions and Western Thought*, London, Oxford University Press, 1940

133a REDFIELD, R., *Peasant Society and Culture*, Chicago, University of Chicago Press, 1956

134   ROBBINS, T., and ROBERTSON, R., 'Studying Religion Today', *Religion*, vol. 21, October 1991, pp. 319–37

135   ROBERTSON, R., *The Sociological Interpretation of Religion*, Oxford, Blackwell, 1969, repr. 1980; New York, Schocken, repr. 1972

136   ROBERTSON, R., and GARRETT, W. R. (eds), *Religion and Global Order*, New York, Paragon House, 1991

137   ROBINSON, E., *The Original Vision*, Oxford, Religious Experience Research Unit, 1977; new edn Oxford, Westminster College, A. Hardy Research Centre, 1991

138   ROBINSON, E., *This Time-Bound Ladder*, Oxford, Religious Experience Research Unit, 1977

139   ROYLE, F., *Victorian Infidels: the Origins of the British Secularist Movement 1791–1866*, Manchester, Manchester University Press, 1974

140   SALISBURY, J. E., *Iberian Popular Religion, 600 BC to 700 AD*, New York/Toronto, Edwin Mellen, 1985, 1989

141   SCHIMMEL, A., and FALATURI, A., *We Believe in One God*, New York, Seabury, 1979; London, Burns & Oates, 1980

142   SCHOOLS COUNCIL, *Religious Education in Secondary Schools*, Working Paper 36, London, Evans, 1971

143   SCHUMAKER, J. F. (ed.), *Religion and Mental Health*, Oxford, Oxford University Press, 1992

144   SEGAL, R. A., *Religion and the Social Sciences: Essays on the Confrontation*, Atlanta, Ga, Scholars, 1989

145   SHARPE, E. J., *Comparative Religion: A History*, London, Duckworth, 1975, 1976; New York, Scribner, 1976; 2nd edn London, Duckworth, 1986; La Salle, Ill., Open Court, 1986

146   SHINER, L., 'The Concept of Secularization in Empirical Research', *Journal for the Scientific Study of Religion*, vol. 6(2), 1967, pp. 207–20

147   SILL, G. G., *A Handbook of Symbols in Christian Art*, New York, Collier, 1975

148   SKORUPSKI, J., *Symbol and Theory: A Philosophical Study of Theories of Religion in Social Anthropology*, Cambridge/New York, Cambridge University Press, 1976

149   SMART, N., *Concept and Empathy: Essays in the Study of Religion*, ed. Donald Wiebe, Basingstoke, Macmillan, 1986

150   SMART, N., *Secular Education and the Logic of Religion*, London, Faber, 1968; New York, Humanities, 1969

151   SMART, N., *The Phenomenon of Religion*, London, Macmillan, 1973

152   SMART, N., *Worldviews: Crosscultural Explorations of Human Beliefs*, New York, Scribner, 1983

153   SMITH, W. C., *The Meaning and End of Religion*, New York, New American Library, 1964; New York, Macmillan, 1963; London, SPCK, 1978; New York, Harper & Row, 1978

154   SMITH, W. C., *Towards a World Theology*, London, Macmillan, 1981; new edn 1990

155   SMITH, J. Z., 'The Bare Facts of Ritual', *History of Religions*, vol. 20 (1–2), August, November 1980, pp. 112–27

156   SMITH, J. Z., *To Take Place*, Chicago, University of Chicago Press, 1987; new edn 1992

157   SPILKA, B., HOOD, R. W., and GORSUCH, R. L., *The Psychology of Religion: An Empirical Approach*, Englewood Cliffs, NJ, Prentice-Hall, 1985

158   STRENG, F. J., *Understanding Religious Life*, 2nd edn, Encino, Cal., Dickenson, 1976; Belmont, Cal., Wadsworth, 1984; first publ. as *Understanding Religious Man*, 1969

159 SUTCLIFFE, J. M. (ed.), *A Dictionary of Religious Education*, London, SCM, 1984

159a SUTHERLAND, S., et al. (eds), *The World's Religions*, London, Routledge, 1988, Part 1, 'Religion and the Study of Religions', pp. 1–60

160 TATE, R. B., *Pilgrimages to St James of Compostela from the British Isles during the Middle Ages*, Liverpool, Liverpool University Press, 1990

161 THOMPSON, K., *Emile Durkheim*, Chichester, Ellis Horwood/London, Tavistock, 1982

162 TILLICH, P., *Systematic Theology*, 3 vols, London, SCM, 1978

163 TILLICH, P., *The Encounter of Religions and Quasi-Religions* (ed. T. Thomas), Lewiston/Queenston/Lampeter, Edwin Mellen, 1990

163a TIRYAKIAN, E. A. (ed.), *On the Margin of the Visible*, New York, Wiley, 1974

164 TOWLER, R., *Homo Religiosus: Sociological Problems in the Study of Religion*, London, Constable, 1974

165 TURNER, B. S., *The Body and Society*, Oxford, 1984

166 TYLOR, SIR EDWARD B., *Primitive Culture*, 2 vols, Magnolia, Mass., Peter Smith, n.d.; first publ. London, Murrary, 1871, and often republ.

VOGT, E. A. (ed.), see no. 108 above

167 VRIJHOF, P. H., and WAARDENBURG, J. (eds), *Official and Popular Religion: Analysis of a Theme for Religious Studies*, The Hague/Paris/New York, Mouton, 1979

168 WAARDENBURG, JACQUES (ed.), *Classical Approaches to the Study of Religion*, 2 vols, The Hague/Paris, Mouton, 1973–4

169 WACH, J., *Essays in the History of Religions* (ed. J. M. Kitawa and G. D. Alles), New York, Macmillan/London, Collier-Macmillan, 1988

170 WACH, J., *The Comparative Study of Religions*, New York/London, Columbia University Press, 1958

171 WALLACE, A. F. C., *Religion: An Anthropological View*, New York, Random House, 1966

171a WATTS, F., and WILLIAMS, M., *The Psychology of Religious Knowing*, Cambridge, Cambridge University Press, 1988

172 WEBER, M., *The Protestant Ethic and the Spirit of Capitalism* (tr. Talcott Parsons), London, Allen & Unwin, 1958; New York, Scribner, 1958

173 WEBER, M., *The Sociology of Religion* (tr. Ephraim Fischoff), Boston, Beacon Press, 1963

174 WEBER, M., *On Charisma and Institution Building* (ed. S. N. Eisenstadt), Chicago/London, University of Chicago Press, 3rd imp. 1977

175 WELCH, C., *Religion in the Undergraduate Curriculum*, Washington, DC, Association of American Colleges, 1972

175a WHALING, F., (ed.), *Contemporary Approaches to the Study of Religion*, vol. 1, *Humanities*, vol. 2, *The Social Sciences*, Berlin/New York/Amsterdam, Mouton, 1984

176 WIDENGREN, GEO, *Religionsphänomenologie*, Berlin, de Grutyer, 1969; German tr. of Swedish *Religionens värld*, Stockholm, 1945, 2nd edn 1953, 3rd edn 1971

177 WILSON, B. R., *Contemporary Transformations of Religion*, Oxford, Oxford University Press, 1976

178 WILSON, B. R., *Religion in Secular Society: A Sociological Comment*, London, Watts, 1966

179 WILSON, B. R., *Religion in Sociological Perspective*, Oxford, Oxford University Press, 1982

180 WILSON, A. N., *Jesus*, London, Sinclair-Stevenson, 1992

181   WULFF, D. M., *Psychology of Religion: Classic and Contemporary Views*, New York, Wiley, 1990

182   WUTHNOW, R., *Meaning and Moral Order: Explorations in Cultural Analysis*, Berkeley, University of California Press, 1987

183   YINGER, J. M., *Religion, Society and the Individual*, New York, Macmillan, 1957

[XXXV]   *Tibetan Religions*

Part 1: Compiled by David Stott

1   AMIPA, S. G., *A Waterdrop from the Glorious Sea*, Rikon, Switzerland, Tibet Institute, 1975 (a history of the Sakya-pa tradition)

2   CHANG, G. C. C. (tr.), *Teachings of Tibetan Yoga*, New Hyde Park, NY, University Books, 1963; New York, Citadel Press, 1974

3   CHATTOPADHYAYA, A., *Atīśa and Tibet: Life and Works of Dīpaṃkara Śrījñāna*, Calcutta, Indian Studies, Past and Present, 1967

4   DARGYAY, E., *The Rise of Esoteric Buddhism in Tibet*, Delhi, Motilal Banarsidass, 1977; Livingston, MJ, Orient Book Distributors/Mystic, Conn., Verry, 1977

5   DAVID-NEEL, A., and LAMA YONGDEN (eds and trs), *Gesar: The Superhuman Life of Gesar of Ling*, rev. edn, London, Rider, 1959

6   EVANS-WENTZ, W. Y. (ed.), *Tibetan Yoga and Secret Doctrines*, 2nd edn, London/New York, Oxford University Press, 1958: bk v, Jigme Lingpa, *The Awesome Mirth of the Dakinis*; new edn, Galaxy, Oxford University Press (NY), 1967

7   FREMANTLE, F., and TRUNGPA, C. (trs), *The Tibetan Book of the Dead: The Great Liberation through Hearing in the Bardo*, Berkeley, Cal., London, Shambhala, 1975

8   GUENTHER, H. V., *The Tantric View of Life*, Berkeley, Cal., Shambhala, 1972, 1976

9   KARMAY, S. G. (ed. and tr.), *The Treasury of Good Sayings: A Tibetan History of Bon*, London/New York, Oxford University Press, 1972

10   KLONG-CHEN RAB-'BYAMS-PA, *Kindly Bent to Ease Us*, vols 1–3 (tr. and ann. H. V. Guenther), Berkeley, Cal., Dharma, 1975–6

11   LAUF, D. I., *Secret Doctrines of the Tibetan Books of the Dead*, Boulder, Colo, Shambhala, 1977

12   LLALUNGPA, L. (tr.), *The Life of Milarepa*, New York, Dutton, 1977

13   MKHAS GRUB RJE, *Fundamentals of the Buddhist Tantras* (tr. F. D. Lessing and A. Wayman), The Hague, Mouton, 1968

14   NEBESKY-WOJKOWITZ, R. DE, *Oracles and Demons of Tibet*, London, Oxford University Press/The Hague, Mouton, 1956; New York, Gordon Press

15   RICHARDSON, H., 'A Tun Huang Fragment', in KAWAMURA, L. S., and SCOTT, K. (eds), *Buddhist Thought and Asian Civilization: Essays in Honor of H. V. Guenther*, Berkeley, Cal., Dharma, 1977

16   RUEGG, D. S., 'The Jo Nan Pas: A School of Buddhist Ontologists', *Journal of the American Oriental Society*, vol. 83, 1963, pp. 73–91

17   SGAM-PO-PA, *The Jewel Ornament of Liberation* (tr. H. V. Guenther), 2nd edn, London, Rider, 1970, 1971; Berkeley, Cal., Shambhala, 1971; this tr. first publ. 1959; new edn Shambhala, 1991

18   SHAKABPA, T. D., *A Political History of Tibet*, New Haven, Conn., Yale University Press, 1967

19 SNELLGROVE, D. L., *Hevajra-Tantra: A Critical Study*, 2 vols, London, Oxford University Press; repr. 1976; first publ. 1959

20 SNELLGROVE, D. L. (ed.), *The Nine Ways of Bon: Excerpts from gZi-brjid*, Boulder, Colo, Prajna, 1980; new edn Shambhala, 1980

21 THINLEY, KARMA, *The History of the Sixteen Karmapas of Tibet* (ed. with an essay by David Stott), Boulder, Colo, Prajna, 1980; Shambhala, 1981

22 TSOGYAL, YESHE, *The Life and Liberation of Padmasambhava* (tr. G. C. Toussaint and K. Douglas), 2 vols, Berkeley, Cal., Dharma, 1977

23 TSONG-KHA-PA, *Tantra in Tibet: The Great Exposition of Secret Mantra* (tr. and ed. J. Hopkins), London, Allen & Unwin, 1977, 1978

24 TUCCI, G., *The Religions of Tibet* (tr. G. Samuel), London, Routledge/ Berkeley, Cal., University of California Press, 1980

25 WANGYAL, GESHE, *The Door of Liberation*, New York, M. Girodias, 1973; rev. edn New York, Lotsawa, 1979, 1987

26 WAYMAN, A., *Yoga of Guyasamaja Tantra: The Arcane Lore of Forty Verses*, Delhi, Motilal Banarsidass, 1977, new edn 1992; Livingston, NJ, Orient Book Distributors

Part 2: Compiled by Paul Williams

27 BEYER, S., *The Cult of Tārā: Magic and Ritual in Tibet*, Berkeley/Los Angeles/London, University of California Press, 1973; new edn 1978

28 BÄRLOCHER, D., *Testimonies of Tibetan Tulkus: A Research among Reincarnate Buddhist Masters in Exile* (Opuscula Tibetana), Rikon, Tibet-Institut, 1982

29 CHANG, G. C. C. (tr.), *The Hundred Thousand Songs of Milarepa*, 2 vols, Boulder/London, Shambhala, 1977

30 DALAI LAMA, THE, *Freedom in Exile: The Autobiography of the Dalai Lama of Tibet*, London/Sydney/Auckland/Toronto, Hodder & Stoughton, 1990

31 PABONGKA RINPOCHE, *Liberation in the Palm of Your Hand* (tr. M. Richards), Boston/London/Sydney, Wisdom Publications, 1991

32 RHIE, M. M., and THURMAN, R. A. F., *Wisdom and Compassion: The Sacred Art of Tibet*, London, Thames and Hudson, 1991

33 THONDUP, T., RINPOCHE, *Hidden Teachings of Tibet* (ed. H. Talbott), London, Wisdom Publications, 1986

34 WILLSON, M., *In Praise of Tārā: Songs to the Saviouress*, London, Wisdom Publications, 1986

[XXXVI] *Zoroastrianism*

Compiled by John R. Hinnells

Two outstanding series of publications merit particular mention:

1 *The Cambridge History of Iran*, ed. A. J. Arberry, vols 1–7, Cambridge, Cambridge University Press, 1968–91, provides substantial scholarly accounts of Zoroastrians at different periods of Iranian history;

2 YARSHATER, E. (ed.), *Encyclopaedia Iranica*, originally London, Routledge, now Costa Mesa, Cal., Mazda Publishers, commenced in 1982, appearing quarterly, covers anything Iranian, not least Zoroastrianism, and will take many years to complete.

3   AMIGHI, J. K., *The Zoroastrians of Iran – Conversion, Assimilation, or Persistence*, New York, AMS, 1989 (Studies in Anthropology, 3)
4   ANKLESARIA, B. T., *Zand-Akāsīh, Iranian or Greater Bundahišn* (English tr.), Bombay, publ. privately, 1956
5   ANKLESARIA, B. T., *Zand-ī Vohūman Yasn . . . with Text, Transliteration and Translation in English*, Bombay, publ. privately, 1957; prev. printed for private circulation, 1919
6   BAILEY, SIR HAROLD W., *Zoroastrian Problems in the Ninth-Century Books*, Oxford, Clarendon Press, 1943; repr. with new introduction, 1971
7   BIVAR, A. D. H., et al. (eds), *Papers in Honour of Professor Mary Boyce*, 2 vols, Leiden, Brill, 1985 (*Acta Iranica* 2ᵉ sèr., Hommages et Opera Minora, X and XI, AI 24, 25)
8   BOYCE, M., *A History of Zoroastrianism*, Leiden, Brill, vol. 1, 1975, (repr. with corrections 1989); vol. 2, 1982; vol. 3, by M. BOYCE and F. GRENET, with a contribution by R. BECK, 1991; vol. 1, 2nd rev. repr. 1989 (*Handbuch der Orientalistik* vol. 8, part 1)
9   BOYCE, M., *A Persian Stronghold of Zoroastrianism*, Oxford, Clarendon Press, 1977; new edn University Press of America, 1990
10   BOYCE, M., *Zoroastrians: Their Religious Beliefs and Practices*, London/Boston, Mass., Routledge, 1979; rev. repr. 1988
11   BOYCE, M., *Textual Sources for the Study of Zoroastrianism*, Manchester, Manchester University Press, 1984; repr. Chicago University Press, 1990
     BOYCE, M. see also no. 7 above
12   BOYCE, M., 'Zoroastrian (Parsi) Festivals', in BROWN, A. (ed.), *Festivals in World Religions*, London/New York, Longman, 1986
13   BOYCE, M., *Zoroastrianism: Its Antiquity and Constant Vigour*, Costa Mesa, Cal., Mazda Publishers, 1992
14   CHOKSEY, K., *Purity and Pollution in Zoroastrianism*, Austin, Tex., University of Texas Press, 1989
15   COHN, N., *Cosmos, Chaos and World to Come*, New Haven, Conn., Yale University Press, 1993
16   DARMESTETER, J., (tr.), *Zend-Avesta: Vendīdād*, repr. Delhi, Motilal Banarsidass, 1965, 1987 (Sacred Books of the East, vol. 4); Mystic, Conn., Verry/New York, Krishna, 1974; first publ. Oxford, Clarendon Press, 1880–87, new edn London, Greenwood, 1972, Delhi, Motilal Banarsidass, 1987–8
17   DARMESTETER, J. (tr.), *Zend-Avesta: Yashts*, repr. as no. 16 above (*Sacred Books of the East*, vol. 23)
18   DHALLA, M. N., *The Nyaishes, or Zoroastrian Liturgies*, New York, Columbia University Press, 1908; repr. New York, AMS, 1965
19   DUCHESNE-GUILLEMIN, J., *The Hymns of Zarathustra* (tr. from the French by M. Henning), London, Murray, 1952, 1993
20   DUCHESNE-GUILLEMIN, J., *La Religion de l'Iran ancien*, Paris, Presses Universitaires de France, 1962; English tr. by K. M. JamaspAsa, *The Religion of Ancient Iran*, Bombay, Tata Press, 1973
21   FIRBY, N. K., *European Travellers and their Perceptions of Zoroastrians in the 17th and 18th Centuries*, Berlin, Dietrich Reimer, 1988 (Deutsches Archäologisches Institut Abt. Teheran, Archäologische Mitteilungen aus Iran, Ergänz. 14)
22   FRYE, R. N., *The Heritage of Persia*, London, Weidenfeld, 1962; 2nd edn London, Sphere, 1976
23   FRYE, R. N., *The History of Ancient Iran*, Munich, Beck, 1984

24 GERSHEVITCH, I. (ed. and tr.), *The Avestan Hymn to Mithra*, Cambridge, Cambridge University Press, 1959

24a GIGNOUX, P. (ed. and tr.), *Le Livre d'Ardā Vīrāz*, Paris, 1984

25 GNOLI, G., *Zoroaster's Time and Homeland: A Study on the Origins of Mazdaism and Related Problems*, Naples, Istituto Univ. Orientale, Seminario di Studi Asiatici, 1980

26 HENNING, W. B., *Zoroaster: Politician or Witchdoctor?*, London, Oxford University Press, 1951

27 HERRMANN, G., *The Iranian Revival*, Oxford, Elsevier–Phaidon, 1977

28 HINNELLS, J. R., *Persian Mythology*, 2nd rev. and expanded edn, Feltham, Middlesex, Newnes, 1985; first publ. New York/London, Hamlyn, 1973

29 HINNELLS, J. R., *Spanning East and West*, Milton Keynes, Open University, 1978

30 HINNELLS, J. R., *Zoroastrianism and the Parsis*, London, Ward Lock Educational, 1981

31 HINNELLS, J. R., 'Parsi Attitudes to Religious Pluralism', in COWARD, H. (ed.), *Modern Indian Responses to Religious Pluralism*, New York, State University of New York Press, 1987, pp. 195–234

32 HINNELLS, J. R., 'Modern Zoroastrian Philosophy', in CARR, B., and MAHALINGAM, I., *Modern Asian Philosophy*, London, Routledge, 1995

33 HINNELLS, J. R., 'The Modern Zoroastrian Diaspora', in BROWN, J., and FOOT, R., *Migration: The Asian Experience*, London, Macmillan, 1994

34 HINNELLS, J. R., *Zoroastrians in Britain*, Oxford, Oxford University Press, 1996 (forthcoming)

35 INSLER, S., *The Gāthās of Zarathustra*, Leiden, Brill, 1975 (*Acta Iranica*, vol. 8)

36 JAMASPASA, H. (ed.), and HAUG, M. (tr.), ARDA VIRAZ NAMAG, *The Book of Arda Viraf* (Pahlavi text prepared by H. Jamaspji Asa, with English tr. by M. Haug), repr. of Bombay/London, 1872 edn; Amsterdam, Oriental Press, 1971

37 KARKAL, M., *Survey of Parsi Population of Greater Bombay – 1982*, Bombay, 1983

38 KOTWAL, F. S., and BOYD, J. W., 'The Zoroastrian Paragna', *Journal of Mithraic Studies*, vol. 2(1), 1977, pp. 18–52

39 KOTWAL, F. M., and KREYENBROEK, PH. G., *The Herbedestan and Nerangestan*, with contributions by J. R. Russell, vol. 1, *Studia Iranica*, Cahier 10, Paris, 1992

40 KREYENBROEK, G., *Šraosa in the Zoroastrian Tradition*, Leiden, Brill, 1985

41 KULKE, E., *The Parsees in India: A Minority as Agent of Social Change*, Munich, Weltforum Verlag, 1974

42 LEVY, R. (tr.), FIRDAWSI, *The Epic of the Kings, Shāh-Nāma*, London, Routledge/Chicago, Ill., University of Chicago Press, 1967

43 LITTLETON, C. S., *The New Comparative Mythology: An Anthropological Assessment of the Theories of Georges Dumézil*, Berkeley, Cal., University of California Press, 1966; 3rd edn 1980

44 MENASCE, J. DE (tr.), *Le Troisième Livre du Dēnkart*, Paris, Klincksieck, 1973 (Travaux . . . de L'Université de Paris)

45 MILLS, L. H. (tr.), *Zend-Avesta: Yasna*, repr. Delhi, Motilal Banarsidass, 1965 (*Sacred Books of the East*, vol. 31); and as no. 16 above

46 MISTREE, K. P., *Zoroastrianism: An Ethnic Perspective*, Bombay, London, Zoroastrian Studies, 1982

47 MODI, J. J., *Religious Ceremonies and Customs of the Parsees*, 2nd edn,

Bombay, J. B. Karani's Sons, 1937; Bombay, British India Press, 1922, repr. New York, Garland, 1980

48　MOULTON, J. H., *Early Zoroastrianism*, London, Williams & Norgate, 1913, repr. Amsterdam, Philo Press, 1972; New York, AMS, 1980

49　PAVRY, J. D. C., *The Zoroastrian Doctrine of a Future Life: From Death to the Individual Judgment*, 2nd edn, New York, Columbia University Press, 1929, repr. New York, AMS

50　PEARSON, J. D. (ed.), *A Bibliography of Pre-Islamic Persia*, London, Mansell, 1975

51　RUSSELL, J. R., *Zoroastrianism in Armenia*, New Haven, Conn., Harvard University Press, 1987

52　SHAHBAZI, A. SH., *Ferdowsi: A Critical Biography*, Costa Mesa, Cal., Mazda Press, 1991

52　SHAKED, S., *Wisdom of the Sasanian Sages, Dēnkard, VI*, Boulder, Colo, Westview Press, 1979

53a　SHAKED, S., *Dualism in Transformation: Varieties of Religion in Sasanian Iran*, London, School of Oriental and African Studies, 1994 (Jordan Lectures no. 16)

54　SMITH, MARIA WILKINS, *Studies in the Syntax of the Gāthās of Zarathustra, together with Text, Translation and Notes*, Philadelphia, Pa, Linguistic Society of America, 1929; repr. New York, Kraus, 1966

55　SPULER, B., *Iranian Literature* (Mainly in English), Leiden, Brill, 1968 (*Handbuch der Orientalistik*, vol. 4, part 1)

56　WEST, E. W. (ed. and tr.), *Dēnkard*, bks VII and V, in *Pahlavi Texts*, V (*Sacred Books of the East*, vol. 47), repr. Delhi, Motilal Banarsidass, 1965, 1987–8; New York, Krishna, 1974; Mystic, Conn., Verry; *Pahlavi Texts*, I–V, first publ. Oxford, Clarendon Press, 1882–92

57　WEST, E. W., (ed. and tr.), *Dēnkard*, bks VIII and IX, in *Pahlavi Texts*, IV (*Sacred Books of the East*, vol. 37); as no. 56 above

58　WEST, E. W. (ed. and tr.), *Dādistan-ī Dīnīk*, in *Pahlavi Texts*, II (*Sacred Books of the East*, vol. 18); as no. 56 above

59　WEST, E. W. (ed. and tr.), *Dinā-ī Māinōg-i Khirad, Šikand-Gūmānik Vigār, Sar Dar*, in *Pahlavi Texts*, III (*Sacred Books of the East*, vol. 24); as no. 56 above

60　WILLIAMS, A. V., *The Pahlavi Rivayat Accompanying the Dadestan i Denig*, 2 vols, Copenhagen, Royal Danish Academy of Sciences and Letters, 1990

61　YAMAMOTO, Y., 'The Zoroastrian Temple Cult of Fire in Archaeology and Literature', *Orient*, vols 15–16, 1979, 1981

62　ZAEHNER, R. C., *Zurvan: A Zoroastrian Dilemma*, Oxford, Clarendon Press, 1955; repr. New York, Biblo, 1973

63　ZAEHNER, R. C., *Teachings of the Magi*, London, Allen & Unwin, 1956; London, Sheldon, 1975; New York, Oxford University Press, 1976

64　ZEHNER, R. C., *The Dawn and Twilight of Zoroastrianism*, London, Weidenfeld, 1961, repr. 1975; New York, Putnam, 1961

Index

References are given to the page on which a term actually appears, not to where the relevant entry begins: (2) or (3) after the page number indicates that the term appears in a number of different entries on that page.

In entries containing many page references, 'main' entries are printed in **bold type**. This is necessarily only a guide, because of the subjective nature of the judgement as to what constitutes a main entry.

There are variant spellings of many technical terms. Where this involves little difference in alphabetical order, the variants are noted in brackets. Where there is a substantial difference, both terms appear separately. An oblique stroke indicates alternative forms of a word in allied languages, e.g. in Sanskrit and Pali.

690 Index

Chela (Cela) 148, 199
chemistry 18
Chen Wo (Zhen Wo) 102
Chen Yen (Zhen Yan) **99**, 102, 470
Ch'eng Huang (Cheng Huang) 103
Cheng I (Zheng Yi) 514
Ch'eng-Shih (Cheng Shi) 340
Cheng Wei Shih Lun 165
Chenrezik 127
Cherem 99
Cherokee 9
Cherubim and Seraphim Societies 1
Chewa 357
Cheyenne 99
Chi (Igbo) 232
Ch'i (Qi) 19, 20, 167, 308
Ch'i (Ji) 346
Chi Li (Ji Li) 100, 271
Chi T'sang (Ji Zang) 447
Chiao (Jiao) 101
Chiba, Japan 85, 353
Chibcha 263
Chicago 112, 215, 371, 420, 421
Chichén Itzá 310 (2), 404
Chicomoztoc 223
Chief Khālsā Dīwān 481
Chief Speaker *see* Tlatoani
chieftainship 16, 288, 306, 509–10
Chieh Chi (Jie Ji) 167
Chien Ai (Juin Ai) 318
Chih Ch'an (Zhi Chan) 102
Chih I (Chih K'ai/Zhi Yi) 527
childbirth *see* birth
children 214, 266, 301, 302, 344, 394, 397, 426, 469, 510, 518, 530
Children of God 165–6, 250, 350; *see also* Family, The
Chilembwe, John 393
Ch'in Shih Huang Ti (Qin Shi Huang Ti), Emperor 19, 115
Chin Wen Chia 115
China 51, 53, 58, 84, 97, 99 (2), **99–100**, 110–11, 112, 146, 147, 220, 239, 257, 266, 285, 287, 294, 295, 340, 353, 357, 363–4, 366, 373, 390, 441, 449, 526 (2), 549; *see also under* List of Contents by Subject Area, Chinese Religions (XII)
China, Republic of (Taiwan) *see* Taiwan
Chineke 231
Chinese Āgamas 354
Chinese language 112, 363, 542
Chinese Buddhist Association 100
Chinese Muslim Association 100
Chinese Taoist Association 100
Chinese Tripiṭaka 84, 528
Chinese Turkestan 536; *see also* Sinkiang
Ch'ing dynasty 100, 116, 271
Ch'ing Ming (Ching Ming) 168
Ch'ing T'an (Ching Ten) 222
Ching T'u School 101, 102, 103, 266

Chinmoy Kumar Chose, Sri 496
Chinvat Bridge (Cinvato Perety) 30, **104**, 573
Chion-in 31
Chippewa 311
Chiradzulu 393
Chishin 31
Chisungu 104
Chitsu, priest 340
Chöd (gCöd) 104
Choga-Zanbil 150, 571
Chogyal Phagpa (Chos.rgyal 'phegs.pa) 442
Chogyur Dechen Lingpa (mChog.'gyur bDe.chen gLing.pa) 424
choir 91, 274, 322
Cholollán **104–5**, 310, 404
Cholula *see* Cholollan
Chorten (mChod.rten) 501; *see also* stupa
Choshen Mishpat 477
Chotki 431
Chou dynasty 34, 102, 115, 226, 271, 468
Chou Li (Zhou Li) 115
Chou Tun I (Zhou Dun-yi) 346
Choukoutien 390
Chrēstērion 297
chrism, chrismation 332
Christ *see* Jesus Christ
Christ (Khlyst), sect 434
Christ Apostolic Church 17
Christadelphians 105
Christian Coalition 177
Christian Council of Trinidad and Tobago 493
Christian Faith, The (F. D. E. Schleiermacher) 456
Christian Fellowship Church 51, **105**, 141
Christian Kabbalah 105–6
Christian marriage 301–2
Christian mysticism 334–7; *see also* mysticism
Christian perfection 311
Christian philosophy 380
Christian pilgrimage 383–4
Christian prophecy 392–3
Christian Sabbath 464
Christian sacraments 436–7
Christian salvation (doctrine) 443–4
Christian Science 22, **106**, 184, 457
Christian Science Monitor 106
Christian sects 457
Christian Socialism 486
Christian spirituality 494–6
Christian theology **106**, 107, 456, 507, 526
Christian World Liberation Front 250
Christian worship 353; *see also entries on* baptism; church music; drama (Christian); eucharist; liturgical